THE WORLD
AND THE WORD

THE WORLD
AND THE WORD

An Introduction to the Old Testament

Eugene H. Merrill
Mark F. Rooker
Michael A. Grisanti

ACADEMIC

Nashville, Tennessee

The World and the Word: An Introduction to the Old Testament

Copyright © 2011 by Eugene Merrill, Mark F. Rooker, & Michael A. Grisanti

ISBN: 978-0-8054-4031-7

Published by B&H Publishing Group
Nashville, Tennessee

Dewey Decimal Classification: 221.07
Subject Heading: BIBLE. O.T.—STUDY \ DOCTRINAL THEOLOGY \ CHRISTIANITY—
DOCTRINE

Printed in the United States of America

6 7 8 9 10 11 12 • 18 17 16 15 14
BP

CONTENTS

DEDICATION

The impetus for this work has come largely from interacting with students for nearly fifty years in the classroom and outside it about issues pertaining to the Bible—its origins, development, character, authority, and meaning. An outflow of intense engagement with these budding scholars in an attempt to deal with their concerns has sharpened my own sense of curiosity, reflection, and research. I therefore dedicate my portion of this project to these committed servants of Christ and students of His word.

Eugene H. Merrill

To former and current students whom I have had the privilege to teach at Southeastern Baptist Theological Seminary.

Mark F. Rooker

I am supremely grateful for the greatest blessing in my life, besides my salvation: my loving and faithful wife, my אֵשֶׁת־חַיִל (Prov. 31:10).

Michael A. Grisanti

Abbreviations

AB	Anchor Bible
ABD	*Anchor Bible Dictionary*
ACORN	*The American Center of Oriental Research Newsletter*
AEHL	*Encyclopedia of Archaeological Excavations in the Holy Land*
Ag. Ap.	*Against Apion* (Josephus)
ANE	Ancient Near East(ern)
ANET	*Ancient Near Eastern Texts Relating to the Old Testament*
Ant.	*Jewish Antiquities* (Josephus*)*
AOAT	*Alter Orient und Altes Testament*
AUSS	*Andrews University Seminary Studies*
BA	*Biblical Archaeologist*
BAR	*Biblical Archaeology Review*
BASOR	*Bulletin of the American Schools of Oriental Research*
BBR	*Bulletin of Biblical Research*
BBR Sup	*Bulletin of Biblical Research Supplement*
BCOT	Baker Commentary on the Old Testament
BCOTWP	Baker Commentary on the Old Testament Wisdom and Psalms
BI	*Biblical Interpretation*
Bib	*Biblica*
BibOr	*Biblica et orientalia*
BIOSCS	*Bulletin of the International Organization for Septuagint and Cognate Studies*
BJS	*Brown Judaic Studies*
BR	*Biblical Research*
BRev	*Bible Review*
BSac	*Bibliotheca Sacra*
BSC	*Bible Student's Commentary*
BST	*Bible Speaks Today*
BT	*Babylonian Talmud*
BTB	*Biblical Theology Bulletin*
BTS	*Bible et terre sainte*
BZAW	*Beihefte zur Zeitschrift für die alttestamentliche Wissenschaft*
CB	*Cultura biblica*
CBC	Cambridge Bible Commentary
CBQ	*Catholic Biblical Quarterly*

CHE	*The Chronicle of Higher Education*
COS	*Context of Scripture*
CTR	*Criswell Theological Review*
DJD	*Discoveries in the Judean Desert*
DSB	Daily Study Bible
DSBOT	Daily Study Bible: Old Testament
DSS	*Dead Sea Scrolls*
DOTP	*Dictionary of the Old Testament: Pentateuch*
EBC	*The Expositor's Bible Commentary*
EQ	*Evangelical Quarterly*
EJ	*Encyclopedia Judaica*
EJT	*European Journal of Theology*
ET	*The Expository Times*
ETL	*Ephemerides theologicae lovanienses*
EvJ	*Evangelical Journal*
FM	*Faith and Mission*
FOTL	*Forms of the Old Testament Literature*
GJ	*Grace Journal*
GTJ	*Grace Theological Journal*
HALOT	*Hebrew and Aramaic Lexicon of the Old Testament*
HAR	*Hebrew Annual Review*
HB	Hebrew Bible
Hb.	Hebrew language
HCOT	*Historical Commentary on the Old Testament*
HCSB	*Holman Christian Standard Bible*
HOTE	*Handbook of Old Testament Exegesis*
HSM	Harvard Semitic Monographs
HTR	*Harvard Theological Review*
HUCA	*Hebrew Union College Annual*
ICC	International Critical Commentary
IDB	*The Interpreter's Dictionary of the Bible*
IDBS	*Interpreter's Dictionary of the Bible Supplements*
IEJ	*Israel Exploration Journal*
Int	*Interpretation*
IOSCS	*International Organization for Septuagint and Cognate Studies*
ISBE	*International Standard Bible Encyclopedia*
ISBL	Indiana Series in Biblical Literature
ITC	*International Theological Commentary*
JANES	*Journal of the Ancient Near Eastern Society*
JAOS	*Journal of the American Oriental Society*
JATS	*Journal of the Adventist Theological Society*
JBL	*Journal of Biblical Literature*
JBQ	*Jewish Bible Quarterly*
JBR	*Journal of Bible and Religion*
JETS	*Journal of the Evangelical Theological Society*

JNES	*Journal of Near Eastern Studies*
JPS	*Jewish Publication Society*
JPSTC	*Jewish Publicaton Society Torah Study*
JQR	*Jewish Quarterly Review*
JSOT	*Journal for the Study of the Old Testament*
JSOTSup	Journal for the Study of the Old Testament: Supplement Series
JSS	*Journal of Semitic Studies*
JTS	*Journal of Theological Studies*
JTT	*Journal of Translation and Textlinguistics*
JTVI	*Journal of the Transactions of the Victoria Institute*
KAI	*Kanaanäische und aramäische Inschriften*
LBC	Layman's Bible Commentaries
LXX	Septuagint
MSJ	*Master's Seminary Journal*
MT	Masoretic Text
NAC	New American Commentary
NACSBT	New American Commentary Studies in Bible and Theology
NCB	New Century Bible
NCBC	New Century Bible Commentary
NCBCOT	New Century Bible Commentary: Old Testament
NEA	*Near Eastern Archaeology*
NEASB	*Near East Archaeological Society Bulletin*
NET	New English Translation
NIBC	New International Biblical Commentary
NICNT	New International Commentary on the New Testament
NICOT	New International Commentary on the Old Testament
NIDOTTE	*New International Dictionary of Old Testament Theology and Exegesis*
NIV	New International Version
NIVAC	*New International Application Commentary*
NRSV	New Revised Standard Version
NT	New Testament
NTC	New Testament Commentary
OT	Old Testament
OTL	Old Testament Library
OTS	Old Testament Studies
OTSB	Old Testament Study Bible
PTR	*Princeton Theological Review*
RB	*Revue Biblique*
RevQ	*Revue de Qumran*
RQ	*Restoration Quarterly*
RTR	*Reformed Theological Review*
SBL	*Society of Biblical Literature*
SBLDS	Society of Biblical Literature Dissertation Series
SBLSP	*Society of Biblical Literature Seminar Papers*
SBT	Studies in Bibilical Theology

SBTS	Sources for Biblical and Theological Study
SJOT	*Scandinavian Journal of the Old Testament*
SJT	*Scottish Journal of Theology*
ST	*Studia theologica*
TA	*Tel Aviv*
TB	Theologische Bücherei: Neudrucke und Berichte aus dem 20. Jahrhundert
TCC	The Communicator's Commentary
TJ	*Trinity Journal*
TLOT	*Theological Lexicon of the Old Testament.* Edited by E. Jenni, with assistance from C. Westermann. Translated by M. E. Biddle. 3 vols. Peabody, MA, 1997.
TOTC	Tyndale Old Testament Commentary
TTZ	*Trierer theologische Zeitschrift*
TynBul	*Tyndale Bulletin*
VT	*Vetus Testamentum*
VTSup	Supplements to Vetus Testamentum
WBC	Word Biblical Commentary
WEC	Wycliffe Exegetical Commentary
WTJ	*Westminster Theological Journal*
ZAW	*Zeitshrift für die alttestamentliche Wissenschaft*
ZIBBC	Zondervan Illustrated Bible Backgrounds Commentary

PREFACE

The Hebrew Scriptures, which Christians call the Old Testament, have been devalued down through the ages. The heretic Marcion (2nd cent.) drew a contrast between the inferior God of the Old Testament and the superior God of the New Testament. From Origen (3rd cent.) the predominant mode of interpretation through the Middle Ages was an allegorical hermeneutic, which paid scant attention to the background and meaning of the Hebrew text. The eighteenth-century Enlightenment led to a questioning of the traditional attitudes toward Scriptures. In the ninteenth century the Higher Criticism of the Old Testament, as articulated by Julius Wellhausen in his *Documentary Hypothesis,* undermined the Mosaic authorship of the Pentateuch. The antisupernaturalist, academic study of Scripture in universities and liberal seminaries, now supplemented by such approaches as Feminist critiques, has thoroughly undermined confidence in the Old Testament as inspired and trustworthy Scriptures.

But even evangelicals who believe in the inspiration of Scriptures and in the inerrancy of their original autographs may fail to grasp the significance of the Old Testament, which constitutes 80 percent of their Bibles. This was, after all, the only Bible of Jesus and His original followers. One cannot fully understand the prophecies quoted in Matthew, the epistles of Paul, or the allusions to the high priesthood of the exalted Christ in Hebrews without a full knowledge of the Old Testament.

It is to introduce readers to the background and the interpretation of the Old Testament that three well qualified scholars have written *The World and the Word*: Eugene H. Merrill is the author of numerous books, most notably *Everlasting Dominion: A Theology of the Old Testament* (2006) and *Kingdom of Priests* (2008), as well as commentaries on Deuteronomy, Haggai, Zechariah, and Malachi. Mark F. Rooker is the author of a commentary on Leviticus and a monograph on the Hebrew of Ezekiel. Michael A. Grisanti is the author of a commentary on the book of Deuteronomy and the books of Samuel and Kings.

While maintaining traditionally conservative positions on such issues as the interpretation of Genesis 1–2, the date of the exodus, the unity of Isaiah, the date of Daniel, and the historicity of Jonah, they do so with a broad knowledge of the Ancient Near Eastern background of the Old Testament as well as the views of past and current biblical critics. What is distinctive about this Introduction is their presentation of alternative evangelical interpretations of these issues, and their engagement with these views.

With its exploration of the historical and cultural world of the Old Testament, its discussion of the composition and canonicity of the individual books, its survey of interpretive approaches both liberal and evangelical, its succinct summary of each book's content and theology, and of their relevance to the New Testament, *The World and the Word* should become a standard textbook at many evangelical colleges and seminaries, as well as a welcome resource for lay persons interested in the Old Testament.

Edwin Yamauchi
Professor of History Emeritus, Miami Universitiy

Acknowledgments

As authors of a work as lengthy and laborious as this, we acknowledge that it could never have been accomplished without the tireless work and considerations of many others whose names do not otherwise appear in the volume. These include Bill Barrick, Professor of Old Testament, and Anna Kroll, Technical Service Librarian, of the Masters Seminary; Daniel Akin, Ken Keathley, and the Board of Southeastern Baptist Theological Seminary, whose generous sabbatical policy makes possible the time for such a project; and the faculty, administration, and students of Dallas Theological Seminary, whose encouragement and enthusiasm as both teachers and learners provided impetus to initiate the project and to bring it to its conclusion. These include especially Dr. Liling Hou and Jeffrey Niles, who prepared the hundreds of slides for the Power Point auxiliary. We also express thanks to our families who patiently endured our frequent neglect of them and to Ray Clendenen, Jim Baird, Dean Richardson, and the entire publishing staff of B&H who had a vision for this work and prioritized it in the midst of a hectic schedule of publications.

Eugene H. Merrill, Dallas Theological Seminary
Mark F. Rooker, Southeastern Baptist Theological Seminary
Michael A. Grisanti, The Masters Seminary

THE OLD TESTAMENT TIME LINE

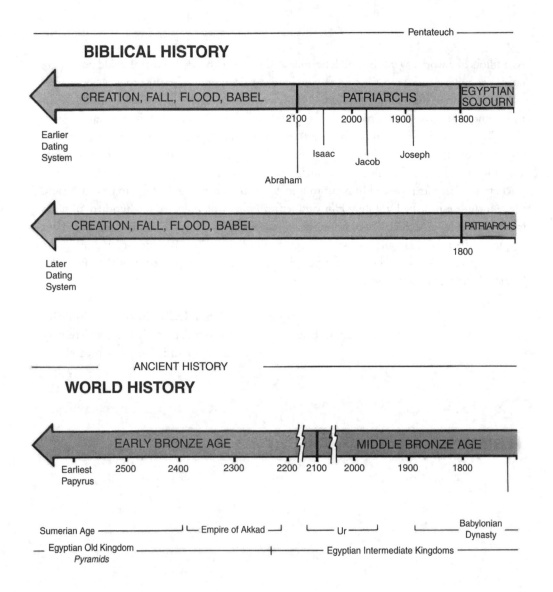

Pentateuch

BIBLICAL HISTORY

CREATION, FALL, FLOOD, BABEL | PATRIARCHS | EGYPTIAN SOJOURN

2100   2000   1900   1800

Earlier
Dating
System

Isaac
Jacob
Joseph

Abraham

CREATION, FALL, FLOOD, BABEL | PATRIARCHS

1800

Later
Dating
System

ANCIENT HISTORY

WORLD HISTORY

EARLY BRONZE AGE | MIDDLE BRONZE AGE

Earliest   2500   2400   2300   2200   2100   2000   1900   1800
Papyrus

Sumerian Age ————————⌐ ⌐— Empire of Akkad —⌐   ⌐— Ur —⌐   ⌐— Babylonian Dynasty

⌐ Egyptian Old Kingdom ———————————— Egyptian Intermediate Kingdoms ————
     Pyramids

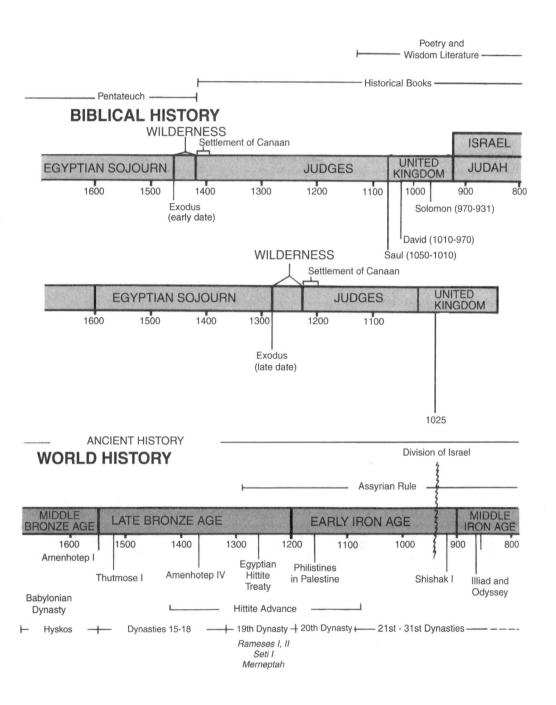

Poetry and
Wisdom Literature

Historical Books

Pentateuch

BIBLICAL HISTORY

WILDERNESS
Settlement of Canaan

ISRAEL

| EGYPTIAN SOJOURN | JUDGES | UNITED KINGDOM | JUDAH |

1600   1500   1400   1300   1200   1100   1000   900   800

Exodus
(early date)

Solomon (970-931)

David (1010-970)

Saul (1050-1010)

WILDERNESS
Settlement of Canaan

| EGYPTIAN SOJOURN | JUDGES | UNITED KINGDOM |

1600   1500   1400   1300   1200   1100

Exodus
(late date)

1025

ANCIENT HISTORY

WORLD HISTORY

Division of Israel

Assyrian Rule

| MIDDLE BRONZE AGE | LATE BRONZE AGE | EARLY IRON AGE | MIDDLE IRON AGE |

1600   1500   1400   1300   1200   1100   1000   900   800

Amenhotep I

Thutmose I   Amenhotep IV   Egyptian   Philistines   Shishak I   Illiad and
                                Hittite   in Palestine   Odyssey
                                Treaty

Babylonian
Dynasty

Hittite Advance

Hyskos   Dynasties 15-18   19th Dynasty   20th Dynasty   21st - 31st Dynasties

Rameses I, II
Seti I
Merneptah

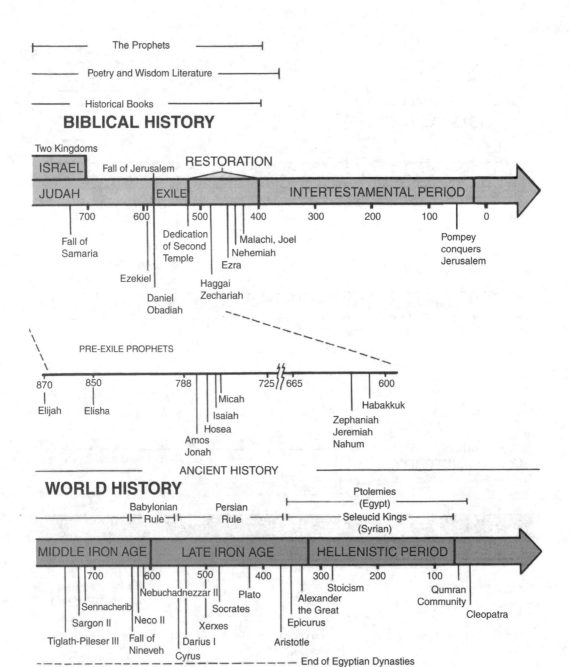

The Prophets

Poetry and Wisdom Literature

Historical Books

BIBLICAL HISTORY

Two Kingdoms

ISRAEL

Fall of Jerusalem

RESTORATION

JUDAH | EXILE | INTERTESTAMENTAL PERIOD

700 | 600 | 500 | 400 | 300 | 200 | 100 | 0

Fall of Samaria

Dedication of Second Temple

Malachi, Joel

Nehemiah

Ezra

Pompey conquers Jerusalem

Ezekiel

Daniel Obadiah

Haggai Zechariah

PRE-EXILE PROPHETS

870 | 850 | 788 | 725 | 665 | 600

Elijah | Elisha

Micah

Isaiah

Hosea

Amos Jonah

Habakkuk

Zephaniah Jeremiah Nahum

ANCIENT HISTORY

WORLD HISTORY

Babylonian Rule

Persian Rule

Ptolemies (Egypt)

Seleucid Kings (Syrian)

MIDDLE IRON AGE | LATE IRON AGE | HELLENISTIC PERIOD

700 | 600 | 500 | 400 | 300 | 200 | 100

Nebuchadnezzar II

Plato

Stoicism

Qumran Community

Sennacherib

Socrates

Alexander the Great

Sargon II

Neco II

Xerxes

Epicurus

Cleopatra

Tiglath-Pileser III

Fall of Nineveh

Darius I

Aristotle

Cyrus

End of Egyptian Dynasties

Chapter 1

INTRODUCTION

Eugene H. Merrill

A DEFINITION OF TERMS

The curricula of nearly all seminaries and graduate schools of religion include courses in subjects called "Old Testament Introduction" (or "Criticism"), "New Testament Introduction" (or "Criticism"), and the like, but few beginning students understand the various nuances of these terms. Usually the assumption is that "introduction" refers to a preliminary study of Bible content and "criticism" refers to an assessment of the nature of the Bible, one that is commonly negative if not destructive. However, as used in biblical scholarship the words "introduction" and "criticism" have meanings quite different from these or at least more refined. Though used interchangeably by some practitioners—and with some justification—the terms should nevertheless not be construed as synonyms but rather as symbols suggesting different emphases. It will be helpful to look at definitions of each as revealed by both etymology and long-standing usage.

"Introduction" may be defined as "a part of a book or treatise preliminary to the main portion" or (and more relevant to our subject) "a preliminary treatise or course of study."[1] That is, an introduction to the Bible is composed as a work preliminary to the study of the Bible itself. According to its Latin etymology (*introducere*), its purpose is "to lead (*ducere*) into (*intro*)," that is, to conduct the student from a position outside the Bible to one inside it. The desired end is that the reader, having been introduced to the Bible, will feel at home with it and come to be on friendly terms with it.

The focus of an "introduction" is thus on familiarity and understanding and not so much on evaluation. The latter is properly the province of criticism, "the art of evaluating or analyzing works of art or literature."[2] A less prejudicial definition, one more in line with traditional use in biblical scholarship as a virtual synonym of "introduction," is "the scientific investigation of literary documents (as the Bible) in regard to such matters as origin, text, composition, or history."[3]

---

[1] *Webster's Eleventh New Collegiate Dictionary* (Springfield, MA: Merriam-Webster, 2004), 657.
[2] Ibid., 297.
[3] Ibid.

"Criticism" is therefore an inherently neutral term, but because of its association with more than 300 years of essentially negative assessment of the biblical writings it has become pejorative in conservative circles and will generally be avoided as a proper term for describing the subject matter of this book as a whole. Indeed, works on this subject, even outside conservative circles, are now universally described as "introductions."

Scholars differ in their opinions on the nature of what we are calling "introduction." The following few examples demonstrate the broad spectrum of understanding that attends the subject.

In a statement not intended to define introduction as an entire genre, Brevard S. Childs offers a succinct description of his own work as one that "seeks to describe the form and function of the Hebrew Bible in its role as sacred scripture for Israel."[4] S. R. Driver, explaining the significance of the title of his book—*An Introduction to the Literature of the Old Testament*—says that what he "conceived this to include was an account of the contents and structure of the several books, together with . . . an indication of their general character and aim."[5] Otto Eissfeldt suggests that whereas at one time "introduction" could consist of anything necessary or desirable for the understanding of the OT, by his time (1965) it had "limited itself to areas covered by these three questions: the origin of the individual books, the growth of the canon, and the history of the text." Of these the first "takes decidedly the largest place."[6]

Horace Hummel proposes that "introduction" "occupies somewhat of a *middle* position *between* Bible survey and exegesis."[7] He asserts that "misunderstanding at this point would be greatly lessened if we could revive the more technical term, 'isagogics'," a term that "concerns itself primarily with questions of date, authorship, occasion, and purpose of writing."[8] J. Alberto Soggin provides the following definition: "We may term that discipline Introduction to the OT, which sets out to present, where possible, the information needed to identify the authors of a text, its literary genre, the milieu from which it derives and so on, making it comprehensible against the background of the events and the problems which have shaped it."[9] In keeping with more modern trends, Walter Brueggemann defines introduction as "a study of the *literature* of the OT and a consideration of the *theological* claims it makes."[10] E. J. Young, a leading conservative scholar of a generation ago, defines introduction as "that science or discipline which treats of certain subjects that are preliminary to the study and interpretation of the contents of the Bible."[11] This last definition best squares with both the etymology of the English word and with the thrust of this present volume.

Though the term "criticism" is synonymous to some people with certain destructive approaches to the OT, and therefore is inappropriate as a synonym for "introduction," it cannot and must not be avoided as a legitimate and evangelically appropriate way of viewing various aspects of introduction. Each type of criticism must be judged on its own merits. Thus if classical "source" criticism is deemed invalid (for reasons to be discussed later), other criticisms such as form, redaction, rhetorical, and "new literary" will be seen as not only frequently tolerable but positively essential to a correct assessment of the purpose and message of the OT.

---

[4] B. S. Childs, *Introduction to the Old Testament as Scripture* (Philadelphia: Fortress, 1979), 16.

[5] S. R. Driver, *An Introduction to the Literature of the Old Testament* (1897; reprint, Cleveland: World, 1956), iii.

[6] O. Eissfeldt, *The Old Testament: An Introduction*, trans. Peter R. Ackroyd (New York: Harper & Row, 1965), 3.

[7] H. Hummel, *The Word Becoming Flesh* (St. Louis: Concordia, 1979), 11 (italics his).

[8] Ibid.

[9] J. A. Soggin, *Introduction to the Old Testament* (Philadelphia: Westminster, 1980), 5.

[10] W. Brueggemann, *An Introduction to the Old Testament* (Louisville: WJK, 2003), 3 (italics his).

[11] E. J. Young, *An Introduction to the Old Testament* (Grand Rapids: Eerdmans, 1958), 17.

Far from resisting the term "criticism," then, this introduction will attempt to show just how important a sound and "sacred" criticism is to the whole task of providing an introduction to the OT Scriptures.

THE SUBJECT MATTER OF OLD TESTAMENT INTRODUCTION

Many of the definitions of "introduction" in the preceding section include topics found in standard textbooks, such as biblical backgrounds; the setting, authorship, and dates of individual books; canon; text criticism; and so forth. Lately other kinds of literary analysis have come to the fore, ranging from classical literary criticism to rhetorical criticism to modern theories of social-scientific criticism, structuralism, narrative criticism, reader-response hermeneutics, and feminist and socioeconomic criticism.[12] Some practitioners of these new methods have come to the task with overarching ideological or theological schemes within or against which the biblical data are viewed. Brevard Childs, with his "canonical" criticism, is a notable case in point. Another (and much more idiosyncratic) approach is by Richard E. Friedman who, in his book *Who Wrote the Bible?*, answers the question by suggesting that it was Ezra in the final analysis, a solution he offers in order to explain the Bible as "a continuous story."[13] Generally speaking, not only the subject matter of an introduction but also the shape it takes and the way it interprets the biblical text will be dictated largely by the assumptions brought to the task by the scholars who undertake it. Thus the critic who views the OT as merely ancient Near East (ANE) religious literature will reach certain predictable conclusions about the nature of the material, whereas the proponent of a more traditional stance will see it in an altogether different light. Both may claim objectivity, but the same data read against different premises will inevitably result in different conclusions or even in what should or should not be included in a book on introduction. A glance at the tables of contents of books on the subject from across the confessional spectrum clearly supports this observation.

Despite the mixed situation just discussed, it is still customary to speak of a distinction between so-called "higher" criticism and "lower" criticism and between "general" introduction and "special" introduction. To deal with the latter first, the concern here is with the issues that affect the entire OT—canon, text, the variety of literary-critical approaches, etc.—as opposed to those that pertain to the individual books or collections of books—authorship, date, provenance, contents, and the like. At a practical level this time-honored way of addressing the subject is sound and, indeed, indispensable.

As for "higher" versus "lower" criticism, such loaded terminology might better be replaced by something like "literary" as opposed to "textual" criticism. On the other hand "higher" is helpful in distinguishing the relatively subjective enterprise of seeking to reconstruct processes of origination, transmission, redaction, and formation of biblical texts (on the basis of little or no objective evidence sometimes), and the comparatively scientific integration of manuscript and version data that can be seen and therefore can be more objectively analyzed and synthesized.

Moreover, "literary" also has fallen on hard times because of its association with early criticisms—now largely abandoned—such as the documentary hypothesis, which also was designated "literary criticism." Many scholars therefore opt for something other than "literary" as a descriptor, choosing instead the awkward "new literary criticism," the rather limited and/

---

[12] S. L. McKenzie and S. R. Haynes, ed., *To Each Its Own Meaning*, rev. ed. (Louisville: WJK, 1999).

[13] R. E. Friedman, *Who Wrote the Bible?* (New York: Summit, 1987), 242.

or misunderstood "rhetorical criticism," or, as in Childs's case again, "canonical criticism," a phrase that implies a particular agenda.

As a result of such a conundrum in terminology, the present work attempts to avoid misleading terms and, by default perhaps, to deal only with text criticism on the one hand and "everything else" on the other.

A RATIONALE FOR THE GENRE "INTRODUCTION TO THE OLD TESTAMENT"

Authors must always seek to justify their works. Throughout the centuries OT introductions have been produced to meet a host of real or perceived needs, some of which are patently obvious and self-commending and others more subtle. The present work incidentally addresses most of the traditional topics associated with the genre, but it also consciously attempts to meet three additional particular concerns: (1) the neglect of the OT in contemporary life, even in the life of the church; (2) the importance of the OT as a revelation of God with abiding relevance to the modern world; and (3) difficulties in or with the OT that frequently exacerbate these other two problems.

One need only review the curricula of most denominational publishers or regularly attend the preaching services of the average church to realize the dearth of teaching and preaching of the Old Testament. The omission is all the more astounding (and disturbing) given the fact that the Old Testament constitutes nearly 80 percent of the Bible. This lack is not redressed even by churches that claim to have a "high view" of the Bible and that confess the ongoing authority and relevance of the OT as Scripture. Any effort to retrieve the OT from the dustbin of benign neglect and rehabilitate it as the major part of the living revelation of God is well worth undertaking.

The neglect of the OT is obviously best remedied by recognizing its importance to modern life and faith. Even superficial familiarity with the New Testament yields the unmistakable conviction that the OT forms the platform and matrix from which sprang the life, ministry, and teachings of Jesus and the apostolic church. A perusal of Wilhelm Dittmar's *Vetus Testamentum in Novo* reveals the astounding permeation of the New Testament by Old Testament allusions and citations.[14] To fail to understand the very source of the New Testament witness is to throw into jeopardy sound theology and practice. In a more practical sense, perhaps, one can argue that the worldview of the NT can only poorly be understood if the OT womb in which it was nurtured and which gave it birth should itself be undercut or ignored as irrelevant. A purpose of this book is to underscore the importance of the OT to NT faith and witness.

Without doubt, one of the major reasons for jettisoning the OT in the modern world and church is its perceived difficulty. It is, after all, a collection of writings in an ancient Semitic language, spanning a period of a millennium, and addressing and describing a world distant in geography as well as in time. In a day when most persons are loath to be conversant with events even in their own familiar communities, how, it may be asked, can they be expected to fathom such a foreign and (to many of them) irrelevant literature of a bygone day?

The question has validity to the extent that the cultural, linguistic, and chronological chasm between the BC world of the ANE and the AD world of the modern reader remains unbridged, at least to his or her satisfaction. It is therefore necessary to make attempt after attempt to link these worlds in fresh, effective, and even enjoyable ways. That has never been done perfectly

---

[14] W. Dittmar, *Vetus Testamentum in Novo* (Göttingen: Vandenhoeck & Ruprecht, 1903).

(nor will it be here), but the approach to be followed will, we trust, contribute to that goal in ways not undertaken in precisely this way before.

A HISTORY OF OLD TESTAMENT INTRODUCTIONS

The first work that set out consciously to address the concerns of what is now known as "biblical introduction" and to do so with that term in its title is apparently J. D. Michaelis's *Einleitung in die göttlichen Schriften des Neuen Bundes* (*Introduction to the Sacred Literature of the New Testament*), published in 1750. This *Einleitung* ("Introduction"), as the title suggests, was devoted to the New Testament alone. It was not until 1783 that a comparable study was done on the Old Testament, this by the eminent German scholar J. G. Eichhorn (*Einleitung in das Altes Testament*). Since then hundreds of books bearing similar titles have been published.

However, attention to matters pertinent to introduction is apparent as early as OT times, a fact clear from the frequent references in the Bible itself to questions of authorship, setting, occasion, and the like. The book of Deuteronomy, for example, opens with introductory information such as authorship (Moses), recipients ("all Israel"), setting ("across the Jordan"), date ("the fortieth year [after the exodus]"), and even occasion (after Yahweh had smitten Israel's enemies) (Deut 1:1–5). The titles of many of the psalms provide similar information, clearly in an attempt to apprise the reader of introductory matters (see, e.g., Psalms 3, 7, 18, 34, 51, 52, 54). As a third example the prophet Ezekiel was particularly careful to speak of circumstances surrounding the composition of his writings. He identified himself by lineage and profession, dated the commencement of his ministry (1:1) and other highlights (8:1; 20:1; 24:1; 26:1, etc.), described the geographical and political setting of his activity (1:1,3), and related the facts of his call by God (1:3).

While these examples may appear at first glance to be only incidental to the writings of which they are a part, they in fact meet the definitions of biblical introduction by revealing information about ancient texts impossible for later generations to recover with absolute reliability. In other words they provide comments about the external nature of the composition rather than interpretations of the contents of the composition. Such information must be supplied either by the author, compiler, or editor of texts or by persons not greatly removed from the time of their creation. The further removed the "introducer," the less reliable the information he imparts. Unfortunately much modern criticism has failed to understand this principle and has arrogantly presumed a knowledge of such matters greatly superior to that of the authors or compilers of the texts themselves.

Attention to introductory concerns did not end with the canonization of the biblical writings. To the contrary, once these writings were recognized as canonical by virtue of their supernatural origin and quality it seemed all the more necessary to understand as much as possible about them in order to safeguard the traditions about their production and to gain greater insight as to their meaning and continuing authority and relevance. The result was a prodigious production of oral and written commentary on all facets of these sacred books, works that find expression in the Talmud (see *Baba Bathra* 14a–15b) and other early Jewish writings. The church, too, was aware of the need to authenticate and clarify its New Testament canonical traditions and thus apostolic and postapostolic treatises began to emerge that dealt with all kinds of introductory matters.[15]

---

[15] M. S. Enslin, *The Literature of the Christian Movement* (New York: Harper & Brothers, 1956), 455–74.

In unbroken succession works on introduction continued to appear but generally as isolated and brief comments on various aspects of the subject.[16] Occasionally they took more organized and comprehensive form such as the fifth-century document by Adrianus, *Eisagōgē eis tas theias graphas* (*Introduction to the Divine Scriptures*). It was the term *eisagōgē* that gave rise to the German *Einleitung* and English "Introduction." The Middle Ages witnessed works on introduction by rabbis and other Jewish scholars such as Ibn Ezra, Kimchi, Rashi, and Maimonides; and by Christians including Isidorus Hispalensis and Nicholas de Lyra. For the most part these were not systematic in their approach and reflected the peculiar dogmatic, theological presuppositions of their particular traditions.

The Reformation and early post-Reformation era saw increasing interest in the Bible as a literary corpus as well as holy Scripture. Luther, though largely consumed by his interests in exegesis and theology, did offer his opinion on matters of introduction. Calvin did also, but even more so. More critical investigation of such things occupied the labors of Philip Melanchthon, Andrea Carlstadt, Martin Bucer, and Petro Vermigli. However, even these men worked within the framework of a strong confessional orthodoxy.

With the Enlightenment of the seventeenth century came a more adversarial criticism, one that challenged the traditional authority of the church and the Bible and that felt free, in the spirit of scientific inquiry, to arrive at conclusions based on rational, empirical evidence alone. This obviously impacted the subject of introduction, resulting in both radically new ways of interpreting the data of Scripture and efforts at categorizing and systematizing the issues involved. Among the proponents of "enlightened" criticism, none was more influential than the Jewish-Christian philosopher Baruch (Benedict) Spinoza. Spinoza never wrote an introduction in the proper sense of that term but the assumptions and methodology evidenced in his most relevant work on the subject—*Tractatus Theologico-Politicus* (1670)—set the tone for a flood of works by other scholars that soon followed. Spinoza's impact will receive full attention in chap. 8, but for now it is important to note that his work was permeated by a spirit of skepticism and rationalism that refused to trust the orthodox tradition based, as it was, on a platform of supernaturalism. The line was thus drawn in the sand between those who continued to view Introduction as a descriptive topic and those who now saw it as a reassessment and correction of traditional understandings.

We have already noted that the first of the new genre to bear the title "Introduction" was the German work by J. D. Michaelis. But it was Johann Eichhorn who fully incorporated the new criticism into an introduction, building on the labors of critics such as R. P. Richard Simon (1685), Johann Semler (1771–76), and Johann von Herder (1774–76). Eichhorn pioneered the way in which introductions from his day to the present have been arranged and the topics they have covered—general and special introduction, text criticism, literary criticism, canon, and so forth. His intellectual and critical heirs have included such luminaries as Wilhelm De Wette, Heinrich Ewald, Julius Wellhausen, W. Robertson Smith, S. R. Driver, Hermann Gunkel, Sigmund Mowinckel, Robert Pfeiffer, Artur Weiser, Otto Eissfeldt, Otto Kaiser, Rolf Rendtorff, and Alberto O. Soggin. Not all of these have authored full-fledged introductions to the OT, but they (and others too numerous to include here) have contributed to the genre from what might loosely be called the "critical" perspective.

---

[16] For helpful surveys see C. Cornill, *Introduction to the Canonical Books of the Old Testament*, trans. G. H. Box (London: Williams and Norgate, 1907), 3–11; R. K. Harrison, *Introduction to the Old Testament* (Grand Rapids: Eerdmans, 1969), 3–18.

Conservative or traditional efforts have not been lacking either. As far back as the day of Eichhorn, a reaction to his method appeared in the work of J. Jahn (1802). This was followed by the contributions of Hengstenberg who, though never having written an introduction proper, stimulated other scholars who did, such as Heinrich Hävernick, C. F. Keil, and Moses Stuart. Major twentieth-century conservative introductions reflect the labors of W. H. Green, R. D. Wilson, E. J. Young, R. K. Harrison, Gleason Archer, Tremper Longman, and Raymond Dillard. Now, as in the past, the difference between these works and those of a more "critical" stance is fundamentally at the level of assumptions about the nature of the Bible itself. Is it or is it not a divinely revealed and supernaturally preserved Word of God, a word that not only contains a saving message but is a saving message as a whole and in all of its parts?

THE APPROACH OF THE PRESENT WORK

A publication must justify its existence, this present effort being no exception. Many quality works on OT introduction have appeared in the last few decades, most of which have been referred to above. Why then should still another be undertaken? What must be the features of such a volume that will set it off from the rest and thereby commend itself to its intended readership?

As longtime teachers of the subject of OT introduction, the authors have discovered that the data relevant to the field and the interpretations of the data are often confused, even by scholars. Beginning students therefore find it almost impossible to distinguish between the two. Thus the approach undertaken here will first lay out clearly the relevant verifiable data (both biblical and extrabiblical) for each topic (i.e., each chapter or major section within a chapter), and then move to the various interpretations of these data. These will include dominant views within biblical scholarship as a whole but will focus primarily on our own evaluation and interpretation of the evidence. The net result will be an unfolding of the pertinent information coupled with constant and (hopefully) consistent interpretation consonant with a strongly evangelical view of the OT as the Word of God. This has been neglected by most textbooks in this field.

Another unique aspect of this book has been a concerted effort to draw theological issues into the open as they naturally present themselves. This has been undertaken at every stage and in every part in such a way as to highlight the theological value of the OT—which, after all, is its highest value—without falling victim to sensational popularizing or trite applications. In this way the reader will be able to connect serious academic study of the OT with an integrative theology that can profoundly shape the way he or she thinks about God's revelation and then acts on it.

With this set of preliminary observations in mind, it will be helpful to look briefly at the overall plan and pattern that fleshes out the approach just suggested. Of seven sections, the first three fall loosely under the rubric "general introduction"; that is, they deal with issues that relate to the Old Testament as a whole. The first section—The World of the Old Testament—is fundamental to all that follows, for it is obvious that one cannot hope to understand the Hebrew Scriptures properly without viewing them against the geographical, historical, and cultural context in which they originated. These elements therefore must be addressed and with attention to the latest findings of the best contemporary scholarship.

Part 2 focuses on the text of the OT. This includes such aspects as the composition of its various books and sections, its canonicity, and the transmission and textual criticism of the writings that eventually emerged as the Hebrew Bible. The OT not only originated in the environment of the ANE, but it has its own history as a collection of texts, a history that frequently is convoluted and, indeed even opaque, and which in any case poses problems much more serious than might occur to the casual reader. When and under what conditions did the inspired message come to the prophets? How did they record what they received? Did they do so at all or to any extent or were they merely sources of truth whose teachings were transmitted to others who wrote, collected, or redacted them into their canonical form? How were these writings identified as Holy Scripture as opposed to the plethora of other writings that made up ancient Israel's literary legacy? In other words what were the principles and procedures the community of faith followed in determining the content and extent of the literature that by consensus would be sanctioned as "the Bible"? Moreover, once these writings were complete, how were they transmitted to later generations and to what degree were they preserved from error in copying? With the dispersion of the Jewish people to distant lands at the end of the Old Testament era and later, how could they retain their sacred writings, especially when the need rose for them to be translated into the various languages of the dispersion?

The problems of text transmission and translation give rise to the need by the contemporary student of Scripture to recover the original reading of the OT if at all possible. The original manuscripts have long since disappeared and are reflected now only by imperfect copies far removed from the earliest Hebrew text or the ancient versions. If the word delivered to the prophets was inspired and inerrant, what may be said of the word that comes to us today through the filter of centuries of transmission? In what sense is it still authentic and to what extent does it reflect that form that issued from the inspired writer himself? The science of textual criticism addresses these and many similar concerns and therefore is an indispensable subject of Old Testament introduction.

Part 3 deals with the various approaches to the study of the OT from the earliest times until today. This is predicated on the history of speculative thought in general, beginning with ancient Near Eastern myth and continuing to philosophy, rationalism, empiricism, existentialism, and finally to the hermeneutics of meaning in modern linguistic philosophy. It is important to see how all of these have affected current understandings of the Bible. Even more important is the Bible's own inner witness to itself as a phenomenon and a conveyor of truth. What does the OT say about itself, and what is added to that self-understanding by postbiblical Jewish literature as well as the NT and beyond? This section, in other words, will seek to provide a brief history of exegesis and hermeneutics.

Special attention is devoted to developments in the past 300 years, that is, since the rise of the so-called "higher critical method." This present chapter has provided a brief summary of the production of works on OT introduction, but it is important that the currents that generated this new method be thoroughly examined. Without this background it is impossible to understand the issues that dominate contemporary OT scholarship.

Post-Renaissance freedom from dogmatic presuppositions paved the way to new avenues of looking at the Judeo-Christian tradition, particularly that pertaining to the nature and authority of the Bible. For the first time it seemed possible to step back from an externally imposed bibliology to one that could inductively and objectively be derived on the basis of reason—that is, what could or could not be believed rather than what should or should not be believed. This opened the Bible to new methods of literary analysis, methods appropriate to the study of any ancient texts, and also to new ways of viewing history.

The new rationalism led to a rejection of traditional views of the authorship, dates, and settings of the OT writings and, indeed, to a repudiation of the idea that they were supernaturally revealed and inspired. To some, the Bible is just another book despite its own extravagant claims and the claims of those who promoted it as holy Scripture. The new way of viewing history stemmed primarily from the historiosophy of G. F. W. Hegel and was profoundly shaped by evolutionary developmentalism that posited a process of religious refinement diametrically opposed to the witness of the OT. The combination of alleged late sources and their rearrangement according to evolutionary patternism resulted in the present state of the discipline of OT studies.

Part 3 thus deals with both the process by which the present state of affairs came to pass and a discussion of what that means for contemporary study, particularly by evangelicals. That discussion includes a description of the contours of the present field of the scholarly study of the OT, especially as expressed in such forms as canonical and new literary criticism. With this it is imperative that a legitimate evangelical posture be presented, one that embodies a reverent but well-established approach to the biblical text and its study.

Parts 4 through 7 address so-called "special introduction," that is, a study of introductory matters relative to each of the OT books. There are different ways of approaching this material depending on the canonical order one chooses to follow. The Hebrew arrangement, for example, consists of three major parts—the Law, the Prophets, and the Writings—and presents a different sequence of the books from that familiar to most readers of the English Bible. The Hebrew canonical tradition will receive full attention at the appropriate place, but it seems best for students of modern Protestant translations to work from the shape most well known to them. Thus Part 4 will address the books of the Pentateuch, Part 5 the historical books, Part 6 those of prophecy, and Part 7 the poetic books. The books of prophecy embrace both the so-called major and minor prophets, and the poetic books include the wisdom literature.

In addition to presenting such standard information as the authorship, date, setting, unity, and integrity of the individual OT books, each of these sections contains at least a brief introduction to the literary features of the respective genres included within them. Thus introduction to the Pentateuch requires some attention to its unity of composition; to matters such as myth, saga, legend, and legal texts; and to covenant form and meaning. Study of the historical books necessitates a look at historiography, chronological and other sequential relationships among the books, and a consideration of features such as the OT "synoptic problem" (that is, Israel's history as presented by Samuel and Kings as opposed to the account of Chronicles) and the theological or ideological "slant" of the various historical accounts.

The works of the prophets are rich in literary variety and their messages to a great extent find meaning only as the characteristics of their literary forms are understood. At least brief analysis of such characteristics is provided for in Part 6 as well as some introductory comments on prophetism as an Israelite institution and prophecy as proclamation and/or prediction. Finally, the rich and rewarding insights of form- and genre-critical method receive attention in the approach to the Psalms and the wisdom literature. Moreover, the development of this kind of literature within the context of the ANE world also deserves consideration. How was Israel's poetic and wisdom tradition akin to that of her neighbors and how was it different? What role did the Psalms and wisdom literature play with respect to Israel's own political, cultural, and religious institutions? These and other similar matters must receive at least passing attention.

THE OLD TESTAMENT AND THE CHRISTIAN

The very neglect and ignorance of the OT by great numbers of Christians might suggest that that part of the Bible is unimportant or irrelevant to the modern believer. Besides being illogical (because based on the wrong premise), such a conclusion is injurious to Christian faith and life for it dismisses 80 percent of God's revelation from consideration, a revelation whose timeliness and efficacy cannot be challenged on any biblical, theological, cultural, historical, or practical grounds. We suggest three areas illustrative of the abiding value of the OT to contemporary times.

First, the OT is a rich source of theology and doctrine that is presupposed by the NT and without which Christian theology would be seriously deficient. The prime example, perhaps, is theology proper, that is, the doctrine of God and His character and attributes. The New Testament indeed has much to say about God but primarily in His persons as Son and Spirit. But apart from a number of references to God as Father (Matt 5:16,45; 6:9; Mark 13:32; Luke 10:22; John 1:14; Acts 1:4; 1 Cor 8:6, etc.) and scattered allusions to His nature and works (Rom 1:19–28; 1 Cor 1:25; Gal 3:20; Phil 2:6, etc.), there is little to be learned there about those qualities that dominate the OT witness. If one is to penetrate the wonders and mysteries of theology proper, he must do so on the basis of the Hebrew Scriptures.

There God appears as Creator, Redeemer, and Covenant-Maker. He is the divine warrior who leads His heavenly and earthly hosts into battle, guaranteeing them inevitable success. He is the One who makes promises and, through His servants the prophets, predicts their fulfillment. He is portrayed as the absolutely holy One, the omnipotent, omniscient, and omnipresent One who never changes. He inspires awe and fear but also confidence, trust, and submission. He epitomizes love, grace, mercy, and loyalty, but also shows Himself to be the sovereign Lord and Judge to whom all the earth is accountable. To fail to know these things about God immeasurably impoverishes the body of Christian truth, and such would be the case were the OT not a part of the Judeo-Christian canon. Surely this alone is sufficient justification to encourage careful and reverent study of the Old Testament.

Second, mastery of the OT is crucial to an understanding of the New Testament. We have already suggested that the NT understanding of God is predicated on the prior revelation by God of His person and attributes as found in the Old Testament. Indeed, there is not a single teaching in the NT that is not presupposed or at least dimly preshadowed by the Old. All this is to say that the OT was the Bible of Jesus, the apostles, and the early church, and the writers of the Gospels and Epistles drew on it almost exclusively for the source of their authority. To them, what they taught and wrote was an extension and fulfillment of God's earlier Word. They therefore felt free to quote, cite, or otherwise allude to it, frequently without elaboration, for they assumed that their hearers and/or readers were already well versed in its teachings.

Sadly, many contemporary Christians believe that the NT is enough, that it has, in fact, superseded the OT and rendered it obsolete. It is ironic, to say the least, that the very Bible of Jesus, which He quoted and from which He preached, and, furthermore, which He never annulled, should be consigned to irrelevance by those who call themselves His disciples. When Jesus said He fulfilled the Scriptures, He did not mean that He had thereby evacuated them of their authority and canonicity. What He meant, in fact, was exactly the opposite—He had completed the message of the OT, making it part and parcel of the whole revelation of God. To paraphrase the familiar slogan, "The NT is in the Old concealed, and the OT is in the New revealed." To ignore either part is to truncate the revelation and reduce it to confusion.

Third, the OT offers, by teaching and example, practical principles of belief and behavior for contemporary times. The great stories of creation, the flood, and Babel; the intriguing and entertaining vignettes about the Hebrew patriarchs; the mighty acts of Yahweh in exodus deliverance and in the conquest of Canaan—all reveal a God and providential purpose that have much to do with people caught up in the perils and perplexities of a world not much different from that of OT times. Who He was and what He did then can be replicated in the lives of men and women of today.

Even the principles of ancient Israelite law can and must find application to the modern life situation. The Ten Commandments, particularly, were not time-bound expressions of the divine will for only Israel. Rather, they are reflective of the very essence of God Himself, eternal in their origination and unending in their truth and applicability. To violate them in any age is to go counter to the very fabric of righteousness inherent in God's own nature and concomitant with His own unchanging purposes.

Christians have long delighted in the Psalms and wisdom literature of the OT, for if anything in the Hebrew Scriptures seems fresh and practical it is that found in their poetic and aphoristic sentiments. No wonder many NTs are published with the book of Psalms. The reason for the popularity of this literature and for its immediate appearance of relevance is precisely because it is so existentially personal. Everyman and Everywoman can see themselves here. The struggles, tensions, joys, sorrows, praise, and laments of the psalmists are the stuff of everyday Christian life. How the psalmists confronted them and responded to them can model behavior for the modern reader. And when it seems that life has dead-ended and the believer despairs of knowing which way to turn, he can open the treasure chest of OT wisdom and find solutions to his dilemmas, or failing that, how to live successfully in spite of them.

Among other purposes, then, this book is designed to introduce the student to the Old Testament as a living Word of God, one whose serious and devout study will yield not only cognitive satisfaction but—and more important—entrée into the very heart and design of God who loves him and wishes to make him the special object of His grace.

Part 1

THE WORLD OF THE OLD
TESTAMENT

Michael A. Grisanti

THE GAP BETWEEN THE MODERN WORLD
AND THE OLD TESTAMENT WORLD

Average modern-day readers have relatively few difficulties understanding a book written in their own culture and time. They can generally relate to contemporary expressions, institutions, and ideologies. The OT represents a collection of "books" written over a period of 1,000 years (c. 1400 BC to 400 BC)[1] by many divinely appointed individuals.[2] These books are not intrinsically more difficult than modern books, but they seem out of place in the modern world. In addition, the OT records God's revelation to and through Israel during those centuries. However, this collection of divinely authoritative writings was not produced in a vacuum. It came into existence in certain times and places, was composed against the backdrop of a unique culture, and was written to real people facing significant issues in that setting.

The fact that the OT was given by God through chosen spokesmen is an important assumption (or belief). Although it came into existence in the midst of circumstances quite different from the modern world, the OT is not *primarily* a product of Israel or the surrounding ANE milieu. The eternally significant and divinely authoritative message of the OT originated with God and was imparted to Israel in order to impact God's servant nation as well as the surrounding nations. So, the message of the OT does not depend *entirely* on the reader's understanding of the culture and history of the times in which these messages were given. An injustice is done to the Old Testament if one simply identifies institutions, practices, or ideologies in the ANE world that somehow parallel those found in the Bible and then proceeds to understand the biblical phenomena on the basis of those found in the ANE. The belief that God revealed the OT writings as divinely authoritative texts signifies that the meaning of the Old Testament will not always parallel practices, ideologies, and institutions in the ANE. Some statements, like

---

[1] For justification of the date of 400 BC, see chap. 20, p. 336.

[2] See Part 2, "The Text of the Old Testament" (pp. 73–121), for an overview of the development of the Old Testament.

theological affirmations of God's character, easily transcend cultural and historical boundaries. Understanding the character and activity of the God of the Bible cannot be mediated through the ideology of the ANE.

Yet, if the modern reader is to understand the message of the Old Testament correctly, he must learn as much as possible about the archaeology, culture, geography, history, languages, and ideology of the ancient Near East, especially of the land of Palestine. Imagine getting to know people in the modern world who come from a different country with a different history, language, and culture. What does it take to understand what they say and how they think? Attention must be paid to aspects of their world even though they are contemporaries. Much more is this the case when dealing with cultures predating modern times by 4,000 years or more. For example who were the Hittites, Jebusites, Philistines, and Amorites, to name only a few people groups? In what way did they interact with the covenant nation Israel? What did a journey from Ur of the Chaldees to the land of Canaan represent? How is it that the law of Moses provides regulations for slavery, as if that were something acceptable? Why was the prophet Isaiah so careful in providing the historical backdrop that paved the way for the Immanuel prophecy in Isa 7:14? What is the significance of boundary stones and moving them? What was daily living in the ancient world like?

The following represent some key differences between modern Western and ancient Near Eastern perspectives:[3]

Modern Western World	*Ancient Near Eastern World*
Promote independence	Promote interdependence
See the parts	See the whole
Urge uniqueness	Urge conformity
Private autonomy	Corporate solidarity
Strong personal identity	Strong familial identity

In light of these and other differences the student of the OT is obliged to learn as much as possible about the world of the OT.

THE VALUE OF UNDERSTANDING THE WORLD OF THE OLD TESTAMENT

Imagine the world of the OT as "their town" and the modern world as "our town."[4] A multitude of data related to the biblical text can cause distance between the modern reader and the time envisioned by an Old Testament book. An understanding of the life and times of the ancient world inevitably will therefore generate a better comprehension of the message of the OT. A sampling of this assertion follows.

Abraham and Sarah Selecting Hagar as a Surrogate Mother

Ten years after God promised Abraham that he would make Abraham the father of a nation, Abraham and Sarah were still childless (Genesis 16). Sarah's suggestion that Abraham should have sexual relations with Hagar, Sarah's handmaiden, in order to provide them with the long-desired heir shocks the average reader. In light of certain ancient Near Eastern law codes (from

---

[3] These are taken from J. Pilch, *Introducing the Cultural Context of the Old Testament* (Mahweh, NJ: Paulist, 1991), 97.

[4] See J. S. Duvall and J. D. Hays, *Grasping God's Word*, 2nd ed. (Grand Rapids: Zondervan, 2005), 19–24, for an overview of this analogy of "their town" and "our town" as the two ends of the interpretive process.

the third to the first millennia BC), families from various nations around Israel utilized the practice of surrogate motherhood to provide children for childless couples.[5]

Baalism in the Old Testament

The discovery of clay tablets from Ugarit, a city on the northeastern coast of the Mediterranean Sea, provides a clear glimpse of the Canaanite religion that Israel sometimes fought but more often assimilated.[6] After Ahab (and his wife Jezebel) began his reign over the northern kingdom and encouraged the worship of Baal, Elijah the prophet announced; "As the LORD God of Israel lives, I stand before Him, and there will be no dew or rain during these years except by my command!" (1 Kgs 17:1). Why did Elijah make this pronouncement and declare that God lives? Withholding rain would cause problems for any society, but Elijah's interaction with Ahab and Jezebel was an attack on Baalism. Why? Because as Ugaritic mythological literature demonstrates, Baal was regarded as the god who controlled storms, lightning, and rain, and hence he was the god of fertility.[7] One of Baal's enemies, Mot ("death"), eventually killed Baal. Later Baal returned to life and restored fertility on the earth. These enemies continued in a perpetual struggle, evidenced in the dry season (when Mot rules) and the rainy season (when Baal rules).[8] Thus, the regular occurrence of the rainy season demonstrated Baal's rule as the fertility god.

What did Elijah demonstrate about God by making this pronouncement? He clearly proved that He lives at all times and that He—not Baal—is the one who determines when the rain falls! Through the prophet, God directly challenged the authority of Baal. In 1 Kings 18, the contest between Elijah (and God) and the Baal prophets communicates a similar message. Baal, the god of fire (lightning) and storm, is unable to consume the sacrifice offered by his worshippers, even in light of their fervent coaxing. God left no doubt about who actually controls the elements by totally consuming the drenched sacrifice as soon as Elijah asked Him to respond. Being aware of the pagan backdrop of Israel's idolatry adds to a clear understanding of the passage.[9]

Supplemental Information about Israelite Kings

Ahab ruled over Israel, the northern kingdom, from 874 to 853 BC. During his reign he fought three times with Ben-hadad, the king of Syria, for control of the city of Ramoth-gilead. He died in the third of those battles (1 Kgs 22:29–40). Assyrian historical annals state that Ahab set aside his differences with Syria to participate in an important battle that took place at Qarqar (853 BC). In that battle he joined 11 other rulers in a battle against Shalmaneser III, the Assyrian king who wanted to extend his dominion to the western seaboard of the Mediterranean. In fact the Kurkh Monolith states that Ahab contributed 2,000 chariots and 10,000

---

[5] V. P. Hamilton, *The Book of Genesis: Chapters 1–17*, NICOT (Grand Rapids: Eerdmans, 1990), 444–45; G. J. Wenham, *Genesis 16-50*, WBC (Dallas: Word, 2002), 7

[6] For some helpful sources on Ugarit and the Old Testament see W. T. Pitard, "Voices from the Dust: The Tablets from Ugarit and the Bible," in *Mesopotamia and the Bible: Comparative Explorations*, ed. M. W. Chavalas and K. L. Younger Jr. (Grand Rapids: Baker, 2002), 251–75; P. C. Craigie, *Ugarit and the Old Testament* (Grand Rapids: Eerdmans, 1983); A. Curtis, *Ugarit*, Cities of the Biblical World (Cambridge, UK: Lutterworth, 1985).

[7] Pitard, "Voices from the Dust," 256; Craigie, *Ugarit and the Old Testament*, 61; Leah Bronner, *The Stories of Elijah and Elisha as Polemics against Baal Worship* (Leiden: Brill, 1968), 40–42.

[8] Pitard, "Voices from the Dust," 256–57; Bronner, *The Stories of Elijah and Elisha*, 36–37.

[9] For other points of comparison see Bronner, *The Stories of Elijah and Elisha*, 50–77; and G. E. Saint-Laurent, "Light from Ras Shamra on Elijah's Ordeal upon Mount Carmel," in *Scripture in Context: Essays on the Comparative Method*, ed. C. D. Evans, W. W. Hallo, and J. B. White (Pittsburgh: Pickwick, 1980), 123–39.

soldiers to the allied forces.[10] Although Shalmaneser claimed to have enjoyed a great victory, history demonstrates that he was not able to control this region until over a decade later. Apparently, soon after returning from this battle with Assyria, Ahab and Ben-hadad engaged once again in the battle for the control of Ramoth-gilead that resulted in Ahab's defeat and death. In light of what is told in 1 Kings about the length of Ahab's reign, one can conclude that this important battle (not recorded in Scripture) occurred in the last year of Ahab's reign. It provides a synchronism between Israelite chronology and Assyrian chronology.

Features of Daily Life in Israel

The OT makes numerous references to tools, weapons, customs, and musical instruments unfamiliar today. For example what did the prophet Amos mean when he accused his fellow Israelites of depriving "the poor of justice at the [city] gates" (5:12) and then challenged them to establish or promote "justice in the gate" (v. 15). Some have gates for their homes, but few think of gates to a city as a place for justice or injustice. However, in ancient Israel legal disputes were resolved at the city gate because this is where the town elders met. Most ancient cities had two or more rooms with benches along the walls just inside their gates.[11]

AN OVERVIEW OF PART 1: THE WORLD OF THE OLD TESTAMENT

The three chapters of this section introduce the reader to the world of the OT. Chapter 2 is an overview of the historical backdrop of the events of the OT. The rich account of God's dealings with His covenant nation did not take place in a vacuum. Although the biblical narrative focuses on God's interaction with the nation Israel, His ultimate concern is for the world as a whole. The events of the OT regularly interact with or need to be understood in relation to the ebb and flow of the history of the ancient Near Eastern world. Chapter 2 considers the flow of history from the third millennium until around 400 BC, giving attention to events and developments in Mesopotamia, Egypt, Syria-Palestine, and Israel. After surveying the geographical features of the land of Palestine, chap. 3 summarizes key archaeological discoveries and their contribution to Old Testament studies. It concludes by considering the development of writing and religion in the ancient Near East.

---

[10] K. L. Younger Jr., "Kurkh Monolith (2.113A)," in *The Context of Scripture*, ed. W. W. Hallo and K. L. Younger Jr. (Leiden: Brill, 2000), 2:263.

[11] P. J. King and L. E. Stager, *Life in Biblical Israel* (Louisville: WJK, 2001), 234–36; V. H. Matthews and D. C. Benjamin, *Social World of Ancient Israel: 1250–587 BCE* (Peabody, MA: Hendrickson, 1993), 122–24.

THE HISTORICAL SETTING OF THE OLD TESTAMENT

EUGENE H. MERRILL

ONE OF THE most distinctive features of the Judeo-Christian faith—and one noted by virtually all students of comparative religion—is its orientation to history.[1] The religion of the Bible cannot be reduced to an abstraction of principles or a collection of doctrinal tenets alone; rather, it is rooted and grounded in space and time, deriving much of its meaning from its environmental contexts. "But when the completion of the time came," Paul wrote, "God sent His Son, born of a woman, born under the law, to redeem those under the law" (Gal 4:4–5). The incarnation of Jesus Christ thus took place at a predetermined point in human history, a paradigm typical of all the mighty acts of God who works out His creating and saving purposes against the backdrop of places and events.

Understanding those purposes therefore demands attention to the world that lies behind them, a world in the case of the Old Testament that is commonly called the ancient Near East. This rather arbitrary term refers to an area from the Caspian Sea in the northeast to the Persian Gulf in the southeast and from northern and central Egypt in the southwest to Anatolia (north-central Turkey) in the northwest. Altogether this region covers approximately 1.5 million square miles (including water), an area half the size of the continental United States. On this limited stage virtually the entire drama of OT history was played out.

Even more arbitrary is the selection of chronological parameters within which to recount the OT story. This is primarily a problem for the beginning point because the completion of the latest of the OT writings no later than 400 BC provides a suitable *terminus ad quem*.[2] The Bible's own story commences with creation, an event impossible to date with precision because

---

[1] E. Breisach "Historiography," in *The Encyclopedia of Religion*, ed. Mircea Eliade (New York: Macmillan, 1987), 6:374–75; R. G. Collingwood, *The Idea of History* (Oxford: Clarendon, 1946), 17, 48–49.

[2] For justification of this date see chap. 20, p. 336.

of the absence of indisputable biblical, archaeological, and historical benchmarks.[3] The brief and oblique remarks about the world of prepatriarchal times (before 2000 BC) prove historically reliable when testable, but the biblical record makes no attempt to provide a sustained account of human history on even a limited scale. It is necessary, therefore, to turn to extrabiblical sources to secure the data with which to attempt a comprehensive reconstruction.

Scholars commonly refer to ancient eras by terms such as Paleolithic, Mesolithic, Neolithic, and Chalcolithic, thus describing preliterary times known exclusively through archaeological, anthropological, and other nonliterary evidences. Using such means, they posit the rise of primitive urbanism in the ancient Near East as early as 7000 BC in such sites as Jericho, Jarmo, Hassuna, Tepe Siyalk, Çatal Hüyük, and others.[4] While the dates and cultures of these sites may be accepted with caution, they cannot properly contribute to an understanding of intellectual, conceptual history in the absence of texts, that is, of written documentation. To try to understand the Old Testament against the inconclusive evidence yielded by nonliterary sources is clearly unproductive.

This limitation demands that we begin our account with the beginning of Sumerian written records at approximately 3100 BC. Such dates precede Abraham by a millennium, but that millennium is so crucial to providing the patriarchal setting that at least brief attention must be paid to it. The time frame within which the OT narrative occurs is thus from 3000 to 400 BC. The following survey sketches the historical and cultural context within which the story of Israel and her ancestors takes place, and it attempts to relate that story to its background in ways that show the significance of an understanding of that world to an adequate interpretation of the Old Testament message.

THE WORLD OF THE THIRD MILLENNIUM

Mesopotamia

The earliest texts so far known derive from Uruk, a site in lower Mesopotamia known today as Warka and in the Old Testament as Erech (Gen 10:10). The language of these documents is largely Sumerian, which suggests that the peoples of Uruk and elsewhere in that region were Sumerians.[5] Their ultimate origins are shrouded in mystery; but these non-Semitic dwellers of the marshlands were clearly endowed with cultural, technical, and political skills that enabled them to create a high urban civilization that flourished in what is now southern Iraq and Kuwait from 3200 (or earlier) to 2360 BC and then again from 2100 to 1800 BC.[6]

The contributions of the Sumerians included city-state forms of government reflecting a primitive democracy; a highly advanced, if cumbersome, script, language, and literature; a complex religious and theological worldview; and arts and crafts that were seldom if ever excelled by later Mesopotamian civilizations. Particularly striking were their mythic and epic traditions that at least superficially resemble those of later OT times, especially their tales of creation, the deluge, and the like. In addition to Uruk, the Sumerians erected city-states at

---

[3] For some of the complex issues involved see K. A. Kitchen, *On the Reliability of the Old Testament* (Grand Rapids: Eerdmans, 2003), 421–27.

[4] A. Falkenstein, "The Prehistory and Protohistory of Western Asia," in *The Near East: The Early Civilizations*, ed. J. Bottéro, E. Cassin, and J. Vercoutter (New York: Delacorte, 1967), 1–51; R. W. Ehrich, ed., *Chronologies in Old World Archaeology* (Chicago: University of Chicago Press, 1954).

[5] A. Falkenstein, *Archaische Texte aus Uruk* (Berlin: Ausgrabungen der Deutschen Forschunggemeinschaft im Uruk-Warka 2, No. 111), 1936.

[6] See S. N. Kramer, *The Sumerians: Their History, Culture, and Character* (Chicago: University of Chicago Press, 1963); D. Schmandt-Besserat and S. M. Alexander, *The First Civilization: The Legacy of Sumer* (Austin: University of Texas Press, 1975).

other famous sites such as Nippur, Eridu, Lagash, Kish, and, most notably, Ur, the birthplace of the patriarch Abraham. Excavations of these and other Sumerian cities have yielded evidence of an amazingly sophisticated manner of life.

However, lower Mesopotamian culture was not exclusively Sumerian, for as early as 2800 BC other ethnic elements began to infiltrate, especially from the Upper Euphrates region to the northwest. These groups, known popularly and collectively to the Sumerians as Martu ("Westerners") are called in their own Semitic language Amurru (OT "Amorite"). The fact that Abraham bore an Amorite name suggests that he descended from these Semitic elements that must have arrived in Lower Mesopotamia several centuries before his time. Sumerian culture was thus more accurately a blending of Sumerian and Semitic.

Sumerian political domination of Mesopotamia began to erode with the rise of a Semitic (Amorite?) power base at Agade (or Akkad), a place in central Mesopotamia not yet identified. The leader of this movement, which resulted in the Akkadian Empire, was Sargon the Great (2360–2305), celebrated in legend and history as the world's first imperialist.[7] His sons and grandson succeeded him in a dynasty that controlled most of the central and southern river basins for 125 years. Based on the earlier and contemporary Sumerian models of statecraft and ideology, Sargon carved out a far-flung sphere of influence that penetrated as far west and northwest as present-day central Turkey. More important, he exposed surrounding peoples to the rich Sumerian legacy of arts and literature that would shape their respective civilizations for centuries.

Table 1: Rulers of the Akkadian Dynasty

Sargon (2360–2305)
Rimush (2304–2296)
Manishtusu (2295–2281)
Naram-Sin (2280–2244)
Sharkalisharri (2243–2219)

Eventually Akkadian dominance collapsed under the blows of barbarous mountain people from the east known as the Guti. For a century or more they prevailed over the southern half of Mesopotamia until they too were supplanted by a revival of Sumerian fortunes known to historians as the Neo-Sumerian (or Ur III) period. In many respects the crowning glory of Sumerian culture, the city states of this era (c. 2100–1900 BC), including Kish, Larsa, Umma, Lagash, and Ur, produced a literary and artistic heritage that remained for 2,000 years the model emulated by successive Mesopotamian (and even more-distant) civilizations. Law codes, mythic and epic texts, hymns and prayers, omen and other "scientific" literature—all reached a level of finesse and abundance seldom equaled thereafter. Of significance to OT history, this was the period of Abraham; from the urbanity of Ur he responded to the call of Yahweh and moved out to a land yet unknown to him.

Egypt

Canaan, the land to which Abraham eventually came, was en route to Egypt, the only other great political and cultural entity of the third millennium. Like Mesopotamia, its origins are shrouded in the mists of antiquity, and also like Mesopotamia Egypt's documentable history

---

[7] B. Lewis, *The Sargon Legend* (Cambridge, MA: American Schools of Oriental Research, 1980).

began to emerge only with the stumbling steps of crude pictographic writing at about 3000 BC.[8] At that time Egypt consisted of a string of villages and small city-states strung out for 500 miles along the Nile valley and even then divided between Lower Egypt (or Delta Egypt) in the north and Upper Egypt in the south (see map 1). Unification of these scattered sites and of the whole nation occurred around 3000 BC in connection with what Manetho, an early Egyptian historian, described as Dynasty 1.

Table 2: The Major Eras of Egyptian History

Protodynastic	Dynasties 1-2 (c. 3100–2700)
Old Kingdom	Dynasties 3-5 (c. 2700–2350)
First Intermediate	Dynasties 6-11 (c. 2350–2000)
Middle Kingdom	Dynasty 12 (c. 2000–1750)
Second Intermediate	Dynasties 13-17 (c. 1750–1570)
New Kingdom	Dynasties 18-20 (c. 1570–1100)
Third Intermediate	Dynasties 21-26 (c. 1100–650)
Assyrian-Hellenistic	Dynasties 27-31 (c. 650–330)

This dynasty, the first of some 30 to follow, was founded by Menes (or Narmer), a ruler of the south. His successors and the rulers of Dynasty 2 comprise the so-called Protodynastic period about which very little is known. There then burst on the scene the brilliant Old Kingdom era which consisted of Dynasties 3–8 and lasted from about 2700 to 2200. This was the age of the pyramids and other colossal achievements, especially in building. Literary and graphic arts were not much behind. The contributions of the Old Kingdom period became integral to all successive Egyptian life and were fondly recalled by later romantics.

Sphinx at Giza with Pyramid of Khafre in the background.

Because of internal strife and disintegration the blaze of glory began to fade, and the next two centuries of Egypt's life (2200–2000) reflected the decline labeled "The First Intermediate Period." This interval, consisting of Dynasties 6–11, was preoccupied not only by domestic unrest but also by the beginnings of foreign inroads, especially by peoples popularly known as "Asiatics." Much of the royal literature of the time consists of warnings by prophets and sages about the uncivilized barbarians from the northeast who, while welcome as trading partners, had the potential of corrupting the pure and superior Egyptian way of life.[9] The biblical chronology locates Abraham in Egypt during this period, probably in Dynasty 10, so the story of his ambivalent reception by the pharaoh takes on new light in view of the times (Gen 12:10–20).

---

[8] B. J. Kemp, *Ancient Egypt: Anatomy of a Civilization* (London: Routledge, 1989).

[9] For inscriptions reflecting these concerns, see Miriam Lichtheim, *The Old and Middle Kingdoms*, vol. 1 of *Ancient Egyptian Literature* (Berkeley: University of California Press, 1973).

Syria-Palestine

Though this region (from the Orontes-Upper Euphrates in the north to the Wadi el-Arish in the south) traces its history back to Neolithic times (7500 BC at Jericho), the absence of any substantial texts from or about the whole area of the Levant leaves its third millennium phase almost totally unknown.[10] Thanks to documents recovered from Ebla in upper Syria, the ancient tradition that Canaanites lived in much of the area can be confirmed as can the names of certain Canaanite city-states.[11] On the whole the peoples of the northern section were known as Amurru and (later) Aramu (or Arameans) whereas those of the south—Canaan proper—were, generically at least, Canaanites.

The period from 3000 to 2500 is largely a blank page, historically speaking. The Ebla texts throw some light on the scene from 2500 to 2200, but mainly on the vicinity of Ebla itself and the Mesopotamian world to the east. The final two centuries of the millennium embrace a period known archaeologically as Early Bronze IV or, by some scholars, as Early Bronze–Middle Bronze (EB–MB), so-called because it marks a cultural transition. According to proponents of this view, the transition, characterized by artifactual differences reflecting new populations, was brought about by the penetration of the Amorites from the Upper Euphrates region into Canaan proper.[12] This penetration, perhaps relatively peaceful at the beginning, became increasingly violent as it was resisted and eventually resulted in massive destruction of population centers and dislocation of their inhabitants.

This information, though not enjoying consensus by any means, provides an explanation of the Genesis stories of patriarchal migration and settlement.[13] As already noted, the Old Testament chronology locates Abraham in Egypt (and Canaan) at 2100–2000 BC, precisely during the EB–MB period during which cultural transition in Canaan allegedly occurred. Thus, Abraham's ability to move freely throughout the Canaanite hill country is most understandable since the Canaanites, according to the hypothesis, had been uprooted from that area. On the other hand the biblical narrative makes clear the fact that the Canaanites were living in the plains and valleys, regions that Abraham avoided (Gen 13:11–12; Num 13:29; Josh 10:6; 17:16). In short, the "Amorite hypothesis" is most amenable to the Bible's own depiction of the late third-millennium history of Syria-Canaan.[14]

THE SECOND MILLENNIUM

Old Babylonian Mesopotamia

The glorious resurgence of Sumerian civilization in the Ur III period (2100–1900 BC) gave way gradually (and for the most part peacefully) to the flourishing of Semitic dynasties in central Mesopotamia, notably those of Larsa, Isin, and Babylon. Descendants of Amorite immigrants, the rulers of these and other jurisdictions capitalized on the foundations provided by the Sumerians to erect even more impressive edifices of cultural and political domination.

Founded as early as 2000, the Larsa and Isin dynasties jockeyed for power and influence until both were eventually brought under the hegemony of Babylon, most especially of its sixth ruler, the famous Hammurabi (1792–1750). Though perhaps overrated in some ways,

---

[10] G. W. Ahlström, *The History of Ancient Palestine* (Minneapolis: Fortress, 1993), 56–157.

[11] G. Pettinato, *The Archives of Ebla* (Garden City, NY: Doubleday, 1981), 56, 226.

[12] See especially K. M. Kenyon, *Amorites and Canaanites* (London: Oxford University Press, 1966).

[13] For a critique of the so-called "Amorite hypothesis" see J. M. Miller and J. H. Hayes, *A History of Ancient Israel and Judah* (Philadelphia: Westminster, 1986), 70–71.

[14] E. H. Merrill, *Kingdom of Priests: A History of Old Testament Israel*, 2nd ed. (Grand Rapids: Baker, 2008), 48–51.

Hammurabi was a major player in the extension of Babylonian influence near and far. His codification of legal custom in the celebrated "Code of Hammurabi" is sufficient to guarantee his historical immortality.

The Stele of Hammurabi.

By that time Assyria, which lay to the north and northeast of Babylon, had become a mighty political and military machine under its ruler Shamshi-Adad. When Shamshi-Adad died, Hammurabi remained unchallenged and began to enlarge his sphere of influence from Assyria to the Persian Gulf and from the Zagros Mountains on the east to Mari on the Upper Euphrates. His own death brought the demise of his empire, and in 1595 BC the capital city fell to the Hittites. Overextended as they were, the Hittites could not retain their hold on Babylon, so they sacked the city and withdrew, leaving the capital and indeed the empire in the hands of people from the eastern mountains, the Kassites, who would hold sway for 450 years (1595–1150).

Middle Kingdom Egypt

Table 3: Major Pharaohs of Dynasty 12

| Amenemhet I (1991–1962) |
| Sesostris I (1971–1928) |
| Amenemhet II (1929–1895) |
| Sesestris II (1897–1879) |
| Sesostris III (1878–1843) |
| Amenemhet III (1842–1797) |

The First Intermediate Period, with its turbulence and decay, passed from the scene with the appearance of a brilliant Theban, Ammenemes (or Amenemhet) I, who founded Dynasty 12, the longest in Egyptian history (1991–1786) except for Dynasty 18 (1570–1320). Though not as impressive in its architecture as the Old Kingdom or in its military might as the New Kingdom, this era of rulers (all but one, named Ammenemes or Sesostris), was one of consolidation, peace, and economic development.

The period under review is of special interest to the reader of the Old Testament because it encompasses the lives and affairs of the great Hebrew patriarchs Jacob and Joseph and their descendants who first settled in Egypt.[15] The chronology of the Bible suggests that Joseph was sold into Egyptian slavery rather early in the Middle Kingdom period, probably in the reign of the fourth ruler, Sesostris II (c. 1900–1880). By then trade had been opened up with Western Asia, agricultural and economic prosperity had begun to prevail, and Egypt was entering a period of unparalleled internal stability. Though Joseph and the Hebrew people are never

---

[15] Ibid., 64–72.

mentioned in ancient Egyptian texts, the setting shared both by those texts and the biblical account favors this as the period for Joseph's life in Egypt.

Especially striking in this connection are the indications of close and peaceful relationships between the Egyptians and their "Asiatic" neighbors to the northeast. Extensive trade existed and there appear to be signs of mutual appreciation of one another's culture and ethnicity. The agricultural reforms that took place early in the period are also compatible with the measures described in the biblical text (Gen 41:46–49; 47:13–26), measures that not only saved Jacob and his family but that also brought about a centralization of Egyptian government hitherto unknown.

In this newly introduced structure, the official next in position beneath the pharaoh was the vizier, a kind of prime minister. He in turn was over three administrators of the three "departments" of Egypt—Upper, Middle, and Lower. Some autonomy of the traditional districts was thus retained but only loosely, for the pharaoh and his vizier were over all Egypt and held tightly to their reins of power. As for the rulers of the nomes (or individual city-states), they lost virtually all independence, exercising authority in name only.[16]

As a concomitant, there arose a large and increasingly influential middle class of tradesmen, craftsmen, and farmers. While still firmly under the control of the central government, this class had freedom to develop new and creative ways of enhancing their own and the national economy. The tax revenues generated thereby brought new levels of prosperity to the royal family and the bureaucracies that served it.

Kassite Mesopotamia

The vacuum left by the fall of the Old Babylonian Empire to the Hittites in 1595 BC was filled by the Kassites, apparently an Indo-European people whose residence was principally in the Zagros Mountains east of Babylonia and in the Habur River valley, a northern tributary of the Euphrates.[17] First attested to in Babylonian texts as early as 1740 BC, the Kassites dominated most of Mesopotamia from 1595 to about 1150. The few native inscriptions they produced, plus several hundred royal and divine names, suggest that their language was akin in certain respects to those of the Hittites and Hurrians. Once more, then, the Semitic world of the Land between the Rivers (Mesopotamia) was in the hands of the sons of Japheth.

Though the Kassites appear not to have been greatly creative, they were not the cultural barbarians that some scholars have made them out to be. In fact they were amazingly adept and prolific in transmitting the Akkadian classics to their own and subsequent generations. Many of the epic, mythic, and poetic texts that form such a profound background to the study of the ancient Near Eastern and biblical world are extant, thanks to the painstaking work of Kassite scribes and scholars who recognized the valuable legacy of which they had at least temporary custody.

However, Kassite rule was not without its problems. By the sixteenth century Assyria began to exert pressure from the northeast and the so-called Sealands people did so from the south. The Assyrians, after a hiatus of several centuries, came to life under the famous Ashur-uballit (1365–1330), who conquered the city of Babylon itself. Subsequent Assyrian kings engaged in battle not only the Kassites but also the Hittites, Mitanni, and various peoples of northern Syria. At last the Kassite dynasty collapsed, a demise brought about by the conquest of Babylon

---

[16] W. C. Hayes, "The Middle Kingdom in Egypt," *The Cambridge Ancient History*, 3rd ed. (Cambridge: Cambridge University Press, 1971), I/2: 505–12.

[17] A. Kuhrt, *The Ancient Near East c. 3000—330 BC* (London: Routledge, 1995), 1: 332–48.

by the Assyrian Tukulti-Ninurta I (1244–1208) and followed a half century later by the permanent eviction of the Kassites by the Elamites, peoples from the southwestern Iranian plateaus.

The Hyksos and New Kingdom Egypt

Meanwhile the Middle Kingdom of Egypt was supplanted by a gradually infiltrating people known as the Hyksos, a term meaning roughly "foreign chieftains."[18] The ultimate origins of the Hyksos are unknown, but the consensus is that they were Semites who migrated into the delta region of Egypt from Palestine in the eighteenth century. By 1720 they were numerous and powerful enough to have founded a capital city of their own, a place named by them Avaris and later, by the Egyptians, Rameses. The site, presently under extensive excavation, is now identified as Tell edh-Dhaba.[19]

Many scholars are of the opinion that the arrival in Egypt of the Hyksos and Hebrews was closely linked and that Joseph rose to prominence while serving a Hyksos pharaoh.[20] However, not only does the Old Testament chronology preclude this, but so does the entire flavor and color of the Egyptian background of the Joseph narratives. If anything is clear, it is that the Israelite patriarchs lived and labored in a native Egyptian environment.

The Egyptian historian Manetho assigned Dynasties 15 and 16 to the Hyksos and Dynasties 13, 14, and 17 to Egyptian rulers of various parts of the country, especially in the south. Many of these were contemporaneous, a fact that illustrates the fractured nature of Egypt from around 1700 to 1570, a period known, for that reason, as the Second Intermediate. Like the Kassites of Mesopotamia the Hyksos were comparatively unresourceful in literary and artistic creativity, but also like them they were in great admiration of their host nation and its culture, and thus they imitated and transmitted it in the interim of their political hegemony.

By 1570 the Egyptians, weary of Hyksos occupation of their Delta garden-land, marched north from Thebes as Dynasty 18 and, under their brilliant ruler Ahmose and his military commander of the same name, laid siege to Avaris and quickly expelled the Hyksos from it and the rest of the Delta. This marked the beginning of a new and glorious epoch in Egyptian history, known in retrospect as the New Kingdom. Embracing Dynasty 18, the so-called Thutmoside, and the 19th and 20th, the Ramesside, the New Kingdom lasted for more than 450 years (1570–1100).[21]

This span of time is of more than usual interest to students of the Old Testament for in it the momentous events of the exodus, the Sinai revelation, and the conquest occurred. These events and the matters of their historicity and theological significance will receive detailed attention later on; the present discussion focuses on the New Kingdom and its own inherent importance.

Ahmose (1570–1546), founder of Dynasty 18, undertook very little foreign activity, choosing rather to consolidate his kingdom internally. He rewarded the loyal local nomarchs by increasing their strength, reorganized the canal and dike systems indispensable to Egypt's agricultural prosperity, expanded industry and trade, and achieved a high level of finesse in such cultural expressions as public building and the arts. Not least of his contributions was the restoration of the worship of Amon-Re as the state deity.

---

[18] J. Van Seters, *The Hyksos. A New Investigation* (New Haven, CT: Yale University Press, 1966).

[19] J. D. Currid, *Ancient Egypt and the Old Testament* (Grand Rapids: Baker, 1997), 127–29.

[20] See, e.g., W. F. Albright, *From the Stone Age to Christianity* (Garden City, NY: Doubleday, 1957), 241–42.

[21] A. Gardiner, *Egypt of the Pharaohs* (London: Oxford University Press, 1964), 177–315.

Table 4: Pharaohs of Dynasty 18

| Ahmose (1570–1546) |
| Amenhotep I (1546–1526) |
| Thutmose I (1525–1512) |
| Thutmose II (1512–1504) |
| Thutmose III (1504–1450) |
| Amenhotep II (1450–1425) |
| Thutmose IV (1425–1417) |
| Amenhotep III (1417–1379) |
| Amenhotep IV= Ikhnaton (1379–1362) |
| Smenkhare (1364–1361)[22] |
| Tutankhamon (1361–1352) |
| Ay (1352–1348) |
| Horemhab (1348–1320) |

The next ruler, Amenhotep I (1546–1526), reflects in his throne name this religious reformation of Amon-Re. He was more aggressive than his predecessor in pursuing foreign military and commercial enterprises, numbering among his enemies Qedmi (the Transjordan) and Mitanni, the upper Euphrates Hurrian kingdom. His sparse texts attest some major construction projects, especially at Karnak, and he may be the first king of Egypt to locate his tomb in the Valley of the Kings, thus separating the temple from the tomb.

Commencing with Thutmose I (1525–1512), the glorious Thutmoside era supplanted the brief tenure of Ahmose and Amenhotep. There was a linkage between the two periods, however, for Thutmose, though a commoner, married the sister of Amenhotep I, a move that elevated him to a status sufficient for his succession. Thutmose I transformed Egypt into a militaristic, imperialistic state, one that terrorized all her surrounding neighbors. His son Thutmose II (1512–1504) set out to continue these policies but died prematurely after a brief reign. His sister/wife Hatshepsut, though disqualified by her gender from ruling in her husband's place, did so at least indirectly through her son-in-law Thutmose III (1504–1450) until he reached full adulthood.

Hatshepsut was perhaps the most powerful woman who ever lived in ancient Egypt.[23] The inscriptions describing her exploits are copious and are validated by the enormous building projects and impressive monuments that she commissioned and that still remain. And this occurred despite the efforts of Thutmose to eradicate them. These reactions to the queen reflect the chafing Thutmose felt while she was still alive. Once he became free of her, he struck out in all directions, leading no fewer than 18 military campaigns into Palestine and Asia alone. At his prime, Thutmose headed a nation that was the fear and envy of the entire world.

A steep decline in Egypt's international fortunes set in with the accession of Amenhotep II (1450–1425) to the throne. Though he undertook a few campaigns into Canaan, his interests were primarily domestic, including possibly the introduction of the Aten cult which focused on the worship of the sun in its manifestation as a disk. The decline was not reversed by the

---

[22] The reign of Smenkhare overlapped the reign of Amenhotep IV by a two-year coregency.

[23] E. Wells, *Hatshepsut* (Garden City, NY: Doubleday, 1969).

next two rulers either, Thutmose IV (1425–1417) and Amenhotep III (1417–1379). Yet it would be incorrect to view Egypt as an impotent second-rate power, for Thutmose married a daughter of the very powerful Mitannian king Artatama, and Amenhotep distinguished himself and Egypt by grand and glorious works of art and architecture.

The period from 1379 to the inauguration of the Ramesside dynasty in 1320 is known as the Amarna Age, so-called because of the shift of the center of Egyptian political and religious life from Thebes to Akhetaton, the modern name of which is Tell el-Amarna. This move was led by the highly eccentric philosopher-king Amenhotep IV (1379–1362), son of Amenhotep III and his Mitanni princess Tiy. Having undergone a religious "conversion" from the worship of Amon-Re to that of Aten, the sun-disk, Amenhotep changed his name to Akhnaton and built a new city and temple where he could carry out his quasi-monotheistic faith. So devoted was he to these matters of the spirit Akhnaton and his beautiful wife Nefertiti had little time for international relations or even domestic affairs. It was inevitable that Egypt should become ever weaker and less and less a factor in the larger world.

The minor rulers who followed—Smenkare (1364–1361), Tutankhamon (1361–1352), and Ay (1352–1348)—could do little to stem the tide of mediocrity. Tutankhamon, as his very name attests, reverted back to the worship of Amon and, in so doing, relocated the capital to Memphis. Only Horemhab (1348–1320), the last king of Dynasty 18, exercised any powerful leadership at all. He undertook great building projects, including his royal tomb in the Valley of the Kings; centralized the government and increased the revenues; and recovered much of the military power that had slipped away in the previous century.

Table 5: Pharaohs of Dynasty 19

Rameses I (1320–1318)
Seti I (1318–1304)
Rameses II (1304–1236)
Merneptah (1236–1223)

The death of Horemheb without a male heir paved the way for his vizier Rameses I (1320–1318) to succeed him as king. This marks the beginning of Dynasty 19, known, along with Dynasty 20, as the Ramesside era because of the predominance of the name Rameses throughout. Having come to power late in life, Rameses I appointed his son Seti I (1318–1304) as his co-regent, a move that ensured a smooth transition. Seti engaged in many foreign campaigns, mainly in Syria-Palestine, and also erected great temples to Amon and other public buildings in places such as Abydos and Karnak. What he began was fully implemented by his illustrious son Rameses II (1304–1236), considered by many historians to be the greatest ruler in the magnificent and lengthy history of Egypt.

Rameses made his principal residence in Memphis, and from there he launched his various foreign enterprises. His major preoccupation was with the Hittites, who, under their several kings whose reigns paralleled his, threatened Rameses by encroaching on Syrian territories claimed by both Hatti and Egypt. By the thirteenth century the New Kingdom Hittites had become so powerful that neither Egypt nor any other neighboring states were able to subdue them. Thus there existed a virtual stalemate of the major nations throughout this period, a stalemate documented in the case of Hatti and Egypt by the survival of treaty texts that attest to their equality as signatories.[24]

Rameses did not neglect domestic matters either, distinguishing himself most impressively in temple construction. The edifices at places such as Abydos, Karnak, Luxor, Thebes, and Abu Simbel are breathtaking in their scope and beauty, bespeaking a wealth and power hardly equaled in human history. But such achievements seem to have been centered so much around the personality himself that when Rameses passed from the scene Egypt's glory largely passed away with him.

The temple of Luxor at Thebes. This view of the first pylon shows several statues of Rameses II.

Dynasty 19 ended with the reign of Merneptah (1236–1223) and several minor kings (1223–1200). Merneptah, a son of Rameses II, managed some Asian military adventures—including the defeat (so he claims) of a people called Israel. But Egypt was slipping badly and with the exception of the reigns of one or two kings in Dynasty 20 Egypt went into political and military eclipse for several centuries.

The major figure in the century from 1200 to 1100 was Rameses III (1198–1166). Beset by many foes, perhaps the most threatening were the so-called Sea Peoples, invaders from the Aegean and other islands who attempted to invade and occupy coastal Egypt. Rameses managed to repel them, and so they moved to the northeast and became an element in the population of the lower Palestine coast known as the Philistines. The remainder of the dynasty was ruled by a succession of kings named Rameses (up through Rameses XI), none of whom, except possibly Rameses IV, is notable, and he is known only for the restoration of earlier building projects.

The New Kingdom Hittites

Hittite history, though traceable as early as 1500 BC, emerges into the clear light of contemporary documentation with the rise of the New Kingdom or Empire period at about

Table 6: New Kingdom Hittite Kings

Shuppiluliuma (1380–1346)
Arnuwanda (1346–1340)
Murshili II (c. 1340–1320)
Muwatalli (c. 1320–1294)
Urkhi-Teshub (1294–1286)
Hattushili III (1286–1265)

[24] For the most important of these, see *ANET*, 199–203.

1380 BC.[25] Credit for the ascendancy of this Indo-European state, centered in Hattushash on the Halys River (now north-central Turkey), lies with Shuppiluliuma (1380–1346), a contemporary for most of his reign with Akhnaton of Egypt. Having recovered and reorganized the homeland following inroads made there by various enemies, Shuppiluliuma launched an attack on Syria, an event attested by Tushratta, king of Mitanni, in a letter addressed to Amenhotep III of Egypt. Shuppiluliuma also made a series of treaties with small neighboring states that had broken their alliances with their overlords in the face of increasing Hittite pressure.

By 1365 the Hittites felt confident enough to launch a full-scale attack on the Hurrian kingdom of Mitanni, a conquest that resulted in Hittite occupation of all Syria north of Ugarit. Since the latter city-state was apparently under Egyptian protection, Shuppiluliuma ventured no farther for the moment. Other jurisdictions such as Halab (Aleppo), Tunip, and Alalakh were made Hittite vassals. Ugarit, Amurru, and Byblos, caught in the middle between Hatti and Egypt, tried to exploit their situation to their own best advantage by playing each of the great powers against the other. Meanwhile Assyria was rising to the east and Shuppiluliuma's misguided policies toward that threat nearly brought his own empire to an end. His two sons who succeeded him—Arnuwanda (c. 1346–1340) and Murshili II (c. 1340–1320)—were able to do no more than maintain the status quo.

By the time Muwatalli (c. 1320–1294) came to power, Hatti, though revived somewhat, began to feel the baleful influence of Egypt under the newly established Dynasty 19. Both Seti I and Rameses II pushed north into Syria but in two major encounters—near Byblos in 1301 and Kadesh in 1300—Rameses II was decisively defeated and the Hittites regained the territory they had recently lost.

After a brief reign by Urkhi-Teshub (1294–1286), the mighty Hattushili III (1286–1265) sat on the Hittite throne. Forced by continuing pressures by the Assyrians to seek allies, Hattushili made treaties with the Kassites of Babylonia and with Egypt, still under Rameses II. These friendly relations were maintained between subsequent Hittite and Egyptian rulers, for both feared the awesome might and imperialist ambitions of the ever-expanding Assyrians. However, at last Hatti came to an end, and a rapid and unexpected end at that. Elements of those same Sea Peoples who had harassed Egypt in the days of Rameses III swept across the upper Mediterranean coast as well, destroying everything in its wake including the last vestiges of the once formidable Hittite Empire.

Late Bronze Syria-Palestine

During this period (1550–1200) Syria consisted of a number of city-states and other small political entities that usually found themselves in vassalship to the major world powers such as Hatti, Egypt, or Mitanni. With a few exceptions like Alalakh and Ugarit, documentary knowledge of these places is indirect, depending almost exclusively on references to them in texts originating from the dominant nations, especially Egypt. However, the exceptions are very important, for both Alalakh and Ugarit have surrendered copious archives that brilliantly illuminate at least those places and their vicinities.[26]

The same may be said of Palestine to the south and even more so, for except for the Amarna texts of around 1375–1350 (and, of course, the Old Testament) next to nothing can

---

[25] H. A. Hoffner, "Hittites" in *Peoples of the Old Testament World*, ed. A. J. Hoerth, G. L. Mattingly, and E. M. Yamauchi (Grand Rapids: Baker, 1994), 127–55.

[26] See respectively Sir L. Woolley, *Alalakh: An Account of the Excavations at Tell Atchana in the Hatay, 1937–1949* (London: Society of Antiquaries, 1955); A. Curtis, *Ugarit (Ras Shamra)* (Grand Rapids: Eerdmans, 1985).

be known of the region for this whole period apart from nonliterary archaeological data. The Amarna texts, originating mainly from sites throughout Canaan but also from as far north as Byblos, are indeed informative, but inasmuch as most of them are preoccupied with a single issue—the inroads and disruptions of the *'apiru* people—they hardly present a comprehensive and informative picture. What they do yield is evidence of great turmoil in areas surrounding and adjacent to the Canaanite highlands where the Old Testament locates the recently settled tribes of Israel.[27] (See map 2.)

The Bible affords the bulk of historical sources for Syria-Canaan during this period. This is true whether one accepts the essentially historical character of the biblical texts or not and however one dates the exodus and conquest, the major events described in those texts. Naturally the more confidence one has in the record as reliable history the more it sheds light on the world it reflects. Similarly the traditional date of 1446 for the exodus allows for a broader, more comprehensive chronological range than does the later, mid-thirteenth century date espoused by many scholars.

The view of this book, one defended at greater length in subsequent discussion, is that the Old Testament narrative recounts a fully reliable story of Israel's history in its Late Bronze Age environment, even if we grant (as we do) that its primary thrust is salvation history and not history as commonly conceived. Moreover, the exodus itself fits best, we believe, an eighteenth-dynasty milieu, specifically that surrounding the reigns of Thutmose III and Amenhotep II.[28]

The biblical witness is that Moses was born in 1526, perhaps in the reign of Pharaoh Amenhotep I. Forced into Midianite exile, he remained there until the death of the king who sought his life, namely, the great Thutmose III. The exodus pharaoh must therefore have been Amenhotep II, and the ruler contemporary with Joshua's conquest of Canaan 40 years later would have been Amenhotep III. The years of largely unsuccessful settlement that ensued were those of the so-called Amarna Age described above. Thus it appears that the chaotic times described in those texts find their literary counterpart in the book of Judges, especially the first two chapters.[29] Only when Othniel came to judgeship in the mid-fourteenth century did a measure of stability come to interior Canaan, a time somewhat later than the last of the Amarna texts. There is no real incompatibility between the state of affairs in fourteenth-century Syria-Palestine as recounted in the Old Testament and that brought to light by the available extrabiblical texts and other archaeological data.

This is also true of the period from 1350 to 1100, the era of the judges. The turbulence that characterizes the judges narratives is amply attested by archaeological evidence of population upheavals and redistributions. The relatively replete literary legacy of the surrounding nations, especially Hatti and Egypt, also dovetails with the biblical history both in what it says and what it does not say. As observed above, the Hittites and Egyptians maintained a standoff through much of this period, thus creating a vacuum in which interior Canaan (Israel in our view) was allowed to conduct its own affairs or, as was the case for much of the time, to be ravaged by hostile minor states without the protection or interference of either major power. All of Palestine, it is true, was theoretically under Egyptian hegemony, but none of the royal inscriptions of any Egyptian king, including Rameses II, ever drops even a hint of involvement in Palestinian hill country affairs. And it is worth mentioning that the book of Judges studiously avoids

---

[27] W. J. Murnane, *Texts from the Amarna Period in Egypt* (Atlanta: Scholars, 1995).

[28] Merrill, *Kingdom of Priests*, 74–96.

[29] For a vivid picture of the early fourteenth-century Canaanite environment of this period see M. Greenberg, *The Hab/piru* (New Haven, CT: American Oriental Society, 1955).

The Merneptah Stele that contains the first mention of Israel.

any reference to Hatti or Egypt, thus confirming from the biblical side the absence of major power activity in the region associated with Israel's settlement. Not until the reign of Rehoboam of Judah, in fact, is there much of any evidence of threat to the people of the Lord from any of the first-rate nations of the eastern world.

The apparent exception to this is the foray of Merneptah of Egypt into Syria-Palestine about 1230 BC. The Merneptah Stele, which documents this campaign, speaks of the "scattering of Israel" which resulted. The structure of the text and its geographic setting suggest, however, that Merneptah was not in Israel proper, but in the Plain of Jezreel to the north.[30] Furthermore the use of the Egyptian determinative for "people" rather than "nation" comports well with the situation in the period of the judges when there was clearly no sense of nationhood or centralized government.

THE FIRST MILLENNIUM

The Assyrian Empire

It is conventional to assign the commencement of the (Neo-) Assyrian Empire to Adad-Nirari II (912–889), but its roots must be traced to a much earlier period. Following the long dormancy occasioned by the collapse of the Old Kingdom at about 1700 BC, Assyrian fortunes rose under Assur-uballit (1365–1330). His reign and those of his successors until 1200 or so were characterized by an uneasy coexistence with the other major powers of the region such as Hatti, Mitanni, Kassite Babylonia, and Egypt. His relationships with the Kassites were particularly complex and fraught with danger, for on occasion Babylonia would submit to Assyrian overlordship only to break free and go its own way.

Particularly noteworthy among these early Assyrian kings were Adad-Nirari I (1307–1275), who annexed much of the upper Euphrates territory and threatened Hatti itself; Shalmaneser I (1274–1245); and Tukulti-Ninurta I (1244–1208). The last of these is distinguished for subjugating Babylonia from the Persian Gulf to Mari but also for having made the fatal mistake of attacking the Hittites and thereby weakening the Assyrian military and economic power, a policy that resulted in his assassination and the rapid decline of the Middle Assyrian Empire.

For nearly a century Assyria was virtually moribund, but at least temporary revival took place under the illustrious Tiglath-Pileser I (1115–1077). Availing himself of the vacuum left in the wake of the Hittite collapse, he penetrated and placed under tribute vast areas to the northwest, terrorized much of the east Mediterranean coastlands, and conquered Babylon. However, such success was not to be sustained, for even though there was not much threat to Assyria from the outside apart from token Elamite and native Babylonian elements, internal upheavals ushered in a century and a half (c. 1050–900) of weakness.

---

[30] R. de Vaux, *The Early History of Israel* (Philadelphia: Westminster, 1978), 390–91. For another view see G. W. Ahlström and D. Edelman, "Merneptah's Israel," *JNES* 44 (1985):59–61.

Table 7: Rulers of the Neo-Assyrian Empire

Adad-Nirari II (912–889)
Tukulti-Ninurta II (889–884)
Asshur-Nasirpal II (883–859)
Shalmaneser III (859–824)
Shamshi-Adad V (824–811)
Adad-Nirari III (811–782)
Shalmaneser IV (782–772)
Asshur-Dan III (772–754)
Asshur-Nirari V (754–746)
Tiglath-Pileser III (745–727)
Shalmaneser V (727–722)
Sargon II (722–705)
Sennacherib (705–681)
Esarhaddon (681–669)
Asshur-Banipal (669–626)
Asshur-Etil-Ilani (626–623)
Sin-Shar-Ishkun (623–612)
Asshur-Uballit (612–609)

At this point the Assyrian Empire proper came to the fore, thanks to the vision and energy of Adad-Nirari II (912–889). For 300 years Assyria dominated the Near Eastern world, an era lavishly documented by both Assyrian and foreign texts of all kinds.[31] Moving quickly, Adad-Nirari conquered Babylon and then proceeded to add the Mitanni kingdom of Hanigalbat to his realm. His immediate successors Tukulti-Ninurta II (889–884) and Assur-Nasirpal II (883–859) continued the policy of expansion and consolidation, but most notable was Shalmaneser III (859–824), celebrated because of both military and domestic successes. Of particular interest to the biblical story is Shalmaneser's fixation on the West, a preoccupation that led to numerous campaigns in that region including at least two that encountered kings of Israel—Ahab and Jehu—whom he mentioned by name. Though he accomplished no more than the exaction of tribute from those lands, Shalmaneser set the stage for ongoing Assyrian pressures on the West, pressures that at last resulted in the conquest and occupation of Israel itself. (See map 3.)

Jehu or one of his representatives appears prostrated before the Assyrian king in this register.

---

[31] For a rather full selection see A. K. Grayson, *Assyrian Royal Inscriptions,* 2 vols. (Wiesbaden: Harrassowitz, 1972, 1976).

The primacy of Assyria continued under Shamshi-Adad V (824–811) but only briefly, for a rebellion led by his own son, coupled with Babylonian insurgence, brought a swift deterioration of Assyrian domination. Adad-Nirari III (811–782) led a few campaigns to the West, including one in which he exacted tribute from King Jehoash of Israel, but otherwise he and his successors until Tiglath-Pileser III were weak and ineffectual.

Tiglath-Pileser III (745–727), also known as Pulu or Pul, had three major objectives: restore order in Babylonia, defend his northern frontier against the powerful nation Urartu, and regain control of the western provinces and dependencies. The latter he addressed in several campaigns climaxed by the capture of Damascus in 732 and the appointment of Hoshea as king over Israel in the same year. This presupposes at least nominal jurisdiction over the northern kingdom of Israel.

After the brief reign of Shalmaneser V (727–722), whose major achievement was the capture of Samaria in 722, Sargon II (722–705) maintained Assyrian interest in the West by launching several invasions of that region, finally arriving at somewhat of a stalemate with Egypt, which also had designs on Palestine. However, Sargon's attention was diverted toward Babylonia for the most part under the leadership of the renegade Chaldean Merodach-Baladan.

Clear subjugation of Merodach-Baladan fell to Sennacherib (705–681), who set about to recover Assyria's glory days by wars against Babylonia, Elam, Egypt, and, most important, Judah. As a result Assyria scaled new heights of imperialism and international respect except for the humiliating inability to follow up on the siege of Jerusalem in 701. In addition, Sennacherib rebuilt and aggrandized Nineveh, making it the capital in place of Dur-Sharrukin (Khorsabad), the site established by his father.

Relief of the details of the siege of Lachish.

Sennacherib's assassination at the hands of his own sons cleared the way for another son, Esarhaddon (681–669), to take his place. In this last glorious period of Assyrian history Esarhaddon consolidated his father's gains and even exceeded them. The Sealands dynasty, Sidon, Babylonia, and even Egypt all succumbed, at least for a time. However, Esarhaddon's passing triggered a collapse of the Assyrian house of cards. Under Asshur-Banipal (669–626) Egypt rebelled, the Sealands Chaldeans sniped away, Tyre and Judah broke away, and the Medes of western Iran loomed large as a potentially lethal threat. Esarhaddon did manage to reverse most of these hostile actions, but by the time he died Assyria clearly was on its last legs. The emergent Neo-Babylonian Empire of Nabopolassar, aided greatly by Media, made rapid and drastic inroads. Nineveh fell in 612, Haran in 609, and finally the last vestiges of once mighty Assyria were crushed at Carchemish in 605 by a Babylonian army under the command of Nabopolassar's own brilliant son, Nebuchadnezzar.

Third Intermediate Egypt

This term encompasses Dynasties 21 through 25, embracing the long period from 1100 to 650 BC.[32] As "intermediate" suggests, this was an era of decline in Egypt's internal and international fortunes, briefly alleviated near the end with the infusion of new energy from the twenty-fifth or so-called "Nubian" dynasty. The center of power was in Tanis, the old Hyksos capital in the East Delta region. The relatively uneventful years of the seven kings of Dynasty 21 (c. 1085–945) gave way to persons and events of much greater import to the biblical story. In fact Shoshenq (Shishak in the OT), founder of Dynasty 22, numbered among his achievements a campaign against Israel in 925 BC, near the end of his reign. Osorkon I (924–889), who followed him, also sent an expedition north, this time against Judah, but this adventure failed when Asa, king of Judah, defeated the Nubian commander of Egypt's army.

Subsequent rulers witnessed the splitting of Egypt into its ancient North and South bifurcation and for a time Dynasties 22 and 23 shared governance. Meanwhile Nubian forces to the south and Libyan forces in the west began to assert themselves, keeping central Egypt in a most tenuous and threatened state of affairs well through the eighth century.

For more than a century (780–656) the Nubian conquerors from the distant land south of Egypt dominated their northern neighbors, at first only in the south (780–715) and then throughout the land. Bold and energetic, these kings, with names like Piankhi and Shabako, consolidated the nation once more under central control and then began to make foreign alliances, especially with Assyria. The pro-Assyria sentiment changed under Shebitku (702–690) who, it seems, began to perceive Assyria as more a threat than an ally. He therefore joined forces with Hezekiah of Judah to repel the Assyrian conquest of Judah in 701. These Nubian troops were commanded by Taharqa (690–664), brother of the king, who himself went on to become king.

After a peaceful respite Taharqa suffered the inroads of Esarhaddon of Assyria in 674, a campaign he was able to counteract. However, three years later Esarhaddon drove the Nubian from his capital Memphis, and Asshur-Banipal, the next Assyrian king, evicted him even from Thebes (667–666). The Nubians recovered under Tantamani (664–656), but only briefly, for once more Asshur-Banipal pushed them south of Thebes.

Dynasty 26, a continuation of 25, was marked by constant political ambivalence. Its founder, Psammeticus I (664–610), was first an Assyrian vassal but then he broke free and reunited his nation. However, Necho II (610–595), fearing a rising Babylonia far more than a receding Assyria, made a forced march north to Haran in 609 with the objective of joining Assyria in its military showdown with the Babylonians. He was intercepted by King Josiah of Judah along the way, an interruption that may have prevented him from suffering the humiliating defeat experienced by his Assyrian allies.

The end of Egyptian might came quickly after this fiasco. First under the Babylonians and then the Persians, the remnants of the Nubian dynasties found themselves under occupation. To the end of the OT period and long beyond it Egypt remained a second-rate nation, a mere shadow of what it had been for more than two and a half millennia.

Israel's United Monarchy

The crises of the era of the judges reached a crescendo with the rise of the Philistines, a foe too powerful and widespread to be contained by local judges alone. Thus there began a clamor

---

[32] K. A. Kitchen, *The Third Intermediate Period in Egypt (1100-650 B.C.)* (Warminster, UK: Aris & Phillips, 1986).

in Israel for a king, a ruler who from a central place could stabilize the nation and raise an army adequate to meet the peril from the Philistines.

The idea of kingship for Israel was not in itself inimical to God's purposes. Moses had already anticipated such human sovereignty (Gen 17:16) and in fact had prepared a royal protocol as it were, a text that formed part of the Deuteronomic covenant and that must be regularly recited and constantly observed by the kings to come (Deut 17:14–20). The problem as Samuel saw it was the prematurity of the appeal for a king and the less-than-godly motive that lay behind it. The Lord made this fact clear to the prophet when He reminded him that "they have not rejected you; they have rejected Me as their king" (1 Sam 8:7). That this refers only to the impropriety of kingship then and there is clear from Samuel's later pronouncement that the Lord was rejecting Saul's dynasty in favor of "a man after his [God's] own heart" (13:14 NIV). That is, David had already been elected by God to kingship, and when the proper time came He would enthrone him according to His eternal purposes.[33]

Meanwhile the Lord permitted the people to have their way, and through Samuel He chose Saul. Josephus and Paul (Acts 13:21) agree that Saul reigned for 40 years, having therefore come to power around 1050 BC. This was immediately after the time of Samson, Israel's last major judge, and at the time of a Philistine resurgence.[34] Surely enough, Saul provided deliverance as the people had hoped, but at the cost of widening the nascent breach between Israel's northern and southern tribes. The insertion of David into the equation about half way through Saul's reign only exacerbated an already fragile state of affairs.

Saul's tragic death in 1010 BC paved the way for David to become king, first at Hebron over Judah alone for seven years, and then over all Israel for 33 more. Under this chosen one, with whom a dynastic and even messianic covenant was made, Israel reached sublime heights of internal and international glory. Protected from the surrounding world powers because of their own political and military paralysis during this period, Israel, under David, became a potent and even dominating entity in its own right. This situation continued and in fact was moved far forward by David's illustrious son Solomon (see map 4). Only toward the end of his long reign (971–931) did cracks in Israelite solidarity become apparent, fissures that were ancient in origin but that opened wide and led to the bifurcation of the nation itself following Solomon's death.

The Divided Monarchy and History of Judah

Table 8: The Kings of Israel and Judah

Israel	Judah
Jeroboam (931–910)	Rehoboam (931–913)
Nadab (910–909)	Abijah (913–911)
Baasha (909–886)	Asa (911–870)
Elah (886–885)	
Zimri (885)	
Omri (885–874)	
Ahab (874–853)	Jehoshaphat (873–848)
Ahaziah (853–852)	

---

[33] For this interpretation see P. K. McCarter Jr., *I Samuel*, AB (Garden City, NY: Doubleday, 1980), 230.

[34] Merrill, *Kingdom of Priests*, 223–25.

Joram (852–841)	Jehoram (848–841)
Jehu (841–814)	Ahaziah (841)
	Athaliah (841–835)
Jehoahaz (814–798)	Joash (835–796)
Jehoash (798–782)	Amaziah (796–767)
Jeroboam II (793–753)	Uzziah (792–740)
Zechariah (753)	
Shallum (752)	
Menahem (752–742)	Jotham (750–731)
Pekahiah (742–740)	
Pekah (752–732)	Ahaz (735–715)
Hoshea (732–722)	Hezekiah (729–686)
	Manasseh (696–642)
	Amon (642–640)
	Josiah (640–609)
	Jehoahaz (609)
	Jehoiakim (608–598)
	Jehoiachin (598–597)
	Zedekiah (597–586)

Solomon's son Rehoboam, having rejected the counsel of the elders to ease up on Solomon's onerous conscription and taxation policies, witnessed the separation of most of his kingdom from his control (see map 5). The separated element—Israel, or the northern kingdom—remained independent for nearly 200 years (931–722 BC), finally succumbing to the Assyrians. The record of the successive dynasties of this kingdom is bleak indeed. Without exception the kings were evil and despite the ministry of many prophets sent to them, they turned aside, walking in the manner of their pagan neighbors.

The Davidic kingdom of Judah was not much better but because of God's inviolate promise to its founder and the periodic reigns of godly kings who led the people to revival and reformation, grace was extended at least a little longer. Spared from the hostilities of her sister nation to the north and even the threats of conquest and captivity by Assyria, Judah at last exhausted even divine patience and fell in 586 BC to the Babylonian king Nebuchadnezzar. However, this was not the utter end, for the covenant with David, reinforced by unremitting prophetic promise, guaranteed the return and restoration of Judah, a regathering with both historical and eschatological significance.

The Neo-Babylonian Empire

Table 9: Rulers of the Neo-Babylonian Empire

Nabo-Polassar (626–605)
Nebuchadnezzar II (605–562)
Evil-Merodach (562–560)
Neriglissar (560–556)
Labashi-Marduk (556)
Nabonidus (555–539)

The last two centuries of Assyrian history were paralleled by the increasing ascendancy of central and lower Mesopotamian tribal peoples with names such as Bit-Yakin, Bit-Dakkuri, Bit-Amukani, and, most important, Kaldu. The last came to be known in the Bible as Chaldeans, a term synonymous it seems with the Neo-Babylonians of secular history. They, in concert with heterogeneous coastal peoples loosely called the "Sealands Dynasty," evolved into a unified nation under the governor of the Sealands, Nabo-Polassar (see map 6). He was able to expel the Assyrians from Babylon in 626 BC, and with Median and other assistance he finally crushed the last remnants of Assyrian might in 605.

This last conquest was actually carried out by Nabo-Polassar's son and chief military officer, the famous Nebuchadnezzar II (605–562). Babylonia had already driven Egypt out of Syria in 609, and after dealing with the Assyrians Nebuchadnezzar routed the Egyptians from Palestine as well, forcing them to retreat to their own country. Meanwhile Nabo-Polassar died, necessitating Nebuchadnezzar's hasty return to Babylon in order to secure his succession. En route he took Jewish captives, including Daniel, and on his return he solidified his hold on Judah, elevating and deposing her kings as he saw fit.

Judah clearly was not pleased with this arrangement and, despite the warnings of the prophet Jeremiah to the contrary, Judah embarked on a program of independence under King Jehoiakim. Nebuchadnezzar, having dealt with problems that had allowed Jehoiakim's intemperate action, returned to Jerusalem to bring the kingdom of Judah to heel. Jehoiakim died in the interim, and it fell to his unfortunate son Jehoiachin to face the Babylonian fury. The young king was captured and sent to Babylon, and his uncle Zedekiah was placed on the Davidic throne. Within a decade he also rebelled. This time there was no mercy when the Babylonians returned, and in 586 Jerusalem and the temple were demolished and the cream of Judean political, religious, and cultural society was carried off to Babylon.

Babylon, under Nebuchadnezzar's despotic leadership, reached new heights of power and glory. Virtually all the eastern world, including Palestine and even Egypt, lay in abject submission to him. But his arrogance and pride—traits so well attested in the book of Daniel—began to erode his position of seeming invincibility. His weak successors, including Nabonidus and his son Belshazzar, could not reverse the tide, and in 539 Babylon fell to a coalition of Medes and Persians led by the mighty Cyrus the Great (559–530). After more than two millennia, Semitic domination of the Mesopotamian valleys yielded to Aryan rulers, a situation that would not be redressed for centuries to come.

The Persian Empire

Table 10: Rulers of the Persian Empire

Cyrus II (559–530)
Cambyses II (530–522)
Gaumata (522)
Darius Hystaspes (522–486)
Xerxes (486–465)
Artaxerxes I (464–424)
Darius II (423–404)
Artaxerxes II (404–358)

Just as Assyria and Babylonia were the means whereby Israel and Judah respectively met judgment and deportation, Persia was the instrument of Judah's deliverance and restoration. The Bible makes clear that all this was in line with divine purpose and strategy. Persian texts—especially those of Cyrus the Great—also view Persia's role as fulfilling manifest destiny, a role from their perspective as providential as that of Israel in the OT theological context of *Heilsgeschichte*.

The Persian Empire arose from the twin streams of Persia and Media, ancient cultural groups of west central Iran.[35] (See map 7.) At first under Median domination, Persia, led by Teispes (675–640), broke free. Teispes placed Cyrus I (640–600) over the northern part of his realm, but a Median king, Cyaxares (625–585), put an end to Persian independence, at least for a time. The next ruler of Media, Astyages (585–550), appointed Cambyses I (600–559) as regent over Persia, cementing the arrangement by marrying him to his daughter. The offspring of this marriage was Cyrus II (559–530), "the Great" as he has appropriately come to be known.

The Cyrus Cylinder. The inscription portrays Cyrus as the liberator of Babylon.

When Cyrus came of age, his grandfather Astyages named him vassal king of Anshan, the southwestern Iranian region that was at the heart of the later Persian kingdom. No sooner was he in place than he unified the Persian tribes, made an alliance with Nabonidus of Babylonia, and rebelled against Astyages. Having overcome the latter, Cyrus claimed all Median territories, setting himself on a collision course with Babylonia, Egypt, and

---

[35] E. M. Yamauchi, *Persia and the Bible* (Grand Rapids: Baker, 1990).

even faraway Lydia in Asia Minor. Croesus, king of Lydia, launched an eastward attack but fell back to his capital Sardis in the face of superior Persian troops.

The main focus of Cyrus's imperialism was Babylonia. When Nabonidus, as was his custom, left his capital in the hands of his son Belshazzar, Cyrus took advantage of the situation to attack Babylon itself in 539. By the stratagem of the diversion of the Euphrates, the Persians entered the capital and seized it with virtually no opposition. All that remained was the Mediterranean Levant, an area, including Palestine, that soon became part of the satrapy of Babylon under Gubaru, the governor appointed by Cyrus.

Within the year Cyrus decreed that all peoples captive in Babylonia were free to return to their homelands, an opportunity quickly seized by the exiled Jews. The beneficent policies of Cyrus continued in effect—at least where the Jews were concerned—throughout the remainder of Persian Empire history. After he died, Cyrus was succeeded by his son Cambyses (530–522), most celebrated for his conquest of Egypt. His death by suicide opened the way for Darius Hytaspes (522–486), descendant of Teispes through another line, to come to power. This provoked many coups and rebellions, all of which Darius was able to overcome. In fact he greatly enlarged the empire while undertaking enormous and elaborate building programs, especially in his new capital city, Susa.

Finally Darius overextended himself by launching a massive attack on Greece, an adventure that ended in the dismal defeat of Persia at Marathon. Four years later Xerxes (486–465) succeeded Darius. Though successful in many efforts, he too underestimated the might of the Aegean world. He did defeat the Spartans at Thermopylae but then was thrashed in a great sea battle at Salamis.

Artaxerxes I (464–423), son of Xerxes, was able to accomplish what his predecessors could not do—contend with and even partially defeat Athens—thanks to the Greek Peloponnesian war of 431. More important to biblical history was his interest in the well-being of the Jewish state (see map 8), an interest, admittedly, that was not without self-interest in that Persia needed a compliant buffer between herself and a refractory and dangerous Egypt. Still the OT story views Artaxerxes with favor, closing as it does with the Pax Persiaca that he and his forebears had brought to the postexilic Jewish community.

Exile and Postexile Judah

Attendant to the capture and destruction of Jerusalem was the deportation of several thousands of its citizens to Babylon and other places in Mesopotamia. Life there was not particularly difficult—easier, in fact, than for the peasant classes left behind in Palestine—but the psychological and spiritual trauma was immeasurable. A major element of the patriarchal covenants was the land of promise; in fact those covenants were theologically incomprehensible without the land. How then could there be a covenant community without temple, king, and territory?

These matters were addressed by prophets such as Jeremiah, Ezekiel, and Daniel in exilic times (586–538) and Haggai, Zechariah, and Malachi later (520–470). All held out the hope that the exile was temporary and that the essential ingredients of covenant life would be reinstituted. There would be a return to the land, the temple and city would be rebuilt, and a scion of David would occupy the ancient throne.

The reconstitution of the state commenced with the return of the Jews to Palestine in 538 in response to the decree of Cyrus. The returnees together with the already existing population quickly laid the foundations of Jerusalem and the temple, but then after the first flush of enthusiasm they turned their attention to more personal affairs of business and industry. Even their leaders Sheshbazzar and Zerubbabel could not redirect their energies back to what mattered most—the renewal of the covenant community.

It fell therefore to Haggai and Zechariah to reinspire the Jews to take up the task of spiritual nation building. By 520 work resumed on the temple, and within five years it was completed. Meanwhile opposition developed from without, especially from Judah's near neighbors who out of a spirit of jealousy and properly perceived exclusion launched a series of tactics designed to retard if not totally bring to an end the work of restoring the city. Thanks to the sympathies of the successive Persian kings these interdictions were in vain. When Ezra returned from Babylon in 458 BC, he did so with the blessing and support of Artaxerxes II. And Nehemiah, 13 years later, enjoyed the favor and protection of the same king. Resistance from foes without and faithless, disobedient friends within did not cease, but the work went forward in any case and by the end of the OT period (c. 400 BC) there was every hope that God's ancient promises—interrupted as they appeared to be for a time—were well on their way to glorious fulfillment.

STUDY QUESTIONS

1. Where and when did writing first originate?
2. Who founded the world's first empire and where?
3. During which dynasties were the great pyramids of Egypt built?
4. Identify the Hyksos and explain their relationship to Israel.
5. What key biblical text provides information about the date of the exodus?
6. What is the major significance of the Amarna texts?
7. What empire succeeded the Neo-Assyrian regime?
8. Whose army was destroyed in an attempt to conquer Jerusalem?
9. Who was the first king of Israel after the division of the monarchy?
10. Identify Merodach-Baladan.
11. Israel is first mentioned in which extrabiblical inscription?
12. Who issued a decree permitting the Jews to return home from the exile?
13. The Tel Dan inscription provides what kind of important information?
14. Who is the pharaoh of the exodus according to the "late" date?
15. Identify the Ugaritic texts and explain their relevance to the Old Testament.

FOR FURTHER STUDY

History of the ANE

Arnold, B. T., and B. E. Beyer, eds. *Readings from the Ancient Near East*. Grand Rapids: Baker, 2002.

Currid, J. D. *Ancient Egypt and the Old Testament*. Grand Rapids: Baker, 1997.

Dothan, T. *The Philistines and Their Material Culture*. New Haven, CT: Yale University Press, 1982.

Finegan, J. *Handbook of Biblical Chronology*. Peabody, MA: Hendrickson, 1998.

Hallo, W. W., and W. K. Simpson. *The Ancient Near East: A History*. 2nd ed. Belmont, CA: Wadsworth, 1998.

Hallo, W. W., and K. L. Younger, eds. *The Context of Scripture*. 3 vols. Leiden: Brill, 1997–2002.

Hoerth, A., G. Mattingly, and E. M. Yamauchi, eds. *Peoples of the Old Testament World*. Grand Rapids: Baker, 1994.

Kemp, B. *Ancient Egypt*. London: Routledge, 1989.

Kuhrt, A. *The Ancient Near East*. 2 vols. London: Routledge, 1995.

Noth, M. *The Old Testament World*. Trans. Victor I. Gruhn. London: Adam & Charles Black, 1964.

Oates, J. *Babylon*. New York: Thames & Hudson, 1986.

Olmstead, A. T. *History of the Persian Empire*. Chicago: University of Chicago Press, 1948.

Oppenheim, A. Leo. *Ancient Mesopotamia*. Chicago: University of Chicago Press, 1964.

Pritchard, J. B., ed. *Ancient Near Eastern Texts Relating to the Old Testament*. 3rd ed. Princeton, NJ: Princeton University Press, 1968.

Roux, Georges. *Ancient Iraq*. Harmondworth, UK: Penguin, 1966.

Sasson, Jack M., ed. *Civilizations of the Ancient Near East*. 4 vols. New York: Scribner's Sons, 1995.

Soden, Wolfram von. *The Ancient Orient*. Grand Rapids: Eerdmans, 1994.

Van der Woude, ed. *The World of the Bible*. Translated by Sierd Woudstra. Grand Rapids: Eerdmans, 1986.

Wiseman, D. J., ed. *Peoples of Old Testament Times*. Oxford: Clarendon, 1973.

History of Israel

Albright, W. F. *From the Stone Age to Christianity*. Garden City, NY: Doubleday, 1957.

Bright, J. *A History of Israel*. 3rd ed. Philadelphia: Westminster, 1981.

Clements, R. E., ed. *The World of Ancient Israel*. Cambridge: Cambridge University Press, 1989.

Finkelstein, I. *The Archaeology of the Israelite Settlement*. Jerusalem: Israel Exploration Society, 1988.

Fritz, V., and P. R. Davies. *The Origins of the Ancient Israelite States*. Sheffield: Sheffield Academic Press, 1996.

Hayes, J. H., and J. M. Miller, eds. *Israelite and Judaean History*. Philadelphia: Westminster, 1977.

Kaiser, W. C. *A History of Israel*. Nashville: B&H, 1998.

Kallai, Z. *Historical Geography of the Bible*. Jerusalem: Magnes, 1986.

Kitchen, K. A. *Ancient Orient and Old Testament*. London: Tyndale, 1966.

———. *On the Reliability of the Old Testament*. Grand Rapids: Eerdmans, 2003.

Long, V. Phillips, ed. *Israel's Past in Recent Research*. Winona Lake, IN: Eisenbrauns, 1999.

———, D. W. Baker, and G. Wenham, eds. *Windows into Old Testament History*. Grand Rapids: Eerdmans, 2002.

Merrill, Eugene H. *Kingdom of Priests: A History of Old Testament Israel*. 2nd ed. Grand Rapids: Baker, 2008.

Millard, A. R., and D. J. Wiseman, eds. *Essays on the Patriarchal Narratives*. Winona Lake, IN: Eisenbrauns, 1983.

Miller, J. M., and J. H. Hayes. *A History of Ancient Israel and Judah*. Philadelphia: Westminster, 1986.

Noth, M. *The History of Israel*. New York: Harper, 1958.

———. *A History of Pentateuchal Traditions*. Englewood Cliffs, NJ: Prentice-Hall, 1972.

Provan, I., V. P. Long, and T. Longman III. *A Biblical History of Israel*. Louisville: Westminster John Knox, 2003.

Tadmor, H., and M. Weinfeld. *History, Historiography and Interpretation*. Jerusalem: Magnes, 1983.

Thiele, Edwin R. *The Mysterious Numbers of the Hebrew Kings*. Grand Rapids: Eerdmans, 1965.

CHAPTER 3

THE CULTURAL WORLD OF THE OLD TESTAMENT

MARK F. ROOKER

T O UNDERSTAND BETTER the historical period of OT Israel requires an acquaintance with the cultural context of the times and the region. Much can be learned of Israel's cultural context through the disciplines of geography and archaeology. Besides describing the physical nature of the earth's surface, geography also addresses features such as climate, plants, and natural resources. Archaeology, on the other hand, is the study of the ancient remains of a civilization. Through the study of geography and archaeology one is in a better position to comprehend the cultural context and thus the message of the OT text.

GEOGRAPHY

The land of Palestine was part of a crescent-shaped strip of land able to support agricultural life between the rugged mountains of Armenia and the great Arabian desert. This land strip, which stretched from Egypt on the southwest up the Mediterranean coast through Palestine and Syria, and down the Tigris-Euphrates valley to the Persian Gulf, was known as the Fertile Crescent. This area was connected by river valleys and coastal plains with sometimes unpredictable but adequate rainfall and agricultural abundance. It was in this region that human civilization began toward the end of the fourth millennium BC.

Located on the bridge of three continents (Asia, Africa, and Europe), Israel's geographic location took center stage in almost every event of importance in the ancient Near East. The following pages provide a general survey of the main geographical features of the ANE with a focus on the land of Israel, the location of the majority of OT events.

Mesopotamia

"Mesopotamia" is from a Greek word meaning "The land between the two rivers," that is, the Tigris and the Euphrates. These two rivers were fed by melting snows in the mountains of eastern Anatolia and made their way southward until they reached the Persian Gulf. The early civilizations of Sumer and Akkad developed along these two rivers as irrigation enhanced the use of farm land and created a surplus for trade. Israel traces its origins to Mesopotamia as Abraham not only migrated from Ur but lived in northern Mesopotamia in the area of Harran of Paddan-aram between the Tigris and Euphrates rivers before he arrived in the land of Canaan (see Ezek 16:3).

Egypt

The other great power of the ancient Near East was Egypt. Like Mesopotamia, Egypt developed along a river, the great Nile River. In contrast to the unpredictable Tigris and Euphrates rivers, the Nile had an established cycle of flooding which continually added new layers of rich soil along its banks. Also in contrast to Mesopotamia, Egypt was geographically isolated. Egypt was cut off from the west by the Sahara, from the south by the Nilotic cataracts, from the east by the Red Sea and the Sinai Peninsula, and from the north by the Mediterranean Sea. These factors contributed in a significant way to making Egypt a stable and unified civilization.

The Land of Palestine

The land of Palestine (or Canaan), south of Syria, was part of the overland route connecting three continents, thus making this tiny region a hub of commerce and the line of march of conquering armies. The latter naturally made an indelible impression on the peoples of the area. The main arteries of commercial travel in the Middle East passed through Palestine as illustrated in the Bible (Gen 37:25; 1 Kgs 4:21–34; 9:15–18; 2 Chr 8:4) and the Amarna letters (EA 7:73; 8:13; 52:37; 225:8; 226:15). Because of its unique location and small size Israel often found itself under the influence of foreign control whether Egyptian, Mesopotamian, Hittite, Persian, Greek, or Roman. Yet its position as a land bridge also allowed the nation to be exposed to many cultural influences carried by foreigners who traversed through the small land strip. This greatly enhanced imports and exports in Palestine, allowing it to become a melting pot of numerous cultures.[1]

The land of Israel is only about 150 miles in length and 75 miles in width at its widest point, making it roughly the size of New Jersey or Vermont, or about 10,000 square miles. Many nations the size of Israel are characterized by a single and uniform terrain and climate. Israel, however, is extremely varied, with alternations from high mountains to flat plains and sub-sea level valleys,[2] and from desert to agricultural conditions, all within an incredibly small land mass. The mountains of Lebanon form a natural northern border, and a 120-mile strip of desert separates Palestine from Egypt in the south. The land is bordered by the desert in the east and the Mediterranean on the west (see map 9).

The westerly winds that blow over Israel are part of a low-pressure weather system from the sea that brings in the winter rains and the summer breezes. From the desert regions on both the east and south on the other hand come dust and dryness along with the hot desert winds. These winds, known as the *khamsin,* normally arrive twice a year near the end of March and in September-October. The arrival of the *khamsin* in the spring signals the end of the blossoming landscape as vegetation quickly becomes desolate and dried up (Isa 40:6–8). Winds originating over the dry areas to the south bring no rain in their passage over the southern section of Israel (Luke 12:54–55). The intermittent rains, usually beginning in October-November and ending in March-April, revive the vegetation. These are the "former and latter rains" so commonly

---

[1] Y. Aharoni, *The Land of the Bible,* rev. ed. (Philadelphia: Westminster, 1979), 6.

[2] The eastern slopes of the Judean mountains well illustrate this diversity. Within 15 miles of the Judean mountains there is a steep descent of more than 3,000 feet.

mentioned in the OT (Jer 5:24; Hos 6:3; Joel 2:23). The end of the rainy season in the spring is normally followed by three to four completely rainless summer months. In biblical times it was only in the spring of the year after the harvests were completed and the rivers could be crossed that wars could be conducted (2 Sam 11:1).

Precipitation varies greatly throughout the area because of varying geographical locations and changes in altitude. Any such change in topography normally causes a change in climate. The coastal strip and the northern mountains receive the most rainfall, whereas the southern and eastern regions bordered by arid desert country receive the least. The rainfall pattern tends to decrease from north to south and from the west to east, averaging as much as 30 inches of rain per year in Galilee, 23 to 25 inches in Jerusalem, and only eight to nine inches in Beersheba. Because of plentiful rainfall and massive limestone rock foundations there is an abundance of springs in Palestine, particularly in those areas marking a transition from mountainous regions to lowlands. Over 100 springs exist along the Jordan Valley north of the Sea of Galilee.

The land of Palestine is often divided longitudinally into four regions or strips: the Coastal Plain, the Central Mountain Range, the Jordan River Valley, and the Transjordan Plateau.[3] The altitudinal differences among these regions is extreme (see map 10). The mountains in the Upper Galilee, in the area of Hebron, and in the Negev of the central mountain region may rise to a height of more than 3,000 feet above sea level while the elevation in the plains and valleys is right at or below sea level.[4]

Coastal plain. The Coastal Plain, narrow in the north, broadens gradually along the Mediterranean Sea as it extends southward. In the north the Plain is interrupted twice by hills jutting into the sea—the Carmel Cape and the Cape of Rosh Haniqra. The shore line consists of sand dunes that forced ancient human settlement and transportation highways farther inland. Unlike Tyre and Sidon in Phoenicia to the north, the coastline was not suitable for harbor facilities.[5] But the major highway connecting Egypt to Damascus, the Via Maris, "the Way of the Sea" (Isa 9:1), passed through the Coastal Plain just east of the dunes and marshes. The existence of this road along with an abundance of natural springs and high water levels enabled this region to be densely populated in biblical times. Being situated near the sea, the Coastal Plain does not have a great variety in temperature, daily or seasonally. Other fertile zones in this region include the Plains of Acco, Sharon, and Philistia.

The Plain of Acco extends north from the foothills of Mount Carmel for about 20 miles with a width ranging from two to ten miles. South of Mount Carmel is the Plain of Sharon which is approximately 50 miles long with a maximum width of 12 miles. The Philistine Plain, which begins just north of Joppa and extends 70 miles south, reaches a width of close to 25 miles near Beersheba.[6]

Central mountain range. The Central Mountain Range is divided into four regions: Galilee, Samaria, the mountains of Judah, and the mountains of the Negev. This region, the "backbone of Palestine," is a watershed since the mountains, which reach heights of 4,000 feet, slope westward toward the Mediterranean Sea and eastward toward the Jordan Valley. Most of the Israelite

---

[3] Small fissures in the land naturally divide the land into four major latitudinal regions: Galilee in the north, Samaria in the north-central area, Judah in the south-central area, and the Negev in the south.

[4] Farther north in Lebanon the mountains rise to 9,000 feet, Mount Hermon being the tallest summit bordering the Fertile Crescent.

[5] The city of Ugarit, modern Ras Shamra, off the Syrian coast also apparently was a thriving coastal town from 1600 to 1200 BC.

[6] For many years the southern part of the Coastal Plain was controlled by the Philistines, the peoples from whose name the word Palestine is derived.

cities were located in this fertile region which contributed to its being the most populated in antiquity. Between the hills of Galilee and Samaria is the Jezreel Valley, not only one of the most agricultural productive areas of all Palestine, but also a vitally strategic location in biblical times as it is today. The city of Jezreel marked the entrance to this valley with Megiddo located near the western end. Megiddo became a strategic city as it shielded a mountain pass along the Via Maris.[7]

Farther south is the Judean hill country, which is more mountainous than the northern Samarian mountains. The mountains of Judah extend south of Bethel for about 60 miles to Beersheba, reaching elevations of 2,500 feet at Jerusalem and over 3,000 feet near Hebron. Jerusalem is located on the northern border of Judah and its territory served an important role as the southernmost thoroughfare to the Transjordan (2 Sam 5:6–12).

Between the mountains of Judah and the Coastal Plain is the Shephelah, a region made up of foothills and valleys where many of the battles between the Israelites and the Philistines took place. In this region the summer days are hot, but there is a measurable cooling off at night. The rainy days in the winter can be harsh. The Central Mountain Range produced an abundance of figs, olives, grapes, and pomegranates as well as oaks, cypresses, and pine trees.

Jordan River Valley. The Jordan River Valley region is actually part of a depression caused by geological faults. The average width of the north-south depression, known commonly as the Rift Valley, is about 10 miles. It contains the Jordan River, the sea of Galilee, the Dead Sea, and the Arabah. The land in the Jordan River Valley is covered with deep alluvial soil washed down from the mountains.

The Jordan River, which originates from waters supplied by springs at the base of Mount Hermon, flows down the center of the valley and empties into the Dead Sea. There is a rapid descent of the Jordan's waters from north of the sea of Galilee to the Dead Sea as most of the Jordan Valley including the Sea of Galilee is below sea level. The surface of the Dead Sea is 1,275 feet below sea level, the lowest point on the surface of the earth.[8] Because of its low elevation, the area enjoys pleasant winter temperatures (c. 70° F), but endures extremely hot summers, not uncommonly over 110° F. South of the Dead Sea is the barren and waste region known as the Arabah. The Jordan River creates a natural boundary between West Jordan (Cisjordan) and the Transjordan to the east.

Transjordan Plateau. The Transjordan Plateau contains the regions of Bashan, Gilead, Moab, and Edom. These regions are set off, from north to south, by four tributaries of the Jordan: the Yarmuk, the Jabbok, the Arnon, and the Zered. The area is most fertile at Bashan, north of the Yarmuk. With sufficient rainfall and rich volcanic soils this area was perhaps the best pastureland along the Fertile Crescent (Ps 22:12; Amos 4:1). A major road running north to south passed through the Transjordan Plateau in ancient times.

The main agricultural products of Palestine are listed in Deut 8:7–8: wheat, barley, vines, figs, pomegranates, olive oil, and honey. The land is described as "a land flowing with milk and honey."[9] This is a general idiomatic description of dairy farming and tree cultivation.[10] The metals of Palestine include copper, bronze, iron, gold, silver, and lead.

---

[7] Armageddon in Rev 16:16 is the Greek transliteration of the phrase *Har Megiddo*, "Mountain of Megiddo."

[8] The Dead Sea is about 45 miles long and 10 miles wide at its widest point. The salt content of the Dead Sea is six times greater than that of other seas in the world since it has no natural outlet.

[9] Exod 3:8,17; 13:5; 33:3; Lev 20; 24; Num 13:27; 14:8; 16:13–14; Deut 6:3; 11:9; 27:3; 31:20; Jer 11:5; 32:22; Ezek 20:6,15.

[10] Honey probably came from dates rather than from bees in biblical times. For an additional ancient attestation of the productivity of Palestine, see the story of Sinuhe (*ANET*, 21).

The great variations of topography from steep mountain slopes to sub-sea level valleys within short distances naturally divided the land into many separate regions. These divisions adversely affected travel and communication. The varied topography was a main cause for fragmentation within the country. It made national and political unity extremely difficult. This is best illustrated by the book of Joshua which describes the division of Canaan into 31 separate kingdoms, each, in fact, becoming individual city-states.

ARCHAEOLOGY

Archaeology may be defined as the "study of the material remains of man's past." These include documents written on stone, clay, parchment, and papyrus, and unwritten discoveries consisting of buildings, fortifications, household vessels, tools, weapons, and personal ornaments.

Storage jars from the palace complex of Knossos.

Scholars differ greatly on the role and value of archaeology in biblical studies in recent times. This discord may be attributed to two opposing but separate factors. The first factor is the enormous amount of archaeological material uncovered in the twentieth century from the ANE as the field of biblical archaeology came into its own as in no previous century. The second factor is the rise of the critical scholarly method that began in earnest late in the nineteenth century and continues to create skepticism regarding the historical reliability of the biblical text. This ongoing conflict is unmistakable in a statement by W. F. Albright, considered by many the foremost biblical archaeologist of the twentieth century. Near the end of his life Albright stated explicitly what seemed to be the philosophical underpinning that motivated his research. "It was no less a scholar than Julius Wellhausen, to whose Hegelian presuppositions we owe the still dominant theory of Israelite religious evolution—which I have opposed throughout my life—who was largely responsible for dating the poetry of the Bible so late."[11]

Fourteenth-century BC pottery at Hazor in Israel.

Archaeologists and ANE historians like Albright, C. Gordon, and G. E. Wright were open to the notion that the written record of Scripture could be harmonized with archaeology data, believing that the events of the Bible could be verified through archaeology. However, since the mid 1970s scholars such as T. Thompson, J. Van Seters, and W. Dever have questioned what earlier had appeared to be a virtual consensus.[12] These scholars believe that earlier scholars like Albright, who believed that archaeology could illuminate events described in

---

[11] W. F. Albright, "Impact of Archaeology on Biblical Research–1966," in *New Directions in Biblical Archaeology*, ed. D. N. Freedman and J. Greenfield (New York: Doubleday, 1971), 13; similarly G. E. Wright, "Biblical Archaeology Today," in *New Directions in Biblical Archaeology*," 169.

[12] T. L. Thompson, *The Historicity of the Patriarchal Narratives* (New York: de Gruyter, 1974); J. Van Seters, *Abraham in History and Tradition* (New Haven, CT: Yale University Press, 1975), 104–12. See also W. G. Dever, in *Israelite and Judaean History*, ed. J. H. Hayes and F. Maxwell (Philadelphia: Westminster, 1977), 99–102.

the Bible, had been presumptuous and had overstated what archaeology had actually revealed in many cases.

Method

Proper archaeological method employs a technique called stratified excavation, which means that excavators begin their digs at the top of a mound (or *tel*) covering an ancient site. The uppermost layer contains the remains of the most recent inhabitants. The archaeological team then works its way downward through earlier periods of civilization, always attempting to keep separate the soil layers and finds within those soil layers. Because pottery is the most common and indestructible item in archaeological digs, it is the most useful item for determining dates at a particular level. In Palestine the method of dating pottery has been perfected to such a degree that there is virtual certainty that pottery fragments can be dated within two centuries or even less of their actual date. Other important techniques and methods that unveil information about ancient people include soil-analysis, pollen-grain analysis, and the uncovering of other human and animal remains.

A modern Middle Eastern potter fashioning pottery in the same manner as in biblical times.

Contribution of Archaeology

For the most part archaeology has verified and illuminated the biblical account to such an extent that one would have to be unduly biased to conclude that the biblical account is based on legend or myth.[13] By contrast, not a single critical theory has been substantiated by archaeological discovery. Although one should avoid taking the position that archaeology "proves" a precise date of a biblical event, archaeology does bring a feeling of intimacy for the modern reader with what is described in the biblical text.

Aspects of OT studies that have been illuminated by archaeological discoveries include Hebrew language, textual criticism, the history of Israel, comparative literature (with the ANE), covenant negotiations, and Hebrew poetry. Moreover, archaeology has yielded a great deal of information about the ancient peoples with whom the Israelites interacted in ancient history. Excavation has also unlocked the mysteries of such previously "dead" languages as Akkadian, Ugaritic, Egyptian, Sumerian, and Hittite.

However, it must be borne in mind that there are inherent limitations to archaeology. It will not at every point substantiate historical records, and furthermore only a small percentage of possible archaeological sites have been excavated.

---

[13] G. E. Wright, *Biblical Archaeology* (Philadelphia: Westminster, 1962), 17–18; M. Unger, *Archaeology and the Old Testament* (Grand Rapids: Zondervan, 1954), 15–18.

To illustrate the contribution archaeology has made to a better understanding of the biblical text, the following seven examples from Egypt, Mesopotamia, and Syria-Palestine are briefly summarized.[14]

Tell El Amarna

In 1887 an Egyptian peasant woman accidentally discovered a large number of tablets at El-Amarna in Middle Egypt. About 150 of these letters were diplomatic correspondences to and from Palestine during the reigns of Amenophis III (1417–1379) and his son Amenophis IV (better known as Akhenaten [1379–1362]). Because most of the letters were written by Canaanite scribes in the Akkadian language, which, though it was the *lingua franca* of the second millennium BC, was not well understood by them, many Canaanite elements in vocabulary, syntax, morphology, and phonology are detectable from the explanatory glosses. These glosses have been extremely valuable in aiding the understanding of the Canaanite language in the middle of the second millennium BC, a language that was a close relative to early biblical Hebrew.

Most of the Amarna letters contain complaints to Egyptian authorities about a certain group of *Apiru* in Palestine who carried out frequent invasions against the native Canaanites. Because the letters were written near the time the Israelites entered Canaan, many scholars were quick to identify the *Apiru* with the Hebrews (*'Ibri*) as the terms seem to be cognate nouns. Based on this identity, it was natural to conclude that what is being described by these *Apiru* attacks in the Amarna letters was the Israelite conquest of Canaan. However, this thesis was later modified because evidence of *Apiru* existence became increasingly attested to in other regions such as Babylon, Mari, Nuzi, and Boghazkoi, even as early as the Old Akkadian period (c. 2360–2180 BC). It is now apparent that the term *Apiru* is not an ethnic designation referring to the Israelites but rather a social designation referring to a class of people who acted much like mercenaries. Yet, it is still possible, if not likely, that Canaanite scribes confused these two groups.[15]

Nuzi

The town of Nuzi, located about 250 miles north of Babylon, was excavated between 1925 and 1931 by Edward Chiera. At this site over 3,500 cuneiform tablets were discovered which were dated to the fifteenth century BC. These tablets refer to customs and practices which seem to parallel many of the customs found in the patriarchal narratives. We find in the Nuzi tablets such practices as adoption and inheritance laws (Gen 15:2), the provision of surrogate mothers for barren wives (16:2), the gift of a female slave as part of a dowry (29:24,29), the sale of birthright (25:29–34), and deathbed blessings (49:3–4). Thompson and Van Seters have challenged the notion that the patriarchal narratives could be dated based on these parallels.[16] While using the tablets for dating the patriarchal narratives should not be forced, customs and practices observed at Nuzi and elsewhere do suggest that the customs and practices observed in

---

[14] When the research has been completed on the thousands of cuneiform tablets discovered at Tell Mardikh (ancient Ebla), this ancient site will surely make a great contribution to the field of biblical studies and its cultural world. For a brief description of what is known to date see M. Chavalas and E. Hostetter, "Epigraphic Light on the Old Testament," in *The Face of Old Testament Studies*, ed. D. Baker and B. Arnold (Grand Rapids: Baker, 1999), 40.

[15] See E. H. Merrill, *Kingdom of Priests*, 2nd ed. (Grand Rapids: Baker, 2008), 117–25.

[16] Thompson, *The Historicity of the Patriarchal Narratives*; Van Seters, *Abraham in History and Tradition*.

the patriarchal narratives were well attested in the second millennium and consequently add to our understanding of the patriarchal way of life.

Mari

In 1933 a group of Arab clansmen were preparing a grave for one of their kin at Mari, about 15 and a half miles north of the Syrian-Iraqi border on the south side of the Euphrates River, when they discovered a statue bearing a cuneiform inscription. Shortly after the inscription was identified, the full-scale excavation of Mari began. Thousands of letters and economic and administrative texts were found dating from 1800 to 1760 BC, the Old Babylonian period. These writings are important for biblical studies if only for the fact that the Harran region where Abraham's family lived figures prominently in the Mari texts. The people of the Mari archives were of Amorite descent, thus making them genetic relatives to the Israelites (Ezek 16:3). Like Abraham, the Amorites were involved in western migrations at the beginning of the second millennium BC. The native language of these people was secondarily related to the Northwest Semitic language group from which Hebrew sprang. At Mari there is also evidence of the concept of the "ban" similar to what is found in the Old Testament as well as possible parallels to Hebrew prophecy.[17]

Ugarit

The Ugaritic cuneiform tablets were discovered by accident in 1929 in modern-day Ras Shamra, Syria. The archives have yielded some 1,400 texts in the Ugaritic language, a Northwest Semitic language very close to Hebrew. Among these finds are mythological texts that have greatly expanded the understanding of Canaanite religion and worship, especially the worship of Baal. Ugaritic has greatly increased knowledge of the lexicography, syntax, and prosody of the Hebrew language.[18] Moreover, Ugaritic contains technical Old Testament terms for sacrifice, such as the peace offering and offerings made by fire.

Dead Sea Scrolls

A shepherd accidentally discovered the first of the DSS in 1947 in a cave at Qumran northwest of the Dead Sea. Often called the most significant archaeological find of the twentieth century, the DSS contained Hebrew manuscripts of the OT that predated the earliest manuscripts by more than a millennium. The DSS have also widened our understanding of Judaism in the first century AD, and they also include themes, motifs, and messianic expectations prevalent in the NT.[19]

Ketef Hinnom

On an encampment identified as Ketef Hinnom overlooking the Hinnom Valley (Gehenna) opposite Mount Zion an inscription on two small cylindrical silver rolls was discovered by Gabriel Barkay in 1979. Inside both rolls were eighteen written lines containing a portion of Num 6:24–26, the priestly benediction. This find, dated to the seventh century BC, is the oldest biblical text ever discovered.

---

[17] See Part 6, "The Prophetic Books," 361–66.

[18] For contribution of Ugaritic regarding the technical term for the vocation of Amos, see 431.

[19] For contribution of the Dead Sea Scrolls to Old Testament textual criticism, see 116–17.

Tel Dan

In the summer of 1993 Avraham Biran discovered a fragment of a stele in northern Galilee which mentions the "king of Israel" and the "house of David." This Aramaic inscription, which is dated to the ninth century BC, represents the first ancient extrabiblical reference to King David.[20]

TRADE AND COMMERCE

In the land of Israel various workshops have been uncovered which provide general information regarding the various occupations of the Israelites in biblical times. Various metal workshops for example have been discovered and in En-gedi a workshop existed where resin was prepared from medicinal and aromatic plants. What are believed to be pottery workshops have been uncovered in other locations. Large quantities of spinning and weaving implements have been discovered in private homes, indicating that Israelites generally wore home-woven garments (Prov 31:13,19,22,24).

During the First Temple period potters lived near "the Potsherd Gate" in Jerusalem (Jer 18:2–4; 19:2). Other Jerusalem gates such as the "Fish Gate" (2 Chr 33:14; Neh 3:3; 12:39; Zeph 1:10), and the "Sheep Gate" (Neh 3:1,32; 12:39) were known for the merchandise that was marketed in their respective vicinities. Similarly in Jerusalem there existed a "street of the bakers" (Jer 37:21 NIV) which was apparently a street where bakers were concentrated.

Merchants involved in marketing their crafts passed their knowledge and skill down to their children who would carry on their business (1 Chr 4:1–23). Apart from a few well-known periods of time, most notably the Solomonic regime, trade in Israel was largely intranational rather than international.[21] It could be argued in fact that there was a derogatory feeling attached to the merchant in that the Hebrew word for "merchant" is the same word translated "Canaanite"[22] (Neh 13:16; Job 40:20; 41:6; Prov 31:24; Isa 23:8; Ezek 17:4; Hos 12:7). Regardless, agriculture was the primary source of livelihood with wine and oil serving as the most important articles of trade in Palestine. As Josephus stated, "Ours is not a maritime country; neither commerce nor the intercourse which it promotes with the outside world has any attraction for us. Our cities are built inland, remote from the sea; and we devote ourselves to the cultivation of the productive country with which we are pleased."[23]

WRITING

Writing, which may be defined as the use of graphic signs for the systematic use of a spoken language, is one of the great cultural achievements of mankind. As the primary means of cultural expression, it reflects individual and collective cultures. The earliest inscribed objects that have been uncovered come from the Mesopotamian and Egyptian regions where writing and civilization developed around the end of the fourth millennium BC. These documents were written in cuneiform and hieroglyphics.

The alphabetic writing system began to develop in Syro-Palestine in the second millennium BC. This is evident from the 24-symbol pictographic writing system discovered at Serabit

---

[20] See A. Biran and J. Naveh, "An Aramaic Stele Fragment from Tel Dan," *IEJ* 43, nos. 2–3 (1993): 81–98.

[21] This might be inferred from the few legal prescriptions regulating trade (e.g., Lev 19:35–36; Deut 25:15–16) when compared with the more numerous Hittite and Mesopotamian regulations addressing merchants and trade.

[22] The term also refers to "the land of purple" because of the purple dye manufactured from the murex shellfish in the region.

[23] Josephus, *Ag. Ap.* I. XII. 160.

el-Khadem in an Egyptian turquoise mine in the Sinai Peninsula. These inscriptions have been dated from 1900 to 1400 BC. Three possibly older inscriptions discovered at Gezer, Lachish, and Shechem use this same script. More recently a Semitic alphabetic text has come to light in Wadi El-Hol in South Egypt.[24] It may have been composed as early as 1900 BC. All these early examples derived from pictographs, which probably developed in turn from Egyptian hiero-glyphs and later evolved into the Phoenician letters of the alphabet. The Greeks borrowed this Phoenician alphabet possibly as early as 1100 BC, as there is evidence of commercial contacts between the Phoenicians and Greeks from this time.[25] Another attestation to this same Proto-Canaanite alphabet was used in cuneiform script at Ugarit before 1300 BC. This language has been attested in Palestine at Beth-shemesh, Taanach, and Nahal Tavor. According to Aharoni, writing was the greatest Canaanite cultural achievement.[26]

RELIGION

Beliefs and Practices

While the introduction of writing was a great accomplishment, many would argue that it is in the area of religion that the ANE and particularly Israel made its greatest cultural contribution.

The earliest writings of the great ANE civilizations demonstrate that these primitive cul-tures were preoccupied with the forces of nature which they often associated with a particular god. The forces of nature were often personified as gods which pagan man would try to placate to avoid an adverse experience or supplicate to derive some positive benefit. The multiplicity of natural forces led to a multiplicity of gods, hence the development of the pagan panthe-ons. The names of about 40 gods and goddesses are known from Egypt, the Hittites referred to their "thousand gods," and Mesopotamia had names for more than 3,000 gods. The gods were given sacrifices in their temples, which for the pagan mind indicated that the gods were being fed. These gods were under no obligation to be ethical or consistent, and in fact the pagan gods were often depicted as extremely immoral. In the Canaanite religion, "worship" of Baal involved sexual intercourse with temple prostitutes to activate their god to fertilize and impregnate the earth.[27]

Pagan Worldview

According to the pagan way of thought the essence of power in the universe was a primor-dial realm that in fact was prior to the gods and to which the gods were dependent.[28] The gods, the primordial realm, and all other aspects of reality were viewed as part of an interlocking reality, which meant that all historical phenomena were somehow related. Since the forces of nature were the expression of a particular god, to influence this god positively one must iden-tify the god responsible for the predicament and placate him through the appropriate ritual or sacrifice. The ritual might involve physical pain and even mutilation (Deut 14:1; 1 Kgs

---

[24] *ACORN* 14/1 (2002):9–10.

[25] The Greek historian Herodotus asserted that according to Greek tradition writing was brought to Greece by the Phoe-nicians by a legendary person known as Kadmos.

[26] Y. Aharoni, *The Archaeology of the Land of Israel*, trans. A. F. Rainey (Philadelphia: Westminster, 1982), 145.

[27] See *ANET*, 3–155, 325–401; J. M. Sasson, ed., *Civilizations of the Ancient Near East* (New York: Scribner's Sons, 1995), 3:1, 685–2094; E. R. Clendenen, "Religious Background of the Old Testament," in *Foundations for Biblical Interpre-tation*, ed. D. Dockery, K. Mathews, and R. Sloan (Nashville: B&H, 1994), 244–305; and J. Walton, "Cultural Background of the Old Testament," in *Foundations for Biblical Interpretation*, 255–73.

[28] Y. Kaufmann, *The Religion of Israel*, trans. M. Greenberg (New York: Schocken, 1972), 21–22.

18:26–29). If a certain phenomenon occurred in conjunction with an event, whether positive or negative, it was assumed that a recurrence of the phenomenon would suggest that the same event would follow. This is the philosophical rationale behind the pagan concept of divination. Mesopotamian scribes in particular made extensive catalogs of all sorts of unusual occurrences with the events that accompanied them. In their divination practices, specialists applied the methods of extispicy (the examination of the entrails of sacrificial animals), hepatoscopy (the reading of animal livers), and astrology. Horoscopes were developed in Babylonia in the fifth century BC and presumably later in Greece and Egypt. And yet the overriding perception was still the cold reality that the will of the gods was mysterious and unknowable.

Israelite Religion

The one concept that transformed Israelite culture and literature was its concept of deity.[29] Unlike the pagan gods the God of Israel revealed Himself and clearly made known His desires and His expectations from His people. He did not need to be fed and maintained by His worshippers; as the all-Sovereign God He needs nothing.

People were not created merely to meet the needs of the gods as seen particularly in Sumerian and Mesopotamian myths. Humans, as the crowns of creation, were created in the image of God and are to exercise dominion as God's representative over the created order. While God does require ritual in His service, this ritual was not a magical spell that could force God to act. It was a form of obedience and was rejected by God if not offered in the spirit of a genuine heartfelt worship and love for God. What was truly distinctive about the Israelite religion was not its cultural or moral superiority—instead its unique monotheistic faith revealed to them the true and living God.

STUDY QUESTIONS

1. What is the difference between geography and archaeology?
2. Israel is located on the bridge of what three continents?
3. Mesopotamia is located between what two rivers?
4. What are the four major land strips of the land of Israel?
5. Who was the foremost biblical archaeologist of the twentieth century?
6. What is the contribution of the Tel Amarna letters to biblical studies?
7. What has been considered the most significant archaeological find of the twentieth century?
8. Where is the location of the earliest biblical verses that have been discovered?
9. What contribution has archaeology made to biblical studies?
10. In what two regions did writing begin?
11. Where did the alphabet emerge?
12. In what way is Israel's view of God different from pagan perceptions?

FOR FURTHER STUDY

Aharoni, Y. *The Land of the Bible: A Historical Geography*. Rev. ed. Translated by A. F. Rainey. Philadelphia: Westminster, 1979.

———, and M. Avi-Yonah. *The Macmillan Bible Atlas*. New York: Macmillan, 1968.

Albright, W. F. "Impact of Archaeology on Biblical Research—1966." In *New Directions in Biblical Archaeology*. Edited by D. N. Freedman and J. C. Greenfield, 1–16. New York: Doubleday, 1971.

Avi-Yonah, M. *The Holy Land: A Historical Geography*. Rev. ed. Grand Rapids: Baker, 1977.

---

[29] J. Walton, "Cultural Background of the Old Testament," 271.

Baly, D. *The Geography of the Bible*. Rev. ed. New York: Harper & Row, 1974.

Beitzel, B. J. *The New Moody Atlas of the Bible*. Chicago: Moody, 2009.

Berrigan, D. *The Kings and Their Gods: The Pathology of Power*. Grand Rapids: Eerdmans, 2008.

Borowski, O. *Daily Life in Biblical Times*. Atlanta: Society of Biblical Literature, 2003.

Chavalas, M. W., and E. Hostetter. "Epigraphic Light on the Old Testament." In *The Face of Old Testament Studies*. Edited by D. W. Baker and B. T. Arnold, 38–58. Grand Rapids: Baker, 1999.

Dever, W., and W. M. Clark. "The Patriarchal Traditions." In *Israelite and Judaean History*. Edited by J. H. Hayes and F. Maxwell, 70–148. Philadelphia: Westminster, 1977.

Dockery, D., K. Mathews, and R. Sloan, eds. *Foundations for Biblical Interpretation*. Nashville: B&H, 1994.

Hoerth, A. J., G. L. Mattingly, and E. M. Yamauchi, eds. *Peoples of Old Testament Times*. Grand Rapids: Baker, 1994.

———. *Archaeology and the Old Testament*. Grand Rapids: Baker, 1998.

Hoffmeier, J. K. *Israel in Egypt: The Evidence for the Authenticity of the Exodus Tradition*. New York: Oxford University Press, 1997.

Kaufmann, Y. *The History of the Religion of Israel*. 4th ed. Jerusalem: Bialik Institute & Dvir, 1937–56 (in Hebrew).

———. *The Religion of Israel*. Translated by M. Greenberg. New York: Shocken, 1972.

Kitchen, K. A. *The Bible in Its World: The Bible and Archaeology Today*. Downers Grove, IL: InterVarsity, 1977.

———. *On the Reliability of the Old Testament*. Grand Rapids: Eerdmans, 2003.

Merrill, E. H. *Kingdom of Priests. A History of Old Testament Israel*. 2nd ed. Grand Rapids: Baker, 2008.

Rogerson, J., and P. Davies. *The Old Testament World*. Englewood Cliffs, NJ: Prentice-Hall, 1989.

Sasson, J. M. *Civilizations of the Ancient Near East*. 4 vols. New York: Scribners, 1995.

Shanks, H. *Abraham and Family: New Insights into the Patriarchal Narratives*. Washington, DC: Biblical Archaeology Society, 2000.

Thompson, T. L. *Early History of the Israelite People from the Written and Archaeological Sources*. Leiden: Brill, 1992.

Unger, M. *Archaeology and the Old Testament*. Translated by S. Woudstra. Grand Rapids: Eerdmans, 1986.

Van der Woude, A. S., ed. *The World of the Old Testament*. Translated by S. Woudstra. Grand Rapids: Eerdmans, 1986.

Von Soden, W. *The Ancient Orient: An Introduction to the Study of the Ancient Near East*. Translated by D. G. Schley. Grand Rapids: Eerdmans, 1994.

Wright, G. E. "Biblical Archaeology Today." In *New Directions in Biblical Archaeology*. Edited by D. N. Freedman and J. C. Greenfield, 167–86. New York: Doubleday, 1969.

CHAPTER 4

ANCIENT NEAR EASTERN LITERATURE AND THE OLD TESTAMENT

MICHAEL A. GRISANTI

A SURVEY OF EXTANT WRITTEN MATERIALS

Major Archives

The texts of the OT and NT, inscribed primarily on leather and parchment, were found in all kinds of conditions. The DSS preserve the oldest remains of biblical books as well as numerous copies of apocryphal and pseudepigraphical writings (see chap. 6) along with various sectarian documents (c. third century BC to first century AD). On the other hand the majority of ancient Near Eastern texts were buried deep beneath earth and rubble until nineteenth- and twentieth-century archaeologists began to unearth them at a great number of locations. Although people from those ancient times most likely kept records on various kinds of materials, only clay tablets by the multiplied thousands have survived the millennia to shed light on life and thought from that distant world. These tablets fall into two categories, based on their function in the ANE. First, libraries located in public buildings such as palaces and temples or in smaller private collections in homes[1] made information (scientific, literary, religious, and historical) available to scholars for reading, consultation, and research. Second, archives associated with administrative sites yielded caches of official documents related to state business.[2] A total of more than 250 libraries and archives from the period between 1500 and

---

[1] These collections were owned by priests, scribes, diviners, exorcists, temple singers, businessmen, and public officials (K. L. Sparks, *Ancient Texts for the Study of the Hebrew Bible: A Guide to the Background Literature* [Peabody, MA: Hendrickson, 2005], 26).

[2] Ibid., 25–26. Sparks also distinguishes between storage and functional archives.

300 BC have been unearthed from 50 different cities.[3] Sparks provides the following table of important archival and library finds.

Important Archival and Library Finds from the Ancient Near East[4]				
	Before 2000	**2000–1500**	**1500–1000**	**1000–300**
Mesopotamia	Uruk, Ur, Nippur, Puzrish-Dagan	Assur, Kish	Assur, Babylon Nippur, Nuzi	Assur, Babylon Kal–u, Sippar, Nineveh, Uruk, Nippur
Syria-Palestine	Ebla	Mari, Alalakh	Emar, Alalakh	
Anatolia		Kaneš (Kultepe)*	–attuša	
Egypt	Abusir	Deir el-Medina, Saqqara	Akhetaton (Amarna)*	Elephantine
Modern names are in parentheses: all dates are BC.				

Overview of Ancient Near Eastern Literature

After introducing some key resources in this area of study, the remainder of this section is an overview of some of the important primary sources represented in ANE literature. That overview is arranged in accord with the nature or content of the primary sources.[5]

Key resources. Several editions and translations of these literatures exist in readily accessible anthologies that enable students of Scripture to engage primary texts from the ANE world. The two most commonly cited and most inclusive are William W. Hallo and K. Lawson Younger, *The Context of Scripture* (*COS*);[6] and James B. Pritchard, ed., *Ancient Near Eastern Texts Relating to the Old Testament* (*ANET*).[7] *COS* offers a more up-to-date translation and bibliography for most of the texts found in *ANET*, but it does not totally replace *ANET*. Each category of primary sources, whether arranged by language or geographical region, has a list of resources that provide translation, commentary, and additional bibliography for that literature. These resources will not be listed here, but a few other convenient works point the reader to publications containing that information.

---

[3] These finds include 28 libraries, 198 archives, and 27 library/archive collections. One of the best sources on this information is O. Pedersén, *Archives and Libraries in the Ancient Near East: 1500-300 B.C.* (Bethesda, MD: CDL, 1998). Pedersén is also working on a second volume covering the earlier period.

[4] Sparks, *Ancient Texts for the Study of the Hebrew Bible*, 27. For a helpful overview of these and other archives and libraries, along with collections of texts, translations, and other key bibliographic sources, see ibid., 33–55.

[5] More extensive treatments of this material can be found in Sparks, *Ancient Texts for the Study of the Hebrew Bible*, 56–476; J. H. Walton, *Ancient Israelite Literature in Its Cultural Context: A Survey of Parallels between Biblical and Ancient Near Eastern Texts* (Grand Rapids: Zondervan, 1989); idem., *Ancient Near Eastern Thought and the Old Testament: Introducing the Conceptual World of the Hebrew Bible* (Grand Rapids: Baker, 2006), 43–83.

[6] W. W. Hallo and K. L. Younger, eds., *The Context of Scripture*, 3 vols. (New York: Brill, 1997–2002).

[7] J. B. Pritchard, ed., *Ancient Near Eastern Texts Relating to the Old Testament*, 3rd ed. (Princeton, NJ: Princeton University Press, 1969).

Two volumes stand out as helpful tools that seek to arrange primary ANE sources with sections of the OT. The first one is Bill T. Arnold and Bryan E. Beyer, *Readings from the Ancient Near East: Primary Sources for Old Testament Study*.[8] In this volume Arnold and Beyer provide excerpts from 90 primary documents in four major sections: Pentateuch, historical books, poetic books, and prophetic books. Under these sections they provide readings from various language groups and regions of the ANE. A brief introduction of a given primary document and a resource that contains the full text of that account introduce each excerpt. No attempt is made to offer parallels to the biblical literatures except through the arrangement of the readings in accordance with the major sections of the OT.

The second volume is Victor C. Matthews and Don C. Benjamin, *Old Testament Parallels: Laws and Stories from the Ancient Near East*.[9] Matthews and Benjamin arrange 61 primary sources in the order of the books of the Bible. They also include brief introductions to each excerpted account along with summaries interspersed in the midst of the longer texts. In several places they cite biblical passages where a biblical parallel occurs. One of the helpful features in this volume is a bibliography of texts in translation, transcription, transliteration, and translation from relatively current resources.[10] Another useful addition is an index of alleged parallels that locates the biblical passage, page number, the ANE text, and the basic idea of the parallel.[11]

Survey of Ancient Near Eastern Literature

The following survey of ANE literature provides only a brief sketch of available materials. It consists of summary statements about the broad content; refers to one, two, or three representative compositions; and makes a few comparative statements with regard to biblical literature.

Wisdom literature. The content of this kind of literature falls into two categories. First, standard or optimistic wisdom assumes predictable patterns that the wise should follow. Second, speculative wisdom implicitly or explicitly questions standard wisdom. In light of their manner of presentation, this category of literature includes short proverbs, longer "instruction" or "admonition" writings, as well as philosophical treatises that deal with theodicy, suffering, and meaning in life.

Babylonian Theodicy is an acrostic dialogue consisting of 27 stanzas of 11 lines each.[12] It presents a dialogue between a man and his friend in which the friend seeks to defend the traditional view of the universe and society against the complaints of the suffering man (like Job's friends). The Egyptian composition *Instruction of Amenemope* is a compilation of Amenemope's words of advice to his son.[13] It consists of a prologue and 30 "sayings" through which the father figure seeks to have his son develop inner virtue. It bears a number of similarities to Prov 22:17–24:22. The following is one example of many that could be cited:

---

[8] B. T. Arnold and B. E. Beyer, eds., *Readings from the Ancient Near East: Sources for Old Testament Study* (Grand Rapids: Baker, 2002). At the end of their work, Arnold and Beyer give the reader footnote references and a bibliography that enable the student to pursue further studies in this area.

[9] V. H. Matthews and D. C. Benjamin, *Old Testament Parallels: Laws and Stories from the Ancient Near East*, 2nd ed. (New York: Paulist, 1997).

[10] Ibid., 338–49. They also include a bibliography of the images that occur throughout the book (ibid., 350–51).

[11] Ibid., 355–84.

[12] *COS*, 1.154, 492–95; *ANET*, 601–4.

[13] *COS*, 1.47, 115–22; *ANET*, 421–25.

Instruction of Amenemope, III, 9–11[14]	**Proverbs 22:17–18**
He says:	
Give your ears, hear the sayings,	Pay attention and listen to the sayings of the wise;
Give your heart to understand them;	apply your heart to what I teach,
It profits to put them in your heart,	for it is pleasing when you keep them in your heart
	and have all of them ready on your lips.

Hymns, prayers, and laments. One of the largest categories of ANE literature,[15] writings of this kind describe ANE worshippers speaking to their gods. The larger genre includes "praise hymns, songs for dying gods, laments over destroyed temples and cities, prayers for healing and protection," as well as other text types.[16] Although most of this literature derives from official settings (e.g., palace or temple), it opens a window into common attitudes, beliefs, and expectations concerning gods in the ANE world.

For example in the "Prayer to Every God" the worshipper addresses no god in particular, but all gods in general.[17] He seeks relief from suffering that he assumes was caused by some violation of divine law. He argues that since humanity is by nature ignorant of divine law and as a result is constantly committing sin, the gods should not single him out for punishment. In similar fashion the "Prayer to Marduk" expresses the frustration of the worshipper whose prayers have gone unanswered for some unknown reason.[18] He begs Marduk to relent in his anger, even calling on other gods to intercede with Marduk on his behalf.

These and other hymns, prayers, and laments demonstrate that ANE worshippers petitioned their gods about problems that are common to all humanity, including Israel, and praised them similarly for positive responses. There are also key differences; for example, the category of declarative praise, though abundantly attested in biblical psalms, is absent in ANE literature. In ANE prayers, the supplicant generally feels compelled to convince the gods to act in his favor through some kind of manipulative device, whereas request in biblical prayers draws on a personal relationship between the supplicant and God.

Rituals and incantations. Rituals generally refer to symbolic religious acts that are repeated, sacral, formalized, and intentional and that regulate contact between the human and divine worlds. They could be related to regular occasions, unusual circumstances, or sacred activities.[19] These rituals accompany the construction of temples, maintain ritual purity, signify the removal of ritual pollution, sanctify priests and priestesses, and address burial and death.

---

[14] *COS*, 1.47, 116. The question of dependency between the texts in this case is hotly debated. The best solution seems to be that each drew from a common fund of wisdom traditions.

[15] Sparks writes that this category "includes thousands of texts from diverse periods and contexts" (*Ancient Texts for the Study of the Hebrew Bible*, 84).

[16] Ibid.

[17] *ANET*, 391–92.

[18] *COS*, 1.114, 416–17.

[19] Sparks, *Ancient Texts for the Study of the Hebrew Bible*, 144; Walton, *Ancient Near Eastern Thought and the Old Testament*, 57.

The Akitu Festival, one of the most famous from Babylonia, was a 12-day enthrone-ment festival that generally took place in association with the New Year.[20] It included the re-enthronement of both the god and the human king. It also involved the recitation of Marduk's victory over Tiamat as described in the great cosmic battle recorded in *Enuma Elish*. During the ceremony the gods declared the fates or destiny of the coming year (pestilence, famine, and military defeat, or the opposite). A number of scholars have identified the Akitu Festival as a fundamental backdrop for the interpretation of the biblical enthronement psalms (Psalms 95–99).[21] Others distance themselves from this ANE connection but suggest that the biblical writers did make use of some phraseology common in the ANE that described the enthrone-ment of pagan gods in order to point to Yahweh as the sole Ruler over the world and over Israel.[22] One of the key differences is that God does not become king but has always been King.

Through a form of sympathetic magic, some ritual practices symbolically attempted to induce desired results. Egyptian execration texts contain names of loathed people, most often enemies of Egypt or some other foreign power (dating from the Old Kingdom through the Roman period).[23] Egyptian priests would ritually curse Egypt's enemies by shattering objects on which they had inscribed the names of their enemies. Some scholars have incorrectly lik-ened prophetic denunciations of Israel's enemies (Isa 13–23; Jer 45–51; Ezek 25–29; Amos 1–2) to these rituals. The biblical denunciations represent more than simple lists of condemned people, but developed presentations of future divine judgment.

Most ANE incantations were magical rituals used to ward off the demons believed to be the cause of some illness or calamity.[24] Many of them were designed to avert existing evil or to prevent or preclude something anticipated like illnesses, snake bites, domestic quarrels, infant mortality, sexual impotence, and threats posed by ominous powers (ghosts, demons, angry gods).[25] Incantations or magical rituals are incompatible with biblical theology (Exod 22:18 [HB, v. 17]; Lev 19:26,31; 20:6,27; Deut 18:10–12,14; 2 Kgs 21:6; Isa 8:19; Ezek 22:28; Mal 3:5).

Omens and prophecies. Kings in the ANE regularly sought guidance from their gods as they made strategic decisions and sought divine favor. This happened through two principal vehicles. First, "omens" communicated the will of the gods through signs that the diviner knew how to interpret (as with the Babylonian diviners in Dan 2). Second, with "prophecy" the prophet was a more direct intermediary. The ANE corpus of omen and prophetic literature is comparatively small with no collections of prophetic texts by particular prophets as in the OT.

The largest portion of ANE omen literature comes from Asshur-Banipal's library, though it is representative of practices from earlier and later periods. The first of the two most important kinds of omens was extispicy, predictions based on the appearance of the entrails of sacrificial

---

[20] Depending on the deity and the city involved, this festival was sometimes celebrated at different times of the year. See Sparks, *Ancient Texts for the Study of the Hebrew Bible*, 166–67, for the variety of ways this festival was celebrated.

[21] S. Mowinckel, *He That Cometh*, trans. G. W. Anderson (Nashville: Abingdon, n.d.), 21–95; idem, *The Psalms in Israel's Worship*, trans. D. R. Ap-Thomas (Nashville: Abingdon, 1962); and R. A. Carlson, *David: The Chosen King* (Stockholm: Almqvist & Wiksell, 1964), 62–77.

[22] C. C. Broyles, *Psalms*, NIBC (Peabody, MA: Hendrickson, 1999), 25–26; Hans-Joachim Kraus, *Psalms 60–150*, trans. H. C. Oswald (Minneapolis: Augsburg, 1989), 268–69.

[23] *COS*, 1.32, 50–52; *ANET*, 328–29.

[24] Walton, *Ancient Israelite Literature in Its Cultural Context*, 149.

[25] Sparks, *Ancient Texts for the Study of the Hebrew Bible*, 176–85.

animals. The second primary category involved astronomical observation, information based on the movements of the sun, moon, planets, and stars.[26]

The Mari prophetic texts represent the largest ANE collection of writings of this genre: more than 50 letters addressed to King Zimri-Lim (eighteenth century BC) in which prophetic oracles or visions were reported to the king.[27] The prophetic statements focus on the king's welfare (warnings of danger and advice for success), and less frequently they address the king's neglect of certain gods (mentioning at least 10 of them). Because the prophets worked in temples and viewed the king as an important benefactor of the worship of those gods, they understandably manifested those concerns in their prophetic writings. All but one of the oracles pertains to the king.

Although there are several points of similarity between ANE and biblical prophetic literature, Walton points out a few clear differences between them.[28] First, Israelite prophets did not focus on religious liturgy or related issues. As a matter of fact, biblical prophets indicted Israelite kings and commoners alike for carrying out the correct form of worship without genuine heartfelt obedience (1 Sam 15:22; Isa 1:10–17; Hos 6:4–6). Second, biblical prophetic predictions do not focus on a specific battle in the near future that will be won or lost. Instead they speak about the long-range political destiny of Israel and the surrounding nations. Third, Old Testament prophecy focuses on the people of Israel rather than Israel's king. This is because God established a unique relationship with all the inhabitants of the nation of Israel.

Epics and legends.[29] The category of epic takes its name from Greek texts like the *Iliad* and the *Odyssey*. They are essentially compositions of extended poetry that narrate the acts of cultural heroes who were usually supported but sometimes opposed by the gods. Although there is more than one way to understand "legend," ANE legends are traditional stories that delineate cultural heroes and institutions.[30] In these epics and legends, the major characters "go on various quests, adventures, and exploits that exhibit their heroism and virtues or; on occasion, expose their folly."[31] Some of the more common epics include the Akkadian *Atrahasis Epic* (combining the creation and flood accounts) and the Ugaritic *Kirta Epic* and the *Legend of Aqhat.*

The *Gilgamesh Epic* is the most widely copied piece of literature in the ANE.[32] Its history of composition is long and complicated.[33] The earliest copies known are Sumerian and date back to the Old Babylonian period (c. 2000–1600 BC). It seems to have reached its final form in the early part of the first millennium BC. It recounts the adventures of Gilgamesh, king of Uruk (mid-third millennium BC). The epic opens by presenting Gilgamesh as a powerful but oppressive king whose subjects cry out to the gods for relief from his domination. The gods respond to the people's cry by creating Enkidu, an uncivilized human living among animals.

---

[26] Ibid., 217.

[27] For some examples see Arnold and Beyer, *Readings from the Ancient Near East*, #79 (207–8); and Matthews and Benjamin, *Old Testament Parallels*, 318–22.

[28] Walton, *Ancient Israelite Literature in Its Cultural Context*, 213–14.

[29] Based on various sources, a key point of distinction between epics and myths is that epics involve heroic humans while myths center on the exploits of the gods. Hence, for example, the Enuma Elish is regarded as a myth and the Gilgamesh Epic is an epic. Historicity is not an issue in either category.

[30] Sparks, *Ancient Texts for the Study of the Hebrew Bible*, 271.

[31] Walton, *Ancient Near Eastern Thought and the Old Testament*, 50.

[32] *COS*, 1.132, 458–60; *ANET*, 44–52, 72–99.

[33] See J. Tigay, *The Evolution of the Gilgamesh Epic* (Philadelphia: University of Pennsylvania Press, 1982). The current Akkadian epic seems to have drawn on at least four separate Sumerian Gilgamesh stories. The most complete version existing today is preserved on 12 clay tablets in the library collection of the seventh century BC Assyrian king Asshur-Banipal.

Enkidu eventually becomes civilized and a friend of Gilgamesh. The punishment for one of their joint exploits is that Enkidu must die. This causes Gilgamesh to embark on a quest to discover immortality. During that endeavor he eventually encounters Utnapishtim and his wife, to whom the gods had granted immortality after they survived a great flood. After failing at a couple of attempts to gain immortality, Gilgamesh returns to Uruk and continues his reign.

The flood account is found on tablet 11 of the epic. For various reasons, the gods had determined to destroy the world with a great flood. They all swore not to reveal this secret to any human. However, Ea (one of the gods who created humanity) told Utnapishtim (in a round-about fashion) of the coming flood and gave instructions for him to build a great boat, as wide as it was long, and to bring all living things on the boat. Utnapishtim completed the boat and loaded it with gold, silver, and all the living things on the earth. The greatness of the flood frightened even the gods who bemoaned their decision to destroy all of humanity. The great flood lasted for seven days and nights, after which the boat came to rest on the top of Mount Nimush and remained there for seven days. On the seventh day Utnapishtim sequentially released a dove, a swallow, and a raven, and only the raven did not return. At that point, he sent every living creature out of the boat and sacrificed a sheep. The smell of the sacrifice caused the gods to gather around Utnapishtim, and Enlil, who had originally proposed to destroy all humans, was furious that a human survived. Eventually his fury subsided, and he made Utnapishtim a god and gave him and his wife immortality.

Since the parallels between the biblical and ANE flood accounts are more significant than those found between the biblical and ANE creation accounts (see the section on myths below), the issue of borrowing is addressed here.[34] The most obvious parallel is the sending out of birds after the flood ended. For many, this indicates that some kind of borrowing, rather than independent development, must have happened.[35] The primary options are that the ANE epics borrowed from the biblical account, the biblical account borrowed from the ANE epics, or they both drew on a common original. A host of scholars have addressed this issue with the majority favoring the second view.[36] However, as Walton correctly points out, one's view of the authority of Scripture plays a key role in the way he or she approaches and answers this question.[37] Since none of the alternatives draws on compelling evidence, other beliefs or assumptions loom large in dealing with this complex issue. Most likely, the similarities between the biblical and ANE flood accounts derive from the fact that God brought the flood to pass as it is described in Genesis. After the rebellion at Babel, various flood traditions developed over time as people migrated in different directions in the wake of the confusion of languages at Babel.

Myths. Although people have defined "myth" in a variety of ways, the term most broadly refers to stories in which the gods are the main characters. Scholars debate whether the readers viewed these stories as fictional or fanciful or as having some concrete reality. The connection various scholars have made between ANE myths and various biblical accounts is the focus on the gods or Yahweh, the God of the Bible. For those who have no strong beliefs about the God of Israel, the differences between ANE myths and biblical accounts are minimal and they view

---

[34] The larger issue of the relationship between biblical and ANE literature is discussed at the end of this section.

[35] A. Heidel affirms, "That the Babylonian and Hebrew versions are genetically related is too obvious to require proof; the only problem that needs to be discussed is the degree of relationship" (*The Gilgamesh Epic and Old Testament Parallels*, 2nd ed. [Chicago: University of Chicago Press, 1949], 260).

[36] J. J. Finkelstein writes that "the dependence of the Biblical story upon the Babylonian to some degree is granted by virtually all schools of thought" ("Bible and Babel," *Commentary* 26 [1958]: 435).

[37] Walton, *Ancient Israelite Literature in Its Cultural Context*, 39–41.

the God of Israel as just as imaginary as the gods of the ANE.[38] For those who regard the God of Israel as the one true God, the differences between these two sets of accounts are significant.

Among the several creation accounts the best known is *Enuma Elish*.[39] Dating to the late second millennium BC, it commemorates Marduk's elevation to the head of the pantheon (by defeating Tiamat). However, the myth employed here comes from the *Baal Cycle* in Ugaritic literature.[40]

This myth has three sections: Baal's conflict with Yamm, Baal's temple, and Baal's conflict with Mot. Of all the gods in the Ugaritic pantheon, Baal was the most active and prominent. He was the god of thunder and rain, and consequently responsible for fertility. In the first section of the cycle, Yamm, the god of the sea and chaos, was having a palace built and was to receive royal power from El, the supreme god of the pantheon. However, Baal battled with Yamm, desiring to have dominion. Armed with magical weapons made by the craftsman god, Kothar, Baal managed to overcome Yamm. In the second section, Baal received permission from El to build a palace for himself and obtained assistance from Asherah and Anath. After Kothar finished the palace, Baal celebrated by inviting the gods to a feast. Among those invited, Baal invited Mot, the god of death, to attend the feast and acknowledge his sovereignty. The final part of the Baal cycle delineates Baal's battle against Mot. After Anath (Baal's sister) heard that Mot had killed Baal, she searched for her brother and then buried him. Attempts were made to find a god adequate to assume Baal's role and to restore fertility to the land, but these attempts failed. She confronted and defeated Mot, grinding up his body like grain and scattering it over land and sea. Eventually both Baal and Mot returned to life and battled once again. The sun goddess warned Mot about the consequences of Baal's defeat. Mot submitted to Baal's rule but retained his area of sovereignty. Both gods played a role in the ongoing cycle of existence.

Among other things, this myth emphasizes the importance of rain to the land. Baal represents the fertility of spring rains, while Mot represents the drought of the summer months. Even the actions taken by Anat against Mot—splitting, winnowing, burning, grinding, and planting—are steps taken by farmers when they harvest wheat. They prepare the grain for use as food during the winter and sow it to create more crops the next year. By defeating the drought (Mot), the rains (Baal) allow life to flourish in the dry Near East.

The idea that Baal was responsible for the fertility of fields, flocks, and herds, as well as sacred sexual activity (a form of sympathetic magic) that was part of the worship of Baal was quite seductive for the people of Israel throughout their history. They believed that Yahweh, the invisible God, would do what He promised and would provide for them abundantly, or they would take things into their own hands and provoke Baal, the god of fertility, into action.

Historical literature. Hundreds of ANE documents fall into this important category[41] of which there are at least two subcategories: royal inscriptions and historical literary texts. Royal inscriptions were generally composed by palace scribes and refer to "monumental" records (written on walls, stone slabs, and even the side of a mountain). Some of the most well-known royal inscriptions are the Black Obelisk, the Sennacherib prism, the Merneptah Stele, the Mesha inscription, the Cyrus cylinder, and the Behistun inscription.[42] They generally focus on

---

[38] Walton, *Ancient Near Eastern Thought and the Old Testament*, 44.

[39] *COS*, 1.111, 390–402; *ANET*, 60–72, 501–3.

[40] *COS*, 1.86, 241–74; *ANET*, 129–42.

[41] A. K. Grayson, "Assyria and Babylon," *Orientalia* 49 (1980): 140–94.

[42] Walton, *Ancient Near Eastern Thought and the Old Testament*, 63–66.

royal achievements, primarily military accomplishments, but they also include building projects. Historical annals involve poetic narratives about activities of kings. Such texts describe
the reigns and exploits of various kings in Mesopotamia and Egypt, as well as in the Hittite
Empire.

The most noteworthy example from Babylonian sources is the *Babylonian Chronicles*.[43] This
series of texts documents in summary form major military campaigns and other significant
occurrences from the beginning of the Neo-Babylonian dynasty to the Seleucid period. The
series is not complete since a number of tablets have never been found. Of interest to the student of the Bible are the accounts of Nabopolassar's accession to the throne, the fall of Nineveh
(612 BC), and the Battle of Carchemish (605 BC).[44]

Law codes. ANE collections of laws demonstrate a significant concern for justice. The oldest
known law code (Laws of Ur-Nammu) dates to the late third millennium BC. These collections of laws focus on civil or criminal offenses rather than moral issues. Most of them have a
prologue and an epilogue that explain the rationale for the laws along with other introductory
and concluding matters. The majority of the laws are casuistic (case laws) in form. They present a case, "If a man does such and such" (the protasis), and then they pronounce the penalty,
"then you must do this" (the apodosis). The laws found in the various ANE law codes share a
number of similarities.

The most extensive and well-known law code, dating to the eighteenth century BC, is the
Code of Hammurabi.[45] This collection of 282 laws addresses offenses against property, land ten-
ure, trade and commerce, family and social institutions, and the like. A comparison of this collection of laws with the Mosaic Law reveals a significant amount of similarities between them.
They address common life issues, employ the same case-law format, and prescribe similar penalties. Many scholars have affirmed that this demonstrates the Bible's wide-scale borrowing of
ANE laws in the composition of the biblical laws (as part of their denial of Mosaic authorship).
What then explains the similarities between ANE law codes and the Mosaic law? First, there
are certain life issues and criminal tendencies that every society must address. Second, in His
revelation of His law through Moses, God saw fit to have Moses write those laws in a fashion
that was understandable in his day. Moses used legal terminology and patterns that were common to his time as a way of clearly explaining God's expectations of His covenant nation in a
manner that was not ambiguous.

Also these two kinds of law codes have many differences. The ANE laws were intended to
insure that justice characterized society. The Mosaic laws include that concern, but they place
much more emphasis on the need to live in accord with them as a way of vividly demonstrating God's character to the surrounding nations (Exod 19:4–6; Deut 26:16–19). Moreover, the
penalty demanded by the Mosaic law for criminal acts is almost always socially blind. In contrast, the ANE law codes assessed penalties for crimes depending on the victim's social status.

---

[43] *COS*, 1.137, 467–68; *ANET*, 563–64 (both anthologies translate only a few of the tablets). See A. K. Grayson, *Assyrian and Babylonian Chronicles* (Winona Lake, IN: Eisenbrauns, 2000), 8–28, 69–124.

[44] A number of studies have discussed the issues related to ANE and biblical historiography, issues that exceed the limita-
tions of this volume. For helpful introductions to some of the key issues and bibliography, see Sparks, *Ancient Texts for the
Study of the Hebrew Bible*, 407–16; Walton, *Ancient Israelite Literature in Its Cultural Context*, 114–27; idem, *Ancient Near
Eastern Thought and the Old Testament*, 217–37.

[45] *COS*, 2.131, 335–53; *ANET*, 163–80.

However, in the end one's view of Scripture plays more of a major role in the attempt to explain the similarities between ANE and biblical laws.[46]

Treaties and covenants. Although these two terms are not synonymous, they share in common the connotation of "agreements enacted between two parties in which one or both make promises under oath to perform certain actions while avoiding others."[47] In addition to the major or core empires of Egypt, Mesopotamia, and Asia Minor, a number of smaller nations also existed. Nations of equal stature entered into *parity treaties*, generally dealing with mutual assistance and nonaggression. *Vassal treaties* outlined the terms of a relationship between a powerful king (suzerain) and his vassal states. Also in *royal grant* treaties/covenants a benevolent king provided property, promises, and blessings on his loyal servants and their descendants. The most prominent examples of ANE treaties are the Hittite treaties (more than half of the extant treaties), the Neo-Assyrian treaties, and the Aramaic treaties from Sefire.

Most of the Hittite covenant texts were vassal treaties in which the Hittite king was the suzerain. In general these treaties consisted of six components:[48]

> *Preamble*—identifies the name, titles, and genealogy of the suzerain
> *Historical prologue*—summarizes the past relationship between the participants that led to this agreement
> *Stipulations/provisions*—details the demands imposed upon the vassal by the suzerain
> *Deposition*—requires that the treaty be placed in the temple of the vassal's chief deity
> *List of divine witnesses*—names the deities of both kings who served as witnesses of the agreement
> *Curses and blessings*—enumerate the punishments meted out for violating the terms of the treaty and the blessings given for keeping the terms.[49]

In addition to shedding light on the relationships between nation, a number of the ANE treaties share features in common with biblical covenants. Many scholars have drawn attention to the structural similarity of the Mosaic covenants in particular and the Hittite and Neo-Assyrian treaties.[50] Although scholars debate this issue, it seems that the Hittite treaties (mid-second millennium BC) provide the best backdrop for comparisons with the Mosaic covenant and support the credibility of a mid-second millennium date for the composition of the Pentateuch.

Although some suggestions have been made in the above survey of the literature of the ANE, what are the key issues to consider in explaining the relationship of ANE literature and the OT? The following section provides a summary of the discussion and offers some suggestions or guidelines relative to that question.

---

[46] For a brief consideration of some of the key issues in this debated area see Walton, *Ancient Israelite Literature in Its Cultural Context*, 74–92; idem, *Ancient Near Eastern Thought and the Old Testament*, 287–302.

[47] Sparks, *Ancient Texts for the Study of the Hebrew Bible*, 435.

[48] G. Beckman, *Hittite Diplomatic Texts* (Atlanta: Scholars, 1996), 2–3.

[49] *COS*, 2.17–18, 87–100; *ANET*, 201–6, 529–30; see also Beckman, *Hittite Diplomatic Texts*.

[50] A few examples are P. Craigie, *Deuteronomy*, NICOT (Grand Rapids: Eerdmans, 1976), 20–44; K. Kitchen, *The Bible in Its World* (Downers Grove, IL: InterVarsity, 1977), 79–85; D. J. McCarthy, *Treaty and Covenant* (Rome: Pontifical Biblical Institute, 1963); M. Weinfeld, *Deuteronomy and the Deuteronomic School* (Oxford: Oxford University Press, 1972).

The Importance of Ancient Near Eastern Literature to Understanding the Old Testament

Archaeological discoveries made in the ANE during the nineteenth and twentieth centuries have significantly impacted the study of the Scriptures on many fronts. The deciphering of ancient Sumerian, Akkadian, and Canaanite languages along with Egyptian hieroglyphics enables us to read texts that predate even Abraham. As one reads different categories of ANE literature, he regularly encounters social patterns, religious practices, and law codes that seem to parallel those found in the OT.[51]

What role should ANE literature play in the interpretation of OT passages? Scholars have debated this point ever since archives from the ANE world were unearthed from the late-nineteenth century to the present time. Scholars have generally dealt with the matter from two perspectives. Some approach ANE discoveries from a confessional standpoint and seek to use the discoveries of ANE literature and artifactual evidence to support the authority of the Bible. They generally focus on the ways in which Israel is distinct from the nations of the ANE. Others interpret the ANE and biblical material from a scientific or secular perspective,[52] viewing parts of the OT as collections of mythologies either borrowed directly from ANE traditions or deeply indebted to them ideologically.[53] Thus Israelite beliefs and practices are viewed as a spin-off from the surrounding ANE world.

How should students of Scripture navigate their way through these complicated issues? Though biblical scholars have approached this question in a variety of ways, the present work can only introduce the reader to some of the key issues and pursue a suggested interpretive course. On the one hand the OT clearly manifests an awareness of cultural and religious traditions of the ANE world and even makes reference to them. Awareness of this fact adds to the vividness and depth of the interpretation of the OT. On the other hand the fact of Israel's distinctive identity in the surrounding world should not be overlooked.[54] What God had in mind for the nation of Israel (and the surrounding nations) was not simply an adapted version of the broad ANE mind-set. Even though the Lord employed various practices and institutions that also occur throughout the ANE, He called His servant nation to function as a distinctive witness in the midst of that world (Exod 19:4–6).

On the one hand the desire to find analogies or make comparisons of social customs can be hazardous. Some foreign cultural practices have no analogy to a given native culture and this fact can lead to misunderstanding that foreign practice by making inappropriate comparisons between the two social customs. On the other hand certain customs are related to indigenous practices that are known and loved. Thus comparing ANE literature and social customs to biblical ones offers a host of both dangers and benefits.

---

[51] For a selection of resources that give attention to several potential parallels between OT and ANE literature see Matthews and Benjamin, *Old Testament Parallels*; J. J. Niehaus, *Ancient Near Eastern Themes in Biblical Theology* (Grand Rapids: Kregel, 2008); Walton, *Ancient Israelite Literature in Its Cultural Context*. See also A. M. Rodríguez, "Ancient Near Eastern Parallels to the Bible and the Question of Revelation and Inspiration," *Journal of the Adventist Theological Society* 12:1 (2001): 43–48; J. H. Walton, "Ancient Near Eastern Background Studies," in *Dictionary for Theological Interpretation of the Bible*, ed. K. J. Vanhoozer (Grand Rapids: Baker, 2005), 40–45.

[52] This "secular" perspective arises from the fact that these scholars rarely give any attention to the concepts of divine revelation or inspiration.

[53] Of course scholars did not approach this area of study from just those two polar standpoints, but populated the spectrum between these two extremes.

[54] P. Machinist refers to 433 Old Testament passages that mention the divinely intended distinctiveness of Israel ("The Question of Distinctiveness in Ancient Israel: An Essay," in *Ah, Assyria . . . : Studies in Assyrian History and Ancient Near Eastern Historiography Presented to Hayim Tadmor*, ed. M. Cogan and I. Eph`al [Jerusalem: Magnes, 1991]: 203–4 n 22).

The study of ancient texts, whether biblical or ANE, must steer clear of arbitrarily assigning meanings to them that are part of the reader's social and cultural heritage. It is wrong to assume that a given practice of another time and place matches something in the modern day. Biblical passages must always be placed in their appropriate contexts literarily, historically, theologically, and culturally.

In the early part of the twentieth century William F. Albright popularized a "comparative method" by means of which he and his students identified a great number of parallels between ANE and biblical literature.[55] Other scholars preferred a "contrastive approach" (e.g., Y. Kaufmann, Frank Moore Cross) that emphasized the differences between them.[56] William Hallo proposed a "contextual approach" by which he examined the "entire Near Eastern literary milieu to the extent that it can be argued to have had any conceivable impact on the biblical formulation."[57] This approach seeks to identify and discuss both similarities and differences that one can observe when comparing the Bible and texts from the ANE (combining the comparative and contrastive approaches). Its goal "is not to find the key to every Biblical phenomenon in some Ancient Near Eastern precedent, but rather to silhouette the Biblical text against its wider literary and cultural environment and thus to arrive at a proper assessment of the extent to which the Biblical evidence reflects that environment or, on the contrary, is distinctive and innovative over against it."[58] It recognizes that traditions will generally be modified as they pass from one culture to another.[59] M. W. Chavalas observes that this kind of approach enables scholars to avoid "parallelomania" (finding numerous inappropriate parallels) and "parallellophobia" (unnecessarily avoiding the recognition that genuine parallels exist).[60]

The general tendency in the past 60 years has followed two stages.[61] In the first flush of discovery, the tendency was to overemphasize the importance of the background material for biblical interpretation. Numerous examples of invalid customs from the archives of Ugarit, Nuzi, and Ebla could be cited as examples of improper comparisons.[62] Later, when some of the flaws in the early interpretations had become apparent, scholars swung to the other extreme of largely ignoring the comparative material.[63]

---

[55] For example C. H. Gordon ("Biblical Customs and the Nuzi Tablets," *Biblical Archaeologist* 3 [1940]: 1–12) and E. A. Speiser (*Genesis*, AB [New York: Doubleday, 1964) focused on parallels between the Nuzi texts and the patriarchal accounts.

[56] W. W. Hallo, "Compare and Contrast: The Contextual Approach to Biblical Literature," in *The Bible in Light of Cuneiform Literature*, ed. W. W. Hallo, B. W. Jones, and G. L. Mattingly (Lewiston, NY: Edwin Mellen, 1990), 2.

[57] W. W. Hallo, "Biblical History and Its Near Eastern Setting: The Contextual Approach," in *Scripture in Context: Essays on the Comparative Method*, ed. C. D. Evans, W. W. Hallo, and J. B. White (Pittsburgh: Pickwick, 1980), 2.

[58] W. W. Hallo, *The Book of the People* (Atlanta: Scholars Press, 1991), 24.

[59] Sparks, *Ancient Texts for the Study of the Hebrew Bible*, 4.

[60] M. W. Chavalas, "Assyriology and Biblical Studies: A Century and a Half of Tension," in *Mesopotamia and the Bible: Comparative Explorations*, ed. M. W. Chavalas and K. L. Younger Jr. (Grand Rapids: Baker, 2002), 43.

[61] J. J. M. Roberts, "The Ancient Near Eastern Environment," in *The Hebrew Bible and Its Modern Interpreters*, ed. D. A. Knight and G. M. Tucker (Philadelphia: Fortress, 1985), 96.

[62] For example M. J. Selman cites several inappropriate Nuzi parallels ("Comparative Customs and the Patriarchal Age," in *Essays on the Patriarchal Narratives*, ed. A. R. Millard and D. J. Wiseman [Winona Lake, IN: Eisenbrauns, 1983], 113–18). See also M. Selman, "The Social Environment of the Patriarchs," *TynBul* 27 (1976): 119–24; P. van der Lugt warned about the dangers of "pan-Ugaritism": ("The "Spectre of Pan-Ugaritism," *Bibliotheca Orientalis* 31 [1974]: 3–26). Various scholars suggested different connections between the Ebla tablets and the Bible that were later withdrawn (see Roberts, "The Ancient Near Eastern Environment," 84–86).

[63] T. L. Thompson (*Historicity of the Patriarchal Narratives* [Berlin: DeGruyter, 1974]) and J. Van Seters (*Abraham in History and Tradition* [New Haven, CT: Yale University Press, 1975]) are examples of those who reject most parallels that scholars had cited as evidence of a legitimate second-millennium backdrop for the Old Testament patriarchal accounts.

Scholars have generally approached this issue from confessional or secular perspectives, often driven by a view of Scripture that logically precedes their examination of the evidence. While prior beliefs about the OT cannot be ignored, it is necessary to be careful not to interact with ANE literature with the intent to prove a given point of view. Whenever comparisons are suggested, there must be extreme care in defining correctly the customs and texts under consideration, paying attention to the cultural and chronological contexts, and understanding the limitations of any conclusions.

Methodology for Comparative Study—Key Definitions

A body of technical terms occurs with some regularity in scholarly discussions of the relationship of the literature of the ANE and the OT. A few of those terms and their explanations follow. First, the goal of *background or cultural studies* is to "examine the literature and archaeology of the ancient Near East in order to reconstruct the behavior, beliefs, culture, values, and worldview of the people."[64] Second, *comparative studies* represent a branch of background or cultural studies. This discipline "attempts to draw from different segments of the broader culture (in time and/or space) into juxtaposition with one another in order to assess what might be learned from one to enhance the understanding of another."[65] In this case the proper approach is to examine ANE culture and Israelite culture and seek to discern the ways in which features of ANE life and culture shed light on Israelite culture (in light of their differences and similarities). Third, one of the most common explanations for similarity between cultures is called "*cultural diffusion.*" Sparks suggests by the term that observable similarities are caused by the transfer of ideas or practices from one culture to another, either indirectly or directly.[66] At the same time, of course, scholars who refer to cultural similarities (transferred via diffusion) must provide a reasonable explanation for where, when, how, and in what direction the influence may have occurred.[67] Fourth, *cognitive environment* refers to the way people thought about themselves and their world.[68] It does not specifically signify something borrowed from another culture but describes a people's cultural heritage that was shaped by various forces. In this regard in light of numerous points of contact between Israel and the larger world the cognitive environment of the ANE appears in biblical literature in several ways.

Methodology for Comparative Study—Guiding Principles

The agenda of scholars when comparing biblical and ANE literature plays a major role in the method they employ. The attempt should not be to employ comparative studies in order to prove or disprove the Bible or to detect literary borrowing (and the direction it occurred). Instead the goal should be to understand how people thought about themselves and their world. When a concept seems to be shared by biblical and ANE literature, the appropriate question is, How is this biblical custom or practice similar to or different from the one found in ANE texts? The point is not to ask how Israel acquired the custom or from where they might have borrowed it.[69]

---

[64] Walton, *Ancient Near Eastern Thought and the Old Testament*, 18.

[65] Ibid.

[66] Sparks, *Ancient Texts for the Study of the Hebrew Bible*, 4. Sparks offers four kinds of diffusion: direct connection, mediated connection, common source, and common tradition (ibid.).

[67] Ibid.

[68] Walton, *Ancient Near Eastern Thought and the Old Testament*, 21.

[69] Ibid.

Selman suggests the following six principles to follow in comparing ANE and biblical social customs:

1. All relevant nonbiblical material should be properly investigated in its own context, and it may have a positive or negative function as far as our modern understanding of the patriarchs is concerned.
2. Comparisons are best drawn from those civilizations which stand in the same historic stream as ancient Israel, though links with their non-Semitic neighbours are by no means ruled out.
3. The means of transmission between the cultures, including linguistic and sociological contacts, must be examined.
4. The different forms of texts are not necessarily a hindrance to a comparison of their contexts.
5. The quality of the contacts is at least as important as their quantity.
6. There must be some basic link between the customs involved if the contact is to be established at all, especially if the biblical custom is being explained by nonbiblical material. [70]

Walton also provides 10 helpful principles of comparative study. These are listed below with slight revisions or additions.

1. Both similarities and differences must be considered. Just pursuing parallels between biblical and ANE literature, whether to buttress or tear down the distinctiveness of Israel, ignores or misinterprets the totality of evidence. Our firm belief in the distinctiveness of Israel requires that we carefully test any alleged similarities [see Selman's principles].
2. Similarities may suggest a common cultural heritage or cognitive environment rather than borrowing. Some degree of similarity does not justify claims of literary dependence or large scale borrowing. It may simply evidence a shared culture.
3. It is not uncommon to find similarities at the surface but differences at the conceptual level and vice versa.
4. All elements must be understood in their own context as accurately as possible before cross-cultural comparisons are made (i.e., careful background study must precede comparative study). Potential parallels found in biblical and ANE literature must first be understood in their native setting before alleging any connection between them. For example, some have compared the biblical concept of "to make atonement" (*kipper*) and the cognate verb in Akkadian, "to wipe off, cleanse" (*kuppuru*). The Akkadian verb in its own context signifies the wiping off of evil in the form of disease that was produced by demonic powers. Through magic and incantations an individual sought to be free of his affliction.[71] In clear contrast to that, the biblical verb (*kipper*) connotes the removal of sin and impurity.[72]

---

[70] Selman, "Comparative Customs and the Patriarchal Age," 133–34. Selman offers a list of 13 legitimate parallels between ANE texts and patriarchal narratives, in which ANE customs provide helpful backdrops to a patriarchal practice in the Pentateuch (ibid., 135–38).

[71] Rodríguez, "Ancient Near Eastern Parallels to the Bible," 51.

[72] Richard E. Averbeck, "כפר (*kapar* II)," in *NIDOTTE*, ed. W. VanGemeren (Grand Rapids: Zondervan, 1997), 2:695–98.

5. Proximity in time, geography, and spheres of cultural contact all increase the possibility of interaction leading to influence. Potential similarities should come from a similar time frame and the closer their geographical proximity the better.

6. A case for literary borrowing requires identification of likely channels of transmission. Are there linguistic and sociological contacts between Israel and the pagan nation with similar practices?

7. The significance of differences between two pieces of literature is minimized if the works are not the same genre. In other words, if two pieces are being compared that are not the same genre, some of the differences that could be observed are merely due to the fact that the genre is different.

8. Similar functions may be performed by different genres in different cultures.

9. When literary or cultural elements are borrowed they may in turn be transformed into something quite different by those who borrowed them. Always be aware of the fact that a practice in one country, though it appears similar, may have an entirely different significance in another culture.

10. A single culture will rarely be monolithic, either in a contemporary cross-section or in consideration of a passage of time.[73]

Walton also offers four goals of background and comparative study.[74] First, students may study the history of the ancient Near East as a means of recovering knowledge of the events that shaped the lives of people in the ancient world. Second, they may study archaeology as a means of recovering the lifestyle reflected in the material culture of the ancient world. Third, they may study the literature of the ancient Near East as a means of penetrating the heart and soul of the people who inhabited the ancient world Israel shared. Fourth, they may study the language of the ANE as a means of gaining additional insight into the semantics, lexicography, idioms, and metaphors used in Hebrew.

Interaction between ANE and Biblical Worlds

In biblical and ANE scholarship there seem to be three broad levels or means of interaction between the biblical and ANE world. First, at the very least, since God revealed Himself to a Semitic world, there could be coincidental references to ANE practices or mythology. Some scholars contend that since the Bible makes no explicit comment on its use of a pagan concept, any connections were not intentional. Second, there could be intentional references to ANE customs and mythology. The next section develops different kinds of intentional interaction with the ANE world by biblical writers. Third, many scholars contend that the OT clearly demonstrates heavy dependence on or borrowing from ANE literature and mythology. Psalm 29 is commonly cited as an example of this. For example, A. Malamat concluded that this psalm "is derived from traditions harking back beyond Late Bronze Age Ugarit, to Old Babylonian, or rather Amorite, times."[75] Frank Moore Cross also suggested that Psalm 29 was a "lightly revised Ba'al hymn" and that it is representative of biblical texts in which "raw

---

[73] Ibid., 26–27. The 10 principles are taken from Walton, but the brief explanations draw on various sources. For additional ideas see Rodríguez, "Ancient Near Eastern Parallels to the Bible," 50–51; Selman, "Comparative Customs and the Patriarchal Age," 133–34.

[74] Ibid., 27–28. Walton also suggests three roles for comparative studies: critical analysis, defense of the biblical text, and exegesis of the biblical text (ibid., 38–40).

[75] A. Malamat, "The Amorite Background of Psalm 29," *ZAW* 100 (1988): 160.

mythology" survives.[76] This is the least likely option and generally draws on an assumption about Scripture that rejects divine revelation and inspiration.

As Elmer Smick concluded, various biblical passages demonstrate that the biblical authors "were not committed to myth but were keenly aware of contemporaneous mythology from which they drew colorful figures to enrich their theological expression."[77] Biblical writers interacted with the ANE world through basic lexical similarity, by drawing on different aspects of shared cognitive environments, and by providing clarification or background for biblical passages.

Lexical similarity. A number of translations have rendered the first line of Job 28:11, "He dams up the streams from flowing."[78] However, in light of several Ugaritic texts, an almost exact parallel suggests this line should be translated "the sources of the rivers."[79] That is a simple example of lexical parallels that arise from biblical Hebrew functioning as a Semitic language.

Shared cognitive environment. A. M. Rodriguez suggests four ways in which the cognitive environments of biblical and ANE literature intersect.[80] First, at times the Old Testament incorporates concrete ideas of literary techniques from the ANE that were compatible with the values and principles of the covenant relationship God established with Israel. For example a number of scholars have pointed out that Prov 22:17–24:22 seems to be modeled after the Egyptian teachings of Amenemope, also involving 30 sayings. Much of the book of Deuteronomy seems to follow the structure of a Hittite treaty. In each instance the Lord may have seen fit to make use of a set of ideas or a manner of arrangement to enhance the understanding and impact of his intended message.

Second, the OT adapts various social structures and practices. Consider the institution of king as one example. In the ancient world the king stood between the divine and human realms, mediating the power of the deity in his city and beyond. The king of Egypt was divinized to a higher degree than kings in other ANE cultures.[81] In Israel the king was the vassal of God, the one and only God and the true king of Israel. Other examples of shared practices involve sacrifice, circumcision, slavery, temples, as well as the wording of the Mosaic law (numerous similarities with ANE law codes).

Third, certain passages engage in a polemical attack against a pagan belief or practice. A variety of Old Testament passages soundly condemn the worship of other gods or any image of those gods. Unfortunately Israel regularly turned to some form of idolatry. The prophets often referred to idolatry with a polemical tone that demonstrated the absurdity of worshiping idols (Isa 40:18–20; 44:9–20; 46:6–7). The prophet Hosea depicted the nation Israel as a woman who says, "I will go after my lovers, the men who give me my food and water, my wool and flax, my oil and drink" (Hos 2:5). This statement alludes to the practice of sexual rites as part of the Canaanite fertility cult that attempted to secure agricultural fertility (i.e., wool, flax, olive oil, and wine) from Baal. The sad reality is that Israel failed to recognize that Yahweh, rather than Baal, is the one who blessed the land, animals, and people out of covenant love (Hos 2:8).[82]

---

[76] F. M. Cross, "The Development of Israelite Religion," *BRev* 8, no. 5 (October 1992): 19.

[77] E. B. Smick, "Mythopoetic Language in the Psalms," *WTJ* 44:1 (1982): 88.

[78] ESV, HCSB, NASB, NKJV, NLT.

[79] J. E. Hartley, *The Book of Job*, NICOT (Grand Rapids: Eerdmans, 1988), 375 n 20. See also NET, NIV, NRSV, Tanakh.

[80] Rodríguez, "Ancient Near Eastern Parallels to the Bible," 62–63.

[81] Walton, *Ancient Near Eastern Thought and the Old Testament*, 278–79.

[82] For other examples of polemics see E. H. Merrill, "Isaiah 40–55 as Anti-Babylonian Polemic," *GTJ* 8 (1987): 3–18.

Fourth, a large number of pagan practices were blatantly rejected by Yahweh. A few examples of pagan customs that were an abomination to the Lord include: consulting spirits of the dead (Lev 20:6; Deut 18:10–12); body markings or piercings (Lev 19:28), and child sacrifice (Lev 20:1).

Clarification/background for biblical passages. Isaiah 14:4b–21 functions as a taunt song against the king of Babylon. These verses mock the formerly powerful king, who had died and was soon to arrive in Sheol. The arrogance of the king is epitomized by five self-laudatory statements (vv. 13–14). One of them declares, "I will ascend to the heavens. I will set up my throne above the stars of God ['de]. I will sit on the mount of the assembly, in the remotest parts of the North [lit. *Zaphon*]." The name for God used here, *'el*, is not the usual name for God (*'elōhîm*). It is the short form that is also the name of the high god of the Canaanite pantheon. Also the Hebrew for "North" also serves in Ugaritic literature as the Canaanite version of Olympus. This was "the mountain of the assembly" where the gods met.[83] Since the king described here was a Gentile king, Isaiah used terms against that broader backdrop. He depicted the king of Babylon as one who mistakenly thought that he could join or replace El as the one who rules the world from Zaphon. An understanding of that backdrop makes more vivid the extremity of his arrogance.

A Word of Caution

Any consideration of potential interaction between the ideology, practices, and institutions of the ANE and the Bible demands the recognition that no alleged literary connections when properly understood can negate the inspiration of Scripture.[84] The tendency of critical scholarship has been to demonstrate that the OT is "derivative literature, a disadvantaged stepsister to the dominant cultures of the ancient Near East."[85] The idea is that the OT is simply a human book that converted ANE mythology into another version, the concoction of Israelite poets and theologians. While that view of the OT must be avoided at all costs, an appreciation for some kind of connection between the world of the ANE and the Bible need not occasion a low view of Scripture. If the Bible was to impact the world to which it was given, it had to interact in some way with the culture and background of its recipients. For the biblical worldview to correct or confront (polemically) the surrounding culture or cognitive environment, the biblical writers would have been aware of that culture and interacted with it. As God had biblical writers make use of the language, culture, and ideology of the surrounding world, He invested it with the meaning and message He wanted to communicate to His people by divesting them of their pagan distortions.[86]

STUDY QUESTIONS
1. What are the most commonly used sources for studying ANE literature?
2. What are the key categories of ANE literature (based on genre and content)?
3. To which Egyptian wisdom composition do scholars often compare Prov 22:17–24:22, and why do they do this? What should we learn from this?
4. What are some key differences between ANE incantations and rituals and activities of biblical priests and prophets?

---

[83] J. N. Oswalt, *The Book of Isaiah: Chapters 1–39*, NICOT (Grand Rapids: Eerdmans, 1986), 322.

[84] Walton, "Ancient Near Eastern Background Studies," 43.

[85] Ibid.

[86] Rodríguez, "Ancient Near Eastern Parallels to the Bible," 62.

5. What are some key differences and similarities between ANE and biblical creation and flood accounts?

6. How do we explain the abundant similarities between the Law of Moses and ANE law codes (e.g., Code of Hammurabi) that predate the Mosaic law?

7. What are the extremes of explaining the relationship of the Bible and ANE literature?

8. What are the three broad levels of interaction between the biblical and ANE world?

9. What is the first of three key areas in which biblical writers interacted with the surrounding ANE world?

10. What is the second of three key areas in which biblical writers interacted with the surrounding ANE world?

11. What is the third of three key areas in which biblical writers interacted with the surrounding ANE world?

FOR FURTHER STUDY

Arnold, B. T., and B. E. Beyer. *Readings from the Ancient Near East: Primary Sources for Old Testament Study.* Grand Rapids: Baker, 2002.

Chavalas, M. W., and K. L. Younger Jr., eds. *Mesopotamia and the Bible: Comparative Explorations.* Grand Rapids: Baker, 2002.

Grayson, A. K. *Assyrian and Babylonian Chronicles.* Winona Lake, IN: Eisenbrauns, 2000.

Finkelstein, J. J. "Bible and Babel: A Comparative Study of the Hebrew and Babylonian Religious Spirit." In *Essential Papers on Israel and the Ancient Near East.* Edited by F. E. Greenspahn, 355–80. New York: New York University Press, 1991.

Hallo, W. W. "New Moons and Sabbaths: A Case Study in the Contrastive Approach." *HUCA* 48 (1977): 1–18.

———. "Biblical History in Its Near Eastern Setting: The Contextual Approach." In *Scripture in Context.* Edited by C. Evans et al., 1–26. Pittsburgh: Pickwick, 1980.

———. "Compare and Contrast: The Contextual Approach to Biblical Literature." In *The Bible in Light of Cuneiform Literature: Scripture in Context III.* Edited by W. W. Hallo, B. Jones, and G. Mattingly, 1–19. Lewiston, NY: Edwin Mellen, 1990.

Hallo, W. W., and K. L. Younger Jr., eds. *Context of Scripture.* 3 vols. New York: Brill, 1997–2002.

Huffmon, H. B. "Babel und Bibel: The Encounter between Babylon and the Bible." In *The Bible and Its Traditions.* Edited by M. P. O'Connor and D. N. Freedman, 309–20. Ann Arbor: University of Michigan Press, 1983.

Kitchen, Kenneth. *The Bible in Its World.* Downers Grove, IL: InterVarsity, 1977.

Machinist, P. "The Question of Distinctiveness in Ancient Israel." In *Essential Papers on Israel and the Ancient Near East.* Edited by F. E. Greenspahn, 420–42. New York: New York University Press, 1991.

Malul, M. *The Comparative Method in Ancient Near Eastern and Biblical Legal Studies.* AOAT 27. Neukirchen-Vluyn: Neukirchener, 1990.

Matthews, V. H., and D. C. Benjamin. *Old Testament Parallels: Laws and Stories from the Ancient Near East.* 2nd ed. New York: Paulist, 1997.

Millard, A. R. "Methods of Studying the Patriarchal Narratives as Ancient Texts." In *Essays on the Patriarchal Narratives.* Edited by A. R. Millard and D. J. Wiseman, 35–51. Winona Lake: Eisenbrauns, 1983.

Niehaus, J. J. *Ancient Near Eastern Themes in Biblical Theology.* Grand Rapids: Kregel, 2008.

Oswalt, J. N. *The Bible among the Myths: Unique Revelation or Just Ancient Literature?* Grand Rapids: Zondervan, 2009.

Pritchard, J. B., ed. *Ancient Near Eastern Texts Relating to the Old Testament.* 3rd ed. with supplement. Princeton, NJ: Princeton University Press, 1969.

Ringgren, H. "The Impact of the Ancient Near East on the Israelite Tradition." In *Tradition and Theology in the Old Testament.* Edited by D. A. Knight, 31–46. Sheffield: Sheffield Academic Press, 1977.

Roberts, J. J. M. "The Ancient Near Eastern Environment." In *The Hebrew Bible and Its Modern Interpreters.* Edited by D. A. Knight and G. M. Tucker, 75–122. Philadelphia: Fortress, 1985.

———. "The Bible and the Literature of the Ancient Near East," 44–58. In *The Bible and the Ancient Near East.* Winona Lake, IN: Eisenbrauns, 2002.

————. "Myth versus History: Relaying the Comparative Foundations." *CBQ* 38 (1976): 1–13.

Rodriguez, A. M. "Ancient Near Eastern Parallels to the Bible and the Question of Revelation and Inspiration," *JATS* 12:1 (2001): 43–48.

Saggs, H. W. F. *The Encounter with the Divine in Mesopotamia and Israel.* London: Athlone, 1978.

Selman, M. J. "Comparative Customs and the Patriarchal Age." In *Essays on the Patriarchal Narratives.* Edited by A. R. Millard and D. J. Wiseman, 93–138. Winona Lake, IN: Eisenbrauns, 1983.

Sparks, K. L. *Ancient Texts for the Study of the Hebrew Bible: A Guide to the Background Literature.* Peabody, MA: Hendrickson, 2005.

Talmon, S. "The Comparative Method in Biblical Interpretation: Principles and Problems." In *Congress Volume—Göttingen 1977. Vetus Testimentum* Supp. 29. Edited by J. Emerton, 320–56. Leiden: Brill, 1978.

Tigay, J. H. "On Evaluating Claims of Literary Borrowing." In *The Tablet and the Scroll.* Edited by M. Cohen et al., 250–25. Bethesda, MD: CDL, 1993.

Toorn, K. van der. *Sin and Sanction in Israel and Mesopotamia.* Assen: Van Gorcum, 1985.

Walton, John H. *Ancient Israelite Literature in Its Cultural Context: A Survey of Parallels between Biblical and Ancient Near Eastern Texts.* Grand Rapids: Zondervan, 1989.

————. "Ancient Near Eastern Background Studies." In *Dictionary for Theological Interpretation of the Bible.* Edited by Kevin J. Vanhoozer, 40–55. Grand Rapids: Baker, 2005.

————. *Ancient Near Eastern Thought and the Old Testament: Introducing the Conceptual World of the Hebrew Bible.* Grand Rapids: Baker, 2006.

Part 2

THE TEXT OF THE OLD TESTAMENT

Michael A. Grisanti

JUST AS AN understanding of the *world* of the OT is important to a correct interpretation of the OT (see Part 1), so the student of Scripture should also be aware of matters relating to the *text* of the OT. As an introduction to the larger section that follows, this unit gives attention to issues raised by the sheer temporal distance between the modern day and the completion of the oldest and even latest OT books. In addition to ancient customs and practices, it focuses on a consideration of factors regarding the transmission of the OT text and the role of oral tradition in that process. Such matters provide an entrée to the subject matter of the subsequent chapters in this section.

TIME FRAME OF THE COMPOSITION OF THE OLD TESTAMENT

Based on an early date for the exodus from Egypt (c. 1446 BC)[1] and the belief in a fourth-century BC close of the OT canon, the 39 books of the OT were written during a period of about 1,000 years. Some of the authors are identified while others are unknown. In contrast to this, the books of the NT were written during a much shorter period of time, about 50 years. Changes in language, geographical designations, and cultural practices, to name a few categories, represent a potentially greater challenge for the interpreter with regard to biblical books composed over a millennium compared to those written during a half century.

THE IMPACT OF VARYING CUSTOMS

The NT was composed in a 50-year period, written by Jewish men (except for Luke) in a time of Roman domination of the world. Apart from the book of Revelation, all the books of the NT were written before the destruction of the Temple at Jerusalem in AD 70. It is not entirely accurate to say the NT was written against a monocultural backdrop, but it was created in a time when the relatively uniform Greco-Roman world system was in place. There were differences among Jewish, Greek, and Roman customs, but those customs are more narrow in

---

[1] In light of this date the Pentateuch was substantially completed by 1406 BC.

breadth than those found in the OT. The books of the OT interact with Egyptian, Canaanite, and Mesopotamian milieus, in addition obviously to the cultural world of Israel itself. The people of Egypt, Ugarit, Babylon, Moab, Ammon, Phoenicia, and Aram (Syria) are just a few of the groups that provide part of the fabric against which the OT was written. This should not discourage students of Scripture, but rather should motivate them to be careful about importing a worldview or customs from the modern day when interpreting OT passages.[2]

THE TRANSMISSION OF THE OLD TESTAMENT TEXT

The oldest books of the OT (the Pentateuch) were initially composed well over 3,000 years ago (c. 1400 BC). Are modern translations of the OT based on these ancient texts or others? Who copied these texts during those centuries? What kind of care did they give to this important task? How close are the latest extant copies to those original texts? How did they become part of the authoritative collection of books known as the OT?

Where Did All the Copies Go?

In addition to stone, clay, wood, ivory, potsherds (ostraca), and precious metals, the writing materials most commonly used in the ancient world for the transmission of biblical texts were papyrus, leather, and parchment.[3] Papyrus is a reed plant that grows in swamps along the Nile River. Narrow strips of the pith of the reed were laid in two layers, alternating horizontally and vertically, and then left to dry on a flat surface underneath a weight. Although it was inexpensive and abundant, it could survive only in dry climates.[4] Most scholars assume that the autographs of the biblical writers were written on papyrus, none of which survived.[5] Leather was obtained from the hides of various animals and was dried, shaved, and scraped clean for writing. It was much more durable than papyrus, but still would dry out, crack, and eventually crumble away. Most of the DSS were made of leather.[6] Parchment was a higher quality of leather that came into widespread use in the second century BC; only a few of the DSS were written on that medium.[7]

In light of the passage of centuries from 1400 BC to the time of the Qumran scrolls and beyond and because of the relatively damp climate of Palestine, most of the copies of these biblical texts did not survive, let alone the autographa. This led to the copying of each biblical book numerous times over those centuries. That passage of time and limited number of manuscripts of Old Testament (compared to the vast number of NT manuscripts) gives rise to the importance of the art of textual criticism (see chap. 7).

How Faithfully Were Copies Made?

One of the most important discoveries of the twentieth century relative to the OT was that of the DSS at Qumran.[8] Over several years and in 11 different caves, various people found evidence of about 200 biblical texts (out of the approximately 800 texts or parts of texts found at

---

[2] Part 1 of this volume offers various insights into the world of the OT.

[3] P. D. Wegner, *The Journey from Texts to Translations: The Origin and Development of the Bible* (Grand Rapids: Baker, 1999), 87–95.

[4] Ibid., 90–92.

[5] F. F. Bruce, *The Books and the Parchments*, rev. ed. (Westwood, NJ: Revell, 1963), 14.

[6] Wegner, *The Journey from Texts to Translations*, 92–93.

[7] Ibid., 93.

[8] The first set of scrolls was discovered by Bedouin shepherds in 1947 on the northwest side of the Dead Sea.

Qumran).[9] The primary reason this discovery was so astounding is that it has provided copies of various biblical books that are almost 1,000 years older than any texts known before that time![10]

What can be learned from the comparison of texts on hand prior to 1947 and the ones discovered at Qumran? Although the DSS do not unanimously support every reading of the modern OT (based on the Masoretic Text—MT),[11] the degree of agreement between the two is amazing.[12] Despite the fact that the DSS are much older than the MT, they generally "support the fidelity with which the Masoretic Text was copied."[13]

Waltke points out that "in every era there was a strong *tendency to preserve the text*."[14] The DSS suggest this, but also the grammar of the MT conforms to the framework of ancient Semitic philology, even preserving rare words that were not understood later on in the transmission of the text.[15] Also over 90 percent of the OT is textually sound and uniformly witnessed to by significant manuscripts. The variants found in the remaining 10 percent are relatively insignificant; only a few have any bearing on any key doctrinal matters.[16] In light of these and other evidences the centuries that have passed since the composition of the earliest biblical texts need not provide grounds for any skepticism about the reliability of contemporary OT texts.

Should We Be Worried?

As Waltke points out, the "very fact that the Scripture persistently survived the most deleterious conditions throughout its long history demonstrates that indefatigable scribes insisted on its preservation."[17] In spite of perishable writing materials and a very long compositional history, the text of the OT has survived with amazing accuracy. Also various biblical passages (e.g., Deut 4:2; 17:18–19; 31:9–13) and ANE texts that warn against tampering with texts[18] suggest that the ANE world maintained a diligent concern for care and accuracy in transmitting sacred writings. Also, various scholars have questioned the integrity of most OT books, regarding them as documentary or literary fabrications, after the analogy of Greco-Roman practice. Albright points out that his careful study of thousands of relevant ANE documents

---

[9] E. Ulrich, "The Bible in the Making: The Scriptures Found at Qumran," in *The Bible at Qumran: Text, Shape, and Interpretation*, ed. P. W. Flint (Grand Rapids: Eerdmans, 2001), 52–53. Some of these involve entire biblical books, parts of books, and even tiny fragments. See chap. 7 for a more complete overview of these discoveries.

[10] Before the Qumran discoveries, the earliest complete copies of various OT books dated to the tenth century AD and the oldest complete copy of the OT dated from the early eleventh century AD. Scholars date these manuscripts from the mid-third century BC to AD 135. (B. K. Waltke, "Old Testament Textual Criticism," in *Foundations for Biblical Interpretation*, ed. D. S. Dockery, K. A. Matthews, and R. Sloan [Nashville: B&H, 1994], 162).

[11] In addition to the DSS that serve as witnesses to the MT as a base text, certain scrolls attest to the textual tradition witnessed by the Samaritan Pentateuch and the LXX as well as nonaligned and "Qumran" texts (E. Tov, *Textual Criticism of the Hebrew Bible*, rev. ed. [Minneapolis: Fortress, 2001], 114–17, 158–63).

[12] E. R. Brotzman, *Old Testament Textual Criticism: A Practical Introduction* (Grand Rapids: Baker, 1994), 95. According to M. Burrows; "It is a matter for wonder that through something like a thousand years the text underwent so little alteration" (*The Dead Sea Scrolls*, reprint [New York: Gramercy, 1986], 304).

[13] Brotzman, *Old Testament Textual Criticism*, 95.

[14] B. K. Waltke, "How We Got the Hebrew Bible: The Text and Canon of the Old Testament," in *The Bible at Qumran*, 47.

[15] Ibid., 47–48.

[16] Ibid., 157–58. Waltke affirms that "95 percent of the OT is therefore textually sound" (ibid., 158).

[17] B. K. Waltke and M. O'Connor, *An Introduction to Biblical Hebrew Syntax* (Winona Lake, IN: Eisenbrauns, 1990), 16.

[18] For example in the epilogue of the Code of Hammurabi, a series of imprecations is directed at anyone who dared change the written laws (Martha Roth, "The Laws of Hammurabi (2.131)," in *COS*, ed. W. W. Hallo and K. L. Younger Jr. [New York: Brill, 2000], 2:351–53). See also *ANET*, 205–6.

clearly demonstrates that "sacred and profane documents were copied with greater care than is true of scribal copying in Greco-Roman times."[19]

ORAL TRADITION VERSUS WRITTEN TEXT?

The previous sections of this chapter have shown ways in which the text of the OT is quite distant from the modern world and offered suggestions on how to bridge that gap. Some scholars have used that "distance" between the OT and the present to argue for a fairly loose transmission of the OT text. The following questions frame the issue. How did biblical writers gather information for their writing, and how were these books passed down to following generations? Were biblical "books" transmitted with great care in written form, insuring that what one generation received was passed on substantially unchanged? Or did these sacred writings have a somewhat extended oral or preliterary stage before they reached written form, during which time numerous changes were introduced to them?

In light of the "antiquity" of the OT and the long period of its composition, scholarship at large has suggested that the text of the OT went through numerous transformations over time. Some even proposed that literacy was a somewhat late development in Israelite society; thus the transmission of biblical "books" over the centuries would have opened them up to significant changes.[20] As new sets of circumstances emerged and the community of faith had different needs or challenges, the message of a given biblical book was likely massaged to accommodate new ideological and theological circumstances. According to this view biblical passages were therefore redacted regularly to meet various challenging situations over the centuries. These critics, sometimes referred to as tradition historians, also assume the existence of a long oral prehistory before a biblical "book" reached written form.[21] They maintain that the OT perception of literature or books was quite different from that of modern times. In fact "the concept of a book would have included, in addition to written pieces, the consciousness of something which had been passed on for generations beforehand, often by word of mouth."[22] In light of the "evidence" of the literature of the ANE, two very important lines of argument are posited. In the first place most of the literature of the OT had a long oral prehistory before being written down.[23] Second, during this oral stage the "literature" was often transposed into new settings with new meanings.[24]

At the outset it must be noted that the tradition historian's use of terminology is unclear. "Oral tradition" is used for the oral composition of a work, oral dissemination to contemporaries, and oral transmission through time. Also their conclusions concerning "oral tradition" involve major misunderstandings of oral tradition in the ANE. Oral tradition existed, but it was normally accompanied by written documents. Mustering evidence from the "thousands of Mesopotamian tablets and acres of hieroglyphic texts," Kitchen contends that for the transmis-

---

[19] W. F. Albright, *From the Stone Age to Christianity: Monotheism and the Historical Process*, 2nd ed. (Garden City, NY: Doubleday, 1957), 78–79. This care is also suggested by an Egyptian scribe's boast: "[The book] is completed from its beginning to its end, having been copied, revised, compared and verified sign by sign" (K. A. Kitchen, *Ancient Orient and the Old Testament* [London: Tyndale, 1966], 140).

[20] W. E. Rast, *Tradition History and the Old Testament* (Philadelphia: Fortress, 1972), 5–16; R. Gnuse, "Tradition History," in *Dictionary of Biblical Interpretation*, ed. J. H. Hayes (Nashville: Abingdon, 1999), 2:583–85.

[21] R. Gnuse, "Tradition History," in *Methods of Bible Interpretation*, ed. J. H. Hayes (Nashville: Abingdon, 2004), 127–32.

[22] Rast, *Tradition History and the Old Testament*, 1.

[23] Ibid., 1–14.

[24] Ibid., 16–18.

sion of anything important the ANE employed writing.[25] Waltke demonstrates that evidence from Mesopotamia, the Hittites, Ugarit, Egypt, and Northwest Semitic literature in general supports the contention that oral and written tradition existed side by side. Beyond that, it seems that the written material was intended to preserve a given nation's religious treasure, while the oral form was designed to disseminate it.[26] For example the city of Ebla, which antedates the Hebrew patriarchs by three to five centuries and Moses by about a millennium, was highly literate and preserved its culture and heritage in writing.[27] So, by the mid-third millennium BC (c. 2500 BC), Semitic culture was quite literate.[28]

The millennium in which the OT came into being does not demand an acceptance of the notion that careful written transmission of biblical books took place only after a long and changing period of oral transmission. The evidence of ANE literary practices as well as the claims of the OT and NT argues against this idea. The "distance" between the text of the OT and the modern world does not undermine a conservative view of textual reliability.[29]

Summary

The passing of centuries between the composition of the oldest OT writings and the modern day need not generate skepticism concerning the OT text. In spite of the frailty of the materials used by God's appointed spokesmen, numerous indications exist that great attention was given to the careful and accurate copying of those biblical books. In addition the admittedly long ages of transmission need not support the notion that the biblical writings were passed on by means of oral tradition and underwent numerous transformational changes. ANE practices concerning sacred writings demonstrate that written texts *preserved* important information (including sacred writings) and orality served primarily to *disseminate* that information.

AN OVERVIEW OF PART 2: THE TEXT OF THE OLD TESTAMENT

The next three chapters examine important issues that relate to the manner in which the Old Testament was written and passed down over the ages, some of the issues addressed briefly above. Chapter 5 reviews the biblical teaching on inspiration that supports a high view of Scripture. It also considers the potential problems of editorial updating, redaction, and *theological tendenz*. Chapter 6 examines the manner in which ancient writings became viewed as authoritative Scripture by considering canonicity. After considering the biblical input on the concept of canonical writings, the chapter also surveys the debate on which books belong in the canon. Chapter 7 discusses the transmission of the Old Testament writings and the practices of textual criticism. Dealing with the period from the earliest manuscripts of biblical texts (Qumran) through the time when the early versions and translations were completed, this section wrestles with the manner in which biblical books were copied and passed on and also summarizes fundamental principles of textual criticism.

---

[25] Kitchen, *Ancient Orient and the Old Testament*, 136.

[26] B. K. Waltke, "Oral Tradition," in *A Tribute to Gleason Archer*, ed. W. C. Kaiser Jr. and R. F. Youngblood (Chicago: Moody, 1986), 20–27.

[27] Ibid., 20. Waltke examines five other regions in the biblical world and shows that each region preserved important information in written form, carefully transmitting it with accuracy.

[28] Waltke concludes that after having examined literature from various ANE peoples (and other literature as well), "no evidence has been found in any Semitic cultures, including Islam, that tradents molded an oral tradition to meet changing situations over the centuries" (ibid., 29–30).

[29] Ibid. See chap. 5 for further consideration of the biblical writers use of sources.

STUDY QUESTIONS

1. What do conservative evangelicals suggest as the time frame for the composition of the OT?
2. What are some of the nations or cultures with which the biblical writers interacted?
3. What are some of the key writing materials used in composing and copying biblical books?
4. What did the discovery of the Dead Sea Scrolls at Qumran indicate about the way in which the OT books were transmitted?
5. What are some evidences of a very faithful transmission of OT books?
6. Did writing develop fairly late in biblical history, creating the need for oral transmission as the primary means for passing on biblical traditions?
7. What are some of the ways people define the expression "oral tradition"?
8. Archaeological work at what location demonstrates the existence of a highly literate *pre-patriarchal* society?

FOR FURTHER STUDY

Brotzman, E. R. *Old Testament Textual Criticism: A Practical Introduction*. Grand Rapids: Baker, 1994.

Bruce, F. F. *The Books and the Parchments*. Rev. ed. Westwood, NJ: Revell, 1963.

Kitchen, K. A. *Ancient Orient and the Old Testament*. London: Tyndale, 1966.

Tov, E. *Textual Criticism of the Hebrew Bible*. 2nd rev. ed. Minneapolis: Fortress, 2001.

Waltke, B. K. "How We Got the Hebrew Bible: The Text and Canon of the Old Testament." In *The Bible at Qumran: Text, Shape, and Interpretation*. Edited by Peter W. Flint, 27–50. Grand Rapids: Eerdmans, 2001.

———. "Oral Tradition." In *A Tribute to Gleason Archer*. Edited by Walter C. Kaiser Jr., and Ronald F. Youngblood, 17–34. Chicago: Moody Press, 1986.

———. "Old Testament Textual Criticism." In *Foundations for Biblical Interpretation*. Edited by D. S. Dockery, K. A. Matthews, and R. Sloan, 156–86. Nashville: B&H, 1994.

Wegner, P. D. *The Journey from Texts to Translations: The Origin and Development of the Bible*. Grand Rapids: Baker, 1999.

CHAPTER 5

THE COMPOSITION
OF THE OLD TESTAMENT

MICHAEL A. GRISANTI

H OW DID AN OT book come into existence? Did God reveal everything a prophet wrote, or did the writer draw on various sources from the world around him? How did OT believers view these writings that came from the hands of God's representatives? What happened in light of potential geographic or linguistic changes that may have occurred in the thousand years between the composition of the Pentateuch and the close of the canon? After briefly summarizing key issues of inspiration and canonicity from an OT perspective, it will be helpful to consider the role of sources in the process of inscripturation[1] and to determine whether there was any inspired editorial activity after the initial "completion" of a biblical book. Since "redaction" has some distinctly negative overtones in some circles, it is important also to give it brief attention. The question of the evidence of bias in the OT and whether it detracts at all from the reliability of biblical writings because of its perceived lack of objectivity deserves serious reflection.

ISSUES OF INSPIRATION AND CANONICITY: BASIC DEFINITIONS

The assumption that the OT is not simply a human product but the very word of God demands the corollary consideration of its authority and infallibility. More precisely, attention must focus on three key concepts: inspiration, the autographs, and the canon.

Inspiration

The Bible, as both a human and a divine product, is God's self-revelation, His meaningful and authoritative communication to human beings.[2] Millard Erickson defines inspiration as

---

[1] "Inscripturation" refers to the issues involved in a biblical book coming into existence, from the Lord impressing ideas on the mind of a biblical writer to that writer editing and crafting the writing as he was guided by the Holy Spirit. "Inspiration" refers to the work of the Holy Spirit that guarantees the authority and infallibility of what a given biblical spokesman wrote.

[2] M. Strauss, "Introducing the Bible," in *The IVP Introduction to the Bible*, ed. P. S. Johnson (Downers Grove, IL: IVP, 2006), 1–2.

"that supernatural influence of the Holy Spirit upon the Scripture writers which rendered their writings an accurate record of the revelation or which resulted in what they wrote actually being the Word of God."[3] The apostle Paul affirmed that "all Scripture is given by inspiration of God" (2 Tim 3:16 NKJV) and Peter wrote that "prophecy never came by the will of man, but holy men of God spoke as they were moved by the Holy Spirit" (2 Pet 1:21 NKJV). The "inspiration" or "spiration" of Scriptures—the fact that they are God-breathed—emphasizes "the divine source and initiative rather than human genius or creativity."[4] God's involvement in the process of "inscripturation" demonstrates that those Scriptures ultimately came from Him.

The divine-human authorship of the Scriptures raises the question as to how those Scriptures came into being. Most scholars contend that the Holy Spirit superintended the biblical writers throughout the process of inscripturation. Whether it concerns a biblical book or books with a stated author (like the Pentateuch) or a book or books that went through a longer period of composition and could have involved more than one writer (such as Samuel, Kings, and the Psalms), the biblical doctrine of inspiration guarantees the accuracy and infallibility of the biblical writings until they reached the final stage of composition.

Autographs

Building on the concept of inspiration, the Chicago Statement on Biblical Inerrancy states, "We affirm that inspiration, strictly speaking, applies only to the autographic text of Scripture."[5] This brings up the question: What constitutes an autograph or the autographa? In general, scholars use the term "autographa" to refer to the first or original copies of the biblical documents, that is, what the author himself actually wrote.[6] Its inspiration connotes the idea of the *original writing* of a biblical book. The "autographa," then, refer to unchanging forms of the text of God's Word in which the original document is identical to the final canonical form of a given OT biblical book. In light of this understanding of the autographa and because of the significant role it plays in the inerrancy debate, the writings designated as autographa would not seem capable of being in flux or susceptible to change.

Canon

The "canon" of Scripture involves "the list of all the books that belong in the Bible"[7] or "the list of books that are reckoned as Holy Scriptures . . . reckoned as supremely authoritative for

---

[3] M. Erickson, *Christian Theology* (Grand Rapids: Baker, 1983), 199. C. Hodge affirms that inspiration was "an influence of the Holy Spirit on the minds of certain select men, which rendered them the organs of God for the infallible communication of His mind and will. They were in such a sense the organs of God that what they said, God said" (*Systematic Theology* [New York Scribner, Armstrong, and Co., 1872], 1:154). B. B. Warfield proposed that "the Bible is the Word of God in such a sense that its words, though written by men and bearing indelibly impressed upon them the marks of their human origin, were written, nevertheless, under such an influence of the Holy Ghost as to be also the words of God, the adequate expression of His mind and will. It has always recognized that this conception of co-authorship implies that the Spirit's superintendence extends to the choice of the words used by the human authors (verbal inspiration), and preserves its product from everything inconsistent with a divine authorship—thus securing, among other things, that entire truthfulness which is everywhere presupposed in and asserted for Scripture by the Biblical writers (inerrancy)" (*The Inspiration and Authority of the Bible*, ed. S. Craig [Philadelphia: Presbyterian and Reformed, 1948], 173).

[4] D. S. Dockery, "The Divine-Human Authorship of Inspired Scripture," in *Authority and Inspiration: A Baptist Perspective*, ed. Duane A. Garrett and Richard R. Melick Jr. (Grand Rapids: Baker, 1987), 20.

[5] Article X. The entire statement is included as an appendix in *Inerrancy*, ed. N. Geisler (Grand Rapids: Zondervan, 1980), 493–502.

[6] W. Grudem, *Systematic Theology* (Grand Rapids: Zondervan, 1994), 96.

[7] Ibid., 54.

belief and conduct."[8] Theologically inspiration serves as the foundation for the canonicity of a biblical book. In other words God's activity determines canonicity. As E. J. Young points out, "That which determines the canonicity of a book, therefore, is the fact that the book is inspired of God. Hence a distinction is properly made between the authority which the OT books possess as divinely inspired, and the recognition of that authority on the part of Israel."[9] Practically speaking, God's people recognized canonicity primarily on the basis of the authority of the prophetic spokesmen through whom the book was given.[10] Once a book was understood to be canonical, God's people sought to safeguard that portion of sacred Scripture. During the thousand years or so of OT compositional history just a few written works (22 or 24 books according to the Jewish canon and 39 according to the Protestant canon) gained canonical status.

IS INSPIRATION COMPATIBLE WITH THE USE OF SOURCES?

Certain OT books are replete with references to God speaking or God appearing to His spokesmen. Other books record information about His dealings with His chosen nation and their interrelationships with other peoples. Some books record eyewitness accounts, while others were written long after the events took place (e.g., Genesis written by Moses). What were the potential sources from which a biblical writer might draw?

Direct Revelation

The writer of the book of Hebrews affirmed, "In the past God spoke to our forefathers through the prophets at many times and in various ways" (Heb 1:1 NIV). God spoke directly to Moses at times ("face to face," Num 12:8 NIV). He directed the psalmists as they composed their songs. He worked through the wisdom writers as they observed the world around them and wrote of the manner in which life fit into God's plan. He spoke to the prophets through visions and dreams and revealed His will to them more directly as well.[11] The Holy Spirit guided each biblical writer to put God's message through them into concrete, propositional form. Were there any other sources on which a biblical writer could draw besides divine revelation?

Canonical or Noncanonical Written Records

The books of Chronicles draw on the narratives in Samuel and Kings,[12] but the Chronicler also makes extensive use of noncanonical books in compiling his history of Israel.[13] In addition to the written sources conjectured by proponents of source criticism regarding the composition

---

[8] F. F. Bruce, *The Books and the Parchments*, rev. ed. (New York: Revell, 1963), 95.

[9] E. J. Young, "The Canon of the OT," in *Revelation and the Bible*, ed. C. F. H. Henry (Grand Rapids: Baker, 1958), 156. Cf. René Pache, *The Inspiration and Authority of Scripture*, trans. H. Needham (Chicago: Moody, 1969), 159–62.

[10] This is the primary criterion identified by R. L. Harris, *Inspiration and Canonicity of the Scriptures* (Greenville, SC: A Press, 1995), 154–77. F. F. Bruce (*The Canon of Scripture* [Downers Grove, IL: InterVarsity, 1988], 255–69) and N. Geisler and W. Nix (*A General Introduction to the Bible: Revised and Expanded* [Chicago: Moody, 1986], 221–34) offer other criteria for recognizing a given book's canonicity.

[11] Phrases like "Thus says the Lord," and "The word of the Lord came to" highlight this divine causation.

[12] More than half of 1 and 2 Chronicles parallels 1 and 2 Samuel and 1 and 2 Kings. However, it does not seem that Chronicles contains any direct quotations from any of these canonical books.

[13] The following list of these sources is taken from A. E. Hill and J. H. Walton, *A Survey of the Old Testament*, 3rd rd. (Grand Rapids: Zondervan, 2009), 312–13: (1) genealogical records (1 Chr 4:33; 5:17; 7:9,40; 9:1,22; 2 Chr 12:15); (2) letters and official documents (1 Chr 28:11–12; 2 Chr 32:17–20; 36:22–23); (3) Poems, prayers, speeches, and songs (1 Chr 16:8–36; 29:10–22; 2 Chr 29:30; 35:25); (4) Other histories, including the Book of the Kings of Israel and Judah (2 Chr 27:7; 36:8), the Book of the Kings of Judah and Israel (2 Chr 16:11; 25:26; 28:26; 32:32), the Chronicles of David (1 Chr 27:24), the Commentary on the book of Kings (2 Chr 24:27), the Directions of David, King of Israel, and the Directions of Solomon his son (2 Chr 35:4); and (5) Prophetic writings, including the Chronicles of Samuel, Nathan, and Gad

of the Pentateuch,[14] many scholars contend that Moses drew on preexisting written records to write the history that predated his life.[15]

Oral Tradition

Oral tradition is a more controversial source of the biblical writings. One of the reasons for the negative reaction to the notion of oral tradition in the composition of the Bible is its use by biblical critics to argue against the Bible's accuracy or infallibility. These critics generally suggest that the traditions included in the final form of the written text were the result of a long period of oral tradition. Over the centuries of the oral tradition's development, each tradition took new shapes, changing to meet the challenging situations that confronted it and its custodians.[16]

As stated in the introduction to Part 1, the historical-critical view of how oral tradition enabled biblical passages to morph into different "shapes" (i.e., presented different messages over time as each new generation faced different circumstances) does not square with biblical or ANE evidence. The mere possibility that biblical writers used oral tradition as a potential source for their writing of a biblical book is not the kind of oral tradition in view here. In fact the concept of oral tradition in the proper sense should not lead to the fallacious conclusion that information transmitted thereby is unreliable or even erroneous. From the time of the OT to the present day, cultures of all kinds have made use of oral tradition as a way of passing on information, exhibiting most careful attention to detail. Whereas written documents from the ANE world preserved important recollections of the past in concrete form, oral tradition was the most common means of disseminating that information to a largely illiterate populace. The point with regard to oral tradition as a potential mechanism for biblical writers is not that this was in fact the practice of the prophets and apostles, but only that they could have done so and to explain what is at stake in their having done so.

Regardless of whether the Lord spoke directly or indirectly to the prophet or the prophet drew on written or oral sources, what the biblical writer selected, edited, and composed based on a given source was authoritative Scripture. What they wrote became part of "God-breathed" Scripture (2 Tim 3:16 NIV). Regardless of the source they used, they wrote "as they were carried along by the Holy Spirit" (2 Pet 1:21 NIV). Divine inspiration does not lie with any source or tradition that lies behind the biblical text. God Himself directed the writers as they incorporated material from revelation, written records, or oral tradition. This resulted in a "complete tapestry of divine revelation in that book, [and] the resulting total composition was exactly what God had intended and wanted preserved for posterity as well as that day."[17]

(1 Chr 29:29), the prophecy of Ahijah and the visions of Iddo the Seer (2 Chr 9:29), and the records of Shemaiah, Jehu, and Isaiah (2 Chr 12:15; 20:34; 32:32).

[14] See chap. 9, "The Present State of Old Testament Scholarship."

[15] R. K. Harrison, *Introduction to the Old Testament* (Grand Rapids: Eerdmans, 1969), 543-51; K. A. Mathews, *Genesis 1–11:26* (Nashville: B&H, 1996), 31–35; P. J. Wiseman, *Ancient Records and the Structure of Genesis: A Case for Literary Unity*, ed. D. J. Wiseman (Nashville: Thomas Nelson, 1985).

[16] R. Gnuse, "Tradition History," in *Methods of Bible Interpretation*, ed. J. H. Hayes (Nashville: Abingdon, 2004), 127.

[17] W. C. Kaiser Jr., *The Old Testament Documents: Are They Reliable & Relevant?* (Downers Grove, IL: InterVarsity, 2001), 16.

SCRIBAL OR EDITORIAL UPDATING

Duration of Composition of the OT

Unlike the NT books that were composed within a 50-year period, the books of the OT canon came into existence over a period of about 1,000 years, from Moses to the close of the canon around 400 BC.[18] During that millennium doubtless multitudes of linguistic, cultural, and geopolitical alterations were introduced into the biblical texts. This possibility gives rise to the question, Did this long compositional history in an ever-developing political and cultural environment affect the fundamental accuracy of the writings of the OT?

Beckwith points out that the concept of canonicity was not merely punctiliar but was part of a process as well. For example, when the Psalter was composed over a number of years, individual psalms were gathered into collections that were then complied into books and eventually brought together into the entire Psalter. At all points along the way an individual psalm had canonical status as part of the OT Scriptures.[19] The book of Kings most probably was composed over a long period of time by more than one historian.[20] If more than one writer or editor participated in the composition of the book, each unnamed prophetic figure delivered to the next writer an authoritative piece. The fact that these books were assembled over a period of time and underwent editorial reshaping does no harm to a conservative understanding of the inspiration of the Scriptures. The book of Proverbs, for example, is primarily Solomonic, but has "pieces" added by someone after Solomon (e.g., other Solomonic proverbs copied by officials of King Hezekiah, chaps. 25–29; words of Agur, chap. 30; words of King Lemuel, chap. 31). In each case an unnamed editor added these words to the book of Proverbs. There can be no doubt that the faithful of Israel would have considered the proverbs of Solomon canonical both before and after the non-Solomonic sections of proverbial material were added.[21]

Basic Propositions

The proposition argued here is that the time span between the initial composition of certain biblical books and the close of the OT canon occasioned the need for various editorial revisions, although on a relatively small scale. The following five propositions buttress this point with reference to the relationship between textual updating on the one hand and inspiration and canonicity on the other. The first image relates to the first two propositions and the second image to the last three.

---

[18] The following section is excerpted, with revisions, from M. A. Grisanti, "Inspiration, Inerrancy, and the OT Canon: The Place of Textual Updating in an Inerrant View of Scripture," *JETS* 44, no. 4 (December 2001): 577–98.

[19] R. Beckwith, *The Old Testament Canon of the New Testament Church* (Grand Rapids: Eerdmans, 1985), 68.

[20] The books of the Kings cover a time period from the end of King David's life until the time of King Jehoiachin's release from Babylonian prison (c. 550 BC).

[21] For a more detailed overview of the OT canon, see chap. 6 of this volume, "The Canonicity of the Old Testament."

Figure 5.1
The Process of Inscripturation

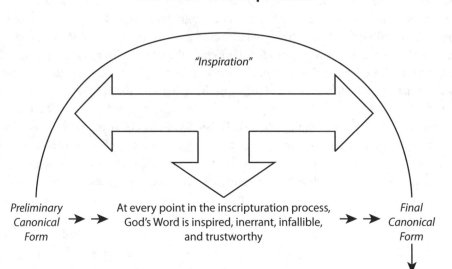

Proposition 1: The customary concept of the OT canon is locked in too tightly with the original or initial form of a biblical book. In light of the various editorial revisions that seem to be present in the text of the OT (to be examined presently), an important distinction must be made between the preliminary and final canonical forms of a biblical book.[22] The word "preliminary" does not suggest a deficient canonical form, but a canonical status that *has not yet been finalized.* During the entire period in which God was giving His Word to mankind, the people of God regarded a given biblical book as canonical (see figure 5.1). In other words throughout the composition history of the OT, the God-breathed nature of each biblical book gave that book canonical status in the eyes of the believing community.

Proposition 2: The doctrine of biblical inspiration is linked to a corollary truth, namely, that God guarantees the accuracy of everything involved in the process of inscripturation. The latter term may be viewed metaphorically as the umbrella that describes the whole process by which God revealed His Word through His prophetic spokesmen. The following remarks aim to demonstrate that the initial composition of a biblical book *and* any editorial revisions of a biblical book before the finalization of the OT canon are part of God-breathed Scripture (see figure 5.2). Their inerrancy, canonicity, and "*autographa*-like" status derive entirely from divine inspiration.

---

[22] R. D. Bergen calls my "preliminary canonical form" "precanonical text" (*1, 2 Samuel* [Nashville: B&H, 1996], 31).

Figure 5.2
**The Dividing Point between Inspired Textual Updating
and Noninspired Textual Transmission**

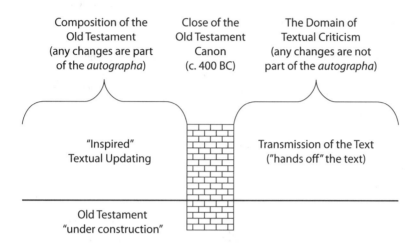

Proposition 3: The *autographa* (i.e., the "original" writings) refers to the final form of the OT. It is that text-form transmitted by the scribes (after the close of the OT canon) without any divinely endorsed content changes.

Proposition 4: The close of the OT canon is the dividing line between inspired editorial activity and uninspired scribal activity. Modernizations, explanatory glosses, and any other similar phenomena can be described as inspired editorial activity only if they are part of the compositional history of the OT, that is, before the close of the OT canon. In other words editorial updating that took place before the close of the canon belongs to the process of inscripturation and is part of the inspired, inerrant text of Scripture. Any updating that occurred after that juncture belongs to the domain of textual criticism and represents a variant from the *autographa*.

Proposition 5: Only recognized individuals (i.e., prophetic figures, whose adjustment of the biblical text would have been accepted by the Israelite community of faith) would have been able to participate in this "updating" process.

To summarize, within the canonical process, and subsequent to the initial writing of a biblical book or books, a God-chosen individual under the superintendence of the Holy Spirit could adjust, revise, or update pre-existing biblical material in order to make a given Scripture passage understandable to succeeding generations. Those revisions, which occurred within the compositional history of the OT, are also inspired and inerrant.

Possible Examples of Inspired Textual Updating[23]

Deuteronomy 34:5–12. Unger (and most OT scholars) points to the narration of Moses' death, burial, and final tribute to his prophetic ministry in Deut 34:5–12 as "an obvious post-Mosaic addition."[24] G. L. Archer concludes that these verses of the final chapter of Deuteronomy

---

[23] In addition to the examples cited below, see Grisanti, "Inspiration, Inerrancy, and the OT Canon, 584–88.

[24] M. F. Unger, *Introductory Guide to the OT* (Grand Rapids: Zondervan, 1951), 239. He also cites Exod 11:3 and Num 12:3 as possible post-Mosaic glosses since they praise Moses in such a manner that Moses might not have written them (ibid.). On Deut 34:5–12 and ancient rabbinic tradition, see Baba Bathra 14b.

are "demonstrably post-Mosaic."[25] An unnamed prophetic figure added them sometime after Moses completed his work on the Pentateuch. Both before and after the addition of the verses, the Pentateuch was fully inspired, authoritative, and inerrant.

Genesis 11:28,31. This passage records Abraham's place of origin as "Ur of the Chaldeans."[26] The annals of Asshur-Nasirpal II contain the first documentary evidence of the presence of Chaldeans in southern Babylon.[27] Although well established when they first appeared on the historical scene, there is no written documentation for the early history of the Chaldeans when they rose to power in southern Babylonia.[28] The Chaldeans did not become contenders for the Babylonian throne until the middle of the eighth century BC.[29] So the expression "Ur of the Chaldeans" could represent a scribal gloss supplied to distinguish Abraham's Ur from other cities carrying the same name.[30]

Genesis 14:14. The place name "Dan" often appears in the historical books as a reference to the northernmost point of the promised land (Judg 18:29; 20:1; 1 Kgs 12:29–30; 15:20) and is part of the common geographical expression, "from Dan to Beersheba" (1 Sam 3:20; 2 Sam 3:10; 17:11; 24:2,15; 1 Kgs 4:25). It is customarily identified with Tell el Qadi. This ancient city was known as Laish in the Egyptian Execration Texts and in Mari texts.[31] The city of Dan received its name in the settlement period when the Danite tribe migrated north and conquered the city of Laish (Gen 14:14)/Leshem (Josh 19:47–48). Thus, it seems that this place did not receive the name of Dan until over a century after the Mosaic period (Judg 18:29).[32]

---

[25] G. L. Archer Jr., *A Survey of Old Testament Introduction*, rev. ed. (Chicago: Moody, 1994), 276.

[26] The Hebrew term for "Chaldees/Chaldean" is *kaśdîm*. The shift from the Hebrew form to the form that serves as the basis for the English translation (*kaldu*) was part of a common phonetic shift of the sibilant (ś) to a lamed (l) when it was followed by a dental (d) (A. R. Millard, "Daniel 1-6 and History," *EQ* 49 [1977]: 70–71; cf. W. von Soden, *Grundriss der Akkadischen Grammatik* [Rome: Pontifical Biblical Institute, 1969], §30g).

[27] The annals refer to the Chaldeans in passing in relationship to the Assyrian campaign of 878 BC (J. A. Brinkman, *A Political History of Post-Kassite Babylonia, 1158-722 B.C.* [Rome: Pontifical Biblical Institute, 1968], 260). The annals of Shalmaneser III preserve the earliest description of Chaldean tribes (in 850 BC) (J. Brinkman, "Merodach-Baladan II," in *Studies Presented to A. Leo Oppenheim*, ed. R. D. Biggs and J. A. Brinkman [Chicago: University of Chicago Press, 1964], 8).

[28] J. A. Brinkman, "Babylonia c. 1000–748 B.C.," in *Cambridge Ancient History* (Cambridge: Cambridge University Press, 1982), 3/2:287.

[29] B. T. Arnold, "Babylonians," in *Peoples of the OT World*, ed. A. Hoerth, G. Mattingly, and E. Yamauchi (Grand Rapids: Baker, 1994), 57.

[30] B. T. Arnold, *Encountering the Book of Genesis* (Grand Rapids: Baker, 1998), 78; U. Cassuto, *A Commentary on the Book of Genesis, Part Two* (Jerusalem: Magnes, 1964), 272; J. D. Davis, *Paradise to Prison: Studies in Genesis* (Grand Rapids: Baker, 1975), 166; A. Hoerth, *Archaeology and the OT* (Grand Rapids: Baker, 1998), 59; E. H. Merrill, *Kingdom of Priests: A History of Old Testament Israel*, 2nd ed. (Grand Rapids: Baker, 2008), 42 n 15; H. W. F. Saggs, "Ur of the Chaldees: A Problem of Identification," *Iraq* 22 (1960): 209; G. Wenham, *Genesis 16–50* (Dallas: Word, 1994), 272. Those who reject the idea that this reference to the Chaldeans represents a later editorial insertion contend that the phonetic shift (*kaśdîm* > *kaldu*) that occurred in the mid-second millennium BC fits Mosaic authorship (W. D. Barrick, "'Ur of the Chaldeans' (Gen. 11:28–31): A Model for Dealing with Difficult Texts," *MSJ* 20:1 [Spring 2009]: 7–18). Some embrace the idea that Abraham's nephew Kesed may have been the ancestor of the Chaldeans (*kaśdîm*), a connection rejected by D. Wiseman ("Chaldea; Chaldeans; Chaldees," *ISBE*, ed. G. W. Bromiley [Grand Rapids: Eerdmans, 1979], 1:630).

[31] N. M. Sarna, *Genesis* (New York: Jewish Pub. Society, 1989), 108. There are five other examples of scribal glosses in Genesis 14 where an updated place name is given after an outdated place name: 14:2, "Bela (that is, Zoar)"; 14:3, "the valley of Siddim (that is, the Salt Sea)"; 14:7, "En-mishpat (that is, Kadesh)"; 14:8, "Bela (that is, Zoar)"; 14:17, "the valley of Shaveh (that is, the King's Valley)." This updating of the onomastic entries indicates the antiquity of the source document and was done to make the text intelligible to the reader. Although this updating could have been done by Moses, most scholars regard these examples as post-Mosaic additions. See D. Garrett, *Rethinking Genesis: The Sources and Authorship of the First Book of the Pentateuch* (Grand Rapids: Baker, 1991), 86; Davis, *Paradise to Prison*, 166; M. F. Unger, *Archaeology and the OT* (Grand Rapids: Zondervan, 1954), 116–17.

[32] At the very least this migration took place some time after Joshua allocated the land to the tribes around 1399 BC.

Several scholars argue that this mention of Dan is indeed Mosaic. Leon Wood points to a city named Dan Jaan, mentioned in 2 Sam 24:6, which he locates in Gilead.[33] Gleason Archer points out that the place name "Dan" appears as early as the second Egyptian dynasty[34] (which ended c. 2700 BC).[35] Three facts argue against the Mosaic authorship of this place name. First, the presence of a place name in ancient Egyptian literature does not demonstrate that the name Dan in Genesis 14 is Mosaic. It simply indicates that the place name of Dan was attested in pre-Mosaic times. Second, that a city named Dan existed in David's day does not mean it existed in Abraham's time. Third, the precise location of this Dan Jaan is unknown. A number of scholars equate it with Israelite Dan, located at the northern extremity of Israel's boundaries.[36]

Genesis 14:14 mentions Dan as the ending point of the first phase of Abram's pursuit of Lot's captors. From Dan, Abraham and his men divided into two groups and pursued the enemy as far as the region to the north of Damascus. One may assume that Moses originally wrote Laish, which was later changed to Dan when that place name was changed.[37]

The expression "until this day." The expressions "until today," "until this day," "as is the case today" are translations of three different Hebrew expressions: `ad hayyôm hazzeh,[38] kayyôm hazzeh,[39] or kʰayyôm hazzeh.[40] They often occur to direct the attention of the audience to an event whose impact is still obvious. For example Moses reminded the Israelites that Egypt was still in shambles at the time of the Israelite conquest of Canaan (Deut 11:4; cf. 4:20; 29:2). He told them they had witnessed or were witnessing the things of which he spoke (Deut 1:19; 2:30; 11:1–19). In addition to this usage of the phrase "until this day," which does not carry any chronological or compositional implications, eight occurrences may represent a post-Mosaic editorial note (Gen 26:33; 32:32 [HB, v. 33]; 47:26; Deut 2:22; 3:14; 10:8; 29:28 [HB, v. 27]; 34:6). The following section briefly considers only one of the most likely examples.

The statement that Bashan was called Havvoth-jair ("Jair's Villages") to this day in honor of Jair, a descendant of Manasseh, who was influential in the conquest of that region (Deut 3:14), would have made little sense in the time of Moses when that region was first taken over by Israel. This phrase suggests a lapse of some time. According to the chronology of this period before the conquest of Canaan, Moses arrived at the plains of Moab approximately

---

[33] Leon Wood, *A Survey of Israel's History*, rev. ed. (Grand Rapids: Zondervan, 1986), 40; cf. H. C. Leupold, *Exposition of Genesis* (Grand Rapids: Baker, 1942), 1:459. Wood does add that a later scribe might have substituted "Dan" for the city's older, less familiar, name in the interest of clarity (Ibid, 40).

[34] Archer, *A Survey of Old Testament Introduction*, 228.

[35] J. K. Hoffmeier, "Egyptians," in *Peoples of the Old Testament World*, ed. A. J. Hoerth, G. L. Mattingly, and E. M. Yamauchi (Grand Rapids: Baker, 1994), 255–56.

[36] A. Anderson, *2 Samuel*, WBC (Dallas: Word, 1989), 284; P. K. McCarter Jr., *II Samuel* (New York: Doubleday, 1984), 510; R. Youngblood, "1, 2 Samuel," in *EBC*, ed. T. Longman III and D. E. Garland (Grand Rapids: Zondervan, 2009), 3:607–8.

[37] G. C. Aalders, *Genesis*, trans. W. Heynen (Grand Rapids: Zondervan, 1975), 1:288; Davis, *From Paradise to Prison*, 181; W. C. Kaiser Jr., *A History of Israel* (Nashville: B&H, 1998), 86; D. Kidner, *Genesis* (Downers Grove, IL: InterVarsity, 1967), 15–16, 178; J. Ridderbos, *Deuteronomy*, trans. E. van der Maas (Grand Rapids: Zondervan, 1984), 315; D. J. Wiseman, "Abraham Reassessed," in *Essays on the Patriarchal Narratives*, ed. A. R. Millard and D. J. Wiseman (Downers Grove, IL: InterVarsity, 1980), 141; Ronald Youngblood, *The Book of Genesis: An Introductory Commentary*, 2nd ed. (Grand Rapids: Baker, 1991), 156. The geographical parameter of "Gilead as far as Dan" in Deut 34:1 and the placement of the blessing for the tribe of Dan (Deut 33:22) after the blessings promised to Zebulun, Issachar, Gad, and before the blessings promised to Asher (all northern tribes) suggests a similar updating.

[38] This phrase occurs 84 times in the OT: 12 times in the Pentateuch (Gen 26:33; 32:32 [HB, v. 33]; 47:26; 48:15; Exod 10:6; Num 22:30; Deut 2:22; 3:14; 10:8; 11:4; 29:3; 34:6).

[39] This phrase occurs 24 times in the OT: seven times in the Pentateuch (Gen 50:20; Deut 2:30; 4:20,38; 8:18; 10:15; 29:28 [HB, v. 27]).

[40] This expression occurs six times in the OT, twice in the Pentateuch (Gen 39:11; Deut 6:24).

three months before Joshua led the Israelites across the Jordan River. In that brief time frame, Moses wrote the bulk of the book of Deuteronomy, he died, Israel mourned for him for 30 days, and preparations were made for the conquest. This hardly leaves time for Jair to have become memorialized "until this day" as the great conqueror of Bashan.

Other Proponents of Inspired Textual Updating

For illustrative purposes the following scholars[41] serve as examples of those who connect the idea of textual updating with inspiration.

Bruce Waltke. Waltke suggests that the problem of explaining the conventional definition of the original autographa "is occasioned by the phenomenon that books of the Bible seem to have gone through an editorial revision after coming from the mouth of an inspired spokesman."[42] After considering some examples of intentional editorial activity, Waltke concludes, "If this be so, then the notion of an original autograph should also take account of later inspired editorial activity. From this perspective it is important to distinguish inspired scribal activity from non inspired scribal changes introduced into the text."[43] The distinction Waltke suggests here relates to the figure provided above that is titled "The Dividing Point between Inspired Textual Updating and Noninspired Textual Transmission." Any reference to inspired editorial activity signifies a divinely guided addition to the existing biblical text that occurred *before* the completion of the Old Testament canon. Any changes introduced *after* the Old Testament reached completion is not part of the process of inscripturation and is a textual variant (and not part of the inspired and inerrant *autographa*).

Herbert Wolf. After dealing with several examples of post-Mosaic additions, Wolf points out that possible post-Mosaic additions to the Pentateuch are relatively minor.[44] He affirms that the work of individuals who added to or modified the work of Moses was superintended by the same Holy Spirit whose ministry superintended all writers of Scripture. Any changes made by Joshua, Samuel, Ezra, or anyone else were prompted by the Holy Spirit and conveyed exactly what He intended (2 Pet 1:21).[45]

Summary

The above explanation represents a way of dealing with the phenomena of the biblical text in light of the hundreds of years involved with the composition of the OT (compared to 50 years of NT composition). From the standpoint of an orthodox position on the inspiration and inerrancy of Scripture, examples from the Pentateuch are particularly relevant since it is traditionally regarded as Mosaic in its parts and in its whole. What must be carefully considered is the way inspiration and inerrancy as defined by systematic theology coheres with the hard data in OT passages. The best resolution lies in the likelihood that on a limited scale the Lord saw fit to use later writers to rework given biblical passages to make clear and current

---

[41] Besides the ones listed here, see also R. D. Wilson, *A Scientific Investigation of the Old Testament* (Philadelphia: Sunday School Times, 1926), 11; E. J. Young, *An Introduction to the Old Testament* (Grand Rapids: Eerdmans, 1949), 33; M. F. Unger, *Introductory Guide to the Old Testament*, 237–40; C. Pfeiffer, *The Book of Genesis: A Study Manual*, 7; J. Ridderbos, *Deuteronomy*, trans. E. van der Maas (Grand Rapids: Zondervan, 1984), 22; D. Garrett, *Rethinking Genesis: The Sources and Authorship of the First Book of the Pentateuch*, 85–86; R. Youngblood, *The Book of Genesis: An Introductory Commentary*, 241.

[42] B. K. Waltke, "Historical Grammatical Problems," in *Hermeneutics, Inerrancy, and the Bible*, ed. E. Radmacher and R. Preus (Grand Rapids: Zondervan, 1984), 78.

[43] Ibid., 79.

[44] H. M. Wolf, *An Introduction to the Old Testament Pentateuch* (Chicago: Moody, 1991), 60.

[45] Ibid.

the revelation of His intentions for the world through Israel. What they wrote was part of the process of an ongoing composition of the inspired, infallible, and inerrant text of Scripture.

WHAT ABOUT REDACTION?

Basic Editing

Since the term "redaction" basically means "editing," it need not be intrinsically offensive or problematic. Given that biblical writers carefully crafted their messages for vividness and clarity, part of their work doubtless involved some form of editing. Whether Moses edited preexisting written or oral sources or a prophet edited an earlier version of a message he preached to his fellow Israelites, redaction of some sort almost certainly took place. To receive a preexisting text and rearrange it (for example) into a chiastic structure, an acrostic, or an enveloping structure (*inclusio*) represents redaction, but as long as both the received text and its editorializing are divinely directed the whole together is the very word of God.

Redaction as Part of Source Criticism

Virtually all critical scholars have perpetuated the framework introduced by J. Wellhausen, who regarded Genesis–Numbers as a composite of the J(ehovistic) and E(lohistic) sources redacted during monarchic times (c. 850 and 750 respectively) and later redacted to the seventh-century D source. The Priestly work (P) developed as a parallel tradition to J and E. Eventually J and P were interwoven in the postexilic era, forming the extant text (c. 450 BC).[46] More recent examples of pentateuchal criticism could be cited as well,[47] but the point is the same. Redaction as a tool of source criticism requires extensive conjecture and often betrays a false sense of confidence. Generally source critics make sweeping conclusions about the literary development of a biblical book, almost always to the neglect of a high view of Scripture.

Redaction Criticism

This form of criticism seeks to understand how a particular biblical tradition reached its present shape.[48] Proponents seek to identify the logic and motivations of the redactor (or author) who gathered the sources together to produce the biblical text in its final form. While source criticism focuses on documentary sources, redaction criticism focuses on the formation of the final form of the text.[49] It assumes that the biblical text has circulated in various forms at earlier stages.[50] The redactors envisioned were not merely collectors and assemblers of traditions, but "creative literary and theological contributors."[51] Proponents of this approach attempt to discern redactional intention. While redaction criticism does examine the final

---

[46] S. R. Driver, *An Introduction to the Literature of the Old Testament*, rev. ed. (New York: Scribner's Sons, 1950), 118–31; O. Eissfeldt, *The Old Testament: An Introduction*, trans. P. R. Ackroyd (New York: Harper and Row, 1965), 164–66; A. F. Campbell and M. A. O'Brien, *Sources of the Pentateuch: Texts, Introductions, and Annotations* (Minneapolis: Fortress, 1993), 4–6; see also J. Wellhausen, *Prolegomena to the History of Ancient Israel* (reprint, Eugene, OR: Wipf and Stock, 2003), 6–10, 13.

[47] R. N. Whybray, *The Making of the Pentateuch* (Sheffield: JSOT Press, 1987), 221–42; R. Rendtorff, *The Problem of the Process of Transmission in the Pentateuch*, trans. J. J. Scullion (Sheffield: JSOT Press, 1990).

[48] P. E. Hughes, "Compositional History: Source, Form, and Redaction Criticism," in *Interpreting the Old Testament: A Guide for Exegesis*, ed. C. C. Broyles (Grand Rapids: Baker, 2001), 237.

[49] M. Biddle, "Hebrew Bible Redaction Criticism," in *Methods of Bible Interpretation*, 135. See also R. Knierim, "Criticism of Literary Features, Form, Tradition, and Redaction," in *The Hebrew Bible and Its Modern Interpreters*, ed. D. A. Knight and G. M. Tucker (Philadelphia: Fortress, 1985), 150–53.

[50] Hughes, "Compositional History: Source, Form, and Reduction Criticism," 238.

[51] Ibid.

form of the biblical text, it does so by considering how the redactor "has reworked, reinterpreted, or in any way reshaped the sources to achieve his or her purposes."[52] Unless the sources are clearly identified in the biblical text and there is clear evidence for reshaping (as in a comparison of the Chronicler's treatment of a Judean king as opposed to the composer of Kings), this use of redaction is quite problematic and subjective.

TENDENZ (BIAS) AND OBJECTIVITY (RELIABILITY)

Biblical writers were not merely stenographers who recorded data without color, passion, or bias. All of them were men who viewed themselves as the servants of the one and only God of the universe, the Suzerain of Israel, and the One who provided for their forgiveness from sin. Whether they composed narratives, spoke oracles, sang psalms, or created works of wisdom, they were moved by the Spirit to select carefully what they included and excluded, and they employed ordinary literary craft to make their messages gripping and understandable.

Their writings manifest theological biases. Intentional theological purposes, aims, or tendencies impacted what and how they wrote what they did. Scholars call this *Tendenz*, a theological tendency or burden. Does this *Tendenz* contribute to or detract from the message of the OT?

Does *Tendenz* Corrupt the Message of Biblical Writers?

Many OT scholars argue that since biblical narratives, for example, are ideologically biased, they cannot reflect actual historical events. Kitchen suggests that these scholars affirm that one cannot properly know what happened in a given biblical event because the writer warped his presentation of historical fact or worse, the ancient writer, in order to express his *Tendenz*, actually manufactured "history" in order to communicate his message.[53] The idea seems to be that whenever "gods" become actors in the events, mythology rather than history has been written.[54] Ahlström dismisses the historical value of the biblical records, stating that "the historiography of certain periods for which there are no other sources available than those of the biblical writers will rest on shaky ground because of the subjective presentation and religious *Tendenz* of the material."[55] For example, the purpose of the book of Judges is "not to present history but to advocate a religious ideal."[56] Since the biblical historian "attempted to present his narrative in such a way that it advanced his own cause," we should not expect that it is possible to rediscover the "objective" or "actual" historical events.[57] Ahlström suggests that ideology (or *tendenz*) and facts (and/or objectivity) are mutually exclusive. "Biblical historiography is a literary phenomenon whose primary goal is not to create a record of factual events. . . . Because the authors of the Bible were historiographers and used stylistic patterns to create a 'dogmatic' and, as such, tendentious literature, one may question the reliability of their product."[58]

---

[52] A. E. Hill and J. H. Walton, *A Survey of the Old Testament,* 3rd ed. (Grand Rapids: Zondervan, 2009), 756.

[53] K. A. Kitchen, "Israel Seen from Egypt: Understanding the Biblical Text from Visuals and Methodology," *TynBul* 42,1 (May 1991): 123.

[54] G. W. Ahlström, *Who Were the Israelites?* (Winona Lake, IN: Eisenbrauns, 1986), 46.

[55] G. W. Ahlström, *The History of Ancient Palestine* (Minneapolis: Fortress, 1993), 32. He suggests that biblical writers had a totally different goal than modern historians. Thus it is almost impossible to discern what real events, if any, can be found in biblical writings (ibid.)

[56] Ibid., 376.

[57] N. P. Lemche, *Ancient Israel: A New History of Israelite Society* (Sheffield: Sheffield Academic Press, 1988), 54.

[58] G. Ahlström, "The Role of Archaeological and Literary Remains in Reconstructing Israel's History," in *The Fabric of History: Text, Artifact, and Israel's Past,* ed. D. Edelman, JSOTSup 127 (Sheffield: Sheffield, 1991), 118. Later in this essay Ahlström states that "Biblical historiography is not a product built on facts. It reflects the narrator's outlook and ideology

Does *Tendenz* Enhance the Message of Biblical Writers?

Without denying the presence of bias in biblical literature, the key question is whether narratives with a didactic or propagandistic intent can also be viewed as history writing.[59] Younger and Millard demonstrate that a definition of history that excludes ideological or propagandistic tendencies is unrealistically narrow.[60] Chavalas examines a number of historiographic records from various ancient civilizations and concludes that "the fact that a work is propagandistic does not preclude it from having historical value."[61] As a matter of fact one could ask if "it is even possible, much less desirable, to write history apart from some angle or point of view that informs the historian's thesis. Historiography reflects intention, and intention requires selectivity and purpose."[62] Biblical history does not have to be without bias to be regarded as history writing.[63]

To interpret the OT properly, the reader must appreciate the fact that biblical writers did not always incorporate everything that happened with respect to events they described. They chose to include certain information and exclude others in order to make their point, the one that God's Spirit directed them to make. This selective presentation of data enabled them to place the focus on God and His actions. Also the fact that biblical writers left out information should caution modern readers about making sweeping conclusions based on what is *not* said. One cannot know why a writer failed to provide this or that bit of information, so the focus must be on what the text actually says. A proper study of OT passages must involve an intentional attempt to understand the writer's theological agenda. The authors did not simply relate information; they wrote about eternally significant truth.

Summary

God made use of "prophetic" figures to communicate His plan for the world He created. What they wrote was divinely authorized, infallible, and without error. Israel regarded these writings as authoritative soon after their completion, and it was to conduct itself according to the truths found there. If the biblical writers availed themselves of extrabiblical sources, they made use of them under the guidance of the Holy Spirit, thereby guarding themselves from inaccuracy of fact or interpretation. God also saw fit to employ inspired redactors to integrate into the sacred text necessary linguistic, geographic, and other alterations to guarantee ongoing understanding of His Word by the generations of His people throughout the thousand years of OT transmission.

---

rather than known facts . . . . Most of the writings about the premonarchic time are of dubious historical value" (ibid., 134–35).

[59] J. J. Bimson, "Old Testament History and Sociology," in *Interpreting the Old Testament: A Guide for Exegesis*, 135.

[60] K. L. Younger, *Ancient Conquest Accounts: A Study in Ancient Near Eastern and Biblical History Writing*, JSOTSup 98 (Sheffield: Sheffield, 1990), 31–35; A. R. Millard, "Story, History, and Theology," in *Faith, Tradition, and History: Old Testament Historiography in Its Near Eastern Context*, ed. A. R. Millard, J. K. Hoffmeier, and D. W. Baker (Winona Lake, IN: Eisenbrauns, 1994), 54–60.

[61] M. Chavalas, "Genealogical History as 'Charter': A Study of Old Babylonian Period Historiography and the Old Testament," in *Faith, Tradition, and History: Old Testament Historiography in Its Near Eastern Context*, 107.

[62] G. H. Reid, "Minimalism and Biblical History," *BSac* 155 (1998): 407.

[63] Younger, *Ancient Conquest Accounts*, 33; see also J. Goldingay, "That You May Know That Yahweh Is God—A Study in the Relationship between Theology and Historical Truth in the Old Testament," *TynBul* 23 (1972): 82–84; M. A. Grisanti, "Old Testament Poetry as a Vehicle for Historiography," *BSac* 161, no. 642 (April–June 2004): 164–66.

STUDY QUESTIONS

1. How have evangelicals customarily defined the following: inspiration, autographa, and canon?
2. What are some of the ways God revealed what He wanted biblical writers to record?
3. Could biblical writers make use of non-canonical written records or oral tradition in writing a biblical book? Why or why not?
4. What is the significance of a thousand-year period during which time biblical writers composed OT books?
5. What are the five propositions offered in this chapter?
6. What are two examples of inspired textual updating?
7. What is the basic idea of "redaction"?
8. What kinds of redaction do evangelicals have concerns with and why?
9. Were biblical writers totally objective or given to bias (*tendenz*)?
10. Does any bias by biblical writers undercut the infallibility of the biblical books they authored?
11. How does recognizing the theological agenda of a biblical writer enhance our exegesis of a biblical text?

FOR FURTHER STUDY

Beckwith, Roger. *The OT Canon of the NT Church*. Grand Rapids: Eerdmans, 1985.

Dockery, David S. "The Divine-Human Authorship of Inspired Scripture." In *Authority and Inspiration: A Baptist Perspective*. Edited by Duane Garrett and Richard Melick Jr., 13–23. Grand Rapids: Baker, 1987.

Erickson, Millard. *Christian Theology*. 2nd ed. Grand Rapids: Baker, 1998.

Garrett, Duane. *Rethinking Genesis: The Sources and Authorship of the First Book of the Pentateuch*. Grand Rapids: Baker, 1991.

Grisanti, Michael A. "Inspiration, Inerrancy, and the OT Canon: The Place of Textual Updating in an Inerrant View of Scripture." *JETS* 44, no. 4 (December 2001): 577–98.

———. "Old Testament Poetry as a Vehicle for Historiography." *BSac* 161, no. 642 (April-June 2004): 163–78.

Grubbs, Norris C., and Curtis Scott Drumm. "What Does Theology Have to Do with the Bible? A Call for the Expansion of the Doctrine of Inspiration." *JETS* 53, no. 1 (March 2010): 65–79.

Grudem, Wayne. *Systematic Theology*. Grand Rapids: Zondervan, 1994.

Kaiser, Walter C., Jr. *The Old Testament Documents: Are They Reliable and Relevant?* Downers Grove, IL: InterVarsity, 2001.

Millard, A. R. "Story, History, and Theology." In *Faith, Tradition, and History: Old Testament Historiography in Its Near Eastern Context*. Edited by A. R. Millard, J. K. Hoffmeier, D. W. Baker, 37–64. Winona Lake, IN: Eisenbrauns, 1994.

Reid, Garnett H. "Minimalism and Biblical History," *BSac* 155 (1998): 394–410.

CHAPTER 6

THE CANONICITY
OF THE OLD TESTAMENT

EUGENE H. MERRILL

INTRODUCTION

Practical Considerations

A religion (such as Judaism, Christianity, or Islam) that bases its claims to authenticity and authority on sacred texts must be prepared to defend those texts against the charge that they are merely human reflections on metaphysical possibilities or philosophical speculations about life's mysteries and meaning. That is, it must be able to show that the writings it holds to be indispensable to its very justification—and only these—are in some sense beyond the pale of ordinary human origination.

Biblical Considerations

This sense of the significance of sacred texts everywhere underlies biblical thought, both OT and NT. Judaism and Christianity, if nothing else, are religions of "the Book," expressions of faith rooted in and understandable only against the notion of a body of revealed literature. So much is this the case and so intuitive the recognition that some texts are inherently divine and others not, that the Scriptures themselves give no attention to any discussion of the issue. Only after the completion of their respective collections of texts did the communities that produced them engage in any kind of debate as to the inclusion or exclusion of any part of them. The biblical witness itself is univocal: The writings that make up its corpus are from God and therefore are to be heeded.

Theological Considerations

The character and content of a body of texts deemed to be of supernatural origin obviously has profound theological implications for the religious communities that find their sanction in those texts and that attempt to systematize the truths derived from them. They must be absolutely certain that these writings and these alone provide at least the grounding for their understanding and practice. Any question about such matters will, to that extent, vitiate the theological authority of the writings to which the community appeals. Therefore one cannot disconnect theology and canon, for theology, most certainly in the Christian tradition at least, finds its roots and circumference in the canon of Scripture, the OT and NT.

DEFINITION OF TERMS

The English word "canon" derives most immediately from Greek *kanōn*, "rule, standard,"[1] indirectly from Hebrew *qaneh* "(measuring) reed,"[2] and ultimately Akkadian *qanû*, "reed."[3] The semantic development is from the idea of a literal staff used to measure length and/or straightness to a metaphorical standard by which literary compositions were compared to determine their fitness for inclusion within a given corpus of literature. The term is still used in the same manner to speak of works that by sanction of critical consensus and longevity are considered to be classics and worthy of recognition as such.[4]

When applied to the Bible, "canon" refers to "a book which derives from divine revelation and provides the normative rule for the faith and life of the religious man."[5] As such the literature of the Bible must measure up to certain criteria established by ancient Judaism and the church, failing which it was considered sub- or deuterocanonical and unworthy of providing an authoritative basis for belief. These criteria and their application to the Old Testament writings are addressed below.

HISTORY OF TERMS

The word "canon" as a term describing the biblical writings is not attested earlier than about AD 300, though cognate forms and conceptual synonyms occur in the NT, Philo, Josephus, the Mishnah, and ante-Nicene fathers such as Origen.[6] Thus, though the technical language was either lacking or imprecise, the idea conveyed by the various terminologies and descriptions leads to no other conclusion than that the OT consisted of a collection of texts to be considered the very Word of God because they measured up to the rigid standards of canonicity. The idea of canon is thus ancient even if the word used to describe it is postbiblical and relatively late. In fact the concept, as already suggested, is inherent in the OT itself.[7] This should hardly be surprising, for canonicity is an almost self-evident corollary to revelation and inspiration. If the theologians of Israel understood and confessed the supernatural origin of the Scriptures (which they did), it is inconceivable that they would fail to recognize and articulate the proposition that the Scriptures, and only the Scriptures, were sufficient for faith and life. All other writings, including their own (to say nothing of the writings of the "pagans"), fell outside the parameters that circumscribed these texts.

---

[1] W. F. Arndt and F. W. Gingrich, eds., *A Greek-English Lexicon of the New Testament and other Early Christian Literature*, 2nd ed. rev. by F. W. Beaver, W. Danker (Chicago; University of Chicago Press, 1979), 403.

[2] L. Koehler and W. Baumgartner, eds., *The Hebrew and Aramaic Lexicon of the Old Testament* (Leiden: Brill, 2001), 2: 1113.

[3] J. A. Brinkman et al., eds., *The Assyrian Dictionary* (Chicago: Oriental Institute, 1982), 13:86.

[4] A lively discussion is currently underway in American higher education as to whether the "canon" of literature long dominated by male authors of European extraction should be changed or at least opened up to the inclusion of works by women and by ethnic and racial minorities. See, e.g., J. Bacon, "Impasse or Tension? Pedagogy and the Canon Controversy," *College English* 55 (1993): 501–14.

[5] O. Eissfeldt, *The Old Testament: An Introduction*, trans. Peter Ackroyd (New York: Harper and Row, 1965), 560.

[6] E. E. Ellis, *The Old Testament in Early Christianity* (Grand Rapids: Baker, 1991), 3–5.

[7] R. I. Vasholz, *The Old Testament Canon in the Old Testament Church* (Lewiston, NY: Mellen, 1990), 2, 9–19.

CONCEPT OF TERMS

The Old Testament Concept

If the word "canon" is missing in the OT, how do the Hebrew Scriptures attest to their own canonicity? Are there indicators in the ancient tradition that point to such a notion or is this a postbiblical theological retrojection, a reading into the text of something that is not really there?

Many scholars begin their investigation of the witness to OT canonicity with the NT evidence or, at the earliest, with late second-temple Jewish deliberations. However, in a major treatment of the issue, one sensitive to the OT's own self-testimony, R. Vasholz argues that the Hebrew Scriptures provide their own canonical authentication; that is, their authors and the communities for whom they wrote these texts were consciously aware that what was written was revelation and, by necessary implication, canon.

> The substance of the matter is that writings with the force of canonical authority are based on eyewitness testimony of God's approval of the writer of scripture by a sizable number in the community. This kind of testimony is open and sufficient. They saw, they heard. An awesome theophany, a manifestation of God's presence, permitted that no question be entertained that God had not spoken. Here is where the rationale for canonicity resides and it will be shown that the Old Testament does not shift from this position. Canonicity is rooted in a measurable visual/audible demonstration of God's approval upon an author of scripture to his contemporaries.[8]

This observation is buttressed by the recurring use of technical or semi-technical words and terms such as "the word of the Lord came," "thus says the Lord," and the like. Eissfeldt identifies six kinds of words that he says "rank as divine words," that is, words indicative of revelation and thus of canonical authority: (1) the judgment (*mišp*) of the lawgiver and judge; (2) the word (*dābār*) which appears as command or prohibition from the proclaimer of the divine will; (3) the directive (*tôrâ*) of the priest; (4) the saying (*dābār*) of the prophet; (5) the song (*šîr*) of the singer; and (6) the proverb (*māšāl*) of the wise.[9] Beyond mere terminology are the passages that reflect a keen awareness that what is being composed, transmitted, and collected is more than ordinary literature—it is the very word of God.[10]

While the development of the canonical corpus was in process, its recognition as such was also in flux. Until the sacred collection reached its completion, the Jewish community was unable to achieve the necessary distantiation and objectivity to be able to look at what had been done and to pronounce a final verdict as to its canonicity in part and as a whole. It thus remained for the postbiblical community to reflect on its literary and theological legacy and to wrestle with issues of what was and what was not religiously authoritative.[11]

---

[8] Ibid., 13.

[9] Eissfeldt, *The Old Testament: An Introduction*, 560.

[10] For many of these see S. Z. Leiman, *The Canonization of Hebrew Scripture: The Talmudic and Midrashic Evidence* (Hamden, CT: Archon, 1976), 16–26.

[11] An ancient and strong Jewish tradition associates Ezra with the collection and sanctioning of the OT canon. See G. Wildeboer, *The Origin of the Canon of the Old Testament*, trans. B. W. Bacon (London: Luzac, 1895), 25–30.

The Second Temple Concept

Among the earliest and most important witnesses to the extent, content, and even division of the canon is the prologue to the apocryphal book Ben Sirach (or Ecclesiasticus). There the grandson and translator of the original author, Jeshua ben Sirach, relates in 132 BC how his grandfather had set out 50 years before to author "something in the line of instruction and wisdom" to assist readers of the Mosaic law in their understanding. He begs the readers' indulgence for his translation from Hebrew into Greek, noting, with a reference to the Septuagint of about 200 BC, that "the Law itself, and the prophecies, and the rest of the books, differ not a little in translation from the original."[12] The identity of "Law" and "prophecies" is clear enough (the Torah and Nebi'im of later nomenclature) and by "the rest of the books" is certainly intended—though here imprecisely—the third part of the canon, the "writings" (Kethubim). By the early second century there clearly existed the notion of a tripartite canon, a collection that already precluded such works as Ben Sirach's own worthy composition.[13]

A second voice, though not contemporary to the pre-Christian period, is that of Josephus, the famed Jewish historian, who, in a treatise titled *Ad Apionem* (c. AD 100), limits the canon to 22 books "which are justly believed to be divine." Five are by Moses; four by the prophets (none after Artaxerxes II, c. 424 BC); and the remaining 13, which "contain hymns to God, and precepts for the conduct of human life," are clearly a reference to the Kethubim. The order and arrangement of the books in the canon familiar to Josephus (later to be known as the Masoretic canon) differ from modern Protestant canons, but the contents are exactly the same.[14] Again, Josephus was aware of a three-part canon as was Ben Sirach, and, indeed, Jesus Himself spoke of such a division: "the Law of Moses, the Prophets, and the Psalms" (Luke 24:44).

The New Testament Concept

The testimony of Jesus just cited makes clear that by the early first century AD the fact of an OT canon and its components was undisputed. Though no formal lists of books from that period and earlier are extant, the presence or absence of various texts and their frequency at Qumran, along with the caveats of Ben Sirach and other ancient traditions, points strongly to the canon collection as Josephus understood it.[15] It is true the NT does not quote or otherwise allude to several of the OT books, but it never clearly cites any of the apocryphal works either.[16] While this fact alone cannot support the claim that the 22 (or 39) books of our canon

---

[12] E. J. Goodspeed, *The Apocrypha: An American Translation* (New York: Vintage, 1959), 223.

[13] R. T. Beckwith, "The Canon of the Old Testament," in *The Origin of the Bible*, ed. P. W. Comfort (Wheaton, IL: Tyndale, 1992), 59.

[14] It is impossible to determine the order of the books within the larger groupings, and in fact there might not have been any particularly sanctioned order. See M. Haran, "Archives, Libraries, and the Order of the Biblical Books," *JANES* 22 (1993): 51–61.

[15] The earliest such list seems to be that of the Talmudic tractate *Baba Bathra*, composed in the second century AD. It no doubt rests on a much earlier, pre-Christian oral tradition as to the number (24) and order of the books. See H. E. Ryle, *The Canon of the Old Testament* (London: Macmillan, 1899), 243. One should also not overlook Jesus' reference to the martyrs of the OT from Abel to Zechariah (Matt 23:35). The Zechariah here is probably the prophet of 2 Chr 24:21, so the intent is to trace the history of the death of the righteous from the first to the last of the OT. This presupposes the familiar Jewish order of the canon (ibid., 151). For the evidence from Qumran see C. A. Evans, "The Dead Sea Scrolls and the Canon of Scripture in the Time of Jesus," *The Bible at Qumran. Text, Shape, and Interpretation*, ed. P. W. Flint (Grand Rapids: Eerdmans, 2001), 67–79.

[16] Leiman makes the following observation: "Most significant is the fact that no books of the Apocrypha . . . are ever cited as Scripture in the New Testament. This despite the fact that LXX influence is evident throughout the New Testament" (*The Canonization of Hebrew Scripture*, 40–41). Leiman is distinguishing between references to apocryphal works as authoritative as opposed to those that are illustrative. As to the latter, it is apparent that Heb 11:34–35, for example, alludes

were recognized as canonical by the first-century church, it is presumptively adversarial to the notion that the church received the apocryphal literature as such.

More positively, both Jesus and the apostles regularly presupposed the concept of OT canonicity by asserting the authoritative nature of the writings of that collection.[17] In fact both they and their Jewish antagonists never dispute the linkage between Scripture and canon, between the text as the Word of God and the necessary corollary that it exists in a clearly definable corpus of texts outside of which there is no written authority. The word "canon" may not have been the chosen way to speak of this corpus but, as already argued, the idea of canon is the only way to explain the first-century Christian consensus that God had spoken through certain ancient Hebrew writings and only through them.

THE HISTORY OF THE DEBATE

Recognition of the concept of canonicity in both Judaism and the church did not automatically translate into unanimity as to the extent and content of the canonical collection.[18] Granted there was a body of revealed and inspired texts, how could it be determined that precisely those and no others constituted the authoritative corpus? Or to ask it another way, what were the criteria of canonicity and how did the various believing communities come to embrace these criteria and the canon that resulted from their application?

The Debate in Pre-Christian Judaism

As noted earlier, the prologue to Ben Sirach (132 BC) has at least an implicit recognition of a three-part canon of the Hebrew OT: the Law, the Prophecies, and "the rest of the books." This description already precludes Ben Sirach's own work from canonical consideration, for despite its antiquity (180 BC in Hb) and eventual popularity its author (technically, translator) distinguishes it from what he clearly intends to be understood as the Word of God.

Absolutely no evidence exists in the oldest oral and written Jewish traditions that the canonicity of Moses' law, the Torah, was ever disputed. As for the Prophets, the testimony of Josephus, which apparently represents ancient, normative Jewish opinion, is unequivocal. "It is true," he wrote, "our history hath been written since Artaxerxes [II, 464–424 BC] very particularly, but hath not been esteemed of the like authority with the former by our forefathers, because there hath not been an exact succession of prophets since that time."[19] What Josephus had in mind is the "former" and "latter" prophets, the authors of Joshua through 2 Kings and of the named prophetic books, respectively. The last of those would be Malachi, of the mid-fifth century BC. The historian thus draws a clear line between the *Nebi'im* ("Prophets") of the present canon and all other, later prophetic works that were consequently deemed noncanonical.

As for the third part, the "Writings," the very imprecision of the term is indicative of the fluidity attendant to their definition. Though the dates of the works in this section cannot be ascertained with certainty, the various ancient Jewish traditions allow no date later than

---

to 2 Macc 6:18–7:42. For other examples (most of which come from the pseudepigrapha, not the apocrypha) see Wildeboer, *The Origin of the Canon*, 52–53.

[17] "Jesus' use of the Old Testament rests on his conviction that these writings were the revelation of God through faithful prophets" (Ellis, *The Old Testament in Early Christianity*, 126). See also L. M. McDonald, *The Biblical Canon: Its Origin, Transmission, and Authority* (Peabody, MA: Hendrickson, 2007), 190–98.

[18] For a helpful review of this aspect see L. M. McDonald and J. A. Sanders, *The Canon Debate* (Peabody, MA: Hendrickson, 2002).

[19] Josephus, *Ad Apiconem* 8:41.

400 BC for any of them.[20] But the date of their composition (and of the prophetic works for that matter) must not be confused with the date of their recognition as canon. Though works later than 400 appear for that reason to be excluded from canonical consideration, not all the writings earlier than that date found automatic acceptance.

The debate therefore centered around a handful of compositions whose canonicity, for a variety of reasons, was suspect. Though the idea that these issues remained unresolved until the Council of Jamnia (c. AD 100) is no longer tenable,[21] probably that resolution was not achieved until nearly the dawn of the Christian era. Meanwhile the disputed texts found wide currency along with those of undebatable merit and others never seriously considered canonical by the Jewish community. The writings of dubious qualification have come to be known as the Antilegomena, those "written against."[22] The standard list of these is Ezekiel, Ecclesiastes, Proverbs, Song of Songs, and Esther. Of these, all but Ezekiel belong to the third section of the Hebrew canon, the Kethubim ("Writings"), and three of these are in the subsection known as Megilloth (or "Scrolls"). Proverbs is technically poetic, part of the section called Emeth ("truth"), with Psalms and Job. Given the relative instability or imprecision of thought regarding the Kethubim, it is not surprising that several of its books should have been questioned.

The reasons for the challenge to canonicity differ with each of the Antilegomena, and from our perspective, seem sometimes arbitrary and perhaps even silly. But careful attention to the tenor of the rabbinical debates as recorded in the various Talmudic tractates reveals that these were serious, godly men whose objective was not to diminish the Word of God but rather to guard it against unwarranted intrusions by literature of questionable character. And in debating the issues of canonicity they provided criteria by which all such matters must be judged.

In the case of Ezekiel, it was alleged that it contradicted Moses, referring no doubt to the inconsistencies between the tabernacle and the Ezekel temple. Were it not for a certain Hananiah, an older contemporary of Jesus, the book would have been withdrawn (*ganaz*) from the sacred collection. He was able to prove that there was no contradiction.[23] Some said Ecclesiastes was also suspect because of self-contradictions and contradiction with David (i.e., Psalms), mainly in areas of doctrine (e.g., views of the resurrection). But the fact that the book began and ended with reference to the Law spared its inclusion in the canon.[24] Proverbs was also charged with self-contradiction (Prov 26:4–5), but it was given a "stay of execution" until it (like Ecclesiastes) could be given more study. As for Esther, the Jerusalem Talmud records that it was rejected by many because it introduced Purim, a festival not sanctioned in the Law. It is possible also that it was challenged because it does not mention God.[25] It should be noted that Esther is the only OT book unattested thus far among the DSS. The Song of Songs was debated because it seemed to some to be parabolic. The issue was settled when the famous rabbi Akiba pronounced; "No day in the history of the world is worth the day when the Song of Solomon was given to Israel. For all the Hagiographa [the Kethubim] are holy, but the Song of Solomon is a holy of holies."[26]

---

[20] W. H. Green, *General Introduction to the Old Testament. The Canon* (New York: Scribner's Sons, 1989; reprint, Grand Rapids: Baker, 1980) 37–38.

[21] J. P. Lewis, "What Do We Mean by Jabneh?" *JBR* 32 (1964): 132.

[22] These are sometimes referred to as the books to be "withdrawn" (HB, *gnaz*), that is, writings that posed problems to their canonicity. See especially Leiman, *The Canonization of Hebrew Scripture*, 72–86.

[23] Sabbath 13b, Hagigah 13a.

[24] Sabbath 30b.

[25] Ryle, *The Canon of the Old Testament*, 211.

[26] Yadaim iii5.

Some readers may find it disconcerting to learn that many OT books achieved canonical recognition on what appear to be such tenuous and capricious bases. However, it is important to know that the Talmudic records contain but the distillation of long and arduous sessions of discussion and prayer by men who truly sought to know the mind of God in such important matters as the extent of divine revelation. These were not trivial conversations, a mere splitting of theological hairs. Rather they were intense wrestlings with issues of life and death. But it is even more important to recognize that the inclusion or exclusion of debated texts was, in the final analysis, a matter of divine oversight. Men might argue over criteria of canonicity, but the God who revealed and inspired the sacred texts prevailed to secure them—and only them—within the confines of the canon that finally emerged.[27]

Coexistent with the emergence of the Hebrew canon was the translation of the OT into a Greek version called the Septuagint (LXX). This project, which commenced around 250 BC and continued for at least 50 years, was undertaken at Alexandria, Egypt, by Palestinian Jews under the aegis of King Ptolemy II Philadelphus. The intent was twofold: (1) to render the holy writings of the Jews into Greek, the lingua franca of the Mediterranean world, so they could be incorporated into the great library at Alexandria in understandable form; and (2) to provide the Greek-speaking Jews of the Diaspora a version of the Scriptures they could read. Though fraught in places with many translational inaccuracies, the LXX served well enough its intended purposes, so much so that translations of other important Jewish writings quickly followed suit. It is impossible to trace the trajectory that followed this flourish of activity but one fact is clear: At the end of the process there was a blurring of the distinction between the books of the Hebrew canon and other Hebrew and even originally Greek texts. A result was the production of what is sometimes called the Alexandrian (or Hellenistic) Canon—the 22 books of the Masoretic canon plus 14 others commonly referred to by the Jewish and Protestant traditions as apocryphal ("hidden," i.e., of noncanonical status).[28] This "accident" (if such it was) of confusing canonical and extracanonical writings was to have serious repercussions in the development of various Christian canons.

The Debate in the New Testament

As I have previously noted, the NT has not a single clearly attested example of citation—or even an indisputable indirect allusion—to an apocryphal writing as authoritative Scripture. This is amazing when one considers that the LXX was the favorite Bible of the apostolic church and that the authors of the various NT writings were demonstrably aware of the existence of the Alexandrian canon. All that can be reasonably deduced is that Jesus and the Apostles—along with mainstream Judaism—rejected the deuterocanonical books as nonscriptural.

Equally significant is the fact that the NT is not above referring to other noncanonical works such as the pseudepigraphical *Assumption of Moses* (in Jude 9) and the *Book of Enoch* (in Jude 14). Paul even quoted pagan Greek poets in his address to the Athenians at the Areopagus (Acts

---

[27] Green puts it well: "Those books, and those only, were accepted as the divine standards of their faith and regulative of their conduct which were written for this definite purpose by those whom they believed to be inspired of God. It was this which made them canonical. The spiritual profit found in them corresponded with and confirmed the belief in their heavenly origin. And the public official action, which further attested, though it did not initiate, their canonicity, followed in the wake of the popular recognition of their divine authority" (*General Introduction to the Old Testament*, 35–36).

[28] For important caveats on the extent of the Alexandrian canon, see Beckwith, *The Old Testament Canon of the New Testament Church* (Grand Rapids: Eerdmans, 1985), 382–86.

17:28).[29] Sparceness of reference to the apocryphal books is not therefore because of reticence to cite noncanonical literature. Rather, the reason seems to be precisely to foreclose any possibility that NT speakers and writers might appear to sanction the Alexandrian canon by doing so. Since no one claimed canonicity for the pseudepigraphical writings—and certainly not for Greek philosophical treatises—there was no danger in quoting them. It was probably because certain of the apocryphal texts were gaining at least quasi-canonical status in some quarters that the apostles studiously avoided them lest they send the wrong message.

The Debate in the Postapostolic Fathers

Having attached itself firmly to the Jewish (Masoretic) canonical tradition, the early post-apostolic church was never in doubt as to the extent of the OT canon. There were, to be sure, critics of the traditional position, mainly those who wished to subtract from and not add to the canon, but these were considered heretics whose position on this as well as other matters was to be soundly repudiated.[30] But it is important to note that this adherence to the "short canon" of Judaism was for the most part limited to the "Jewish" church, that is, to the church of the Syro-Palestinian world and then only for a relatively brief period of time. With the voluntary and forced dispersion of the church to "the ends of the earth" came a corresponding introduction to and influence from other intellectual and doctrinal currents emanating from places other than the Levant.

This scattering went to and from places like Alexandria and Antioch, the former with its Greek "Alexandrian canon" and the latter with its Syriac Bible, the Peshitta, which was heavily influenced by the LXX and its concomitant longer canon.[31] Thus those churches most indebted to the Alexandrian text and canon tradition (Rome and other Western churches) adopted a canon derived from Alexandria, one including the Apocrypha, and those springing from Syria (Constantinople and the Eastern churches) reflected the Syriac canon, a collection also ultimately original to Alexandria. The result was a canon in both West and East that contained at least seven more books than the Jewish Masoretic canon.[32]

The Debate in the Eastern Church

The central issue with regard to the canon of the Eastern churches was not whether the apocryphal (or even pseudepigraphical) literature should be included but exactly which writings. Another concern was with the Antilegomena, those OT books whose canonicity had been debated even within normative Judaism. On the whole the Syrian church and its Ethiopian, Armenian, and Georgian "daughters" followed the Jewish lead in eventually accepting all 22 books but not without serious question for a time about Ecclesiastes, Song of Songs, and Esther. The cause for the acceptance of these books was not at all abetted by the weighty opinion of Theodore of Mopsuestia who challenged them and also Ezra–Nehemiah and Chronicles.[33]

The earliest Eastern church fathers refused to include the apocryphal literature in the canon. They recognized its value in some instances but denied its canonicity. Eventually, however, the

---

[29] Paul referred to the Stoic poet Aratus (c. 275 BC), who may himself have been quoting from a hymn to Zeus composed by another poet, Cleanthes (J. B. Polhill, *Acts*, NAC (Nashville: Broadman, 1992), 376.

[30] Éric Junod, "La Formation et la Composition de L'Ancien Testament dans L'Église Grecque des Quatre Premier Siècles," in *Le Canon de L'Ancien Testament*, ed. Jean-Daniel Kaestli et Otto Wermelinger (Genève: Labor et Fides, 1984), 107.

[31] For the complicated question of the relationship between the Syriac and Alexandrian canons, see Beckwith, *The Old Testament Canon of the New Testament Church*. 195–97.

[32] McDonald, *The Biblical Canon*, 200-206.

[33] Beckwith, *The Old Testament Canon of the New Testament Church*, 308.

Syriac Peshitta, under LXX influence, began to appear with apocryphal additions as did other translations based on it. For the most part they were considered deuterocanonical, though in a few traditions such books as Sirach, Judith, 1 and 2 Maccabees, and Wisdom were accorded full canonicity or at least intermediate authority. The Ethiopic Bible went so far as to accept the entire Alexandrian canon and several pseudepigraphical works such as *Enoch, Jubilees*, and the *Ascension of Isaiah*. The present Orthodox situation is not uniform, but the Greek Church, for example, considers only the Hebrew 22 books to be fully canonical with 3 Esdras, Tobit, Judith, Wisdom, Sirach, the Epistle of Jeremiah, Baruch, and 1–3 Maccabees as of secondary but useful value. The entire Apocrypha is printed in most Greek Orthodox Bibles.

The Debate in the Western Church

The question of the extent of the OT canon was greatly complicated by the fact that the Western church, for the most part, was an offspring of the Alexandrian ecclesiastical and canonical tradition by virtue of the Latin versions having been translated from the LXX and not the Hebrew Scriptures. The longer Alexandrian canon (the Hebrew 22 books plus 14 apocryphal books) was thus incorporated into the earliest Latin Bible, the so-called Itala, with apparently little or no dissent except for the omission of 3 and 4 Maccabees and the addition of 2 Esdras (= 4 Ezra).[34]

In AD 385 Jerome undertook a new Latin version (the Vulgate) that was initially a revision of Itala and then a fresh translation of the Hebrew. Having come to recognize the intrinsic worth and authority of the Hebrew text, Jerome also felt compelled to limit his canon to the 22 books of the Jewish canon. He did not entirely repudiate certain apocryphal writings, however. In fact, he grudgingly approved at least an intermediate status for Judith, Tobit, Maccabees, Wisdom, and Sirach, and even allowed the Additions to Daniel and Additions to Esther to be added to his list though clearly as subcanonical works.[35] Jerome's willingness to countenance even part of the apocryphal literature paved the way for the inclusion of more of it in years to come. The principal manuscript of the Vulgate (Amiatinus, c. AD 700) contains all the books of Jerome plus others he had clearly rejected and claimed that all of them carried his sanction.[36] This collection received its final stamp of approval at the Council of Trent (1546) and to this day is the canon followed by the Roman Catholic Church.

Other voices also contributed to the debate and must be given at least brief mention. The first of these is Melito of Sardis, who in the second century (c. 160) compiled a canon lacking Esther and all of the Apocrypha. Origen (c. 250) embraced all the Hebrew canon (including Esther) and also apparently the Epistle of Jeremiah, Susanna, Tobit, and Judith. Hilary of Poitiers (c. 350) followed Origen's lead, but Rufinus (c. 400) agreed with Jerome that the apocryphal works in their entirety should be relegated to secondary status. Augustine (c. 400), however, brought his considerable prestige to bear and, against Jerome, he regarded Tobit, Judith, 1 and 2 Maccabees, Wisdom, and Sirach as fully canonical, though in his latest writings he gathered the apocryphal writings together and placed them at the end of the Jewish canon. This apparent equivocation by Augustine characterized the Roman Catholic debate until the Council of Trent once and for all put its imprimatur on the apocryphal books that had most

---

[34] F. C. Porter, "Apocrypha," in *A Dictionary of the Bible*, ed. J Hastings (New York: Scribner's Sons, 1898), 1:121.

[35] Ellis succinctly traces Jerome's painful struggles to limit the canon to the Jewish collection (*The Old Testament in Early Christianity*, 30–33).

[36] Thus Porter, "Apocrypha," 1:122.

commonly been considered canonical—Tobit, Judith, 1 and 2 Maccabees, Wisdom, Sirach, and Baruch (including the Letter of Jeremiah).

The Debate among the Reformers

Repudiation of the authority of the Roman Church by Protestant Reformers was inextricably linked to their rejection of its canon. As early as Andreas Carlstadt (1520) the apocryphal books came under attack, vigorously in some quarters, more cautiously in others. Martin Luther, for example, preferred 1 Macabees to Esther (though only theoretically) and viewed all others but Baruch and 2 Macabees with favor.[37] In the Luther Bible of 1534 the Apocrypha appear between the Testaments with the caveat "Apocrypha, that is books which are not held equal to the sacred Scriptures, and nevertheless are useful and good to read." Similarly John Calvin's Bible of 1535 placed these writings in the same place with the wording, "The volume of the apocryphal books contained in the vulgate translation, which we have not found in Hebrew or Chaldee."[38]

The English versions from Miles Coverdale (1536) to the Authorized (King James) Version (1611) contained the Apocrypha but always with disclaimers as to their canonicity. The Synod of Dort (1618) argued the matter in the Lutheran traditions and concluded that the Apocrypha should remain in the Bibles under their jurisdiction. In England the Westminster Confession (1648) repudiated the Apocrypha, but the Anglican Church continued to retain some of the books and to use them in parts of the liturgy (mainly Wisdom, Sirach, Baruch, and occasionally Tobit). By and large, however, the Apocrypha is denied canonical status by the Protestant communions and in fact is totally ignored by most as having any value whatsoever.

THE CONTENT AND ORDER OF THE MAJOR CANONS

The extant examples of canon lists reflect such a bewildering array of options that it is impossible to do more here than to identify the most important and representative.

The Jewish (or Masoretic) Canon

The Jewish canon, as already noted, was viewed as a tripartite collection, the Torah (Pentateuch), the Nebi'im (the Prophets, both Former and Latter), and the Kethubim (the Writings). The whole is popularly known today as the Tanak, an acronym formed from the first letters of the three sections, T, N, and K. The total of 22 books (as opposed to the Protestant 39) is obtained by attaching Ruth to Judges; combining 1 and 2 Samuel, 1 and 2 Kings, 1 and 2 Chronicles, and Ezra–Nehemiah; joining Lamentations to Jeremiah; and by considering the 12 "minor" prophets as one document. The only other major variant separates Ruth from Judges and Lamentations from Jeremiah, steps taken so that Ruth and Lamentations could be relocated for liturgical purposes.

---

[37] Ibid., 37.
[38] Ibid., 123.

Table 1: The Jewish (Masoretic) Canon

The Torah	The Nevi'im	The Kethubim
Genesis	The Former Prophets	Poetry
Exodus	Joshua	Psalms
Leviticus	Judges	Proverbs
Numbers	Samuel	Job
Deuteronomy	Kings	The Megilloth
	The Latter Prophets	Song of Songs
	Isaiah	Ruth
	Jeremiah	Lamentations
	Ezekiel	Ecclesiastes
	The Twelve	Esther
		History
		Daniel
		Ezra–Nehemiah
		Chronicles

The Septuagint Canon

The major codices of the Greek version differ as to arrangement and even extent of the canon as do other ancient sources.[39] This must be at least partially attributed to the uncertainty of the early Jewish (and Christian) communities, especially at Alexandria, as to the status of these writings. Their openness to or rejection of them in various circles would, of course, determine the shape of the LXX canon lists. The following is somewhat a consensus arrangement that eventually took on at least a nominally authoritative character. The apocryphal works are indicated by asterisks.

Table 2: The Septuagint (Alexandrian) Canon

The Pentateuch	History	Poetry	Prophecy
Genesis	Joshua	Psalms	Hosea
Exodus	Judges	*Odes of Solomon	Amos
Leviticus	Ruth	Proverbs	Micah
Numbers	1 Kingdoms (Samuel)	Ecclesiastes	Joel
Deuteronomy	2 Kingdoms (Samuel)	Song of Songs	Obadiah
	3 Kingdoms (Kings)	Job	Jonah
	4 Kingdoms (Kings)	*Wisdom of Solomon	Nahum
	1 Paralipomena(Chronicles)	*Sirach (Ecclesiasticus)	Habakkuk
	2 Paralipomena (Chronicles)	*Psalms of Solomon	Zephaniah
	1 Esdras (Ezra)		Haggai
	2 Esdras (Nehemiah)		Zechariah

---

[39] H. B. Swete, *An Introduction to the Old Testament in Greek* (Cambridge: The University Press, 1902), 219–30.

	Esther		Malachi
	*Judith		Isaiah
	*Tobit		Jeremiah
	*1 Maccabees		*Baruch
	*2 Maccabees		Lamentations
	*3 Maccabees		*Letter of Jeremiah
	*4 Maccabees		Ezekiel
			*Susanna
			Daniel
			*Bel and the Dragon

The Eastern Christian Canon

No unanimity exists among the various Eastern Orthodox confessions—Russian, Ukrainian, Romanian, Armenian, Syrian, and the like—as to the definition of the OT canon. Space does not allow opportunity to explore the reasons for the differences, nor can even the list of each communion be presented. Since the Greek Orthodox Church and its traditions are most familiar to the Western world, the following chart presents its official canon. Once again the apocryphal writings are indicated by an asterisk.

Table 3: The Greek Orthodox Canon

The Pentateuch	History	Poetry	Prophecy
Genesis	Joshua	Psalms	Hosea
Exodus	Judges	Proverbs	Amos
Leviticus	Ruth	Ecclesiastes	Micah
Numbers	1 Kingdoms	Song of Songs	Joel
Deuteronomy	2 Kingdoms	Job	Obadiah
	3 Kingdoms	*Wisdom of Solomon	Jonah
	4 Kingdoms	*Sirach	Nahum
	1 Paralipomena		Habakkuk
	2 Paralipomena		Zephaniah
	1 Esdras		Haggai
	2 Esdras		Zechariah
	*3 Esdras		Malachi
	Esther		Isaiah
	*Judith		Jeremiah
	*Tobit		*Baruch
	*1 Macabees		Lamentations
	*2 Macabees		*Letter of Jeremiah
	*3 Macabees		Ezekiel
			Daniel

The Roman Catholic Canon

The Roman Catholic Church established its authoritative canon at the Council of Trent in 1546. This is not to say that there has been no dissent in Catholic scholarship and hierarchy, but objections have done nothing to prevent the consensus achieved at Trent. The apocryphal works retained by the action of that Council are marked by an asterisk.

Table 4: The Roman Catholic Canon

The Pentateuch	History	Wisdom	Prophecy
Genesis	Joshua	Job	Isaiah
Exodus	Judges	Psalms	Jeremiah
Leviticus	Ruth	Proverbs	Lamentations
Numbers	1 Samuel	Ecclesiastes	*Baruch (+ Letter of Jeremiah)
Deuteronomy	2 Samuel	Song of Songs	Ezekiel
	1 Kings	*Wisdom	Daniel (+ additions)
	2 Kings	*Ecclesiasticus	Hosea
	1 Chronicles		Joel
	2 Chronicles		Amos
	Ezra		Obadiah
	Nehemiah		Jonah
	*Tobit		Micah
	*Judith		Nahum
	Esther		Habakkuk
	*1 Macabees		Zephaniah
	*2 Macabees		Haggai
			Zechariah
			Malachi

The Anglo-Protestant Canon

The term "Anglo-Protestant" is used here not to suggest a commonality of viewpoint regarding the nature and extent of the OT canon but to mark the formal distinction between the Protestant and (non-Roman-) Catholic communities such as Anglicanism. The two do in fact embrace the Jewish canon exclusively but as noted, some forms of Anglo-Catholicism continue the practice of reading certain apocryphal texts as part of this liturgy. The Protestant canon is well known to many of the readers of this book, but for the sake of completeness it too is included here. Its content is precisely that of the Jewish canon, though its arrangement and number of books differ.

Table 5: The Anglo-Protestant Canon

The Pentateuch	History	Poetry and Wisdom	Prophets
Genesis	Joshua	Job	Major Prophets
Exodus	Judges	Psalms	Isaiah
Leviticus	Ruth	Proverbs	Jeremiah/Lamentations
Numbers	1 Samuel	Ecclesiastes	Ezekiel
Deuteronomy	2 Samuel	Song of Songs	Daniel
	1 Kings		Minor Prophets
	2 Kings		Hosea
	1 Chronicles		Joel
	2 Chronicles		Amos
	Ezra		Obadiah
	Nehemiah		Jonah
	Esther		Micah
			Nahum
			Habakkuk
			Zephaniah
			Haggai
			Zechariah
			Malachi

CANONICAL CRITICISM

The term "canonical criticism" somewhat misleadingly implies a connection with the subject of this chapter, that is, the search for the shape and content of the OT canon. This is not the case at all except for the fact that the criticism in question takes its point of departure from the canonical collection esteemed as sacred Scripture by the Jewish and Protestant traditions. It is a new attempt to trace the development of the OT to its completed form and to determine how the Jewish and Christian communities used it in that form as the basis for their own beliefs and practice. From such a perspective related approaches—such as "canonical theology"—have sprung.

Chapter 8 of this book deals with the various critical methods currently employed in the study of the literature and theology of the OT, including canonical criticism.

CONCLUSION

The issue of canon cannot be divorced from other questions relative to the nature and authority of Scripture. If the OT is not revelation safeguarded by inspiration and reliable text transmission, then it matters little whether the writings that comprise its contents are, indeed, the only writings that should be there, or on the other hand whether some works included in the collection should be removed. The only redeeming virtue of the traditional canon is its function as the major source of tradition on which the Judeo-Christian faith has been erected.

However, if the OT is God's Word in the fullest sense, the question of canon logically and theologically follows as a matter of the most urgent and serious concern. It then becomes an issue of virtual life-and-death dimensions; for to add to the completed revelation is to impose human judgment and opinion on the reader, and to eliminate portions from the revelation is to deny to the reader a Word from God. As noted, it is impossible from the modern vantage point to discern the currents at work in the ancient world to achieve canonical consensus. But it is theologically imperative that the modern church recognize that the consensus was God-driven and that the OT Scriptures we hold in our hands is the very Word of God fully and in all its parts.

STUDY QUESTIONS

1. What are the Hebrew and Greek etymologies of the term "canon"?
2. What early Jewish council was alleged to have dealt with the issue of the OT canon?
3. What is meant by the Antilegomena?
4. When was the issue of the extent of the canon settled by Roman Catholicism?
5. Define the term "apocryphal."
6. How many books are in the Hebrew canon?
7. Name three of the five books whose canonicity was questioned by early Judaism.
8. In the Hebrew canon what is meant by the "Former Prophets"?
9. What is another name for the book Ben Sirach?
10. What is meant by the term "pseudepigraphical"?
11. To which book is Ruth attached in some lists of the Hebrew canon?
12. What was troublesome to the rabbis about the book of Proverbs?
13. Identify Melito.
14. List at least two criteria by which a book was tested for canonicity.
15. The order of the "English" canon is based on which ancient canon?

FOR FURTHER STUDY

Batto, B. F. *The Biblical Canon in Comparative Perspective*. Lewiston, NY: Mellen, 1984.

Beckwith, R. *The Old Testament Canon of the New Testament Church*. Grand Rapids: Eerdmans, 1985.

Evans, C. A. *Exploring the Origins of the Bible*. Grand Rapids: Baker, 2008.

Green, W. H. *General Introduction to the Old Testament: The Canon*. London: J. Murray, 1899.

Helmer, C. *One Scripture or Many?* Oxford: Oxford University Press, 2004.

McDonald, L. M. *The Biblical Canon*. Peabody, MA: Hendrickson, 2007.

Ryle, H. E. *The Canon of the Old Testament*. London: Macmillan, 1895.

Sanders, J. A. *Canon and Community. A Guide to Canonical Criticism*. Philadelphia: Fortress, 1984.

Steinmann, A. E. *The Oracles of God*. Saint Louis: Concordia, 1999.

Thomassen, E. *Canon and Canonicity*. Copenhagen: Museum Tusculanum, 2010.

Vasholz, R. I. *The Old Testament Canon in the New Testament Church*. Lewiston, NY: Mellen, 1990.

Zaman, L. *Bible and Canon*. Leiden: Brill, 2008.

CHAPTER 7

THE TRANSMISSION AND
TEXTUAL CRITICISM
OF THE OLD TESTAMENT*

MARK F. ROOKER

DEFINITION AND BACKGROUND

The textual criticism of an ancient document involves the critical study of the available manuscripts and translations in order to determine the original reading of the text. This endeavor is sometimes referred to as lower criticism, implying that it must be addressed first before one endeavors to do exegetical and literary analysis. Textual criticism tries to uncover the original copy (autograph) of a piece of literature by comparing available copies, all of which inevitably contain transmission errors or mistakes.[1] Through analysis and examination, sound principles (see below) are applied to these copies that result in the confident recognition of the original text. With regard to the textual criticism of the OT the serious study of the text is intrinsically related to the issue of canon. The determination of books designated as canonical over against all other extant writings was a prerequisite for which books should be examined for exact wording.

The focus on the canon of Scripture and exegesis was especially important during the Protestant Reformation and led to a new level of textual inquiry. Later polyglot Bibles were published, which placed the Hebrew OT next to translations in various languages in separate columns. Viewing the Hebrew text next to its translations naturally led to the critical investigation of the relation of the Hebrew text to the various witnesses.

---

* An earlier version of this chapter was published in M. F. Rooker, *Recent Studies in Hebrew Language, Intertextuality, and Theology* (New York: Edwin Mellen, 2003), and is used by permission.

[1] R. W. Klein, *Textual Criticism of the Old Testament* (Philadelphia: Fortress, 1974), vii.

NEED FOR TEXTUAL CRITICISM

Except in the case of photographic reproductions of the same text, no two printed editions of the Hebrew Bible (or any ancient document for that matter) are identical. Copying thus becomes the source of survival and corruption for a text; the very process that preserves the text also exposes it to danger.[2]

The Jewish sages knew that there were variant readings in biblical manuscripts as they often argued against the use of a text that contained errors. These texts were banned from public worship and official text-transmission but were often used for midrashic exposition.[3] There is a tradition that the Sadducees had sacred texts that were not regarded as worthy, implying that they may contain variant readings (*b. Šabb.* 116a). Moreover, Rabbi Akiba warned against teaching from uncorrected manuscripts (*b. Pesaḥ* 112a). But even authoritative Torah manuscripts were known to contain variant readings as the Torah of Rabbi Meir and the Severus scroll were known to disagree in 30 cases.[4]

Another attestation of the early awareness of variant readings even from among Masoretic manuscripts is the existence of the 1,300 *Kethib/Qere* variants which may have originated as optional corrections of the consonantal text. These alternative readings became obligatory notations by the time of the Masoretes.[5] Moreover, it is likely that the origin of the Rabbinic *Seberin* notes, which suggest alternative readings for 70 to 200 passages depending on the manuscript, also reflects ancient variants although certainty is not possible.[6] It is probable that the great majority of the textual errors crept into the manuscript copies before the first century AD.

The Babylonian Talmud refers to temple officials who had the task of revising manuscripts and restoring mistakes (*b. Ketub.* 106a). Once a year texts were taken to the temple for revision (*b. Moʿed Qat.* 18b) and compared to the three authorized manuscripts (*y. Taʿan.* 4:2). An official temple scroll (Sefer ha-Azarah) enjoyed a special prestige. The scribes treated what came to be the authorized Masoretic text (MT) with reverence and did not alter its orthography as did the scribes of the Samaritan Pentateuch (SP) and many of the scribes who copied the Dead Sea Scrolls (DSS). The temple scribes particularly were entrusted with the task of preserving the MT.[7]

PERSPECTIVE

Obviously copying errors have occurred in the thousand years of copying manuscripts. However, the variant readings that do exist are certainly not so numerous as to destroy the text's credibility. On the whole the incidents of scribal errors are very few. Ninety percent of the texts contain no variants, and none affects any doctrinal issue. As Stuart stated, "It is fair to say that the verses, chapters, and books of the Bible would read largely the same, and would leave the same impression with the reader, even if one adopted virtually every possible alternative reading

---

[2] P. K. McCarter, *Textual Criticism* (Philadelphia: Fortress, 1986), 12.

[3] S. Talmon, "The Old Testament Text," in *Qumran and the History of the Biblical Text*, ed. F. M. Cross and S. Talmon (Cambridge: Harvard University Press, 1975), 29.

[4] See M. Bar-Ilan, "Part Two: Scribes and Books in the Late Second Commonwealth and Rabbinic Period," in *Mikra*, ed. M. J. Mulder (Philadelphia: Fortress, 1988), 30. The Severus scroll is allegedly an official scroll taken from Jerusalem after the Roman conquest in AD 70 and donated to a Jewish synagogue by Emperor Severus in AD 220.

[5] However, J. Barr has noted that the *Qere* is never a totally different word from the *Kethib*, but is rather a minimal variation normally of one letter, most commonly *waw* or *yod* ("A New Look at *Kethibh-Qere*," *OTS* 21 [1981]: 27).

[6] E. Tov, *Textual Criticism of the Hebrew Bible*, rev. ed. (Minneapolis: Fortress, 2001), 64.

[7] Ibid., 28.

to those now serving as the basis for current English translations."[8] The same kind of variants we observe today existed in the first century, and yet Christ and the apostles did not waver in their clear affirmation of the authority of Scripture.

WITNESSES TO THE OLD TESTAMENT

All the available Hebrew manuscripts as well as the translations of the OT are called "witnesses" as they give evidence to the original form of the OT text. Hebrew manuscripts are the most important witnesses to the OT text. The four Hebrew witnesses to the Old Testament are the Masoretic text, the Samaritan Pentateuch, scrolls from the Judean Desert, and minor Hebrew witnesses.

Hebrew Witnesses

During the First- and Second-Temple periods documents were written on stone, clay, wood, pottery, papyrus, metal, and skins (leather). For biblical manuscripts the main materials used were papyrus and leather, with papyrus being the main writing material before Israel's exile. After the Israelites returned from exile leather took the place of papyrus as the main writing material (see *b. Šabb.* 108a). Not until the first century AD was the codex invented. The codex allowed for writing on both sides of the page with each page held in place by a binding. Ritual reading continued to be carried out from scrolls while manuscripts written on codices could be used for teaching and studying.

The Masoretic Text. The terms "Masorah" and "Masoretic" stem from a comment by Rabbi Akiva when he explained that scribal tradition was a fence around the Law (*m. ʾAbot* 3:14). The Hebrew word *masorah* is translated "tradition," hence the use of the adjective "Masoretic" in the expression "Masoretic text."

The MT is made up of five basic components: (1) the consonantal text; (2) para-textual elements like verses,[9] paragraph divisions, and ancient textual corrections; (3) the Masorah; (4) vocalization,[10] and (5) Cantillation signs. The Masorah was prepared sometime between AD 500 and 1000 by several generations of scribes. The Masoretic scribes were both technicians and innovators. They copied and counted letters, words, and verses, but they were creative in that they invented a scheme for vocalization and accents.[11] The Masoretes continued the work of the scribes who had devoted themselves to the maintaining of the text of Scripture, but it is not possible to precisely know how much they borrowed from previous scribes.

The Babylonian, Palestinian, and Tiberian schools represent three Masoretic traditions. Of these three only the Tiberian system of accentuation is a complete system consisting of disjunctive and conjunctive accents. The Tiberian system became the standard. The vocalization

---

[8] D. Stuart, "Inerrancy and Textual Criticism," in *Inerrancy and Common Sense*, ed. R. R. Nicole and J. R. Michaels (Grand Rapids: Baker, 1980), 98.

[9] R. H. Pfeiffer maintains that verse divisions originated in the practice of reading brief sections of the Hebrew Scriptures in the synagogue and translating them into Aramaic (*Introduction to the Old Testament* [London: Adam and Charles Black, 1948], 80).

[10] The signs for vocalization were created between AD 500 and 700 and were later developed into the full-fledged system. Aquila (2nd century AD) and Jerome (4th century AD) were aware of a vowel system particularly as it pertained to pronunciation. Not until the sixteenth century was the notion that the vowels were as old as the consonants challenged by Elias Levita. Yet even in Switzerland in 1678 a law was passed that no person could preach the gospel in churches unless he held to the divine origin of the vowel points and accents.

[11] E. Tov, "Textual Criticism," in *ABD*, ed. D. N. Freedman (New York: Doubleday, 1992), 6:396. Early vocalization by dots is attributed to the system used by Syriac writers (B. J. Roberts, *The Old Testament Text and Versions* [Cardiff: University of Wales Press, 1951], 51).

system developed to guard the traditional reading and interpretation of the text when Hebrew was no longer the dominant spoken language among many Jews.

The oldest complete MT manuscript is the Leningrad B 19a (Codex L) dated AD 1009. It served as the basis of the last two critical editions of the Old Testament, BHK (1937) and BHS (1967–77). Codex L is the closest to the Ben Asher tradition, the tradition authorized by M. Maimonides (1135–1203). The Ben Asher family played a leading role in the Masoretic work at Tiberias for five or six generations, in the latter half of the first millennium AD. The Aleppo Codex, the oldest complete codex of the Tiberian system, is the earliest complete codex of the Masoretic system developed by the Ben Asher family. It is the manuscript used in the Hebrew University Bible edition currently being produced in Jerusalem. Besides the BHK and BHS editions two earlier editions based on the Rabbinic ben Hayyim text printed by Daniel Bomberg in Venice in 1524–25 were produced earlier in the twentieth century.[12]

The Samaritan Pentateuch. The second major Hebrew witness of the OT is the Samaritan Pentateuch (SP). The Samaritans, who had intermarried with foreigners after the Assyrian defeat (2 Kgs 17:14–21), separated from the Israelites and restricted their Scriptures to the Pentateuch. They rejected the Prophets and the Writings sections of the OT since these Scriptures acknowledged Jerusalem as the designated holy city (the Samaritans had chosen Mount Gerizim as their holy place). The SP is an expansionistic text containing numerous additions that attempt to smooth-over some of the grammatical difficulties represented in the MT. It thus represents a popular or vulgar text (i.e., a text used by the public at large). There are approximately 6,000 differences between the SP and the MT, but most of these are superficial, reflecting changes only in orthography (spelling). For example the SP includes more use of the *matres lectionis* (vowel letters) than the MT, suggesting that it is a later text than what is represented by the MT. According to Talmon, the SP should be viewed as a revision of the same text exhibited by the MT.[13] Roberts believed the SP bears witness to a text form which was in existence in the fourth century BC and earlier.[14] The SP frequently agrees with the LXX against the MT, but the agreements often reveal a shared exegetical method.[15]

Dead Sea Scrolls. One of the greatest archaeological discoveries of the last millennium was certainly the discovery of the DSS in 1947. To date, 221 texts and fragments from the Old Testament have been uncovered with sections of all OT books except Esther.[16] These texts have been dated from 250 BC to AD 135. Before the discovery of the DSS the earliest known Hebrew text was the Nash Papyrus, which contained only a version of the Decalogue and was dated between 150 BC and AD 68.

E. Tov has identified five different types of biblical manuscripts found among the DSS.[17] These include those of the Masoretic type, which account for at least 35 percent of the manuscripts, those of a Pre-Samaritan text type (5 percent), those that have readings similar to the LXX variants (5 percent of texts), those texts that have no parallels in their variant readings (35

---

[12] The Cairo Genizah fragments discovered in 1890 in an old synagogue are mainly codices of Masoretic Hebrew manuscripts. They consist of fragments of over 200,000 texts, which while not official synagogue scrolls were used by cantors, worshippers, and possibly children. A *genizah* was a place for storing old manuscripts that were to be destroyed because they could no longer be used.

[13] Talmon, "The Old Testament Text," *Qumran and the History of the Biblical Text*, 14, and Tov, "Textual Criticism," 406.

[14] Roberts, *The Old Testament Text and Versions*, 181.

[15] E. Tov, *The Text-Critical Use of the Septuagint in Biblical Research* (Jerusalem: Simor, 1991), 269.

[16] P. W. Flint, *The Dead Sea Psalms Scroll and the Book of Psalms*, Studies on the Texts of the Desert of Judah, vol. 17, ed. F. Garcia Martinez and A. S. Van Der Woude (New York: Brill, 1997), 1.

[17] Tov, *Textual Criticism of the Hebrew Bible*, 114–17.

percent), and those texts written by the unique Qumran practice which is characterized by a free approach to the biblical text (20 percent).

If the Qumran scrolls display a trustworthy picture, it appears that from the third century BC onward, the proto-Masoretic text[18] was more abundant than any other type of text. The Qumran scribes displayed painstaking efforts to produce exact copies of the proto-Masoretic text. The predominance of the Masoretic text at Qumran also suggests that the Masoretic text type was considered to have an authoritative status.[19]

The same can be said for texts found in the Judean Desert at Masada (AD 73), and Naḥal Ḥever and Wadi Murabba'at (AD 132–135). These texts clearly reflect the standard MT.

Additional Hebrew witnesses. The oldest Hebrew witness of any kind is the silver roll found in Ketef Hinnom, discovered in 1979. This ornament is dated to around seventh century BC. This text contains a portion of the priestly prayer of Num 6:24–26 and is largely in agreement with the MT.

EARLY VERSIONS OF THE OLD TESTAMENT

Greek Versions

The collection of the Greek translation of the Old Testament is called the Septuagint (LXX). The name "Septuagint" is derived from the legendary Letter of Aristeas that claimed that 72 scholars from Palestine miraculously translated the Torah into Greek. According to Aristeas and Aristobulus (c. 170 BC) the translation of the Pentateuch into Greek was carried out in the third century BC. The remainder of the biblical books were translated in the third and second centuries.[20] This version represents the first translation of a complete corpus of literature of a Semitic language into Greek. The impetus for the translation was the existence of a Jewish community in Egypt that was losing its ability to read Hebrew and desired to have an OT in Greek, the dominant language in Egypt after Alexander the Great. The use of the Greek translation quickly became widespread as a man named Demetrius cited the book of Genesis in Greek at the end of the third century BC. The author of 1 Maccabees in the Apocrypha knew the Greek translation by the first century AD. It was also quoted by Philo, the NT writers, and Josephus.

The translation techniques in the LXX vary from book to book and even between sections of individual books indicating different translators within individual books. Some of the translations are literal, some are free, while others are interpretive. Moreover, before the books had been completed revisions had taken place at various stages of the individual translations.[21] The LXX also betrays Greek influence on occasion as well as a general tendency to avoid anthropomorphisms. In Ptolemaic Egypt two different types of translation techniques were used, precise translations for commercial and judicial actions and freer translations for literary works.[22]

The most striking differences between the Greek translation and the Hebrew Bible include the Greek additions to the books of Esther and Daniel. There are six additions to the Book of

---

[18] The proto-Masoretic text refers to a text that had the same basic consonantal text of what later became the traditional Masoretic text. The proto-text would thus not have the vocalization, accentuation, and Masoretic notes found in the later Masoretic text.

[19] Tov, *Textual Criticism of the Hebrew Bible*, 117.

[20] The first Greek translation is called "the Old Greek" (Tov, "The Septuagint," in *Mikra*), 161.

[21] See P. Gentry, "The Text of the Old Testament," *JETS* 52 (March 2009): 24.

[22] Tov, "The Septuagint," *Mikra*, 169.

Esther, while the Prayer of Azariah and the Three Young Men, the Story of Susana, and the Story of Bel and the Dragon are adjoined to Daniel. Most agree that these all represent later additions and are to be deemed as examples of theological embellishment. Other significant differences between the LXX and the MT include the fact that the Greek text of Jeremiah is one-eighth shorter than the MT, the Greek text of Job is one-sixth shorter, and a number of differences exist between the Hebrew and Greek texts of Samuel–Kings. The LXX of Jeremiah exhibits a sequence of chapters different from the MT, and in Proverbs a number of individual proverbs in the Hebrew and Greek versions have no correspondent in the other. The phenomenon of quoting verses from another passage for explanatory purposes is quite common in the LXX. The LXX quotes Jer 9:23 after 1 Sam 2:10, includes Exod 19:5–6 at Exod 23:22, and adds Deut 5:14 after Exod 20:10.

At the end of the first century AD the Jews stopped using the LXX, which apparently had been adopted by the early Christians as their Bible. The ongoing dialogue with the Christians who defended Jesus' messiahship from the LXX caused the Jews to abandon the LXX and adopt new Greek translations which were in fact closer to the MT. Thus in the second century AD there arose the Greek translations of Aquila, Symmachus, and Theodotian. Aquila's translation was extremely literal almost at the point of being absurd in places. Theodotion desired to correct the LXX, bringing it closer to the MT, while Symmachus's translation was designed to conform to the Hebrew while reflecting good Greek style.

In the nineteenth century it was common for Old Testament textual critics to emend the MT based on an alleged different reading in the LXX. This practice is well illustrated in the textual apparatus of BHK. In BHK there are a number of unwarranted cases where the MT was corrected by the process of retroversion based on the reading of the LXX.[23] Scholars are now realizing that the text used as the Vorlage for the LXX translation was much closer to the proto-Masoretic text than was previously assumed.[24] The alleged differences between the Greek texts and the Masoretic texts should be attributed more to translation issues than to an alleged non-Masoretic text as the basis for the Greek translation.[25] Yet even so the LXX is not a uniform translation. Appropriate use of the LXX for textual criticism of the OT first requires that the original text of the LXX be established—no small task.[26] While the use of the LXX to correct the MT has been overdone, the LXX does contain more significant variants from the MT than all of the other versions combined.[27]

Aramaic Targums

Part of early synagogue worship included an oral translation of the reading of OT into Aramaic. This practice traces its origin to biblical times when Ezra and other Israelite leaders translated the Law into Aramaic as recorded in Neh 8:8. The practice probably started as early as

---

[23] See M. Goshen-Gottstein, "The History of the Bible-Text and Comparative Semitics. A Methodological Problem," *VT* 7 (1957): 195.

[24] See A. Wolters, "The Text of the Old Testament," in *The Face of Old Testament Studies*, ed. D. Baker and B. Arnold (Grand Rapids: Baker, 1999), 23.

[25] Gentry, "The Text of the Old Testament," 28.

[26] See J. Lust, "Textual Criticism of the Old and New Testaments: Stepbrothers?" in *New Testament Textual Criticism*, ed. A. Denaux (Leuven: University Press, 2002), 18–19.

[27] For issues that need to be resolved and addressed before one can argue that the LXX has priority over the MT, see the helpful discussion by P. J. Gentry, "The Septuagint and the Text of the Old Testament," *BBR* 16 (2006): 193–218.

the Babylonian exile.[28] In the synagogue the Law was translated after the reading of each verse, while the translation of the prophets took place after the reading of three verses (*m. Meg.* 4:4).

There was a natural resistance to writing down these oral translations, however, since only biblical texts were seen as sacred and worthy of transmission (*b. Git.* 60a). But as the knowledge of Hebrew abated and as Aramaic became the *lingua franca* of the Assyrian Empire, reducing the oral translations to writing could no longer be avoided. This inevitably led to the practice of writing the translations of biblical books into Aramaic sometime in the late Second Temple period. All of the books of the Bible occur in at least one Targum translation apart from Daniel and Ezra–Nehemiah which are the only books of the MT that contain significant Aramaic sections.

Of all the Old Testament versions the Aramaic Targums are known as the most interpretive or paraphrastic translations, although clearly based on the proto-MT.[29] Aramaic Targum fragments found among the DSS are somewhat distinctive among Aramaic Targums exhibiting both free and literal translations.

Syriac Peshitta

The OT and NT were translated into the Aramaic dialect of Syriac perhaps as early as the first century AD. Of all of the versions of the Bible the Syriac shows the greatest variety of translation methods, indicating that a number of individuals were involved with the translation. The evidence suggests that the Syriac translation must have taken place over a number of generations.[30] Because the translation reveals such an excellent acquaintance with Jewish traditions from the Talmud, midrash, and Aramaic Targums, many have felt compelled to conclude that the translation was done by a Jewish person or perhaps a Jewish convert to Christianity. The translators translated a text that was virtually identical to the MT type but also occasionally consulted early Aramaic translations that existed in a slightly different form than in their final crystallization.[31] However, the further one goes from the Pentateuch in the Peshitta the more detectable is the influence of the LXX translation.

Vulgate

The earliest evidence of a Latin version of the Bible dates back to the middle of the second century AD when Christian writers would cite Scripture in Latin. Jerome was commissioned to make the official Latin translation in AD 382. Though Jerome translated a text that was essentially the Masoretic text type, his translation method was not consistent. In 1546 the Council of Trent made this text the official Bible of the Roman Catholic Church. While the Vulgate was translated directly from the Hebrew text, there is some evidence that it was influenced by the Septuagint, and particularly the Symmachus revision.[32]

---

[28] The Aramaic oral translations thus preceded the Greek translations by centuries. See J. Myers, *Ezra Nehemiah*, AB 14 (Garden City, NY: Doubleday, 1965), 154; F. Fensham, *The Books of Ezra and Nehemiah*, NICOT (Grand Rapids: Eerdmans, 1982), 217–18; and E. Meyers, "Synagogue," *ABD*, ed. D. N. Freedman (New York: Doubleday, 1992), 6:252.

[29] See Gentry, "The Text of the Old Testament," 26.

[30] See Roberts, *Old Testament Text and Versions*, 214, and P. B. Dirksen, "The Old Testament Peshitta," in *Mikra*, 260.

[31] See P. Wernberg-Moller, "Some Observations on the Relationship of the Peshitta Version of the Book of Genesis to the Palestinian Targum Fragments," *ST* 15 (1961): 149.

[32] Gentry, "The Text of the Old Testament," 25.

The Aramaic Targums, the Syriac Peshitta, and the Vulgate normally agree with the MT. Indeed, it has become increasingly clear that the proto-Masoretic text was the textual base for all of the ancient versions.[33]

HISTORY OF THE TEXT

From Original Composition to Third Century BC

During this period the scribes were responsible for copying the biblical texts. Scribes are mentioned as early as the time of David and Solomon as part of the royal chanceries (2 Sam 8:16–18; 1 Kgs 4:1–6) and were also mentioned in association with Joash and Hezekiah (2 Kgs 18:18,37; 2 Chr 24:11;).[34] There is more than ample evidence of scribal activity throughout the ANE, beginning in Sumer in the third millennium BC, to suggest that the Israelites were involved in copying manuscripts soon after they were inscribed. In Mesopotamia scribal activities included the copying, collating, and annotating of manuscripts.[35]

Israelite scribes normally copied manuscripts from other scrolls, though at times they wrote from dictation and possibly memory (*t. Meg.* 2:5). If scribes omitted a letter, they often "hung" it above the script (*Sop.* 8:2) and indicated errors by dotting letters above the script or alternatively they made corrections in the margin. Their main task was to preserve the text by faithfully copying the Hebrew manuscripts; for the OT was not only the source of their national tradition but was viewed as having been revealed by God. This mind-set of canonicity existed not only in Israel but also among the Mesopotamians as demonstrated by the Code of Hammurabi and Hittite treaties of the second millennium BC. The scribes of the ANE went about their work in a more careful manner than was practiced by the Greeks.[36] The tenacious efforts of the Israelite scribes in particular is unparalleled in history.

Much of what is known about Israelite scribal practice comes from rabbinic literature. Evidence of scribal practice is indicated by several rabbinic texts. One technique used was that of the *tiqqune sopherim*, "scribal corrections." According to tradition, in 18 passages the scribes corrected the text to soften anthropomorphisms and to supply euphemisms for troubling statements.[37] Sometime during this period the script of the biblical manuscripts was changed from the old Paleo-Hebrew script to the Aramaic square script still used in Bible editions today (*b. Sanh.* 21b).[38] The script is called the square script because it appears to be written within an imaginary square frame. According to Jewish tradition Ezra, "a scribe skilled in the Law of Moses" (Ezra 7:6), is credited with establishing this change of script. Rabbinic literature confines the work of the scribes from the period of Ezra to the second century BC.[39] From this rabbinic material we discover that the temple employed professional *magihim* or "correctors,"

---

[33] Wolters, "The Text of the Old Testament," *The Face of Old Testament Studies*, 23.

[34] See also Jer 8:8.

[35] See M. Fishbane, *Biblical Interpretation in Ancient Israel* (Oxford: Clarendon, 1985), 24–27.

[36] See W. F. Albright, *From Stone Age to Christianity*, 2nd ed. (New York: Doubleday, 1957), 78–79. The OT has no fewer than 429 references to writing. This should be contrasted with the *Iliad* that has only one reference to writing and the *Odyssey* that has none.

[37] The list in the *Mekilta* includes 11 passages in the following order: Zech 2:12; Mal 1:13; 1 Sam 3:13; Job 7:20; Hab 1:12; Jer 2:11; Ps 106:20; Num 11:5; 2 Sam 20:1; Num 2:12; and Ezek 8:17.

[38] Before the use of the paleo-Hebrew script was used, the manuscripts were probably written in a proto-Canaanite alphabet that was a pictographic alphabet. Changes of script caused no real difficulty as there was a clear one-to-one correspondence between the different alphabetic scripts.

[39] M. Greenberg, "The Stabilization of the Text of the Hebrew Bible Reviewed in the Light of the Biblical Materials from the Judean Desert," *JAOS* 76 (1956): 159.

who oversaw the writing and copying of biblical manuscripts *(b. Ketub.* 106a).[40] Because many of the scribes worked in the temple where the authoritative manuscripts were kept, many of the scribes were also priests.[41]

Third Century BC to First Century AD

Knowledge of this period has been particularly impacted by the study and analysis of the DSS.[42] The settlement at Khirbet Qumran was a community that had broken with the authorities in Jerusalem. The members of the sect were irreconcilably hostile to Jerusalem and the religious establishment, but they too claimed that the OT was their authority. Hence they were very much involved in the copying and preserving of biblical manuscripts. Based on the diversity of text types at Qumran, many scholars have followed Frank Moore Cross and have argued for a plurality of nonstandard text types. But because the Qumran scribes demonstrate an uncritical acceptance of all text types, one should perhaps be reluctant to build a strong case for plurality of text types (see discussion below). The sensibility of the Qumran scribes certainly did not reflect that of Israelite copyists in official Jewish circles.[43]

Thus other scholars have presented an alternative view and focus on what appears to be a vigorous process of textual standardization during this time period. They find evidence of efforts to make all types of texts conform to what came to be the authorized MT. The earliest attestation to the consonantal framework of the MT (apart from the Ketef Hinnom roll) is found in the Qumran texts around 250 BC. As mentioned, 35 percent of the biblical manuscripts at Qumran are classified as the Masoretic-type of texts. The resemblance especially of 1QIsa[b] to the MT shows how accurate the transmission of the MT had been through the centuries. But since the text which gained hegemony was already in existence at Qumran, the history of that text should be considered much older.[44] Moreover, because of our lack of knowledge regarding the viewpoint of the Qumran community with regard to their collecting of differing text types, it may be accidental that only 35 percent of the texts were of the MT type. The collection may not reflect a library at all but a place to preserve discarded texts.[45]

Hebrew biblical manuscripts were also found at Wadi Murabbaʿat where Jews had congregated to form an outpost during Bar Kochba's revolt against Rome (AD 132–35). Among the group were eminent rabbis, and thus as expected, no heterodox literature was found and the biblical manuscripts agree in every detail with the proto-Masoretic text type. Biblical texts from Masada (AD 73) also provide another early example of the preeminence of the MT type.

At the beginning of the Hellenistic period biblical texts were extant in two main types, a fuller text and a shorter text. The "vulgar" texts were usually expansionistic and could be used by the public at large while the nonvulgar texts like the MT gained a special and authoritative

---

[40] A similar practice was carried out by Mesopotamian and Syrian scribes in the second millennium BC (A. R. Millard, "In Praise of Ancient Scribes," *BA* 45 [1982]: 144–45).

[41] Bar-Ilan, "Part Two: Scribes and Books in the Late Second Commonwealth and Rabbinic Period," *Mikra*, 22. See also Fishbane, *Biblical Interpretation in Ancient Israel*, 84.

[42] The time span is because the biblical manuscripts discovered at Qumran date from the third century BC to the first century AD.

[43] Greenberg, "The Stabilization of the Text of the Hebrew Bible Reviewed in the Light of the Biblical Materials from the Judean Desert," 165.

[44] N. M. Sarna, "Bible," *EJ* 4 (1971): 833. See also N. M. Sarna and S. O. Sperling, "Bible," *EJ* 3, 2nd ed. (2007): 584.

[45] Sarna, "Bible," 4: 834.

status within mainstream Judaism. The scribes at Qumran may provide the best illustration of this vulgar approach to the text.[46]

Normative or "mainstream" Judaism rejected the textual tradition of the LXX very early. This is demonstrated by a Greek manuscript of the Minor Prophets found in the Judean desert at Naḥal Ḥever copied sometime between 50 BC and AD 50 and placed in a cave at the time of the Bar Kochba rebellion against the Romans. This Greek text is aligned with the proto-Masoretic text. Also the Aquila, Symmachus, and Theodotian translations were attempts to harmonize the LXX with the proto-MT tradition already deemed authoritative in Jerusalem.[47] Textual variety may have been characteristic of Palestine as a whole, but apparently only the MT type was used in temple circles.[48] This concept of a temple library where official texts were kept was commonplace in the ANE. Thus several authoritative biblical scrolls were in the temple archive, and their use in the editorial process was a continuing practice.[49]

From Third Century AD to Medieval Times

The biblical quotations in the Talmud and rabbinic literature generally reflect the MT, although there are some differences in details.[50] Kennicot and de Rossi compiled a compendium of variants of medieval manuscripts of the Hebrew Bible and concluded that every manuscript presupposed one single archetype. Thus medieval manuscripts lack real variants and are without practical value for any attempt to reach back into the early history of the Hebrew text.

LOCAL TEXT THEORY OR LINEAR DEVELOPMENT?

Local Text Theory

For many years now introductions to the OT by Western scholars have described the history of the transmission of the Hebrew Bible based on the model developed by F. M. Cross, professor emeritus at Harvard University. The local-text theory maintains that the variant manuscripts can be explained by noting that biblical manuscripts were copied in three locations. This led to the development of three recensions: one in Babylon, one in Egypt, and one in Palestine. Generally speaking the MT derives from the Babylonian recension, the LXX from the Egyptian, and the SP from the Palestine. The existence of these so-called text types at Qumran has bolstered this theory.

Some scholars have always opposed the local texts theory, particularly among the Israeli scholars. E. Tov, esteemed LXX scholar and now editor-in-chief of the DSS publication project, vehemently argued that texts from the DSS that were thought to reflect the LXX should not be seen as part of the same family. It is not possible to prove that the Vorlage[51] of the LXX in any way reflects a family of manuscripts, a recension (work of adaptation to a Hebrew original) or a revision. It was wrong, Tov argued, to refer to the MT, LXX, and SP as recensions or text types. They do not show distinctive features of recensional activity, that is, a conscious effort to change an earlier text systematically in a certain direction. The DSS do not attest to

---

[46] See Tov, "Textual Criticism," *ABD,* 6:406.

[47] See A. S. Van Der Woude, "Tracing the Evolution of the Hebrew Bible," *BR* 11 (1995): 45.

[48] Tov, "Textual Criticism," 406.

[49] Greenberg, "The Stabilization of the Text of the Hebrew Bible Reviewed in the Light of the Biblical Materials from the Judean Desert," 160.

[50] For a study of the variations see V. Aptowitzer, *Das Schriftwort in der Rabbinischen Literatur* (New York: KTAV, 1970).

[51] A Vorlage is the text a scribe is using for a translation or to copy.

three groups of textual witnesses.[52] These texts rather relate to each other in an intricate web of agreements, disagreements, and exclusive readings.[53] No published scroll at Qumran with the possible exception of 4QJer[b] agrees with the LXX in the majority of its details.[54] The labeling of 4QSam[a] as Septuagintal does not take all evidence into account, as the scroll differs from the LXX almost as often as it agrees with it.[55]

How can it be determined that the MT is Babylonian and that not only the translation but also the Vorlage of the LXX is Egyptian? There is no evidence for making these general statements about the nature of these local traditions.[56] Practically nothing is known about the literary vitality of Babylonian Judaism in the period from Ezra to Hillel.[57] Nor is anything known about the literary competence of the Egyptian Jews in the field of Hebrew. Moreover, the very existence of so-called separate text-types at Qumran over long periods raises questions about postulating geographical isolation as the key to the emergence of distinct textual traditions.

Linear Text Development

The textual evidence points in the direction of one original text. Thus most of the textual variation should be viewed as genetic, that is the text developed in one direction only, and in a linear direction. Very little evidence points exclusively to the existence of ancient parallel texts. The Hebrew text presupposed by the LXX represents a tradition close to the MT, or alternatively could be viewed as a descendant of it.

The MT is the medieval representative of an ancient text that already existed at the earliest stage of manuscript evidence. And at an early stage the MT was accepted as the sole text by a central stream of Judaism. The final form of this text developed in the Middle Ages, and it is this final form that is called the MT. The MT is limited to a segment of representations of the textual tradition of the MT, the textual tradition given by Aaron ben Asher of the Tiberian group of Masoretes. Although the medieval form of the MT is late, its consonantal framework reflects an ancient tradition that was in existence at least a thousand years earlier, especially evident among the finds in the Judean Desert. From 4QSam[b] Andersen-Freedman infer that the Masoretic system was firmly in place in the third century BC.[58] More than 6,000 manuscripts are witnesses to this tradition. And the proto-Masoretic tradition is the text translated in the Aramaic Targum, the Peshitta, the revisions of the LXX (the kaige-Theodotian, Aquila, Symmachus, and the fifth column of the Hexapla), and the Vulgate. It is also quoted in the rabbinic literature and is the text used in the vast majority of the DSS. But still, while engaging in the practice of textual criticism, one should not assume in advance that the MT reflects the original text better than other texts or that it is the original text.[59]

---

[52] Tov, *Textual Criticism of the Hebrew Bible*, 160–63. Recensions show recognizable textual characteristics such as expanding, abbreviating, harmonizing, Judaizing, or Christianizing, or a combination of these.

[53] E. Tov, "Determining the Relationship between the Qumran Scrolls and the LXX: Some Methodological Issues," *BIOSCS* (1980): 64.

[54] E. Tov, *The Text-Critical Use of the Septuagint in Biblical Research*, 261.

[55] See Tov, "Determining the Relationship between the Qumran Scrolls and the LXX: Some Methodological Issues," 54, 64.

[56] Tov, "Textual Criticism," 405.

[57] D. Barthelemy, "Text, Hebrew, History of," *IDBS*, ed. K. Crim (Nashville: Abingdon, 1976), 879.

[58] Tov, *Textual Criticism of the Hebrew Bible*, 32.

[59] Ibid., 11.

THE PRACTICE OF TEXTUAL CRITICISM

Broadly speaking, two types of variants can be noted: intentional and unintentional. Intentional variants are those that have arisen for correctional and tendentious purposes as found for example in the SP when rough grammatical forms are smoothed-over and worshipping on Mount Gerizim is made into the tenth commandment. Other examples of deliberate changes include the changing of the seventh day in Gen 2:2 to the *sixth* day in the SP, LXX, and Peshitta to avoid the possible interpretation that God worked on the Sabbath, as well as adding an additional *nun* in some MT manuscripts to the name Moses in Judg 18:30 so as to disassociate Moses' family from idolatry. These changes are quickly recognized as secondary and thus not part of the original text.

The unintentional errors are the primary concern of textual criticism. These errors have arisen in the process of transmission through a mistake by a scribe. Some of the more common causes of variant readings arise through confusion of letters, haplography, dittography, and metathesis.

Confusion of Letters

Letters that are similar in shape were sometimes confused in the copying of manuscripts. Letters which were most often confused included: ב and ר, א and ח, נ and פ, ה and ח, ד and ר, ח and ת, י and ו, and כ and ב. One classic example of the confusion occurs in Gen 10:4, which reads Dodanim with the ד, while some MT manuscripts, the SP, the LXX, and 1 Chr 1:7 read Rodanim with the ר.

Haplography

Haplography occurs when a copyist fails to repeat a letter, a group of letters in a word or a whole word, writing the letter, letters, or words only once. *B. Ned.* 37b–38a records a list of haplographies the rabbis were aware of in the Hebrew Bible. First Samuel 17:46 is often cited as an example; the Hebrew word for "corpse" (פֶּגֶר) is written only once in the MT:

LXX   I will leave *your corpse and the corpses* of the Philistine army.

MT   I will leave *the corpses* of the Philistine army.

Dittography

Dittography is the antithesis to haplography where the letter, series of letters, or words, was written twice when it should have been written only once. One example comes from the 1QIsaᵃ scroll that is known for scribal mistakes:

MT   The Lord shall make heard.

1QIsaᵃ   The Lord shall make heard, make heard.

Metathesis

Metathesis occurs when letters have been erroneously exchanged. The following example shows the interchange of the two letters k and l in Deut 31:1:

MT   So Moses *went* [wāyēlek] and spoke these words to all Israel.

LXX   So Moses *finished* [*sunetelesen* Gr translation of *wykl*] speaking these words to all Israel.

THE PROCESS OF TEXTUAL CRITICISM

The process of textual criticism involves three steps: listing variants, evaluating variants, and explaining variants.

Listing of Variants

This initial step involves listing and lining up the various witnesses to a particular reading. The variants should be translated, and then it should be determined if possible which Hebrew word(s) the variant reading was translating.

Evaluating Variants

This step involves determining which witnesses belong together and if there is any significance to the range of witnesses that share a particular reading. This step should seek to determine which reading the various witnesses seem to support more strongly.

Evaluating a textual variant according to its intrinsic probability involves considering an author's style and immediate context. The discussion of context leads to a complete exegesis of the passage as well as analysis of the language and style of the OT as a whole and the specific unit under consideration. *Lection difficilior* ("the most difficult reading is preferred") and *lection brevior* ("the shortest reading is preferred") must be applied only to a small percentage of readings. To some extent textual evaluation cannot be bound by any fixed rules. This is as much art as it is a science.[60]

Variant readings in the versions should be examined on a case-by-case basis. When evaluating an early version, it is essential that not just the passage with the alternative reading be examined. The entire character of the version must be taken into account, including its translation method, number of translators, and so forth. Manuscripts and translations must be weighed, not just counted.

While vulgar texts contain many secondary readings in comparison to non-vulgar texts, on occasion they may preserve more original readings.[61] Caution should always be exercised, however. Even with the LXX, which apart from the MT is the most valuable witness to the OT text, serious considerations should be exercised before one suggests that the LXX reading is superior or more original than the MT. Hardly any translation unit in the LXX is consistent in its choice of translation equivalents; thus one is always on unsure ground in suggesting individual reconstructions.[62] The more one knows about the nature of any given translation and the more thoroughly inner-translational deviations are analyzed the less one is inclined to suggest that the translator had a different Hebrew text before him.[63]

Explaining Variants

In the final procedure a determination should be made as to how the various variant readings arose. The essence of textual evaluation is to select from the different transmitted readings the one reading that is most appropriate to its context and that is more likely to have given rise to the alternatives. Thus the final step, based on the external and internal evidence, is to determine which reading is the original.

---

[60] Ibid., 307, 309.

[61] Greenberg, "The Stabilization of the Text of the Hebrew Bible Reviewed in the Light of the Biblical Materials from the Judean Desert," 164.

[62] E. Tov, "'Pseudo-variants' Reflected in the Septuagint," *JSS* 20 (1975): 166.

[63] Tov, *The Text-Critical Use of the Septuagint in Biblical Research*, 80. To emend the Hebrew based on the Septuagint even in the case of Jeremiah would be a risky business according to Millard ("In Praise of Ancient Scribes," 152).

CONCLUSION

On the whole the MT is without doubt to be more highly valued than all the other textual sources. The MT has been repeatedly demonstrated to be the best witness to the original text.[64] Where Hebrew manuscripts and ancient versions offer sensible readings in harmony with the MT, one should allow the MT to stand. If a reading of the MT is to be rejected, every possible interpretation of it must have been thoroughly examined. The reading in question must be taken through a comprehensive philological treatment elucidating meanings through the application of linguistic evidence previously ignored. By removing difficulties in the Hebrew text the necessity of further text critical analysis is undercut. This involves especially exploring the forms and meanings of the words in cognate languages as well as examining the words and forms in postbiblical Hebrew.[65] Because of the meticulous practice of ancient scribes in the ANE, caution should accompany every suggestion of glosses or changes in the biblical text.[66] When the scales are balanced, there is much to be said for retaining the MT.

STUDY QUESTIONS

1. How can textual criticism be defined?
2. The most important witnesses of the OT text are written in which language?
3. Who were the Masoretes?
4. What is the Masoretic text?
5. Does the existence of textual variants undermine the authority of the OT text?
6. What is the contribution of the DSS to the field of OT textual criticism?
7. What is the Septuagint?
8. How valuable are the Aramaic Targums to textual criticism?
9. Which church father was especially involved with the Latin Vulgate translation?
10. What is the Vorlage?
11. Describe haplography, dittography, and metathesis.
12. How should a variant reading be evaluated?

FOR FURTHER STUDY

Bar-Ilan, M. "Part Two: Scribes and Books in the Late Second Commonwealth and Rabbinic Period." In *Mikra*. Edited by Martin Jan Mulder. Philadelphia: Fortress, 1988.

Barr, J. *Comparative Philology and the Text of the Old Testament*. Winona Lake, IN: Eisenbrauns, 1987.

Brotzman, E. R. *Old Testament Textual Criticism: A Practical Introduction*. Grand Rapids: Baker, 1994.

Cross, F. M., and S. Talmon, eds. *Qumran and the History of the Biblical Text*. Cambridge, MA: Harvard University Press, 1975.

Dirksen, P. B. "The Old Testament Peshitta." In *Mikra*. Edited by Martin Jan Mulder, 255–97. Philadelphia: Fortress, 1988.

Fishbane, M. *Biblical Interpretation in Ancient Israel*. Oxford: Clarendon, 1985.

Jobes, Karen H., and Moisés Silva. *Invitation to the Septuagint*. Grand Rapids: Baker Academic, 2000.

Klein, R. W. *Textual Criticism of the Old Testament*. Philadelphia: Fortress, 1974.

McCarter, P. K. *Textual Criticism*. Philadelphia: Fortress, 1986.

Rooker, M. F. *Recent Studies in Hebrew Language, Intertextuality, and Theology*. Lewiston, NY: Edwin Mellen, 2003.

Tov, E. *Textual Criticism of the Hebrew Bible*. Rev. ed. Minneapolis: Fortress, 2001.

———. *The Text-Critical Use of the Septuagint in Biblical Research*. Jerusalem: Simor, 1991.

Wolters, A. "The Text of the Old Testament." In *The Face of Old Testament Studies*. Edited by D. Baker and B. Arnold, 19–37. Grand Rapids: Baker, 1999.

Würthwein, E. *The Text of the Old Testament*. Translated by E. F. Rhodes. Grand Rapids: Eerdmans, 1979.

---

[64] E. Würthwein, *The Text of the Old Testament*, trans. E. F. Rhodes (Grand Rapids: Eerdmans, 1979), 113.

[65] J. Barr, *Comparative Philology and the Text of the Old Testament* (Winona Lake, IN: Eisenbrauns, 1987), 6–7, 43.

[66] Millard, "In Praise of Ancient Scribes," 153.

Part 3

APPROACHES TO THE STUDY OF THE OLD TESTAMENT

Michael A. Grisanti

THIS SECTION GIVES an overview of the ways various scholars have explained the composition and meaning of the OT. Chapter 8 examines the historical critical method more broadly. After considering the historical and philosophical backdrop to the eigtheenth century (the Enlightenment in particular), this chapter tracks the development of source criticism, first in the Pentateuch and then in the rest of the OT. It concludes by summarizing form criticism, tradition criticism, canonical criticism, and rhetorical criticism. Chapter 9 focuses on the state of affairs in biblical scholarship, primarily in the past 50 years. It considers several diachronic and synchronic critical methodologies that are part of the scholarly study of the OT. This includes historical criticism, literary criticism, narrative criticism, and reader-response methods.

DOES THE OLD TESTAMENT RECORD RELIABLE HISTORY?

How do critical methodologies explain the historical reliability of the OT? Biblical scholarship offers five answers to this question that can be charted chronologically by tracing the history of consensus positions. At times these methods have coexisted to some extent and all are embraced across the spectrum of biblical scholarship in modern times as well.

First, during the first 17 centuries of the Christian era, the vast majority of biblical scholars accepted the inspiration and authority of the Bible. They viewed the Bible's descriptions of various events as reliable, actual history and regarded the biblical text as divinely given. Of course there were a few detractors along the way, but even they did not abandon wholesale the general reliability of the biblical tradition. Modern biblical critics regard (and generally discount) this era as a "precritical" period of biblical scholarship.

Second, the Renaissance and Enlightenment periods fostered a significant degree of skepticism toward beliefs and practices that had been the consensus for centuries.[1] A growing

---

[1] The Protestant Reformation was one of the fruits of this willingness to question papal authority and Roman Catholic Church tradition.

number of scholars sought to explain God, the Bible, and science primarily through the perspective of a man-centered rationalism. The idea of the Bible being divinely revealed and authoritative became much less acceptable. By the end of the eighteenth century, Jewish and Christian scholars began to subject the OT to wholesale critical analysis. This led to a broad consensus in Europe and then America that viewed the OT as a written work that drew on various sources and demonstrated, in general, sloppy editing. The events and truths presented by the OT were considered untrustworthy and therefore not historical. Rather than granting divine revelation as the basis of Israel's function as a holy nation, these scholars viewed OT religion as the product of a long period of evolution from primitive paganism to monotheism (by the postexilic period).

Third, as scholars at the end of the nineteenth century began to discover and study literary and nonliterary artifacts from the ANE world, they began to realize that the world described by the Bible was not totally out of touch with the world depicted by the recently unearthed artifactual evidence. W. F. Albright and his protégés introduced an understanding of the OT that viewed the biblical text as generally reliable. Rather than creating fictional traditions, they suggested that the Bible preserved believable historical events and traditions. They may not have believed the Bible to be divinely inspired and authoritative, but they did conclude that it was a credible and reasonably accurate tool for reconstructing the history it described.

Fourth, the consensus of modern biblical scholarship is that the Bible is unreliable as a source for reconstructing the history of the events and characters it describes, especially when there is the absence of abundant archaeological evidence.[2] Since the amount of archaeological evidence significantly increases from Israel's divided monarchy period, critics are much more willing to view the biblical narratives from that period as having greater potential historicity. However, even when understood in conjunction with compelling archaeological evidence, most scholars still do not view the OT with much credence. To them it came into existence through a long oral prehistory, during which time various "communities" changed and reshaped the message of the OT to fit the needs and challenges of their own historical setting. A more radical subcategory of this last broad perspective on the OT (known as minimalism) dates the OT to the Persian or Hellenistic periods and rejects any thought of the OT having historical credibility.

Fifth, the evangelical wing of scholarship (like the authors of this volume and scores of others) regard the Bible as God's Word, divinely revealed and inspired, presenting its readers with an inerrant and authoritative message. The Bible gives an authoritative redemptive message, and also delineates credible and reliable history. Although it does not "prove" anything in the Bible, archaeology illuminates, illustrates, supplements, and confirms the biblical record. The following section offers a few examples of recent discoveries that demonstrate that the historical context presented by the OT matches that suggested by artifactual evidence.

---

[2] For example these scholars have absolutely no confidence that the biblical description of Israel's exodus from Egypt and conquest of Canaan has any credibility. See, e.g., N. P. Lemche, *Prelude to Israel's Past: Backgrounds and Beginnings of Israelite History and Identity*, trans. E. F. Maniscalco (Peabody, MA: Hendrickson, 1998), 58; cf. 45–61; W. G. Dever, "Is There Any Archaeological Evidence for the Exodus," in *Exodus: The Egyptian Evidence*, ed. E. S. Frerichs and L. H. Lesko (Winona Lake, IN: Eisenbrauns, 1997), 81.

RECENT DISCOVERIES AND THE HISTORICAL CREDIBILITY OF THE OLD TESTAMENT

The way higher critics have dealt with the OT has caused many students of Scripture to wonder about their cherished belief that God revealed His will to humanity through prophetic spokesmen over the centuries and whether this message carries divine authority. Is the long and complicated development of traditions that are the creations of authors, editors, tradents, and writers really how things happened? Was the nation Israel generally an illiterate society for much of its history until the period of the exile? Was actual writing limited to a tiny slice of Israelite society (those composing royal historical annals) that could not have facilitated the composition and passing along of God's revelation to His people in written form? Were any of the individuals mentioned in the Bible ever recorded in texts and cultures outside of Israel in a way that demonstrates some degree of credibility for Scripture?

Three recent discoveries may shed some light on the matter of the nexus of archaeological discovery and the reliability of the OT witness: the Ketef Hinnom scrolls, the Tel Dan inscription, and the Khirbet Qeiyafa inscription.

Ketef Hinnom Scrolls

Discovery of the scrolls. In 1979 archaeologist Gabriel Barkay discovered two silver scrolls beneath a burial chamber just southwest of the old city of Jerusalem.[3] Silver scrolls like these would have been worn as amulets by the owner. After these scrolls were unrolled (a three-year process), they revealed on their inside surfaces very delicately scratched paleo-Hebrew characters that eventually were read as part of the Aaronic blessing (Num 6:24–26): "The LORD bless you and protect you; the LORD make His face shine on you, and be gracious to you; the LORD look with favor on you and give you peace." Scholars have dated these silver scrolls to the late-seventh or early-sixth centuries BC. So, these verses predate the DSS by approximately four centuries. They are the only extant *biblical verses* from the First Temple period.

Key point of interest. All would agree that the discovery of these amulets does not prove that the Pentateuch was written by the seventh century. However, Barkay has pointed out that the confessional language of these amulets indicates that, *at the very least*, there was the preexilic presence of formulations also found in the canonical text.[4] Waaler suggests that the presence of the priestly blessing in two amulets and the Hebrew OT (with little variation in the text of both) indicates a continuous written tradition before the inscription of the amulets (c. 700–650 BC). He also believes that the accidental character of an amulet and the sparse material from this time suggest that the amulets are not the earliest use of this text. In other words it would seem that the text included in a personal amulet would have had somewhat widespread usage at that time.[5] Since these amulets belong to the preexilic period, they provide a clear challenge to an exilic or postexilic date of the combination of pentateuchal sources as is customarily maintained by critical scholars.

Tel Dan Inscription (TDI)

Discovery of the TDI. Tel Dan (formerly known as Tell el-Qadi) is located at the foot of Mount Hermon in northern Israel. After the end of the 1993 digging season, Abraham Biran

---

[3] G. Barkay, "The Riches of Ketef Hinnom," *BAR* 35, no. 4 (July–Oct 2009): 22–35, 122–26.

[4] G. Barkay, M. J. Lundberg, A. G. Vaughn, and B. Zuckerman, "The Amulets from Ketef Hinnom: A New Edition and Evaluation," *BASOR* 334 (May 2004): 68.

[5] E. Waaler, "A Revised Date for Pentateuchal Texts? Evidence from Ketef Hinnom," *TynBul* 53, no. 1 (2002): 53–54.

and the dig surveyor, Gila Cook, discovered on July 31, an inscribed basalt stone (an expensive stone in antiquity), which was a fragment of a larger monumental inscription.[6] Two other fragments that seem to be part of the same basalt monument were found during the next digging season. The main fragment contains 13 lines of text written in a dialect of early or old Aramaic.[7]

Scholars are unable to date exactly the composition of the inscription itself because it was not found whole or in its original setting. In light of other evidence found near these fragments, Biran and Naveh conclude that the basalt monument must have been smashed around the middle of the ninth century BC and would have been erected before that time.[8] Other scholars have dated it to the late ninth or the eighth century BC as well.[9]

Key point of interest. For understandable reasons, scholars have focused on the meaning of the expression *bytdwd* in line nine. One of the factors favoring a reference to David's dynasty is the fact that this expression parallels the phrase "king of Israel" in line eight.[10]

Potential significance of this discovery. Although the contents of this inscription have triggered various debates on how to correlate the inscription with OT historical narratives, one of the primary contributions of the TDI was that its discovery marked the first time the royal name "David" or the expression "House of David" has been found outside the Bible. Of course this discovery and its potential function as a confirmation of biblical narratives has triggered a storm of controversy among biblical scholars.[11] There is no need to discuss the various interpretive suggestions that have been offered since the discovery of these fragments. A number of them were offered by minimalists who sought to reject any historical value the inscription might have.[12] Regardless of this debate, the strong consensus of scholars across the board is that the expression "the house of David" refers to "the dynastic name of the kingdom of Judah."[13] This expression may refer specifically to the Davidic dynasty. Knoppers suggests that since the inscription comes from an Aramaic context, it more likely refers to "the state of Judah

---

[6] A. Biran and J. Naveh, "An Aramaic Stele Fragment from Tel Dan," *IEJ* 43, no. 2–3 (1993): 81; H. Shanks, "Happy Accident: David Inscription," *BAR* 31, no. 5 (Sept/Oct 2005): 46.

[7] C. S. Ehrlich, "The *bytdwd*-Inscription and Israelite Historiography: Taking Stock after Half a Decade of Research," in *The World of the Aramaeans II: Studies in History and Archaeology in Honour of Paul-Eugène Dion*, ed. P. M. Michèle Daviau et al., JSOTSup 325 (Sheffield: Sheffield Academic, 2001), 59.

[8] Scholars debate the time of the original composition of the TDI based on the correlations they make between the inscription itself and biblical historical narratives.

[9] For example, S. L. McKenzie, *King David: A Biography* (New York: Oxford University Press, 2000), 12; G. Athas, *The Tel Dan Inscription: A Reappraisal and a New Interpretation* (London: T & T Clark, 2005), 5–17.

[10] The transcription and translation are taken from Ehrlich, "The *bytdwd*-Inscription and Israelite Historiography," *The World of the Aramaeans II*, 67.

[11] The purpose here is not to provide a listing of the numerous articles and essays written on this issue. For such listings see the following resources: I. Provan, V. P. Long, and T. Longman III, *A Biblical History of Israel* (Louisville: WJK, 2003), 355 n 122. For a concise summary of the contentious debate over this issue see C. Shea, "Debunking Ancient Israel: Erasing History or Facing the Truth?" *CHE* 44, no. 13 (November 21, 1997): A12–A14. H. Hagelia writes that he has come across 170 articles and books on this debate, including 13 editions of fragment A and 20 editions of the joint fragments A and B, ("The First Dissertation on the Tel Dan Inscription," *SJOT* 18 [2004]: 135).

[12] B. D. Halpern describes the refusal (on the part of the minimalists) to accept that the TDI supports the historical existence of David as king of Israel as a matter of "fighting a rear-guard action for their original denials of the historical value of 2 Samuel and 1 Kings 1–11" ("Erasing History: The Minimalist Assault on Ancient Israel," *BAR* 11, no. 6 [December 1995]: 32).

[13] Biran and Naveh, "An Aramaic Stele Fragment," 93, 95–96.

headed by the Davidic dynasty."[14] The TDI commemorates the triumph of a Syrian king over the kings of Israel and Judah.[15]

Knoppers notes that the publication of TDI is important in at least two ways. First, although this inscription "proves neither the existence of the united monarchy nor the existence of Solomon, it does point to David as a historical figure."[16] The expression "the house of David" points to the importance of David as the founder of a dynasty. The expression also suggests that this dynasty would have to go back at least a few generations. Second, the inscription militates against the suggestion that Jerusalem (or Judah) was not a regional state in the ninth century BC.[17]

What conclusions can be drawn from the discovery of TDI? First, it seems fair to assert that the inscription confirms a Davidic dynasty. Second, it does not *prove* that King David existed or that he had a reign exactly like that described in the Bible. Third, it demonstrates that it is feasible that the biblical description of David's existence is credible.[18]

Khirbet Qeiyafa Inscription (KQI)

Discovery of the inscription. In 2008 archaeologists uncovered an inscription that dates to around 1000 BC at Khirbet Qeiyafa in the Shephelah, near Azekah and Socoh (location of the battle between David and Goliath).[19] The inscription includes five lines of text written in ink on a broken piece of pottery. Scholars debate whether the language of the inscription is Hebrew, Phoenician, Moabite, or an early form of these languages. Although a rough translation has been offered by Haggai Misgav, the official Khirbet Qeiyafa epigrapher, work on the translation and meaning of the inscription continues.

Key point of interest. This inscription is the oldest extant Hebrew text. It does not refer to any known historical events or persons. It does not "prove" anything about the composition or historicity of the OT. Yet, it does demonstrate an important reality. Scribal activity was taking place in ancient Israel, even in frontier posts. Though KQI does not establish the nature of literacy in Israel in the eleventh or tenth centuries, it clearly speaks against the common rejection by minimalists of any credible literacy this early. Also the discovery of a fortified city from the eleventh or tenth centuries argues against the common minimalist suggestion that the time of David and Solomon involved a collection of unfortified villages. KQI would seem to indicate that in the tenth century the Israelite kingdom was organized enough to have fortified cities at important border locations.

---

[14] G. N. Knoppers, "The Vanishing Solomon: The Disappearance of the United Monarchy from the Recent Histories of Ancient Israel," *JBL* 116 (1997): 36.

[15] N. P. Lemche and T. L. Thompson have sought to disassociate the expression "the house of David" from any connotations of dynasty in the OT historical books ("Did Biran Kill David? The Bible in Light of Archaeology," *JSOT* 64 [1994]: 15); T. L. Thompson, "'House of David': An Eponymic Referent to Yahweh as Godfather," *SJOT* 9 [1995]: 59–74). After pointing out several dynastic occurrences of *byt*, Knoppers concludes, "There are associations between *byt*, patronage (divine and human), allegiance, and kinship in various biblical texts, but precisely because establishing a royal house inevitably involves developing a line of succession, maintaining a network of allegiances, and orchestrating a system of patronage, such associations complement, rather than exclude, the dynastic connotations of *byt*" ("Vanishing Solomon," 37 n 103).

[16] Knoppers, "The Vanishing Solomon," 39.

[17] Ibid., 40.

[18] This evidence should (but does not) prevent minimalists from making sweeping statements about David being only a legendary figure.

[19] H. Shanks, "Newly Discovered: A Fortified City from King David's Time," *BAR* 35, no. 1 (Jan/Feb 2009): 38–43; idem, "Prize Find: Oldest Hebrew Inscription Discovered in Israelite Fort on Philistine Border," *BAR* 36, no. 2 (March/April 2010): 51–54.

CONCLUSION

Chapters 8 and 9 in this work introduce the reader to ways scholars have explained the composition of the OT as well as various interpretive methods used in studying the Bible. Many of the modern critical approaches stem from a rejection of the divine character of Scripture. They also pay little attention to authorial intention and place emphasis on the reader as an important part of the interpretive process. These chapters also review the philosophical underpinning of the various critical methods together with some suggestions as to whether they help offer a proper interpretation of the OT.

CHAPTER 8

THE DEVELOPMENT OF THE HISTORICAL CRITICAL METHOD

EUGENE H. MERRILL

A NCIENT AUTHORS, UNLIKE modern ones, were little concerned about providing information on the composition of their texts. Such matters as place, time, and occasion—and even authorship—were either ignored entirely or given only passing and imprecise notice. What mattered most was the literary piece itself and not who wrote it and for what purpose.[1]

This is largely true of the OT as well, though concerns about their character as revelation and their qualification for canonicity often mandated that some such introductory information accompany the text. Thus all 16 of the books of prophecy (including Daniel) record the names of their authors and frequently the times and settings of their origin. This is true as well of many of the psalms, much of the Wisdom literature, and of course the Pentateuch (except for Genesis). On the other hand none of the books of history bears its author's/authors' names and circumstances, nor do many of the psalms and others of the Writings. This lack of documentation clearly attests to the apparently inconsequential nature of such data to the ancient Israelite community.

However, as the issue of the canonical status of the various texts began to emerge, the need became increasingly apparent to ascertain the source(s) of these texts in order to justify their inclusion within the sacred corpus. Hence Jewish tradition, first oral and then written, advanced arguments and evidences to establish actual authorship and other compositional details for all parts of the OT collection that hitherto had lacked such information.[2] In this

---

[1] D. G. Meade points out that the notion of *geistiges Eigentum* ("intellectual/creative property"), a matter of great concern today, was known already in the sixth century BC Greek world. However, it was introduced to the Jewish culture much later, sometime in the Hellenistic era (*Pseudonymity and Canon* [Grand Rapids: Eerdmans, 1987], 4. See also W. Speyer, *Die literarische Fälschung im Altertum* [Melnich: C. H. Beck, 1971]).

[2] *Baba Bathra* 14b–15a. The unusual attention paid in this tractate of the Talmud to establishing authorship and other information about the origins and organization of the OT need not mean that these facts were unknown before, but only that questions and challenges about them had begun to surface and needed

manner the first tentative steps were taken toward what would eventually be known as "the historical-critical method."[3]

PRE-ENLIGHTENMENT CRITICISM

For more than 2,000 years Judaism and then Christianity held almost univocally to the notion that their sacred Scriptures were in every sense the Word of God in whole and in part. But dissenting voices arose, voices that for various reasons questioned the divine quality and full authority of the biblical writings, sometimes because of their lack of authorial attestation. At the outset one should note that these voices were few and far between and were almost always from those who stood apart from the Judeo-Christian tradition. They were "outsiders" who for a variety of reasons attempted to discredit the Bible and the religious movements derived from it.

The impetus for such criticism most likely accompanied the first serious struggles with the issues of canonicity. Unless and until such issues could be resolved—those dealing with authorship, dating, unity, and the like—a shadow could be cast over the admission of literature lacking some or all of this information.[4] The absence of debate surrounding canonicity is surprising in early translation efforts (such as the LXX) and in such pre-Christian Jewish literature as the Apocrypha, Pseudepigrapha, and the community texts of Qumran. As suggested earlier, this implies perhaps a relative disinterest in canonicity or a general consensus about it and other matters of an introductory nature.

The cultural conquest of Hellenism, augmented later by Roman political domination, opened the Jewish world to new currents of thought. For the first time the OT began to be examined critically by outsiders who had no predisposition to consider it a sacred book. Thus the rationalistic humanism that led Greek skeptics to challenge their own ancient myths and religious traditions turned toward the Bible and was quick to point out its alleged fallacies despite its claims and those of its adherents to be divine revelation.[5]

Two examples must suffice. The first was an Alexandrian rhetorician—Apion by name— who led a delegation to Rome in the first Christian century, the purpose of which was to discredit Judaism in the eyes of the Roman Emperor Gaius. His attack obviously necessitated a challenge to the Jewish Scriptures. Both Philo (25 BC–AD 40) and Josephus (c. AD 37–100) responded to Apion, the latter in a treatise titled *Ad Apionem (Against Apion)*. In it the famous historian, speaking of the writings of the OT, makes the observation that "we [Jews] have not an innumerable multitude of books among us, disagreeing from and contradicting one another [as the Greeks have], but only twenty-two books . . . justly believed to be divine."[6] So intense was Josephus' devotion to the Bible as written that he added, "It becomes natural to all Jews,

---

response. For arguments along this line see D. Barthélemy, "L'État de la Bible Juive depuis le Début de Notre Ère jusqu'a la Deuxième Révolte contre Rome (131–135)," *Le Canon de L'Ancien Testament*, ed. S. Amsler, Genea: Labor et Fides, 1984), 14, 17–18.

[3] For surveys of the so-called "historical-critical method" see A. Duff, *History of Old Testament Criticism* (London: Watts, 1910); H. F. Hahn, *The Old Testament in Modern Research* (Philadelphia: Fortress, 1966); J. W. Rogerson, *Old Testament Criticism in the Nineteenth Century* (Philadelphia: Fortress, 1984); S. L. McKenzie and S. R. Haynes, ed., *To Each Its Own Meaning* (Louisville: WJK, 1999).

[4] L. M. McDonald, *The Biblical Canon: Its Origin, Transmission, and Authority* (Peabody, MA: Hendrickson, 2007), 214–23.

[5] Plato's *The Apology of Socrates* provides insight into the inroads of philosophical skepticism regarding the existence of the gods and/or their role in human affairs. See "The Apology, Phaedo and Crito of Plato," trans. Benjamin Jowett, in *The Harvard Classics*, ed. C. W. Eliot (New York: Collier & Son, 1937), 14–15.

[6] W. Whiston, trans., *Josephus: Complete Works* (Grand Rapids: Kregel, 1960), 609.

immediately and from their very birth, to esteem those books to contain divine doctrines, and to persist in them, and, if occasion be, willingly to die for them."[7]

A very specific critique of the Bible was made by Porphyry (232–304), the important Neo-Platonist philosopher and pupil of Plotinus, who in his *Against the Christians,* argued that the book of Daniel must have been written in the second century BC, not the sixth.[8] His principal evidence was that prediction in such detail as is found, for example, in Daniel 11 is impossible on rational grounds and that the historical Daniel could therefore not have been its author. The true second century BC author remains anonymous according to Porphyry, and the alleged Daniel authorship must be rejected as having no authentic historical value.[9]

The skepticism displayed in these two instances paved the way for much more to follow, most outside the Judeo-Christian confession but increasingly more from within. The ancient opinions in these matters prevailed throughout the Middle Ages and up to the dawn of the Renaissance and Enlightenment eras. Then a major reassessment began to take place.

PHILOSOPHICAL FOUNDATIONS OF THE ENLIGHTENMENT

The period of the Enlightenment (sometimes referred to as "the Age of Reason") speaks of that era in Europe following the Renaissance when art, literature, philosophy, and other cultural expressions sought to return to their classical roots on the one hand and to pursue the newly discovered "scientific method" on the other. As a result, skepticism toward and a challenge to existing modes of life and thought including that of established religion came to the fore. The Protestant Reformation, in fact, capitalized on this iconoclastic spirit though its interest was not the rediscovery of the Greco-Roman civilizations but rather a return to the purity of the primitive church and its teachings.[10]

The Renaissance and its intellectual legacy had a devastating impact on the Bible, for the scientific method demanded that no point of view, no dogma of the church, was above re-examination to determine whether it met the criteria of rationality and scientific analysis. Judged by such arbitrary standards, the Bible was believed to be invalid with its claims to prophecy, miracles, and the supernatural. Its self-attestation as revelation, its teachings as to its own inspiration, and its accounts of events that stood outside the realms of contemporary experience and empirical investigation rendered the Bible to the skeptic an unbelievable collection of ancient myths and legends.

These viewpoints were not of course embraced by the common people or even in the beginning by the theologians and ecclesiastics of the church. They were the grist of philosophical discourse argued on the plane of theoretical speculation. But the climate was set for the toleration of such thought, and by the dawn of the nineteenth century Enlightenment rationalism dominated theological education in Europe and had begun to do so in America as well.[11]

---

[7] Ibid.

[8] For the life and thought of Porphyry see K. O. Wicker, *Porphyry the Philosopher: To Marcella* (Atlanta: Scholars Press, 1987).

[9] T. D. Barnes, "Porphyry *Against the Christians*: Date and Attributions of the Fragments," *JTS* 24 (1973): 435, 441. Porphyry's position is known primarily through the writings of Eusebius and Jerome.

[10] The Renaissance, ironically, provided the intellectual stimulus for the Reformation while at the same time supplying the tools for the demolition of the Scriptures upon which the Protestant movement laid its foundation. See B. Thompson, *Humanists and Reformer* (Grand Rapids: Eerdmans, 1996), 372–73; W. Manchester, *A World Lit Only by Fire* (Boston: Little, Brown and Co., 1992), 106–25.

[11] For the scene in America see J. W. Brown, *The Rise of Biblical Criticism in America, 1800–1870* (Middletown, CT: Wesleyan University Press, 1969).

Enlightenment Thought in England[12]

Thomas Hobbes (1588–1679),[13] a student of the famous English scientist and philosopher Francis Bacon (1561–1626), thoroughly imbibed the scientific method of such Renaissance luminaries as Leonardi da Vinci (1452–1519), Nicolaus Copernicus (1473–1543), Galileo Galilei (1564–1642), and of course Bacon himself. To Hobbes religion was just a natural human drive like sex, sleep, or hunger, and no one religion was better than another for it is all sheer superstition. In his classic work *Leviathan* (1651) Hobbes addressed the Bible specifically. On purely rational grounds alone he concluded that Moses wrote much of the Pentateuch, with the exception of references to his own death, anachronisms, and other similar details. Though departing at many points from traditional opinion about authorship, dating, and unity of the biblical books, Hobbes's criticism was remarkably restrained, given his general philosophical outlook.

David Hume (1711–1776)[14] represents a thorough-going skepticism about God and the Bible that provided considerable aid and comfort to eighteenth-century attempts in England to discredit the Bible and its authority. His treatise *Dialogues* makes clear his objections to the standard arguments for the existence of God such as ontological and causal proofs and the argument from design. Having precluded the Scriptures entirely as a source of authentic information about God, Hume (ironically, it seems) wistfully yearned for a revelation that would once and for all clarify questions of ultimate reality. This, he said, was preferable to the stance of the philosopher (i.e., himself) who maintains that "to be a philosophical skeptic is, in a man of letters, the first and most essential step towards being a sound, believing Christian."[15] In reality, of course, Hume denied that such a revelation could or would exist.

Enlightenment Thought in France[16]

The Age of Reason in France is epitomized by René Descartes (1596–1650)[17] who, though theistic to the core, had no room in his system of thought for God-initiated special revelation. What could be known of God must be known rationally. "We should never," he said, "allow ourselves to be persuaded of anything excepting by the evidence of our reason."[18] However, to Descartes, reason was only relative and was reliable only to the extent that it harmonized with divine reason, that is, with the very mind of God. To put it in more Platonic terms, there is an absolutely perfect and divine reason in heaven of which the best human rational process is only a dim reflection. Human beings have an intuitive capacity to tap into the reason from above through a process of illumination. Descartes described it this way: "Intuitive knowledge is an illumination of the mind by which it sees in the light of God those things which it pleases Him

---

[12] The following surveys must restrict themselves to only one or two representative figures and only to England, France, and Germany. They are intended to provide a sample of the philosophic underpinnings of the later historical-critical approaches to the Bible. Other English philosophers of the time include John Locke (1632–1704) and George Berkeley (1685–1753), both of whom contributed to the skeptical spirit of the age. See I. Tipton, "Locke: Knowledge and Its Limits," and D. Berman, "George Berkeley," both in S. Brown, ed., *British Philosophy and the Age of Enlightenment* (London: Routledge, 1996), 69–95 and 123–49, respectively.

[13] S. Priest, *The British Empiricists. Hobbes to Ayer* (London: Penguin, 1990), 17–49.

[14] Ibid., 132–72.

[15] D. Hume, *Dialogues Concerning Natural Religion* (reprint, Edinburgh: Blackwood, 1907), 191.

[16] Other important French philosophers of the Enlightenment were F. Voltaire (1694–1778), B. Montesquieu (1689–1755), and J. J. Rousseau (1712–78). See P. Gay, *The Party of Humanity: "Essays in the French Enlightenment"* (New York: Norton, 1954).

[17] P. A. Schouls, *Descartes and the Enlightenment* (Kingston, Ont: McGill-Queen's University Press), 1989.

[18] W. T. Jones, *A History of Western Philosophy* (New York: Harcourt, Brace, 1952), 673.

to have the mind discover, by a direct impression on our understanding of the divine light. So far, the mind cannot be considered as an agent; it only receives the rays of divinity."[19]

Such a view, while allowing for the Transcendent and for a "private" form of divine communication, stands outside the classical tradition that God has revealed Himself propositionally through texts known as the Bible. Descartes in fact gave little or no attention to the Scriptures one way or the other. To him it was virtually a nonissue. What did come of his form of rationalism was an openness to existential mysticism, an approach that encouraged later expressions of pietism and eventually neoorthodoxy.

Enlightenment Thought in Germany[20]

A brief survey of the thought of Gottfried Leibniz (1646–1716)[21] must suffice for German criticism of this period. His philosophy at every level presupposed and argued for the existence of God.[22] At the heart of his understanding of reality was the Aristotelian idea of monads, indivisible units of force that are inherently independent of each other and incapable of penetrating one another. The fact that the universe exhibits harmony and teleological purpose despite its consisting of these unrelated monadic building blocks attests to a transcendent and personal God who alone is sufficient to account for it. Having argued that God is possible, Leibniz concluded that He therefore exists.[23] His famous analogies of a universe consisting of innumerable clocks, all of which keep perfect time because a perfect clock-maker made them, and of a symphony that plays harmoniously, if occasionally in solo or contrapuntally, because of a score composed by a single composer before the symphony began make clear Leibniz's understanding of the relationship of God and creation.

Again, however, Leibniz's "theology" is one bereft of Scripture and its special revelation. Rationalism alone—especially one open to the reality of God as its fundamental premise—is sufficient. Leibniz as a critic is therefore not to be seen so much as an enemy of the Bible intent on its destruction as one who, by benign neglect, made it appear irrelevant. When destructive higher criticism did emerge, it found a soil of indifference toward the Bible, at least in some circles, an indifference that provided little impetus to resist the inroads of increasing skepticism and unbelief toward the Word of God.

THE ENLIGHTENMENT AND OLD TESTAMENT CRITICISM

This brief survey of the philosophical currents of post-Renaissance thought in Europe through some of its main representatives reveals that either by blatant attack on the Bible or more commonly by ignoring it, skeptics and critics paved the way for a view of Scripture that challenged its authority and questioned time-honored traditions as to its authorship, dating, and literary integrity. By the end of the seventeenth century the charge was led no longer by disinterested "secularists" but by Jews and Christians within the camp who, in the liberating spirit of rationalism, began to subject the Bible to wholesale critical analysis in which little was taken for granted and everything was negotiable.

---

[19] Ibid.

[20] In addition to Leibniz, the prominent German Enlightenment thinkers included C. Wolff (1679–1759), G. Lessing (1729–81), and I. Kant (1724–1804). For the movement in general see P. H. Reill, *The German Enlightenment and the Rise of Historicism* (Berkeley, CA: University of California Press, 1975).

[21] B. Mates, *The Philosophy of Leibniz: Metaphysics and Language* (New York: Oxford University Press, 1986).

[22] Ibid., 244.

[23] Ibid., 154–55.

The Pentateuch, perhaps because of its antiquity and inherent interest, was first to undergo the searching scrutiny of Enlightenment investigation. It is true, of course, that the first serious challenge to the Mosaic provenience of the Pentateuch long antedated the Enlightenment.[24] Medieval thinkers such as Isaac ben Jasos (c. 982–1057) and Ibn Ezra (c. 1092–1167) had challenged the Mosaic tradition but only to the extent of suggesting that there were late additions to the basic Mosaic text. Later Reformation and post-Reformation Christian scholars, including Andreas Carlstadt (1480–1541), Andreas Masius (1514–73), Benedict Pereira (c. 1535–1610), and Isaac de la Peyrère (1594–1676), broke free of these limitations and while conceding a Mosaic core to the Pentateuch, they argued that it was largely post-Mosaic, reflecting the time of its composition. This laid the foundation for the abandonment of the view of a unified Pentateuch written by Moses.

These challenges increased when infused by the spirit of the Enlightenment which, as noted above, questioned traditional authority including that of the church and the Scriptures. Rationalism began to supplant faith, and humanism undercut belief in the supernatural. The Bible was no longer accepted as the Word of God on purely dogmatic or confessional grounds, but like any ancient document or artifact it came to be an object of study susceptible to the ordinary canons of analysis and criticism. Traditional view on authorship, unity, and dating were scuttled in the interests of an "objectivity" that maintained, in effect, that only a scientific, "nonbiased" approach could yield the true facts in the case.

Baruch (Benedict) Spinoza

Foremost in the new critical appraisal of the Pentateuch was Baruch (Benedict) Spinoza (1632–77), the brilliant Jewish philosopher from Amsterdam.[25] Spinoza expressed his aversion to the rigid hierarchical and traditional structures of his Jewish faith, structures that in his view stifled true religious feeling and practice.[26] His excommunication from Judaism and conversion to nominal Roman Catholicism did nothing to help free him from this confinement, for he saw in his new religion the same intrusion of dogma between God and humankind.[27] He was then led to investigate the biblical text philosophically and not theologically; that is, he read the Bible as an open book and not one whose message was filtered through a corrupt clerical hierarchy whose only objective, as he saw it, was self-advancement.

Spinoza, having thus rejected the authority of the church as a whole, rejected also its claims about the Bible, including its particular formulation of inspiration. If the Bible is inspired, he said, its inspiration must be evident from its own nature and self-attestation and not as a fiat declaration of the church. After a lengthy discourse on prophecy, law, miracles, and the interpretation of Scripture, he tested the Pentateuch inductively and drew several conclusions. First, the Pentateuch and the historical books that follow (Joshua–2 Kings) contain many inconsistent and conflicting statements and could not therefore be from the hands of their alleged, contemporary authors. Second, citing Ibn Ezra (not always accurately), Spinoza denied the Mosaic authorship of the Pentateuch by adding to I. Ezra's list of non-Mosaic elements several others such as (1) frequent references to Moses in the third person, (2) the account of his death

---

[24] For a brief treatment of this development see R. H. Pfeiffer, *Introduction to the Old Testament* (London: Adam and Charles Black, 1952), 44–46.

[25] R. Kayser, *Spinoza: Portrait of a Spiritual Hero* (New York: Greenwood, 1968).

[26] B. Springs, *Tractatus Theologico-Politicus (1670).*

[27] B. de Spinoza, *Tractatus Theologico-Politicus, Tractatus Politicus,* trans. R. H. M. Elwes (London: Routledge and Sons, n.d.), 4–8.

in Deuteronomy; (3) anachronistic place names (e.g., Dan in Gen 14:4); and (4) references to historical events that postdated Moses. His conclusion was that the Pentateuch was finally collected and composed by Ezra the scribe of postexilic times.[28]

Because of his immense intellectual prowess and reputation in philosophical circles Spinoza almost singlehandedly broke down further resistance to similar "objective" approaches to the Scriptures. The crack in the façade of Mosaic authorship of the Pentateuch as well as fissures that appeared in other areas of Old Testament research soon opened into a broad gate through which all kinds of destructive criticism could pass.

Jean Astruc

The next major figure in the development of the higher critical method seemed innocent enough. He was Jean Astruc (1684–1766), a French physician to King Louis XV. In the interest of sharing some of his own observations and concerns about the book of Genesis, he published a little work in 1753 known popularly as *Conjectures*.[29] In it he set forth his case for a position which, while not denying Mosaic authorship, drew attention to Moses' use of sources. These came to be the putative documents that form the starting point for the so-called Documentary Hypothesis of the Pentateuch.

Despite Astruc's analysis and conclusions, he did not set out to undermine traditional views of the unity and Mosaic authorship of the Pentateuch. He did suggest that Moses never claimed to have written Genesis, for he (Moses) was not an eyewitness to the events of that book. Astruc's opinion was that Moses did in fact write it, but he did so on the basis of either oral or written traditions handed down to him through his ancestors who were witnesses.

Astruc rejected the oral tradition option because of the difficulties inherent in memorizing materials so filled with names and numbers. He concluded that Moses gathered the written texts of his fathers, divided them up according to their content, and then arranged them *seriatim* in their entirety. The result, he maintained, was repetition of the same events (e.g., two creation and two flood stories), the use of different divine names in different sources, and chronological disarrangement in which later events are sometimes placed before earlier ones (e.g., the Table of Nations in Genesis 10 before the Tower of Babel record in Genesis 11).

The last stage of Astruc's analysis—what he called decomposition—was most important to later critical hypotheses. He set out to isolate and then gather together the documents he had identified by means of the criteria listed above. Thus the stories in which God was called Elohim were linked together in column A. Those with the divine name Yahweh were listed under B. Sections repetitious of A, B, or both were placed under C. Stories that appeared to be extraneous to the Hebrew tradition were categorized as D. Even these larger units could not account for all the variety of material in Genesis, so Astruc ended up with a dozen or more sources in all.

The implications of Astruc's work are obvious. He had clearly pioneered the way to a source-critical analysis of Genesis, an approach that predictably found its way throughout the Pentateuch and beyond. In fairness it must again be repeated that Astruc did not deny that Moses was the author of Genesis and the rest of the Pentateuch. He only posited that the great

---

[28] Ibid., 120–32.

[29] The full title is "Conjectures sur les Memoires Originaux dont il paroit que Moyse s'est servi pour composer le livre de la Genese." Extensive quotations from and comments on the essay may be found in E. M. Gray, *Old Testament Criticism: Its Rise and Progress* (New York; Harper & Brothers, 1923), 129–47.

law-giver did so on the basis of documents that came to him and that he attempted to incorporate them together as well as he could under the direction of the Spirit of God.

THE DOCUMENTARY HYPOTHESIS

His noble intentions not withstanding, Astruc had set the stage for other critics such as J. G. Eichhorn who extended the method through the remainder of the Pentateuch.[30] Eichhorn added to Astruc's criteria for diversity of sources elements such as style, vocabulary, and repetitions and eventually concluded that an unknown redactor—not Moses—composed the Pentateuch long after Moses' time. Heinrich Ewald[31] proposed the theory that the materials of the Pentateuch must not be viewed as just so many originally unrelated fragments but that there must be an underlying organization, a source that can be identified as the foundational story to which the others were supplements. This he designated E since it appeared to him that the Elohistic document was longest and most intelligible by itself. J, the source that preferred the name Jahveh (German for Yahweh), Ewald considered to be a continuous though secondary and later composition. However, his successors rejected J as a complete document and viewed it as only a supplement to E.

The basic E + J construction was shattered particularly by W. M. L. DeWette[32] who in 1805 set forth the position that Deuteronomy (D) had nothing to do with the J and E sources and indeed was to be identified with "the book of the law in the LORD's temple" of the era of King Josiah of Judah (622 BC; cf. 2 Kgs 22:8; 23:2,21). The reason for this ripping of Deuteronomy from its JE connection was that the reformation of Josiah seems to have followed Deuteronomic prescriptions point by point. That is, the freshness of approach taken by the zealous young king reflects a new way of understanding the requirements of the Lord in these matters, a way unknown to the old JE sources.

Meanwhile it had become apparent to many critics that E itself was not an original unity. Therefore in 1853 Hermann Hupfeld[33] divided E into E and P (Priestly) on linguistic and theological grounds. He drew attention to the fact that where these features most diverge is precisely in the areas where matters of the cult and priesthood are most concerned. That is, P was an independent (and to Hupfeld the oldest) source to which was redacted the material of E and (later) J. It was P's preference for the name Elohim that had led earlier scholars to fail to distinguish E from P.

A result of this century of labor was a growing consensus that the Pentateuch consisted of four major sources—PEJD—and in that chronological order. None of it was attributed directly to Moses, and in fact all of it was thought to have originated in post-Davidic times. Then concomitant with the rise of evolutionary hypotheses in general and the Hegelian philosophy of history in particular, the next major development in pentateuchal criticism took place, a development associated especially with K. H. Graf.[34] Graf urged, in line with current

---

[30] For a brief but enlightening assessment of Eichhorn's life and impact see T. K. Cheyne, *Founders of Old Testament Criticism* (New York: Scribner's Sons, 1893), 13–26.

[31] Rogerson, *Old Testament Criticism in the Nineteenth Century,* 91–103.

[32] J. W. Rogerson, *W. M. L. de Wette: Founder of Modern Biblical Criticism,* JSOTSup (Sheffield: Sheffield Academic Press, 1992).

[33] Rogerson, *Old Testament Criticism,* 131–34.

[34] O. Eissfeldt, *The Old Testament: An Introduction* (New York: Harper and Row, 1965), 165–66. Eissfeldt denies Hegel's influence on Graf. However, Wellhausen, who stood in debt to Graf's observations on P, confessed his further debt to W. Vatke who was Hegelian. This suggests that Wellhausen and Graf both imbibed at least some Hegelian developmentalism. See R. E. Clements, *One Hundred Years of Old Testament Interpretation*

understandings of social and religious developmentalism, that highly organized cultic religion such as that outlined in the P texts is always the last stage of expression and not the earliest. Religion—so the prevailing theory went—always progresses from primitive animism, to pantheism, to polytheism, to henotheism, and finally to monotheism. Moreover, it moves from an intensely personal and private encounter with the divine to an increasingly societal, structured, and hierarchical form in which the individual worshipper recedes in importance and the cult becomes important in its own right. For OT Israel this religious evolutionism meant that the personal though polytheistic faith of the patriarchs gave way to the quasi-monotheism of Moses, which in turn found full expression in the ethical monotheism of the great prophets. From there, however, Israelite religion deteriorated into mere ritual and ceremony at the hands of a professional priesthood, a development that found florescence in the postexilic period. The direct encounter of a human being with his or her God became subverted by a religious hierarchy that operated out of self-interest and placed itself and its cult in a position of mediation.

Graf therefore needed to place P where it properly belonged according to this pattern, namely, at the end of OT times. Thus P became postexilic, a product of the priesthood that dominated Judah's community life following the destruction of Jerusalem and the virtual cessation of prophetism. Meanwhile the chronological priority of J over E was gradually gaining favor so that the order of documents became JEDP, the order still favored by the majority of scholars.

Abraham Kuenen,[35] though recognizing that P may have used older materials, accepted the Graf hypothesis and transmitted it to Julius Wellhausen[36] who is generally regarded as the synthesizer of the documentary and developmental hypotheses. His classic work, *Prolegomena to the History of Ancient Israel* (English edition, 1885),[37] provided the definitive statement of the matter to which all subsequent discussions have been compared. In it Wellhausen propounded the order JEDP, dating J in the ninth century BC, E in the eighth, D in the seventh, and P in the fifth. He commenced his history with the exodus, relegating the patriarchal narratives to mere legend on the grounds that they contained religious ideas that were too early in the development of Israel's religion and that moreover reflected the time of their composition, not that of their historical setting.

The conclusions of Wellhausen, while modified here and there in details, have remained to this day the point of departure for pentateuchal studies by liberal scholars (see figure 8.1). But the objections raised to the hypothesis through archaeological discovery and comparative ANE languages and literatures have created serious problems for scholars who embrace it. The evolutionary premises on which it is based have been totally discredited and even the antiquity of the contents of the documents has had to be reassessed.[38] The result has been the introduction of new methods of investigation that can allow the Graf-Kuenen-Wellhausen structure to stand but be invested with new content and meaning.

(Philadelphia: Westminster, 1976), 3. One is reminded of J. Wellhausen's own tribute: "My inquiry proceeds on a broader basis than that of Graf, and comes nearer to that of Valke, from whom indeed I gratefully acknowledge myself to have learnt best and most" (Julius Wellhausen, *Prolegomena to the History of Ancient Israel* [Gloucester, MA: Peter Smith, 1983], 13).

[35] Cheyne, *Founders of OT Criticism*, 185–94.

[36] For an overview of Wellhausen's life and scholarly endeavors see the entire issue of *Semeia* 25 (1982).

[37] This was originally published in 1883 as *Prolegomena zur Geschichte Israels*. For an English translation, see J. Wellhausen, *Prolegomena to the History of Ancient Israel* (Cleveland: World, 1957).

[38] See R. N. Whybray, *Introduction to the Pentateuch* (Grand Rapids: Eerdmans, 1995), 134–35.

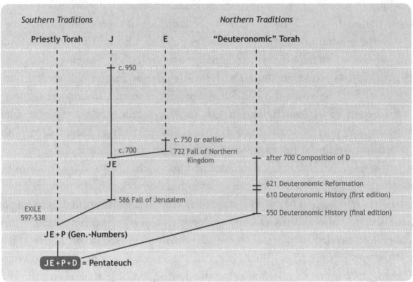

Figure 8.1

SOURCE CRITICISM BEYOND THE PENTATEUCH

Though the technical term "source criticism" is normally limited to study of the Mosaic literature—and certainly such is the case with the synonymous idea "The documentary hypothesis"—the methods and conclusions of source criticism have been applied to virtually the entire OT canon. Thus it is customary to speak of the core and supplementary materials of historical books such as Joshua and Judges, the "authentic" writings (if any) of the great classical prophets (as opposed to later redactions or collections of these works), or the several constituent elements of poetic and wisdom texts such as Job and Proverbs. All these genres and individual compositions receive full treatment later in this book so there is no need now to look at each in particular. It may be helpful, however, at least to review the criteria by which judgments are made as to authorship, date, and unity of the various OT texts.

Classic source criticism of the Pentateuch made much of the use of divine names, doublets, repetitions, lexical variation, shifts in style, differing theological and ideological viewpoints, and the like in determining such matters. To a lesser extent, these same features inform its current practice. In addition there was at least implicit adherence to the notion of religious developmentalism in positing the temporal sequence of the alleged sources, a philosophical idea that does not find quite so much favor today.

Many of these criteria (notably divine name distinction and repetitions) are lacking in the analysis of non-pentateuchal literature, either because the features themselves are missing or they can be explained in some way other than differing sources. Others are retained, however, and augmented by still others that find little or no significant place in the study of the Pentateuch. These include the impossibility of detailed predictive prophecy (at least as it has been classically articulated), shifts of viewpoint and/or theological agenda within literary corpora, and a general disinclination to take any of the historical, cultural, and ideological self-attestations of the OT seriously. It is common in at least more radical forms of modern criticism to view the entire canon as a postexilic production designed to promote the interests of a self-serving Jewish community.[39] Rather than accepting these writings as authentic texts

---

[39] So, for example, J. Van Seters, *Prologue to History* (Louisville: WJK, 1992), 332.

deriving from the persons, times, and circumstances that they intrinsically profess, it is fashion-able now to see them as largely propagandistic compositions created *de novo* in order to bolster the claims of the Second Temple Jewish community to religious and political independence in the land of Palestine.[40]

Less extreme criticism puts much more stock in the reliability of the traditions concern-ing the origin and transmission of the biblical texts, but it is still beholden to a philosophi-cal framework that precludes certain elements of the tradition (such as miracles and fulfilled prophecy) from serious—or at least literal—consideration. According to much contemporary criticism, any text asserting such elements must be interpreted or reinterpreted along histor-ical-critical lines that allow their basic veracity and religious value to be retained though not at the cost of believing the unbelievable. To put it in more pithy epistemological terms, the task of criticism is to discover and assert the truth of ancient biblical texts without necessarily buying into the idea that they communicate factual reality.[41] How this shift has occurred must now be traced historically.

FORM CRITICISM[42]

A developing and increasing disillusionment with the results of source criticism emerged by the end of the nineteenth century, especially as that method was applied to the Pentateuch. This gave rise to new ways of looking at the biblical traditions and their literary expressions. The first of these "new criticisms" sprang from the work of Hermann Gunkel,[43] common-ly regarded as the "father" of so-called "form criticism." Having recognized that the source-critical approach to the Pentateuch espoused by Wellhausen had run its course and, moreover, was clearly contrary to all that was being learned from the ANE, Gunkel sought to explain not the differences among the alleged sources but their similarities. He had begun to see that the biblical literature represented a wide variety of genres and forms and that these forms were nearly inflexible throughout the biblical record regardless of the postulated sources.

Gunkel therefore shifted his attention from the JEDP documents as separate sources to the background and history of the literary types of which they consisted and which they shared in common. He attempted to identify these types by their structural and stylistic patterns, to

---

[40] As G. Garbini states it, "What the Old Testament gives us is a history of the religious evolution of Israel from the point of view of the priestly class of Jerusalem in the post-exilic period: a history with irritat-ingly nationalistic connotations, characterized by an increasingly marked exclusivism" (*History and Ideology in Ancient Israel* [New York: Crossroads, 1988)], 62).

[41] This is the thrust, for example, of the moderately critical work by W. L. Humphreys, *Crisis and Story: Introduction to the Old Testament* (Palo Alto, CA: Mayfield, 1979). See esp., 1–13.

[42] Old Testament form criticism exhibits an enormous literature. For significant studies see H. Gunkel, *The Psalms. A Form-Critical Introduction*, trans. T. M. Horner (Philadelphia: Fortress, 1967); J. H. Hayes, *Old Testament Form Criticism* (San Antonio: Trinity University Press, 1974); K. Koch, *The Growth of the Biblical Tradition. The Form-Critical Method*, trans. S. M. Cupitt (New York: Scribner, 1969); R. Knierim, "Old Testa-ment Form Criticism Reconsidered," *Int* 27 (1973): 435–68; E. V. McKnight, *What Is Form Criticism?* (Phila-delphia: Fortress, 1969); J. Muilenburg, "Form Criticism and Beyond," *JBL* 88 (1969): 1–18; E. Norden, *Agnostos Theos: Untersuchungen zur Formengeschichte religiöser Rede* (Stuttgart: B. G. Teubner, 1956); G. Rad, "The Form-Critical Problem of the Hexateuch," in *The Problem of the Hexateuch and Other Essays* (London: SCM, 1984), 1–78; M. A. Sweeney, "Form Criticism," in *To Each Its Own Meaning*, ed. S. L. McKenzie and S. R. Haynes (Louisville: WJK, 1999), 58–89; G. M. Tucker, *Form Criticism of the Old Testament* (Phila-delphia: Fortress, 1971); C. Westermann, *Basic Forms of Prophetic Speech*, trans. H. C. White (Philadelphia: Westminster, 1967).

[43] See especially H. Gunkel, *The Legends of Genesis*, trans. W. H. Carruth (New York: Schocken, 1964); idem, *The Folktale in the Old Testament*, trans. M. D. Rutter (Sheffield: Almond, 1987).

determine the kinds of sociocultural-religious settings (*Sitz im Leben*) that gave rise to them, and to trace the transmission of the individual compositions from their (oral) creation to their present place in the sacred text.

Gene Tucker suggests the following four steps in the form-critical analysis of a biblical text: (1) analysis of the structure; (2) description of the genre; (3) definition of the setting or settings; and (4) statement of the intention, purpose, or function of the text.[44]

Analysis of structure requires a means of determining the limits of the literary piece itself. Frequently stock formulae indicate the beginning and end of a given literary unit even if these are lacking internal clues such as changes in content, style, mood and tone, or grammatical person and tense. Genre, the *type* of composition, can be divided first between poetry and prose and then each of these can be further subdivided. For example, some psalms are classified as hymns, others as individual or community laments, and still others as proclamations of salvation. Prose types may be legal texts, disputation speeches, or prophetic call narratives. When these appear regularly throughout the Bible, they can be compared and contrasted so that their invariable points in common as well as their individual uniquenesses can be identified.

The setting of a text can sometimes be obvious from the historical circumstances most likely to have produced it (e.g., Deuteronomy on the eve of conquest or Esther at the time of a miraculous deliverance of the Jews). Other times the genre of the piece itself suggests the setting. This is particularly true of the psalms, which generally do not appear in any kind of discernible historical context but whose *Sitz im Leben* can still be surmised. For example the "Psalms of Ascent" (Psalms 120–134), because of their pervasive imagery of pilgrimage and temple, may have been composed against the background of the thrice-annual celebrations of the great festivals of Israel (see also Psalm 63).[45] Frequently, however, attempts to discover settings for individual compositions apart from clues within their literary context are subjective and misleading. This is one of the liabilities of the form-critical approach and the source of much abuse of the method.

Tucker's fourth step in the form-critical process—the statement of the intention, purpose, or function of a text—is even less susceptible of scientific control, especially again in a piece that has no literary/historical context. The purpose of the flood narrative, for example, is abundantly clear for there are clues within and surrounding the pericope to clarify its purposes (Gen 6:1–6,13; 8:21–22; 9:11–17). On the other hand guessing the intention of noncontextualized compositions such as many of the psalms on form-critical lines alone is extremely hazardous, for it forces these compositions into a functional straitjacket that allows their authors no room for creativity. In other words one must allow a biblical (or any other) writer to employ a literary form in any way he or she chooses without drawing hasty conclusions as to how the author inevitably *must* have used it. For example one should not conclude that because a writer speaks of human life in the allegory of a baseball game ("three strikes and you're out!") the piece originated in the sports pages of the local newspaper or was intended to describe a literal game.

There is no doubt that form criticism has yielded great benefits to OT scholarship. To see that the genealogies of Genesis have a particular function based on their form (i.e., to represent connections between covenant promises and to highlight specific links) is exegetically and

---

[44] Tucker, *Form Criticism of the Old Testament*, 11.

[45] E. S. Gerstenberger, *Psalms, Part 2, and Lamentations*, FOTL XV (Grand Rapids: Eerdmans, 2001), 320–21.

theologically useful.[46] Likewise, to know that the covenant texts associated with Abraham and the patriarchs are, by form, in the pattern of royal land-grant treaties is to give the Abrahamic covenant a rich theological dimension.[47] This is even more the case with the impressive evidence that the book of the covenant (Exod 20:1–23:33) and the book of Deuteronomy are literarily patterned after classic Hittite sovereign-vassal treaty texts of the Late Bronze Age (c. 1550–1200 BC).[48] Form criticism, judiciously employed, has self-evident value.

TRADITION CRITICISM[49]

The attempts of Gunkel and subsequent generations of form critics to trace the source and history of the oral and written traditions that gave rise to the present literary compositions of the OT led inevitably to still another method—traditiohistorical criticism. As J. Coert Rylaarsdam says, tradition criticism's "intentions are synthetic and presuppose the analytic work of both literary and form criticism. Since it follows in the wake of both, it assumes that both oral and written continuities play a role in the shaping of the traditions that finally culminated in Scripture."[50]

Gunkel's form critical work first initiated the notion that oral tradition lay behind the written text. This was largely based on the assumption (for which there is no real evidence) that ANE and classical literature existed in its earliest form as oral poetry and was transmitted orally. Capitalizing on this suggestion and drawing on analogies from more modern examples, particularly from their own culture, Scandinavian scholars such as H. S. Nyberg[51] and Ivan Engnell[52] proposed that all of Israel's "literature" was oral until the period of the exile and later. Such a view obviously contradicted and totally rejected any sort of a source-critical (documentary) hypothesis of the JEDP variety, and it also called into question the standard methods and conclusions of form criticism.

Sigmund Mowinckel[53] and Eduard Nielsen[54] went even beyond their colleagues by an assiduous attempt to trace down the origination and development of every oral tradition from the hands (or mouths) of the ancient Israelite poets and prophets and their circles of disciples. This was an exercise in futility and was recognized as such by a host of critics across the theological

---

[46] R. R. Wilson, *Genealogy and History in the Biblical World* (New Haven, CT: Yale University Press, 1977), 193–95.

[47] M. Weinfeld, "The Covenant of Grant in the Old Testament and in the Ancient Near East," *JAOS* 90 (1970): 184–203.

[48] E. H. Merrill, *Deuteronomy,* NAC (Nashville: B&H, 1994), 27–32.

[49] The following is a sampling of the available literature: W. Brueggemann and H. W. Wolff, *The Vitality of Old Testament Traditions* (Atlanta: John Knox, 1975); R. A. Di Vito, "Tradition-Historical Criticism," in *To Each Its Own Meaning,* 90-104; N. C. Habel, "Appeal to Ancient Tradition as a Literary Form," *ZAW* 88 (1976): 253–72; J. Hempel, "The Forms of Oral Tradition," *Record and Revelation,* ed. H. W. Robinson (Oxford: Clarendon, 1938), 28–44; R. Knierim, "Criticism of Literary Features, Form, Tradition, and Redaction," in *The Hebrew Bible and Its Modern Interpreters,* ed. D. A. Knight and G. M. Tucker (Philadelphia: Fortress, 1985), 123–65; D. A. Knight, *Rediscovering the Traditions of Israel,* SBL Diss. Series (Missoula, MT: Scholars, 1975); W. E. Rast, *Tradition History and the Old Testament* (Philadelphia: Fortress, 1972).

[50] Rast, *Tradition History, and the Old Testament,* vii.

[51] Knight, *Rediscovering the Traditions of Israel,* 233–39.

[52] Ibid., 260–74.

[53] A. Kapelrud, "Sigmund Mowinckel and Old Testament Study," in *Sigmund Mowinkel's Life and Works,* ed. D. Kvale and D. Rian (Oslo: Smaskrifter Utgitt av Institutt for Bibelvitenskap, 1984).

[54] E. Nielsen wrote, "The Old Testament as *written* literature may in all probability be ascribed to the period between the destruction of Jerusalem in 587 B.C. and the time of the Maccabees" (*Oral Tradition* [London: SCM, 1954] 39, italics his).

spectrum. Not least among them was G. Widengren,[55] a fellow Scandinavian and an esteemed Assyriologist, who showed by comparative Semitics study that the very notion of such an extensive oral tradition in Israel was anomalous.

Though tradition-critics differ among themselves as to approach and method, the following steps are typical:[56]

First, there must be an investigation of the community or group responsible for the shaping and transmission of a particular tradition or cycle of traditions. Those pertaining to sacrifice, offering, cult, and certain historical accounts favorable to the priesthood (the so-called P sections) must have originated in priestly circles. Any texts that present old sacral and legal traditions in a homiletical style should be attributed to a "Deuteronomic school" for that is the tone and flavor of the "Deuteronomic history" (Deuteronomy–2 Kings). Wisdom materials clearly arose from sapiential sources such as the wisdom schools and royal courts, and obviously prophetic writings were produced by the prophets and/or their intellectual heirs.

Second, attention must be given to the significance of the geographical locale of a tradition. For example, Bethel, as a site associated with Jacob and oracles received by and cultically acted out by him, must, according to tradition criticism, have cultic importance from the dawn of history. Likewise Shechem as a covenant center must have been a source of certain covenant traditions, especially in the D materials. Jerusalem, according to this approach, originated much of the royal ideological tradition because of its obvious association with Israel's monarchy. If royal theology was the product of Jerusalem or the south in general, then the Mosaic covenant traditions, which appear to tradition critics to be at odds with royal theology, must, with the whole exodus complex, be associated with the north. Obviously such reconstructions rest on the premise that these various sites gave rise to the traditions and not that the "traditions" themselves are reliable historical accounts that occurred precisely at or in connection with these places.

Third, one must be aware of sociological, political, or cultural influences that might have given impetus to certain kinds of literature. That is, one must recover the *Sitze im Leben* of the underlying traditions. The possibilities here are nearly endless since tradition critics generally deny the Bible's own understanding of the settings from which the literature sprang. In its place they postulate the most likely set of circumstances that could have led the biblical tradents to create their material as they did without respect to its actual historicity. Thus, Mowinckel centers nearly everything on the cult, suggesting that Israel was fundamentally a worshipping people whose every tradition finds its expression in its places, times, and modes of worship and takes on meaning with reference to them.[57] Gerhard von Rad, on the other hand, focuses on so-called holy war, a reflection of the turmoil of the Assyrian onslaught against Judah in 701 BC, and the immediate occasion for the composition of Deuteronomy, which of course deals extensively with holy war themes. As for Deuteronomy's form, von Rad argues that it was based on ancient covenant patterns thus giving it the appearance of being Mosaic in origin.[58]

Fourth, one must search for the various themes of the OT, how they came to be formulated, and the ongoing role they played. Von Rad, in his important article "The Form-Critical Problem of the Hexateuch," assumed that the basis of the Hexateuch (Genesis–Joshua) was

---

[55] Knight, *Rediscovering the Traditions of Israel*, 303–16.

[56] For the following see especially Rast, *Tradition History and the Old Testament*, 19–29.

[57] S. Mowinckel, *The Psalms in Israel's Worship*, trans. D. R. Ap-Thomas (New York: Abingdon, 1967), I:15–22.

[58] G. von Rad, *Deuteronomy: A Commentary* (Philadelphia: Westminster, 1966), 11–30.

cultic and centered in three passages containing cultic confessions—Deut 6:20–24; 26:5b–9; and Josh 24:2b–13.[59] Because these passages refer to the exodus, wilderness, and conquest (and not Sinai and the covenant), von Rad concluded that these must be the foundational traditions concerning Israel's cultic faith and celebration. The patriarchal and Sinai traditions, he said, were taken over from the Yahwist in later formulations.[60] Martin Noth, whose impact as a tradition-critic is enormous, attempted to demonstrate that there were five major themes around which the pentateuchal traditions developed and which eventually were interwoven.[61] These were deliverance from Egypt, settlement in the land, promise to the patriarchs, leadership in the wilderness, and revelation at Sinai. According to Noth these various themes were originally known only to individual tribes or tribal associations, which over a long period of time began to form a 12-tribe sacral confederation (an amphictyony, to use Noth's term). What had been separate and unrelated traditions then came to be the common property of all Israel. The Pentateuch as it now exists is, in Noth's view, the final collection and synthesis of these themes.

REDACTION CRITICISM[62]

If there is a synthesis of themes—or of the literature containing those themes—there must be a synthesizer, someone responsible for having arranged the material into its present form. That anonymous someone is, in the parlance of biblical scholarship, the redactor. The identification of the redactor's hand in accomplishing his work and the attempt to recover the boundaries of the pre-redacted texts is the task of redaction criticism.

The Talmud itself recognizes the existence of redaction when it speaks, for example, of "Hezekiah and his colleagues" who "wrote Isaiah, Proverbs, the Song of Songs and Ecclesiastes" (*Baba Bathra* 15a). Clearly the intent is not to claim authorship of these works by King Hezekiah and his scribes but to credit them with having edited or at least collected them into their present arrangement. This tradition of redaction is actually spelled out in the case of Proverbs which, in Prov 25:1, says: "These too are proverbs of Solomon, which the men of Hezekiah, king of Judah, copied." The verb rendered "copied" (*ʿtq*) can just as well mean "removed,"[63] that is, brought from one place to another. Thus Proverbs, as is commonly recognized, is an anthology of wisdom texts redacted into the present order.

This "older" understanding of redaction made the editor merely a compiler or even combiner of preexistent texts, without having any personal input in *changing* those texts in any manner. With the emergence of nineteenth-century source criticism, critics began to attribute to redactors much more independence and creativity. They began to see the hand of the redactor as reaching beyond the arrangement of the literature to making significant changes in it. This ranged all the way from composing verbal linkages between texts to statements of interpretation, interpolations, excisions, internal rearrangement of source texts, and complete rewriting of such documents to invest in them new ideological or theological content.

---

[59] Von Rad, "The Form-Critical Problem of the Hexateuch," *The Problem of the Hexateuch and Other Essays*, 1–78.

[60] Ibid., 53–54.

[61] M. Noth, *A History of Pentateuchal Traditions* (Englewood Cliffs, NJ: Prentice-Hall, 1972), 46–62.

[62] See Knierim, *The Hebrew Bible and Its Modern Interpreters*, 150–53; J. Nogalski, *Redactional Processes in the Book of the Twelve* (Berlin: de Gruyter, 1993); N. Perrin, *What Is Redaction Criticism?* (Philadelphia: Fortress, 1969); G. A. Rendsburg, *The Redaction of Genesis* (Winona Lake, IN: Eisenbrauns, 1986); Gail P. C. Streete, "Redaction Criticism," in *To Each Its Own Meaning*, 105–21; G. A. Yee, *Composition and Tradition in the Book of Hosea: A Redaction-critical Investigation* (Atlanta: Scholars, 1987).

[63] L. Koehler and W. Baumgartner, *Lexicon in Veteris Testamenti Libros* (Leiden: Brill, 1958), 748.

The implications of this for the inspiration and inerrancy of the Scriptures are most evident. Evangelicals insist that if redaction this broad in scope actually took place, it had to have done so with as much superintendence of the Holy Spirit as the initial composition of the original texts themselves. While this is theoretically possible, there is no biblical evidence to support it. In fact there is no evidence that such sweeping additions (or editions) ever occurred in the first place. To use the transparently clear indication of redactional activity in such anthological works as Psalms, Proverbs, and (perhaps) Ecclesiastes and in historiographical compositions such as Samuel, Kings, and Chronicles (or even Joshua through Kings, the so-called "Deuteronomic history") as proof for such activity throughout the biblical literature is to engage in question-begging. These works never profess to be from a single hand—in fact they contain inner witness to redaction—whereas the Pentateuch, the Prophets, and other sections yield redactional evidence only to those who look for it there. For example, for von Rad to describe the Yahwist (the alleged redactor of the "Hexateuch") as having "creative genius" and to credit him with achieving "one of the greatest accomplishments of all times in the history of thought"[64] is somewhat disingenuous, given the lack of objective evidence of a Yahwist to begin with. And to assert that the redactor (for such the Yahwist is) outweighs the author(s) of his texts in importance indicates the extent to which current redaction criticism has gone.

One would be cavalier to dismiss the reality and importance of redaction criticism where the biblical evidence clearly allows or even mandates it. However, to argue for its existence—and even necessity—on the basis of a certain critical presuppositional stance is neither methodologically sound nor theologically safe. As John Barton has noted, redaction criticism frequently is open to the charge of (1) exaggerating the importance of small details, attributing them incorrectly to redaction; (2) attempting to identify the raw materials with which the redactors worked; and (3) failing to recognize the impossibility of checking the accuracy of redactional reconstruction against any external controls.[65] It can be a method by which the sensitive Bible reader can grasp the importance of the arrangement of biblical texts to their meaning or, used without restraint, it can reduce the Bible to a collection of texts, no matter how well synthesized, that reflects only the theological viewpoint of the last redactors who worked them over.

CANONICAL CRITICISM[66]

Redaction criticism of the kind that sees the OT in its present form as the result of a massive redactionary process has resulted in an approach known popularly as "canonical" or "canon" criticism. According to its proponents—most notably Brevard S. Childs and James A. Sanders—what is most important in understanding the function and meaning of the OT texts is what exists, namely, the OT in its present (HB) canonical form. This is not to say that source-, form-, tradition-, and redaction-criticism are unimportant, but only that the sources on which they are based are irrecoverable and therefore all that is left is the canonical collection representing the final stage of redaction. As Sanders puts it, "The model canonical criticism sponsors

---

[64] G. von Rad, *Genesis: A Commentary*, trans. John H. Marks, OTL (London: SCM, 1961), 24.

[65] J. Barton, "Redaction Criticism," in ABC, 5:645.

[66] D. A. Brueggemann, "Brevard Childs' Canon Criticism: An Example of Post-Critical Naiveté," *JETS* 32 (1989): 311–26; M. C. Calloway, "Canonical Criticism," in *To Each Its Own Meaning*, 142–55; B. S. Childs, "The Exegetical Significance of Canon for the Study of the Old Testament" *VT*Sup (Leiden: Brill, 1978), 66–80; E. S. Gerstenberger, "Canon Criticism and the Meaning of *Sitz im Leben*," in *Canon, Theology, and Old Testament Interpretation*, ed. G. M. Tucker, D. L. Petersen, and R.R. Wilson (Philadelphia: Fortress, 1988), 20–31; J. H. Sailhamer, "The Canonical Approach to the OT: Its Effect on Understanding Prophecy," *JETS* 30 (1987): 307–15; J. A. Sanders, *Torah and Canon* (Philadelphia: Fortress, 1972).

. . . is that of the Holy Spirit at work all along the path of the canonical process: from original speaker, through what was understood by hearers; to what disciples believed was said; to how later editors reshaped the record, oral and written, of what was said; on down to modern hearings and understandings of the texts in current believing communities."[67]

Childs suggests that "the significance of the final form of the biblical text is that it alone bears witness to the full history of revelation. Within the Old Testament neither the process of the formation of the literature nor the history of its canonization is assigned an independent integrity. This dimension has often been lost or purposely blurred and is therefore dependent on scholarly reconstruction."[68]

These citations of two of its leading advocates are self-explanatory and provide an entrée into the rationale for and the leading ideas of the canonical-critical method. Though welcomed by many in the evangelical community who perceive it as a return to a precritical approach to the Bible, such a reading would be incorrect. Sanders is quick to note that "literalists and fundamentalists . . . should not be deceived into thinking that critical scholarship has come to its senses in repentance of its errant ways. Far from it. What is happening [in canonical criticism] is an extension of biblical criticism as it has developed to date."[69] Moreover, canonical criticism fails to take seriously the diachronic dimensions of the divine self-disclosure in the OT. In its desire to camp on the finished product it dismisses too easily the canon's own witness as to how it achieved its present shape.

Critical scholarship on the other hand perceives canonical criticism as having capitulated to a fundamentalist mind-set. John Barton, for example, while admitting that Childs cannot be called a fundamentalist, charges that the structure of his arguments bears an analogy to those used by fundamentalists.[70] In a serious misreading of Childs he asserts that Childs's method is not really canonical at all, for a canonical reading would be open to the obvious inconsistencies and incompatibilities in the biblical account and Childs's method is not. To the contrary, Childs sees in the development of the canonical process a constant struggle with conflicting viewpoints the sublimation of which was never entirely successful.[71] Yet there may be some justification for the criticism of the canonical method that it attempts to have its (critical) cake and eat it (the final canonical form) too.

THE NEW LITERARY (RHETORICAL) CRITICISM[72]

The past generation has witnessed the development of a plethora of new ways of addressing the nature and meaning of the OT as literature. It is impossible here to enter the discussion of

---

[67] J. A. Sanders, *Canon and Community* (Philadelphia: Fortress, 1984), xvii.

[68] B. S. Childs, *Introduction to the Old Testament as Scripture* (Philadelphia: Fortress, 1979), 75–77.

[69] Sanders, *Canon and Community*, 2.

[70] J. Barton, *Reading the Old Testament* (Philadelphia: Westminster, 1984), 98.

[71] Childs, *Introduction to the Old Testament as Scripture*, 76.

[72] Representative of the burgeoning literature in this area are the following: R. Alter, *The Art of Biblical Narrative* (New York: Basic, 1981); Barton, *Reading the Old Testament*, 140–57; A. Berlin, *Poetics and Interpretation of Biblical Narrative*, ISBL (Sheffield: Almond, 1983; repr., Winona Lake, IN: Eisenbrauns, 1994); D. J. A. Clines and J. C. Exum, "The New Literary Criticism," in *The New Literary Criticism and the Hebrew Bible*, ed. J. C. Exum and D. J. A. Clines, JSOTSup (Sheffield: JSOT Press, 1993), 11–25; D. A. Dorsey, "Can These Bones Live? Investigating Literary Structure in the Bible," *Evangelical Journal* 9 (1991): 11–26; P. R. House, ed., *Beyond Form Criticism: Essays in Old Testament Literary Criticism* (Winona Lake, IN: Eisenbrauns, 1992); D. M. Howard Jr., "Rhetorical Criticism in Old Testament Studies," *BBR* 4 (1994): 87–104; M. Kessler, "An Introduction to Rhetorical Criticism of the Bible: Prolegomena," *Semitics* 4 (1980): 1–27; T. Longman III, *Literary Approaches to Biblical Interpretation* (Grand Rapids: Zondervan, 1987); D. Patrick and A. Scult,

such methods (or even movements) as structuralism, text- versus reader-centered hermeneutics, or text as artifact, as important and interesting as these approaches might be. Rather "new literary" here suggests a reading of biblical texts that presupposes a communication linkage between their divine and human authors on the one hand, the reader on the other; and that is sensitive to their rhetorical functions, structures, and derivative meaning.

Like canonical criticism, this entrance into the literature concerns itself with texts as they stand and not as they may or may not have evolved into their present dimensions. Thus it is a logical extension in some ways of the canonical approach. On the other hand there has been a long and venerable history of "literary" readings of the Bible—readings that appreciate the Bible not only as the written Word of God but also as literature worthy of study as such. Robert Lowth,[73] J. G. Herder,[74] and G. B. Gray,[75] among a host of others, suggested decades ago that attention to the Scriptures as artistic works could yield not only an enhanced appreciation for the genius and beauty of their composition but also give exegetical and hermeneutical insights into the truths they communicate.

Recent renewal of interest in the "Bible-as-literature" movement is largely attributed to an article written by James Muilenburg in 1968 in which he coined the term "rhetorical criticism" to refer to the specific aspect of the new literary criticism under discussion here.[76] Seizing on some of the methods and proposals he brought to the fore, as well as those long practiced by both secular and biblical scholars, a new generation of critics has launched a massive program of reinvestigating the biblical texts as objective entities capable and worthy of being analyzed with every tool and skill available to rhetorical technique. The results are only now beginning to emerge, but it is well nigh a consensus among both critical and conservative scholars that untold benefits await its ongoing and more-refined practice.

Though his detractors should be heard and taken seriously, Muilenburg's program of rhetorical criticism must suffice for the present overview. First, he addressed method including making observations on the text (empirical data), identifying from the data certain stylistic devices (quantitative recovery), giving titles to these devices and explaining their meaning and/or function (qualitative recovery), and stating the meaning of the text consistent with the author's intent.

Next Muilenburg listed various devices that indicate text limitations. These include acrostics, breakup of stereotyped phrases, chiasm/inclusio, meter, refrain, repetition, and shifts of speaker or motif. Within major units one can also isolate inner substructures by still other devices such as alliteration, paronomasia, grammatical particles, pivot-pattern, and rhetorical questions.

The major benefits of this form of new literary criticism are (1) an appreciation of Old Testament texts as highly skilled, aesthetically pleasing *belles lettres*; (2) a recognition of the wholeness of texts once thought by older criticism to be composites or even today to be hopelessly at odds; (3) new or reinforced exegetical, hermeneutical, and theological ways of looking at texts and at relationships between texts; (4) explanations for the present arrangements of texts that

---

Rhetoric and Biblical Interpretation, JSOTSup (Sheffield: Almond, 1990); D. Robertson, *The Old Testament and the Literary Critic* (Philadelphia: Fortress, 1977); M. Sternberg, *The Poetics of Biblical Narrative* (Bloomington, IN: Indiana University Press, 1985); P. Trible, *Rhetorical Criticism* (Minneapolis: Fortress, 1994); P. K. Tull, "Rhetorical Criticism and Intertextuality," in *To Each Its Own Meaning,* 156–80; W. Wuellner, "Where Is Rhetorical Criticism Taking Us?" *CBQ* 49 (1987): 448–63.

[73] R. R. Lowth, *De Sacra Poesi Hebraeorum* (Lipsiae: Gottl. Weigel, 1815).

[74] J. G. Herder, *Vom Geist der Hebräischen Poesi,* 2 vols. (Dessau: N. p., 1782–83).

[75] G. B. Gray, *The Forms of Hebrew Poetry* (London: Hodder and Stoughton, 1915).

[76] J. Muilenburg, "Form Criticism and Beyond," *JBL* 88 (1969): 1–18.

otherwise appear to violate chronological, topical, or thematic sequences. There are, of course, risks in and abuses of the method, not least of which is the imposition of preconceived patterns on texts, forcing them to yield structures, functions, or meanings never intended by their authors. It is also possible for one to become so enthralled by the setting of the gem (i.e., the literary form) that one loses sight of the gem itself (the truth it communicates). However, properly used, so-called rhetorical criticism holds great promise as a God-honoring critical method.

CONCLUSION

The foregoing, while not an exhaustive treatment of the critical approaches to the OT, presents the dominant ones.[77] No one can deny that certain benefits have accrued from such endeavors, particularly in the areas of form and new literary criticism. Yet, these methods on the whole are founded on the Enlightenment mentality that (1) denies the verbal, plenary inspiration of the Bible; (2) rejects the notion of direct, propositional revelation; (3) insists on treating the biblical text as the product of human reflection on the acts of God in history and experience; and (4) assumes that the biblical record is not historically reliable but is a theological interpretation of real or imagined events by succeeding generations of Israelite traditionists. The OT thus is not the work of its self-ascribed authors, but in its present form it is the final edition of a centuries-long accumulation of texts and traditions that may or may not conform to the realities to which they testify. As research continues, however, it is becoming increasingly clear that the traditional (and biblical) understanding of the OT as the revelation of God to Israel rests on excellent literary, historical, and theological bases.

STUDY QUESTIONS

1. In modern biblical studies what is the most common understanding of the term "critical"?
2. What larger philosophical movement spawned historical critical thought and method?
3. Who was the seventeenth-century Jewish philosopher often referred to as the "father of higher criticism"?
4. What was Jean Astruc's contribution to the study of Genesis?
5. Describe briefly what is meant by JEDP.
6. Who formulated the hypothesis of JEDP in its final form?
7. Name at least one conservative scholar of the nineteenth century who resisted the critical hypotheses advocated by most OT scholars.
8. What is the principal argument in favor of the multiple authorship of Isaiah?
9. What is the best response to this argument?
10. What is the major critical issue relative to the book of Daniel?
11. What is meant by "Form Criticism"?
12. Briefly define "Tradition Criticism."
13. With what kind of modern criticism is Brevard Childs associated?
14. Who was mainly responsible for the so-called "Rhetorical Criticism"?
15. Define "chiasm."

---

[77] For a number of other modern literary methods see D. G. Firth and J. A. Grant, eds., *Words and the Word* (Downers Grove, IL: IVP Academic, 2008); D. B. Sandy and R. L. Giese Jr., ed., *Cracking Old Testament Codes* (Nashville: B&H, 1995); K. A. Mathews, "Literary Criticism of the Old Testament," in *Foundations for Biblical Interpretation*, ed. D. S. Dockery, K. A. Mathews, and R. B. Sloan (Nashville: B&H, 1994), 205–31.

FOR FURTHER STUDY

Adam, A. K. M. *What Is Postmodern Biblical Criticism?* Minneapolis: Fortress, 1995.

Dockery, D. S., K. A. Mathews, and R. B. Sloan, eds. *Foundations for Biblical Interpretation.* Nashville: B&H, 1994.

Gray, E. M. *Old Testament Criticism: Its Rise and Progress.* New York: Harper & Brothers, 1923.

Habel, N. C. *Literary Criticism of the Old Testament.* Philadelphia: Fortress, 1971.

Hahn, Herbert F. *The Old Testament in Modern Research.* Philadelphia: Fortress, 1966.

Haynes, S. R. and S. L. McKenzie, eds. *To Each Its Own Meaning: An Introduction to Biblical Criticisms and Their Application.* Louisville: Westminster John Knox, 1993.

House, P. R., ed. *Beyond Form Criticism: Essays in Old Testament Literary Criticism.* Winona Lake, IN: Eisenbrauns, 1992.

Knight, D. A. and G. M. Tucker, eds. *The Hebrew Bible and Its Modern Interpreters.* Philadelphia: Fortress, Scholars, 1985.

Krentz, Edgar. *The Historical-Critical Method.* Philadelphia: Fortress, 1975.

Levenson, J. D. *The Hebrew Bible, the Old Testament, and Historical Criticism.* Louisville: Westminster/John Knox, 1993.

Maier, G. *The End of the Historical-Critical Method.* St. Louis: Concordia, 1977.

McKenzie, S. L., and M. P. Graham, eds. *The Hebrew Bible Today: An Introduction to Critical Issues.* Louisville: Westminster John Knox, 1998.

Miller, J. M. *The Old Testament and the Historian.* Philadelphia: Fortress, 1976.

Rast, W. E. *Tradition History and the Old Testament.* Philadelphia: Fortress, 1972.

Robertson, D. *The Old Testament and the Literary Critic.* Philadelphia: Fortress, 1977.

Rogerson, J. W. *Old Testament Criticism in the Nineteenth Century.* Philadelphia: Fortress, 1984.

Sanders, J. A. *Canon and Community: A Guide to Canonical Criticism.* Philadelphia: Fortress, 1984.

Sandy, D. B. and Ronald L. Giese Jr. *Cracking Old Testament Codes.* Nashville: B&H, 1995.

Trible, P. *Rhetorical Criticism:Context, Method, and the Book of Jonah.* Philadelphia: Fortress, 1994.

Tucker, G. M. *Form Criticism of the Old Testament.* Philadelphia: Fortress, 1971.

CHAPTER 9

THE PRESENT STATE OF OLD TESTAMENT SCHOLARSHIP

MICHAEL A. GRISANTI

AFTER PROVIDING A broad overview of critical methodology in general, this chapter categorizes a number of the current critical methodologies under two broad headings: diachronic and synchronic (defined below). After summarizing and evaluating the most important or common of those approaches, the impact of "minimalism" on biblical scholarship is considered. The chapter concludes by offering some suggestions for an evangelical posture toward the OT.

OVERVIEW OF THE SCHOLARLY STUDY OF THE OLD TESTAMENT

Andrew Hill and John Walton have provided a chart that offers a helpful summary of the primary critical methodologies.[1] A few points of clarification will facilitate a correct understanding of the chart. First, "critical" methodologies do not necessarily refer to unacceptable or non-Evangelical approaches to the Bible. The terms "critical" and "criticism" refer to the "exercise of an expert sense of judgment about the text," and it should not be confused with "criticism" in the sense of making negative statements.[2] Also important is the contrast between "critical scholarship" and "evangelical scholarship." This does not imply that evangelical scholarship represents *uncritical* or *precritical* study of Scripture. It does signify that certain scholars make wide-scale use of a number of critical methodologies because they are not bound by the same set of beliefs about the nature of Scripture.[3] But conservatives do indulge in certain "critical" methodologies.

Second, evangelical scholars reject certain critical methodologies (as systems) because they sometimes represent a rejection of belief about the nature of Scripture (inspired and authori-

---

[1] A. E. Hill and J. H. Walton, *A Survey of the Old Testament*, 3rd ed. (Grand Rapids: Zondervan, 2009), 758. See chart below.

[2] Ibid., 753.

[3] Ibid., 754.

tative). For example because tradition history seeks to trace the reworking of Scripture over centuries until it reaches a written form, and it posits that the message of Scripture is changed many times during that reworking, tradition history offers little benefit to evangelicals *as a system*. Critics of this persuasion assume a long preliterary stage of Scripture, view human involvement as primary, and do not accept divine involvement in the process of inscripturation.

Third, evangelicals vary in their use of these methodologies. The term "evangelicals" describes individuals who embrace the inspiration and authority of the Bible and affirm that salvation from sin can be enjoyed only through faith that the work of Christ on Calvary is totally sufficient for the forgiveness of their sins. Yet some "evangelicals" make use of certain critical methodologies. For example some enthusiastically view Moses as the substantial author of the Pentateuch while other evangelicals see the Pentateuch as the work of a later editor who made use of Mosaic writings or traditions.[4]

Fourth, evangelicals can benefit from observations made by certain objectionable methodologies that might not be acceptable to them as a system. For example as a system form criticism operates on certain presuppositions about Scripture that are problematic to evangelicals. Attempts to conjecture the original *Sitz im Leben* of a given genre or subgenre, which often carries more significance than the content of the passage itself as it relates to the ultimate meaning of the passage, is problematic for evangelicals. However, form critics have offered many helpful observations about OT genres that contribute to a clearer understanding of OT passages.

In light of the above explanation, even evangelicals do not agree on what critical methodologies are acceptable or what aspects of a critical methodology offer legitimate benefits to the evangelical interpreter of Scripture. The following overview of critical methodologies suggests an evangelical posture toward OT criticism from one perspective only, recognizing that other models are also possible.

The following chart summarizes several critical methodologies according to two areas of focus. The column headings at the top of the chart pertain to the text itself. *Diachronic* approaches attempt to reconstruct the way the biblical text reached its current form. These approaches explore the history of the text and look for meaning in previous forms and settings of portions of the text. *Synchronic* approaches primarily seek meaning in the current or final form of the biblical text.[5] Proponents of these approaches view the text as self-sufficient, requiring no outside information in order to interpret it correctly. The headings on the left side of the chart identify the primary object of a given method: the author and his intended meaning, the text and the signals found in the text, or the reader and the way a reader can interact with the text in light of his current situation.

---

[4] See the Part 4 summary (pp. 163–69) below for examples of evangelicals who demonstrate this point.

[5] Proponents of synchronic approaches do not reject the idea that the biblical text had a history of development. They simply do not focus on that history or its process.

	Diachronic (Reading in light of historical development)	Intermediary	Synchronic (Reading in light of context)
Author Intended Meaning: Words/Ideas/Message	**Historical Criticism*** **Literary Criticism**	**Form Criticism** **Redaction Criticism**	
	Tradition Criticism	**Rhetorical Criticism**	Structuralism
Text Represented Meaning: Symbols/Structure	**Textual Criticism** **Source Criticism**		New Criticism **Canonical Criticism**
			Narrative Criticism
Reader Interpreted Meaning: Decoding Symbols/ Structure			Ideological Criticism Post-Structural Criticism **Reader-Response**

*Methodologies in bold copy are discussed in the following sections.

BRIEF SUMMARY OF CRITICAL METHODOLOGIES

The Diachronic

To repeat, this broad category seeks to reconstruct the way the OT text came into being (ultimately focusing on its final form). To avoid undue repetition, those approaches in this category that are summarized elsewhere will receive only brief attention here.

Text criticism seeks to recover the Hebrew text of the OT that most closely approximates the likely text-form of the original copies (*autographa*).[6] This methodology (also called "lower criticism") offers no intrinsic problems to the evangelical and in fact is an important part of the exegetical process.

Source criticism attempts to identify which units of the biblical writings belong to hypothetical sources and to analyze those sources.[7] The section of the Bible most often considered in light of source criticism is the Pentateuch. Though no one denies that biblical authors made use of preexisting literary sources as part of the process of composing biblical texts, evangelicals generally struggle with many of the assumptions behind source criticism.

---

[6] See chap. 7 in this volume for fuller discussion of the transmission and textual criticism of the Old Testament.

[7] See chap. 8 as well as Part 4 for a fuller explanation and evaluation of source criticism.

Form criticism attempts to get behind the literary sources to discern the original life setting that gave rise to the various genres of Scripture.[8] Ascertaining the life settings is a fundamentally important part of understanding the message of a biblical pericope. On the one hand form critics have provided helpful observations about biblical genres that add luster to a passage's meaning. However, they usually reject the idea of divine inspiration of texts, thus undermining their authority. Their attempt to reconstruct this life setting is quite subjective as well.

Redaction criticism attempts to identify the logic and motivation of authors and editors who gathered disparate sources together to generate the final form of the biblical texts.[9] Those who utilize this method generally accept the sources identified through source criticism, but they try to explain how the author/editor reworked, reshaped, or reinterpreted that material in the process. Redaction criticism draws on source criticism but is not identical to it. Certainly biblical writers included and arranged information from other sources with a purpose in mind. The larger context often helps make obvious the agenda or ideology of the biblical writer or editor. However, much of the work of redaction criticism is based on a low view of Scripture and a high confidence in the critic's ability to identify motives behind the changes the putative author or editor might have made.

Tradition (history) criticism functions between form and source criticism.[10] A tradition historian builds on the original setting for a given genre (identified by form criticism) and tries to unravel the layers of tradition that led to the written form of the biblical text (at which time source criticism came into play). The work of the tradition critic builds on the preliterary stage of the biblical text. It seeks to suggest the development of a tradition based on clues identified in a passage. This approach assumes that the Scriptures were passed along in a primarily oral form for centuries, during which time various communities reshaped the message or traditions of a given passage according to the varying needs of those communities. As a system, this methodology offers little help to the interpretation of Scripture.

The Synchronic

This category of historical-critical method focuses on the text itself without giving much attention to "outside" information.

Canonical criticism seeks to examine biblical texts in their final form.[11] Most nonevangelical proponents of this approach believe the idea that a given text has a long prehistory and is not divinely inspired or authoritative. Generally proponents of this method seek to understand a given passage as part of a book which is also part of the larger canon. They have little interest in historical, cultural, or archaeological contexts as important parts of the exegetical process.[12]

Rhetorical criticism focuses on biblical texts as they stand.[13] It gives attention to the structure and arrangement of a passage, put there intentionally by an author or editor, as tools to enhance the message of a text (and to assist the reader in grasping that message). Rhetorical

---

[8] See chap. 8 and Part 4 for a fuller explanation and evaluation of form criticism.

[9] See chap. 8 for a fuller explanation of redaction criticism.

[10] See Part 2, chap. 8, and Part 4 for a fuller explanation and evaluation of tradition criticism.

[11] See chap. 8 for a fuller explanation of canonical criticism.

[12] Evangelical scholar J. Sailhamer embraces a form of this method. For examples of his approach see his *Introduction to Old Testament Theology: A Canonical Approach* (Grand Rapids: Zondervan, 1995); and idem, *The Meaning of the Pentateuch: Revelation, Composition and Interpretation* (Downers Grove, IL: InterVarsity, 2009).

[13] See chap. 8 for a fuller explanation of rhetorical criticism. In Walton's chart above, he places rhetorical criticism in the intermediary category. It could just as well fit in the synchronic category because this method does not generally ask how a given passage came to be arranged in a certain way.

criticism considers the role of rhetorical tools such as acrostics, alliteration, inclusios, chiasms, refrains, repetition, and the like as they relate to a passage's meaning. This approach assumes that biblical writers employed literary craft or artistry as part of their God-given (and divinely guided) role. Most evangelical scholars make use of this helpful interpretive method.

REMAINING CRITICAL METHODOLOGIES

Though many other critical methodologies exist, only those that have made a significant impact on OT studies can be considered here. Like those treated above, these are categorized according to their diachronic or synchronic focus.

Diachronic Methodologies

Historical criticism. Though the historical-critical method serves as an umbrella term for all critical methodologies, the term "historical criticism" describes by itself a narrowly specific approach by which an attempt is made to reconstruct the events that lie behind the biblical narratives.[14] For example such an approach may seek to reconstruct what *actually* happened "behind" the biblical description of Israel's crossing of the Red Sea. It generally offers natural explanations for anything the Bible presents as divine intervention into history, and it tends to regard such passages as legendary or ideological (e.g., David fighting Goliath) while seeking to uncover the "historical kernel" located at the heart of the biblical construal. Also historical criticism regards the biblical text as a source for reconstructing the ancient past rather than as a literary text whose original meaning has intrinsic value or even divine authority.[15]

Literary criticism. This is a descriptive term that is defined in different ways.[16] In the nineteenth century it was another term for source criticism or the JEDP theory.[17] By the mid-twentieth century it referred to the "Bible as Literature" movement, which focused on the text's rhetorical elements and literary structure.[18] Since the latter part of the twentieth century, the term has been applied broadly to any attempt to understand biblical literature in accord with the interests of modern literary critics and theorists. It encompasses a number of critical methodologies including structuralism, narrative criticism, deconstruction, reception theory, reader-response criticism, and feminist criticism.[19] This type of literary criticism includes several basic features. First, though proponents recognize that the biblical stories were written for a certain purpose or function ("applied literature"), they seek to examine biblical literature as "pure literature."[20] That is, they may consider a given story as a good one, regardless of any alleged function for which it had been written.[21] Second, this kind of literary criticism is not viewed as superior to other methodologies; it is just different. Its proponents sometimes call it "agglutinative" in that two readings of a text that arise based on different critical methodologies are not mutually

---

[14] See E. Krentz, *The Historical-Critical Method* (Philadelphia: Fortress, 1975), 34–61.

[15] R. N. Soulen and R. K. Soulen, *Handbook of Biblical Criticism*, 3rd ed. (Louisville: WJK, 2001), 79.

[16] Ibid., 105.

[17] See chap. 8 and Part 4 for a fuller explanation and evaluation of source criticism. See also N. Habel, *Literary Criticism of the Old Testament* (Philadelphia: Fortress, 1971).

[18] Chap. 8 treats this methodology under the heading "The New Literary (Rhetorical) Criticism." See various representative resources for this methodology there.

[19] For an overview as well as examples of the varied methodologies under this broad category see the essays in J. C. Exum and D. J. A. Clines, eds., *The New Literary Criticism and the Hebrew Bible* (Valley Forge, PA: Trinity, 1993), and the essays and abundant bibliographies in *Methods of Biblical Interpretation* (Nashville: Abingdon, 2004), 147–208.

[20] For example rhetorical criticism is a method that treats the biblical accounts as "applied literature."

[21] D. Robertson, *The Old Testament and the Literary Critic* (Philadelphia: Fortress, 1977), 3.

exclusive.[22] Third, proponents of this broad approach define "truth" as "appropriateness." The biblical text creates a "narrative world" that the literary critic seeks to understand. The question of whether a story fits within the world created by that story is one of their primary concerns.[23] Fourth, the text is regarded as primarily an object, a product, not as a window into historical actuality.[24] Proponents are not concerned with whether a biblical event happened, but whether the narrative accomplishes its goal as a story. This version or phase of literary criticism (like those that preceded it) generally rejects God's involvement in the giving of Scripture to His people.[25] Biblical passages offer no intrinsic meaning, it is alleged, and whatever "meaning" one might glean from a passage through literary criticism is not truth nor is it exclusive in any fashion. According to this approach the biblical events described in the OT have no intrinsic historical value but are simply part of the narrative world created by a writer.

Synchronic Methodologies

Narrative criticism. Since the 1970s a number of scholars have defined, described, and applied *narrative criticism* to biblical studies (more so in the NT than in the OT originally).[26] Proponents of this approach affirm that understanding literary features like plot, characterization, and point of view are necessary to understanding the meaning of a passage.[27] Narrative criticism was part of a movement away from the idea that authorial intent should play a primary role in the interpretive process. Narrative critics generally view the biblical text as a piece of literature rather than as a text that has some larger meaning. They read biblical stories with insights drawn from the secular field of modern literary criticism. Their primary aim is to determine the effects the stories are expected to have on their audiences.[28] Although some narrative critics grant that biblical stories *may function* referentially as records of significant history, they focus on the narrative's function to fire the imagination of the readers.[29] For example W. Randolph Tate defines this methodology as the study of narratives, focusing not only on traditional narrative elements such as plot, setting, and characterization, but also on the role of the reader.[30] After the introduction and development of this approach,[31] a number of narrative critics devised reader-response criticism (see below). Like reader-response criticism, the narra-

---

[22] Ibid., 4, 11.

[23] Ibid., 11–12.

[24] D. J. A. Clines and J. C. Exum, "The New Literary Criticism," in *The New Literary Criticism and the Hebrew Bible*, 11.

[25] As will be seen below, some evangelicals advocate using literary approaches when interpreting Scripture. They seek to maintain a high view of Scripture as they apply customary rules of literature to biblical passages. Most proponents of literary criticism as a system are nonevangelical.

[26] For an overview of the history of narrative criticism from the perspective of a critic see R. C. Heard, "Narrative Criticism and the Hebrew Scriptures: A Review and Assessment," *RQ* 38 (1996): 29–43.

[27] D. W. Gunn, "Narrative Criticism," in *To Each Its Own Meaning: An Introduction to Biblical Criticisms and Their Application*, rev. ed., ed. S. L. McKenzie and S. R. Haynes (Louisville: WJK, 1999), 201.

[28] M. A. Powell, "Narrative Criticism," in *Dictionary of Biblical Interpretation*, ed. J. H. Hayes (Nashville: Abingdon, 1999), 2:201.

[29] Ibid. They make this comparison to emphasize this point: "Historical criticism treats biblical narratives as windows that enable readers to learn something about another time and place, while narrative criticism treats these same texts as mirrors that invite audience participation in the creation of meaning" (ibid., 202).

[30] W. R. Tate, *Interpreting the Bible: A Handbook of Terms and Methods* (Peabody, MA: Hendrickson, 2006), 231.

[31] Some examples of work by narrative critics include R. Alter, *The Art of Biblical Narrative* (New York: Basic, 1981); A. Berlin, *Poetics and Interpretation of Biblical Narrative* (Sheffield, Almond, 1983; repr., Winona Lake, IN: Eisenbrauns, 1994); M. Sternberg, *The Poetics of Biblical Narrative: Ideological Literature and the Drama of Reading* (Bloomington, IN: University of Indiana Press, 1985); S. Bar-Efrat, *Narrative Art in the Bible* (Sheffield: Almond, 1989); R. Alter and F. Kermode, eds., *The Literary Guide to the Bible* (Cambridge, MA: Harvard University Press, 1987); D. M. Gunn and D. N. Fewell, *Narrative in the Hebrew Bible* (Oxford: Oxford University Press, 1993).

tive critic assumes that the story does not exist autonomously within the text, but comes into being through the interaction between the text and the reader.[32]

Should evangelicals, who believe the biblical texts to be divinely inspired and authoritative, use narrative criticism as part of their interpretive toolbox? Carl F. H. Henry examined narrative criticism and concluded, "The narrative approach seems not fully befitting the historic Christian faith. . . . One discerns here an enchantment with the affective, a flight from history to the perspectival that enjoins no universal truth claims, a reflection of the revolt against reason, a reliance on 'symbolic' truth and imagination, and an interest in earthly theatre more than revealed theology."[33] It is valid to keep Henry's point in mind. As it was articulated by higher critics, narrative criticism rules out divine revelation, inspiration, and authority.[34] However, much of its methodology does not depend on antisupernatural assumptions.[35] Evangelical scholars have increasingly made use of narrative criticism in ways that have enhanced their understanding of God's message as communicated through biblical narrators.[36] When considering the viability of using this critical approach, one should ask, Were biblical writers *doing* literary art rather than writing narratives of theological significance or *using* literary art as a way of enhancing their communication of theological truth?[37]

Reader-response criticism. This is a literary approach to the Bible concerned primarily with the reader and the process of reading rather than with the author or the text as a self-contained unit.[38] Proponents of this approach view the reader[39] as the source of the meaning of a given text[40] or at least as having a share in the act of literary communication.[41] This contrasts with the approach that seeks to understand the author's world and his intended meaning, one to be found in the biblical text and that shares the same place and perspective of the biblical author.[42] Some evangelical scholars engage in this approach. For example Robert Morgan and John

---

[32] W. R. Tate, *Biblical Interpretation: An Integrated Approach*, 3rd ed. (Peabody, MA: Hendrickson, 2008), 335.

[33] C. F. H. Henry, "Narrative Theology: An Evangelical Appraisal," *TJ* 8 (1987): 19.

[34] See G. R. Osborne, *The Hermeneutical Spiral: A Comprehensive Introduction to Biblical Interpretation*, rev. ed. (Downers Grove, IL: InterVarsity, 2006), 212–16, for a number of weaknesses of narrative criticism.

[35] For example even a nonevangelical proponent of narrative criticism (M. Sternberg) argues strongly for authorial intent and for the importance of history; cf. *The Poetics of Biblical Narrative*.

[36] T. Longman III, *Literary Approaches to Biblical Interpretation* (Grand Rapids: Zondervan, 1987); S. D. Mathewson, *The Art of Preaching Old Testament Narrative* (Grand Rapids: Baker, 2002); Osborne, *The Hermeneutical Spiral*, 200–21; J. S. Duvall and J. D. Hays, *Grasping God's Word; A Hands-On Approach to Reading, Interpreting, and Applying the Bible*, 2nd ed. (Grand Rapids: Zondervan, 2005); R. B. Chisholm, *Interpreting the Historical Books: An Exegetical Handbook*, HOTE (Grand Rapids: Kregel, 2006); G. Schnittjer, *The Torah Story* (Grand Rapids: Zondervan, 2006); J. A. Beck, *God as Storyteller: Seeking Meaning in Biblical Narrative* (St. Louis, MO: Chalice, 2008); J. D. Hays, "An Evangelical Approach to Old Testament Narrative Criticism," *BSac* 166 (Jan–Mar 2009): 3–18.

[37] I have revised this question from a point made in Hill and Walton, *A Survey of the Old Testament*, 757.

[38] Soulen and Soulen, *Handbook of Biblical Criticism*, 156.

[39] Various subcategories of this approach describe the reader with different terms: real reader, implied reader, informed reader, ideal reader, optimal reader, and even super-reader. R. M. Fowler, "Who Is 'the Reader' in Reader Response Criticism," *Semeia* 31 (1985): 10, 15.

[40] W. R. Tate, *Interpreting the Bible: A Handbook of Terms and Methods* (Peabody, MA: Hendrickson, 2006), 303.

[41] As we will see below, some proponents of this approach give ultimate significance to the reader, while others coordinate the biblical text with the reader. For the latter group, the reader being the subject (acting upon the text) and the reader as object (being acted upon by the text) are not viewed as in opposition but as two sides of the coin. E. V. McKnight, *The Bible and the Reader: An Introduction to Literary Criticism* (Philadelphia: Fortress, 1985), 128.

[42] K. J. Vanhoozer, "The Reader in New Testament Interpretation," in *Hearing the New Testament: Strategies for Interpretation*, ed. J. B. Green (Grand Rapids: Eerdmans, 1995), 305.

Barton write, "Texts, like dead men and women, have no rights, no aims, no interests. They can be used in whatever way readers or interpreters choose."[43]

The author of a biblical text is regarded as dead and irrelevant to whatever meaning(s) the text might offer its reader. An evangelical approach to Scripture challenges Bible interpreters to leave their prejudices behind as much as possible. However, the reader-response approach declares that the death of the author "deregulates" interpretation.[44] So, this encouragement for readers to bring their aims and agendas with them has generated numerous "interested" (rather than disinterested) readings of the biblical text (feminist, Marxist, Freudian, liberation, etc.). Another important feature of this angle is that meaning is indeterminate.[45] Whatever a text might mean in one context, it may mean something different in another setting.[46] Some would even prefer dropping the term "meaning" altogether and speaking instead of what readers wish to do with a biblical text.[47]

This methodology encompasses a wide variety of subtheories. The three most common can be described with the phrases "reader over the text" (the most radical version), "reader with the text," and "reader in the text."[48] The first of these affirms that biblical texts have absolutely no intrinsic value apart from their use by a given reader in a particular community and context.[49] At the other end of the spectrum, certain proponents of this critical methodology find it useful to investigate a text's original meaning for its original audience. However, that investigation involves the application of higher criticism methodologies that reject the divine character of Scripture.[50] Most proponents of reader-response criticism subscribe to two fundamental premises. First, the meaning of a literary text does not reside within the text as a self-contained unit but is actualized or created by the interaction of the reader with the text. Second, the meaning of a text can differ from reader to reader (when a given story is read in different times, facing different circumstance, or for different purposes).[51] Most nonevangelical scholars (and some evangelicals) have made this approach one of several they employ.[52]

---

[43] R. Morgan with J. Barton, *Biblical Interpretation* (Oxford: Oxford University Press, 1989), 7.

[44] Vanhoozer, "The Reader in New Testament Interpretation," 305.

[45] Some proponents of this approach view their task as filling in the gaps left by the original author; i.e., finishing an unfinished meaning while drawing on signals in the text. Other proponents present the reader as the one who determines what to make of the text (ibid., 305–6).

[46] D. J. A. Clines, "Possibilities and Priorities of Biblical Interpreters in an International Perspective," *BI* 1 (1993): 78–82. Clines calls his approach "an end-user theory of interpretation" (ibid., 78).

[47] J. Stout, "What Is the Meaning of a Text?" *New Literary History* 14 (1982): 6.

[48] M. A. Powell, *What Is Narrative Criticism?* (Minneapolis: Fortress, 1990), 16. See also K. J. Vanhoozer, *Is There a Meaning in This Text? The Bible, the Reader, and the Morality of Literary Knowledge* (Grand Rapids: Zondervan, 1998), 151–54.

[49] E. V. McKnight, "Reader-Response Criticism," in *Dictionary of Biblical Interpretation*, 2:371. This more radical approach manifests itself in an interpretive movement called deconstruction (Powell, *What Is Narrative Criticism?* 17).

[50] Some call this version of the reader-response approach "audience criticism" (Soulen and Soulen, *Handbook of Biblical Criticism*, 15, 157).

[51] Ibid., 156–57. See Tate for his delineation of four assumptions that guide reader-response critics (*Interpreting the Bible*, 304–5).

[52] In his book on Isaiah 53 (*I, He, We and They: A Literary Approach to Isaiah 53* [Sheffield: JSOT Press, 1983]), D. J. A. Clines approaches this passage from four vantage points. In his view each vantage point generates distinct meanings that are mutually compatible. Clines also offers an example of this critical method in his explanation of Psalm 24 ("A World Established on Water [Psalm 24]: Reader-Response, Deconstruction and Bespoke Interpretation," in *The New Literary Criticism and the Hebrew Bible*, ed. J. Cheryl Exum and David J. A. Clines [Valley Forge, PA: Trinity, 1993], 80–83). In his appendix B, Tate provides an example of a reader-response analysis of the Gospel of Mark to illustrate this critical approach (*Interpreting the Bible*, 435–65).

Anthony Thiselton offers some significant warnings about the results of a reader-response approach to the Bible.[53] To him, if the biblical text does not significantly impact the reader, the historical Reformation (which plays such a primary role in evangelicalism) becomes nothing more than a dispute over alternative community lifestyles.[54] The reader-response approach rules out revelation, grace, and mercy as concrete truths. It changes the message of the cross into a linguistic construct of a tradition. And, it makes any and all doctrinal conclusions acceptable. Whatever is called "truth" is the belief that has the most readers or proponents.[55] Gordon Fee adds a few important points as well. First, if a variety of "meanings" are equally valid, there is no way to arbitrate between competing meanings.[56] Reader response also rejects the belief that there is one true God who revealed Himself to His creation in propositional terms. Second, if meaning lies only or primarily with the reader rather than in the text or with the author of the text, there is no possibility for the Christian community to hear God's message through sacred Scripture.[57]

Some evangelicals use reader-response criticism in their interpretation of Scripture, but none who label themselves as such employ the more radical version of this approach, one in which the reader creates meaning unilaterally. Some go so far as to contend that aspects of this approach must be part of proper interpretive methodology. For example John Barton, who places himself in the camp that believes that biblical texts have definite meanings, finds the "softer" version of reader-response criticism as intuitively convincing.[58] He suggests that through "creative transcriptions" words that *meant* one thing in one setting (and to one audience) can be made to *mean* something else in a different setting.[59] In their volume on hermeneutics William Klein, Craig Blomberg, and Robert Hubbard write about legitimate reader-response interpretation.[60] Although they are much more conservative than Barton, these authors contend that in a limited fashion biblical text readers do "construct" meaning.[61] They point to two examples that demonstrate for them this limited benefit of a reader-response approach: the way NT writers sometimes explain OT texts in ways not obvious in the OT texts themselves, and the varied interpretations on baptism and the millennium that exist among evangelical interpreters. They also say that "readers do not change an author's meaning, but different readers will understand it differently."[62] Although these writers seem to legitimize a limited use of this methodology, they seem to have confused different significances or interpretations with different meanings.

---

[53] A. C. Thiselton, *New Horizons in Hermeneutics* (Grand Rapids: Zondervan, 1992), 549–50.

[54] Ibid., 549.

[55] For further critique of a reader-response approach see Vanhoozer, *Is There a Meaning in This Text?* 148–95; and A. C. Thiselton, "Reader-Response, Hermeneutics, Action Models, and the Parables of Jesus," in *The Responsibility of Hermeneutics* by R. Lundin, A. C. Thiselton, and C. Walhont (Grand Rapids: Eerdmans, 1985), 79–113.

[56] G. D. Fee, *New Testament Exegesis: A Handbook for Students and Pastors*, 3rd ed. (Louisville: WJK, 2002), 182.

[57] Ibid., 184. Fee points out the self-contradictory nature of the fact that reader-response critics hope that their readers will understand and accept their intended meanings and do not authorize their readers to conclude whatever they might determine to be the meaning themselves (ibid., 183–84).

[58] J. Barton, "Thinking about Reader-Response Criticism," *ET* 113:5 (February 2002): 150–51.

[59] J. Barton, *The Nature of Biblical Criticism* (Louisville: WJK, 2007), 85. He also contends that since biblical texts have been used and reused numerous times, any attempt to fix an "original" meaning will likely fail (ibid., 79).

[60] W. W. Klein, C. L. Blomberg, and R. L. Hubbard, *Introduction to Biblical Interpretation*, rev. ed. (Nashville: Thomas Nelson, 1993), 192–201.

[61] Ibid., 192–93.

[62] Ibid., 193. Earlier in the same volume these authors write; "Original *meaning* remains fixed, even as contemporary *significance* varies" (ibid., 75, italics added).

The fact that a solid evangelical approach to Scripture is author- and text-focused does not mean the reader of Scripture is a totally passive participant. Instead, a reader should be active and passive. Interpretation always involves the interpreter. As K. J. Vanhoozer points out, "by scanning the page and deciphering the marks, they receive something not of their own making."[63] Readers of Scripture must recognize that they inhabit a different world from that of the writers of Scripture. The interpretive process involves the engagement of two horizons, that of the ancient writer and that of the modern reader.[64] Thus, the meaning of a biblical passage (from the perspective of its world) must be grasped before its significance and application can be appropriated.

Summary

In addition to the critical methodologies summarized in chap. 8, four others have been brought to the fore here, two under the rubric diachronic and two under synchronic. Of the former two, historical criticism seeks to get "behind" a historical event in order to reconstruct what *actually* happened. Obviously, this approach does not attribute historical credibility to the biblical text as it stands. The second, literary criticism, represents the attempt to apply theories of modern literary analysis to the OT. A focus on the Bible's literary features is commendable, but this methodology looks at the function of a story without recognizing any divine authority in the message.

The two synchronic approaches, narrative and reader-response, are related in such a manner that one could say that narrative criticism is the womb that gave birth to reader-response criticism. In its standard presentation, narrative criticism views biblical accounts as a piece of literature rather than a vehicle for divine truth. Because it gives attention to literary signals included by a biblical author as part of the presentation of his divinely occasioned message, evangelicals can benefit from several observations of narrative critics. Since reader-response approaches separate "meaning" and "truth" from the author and text and primarily or exclusively connect them with the reader, it offers little assistance to the conservative student of Scripture.

THE DEVELOPMENT AND IMPACT OF BIBLICAL "MINIMALISM"

Brief Overview

An approach to the OT that also deserves attention has been called "minimalism" or "historical revisionism." Since the mid-1970s a number of influential scholars have demonstrated a throughgoing skepticism toward the historical validity of the OT.[65] They suggest that the OT books were composed no earlier than the exile, and most likely in the Persian (c. fifth to third centuries BC)[66] or Hasmonean (c. 166–64 BC)[67] period. Almost all minimalists totally reject the OT as a credible source for historical reconstruction. For example, Niels Lemche proposes that one should regard the biblical account "like other legendary materials, as essentially ahis-

---

[63] Vanhoozer, *Is There a Meaning in This Text?* 149.

[64] A. Thiselton, *The Two Horizons: New Testament Hermeneutics and Philosophical Description with Special Reference to Heidegger, Bultmann, Gadamer, and Wittgenstein* (Grand Rapids: Eerdmans, 1980), 15.

[65] Most of the key minimalist scholars are professors at the University of Copenhagen in Denmark (e.g., G. W. Ahlström, N. P. Lemche, and T. Thompson) and Sheffield University in England (e.g., P. Davies and K. Whitelam).

[66] P. Davies dates most of the OT to the Persian period (*In Search of "Ancient Israel,"* JSOTSup 1 [Sheffield: Sheffield Academic, 1992], 86–89).

[67] J. Strange, "The Book of Joshua: A Hasmonean Manifesto?," in *History and Traditions of Early Israel: Studies Presented to Eduard Nielsen, May 8th, 1993,* ed. A. Lemaire and B. Otzen, VTSup 50 (Leiden: Brill, 1993), 136–41; G. Garbini, *History and Ideology in Ancient Israel* (New York: Crossroad, 1988), 132.

torical, that is, as a source which only exceptionally can be verified by other information."[68] Thomas Thompson affirms that "not only is the Bible's 'Israel' a literary fiction, . . . [w]e can now say with considerable confidence that the Bible is not a history of anyone's past."[69] The following are a few comments illustrating minimalist thinking. "The writers of the Hebrew Scriptures knew little or nothing about the origin of Israel. . . . The period under discussion [i.e., the scriptural period], therefore, does not include the periods of the patriarchs, exodus, conquest, or judges, as devised by the writers of the Scriptures. These periods never existed."[70] Lemche adds that the Bible presents a situation "where Israel is not Israel, Jerusalem is not Jerusalem, and David not David. No matter how we twist the factual remains from ancient Palestine, we cannot have a biblical Israel that is at the same time the Israel of the Iron Age."[71] In fact about the only thing shared by biblical and historical Israel is the name of the god Yahweh.[72] The people of ancient Palestine occupied history in a way that totally contrasts with that presented in the Bible. For Lemche biblical Israel is constructed in biblical literature (i.e., a literary reality and not a historical reality) while that same literature tells almost nothing credible about the Israel of the Iron Age. In a more recent volume John Van Seters suggests that the biblical story of David is a saga composed in the late Persian period.[73] Although he regards these accounts as a beautifully crafted and highly realistic portrayal of a typical ANE monarch of that time, those accounts have little to do with history.[74] According to Van Seters, in contradiction to the earlier version of the David story by the Deuteronomic historian (who had presented a completely idealized David as the king and founder of a unified state of the people of Israel), the writer of the saga in the Bible undercuts that ideology and describes David and his heirs (including Solomon) as rulers unfit for rule. The saga has nothing to do with history but is part of a battle between ideologies.

Brief Response

Scholars from numerous perspectives have criticized and in some cases rejected the minimalist perspective. This negative reaction includes liberal (Jewish and Protestant) scholars[75] as

---

[68] N. P. Lemche, *Early Israel: Anthropological and Historical Studies on the Israelite Society before the Monarchy*, VTSup (Leiden: Brill, 1985), 415.

[69] T. L. Thompson, *The Mythic Past: Biblical Archaeology and the Myth of Israel* (New York: Basic, 1999), xv.

[70] R. B. Coote, *Early Israel: A New Horizon* (Minneapolis: Fortress, 1990), 2–3.

[71] N. P. Lemche, *The Israelites in History and Tradition* (Louisville: WJK, 1998), 166.

[72] Ibid. However, according to Lemche not even the character or locale of that god is the same.

[73] J. Van Seters, *The Biblical Saga of King David* (Winona Lake, IN: Eisenbrauns, 2009), 345–60.

[74] With regard to the Tel Dan Stele that cites "the house of David" (A. Biran and J. Naveh, "An Aramaic Stele Fragment from Tel Dan," *IEJ* 43 [1993]: 81-98; idem, "The Tel Dan Inscription: A New Fragment," *IEJ* 45 [1995]: 1–18), Van Seters seems to assume (with little comment) that this stele refers to some David other than the king of Israel described in 1 and 2 Samuel. Van Seters suggests that the deuteronom historian added this reference to a David as he created his history of Israel (*The Biblical Saga of King David*, 230). One example of a liberal scholar's critique of the contortions minimalists have gone through to dismiss the relevance of this inscription to the general historicity of the biblical historical accounts is B. Halpern, "Erasing History: The Minimalist Assault on Ancient Israel," in *Israel's Past in Present Research*, ed. V. P. Long (Winona Lake, IN: Eisenbrauns, 1999), 415–26.

[75] J. M. Miller, "Is It Possible to Write a History of Israel without Relying on the Hebrew Bible?" in *The Fabric of History: Text, Artifact and Israel's Past*, ed. D. V. Edelman, JSOTSup 127 (Sheffield: Sheffield Academic, 1991), 93–102.; C. Isbell, "Minimalism: the Debate Continues (Part 1)," *JBQ* 32 (July–Sept 2004): 143–47; idem, "Minimalism: the Debate Continues (Part 2)," *JBQ* 32:4 (Oct–Dec 2004): 211–23; W. G. Dever, *What Did the Biblical Writers Know, and When Did They Know It? What Archaeology Can Tell Us about the Reality of Ancient Israel* (Grand Rapids: Eerdmans, 2001); idem, *Who Were the Early Israelites, and Where Did They Come From?* (Grand Rapids: Eerdmans 2003).

well as evangelical scholars.[76] The following are a few of the reasons proposals offered by mini-malists are not compelling. First, they operate with a "hermeneutics of suspicion" in which they assume that the biblical text is erroneous and unreliable until it is proven correct by some independent means of verification. At the same time, they regard their broad conclusions about the biblical accounts to be convincing and accurate. For example Van Seters rejects the sug-gestion of Halpern that 2 Samuel 8 was the product of David's own scribes and was therefore credible history. He rejects Halpern's suggestion because he (Van Seters) has already demon-strated that these "historical" accounts are nothing but fictitious compositions.[77] Second, since biblical texts involve the intervention of a deity and have an ideology or theology, they have no value for historical reconstruction. For example Ahlström writes, "Since the biblical text is concerned primarily with divine actions, which are not verifiable, it is impossible to use the exodus story as a source to reconstruct the history of the Late Bronze and Early Iron I periods. The text is concerned with mythology rather than with a detailed reporting of historical facts. As soon as someone 'relates' a god's actions or words, mythology has been written."[78] Thus, the Bible, which describes God's intervention in human affairs, is methodologically ruled out as a reliable source for reconstructing actual history. Third, though minimalists suggest that they view archaeological data as objective and untainted, they fail to realize that most sites offer only sketchy information without literary artifactual evidence (as opposed to biblical literature).[79]

SUMMARY

Though minimalist scholars represent a minority of biblical scholarship, their conclusions have impacted the world of biblical scholarship. Scholars who regard themselves as maximalists (even though they may be theologically liberal) are more reticent to write about the credibility of the biblical presentation of history. In light of the loud and sweeping statements made by minimalists in general, the larger population has even less confidence in the credibility of the OT as it stands. OT scholars must indeed be careful about overstating what is clearly estab-lished by artifactual evidence. And, they should not shy away from affirming confidence in the message and history of the Bible in general and the OT in particular.

EVANGELICAL POSTURE TOWARD THE TEXT AND ITS STUDY

In light of what the preceding chapters have addressed, there exist many minefields through which the OT interpreter must navigate. What are the methodologies totally acceptable to evangelicals, which offer some helpful observations, and do some offer little to nothing of

---

[76] Some helpful summaries and evaluations of minimalism by evangelicals include E. M. Yamauchi, "The Current State of Old Testament Historiography," in *Faith, Tradition, and History: Old Testament Historiography in Its Near Eastern Context*, ed. A. R. Millard, J. K. Hoffmeier, and D. W. Baker (Winona Lake, IN: Eisenbrauns, 1994), 21–36; D. M. Howard Jr., *Joshua*, NAC (Nashville: B&H, 1998), 40–46; G. H. Reid, "Minimalism and Biblical History," *BSac* 155 (Oct–Dec 1998): 394–410; K. L. Younger Jr., "Early Israel in Recent Biblical Scholarship," in *The Face of Old Testament Studies: A Survey of Contemporary Approaches*, ed. D. W. Baker and B. T. Arnold (Grand Rapids: Baker, 1999), 185–91; K. A. Kitchen, *On the Reliability of the Old Testament* (Grand Rapids: Eerdmans, 2003), 450–72.

[77] Van Seters, *The Biblical Saga of King David*, 230. It is almost like saying, "I said that it was fiction, so any view that says otherwise is obviously wrong."

[78] G. Ahlström, *Who Were the Israelites?* (Winona Lake, IN: Eisenbrauns, 1986), 46.

[79] Howard points out that the discovery of the library at Ebla revolutionized our understanding of their life and culture (*Joshua*, 44). Before that discovery, only the barest of details were known.

eternal value to the interpreter of Scripture? After the summation of some basic guidelines, attention will turn to the text of the OT directionally ("behind," "within," and "in front of").[80]

Fundamental Guidelines. Among other bedrock guidelines to assist the OT student to mine the rich, eternal truths found therein are four foundational suggestions. First, the divine inspiration of the inerrant text of Scripture, gives the message of the OT authority and infallibility. This theological belief pushes toward as well as away from various methodologies and interpretive conclusions offered by certain scholars. Second, the historical, cultural, and archaeological context of biblical passages must be noted. Those did not emerge in a vacuum; instead they depend on the context of an original setting, a factor essential to the understanding of any application and relevance to a modern audience. Part of this contextual awareness deals with the larger ANE world in which the Bible is situated. As spelled out in chaps. 2–4 of this volume, that world and literature are quite distinct from what one finds in the OT. The two must not be equated. However, numerous points of similarity do exist between those two "worlds," and those ANE factors can assist in interpreting the OT text. The degree of similarity that an interpreter identifies and the way that similarity impacts exegesis generates some of the interpretive variety even within evangelicalism, let alone the larger world of scholarship. Third, attention must be given to which methods enhance the Bible's inspiration and authority and which ones undercut it. If a specific feature of a methodology is based on an antisupernatural assumption, then it affords no value. However, if a given methodology does not spring from a flawed bibliology, it can offer assistance to the interpreter of the OT. Fourth, along with the fact that the OT was composed by many prophetic authors over a period of about 1,000 years, it is important to recognize that linguistic, geographic, cultural, and related adjustments may have been introduced into the text of Scripture by other prophetic figures before the OT reached its final form (see chap. 5 of this volume).

Summary of Directional Approaches to the Text

A serious approach to the OT calls for careful attention to issues *"behind" the text*. This first includes awareness of the historical, cultural, and archaeological context of a passage along with similarities to and differences from the ANE world. More subjectively, some suggest that source criticism, form criticisms, and tradition history assist the biblical scholar in identifying the process through which the Bible came into being. Other critical methodologies also attempt to recreate the sociological and anthropological background for biblical texts as well. In general, this latter group offers little help to evangelicals. As stated elsewhere, that does not rule out the importance of recognizing that biblical authors may have used preexisting sources or that they arranged some of their writings in accord with common patterns or genres.

Any reconstruction of the situation "behind" the text of the OT is based on sketchy information and involves a degree of subjectivity. Value is to be gained from considering concrete information about the culture and history behind a passage. However, the methodologies in the second category increase in their subjectivity and significantly decrease in any objective value that they might offer in relation to the meaning of OT texts.

"Within" the text methods focus on what is actually written in the extant, biblical text. In addition to customary grammatical-historical exegesis, this involves a version of narrative criticism that operates under the acceptance of the Scriptures as inspired, inerrant, and authoritative.

---

[80] R. R. Lessing presents these three directional approaches to the biblical text as part of his summary of critical views of the prophet Amos (*Amos*, Concordia Commentary [St. Louis: Concordia, 2009], 6–8).

Based on what may be gleaned from the OT by working behind and within the text, one can then focus on issues *"in front" of the text*. Based on what a biblical passage *means*, it is possible to consider the *significance* and *application* of that text to a modern situation and audience. In general the determination of a passage's modern significance draws heavily on careful attention to its original setting. For example a prophetic oracle spoken by God to rebellious Israel that promises national destruction because of injustice and social inequity does not become a direct exhortation to a modern people, promising their destruction as well.

CONCLUSION

The world of OT scholarship today presents the student of the Bible various promises as well as pitfalls. Scholars today have built on the work of scholars of previous centuries. Thus by means of a greater awareness of ANE literature in general it is possible to have a clearer idea of literary and genre tools used by biblical authors and to communicate with greater clarity, vividness, and potential impact the message God gave through them. As they wrote, they provided narrative and rhetorical signals that aid readers in comprehending their message.

Besides these positive contributions, critical scholars continue their rejection of the divinely authorized message of the Bible. Many of their methodologies assume that God was not involved in revealing His message to His people through prophetic spokesmen (revelation) or that the Holy Spirit superintended the process through which these prophets wrote down that message (inspiration). In light of those important assumptions, observations made by proponents of these methodologies as well as the methodologies themselves offer little assistance to the evangelical interpreter. The task of an evangelical interpreter is to comprehend the biblical text as the God-given message it is. Evangelical interpreters can benefit from critical methodologies that are not integrally based on antisupernatural assumptions. And evangelicals must discard those methodologies based on a rejection of divine revelation and inspiration.

Part 4

THE PENTATEUCH

Michael A. Grisanti

T HE TERM "PENTATEUCH" derives from the Greek *pentateuchos*, literally, "five implements," following the Jewish designation, "the five-fifths of the Law."[1] The Greek term was apparently popularized by the Hellenized Jews of Alexandria, Egypt, in the first century AD. The Jewish canon designates the five books of the Pentateuch as the "Torah."

MODERN SCHOLARSHIP AND THE COMPOSITION OF THE PENTATEUCH

According to Gordon I. Wenham, studies on the Pentateuch seem to have arrived at a comfortable consensus by 1970, and though major challenges had till then been offered to the documentary hypothesis, those had been largely forgotten and JEDP still served as a badge of academic respectability.[2] However, since 1970 cracks have begun to appear in this apparently solid wall, ranging from suggesting minor revisions to a total rejection of the approach. A majority of scholars still regard the documentary hypothesis as the "default" understanding of the OT,[3] but the model is held much more tentatively than before. Wenham summarizes

---

[1] R. K. Harrison, *Introduction to the Old Testament* (Grand Rapids: Eerdmans, 1969), 495.

[2] G. J. Wenham, "Pondering the Pentateuch: The Search for a New Paradigm," in *The Face of Old Testament Studies: A Survey of Contemporary Approaches*, ed. D. W. Baker and B. T. Arnold (Grand Rapids: Baker, 1999), 116. R. Rendtorff has also written about the widespread acceptance of the documentary hypothesis at institutions of higher learning: "Current international study of the Pentateuch presents at first glance a picture of complete unanimity. The overwhelming majority of scholars in almost all countries where scholarly study of the Old Testament is pursued, take the documentary hypothesis as the virtually uncontested point of departure for their work; and their interest in the most precise understanding of the nature and theological purposes of the individual written sources seems undisturbed" (*The Problem of the Process of Transmission in the Pentateuch*, JSOTSup [Sheffield: JSOT Press, 1990], 101).

[3] C. Westermann cites numerous scholars who still maintain much of the JEDP theory (*Genesis 1–11: A Commentary*, trans. J. J. Scullion [Minneapolis: Augsburg, 1984], 569–73). For example O. Kaiser affirms that form criticism and tradition-historical method "not only presuppose the results of literary criticism, but in their turn can contribute a clarification of the literary-critical evidence" (*Introduction to the Old Testament: A Presentation of Its Results and Problems*, trans. J. Sturdy [Minneapolis: Augsburg, 1975], 42). Westermann correctly observes that this observation implies that the new methodologies have left literary criticism "completely unscathed" (*Genesis 1–11: A Commentary*, 578–80). Numerous scholars regard the divine name criterion for discerning sources in the Pentateuch as totally acceptable (ibid., 1–11, 572).

the situation well: "Today there is . . . no consensus. 'Every man does what is right in his own eyes.'"[4]

The background to the rise of the historical-critical method is explored elsewhere (chap. 9) so all that remains to do here is to sample the views of two so-called "minimalists" and then the approaches of two leading contemporary critical scholars, Rolf Rendtorff and R. N. Whybray.

Thompson, Van Seters, and "Minimalism"

A growing group of scholars are offering another proposal about the authorship of the Pentateuch (and other OT books as well). They are designated "minimalists" by many because they accept little that is found in the OT as historical or credible.[5] Andrew Hill and John Walton provide a helpful summary of this proposal: "A group of editors collected and arranged Hebrew stories, folktales, and other literary materials and traditions (oral and written) into the five books of the Pentateuch during the Babylonian exile and postexilic periods of Hebrew history. The traditions collected are considered largely nonhistorical and shaped by later editors for specific religious and nationalistic purposes."[6] So, students of the Bible should approach the Pentateuch with a certain degree of skepticism because they cannot trust the sources or the motivations of the editors. In this view the Pentateuch is a thoroughly late composition with respect to both the time of its writing and the traditions it preserves. Since the pentateuchal traditions have been so thoroughly reshaped, they are not reliable for reconstructing Israel's history.[7]

John Van Seters[8] and Thomas Thompson[9] have introduced a fresh paradigm for understanding the Pentateuch. Van Seters rejects most of the traditional criteria for source analysis (except for alleged "doublets") and proposes that the books of the Pentateuch should be understood as ideological fiction rather than history.[10] In his view the Yahwist lived and wrote in the exilic period, creating Israel's history by drawing on the mythology and history of that time, while the Elohist lived in the postexilic period.[11] Like both Wellhausen and Vatke before him, Van Seters affirms that the entire Pentateuch (laws and narrative) were based on and written after the prophets (by about 300 BC).[12]

---

[4] Wenham, "Pondering the Pentateuch," *The Face of Old Testament Studies*, 119. R. N. Whybray also concludes: "There is at the present moment no consensus whatever about when, why, how, and through whom the Pentateuch reached its present form, and opinions about the dates of composition of its various parts differ by more than five hundred years" (*Introduction to the Pentateuch* [Grand Rapids: Eerdmans, 1995], 12–13).

[5] As a concrete approach minimalism developed, in part, in the wake of the work of Van Seters, Thompson, and others. When Van Seters and Thompson wrote about the historicity of the patriarchs and the composition of the Pentateuch, minimalism was not recognized as an identifiable approach to the OT.

[6] A. E. Hill and J. H. Walton, *A Survey of the Old Testament*, 3rd ed. (Grand Rapids: Zondervan, 2009), 768.

[7] Van Seters and Thompson are examples of minimalists.

[8] J. Van Seters, *Abraham in History and Tradition* (New Haven, CT: Yale University Press, 1975); idem, *Prologue to History: The Yahwist as Historian in Genesis* (Louisville: WJK, 1992); idem, *The Life of Moses: The Yahwist as Historian in Exodus–Numbers* (Louisville: WJK, 1994).

[9] T. L. Thompson, *The Historicity of the Patriarchal Narratives: The Quest for the Historical Abraham*, BZAW (New York: de Gruyter, 1974).

[10] Ibid., 120–22.

[11] Ibid., 104–22.

[12] Ibid., 304–8. Van Seters applies his approach to the entire Pentateuch (*The Pentateuch: A Social-Science Commentary* [New York: T&T Clark, 2004]). He also reaffirms his belief that the Pentateuch reached its completion in the Hellenistic/Maccabean period as a result of the religious control enjoyed by the priests in Jerusalem (ibid., 213).

Rolf Rendtorff

Rendtorff offered a direct challenge to the documentary hypothesis by disputing the general consensus that source criticism and form and tradition criticism are compatible.[13] He also pointed out a number of inconsistencies in the way scholars explain their version of source analysis[14] as well as the inconsistent use of certain linguistic arguments to assign material to a particular source.[15] He rejected the idea that two different authors, a Yahwist and Elohist, generated continuous and coherent documents as part of the composition of the Pentateuch.[16] Although he grants the existence of smaller text units, he focuses on larger units that eventually made up the Pentateuch. He suggests that these larger units were reworked theologically over time by various individuals.[17] The Deuteronomist editor was finally responsible for producing the overall shape of the Pentateuch.[18]

R. N. Whybray

Drawing on Rendtorff and Van Seters, Whybray offers several primary objections to the documentary hypothesis. First, he argues that repetition as well as varying literary style does not necessarily mean that different original sources existed. Numbers of ancient documents make use of these "features for aesthetic and literary purposes."[19] It does seem odd that early writers of the original sources totally avoided repetition and any changes in literary style while the later writers and editors were glad to tolerate those tendencies.[20] Second, Whybray rejects the suggestion that each alleged source document manifests a single style, purpose, and point of view or theology as well as an unbroken narrative thread.[21] Recognizing that the Pentateuch is a unified, integrated work, he concludes that it had a single author who composed it no earlier than the sixth century BC.[22] One of the factors behind this conclusion is Whybray's assertion that there are almost no references to the Pentateuch in preexilic writings.[23] In contrast to that, in Second-Temple Judaism the consensus is that Moses is the author of the Law. This author sought to forge a national identity for the Israelites by drawing on a loose collection of sources, but especially by inserting his own imaginative reconstructions.[24]

In the latter part of the twentieth century a host of critical scholars have perpetuated a revised version of the documentary hypothesis (source criticism). In addition to this long-standing view, scholars have pursued form- and tradition-history criticism as a way of explaining how the OT reached its written form. Some of them utilize these methods in conjunction with source criticism, while others view them as totally incompatible and have rejected the source-critical model as they have offered different models for explaining the composition of the Pentateuch.

---

[13] R. Rendtorff, *The Problem of the Process of Transmission in the Pentateuch*, trans. J. J. Scullion (Sheffield: JSOT Press, 1990), 11–12, 24–31.

[14] Ibid., 28–29, 101–17.

[15] Ibid., 119–36.

[16] Ibid., 108–36.

[17] Ibid., 82–83.

[18] Ibid., 203.

[19] R. N. Whybray, *The Making of the Pentateuch* (Sheffield: JSOT Press, 1987), 130. See also idem, *Introduction to the Pentateuch*, esp. 12–27, 133–43.

[20] Whybray, *The Making of the Pentateuch*, 49–50.

[21] Ibid., 130.

[22] Ibid., 221–42.

[23] Ibid., 48–49.

[24] Ibid., 225–30.

LATE TWENTIETH CENTURY EVANGELICAL SCHOLARSHIP ON THE COMPOSITION OF THE PENTATEUCH

Evangelical scholars of many persuasions have offered a much different view of the composition of the Pentateuch alongside the critical views summarized above.[25] Once again, only representative views and proponents receive attention in this brief overview.

Biblical Information

Although the book of Genesis contains no statements of authorship, its presence in the Torah implies Mosaic involvement. In addition to abundant references in the Pentateuch that associate the Torah with Moses, the NT refers to the biblical teaching on circumcision (found in Genesis) as from Moses (John 7:22–23; Acts 15:1). It is also true that early Jewish and Christian sources manifest an almost uncontested acceptance of Mosaic authorship of the Pentateuch.[26] Philo,[27] Josephus,[28] various NT passages (e.g., Luke 24:27), sections of the Talmud (*b. Sanh.* 21b–22a; *b. B. Bat.* 14b), and Mishnah (*m. 'Abot* 1:1) seem to assume Mosaic authorship.

Other Old Testament passages refer to these books or a passage in them as "the Book of Moses" (2 Chr 25:4; 35:12; Neh 13:1); "the Law of Moses" (1 Kgs 2:3; 2 Kgs 23:25; 2 Chr 23:18; 30:16; Ezra 3:2; 7:6; Dan 9:11,13; "the instruction of Moses" (Mal 4:4); "book of the Law of Moses" (Josh 8:31–32; 23:6; 2 Kgs 14:6; Neh 8:1); "this book" (2 Kgs 22:13; 23:3); or "the book" (2 Kgs 22:8,16; 23:24; Neh 8:5). The preface of *Ecclesiasticus* (2nd century BC) refers to the "Law and the Prophets." Various NT books refer to the entire OT as "the Law and the Prophets" (Matt 7:12; 22:40), "Moses and [all] the prophets" (Luke 16:31; 24:27), or "Moses, the Prophets, and the Psalms" (Luke 24:44). God also commanded Moses to record certain historical events (Exod 17:14; Num 33:2) and laws (Exod 24:4; 34:27), as well as a song (Deut 31:22).

Primary Evangelical Views

The major views proposed by evangelicals fall into three categories. The first two present Moses as the author, and the third emphasizes the anonymous nature of Genesis (and the Pentateuch). All these proponents view Genesis as inspired Scripture with an infallible message. Even those who embrace the second view recognize that it is a complicated question.[29]

Moses is the exclusive author. Held now by a minority of evangelicals, this claim contends that Moses penned every word in the Pentateuch, including Deuteronomy 34.[30]

Moses is the substantial author. Although proponents of this position do not agree on exactly how much non-Mosaic material occurs in the Pentateuch[31] and the degree or purpose of post-

---

[25] A mere sampling of these resources include: E. W. Hengstenberg, *Dissertations on the Genuineness of the Pentateuch*, trans. J. E. Ryland, 2 vols. (Edinburgh: J. D. Lowe, 1847); R. D. Wilson, *A Scientific Investigation of the Old Testament* (Philadelphia: Sunday School Times, 1926); E. J. Young, *An Introduction to the Old Testament* (Grand Rapids: Eerdmans, 1949); O. T. Allis, *The Five Books of Moses* (Phillipsburg, NJ: Presbyterian & Reformed, 1949).

[26] Harrison, *Introduction to the Old Testament*, 497; B. T. Arnold, "Pentateuchal Criticism, History of," in *DOTP*, ed. T. D. Alexander and D. W. Baker (Downers Grove, IL: InterVarsity, 2003), 622.

[27] Philo, *Vita Mosis*, 3:39.

[28] Josephus, *The Antiquities of the Jews*, 4.8.48, §326.

[29] Hamilton says that finding an author and date for Genesis is "an exercise in futility."

[30] E.g., W. D. Barrick, "The Authorship of Deuteronomy 34: Moses or a Redactor" (paper presented at the National Evangelical Theological Society meeting, Colorado Springs, November 15, 2001).

[31] Some of the commonly cited examples of post-Mosaica are the narration of Moses' death (Deut 34:5–12), mention of the phrase "of the Chaldees" (Gen 11:31), the presence of "Dan" (Gen 14:14), certain "until this day" statements. For other

Mosaic editorial activity (see below),[32] these scholars regard Moses as the compiler and author of Genesis (and the Pentateuch), that is, he was the essential or principal "author." He gathered preexisting written sources, carefully drew on established oral traditions, and received divine revelation in writing the book of Genesis. Proponents suggest that Moses completed his writing of the Pentateuch before his death.[33] They affirm that the final form of Genesis passed down to the modern day is not exactly identical of the Genesis of Moses' time. Some reserve the term *autographa* for the final form of Genesis, the form of the book that existed at the close of the OT canon.[34] Others refer to "Ur-Genesis," that is, an early form of Genesis, to designate the form of Genesis that was not totally finished (in Moses' time).[35] All who believe that Moses was the substantial author of the Pentateuch uphold the inspiration of Scripture.[36]

Reference to Moses as the *substantial* author of the Pentateuch can mean different things to various scholars. First, some who refer to Moses as the substantial author of the Pentateuch emphasize his role as author, compiler, or editor[37] for the *vast majority* of these five biblical books.[38] The reference to "Dan" in Gen 14:14, various "until this day" statements (e.g., Deut 3:14), and the narrative describing Moses' death and burial (Deut 34:4–12) are examples of texts added after the death of Moses.[39] Second, other evangelical scholars who view Moses as the *predominant* author of the Pentateuch suggest that examples like those just cited "could just be the tip of a large iceberg. There could be considerable later redactional activity that could extend to the latest period of Old Testament history."[40] Regarding the book of Exodus, Hill and Walton point to four literary units that were clearly Mosaic (15:1–21; 17:8–16; 19:1–24:18; 34:1–28). The extensive third-person narratives of Exodus along with various parenthetical insertions were added by someone other than Moses. Even though a relatively small portion of Exodus was clearly written by Moses, Hill and Walton affirm that the book of Exodus "stands substantially as the literary product of Moses."[41] As stated above, all those who view Moses as

---

possible examples see M. H. Segal, *The Pentateuch: Its Composition and Its Authorship and Other Biblical Studies* (Jerusalem: Magnes, 1967), 34–35. For a proposal of how this relates to an acceptance of inspiration and inerrancy, see M. A. Grisanti, "Inspiration, Inerrancy, and the Old Testament Canon: The Place of Textual Updating in an Inerrant View of Scripture," *JETS* 44:4 (December 2001): 577–98, chap. 5 in this volume.

[32] D. Garrett suggests that any post-Mosaic redaction did not take place to substantially change Genesis in any way, but was done to make it intelligible to a later generation of readers. He limits the editorial activity to minor revisions (*Rethinking Genesis: The Sources and Authorship of the First Book of the Pentateuch* [Grand Rapids: Baker, 1991], 85–86).

[33] The precise date they give to the completion of Moses' work depends on their view of the date of the Exodus from Egypt and the conquest of Canaan, either late fifteenth or the mid-thirteenth centuries BC. For a survey of that issue see chap. 11, "The Book of Exodus," in this volume.

[34] See chap. 5 of this volume.

[35] Garrett, *Rethinking Genesis*, 237; B. K. Waltke, *Genesis: A Commentary* (Grand Rapids: Zondervan, 2001), 22–29.

[36] Harrison, *Introduction to the Old Testament*, 542–65; idem, "Genesis," in *ISBE*, ed. G. Bromiley (Grand Rapids: Eerdmans, 1986), 2:437–38; K. A. Kitchen, *Ancient Orient and the Old Testament* (Chicago: InterVarsity, 1966), 112–46; idem, *The Bible in Its World* (Downers Grove, IL: InterVarsity, 1978), 56–74; Garrett, *Rethinking Genesis*, 91–93, 237; A. P. Ross, *Creation and Blessing: A Guide to the Study and Exposition of the Book of Genesis* (Grand Rapids: Baker, 1988), 34–36; T. Longman III and R. Dillard, *An Introduction to the Old Testament*, 2nd ed. (Grand Rapids: Zondervan, 2006), 40–42, 50–51; K. A. Mathews, *Genesis 1:1–11:26*, NAC (Nashville: B&H, 1996), 76–81; Mark F. Rooker, *Leviticus*, NAC (Nashville: B&H, 2000), 38–39; J. H. Walton, *Genesis*, NIVAC (Grand Rapids: Zondervan, 2001), 41–42.

[37] Since Moses' task in writing the Pentateuch involved events and people who lived before his time, he likely used existing sources (written or oral) for writing Genesis (along with direct revelation). That is why Moses functioned as author, editor, or compiler in different parts of the Pentateuch. The Holy Spirit superintended the work of Moses in all these functions.

[38] That is the consensus view of the authors of this volume. See C. Dyer and G. Merrill, *Old Testament Explorer*, ed. R. B. Zuck (Nashville: Word, 2001), 1–3; Rooker, *Leviticus*, 38–39.

[39] See chap. 5 in this volume for a more extended explanation of this issue.

[40] Longman and Dillard, *An Introduction to the Old Testament*, 42.

[41] Hill and Walton, *A Survey of the Old Testament*, 104.

the *substantial* author of the Pentateuch view the biblical text of the Pentateuch as inspired Scripture.[42] Of course, as noted, scholars who refer to Moses as the *substantial* author of the Pentateuch can mean widely different things.

Anonymous author. Along with continuing proposals from the nonevangelical world, some evangelical scholars, who do not accept the anti-supernatural assumptions of most critical methodologies, draw on some source-critical categories in their explanation of the composition of Genesis without defining these categories in exactly the same way as critical scholars. Their proposals should not be equated with those of liberal critical scholars who reject Mosaic authorship of the Pentateuch. Proponents of this broad view affirm that Moses wrote narrative, legislative, and poetic literature found in the Pentateuch (and Genesis). Although his work was highly formative, they do not believe that he wrote the Pentateuch (or Genesis) as it exists in its final form. Various writers and editors compiled and edited the materials, and the Pentateuch reached its final form several centuries after Moses. Proponents of this view prefer an anonymous author for various reasons. Some scholars contend that the complexities of the text of the Pentateuch and information presented by some critical methodologies demands a later composition that involved various authors and editors/redactors in some significant fashion.[43]

For example LaSor, Hubbard, and Bush affirm that the Pentateuch is the "final result of this long process, produced by the inspired authors, editors, and tradition-bearers of God's chosen people."[44] Sailhamer recognizes Mosaic involvement in the content of the Pentateuch but advocates a final composition of the Pentateuch (no date given) when the anonymous author shaped the Pentateuch to accomplish his theological agenda.[45] His view draws on his conclusions concerning the canonical shaping of the Old Testament in general.[46] Allen Ross grants the possibility that Moses wrote the sections customarily assigned to P and compiled the old traditions generally identified as J and E.[47] Gordon Wenham agrees with the basic parameters of Whybray's view of the composition of the Pentateuch: one major author using a variety of sources.[48] The Pentateuch was essentially completed sometime between 1250 and 950 BC by one primary author/editor, drawing heavily on J and P source materials (which would have involved Mosaic writings and traditions).[49] Wenham is vague about Moses' direct involvement in the composition of the Pentateuch. In his commentary on Genesis, Bill Arnold suggests that "Genesis is a carefully structured composite text of ancient Yahwistic and priestly materials, edited and joined together by a redactor of the Holiness tradition, who also incorporated a Joseph Novel near the conclusion."[50] The final edition of Genesis was accomplished by an editor

---

[42] E.g., Walton, *Genesis*, 41–42.

[43] Hamilton, *The Book of Genesis: Chapters 1–17*, 36–38; B. T. Arnold, *Genesis* (Cambridge: Cambridge University Press, 2009), 12–18; idem, *Encountering the Book of Genesis: A Study of Its Content and Issues* (Grand Rapids: Baker, 1998), 168–75; W. S. LaSor, D. A. Hubbard, and F. W. Bush, *Old Testament Survey: The Message, Form, and Background of the Old Testament*, 2nd ed. (Grand Rapids: Eerdmans, 1996), 8–9, 12–13; J. E. Hartley, *Genesis*, NIBC (Peabody, MA: Hendrickson, 2000), 15–17; J. McKeown, *Genesis* (Grand Rapids: Eerdmans, 2008), 8–12.

[44] LaSor, Hubbard, and Bush, *Old Testament Survey*, 13.

[45] J. Sailhamer, "Genesis," in *EBC*, rev. ed., ed. T. Longman III and D. E. Garland (Grand Rapids: Zondervan, 2008), 1:30–37.

[46] J. Sailhamer, *The Pentateuch as Narrative* (Grand Rapids: Zondervan, 1992), 35–37.

[47] Ross, *Creation and Blessing*, 35, n. 12. Although he offers no clear date for the composition of Genesis, he seems to regard Moses as the primary author of Genesis.

[48] Wenham, "Pondering the Pentateuch," 133; see also idem, *Genesis 1–15*, WBC (Waco, TX: Word, 1987), xliii–xlv.

[49] Wenham, *Genesis 1–15*, xliv.

[50] Arnold, *Genesis*, 17, Although Arnold uses J and P designations, he rejects the customary source-critical criteria for definitions of those designations.

of the Holiness school of preexilic Israel.[51] Regardless, the panorama of views on the composition of the Pentateuch in general (and Genesis in particular) is intricate.

According to T. Desmond Alexander, biblical scholars (both evangelical and nonevangelical) agree that the Pentateuch, as it now stands, is an edited work and is not a piece of literature that was written in the beginning by one individual.[52] He suggests that the Pentateuch "was created through a process involving the editing of already-existing material, regardless of whether the editor was Moses or someone else."[53] So, according to this view the Pentateuch is a literary collage.

The authors of this volume affirm that Moses is the substantial author of the Pentateuch, recognizing that he could and did draw on various preexisting sources. In that sense the Pentateuch (and Genesis in particular) represents a kind of literary collage.[54] On the one hand we can say that Moses is its *primary* editor, arranger, and author. However, on the other hand, references in this volume to Moses as the *substantial* author of the Pentateuch presents him as the author of the vast majority of those five biblical books.

CONCLUSION

Beliefs about the composition of the Pentateuch (who wrote, when, and how) are quite varied. For the first 18 centuries of the Christian era, the general consensus viewed the Pentateuch as something Moses had written. In the eighteenth century significant changes took place in biblical scholarship that eventually led to the suggestion that later editors combined various "documents" (J, E, D, and P) together resulting in the five books of the Pentateuch. Proponents of this view generally viewed the pentateuchal narratives as historically flawed and poorly edited. Amazing archaeological discoveries at the end of the nineteenth and beginning of the twentieth century AD began to provide a picture of life in the ANE that did not correspond to that proposed by the source critics. In conjunction with this observation, numerous scholars began noticing similarities between the OT and recently discovered ANE literary accounts. This triggered the suggestion that scholars needed to discover the original, preliterary setting and function of biblical narratives in order to understand them correctly. This also led to the belief that those stories were reworked repeatedly over the ensuing centuries until they reached written form. In the last several decades critical scholars have added other proposals to explain the composition of the Pentateuch. Some of these suggestions draw on the conclusions of source criticism, while others reject that approach and draw more heavily on form and tradition history criticism.

From the eighteenth century to the present, evangelical scholars have sought to demonstrate the viability of their belief in the inspiration and authority of the OT text and their view that Moses was the "substantial" author of the Pentateuch.[55] Although evangelical scholars vary in how they explain the composition of the Pentateuch, they have sought to offer a model quite different from that of critical scholars.

---

[51] Ibid., 18.

[52] This basic idea is the standard view among critical scholars and seems to be the majority position among evangelicals as well, although the way that critical and evangelical scholars explain the composition of the Pentateuch is quite different.

[53] T. D. Alexander, "Authorship of the Pentateuch," in *DOTP*, 63.

[54] Mathews, *Genesis 1:1–11:26*, 25.

[55] See the above discussion on the meaning of the "substantial" author of the Pentateuch.

CHAPTER 10

THE BOOK OF GENESIS

MICHAEL A. GRISANTI

THE BOOK OF Genesis, the first book of the Bible, deals with themes and events that lay the foundation for the rest of Scripture. As the first words of the book suggest ("In the beginning"), Genesis introduces many theological threads that are woven throughout the tapestry of the entire Bible. It *begins* answering questions like "Where did our world come from?" "How did sin enter our existence?" "How did Israel gain such prominence?" "What does God have in mind for Israel?" and "What does God have in mind for the world?"

THE TITLE OF THE BOOK

Hebrew titles of biblical books derive either from their first words (or incipit), their content, or both. The Hebrew text of Genesis begins with the phrase *bᵉrēʾšît*, which means "in the beginning."[1] The English title comes from Jerome's Vulgate, *Liber Genesis*, which obviously derives from the LXX title, *genesis*.[2]

THE CANONICITY OF THE BOOK

Genesis is the first book of the Hebrew canon and as such is the first in the section of the canon known as "Torah." Although Genesis is one of five books that make up the Torah, these five were not originally regarded as separate, individual works. Many OT texts refer to them or to passages in them as "the book of Moses" (2 Chr 25:4; 35:12; Neh 13:1), "the law of Moses" (1 Kgs 2:3; 2 Kgs 23:25; 2 Chr 23:18; 30:16; Ezra 3:2; 7:6; Dan 9:11,13), "the book of the law of Moses" (Josh 8:31–32; 23:6; 2 Kgs 14:6; Neh 8:1), "this book" (2 Kgs 22:13; 23:3), or "the book" (2 Kgs 22:8,16; 23:24; Neh 8:5). The preface of Sirach (or Ecclesiasticus) (2nd century BC) speaks of "the Law and the Prophets." The NT refers to the entire OT as "the Law

---

[1] The Hebrew title for the book, as is true of all Hebrew titles for OT books, involves the first set of words in the Hebrew text, here *bᵉrēʾšît*.

[2] A genitive plural form of *genesis*, *geneseōs*, which is a translation for the Hebrew *tôledôt*, "generations," occurs in 2:4a and 10 other times in the book as part of a literary formula (see the outline section below).

and the Prophets" (Matt 7:12; 22:40), "Moses and [all] the Prophets" (Luke 16:31; 24:27), or "Moses, the Prophets, and the Psalms" (Luke 24:44). This evidences the common view that the Torah was viewed as one literary piece. Sometime before the Christian era, the tradition arose of describing Torah as the five books of Moses, thus granting them individual identities.[3]

No extant Christian or Jewish source has ever raised questions about the legitimacy of the canonicity of Genesis.[4] However, only scraps of Genesis have been discovered among the DSS. The best known of these Qumran documents relating to Genesis is the Genesis Apocryphon (1QapGen), a writing that gives evidence of the popularity of Genesis among the Qumran community. Also, despite its foundational role with respect to the rest of the OT, the book of Genesis never received widespread usage in the literature of post-biblical Judaism, its greatest attention being devoted to Leviticus.

THE COMPOSITION OF THE BOOK[5]

Discussions about the composition of Genesis (and the Pentateuch as a whole) have had two primary phases. For the first 1,800 years of the Christian era, the scholarly consensus was that Genesis was a unified composition by Moses.[6] Modern scholars generally regard that scholarly consensus as "pre-critical," i.e., before the application of critical methodologies that came into use during the Enlightenment and later.[7] In the mid-eighteenth century, in the wake of major changes in the world of biblical scholarship, a second phase of explanation of the composition of Genesis (and the Pentateuch) developed, one that has become the standard or consensus position in mainstream study of the OT.[8] The next sections briefly consider the impact of three critical methodologies on the book of Genesis.

Impact of Source Criticism on Genesis

All critical (nonevangelical) commentaries apply the various criteria of source criticism to this biblical book.[9] They identify two creation accounts (chaps. 1–2), two flood accounts (chaps. 6–9), various duplicate accounts (Abraham and Isaac lying), as well as alleged vocabulary and linguistic style arguments to demonstrate the validity of their division of Genesis into J and E "documents" primarily.[10]

---

[3] Josephus (*Ag. Ap.*, 1.8) and Philo (*On Abraham*, 1.1) both refer to five books of Moses.

[4] V. P. Hamilton, *The Book of Genesis: Chapters 1–17*, NICOT (Grand Rapids: Eerdmans, 1990), 71.

[5] Some of this information overlaps with material presented in chaps. 8–10 and the introductory chapter for section 4. This section summarizes information that receives fuller attention in R. K. Harrison, *Introduction to the Old Testament* (Grand Rapids: Eerdmans, 1969), 1–82; Hamilton, *The Book of Genesis: Chapters 1–17*, 11–38; and B. T. Arnold, *Encountering the Book of Genesis: A Study of Its Content and Issues* (Grand Rapids: Baker, 1998), 187–91.

[6] A few scholars dissented from this tradition, but their views did not approximate in scope and intensity the views popular in the next phase of scholarly discussion. For some examples of this dissent see Harrison, *Introduction to the Old Testament*, 5–11.

[7] Modern scholars usually regard the views from the pre-critical period as somewhat archaic and of little use.

[8] See chaps. 8 and 9 for a fuller development of the factors involved in these changes.

[9] Here is a sampling of some evangelical commentaries that also refer to sources like J and E as part of their explanation of the composition of the Pentateuch (or a book in the Pentateuch): G. J. Wenham, *Genesis 1–15*, WBC (Waco, TX: Word, 1987), xxxix–xlv; B. K. Waltke with C. J. Fredricks, *Genesis: A Commentary* (Grand Rapids: Zondervan, 2001), 21–29, esp. 27–28; B. T. Arnold, *Genesis* (New York: Cambridge University Press, 2009), 12–18; T. R. Ashley, *The Book of Numbers*, NICOT (Grand Rapids: Eerdmans, 1993), 3–7.

[10] See various examples of this in the introduction to Part 4, p. 163.

Impact of Form Criticism on Genesis

In his Genesis commentary Hermann Gunkel divided the book into two sections. Chapters 1–11 are mythical in nature, and chaps. 12–50 contain the legends of the patriarchs, none of which have any connection to Moses.[11] Klaus Koch examined the "she is my sister" narratives form-critically, and identifies them as "sagas," a genre that presents prehistoric historiography in popular form.[12] He further identifies them as "ethnological sagas" and identifies their original function as some kind of Bedouin tale that emphasized God's role in relation to a particular people group (as well as explaining subsequent relations between other nomadic or ethnic groups).[13]

Impact of Tradition History on Genesis

Jacob's treaty with Laban (31:44–54) is an example of a passage viewed from a tradition-history view. This narrative, according to Noth, is based on the historical fact of a treaty between the Ephraimite settlers, who lived on the west side of the Jordan, and the Arameans in the Transjordan.[14] According to tradition-history it is unknown whether Laban was a historical person or a figure developed by the Israelites to characterize their Aramean neighbors. The terms of the treaty in Genesis suggests that the original treaty was a mutual agreement with essential fidelity.[15] Noth affirms that "the Pentateuchal tradition which came to be the common Israelite epic was that form shaped by the particular memories and traditions of the central Palestinian tribes and reflective of their point of view."[16]

Preferred view. As presented in the introductory chapter for the Pentateuch volume, Moses was the substantial author of the book of Genesis as well as the Pentateuch. This does not rule out the possibility that Moses could have drawn on oral traditions or existing written records (in addition to direct revelation) for his composition of the book of Genesis; whatever he included in the book of Genesis is part of the inspired text of Scripture and is infallible and inerrant.

Of course, the fact that Moses was not alive during the time of the events described in Genesis serves as one of the reasons this question of authorship receives attention. However, the multiple references to the five books of the Pentateuch as the Law of Moses (see above section on canonicity) and the way the NT quotes passages from Genesis and attributes them to Moses supports this view of the authorship of Genesis.

THE LITERARY FORMS AND GENRES OF THE BOOK

The majority of Genesis involves prose narrative. This narrative has prayers, speeches, and other types of direct discourse interspersed throughout it. There are genealogies (chaps. 5, 10, 11, 36, etc.) and poetry (the blessing of Rebekah [24:60] and Jacob's blessing of his 12 sons [chap. 49]). A few prophetic statements can be found as well. God predicted the oppression

---

[11] H. Gunkel, *The Legends of Genesis: The Biblical Saga and History* (New York: Schocken, 1964), 160.

[12] K. Koch, *The Growth of the Biblical Tradition: The Form-Critical Method*, trans. S. M. Cupitt (New York: Scribner, 1969), 118–19.

[13] Ibid., 119–28. For a form-critical treatment of Jacob's struggle at Jabbok (Gen 32:22–32), see G. M. Tucker, *Form Criticism of the Old Testament* (Philadelphia: Fortress, 1971), 41–54.

[14] M. Noth, *A History of Pentateuchal Traditions*, trans. B. W. Anderson (Englewood Cliffs, NJ: Prentice-Hall, 1972), 92.

[15] Ibid.

[16] Ibid., 57.

of Abraham's descendants (15:12–16) and introduces the idea of a coming king from Judah in Jacob's blessing on his sons (49:8–12).

THE STRUCTURE OF THE BOOK

Mathews likens the literary structure of Genesis to a stained-glass window adorning an edifice. At a distance, one views the window holistically, observing its collective beauty. At closer distance, the intricate design becomes more apparent, involving different pieces of different sizes, shapes, and colors. Similarly Genesis is an intricate literary composition "with symmetrical unity but a diversity of genres."[17] Although the pieces may not always blend together to the satisfaction of a later reader, together they form an "unmistakably coherent, unified story line."[18]

Various scholars have suggested that Genesis falls into two general sections: Primeval history (chaps. 1–11) and patriarchal history (chaps. 12–50). The first section encompasses four significant events: creation, the fall, the flood, and the rebellion at Babel. The second section, though it gives attention to five people (Abraham, Isaac, Esau, Jacob, and Joseph), involves three narrative collections dealing with Abraham, Jacob, and Joseph.[19]

The structure of the book is comprised of an initial section that concerns the creation of the universe and mankind (1:1–2:3), followed by 11 (or 10) sections,[20] each introduced with the same word.[21] The major structural word of the book is *tôledôt*, literally, "these are the generations of. . . ." The word is a feminine plural noun from the verb *yālad* ("to give birth" or "to beget"). It is often translated as "generations" or "descendants." The term is part of a heading for each section of Genesis (after the creation account). It serves "as a linking device that ties together the former and the following units by echoing from the preceding material a person's name or literary motif and at the same time anticipating the focal subject of the next."[22] The *tôledôt* heading could be freely rendered, "this is what became of." For example the *tôledôt* of Terah is not so much *about* Terah; it is primarily concerned with *what became of* Terah, that is, Abraham and his kin. The person named after *tôledôt* is usually not the central character in the narrative but the person of origin.[23] Via the *tôledôt* sections Genesis involves a narrowing in the focus of God's program, from all of creation (first section of the book) and Adam in particular (first *tôledôt* section), to the 12 sons of Jacob (final *tôledôt* section), one of a myriad of descendants of Adam.

---

[17] K. A. Mathews, *Genesis 1:1–11:26*, NAC (Nashville: B&H, 1996), 25.

[18] Ibid. This obvious diversity does not preclude unified authorship/compilation by Moses.

[19] Isaac holds an important, though transitional, role in the book. Abraham and Jacob seem to overshadow him.

[20] The expression, "these are the generations of," occurs 11 times as a formula (2:4; 5:1; 6:9; 10:1; 11:10,27; 25:12,19; 36:1,9; 37:2). It also occurs in 36:1 and 36:9, and scholars are not agreed whether the second occurrence introduces a new section. This affects whether Genesis has 11 or 12 sections. The term *tôledôt* also occurs in 10:32 and 25:13 as part of a prepositional phrase and not as a structural formula.

[21] Some scholars point to this formulaic use of *tôledôt* as an indication that Moses made use of preexisting written sources (see chap. 5).

[22] Mathews, *Genesis 1:1–11:26*, 33–34.

[23] Because most of the information about the person named in the *tôledôt* formula precedes the phrase, some scholars view the *tôledôt* phrase as a summarizing formula that ends a unit rather than introducing a new unit. See P. J. Wiseman, *Ancient Records and the Structure of Genesis: A Case for Literary Unity*, ed. D. J. Wiseman (Nashville: Thomas Nelson, 1985); and Harrison, *Introduction to the Old Testament*, 543–47.

AN OUTLINE OF THE BOOK

The following outline draws on the prominent *tôledôt* structure as well as key thematic/
topic shifts. However, the words "primeval" and then "patriarchal" do not signify legendary
or nonhistorical material followed by historical narratives, as suggested by some scholars. The
term "primeval" simply describes an early period (for which there are no clear dates) before the
more clearly dated patriarchal narratives.

I. **Primeval History: Creation of the Universe and Preparation for the Establishment of the
Covenant People (1:1–11:26)**
Four Great Events: Creation, Fall, Flood, Babel
A. Creation (1:1–2:3)
B. The *Tôledôt* of the Heavens and the Earth (2:4–4:26)
C. The *Tôledôt* of Adam (5:1–6:8)
D. The *Tôledôt* of Noah (6:9–9:29)
E. The *Tôledôt* of Shem, Ham, and Japheth (10:1–11:9)
F. The *Tôledôt* of Shem (11:10–26)

II. **Patriarchal History: The Establishment of the Covenant People (11:27–50:26)**
Four Great Men: Abraham, Isaac, Jacob, Joseph
A. Patriarchal Narratives about Abraham (11:27–25:18)
    1. The *Tôledôt* of Terah (11:27–25:11)
    2. The *Tôledôt* of Ishmael (25:12–18)
B. Patriarchal Narratives about Abraham's Descendants (Primarily Jacob) (25:19–37:1)
    1. The *Tôledôt* of Isaac (25:19–35:29)
    2. The *Tôledôt* of Esau, the Father of Edom (36:1–37:1)[24]
C. The Story of Joseph (37:2–50:26)

KEY INTERPRETIVE ISSUES IN THE BOOK

Is Genesis 1–11 Myth, Fiction, or History?

Possible points of similarity between ANE and biblical creation and flood accounts. For decades,
scholars of various theological persuasions have debated the meaning and significance of Genesis
1–11 (and chaps. 1–2 in particular). Should these chapters be understood as history or myth?
A key issue that gives rise to this discussion involves a comparison of the biblical accounts of
creation (chaps. 1–2) and the flood (chaps. 6–9) with various ANE creation and flood accounts.
Although scholars discuss Egyptian and Ugaritic literature, most attention is given to Mesopotamian myths, focusing on the *Enuma Elish*, the *Atrahasis Epic*, and the *Gilgamesh Epic*. Scholars
commonly point out several points of similarity. First, ANE and biblical accounts present a
period of chaos (involving water) followed by creation, bringing the world into order, and establishing function and purpose.[25] Second, the "primal chaotic condition" involved water and darkness.[26] In both ANE and biblical passages, the supreme God exerted power and authority over
the deep (Tiamat/*tᵉhôm*) and darkness. Third, the divine being demonstrates His authority by
dividing the water. In the Bible God creates a firmament between water that is above and below
the firmaments. In *Enuma Elish* Marduk splits the corpse of the vanquished Tiamat, dividing

---

[24] As stated above, this section includes two *tôledôt* statements, which this outline point (II. B. 2) binds together.

[25] J. H. Walton, "Creation," in *DOTP*, ed. T. D. Alexander and D. W. Baker (Downers Grove, IL: InterVarsity, 2003),
156.

[26] Ibid., 157.

her waters in half. Fourth, in the ANE myths, the gods mix blood and spit with clay as part of bringing humanity into existence (combination of elements). In Genesis 1 God creates mankind by combining the dust of the ground with His breath. Eve is later created from Adam's rib.

Genesis 1–2 as myth. In light of the above points of similarity (and others), critical or nonevangelical scholars almost exclusively categorize these chapters as myth.[27] Although it is difficult to define "myth,"[28] the basic understanding is that a myth involves "an ancient, premodern, prescientific way of addressing questions of ultimate origins and meaning in the form of stories: Who are we? Where do we come from?"[29] In many instances by "myth" these scholars mean something fictional or nonhistorical. However, some scholars are careful to distinguish myth from free-ranging fantasy and contend that myth can conjure up or point to history.[30] To the question, "Is Genesis 1 a Creation Myth?" Mark Smith answers "yes and no."[31] In light of the context of Genesis 1 (both biblical and ANE), Smith concludes that Genesis 1 is certainly mythic. However, its placement at the beginning of Genesis and certain phrases in the chapter suggest that it is linked to historical time. Smith grants that the answer to the question depends on how a person defines "myth."

Evangelicals also wrestle with this question, and several agree that the first section of Genesis (chaps. 1–11) belongs to the genre of myth rather than history.[32] Unlike the nonevangelical scholars who reject the idea of divine revelation and inspiration, evangelical proponents of the myth view believe that careful attention to the ANE context of chaps. 1–2 occasions their interpretation. Also, they do not discount that these chapters present "facts" (e.g., God is one and not many, human beings are made in God's image, etc.). They are concerned about the form in which Genesis presents these facts.[33] In various ways they seek to answer the question, Did the creation of Adam literally take place the way it is narrated, or is the creation of Adam shaped to teach us things about the nature of humanity?[34] Walton suggests that in the ancient world, mythology was like science in the modern world—it represented their explanation of how the world came into being and how it worked. So mythology served as a window to culture, that is, as a reflection of the worldview and values of the culture that forged it. Walton believes that many parts of the OT performed the same function as mythology did in

---

[27] Here is a selection of non-evangelical scholars who regard Genesis 1–11 as myth: B. S. Childs, *Myth and Reality in the Old Testament*, SBT (Naperville, IL: Alec R. Allenson, 1960), 30–42; E. A. Speiser, *Genesis*, AB (New York: Doubleday, 1964), liv–lv; N. M. Sarna, *Understanding Genesis* (New York: McGraw-Hill, 1966), 1–36; G. Von Rad, *Genesis: A Commentary*, rev. ed., OTL (Philadelphia: Westminster, 1972), 31–43; C. Westermann, *Genesis 1–11: A Commentary*, trans. J. J. Scullion (Minneapolis: Augsburg, 1984), 22–47; T. L. Thompson, "Historiography in the Pentateuch: Twenty-five Years after Historicity," *SJOT* 13 (1999): 280; M. S. Smith, *The Priestly Vision of Genesis 1* (Minneapolis: Fortress, 2010), 139–59.

[28] For example J. W. Rogerson offers four definitions for myth: "Slippery Words V: Myth," *ET* 90 (1978): 10–14. See J. N. Oswalt, *The Bible among the Myths: Unique Revelation or Just Ancient Literature* (Grand Rapids: Zondervan, 2009), 29–46, for a discussion of this problem of defining myth.

[29] P. Enns, *Inspiration and Incarnation: Evangelicals and the Problem of the Old Testament* (Grand Rapids: Baker, 2005), 40. T. S. Beall defines myth as "a traditional pre-scientific story normally revolving around gods and heroes, which explains the origin of something" ("Contemporary Hermeneutical Approaches to Genesis 1–11," in *Coming to Grips with Genesis: Biblical Authority and the Age of the Earth*, ed. T. Mortenson and T. H. Ury [Green Forest, AR: Master, 2008], 132–33).

[30] Von Rad, *Genesis*, 33.

[31] Smith, *The Priestly Vision of Genesis 1*, 156–59.

[32] Here is a selection of evangelical scholars who regard Genesis 1–11 as myth: J. H. Walton, *Genesis*, NIVAC (Grand Rapids: Zondervan, 2001), 27–31; idem, "Creation," *Dictionary of the Old Testament*, 155–68; T. Longman III, *How to Read Genesis* (Downers Grove, IL: InterVarsity, 2005), 71–87; Enns, *Inspiration and Incarnation*, 39–56; I. Provan, "'How Can I Understand Unless Someone Explains It to Me?' (Acts 8:30–31): Evangelicals and Biblical Hermeneutics," *BBR* 17 (2007): 15–20; Kenton L. Sparks, *God's Word in Human Words: An Evangelical Appropriation of Critical Biblical Scholarship* (Grand Rapids: Baker, 2008), 97–99.

[33] Provan, "'How Can I Understand Unless Someone Explains It to Me?' (Acts 8:30–31)," 15.

[34] Longman, *How to Read Genesis*, 78.

other cultures. It gave the Israelites a literary mechanism for preserving and transmitting their worldview and values. Here Walton proposes an important connection between the biblical and ANE worlds. As with ANE literature he suggests that the accounts in chaps. 1–11 help readers understand what the Israelites thought about themselves, their world, and their gods.[35] Evangelical proponents of the myth view of the first section of Genesis also contend that the text of chaps. 1–2 is not narrative in form and has no interest in chronology.[36] They affirm that the biblical creation account was written against the backdrop of and alludes to a common ANE cosmogony (primarily that found in Mesopotamia).[37] They correctly believe that the biblical authors (of various biblical accounts that deal with creation) propose things about the nature of reality (about God, the world, and the nature and vocation of human beings in that world) that clearly differs from that found in the ANE world.[38] However, they affirm that those propositions are embedded in the myth language of the day. Longman suggests that the biblical writers took an ANE myth/tradition and substituted God's breath for either the divine spit or blood. He concludes that this communicates the truth that humans are creatures connected to earth and beings who have a special relationship with God.[39]

Genesis 1–2 as history. Also numerous evangelicals, whether they interpret the details of chaps. 1–2 in a predominantly literal fashion (early earth) or nonliteral fashion (late earth), reject the notion that these chapters are to be regarded as mythological.[40] Several arguments stand in favor of regarding chaps. 1–11 as history.

First, it seems that a person should be able to apply their hermeneutical approach uniformly to chaps. 1–11 as well as to the rest of the book.[41] Whether they regard chaps. 1–11 or just chaps. 1–2 as myth, several critical and all evangelical scholars treat chaps. 12–50 as historical narrative in contrast to their treatment of the earlier chapters of Genesis. Just like Genesis 12–50, Genesis 1–11 is clearly written in narrative form[42] and is not poetic.[43] This is important because most of those who argue for a mythological understanding of chaps. 1–11 view chaps. 1–2 as poetic.

Second, Walton's suggestion that the biblical creation account (like ANE mythology) teaches what Israelites believed about themselves and the world around them seems to misun-

---

[35] Walton, *Genesis*, 27.

[36] Provan, "'How Can I Understand Unless Someone Explains It to Me?' (Acts 8:30–31)," 16, and n. 21. Provan (16–20), along with other proponents, points to the customary chronological and scientific problems that are part of viewing the biblical creation account as history (ibid., 16–20).

[37] Ibid., 16. Walton provides a lengthy chart of comparisons between biblical accounts of creation and flood and those of the ANE (*Genesis*, 29–31).

[38] Provan, "'How Can I Understand Unless Someone Explains It to Me?' (Acts 8:30–31)," 17.

[39] Longman, *How to Read Genesis*, 78. See also Enns, *Inspiration and Incarnation*, 49–56.

[40] Here is a selection of evangelical scholars who do not regard Genesis 1–11 as myth: G. F. Hasel, "The Significance of the Cosmology in Genesis 1 in Relation to Ancient Near Eastern Parallels," *AUSS* 10 (1972): 1–20; idem, "Polemic Nature of the Genesis Cosmology," *EQ* 46 (April–June 1974): 81–102; G. C. Aalders, *Genesis*, trans. W. Heynen, BSC (Grand Rapids: Zondervan, 1981), 44–47; Mathews, *Genesis 1–11:26*, 85–89; C. J. Collins, *Genesis 1–4: A Linguistic, Literary, and Theological Commentary* (Phillipsburg, NJ: P & R, 2006), 237–67; Beall, "Contemporary Hermeneutical Approaches to Genesis 1–11," 132–40; Oswalt, *The Bible among the Myths*, 85–107, esp. 99–104.

[41] Beall, "Contemporary Hermeneutical Approaches to Genesis 1–11," 132.

[42] The *wayyiqtol* verbal form, the customary narrative verb form, abounds throughout Genesis, including chaps. 1–11.

[43] S. W. Boyd argues convincingly on linguistic grounds that Gen 1:1–2:3 is historical narrative ("The Genre of Genesis 1:1–2:3: What Means This Text?" in *Coming to Grips with Genesis: Biblical Authority and the Age of the Earth*, ed. T. Mortenson and T. H. Ury (Green Forest, AR: Master Books, 2008), 163–92; idem, "Statistical Determination of Genre in Biblical Hebrew: Evidence for an Historical Reading of Genesis 1:1–2:3," in *RATE II: Radioisotopes and the Age of The Earth: Results of a Young-Earth Creationist Research Initiative*, ed. L. Vardiman et al. (San Diego, CA: Institute for Creation Research, 2005), 631–734.

derstand the nature of Scripture, especially in chaps. 1–2. This is an instance where genre identification has a significant impact on the interpretation of a passage. It is true that mythology does demonstrate what a people or culture believes about something. However, if these chapters are narrative presentations, they do not serve to present Israel's self-understanding, instead they state what God wanted to tell His people about those ancient events and individuals.

Third, while it is valid that there seem to be similarities between the biblical and ANE accounts of creation and flood, many scholars suggest that the biblical account alludes to the ANE mythologies for polemical purposes. As Mathews points out, "Instead of a borrowing or a historicizing of ancient myth, it is fairer to say that Genesis comes closer to a repudiation of pagan ideas about origins, mankind, civilization, and the flood. . . . Rather than true polemic, however, in general the Genesis accounts are inferentially undermining the philosophical basis for pagan myth."[44]

Fourth, although proponents of the myth view recognize that there are differences between the ANE and biblical accounts of creation and the flood, they emphasize the similarities and minimize those differences. Myth proponents offer various charts that compare biblical and ANE creation and flood accounts.[45] On the surface the similarities in these lists seem convincing. However, when one reads the two passages side by side, they will reach quite different conclusions. The following reveals what receives emphasis in the *Enuma Elish*.[46]

Comparison of *Enuma Elish* and Genesis Creation Account

Tablets #1–5	Basic content	Relevance to Genesis
First 160 lines	An account of the emergence of the gods from chaos, their multiplication, the plan of the chaos monster, Tiamat, and her consort Apsu, to kill the gods, and the war that results.	None
Second 130 lines	The selection of Marduk as the champion of the gods	None
Next 138 lines	The reason for Marduk's supremacy	None
Next 134 lines	The destruction of Tiamat	None
Next 5 lines	Marduk hangs up half of Tiamat's body to be the sky separating upper waters from lower waters	Firmament dividing waters above and below the firmament
Next 27 lines	The placement of the gods in heaven	None
	Remaining 120 lines are broken/incomplete	
Tablet #6 First 44 lines	Marduk makes humans from mud and the blood of one of Tiamat's monsters in order for those humans to serve the gods and allow them to be at ease.	Formation of Adam from dust?
Next 86 lines	Building a heavenly sanctuary for Marduk	None
Next 214 lines	Proclaiming the 50 names of Marduk	None

[44] Mathews, *Genesis 1–11:26*, 89; cf. Hasel, "Polemic Nature of the Genesis Cosmology," 81–102.

[45] Walton, *Genesis*, 29–31; Speiser, *Genesis*, 10.

[46] Oswalt, *The Bible among the Myths*, 100–101.

Although Speiser wrote that "on the subject of creation biblical tradition aligned itself with the traditional tenets of Babylonian 'science,'" the evidence suggests something quite different.[47] The similarities are relatively minor in comparison to the distinctive focus and purpose of the Babylonian creation account. In fact, another nonevangelical scholar offers a very different assessment: "Direct influence of the Babylonian creation epic on the Biblical account of creation cannot be discerned."[48] As stated above, it seems more accurate to affirm that chaps. 1–2 were composed as a polemic *against* the Mesopotamian understanding of creation or origins.[49]

Fifth, Oswalt also points out that the key elements of myth are conspicuously absent in the biblical creation account. For example, in the biblical accounts there are no gods, no continual creation on the primeval plane that this world only reflects, no conflict between good and evil (or between order and chaos) on the metaphysical level as the precursor to creation, and sexuality plays no role in creation. Also the biblical creation accounts demonstrate a high view of humanity.[50]

The genre of chaps. 1–11 (and chaps. 1–2 in particular) has consumed much scholarly attention for decades. The consensus of critical scholarship is that these chapters should not be regarded as history. Instead, since they draw heavily on imagery and thinking common in ANE creation and flood accounts, scholars should treat them as mythological literature, delineating how people understood those "events." Various evangelical scholars who enthusiastically embrace divine inspiration of Scripture agree that these early chapters of Genesis must be regarded as myth if one desires to understand those chapters correctly against their ANE backdrop. However, even though the Genesis account does allude to various aspects of ANE mythology, those references have a polemical function rather than serving as indications of heavy reliance. These chapters provide a reliable presentation of what happened during the creation week and in the worldwide flood.

DOES GENESIS 1–2 DESCRIBE AN EARLY EARTH OR A LATE EARTH?

Biblical scholars and scientists have offered various interpretations of chaps. 1–2 as it relates to the creation of the universe. The consensus view in today's world is Neo-Darwin evolution or atheistic evolution.[51] This view of evolution proposes that everything in the universe has come into existence and has evolved into its present form as a result of natural processes, totally apart from any divine involvement. The following overview pays attention to views held by evangelicals who believe that God had some role to play in the universe and humanity coming into being. "Young earth" refers to views that regard the age of the earth as between c. 6,000 and 20,000 years BC.[52] An "old earth" view accepts evolution as a vehicle that led to the earth and the animal world and describes "creation" as taking place over the past millions or even billions of years ago. "Intelligent design" counters the arguments of Neo-Darwin evolu-

---

[47] Speiser, *Genesis*, 11.

[48] W. von Soden, *The Ancient Orient: An Introduction to the Study of the Ancient Near East*, trans. D. G. Schley (Grand Rapids: Eerdmans, 1994), 213.

[49] Hasel, "Polemic Nature of the Genesis Cosmology," 81–102.

[50] Oswalt, *The Bible among the Myths*, 99.

[51] The adjective "atheistic" is not meant primarily as a pejorative term but to distinguish this view of evolution from those views held by evangelicals who believe God played a part in the universe and humanity coming into being.

[52] If the genealogies of Genesis 5 and 11 are exhaustive, creation can be dated to c. 4004 BC. If those genealogies are not exhaustive (with missing generations intentionally left out for stylistic reasons), the date of creation cannot be determined precisely. An important distinction is that a "young-earth" date for the earth's creation is in the thousands or tens of thousands of years, not in millions or billions of years.

tion, which assumes an undirected process such as natural selection. Its primary claim is that "intelligent causes are necessary to explain the complex, information-rich structures of biology and that these causes are empirically detectable."[53] Advocates of intelligent design are adamant that their view is not creationism, although most (but not all) adherents are theists.[54] Various proponents of intelligent design vary in their explanation of the manner and degree of divine involvement in the process of creation. The three categories of views regarding creation summarized below are not exhaustive or monolithic.[55]

Figure 10.1
Three Major Views on the Creation of the Universe

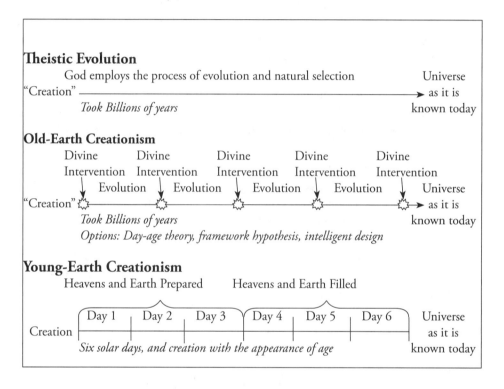

[53] W. A. Dembski, *Intelligent Design: The Bridge between Science and Theology* (Downers Grove, IL: InterVarsity, 1999), 106.

[54] R. B. Stewart, "What Are We Talking About?" in *Intelligent Design: William A. Dembski and Michael Ruse in Dialogue*, ed. R. B. Stewart (Philadelphia: Fortress, 2007), 7.

[55] Different listings have been offered by various sources. The three categories presented here offer a basic summary of the key positions in modern scholarship. For example it does not include the gap theory. These categories are taken from *Three Views on Creation and Evolution*, ed. S. N. Gundry, J. P. Moreland, and J. M. Reynolds (Grand Rapids: Zondervan, 1999).

Theistic evolution (fully gifted creation). Proponents of this view affirm that classical religious teachings about God are compatible with the modern scientific understanding about biological evolution. They propose that God created the universe and all life by utilizing the process of evolution and natural selection as a tool to accomplish His will.[56] According to this view chap. 1 states that God created the world but did not tell how He did it. Therefore people today must learn from science how creation took place. Genesis 1 should be understood in nonliteral terms, and the language there should be regarded as a figurative way of presenting God as the moving force behind "creation."

Old-earth creationism (progressive creationism). According to this view God used some combination of supernatural intervention and providential guidance to create the universe and all its inhabitants.[57] The descriptive adjective "progressive" refers to their belief that "creation" involved numerous steps over a long period of time. Each of these steps progressed to a higher level. The "creation" of the earth and various forms of life took place over a period of hundreds of millions of years. However, any new kinds of plants and animals that appeared successively during earth's history serve as examples of God's direct intervention. Progressive creationists reject macroevolution (evolution from one species to another species) because they believe that it is untenable biologically and there is no evidence of that kind of evolution in the fossil record. They rely on scientific dating methods to demonstrate that the age of the earth requires a date of origin millions or billions of years ago.[58] They argue that God created mankind, as described in the creation account, between 8,000 and 24,000 years ago.[59]

Proponents of old-earth creationism contend that most of the details in the account of creation in Genesis 1 should not be understood literally. Here is where progressive creationists differ in how they explain this long process of "creation."[60] Some scholars explain the days of chap. 1 with some version of a "day-age" approach. The customary "day-age" view understands each "day" in the creative week as long periods of time (millions of years). During those periods development occurred by natural process between times of special fiat creation.[61] The "intermittent day-age" view understands the days of Genesis 1 as literal days separated by long periods.[62] The framework hypothesis regards the days of Genesis 1 as a literary device that encompasses the events of creation in topical order.[63]

---

[56] H. J. Van Til, "The Fully Gifted Creation ('Theistic Evolution')," in *Three Views on Creation and Evolution*, 161–218.

[57] R. C. Newman, "Progressive Creationism ('Old Earth Creationism')," in *Three Views on Creation and Evolution*, 105–33. H. Ross is a key proponent of this theory (*A Matter of Days: Resolving a Creation Controversy* [Colorado Springs, CO: NavPress, 2004]).

[58] Ross, *A Matter of Days*, 175–84.

[59] They contend that Neanderthals represent a prehuman, primate species but were morphologically and biochemically distinct from humans. In other words humans could not possibly be descended from Neanderthals (ibid., 224–25).

[60] J. Walton has recently offered what he calls the "cosmic temple inauguration view" (*The Lost World of Genesis One: Ancient Cosmology and the Origins Debate* [Downers Grove, IL: InterVarsity, 2009], 162). He proposes that Genesis 1 has nothing to say about the origin of the material universe. Instead, it focuses on delineating the divinely intended function of the universe, however it came into being. Walton regards the framework hypothesis or intelligent design as feasible efforts to explain the way the universe came into being. However, the intent of Genesis 1 is not to explain the "mechanics" of creation.

[61] D. A. Young, *Christianity and the Age of the Earth* (Grand Rapids: Zondervan, 1982), 57–59.

[62] R. C. Newman and H. J. Eckelman Jr., *Genesis One and the Origin of the Earth* (Grand Rapids: Baker, 1977), 61–66.

[63] For example M. Ross, "The Framework Hypothesis: An Interpretation of Genesis 1:1–2:3," in *Did God Create in Six Days?* ed. J. A. Pipa Jr., and D. W. Hall (Taylors, SC: Southern Presbyterian Press, 1999), 113–30; Wenham, *Genesis 1–15*, 39–40. For a critique of the framework hypothesis from an early-earth perspective, see R. V. McCabe, "A Critique of the Framework Interpretation of the Creation Week," in *Coming to Grips with Genesis: Biblical Authority and the Age of the Earth*, 211–49.

Young-earth creationism (scientific creationism). Proponents of this view regard the text of Gen 1:1–2:3 as a narrative text and so they interpret it literally. They also discount the impact of ANE myths as a primary means of interpreting these verses.[64] They regard days of the creation week as solar days, around 24 hours in length. The fact that the word "days" is preceded by an ordinal number and is accompanied by the phrase "evening and morning" supports this interpretation.[65] During this creative week, God brought into existence the entire universe, including the earth and all forms of plant, animal, and human life that inhabited it. This view of creation allows for "microevolution," that is, developments or changes within a species (size, coloration, features). However, it rejects "macroevolution"—evolution from one species to another (something that is required for Neo-Darwinism and theistic evolution). As a corollary to an early-earth creationism view, proponents also believe that Noah's flood was universal in scope and the rising and receding of the floodwater caused much of the deposition of fossil evidence that is generally pointed to as evidence of the great age of the earth.[66]

Evaluation. Several important issues provide the grounds for the differences between the views on the origins of the universe summarized above. First, there is an important difference in fundamental assumptions about science. For all but the early-earth view, the uniformitarian nature of scientific theories is regarded as reliable. For example, since the speed of light has been established many conclude that this requires a certain date (billions of years ago) for the beginning of the universe. The early-earth view contends that various creative "events" (divine fiat) and "catastrophes" (universal flood) account for much of the evidence that modern science seeks to interpret. Both views seek to interact with science but in different ways.[67] Both theistic evolution and evangelical old-earth views accept numerous scientific conclusions that impact their interpretation of Genesis 1–2. Early-earth proponents interact with the geology relating to the universal flood (focusing on the Grand Canyon, among other sites), arguing that an event rather than a process involving billions of years provides the only feasible answer for the geological evidence.[68] Second, the way scholars identify the literary form of Genesis 1 (whether symbolic, poetic, or literal) and the way they interact with the ANE myths creates some of the interpretive differences. As stated above, it seems best to read Genesis 1–2 as narrative and to reject a close relationship between the biblical and ANE accounts of creation. Third, whether the "days" of chap. 1 should be understood as solar days or symbolic for some long period of

---

[64] This does not discount the idea that polemical references to ANE myths can be found in Genesis 1. However, the biblical account of creation in Genesis 1 is quite different from those ANE myths and so those myths are not similar in genre, content, or intent to the biblical creation account.

[65] G. F. Hasel, "The 'Days' of Creation in Genesis 1: Literal 'Days' or Figurative 'Periods/Epochs' of Time?" *Origins* 21 (1994): 5–38; cf. T. Craigen, "Can Deep Time Be Embedded in Genesis?" in *Coming to Grips with Genesis: Biblical Authority and the Age of the Earth*, 193–210.

[66] For some resources that explain this view more completely and provide references to other supportive resources see the following: D. F. Kelly, *Creation and Change: Genesis 1:1–2:4 in the Light of Changing Scientific Paradigms* (Ross-shire, UK: Christian Focus, 1997); various essays in *Coming to Grips with Genesis: Biblical Authority and the Age of the Earth*; A. S. Kulikovsky, *Creation, Fall, Restoration: A Biblical Theology of Creation* (Ross-shire, UK: Christian Focus, 2009).

[67] An important distinction should be made between *operational science* and *origin science*. *Operational science* refers to the numerous scientific discoveries that have utilized the scientific process in which theories are tested repeatedly, refined, and result in a concrete conclusion. *Origin science* is totally conjectural since there is no way of testing the theories. That inability of testing one's *belief* about creation or evolution is shared by early- and young-earth proponents. So origin science does not offer solid evidence that should compel evangelicals to overturn a literal reading of Genesis 1–2.

[68] A helpful resource that carefully considers the geology of the flood in particular is A. Snelling, *Earth's Catastrophic Past: Geology, Creation, and the Flood*, 2 vols. (Dallas: Institute for Creation Research, 2009).

time also greatly impacts one's view of creation. The presence of numerical modifiers and the expression "evening and morning" favor the early-earth view.[69]

AN OVERVIEW OF THE BOOK

The next section briefly narrates the argument of Genesis.

I. Primeval History (1:1–11:26)

The first half of Genesis presents the impressive divine creation of the universe and then traces the first steps of God extending His rule over all creation. As He deals with human rebellion, the Lord lays the groundwork for the establishment of a servant nation. The four key events of chaps. 1–11 are creation, fall, the flood, and Babel.

A. *Creation (1:1–2:3)*. The God who spoke the heavens and earth into existence is the incomparable God, totally unlike any of the so-called deities of the ANE. Creation demonstrates God's awesome power and majesty, and it also reveals God's intent in creating mankind. He intends that every knee bow to Him and every tongue assent to His absolute sovereignty.[70]

B. *Human sin and divine intervention (2:4–6:8)*. In the wake of creation God made man painfully aware of his incompleteness (2:18–25). Unlike God, who is complete in Himself, man was made with a built-in need for a companion. God provided Eve, a woman who would "complete" Adam and serve as his partner in carrying God's intentions for the world. Adam and Eve's choice to sin interfered, in the immediate sense, with the accomplishment of God's plan. Will man absolutely submit to God's sovereignty or choose his own way (and seek to rule his own kingdom)?[71] In His mercy and grace God provided a symbolic provision of forgiveness with the animal skins.[72] As part of the consequences for their sin, God banished Adam and Eve from the garden of Eden. However, He did not cut them off from Him absolutely and would progressively reveal how they could one day be welcomed back into His presence. In the wake of human sin, two lines of descent appeared—the line of Seth and the line of Cain, godly and ungodly lines, respectively. Although God ensures the continuation of the godly line, the ungodly line makes a powerful impact on the world. The horrific sin of Gen 6:1–4 and its far-reaching consequences provide the occasion for a divine judgment that would exterminate all of humanity except the eight who sought refuge in the ark.

C. *Punishment and renewal (6:9–11:26)*. Noah served as an example of what God wanted mankind to be, and God's deliverance of Noah and his family from the flood pictured the eternal deliverance He would provide for those who rely on the salvation He promises. After the flood, the Lord promised that He would not destroy the earth again in *this fashion*. The genealogy of chap. 10 climaxes in the line of Seth, paving the way for God's introduction of Abraham as His covenant partner in chap. 12. The rebellion at the tower of Babel represents another attempt to defy God's rule (11:1–9). However, the feeble attempts of its builders to

---

[69] This chapter's author holds to the early-earth creation view.

[70] The numerous important and complicated exegetical issues in chaps. 1–2 in particular exceed the more synthetic concerns of this treatment of Genesis.

[71] Satan's involvement in the fall of mankind into sin represented a flagrant attempt to usurp God's sovereignty once again. Nevertheless God promised to deal a mortal blow to Satan and his descendants. Later biblical revelation (Gen 49:10–11; Num 24:17; 1 Chr 17:11–14; Isa 7:14; 9:6 [HB, v. 5]; Matt 1:18–23) makes it clear that the seed of the woman, Christ, would bring fulfillment to God's plan and initiate the end of Satan's flawed striving for absolute sovereignty.

[72] The text does not explicitly say that God's provision of animal skins to clothe Adam and Eve also gave them forgiveness of their sins and salvation. However, the death of that animal prefigured what God would require for their redemption, viz., shedding of innocent blood.

go their own way triggered circumstances that forced the people to carry out what God had already commanded them to do, namely, to spread throughout the world and function as His image-bearers. The "darkness" of the Babel rebellion provides the backdrop for God's introduction of the next step of accomplishing His plan to extend His rule over the entire created world (11:10–26).

II. Patriarchal History (11:27–50:26)

In the preceding chapters the Lord introduced the "what" or big idea, namely, extending His rule over the entire created world. Human sin and rebellion, in the ultimate sense, could not forestall the accomplishment of that divine plan. The ensuing chapters delineate the "how," the way God will bring His intentions into reality.

A. *Patriarchal Narratives about Abraham (11:27–25:18)*. Of all the families of the earth God elected Abraham to "father" a people who would become a servant nation through whom He would impact the world. God made Abraham and his descendants the vehicle for the "seed" of the woman (3:15) that would culminate in the Messiah. God promised to provide Abraham and his offspring with a land, worldwide fame, and the opportunity to be a tool He would use to impact the world (12:1–3). What Abraham (and his descendants) must do is implicitly depend on the Lord to do exactly what He promised. In the subsequent chapters Abraham at times modeled faith, but all too often he resorted to his own devices. In more than one instance the Lord tested Abraham's willingness to live out his belief that God will bring His promises to pass. When God provided Abraham with his long-anticipated son and then, through a painful set of circumstances, spared that son of promise from what seemed like certain death, Abraham faced the need to live by faith in the incomparable God of the universe. He will bring to pass what He promised.

B. *Patriarchal Narratives about Abraham's Descendants (Primarily Jacob) (25:19–37:1)*. Although Jacob receives the bulk of attention in this section, Isaac plays no insignificant role. When Abraham died, God's covenant plan did not come to a screeching halt. No, God continued revealing His covenant plan for Israel (and the world). As He did with Abraham and Sarah, the Lord gave Isaac and Rebekah a child (in fulfillment of His covenant promise) in a way that makes it absolutely clear to all that He alone is responsible for this provision of another son of promise. God's intentions are further narrowed: Isaac and not Ishmael, Jacob and not Esau. God chose to work through Jacob to continue the outworking of His plan for His creation, not because Jacob was a paragon of virtue and submission, but because God had seen fit to do so. After two decades in Paddan-aram, Jacob returned to his homeland, with covenant blessings of his own: wives, children, herds, and flocks. After an unfortunate set of events at Shechem, the Lord told Jacob to move south, first to Bethel and eventually to Hebron, where his father Isaac was still living.

The verses that delineate the family and eventual influence of Esau (chap. 36) tangibly demonstrate that God is interested in impacting nations other than Israel. God intends to bring salvation to the nations (Gen 12:3; 26:4; 28:14). The verses in chap. 36 also pave the way for understanding God's demand for Israel to treat the Edomites properly in later centuries (e.g., Deut 2:1–8; 23:7).

C. *The Story of Joseph (37:2–50:26)*. The God who established His covenant people and guides them will also preserve them. The wickedness of the Canaanites had an impact on Jacob's family. When Jacob first returned to Canaan, his family faced challenges with the inhabitants of Shechem (34:1–17). Reuben had intimate relations with his father's handmaiden (35:22), and Judah eventually chose to marry a Canaanite woman (38:1–2). God Himself orchestrated the transition of Jacob's family from Canaan to Egypt. He allowed Jacob's favored son, Joseph, to experience tragedy after tragedy, a set of circumstances that eventually led to his promotion to the second highest position in the Egyptian government. Malicious intent, outright lies, negligence—all contributed to the humanly challenging circumstances of Joseph. On the other hand God used those circumstances to install Joseph in a position where he would be able to provide a haven for his beloved father Jacob and his entire family. Although his brothers had acted out of malicious evil, God arranged these circumstances to accomplish what He determined to be good (50:20). God was bringing to pass His plan to work in and through the descendants of Abraham for His own glory.

THE THEOLOGY OF THE BOOK

A central purpose of the book of Genesis is to lay the foundation for the theocracy, that is, the rule of God over His creation. The book also explains how and why God chose Abraham to father a nation and make a covenant with that people. House provides a descriptive summary of the theological message of Genesis:

> Genesis acts as foundational prelude to Israel's greatest leader (Moses), Israel's most crucial event (the exodus), Israel's defining moment (Sinai) and Israel's immediate future (the conquest of Canaan). It expresses the roots and results of worldwide rebellion against God and Israel's place in the remedy for that rebellion. Standing serenely above all these vital, defining ideas, though, is the book's portrayal of one God who alone creates and rules all that has been created.[73]

Genesis lays the groundwork for the rest of the OT by giving attention to a number of important truths. The ones summarized below are creation, the rule of God, sin, covenant, and election, to select a few themes from the many in the book.

Creation

The theme of creation begins and ends the Bible. God's plan for His creation spans both testaments and is bracketed by two creations. The Scriptures begin with the creation of the universe (Genesis 1–2) and end with a description of a more glorious creation, that of the new heavens and new earth (Revelation 21–22). God's creation of the universe and all it contains was not for the sake of His handiwork, but for His own purposes. The apostle Paul wrote concerning Christ that "by Him everything created . . . all things have been created through Him and for Him" (Col 1:16).

Imagine the impact of this truth on Moses' immediate audience in addition to those of every following generation. God begins with an earth that is "formless and empty" (Gen 1:2) and he brings order, beauty, and perfection to that world. In a methodical, symmetrical, and beautiful progression, Moses leads his readers through the creative week as each realm of the created universe submits to God's authority. The Lord's power is unparalleled, especially if one were to compare the creation by the God of Israel with the imperfect and somewhat chaotic creation myths of the ANE world. God will bring His chosen nation into the land of Canaan, give them victory, and enable them to receive the land of promise as a divine stewardship.

---

[73] P. R. House, *Old Testament Theology* (Downers Grove, IL: InterVarsity, 1998), 58.

As the great Creator God is worthy of their faith and obedience, He has no limitations that will prevent Him from accomplishing His plan for the entire created world according to His timetable.

Rule of God

A motif that begins in Genesis 1 and continues throughout the Bible is God's intention to extend His rule over all creation. God made man, the crowning jewel of His creation, to function as His image. The statement that the Godhead created man "in Our image, according to Our likeness" (1:26) delineates man's function (what he is to be and do) and not merely his essence (what he is like).[74] According to Merrill, "Man was created . . . to serve as the agent of God in implementing God's sovereign will and sway over the universe."[75] God commissioned mankind, the crowning jewel of His creation, to serve as His vice-regent in the world. He desires that mankind would be a tool for God to bring every part of creation into submission to His rule. God could have easily ruled the world on His own, but He chose to work through representative figures. After He declared that He made mankind to function as His image-bearer, fashioned in accord with God's image, He declares to Adam, His vice-regent: "Be fruitful, multiply, fill the earth, and subdue it. Rule the fish of the sea, the birds of the sky, and every creature that crawls on the earth" (1:28).

Sin

As the image of God, man is to represent God Himself as the sovereign over all creation. Man is to carry out this mediatorial/representative role by means of exercising lordship over all creation (1:28–29). Unfortunately Adam's sin disrupted the accomplishment of God's intentions for His creation (chap. 3). Adam and Eve's sin marred God's perfect order and initiated the human tendency to rebel against God's rule. No longer would the earth and animal world willingly submit to His direction. Adam's sin disrupted the harmony of all man's relationships (with God, with other human beings, with creation). After casting Adam and Eve out of the garden, God initiated the provision of reconciliation for fallen mankind. The salvation provided by this reconciliation would enable Adam (and mankind) to return to his role as God's vice-regent.[76]

Other rebellions against God's rule are recorded in chaps. 4–11. This penchant to rebel against God's sovereignty (whether direct or mediated through His representatives) manifests itself in the abhorrent human conduct leading up to the flood and the rebellion at Babel. God's response to both rebellions was severe judgment (universal flood, worldwide dispersal). This leads to the truth of God initiating a covenant relationship with Abraham and his descendants.

Covenant

In each case of rebellion and judgment referred to above, one could ask, "Does this judgment mean the end of God's redemptive dealings with mankind?" God resolves that tension by raising up other mediators (Noah, Abram) to carry out His purposes for mankind after each judgment. In fact, the textual interweaving of the narratives describing these rebellions

---

[74] E. H. Merrill, "A Theology of the Pentateuch," in *A Biblical Theology of the Old Testament*, ed. R. B. Zuck (Chicago: Moody, 1991), 14.

[75] E. H. Merrill, "Covenant and the Kingdom: Genesis 1–3 as Foundation for Biblical Theology," *CTR* (1987): 298. See also idem, *Everlasting Dominion: A Theology of the Old Testament* (Nashville: B&H, 2006), 135–37.

[76] The "salvation" provided here was accomplished through the redemptive work of Christ, ordained by the Godhead before the foundation of the world.

and God's response with the genealogies in chaps. 5 and 11 carefully delineates the significant role played by these mediatorial figures. Widbin points out that the "genealogical notices (Gen 5:32; 11:10–26) link Adam, Noah, and Abram, each ten generations apart. This literary pattern identifies these individuals as single representatives and bearers of the potential for blessing of human life in history."[77]

The narrative immediately preceding God's call of Abraham out of Ur (11:27–12:3) describes God's judgment against His rebellious creatures at Babel (11:1–9). The historical stage onto which Abraham entered seems to be characterized by chaos and rebellion. Once again God raised up a special individual to function as His vice-regent and to bring equity and order to the world. More than that, in His choice of Abraham God singled out a people to carry out that representative role. Moberly draws attention to the strategic location of 12:1–3, which introduces the subsequent patriarchal accounts, setting them in relation to the record of God's dealings with the whole of humanity in chaps. 1–11. Moberly suggests that this passage provides the context for the subsequent delineation of God's purposes for Israel, "whose existence is to be related to Yahweh's purposes for the whole world."[78]

Both a particularity and a universalism pervades this covenantal arrangement. As was clear since the creation of mankind, God's intentions encompass the entire world. He will establish His rule over all His creation (1:26–28). In 12:1–3 the Lord not only reveals what He will do for Abraham, but He also begins to demonstrate the means by which He will address His universal purposes. God will cause Abraham to father a great nation, not for his (or their) sake, but because Abraham (and the nation) will be the means through whom Yahweh blesses all nations.

Election

God's call for Abraham to leave his home in Ur and set out for a land of God's choosing constitutes God's election of Abraham to father a special people for Himself. In 12:1–3 (the initial expression of the Abrahamic covenant, restated and developed in chaps. 15 and 17) God declared His intentions for Abraham and the means by which He will accomplish His purposes for the world.

This covenant arrangement is unconditional in that it exists, regardless of the behavior of the recipient. Only the *enjoyment* of the covenant benefits is conditioned on the obedience of the subordinate covenant partners. It is unilateral in that the ultimate fulfillment of its provisions rests on God's surpassing character.[79]

The massive transition that exists between chaps. 11 and 12 highlights the significance of covenant and election. In chaps. 1–11 the narrative focuses on the universe and all the inhabitants of the world. There is indeed a narrowing of focus that occurs with Noah and his three sons, but still all humanity is at stake. Genesis 12, somewhat abruptly, narrows the panorama from all humanity to one man and his descendants.[80] Election and God's choice to enter into

---

[77] R. B. Widbin, "Salvation for People outside Israel's Covenant?" in *Through No Fault of Their Own: The Fate of Those Who Have Never Heard*, ed. W. V. Crockett and J. G. Sigountos (Grand Rapids: Baker, 1991), 78 n. 9; see also M. Fishbane, *Text and Texture: Close Readings of Selected Biblical Texts* (New York: Schocken, 1979), 30–31.

[78] R. W. L. Moberly, *The Old Testament of the Old Testament: Patriarchal Narratives and Mosaic Yahwism* (Minneapolis: Fortress, 1992), 141.

[79] Merrill, "Theology of the Pentateuch," *Biblical Theology of the Old Testament*, 26; W. C. Kaiser Jr., *Toward an Old Testament Theology* (Grand Rapids: Zondervan, 1978), 93–94.

[80] Actually, this transition is introduced in 11:27, but the primary impact of the transition is felt in 12:1.

covenant relationship with one man and his descendants is explained well by Baylis in his summary of the transition from Genesis 1–11 to 12–50:

> In Genesis 1–11 we were faced with cosmic issues: the sovereign Creator, the divine order for life, the destructive and debilitating effects of sin, God as sovereign moral ruler, and man as God's designated regent—yet unable to rule himself. Genesis builds on these themes, but focuses our vision on the cosmic importance of one person's life. Genesis 1–11 crunches more than 2000 years of human history—perhaps much more—into less than twenty percent of the book. Genesis 12–50 deals with only four generations. God has focused on one family before. He began with Adam and Eve, but the account quickly moves on through generations to the Flood. He began all over with Noah and his family. But again, from a few critical incidents in their lives the camera scans to the failure of civilization.
>
> With Abraham we are beginning again. Abraham—initially "Abram"—is God's chosen instrument for starting His program of reversal. The development of God's program of redemption begins to take shape in the story of Abraham. God intends the entire world to be in proper relationship with Himself. This universal redemption, however, will come about by selecting not everyone, but a few. This is the Story of Reversal.[81]

CONCLUSION

Genesis, indeed a book of beginnings, lays a marvelous foundation for the history and theology presented in the rest of the OT. It vividly portrays the incomparable one and only God of the universe, who speaks the world into existence. In measured tones it presents the treachery committed by Adam and Eve in a situation where disobedience seems shocking. The book goes on to show, with initial and incomplete information, how God intended to provide redemption for His creation. God intends to extend His rule over every part of His creation, and so He created mankind to function as His vice-regents, that is, to be His tools through whom He will rule over His subjects. The Lord chose Abraham to father a people who will one day become His servant nation, a nation through whom He will demonstrate His unparalleled glory to the world.

STUDY QUESTIONS

1. What is the impact of source, form, and tradition history criticism on the understanding of Genesis?
2. Whom does this volume present as the author of Genesis?
3. What expression serves as a structural key to understand the layout of the book of Genesis?
4. How do evangelicals who believe in divine inspiration of the Bible explain their view of Genesis 1–2 as myth?
5. How do evangelicals who reject the idea that Genesis 1–2 are myth support their view? What similarities and differences exist between the biblical and ANE accounts of creation?

---

[81] A. H. Baylis, *From Creation to the Cross: Understanding the First Half of the Bible* (Grand Rapids: Zondervan, 1996), 79.

6. How should we explain the key terms in the creation/evolution debate: young earth, old earth, intelligent design?
7. What are the fundamental ideas of theistic evolution?
8. What are the fundamental ideas of old-earth creationism?
9. What are some of the subvarieties of old-earth creationism?
10. What are the fundamental ideas of young-earth creationism?
11. What are three key ideas one must consider in evaluating the different options in the creation-evolution debate?
12. What are the key theological ideas in Genesis?

FOR FURTHER STUDY

Arnold B. T. *Encountering the Book of Genesis: A Study of Its Content and Issues*. Grand Rapids: Baker, 1998.

———. *Genesis*. New York: Cambridge University Press, 2009.

Ashley, T. R. *The Book of Numbers*. NICOT. Grand Rapids: Eerdmans, 1993.

Beall, T. S. "Contemporary Hermeneutical Approaches to Genesis 1–11." In *Coming to Grips with Genesis: Biblical Authority and the Age of the Earth*. Edited by Terry Mortenson and Thane H. Ury, 131–62. Green Forest, AR: Master Books, 2008.

Boyd, S. W. "The Genre of Genesis 1:1–2:3: What Means This Text?" In *Coming to Grips with Genesis: Biblical Authority and the Age of the Earth*. Edited by Terry Mortenson and Thane H. Ury, 163–92. Green Forest, AR: Master Books, 2008.

———. "Statistical Determination of Genre in Biblical Hebrew: Evidence for an Historical Reading of Genesis 1:1–2:3." In *RATE II: Radioisotopes and the Age of the Earth: Results of a Young-Earth Creationist Research Initiative*. Edited by L. Vardiman et al., 631–734. San Diego: Institute for Creation Research and the Creation Research Society, 2005.

Collins, C. J. *Genesis 1–4: A Linguistic, Literary, and Theological Commentary*. Phillipsburg, NJ: P & R, 2006.

Craigen, T. "Can Deep Time Be Embedded in Genesis?" In *Coming to Grips with Genesis: Biblical Authority and the Age of the Earth*. Edited by Terry Mortenson and Thane H. Ury, 193–210. Green Forest, AR: Master Books, 2008.

Hamilton, V. P. *The Book of Genesis: Chapters 1–17*. NICOT. Grand Rapids: Eerdmans, 1990.

———. *The Book of Genesis: Chapters 18–50*. NICOT. Grand Rapids: Eerdmans, 1995.

———. *Handbook on the Pentateuch*. 2nd ed. Grand Rapids: Baker, 2005.

Harbin, M. A. *The Promise and Blessing: A Historical Survey of the Old and New Testaments*. Grand Rapids: Zondervan, 2005.

Harrison, R. K. *Introduction to the Old Testament*. Grand Rapids: Eerdmans, 1969.

Hasel, G. F. "The 'Days' of Creation in Genesis 1: Literal 'Days' or Figurative 'Periods/Epochs' of Time?" *Origins* 21 (1994): 5–38.

———. "Polemic Nature of the Genesis Cosmology." *EQ* 46 (April–June 1974): 81–102.

———. "The Significance of the Cosmology in Genesis 1 in Relation to Ancient Near Eastern Parallels." *AUSS* 10 (1972): 1–20.

House, P. R. *Old Testament Theology*. Downers Grove, IL: InterVarsity, 1998.

Kaiser, W. C., Jr. *The Promise-Plan of God: Biblical Theology of the Old and New Testaments*. Grand Rapids: Zondervan, 2008.

Kelly, D. F. *Creation and Change: Genesis 1:1–2:4 in the Light of Changing Scientific Paradigms*. Ross-shire, UK: Christian Focus, 1997.

Kulikovsky, A. S. *Creation, Fall, Restoration: A Biblical Theology of Creation*. Ross-shire, UK: Christian Focus, 2009.

Longman, T., III. *How to Read Genesis*. Downers Grove, IL: InterVarsity, 2005.

Mathews, K. A. *Genesis 1:1–11:26*. NAC. Nashville: B&H, 1996.

———. *Genesis 11:27–50:26*. NAC. Nashville: B&H, 2005.

McCabe, R. V. "A Critique of the Framework Interpretation of the Creation Week." In *Coming to Grips with Genesis: Biblical Authority and the Age of the Earth*. Edited by Terry Mortenson and Thane H. Ury, 211–49. Green Forest, AR: Master Books, 2008.

Merrill, E. H. *Everlasting Dominion: A Theology of the Old Testament*. Nashville: B&H, 2006.

Newman, R. C. "Progressive Creationism ('Old Earth Creationism')." In *Three Views on Creation and Evolution*. Edited by S. N. Gundry, J. P. Moreland, and J. M. Reynolds, 103–33. Grand Rapids: Zondervan, 1999.

Oswalt, J. N. *The Bible among the Myths: Unique Revelation or Just Ancient Literature*. Grand Rapids: Zondervan, 2009.

Ross, A. P. *Creation and Blessing: A Guide to the Study and Exposition of the Book of Genesis*. Grand Rapids: Baker, 1988.

Ross, M. "The Framework Hypothesis: An Interpretation of Genesis 1:1–2:3." In *Did God Create in Six Days?* Edited by J. A. Pipa Jr. and D. W. Hall, 113–30. Taylors, SC: Southern Presbyterian Press, 1999.

Sailhamer, J. "Genesis." In *EBC*. Rev. ed. Edited by T. Longman III and D. E. Garland, 1:21–331. Grand Rapids: Zondervan, 2008.

Schnittjer, G. *The Torah Story*. Grand Rapids: Zondervan, 2006.

Van Til, H. J. "The Fully Gifted Creation ('Theistic Evolution')." In *Three Views on Creation and Evolution*. Edited by S. N. Gundry, J. P. Moreland, and J. M. Reynolds, 161–218. Grand Rapids: Zondervan, 1999.

Waltke, B. K. *An Old Testament Theology*. Grand Rapids: Zondervan, 2007.

———, with Cathi J. Fredricks. *Genesis: A Commentary*. Grand Rapids: Zondervan, 2001.

Walton, J. H. "Creation." In *DOTP*. Edited by T. D. Alexander and D. W. Baker, 155–68. Downers Grove, IL: InterVarsity, 2003.

———. *Genesis*. NIVAC. Grand Rapids: Zondervan, 2001.

———. *The Lost World of Genesis One: Ancient Cosmology and the Origins Debate*. Downers Grove, IL: InterVarsity, 2009.

Wenham, G. *Genesis 1–15*. WBC. Waco, TX: Word, 1987.

———. *Genesis 16–50*. WBC. Waco, TX: Word, 1994.

Young, D. A. *Christianity and the Age of the Earth*. Grand Rapids: Zondervan, 1982.

Youngblood, R. *The Genesis Debate*. Nashville: Thomas Nelson, 1986.

THE BOOK OF EXODUS

MICHAEL A. GRISANTI

T HE BOOK OF Exodus continues the account of God's dealings with the descendants of Abraham that began in Genesis. This continuation of God's dealings with His chosen people is not uneventful or insignificant. Exodus is a book of major transition. God transformed the descendants of Abraham into a fledgling nation. Exodus is also a book of redemption, demonstrating how the Israelites gained their freedom from Egypt by means of divine intervention. It is a book of revelation, a book in which God's character and His covenantal expectations arrive with stark clarity. And Exodus is a book of communion, delineating the means by which a sinful people could have fellowship with a holy God (a theme Leviticus will continue).

THE TITLE AND CANONICITY OF THE BOOK

The title of Exodus in the Hebrew Bible is "And these are the names of," the opening words of Exod 1:1.[1] The Greek translators of the OT gave the book the title 'exódou, "a way out."[2] Obviously this title highlights God's deliverance of His chosen people from slavery in Egypt as part of His plan to bring them into the land of promise.

This seemingly obscure statement at the beginning of Exodus suggests a strong connection with the narrative of Genesis. The conjunction points to the connection of this statement with whatever precedes, in this case the end of the book of Genesis.[3] This book begins where the book of Genesis left off, giving attention to the sons of Israel/Jacob.

THE COMPOSITION AND DATE OF THE BOOK

According to Jewish and Christian traditions, Moses authored the book of Exodus under the direction of God. As with the book of Genesis, the primary options for the composition of

---

[1] The Hebrew phrase is *w'ēlleh š'môt*, but the Hebrew title for Exodus is often limited to *Shemoth*.

[2] This is apparently based on the LXX translation of Exod 19:1.

[3] Even this construction, a conjunction on a non-verb (which often introduces some circumstantial or disjunctive idea), occurs as part of a flowing narrative, not as an introduction of a totally new book.

Exodus fall into two categories. The first category alleges the use of various sources, gathered and edited by someone long after Moses, and the second views Moses as having some responsibility as the author or source of the traditions.

Compiled from Sources through Oral Tradition

Those scholars who subscribe to some form of source criticism suggest that Exodus represents the compilation of at least three sources: J (Yahwist), E (Elohist), and P (Priestly) documents.[4] As an example of this distribution, see the chart below.[5] Concerning Exodus, chaps. 1–34 are viewed as a "splicing together of J, E, and P, while chaps. 35–40 (that deal with the tabernacle) involve P alone.[6] Priestly authors/editors wove together the text of Exodus sometime during or after the exile to Babylon.

Figure 11.1 - Distribution of the JEDP Sources in the Pentateuch

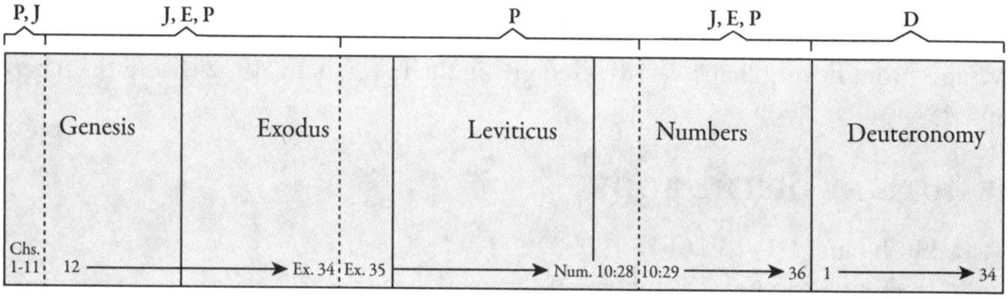

As stated in chap. 10 of this volume, scholars who explain the composition of Exodus as the result of the gathering together of these written sources view this as the end of a very long process. In the "original setting" or *Sitz im Leben*, the passages found in Exodus each had a unique function in the life and culture of Israel (form criticism). From that time until the alleged documents came into existence (several centuries later according to tradition historians), the oral traditions went through various stages of rewriting, adjusting, and even expansion. Thus according to these writers, the accuracy of the Exodus passages is somewhat questionable.

Moses as "Author"

Some view Moses as the exclusive author with every word written by him. Others say Moses was the primary author of Exodus with only minor additions added later for the purpose of clarification in view of the passage of centuries.[7] Some say Moses wrote significant parts of the book with certain sections added by later editors (e.g., the genealogy in 6:14–27).[8] Still others

---

[4] See the chapter that introduces Part 4 and the composition section in chap. 10 on Genesis for a fuller overview of source, form, and traditio-historical criticism.

[5] This chart is based on A. E. Hill and J. H. Walton, *A Survey of the Old Testament*, 3rd ed. (Grand Rapids: Zondervan, 2009), 766.

[6] Even source critics recognize that "the literary relationships [between J, E, and P] are rather more complicated than in Genesis" (M. Noth, *Exodus*, OTL [Philadelphia: Westminster, 1962], 13).

[7] See the discussion of textual updating in chap. 5.

[8] Some have suggested that extensive third-person narrative sections could have been added by someone after Moses to bring a later audience up to date. For example, see Hill and Walton, *A Survey of the Old Testament*, 104–5.

believe that later writers composed the book of Exodus based on oral tradition passed down from Moses and Aaron.

Scholars who take one of the first three views date the book of Exodus in accord with their view of the date of the exodus from Egypt (see section below). Those who regard the book as the result of later individuals gathering together Mosaic traditions do not date the book in light of the events it describes. The text of Exodus provides several explicit references to Mosaic writing activity (17:14; 24:4; 34:4,27–29). See the section on the composition of Genesis for ways evangelical scholars explain the authorship of Exodus as part of the Pentateuch.[9] The present author regards Moses as the author of the book of Exodus (allowing for minor inspired editorial activity).

THE STRUCTURE OF THE BOOK

Exodus does not have clear structural markers as does Genesis (the *tôledôt* formula). But Exodus seems to be laid out along key geographical lines. The outline below delineates the geographic progression of God's dealings with the Israelites (in Egypt, between Egypt and Sinai, at Sinai). Others have outlined the book in a more thematic fashion, focusing on divine deliverance from Egypt (chaps. 1–18), God giving the Law (chaps. 19–24), and the tabernacle (chaps. 25–40).

THE OUTLINE OF THE BOOK

   I. Israel in Egypt (1:1–13:16)
       A. The Oppression of Israel in Egypt (chap. 1)
       B. The Deliverer of Israel from Egypt (chaps. 2–4)
       C. The Struggle of Moses with Pharaoh in Egypt (5:1–13:16)

  II. Israel's Journey from Egypt to Sinai (13:17–18:27)
       A. The Exodus from Egypt (13:17–15:21)
       B. The Journey to Sinai (15:22–18:27)

 III. God's Revelation to Israel at Sinai (chaps. 19–40)
       A. The Establishment of God's Covenant with His People (chaps. 19–24)
           1. A Theophany on Mount Sinai (chap. 19)
           2. The Decalogue (20:1–21)
           3. The Book of the Covenant (20:22–23:33)
           4. The Ratification of the Covenant (chap. 24)
       B. Instructions concerning the Tabernacle (chaps. 25–31)
       C. The Failure and Restoration of God's People (chaps. 32–34)
       D. The Erection of the Tabernacle (chaps. 35–40)

AN OVERVIEW OF EXODUS

Israel in Egypt (1:1–13:16)

The book of Exodus begins with a description of Israel's painful transition from bliss and abundance to slavery. This challenging set of circumstances provides the backdrop for God's intervention in Israel's affairs. Through His glorious deliverance of the people of Israel from slavery in Egypt, God would transform the people of Abraham (the Hebrews) to the nation of Israel. God introduced Moses to the reader and Israel as His chosen instrument of deliverance.

---

[9] See Part 4, which introduces the Pentateuch in this volume.

Moses' request that the Egyptian pharaoh release God's people initiates a "battle" between God and his human deliverer and the powerful ruler of Egypt. Through the 10 plagues (see further explanation below) that ensued, the Lord demonstrated His absolute power over all realms of life, in contrast to the weak and compartmentalized gods of Egypt. This vivid demonstration of God's majesty and authority impacted Egypt, and also presented God as the incomparable God of Israel who does whatever is necessary to bring His plans to pass.

Israel's Journey from Egypt to Sinai (13:17–18:27)

Israel's journey to Mount Sinai represents much more than a change of location. It was an important step in the fulfillment of some of the provisions of the Abrahamic covenant—to become a nation and occupy their own land. Led by the pillar of cloud by day and pillar of fire by night (a visible manifestation of Yahweh's presence), God's people journeyed to the western shore of the "Red Sea." There God delivered His people from the Egyptian army, whom the Pharaoh sent against the Hebrews sometime after their departure from Egypt. The Lord parted the waters of the Red Sea, allowing God's people to cross that body of water on dry land. After the Israelites had crossed to the other side, those same waters crashed on the pursuing Egyptian soldiers, killing them all. In addition to being one of the most impressive miracles of the Old Testament, this divine intervention tangibly demonstrated that Yahweh can do all that is needed to bring His promises to pass.

Unfortunately many Israelites did not seem to believe that God would take care of them. At two locations they grumbled and complained about their need of food and water. In both places Yahweh abundantly took care of them regardless of their shortsightedness. He also delivered them from Amalekites and then brought them to Mount Sinai.

God's Revelation to Israel at Sinai (chaps. 19–40)

After God delineated the rationale for the Mosaic covenant (to be a servant nation; see below), He introduced that covenant with the Decalogue, or Ten Commandments (the heart of the Mosaic covenant; 20:1–21). God made these (and many other) covenantal demands of His people as part of the relationship that already existed between them (initiated in the Abrahamic covenant). His recent impressive deliverance of the Israelites from the clutches of Egypt was only the most recent way God had demonstrated the kind of God He is and His commitment to His relationship with them. He has the right to demand their total allegiance. After setting forth the requirements of the Book of the Covenant (20:22–23:33; see below), God and the leaders of Israel ratified the Mosaic covenant.

The bulk of chaps. 25–40 focuses on the building of the tabernacle (instructions concerning it are in chaps. 25–31, and the erection of it is recorded in chaps. 35–40). This sanctuary was to function as the nexus of God's relationship with His people. The tangible demonstration of God's presence and of most worship functions would be at the tabernacle. Sandwiched between the sections dealing with the tabernacle, chaps. 32–34 record the sad account of Israel's golden calf rebellion and the Lord's gracious forgiveness of His people.

An important transition takes place in the book of Exodus. The book opens with an account of the *descendants of Abraham*. It closes by describing the worship practices of the *nation of Israel*. God's performance of the 10 plagues, Israel's departure from Egypt, God's parting of the waters of the Red Sea, and His giving Israel the Law at Mount Sinai all contributed to the transformation of the people of Abraham to the nation Israel, a nation commissioned to represent the incomparable God of the universe.

THE DATE OF THE EXODUS FROM EGYPT

The question of the date of Israel's departure from Egypt has occupied scholars for centuries.[10] Until the last quarter of the twentieth century the most prominent options were the early (c. 1446 BC) and late dates (c. 1250 BC).[11] Even before then the scholarly consensus was that there was *no* exodus at all as described in the Bible.[12] After providing an overview of the major interpretive views on the Exodus from Egypt, this chapter summarizes the key evidence and suggests that the conventional early date provides the best reading of the evidence.[13]

Basic Views

No exodus at all.[14] In the 1970s a growing number of scholars embraced a thoroughgoing skepticism about the historical credibility of the OT (minimalists).[15] They concluded that the historical books of the OT were not composed until the time of the exile or later. The OT had no value for historical reconstruction. It demonstrated only what some people thought, believed, or wished had happened. Lemche affirms that "the authors of the book of Exodus created the narratives as we know them. These writers—just like the authors of the patriarchal narratives in Genesis—created their own narrative universe. They wrote about places and events that never existed." He adds that the Exodus narratives "describe a literary world, not historical facts."[16] William Dever, who eschews the title "minimalist" and has an antagonistic relationship with most minimalists, wrote, "Not only is there no archaeological evidence for an exodus, there is no need to posit such an event. . . . As a Syro-Palestinian archaeologist, I regard the historicity of the Exodus as a dead issue."[17]

---

[10] For a helpful overview of the primary issues involved in this debate see J. H. Walton, "Exodus, Date of," in *DOTP,* ed. T. D. Alexander and D. W. Baker (Downers Grove, IL: InterVarsity, 2003), 258–72. See also C. G. Rasmussen, "Conquest, Infiltration, Revolt, or Resettlement? What Really Happened during the Exodus–Judges Period?" in *Giving the Sense: Understanding and Using OT Historical Texts,* ed. D. M. Howard Jr., and M. A. Grisanti (Grand Rapids: Kregel, 2003), 138–59; W. H. Shea, "The Date of the Exodus," in *Giving the Sense: Understanding and Using OT Historical Texts,* 236–55; B. G. Wood, "From Ramesses to Shiloh: Archaeological Discoveries Bearing on the Exodus–Judges Period," in *Giving the Sense: Understanding and Using OT Historical Texts,* 256–82.

[11] In the 1950s J. Bright wrote, "There can be little doubt that ancestors of Israel had been slaves in Egypt and had escaped in some marvelous way. Almost no one today would question it . . . . the Biblical tradition a priori demands belief" (*A History of Israel* [Philadelphia: Westminster, 1959], 110).

[12] As K. L. Younger Jr. observes, "As the field of biblical studies enters a new millennium, the only apparent consensus is that the Albrightian 'conquest model' is invalidated" ("Early Israel in Recent Biblical Scholarship," in *The Face of OT Studies: A Survey of Contemporary Approaches,* ed. D. W. Baker and Bill T. Arnold [Grand Rapids: Baker, 1999], 177).

[13] The issues involved in this interpretation are abundant and complex. Three of the five positions summarized below are held by evangelicals. Each position has "weak links" of evidence.

[14] E. H. Merrill calls this view the "Emergence of Israel" model (*Kingdom of Priests: A History of OT Israel,* 2nd ed. [Grand Rapids: Baker, 2008], 145–47).

[15] Two seminal works seemed to provide the foundation and impetus for this approach to the OT: T. L. Thompson, *The Historicity of the Patriarchal Narratives: The Quest for the Historical Abraham,* BZAW (Berlin: de Gruyter, 1974); and J. Van Seters, *Abraham in History and Tradition* (New Haven, CT: Yale University Press, 1975).

[16] N. P. Lemche, *Prelude to Israel's Past: Backgrounds and Beginnings of Israelite History and Identity,* trans. E. F. Maniscalco (Peabody, MA: Hendrickson, 1998), 58, cf. 45–61. Lemche proposed that biblical scholars should treat the biblical account as any other legendary material, "as essential ahistorical; that is, as a source which only exceptionally can be verified by other information" (*Early Israel: Anthropological and Historical Studies on the Israelite Society before the Monarchy,* VTSup [Leiden: Brill, 1985], 415).

[17] W. G. Dever, "Is There Any Archaeological Evidence for the Exodus," in *Exodus: The Egyptian Evidence,* ed. E. S. Frerichs and L. H. Lesko (Winona Lake, IN: Eisenbrauns, 1997), 81.

Limited exodus but no conquest. Discussions of Israel's departure from Egypt are usually related to the conquest and settlement of Canaan.[18] Many scholars believe that only a handful of people came out of Egypt and traveled to the promised land, and joined with other nonindigenous people in the area of Canaan and eventually formed what is known as the people of Israel and then the nation of Israel.[19]

Limited exodus and conquest (Iron Age I; c. 1150 BC). Gary Rendsburg has proposed that a number of Israelites left Egypt sometime during the reign of Rameses III (around the same time the Philistines arrived in the region) where they rejoined Israelites who had never entered Egypt.[20] Excavations that show Iron Age I settlements at cities like Lachish, Gibeon, and Heshbon serve as primary evidence for his view. One of the unique features of his view is that Merneptah's reference to "Israel" on his stele describes Israel as a people still living as slaves *in Egypt.*[21]

Conventional late date (LB IIB, c. 1250 BC). According to this view the Nineteenth Dynasty kings of Egypt oppressed the Israelites, forcing them to build the storage cities of Pithom and Rameses (Exod 1:10). Proponents identify Rameses II as the pharaoh of the oppression as well as the exodus. The reference to Israel as a people in the Merneptah Stele (1207 BC) demonstrates that the exodus and conquest had to occur before that time.[22]

Middle Bronze early date (c. 1470 BC). John Bimson suggested that archaeologists incorrectly dated the end of the Middle Bronze period (hereafter MB) and changed the end date of that period from 1550 to 1430 BC.[23] Many cities destroyed at the "end" of the MB period can now be dated later. He suggests that some of these cities were destroyed as part of the Israelite conquest of Canaan. Also according to the customary dating of MB and Late Bronze periods (hereafter LB), few walled cities were found in LB. This dating change puts numerous walled cities in the same time as Bimson's suggested date for an exodus from Egypt. In summary Bimson rejects the late date of the exodus but proposes 1470 BC as the date for the Exodus (rather than the conventional early date of 1446 BC).

Conventional early date (LB I; c. 1446 BC). This traditional early date for Israel's exodus from Egypt[24] draws heavily on the chronological statement in 1 Kgs 6:1 which affirms that Solomon began building the temple in the fourth year of his reign, 480 years after the exodus. Since most scholars date Solomon's fourth year as 966 BC, the exodus took place in 1446 BC. These scholars also point to Jephthah's statement in Judg 11:26. Involved in "negotiations" with the Ammonites, he affirmed that the Israelites had been in possession of land that used to belong to the Ammonites for 300 years. According to the early date, Israel was in the Transjordan in 1406 BC, the fortieth year of the wilderness sojourn. Three hundred years from then would put the beginning of the Ammonite oppression in 1106 BC.

---

[18] Merrill refers to these views as the "Traditio-Historical" model and the "Sociological" model (*Kingdom of Priests*, 139–45). For some of the alternatives suggested by scholars, see chap. 15 (on Joshua).

[19] Cf. M. Noth, *The History of Israel*, 2nd ed. (New York: Harper & Row, 1960), 53–163; and J. Bright, *A History of Israel*, 4th ed. (Louisville: WJK, 2000), 148–73.

[20] G. A. Rendsburg, "The Date of the Exodus and the Conquest and Settlement: The Case for the 1100s," *VT* 42 (1992): 510–27.

[21] Ibid., 517–20.

[22] Proponents of the conventional late-date view are introduced below.

[23] J. J. Bimson, *Redating the Exodus and the Conquest*, JSOTSup (Sheffield: JSOT, 1978), 143–45; and J. J. Bimson and D. Livingston, "Redating the Exodus," *BAR* 13 (September/October 1987): 40–53, 66–68.

[24] Cf. Merrill, *Kingdom of Priests*, 83–92; Bruce K. Waltke, "Palestinian Artifactual Evidence Supporting the Early Date of the Exodus," *BSac* 129 (1972): 33–47; and Shea, "The Date of the Exodus," *Giving the Sense*, 236–55.

Biblical Statements

Scholars discuss various biblical passages in advocating their views on Israel's exodus from Egypt. This section considers four important biblical passages or issues: 480 years in 1 Kgs 6:1, the Mosaic conquest policy and how Joshua conducted Israel's conquest of Canaan, Jephthah's reference to 300 years in Judg 11:26, and the chronology of the period of the judges.

Input from 1 Kings 6:1. Taken at face value, the chronological data found in this passage, clearly points to 1446 BC as the date of the exodus. However, a number of scholars have correctly observed that the number 40 occurs repeatedly for a set number of days and years. It occurs almost 20 times in the expression "40 days" or "40 nights" and almost 50 times as "40 years." Thus many regard the number 40 as a somewhat symbolic number. The idea that a number in the OT can be approximate or a rounded number is not a problem. Whether 185,000, or some close number (e.g., 184,981), of Assyrian soldiers died does not seem essential or problematic (2 Kgs 19:35). It is also clear that numbers can have a symbolic or metaphorical function as well (1 Sam 18:7; Mic 6:7; 2 Pet 3:8). However, in numerous places a number should be taken at face value. It is also important to recognize that 480 occurs in a historical narrative, rather than a poetic passage.

Numerous scholars, evangelical and otherwise, have suggested that the number 480 should be regarded as a symbolic or schematic number, representing 12 generations of 40 years each.[25] However, since a generation is probably closer to 25 years, this number more accurately reflects 300 years instead of 480. Proponents of this view affirm that their conclusion concurs with an OT or ANE view of history rather than a modern one.[26] Some scholars who do not take an "early date" view of the exodus contend that there is "no convincing basis" for the conclusion that the number 480 in 1 Kgs 6:1 is to be viewed as resulting from calculating 12 generations of 40 years each.[27]

Hoffmeier offers another view on the 480 years. First, he draws on Wiseman's suggestion that 480 years is a nonliteral generalization to refer to the midpoint between the exodus and the exile, 12 generations of 40 years each.[28] In this view 480 is not a symbolic number for 300,[29] but a way to refer to a period of time. Second, Hoffmeier compares this to an ANE custom of "given distances" (*Distanzangaben*).[30] Some ANE texts refer to a certain number of years that elapse between two important events. Scholars have offered various computations

---

[25] Some scholars who advocate this schematic understanding of 480 are J. Gray, *I and II Kings*, 2nd ed., OTL (Philadelphia: Westminster, 1970), 159–60; Bright, *A History of Israel*, 123; M. Cogan, *1 Kings*, AB (New York: Doubleday, 2000), 236; R. K. Harrison, *Introduction to the Old Testament* (Grand Rapids: Eerdmans, 1969), 317; G. E. Wright, *Biblical Archaeology*, rev. ed. (Philadelphia: Westminster, 1962), 84; K. A. Kitchen, *On the Reliability of the Old Testament* (Grand Rapids: Eerdmans, 2003), 307–8.

[26] Commenting on his view that "480 years" should be understood as "300 years," Kitchen notes that in the ANE "the Hebrew Bible's own world (which ours is not!), such procedures were almost certainly in use" (*On the Reliability of the Old Testament*, 307). The problem is that Kitchen offers no evidence to support his conclusion that this procedure was a regular part of computations in the ANE world.

[27] E.g., M. A. Sweeney, *I and II Kings: A Commentary*, OTL (Louisville: WJK, 2007), 108; cf. M. J. Mulder, *1 Kings*, trans. John Vriend, HCOT (Leuven: Peeters, 1998), 1:231.

[28] J. K. Hoffmeier, "What Is the Biblical Date for the Exodus: A Response to Bryant Wood," *JETS* 50 (June 2007): 237–38. Cf. D. J. Wiseman, *1 and 2 Kings: An Introduction and Commentary*, TOTC (Downers Grove, IL: InterVarsity, 1993), 104.

[29] In another work Hoffmeier dismisses the customary symbolic treatment of 480 years for two reasons. First, he affirms this because genealogical lists from the exodus to Solomon's day do not add up to 10 or 11 generations. Second, there is no evidence elsewhere in the Bible for using a large number to symbolize a number of generations (*Israel in Egypt: The Evidence for the Authenticity of the Exodus Tradition* [New York: Oxford University Press, 1996], 125).

[30] Hoffmeier, "What Is the Biblical Date for the Exodus?" 238–39.

to explain the number of years mentioned.[31] In light of this practice Hoffmeier wonders if the reference to 480 years in 1 Kgs 6:1 might be an example of *Distanzangaben*. If so, the number of years mentioned does not give a chronological datum, "but rather [serves] to create a link between the building of Israel's temple and the event that led to YHWH becoming the God of Israel."[32]

Does this understanding mesh with the way the rest of the OT deals with chronological data? Outside of genealogical references (Gen 11:13,15,17) and a reference to Israel's sojourn in Egypt (Gen 15:13), Exod 12:40–41 and 1 Kgs 6:1 are the only times scholars identify the number 40 as a multiple of a chronological reference. This approach is not applied to somewhat large numbers in general. For example the 430 years of Egyptian sojourn (Exod 12:40–41) is not treated as schematic since it does not involve a multiple of 40.[33] Cassuto has pointed out that the OT employs two ways of presenting numbers, an ascending and a descending order.[34] He suggests that when numbers are presented in an ascending order (small numbers followed by larger numbers), the OT is providing technical or statistical data.[35] In 1 Kgs 6:1, the Hebrew text reads "in the eightieth year and four hundredth year" (other examples of this ascending order are in Gen 11:13,15,17; Exod 12:40–41; Num 7:13,19,25,86; 1 Kgs 9:23). Could this indicate that the number 480 was intended to be understood as a credible number? First Chronicles 6:33–37 lists 18 generations between Korah (who likely lived at the time of the exodus) and Heman, a singer in David's time. An assumption of 25 years for a generation results in a period of 450 years (and does not include the generation between David and Solomon). This does not prove the credibility of 480 years, but it does demonstrate its feasibility.

What compels competent scholars to deal with 480 as a schematic or symbolic number? Bright points out that the view that takes 480 at face value "has now been generally abandoned, *chiefly because it is difficult to harmonize with other evidence bearing on the problem.*"[36] In other words his conclusions about the archaeology of Egypt and Palestine drive his interpretation of the chronological data found in 1 Kgs 6:1. Of course significant and legitimate debates about the correct understanding of various archaeological conclusions are ongoing (see below). If a scholar views 480 years as a schematic number, he has not embraced heresy or betrayed evangelicalism. Scholars who hold to a late date of the exodus[37] share with proponents of the early-date view in accepting the credibility of the OT presentation of history. Unfortunately scholars have generally dismissed the validity of a face value understanding of the information in 1 Kgs 6:1 as something patently obvious in light of the archaeological evidence. It would be better for late-date proponents to present their understanding of 480 years as the consequence

---

[31] Not one of these potential examples of "given distances," however, uses the factors of 12 or 40.

[32] Hoffmeier, "What Is the Biblical Date for the Exodus?" 239.

[33] Wright, *Biblical Archaeology*, 84.

[34] U. Cassuto, *The Documentary Hypothesis and the Composition of the Pentateuch*, trans. I. Abrahams (Jerusalem: Magnes, 1961), 52–53.

[35] Cassuto states that "the tendency to exactness in these instances causes the smaller numbers to be given precedence and prominence" (ibid., 52).

[36] Bright, *History of Israel*, 123 (italics his). In the following pages of his volume he develops the archaeological evidence that he suggests supports a late date for the Exodus. K. A. Kitchen calls the face value interpretation of 480 years "lazy man's solution" and contends that "this too simple solution is ruled out by the combined weight of all the other biblical data plus additional information from external data" ("The Exodus," in *ABD*, ed. D. N. Freedman [New York: Doubleday, 1992], 2:702). Elsewhere Kitchen has proposed a more complicated explanation that involves 12 periods that would encompass the "554 + xyz years aggregate, on some principle not stated" (*On the Reliability of the Old Testament*, 308–9). He does not even grant that 480 could mean 480.

[37] That is, "conventional" late-date view.

of decisions they have made elsewhere rather than the obvious view or the one that is most in tune with practices of the ANE world. Though the schematic understanding of 480 years is not intrinsically compelling, it gains its primary strength from conclusions based on Egyptian and Palestinian archaeology. In addition, based on the way the OT presents chronological information, the face value interpretation is intrinsically strong. The conclusion that numbers must be understood metaphorically or schematically should draw on compelling evidence in the immediate passage or be based on other integrally related issues.

Mosaic conquest policy. When most people consider Israel's conquest of Canaan, they envision widespread destruction. Archaeologists consistently point out that the most cities of the LB I age do not manifest layers of destruction. What does the conquest policy presented in the Pentateuch as well as the biblical description of Israel's conquest of the land of Canaan suggest should be found? In a word the clear statement of Scripture concerning conquest destruction and the artifactual evidence of the conquest itself support an early date.[38]

First, the stated Mosaic conquest policy was that the property and structures of the land were to be left virtually intact. God promised to give them a land that would be relatively undamaged. The gods, high places, sacred pillars, inhabitants, and so forth, were to be destroyed or driven out, but no mention is made of widespread destruction of structures or cities (Exod 23:24; Num 33:50–56). Only the idols and whatever utensils were involved in idolatrous worship and the pagan Canaanite inhabitants were to be "devoted to destruction" (*ḥāram*). The Pentateuch also demonstrates that a promised result of the conquest of Canaan would be Israel's enjoyment of cities, houses, cisterns, vineyards, and groves they did not build or plant (Deut 6:10–11; 19:1; Josh 24:13).

Second, Joshua and his armies captured the Canaanite cities in two different ways. They occupied most of them without first destroying them, in accord with the Mosaic conquest policy summarized above. The verb used for "taking" a city (*lākad*) "is a technical term that describes in a general way the capture of a person or place but which in no way implies destruction."[39] When the narrative states that Joshua took a city and put it to the sword, this refers to the inhabitants of the city unless noted otherwise.[40] The verb, "to devote to destruction" (*ḥāram*), refers to the total destruction of the object, whether the inhabitants of a town or the structure and people together (e.g., 10:35,37,39–40; 11:11). Unless specifically stated, the people alone were destroyed in this "devotion to destruction." The focus of Joshua and the army of Israel was to drive out or kill the inhabitants of the land of Canaan, but in the process only three cities were destroyed by burning: Jericho (6:24), Ai (8:28), and Hazor (11:13) (cf. 24:13). For an overview of the archaeological evidence relevant to these cities, see the following section.

Jephthah's statement (Judg 11:26). The Ammonite attack against Israel occasioned Jephthah's rule over Israel as a judge. He sent a message to the Ammonite king in an attempt to negotiate an end to this conflict. One of his arguments was that the Israelites had occupied Ammonite territory for 300 years. During all that time the Ammonites never attempted to retake that land. Since it was gained through battle, it rightly belonged to Israel. Any just claim to the

---

[38] Two especially helpful articles on this argument are B. K. Waltke, "Palestinian Artifactual Evidence Supporting the Early Date of the Exodus," *BSac* 129 (Jan–March 1972): 33–47; and E. H. Merrill, "Palestinian Archaeology and the Date of the Conquest: Do Tells Tell Tales?" *GTJ* 3 (Spring 1982): 107–21.

[39] Merrill, "Palestinian Archaeology and the Date of the Conquest," 113.

[40] A common meaning for the noun "city" is "population" (L. Koehler and W. Baumgartner, *HALOT* [Leiden: Brill, 2001], 821).

land should have been presented long ago. If this chronological reference is valid, it provides strong evidence for an early date view of the Exodus. According to the conventional early-date view, Israel left Egypt in 1446 BC and began the conquest of Canaan in 1406 BC. They conquered the Ammonite region in the months immediately before the conquest, as the Israelites marched through the Transjordan area (Deut 2:24–37). As it stands, the 300-years figure between the conquest and Jephthah's conflict with the Ammonites is totally incompatible with the conventional late-date view. If the exodus were in 1250, a 300-year period would place this set of circumstances in 950 BC, that is, in the reign of Solomon. Also this number cannot be regarded as a schematic number like 480 in 1 Kgs 6:1.

An important reason scholars wonder about the value of Jephthah's chronological statement concerns his words in Judg 11:24: "Isn't it true that you may possess whatever your god Chemosh drives out for you, and we may possess everything the LORD our God drives out before us?" These words present two significant problems. First, Jephthah substituted Chemosh, the god of the Moabites, for Milcom, the god of the Ammonites. Second, he seems to have shown contempt for the bedrock beliefs of Israel. Yahweh presented Himself alone as the one who determines the boundaries of nations (Deut 32:8–9; Amos 9:7), and yet Jephthah seems to have granted Chemosh an equal standing with Yahweh, thereby suggesting a syncretistic perspective.

Scholars have interacted with this issue in three ways. First, as summarized above, various scholars regard the figure as reliable and supportive of an early date of the exodus.[41] Since Jephthah was involved in international diplomacy, he could not be casual about details and still maintain credibility with his enemies. Jephthah demonstrated an understanding of Israel's history, drawing on Numbers 22–24. Second, others affirm that Jephthah spoke erroneously. Kitchen's classic wit expresses this position well: "What we have is nothing more than the report of a brave but ignorant man's bold bluster in favor of his people, not a mathematically precise chronological datum. . . . It is in the same class as other statements that biblical writers may well report accurately but which they would not necessarily expect readers to believe."[42] He adds that for "blustering Jephthah's propagandistic 300 years . . . it is fatuous to use this as a serious chronological datum."[43] Third, some suggest that Jephthah said what he did for rhetorical effect[44] or as propaganda.[45] The Ammonite king was making a claim for land they had never controlled. The regions mentioned had originally been part of Moabite territory and then was conquered by Sihon the Amorite. "By speaking to him as a Moabite king, Jephthah sarcastically reminds him that he could claim the land only if he were Moabite. But even if this were the case, he could only claim what Chemosh granted and the Moabite god had surrendered this area long ago."[46] If Jephthah was able to argue this way possibly for rhetorical impact, he

---

[41] Merrill, *Kingdom of Priests*, 84–85; D. M. Howard, *Joshua*, NAC (Nashville: B&H, 1998), 31, 35; H. M. Wolf, *An Introduction to the Old Testament Pentateuch* (Chicago: Moody, 1991), 170; W. Shea, "Date of the Exodus," in *ISBE*, rev. ed., ed. G. W. Bromiley (Grand Rapids: Eerdmans, 1982), 2:233; C. J. Goslinga, *Joshua, Judges, Ruth*, trans. R. Togtman (Grand Rapids: Zondervan, 1987), 227–30.

[42] Kitchen, *On the Reliability of the Old Testament*, 209. See also A. E. Cundall, *Judges: An Introduction and Commentary*, TOTC (Downers Grove, IL: InterVarsity, 1978), 144; K. Lawson Younger Jr., *Judges and Ruth*, NIVAC (Grand Rapids: Zondervan, 2002), 256–57.

[43] Kitchen, *On the Reliability of the Old Testament*, 308.

[44] R. B. Chisholm Jr., "The Chronology of the Book of Judges: A Linguistic Clue to Solving a Pesky Problem," *JETS* 52 (June 2009): 254–55.

[45] D. I. Block, *Judges, Ruth*, NAC (Nashville: B&H, 1999), 362–63.

[46] Chisholm, "The Chronology of the Book of Judges," 254. Rejection of Jephthah's statement as credible chronological information does not automatically lead to a late-date view, as the rest of Chisholm's article demonstrates.

inflated the number of years that had lapsed since Israel's conquest of that region. Reference to 300 years would have grabbed the attention of his listeners. Block concludes, "Since this is a political speech, Jephthah crafts his comments deliberately for propaganda purposes rather than factual reconstruction."[47]

However, Jephthah's reference to 300 years may be an accurate figure, arguing for an early date for the exodus. The idea that he referred to Chemosh for rhetorical effect does not take away the possibility that the chronological reference is accurate. The point is that Ammon did not have a legitimate claim to that land. The Israelites took it from Sihon the Amorite, who had taken it from Moab. This fits Jephthah's reference to Chemosh (the Moabite god) instead of Milcom (the Ammonite god) and does not totally discredit his chronological statement. However, its accuracy may not be ironclad. Except for Chisholm, those who dismiss the possibility of Jephthah's statement as credible also advocate a late date for the exodus. But as noted, the 300-year figure, when taken at face value, does not fit the chronology of the late-date view. However, whether Jephthah's statement should be regarded as credible does not make the early-date view impossible.

Broad chronology of the Judges period. The chronological notations in the book of Judges total 410 years. If the chronological input of 1 Kgs 6:1 is taken at face value, 480 years elapsed between the exodus from Egypt and Solomon's beginning of the construction of the temple. So, in addition to the 410 years of stated time in the book of Judges, the following events[48] also must fit within that 480-year period:

Wilderness wanderings (Deut 1:3; Josh 5:10)	40 years
Conquest (Deut 2:14; Josh 14:7–10)	c. 7 years
Remaining days of Joshua[49] (33 + ?? years) (Josh 23:1; Judg 2:7) and years leading up to the period of the judges	c. 50–60 years
Period of the Judges	**410 stated years**
Judgeship of Eli (1 Sam 4:18)	40 years
Judgeship of Samuel (1 Sam 7:3–14; 10)	c. 40 years
Reign of Saul	c. 20–40 years
Reign of David[50]	40 years
4 years of Solomon's reign (1 Kgs 6:1)	4 years

Total: 241–271 years outside of the judges period

This results in a total of over 600 years that must "fit" into the 480 years between the exodus and the beginning of the temple construction.[51] Obviously then some of the events must have

---

[47] Block, *Judges, Ruth*, 363.

[48] See Chisholm, "The Chronology of the Book of Judges," 248, 252–53, for the rationale for some of these numbers. Of course, if all numbers that involve multiples of 40 are viewed as schematic, that would change the total. Since some of this information depends on interpretations in various passages, it is presented as a general frame of reference.

[49] Merrill assumes that Joshua was the same age as Caleb and places Joshua's death at 1366 BC, resulting in about 33 years between the conquest itself and Joshua's death (*Kingdom of Priests*, 166). One can only estimate how much time elapsed between Joshua's death and the first judge, Othniel (Josh 23:1; Judg 2:7).

[50] Ibid., 259–65.

[51] Block suggests 593, but does not include the years between the end of the conquest and the first judge (c. 33 years) (*Judges, Ruth*, 59–61). Hoffmeier offers 633 years ("What Is the Biblical Date for the Exodus," 227–28), and Kitchen pro-

overlapped. But the events that precede and follow the period of the judges could not have overlapped. So any overlapping had to involve the rule of the various judges and the times of peace between them.

The proponents of the conventional early-date view recognize some kind of overlapping of judgeships since they regard the chronological data in the book of Judges as credible. If the above numbers are at least representative, there are about 209–239 years in which to place the period of the judges. Various proposals have been made on how to do this. Chisholm's recent proposal offers a fairly streamlined view of the time of the judges, allowing 206 years for the events of the book.[52]

The conventional late-date view allows for 264 years between the conquest (c. 1230 BC) and Solomon's beginning of the construction of the temple. At first glance, especially with the numbers proposed above, there is virtually no time for the period of the judges (20 years!). Of course that is not what any late-date proponent would suggest. How can this tension be resolved? At least two approaches are possible. First, Cundall offers this approximate chronology for the period of the judges:[53]

1230	Entry into Canaan
1200	Othniel
1170	Ehud
1150	Shamgar
1125	Deborah and Barak
1100	Gideon
1080	Abimelech
1070	Jephthah
1070	Samson
1050	Battle of 1 Samuel 4
1020	Accession of Saul

This framework allows 150 years for the period of the judges. The periods of peace that involve a multiple of 40 are viewed as schematic. This seems somewhat close to Chisholm's proposal, with a difference of only 56 years. However, other factors must be considered. This view allows 30 years for the conquest of Canaan, the rest of Joshua's life, the "many days" or "long time" after Joshua's death (Josh 23:1), and the eight years of oppression before Othniel. At the other end of the scheme, the 20 years of Samson's judgeship is coterminous somehow with the 40 years of Eli's ministry, when they appear to be successive ministries. Also this view allows only 50 years for the reigns of Saul, David, and Solomon. The result is that a conventional late-date position has to compress the chronology of the *entire period under consideration* to fit all the events. It also regards any number that involves some multiple of 40 as schematic. Some scholars propose that the author may be suggesting that the calculations should not be forced into a coherent scheme and that he was not concerned about synchronizing the sources he used with external chronological data.[54]

---

vides a "minimal" figure of 591/596 years (*On the Reliability of the Old Testament*, 203).

[52] Chisholm overviews three other approaches and offers his own proposal, which results in 206 years for the time covered by the oppressions, peace, and reign of the judges ("The Chronology of the Book of Judges," 247–53).

[53] Cundall, *Judges*, 32–33.

[54] Block, *Judges, Ruth*, 63.

The conventional late-date view forces its proponents to make numerous other adjustments in the chronology of the time between the conquest and the reign of Solomon. Their schematic view of numbers shows up repeatedly. However, those numbers could be round or approximate numbers just as easily without assuming some schematic function. The general chronology of the period of the judges seems to favor the conventional early-date view.

Archaeological Information

Numerous issues in archaeology relate to one's view on the date of the exodus. This chapter touches on two of those issues: the three cities said to be burned as part of the conquest and the Egyptian storage cities built by the Hebrew slaves (Exod 1:11).

What about Ai, Jericho, and Hazor? Does archaeological evidence confirm what the text of Joshua suggests about these three cities (Josh 6:21–24; 8:18–19; 11:10–11)? Frankly, the evidence is somewhat mixed, and one's perspective on other issues comes to bear on the way they might answer the question. Some of the ambiguity arises from the fact that ongoing archaeological digs are taking place at two of the three sites.

Concerning Ai, evidence from the customary location for Ai (et-Tell), does not give evidence for either date of the exodus. Other suggestions have been made for the location of Ai, and the dig being conducted by Associates for Biblical Research at Khirbet el-Maqatir offers promise. A burn layer and an abundance of LB I pottery have been uncovered.[55] However, it is premature to say that this location is the correct site for the biblical Ai and to cite it as a confirmation of the biblical presentation of the conquest of Canaan.

Scholars have not debated the significance of what has been found at Jericho. The question pertains more to the chronology the evidence supports. The following facts are relevant: The city was strongly fortified (Josh 2:5,7,15; 6:5,20); the attack took place just after harvest (2:6; 3:15; 5:10); the inhabitants were unable to flee and take their supplies (6:1); the siege was brief (6:15); and the walls collapsed (6:20).[56]

In the early 1900s John Garstang found a wall at Jericho that had collapsed and concluded that it had fallen about 1400 BC, with evidence of the city having been burned.[57] However, Garstang's findings and conclusions were disputed by later scholars. In the 1960s Kathleen Kenyon reexamined the evidence and dated the wall to 1550 BC. She concluded that the city was unoccupied from 1550 to 1100 BC (except for a brief period after 1400 BC).[58] Obviously this supports neither the early nor the late date for the exodus.

Bryant Wood has studied the excavation reports of Garstang and Kenyon and has presented some important conclusions.[59] His central concern was that Kenyon gave significant weight to the *absence* of Cypriot bi-chrome pottery (a kind of pottery common in other cities of the LB period) as a key part of her MB dating of the destruction at Jericho.[60] Arguments based on what is not there are always weak. In fact she based her dating of the destruction layers on

---

[55] B. G. Wood, "The Search for Joshua's Ai," in *Critical Issues in Early Israelite History*, ed. R. S. Hess, G. A. Klingbeil, and P. J. Ray Jr., BBR Sup (Winona Lake, IN: Eisenbrauns, 2008), 231–37.

[56] Significant supplies of grain were found in the midst of the destruction. One assumes that much of that would have been consumed in a long siege.

[57] J. Garstang and J. B. E. Garstang, *The Story of Jericho*, 2nd ed. (London: Marshall, Morgan, & Scott, 1948). Garstang dated his "City IV" to 1400 BC, a date that matches the early date of the exodus.

[58] K. M. Kenyon, "Jericho," in *New Encyclopedia of Archaeological Excavations in the Holy Land*, ed. E. Stern (New York: Simon & Schuster, 1993), 2:679–80.

[59] B. Wood, "Did the Israelites Conquer Jericho?" *BAR* 16 (March/April 1990): 45–58.

[60] Ibid., 50.

limited evidence, two 26 x 26 foot squares. Her small excavation area was in an impoverished part of Jericho, a city located a distance from major trade routes.[61] Imported pottery, like Cypriot bi-chrome vessels, was generally along major trade routes, found not in poorer areas.[62] Based on his examination of the "local" pottery (from Garstang's reports), Wood pointed out a number of LB pottery samples that suggest Jericho was indeed occupied in the LB period.[63] Among other things, Wood also highlighted Egyptian scarabs Garstang had discovered in a cemetery northwest of the city, dating from the eighteenth to the thirteenth centuries BC. This also suggests that the city was occupied in the late fifteenth century, the time of the conquest according to the early date view.[64] Wood's work has been generally ignored by most archaeologists but must be seen, at the very least, as important enough to reopen discussions about the date attributed to the destruction of Jericho.

The city of Hazor was one of the most significant cities in Canaan.[65] The tell of the upper and lower city involves about 210 acres, and estimates of its population range upward from 20,000.[66] Scholars date an especially dramatic destruction of the city, which left a thick layer of ash and charred wood as deep as three feet in places, to about 1230 BC (stratum XIII).[67] The current excavation director, Amnon Ben-Tor, dates this destruction less specifically, to sometime in the fourteenth or thirteenth centuries.[68] He leans toward attributing this destruction to the Israelites.[69] Although Ben-Tor does not name Joshua, this would obviously fit a late date of the exodus. It is easy to understand how the massive destruction described above makes one think of the destruction described in Joshua 11.

From the time of the end of MB IIC to the end of the LB age, Hazor was destroyed no less than four times, and at least two of those destructions involved burning.[70] The first option that might relate to the early date for the exodus is a burn layer dated to an MB IIC stratum (stratum XVI). Yigael Yadin, the chief excavator of the original primary dig at Hazor, presented evidence of a major destruction of this city (MB IIC) by fire. Originally he suggested that either Thutmose III or Amenhotep II destroyed the city in the middle of the fifteenth century.[71] A year later he dated this destruction to about 1400 BC (the end of the fifteenth century).[72] With little archaeological support, he once more changed this destruction date to around 1550 BC,

[61] Ibid., 50.

[62] Walton, "Exodus, Date of," 268.

[63] Wood, "Did the Israelites Conquer Jericho?" 51–52; idem, "Dating Jericho's Destruction: Bienkowski Is Wrong on All Counts," *BAR* 16:5 (September/October 1990): 47–49.

[64] P. Bienkowski attempts to dismiss this evidence, affirming that scarabs would remain in circulation as good luck charms long after the king to whom they refer died and do not provide concrete evidence for an LB I occupation of Jericho ("Jericho Was Destroyed in the Middle Bronze Age, Not the Late Bronze Age," *BAR* 16 [September/October 1990]: 46). Wood responds by pointing to scarabs of unpopular kings (e.g., Hatshepsut) whose scarabs would not be kept for good luck for centuries ("Bienkowski Is Wrong," 49). R. K. Hawkins argues for the conventional late-date view based on datable scarabs from the city of Samaria ("Propositions for Evangelical Acceptance of a Late-Date Exodus-Conquest: Biblical Data and the Royal Scarabs from Mt. Ebal," *JETS* 50 [March 2007]: 31–46).

[65] Hazor is listed in an Egyptian execration text, appears in the archives of Mari, and received visits by various ANE ambassadors (A. F. Rainey, "Hazor," in *ISBE*, rev. ed., ed. G. W. Bromiley [Grand Rapids: Eerdmans, 1988]), 2:637.

[66] I. Provan, V. P. Long, and T. Longman III, *A Biblical History of Israel* (Louisville: WJK, 2003), 178.

[67] Y. Yadin, *Hazor: The Rediscovery of a Great Citadel of the Bible* (New York: Random House, 1975), 249–55.

[68] A. Ben-Tor and M. T. Rubiato, "Excavating Hazor, Part Two: Did the Israelites Destroy the Canaanite City?" *BAR* 25 (May/June 1999): 36.

[69] Ibid., 38.

[70] Bimson, *Redating the Exodus and Conquest*, 188–89.

[71] Y. Yadin, "Further Light on Biblical Hazor," *BA* 20 (1957): 44.

[72] Y. Yadin, "The Third Season of Excavating at Hazor," *BA* 21 (1958): 31.

suggesting that the Hyksos had destroyed the city.[73] Bimson, contending that there was no new evidence to justify this change, argues in favor of the 1400 BC date for this destruction.[74]

The second option that could fit the conventional early date of the Israelite exodus from Egypt was not discovered until the 2000 and 2001 excavation seasons at Hazor. While digging in Area M, Ben-Tor's team found a large pit that provided evidence of a burn layer in stratum XV, dated to sometime in the fifteenth century. In the excavator's view, "It is so far the only clear indication of an earlier destruction, still in the Late Bronze Age, pre-dating the final destruction of the city" in about 1300 BC.[75] The excavator attributes this destruction to Thutmose III (c. 1483 BC).[76] In light of the fact that pottery evidence does not allow for a given layer or stratum to be dated precisely, this destruction could just as easily relate to that accomplished by the Israelites under Joshua's leadership around 1400 BC.

Another issue relates to the far-reaching destruction of Hazor in the thirteenth century, the one pointed to as part of Joshua's conquest of Hazor (according to the conventional late date view). After this destruction the city of Hazor was not substantially rebuilt until the time of Solomon. If that is the case, whom did the Israelites fight against and defeat in Judges 4–5?[77] A summary statement by the excavators of Hazor seems to undercut the idea that Judges 4–5 refers to some conflict after Joshua 11. Ben-Tor and Sharon Zuckerman write that the "final destruction of the LB Age city is followed by total abandonment of the lower city. The upper tell is left unoccupied for an unspecified period of time, with no clear evidence of post-destruction activity anywhere in the city prior to its reoccupation in the Iron I period."[78] Some scholars have suggested various ways to explain this lack of evidence for an occupation of Hazor after the late thirteenth century destruction that is associated with the conquest of Canaan by conventional late-date proponents. Kitchen suggests that Jabin ruled as "king of Canaan" (Judg 4:2) from a different location than the city of Hazor itself, even though 4:2 says he ruled "in Hazor."[79] Block and Hess envision a less substantial occupation of Hazor than in the time of the Conquest. This occupation in the time of the Judges did not leave behind substantial archaeological evidence[80] and was "without city walls or substantial public buildings" and did not cover the entire tell.[81] Also the book of Judges says nothing about a destruction of an established city. In response, it does seem odd that the Canaanites, who were able to oppress the Israelites for decades and to field a significant army, would "leave no lasting mark on the archaeological record."[82]

---

[73] Y. Yadin, "Further Light on Biblical Hazor," *BA* 20 (1957): 44; idem, "The Fifth Season of Excavating at Hazor, 1968–69," *BA* 32 (1969): 54–55. Yadin conducted the dig at Hazor for four years (1955–1958) and then it was inactive from 1959 to 1967.

[74] Bimson, *Redating the Exodus and Conquest*, 192–94.

[75] A. Ben-Tor, "Tel Hazor, 2000," *IEJ* 50 (2000): 248–49.

[76] A. Ben-Tor, "Tel Hazor, 2001," *IEJ* 51 (2001): 235–38, esp. 238.

[77] Various scholars have resolved this problem with a number of suggestions that view the biblical text as being in error. For a survey of these suggestions see Bimson, *Redating the Exodus and Conquest*, 196–98.

[78] A. Ben-Tor and S. Zuckerman, "Hazor at the End of the Late Bronze Age: Back to Basics," *BASOR* 350 (May 2008): 1–6. Yadin refers to strata XII and XI for the twelfth and eleventh centuries, but states that no buildings were constructed on the upper city until the tenth century, during the reign of Solomon. He conjectures that Hazor was settled in the twelfth and eleventh centuries by semi-nomads, who lived in tents or huts. "Hazor," in *AEHL*, 3rd ed., ed. M. Avi-Yonah (Englewood Cliffs, NJ: Prentice Hall, 1976), 2:487.

[79] Kitchen, *On the Reliability of the Old Testament*, 213.

[80] Block, *Judges, Ruth*, 189.

[81] R. Hess, *Joshua: An Introduction and Commentary*, TOTC (Downers Grove, IL: InterVarsity, 1996), 214 n. 1.

[82] Block, *Judges, Ruth*, 189. Absence of evidence never establishes that something did not exist. Even so the absence of any substantial evidence of occupation after the 1230 BC destruction does not seem to match what one would expect from

So what can be said about the evidence from Hazor? Once again, both options (which are compatible with a high view of Scripture) have benefits and drawbacks. However, in light of 1 Kgs 6:1 and the broad issue of the chronology of the Judges (see above) and the presence of a burn layer at Hazor that dates to the fifteenth century BC, it seems best to favor correlating the Israelites' conquest of the city of Hazor with the fifteenth century BC burn layer uncovered by Ben-Tor (stratum XV). It follows that the impressive destruction of around 1230 should be associated with the Israelite conquest of the Canaanites in Judges 4–5.

The Egyptian storage cities (Exod 1:11). This verse states that the Egyptians placed taskmasters over the Israelites and forced them to build "Pithom and Rameses as store cities for Pharaoh." Since the middle of the nineteenth century AD numerous scholars have suggested that this construction project took place during the Nineteenth Dynasty of Egypt, more specifically during the reign of Rameses II (1279–1213 BC),[83] one of the most powerful pharaohs of Egypt.[84] This would clearly favor the conventional late date view. Two issues must be addressed with regard to this issue: the significance of the names of these cities and the place of Exod 1:11 in the larger textual and historical context.

First, one must consider the names of these cities and what they signify. Rameses has long been associated with Pi-Ramesses (Tell el-Dab`a-Qantir), although the exact location of Pithom is less clear.[85] The city of Pi-Ramesses was abandoned after 150 years because of the movement of the Nile River away from the city, so it was occupied from around 1270 to 1120 BC (during the reign of Rameses II). After about 1120 BC, this city ceased to exist. A new capital was established 12 miles northeast at Tanis. The potential association of Pi-Ramesses with Rameses II is obvious. Proponents of the late date cite this information as foundational to their view, since Rameses ruled almost 170 years after the time envisioned by the early date. Hoffmeier also points out that several other place names found in Exodus 1 are referred to only in Nineteenth-Dynasty written sources.[86]

Early-date proponents respond to this argument in one of two ways. Some scholars point out that Rameses was also a name used in the Hyksos period when the storage cities were being built in the first place.[87] According to them the Ramaside Nineteenth Dynasty traced its ancestry back to the Hyksos line. Seti I, the father of Rameses II, was apparently named after the Hyksos patron god, Seth. Thus the name Rameses could have been used by the Hyksos long before the Nineteenth Dynasty and was the name given to the city when it was being built for the Hyksos by the enslaved Hebrews. Moses then recorded the actual, original name—the one he probably knew when coming on the scene a few generations later. The more common assertion is that a prophetic figure added the name Rameses later, after the city changed from the ancient name to the new one, that is, it was an anachronism.[88] Kitchen, a proponent of

---

a Canaanite people based at Hazor that dominated this region for several years.

[83] The precise dates of Egyptian pharaohs are debated. The dates here are those provided by B. Wood, "The 13th Century Exodus-Conquest Theory," *JETS* 48 (2005): 475–89.

[84] Hoffmeier, *Israel in Egypt: The Evidence for the Authenticity of the Exodus Tradition*, 116–26. Cf. idem, "What Is the Biblical Date for the Exodus," 231–35; Kitchen, *On the Reliability of the Old Testament*, 255–59. Various late-date proponents regard this as the most important evidence supporting their view.

[85] J. K. Hoffmeier, "Out of Egypt," *BAR* 33 (January/February 2007): 36.

[86] Hoffmeier, "What Is the Biblical Date for the Exodus?" 235.

[87] J. Rea, "The Time of the Oppression and the Exodus," *GJ* 2 (1961): 5–14; G. L. Archer, "An Eighteenth Dynasty Ramases," *JETS* 17 (winter 1974): 49–50; Merrill, *Kingdom of Priests*, 87.

[88] C. F. Aling, "The Biblical City of Ramses," *JETS* 25 (June 1982): 129–37; Wood, "The 13th Century Exodus-Conquest Theory," 479; idem, "From Ramesses to Shiloh," 260–62; A. J. Hoerth, *Archaeology and the Old Testament* (Grand Rapids: Baker, 1998), 166 n. 1.

the late-date view, regards the reference to Rameses in Gen 47:11 as an anachronism,[89] but he rejects that possibility here.

More importantly, the immediate context of Exod 1:11 causes more significant problems for the late-date interpretation. Exodus 1:11–15 presents the following progression of events. In spite of the oppression by the Egyptians, the Hebrews became more numerous. Years passed as the Hebrew slaves built the cities of Rameses and Pithom. Then the pharaoh decreed that the Hebrew midwives were to kill all male babies. They refused to obey and the Israelites continued to experience great population growth. Thus the pharaoh decreed that all male babies were to be killed by throwing them into the Nile River. In the context of this second decree Moses was born (Exod 2:1–8). This passage gives the impression that there was some passage of time that allowed the Israelites to increase in number significantly, after the oppression and the first decree. According to other passages, Moses was 80 years old when he led God's people out of Egypt, having spent 40 years in the wilderness after he chose to identify with the Hebrews. All these events would have taken well over 100 years to reach completion.[90] Here are the problems raised by this sequence of events. First, if the storage cities were built and named for Rameses II, this entire complex of events could not fit into his reign, as long as it was (c. 67 years). Second, if the city of Rameses was built, named after its namesake, and completed in 1270 BC, that leaves just a few years for all the events mentioned above to occur. If 480 years in 1 Kgs 6:1 is regarded as a schematic reference for 300 years, that number of years before Solomon's fourth year reaches back to 1266 BC. Third, late-date proponents generally regard Rameses II as the pharaoh of the exodus. Exodus 2:23 states that the Egyptian king died, clearly referring to the king who was in power when Moses was forced to flee from Egypt. This precludes Rameses from being the pharaoh for whom the storage city was named as well as the pharaoh of the exodus. Merneptah, Rameses' successor, cannot have been the pharaoh of the exodus either. His stele (c. 1208 BC), which records Israel's presence in the land of Canaan as a people, does not allow him time to play that role, for Israel to travel to Sinai, wander in the wilderness, conquer Canaan, and to encounter him there.

Summary

The question of the date of the exodus has captured the attention of scholars for centuries. In the middle of the twentieth century, the two primary options were a late date (c. 1250 BC) and an early date (c. 1446 BC). Since then, numerous archaeologists have affirmed that their discoveries do not support the way the OT narrative describes Israel's conquest of Canaan. So most nonevangelicals have discarded the idea that an exodus of 12 Israelite tribes out of Egypt and some kind of military conquest of Canaan by Israel ever happened. Others dismiss the credibility of the OT narratives altogether. The debate between an early and late date of the exodus has become an "intramural" debate for evangelicals. On the one hand important interpretive issues are involved in the position one takes that have implications for the way one interprets numerous OT passages. In other words the debate is not meaningless or insignificant. Although evangelicals differ in the way they understand OT chronology and certain archaeological discoveries, they share an important common heritage. They together hold that the OT narratives present a credible presentation of 12 Israelite tribes who departed from

---

[89] Kitchen, *On the Reliability of the Old Testament*, 348, 354.

[90] Of course, if every occurrence of some multiple of the number 40 must be regarded as schematic, Moses may have been much younger than 80. In view of the events before Moses birth the reign of Rameses II hardly seems long enough to encompass all that history.

Egypt, wandered in the wilderness, and "conquered" the Canaanites as instruments of the all-powerful God of the universe.

Having said that, the balance seems to tilt in the direction of the early date for the exodus from Egypt, a date that best corresponds to the evidence found in relevant biblical statements. Those statements present various complicated issues, but together they present an exodus from Egypt in about 1446 BC. The archaeological data does not enable early-date or late-date proponents to argue for their position with absolute dogmatism. However, the juncture of biblical statements along with the indications of various archaeological discoveries also seems to favor strongly the early-date position.

THE ROUTE OF THE EXODUS

The precise route of the Exodus is difficult to determine because of a lack of clear knowledge of several of the locations mentioned in the Exodus narrative (see map 11). Of course, some scholars view the account of Israel's crossing of the Red Sea as an important Israelite myth.[91] Yet several of the commonly cited options for the Red Sea crossing are these: the northern end of the Gulf of Suez,[92] Lake Menzaleh (southern bay of the Mediterranean Sea),[93] the vicinity of Lake Timsah or Bitter Lakes,[94] and somewhere near Baal Zaphon.[95] Regardless of where it happened, God enabled the Israelites to cross a body of water that they could not cross on their own.

THE PLAGUES AND THE GODS OF EGYPT

When Moses first met with the pharaoh and asked that he allow the Hebrews to travel into the wilderness to worship Yahweh, the pharaoh refused. Instead he declared: "Who is the LORD that I should obey Him by letting Israel go? I do not know the LORD, and what's more, I will not let Israel go" (Exod 5:2). He knew nothing about Yahweh that would compel him to allow the Hebrews to have this religious pilgrimage. Yahweh introduced Himself to the Egyptian pharaoh and people through the 10 plagues. He was the unparalleled and all-powerful God of the universe. As He explained the tenth plague, the Lord affirmed that through this plague He "will execute judgments against all the gods of Egypt" (Exod 12:12). Looking back on that plague, Moses wrote that the Israelites were marching out of Egypt in full view of the Egyptians who were burying their firstborn children, because Yahweh "had executed judgment against their gods" (Num 33:4).

---

[91] B. F. Batto, "The Reed Sea: Requiescat in Pace," *JBL* 102 (1983): 27–35. Kitchen replied to Batto's view in *On the Reliability of the Old Testament*, 262.

[92] R. L. Overstreet, "Exegetical and Contextual Facets of Israel's Red Sea Crossing," *Master's Seminary Journal* 14 (Spring 2003): 63–86; J. D. Currid, *Ancient Egypt and the Old Testament* (Grand Rapids: Baker, 1997), 123–36; W. C. Kaiser Jr., "Exodus," in *EBC*, rev. ed., ed. T. Longman III and D. E. Garland (Grand Rapids: Zondervan, 2008), 1:438.

[93] K. A. Kitchen, "Exodus, the," in *Zondervan Pictorial Encyclopedia of the Bible*, ed. M. C. Tenney and M. Silva (Grand Rapids: Zondervan, 2009), 2:481–83; idem, "Red Sea," in *Zondervan Pictorial Encyclopedia of the Bible*, 5:61–63; Merrill, *Kingdom of Priests*, 82; H. G. May, ed., *Oxford Bible Atlas*, 2nd ed. (New York: Oxford University Press, 1974), 58–59.

[94] H. G. May, ed., *Oxford Bible Atlas*, 3rd ed., rev. John Day (New York: Oxford University Press, 1984), 58–59; B. J. Beitzel, *The Moody Atlas of the Bible* (Chicago: Moody, 2009), 106–8; J. C. Laney, *Baker's Concise Bible Atlas: A Geographical Survey of Bible History* (Grand Rapids: Baker, 1988), 74–75; C. G. Rasmussen, *Zondervan NIV Atlas of the Bible* (Grand Rapids: Zondervan, 1989), 89. Hoffmeier offers three likely options: Lake Timsah, Bitter Lakes, or Lake Ballah (*Israel in Egypt*, 215).

[95] Y. Aharoni and M. Avi-Yonah, *The Macmillan Bible Atlas*, rev. 3rd ed. (New York: Macmillan, 1993), 45; A. F. Rainey and R. S. Notley, *The Sacred Bridge: Carta's Atlas of the Biblical World* (Jerusalem: Carta, 2006), 118–19.

In what way, then, were the ten plagues directed against the gods of Egypt? Although some reject this notion altogether,[96] the above passages clearly affirm that the plagues had some kind of divine polemical function. Some scholars have made a fairly detailed connection between the plagues and specific Egyptian gods.[97] While some of these connections may have been obvious to the Hebrews and the Egyptians, it seems better to understand the plagues as a judgment against the entire pantheon of Egyptian gods. In addition to this, since the Egyptian ruler was responsible to maintain cosmic order (*ma'at*), these plagues represented a direct front against the pharaoh as one who ruled on behalf of the gods. In this sense they represented an "assault . . . on Egypt's very ideas of creation, order, and harmony in the universe."[98]

THE DECALOGUE AND THE BOOK OF THE COVENANT

The Mosaic law includes two broad categories of law. First, *apodictic* law generally begins with a second-person command that involves a statement of principle. This kind of law does not present conditions or state consequences of nonobservance. Examples of this category occur in Leviticus 19 and Exodus 20. Second, *casuistic* law makes up the majority of the Mosaic law. It usually begins with an expressed or implied condition (protasis) that is followed by a consequence or penalty for nonobservance (apodosis).

Another aspect of Mosaic law (esp., casuistic law) demands attention. A given "law" includes both the protasis and the apodosis. The protasis or condition presents a situation or practice that was current in Israelite life. God desired that His chosen nation conduct distinctive lives in these kinds of circumstances. Technically speaking, the apodosis presents the legislation proper. When considering whether a given law has a normative principle for modern life, the student of Scripture should focus on the apodosis for that principle.

The Decalogue (Ten Commandments)

The Ten Commandments (Exod 20:1–17 and Deut 5:6–21) represent the heart of what God demanded of His servant nation. They serve as an essential part of the Mosaic covenant and must not be separated from that biblical and theological context. Each commandment addressed fundamental or bedrock life issues for Israel. They delineated, with broad strokes, the manner in which God's chosen people could submit to God's covenantal authority as well as impact the world around them.

Historical context. When Moses led the Israelites out of Egypt and the people began their journey toward the land of promise, they were a people without a clear identity and purpose.

---

[96] Even though he refers to the verses mentioned above, V. Hamilton concludes, "We should note that the biblical text gives no indication that the plagues are to be associated with Egyptian religion and deities. The similarities may, therefore, be coincidental" (*Handbook on the Pentateuch*, 2nd ed. [Grand Rapids: Baker, 2005], 160). J. Sailhamer grants the possibility of connecting the plagues to certain Egyptian gods or even between the plagues and the Egyptian *ma'at*, but he affirms that "there is no clear indication that the author intends his readers to see the plagues in this way" (*The Pentateuch as Narrative: A Biblical-Theological Commentary* [Grand Rapids: Zondervan, 1992], 253).

[97] C. Aling, *Egypt and Bible History* (Grand Rapids: Baker, 1981), 103–10; J. J. Davis, *Moses and the Gods of Egypt: Studies in Exodus*, 2nd ed. (Grand Rapids: Baker, 1986), 94–153; G. A. F. Knight, *Theology as Narration* (Grand Rapids: Eerdmans, 1976), 62–79. N. M. Sarna identifies a connection between some of the plagues and certain Egyptian gods, but not for all plagues (*Exploring Exodus: The Heritage of Biblical Israel* [New York: Schocken, 1986], 78–80); Currid, *Ancient Egypt and the Old Testament*, 108–13. Although he questions this detailed connection, J. Walton provides a helpful chart displaying the common associations that have been suggested (*Chronological and Background Charts of the Old Testament*, rev. ed. [Grand Rapids: Zondervan, 1994], 85). Hoffmeier points out some of the problems with the alleged connections (*Israel in Egypt*, 149–51).

[98] Currid, *Ancient Egypt and the Old Testament*, 118; cf. 118–20. See also Hoffmeier, *Israel in Egypt*, 151–53; and idem, "Egypt, Plagues in," in *ABD*, ed. D. N. Freedman (New York: Doubleday, 1992), 2:374–78.

They left behind an Egyptian sojourn of 430 years. At the Red Sea, the Lord orchestrated one of the most stupendous miracles of the OT. The Israelite crossing of this body of water on dry ground represented God's commitment to bring to pass what He had promised to His people and served as a paradigm for God's character and activity in the rest of the OT. Once the people camped at the base of Mount Sinai, God led Israel to a greater depth in their relationship with Him.

Ten Commandments: Core of the law (God's covenant expectations). Moses ascended Mount Sinai as Israel's representative to receive the law from Yahweh. The Lord Himself etched the words of the Ten Commandments (or "Ten Words," hence *Decalogue*) on two stone tablets (Exod 20:2–11; Deut 5:6–21). These 10 far-reaching divine requirements represented the heart of what Yahweh expected of His people. The first four commandments focus on an Israelite's relationship with God (vertical), and the other six commandments give attention to one's relationship with fellow Israelites (horizontal).

The Ten Commandments begin with a preface, something common in ANE treaties. This preface or prologue generally provides the past dealings of the parties of the treaty. In this passage the prologue demonstrates that God did not deliver His covenant demands to Israel in a vacuum but in the context of an intimate relationship, clearly evidenced by His surpassing character and abundant activity on Israel's behalf. His gift of the law was preceded by an act of love and grace. He gave these covenant demands to a people with whom He had already established a relationship, not as a means to enter that relationship (which always was and is by faith).

Mosaic covenant versus Mosaic law. Although these two descriptive titles are appropriately used interchangeably, also key differences exist between them. First, a "covenant" can create a new relationship or maintain or adjust an existing relationship. The Ten Commandments and the rest of the Mosaic law involve requirements anchored in a covenant *relationship*. God began that relationship with the descendants of Abraham (Genesis 12, 15, 17), but He formalized and deepened that relationship with the Ten Commandments and the rest of the law of Moses. Second, "law" arranges or orders life and conduct. In that regard these covenant demands or laws gave concrete direction to Israel's relationship with Yahweh. The Israelites were to obey these stipulations, not purely for the sake of obedience, but to demonstrate God's character to the surrounding nations (Exod 19:4–6; Deut 26:16–19). They were to arrange their lives in a way that turned the attention of the surrounding nations to their majestic and awesome God.

Detailed legislation: Delineation of the Ten Commandments. The detailed rules and regulations that fill much of Exodus, Leviticus, and Deuteronomy are not a free-floating set of rules that have no connection with the Ten Commandments. Rather, they represent the detailed application of the character of God to every area of an Israelite's life. Also these regulations operate in two basic spheres: vertical and horizontal (cf. Christ's summary of the Mosaic law into two spheres in Luke 10:25–28). Some laws, primarily those on worship ritual and requirements that do not directly impact fellow Israelites (dietary regulations), focus on an Israelite's walk with God. They can be summed up as a call to live a life of total allegiance before God. Other laws concern the way an Israelite should treat his fellow citizens. God's chosen people are to treat each other with love, justice, and equity.

Theological function of the Decalogue (and the rest of the Mosaic law). By means of the Abrahamic covenant (Genesis 12, 15, 17), God promised that He would bless the patriarchs with innumerable seed, that this people would inherit a land, and that He would use them to impact the world around them. This promised land represented the "life platform" on which this people could conduct their lives in a way that would impact and bless the surrounding nations. When the Hebrews were slaves in Egypt, God raised up Moses to deliver God's people from bondage and to begin their journey to the land of promise. As an essential part of God bringing His plan for this people to pass, He gave them His law at Mount Sinai. However, before He actually gave them His covenant requirements, He laid out for them the rationale for this law. Using the "if . . . then" construction that is common in the Mosaic law, Yahweh declared that Israel's heartfelt obedience to the requirements of the covenant He was about to reveal would enable them as a nation to represent their great God before the rest of the world (Exod 19:5–6).[99]

The Book of the Covenant

Overview. The expression, "the Book of the Covenant," is based on the expression that is found in Exod 24:7: *sēper habbᵉrît*. Most scholars apply this descriptive phrase to Exod 20:22–23:33, while others include Exodus 19, the Decalogue, and the ratification section in chap. 24 as well.[100] The larger section of Exodus 19–24 presents an interesting variety of genres. Exodus chap. 19; 20:18–21, and chap. 24 are narrative passages. Interspersed between them is legal material: the Ten Commandments (20:1–17) and the specific regulations of "the Book of the Covenant" (20:22–23:33). The laws of "the Book of the Covenant" vary from apodictic law (20:22–26) to primarily casuistic (21:1–22:17; except 21:12,15–17) to primarily apodictic (22:18–23:19; except 22:23–27; 23:4–5).

A prologue (20:18–26 or 20:22–26) and an epilogue (23:14–33 or 23:20–33) introduce and conclude "the Book of the Covenant" proper (21:1–23:19).[101] Both the prologue and epilogue focus attention on the need for Israel to worship Yahweh alone and to worship in a way that He defines. Along with the Ten Commandments, the requirements of "the Book of the Covenant" carried ultimate significance in conjunction with a proper theocentric focus. Yahweh was not merely interested in a well-behaved nation. Instead He wanted a nation with whom He could enjoy an intimate relationship. He desired that Israel would live as loyal citizens and thereby direct the attention of each other as well as the nations around them to their majestic and unparalleled God. The laws by themselves, that is, apart from covenant relationship (or a theocentric focus) had no ultimate significance.

Relationship to the Decalogue. Similar to what occurs in various ANE treaties, the covenant requirements of the Mosaic law may be divided into general and specific stipulations. For example Deuteronomy 5–11 represents the general stipulations of the Mosaic covenant and chaps. 12–26 serve as the specific stipulations. The general stipulations involve broad demands for loyalty and absolute allegiance. They focus on central, far-reaching demands that strike at the heart of a covenant citizen. The Decalogue represents the general stipulations of the Mosaic covenant, as it appears in Exodus. The specific stipulations give the detailed legislation that God wanted to impact every area of Israelite life. The Book of the Covenant delineates a

---

[99] Before and after the predominantly legal section of the Pentateuch (Exod 20:1–Deut 26:15), Moses recorded Exod 19:4–6 and Deut 26:16–19 in order to manifest with great clarity the divine rationale for these covenant requirements—manifesting His great glory to the watching world.

[100] See J. M. Sprinkle, *"The Book of the Covenant": A Literary Approach*, JSOTSup (Sheffield: Sheffield Academic, 1994), 27–34, for a brief discussion of this issue. Sprinkle prefers not to use the term "the Book of the Covenant" to describe Exod 20:22–23:33 (ibid., 27).

[101] B. K. Waltke with C. Yu, *An Old Testament Theology: An Exegetical, Canonical, and Thematic Approach* (Grand Rapids: Zondervan, 2007), 433–35.

number of specific covenant stipulations. These detailed requirements are not exhaustive but were illustrative of the manner in which a loyal Israelite could live out his willing submission to the lordship of Yahweh. These specific stipulations take the broad, far-reaching demands of the Ten Commandments and apply them to daily situations in life.

The Layout of the Tabernacle

Reconstruction of the Tabernacle.

THE THEOLOGY OF THE BOOK

Exodus picks up where the book of Genesis left off. God's people were in a great location (Goshen), enjoying abundance, and they had the respect of the Egyptians. When Exodus opens, Joseph had died, his descendants were still living in Egypt, and then follow the sober words: "A new king, who had not known Joseph, came to power in Egypt" (1:8). From a human perspective trouble was about to begin. However, against that dark backdrop God once again accomplished His purposes for His glory. He would move His plan a few steps forward through the events of this book, that is, His intention to extend His rule over all creation.

Chosen by Deliverance

Yahweh began His covenant relationship with Abraham and His descendants in Genesis and brought initial fulfillment to aspects of that relationship (a people—Gen 12:1–3; 15:13–21; 18:18; 22:18; etc.). The book of Exodus advances God's dealings with his chosen people with an important step forward. By raising up Moses as their mediator/deliverer, performing the 10 plagues, delivering them from slavery, bringing them across the Red Sea with incontestable power, guiding them to Mount Sinai, and giving them His law, the Lord transformed a *people* of His own choosing to His elect *nation*.[102] No longer did the Hebrews share

---

[102] While many of the features that customarily are part of national existence, God put the building blocks in place for His theocratic nation.

only a common ethnic heritage. Through these events and others to come, the Lord was forming a nation that could be His witness before the rest of the world.

His choice of Israel as His chosen nation is clearly displayed when He, the all-powerful God, extricated His oppressed people from slavery under one of the most powerful empires of the world. This was accomplished, not simply to make their lives easier, but also to help them better understand their incomparable God (Deut 4:32–40). By performing the plagues, parting the waters of the Red Sea, and providing for all their physical needs as they journeyed to Mount Sinai, He revealed His character to them and made these things divine tools to transform them from a people to a nation of His own choosing. Their arrival at Mount Sinai laid the groundwork for another, even more impressive, revelation of their great God.

Commissioned to Be a Servant Nation

The next section of Exodus gives readers of Exodus a clear picture of God's intentions for His servant nation. As the nation was gathered at the base of Mount Sinai, before Yahweh revealed His covenant demands to them through Moses, the Lord desired that His chosen people understand the relational dimension of what He was about to reveal, namely, the law. Exodus 19:4–6 gives the divine rationale, not only for His giving of the law, but also for their very existence as a nation.[103]

Verse 4 focuses on Yahweh as the great God who was solely responsible for their deliverance from oppression in Egypt and for guiding them through every obstacle they faced along the way. As the God who had acted on their behalf, He had the credibility to demand what He was about to tell them. Before He gave them the details of this expansion of His covenant relationship with them, He wanted them to grasp the big idea. In vv. 5–6 He presented this rationale in the form of an "if . . . then" statement. The condition entails their absolute loyalty to the demands of the covenant He was about to give them through Moses. And what would be the impact of that kind of allegiance? A nation characterized by covenant loyalty will function as a treasured possession, kingdom of priests, and a holy nation (v. 6), and will represent God vividly and clearly before the surrounding nations.[104] The question is whether this servant nation will be able to function in the way God intended and will impact the world by demonstrating God's unparalleled character to them.

God revealed His demands for His servant nation through the Ten Commandments (20:2–21) and "the Book of the Covenant" (20:22–23:33). The Ten Commandments represent the core or center of what Yahweh demanded of His people. All the detailed legislation in some fashion delineated the values presented in the Ten Commandments. This servant nation could carry out God's intentions for them by enthusiastic loyalty to His covenant demands. This would give them a distinctive witness in a world that talked about justice and compassion but rarely practiced it. The sacrificial system and worship at the tabernacle would give the world a glimpse of the potential of enjoying an intimate relationship with the God of the universe as well as the hope of receiving an eternal resolution to their sin problem.

---

[103] E. H. Merrill calls this "the most theologically significant text in the book of Exodus, for it is the linchpin between the patriarchal promises of the sonship of Israel and the Sinaitic Covenant whereby Israel became the servant nation of Yahweh" ("A Theology of the Pentateuch," in *A Biblical Theology of the Old Testament*, ed. R. B. Zuck [Chicago: Moody, 1991], 32).

[104] For more on the role of this passage on God's intentions for Israel see M. A. Grisanti, "The Missing Mandate: Missions in the Old Testament," in *Missions in a New Millennium: Change and Challenges in World Missions*, ed. W. E. Glenny and W. H. Smallman (Grand Rapids: Kregel, 2000), 50–56.

The concept of servanthood serves as an interesting motif throughout the book of Exodus.[105] The book opens by describing the way the Egyptians forced the Hebrews into slavery. This slavery was nothing but heartless oppression, creating misery for all Israelites.[106] However, this miserable, human servitude paved the way for another kind of relationship, servitude to Yahweh. The first set of covenantal requirements after the Ten Commandments involves a servant's loving relationship to his master (Exod 21:2–6). This conceptually prepares the reader for what God will say in the wake of His demand for redemption in the Year of Jubilee: "For the Israelites are My slaves. They are My slaves I brought out of the land of Egypt; I am the LORD your God" (Lev 25:55). God's calling His chosen people to be His servant nation is not oppression; it is privilege, the opportunity to demonstrate to the surrounding nations the surpassing and incomparable character of the one and only God of the universe.

Access to the God of the Universe

As noted above, Exodus records the redemption of the covenant people from bondage through great miracles and the granting of a charter to them—a commission to represent the incomparable God before the nations. This last important section and theme of Exodus involves establishing the theocratic center of worship, the tabernacle (chaps. 25–40).

Unlike the alleged gods of the Gentile nations, who are spoken about in mythological literature but never seen, God intended to dwell tangibly in the midst of His servant nation. He represented His glory by appearing as a pillar of cloud by day and a column of fire at night, rising above the holy of holies in the tabernacle. His visible presence at the tabernacle would remind the Israelites that He is their covenant lord and deserves their obedience. As He provided them with flawless guidance through the parched and barren wilderness, they would regard him as the God who cares for them as well. Most importantly His presence in the tabernacle gave them the opportunity to have an audience with Him through the sacrificial system.

So the Lord established a priesthood by setting aside one of the tribes of Israel (the Levites) to minister at the tabernacle and teach the law to God's people. They were to have a mediatorial function, serving between God and His covenant nation. As those consecrated for this special ministry, the Levites must offer the appointed sacrifices and also care for the tabernacle. The sacrifices offered by the Israelites represented tribute offered by the vassals to the suzerain, Yahweh. However, unlike worship in many pagan nations, these offerings were not intended to purchase divine favor or move God to action. They were meant to provide a means for forgiveness as well as an outlet for other important relational sentiments: thanksgiving, trust, sorrow, and love. What an Israelite offered as a sacrifice was to be a window into his soul rather than a cloak for what was really there.

God's presence at the tabernacle was also a clear demonstration of God's grace and mercy. Before the tabernacle was constructed, God's people committed covenant treachery by commissioning Aaron to form a golden calf from their donated gold and silver jewelry (Exodus 32). Although this could have served as the just occasion for their demise, the Lord forgave them and remained in their midst. He desires to restore rebellious subjects to an intimate relationship with Him.

---

[105] R. W. L. Moberly, "Exodus," in *Theological Interpretation of the OT: A Book-by-Book Survey*, ed. K. J. Vanhoozer (Grand Rapids: Baker, 2008), 50–51.

[106] The verb "to serve" (*'bd*) and a noun (*ʿbōdāh*) derived from that verb occur five times in Exod 1:13–14.

CONCLUSION

The book of Exodus teaches about God Himself as well as what He has in mind for the world. The book begins with the Hebrews in circumstances that may have seemed "out of place." Had not God promised to give them a land, make them into a great people, and use them as His instruments in the world? God's deliverance of His chosen people out of Egypt and slavery, His astounding intervention at the Red Sea, and His provision of the law at Mount Sinai all served as part of God's formative process. What Israel was to become would not be of their own doing; it would be totally through His sovereignty. He not only delivered His chosen people and gave them His law (thereby welding them into a fledgling nation), but He also made arrangements to dwell in their midst, in visible and tangible form.

STUDY QUESTIONS

1. What are "sources" commonly cited by critics as an important part of the process of the composition of the book of Exodus?
2. What are the six primary views on the date of Israel's exodus from Egypt. Which ones are held by evangelicals?
3. How do late-date Exodus proponents explain the chronological information found in 1 Kgs 6:1?
4. Is there evidence that suggests that the chronological datum in 1 Kgs 6:1 should be understood at face value?
5. What was the Mosaic conquest policy that was to guide Israel in their conquest of Canaan?
6. Summarize the primary debate surrounding Jephthah's chronological statement and the two evangelical interpretations offered?
7. What is the key issue both sides must deal with concerning the broad chronology of the Judges period?
8. What are the key issues related to the destruction of Jericho?
9. What are the key issues related to the destruction of Hazor?
10. Why does the statement about storage cities in Egypt play such a large role in the debate on the date of the Exodus?
11. Did each of the plagues against Egypt address the domain of a particular Egyptian god?
12. What is "the Book of the Covenant," and how does it relate to the Decalogue?

FOR FURTHER STUDY

Beitzel, B. J. *The New Moody Atlas of the Bible.* Chicago: Moody, 2009.

Bienkowski, P. "Jericho Was Destroyed in the Middle Bronze Age, Not the Late Bronze Age." *BAR* 16, no. 5 (September/October 1990): 45–49.

Bimson, J. J. *Redating the Exodus and the Conquest.* JSOTSup. Sheffield: JSOT, 1978.

———, and David Livingston. "Redating the Exodus." *BAR* 13 (Sept/Oct 1987): 40–53, 66–68.

Block, D. I. *Judges, Ruth.* NAC. Nashville: B&H, 1999.

Bright, J. *A History of Israel.* Philadelphia: Westminster, 1959.

Chisholm, R. B., Jr. "The Chronology of the Book of Judges: A Linguistic Clue to Solving a Pesky Problem." *JETS* 52 (June 2009): 247–55.

Cundall, A. E. *Judges: An Introduction and Commentary.* TOTC. Downers Grove, IL: InterVarsity, 1978.

Currid, J. D. *Ancient Egypt and the Old Testament.* Grand Rapids: Baker, 1997.

Grisanti, M. A. "The Missing Mandate: Missions in the Old Testament." In *Missions in a New Millennium: Change and Challenges in World Missions*. Edited by W. Edward. Glenny and W. H. Smallman, 43–68. Grand Rapids: Kregel, 2000.

Hamilton, V. P. *Handbook on the Pentateuch*. 2nd ed. Grand Rapids: Baker, 2005.

Harbin, M. A. *The Promise and Blessing: A Historical Survey of the Old and New Testaments*. Grand Rapids: Zondervan, 2005.

Harrison, R. K. *Introduction to the Old Testament*. Grand Rapids: Eerdmans, 1969.

Hess, R. *Joshua: An Introduction and Commentary*. TOTC. Downers Grove, IL: InterVarsity, 1996.

Hill, A. E., and J. H. Walton. *A Survey of the Old Testament*. 3rd ed. Grand Rapids: Zondervan, 2009.

Hoerth, A. J. *Archaeology and the Old Testament*. Grand Rapids: Baker, 1998.

Hoffmeier, J. K. *Israel in Egypt: The Evidence for the Authenticity of the Exodus Tradition*. New York: Oxford University Press, 1996.

———. "What Is the Biblical Date for the Exodus? A Response to Bryant Wood." *JETS* 50 (June 2007): 225–47.

House, P. R. *Old Testament Theology*. Downers Grove, IL: InterVarsity, 1998.

Howard, D. M. *Joshua*. NAC. Nashville: B&H, 1998.

Kaiser, W. C., Jr. "Exodus." In *EBC*. Rev. ed. Edited by T. Longman III and D. E. Garland, 1:333–561. Grand Rapids: Zondervan, 2008.

———. *The Promise-Plan of God: Biblical Theology of the Old and New Testaments*. Grand Rapids: Zondervan, 2008.

Kitchen, K. A. "Exodus, The." In *Zondervan Pictorial Encyclopedia of the Bible*. Edited by Merrill C. Tenney and Moisés Silva, 2:477–84. Grand Rapids: Zondervan, 1976.

———. "The Exodus." In *ABD*. Edited by D. N. Freedman, 2:700–708. New York: Doubleday, 1992.

———. *On the Reliability of the Old Testament*. Grand Rapids: Eerdmans, 2003.

Longman, Tremper, III, and Raymond Dillard. *An Introduction to the Old Testament*. 2nd ed. Grand Rapids: Zondervan, 2006.

Merrill, E. H. *Everlasting Dominion: A Theology of the Old Testament*. Nashville: B&H, 2006.

———. *Kingdom of Priests: A History of Old Testament Israel*. 2nd ed. Grand Rapids: Baker, 2008.

———. "Palestinian Archaeology and the Date of the Conquest: Do Tells Tell Tales?" *GTJ* 3 (Spring 1982): 107–21.

———. "A Theology of the Pentateuch." In *A Biblical Theology of the Old Testament*. Edited by Roy B. Zuck, 7–87. Chicago: Moody, 1991.

Moberly, R. W. L. "Exodus." In *Theological Interpretation of the OT: A Book-by-Book Survey*. Edited by Kevin J. Vanhoozer, 42–51. Grand Rapids: Baker, 2008.

Overstreet, R. L. "Exegetical and Contextual Facets of Israel's Red Sea Crossing." *MSJ* 14 (Sspring 2003): 63–86.

Provan, I., V. P. Long, and Tremper Longman III. *A Biblical History of Israel*. Louisville: Westminster John Knox, 2003.

Rainey, A. F. "Hazor." In *ISBE*. Rev. ed. Edited by G. W. Bromiley, 2:636–38. Grand Rapids: Eerdmans, 1988.

Rasmussen, C. G. "Conquest, Infiltration, Revolt, or Resettlement? What Really Happened during the Exodus–Judges Period?" In *Giving the Sense: Understanding and Using Old Testament Historical Texts*. Edited by D. M. Howard Jr. and M. A. Grisanti, 138–59. Grand Rapids: Kregel, 2003.

———. *Zondervan Atlas of the Bible*. Rev. ed. Grand Rapids: Zondervan, 2010.

Sailhamer, J. H. *The Pentateuch as Narrative: A Biblical-Theological Commentary*. Grand Rapids: Zondervan, 1992.

Schnittjer, G. *The Torah Story*. Grand Rapids: Zondervan, 2006.

Shea, W. H. "The Date of the Exodus." In *Giving the Sense: Understanding and Using Old Testament Historical Texts*. Edited by D. M. Howard Jr. and M. A. Grisanti, 236–55. Grand Rapids: Kregel, 2003.

Sprinkle, J. M. *"The Book of the Covenant": A Literary Approach*, JSOTSup. Sheffield: Sheffield Academic, 1994.

Waltke, B. K. *An Old Testament Theology: An Exegetical, Canonical, and Thematic Approach*. Grand Rapids: Zondervan, 2007.

———. "Palestinian Artifactual Evidence Supporting the Early Date of the Exodus." *BSac* 129 (January-March 1972): 33–47.

Walton, J. H. "Exodus, Date of." In *DOTP*. Edited by T. D. Alexander and D. W. Baker, 258–72. Downers Grove, IL: InterVarsity, 2003.

Wells, B. "Exodus." In *ZIBBC*. Edited by John H. Walton, 1:160–283. Grand Rapids: Zondervan, 2009.

Wiseman, D. J. *1 and 2 Kings: An Introduction and Commentary*. TOTC. Downers Grove, IL: InterVarsity, 1993.

Wolf, H. M. *An Introduction to the Old Testament Pentateuch*. Chicago: Moody Press, 1991.

Wood, B. "The Biblical Date for the Exodus Is 1446 BC: A Response to James Hoffmeier." *JETS* 50, no. 2 (2007): 249–58.

———. "Dating Jericho's Destruction: Bienkowski Is Wrong on All Counts." *BAR* 16, no. 5 (September/October 1990): 44–58.

———. "Did the Israelites Conquer Jericho." *BAR* 16, no. 2 (March/April 1990): 45–58.

———. "From Ramesses to Shiloh: Archaeological Discoveries Bearing on the Exodus–Judges Period." In *Giving the Sense: Understanding and Using OT Historical Texts*. Edited by D. M. Howard Jr., and M. A. Grisanti, 256–82. Grand Rapids: Kregel, 2003.

———. "The Search for Joshua's Ai." In *Critical Issues in Early Israelite History*. Edited by Richard S. Hess, Gerald A. Klingbeil, and Paul J. Ray Jr., 205–40. BBR Supplements 3. Winona Lake, IN: Eisenbrauns, 2008.

———. The Rise and Fall of the 13th-Century Exodus-Conquest Theory." *JETS* 48, no. 3 (2005): 475–89.

Yadin, Y. *Hazor: The Rediscovery of a Great Citadel of the Bible*. New York: Random House, 1975.

Younger, K. Lawson, Jr. "Early Israel in Recent Biblical Scholarship." In *The Face of OT Studies: A Survey of Contemporary Approaches*. Edited by D. W. Baker and B. T. Arnold, 176–206. Grand Rapids: Baker, 1999.

———. *Judges and Ruth*. NIVAC. Grand Rapids: Zondervan, 2002.

CHAPTER 12

THE BOOK OF LEVITICUS

MICHAEL A. GRISANTI

F OR MANY MODERN Bible readers, the book of Leviticus is like a desert "as barren and unknown as the dry, trackless wilderness" of its envisioned surroundings.[1] Although it may have been the first book Jewish children would read, it is perhaps one of the last ones read by Christians. The customary response to Leviticus may therefore not be excitement. Yet this book is of fundamental importance to both the OT and the NT. Without the book of Leviticus, readers of the OT would be confused by the myriad of details concerning sacrificial ritual encountered in the historical and prophetic books. And they would miss important aspects of the character of Israel's God. Also they would be unprepared for the significance of the sacrificial death of Christ and the meaning of many passages in the book of Hebrews.[2]

THE TITLE AND CANONICITY OF THE BOOK

As is the case with other OT books, the Hebrew title of Leviticus is the first word of the book: "and he called" (*wayyiqrā*).[3] The Septuagint entitled the book *Leuitikon* ("that which concerns the priests").[4] The Latin Vulgate rendered that Greek heading with the phrase *Liber Leviticus*, the basis for the English title. Although the book deals with much more than levitical duties, the title touches an important emphasis of the book. In fact Leviticus has had more impact on Judaism than any other OT book. Rabbinic literature presents it as the first book given to children and about one-half of the Talmud deals with understanding its contents.[5] Its place in the Hebrew canon has never been questioned.

---

[1] J. L. Mays, *The Book of Leviticus: The Book of Numbers*, LBC (Richmond, VA: John Knox, 1963), 7.

[2] R. K. Harrison refers to Leviticus as the "seed-bed of NT theology, for in this book is to be found the basis of Christian faith and doctrine" (*Leviticus: An Introduction and Commentary*, TOTC [Downers Grove, IL: InterVarsity, 1980], 9).

[3] Later rabbinic works and the Syriac Peshitta call the book *tôrat kōhᵃnîm*, "book of the priests."

[4] B. A. Levine, "Leviticus, Book of," in *ABD*, ed. D. N. Freedman (New York: Doubleday, 1992), 4:312.

[5] V. P. Hamilton, "Recent Studies in Leviticus and Their Contribution to a Further Understanding of Wesleyan Theology," in *A Spectrum of Thought: Essays in Honor of Dennis F. Kinlaw*, ed. M. L. Peterson (Wilmore, KY: Asbury College, 1982), 146.

THE TEXT OF THE BOOK

The MT of Leviticus is highly reliable. The book's lengthiest attestation from the DSS was found in Cave 11 at Qumran. Written in the paleo-Hebrew script, it contains portions of Leviticus 22–27.[6] In addition to the scroll, 17 small fragments contain texts from Leviticus 4–21.[7] The MT is regarded as superior to 11QpaleoLev and the rest of the Leviticus fragments found at Qumran.[8] In addition first-century AD fragments found at Masada attest to a text that is identical to the MT.[9] The ancient versions (e.g., Samaritan Pentateuch and LXX), for the most part, support the MT.[10]

THE COMPOSITION OF THE BOOK

Source-Critical View

The customary arguments offered by source critics for other books of the Pentateuch apply to Leviticus as well.[11] However, because Leviticus primarily deals with sacrifices and different aspects of levitical ritual, the P source receives special attention. In review, according to source critics, P contains most of the material in the Pentateuch that concerns sacrifice and priesthood. Because of its meticulous detail and advanced theology, critics present it as the latest of the four foundational documents (JEDP). Earlier source critics dated P as the earliest document, but Abraham Kuenen and Julius Wellhausen dogmatically affirmed that P must be the latest because, in their view, the evolution of religion eventually becomes fossilized in dead ritual.[12] Some scholars have also advanced a Holiness source (H), Leviticus 17–26.[13] According to their reconstruction, editors combined material from P (that includes Leviticus 1–16) with H during the exile, around the time Ezekiel was written. In the standard source critical understanding of Leviticus, P fictitiously presents all the levitical ritual as something revealed by God through Moses in order to give its contents an authoritative tenor. In the critical view, all these practices were fabricated during the postexilic period as if they came from a second millennium BC setting.[14] Israel's religion evolved from the simple, somewhat flexible patterns found in the historical books to the rigid, ritualistic framework of the postexilic priestly code.

There is a mediating position (between the evangelical and customary source critical views) that maintains that P is preexilic but not Mosaic.[15] Since societies have a natural tendency to become more secular, the priestly source was composed before Deuteronomy (c. eighth century BC). Proponents of this view point out that language, laws, and institutions referred to

---

[6] The part of the scroll that survived is only one-fifth of the original height (K. A. Mathews, "The Paleo-Hebrew Leviticus Scroll from Qumran," *BA* 50 [March 1987]: 47).

[7] Other manuscripts of Leviticus have been found at Qumran (9 in Hebrew, 2 in Greek, and 1 Targum), but only as fragments (J. E. Hartley, *Leviticus*, WBC [Nashville: Thomas Nelson, 1992], xxix).

[8] K. A. Mathews, "The Leviticus Scroll (11QpaleoLev) and the Text of the Hebrew Bible," *CBQ* 48 (1986): 196–97.

[9] These fragments contain text from Lev 4:3–9 and 8:31–11:40 (MLev[a] and MLev[b]) (S. Talmon, "Fragments of Two Scrolls of the Book of Leviticus from Masada," *Eretz-Israel* 24 [1993]: 99–110 [Hebrew]). Cf. idem, "Masada: Written Material," in *Encyclopedia of the Dead Sea Scrolls*, ed. L. H. Schiffman and J. C. VanderKam (Oxford: Oxford University Press, 2000), 1:521.

[10] Hartley, *Leviticus*, xxix.

[11] See the introduction to Part 4, and the section in chap. 10 that deals with the composition of Genesis.

[12] J. Wellhausen, *Prolegomena to the History of Israel* (1878; reprint, Eugene, OR: Wipf and Stock, 2003), 10–12.

[13] O. Eissfeldt, *The Old Testament: An Introduction* (New York: Harper & Row, 1965), 238–40.

[14] Wellhausen, *Prolegomena to the History of Israel*, 35–38.

[15] Y. Kaufmann, *The Religion of Israel*, trans. M. Greenberg (Chicago: University of Chicago Press, 1960), 175–200. Cf. J. Milgrom, *Leviticus 1–16*, AB (New York: Doubleday, 1991), 3–13.

in P do not match those of the postexilic period.[16] They also suggest that the ideas of holiness, war, and laws dealing with sacrifices and blood more closely match practices mentioned in Judges and Samuel than in Chronicles.[17]

As suggested, modern critical scholars approach Leviticus in a quest for the original forms that gave rise to the present form of the book (form criticism). They also trace the development of traditions through a long oral prehistory (tradition history) leading to the written documents compiled by various editors, thus creating the present book of Leviticus (source criticism).

Evangelical View

Unlike Exodus (17:14; 24:4; 34:27), Leviticus makes no allusion to Mosaic authorship. Yet, Leviticus attests to direct revelation more than the other books of the Pentateuch. The statement "the LORD said to Moses" occurs 37 times.[18] Most of the book involves "Yahweh speeches" that Moses delivered to God's servant nation.[19] The geographical context of this revelation is clearly presented as Mount Sinai, where the Lord gave Moses His covenant demands (Lev 7:38; 25:1; 26:46; 27:34). The rest of the OT affirms that the levitical ritual came from the hand of Moses (2 Chr 23:18; 30:16; 35:12) as does the NT (Matt 8:2–4; Luke 2:22; Rom 10:5). As part of the continuous presentation of narrative, law, and covenant in the Pentateuch, Leviticus takes its place as a Mosaic composition.[20]

Hess gives five reasons for a second millennium setting for Leviticus, rather than the first millennium setting proposed by critical scholars.[21] First, the form of the tabernacle as well as some of the utensils used in worship most closely resemble building layout or utensils from the West Semitic world of Ugarit as well as Hittite and Egyptian objects found only in second millennium settings. Second, references to the ark, the Urim and Thummim, and anointing oil all appear in early historical narratives. Third, the language of Leviticus includes terms that do not occur in literature that is clearly postexilic. Fourth, Leviticus shares parallels with several texts from ANE cultures, most of which come from the Late Bronze Age (c. 1550–1200 BC). Fifth, a recent analysis of texts from the thirteenth-century BC West Semitic city of Emar reveals literary forms and cultic institutions that are found nowhere else except in Leviticus. The point is that a composition of Leviticus in the middle of the second millennium BC nicely fits the evidence.

As with the other books of the Pentateuch, evangelicals have offered three approaches to the authorship of the book of Leviticus. All three regard the message of Leviticus as inspired and authoritative, and most of them regard the book as substantially completed in the second millennium.[22] First, some say Moses wrote every word found in the present Hebrew text of

---

[16] A. Hurvitz, "The Evidence of Language in Dating the Priestly Code," *RB* 81 (1974): 24–56.

[17] Kaufmann, *The Religion of Israel*, 181–84.

[18] W. C. Kaiser, Jr. affirms that "Leviticus, more than any other OT book, claims to be a divine word for humanity" "The Book of Leviticus: Introduction, Commentary, and Reflections," in *The New Interpreter's Bible*, ed. L. E. Keck (Nashville: Abingdon, 1994), 1:987.

[19] Hartley, *Leviticus*, xxx.

[20] See comments on Mosaic authorship in the introductory chapter to Part 4 and chap. 10 on Genesis.

[21] R. S. Hess, "Leviticus," in *EBC*, rev. ed., ed. T. Longman III and D. E. Garland (Grand Rapids: Zondervan, 2008), 1:566.

[22] This would include all who hold to Mosaic authorship and some of those who believe in anonymous authorship.

Leviticus.[23] Second, other scholars regard Moses as the primary author of the book.[24] They allow for minor adjustments, especially linguistic adjustments that would have developed over the centuries from 1400 to 400 BC. For example Harrison grants the possibility that an editor or scribe of a later generation could have arranged the Mosaic material in its present order or added Mosaic sayings. However, Harrison concludes that more likely the book was organized in its present form at the time of Moses, since Israel desperately needed what he wrote as a manual for priestly times during the encampment at Mount Sinai and for successive genera-tions.[25] Harrison also points out that there is little evidence for scribal updating of ancient "priestly" terminology in Leviticus. Third, some scholars regard the book as anonymous, though its contents are Mosaic traditions. Because the text says nothing about explicit author-ship, they feel it is best to recognize the divine authority of the book, and Moses' immense contribution to the book (as God's mouthpiece), but they refrain from identifying who penned the words found in Leviticus.[26]

THE STRUCTURE OF THE BOOK

The book of Leviticus is part of a larger block of passages that deal with the ritual and sacrificial system ordained by Yahweh (Exodus 25–Num 10:10). It begins at the same "place" where Exodus ends. Exodus closes with a description of Yahweh's visible presence (Shekinah glory) covering the tabernacle and providing guidance to the nation as they traveled through the wilderness toward the land of promise. Leviticus begins with the Lord calling to Moses and speaking to him from that very "tent of meeting" (Lev 1:1).

The overall logic of the argument is especially clear in chaps. 1–16. The first section deals with the major sacrifices in the Mosaic system (chaps. 1–7). The next section focuses on the ordination and installation of priests (chaps. 8–10). Purification ritual receives attention in chaps. 11–16, and the last part (chaps. 17–26) addresses a number of different issues.

Almost every chapter begins with "the LORD spoke to Moses," and this statement occurs numerous times in several chapters. This repeated clause emphasizes that these instructions have divine origin and authority. Many of the divine speeches end with either summary state-ments (e.g., 7:35–36; 11:46–47; 13:59; 14:32) or compliance reports (e.g., 8:36; 10:7b; 21:24; 23:44). These structural markers provide the framework for Yahweh's providing wor-ship instructions for His chosen people.

---

[23] This view does not ignore the fact that only copies of Leviticus are available since the Hebrew text has been copied numerous times over the centuries. Their point is that the autographa of the book has been passed down unchanged since the time of Moses.

[24] J. D. Currid, *A Study Commentary on Leviticus* (Faverdale North, Darlington, UK: Evangelical, 2004), 20–22; C. Dyer and G. Merrill, *Old Testament Explorer: Discovering the Essence, Background, and Meaning of Every Book in the Old Testament* (Nashville: Word, 2001), 71; M. F. Rooker, *Leviticus*, NAC (Nashville: B&H, 2000), 38–39; D. Tidball, *The Message of Leviticus: Free to Be Holy*, BST (Downers Grove, IL: InterVarsity, 2005), 18–20. N. Kiuchi enthu-siastically affirms that Leviticus was written in the time of Moses, whether by Moses or one of his contemporaries. "Leviticus, Book of," in *Dictionary of the OT: Pentateuch*, ed. T. D. Alexander and D. W. Baker (Downers Grove, IL: InterVarsity, 2003), 523; cf. idem, *Leviticus*, Apollos (Downers Grove, IL: InterVarsity, 2007), 18.

[25] Harrison, *Leviticus*, 23. Harrison writes, "The most logical conclusion concerning authorship and date would be to recognize the antiquity and authenticity of Leviticus and to regard it as a genuine second-millennium BC literary product compiled by Moses, with probable assistance of priestly scribes (ibid.)."

[26] R. Gane, *Leviticus, Numbers*, NIVAC (Grand Rapids: Zondervan, 2004), 27–28; Hartley, *Leviticus*, xli–xliii; Hess, "Leviticus," 1:565-67; J. W. Kleinig, *Leviticus*, Concordia (St. Louis: Concordia, 2003), 17–18; A. P. Ross, *Holiness to the Lord: A Guide to the Exposition of the Book of Leviticus* (Grand Rapids: Baker, 2002), 38–42.

The abundant legal material of Leviticus is arranged in the midst of a narrative framework. History and law are intertwined throughout Exodus–Numbers.[27] The giving of the law is anchored to events that describe Israel's interaction with Yahweh. God did not give His people these demanding requirements in a vacuum, He gave them as part of His ongoing relationship with and care for His covenant nation. Reference to tragic events (chap. 10; 24:10–23) demonstrates how important Israel's heartfelt conformity to these covenant stipulations was to Yahweh.

THE OUTLINE OF THE BOOK[28]

I. **The Manual of Sacrifice: Enjoying God's Presence (chaps. 1–7)**
   A. The Offerings from the People's Perspective (1:1–6:7 [HB, 1:1–5:26])
   B. The Offerings from the Priest's Perspective (6:8 [HB, 6:1]–7:38)

II. **The Manual of Priesthood: Entering God's Service (chaps. 8–10)**
   A. The Ordination of the Priests (chap. 8)
   B. The Beginning of Priestly Ministry (chap. 9)
   C. The Violation of Priestly Ministry (chap. 10)

III. **The Manual of Purity: Encountering God's Design (chaps. 11–15)**
   A. Holiness and Daily Food: Clean and Unclean Animals (chap. 11)
   B. Holiness and the Physical Life: Childbirth (chap. 12)
   C. Holiness and Disease: Discerning and Cleansing of Disease (chaps. 13–14)
   D. Holiness and the Body: Cleansing after Discharges (chap. 15)

IV. **The Manual of Atonement: Ensuring God's Forgiveness (chap. 16)**

V. **The Manual of Holiness: Enacting God's Word (chaps. 17–26)**
   A. The Laws (chaps. 17–25)
      1. The Sanctity of Blood (chap. 17)
      2. The Sanctity of Intimacy (chap. 18)
      3. Sanctity of Interpersonal Relationships (chap. 19)
      4. Punishment for Holiness Violations (chap. 20)
      5. Worship and Holiness (chaps. 21–22)
      6. The Worship Calendar (chap. 23)
      7. Holiness at the Sanctuary (chap. 24)
      8. Holiness of the Land: Sabbatical Year and the Year of Jubilee (chap. 25)
   B. The Cursings and Blessings (chap. 26)

VI. **The Manual of Dedication: Enamored by God's Grace (chap. 27)**

THE UNDERLYING RATIONALE OF THE BOOK

In Exodus 25–40 God gave instructions for building the tabernacle. The climax of that section is in 40:34–38 when the Shekinah glory (God's presence manifested in a cloud) swept into residence. *This event* is the clue to what Leviticus is all about. No one can understand the laws and the details of the book without meditating first on what this passage means. These verses

---

[27] Hartley, *Leviticus*, xxxi.
[28] The major outline points are taken from Tidball, *The Message of Leviticus*, 5–6.

describe the holy and eternal God, who chose to dwell in the midst of His servant nation. He is their Immanuel ("God with us"). One can only imagine how dramatic that event must have been for all who witnessed it. Besides that, the arrival of God's presence transformed a structure made up of animal skins and various sacrificial utensils and altars into a holy place, that is, a sanctuary. The tabernacle was set apart from what was sinful and common and was the center of life for every Israelite.

In the wake of the arrival of God's visible presence at the tabernacle, the defining concern of all of Leviticus is the arrangement of life around His presence. *How should people live if the eternal, holy, almighty God lived with them?* Leviticus answers various questions in relation to this important reality.

How should profane and sinful people conduct their lives around such a holy presence?

Leviticus 1–7 provides the answer. As a manual of sacrifice, these chapters provide instructions on how the Israelites were to address various relational breakdowns, whether sins against God or sins against fellow Israelites. These sacrifices were not offered as a means of initiating a relationship with God; they were to enable the Israelites to maintain a life of submission to the covenant.

How can profane people reach the holy God in worship and how shall God reach them?

Leviticus 8–10 offers the answer: through the consecrated mediatorial priesthood. These priests could not give grace or forgiveness, but they facilitated the worship of individual Israelites as well as the nation. By teaching the Mosaic law to God's people, they represented God to the Israelites as well. The fact that they were set apart for this task in various ways demonstrates the sobering nature of approaching God. Yahweh requires that His people be totally consecrated to Him.

How should the holiness of God dominate and sanctify one's profane life?

Leviticus 11–16 is a manual of purification that answers this question. Most moderns do not understand this concept. Here is the basic idea: every Israelite was called to be holy as God was holy (11:44–45; 20:7). They were to lead a distinctive life, consecrated to God's use alone, as a way of demonstrating His unparalleled character to the rest of the world. When an Israelite became ritually unclean or impure, ritual cleansing or purification was necessary for him to pursue holiness.

How should the Israelites obey God so that holiness becomes a way of life?

Leviticus 17–27 gives the answer by delineating the laws of holiness. They lay out what was involved in living out the holiness demanded by God in numerous areas of life. For example, it should impact the way they offer sacrifices (chap. 17) as well as their sexual conduct (chap. 18). Chapter 19 provides an overview of a comprehensive life of holiness, focusing on how Israelites should treat their fellow citizens. Chapters 21–25 and 27 examine the impact of holiness on various parts of theocratic life: priests, offerings, times, land, and so forth. Chapter 26, like Deuteronomy 28, delineates that the consequences of obedience or treachery are blessings or cursings.

Readers of Leviticus must understand this broad rationale that gives the foundation for the details and theology of the book of Leviticus. In this way readers can avoid being overwhelmed by the details of sacrificial ritual that is foreign to most people today.

KEY ISSUES IN UNDERSTANDING LEVITICUS

Three concepts basic to understanding the message of Leviticus are these: the dimensions of the Mosaic law, the covenantal backdrop to that law, and the basic idea of holiness and purity.

Internal, Vertical, and Horizontal Dimensions of the Law

The Mosaic law was not to be carried out in a mindless fashion. The way God's chosen people lived and the manner in which they worshipped Yahweh, in accord with the Mosaic law, was to be a genuine expression of their faith relationship with God. Mere external conformity to the law as well as conformity to certain worship practices was never intended as a thin veneer to hide an Israelite's penchant for rebellion and wickedness. What happened on the "outside" was to be a window into what existed on the "inside." God was never interested in mere external conformity to His covenant demands.

With all the detailed laws it was essential to recognize that the Mosaic law focused on the Israelites' relationship with God (vertical dimension) and their relationships with each other (horizontal dimension). Leviticus addresses both of these dimensions. The book begins by focusing on an Israelite's walk with God by means of the sacrificial system (chaps. 1–7) and then turns to dealing with various issues in the horizontal dimension (esp. chaps. 18–19). Laws in all pentateuchal books address both dimensions. Vertically Yahweh desired that His covenant people would enthusiastically lead lives of undivided loyalty (Deut 6:4–5). Horizontally He demanded that justice and compassion characterize their relationships with others, especially with fellow citizens of the servant nation. By living this way, they could serve as God's representatives on behalf of each other, displaying God's character to each other as fellow Israelites. Obedience in both dimensions of the law would enable the chosen nation to live distinctively before the surrounding nations (Exod 19:4–6; Deut 26:16–19).

Covenant Backdrop

God gave covenant demands to Israel as they were encamped at the base of Mount Sinai. He had delivered them from the clutches of Egypt, one of the most powerful empires of the ancient world at that time. And why did He deliver them from Egypt in such glorious fashion and guide them to Mount Sinai? He intended that they would function as His treasured possession, as a kingdom of priests, and as a holy nation (Exod 19:5–6). Their obedience or disobedience at the national level would determine whether they would experience blessings or cursings (Leviticus 26). To the question, "Who is in charge?" Leviticus clearly answered, "Yahweh, as the covenant Lord is your suzerain."

In normal political/covenantal relationships a vassal ruler would occasionally offend his suzerain and need to sue for peace and the normalization of relationships. The suzerain would also expect regular reaffirmations of loyalty, expressed by periodic appearances at the palace. In light of this covenantal background, Merrill suggests that the sacrifices were designed to demonstrate the subservience of Israel, atone for her offenses against her sovereign, Yahweh, and reflect the harmoniousness and peaceableness of the relationship established (or reestablished).[29]

---

[29] E. H. Merrill, "A Theology of the Pentateuch," in *A Biblical Theology of the Old Testament*, ed. R. B. Zuck (Chicago: Moody, 1991), 57.

Holiness and Ritual Purity

The noun "holiness" and its related forms which occur over 800 times in the OT, are used in many different ways: of God (Isa 6:3, "Holy, holy, holy is the Lord of Hosts"), of persons (priests, Levites, prophets, the nation Israel), of places (tabernacle/temple area, Jerusalem, the burning bush), of things (ark of the covenant, oil and incense to be burned in the temple, sacrifices offered there), and of times (Sabbath, feast days, special days).

In all these uses the central idea is apartness.[30] In the OT this apartness has two facets. First, God is apart from everything that is common, that is, *He is unique*. This first aspect of "apartness" is broad. In the OT, almost everything involved in life fell into one of two categories. It was either defiled or holy, unclean or clean, common or sacred. To put it another way, most things in life were either ordinary or special. However, God is apart from all that is common. He is unique, quite out of the ordinary (Exod 15:11; 1 Sam 2:2). The OT makes it abundantly clear that Yahweh is incomparable (Deut 4:35,39; 1 Kgs 8:60; Isa 45:5–6,14, etc.). Second, God is apart from everything that is sinful, that is, *He is pure*. As the holy God, He has nothing to do with anything that is sinful (Ps 5:4–5). Being holy Israel's God stands distinct from everything that is common and everything that is sinful. He is unique, and He is pure.

Yahweh called His chosen people to be holy. They were to be distinct from whatever was common and sinful. Beyond that, holiness for God's people involved something else, the other side of the coin of the apartness idea. Being apart has negative connotations, but from a positive side the concept involves the idea of "consecration." Why were pieces of furniture in the temple or certain days of the year called "holy"? Those things or those days were holy because they were consecrated or dedicated to the Lord's use alone. So when Yahweh demanded that His covenant nation conduct holy lives, He wanted their lives to be characterized by uniqueness and moral purity. They also were to live as if they had been set apart for His use alone.[31]

The Israelites were commanded to lead holy lives for at least two important reasons. First, it was required if they were to have regular fellowship with God. Only holy people were permitted to enter the presence of God (at the tabernacle and later at the temple). Second, the only way God's servant nation could accurately represent His surpassing character to the surrounding nations was to lead "set-apart" lives.

An important related concept is *ritual purity*. This concept is foreign to most people today. Whether a person was holy was determined by his conduct and his being in fellowship with God through offering the required sacrifices at the tabernacle/temple. People and things were "clean" or "pure" as opposed to "unclean" or "impure."[32] However, someone or something could be "unclean," either through sin or "pollution." Certain Levitical rituals offered purification, while the sacrificial system dealt with holiness.

The following diagram illustrates this relationship of holiness and purity:[33]

---

[30] L. Koehler and W. Baumgartner, *HALOT* (Leiden: Brill, 2001), 1072–73.

[31] Of course, in both the OT and NT God's demand for His people to conduct holy lives was not a demand for perfection. That is one of the reasons He ordained the sacrificial system; He knew His people would sin.

[32] These concepts have negative connotations that may not have been part of their OT meaning. Some things in OT times that caused a person to become "unclean" or "impure" involved sinful conduct, but much of what caused "ritual pollution" did not involve sin. So one should not think negatively of a woman who becomes "impure" through giving birth to a child.

[33] This image slightly revised from Ross, *Holiness to the Lord*, 244, who improved Wenham's diagram (*Leviticus*, 19).

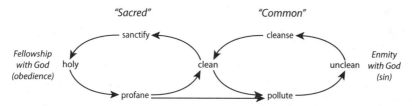

Ritual cleansing was necessary for there to be sanctification or holiness. Profane or sinful living often led to ritual pollution. The one involves movement toward God and the other departure from God.

In a worldview that emphasized God's matchless holiness and His demand for His people to live distinctively, ritual pollution or impurity was a hindrance to that distinctive, God-focused living. Purification rituals (Leviticus 11–15) were not necessarily dealing with sinful conduct; they were dealing with impurity that interfered with the distinctiveness God demanded of His people.

Sacred Space

The OT sacrificial system and life as part of God's theocratic kingdom dealt with this idea of sacred space. From the holy of holies in the tabernacle/temple as far out as the boundaries of the land of promise, God's chosen people were interacting with this concept of space set aside for God's use, use by those appointed by Him (e.g., priests and Levites), or use by His servant nation. Living distinctive lives and conducting worship that honored God in certain ways relates to living in sacred space. In every area of their lives God's people were always in the context, directly or indirectly, of sacred space.

IMPORTANT ASPECTS OF ISRAEL'S WORSHIP REQUIREMENTS

Since the book of Leviticus places such great emphasis on worship ritual, an overview of the fundamental aspects of that system merits brief attention. The following section summarizes the Mosaic sacrificial system, the feast calendar, the concept of Sabbath, as well as the requirement for tithes and offerings. Understanding the big picture can help the reader grasp the details of how God required that His servant nation offer Him worship.

Yahweh originally established a covenant relationship with Abraham and his descendants in Genesis 12. As Abraham had done (Gen 15:6), his descendants were able to enjoy a relationship with God through faith. Through Moses, several centuries later the Lord required that His covenant nation offer certain sacrifices to Him. As with Abraham, salvation was by faith and not works. These sacrifices had nothing to do with persons *beginning* their relationship with God; they had everything to do with *maintaining* that relationship with God. There were two broad categories of sacrifices: voluntary acts of worship and mandatory atonement for sin (see chart "Mosaic Sacrificial System" on p. 228).[34]

Voluntary Act of Worship

The fact that God actually dwelt among the people in the tabernacle (and later in the temple) and wanted to have a relationship with them is the relational foundation for the system of offerings and sacrifices prescribed at Mount Sinai. Three sacrifices (burnt, grain, and fellowship

---

[34] For a helpful overview of the OT sacrificial system see R. E. Averbeck, "Offerings and Sacrifices," in *NIDOTTE*, ed. W. VanGemeren (Grand Rapids: Zondervan, 1997), 4:996–1022, esp. the charts on 1020–21.

offerings) were offered voluntarily, either as an act of consecration or for fellowship.[35] First, for the *burnt offering* (Lev 1:3–17; 6:8–13 [HB, 6:1–6]), the entire (except the skin) bull (1:3–9), ram or goat (1:10–13), or male bird (1:14–17; usually limited to the poor—e.g., 12:8; 14:22) was consumed on the altar to express the devotion of the worshipper (or atonement for unintentional sin).[36] The burnt offering had an atoning effect as a gift that appeased or entreated God rather than as a literal cleansing procedure. As the worshipper placed his hand on the head of the sacrificial animal, he was identifying with his offering. Contrary to popular belief, the laying on of the hand did not transfer sin or anything else from the worshipper to the offering. One could not offer something laden with sin on the altar. Also, in addition to providing atonement for the priests and people when the tabernacle was inaugurated (9:7), the burnt offering was part of making atonement for the priests and the people on the Day of Atonement, after the extended series of sin offering rituals as well as the scapegoat ritual (16:11–22,24). Second, a token portion of unleavened cakes or grains was offered as a *meal or grain offering* as an act of worship (Leviticus 2; 6:14–23).[37] The daily offering of a burnt offering by the priests was also accompanied by a grain and drink offering both in the morning and in the evening (9:17; Num 28:3–8). A grain offering could be brought to the Lord in various forms: as sifted grain, baked cakes, baked wafers cooked on a griddle, or fried in a pan, or crushed grits (if it was the first ripe grain of the new harvest (Lev 2:1–16). The priest was to offer a part of it (a handful) on the burnt offering altar as a sign offering or memorial (portion) to the Lord. However, the remainder of all grain offerings could be consumed only by the priests within the tabernacle precincts (2:3,10; 6:16–18 [HB, vv. 9–11]; 10:12–13; etc.). Third, any animal from the herds of flocks (without blemish) could be offered as a *peace or fellowship offering* (chap. 3; 7:11–34). Only the fat portion of the animal would be burned and the rest would be shared in a fellowship meal by the priest and the worshipper's family. This category of sacrifice emphasizes the fact that all the people of ancient Israel had opportunity for close communion with the Lord. They could eat the flesh of an animal that had been presented, identified, and consecrated as an offering to the Lord (3:1–2; 7:11–21).[38]

Mandatory Atonement for Sin

Basic overview. The sin and guilt offerings overlap in some respects while retaining distinct identities. Depending on the circumstances, a young bull, male or female goat or lamb, a dove or pigeon, or a prescribed portion of flour would be offered as part of a sin offering (Leviticus 4), and the priests were allowed to eat all but the fat portions. The guilt offering involved an unblemished ram, and the priests were able to eat all but the fat portions (5:1–6:7).

Brief comparison. Since these two offerings occur in juxtaposition in several passages (6:17 [HB, v. 10]; 7:7,37; 14:13; Ezek 46:20), scholars have offered various suggestions on how to distinguish these sacrifices. First, and most broadly, the guilt offering represented the guilty person's attempt to absolve wrongdoing by making restitution.[39] One way this offering was distinct from a sin offering is that it addressed an offense that created a debt, calling for compensation

[35] These three sacrifices are treated as a literary unit (chaps. 1–3), distinct from the next two sacrifices: guilt and sin offerings (chaps. 4–5).

[36] R. E. Averbeck, " עלָה " in *NIDOTTE*, 3:407–13.

[37] Averbeck, " מִנְחָה " in *NIDOTTE*, 2:983–85.

[38] Averbeck, " שֶׁלֶם " in *NIDOTTE*, 4:136–40.

[39] Hartley, *Leviticus*, 77.

(hence it is also called a reparation offering).[40] Although the guilt offering represented a penalty paid in the form of a sacrificial offering to God, it did not relieve the offender of his duty to make full restitution for any loss he had caused another.[41] In fact, the offender was fined 20 percent above the lost value. This sacrifice "merely squared the offender with his God."[42]

Second, the sin offering has also triggered significant discussion. In several passages (Leviticus 8, 12, 15; Numbers 6), the purpose of this offering was to purify the altar that had become contaminated. Therefore some scholars refer to this offering as the purification offering.[43] However, the repeated reference to sin in Leviticus 5 suggests that forgiveness of sins was also in view in numerous instances where the sin offering was offered.[44]

Third, and more narrowly, the guilt and sin offerings function in relationship to the sanctuary and sacred cult objects (or "sancta"). Milgrom suggests that the guilt/reparation offering dealt with the desecration of "sancta," while the sin/purification offering was offered to remove the contamination of "sancta" arising from inadvertent sins.[45]

Festivals Calendar

Three of the festivals (see chart below) represented part of the homage due to Yahweh: Passover (and Unleavened Bread), Feast of Weeks, and Feast of Tabernacles (or Booths) (Exod 23:14–18; 34:18–26; Leviticus 23; Deut 16:1–17). They formed part of the "sacred rhythm" of Israel's life. The first two framed the spring grain harvest, and the Feast of Tabernacles occurred in the fall when the new grain and wine were stored away for the winter. All three commemorated God's deliverance of His people through the exodus from Egypt and expressed gratitude for the harvest. For these three festivals, all Israelite men were to make the pilgrimage to the central sanctuary to appear before the Lord, the great King. This "national" gathering of Israelites from all parts of the land of promise would remind them of their national identity as God's covenant people.

Sabbath

The Lord required the Israelites to set aside the seventh day of the week for special purposes (Exod 20:8–11; Deut 5:12–15).[46] Unlike an ordinary day of work, the Sabbath was to be set aside for a special function, to celebrate God's activity on behalf of His people. All people (both free and enslaved) and all animals normally used for work were to enjoy this Sabbath rest. No person and no animal was to work on this special day. The Sabbath day was not simply intended as a day of inactivity, but also as a day of celebration. God's people were to take this opportunity to celebrate God's purposes demonstrated in His creative and redemptive work.

---

[40] The various offenses addressed by the guilt offering include the following: (1) the act of misappropriating or misusing an item of sacred value (5:14–16); (2) sinning inadvertently and not knowing it (5:17–19); (3) swearing falsely in regard to damages done to another person (6:1–7 [HB, 5:20–26]); (4) the rite of purification of the leper; (5) the rite of renewing the vow of a Nazirite who had become unclean (Num 6:10–12); (6) having sexual relations with a slave who has been betrothed to another man (Lev 19:20–21). See G. A. Anderson, "Sacrifice and Sacrificial Offerings," in *ABD,* ed. D. N. Freedman (New York: Doubleday, 1992), 5:880–81.

[41] E. Carpenter and M. A. Grisanti, " אשם " in *NIDOTTE,* 1:554.

[42] Ibid.

[43] J. Milgrom, *Studies in Cultic Theology and Terminology* (Leiden: Brill, 1983), 67–73; Anderson, "Sacrifice and Sacrificial Offerings," 5:879.

[44] Cf. W. C. Kaiser Jr., "Leviticus," in *The New Interpreter's Bible,* ed. L. E. Keck (Nashville: Abingdon, 1994), 1:1033.

[45] J. Milgrom, *Cult and Conscience: The Asham and the Priestly Doctrine of Repentance* (Leiden: Brill, 1976), 127–28.

[46] The Sabbath is referred to eighteen times in Leviticus 16–26.

Tithes and Offerings

Building on other tithing passages (Gen 14:20; 28:22), Moses commanded the people of Israel to set aside one-tenth of their produce (grain, new wine, and oil) and the firstborn of their herds and flocks each year and devote them to the Lord (Lev 27:30–32; Num 18:21–28; Deut 14:22-29). The purpose for this practice was to teach God's chosen people to fear Him always (Deut 4:10; 17:19). Their prosperity did not result from their irrigation or advanced agricultural techniques, but was due to Yahweh's fixed commitment to His covenant promises. In addition to tithing, Yahweh encouraged Israelites to give generously on other occasions as well.

Mosaic Sacrificial System				
Voluntary act of worship—Consecration				
Name	**Portion** Burnt	**Description**	**Occasion**	**Reference**
Burnt Offering	Entire animal	Male without blemish; Cattle, sheep, goats, birds*	Propitiation for sin; complete devotion to God	Lev 1:1–17; 6:8–13
Meal Offering	Token portion	Unleavened cakes or grains (salted)	Thanksgiving for first-fruits	Lev 2:1–6; 6:14–23
Voluntary act of worship—Fellowship				
Name	**Portion** Burnt	**Description**	**Occasion**	**Reference**
Peace Offering includes (1) Thank offering (2) Vow offering (3) Freewill offering	Fatty portions⁺	Male or female without blemish*; ox, sheep, or goat (or, can be grain offering	Fellowship with God 22:17–30 (1) Thankfulness for specific blessing (2) for a blessing received related to a vow that had been made (3) General thankfulness; expression of love for God	Lev 3:1–17; 7:11–36;
Mandatory atonement for sin—Expiation				
Name	**Portion** Burnt	**Description**	**Occasion**	**Reference**
Sin Offering	Fatty portions	Male or female without blemish: *Priest/congregation*: bull; *King*: male goat *Individual*: female goat or lamb *Poor*: dove or pigeon *Very poor*: one-tenth an ephah of flour	Purification; particular acts of sin where no restitution was possible	Lev 4:1–5:13; 6:24–30; 12:6–8
Guilt Offering	Fatty portions	Ram without blemish	Deprived someone of rights or desecrated something holy	Lev 5:14–6:7; 7:1–6; 14:12–18
The animal offered was determined by the wealth of the worshippers. ⁺ *The priest and the worshipper's family would eat what was not offered.*				

The Jewish Calendar						
Month	Hebrew Name	Modern Equivalent	Feasts	Day	Scripture	Commemoration
1	**Nisan**	**March/April**	**Passover** (*Pesah*)	**14**	Exod 12:1–4 Lev 23:4–5; Deut 16:1–8	Deliverance from Egypt
			Unleavened Bread	**15–22**	Exod 12:15–20 Lev 23:6–8; Deut 16:1–8	Deliverance from Egypt
2	Iyyar	April/May				
3	**Sivan**	**May/June**	**Feast of Weeks** (*Šabāt*) "Pentecost"	**6**	Lev 23:15–22 Deut 16:9–12	Celebration of harvest
4 5 6	Tammuz Ab Elul	June/July July/Aug. Aug./Sept.				
7	**Tishri**	**Sept./Oct.**	**Feast of Trumpets** (*Roš Hašanah*)	**1**	Lev 23:23–25 Num 29:1–6	Beginning of year
			Day of Atonement (*Yôm Kippūr*)	**10**	Lev 16; 23:26–32 Num 29:7–11	Atonement for the sins of the nation
			Feast of Tabernacles (Booths) (*Sūkkôt*)	**15–22**	Lev 23:33–43 Deut 16:13–17 Nehemiah 8	Wandering in the wilderness
8 9 10 11	Marchesvan Kislev Tebeth Shebat	Oct./Nov. Nov./Dec. Dec./Jan. Jan./Feb.				
12	**Adar**	**Feb./March**	**Purim**	**13–14**	Esther 9	Deliverance from death

THE THEOLOGY OF THE BOOK[47]

The book of Exodus ends and Leviticus begins with God speaking to Moses from "the tent of meeting," that is, the tabernacle. The reason God spoke to Moses from there is that He had determined to dwell in the midst of them. By installing His Shekinah glory above the ark of the covenant in the holy of holies, God provided a visible demonstration of His presence for his people to see. Wherever they were in the camp of Israel throughout the wilderness wanderings, they simply had to look up and they could see this visible reminder that the all-powerful God of the universe was with them! He guided them flawlessly throughout their wilderness travels. He provided for all their physical needs. He also demanded and deserved their heartfelt obedience.

---

[47] Some of the truths presented earlier in this chapter are also part of the theology of Leviticus; thus this section presents an overview of only a few other key concepts.

His presence at the tabernacle was also a visible reminder of the serious challenge before them. How do sinful people live near a God this majestic? The book of Leviticus delineates how God's people can live in proximity with the holy God who had formed them as a nation, had repeatedly intervened on their behalf, and demanded their total allegiance. He longed that they too would be holy.

In Exod 19:5–6, God explained His rationale for establishing the Mosaic covenant[48] with His servant nation. He established His covenant and gave His law to them for a number of reasons, but the central reason was to help them understand how they could accurately and vividly demonstrate His incomparable character to the entire world. By conforming their lives to Yahweh's covenant demands, they had opportunity to function, as noted earlier, as His treasured possession, a kingdom of priests, and holy nation (v. 5).

The book of Leviticus focuses on the cleansing, worship, and service of God's servant nation that was necessary for the realization of this priestly calling. Since sin was part of human life and clouded Israel's ability to "advertise" God's unparalleled identity, this book explains the means by which His people were to receive forgiveness and restoration to that lofty function.

CONCLUSION

Many Christians, when they begin reading the book of Leviticus, may feel that they have entered a foreign land. They often regard it as a myriad of incomprehensible and irrelevant details, what might be called a levitical minutiae. But to view Leviticus this way is to abuse the book and to overlook its significance. Jacob Milgrom was correct when he wrote, "Theology is what Leviticus is all about. It pervades every chapter and almost every verse."[49] It deals with how God defines sin, how He forgives sin, and how He helps people avoid sin—highly relevant truths.[50] Leviticus gives a glimpse of the one and only God who is holy and who requires that His subjects be holy. In Leviticus He sets before His people the way they can pursue that holiness. In addition, Leviticus profoundly lays a foundation for the life and ministry of Jesus Christ.

STUDY QUESTIONS
1. Which of the sources cited by critics receives the most attention in critical explanations of the composition of the book of Leviticus?
2. What evidence is there for a second-millennium setting for the writing of Leviticus?
3. What is the underlying rationale for the book (and theology) of Leviticus?
4. What are three key *dimensions* of the Mosaic law?
5. What is holiness and ritual purity, and how do these two important concepts relate to each other?
6. What is the concept of "sacred space"?
7. What are the two broad categories of OT sacrifices and what was the primary function for the sacrifices in these two categories (generally speaking)?
8. Which three sacrifices fell under the first category of OT sacrifices?
9. What were the three pilgrimage festivals that all Israelite men were required to attend?

---

[48] Since this covenant was made with the nation Israel, it might be better to call it the Israelite covenant.

[49] Milgrom, *Leviticus 1–16*, 42.

[50] P. R. House, *Old Testament Theology* (Downers Grove, IL: InterVarsity, 1998), 126.

FOR FURTHER STUDY

Averbeck, R. E. "Offerings and Sacrifices." In *NIDOTTE*. Edited by Willem VanGemeren, 4:996–1002. Grand Rapids: Zondervan, 1997.

Baylis, A. H. *From Creation to the Cross: Understanding the First Half of the Bible*. Grand Rapids: Zondervan, 1996.

Currid, J. D. *A Study Commentary on Leviticus*. Faverdale North, Darlington, UK: Evangelical, 2004.

Dyer, C., and G. Merrill. *Old Testament Explorer: Discovering the Essence, Background, and Meaning of Every Book in the Old Testament*. Nashville: Word, 2001.

Gane, R. E. "Leviticus." In *ZIBBC*. Edited by J. H. Walton, 1:284–337. Grand Rapids: Zondervan, 2009.

Hamilton, V. P. *Handbook on the Pentateuch*. 2nd ed. Grand Rapids: Baker, 2005.

Harbin, M. A. *The Promise and Blessing: A Historical Survey of the Old and New Testaments*. Grand Rapids: Zondervan, 2005.

Harrison, R. K. *Introduction to the Old Testament*. Grand Rapids: Eerdmans, 1969.

———. *Leviticus: An Introduction and Commentary*. TOTC. Downers Grove, IL: InterVarsity, 1980.

Hartley, J. E. *Leviticus*. WBC. Nashville: Thomas Nelson, 1992.

Hess, R. S. "Leviticus." In *EBC*. Rev. ed. Edited by T. Longman III and D. E. Garland, 1:563–826. Grand Rapids: Zondervan, 2008.

Hill, A. E., and J. H. Walton. *A Survey of the Old Testament*. 3rd ed. Grand Rapids: Zondervan, 2009.

House, P. R. *Old Testament Theology*. Downers Grove, IL: InterVarsity, 1998.

Kaiser, W. C., Jr. *The Promise-Plan of God: Biblical Theology of the Old and New Testaments*. Grand Rapids: Zondervan, 2008.

———. "The Book of Leviticus: Introduction, Commentary, and Reflections." In *The New Interpreter's Bible*. Edited by Leander E. Keck, 1:983–1191. Nashville: Abingdon, 1994.

Kaufmann, Y. *The Religion of Israel*. Translated by M. Greenberg. Chicago: University of Chicago Press, 1960.

Kiuchi, N. "Leviticus, Book of." In *Dictionary of the OT: Pentateuch*. Edited by T. D. Alexander and D. W. Baker, 522–32. Downers Grove, IL: InterVarsity, 2003.

———. *Leviticus*. Apollos. Downers Grove, IL: InterVarsity, 2007.

Kleinig, J. W. *Leviticus*. Concordia Commentary. St. Louis: Concordia, 2003.

Levine, B. A. "Leviticus, Book of." In *ABD*. Edited by D. N. Freedman, 4:311–21. New York: Doubleday, 1992.

Longman, T., III, and R. Dillard. *An Introduction to the Old Testament*. 2nd ed. Grand Rapids: Zondervan, 2006.

Merrill, E. H. *Everlasting Dominion: A Theology of the Old Testament*. Nashville: B&H, 2006.

———. "A Theology of the Pentateuch." In *A Biblical Theology of the Old Testament*. Edited by Roy B. Zuck, 7–87. Chicago: Moody, 1991.

Milgrom, J. *Cult and Conscience: The Asham and the Priestly Doctrine of Repentance*. Leiden: Brill, 1976.

———. *Leviticus 1–16*. AB. New York: Doubleday, 1991.

———. *Studies in Cultic Theology and Terminology*. Leiden: Brill, 1983.

Moberly, R. W. L. *The Old Testament of the Old Testament: Patriarchal Narratives and Mosaic Yahwism*. Minneapolis: Fortress, 1992.

Rooker, M. F. *Leviticus*. NAC. Nashville: B&H, 2000.

Ross, A. P. *Holiness to the Lord: A Guide to the Exposition of the Book of Leviticus*. Grand Rapids: Baker, 2002.

Schnittjer, G. *The Torah Story*. Grand Rapids: Zondervan, 2006.

Tidball, D. *The Message of Leviticus: Free to Be Holy*. BST. Downers Grove, IL: InterVarsity, 2005.

Waltke, B. K. *An Old Testament Theology*. Grand Rapids: Zondervan, 2007.

CHAPTER 13

THE BOOK OF NUMBERS

MICHAEL A. GRISANTI

ISRAEL'S SITUATION AT the beginning of the book of Numbers is quite different from her experience at the end of the book. God had redeemed His chosen nation from slavery in Egypt and had performed one of the greatest OT miracles, the crossing of the Red Sea. He had given them His law through a set of events that heightened Israel's awareness of His majesty. Israel had built the tabernacle, and God dwelt in their midst. Throughout the year since they had left Egypt, God had provided all their needs for food and drink. Now they were ready to depart from Mount Sinai and travel to the long-anticipated land of promise. The events of the book of Numbers, though humanly shocking, serve as clear demonstrations of numerous realities: the fickleness of the human heart, the patience of God, and the painful reality of judgment against rebellion. Regardless of "bad news," God will still bring His promises to pass.

THE TITLE AND CANONICITY OF THE BOOK

The Hebrew title for Numbers, "in the desert" (*bᵉmidbār*), correctly describes the setting for the book.[1] The Septuagint title for the book, *arithmoi* (probably because of the two census lists in the book), is the basis for the title of the book in the Latin Vulgate, *Numeri*. As part of the Pentateuch, the canonicity of Numbers has been largely unquestioned.

THE TEXT OF THE BOOK

The Hebrew text of Numbers is generally well preserved and free from problems. About eight fragments of Numbers were found at Qumran as well as two fragmentary texts.[2] The most complete text of Numbers found at Qumran (4QNum[b]) does not differ substantially from the MT.

In 1979 in a tomb on the west side of the Hinnom Valley in Jerusalem, archaeologists unearthed a previously covered collection of ancient items. Included among these were two

---

[1] The Hebrew title comes from the fifth Hebrew word in Num 1:1.
[2] R. D. Cole, *Numbers*, NAC (Nashville: B&H, 2000), 27 n. 15.

silver scrolls, likely worn as amulets. Once discovered, scholars had the daunting task of unrolling and deciphering the text. It took three years to unroll the larger scroll. Once unrolled, it disclosed a text written with very delicately scratched paleo-Hebrew characters.[3] The first word to be deciphered was "YHWH." Until this time no inscriptions with the name of God had been found in Jerusalem. The epigraphers eventually determined that the two tiny silver scrolls recorded part of the Aaronic blessing (Num 6:24–26) and perhaps a couple of lines from Deut 7:9.[4] Scholars have generally dated these silver scrolls to the late seventh or early sixth centuries BC.[5] Thus, these verses predate the famous DSS by approximately four centuries and are the only biblical verses known from the time of the First Temple period (see next section). Thus they are the earliest known artifacts from the ancient world that document passages from the Hebrew Bible.

THE LITERARY FORMS AND GENRES OF THE BOOK

Although the book of Leviticus is primarily legal material, the book of Numbers attests a wide variety of genres. In addition to two census lists (chaps. 1 and 26) the book includes summaries of levitical laws and rituals (chaps. 8, 15, 18, etc.), an itinerary of Israel's wandering in the wilderness (chap. 33), short sections of poetry (10:35–36; 21:14–15,17–18,27–30), and prophetic utterances from a pagan prophet (chaps. 22–24). This diversity adds to the complexity of outlining the book, but this does not suggest that numerous sources were gathered together through a long oral and written process to form the book.[6]

THE COMPOSITION OF THE BOOK

As with the other books in the Pentateuch, the book of Numbers is commonly viewed as the result of a long oral process that eventually led to various documents woven together by different editors with the Pentateuch reaching a final form in the fourth century BC.[7] Unlike Leviticus, Numbers has clear chronological references. It must have been compiled after the 38 years of wandering in the wilderness because it traces Israel's history from the time of the end of the book of Exodus to Israel's presence on the brink of the promised land. Wenham delineates various ways that ANE documents from the second millennium BC parallel several of the features of Numbers, thus suggesting the viability of its composition close to the time of the events it describes.[8]

Although some scholars have attempted to date the Ketef Hinnom scrolls as late as the postexilic and even the Hellenistic period, the scholarly consensus dates these scrolls to the late seventh or early sixth centuries BC. What does this signify for the date of composition for the Pentateuch in general and the book of Numbers in particular? Various scholars have affirmed that "the presence of the Priestly Blessing in this late preexilic context does not in and

---

[3] G. Barkay et al., "The Challenges of Ketef Hinnom: Using Advanced Technologies to Reclaim the Earliest Biblical Texts and Their Context," *NEA* 66 (2003): 162–71.

[4] G. Barkay, "The Priestly Benediction on Silver Plaques from Ketef Hinnom in Jerusalem," *TA* 19 (1992): 154–55.

[5] G. Barkay et al., "The Amulets from Ketef Hinnom: A New Edition and Evaluation," *BASOR* 334 (2004): 52.

[6] The problem does not concern whether Moses used sources, but whether the diversity requires a long and complicated process of composition.

[7] See the chapter that introduces Part 4 on the Pentateuch for a more detailed consideration of the composition of the Pentateuch (and Numbers).

[8] G. J. Wenham, *Numbers: An Introduction and Commentary*, TOTC (Downers Grove, IL: InterVarsity, 1981), 24. Wenham does not hold to Mosaic authorship of Numbers, but he agrees that the traditions found in the book originated in the Mosaic period. He concludes that the book reached its final form in the early days of Israel's monarchy period.

of itself prove that the biblical context in which the blessing appears in the MT had already been consolidated."[9] At the very least, it does point to the preexilic presence of formulations that are also found in the canonical text. Some critical scholars, before the discovery of these scrolls, suggested that the priestly blessing existed before the editor of P chose to include it in his work.[10]

If Gabriel Barkay, the archaeologist who discovered the scrolls, is correct, they witness to texts that are found in two pentateuchal passages, Numbers 6 and Deuteronomy 7. While it is true that this discovery does not prove a preexilic composition of Numbers or the Pentateuch, perhaps the presence of two texts from the Pentateuch in one amulet speaks for a written tradition that included these two texts prior to its inscription.[11] Their inclusion in a personal amulet also suggests that the written material from which they were taken had been in existence long enough for its contents to become well known. In the end, belief about the composition of the Pentateuch does not depend on these silver amulets.

THE STRUCTURE OF THE BOOK

Scholars disagree on the literary structure of the book. One approach is geographical, which sees movement taking place throughout the book. The book opens with the nation camped at Mount Sinai, preparing for the next phase of their journey to the land of promise. Then Israel traveled from Sinai to Kadesh-barnea, where a rebellion took place. They wandered in the wilderness for almost 40 years and then, at God's instruction, headed toward the land of promise. This time they travelled up the east side of the Jordan Rift valley and ended their journey when they arrived at the plains of Moab, overlooking the promised land on the other side (west) of the Jordan River. Almost everyone agrees on a break between 10:10 and 10:11 because that is where the text describes Israel's departure from Mount Sinai. What scholars do after that is quite varied.[12]

Another approach to the book's structure focuses on the two censuses (chaps. 1 and 26), suggesting the book falls into two large sections with the break between chapters 25 and 26.[13] This structure places emphasis on the transition from the old generation to the new generation of Israel. The second census follows the period of wilderness wandering, during which time thousands of Israelites died as part of God's punishment of their rebellion at Kadesh-barnea. Olson also provides an impressive list of 13 topical/thematic parallels, events, subjects, or activities that occur in both halves of the book.[14] He also points out that in the second half of the book and after the second census (chap. 26), the question of land inheritance by the daughters of Zelophehad (chaps. 27 and 36) forms an inclusio that frames the material of chaps. 28–35.

---

[9] Barkay et al., "The Amulets from Ketef Hinnom," 68. A. Yardeni adds that this discovery does not prove the existence of a written Pentateuch in the preexilic period or even that the blessing was already incorporated into the Pentateuch in that time frame ("Remarks on the Priestly Blessing on Two Ancient Amulets from Jerusalem," *VT* 51 [1991]: 181, 185).

[10] G. B. Gray, *A Critical and Exegetical Commentary on Numbers*, ICC (Edinburgh: T&T Clark, 1903), 71; M. Noth, *Numbers: A Commentary*, trans. J. D. Martin, OTL (Philadelphia: Westminster, 1968), 58.

[11] E. Waaler, "A Revised Date for Pentateuchal Texts: Evidence from Ketef Hinnom," *TynBul* 53 (2002): 53.

[12] D. Olson observed that 33 commentators who outlined the book of Numbers in accord with geographical movement offered no fewer than 18 different proposals! (*The Death of the Old and the Birth of the New: The Framework of the Book of Numbers and the Pentateuch*, BJS 71 [Chico, CA: Scholars, 1985], 35).

[13] D. T. Olson, "Numbers, Book of," in *Dictionary of the OT: Pentateuch*, ed. T. D. Alexander and D. W. Baker (Downers Grove, IL: InterVarsity, 2003), 612–17; idem, *Numbers*, Interpretation (Louisville: John Knox, 1996), 3–7. Cf. R. B. Allen, "Numbers," in *EBC*, ed. F. Gaebelein (Grand Rapids: Zondervan, 1990), 2:673–75; T. Longman III and R. Dillard, *An Introduction to the Old Testament*, 2nd ed. (Grand Rapids: Zondervan, 2006), 96–98; R. Gane, *Leviticus, Numbers*, NIVAC (Grand Rapids: Zondervan, 2004), 476–78.

[14] Olson, *Numbers*, 5–6.

Chronology of Israel's Journey from Egypt to Canaan					
Yr.	Mo.	Day	Reference	Event	Elapsed Time Since Previous Event
1	**1**	**14**	Exod 12:1–6	Passover and death Angel; beginning of the Exodus	
1	2	15	Exod 16:1	Arrival at the Wilderness of Sin	1 mo., 1 day
1	3	14	Exod 19:1	Arrival at the Wilderness of Sinai, at base of Mount Sinai	29 days
2	1	1	Exod 40:17	Tabernacle erected; events of Leviticus begin	9 mos., 16 days
2	2	1	Num 1:1–2	Events of Leviticus conclude; instruction to number the people	1 mo.
2	2	20	Num 10:11–12	Numbering finished; departure from Wilderness of Sinai	20 days
40	1	?	Num 20:1	The death of Miriam	
40	5	1	Num 20:23–29; 33:38	The death of Aaron	
40	11	1	Deut 1:3	Moses' last words *39 yrs., 9 mos., 17 days since Passover*	38 yrs., 8 mos., 11 days
41	1	10	Josh 4:19	Crossing of the Jordan *39 yrs., 11 mos., 26 days since the Passover*	1 mo., 9 days
41	**1**	**14**	Josh 5:10	Celebration of the Passover	4 days
Total time elapsed between the celebration of the first and second Passovers: 40 years to the day					

AN OUTLINE OF THE BOOK

Though there is clear geographical movement in the book of Numbers, the two census lists and the parallels between these two sections favor an outline that arranges the book into two major sections. These censuses mark the transition from the old generation to the new.

I. **The Experience of the Old Generation in the Wilderness (chaps. 1–25)**
  A. The Preparation and Inauguration of Israel's March to the Promised Land (chaps. 1–10)
  B. An Abrupt Slide into Rebellion (chaps. 11–20)
  C. The End of the First Generation: Signs of Hope Coupled with Failure (chaps. 21–25)

II. **The Prospects for the New Generation to Enter the Promised Land (chaps. 26–36)**
   A.   A Second Census: The Rise of a Generation of Hope (chap. 26)
   B.   The Daughters of Zelophehad and Land Inheritance (27:1–11)
   C.   Succession of Leadership from Moses to Joshua (27:12–23)
   D.   Appointed Offerings and Voluntary Vows (chaps. 28–30)
   E.   War of Vengeance against the Midianites (chap. 31)
   F.   Allocation of Transjordanian Land to Reuben, Gad, and Half of Manasseh (chap. 32)
   G.   Summary of Israel's Journey from Egypt to Canaan (33:1–49)
   H.   Final Instructions about Conquest and Inheritance (33:50–35:34)
   I.   The Daughters of Zelophehad and Land Inheritance (chap. 36)

AN OVERVIEW OF NUMBERS

As stated above, the two census lists (in Numbers 1 and 26) emphasize the transition from the old generation to the new generation of Israel. These censuses also count the soldiers of Israel, focusing on the upcoming conquest. Thus Numbers represents a transition from pilgrimage (wandering in the wilderness) to the conquest and occupation of the land of promise.

The Experience of the Old Generation in the Wilderness (chaps. 1–25)

The first half of Numbers focuses on the older generation, from the time of their departure from Mount Sinai to their dealings with compromise in the region of Moab. The first 10 chapters take place in the region of Mount Sinai. After the counting of the men of war, chaps. 2–4 record the numbering of the Levites, and the arrangement of the tribes in camp and during travel, and also list the duties of Levites and priests. Chapters 5–6 concern various issues of uncleanness and sin, including the jealousy ordeal (see below), as well as the Nazirite vow. Chapters 7–8 summarize the dedication of the bronze altar and the consecration of the Levites for their God-given tasks. After some remaining instructions about the Passover (chap. 9) and instructions for travel (10:1–10), the nation resumes its journey toward the promised land (10:11–36).

Chapters 11–20 records a chain of rebellions. Although various acts of treachery precede and follow chaps. 13–14,[15] Israel's rebellion at Kadesh-barnea represents the most serious act of rebellion. The chosen nation stood at the moment of promise (and decision) when the 12 spies returned from their journey through the land of promise. Even though 10 of the spies declared that the obstacles before the nation were too great, the nation had seen God demonstrate His unmatched power in numerous settings. Yet, the nation rejected God's direction to advance toward Canaan. Yahweh's punishment for their foolish rebellion was swift and drastic. The generation that made that decision/act of rebellion (those 20 years old and older) would not live to see the land of promise. For the next 38 and a half years, the nation wandered in the wilderness, during which time that generation ceased to exist.

After God instructed His people to resume their journey to the land of promise, this time toward the region west of the land of Canaan, the nation enjoyed several military victories, along with episodes of divine judgment (chap. 21). Once the nation settled on the plains of Moab, Balak (king of Moab) hired the prophet Balaam to curse the nation Israel. Although God prevented that from happening (see summary below on the oracles of Balaam), Balaam suggested a way to devastate the nation: have Moabite women intermarry with Israelite men

---

[15] Even Aaron and Miriam, the brother and sister of Moses, rebelled against Moses (and Yahweh) (11:35–12:16).

and turn their hearts to idolatry (chaps. 22–25). Obviously the nation Israel was unprepared to conquer the promised land.

The Prospects for the New Generation to Enter the Promised Land (chaps. 26–36)

This second section of Numbers concerns the generation that would enter the land of promise. In these chapters Moses recorded various issues related to the conclusion of pilgrimage and the beginning of the conquest of Canaan. In addition to handling unique inheritance problems, Moses explained various offerings and vows that God required. Also Moses gave the nation final instructions about the imminent conquest of the land of promise.

Figure 13.1
The Arrangement of the Twelve Tribes around the Tabernacle

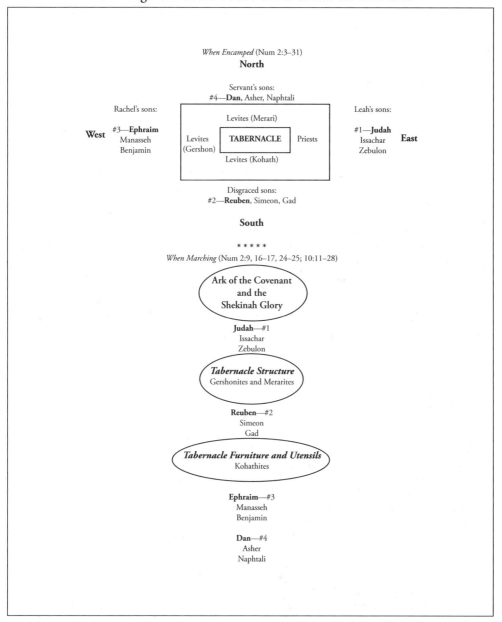

When Encamped (Num 2:3–31)
North

Servant's sons:
#4—**Dan**, Asher, Naphtali

Rachel's sons: Leah's sons:
#3—**Ephraim**   #1—**Judah**
West   Manasseh   Levites (Merari)   Issachar   **East**
         Benjamin   Levites   TABERNACLE   Priests   Zebulon
                     (Gershon)
                              Levites (Kohath)

Disgraced sons:
#2—**Reuben**, Simeon, Gad

South

* * * * *

When Marching (Num 2:9, 16–17, 24–25; 10:11–28)

Ark of the Covenant
and the
Shekinah Glory

Judah—#1
Issachar
Zebulon

Tabernacle Structure
Gershonites and Merarites

Reuben—#2
Simeon
Gad

Tabernacle Furniture and Utensils
Kohathites

Ephraim—#3
Manasseh
Benjamin

Dan—#4
Asher
Naphtali

THE JEALOUSY ORDEAL

This jealousy ordeal (Num 5:11–28) is the third passage in Numbers 5 that deals with Israel's "holiness" or distinctiveness.[16] It presents a "case law" that deals with a woman suspected of marital unfaithfulness. This misconduct is probably singled out because marital fidelity is foundational to the stability of any society (cf. Exod 20:14). The "jealousy" (*qin'āh*) described here does not signify some petty bickering. In the context of marriage it signifies the legitimate desire to maintain the purity or exclusive relationship between a husband and a wife (repeatedly in Numbers 5; cf. Prov 6:34; 27:4).[17]

If a husband suspects that his wife has been sexually unfaithful but he has no evidence or witnesses, he can bring his wife and a grain offering to the priest in order to discern the truth.[18] The priest takes some "holy water" (probably water from the bronze basin in the courtyard of the tabernacle) and mixes in it dust from the floor of the sanctuary. After the priest (and the woman) present the grain offering on the altar, the woman will drink the "bitter water" and either experience serious consequences or be free of ill effects. Scholars have offered numerous interpretations of the "ill effects" of drinking this water, the most common being miscarriage[19] or sterility.[20] Regardless of exactly what the negative consequences were, she became a "curse" among the Israelites (Num 5:27).

Numerous scholars have called this procedure a "trial by ordeal," a procedure that was somewhat common in the ancient world (found esp. in Mari, Hittite, and Babylonian texts).[21] This method involved "an appeal to divine judgment to decide otherwise insoluble cases that cannot be allowed to remain unsolved."[22] The most common ordeals in the ancient world involved water (e.g., plunging into rivers), heat (e.g., plunging the hand into boiling liquid), or some potion.[23] Although there are some similarities between this passage in Numbers and these ordeals, the differences are even more obvious.[24] First, unlike the ANE ordeals in which the agent (water, poison, etc.) was dangerous to the guilty and innocent alike, the "bitter water" only endangers the guilty party. Second, in the ANE ordeals the accused had to *survive* something inherently harmful. In a way the accused was guilty until proven innocent. In this example in Numbers 5, the fate of the accused is left totally open. Third, in most ANE ordeals the penalty was pronounced separately by the court, but in Numbers 5 the penalty was the outcome of the ritual. This procedure in Numbers 5 is not an example of magic; it is a procedure through which God punishes the guilty.

---

[16] For a list of the many scholarly resources devoted to this difficult passage see P. J. Budd, *Numbers*, WBC (Dallas: Word, 1984), 62–66.

[17] G. Sauer, "קִנְאָה *qin'â* fervor," in *TLOT*, 1146.

[18] One would assume that a husband would not do this casually, without deep, nagging concerns about his wife's faithfulness.

[19] R. K. Harrison, *Numbers* (Chicago: Moody, 1990), 110–13.

[20] J. Milgrom, *Numbers*, JPS Torah Commentary (Philadelphia: Jewish Publication Society, 1990), 41, 349; T. R. Ashley, *The Book of Numbers*, NICOT (Grand Rapids: Eerdmans, 1993), 131–33. If the punishment is sterility, her punishment represents divinely caused inability to bear children and to participate in one of the central blessings of the Abrahamic covenant (Gen 12:2; 22:17).

[21] Wenham, *Numbers*, 80. T. H. Gaster also provides numerous examples of "the poison ordeal" from various cultures (*Myth, Legend, and Custom in the Old Testament* [New York: Harper & Row, 1918], 280–300). Milgrom surveys various examples of judicial ordeal in ANE literature and the Bible (*Numbers*, 346–48).

[22] T. S. Frymer, "Ordeal, Judicial," in *IDBS*, ed. K. Crim (Nashville: Abingdon, 1976), 639.

[23] Ashley, *The Book of Numbers*, 123.

[24] These differences are summarized from Ashley, *The Book of Numbers*, 123–24.

THE TRANSJORDAN CONQUEST

After Israel's arrogant rebellions against their covenant Lord at Kadesh-barnea (Numbers 13–14), the Lord judged them with almost 40 years of wilderness wandering. During that period of wandering they stopped at over 20 locations and experienced the death of the entire generation of adults (20 years old and older, except Moses, Joshua, and Caleb). At the Lord's direction (Deut 2:1–3), the Israelites began their second approach to the land of promise (Num 20:14–29). Moses' brother, Aaron, died at Mount Hor before the nation departed for Edom. When the Israelites along the way to Edom complained again about God's wisdom and His care for them, this triggered a plague of poisonous snakes. God directed Moses to provide relief from the plague by erecting a brass serpent (Num 21:4–9).[25] Avoiding any military conflict with the Edomites, Moabites, and the Ammonites (Num 20:14–21; 21:10–13; Deut 2:4–25),[26] the Israelites arrived at the Wadi Arnon on the southern boundary of the Amorites. Sihon, ruler of Heshbon, and Og, king of Bashan, both refused Israel passage through their territories. The Israelites conquered both groups of Amorites and took possession of their land (much of the Transjordan region; Num 21:21–35). Moses allocated this land on the east side of the Jordan River to the tribes of Reuben, Gad, and half the tribe of Manasseh (32:1–5, 33–42). Even though they were occupying their tribal inheritance before the land of Canaan was conquered, Moses demanded that they send their men with the entire army of Israel for the conquest of the land on the west side of the Jordan (32:6–32). (See map 12.)

THE BALAAM ORACLES

After conquering most of the Transjordan, the Israelites set up camp on the plains of Moab, just across the Jordan River from the promised land. Their proximity to the territory of Moab apparently prompted Balak, the king of Moab, to hire the prophet Balaam[27] to pronounce a curse against Israel (22:1–7).[28] At first the Lord commanded Balaam not to return with the emissaries from Moab. However, after the second request the Lord allowed Balaam to travel to Moab but demanded that he say only what the Lord commanded him to say (22:8–20).[29] To Balak's dismay, Balaam pronounced only blessing rather than curses on God's chosen nation (through four oracles), but he uttered curses against Moab, Edom, and Amalek (24:15–24). In the climactic fourth oracle Balaam declared that Yahweh's sovereign control over world affairs extends to His future provision of a Messiah (24:17; cf. Gen 49:10).

Although Balaam refused to pronounce a curse against Israel, it seems that he gave Balak, the king of Moab, some powerful advice, recommending that Moabite women seduce Israelite men

---

[25] Hezekiah later destroyed this brass serpent because the Israelites eventually made it into an object of worship (2 Kgs 18:4).

[26] The Edomites (through Esau), Moabites, and Ammonites (through Lot and his two daughters) were all distant relatives of the Israelites.

[27] Balaam lived near the Euphrates River (Num 22:5) and apparently was well-known as a diviner and prophet. Another story of a prophet named Balaam (which may or may not refer to the same Balaam) conveying a message from the gods to a disobedient nation is found in the Deir 'Allah texts (J. Hoftijzer and G. van der Kooij, eds., *Aramaic Texts from Deir Alla* [Leiden: Brill, 1997], 268–70).

[28] Balak seems to have been unaware that God had instructed the Israelites not to attack or harass the Moabites or the Ammonites (Deut 2:16–19), apparently because they were distant relatives of the Israelites (through Abraham's nephew, Lot; Gen 19:30–38).

[29] Scholars have debated the exact relationship of Yahweh and Balaam. Balaam listened to Yahweh and referred to Him as "the Lord my God" (Num 22:18). Also he inquired of Yahweh after he arrived in Moab (Num 23:1–12). The NT presents Balaam as a false prophet (2 Pet 2:15; Jude 11). It seems that Balaam had some kind of relationship with Yahweh, but his treachery eventually led to his death (Num 31:8).

and convince them to practice idolatry with them (worshipping Baal of Peor; Num 31:16). Thus many Israelite men began worshipping Baal, and their covenant treachery led to the nation's experience of a plague, resulting in the death of 24,000 Israelites (Num 25:1–9).

Balak had also entered into an alliance with the Midianites against Israel (Num 22:4). After the Lord removed the plague experienced by Israel, He commanded His chosen people to attack the Midianites, the allies of Moab (31:1–6). As part of their victory over the Midianites (killing every soldier and all five Midianite kings), the Israelites also killed Balaam the prophet (Num 31:7–8). God once again demonstrated His absolute sovereignty over the nations and false prophets. He also reminded His servant nation that He demands their exclusive loyalty.

LARGE NUMBERS IN THE OLD TESTAMENT

The censuses in Numbers 1 and 26, taken before and after Israel's wilderness wanderings, present a total number of over 600,000 Israelite men old enough to be soldiers in the upcoming conquest of Canaan.[30] Based on those figures, the traditional view posits a total population of 1.5 to 2.5 million. Of course a number this great raises questions. How could Moses manage such a large group of people and how would they survive in the desert? What about the armies of other nations in that region that seem to have been much smaller in number? How did that many people travel through the rugged terrain of the wilderness? How much food and water was necessary to feed that number? How does this number compare with what the archaeology of Canaan suggests about the population of Canaan at the time of the conquest?[31] How does this cohere with Deut 7:7 that suggests that Israel was "the smallest of all nations"? These and other questions have caused scholars to offer various suggestions that attempt to resolve the tension that exists between the stated numbers and what might be reasonably expected. To many, the census numbers seem to be impossible and un-historical. The following are the principal suggested alternatives.[32]

Option 1: The Census Numbers Were Not Meant to Be Understood

First, some have proposed that these large numbers are totally fabricated and not historical—they have no relation to fact.[33] Second, some have suggested that the numbers in Numbers 1 and 26 are accurate for a later period in Israel's history and were transposed to the wilderness period to show that, in a theological sense, all Israel was present.[34] Philip Budd writes that the "historical difficulties in accepting this figure as it stands are insuperable."[35] He concludes that the census figures were imported from the postexilic period.[36] Others view the

---

[30] Numbers 1:46 puts the total at 603,550 and 26:51 gives 601,730.

[31] D. Merling Sr. contends that the population of Canaan never exceeded 150,000 (*The Book of Joshua: Its Theme and Role in Archaeological Discussions* (Berrien Springs, MI: Andrews University Press, 1997), 214–18. Cf. idem, "Large Numbers at the Time of the Exodus," *NEASB* 44 (1999): 15–27.

[32] This section cannot provide an exhaustive overview of the issues or provide a convincing argument for a position. The goal here is to provide a helpful overview of what has been suggested (with references) and offer a preferred solution. Overviews of this debate are given in T. R. Ashley, *The Book of Numbers*, NICOT (Grand Rapids: Eerdmans, 1993), 61–66; C. J. Humphreys, "The Number of People in the Exodus from Egypt: Decoding Mathematically the Very Large Numbers in Numbers I and XXVI," *VT* 48 (1998): 197–99.

[33] Gray, *Numbers*, 13; R. de Vaux, *The Early History of Israel to the Period of the Judges*, trans. D. Smith (London: Darton, Longman & Todd, 1978), 725; J. Sturdy, *Numbers*, CBC (New York: Cambridge University Press, 1976), 16.

[34] W. F. Albright, *From the Stone Age to Christianity*, 2nd ed. (New York: Doubleday, 1957), 253, 290–91; N. M. Sarna, *Exodus*, JPS Torah Commentary (Philadelphia: Jewish Publication Society, 1991), 62.

[35] P. J. Budd, *Numbers*, WBC (Waco, TX: Word, 1984), 6.

[36] Ibid., 8–9.

numbers as "grossly inflated numbers" with a theological rationale.[37] These numbers were not meant to be understood propositionally. For example Bellinger affirms that these censuses "are not attempting to give a detailed account of the past but are rather proclaiming the theological message of God's blessing and promise."[38]

Option 2: The Noun *'elep* Must Mean Something Other Than "Thousand"

Some attempts to solve the conundrum of large numbers deal with the semantic range of the noun *'elep*. These views share the common thread that the biblical writer did not intend for this noun to signify some number. The most common suggestions are that *'elep* means "group" or "clan," "chieftain," or "troop."

"Group" or "clan." This view was first suggested by Flinders Petrie, who understood *'elep* to mean a "group" or "clan."[39] For example the census figure for Reuben in Num 1:21 is 46,500. According to Petrie, the reference is to 46 *'elep* and 500, that is, 46 groups with a total of 500 men. A total of all the "groups" and "men" categories in Numbers 1 yields 5,550 men in 598 groups whereas Numbers 26 records 5,730 men in 596 groups. Based on that, Flinders Petrie suggested a population for Israel of about 20,000.[40] However, this suggestion does not work for the Levites, of whom it is said there were 22,000 of them (Num 3:39)—22 groups and no men! To deal with this problem, Petrie affirmed that the Levite passages were added to the text later.[41] George Mendenhall revived Petrie's thesis and affirmed that the census lists contained the quotas sent to war from each group rather than the whole number of fighting men.[42]

"Chieftain." John Wenham pointed out that the consonants that make up *'elep* could be vocalized as *'elep* or *'allûp*, "chieftain."[43] He combines the "chieftain" with the word for "hundred," the unit which he commanded. For example Reuben would have had 45 "chieftains" (*'allûpîm*) and 1,500 men. According to his complicated calculations, Israel had 18,000 soldiers and a population of about 72,000.[44] Once again, this approach cannot answer the numbers assigned to the Levites, who were not fighting men.

"Troop." Humphreys has more recently proposed a solution that has caught the interest of a number of scholars.[45] His study is founded on his viewing the following statement in Num 3:46 as correct: "the 273 firstborn Israelites who outnumber the Levites." Based on various assumptions and calculations, he determined that the figures of 603,550 men over 20 (Num 1:46) and 22,000 Levites (Num 3:39) are incorrect "interpretations." His interpretation of *'elep* leads him to the conclusion that in the censuses there were 598 troops (by totaling the

---

[37] E. W. Davies, "A Mathematical Conundrum: The Problem of the Large Numbers in Numbers I and XXVI," *VT* 45 (1995): 467–68.

[38] W. H. Bellinger, *Leviticus and Numbers*, NBCOT (Peabody, MA: Hendrickson, 2001), 183. Cf. B. E. Scolnic, *Theme and Content in Biblical Lists* (Atlanta: Scholars, 1995), 65; Olson, *Death of the Old*, 79.

[39] W. M. F. Petrie, *Researches in Sinai* (London: Murray, 1906), 208–21.

[40] Each of these views that translate *'elep* with something other than "thousand" ignore the total figure given at the end of the census.

[41] Petrie, *Researches in Sinai*, 215–16.

[42] G. E. Mendenhall, "The Census Lists of Numbers 1 and 26," *JBL* 77 (1959): 60. Mendenhall examined Mari materials as a paradigm for his suggestions. He dated the census lists to the time of the Judges (ibid., 53–59).

[43] J. W. Wenham, "The Large Numbers in the OT," *TynBul* 18 (1967): 19–53.

[44] Wenham based his approach on the suggestions of R. E. D. Clark, "The Large Numbers of the OT," *JTVI* 87 (1955): 82–92, who suggested that Israel's total population was 140,000.

[45] K. A. Kitchen, *On the Reliability of the Old Testament* (Grand Rapids: Eerdmans, 2003), 265; G. A. Rendsburg, "An Additional Note to Two Recent Articles on the Number of People in the Exodus from Egypt and the Large Numbers in Numbers I and XXVI," *VT* 51 (2001): 392–96.

'elep numbers) involving 5,550 men of war (by totaling the numbers measured in hundreds) and that the total population of Israel was 20,000.[46] Then, he offers a solution as to why his final number for the census does not match the one found in Num 1:46 ("All those registered numbered 603,550"). The biblical text has 600 *'elep*, and 3 *'alāpîm*, and 550; and Humphreys has 598 troops and 5,550 men.

Humphreys suggests this: "At a later date, when the original meaning was lost, a scribe collated the numbers and ran together the two *'lp* figures (598 + 5), to yield 603 thousand, not realising (*sic*) that two different *'lp* meanings were intended."[47] Of course, the "5" *'lp* that is conflated with the 598 is not in the Hebrew text, but is an assumption as to what was there originally as the total of the numbers of the men from the 12 tribes. The same thing happens with his explanation of the encampment numbers in Numbers 2. He cites the tribes located on the east side of the tabernacle as his example (Num 2:1–9):

	Total Numbers	Troops	Men
Judah	74,600	74	600
Issachar	54,400	54	400
Zebulon	57,400	57	400
Totals:	*186,400*	*185*	*1,400*

Humphreys concludes that "the correct interpretation is [the above figures] yielding a total of 185 *'lp* (troops) and 1 *'lp* (thousand) and 400 men. This was later conflated to 186,400 men, although a total of 1,400 men was originally intended."[48] After giving the totals for the other three sides of the encampment, Humphreys concludes, "These figures are plausible and reasonable, and we have explained how the misinterpretation has arisen."[49] Again, the one *'lp* ("thousand"), which is "conflated" with the 185 *'lp* ("troops"), is not in the Hebrew text. According to Humphreys's view, the original text did not give any totals. Later some scribe who added up the two sets of numbers misunderstood the distinction between the two kinds of *'lp* terms in the list and calculated the total incorrectly. Besides the fact that the absence of totals would seem odd in a census, Klingbeil puts the matter to rest when he writes, "The suggestion of systematic textual corruption in the total numbers debilitates the semantic-interpretation approach."[50]

In addition to these problems Humphreys's approach to this issue draws on several important presuppositions. First, his calculations require that each family have a large number of children. He answers that concern by suggesting that the pharaoh's decree that all male children be killed drastically reduced the male population until they were no longer viewed as a threat by the pharaoh. This, however, created a male-female imbalance in the population that led to widespread polygamy. This would have enabled each family to have a larger than normal number of children (c. 17 children per family).[51] Second, he assumes that half the population was under 20 years old, based on figures from other countries with high birth rates.[52] These two assumptions lead to another calculation that affirms that there were about 1,000 Levites

---

[46] Humphreys, "The Number of People in the Exodus from Egypt," 196. See his Table 2, p. 212.

[47] Ibid., 207.

[48] Ibid.

[49] Ibid.

[50] Klingbeil, "Historical Criticism," 410. Klingbeil ends the sentence with "although it still presents a viable possibility."

[51] C. Humphreys, "Response by Colin J. Humphreys," *Science and Christian Belief* 13 (2001): 66.

[52] Humphreys, "The Number of People in the Exodus from Egypt," 202.

at the time of the census in Numbers.[53] This is important because he rejects the biblical text's statement that there were 22,000 Levites (Num 3:39) because his multi-step calculations established that there were only 1,000 of them.[54] By defining *'elep* as "troop" he dismisses the total given in Numbers of over 600,000 men. However, his rejection of the 22,000 number has nothing to do with the "troop" definition, but is the consequence of his mathematical computations based on various assumptions.

Problems with a Nonnumerical Meaning of *'elep (Semantic view)*[55]

Because this view generally receives so much attention, direct response seems appropriate. First, in Numbers 1 and 26, numeric units down to hundreds and tens follow *'elep*. If *'elep* means something other than a numeric unit, how does this term relate to the following numeric units? For example, Num 1:46 states, "All those registered numbered 603,550." This literally reads, "The total number was six hundred *'elep* and three *alāpîm* and five hundred and fifty" or "six hundred three *'elep* and five hundred fifty." In what way are the 603 *'elep*, that is, clans, troops, and so forth, related to the number 550? The general assumption of the semantic interpretation seems to be that the first number signifies how many units there were and the second unit states how many people belonged to those units. So does this mean that there were 603 units that involved 550 men?

Second, since the 22,000 Levites mentioned in 3:39 did not function in a military setting, the semantic suggestions of troop, chieftain, and so forth, are not relevant (at least in these instances). When used with reference to the Levites, *'elep* seems to have a clear numeric value.

Third, Num 3:43 relates that "The total number of the firstborn males one month old or more listed by name was 22,273." This number seems to be drawn from the total population of Israel at the time of the census. Since not every family had sons (e.g., daughters of Zelophehad—Numbers 27, 36), this number would not include certain families. However, it would include most families since most families would have at least one son.

On the one hand, this number causes problems for those who suggest a different meaning for *'elep* than "thousand." Since these are not soldiers, the conventional word "troop" does not work. Twenty-two "clans" involving 273 firstborn males would be an amazingly small number as well (273 family units?). Also other scholars who advocate another meaning for *'elep* suggest a total population of about 20,000.[56] But this number of firstborn males is larger than the total population of Israel! This is not a rounded number but is precise to the last digit.[57] This number of firstborn can work, however, with the hyperbolic interpretation that suggests a total population of around 200,000 to 250,000.

On the other hand, this number also presents a potential problem for scholars who maintain a face value meaning of large numbers (those that use *'elep*). If there were 22,273 firstborn males out of a population of about 2.5 million, the result is over 112 children per family. This number divided into 600,000, the approximate number of fighting men, according to the censuses in Numbers 1 and 26, results in about 27 children per family. One of the suggested

---

[53] Ibid., 205.

[54] Humphreys says, "We can eliminate this interpretation because the figures are totally inconsistent with Table 1" (i.e., his calculations) (ibid., 203). Table 3, where he concludes that there were only 1,000 Levites, builds on the data from Table 1 (ibid., 213).

[55] Several of these are drawn from Gane, *Leviticus, Numbers*, 497–98.

[56] Humphreys, "The Number of People in the Exodus from Egypt," 196; J. H. Walton, V. H. Matthews, and M. W. Chavalas, *The IVP Bible Background Commentary: Old Testament* (Downers Grove, IL: InterVarsity, 2000), 144.

[57] Most of the numbers in the recorded census figures go only as far as the hundreds.

solutions is that this number refers only to firstborn males born after the exodus, since all the other firstborn would have been redeemed on the occasion of the first Passover (Exod 12:22–23) when the Egyptian firstborn perished in the tenth plague. Once those born since that Passover celebration were redeemed, God's claim to the firstborn would be complete.[58]

Fourth, in Exod 38:25–26, a census tax of one-half shekel ("sanctuary shekel") for each Israelite male was collected. This tax generated 100 talents and 1,775 shekels, payment for 603,550 men. Since a talent equaled 3,000 shekels,[59] this totaled about 301,775 shekels. At a half shekel per Israelite male qualified to be a warrior (20 years or older), the result is quite close to the stated number of 603,550 male Israelites (cf. Num 1:46). It is difficult to dismiss this number when evaluating the meaning of 'elep in large numbers.[60]

Fifth, Num 31:31–40 records animals and persons captured in Israel's war with the Midianites. On the one hand with regard to the "troop" or "clan" interpretation of 'elep, the term here cannot refer to some military subunit of animals. The formatting of the numbers is exactly the same as that found in the censuses. On the other hand the numbers here are astounding. Twelve thousand Israelite soldiers (1,000 from each tribe, 31:6) won this victory for Israel. They had to deal with almost 700,000 sheep, 133,000 cattle and donkeys, and 32,000 young women.

The Large Numbers Are Intentionally Exaggerated

Ronald Allen has suggested that "the large numbers in the census lists in the Book of Numbers are deliberately and purposefully exaggerated as a rhetorical device to bring glory to God, derision to enemies, and point forward to the fulfillment of God's promise to the fathers that their descendants will be innumerable, as the stars."[61] This suggestion has nothing to do with skepticism about what God could do, whether He could get a group of two million Israelites across the Red Sea or provide food and water for them as they wandered through the wilderness. Also its proponents do not diminish the historical reality of the biblical record. David Fouts proposed that numerical hyperbole was a "common ancient Near Eastern literary convention appearing in royal inscriptions."[62] The point of this convention of providing hyperbolic numbers (with a factor of 10 or 60, depending on the numerical system in use) in historical annals was to "glorify a reigning monarch."[63] A scribe would write larger numbers in order to "puff" the majesty of the king.

---

[58] Harrison, *Numbers*, 74. C. F. Keil and F. Delitzsch, *The Pentateuch*, Biblical Commentaries on the Old Testament (n.d.; reprint, Grand Rapids: Eerdmans, 1968), 9–11.

[59] M. A. Powell, "Weights and Measures," in *ABD*, ed. D. N. Freedman (New York: Doubleday, 1992), 6:905; B. Wells, "Exodus," in *ZIBBC*, ed. J. H. Walton (Grand Rapids: Zondervan, 2009), 1:258.

[60] D. Stuart assumes that this count given for 1,775 shekels and 100 talents was based on the meaning of 'elep used in counting the troops (i.e., not 1,000) (*Exodus*, NAC [Nashville: B&H, 2007], 773 n. 303). So the actual amount of silver was considerably lower than what a face value reading of the numbers would suggest. This suggestion faces two problems. First, the explanation of "troop" works with soldiers but not with money/weight measures. Second, the 'elep only impacts the smaller number (1,775 shekels = .6 talent), not the 100-talent figure.

[61] R. B. Allen, "Numbers," in *EBC*, 2:688. Cf. D. M. Fouts, "The Use of Large Numbers in the Old Testament with Particular Emphasis on the Use of 'elep," (Th.D. diss., Dallas Theological Seminary, 1992); idem, "A Defense of the Hyperbolic Interpretation of Large Numbers in the Old Testament," *JETS* 40 (1997): 377–87; idem, "The Incredible Numbers of the Hebrew Kings," in *Giving the Sense: Understanding and Using Old Testament Historical Texts*, ed. D. M. Howard Jr. and M. A. Grisanti (Grand Rapids: Kregel, 2003), 283–99.

[62] Fouts, "The Incredible Numbers of the Hebrew Kings," 290.

[63] Ibid., 295.

Yet this approach to large numbers faces several challenges. First, Fouts himself points out that the census of David and that of the book of Numbers "do not share as many affinities with the royal-inscription genre" as passages like 2 Sam 8:1–18 and 1 Kgs 4:21–5:16 might.[64] Second, various ANE scholars recognize numerical hyperbole in only a relatively small number of historical annals.[65] Third, and related to the preceding point, was this "hyperbolic" use of large numbers in ANE historical annals embedded so firmly in that genre that this hyperbolic convention was utilized by biblical writers? Fouts's proposal suggests that the hyperbolic use of large numbers was a function of genre. If that use of numbers was not a fundamental part of the ANE practice of writing annals, it is doubtful that it would come across in a biblical setting whenever biblical writers used that same genre.[66] Fourth, there might be another reason why ANE scribes employed hyperbolic numbers in certain historical annals. Gregory McMahon has pointed out several differences between early Hebrew and Hittite historical writings. Hittite scribes placed more emphasis on the activities of the king and queen for political purposes.[67] There was also the somewhat legendary presentation of the accomplishments of the kings.[68] Thus before equating the function of conventions of writing history annals in the ANE and the OT, one must pay careful attention to their distinct audiences and focus.[69] Fifth, since this approach is based on a more subjective understanding of the numbers, it lacks clear signals to guide the reader in knowing when numbers should be understood literally and when they should be understood more symbolically or rhetorically. Sixth, the rationale that exaggerated numbers functioned "as a rhetorical device to bring glory to God" seems less than convincing. In repeated biblical narratives the Lord minimized the grounds for human credit to make sure that His people were forced to recognize that He alone accomplished what was otherwise impossible. To multiply the numbers by 10 would seem to function like "stroking" God, much like the larger numbers would have boosted the ego of an ANE king. However, God needs no such affirmation or better press.

The Large Numbers Are Accepted at Face Value

Many scholars, aware of the "problems" with an Israelite population of two million, still understand the noun 'elep as signifying the conventional meaning of "thousand."[70] Since the suggested solutions for large numbers seem to create more significant problems than a face-value understanding, these scholars assume that OT large numbers were meant to be understood as such (until some more adequate solution can be found).

---

[64] Ibid., 296.

[65] A. R. Millard, "Large Numbers in Assyrian Royal Inscriptions," in *Ah, Assyria . . . Studies in Assyrian History and Ancient Near Eastern Historiography Presented to Hayim Tadmor*, ed. M. Cogan and I. Eph'al, Scripta Hierosolymitana 33 (Jerusalem: Magnes, 1991), 213–22. For Fouts's response to Millard see D. M. Fouts, "Another Look at Large Numbers in Assyrian Royal Inscriptions," *JNES* 53 (1994): 205–11.

[66] The issue is not whether or not ANE historical annals ever used hyperbolic numbers, but whether it was so fundamental to that genre that everyone understood that when they read things like censuses and annals they had to reduce the numbers by a factor of 10.

[67] G. McMahon, "History and Legend in Early Hittite Historiography," in *Faith, Tradition, and History: Old Testament Historiography in Its Near Eastern Context*, ed. A. R. Millard, J. K. Hoffmeier, and D. W. Baker (Winona Lake, IN: Eisenbrauns, 1994), 156.

[68] Ibid., 157.

[69] Klingbeil, "Historical Criticism," 408.

[70] Keil, *The Pentateuch*, 3:5–15; Wolf, *An Introduction to the Old Testament Pentateuch* (Chicago: Moody, 1991), 177–80; W. C. Kaiser Jr., *A History of Israel from the Bronze Age through the Jewish Wars* (Nashville: B&H, 1998), 102; G. Archer Jr., *A Survey of OT Introduction*, rev. ed. (Chicago: Moody, 2007), 219–22; Gane, *Leviticus, Numbers*, 497–98.

Evaluation and Suggestion

So what must be done with these large numbers? As already noted, some writers do not accept the historical credibility of the biblical record. The views that offer another meaning for *'elep* share similar challenges. First, the text of Numbers seems to view this debated term as a number, that is, as "thousand." Second, to understand *'elep* as anything other than "thousand" assumes some kind of misunderstanding of the term and poor transmission of the text in all the census lists of Exodus and Numbers, not to mention the LXX and Samaritan Pentateuch, both of which basically agree with the Hebrew text. If this is true, this misunderstanding had to have taken place as early as the fifth or fourth centuries BC. As stated above, the hyperbolic view, though commendable for its recognition of *'elep* as a number and its high view of Scripture, falls short since a larger number would not bring God greater glory than a realistic number.

Hartley gives a good summary: "In short, we lack the materials in the text to solve this problem. When all is said and done one must admit that the answer is elusive. Perhaps it is best to take these numbers as R. K. Harrison has done—as based on a system familiar to the ancients but unknown to the moderns. According to Harrison the figures are to be taken as 'symbols of relative power, triumph, importance, and the like and are not meant to be understood either strictly literally or as extant in a corrupt textual form.'"[71]

These cautions are prudent as they relate to understanding large numbers in the OT. However, until there arises a solution that has fewer problems than it creates, it is best to maintain a face-value understanding of large numbers in the OT and, at the same time, make sure that students understand the problems that face this view (e.g., the demographics of the land of Canaan).[72]

THE THEOLOGY OF THE BOOK

At the outset of Numbers, all seemed ready for Israel's last leg in their journey to the promised land. God had delivered them from Egypt and had provided a climactic expression of His absolute power by making it possible for them to cross the Red Sea. He gave them His law, which represented more than burdening His people with innumerable requirements. The Lord had deepened and broadened His relationship with His covenant people by establishing the Mosaic covenant with them. He had committed to be their God and demanded that they conduct themselves as His people. He had provided a sacrificial system and a dwelling place for His presence that would enable His covenant nation to find forgiveness and maintain ritual purity. He had provided all that was necessary for His people to be able to broadcast His surpassing character to all those beyond their borders. Now it was time to leave Mount Sinai (after almost a year there) and head toward Canaan and experience the realization of God's promise to give them a land. However, at Kadesh-barnea the timing of that experience was delayed by Israel's incomprehensible rebellion. What does the book of Numbers teach about God and His plan for Israel (and the world)?

---

[71] Ashley, *Numbers*, 66. Cf. R. K. Harrison, *Introduction to the Old Testament* (Grand Rapids: Eerdmans, 1969), 633.

[72] M. Broshi and R. Gaphna, "The Settlements and Population of Palestine during the Early Bronze Age II–III," *BASOR* 253 (Winter 1984): 41–53; M. Broshi and R. Gophna, "Middle Bronze Age II Palestine: Its Settlements and Population," *BASOR* 261 (Fall 1986): 73–90; M. Broshi and I. Finkelstein, "The Population of Palestine in Iron Age II," *BASOR* 287 (August 1992): 47–60.

Yahweh, Faithful and Present

God's presence. Building on the end of the book of Exodus, when the Lord installed a visible manifestation of His presence at the tabernacle (Exod 40:34–38), Numbers continues this emphasis that Yahweh is with His people. Seen as a pillar of cloud by day and fire by night, the Lord's presence transformed the tabernacle into a sanctuary, the dwelling place of God. This made the tabernacle a potential nexus between God and His people. Balaam, the pagan prophet, declared: "The LORD their God is with them, and there is rejoicing over the King among them" (Num 23:21). Also God's visible presence provided flawless guidance throughout their wilderness wanderings, both before and after Israel's rebellion at Kadesh-barnea (9:15–23). His presence with them assured them of victory over their foes (10:33–36). Finally, his presence should have motivated the Israelites to conduct themselves as loyal citizens during these wanderings and once they have settled in the land of promise (35:34).

God's holiness. God's visible presence and the sacrificial ritual gave His people a stark reminder of His holiness. Just as He is like no other alleged god and His tabernacle and the various utensils were set apart for God's use (through the priests), so His people were to model their lives after His holiness, pursuing moral purity and distinctive lives. God's holiness is the basis for His judgment of the nation in the wake of their rebellion at Kadesh-barnea (chaps. 13–14).

God's grace and faithfulness. Just as God's judgment of Israel's rebellion manifested His holiness, so His treatment of His covenant people before and after that rebellion demonstrated His grace. He provided the tabernacle, priests, and a sacrificial system as a means for His people to maintain an intimate relationship with Him. Even after His people refused to enter the land of promise in spite of all His demonstrations of absolute power and His willingness to intervene on their behalf to bring to pass what He promised, the Lord did not depart from His plan for the nation and the world. In 15:2, He referred to "the land where you are to live, which I am giving you" (NASB). This should have caused the Israelites to be grateful. They deserved extermination, but God was determined to bring them to the land of promise, and He was gracious in giving them what they did not deserve.

The Inheritance and Occupation of the Land

Every part of the book of Numbers anticipates the nation's entrance into the land of Canaan. This future reality represents the potential fulfillment of what God had first promised to Abraham (Gen 12:1–3). The Lord repeatedly affirmed that He had given this land to His servant nation (nine times; Num 13:2; 14:8; 15:2; 20:12,24; 27:12; 32:7,9; 33:53). As Eugene Merrill points out, Israel's occupation of the land of Canaan was a stage in the process of claiming all creation for the Creator. Canaan represents a microcosm of the earth that lay under the control of anti-god forces.[73] "Like the Tabernacle, Canaan would be the focal point of Yahweh's residence among men, the place where His sovereignty would find historical expression through His specially chosen people."[74]

This land was to be holy, sanctified by God's presence in Israel's midst (33:54). In order to achieve this divinely authorized objective, God's people must destroy all aspects of idolatry and drive out or kill all the pagan inhabitants. This land, as their divine inheritance, was also to be theirs for perpetuity. It was part of covenant blessing for His chosen people (cf. Deut 28:1–14).

---

[73] E. H. Merrill, "A Theology of the Pentateuch," in *A Biblical Theology of the Old Testament*, ed. R. B. Zuck (Chicago: Moody, 1991), 59–60.

[74] Ibid., 60.

Numbers also provides the cultic laws for the camp "in motion." For the sake of the next generation the book provides the instructions for God's people as they journeyed to the promised land. Numbers offered instruction for the arrangement and census of the tribes and the transport of the ark of the covenant. The book also shows that the promised blessing cannot be frustrated from within (through their unbelief) or from without (through Balak and Balaam).

Human Rebellion in Spite of Divine Faithfulness

In light of all that God had done for His people, the book of Numbers is clearly "a study in the contrast between God's faithfulness and human disobedience."[75] The sad aspect of this book is man's penchant for rebellion. In spite of the repeated times God had demonstrated His awe-inspiring power and willingness to act on behalf of His people, they were easily swayed by immediate circumstances. The rebellion of the Israelites reminds each reader of Numbers that human hearts are dark and no one is far from rebellion.

CONCLUSION

The God who established His covenant with Israel, commissioning them to broadcast His incomparable character to the entire world through their enthusiastic obedience of His requirements, brought that people one step closer to the realization of their possession of the land of promise. In spite of their rebellion the faithful and gracious God (who punished His rebellious subjects) continued guiding and sustaining His servant nation. Although Israel's rebellion impacted whether any given generation enjoyed the blessings offered through covenant, the ultimate fulfillment of those covenant promises rests squarely on God's character alone.

STUDY QUESTIONS

1. How does the discovery of the Ketef Hinnom scrolls relate to the canonicity and composition of the book of Numbers? What does this discovery not *prove*?
2. What is the agenda of the "jealousy ordeal"? How is it distinct from ANE "ordeals"?
3. What Israelite tribes occupied the region of the Transjordan?
4. What did Balak hope Balaam would do, and what did Balaam end up doing?
5. What are the four primary views of large numbers in the OT, and what is the "big idea" of each view?
6. Which of the views on large numbers clearly rejects the historicity of biblical texts?
7. What are the strengths and weaknesses of the "semantic" view on large numbers?
8. What are the strengths and weaknesses of the "intentional exaggeration" view on large numbers?
9. What are the strengths and weaknesses of the "face value" view on large numbers?

FOR FURTHER STUDY

Albright, W. F. *From the Stone Age to Christianity*. 2nd ed. New York: Doubleday, 1957.

Allen, R. B. "Numbers." In *Expositor's Bible Commentary*. Edited by F. Gaebelein, 2:655–1008. Grand Rapids: Zondervan, 1990.

Ashley, T. R. *The Book of Numbers*. NICOT. Grand Rapids: Eerdmans, 1993.

Barkay, G., et al. "The Amulets from Ketef Hinnom: A New Edition and Evaluation." *BASOR* 334 (2004): 41–71.

———. "The Challenges of Ketef Hinnom: Using Advanced Technologies to Reclaim the Earliest Biblical Texts and Their Context." *NEASB* 66 (2003): 162–71.

---

[75] Harrison, *Numbers*, 25.

Baylis, A. H. *From Creation to the Cross: Understanding the First Half of the Bible*. Grand Rapids: Zondervan, 1996.

Bellinger, W. H. *Leviticus and Numbers*. NIBCOT. Peabody, MA: Hendrickson, 2001.

Budd, P. J. *Numbers*. WBC. Dallas: Word, 1984.

Clark, R. E. D. "The Large Numbers of the OT." *JTVI* 87 (1955): 82–92.

Cole, R. D. *Numbers*. NAC. Nashville: B&H, 2000.

———. "Numbers." In *ZIBBC*. Vol. 1. Edited by John H. Walton, 1:338–417. Grand Rapids: Zondervan, 2009.

Davies, E. W. "A Mathematical Conundrum: The Problem of the Large Numbers in Numbers I and XXVI." *VT* 45 (1995): 449–69.

de Vaux, R. *The Early History of Israel to the Period of the Judges*. Translated by David Smith. London: Darton, Longman & Todd, 1978.

Fouts, D. "Another Look at Large Numbers in Assyrian Royal Inscriptions." *JNES* 53 (1994): 205–11.

———. "A Defense of the Hyperbolic Interpretation of Large Numbers in the Old Testament." *JETS* 40 (1997): 377–87.

———. "The Incredible Numbers of the Hebrew Kings." In *Giving the Sense: Understanding and Using Old Testament Historical Texts*. Edited by David M. Howard Jr. and Michael A. Grisanti, 283–99. Grand Rapids: Kregel, 2003.

Gane, R. *Leviticus, Numbers*. NIVAC. Grand Rapids: Zondervan, 2004.

Gaster, T. H. *Myth, Legend, and Custom in the Old Testament*. New York: Harper & Row, 1918.

Hamilton, V. P. *Handbook on the Pentateuch*. Grand Rapids: Baker, 2005.

Harbin, M. A. *The Promise and Blessing: A Historical Survey of the Old and New Testaments*. Grand Rapids: Zondervan, 2005.

Harrison, R. K. *Introduction to the Old Testament*. Grand Rapids: Eerdmans, 1969.

———. *Numbers*. Chicago: Moody, 1990.

Hill, A. E., and J. H. Walton. *A Survey of the Old Testament*. 3rd ed. Grand Rapids: Zondervan, 2009.

House, P. R. *Old Testament Theology*. Downers Grove, IL: InterVarsity, 1998.

Humphreys, C. J. "The Number of People in the Exodus from Egypt: Decoding Mathematically the Very Large Numbers in Numbers I and XXVI." *VT* 48 (1998): 196–213.

Kaiser, W. C., Jr. *The Promise-Plan of God: Biblical Theology of the Old and New Testaments*. Grand Rapids: Zondervan, 2008.

Keil, C. F. *The Pentateuch*. Biblical Commentary on the Old Testament. N.d. Reprint, Grand Rapids: Eerdmans, 1968.

Kitchen, K. A. *On the Reliability of the Old Testament*. Grand Rapids: Eerdmans, 2003.

Klingbeil, G. A. "Historical Criticism." In *Dictionary of the OT: Pentateuch*. Edited by T. D. Alexander and D. W. Baker, 401–20. Downers Grove, IL: InterVarsity, 2003.

Longman, T., III, and R. Dillard. *An Introduction to the Old Testament*. 2nd ed. Grand Rapids: Zondervan, 2006.

McMahon, G. "History and Legend in Early Hittite Historiography." In *Faith, Tradition, and History: Old Testament Historiography in Its Near Eastern Context*. Edited by A. R. Millard, J. K. Hoffmeier, and D. W. Baker, 149–57. Winona Lake, IN: Eisenbrauns, 1994.

Mendenhall, G. E. "The Census Lists of Numbers 1 and 26." *JBL* 77 (1959): 52–66.

Merling, D., Sr. "Large Numbers at the Time of the Exodus." *NEASB* 44 (1999): 15–27.

Merrill, E. H. "A Theology of the Pentateuch." In *A Biblical Theology of the Old Testament*. Edited by Roy B. Zuck, 7–87. Chicago: Moody, 1991.

———. *Everlasting Dominion: A Theology of the Old Testament*. Nashville: B&H, 2006.

Milgrom, J. *Numbers*. JPS Torah Commentary. Philadelphia: Jewish Publication Society, 1990.

Millard, A. R. "Large Numbers in Assyrian Royal Inscriptions." In *Ah, Assyria . . . Studies in Assyrian History and Ancient Near Eastern Historiography Presented to Hayim Tadmor*. Edited by Mordechai Cogan and Israel Eph'al, 213–22. Scripta Hierosolymitana 33. Jerusalem: Magnes, 1991.

Noth, M. *Numbers: A Commentary*. Translated by James D. Martin. OTL. Philadelphia: Westminster, 1968.

Olson, D. T. *The Death of the Old and the Birth of the New: The Framework of the Book of Numbers and the Pentateuch*. BJS. Chico, CA: Scholars, 1985.

———. "Numbers, Book of." In *Dictionary of the OT: Pentateuch*. Edited by T. D. Alexander and D. W. Baker, 611–18. Downers Grove, IL: InterVarsity, 2003.

———. *Numbers*. Interpretation. Louisville: John Knox, 1996.

Rendsburg, G. A. "An Additional Note to Two Recent Articles on the Number of People in the Exodus from Egypt and the Large Numbers in Numbers I and XXVI." *VT* 51 (2001): 392–96.

Schnittjer, G. *The Torah Story*. Grand Rapids: Zondervan, 2006.

Sturdy, J. *Numbers*. CBC. New York: Cambridge University Press, 1976.

Waaler, E. "A Revised Date for Pentateuchal Texts: Evidence from Ketef Hinnom." *TynBul* 53 (2002): 29–55.

Waltke, B. K. *An Old Testament Theology*. Grand Rapids: Zondervan, 2007.

Walton, J. H., V. H. Matthews, and M. W. Chavalas. *The IVP Bible Background Commentary: OT*. Downers Grove, IL: InterVarsity, 2000.

Wenham, G. J. *Numbers: An Introduction and Commentary*. TOTC. Downers Grove, IL: InterVarsity, 1981.

Wenham, J. W. "The Large Numbers in the OT." *TynBul* 18 (1967): 19–53.

Wolf, H. M. *An Introduction to the Old Testament Pentateuch*. Chicago: Moody, 1991.

Chapter 14

The Book of Deuteronomy

Eugene H. Merrill

TITLE OF THE BOOK

The name "Deuteronomy" for the last book of the Pentateuch derives from the Latin Vulgate *Deuteronomium*, which in turn is a transliteration of the Greek Septuagint's *Deuteronomion*. This term arose from the translation of the Hebrew of Deut 17:18 ("a copy of this instruction"), which implies that the book was a "second law" (the meaning of *deuteronomion*). Deuteronomy is not in fact a second law but an amplification of the first given at Mount Sinai, so the Greek (and hence English) title is somewhat misleading. The Hebrew title, *ʾēlleh haddĕbārîm* ("these are the words"), is simply the first two words of the first verse of the book.

DATE AND AUTHORSHIP OF THE BOOK

The Traditional View

Until 200 years ago the date and authorship of Deuteronomy were matters of little dispute.[1] Based on the book's own testimony as well as that of Jewish tradition, the NT, and pre-Enlightenment consensus, Moses was the author, having composed the book just before his death in 1400 BC or thereabouts. After the first two words (see the preceding paragraph), the book adds, "which Moses spoke" (NASB), clearly ascribing the following words and by implication the entire book to him (see also 1:5; 4:44; 29:1; 31:1,9,14,22,24; 32:45; 33:1,4). The remainder of the OT (Josh 1:7,13; 8:31–35; 23:6; 1 Kgs 2:3; 2 Kgs 14:6; 21:8; 23:25; 2 Chr 23:18; 25:4; 33:8; 34:14; Ezra 3:2; Neh 9:14; 10:29; 13:1; Dan 9:13) as well as the NT (Matt 19:7–8; 22:24; Mark 12:19; Acts 3:22; Rom 10:19; 1 Cor 9:9; Rev 15:3) concur and, in fact, never raise the possibility of alternative authorship.

The Talmudic tradition invariably links the Torah (the five books of the Pentateuch) with Moses in whole and in its parts. The pertinent tractate, *Baba Bathra*, makes the general observation that "Moses wrote his own book and the portion of Balaam and Job" (14b), and then,

---

[1] See chap. 8, "The Development of the Historical Critical Method," p. 129.

more specifically, adds that Joshua wrote the book bearing his name and "[the last] eight verses of the Pentateuch" (14b). The famous Rabbi Judah adds, "The truth is, however, that up to this point [in Deuteronomy, about his own death] Moses wrote, from this point Joshua wrote" (15a).

Toward the end of the first century AD, the Jewish general and historian Josephus, in a polemical dialogue with the skeptic Apion, took pains to describe the canon of sacred Scripture and to buttress arguments for its authenticity by appealing to the authorship and dating of its three major parts. Of the Pentateuch Josephus said, "Of them [i.e., the 22 books of the canon] five belong to Moses, which contain his laws and the traditions of the origin of mankind till his death. This interval of time was little short of three thousand years."[2] Josephus was clearly expressing a point of view shared by adherents of Judaism and Christianity of his time.

The Post-Enlightenment View

Cracks in the façade of Mosaic authorship of Deuteronomy began to appear as early as the seventeenth century, thanks to the penetrating critiques of skeptics such as Richard Simon[3] and Benedict de Spinoza,[4] to name but two. The latter quoted Ibn Ezra, the medieval rabbi, to the effect that Moses could not have written Deuteronomy because of many apparent allusions by its true author to the distant past in which Moses actually lived. Spinoza elaborated by pointing out that Moses would not have referred to the Transjordan as "beyond the river [Jordan]"; that the whole Torah could not have been inscribed on Joshua's altar (Deut 27:4–8; Josh 8:30–32), thus presupposing a much smaller work; that Moses would not have referred to himself in the third person (as in Deut 31:9); and that he could not have written of his own death with the statement that he surpassed all the prophets who came after him (Deut 34:5–12). Spinoza concluded by asserting that "it is thus clearer than the sun at noonday that the Pentateuch [including Deuteronomy, of course] was not written by Moses, but by someone who lived long after Moses."[5]

One hundred thirty-five years after the publication of Spinoza's Tractatus, W. M. L. de Wette wrote a dissertation,[6] the purpose of which was to demonstrate that Deuteronomy was the latest of the books of the Pentateuch, a conclusion that of necessity precluded its authorship by Moses.[7] In the six parts of this 16-page treatise de Wette argued that (1) Moses did not write the Pentateuch, Genesis through Numbers being a complete but composite work produced by later hands; (2) the beginning of Deuteronomy is only a paraphrase of Numbers; (3) Deuteronomy is an expansion of earlier material and has its own peculiar phraseology; (4) Deuteronomy manifests a sophisticated theology similar to that of later Judaism; (5) Deuteronomy first introduces the idea of a single legitimate central sanctuary and emphasizes the role of the Levites, monarchy, and prophets; and (6) Deuteronomy frequently contradicts, supplements, and corrects the earlier writings.[8]

---

[2] Josephus, *Ad Apionem* 1:8.

[3] R. Simon, *Histoire critique du Vieux Testament* (Rotterdam: Chez Reinier Leers), 1685.

[4] B. de Spinoza, *Tractatus Theologico-Politicus, Tractatus Politicus*, trans. R. H. M. Elwes (London: Routledge and Sons, n.d.), 121–24.

[5] Spinoza, *Tractatus*, 124.

[6] "Dissertatio critica qua a prioribus Deuteronomium pentateuchi libris diversum, alius cuiusdam recentioris auctoris opus esse monstratur" (University of Jena, 1805).

[7] For a very helpful account of de Wette's life and influence see J. W. Rogerson, *W. M. L. de Wette, Founder of Modern Biblical Criticism*, JSOTSup (Sheffield: Sheffield Academic, 1992).

[8] Rogerson, *W. M. L. de Wette*, 40–42.

Perhaps the most farreaching consequence of this study was the suggestion that the scroll found in the temple in the course of King Josiah's reformation of 622 BC was the book of Deuteronomy (2 Kgs 22:8–23:3; 2 Chr 34:14–33). Evidence for this was (1) the description of the scroll as "the book of the law" (2 Kgs 22:8,11) or "the book of the covenant" (2 Kgs 23:2), terms reminiscent of Deuteronomy (Deut 31:26); (2) the insistence on one central sanctuary (2 Kgs 23:4–20; Deut 12:1–14; 2 Chr 34:3–7); and (3) the alleged contradiction between Deuteronomy, on the one hand, and, on the other hand, Exod 20:24–25 (which allows multiple altars) and the practice of Samuel, Saul, David, and Solomon, all of whom worshipped at many places with impunity.

In addition to removing Deuteronomy from Mosaic authorship and provenance, de Wette's hypothesis proved to be the cornerstone for a radically new way of looking at the composition of the Pentateuch as a whole. Deuteronomy, it was argued, presupposes the Yahwist and Elohist sources, and though de Wette personally dated the Priestly material earlier than Deuteronomy (D) it was not long before other critics began to date it later, largely because of evolutionary views of Israel's religious development that were then coming into vogue.[9]

Fig. 14:1
Classic Form of the Documentary Hypothesis

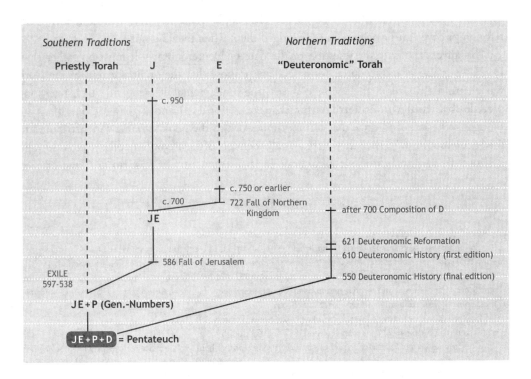

[9] E. Reuss (1833), K. Graf (1866), A. Kuenen (1869-70), J. Wellhausen (1878). O. Eissfeldt, *The Old Testament. An Introduction,* trans. P. R. Ackroyd (New York: Harper and Row, 1965), 165–66.

The Modern View

From de Wette's day to today, historical-critical scholars have differed little if at all from the preceding presentation of the authorship and setting of Deuteronomy.[10] It is almost dogma that the book as a whole was the product of a seventh century reform movement that was based either in fact on ancient—perhaps even Mosaic—covenant principles, or more likely on ideologies of more contemporary vintage.[11] However, responsibility for its ideas and promulgation is a matter of considerable debate. Some scholars suggest a northern, prophetic source, while others argue for a southern levitical origin, depending primarily on the date of its central concepts. Those open to greater antiquity propose that the work was originally intended as a means of addressing Israelite idolatry in the northern kingdom.[12] Those who view it as a text composed precisely to achieve reformation of the cultus in Judah naturally favor a later date.[13]

In modern times Deuteronomy has been linked to what has been described as the "Deuteronomic history" (also known as "Deuteronomistic history").[14] This is a way of viewing Joshua through 2 Kings as a massive theological or ideological history work whose purpose is to explain how and why Israel and Judah came to ruin despite being the covenant people of Yahweh. Some scholars suggest that this composition (DtrH) was completed some time in the period of the exile (c. 562 BC, in the time of Jehoiachin's release from prison),[15] while others see a later redaction in the postexilic era, one that allows at least vestiges of hope to be entertained.[16] All agree, however, that the history was composed with Deuteronomy in mind. That is, its central thrust is that God blessed His people when they lived in accord with Deuteronomy's covenant principles, but He judged them when they did not.[17]

This affects not only the question of the date of Deuteronomy—it must be earlier than DtrH—but also of its structure. Most scholars propose that the original extent of the work was chaps. 5–26. This is the "Mosaic" heart, the fundamental elements of which may long precede the actual written text. As for chaps. 1–4 (or 1–3) and 27–30 (or 34), they are thought to be later additions that form a framework to the book, a framework attributed to the "deuteronomist."[18] Thus the DtrH actually consists of Deuteronomy plus Joshua through 2 Kings. Besides anchoring Deuteronomy, in its present form at least, to an exilic or even

---

[10] For important essays and periodical literature addressing all aspects of Deuteronomies study see D. L. Christensen, ed. reprint, *A Song of Power and the Power of Song: Essays on the Book of Deuteronomy* (Winona Lake, IN: Eisenbrauns, 1993).

[11] J. Blenkinsopp, *The Pentateuch* (New York: Doubleday, 1992), 214–17. For a more moderate position advocating the presence of ancient oral and written traditions in Deuteronomy see J. H. Tigay, *Deuteronomy, JPS Torah Commentary* (Philadelphia: Jewish Publication Society, 1996), xxiv–xxvi.

[12] E. W. Nicholson, *Deuteronomy and Tradition* (Philadelphia: Fortress, 1967), 122–24.

[13] G. von Rad, *Studies in Deuteronomy* (London: SCM, 1953), 60–69.

[14] The terminology and associated hypothesis find their source primarily in M. Noth. See his *Überlieferungsgeschichtliche Studien* (Tübingen: Niemeyer, 1957); now in English as *The Deuteronomistic History*, JSOTSup (Sheffield: JSOT Press, 1981). See also A. F. Campbell and M. A. O'Brien, *Unfolding the Deuteronomistic History* (Minneapolis: Fortress, 2000); B. Peckham, *The Composition of the Deuteronomistic History* (Atlanta: Scholars, 1985); and R. Polzin, *Moses and the Deuteronomist: A Literary Study of the Deuteronomistic History* (New York: Seabury, 1980).

[15] Noth, *The Deuteronomistic History*, 6–11, 73–74.

[16] F. M. Cross, "The Themes of the Book of Kings and the Structure of the Deuteronomistic History," in *Canaanite Myth and Hebrew Epic* (Cambridge, MA: Harvard University Press, 1973), 287–89.

[17] E.g., Nicholson, *Deuteronomy and Tradition*, 114–15.

[18] A. D. H. Mayes, "Deuteronomy 4 and the Literary Criticism of Deuteronomy," *JBL* 100 (1981): 23–51; reprinted in Christensen, *A Song of Power and the Power of Song*, 195–224.

postexilic setting, such a reconstruction effectively removes the book from the Pentateuch, leaving what some scholars call a "Tetrateuch" (Genesis–Numbers).[19]

Assessment of Critical Views

This construal of the tradition concerning the Mosaic authorship of Deuteronomy and the Pentateuch (or at least their antiquity) has met with detailed refutation elsewhere.[20] All that is necessary here is to point out a few of the deficiencies of the critical model and to offer arguments supportive of the precritical point of view.

First, with only a token dissent, more than 2,000 years of reflection on the matter prior to the Enlightenment led to no other conclusion than that Moses was the author of Deuteronomy, his own obituary perhaps being a notable exception. To reject such consensus is to call into question the integrity or intelligence of those who maintained it, to assume canons or standards of authorship in ancient times that vary from modern convention (for which there is no real evidence), and/or to disregard the consensus as only a product of pious but unenlightened tradition.

Second, no objective evidence supports the idea that Deuteronomy originated and developed in the manner adduced by modern criticism. No ancient texts have been found, no contemporary corroboration unearthed, that substantiates a late, non-Mosaic setting for the book. One could argue, of course, that evidence of this kind is lacking also for the Mosaic tradition, but as has been shown, authorship by Moses is attested to in Deuteronomy itself and was embraced by virtually all pre-Enlightenment thinkers. Moreover, as is well known, the burden of proof in such a matter always falls on those who challenge the tradition. Unless and until there are insuperably compelling reasons to deny the Mosaic date and authorship, they must be allowed to stand.

Third, the evidence put forward in support of a non-Mosaic provenance is circular in nature, being based on hypothetical source-critical analyses of the Pentateuch as well as (in its original formulation at least) a postulated religious evolutionism. Thus it is argued that the Pentateuch is a composite of originally independent oral and written sources that betray not a Late Bronze Age milieu but one much later, the product of redactional activity reflecting the time and circumstances of the redactors themselves.[21] As for Deuteronomy (so continues the argument), since it presupposes the J (950–850 BC) and E (750 BC) sources, it must be later than them; but since it is presupposed by postexilic P (450 BC), it must be earlier then that source. However, since the Pentateuch's own witness is that Deuteronomy presupposes the patriarchal and exodus traditions, that is a rather moot point. It is only when the so-called J and E narratives themselves are divorced from Moses and his time that Deuteronomy also must be severed from its traditional roots.

---

[19] This term originated with M. Noth, but its implications are rejected by most critics who see J and E as well as D, looking forward to the gift of the land and thus not separated in concept (*A History of Pentateuchal Traditions*, trans. B. W. Anderson [Atlanta: Scholars, 1981], 228–47).

[20] O. T. Allis, *The Five Books of Moses* (Philadelphia: P&R, 1949); U. Cassuto, *The Documentary Hypothesis*, trans. I. Abrahams (Jerusalem: Magnes, 1961); P. C. Craigie, *The Book of Deuteronomy*, NICOT (Grand Rapids: Eerdmans, 1976), 20–32; K. A. Kitchen, *On The Reliability of the Old Testament* (Grand Rapids: Eerdmans, 2003), 299–304; H. M. Wolf, *An Introduction to the Old Testament Pentateuch* (Chicago: Moody, 1991), 51–78, 207–22; E. J. Young, *An Introduction to the Old Testament* (Grand Rapids: Eerdmans, 1958), 101–14.

[21] For a response to this particular point, see E. H. Merrill, "Deuteronomy and History: Anticipation of Reflection?" *FM* 18 (2000): 57–76.

This is where the nineteenth century notion of gradually developing religious and theological sophistication enters the debate. Since it appears that the J and E sources reflect a comparatively primitive, undeveloped cultus compared to that of D and P, then D must be later and P, which tends toward an institutionalizing of the more spontaneous and purer faith of the preexilic era, later still.[22] The scenario just described admittedly stems more from that of a previous generation of scholarship than today's. However, the location of D in the seventh century, a fruit of earlier criticism, still prevails, though newer objective evidence to support it is still totally lacking.[23]

Fourth, the principal objective datum on which the seventh century date of Deuteronomy rests is identifying the "book of the law" of Josiah's reformation with Deuteronomy.[24] More specifically, it is Josiah's insistence on a central, unrivaled sanctuary and, correspondingly his destruction of all other worship sites that constitute the nub of the argument. In response it is true that the scroll found by Hilkiah the priest is called the "book of the law" (2 Kgs 22:8, 11; 2 Chr 34:14–15) and that this term occurs in Deuteronomy as well to describe that book (Deut 28:61; 29:21; 30:10; 31:24–26). However, the Hilkiah scroll is also called "the book of the covenant" (2 Kgs 23:2–3; 23:21; 2 Chr 34:30–31), a term of description never used in Deuteronomy but found in Exod 24:7. Thus a case can be made for a more extensive literature than just Deuteronomy.

Even if it be conceded that the scroll in question is Deuteronomy, there is nothing in the Josiah narratives to suggest that it had only recently been composed or that its contents had not previously been known. Granted, the account in 2 Kings suggests that Josiah's apparent centralizing of the cultus and his eradication of pagan shrines commenced only after the discovery of the scroll (2 Kgs 23:4–20). In 2 Chronicles, however, the young king is said to have begun the purge in the twelfth year of his reign, a full six years before the scroll's recovery (2 Chr 34:3, 8). The best understanding of this apparent discrepancy is that the newly found scroll simply reinforced the determination of the king to do what he already knew the Law teaches. That is, the instructions in Deuteronomy—and hence Deuteronomy itself—were already known. What Hilkiah did was to locate a copy of Deuteronomy, a book that had been suppressed or even eradicated (except for this copy) during the reigns of Josiah's wicked predecessors, Manasseh and Amon.

Support for this supposition may be found in the similar reformation of Hezekiah a century earlier.[25] This good king faced precisely the same problems as did Josiah—idolatry and a multitude of pagan shrines (2 Kgs 18:3–6; 2 Chr 31:1)—and he addressed them in the same manner, in connection with reformation and temple restoration (2 Chr 29:3–19). To the objection that there is no reference to centralizing the cult exclusively in Jerusalem in the Hezekiah narratives—a major tenet of Deuteronomy (e.g., Deut 12:2–14)—one should note that such a demand is lacking in the Josiah reformation as well. In both cases what is commanded is the obliteration of pagan or other illicit shrines. To infer from this that worship was to be limited to one place only—the Jerusalem temple—is to go beyond the evidence.[26] The

---

[22] J. Wellhausen, *Prolegomena to the History of Ancient Israel* (Cleveland: World, 1957 [1878]), 1–13.

[23] R. D. Nelson. *Deuteronomy: A Commentary,* OTL (Louisville: WJK, 2002), 6–7.

[24] J. Blenkinsopp, *The Pentateuch* (New York: Doubleday, 1992), 4–9.

[25] M. Cogan and H. Tadmor, *II Kings,* AB (Garden City, NY: Doubleday, 1988), 220.

[26] T. R. Hobbs concedes that cult centralization is just an inference from the account, one based on the destruction of pagan shrines and the subsequent celebration of the Passover in Jerusalem (*2 Kings,* WBC [Waco, TX: Word], 322).

text is clear throughout: the high places must be destroyed not because they existed but because they were evil.

This leads to a brief consideration of what is meant by Deuteronomy's insistence on a single central place of worship. In the context of the whole book as a covenant document concerned with the relationship of God with the elect nation Israel, the intention of Deuteronomy 12 is to mandate that the community as a whole limit its corporate worship to one designated site, namely, Jerusalem.[27] This is why worship and sacrifice could be and in fact were carried out privately and for small assemblies by such notables as Samuel (1 Sam 9:12; 10:8; 16:2, 5), David (2 Sam 24:24–25), and Elijah (1 Kgs 18:36–38), all at some place apart from the tabernacle or temple. The insistence that Josiah's reformation included the need to worship at Jerusalem only, a truth he supposedly discovered from the newly turned-up scroll of Deuteronomy, betrays a serious misreading of the narratives themselves.

Fifth, recent archaeological discoveries necessitate a fresh assessment of the antiquity of Deuteronomy and hence the possibility of its Mosaic authorship. In the past few decades scholars have drawn attention to the fact that the book of Deuteronomy—prologue and epilogue as well—is in the form of treaty or covenant texts strikingly similar to secular documents found in Hittite archives dating as early as the Late Bronze Age, the traditional date of Deuteronomy.[28] This has given rise to a new way of looking at not only the structure and meaning of the book but also at its purpose and setting. Since it most closely resembles texts that find no attestation in precisely those forms after 1200 BC, the prima facie case for the antiquity of Deuteronomy and by extension its authorship by Moses, are on firmer ground than ever before.[29] This leads now to a description of the book from the standpoint of its text and literary form.

THE TEXT OF DEUTERONOMY

The Hebrew text of Deuteronomy, based on the Ben Asher Masoretic tradition (Leningradensis, or B19A), is one of the least contested of all the OT books. The major versions, especially the LXX, follow a parent text similar if not identical to the MT. In some cases the SP appears to underlie the LXX and its dependent translation, but this is the exception rather than the rule.[30] It is well known that the SP departs from the normative MT reading at points where theological or sociopolitical *Tendenz* is apparent. A famous example occurs in Deut 27:4 where MT reads "Mount Ebal" but SP has "Mount Gerizim." The latter was in the interest of defending Gerizim as the sacred shrine of the Samaritan community.[31]

The Qumran evidence is full and confirms the preceding assessment of the primacy of the Masoretic tradition and integrity of the extant text. As Ulrich, White, and others have shown, the minor deviations from MT attested here and there in the DSS are trivial for the most part and in any case they demonstrate that MT enjoyed pride of place in the communities responsible for the composition and collection of scrolls.[32]

---

[27] G. J. Wenham, "Deuteronomy and the Central Sanctuary," *TynBul* 22 (1971): 109–16.

[28] A vast amount of literature has been written on the general subject of ANE covenants and their relationship to studies of Deuteronomy. For a survey see J. G. McConville, "berît," in NIDOTTE, ed. W. A. VanGemeren (Grand Rapids: Zondervan, 1997), 1:747–55.

[29] Kitchen, *On the Reliability of the Old Testament*, 283–304.

[30] J. W. Wevers, *Notes on the Greek Text of Deuteronomy* (Atlanta: Scholars, 1995), xi–xii.

[31] E. Tov, *Textual Criticism of the Hebrew Bible* (Minneapolis: Fortress, 1992), 94–95.

[32] E. Ulrich et al., eds., *Qumran Cave 4. IX. Deuteronomy, Joshua, Judges, Kings*, DJD XIV (Oxford: Clarendon, 1995); S. A. White, "Special Features of Four Biblical Manuscripts from Cave IV, Qumran: 4 Q Dt^a, 4 Q Dt^e, 4 Q Dt^d, and 4 Q Dt^g," *RevQ* 15 (1991): 157–67; idem, "Three Deuteronomy Manuscripts from Cave 4, Qumran," *JBL* 112 (1993): 23–42.

THE LITERARY FORM AND CHARACTER OF DEUTERONOMY

Since there is a virtual consensus (among conservatives, at least) that Deuteronomy is modeled after well-known ANE (specifically, Hittite) treaty forms, some attention must be paid to the standard elements of such texts and how they comprise the structure and outline of the book. At the same time it is important to emphasize that Moses creatively integrated into the covenant form large blocks of noncovenantal material such as parenesis (exhortation) and poetry, though both of these types are employed in support of the overall covenant document.

Table 2: The Hittite Suzerain-Vassal Treaty Form[33]

1. Title
2. Historical Prologue
3. Stipulations
4. Deposit/Reading
5. Witnesses
6. Curses
7. Blessings

Investigation of the Hittite texts reveals that those of a sovereign-vassal type in which the Great King of the Hittites enjoined treaty requirements upon his conquered or dependent subject rulers contained certain mandatory components.[34] Deuteronomy, as a covenant text of that kind, embodies all these essential parts and in the normal order. In addition of course it adds parenetic discourses and other elaborations appropriate to its larger character as a farewell sermon of Moses addressed to a particular people in special historical and theological circumstances.

The following are the standard elements of Hittite covenant texts and their corresponding place in Deuteronomy.

1. The Preamble (1:1–5). This section is an introduction to the main text and provides the setting in which the text is being presented to the vassal by the Great King.

2. The Historical Prologue (1:6–4:49). The purpose of this element is to rehearse the past relationships between the contracting parties and even their respective forebears.

3. The General Stipulations (5:1–11:32). These are the basic principles of relationship designed to reveal the purposes of the Great King and to alert the vassal regarding the guidelines within which those purposes, as they affect him especially, are to be implemented in time to come.

4. The Specific Stipulations (12:1–26:19). The general stipulations, stated in broad, principal terms, must be further defined by particular cases that have arisen in the past or may be expected to rise in the future. That is, the Great King must not only speak in categories of theoretical behavior or generalized expectation, but he must anticipate peculiar or unique circumstances in which the vassal is unable to extrapolate a particular response either because the principle is too broad or the vassal is incapable of making the proper application without further guidance.

---

[33] Based on Kitchen, *On the Reliability of the Old Testament*, 288.

[34] G. E. Mendenhall, "Covenant Forms in Israelite Tradition," *BA* 17 (1954): 58–60; Kitchen, *On the Reliability of the Old Testament*, 287–88.

5. The Blessings and Curses (27:1–28:68). The result of faithful obedience to the terms of the covenant, that is, to the stipulations, will ensure that the vassal will receive appropriate regard. Conversely, disobedience will bring swift and sure retribution at the hands of the Great King.

6. The Witnesses (30:19; 31:19; 32:1–43). In order for the treaty to have legal validity it must be sworn in the presence of witnesses who can thenceforth testify to its worth and to the commitments made by the contracting parties. Even the Great King acknowledges the need to stand by the promise he has solemnly sworn.

Despite the fact that Deuteronomy is essentially a covenant text, it is evident that it is more than that. It is a covenant statement embedded in the farewell address of Moses, which he delivered to the people of Israel in the plains of Moab just before his death (Deut 1:1–3). The Israelites had completed the wilderness journey from Sinai and were about to enter and occupy the land of Canaan. The old generation had died, so the new generation must for themselves hear and respond to the message of the covenant that God had made with their ancestors at Mount Sinai. Moses thus repeated its terms but with amendments and qualifications appropriate to the new situation of conquest and settlement that lay ahead. In addition he repeated to them the history of God's faithfulness and exhorted them to be obedient and to fulfill the mandates of the covenant to which they had subscribed. Thus Deuteronomy is a sermon centered on covenant, an address that takes its fundamental shape from the pattern of Late Bronze Age covenant documents.

THE PURPOSE AND THEOLOGY OF DEUTERONOMY

The purpose of Deuteronomy is to provide a restatement of the covenant between God and Israel to the generation assembled in the plains of Moab prior to the crossing of the Jordan and conquest of Canaan under Joshua.[35] Most of the people in the generation that had heard and accepted the covenant at Sinai 38 years earlier (Deut 2:14; cf. Num 14:34) had died. Their sons and daughters now needed to hear it for themselves and to make their own affirmation of loyalty to it (Deut 4:1–2; 5:1–5). Moreover, the Sinai statement of the covenant was particularly appropriate to the times and conditions of the wilderness migration. Now with conquest and permanent settlement in view it was necessary that the covenant stipulations be set forth in terms commensurate with the new environment in which Israel would live out its history as a servant people. Thus the covenant text of Deuteronomy is much longer than that of Exodus (plus the legal portions of Lev and Num), and it includes changes and reinterpretations of instruction previously given. These will be noted in detail below.

As noted, Deuteronomy consists of exhortation or parenesis as well as covenant prescription. This suggests that the second major purpose of the book is to record Moses' words of admonition, encouragement, and warning to those about to enter the land of promise. They must learn from the past, he maintained, if they were to fulfill the purposes for which the Lord had created them (Deut 8:11–20).

The theology of Deuteronomy cannot be separated from its form.[36] As a document cast in the structure of a covenant text it becomes the vehicle by which the sovereign God expressed His saving and redemptive purposes to His servant nation, His kingdom of priests whom He elected and delivered from bondage in response to the ancient patriarchal promises. This

---

[35] P. C. Craigie, *The Book of Deuteronomy*, NICOT (Grand Rapids: Eerdmans, 1976), 30–32.

[36] J. G. McConville, *Grace in the End: A Study in Deuteronomic Theology* (Grand Rapids: Zondervan, 1993); E. H. Merrill, "A Theology of the Pentateuch," in *A Biblical Theology of the Old Testament*, ed. R. B. Zuck (Chicago: Moody, 1991), 62–87; idem, *Everlasting Dominion: A Theology of the Old Testament* (Nashville: B&H, 2006), 383–411.

theme—that Israel is the mediator of God's gracious restorative purposes toward fallen mankind—is the great central theological statement of the book. It is that integrative principle that
unifies the book and explains its canonical function within the whole body of divine revelation.

While addressed specifically to ancient Israel, Deuteronomy also consists of timeless principles and theological truths that are very much appropriate to the modern church and world.
The elements of covenant that make up the great bulk of the book are, after all, expressions
of the character of God. God prescribes and commands what He does because of who He is.
This is particularly true of the Ten Commandments, which, though certainly time-bound in
some respects such as the observance of the Sabbath as celebration of the exodus, nevertheless
articulate fundamental notions about the incomparability and uniqueness of God on the one
hand and the expectation of universal human response to Him on the other. Jesus nowhere
abrogated the Ten Commandments and, in fact, when questioned about the greatest of them,
quoted Deut 6:4–5 (Matt 22:37–38), a passage that expresses the quintessence of OT revelation and requirement.

Basic to Deuteronomy is the fact that the God of Israel, who had redeemed them from
bondage and chaos, chose to identify with them in an everlasting covenant bond. This very
God, in and through His Son Jesus Christ, has graciously condescended to do likewise in a
great saving act on behalf of all people everywhere. Deuteronomy, the text of that old covenant, may indeed no longer be directly applicable to the redeemed people of today, but the
undying principles on which it was based are as viable today as they ever were in the days of
God's servant Moses.

Obviously all God's revelation is of ethical significance, for it flows from One who embodies the very idea of righteousness and holiness. When Deuteronomy discloses anything of the
nature and purpose of God, it discloses at the same time patterns of attitude and behavior
commensurate with His own character. Again particular instructions on matters of religious
practice, for example, may not be directly pertinent to Christian worship, but the attitudes
that undergird and presuppose even those practices are attitudes appropriate to a Christian
understanding of God and of what He desires of all His people everywhere and at all times.

AN OUTLINE OF DEUTERONOMY

  I. The Covenant Setting (1:1–5)

 II. The Historical Review (1:6–4:40)
      A. The Past Dealings of Yahweh with Israel (1:6–3:29)
      B. The Exhortation of Moses (4:1–40)

III. The Preparation for the Covenant Text (4:41–49)
      A. The Narrative Concerning Cities of Refuge (4:41–43)
      B. The setting and introduction (4:44–49)

 IV. The Principles of the Covenant (5:1–11:32)
      A. The Opening Exhortation (5:1–5)
      B. The Ten Commandments (5:6–21)
      C. The Narrative Relating the Sinai Revelation and Israel's Response (5:22–33)
      D. The Nature of the Principles (chap. 6)
      E. The Content of the Principles (chaps. 7–11)

AN ANALYSIS OF DEUTERONOMY AS A COVENANT DOCUMENT

I. The Covenant Setting (1:1–5)

At the beginning of Deuteronomy Moses was addressing the assembly of Israel in Moab, just east of the Jordan River. Forty years had transpired since the exodus, the long trek from Sinai had been completed, the enemies in the Transjordan had been defeated, and everything was in readiness for the conquest of Canaan. Moses therefore delivered a farewell address of covenant instruction and pastoral exhortation.

II. The Historical Review (1:6–4:40)

Since all suzerain-vassal treaties included a summation of past relations between the contracting parties, Moses accordingly recited the highlights of God's dealings with His people since the giving of the covenant at Sinai nearly 40 years before. This takes the form of the résumé itself (Deut 1:6–3:29) and a following exhortation (4:1–40).

The Lord had commanded Israel to leave Sinai and to press toward the land of promise (1:6–8). The way had been hard, taxing Moses almost to the limit (1:9–18), but eventually they had arrived at Kadesh-barnea (1:19–25). There the people rebelled, refusing to enter the land (1:26–33), so the Lord condemned them to wander in the wilderness until they died (1:34–40). After futile attempts to penetrate Canaan from the south (1:41–46) the tribes pressed north, bypassing Edom (2:1–8a) and eventually arriving at Moab (2:8b–25). From there they sought permission to pass through Amorite territory but were soundly rebuffed by both Sihon, king of the Amorites, and Og, king of Bashan. These two the Lord delivered into Israel's hands (2:26–37; 3:1–11), thereby giving Israel possession of the entire Transjordan region (3:12–17). From there Moses had requested that he be allowed to lead his people into Canaan, a request the Lord denied because of Moses' sin of impatience in the wilderness (3:18–29; see Num 20:12).

Following this sketch of history, Moses reminded his people of their special privileges as recipients of God's covenant grace (4:1–8), and he urged them to remember what God had done in the past in making Himself known to them (4:9–14). He is the invisible God who cannot be represented in stone or wood or even in His creation (4:15–24). If they try to do so, they will suffer His punishment of destruction and exile (4:25–31). Israel's motive for serving and worshipping Yahweh exclusively lies, as Moses said, in God's uniqueness as the transcendent yet covenant-making God (4:32–40).

III. The Preparation for the Covenant Text (4:41–49)

In a brief interlude Moses set aside three Transjordan cities as places of refuge in the event of manslaughter (4:41–43; see 19:2–13). There then follows an introduction to the covenant document proper, a text that consists of "decrees, statutes, and ordinances" (4:45).

IV. The Principles of the Covenant (5:1–11:32)

After an opening exhortation in which the purpose for the present covenant is stated (5:1–5) Moses listed the Ten Commandments, the very essence of the character of God and of His requirements for Israel and all mankind (5:6–21). Then in a flashback to the Sinai revelation, Moses reflected on that great theophanic experience and Israel's fearful response to it (5:22–33). They had learned there of "every command—the statutes and ordinances" (5:31), which must now be restated to the new generation.

The fundamental nature of the relationship between God and Israel consists of the recognition that He is one (6:4–5) and that His people, if they are to enjoy the benefits of His promises to the fathers, must give Him undivided allegiance and unswerving obedience (6:1–25). This must be reflected in their dispossession of the inhabitants of Canaan and their refusal to enter into any kind of entangling alliance with them (7:1–26). They must acknowledge that Yahweh—not the gods of Canaan—is the source of all blessings (8:1–20) and that those blessings are a product of His grace alone (9:1–10:11). All this is true despite Israel's past disobedience, for the Lord is faithful to His own commitment.

The oneness and exclusivity of Yahweh demand that He be loved by His people, a love synonymous with covenant fidelity. But love for God cannot be divorced from love for man, especially within the covenant community. Thus the center and substance of the covenant relationship is not works but love (10:12–22). Moreover, love must be manifest and in covenant terms that mean obedience. Israel had already seen what disobedience could bring (11:1–7), and now they must understand afresh that the bounties of God's goodness (11:8–12) were theirs only as they loved Him and kept His commandments (11:13–25). Now, and when they later entered the land, Israel would have opportunity to pledge its faithfulness to the Lord (11:26–32).

V. The Specific Stipulations of the Covenant (12:1–26:15)

The broad principles of covenant relationship and responsibility having been expounded (chaps. 5–11), Moses turned to more specific examples of their application.[37] The first of these had to do with the location of the one God among His people in a specified central place, one and only one sanctuary where community worship must be carried out (12:1–14). This could not be at the whim of the people but where Yahweh caused His name to dwell (12:11).

Central to that worship was the offering of animal sacrifice, an offering appropriate to Israel as God's chosen nation (12:15–32). A leading feature of pagan religion was its dependence on soothsayers and enchanters as channels of revelation and power. Since this presupposed the existence of gods other than Yahweh, it was obviously proscribed to Israel. In fact such a prophet, even if he came from within Israel itself, must be put to death if he counseled God's people to defect from Him (13:1–18).

Further differences between Israel and the unbelieving nations around them lay in their perception of the pure and the impure (14:1–21), the need for regular expressions of reverence of the sovereign God by generous offer of tribute to Him in the form of tithes of all their increase (14:22–29), and the observance of every seventh year as a year of release in which poor Israelites were freed of all financial encumbrances that had befallen them as a result of their indenturing themselves to their fellow countrymen (15:1–18).

Because the Lord had saved the firstborn of every house of Israel in the tenth plague (Exod 13:11–16), the faithful of Israel must offer up the firstborn of their herds and flocks annually as an expression of devotion (Deut 15:19–23). This was done as part of the Passover celebration and the Feast of Unleavened Bread that followed immediately thereafter (16:1–8). Other occasions for offering tribute to the Great King as a community of faith were the Feast of Weeks (or Pentecost), seven weeks after Passover (16:9–12), and the Feast of Tabernacles in the seventh month of the year (16:13–17).

The implementation of the demands of the covenant on the part of the community required political and religious officials such as "judges and officials" (16:18–17:13), a king (17:14–20), and priests and Levites (18:1–8). The prophets also were important in shaping the course of Israel's theocratic life (18:9–22). All peoples, including the Canaanites, had their prophets,

---

[37] Many scholars favor the view that Deuteronomy 12–26 consists of detailed exposition and application of the principles elaborated in chaps. 5–11. See G. Braulik, "The Sequence of the Laws in Deuteronomy 12–26 and in the Decalogue," in *A Song of Power and the Power of Song,* 313–35; S. A. Kaufman, "The Structure of the Deuteronomic Law," *Maarav* 1/2 (1978–79): 105–58; J. H. Walton, "Deuteronomy: An Exposition of the Spirit of the Law," *GTJ* 8 (1987): 213–25; A. Rofé, "The Arrangement of the Laws in Deuteronomy," *ETL* 64 (1988): 265–87.

but these practitioners of sorcery and incantation were so evil before God that they and their demonic techniques must be totally repudiated and disavowed (18:9–14). In their place God would raise up an order of prophets in the tradition of Moses, spokesmen who would speak the true word of the Lord (18:15–19). Any among them who defected from this high and holy calling by prophesying falsely must die. The fundamental test of their integrity would be whether their predictive word came to pass (18:20–22).

Though Israel was by definition a religious community, it was also a social community composed of individuals, of citizens, who must live together in peace and order. There was, in other words, a social and civil dimension to life as a covenant people. This dictated the need for civil legislation, for rules of behavior in a social setting (19:1–22:4). These include such issues as homicide (19:1–13), the removal of boundary markers (19:14), and guarantees of justice in the court (19:15–21).

As a nation about to engage the Canaanite nations in wars of conquest, Israel must have guidelines as to its undertaking. This was especially important because some of the campaigns would involve "holy war" or war fought on the Lord's behalf and for covenant principles whereas others would be war of the normal, "secular" type. In the former case the people must know that God was with them (20:1–4) and that He would achieve the victory.[38] This allowed for many kinds of exemption from military service (20:5–9) for sheer numbers of troops would not determine the outcome but only faithfulness to the Lord's commands. In instances of "regular" war, terms of peace must first be offered. If they were accepted the populace would be spared but would be reduced to vassalage (20:10–15). If, however, the cities were devoted to the Lord as part of Israel's inheritance, they must be annihilated lest their people draw Israel away into apostasy (20:16–18). Even in such cases, however, the physical structures, including even the trees, must be preserved since they had no moral culpability (20:19–20).

Other circumstances covered by the covenant law were cases of homicide without witnesses (21:1–9), the proper treatment of prisoners of war (21:10–17), unmanageable children (21:18–21), the disposition of dead corpses (21:22–23; see John 19:31), and the problem of lost property (Deut 22:1–4). Any Israelite who found anything belonging to a fellow citizen must either return it to him or wait for him to come and claim it. If it were an animal that had fallen by the wayside, brotherliness mandated that the beast be lifted up and restored.

As the Mosaic covenant states repeatedly, Israel was a holy people and must live a holy life before the world. Like Leviticus, then (see Leviticus 17–25), Deuteronomy also has its "holiness code," its set of guidelines by which Israel must achieve and maintain its purity (22:5–23:18). Though the reason for the inclusion of some of these may escape the modern reader, in their own time and circumstances they undoubtedly contributed to Israel's understanding of what it meant to be a people peculiar to the Lord and unique among the peoples of the earth.

These matters include transvestitism (22:5); the protection of young birds (22:6–7); the building of roof railings (22:8); sowing mixed seed, plowing with mixed teams, and wearing clothing of mixed material (22:9–11); and wearing garments with tassels (22:12). Sexual purity also comes in for attention. Thus the law addresses accusations about a bride's loss of virginity before marriage (22:13–21), adultery (22:22–24), rape (22:25–29), and incest (22:30).

The holiness of God's people also reveals itself in its rejection of those from its assembly who have been emasculated (23:1), born of mixed marriage (23:2), or who were of Ammonite

---

[38] For the "rules" of holy war see the groundbreaking work of G. von Rad, *Holy War in Ancient Israel*, trans. M. Dawn (Grand Rapids: Eerdmans, 1991), 41–51.

or Moabite descent (23:3–6). On the other hand, Edomites and Egyptians were to be accepted as proselytes because they were brothers and hosts to Israel, respectively (23:7–8). Purification pertained to matters of bodily cleanliness, especially in the context of holy war (23:9–14). Soldiers contaminated by bodily secretions must purify themselves, and they must also bury their defecation. The reason was that the Lord walked in the midst of the camp. Physical impurity was an affront to a holy God and bespoke a cultic and spiritual impurity as well. An escaped slave was welcome, however, and in fact must not be forced to return to his master (23:15–16). Prostitutes and sodomites were strictly forbidden in Israel and obviously their ungodly gain could not serve as offering to the Lord (23:17–18).

Attention to the laws of purity gives rise to an association with precepts governing interpersonal relationships in general (23:19–25:19), for there are areas of societal life which, though not cultic in nature, have moral and ethical implications important to covenant life and faith. Such matters as loans to fellow Israelites and foreigners (23:19–20), vows to the Lord (23:21–23), and the right to help oneself to a neighbor's grapes and grain while passing through his land (23:24–25) are juxtaposed to illustrate the principle that one's fair dealings with both God and man are on the same level. Similarly the covenant addresses the problems of divorce (24:1–4) and the newly wed (24:5); loan security (24:6,10–13); kidnapping (24:7); contagious skin diseases (24:8–9); the charitable care of the poor, weak, and disenfranchised (24:14–15, 17–22); and the principle that one is responsible for his own sin and must therefore expect to be punished for it (24:16).

Justice demanded that the guilty suffer appropriate punishment (25:1–3), that a brother of a deceased and childless Israelite raise up offspring in his name by marrying his widow (25:5–10), that a woman not dishonor a man sexually (25:11–12), and that weights and measures be according to standard (25:13–16). It even extended to the animal world, for the ox must be allowed to eat of the grain it was threshing for its owner (25:4; see 1 Cor 9:9). At the other extreme God's justice demanded that the enemies of His chosen people experience judgment at their hands. Thus, Amalek, who had attacked the elderly and defenseless of Israel in the wilderness journey (Exod 17:8–16), must one day be destroyed from the earth (Deut 25:17–19).

The Specific Stipulations section of Deuteronomy concludes with the laws of covenant celebration and confirmation (26:1–15). When Israel finally entered the land of Canaan, they must acknowledge the Lord's faithful provision by offering their first fruits to Him while reciting the history of His beneficent covenant dealings with them from the ancient days of the patriarchs to the present (26:1–11). This ceremony appears to be a part of the celebration of the Feast of Weeks (or Pentecost or Harvest; Exod 23:16; Lev 23:15–21). Following the offering of the first of the grain harvest to the Lord the farmers of Israel must provide the Levites and other dependent citizens the tithe of their produce (26:12–15). In this manner tribute to God and support of the needy merge into one glorious act of worship.

VI. Exhortation and Narrative Interlude (26:16–19)

The long body of stipulations having been outlined, Moses commanded the people to obey them and not just perfunctorily—they must do so with all their heart and soul (26:16). The very essence of the covenant, he said, was the pledge they had made to be God's people and the Lord's reciprocal promise to be their God. God's will was that Israel continue to be His special people, a holy communion called to be an expression of praise and honor of the Lord.

VII. The Curses and Blessings (chaps. 27–28)

A central element of any bilateral covenant was the section describing the rewards for faithful compliance to its terms and the punishments befitting disobedience to it. As a suzerain-vassal treaty text, Deuteronomy obviously holds only Israel—and not the Lord—accountable, though there is the promise of the Sovereign that He will respond to Israel's obedience with blessing beyond measure.

The ceremony of blessing and curses, to take place once Canaan had been occupied, must occur at Shechem, the site of early patriarchal encounters with God (27:4; Gen 12:6; 35:4; Deut 11:26–29). There they must erect great plastered monuments containing the covenant text and an altar of stone on which appropriate offerings of covenant renewal could be sacrificed (27:1–8). As God's people (27:9–10) they would stand, half on Mount Ebal and half on Mount Gerizim, to affirm their covenant commitment (27:11–14).

The reading of the curses and blessings took the form of an envelopment in which the curses that follow disobedience of specific stipulations (27:15–26) and those that follow disobedience of general stipulations (28:15–68) embrace the list of blessings that follow obedience (28:1–14). As a great antiphonal chorus, tribal representatives would stand on Mount Gerizim to shout "amen" at the listing of the blessings while others, on Mount Ebal, would do so when the curses were sounded.

The first list of curses (27:15–26) deals with representative covenant violations without specifying the form the curses might take. The blessing section (28:1–14) promises prosperity in physical and material ways and reaffirms God's intention to make Israel an exalted and holy people. The second list of curses (28:15–68) threatens loss of prosperity (28:15–19), disease and pestilence (28:20–24), defeat and deportation with all that that would entail (28:25–35), and a reversal of roles between Israel and the nations (28:36–46). Rather than being exalted among them Israel would become their servant. All of this would result in indescribable misery and hopelessness (28:47–57). In effect, covenant violation would undo the exodus and deliver the nation back into the throes of bondage (28:58–68).

VIII. The Epilogic Historical Review (chaps. 29–30)

By way of summary Moses rehearsed God's dealings with Israel in the exodus and wilderness (29:2–9) and exhorted them to pledge themselves to covenant fidelity as the new generation chosen by the Lord to represent Him in the world (29:10–21). Their commitment must be personal and genuine, for if it is not, the time of judgment would come in which the nations would question whether Israel was in fact the people of the Lord (29:22–29).

That this was a foregone conclusion is clear in Moses' promise that God would visit His people in their day of calamity and exile and would cause them once more to reflect on their covenant privileges. He then would exercise His grace and restore them to full covenant partnership with all its blessings (30:1–10). Their pledge to faithful adherence to the terms of the covenant could bring immediate and lasting reward (30:11–16) but disobedience would produce only judgment (30:17–20).

IX. Deposit of the Text and Provision for Its Future Implementation (31:1–29)

Though the ceremony of covenant does not appear in the narrative (except by implication; 29:10–13), it did take place, as is clear from Moses' selection of Joshua to succeed him as covenant mediator (31:1–8) and his delivery of the covenant text to the priests for safekeeping (31:9–13). Moreover, the Lord commanded Moses, who was near the end of his life, to compose a song whose purpose was to remind the nation of the covenant pledges they had made (31:14–23). This certainly presupposes that such pledges had already been confessed. In true covenant fashion the Lord invoked heaven and earth as witnesses to the promises that Israel had sworn (31:24–29).

X. The Song of Moses (31:30–32:43)

This wonderful hymn of covenant commitment (32:1) extols the God of Israel for His greatness and righteousness (32:2–4) despite the wickedness of His people (32:5–6a). He had created them (32:6b) and had redeemed (32:7–9) and preserved them (32:10–14). They rebelled in turn and followed other gods (32:15–18), a course of action that provoked His judgment in the past and would do so in the future (32:19–38). At last, however, He would remember His covenant and bring His people salvation (32:39–43).

XI. Narrative Interlude (32:44–52)

Having sung his song, Moses urged his people to subscribe to its demands as a covenant instrument (32:44–47). Then in response to the command of the Lord, Moses ascended Mount Nebo to await the day of his death (32:48–52).

XII. The Blessing of Moses (chap. 33)

Before he left them, Moses offered to his fellow Israelites a will and testament similar to that with which Jacob had blessed his sons (see Gen 49:2–27). After praising the God of deliverance and covenant (Deut 33:2–5) he listed the tribes by name, assigning to each a prophetic blessing (33:6–25). He concluded with a paean of praise of Israel's Lord (33:26–28) and a promise that His chosen ones would ultimately triumph over all their foes (33:29).

XIII. Narrative Epilogue (34:1–12)

Having ascended Mount Nebo (or Pisgah), Moses viewed all the land of promise, a land promised to the patriarchal ancestors but denied to Moses himself because of his intemperate behavior at the rock in the wilderness (34:1–4). He then died and was buried by the Lord in an unknown and unmarked grave (34:5–6). With great lament the people of Israel mourned his passing, for though Joshua possessed the spirit and authority of Moses, neither he nor any man to come could compare with this giant whom God knew "face to face" (34:7–12).

Mount Nebo and the Jordan Valley.

CONCLUSION

The book of Deuteronomy was a favorite of Jesus and the NT writers and for good reason. It is perhaps the preeminent theological treatise of the OT, a composition that not only articulated for Moses' generation who they were and what was expected of them, but that also provided the standard of belief and behavior against which all subsequent generations were to assess themselves. The debate about its authorship and setting is therefore not a meaningless trivial pursuit, but one that affects the very nature and authority of the book. It was precisely the Mosaic origins of Deuteronomy that gave sanction to the reformations of Hezekiah and Josiah and that provided an authoritative statement of the covenant relationship between God and Israel that issued into the fullness of God's redemptive work on behalf of the whole world through Jesus Christ.

STUDY QUESTIONS

1. What is the setting of the book of Deuteronomy according to historical-critical scholarship?
2. What is the setting of the book according to Judeo-Christian precritical scholarship?
3. Name the scholar who first proposed that Deuteronomy was "the book of the covenant" found in Josiah's temple restoration.
4. What secular treaty model does Deuteronomy most clearly follow?
5. How does the "Sabbath command" in Deuteronomy differ most strikingly from the version in Exodus?
6. Where was Moses when he composed the book of Deuteronomy?
7. What modern scholar has proposed that the Specific Stipulations section of Deuteronomy is a detailed exposition of the General Stipulations section?
8. By form, what kind of a treaty is Deuteronomy?
9. What is meant by the "Shema"?
10. Who is thought to have composed the account of Moses' death?
11. Sihon was king of what people encountered by Israel?
12. Which tribes elected to remain east of the Jordan at the time of the conquest?
13. What seventh century texts are sometimes compared to the covenant form of Deuteronomy?
14. What was the principal test by which a prophet's authenticity could be determined?
15. What is the literal meaning of the word "deuteronomy"?

FOR FURTHER STUDY

Carmichael, C. M. *The Laws of Deuteronomy*. Ithaca, NY: Cornell University Press, 1974.
Christensen, D. L. *Deuteronomy 1–21:9*. WBC. Nashville: Thomas Nelson, 2001.
———. *Deuteronomy 21:10–34:12*. WBC. Nashville: Thomas Nelson, 2002.
Clements, R. E. *God's Chosen People*. Valley Forge, PA: Judson, 1968.
Craigie, P. C. *The Book of Deuteronomy*. NICOT. Grand Rapids: Eerdmans, 1976.
DeRouchie, J. S. *A Call to Covenant Love: Text, Grammar and Literary Structure in Deuteronomy 5–11*. Piscataway, NJ: Gorgias, 2007.
Driver, S. R. *A Critical and Exegetical Commentary on Deuteronomy*. Edinburgh: T. & T. Clark, 1902.
Fokkelman, J. P. *Major Poems of the Hebrew Bible*. Assen: Van Gorcum, 1998.
Hillers, Dilbert. *Covenant: The History of a Biblical Idea*. Baltimore: Johns Hopkins University Press, 1969.
Kitchen, K. A. *Ancient Orient and Old Testament*. Chicago: InterVarsity, 1966.
———. *On the Reliability of the Old Testament*. Grand Rapids: Eerdmans, 2003.
Kline, M. G. *The Structure of Biblical Authority*. Grand Rapids: Eerdmans, 1972.
———. *Treaty of the Great King*. Grand Rapids: Eerdmans, 1963.
Levinson, Bernard. *Deuteronomy and the Hermeneutics of Legal Innovation*. New York: Oxford, 1997.
Manley, G. T. *The Book of the Law*. Grand Rapids: Eerdmans, 1957.
Mayes, A. D. H. *Deuteronomy*. NCBC. Grand Rapids: Eerdmans, 1979.
McCarthy, D. J. *Treaty and Covenant*. Roma: Analecta Biblica, 1963.
McConville, J. G. *Deuteronomy*. AOTC 5. Downers Grove, IL: InterVarsity, 2002.
———. *Grace in the End: A Study in Deuteronomic Theology*. Grand Rapids: Zondervan, 1993.
Merrill, Eugene H. *Deuteronomy*. NAC Nashville: B&H, 1994.
Millar, J. G. *Now Choose Life: Theology and Ethics in Deuteronomy*. Grand Rapids: Eerdmans, 1998.

Miller, Patrick D. *Deuteronomy*. Louisville: John Knox, 1990.

Nelson, Richard D. *Deuteronomy: A Commentary*. Louisville: Westminster John Knox, 2002.

Nicholson, E. W. *Deuteronomy and Tradition*. Philadelphia: Fortress, 1967.

Paul, S. M. *Studies in the Book of the Covenant in Light of Cuneiform and Biblical Law*. Leiden: Brill, 1970.

Rad, G. von. *Deuteronomy: A Commentary*. Philadelphia: Westminster, 1966.

Thompson, J. A. *The Ancient Near Eastern Treaties and the Old Testament*. London: Tyndale, 1963.

———. *Deuteronomy: An Introduction and Commentary*. TOTC. Downers Grove, IL: InterVarsity, 1974.

Tigay, J. H. *Deuteronomy. JPS Torah Commentary*. Philadelphia: Jewish Publication Society, 1996.

Weinfeld, M. *Deuteronomy 1–11*. AB New York: Doubleday, 1991.

Wiseman, D. J. *The Vassal-Treaties of Esarhaddon*. London: British School of Archaeology in Iraq, 1958.

Part 5

THE HISTORICAL BOOKS

Eugene H. Merrill

I N A VERY real sense the OT as a whole is a history book. From beginning to end it is
an account—in generally chronological order—of the outworking of God's creation and
redemption purposes for the world through Abraham and his descendants, particularly
the nation Israel. However, long-standing tradition as well as obvious genre-critical analysis
shows that this is too broad a way of looking at the whole corpus of biblical literature. Hence,
the term "history" has come to be applied in a more restricted, technical sense to a certain
block of the material that more clearly conforms to standard notions of historiography.

THE EXTENT OF THE HISTORICAL BOOKS

The historical books in the so-called "Protestant canon" consist of Joshua, Judges, Ruth,
1 and 2 Samuel, 1 and 2 Kings, 1 and 2 Chronicles, Ezra, Nehemiah, and Esther—nearly
one-third of all the books of the OT. The Jewish (Masoretic) canon, on the other hand, regards
these books (except for Ruth and Esther), along with the writings of the literary prophets,
as constituting the second great part of the inspired collection, the *Nebî'îm* ("Prophets"). To
distinguish between these two kinds of prophetic works, the historical books are sometimes
designated the "Former Prophets" and the others the "Latter Prophets."

This perception of the historical books is instructive in at least two ways. First, it minimizes
the rather facile assumption that they are fundamentally works of history. Second, it suggests
that their authors were prophets. Whether this second point is correct or not (see below), it
does draw attention to the fact that these compositions, while historical in nature, narrate history in theological terms. That is to say, they express a divine account and interpretation of
events through prophetic mediation. While one may properly speak of historical books, one
must be sensitive to the Jewish nuancing of the terms that open up their more deeply theological nature.[1]

---

[1] E. H. Merrill, "Old Testament History: A Theological Perspective," in *NIDOTTE*, ed. W. A. VanGemeren (Grand
Rapids: Zondervan, 1997), 1:68–85.

THE AUTHORSHIP, DATING, AND SETTING
OF THE HISTORICAL BOOKS

First, none of the historical books contains internal attestation of authorship. Opinion on the matter must be based on tradition and in some cases on what is most likely. Second, while some of the books provide a fair amount of information about their provenience, others say little or nothing. Again only tradition and plausibility can afford much help.

The Talmud offers the following information relative to the composition of various writings including the historical books:

> Joshua wrote the book which bears his name and [the last] eight verses of the Pentateuch. Samuel wrote the book which bears his name and the Book of Judges and Ruth. . . . Jeremiah wrote the book which bears his name, the Book of Kings, and Lamentations. . . . The Men of the Great Assembly wrote . . . the Scroll of Esther. Ezra wrote the book that bears his name and the genealogies of the Book of Chronicles up to his own time. . . . Who then finished it [the Book of Chronicles]?—Nehemiah the son of Hachaliah (*Baba Bathra* 14b-15a).

To what extent this can be accepted is a matter of debate, but in some instances at least it has inherent possibility and even probability. To the extent the attribution of authorship is correct, the dates and situations that produced the literature can also be determined with some degree of confidence.

THE LITERARY CHARACTER OF THE HISTORICAL BOOKS

Contemporary study of the OT as history revolves largely around the issue as to whether it conforms to accepted norms of historiographical literature.[2] Part of the problem is ideological and presuppositional and may be stated as follows: Since history writing in the truest sense must be objective, unbiased, closed to the irrational and unique, and limited to the recovery, assessment, and reporting of the "facts," it follows that most of the biblical literature is nonhistorical for it does not meet most of these criteria.[3] Another argument, more literary in nature, questions the historicity of reported biblical events because their accounts appear in story, poetry, conversation, dialogue, and even soliloquy. Even granting that such events and discourses may have taken place, how, the critic asks, could the historian have accessed such sources?[4]

As for the likelihood of supernatural, "unbelievable" occurrences to have taken place in Israel's past, one's predisposition toward such possibilities can be the only guarantor to their having any historical reality.[5] One cannot, of course, believe what one will not believe. As for the lack of conventional literary form in recounting biblical history, scholars recently have begun to recognize that no such thing existed in the ANE. New approaches to literary/

---

[2] V. P. Long, *The Art of Biblical History* (Grand Rapids: Zondervan, 1994), 27–57.

[3] For a criticism of the view of F. H. Bradley (*The Presuppositions of Critical History*, 1874), that the "unbelievable" could not and therefore did not happen, see R. G. Collingwood, *The Idea of History*. (Oxford: Clarendon, 1946), 238–40.

[4] R. Alter, *The Art of Biblical Narrative* (New York: Basic, 1981), 32–36. To Alter, information that could be known only privately or at least not in such a way as to constitute historical sources, is to be understood as the exercise of "narrator omniscience." That is, it is fabricated by the historian as representing what most likely would have been done or said under the given circumstances (ibid., 35–36).

[5] Long, *The Art of Biblical History*, 128–35.

rhetorical criticism make it clear that history can be told in many forms and that no single genre is essential to establishing the credibility of historical accounts.[6]

The historical books of the Old Testament are replete with formal and generic variation. Anecdotes, annals, biographies, chronicles, etiologies, genealogies, inscriptions, itineraries, letters, pareneses, prophecies, reports, and stories—all are the stuff of OT history-writing, and all should be taken seriously as modes of communicating the facts of Israel's past. The historical books are especially and for obvious reasons filled with these and other forms because it is their intention to portray in a faithful and accurate manner the great events of salvation history and to do so in an engaging style.

THE MAJOR THRUST OF THE HISTORICAL BOOKS

The dominating topic of the historical books is the ebb and flow of the affairs of the nation Israel. Whether in its premonarchic infancy (Joshua, Judges, Ruth), its brief fling as a united kingdom (Samuel–1 Kings 1–11), or its tragic days as separate entities (1 Kings 12–Nehemiah), north and south, Israel is the focus of the narrative. But Israel's history is told not just as a sequence of episodes only loosely connected or not connected at all. Rather, it is reflective of a pattern, of an interlinking chain of events that played themselves out within a geographic, cultural, and political context but that also transcended that context at the same time. In other words Israel's history is *Heilsgeschichte*, a record not so much of words spoken and deeds done but of their meaning in terms of God's ultimate design.[7] This is why the description "former prophets" for this literature is so apt.

To characterize the account as "sacred history" is not to vitiate its claims to authentic reportage, however, for in a sense true history is history only as viewed from divine perspective. Without God's evaluation of Israel's historical existence, the story of that existence is essentially meaningless. Thus the record is saturated with overtones of theodicy. Repeatedly it speaks of cause and effect, it offers explanations for what might otherwise be construed as randomness, and it exhorts the attitude and behavior necessary to avoid repeating the sins and failures of the past.

THE HISTORIOGRAPHICAL METHOD OF THE HISTORICAL BOOKS

Readers of the OT historical books come away with one overriding impression—they have been reading and enjoying stories. This includes people who "hate history" because it is so dull and so packed with names, dates, facts, and other irrelevancies. For them, at least, the OT is not history but something different and better. The reason of course is that narrative is the primary vehicle by which the message of Israel's history has been communicated, and narrative is usually interesting no matter its subject matter. "Narrative" refers not just to stories but to accounts, that is, the entire record of the past in whatever form it might take, but one with a discernible theme and pattern.[8] Together and separately the historical books share these narrative features, for they constitute a coherent presentation of God's pursuit of an eternal objective—the election, redemption, and employment of Israel as the instrument of His reconciling grace. As noted above, the very fact that the historical literature is narrative raised questions in a previous generation as to its historicity. Such objections seldom arise anymore, and doubts

---

[6] B. O. Long, *1 Kings with an Introduction to Historical Literature*, FOTL IX (Grand Rapids: Eerdmans, 1984), 4–8.

[7] Merrill, "Old Testament History: A Theological Perspective," 68–75.

[8] A. Berlin, *Poetics and Interpretation of Biblical Narrative* (Sheffield: Almond, 1983), 13–21.

as to historicity now find other justification. However, the peculiar way in which the narrative unfolds at times does call for some attention.

First, the approach in the narratives is primarily thematic, not chronological. Frequently persons or episodes are "collected" or juxtaposed because they share things in common even if in doing so the historian gets things "out of order." Examples may be found in the stories of Elijah and Elisha which do not always conform to chronological sequence.

Second, the record is often tendentious or biased. It is always true and accurate, but not always complete. The story of David in Samuel differs in many respects from the version in Chronicles, mainly because of what the Chronicler does not say. He is silent about David's adultery and murder and their tragic aftereffects. The reason surely was not to attempt a cover-up, for the whole sordid escapade was public knowledge and had been for centuries before the Chronicler came on the scene. Other reasons dictated the omission as will be noted later.

Third, the overriding concern is theological, not mundane. This results in a history-writing in which heavenly concerns outweigh earthly ones and which seems to give inordinate attention to some details and scarcely any or none at all to others that would ordinarily be dominant in a normal approach. For example the book of 1 and 2 Kings devotes an apparently disproportionate amount of space to the ministries of Elijah and Elisha and record nothing about such major international events as the Battle of Qarqar or the demise of the Urartian Empire. Such unevenness can be explained only by purposes that stand outside ordinary history-writing. What is central to its theological concerns appears in the record; what is peripheral or irrelevant does not.

THE "SYNOPTIC PROBLEM" IN THE HISTORICAL BOOKS

This expression, derived from the study of problems pertaining to comparisons of the NT Gospels of Matthew, Mark, and Luke, is applicable to the only instance of such a phenomenon in the OT, the comparison and contrast of Samuel–Kings, on the one hand, with Chronicles, on the other. The two great writings have a few instances of apparent contradiction—mainly of a text-transmission nature—but the differences otherwise have to do with materials included or lacking in one or the other. This is not the place to deal with specifics or to draw conclusions about intent and purpose, but it is worth noting that the very existence of parallel accounts lends support to the notion already advanced that the history related in both sources has an agenda beyond merely human interest or inspiration. The authors and/or compilers of both the Samuel–Kings and Chronicles materials were first and foremost theologians. Their interest was not just in the reporting of facts but in their selection and interpretation in such a way as to provide special theological understandings of God's dealings with His people.

THE CHRONOLOGY OF THE HISTORICAL BOOKS

Ancient Israelite historians did not link the events they recount to a permanent fixed point of reference such as the birth of Christ. True, there are examples of cross-referencing within the text but the benchmarks to which the historians refer are themselves "floating," that is, unconnected to a chronological scheme that enables modern readers to date them. For example Exod 12:40 states, "The time that the Israelites lived in Egypt was 430 years." This is helpful so far as it goes, but it provides no beginning or ending dates. Likewise, 1 Kgs 6:1 notes that Solomon commenced temple construction in the fourth year of his reign which was also the 480th year after the exodus. Unless one knows either the date of Solomon's succession or that of the exodus, this information has only limited chronological value. The same is true of the scores of instances in which the tenures of the kings of Israel and Judah are stated with reference to each other. Thus 2 Kgs 15:1 states, "In the twenty-seventh year of Israel's King Jeroboam, Azariah son of Amaziah became king of Judah." This information is useful in its own context but of no assistance in dating these reigns in terms of modern calendars.

The resolution of this conundrum has been found in the discovery of datable events of ANE history to which those of the OT can be associated.[9] These consist primarily of astronomical phenomena that can be precisely pinpointed and chronographical texts that make reference to them. When these are integrated, a consistent and virtually certain chronological framework emerges for the OT historical books. In fact one of the evidences for the historiographical nature of these writings is precisely their internal chronological consistency as well as their accurate integration into the larger historical environment.

CONCLUSION

The OT historical books are a treasure house of information about ancient Israel's life and times. But they are also far more than this. They reveal that all history is an outworking of divine purpose, a purpose which, though apparently frustrated over and over by human disobedience, inexorably moves forward to a glorious and triumphant resolution.

---

[9] For a detailed discussion see E. H. Merrill, *An Historical Survey of the Old Testament*, 2nd ed. (Grand Rapids: Baker, 1991), 97–100.

CHAPTER 15

THE BOOK OF JOSHUA

MARK F. ROOKER

CULTURAL CONTEXT OF THE BOOK

After the last Hyksos ruler had ruled in Egypt (c. 1570 BC), Egyptian power began to increase along the Fertile Crescent, particularly in the region of Syria-Palestine. Especially prominent in this time period were the numerous incursions of Thutmoses III (1504–1450 BC), who at the time of his death had placed virtually all of Syria under Egyptian control.

Thus during the life of Joshua in the LB age (1550–1200 BC) the land of Canaan was nominally under Egyptian control, while great international powers from Syria, Mesopotamia, and Asia Minor were in no position to become involved in Canaanite affairs. Also the Canaanites internally were unable to present a united front against the Israelites since the land of the Canaanites was divided into 31 separate city-states (Josh 12:9–24). This was due in no small measure to the highly diversified terrain in the small area of the land of Israel.

THE DATE OF THE BOOK

The Critical View

Critical introductions and commentaries on the book of Joshua have typically argued that the alleged sources underlying the Pentateuch, particularly D and P, can also be found in Joshua. A principal argument for the detection of various sources in Joshua is the alleged contradictory report of the conquest reported in the books of Joshua and Judges. According to Joshua the entire land of Canaan was conquered by the united nation of Israel and divided into tribal allotments during Joshua's lifetime. Judges 1, on the other hand, presents the conquest as incomplete after Joshua's lifetime as areas were being conquered by individual tribes. The latter version of the events is thought by the critics to be closer to the actual truth. Thus the narrative accounts in Joshua (especially Joshua 1–11) are viewed as local independent tribal stories. According to such critics as Albrecht Alt and Martin Noth and their followers, the Joshua narratives were originally no more than local etiological legends.[1] These legends allegedly helped

---

[1] A. Alt, *Kleine Scriften zur Geschicht des Volkes Israel* (Munich: C. H. Beck'she, 1953), 176–92; and M. Noth, *Das Buch Josua* (Tübingen: J. C. B. Mohr [Paul Siebeck], 1971), 9–16.

explain the ruins of the walls of Jericho (Josh 6) and the survival of Rahab's house and family (chap. 2; 6:22–25), the sanctuary of stones of Gilgal (4:3,8,20–24) and the twelve stones in the Jordan (4:9), the name Gilgal (5:9) and the "hill of foreskins" (5:2–8), the ruins of Ai (8:28), the pile of stones at Achor (7:26), and the Gibeonite presence at the Israelite sanctuary (chap. 9). These legends, it was argued, were later transformed into a national saga by an unknown literary redactor who gave the book of Joshua the form of a national epic. Thus the stories and records presented in the book were not contemporary to the events but were given shape in later times and reflected the ideology of a particular Israelite group.

While numerous scholars still resoundingly echo this critical dogma, many modern critics have abandoned it because of the current impasse that exists among critics regarding the dating of the sources of the Pentateuch.[2] Also, there is no consensus in the assignment of passages in Joshua to specific pentateuchal sources. In addition, critical scholars such as Alt and Noth admit that the border lists of the tribes in chaps. 13–19 are authentic reflections of life in Canaan before the rise of the Israelite monarchy.

Recent minimalist views are advocated by Robert Coote and John Van Seters. They have argued that the invasion and conquest of Canaan have no historical bearing whatever because they are merely literary inventions.[3] But such views are difficult to maintain since Lawson Younger has demonstrated that records from the second and first millennia BC from Egypt, Mesopotamia, and Anatolia display genres similar to what is found in Joshua 1–11.[4]

The Traditional View

The dating of the events described in the book of Joshua is intricately linked to the date of the exodus, normally viewed as having occurred in either the fifteenth or thirteenth century BC.[5]

The late date of the exodus and conquest is based on the alleged archaeological evidence which does not support a massive destruction of Israelite cities in the fifteenth to thirteenth centuries. However, this appeal to archaeological evidence as conclusive proof for the dating of the conquest is not convincing.[6] The biblical record in the book of Joshua does not claim that the conquest of Canaan by Joshua was accompanied by mass destruction with every military victory. The specific term used to refer to Joshua's military activity is the verb *lākad*, which means "to take," not "to destroy." The Israelites were instructed to demolish pagan cult objects, expel or execute the inhabitants, and occupy the land. But no mention is made of demolishing cities (see Exod 23:24; Num 33:50–56; Deut 20:10–20). John Bimson has argued that the archaeological record in fact may be viewed as quite harmonious with the biblical account

---

[2] E.g., R. N. Whybray, *The Making of the Pentateuch*, JSOTSup (Sheffield: JSOT Press, 1987); and R. Rendtorff, *The Problem of the Process of Transmission in the Pentateuch*, JSOTSup (Sheffield: JSOT Press, 1990).

[3] R. Coote, *Early Israel: A New Horizon* (Minneapolis: Fortress, 1990), 1–3; and J. Van Seters, "Joshua's Campaign of Canaan and Near Eastern Historiography," in *Israel's Past in Present Research*, ed. V. P. Long (Winona Lake, IN: Eisenbrauns, 1999), 170–80.

[4] K. Younger Jr., *Ancient Conquest Accounts: A Study in Ancient Near Eastern and Biblical History Writing*, JSOTSup (Sheffield: JSOT Press, 1990).

[5] The view taken here is that the exodus took place in the fifteenth century and thus the events surrounding the conquest of Canaan took place shortly thereafter. The early dating of the exodus and conquest is supported in the biblical text by such passages as 1 Kgs 6:1 and Judg 11:26.

[6] Bryant Wood is one who has challenged this consensus particularly with regard to Jericho. Wood has returned to Garstung's date of the destruction of Jericho in about 1400 BC based on pottery fragments, stratigraphic considerations, scarab data, and Carbon-14 dating ("Did the Israelites Conquer Jericho?" *BAR* 16 [March/April 1990]: 44–57). See also E. Merrill, "Palestinian Archaeology and the Date of the Conquest: Do Tells Tell Tales?" *GTJ* 3 (1982): 107–21.

of the conquest. The lack of massive destruction in the fifteenth to thirteenth centuries BC is actually consistent with the biblical narrative in the book of Joshua, which does not indicate that Joshua carried out massive destructions. Although the Canaanite people were put to the sword, the cities that were razed were in fact few (see Josh 11:13).[7]

Several reasons suggest that the book of Joshua was composed soon after the occurrence of the events themselves. Three primary passages support an early date for the composition of the contents of the book. First, 13:6 mentions Sidon as the dominant city of Phoenicia. Sidon's superiority over Tyre was true only before the rise of the Israelite monarchy which witnessed the beginning of Tyre's prominent role on the Phoenician coastline. Similarly, 15:63 mentions that the Jebusites were the inhabitants of Jerusalem. The non-Israelite occupation of Jerusalem by the Jebusites was true only in the time before David's rise to power when he conquered Jerusalem and turned it into the national capital. Third, 16:10 mentions that the Israelites failed to drive the Canaanites out of Gezer and that the Canaanites remained in the city at the time of the book's composition: "to this day."[8] This chronological note indicates that the writing of the account and of the book must have taken place before Solomon's lifetime because in Solomon's reign the Canaanites of Gezer were massacred by the Egyptians (1 Kgs 9:16).[9]

THE AUTHORSHIP OF THE BOOK

The authorship of the book of Joshua was attributed to Joshua himself in the Talmud and by some notable Jewish medieval commentators such as Rashi and David Kimchi. Explicit attestation to Joshua's writing (at least of portions of the book) is recorded in Josh 24:26: "Joshua recorded these things in the book of the law of God." The use of the first person in 5:6 supports the premise that Joshua played a part in the writing of the book and suggests that he was an eyewitness to the events. And yet some passages suggest that they were written after Joshua's death. This would include not only the passage which records his own passing (24:29–30), but also 24:31, which indicates that considerable time had passed since Israel was under Joshua's leadership. In addition, 19:47 locates the tribe of Dan in the north. This would seem to be a later addition, because the migration of the Danites to the north of Palestine did not take place until the time of the judges (Judg 18:27–29).[10] It seems, therefore, that a substantial part of the book of Joshua was written by the Israelite leader himself with some supplementary material added possibly shortly after his death.

THE TITLE OF THE BOOK

Joshua, son of Nun, was a grandson of Elishama from the tribe of Ephraim (Num 13:8; 1 Chr 7:26). His name means "the Lord saves/delivers" and in Greek it is the equivalent of the name Jesus. Joshua is first mentioned in Exod 17:9 as a military leader and is noted an

---

[7] J. J. Bimson, *Redating the Exodus Conquest*, JSOTSup (Sheffield: Almond, 1988), 229–37.

[8] This expression occurs in 4:9; 5:9; 6:25; 7:26(twice); 8:28–29; 9:27; 10:27; 13:13; 14:14; 15:63; 16:10; and 9:27 has "as they are today." B. Childs concedes that the use of the phrase in 15:63 and 16:10 indicates a recording of the events in a period not later than the tenth century BC ("A Study of the Formula, 'Until This Day,'" *JBL* 82 [1963]: 279–92).

[9] Moreover, the author of Joshua said nothing about the decline and apostasy of the judges.

[10] Otherwise the book seems to be unaware of Dan's migration to the north, which marked the beginning of the idiomatic territorial description "from Dan to Beersheba." The author must have lived long before Dan's military conquest and relocation had taken place. Y. Kaufmann believes this latter point is of critical significance for the early dating of the book of Joshua (*The Biblical Account of the Conquest of Canaan*, trans. M. Dagut [Jerusalem: Magnes, 1985], 21, 36, 123, 127). Similarly the author placed the tribe of Simeon in the land of Judah and was hence unaware of the tribe's later expansion to Mount Seir (1 Chr 4:42–43).

additional 27 times in the Pentateuch. He served as Moses' personal attendant (Num 11:28) and led Israel in her first battle in the defeat of the Amalekites (Exod 17:8–14). Since Moses was not allowed to accompany the nation into Canaan (Num 20:1–13; Deut 1:37; 3:21–28), Joshua was appointed the leader of the nation who would bring the Israelites into the land promised to her forefathers (Num 27:12–23; Deut 31:1–8).

Many parts of the narrative of Joshua refer to the link between Moses and his successor Joshua. Like Moses, Joshua instructed the people to sanctify themselves before the Lord (Josh 3:5 [Exod 19:10]),[11] interceded for the nation (Josh 7:6–9 [Deut 9:25–29]), instructed the priests (Josh 4:10 [Leviticus 8–10]), and he gave his last will before his death (Josh 23:1–16 [Deut 31:2–8]). Also like Moses he performed the covenant sign of circumcision before work for the Lord was carried out (Josh 5:2–9 [Exod 4:24–26]). His success is contingent on obedience to Moses' law (Josh 1:8). He is also to be viewed as Moses' literary heir as he became the next great literary recorder of the biblical revelation after Moses.

THE PURPOSE AND MESSAGE OF THE BOOK

The purpose of the book of Joshua is to show the fulfillment of God's covenant promise to the patriarchs to give the land of Canaan to their descendants (Gen 12:2; 15:16; Deut 30:20). Not one of his promises to the house of Israel failed (Josh 21:45).

THE OUTLINE OF THE BOOK

I. **Entrance into Canaan (1:1–5:12)**
   A. Introduction and Marching Orders (chap. 1)
   B. Reconnaissance of Jericho (chap. 2)
   C. Crossing into the Promised Land and Remembering God's Acts (chaps. 3–4)
   D. Covenant Sign and Covenant Meal (5:1–12)

II. **Conquest of Canaan (5:13–12:24)**
   A. The Captain of the Lord's Army (5:13–15)
   B. The Capture of Jericho (chap. 6)
   C. The Defeat at Ai (chap. 7)
   D. Ai Conquered and Burned (8:1–29)
   E. Blessings and Curses at Shechem (8:30–35)
   F. The Southern Campaign (chaps. 9–10)
   G. The Northern Campaign (11:1–15)
   H. Summary of Conquest (11:16–23)
   I. The Defeated Kings of Canaan (chap. 12)

III. **Division of Canaan (chaps. 13–21)**
   A. Land Remaining to Be Taken (13:1–7)
   B. Land East of the Jordan (13:8–33)
   C. Distribution of West Jordan Introduced (chap. 14)
   D. Land Given to Judah (chap. 15)
   E. Land Given to Joseph (chaps. 16–17)
   F. Lands Given to Remaining Tribes at Shiloh (chaps. 18–19)
   G. Cities of Asylum Set Aside (chap. 20)

---

[11] The three-day period before the crossing of the Jordan parallels the three days set aside for purification before Mount Sinai (Josh 1:11; 3:2; see also Exod 19:10–11).

H.   Levitical Cities Assigned (21:1–42)
I.   Summary of the Lord's Faithfulness (21:43–45)

IV. **Obedience in Canaan (chaps. 22–24)**
A.   Threat of Civil War and Unity Preserved (chap. 22)
B.   Joshua's Farewell Exhortation (chap. 23)
C.   Renewal of Covenant at Shechem (24:1–28)
D.   Graves in the Promised Land (24:29–33)

THE CONTENTS OF THE BOOK

Each of the four sections in the book is characterized by a prominent verb. The key verbs are ʿābar, "cross" (1:1–5:12),[12] lāqaḥ, "take" (5:13–12:24),[13] ḥālaq, "divide" (chaps. 13–21),[14] and ʿābad, "serve" (chaps. 22–24).[15]

1. Entrance into Canaan (1:1–5:12). In 1:1–9 God initiated the call for Israel to cross over into the land of Canaan. The opening temporal reference, "After the death of Moses," functions as a structural marker, but it also indicates at the outset that Joshua, not Moses, would lead the people into the promised land (Deut 3:23–29). God's presence was promised to Joshua as it had been with Moses (Joshua 1:5), and as a result he should be "strong and courageous" to obey the instruction Moses had given (vv. 6–8; see Deut 31:7). This theme permeates the entire book; Israel's success will depend directly on her obedience to the law of the Lord. This section thus forms a natural transition from the Mosaic teaching in the blessing and cursing sections of the Pentateuch (Leviticus 26; Deuteronomy 27–28). The concluding narrative of this section emphasizes the absolute necessity of obedience as Joshua circumcised the new generation of male Israelites (Josh 5:1–12).[16]

The mission of the spies (chap. 2) recalls an earlier, similar event that proved to be unsuccessful (Numbers 13–14), but the cooperation of Rahab the Canaanite holds out the hope for a better sequel.[17] The entrance into the promised land was initiated by God when He parted the Jordan River, allowing the Israelites to pass over (Joshua 3:1–17). The division of the Jordan parallels the dividing of the Red Sea, which may be considered the formative saving event in the OT. The parting of the Red Sea effected an exit from Egypt, whereas the parting of the Jordan River effected an entrance into the land of Canaan. In both accounts God's people passed through the water on dry ground. After erecting a memorial of 12 stones to commemorate the crossing of the Jordan, the Israelites established their base camp at Jericho (chap. 4).

As mentioned above, the necessity of obedience is reinforced by the concluding narrative of the section wherein Joshua in obedience to the law circumcised the new generation of male Israelites and led them in the celebration of the Passover at Gilgal (5:1–12). This celebration formally concluded the period of wilderness wanderings, and manna was no longer provided. The performance of circumcision links this event with the promises made to Abraham and the covenant relationship with the Lord (Gen 17:9–14). The celebration of the Passover explicitly

---

[12] See Josh 1:2,11(twice),14; 2:23; 3:1–2,4,6,11,14,16–17(twice); 4:1,3,5,7–8,10–13,23(twice); 5:1.

[13] See Josh 6:18; 7:1,11,21,23–24; 8:1,12; 9:4,11,14; 11:16,19,23.

[14] See Josh 13:7; 14:5; 19:2,10,51. The nominal form ḥēleq is also in Josh 14:4; 15:13; 18:5–7,9; 19:9.

[15] See Josh 22:5,27; 23:7,16; 24:2,10,14(twice),15(twice),16,18–19,21–22,24,31. The nominal form ʿebed, "servant," is found in Josh 22:2,4–5; 24:17,29.

[16] Statements about the preparation of Joshua are in Exod 33:11; Num 27:12–23; Deut 3:23–29; 31:1–8; and 34:9.

[17] J. G. McConville, "Joshua," in *Theological Interpretation of the Old Testament*, ed. K. J. Vanhoozer (Grand Rapids: Baker Academic, 2008), 86.

links this event with the deliverance from Egypt. Passover, considered the most holy of Israel's festivals, was celebrated at the beginning of the Israelite journey from Egypt to Canaan and now at the end. Circumcision was required before a male could participate in the Passover celebration (Exod 12:43–49).

2. The Conquest of Canaan (5:13–12:24). Three primary models have been proposed to account for the means by which the Israelites came to be in possession of the land of Canaan. In the traditional model the conquest of Canaan resulted from a large-scale invasion by the Israelites, resulting in major victories in Canaanite cities and towns.[18] The second model, known as the sedentary infiltration model, suggests that the Israelites came to occupy the land of Canaan by a gradual infiltration into the land. Other migrating groups, including possibly Canaanites, may have joined forces with Israelite tribes. The account of the alliance with the Gibeonites (chap. 9) serves as an illustration of this model. This sort of alliance, it is argued, occurred on numerous occasions and is not to be relegated to the single account mentioned in Joshua.[19] The third model for the conquest depicts the conquest as the result of a "peasant revolt" in which many native inhabitants (who may have joined a small number of outsiders) revolted against those in power, leading to a social and political upheaval. The example of Rahab (chap. 2) may serve as a model for this view.[20]

Only the traditional model accurately reflects the narrative description of the conquest in Joshua. The biblical account describes the conquest as resulting from the invasion of the united tribes of Israel from outside the nation of Canaan.

This second major section, like the first, begins with a divine encounter (5:13–15). This encounter indicates that what will subsequently transpire will be at God's initiative as the success of the ensuing battles will be because of His power, not because of Israel's military strategies. In this encounter Joshua is seen as Moses' successor, and he appears as a "second Moses." Like Moses, Joshua had to remove his sandals in God's presence because he was on holy ground (5:15; cf. Exod 3:5). God, as Israel's military commander (Josh 5:14–15), manifested Himself before the invasion of Jericho was to begin. God's appearance before this battle represents His involvement in all of Israel's military campaigns. The conquest of Jericho serves as a paradigm for all other military victories (8:1–2; 10:28,30). Following the divine appearance this second section includes five narratives: the conquest of Jericho, the defeat at Ai, the surrender of Gibeon, victory over the kings of the south, and victory over the kings of the north.

The Israelites conquered Jericho (chap. 6) and then Ai (7:2–8:28), dividing Canaan in two and making it impossible for the Canaanite city-states in the north to form a coalition with those in the south.[21] In response to these victories the Gibeonites tricked the Israelites into forming an alliance (chap. 9),[22] provoking the kings of Jerusalem, Hebron, Jarmuth, Lachish, and Eglon to form a military coalition (10:1–4).[23] Unlike the central Canaan

---

[18] See E. H. Merrill, *Kingdom of Priests*, 2nd ed. (Grand Rapids: Baker, 2008), 110–59; and W. C. Kaiser Jr., *A History of Israel* (Nashville: B&H, 1998), 143–61.

[19] See G. Fohrer, *Introduction to the Old Testament*, trans. David E. Green (Nashville: Abingdon, 1968), 199; and V. H. Matthews and J. C. Moyer, *The Old Testament: Text and Context* (Peabody, MA: Hendrickson, 1997), 70.

[20] See N. Gottwald, *The Tribes of Yahweh: A Sociology of the Religion of Liberated Israel, 1250—1050 B.C.E.* (Maryknoll, NY: Orbis, 1962); and B. Bandstra, *Reading the Old Testament* (Belmont, CA: Wadsworth, 1995), 223.

[21] Moreover, the Israelite forces employed such techniques as decoys, ambushes, deception, surprise (8:6,16; 10:9–10; 11:7–8), the organization of equipment and food supplies (1:10–11), and dispatching intelligence operations (chap. 2).

[22] The Mosaic instruction for forming a peaceful alliance is recorded in Deut 20:10–15. Israel was not to make a covenant with any nation after they settled in Canaan (Exod 23:32; 34:12; Deut 7:2).

[23] In Gen 14:2 and Josh 13:3 five kings joined together to form a military coalition.

campaigns in chaps. 6–9 in which Israel initiated the conquest, the southern Canaan alliance attacked Gibeon, forcing Gibeon's ally, the Israelites, into a conflict (10:5). Joshua surprised the Canaanite coalition at Gibeon and was able to rout the enemy thoroughly as God cast hailstones from heaven and caused the sun to stand still (10:11–13).[24] This miracle parallels the divine protection the Israelites experienced during several of the plagues on Egypt (Exod 9:4,6,26; 10:23). Because of the extraordinary success of the Israelites, Jabin, king of Hazor, forged an alliance with some northern Canaanite kings to fight against the Israelites. Anticipating an attack, Joshua took the offensive, launching a surprise attack. The northern coalition was dispersed, and Hazor, the principal city state of northern Canaan, was burned (Josh 11:1–5). Even though the northern coalition was equipped with horses and chariots, God displayed His power and had the horses hamstrung and the chariots burned (11:4–9).[25] The victories over the kings of Canaan (12:7–24) were a joyful reversal of the tyranny of the Israelites' hardships under the king of Egypt.[26]

3. The Division of Canaan (chaps. 13–21). As with the previous sections this one too opens with a divine encounter (13:1–7). It provides detailed descriptions of the boundaries of the land and the allotments for each tribe. Though the land portions are not identical in size, there is an inherent equality among the tribal portions (1:6). In chaps. 13–14 the lands are apportioned by use of the lot, which suggests that the divisions were ultimately made by divine initiative. This section concludes with references to the cities of refuge (chap. 20) and the cities assigned for the Levites (21:1–42). The provision for the Levites was a reminder once again of the importance the law would play in the life of Israel in the promised land (1:7–8). The law of Moses had established that these special places were to be set aside for the Levites after the Israelites set up residence in the land of Canaan (Deut 1:38; 3:28). This section thus records the fulfillment of the promise of the land given to Abraham (Gen 12:1–3).

4. Obedience in Canaan (chaps. 22–24). This final section of the book addresses the subject of the proper service of God in Canaan. Reverence and love for God required obedience to the law, particularly avoiding the idolatrous influence of the remaining nations of Canaan (Josh 23:7–13). The law also called on the people to recognize that the land was God's gift (23:9–11), to avoid intermarriages (23:12–13), and to be committed to covenant faithfulness (23:15–16). The building of the altar across the Jordan posed a potential threat to the pure worship of God, but the contentious issue was quickly resolved (22:10–34).

Covenant renewal and rededication took place at Shechem (24:1), the first place Abram reached in the promised land. Abram and Jacob built altars at this sacred site (Gen 12:6–7; 33:18–20). The experience of Joshua's generation thus paralleled the worship experience of the forefathers and is a testimony to the Lord's continuous faithfulness. This service and worship of the Lord could be viewed as the ultimate purpose for Israel's occupation of Canaan. It was a response to God's faithfulness.

SPECIAL ISSUES IN THE BOOK

Apiru

As mentioned above, the area of Canaan was subject to various military threats in the mid-second millennium BC. Many have argued that the threat of the "Apiru" mentioned in the

---

[24] See W. C. Kaiser Jr., *More Hard Sayings of the Old Testament* (Downers Grove, IL: InterVarsity, 1992), 123–26.

[25] R. B. Chisholm Jr., *Interpreting the Historical Books* (Grand Rapids: Kregel, 2006), 90.

[26] McConville, "Joshua," 86.

Amarna letters (c. 1400 BC) is the same as the military incursions of the Israelites during the time of Joshua. Several scholars have maintained that the Apiru were the Hebrews and that there is sufficient agreement between the data presented in the Amarna letters and the book of Joshua to see a connection between the two. However, despite this resemblance there is a growing consensus that the Apiru were composed of nonethnic groups linked by social and political factors, and while they caused great difficulties for the Canaanites, they should not be equated with the Israelites. The situations described in the Amarna Letters regarding the problems with the Apiru probably occurred shortly after the Israelite conquest.[27]

Destruction of the Canaanites

A troubling topic for many Christians today is the annihilation of the inhabitants of Canaan by the Israelites. Many contrast this practice with the NT focus on the love of enemies (Matt 5:44) and have concluded that the God of the OT seems to be different from the God and Father of the Lord Jesus Christ. This practice of annihilating the Canaanites and destroying objects used in pagan worship is called a *ḥērem*, based on the Hebrew term used to depict this activity. This term was also used in the ninth-century Mesha inscription, which called for the massacre of the Israelite population of Ataroth in the dedication of the inhabitants of that town to the Moabite god Chemosh.

That God was just in issuing the command to annihilate the Canaanites may be argued on the basis of two reasons. First, the Canaanites received this judgment at the hand of the Israelites as a just payment for their own national sinfulness. God had promised Abraham that the Israelites would not be able to enter the promised land until the iniquity of the Amorite (i.e., Canaanite) was complete (Gen 15:16). The Israelite invasion of Canaan some 600 years after this promise to Abraham indicated that the iniquity of the Canaanites had now reached its saturation point and that they were now to be judged by the Israelite nation (see Lev 20:23; Deut 9:4–5).[28] Thus the conquest was a just act of God's punishment on wickedness and not gross aggression on the part of the nation Israel. Far more generations of Israelites experienced God's wrath at the hand of her enemies when Israel had broken covenant and lived in disobedience to the Lord.[29]

Second, the Israelites were commanded to destroy the Canaanites in order to maintain the preservation of Israel. As Israel was in a covenant relationship with God, the reception of the blessing of God for any particular Israelite generation depended on Israel's obedience to the laws that had been revealed to Moses. If Israel had shared the land with the Canaanites, the purity of the Israelites would be potentially jeopardized, as the Canaanites would lead the Israelites to immorality and idolatry. This would constitute a threat to Israel's purity and hence survival (Leviticus 26; Deuteronomy 28).

Also the command to annihilate the Canaanites was limited to a single generation and to this particular occasion when Israel was to invade and conquer the promised land. It was necessary in Joshua's day for Israel to render to the Canaanites the wages of their sins. Moreover, God was preserving the Israelites from assimilating and adopting foreign and immoral practices. Also while God ordered the Israelites to destroy the Canaanites, the instruction to totally demolish the physical structures of a habitation was directed only toward those Canaanites

---

[27] Bimson, *Redating the Exodus and Conquest*; Merrill, *Kingdom of Priests*. See chap. 3 in this volume, "The Cultural World of the Old Testament."

[28] Moses listed a litany of the offenses of the Canaanites in Lev 18:6–23.

[29] See C. Wright, *Old Testament Ethics for the People of God* (Downers Grove, IL: InterVarsity, 2004), 476–77.

who occupied the three cities of Jericho, Ai, and Hazor. God did not require this comprehensive judgment upon all Israel's pagan enemies. But ultimately even the destruction of the Canaanites will bring praise from the nations (Deut 32:43).[30]

Conflict with Judges

One argument in defense of the gradual infiltration view of the conquest is the supposed discrepancy between the conquest as described in Joshua and the occupation described in the book of Judges. Critics have argued that Judges 1 describes a gradual infiltration by separate tribes and clans. This is particularly evident in Judg 1:1–2:5 and 2:6–3:6, which states that the individual tribes were to complete the conquest by driving out from the Canaanite enclaves those inhabitants the nation had not yet succeeded in displacing. This more gradual occupation of the land, it is argued, is in direct contradiction with the book of Joshua which seems to describe a swift and violent entry of the Israelites into the land of Canaan.

The view that Joshua describes a swift and comprehensive conquest and occupation of Canaan is not totally consistent with the facts of the book of Joshua. While Josh 11:23; 21:43–45 could be understood as indicating that the entire land had been conquered, other passages in Joshua indicate that not every city had come under Israelite control (13:1–6; 15:63; 16:10; 17:12–13; 18:2–3; 23:4–5,13). This is harmonious with what is indicated in the book of Judges. Judges 1 is thus an account of the battles of the individual tribes that followed the period of national warfare described in the book of Joshua. The narratives in the book of Joshua do not describe immediate occupation of the conquered territories by the Israelites. The Philistines for example remained in control of the land along the Mediterranean Sea (13:2–3), while the cities of Tyre, Sidon, and Gebal remained under Phoenician control. The book of Joshua completely separates the national war from the occupation of the territory. Joshua kept the nation in camp for the duration of the war, without occupying a single city. The conquest of the land recorded in Joshua shows that the promise to Abraham's descendants to occupy the land of Canaan was now coming to fruition. The possession of Canaan was now finally decided.

TEXT

The Hebrew text of the book of Joshua has been well preserved. The MT is supported by all the major versions, and there are no variant readings of any significance.

THE THEOLOGICAL THEMES OF THE BOOK

Land

As noted above, the fulfillment of the patriarchal promise that the Israelites would occupy the land of Canaan should be understood as the purpose of the book of Joshua.[31] The focus on the land of Canaan for the Israelites has been the central focus of the pentateuchal narrative beginning with Num 10:11–12 when the Israelites broke camp at Sinai and began their trek toward the promised land. Thus the giving of the land in the book of Joshua is a testimony to God's faithfulness to His promises to both the patriarchs (Josh 1:6; 5:6; 21:43–44) and the nation. The promise of the land to Abraham and the patriarchs of Israel is widely attested (Gen 12:1; 15:18–21; 17:8; 26:3; 28:4,13; 35:12; 48:6,16,21–22; Exod 3:8,17; 6:8; 13:5; 23:23, 28–33; 33:1–3; 34:11; Num 34:29; Deut 1:7–8; 3:21; 7:16,19; 9:1–3; 11:23–25; 31:3–8;

---

[30] Ibid., 474.

[31] References to God giving the land to Israel occur more than 50 times in the book of Joshua.

Josh 1:2–5). Chisholm has stated that the dominant theme of the book of Joshua is the faithfulness of God.[32]

In the same way the exodus of Egypt—the formative act of deliverance in the OT—was a demonstration of God's power, so the conquest of Canaan was because of God's direct intervention. The exodus itself is replicated in a real sense in the experience of the Israelites in the book of Joshua. As in the exodus, Yahweh was to be viewed as a warrior (Exod 15:3). God took the initiative in the conquest, just as He had done in choosing Abraham and his descendants, leading Israel out of Egypt, and establishing a covenant with Abraham's descendants at Mount Sinai. Canaan was delivered into Joshua's hand not because of superior military acumen, but as a gift of the grace of God as Israel responded to God's commands in obedience (Amos 2:10). God used human obedience to accomplish His purposes. Yet the outcome of each military encounter was determined by God's will (Josh 6:2; 8:1; 10:8; 11:6). The Lord even determined the military strategies of the Canaanites to ensure their defeat (11:20). That the outcome of each military victory was directly due to the intervention of Yahweh is apparent in Israel's lone military defeat at Ai. This loss is not attributable to inferior military might but rather to transgression against the Lord (7:11–12). Before further military campaigns could be undertaken, the Israelites did not need to retrain or to revise their strategy; they had to deal with sin (7:24–26).

The conquest of Canaan to occupy the land is one of the most important events in OT history. Much of the legislation in Exodus–Deuteronomy is addressed to the nation Israel settled in the land of Canaan. Occupation of the land is the central theme in the book of Joshua.[33] If the people of God were to live there as God intended, their occupation of the land would result in blessing for all nations. The hope and longing of the postexilic prophets was the return to the land. God gave the land to Israel because it is His land (Lev 25:23; Ps 24:1), and He decided to give the land to Israel for His own purposes.

Joshua and the Law

From the very first encounter Joshua had with God in the book of Joshua, adherence to the law of God is shown to be absolutely essential for Joshua's success (Josh 1:8). In 8:34 Joshua read the blessings and cursings according to Moses' command (Deut 27:1–8). Later he set up cities of refuge in obedience to the law (Josh 20:1–9; cf. Deut 19:1–13). The defeat of the Anakim is depicted as a fulfillment of what had been promised (Josh 11:21; cf. Deut 9:2). Moreover the "hornet" (Josh 24:12) that expels the enemy was promised in Deut 7:20.[34]

Israel's obligation to carry out covenant compliance with the Mosaic law is also stressed in Joshua 22–24. These passages reflect the fact in the Mosaic law that faithfulness to the Mosaic covenant would determine Israel's future (Leviticus 26; Deuteronomy 27–28). Occupation of the land was directly linked to obedience (Deut 4:1,25–27,40; 6:17–18; 8:1; 11:8; 30:15–20; 32:46–47; see Josh 10:40; 11:20,23; 23:9–13,15–16).[35] Failure to obey would result in expulsion (Lev 26:27–35; Deut 28:58–68). Ironically Rahab, the pagan Canaanite, acted in faith and was obedient whereas Achan, the Israelite, disobeyed and was destroyed.

---

[32] Chisholm, *Interpreting the Historical Books*, 89.

[33] W. Brueggemann, *The Land* (Philadelphia: Fortress, 1977), 3.

[34] See B. Childs, *Introduction to the Old Testament as Scripture* (Philadelphia: Fortress, 1979), 245–46.

[35] One perpetual reminder of the consequences of obedience and disobedience can be seen from the two heaps of stones erected after the defeat and then after the victory at Ai (Josh 7:25–26; 8:29). See Chisholm, *Interpreting the Historical Books*, 91.

Fellowship with God

As noted in discussing the organization of the book of Joshua, the worship or service of God is the final and culminating section toward which the book progresses. An important purpose for Israel's occupation of Canaan was to provide a platform for worshipping God. This idea is harmonious with the creation of mankind in the creation week that culminates in sanctification of the seventh day as a holy day for worship. Similarly the exodus itself culminates with the building of the tabernacle, the place of worship. If H. J. Koorevaar's structural arrangement of Joshua 13–21 is accepted, a case could be made that the presence of God in the midst of the land is the central theme. Koorevaar arranges this section as follows:[36]

A.   13:8–33 Transjordan for 2 1/2 tribes
    B.   14:1–5 The principles of the division
        C.   14:6–15 Beginning: Caleb's inheritance
            D.   15:1–17:18 The lot for Judah and Joseph
                E.   18:1–10 **The Tent of Meeting taken to Shiloh and the apportioning of the land**
            D^1.   18:11–19:48 The lot for the seven remaining tribes
        C^1.   19:49–51 Ending: Joshua's inheritance
    B^1.   20:1–6 God's fourth initiative: designating cities of refuge
A^1.   20:7–21:42 Cities of refuge and levitical cities

This focus on the tabernacle, the physical manifestation of the presence of God, explains the preeminence of the ark in the preceding narratives of Joshua. The ark is mentioned in conjunction with the crossing of the Jordan (3:3–4,6,8,11,13–15; 4:5,7,9–11,16,18), the capture of Jericho (6:4,6–9,11–13), the sin of Achan (7:6), and the covenant renewal ceremony at Mount Ebal where the Law was read (8:33). The presence of God is promised to Joshua himself (1:9) and is mentioned also in 8:1; 10:8; 11:6.[37]

And yet in spite of this renewal and the faithfulness of God's presence, there is also the hard reality that the nation would fail to keep God's commands (24:19; see Deut 9:4–7). They would show signs of assimilation to the Canaanite way of life (Josh 23:9–13). This disappointment is recorded repeatedly in the subsequent pages of the OT.

Joshua and Biblical Revelation

The conquest of Canaan is discussed very little in the OT outside the book of Joshua. The victories of the conquest are mentioned in Ps 135:10–11, which emphasizes God's work on Israel's behalf. The focus in the psalm, as in the book of Joshua, is on the Lord who brought about the defeat of the Canaanite peoples. The same conclusion was also drawn by the apostle Paul in Acts 13:19 before the Jews of Antioch of Pisidia.

Joshua shares the same name with Jesus, and he also typifies the work of Christ in the NT. Much as Joshua led the people into the promised land and allotted their territories, Jesus brings believers today into promised rest (Acts 20:32; 26:18; Heb 4:8–9). The temporary entering of rest gained by Joshua was a type of the spiritual and eternal rest given by Christ. The extension of the application of the conquest to the believer's life is anticipated in Ps 95:7–8, which is quoted by the author of Hebrews (Heb 4:7).

---

[36] H. J. Koorevaar, cited in J. Robert Vannoy, "Joshua, Theology of," in *NIDOTTE*, 4:814.
[37] Ibid., 4:818–19.

Moreover, the account of Rahab, a type of all non-Israelites who embrace Israel's God and who even became a member of the messianic line (Matt 1:5), is recorded in Josh 2:1–24.

STUDY QUESTIONS

1. What was the nature of the international scene at the time of Joshua?
2. What seems to be the difference between the account of the conquest in Joshua and Judges?
3. What are the parallels between Moses and Joshua?
4. What event does the dividing of the Jordan River evoke?
5. What are the three models for the conquest of Canaan?
6. Where did the covenant renewal ceremony take place in the book of Joshua?
7. Where do we find references to the Apiru?
8. Are the Apiru to be identified with the Hebrews?
9. Why were the Israelites commanded to annihilate the Canaanites?
10. What does the book of Joshua say about the total and comprehensive defeat of the Canaanites?
11. How important is the occupation of the land of Canaan for God's purposes for Israel?
12. What does the book of Joshua have to do with the worship of God?

FOR FURTHER STUDY

Bimson, J. J. *Redating the Exodus and Conquest*. Sheffield: JSOT Press, 1978.

Boling, R. *Joshua*. Garden City, NY: Doubleday, 1982.

Brueggemann, W. *The Land*. Philadelphia: Fortress, 1977.

Childs, B. "A Study of the Formula, 'Until This Day.'" *JBL* 82 (1963): 279–92.

———. *Introduction to the Old Testament As Scripture*. Philadelphia: Fortress, 1979.

Chisholm, R. B., Jr. *Interpreting the Historical Books*. Grand Rapids: Kregel, 2006.

Cragie, P. C. *The Problem of War in the Old Testament*. Grand Rapids: Eerdmans, 1978.

Hess, R. S. *Joshua*. Downers Grove, IL: InterVarsity, 1996.

Howard, D. M., Jr. *Joshua*. Nashville: B&H, 1999.

Kaufmann, Y. *The Biblical Account of the Conquest of Palestine*. Jerusalem: Magnes, 1953.

Longman, T. III, and D. Reid. *God Is a Warrior: Studies in Old Testament Biblical Theology*. Grand Rapids: Zondervan, 1995.

Mattingly, Gerald. "The Exodus-Conquest and the Archaeology of Transjordan: New Light on an Old Problem." *GTJ* 4: 245–62.

McConville, J. G. "Joshua." In *Theological Interpretation of the Old Testament*. Edited by K. J. Vanhoozer, 83–91. Grand Rapids: Baker Academic, 2008.

Merrill, E. H. *Kingdom of Priests*. 2nd ed. Grand Rapids: Baker, 2008.

Rooker, M. "Conquest." In *NIDOTTE*. Edited by W. VanGemeren, 4:487–91. Grand Rapids: Zondervan, 1997.

Wenham, Gordon. "The Deuteronomic Theology of the Book of Joshua." *JBL* 90 (1971): 140–48.

Wiseman, D. J. *Peoples of Old Testament Times*. Oxford: Oxford University Press, 1973.

Wood, B. G. "Did the Israelites Conquer Jericho? A New Look at the Archaeological Evidence." *BAR* 16 (1990): 44–58.

———. "Dating Jericho's Destruction: Bienkowski Is Wrong on All Counts." *BAR* 6 (1990): 45–49, 69.

Woudstra, Martin. *The Book of Joshua*. NICOT. Grand Rapids: Eerdmans, 1981.

Wright, Christopher. *Old Testament Ethics for the People of God*. Downers Grove: InterVarsity Press, 2004.

Yadin, Yigael. "Is the Biblical Account of the Israelite Conquest of Canaan Historically Reliable?" *BAR* 8 (1982): 16–23.

Young, Edward J. "The Alleged Secondary Deuteronomic Passages in the Book of Joshua." *EvQ* 25 (1953): 142–57.

Younger, K. L., Jr. *Ancient Conquest Accounts*. JSOTSup. Sheffield: JSOT Press, 1990.

Zevit, Ziony. "Problems of Ai." *BAR* 11 (1985): 56–69.

CHAPTER 16

THE BOOK OF JUDGES

MARK F. ROOKER

THE TITLE OF THE BOOK

The English title Judges, like the LXX and Vulgate translations, is based on the literal translation of the Hebrew name *šōpeṭîm*.

Reference to "the time of the judges," as described in the book, became so commonplace so as to mark a certain epoch in Israel's history (see Ruth 1:1; 2 Kgs 23:22).

THE COMPOSITION OF JUDGES

Early in the twentieth century many scholars argued that the book of Judges passed through a lengthy process of development. First, there was an oral stage when many of the individual stories about the judges were developed. Later these oral traditions were committed to writing by the authors often identified as the authors of the pentateuchal sources (J and E). Then a Deuteronomic editor reworked the material in Judg 2:6–16:31 to show that the punishment of the exile had resulted from violating the Deuteronomic code.[1] This was followed by a final redaction of the book in the postexilic period which included the introduction (1:1–2:5) and the appendixes (17:1–21:25), both of which included much earlier material.

Though this was the general explanation for the composition of the book of Judges, there were differences of opinion among the critics regarding the pentateuchal sources that were used in Judges. Otto Eissfeldt, for example, argued that the L, J, and E narratives found in the Pentateuch continued through the book of Judges. Sellin and Fohrer maintained that J and E were used only up to 2:5. They argued that 1:1–2:5 was extracted from the Hexateuch and inserted at the beginning of Judges in the postexilic period.[2]

---

[1] The characteristics of the deuteronomist include the sermonic style and emphasis on the word of God spoken through His spokesman, whether Moses, Joshua, or a judge.

[2] J. Sellin and G. Fohrer, *Introduction to the Old Testament*, trans. D. E. Green (Nashville: Abingdon, 1968), 197–98.

The approach that attempts to find pentateuchal sources in the book of Judges has been largely abandoned beginning with the seminal work of Martin Noth.[3] Noth proposed that Deuteronomy through 2 Kings formed a literary and theological unity that contained the narrative from the exodus to the exile. This analysis was at odds with those who argued that the contents of the book were based on the pentateuchal sources, particularly J and E. For Judges Noth claimed that a Deuteronomic compiler had united the narratives of early tribal heroes (the major judges) with the minor judges who were actual individual leaders of an amphictyony and responsible for sacral duties at a central shrine. The analogy was based on the actual tribal organization of ancient Greece in the first millennium BC.

Noth's hypothesis, which removed the need for positing the pentateuchal sources in Judges, has been modified in recent times, especially through the efforts of Frank Cross. Unlike Noth, Cross argued for two redactional layers in the Deuteronomic history, including layer 1 from the time of Josiah and layer 2 from the time of the exile. The first layer was responsible for passages that seem to contain unconditional promises composed at the time of Josiah, while the second layer focused on the conditional nature of Israel's relationship to God and was composed in the exile. In addition, Noth's position on the organization of the Israelite tribes has come under fire. For Noth's position to be valid the Israelite tribes had to have gone through a substantial period as independent tribes. However, there is no textual evidence in the book of Judges that the individual Israelite tribes viewed themselves as autonomous. The book of Judges in its entirety clearly indicates that tribes had a consciousness of belonging to one nation. This is supported by the fact that the name "Israel" occurs more frequently in the book of Judges than in any other OT book.[4] None of the Greek amphictyonies had anything that closely paralleled the Sinaitic covenant, the key component for the unity of the Israelite tribes.

Modern scholarship is continuing to distance itself from the earlier critical views including the position that Deuteronomic authors played a major role in the composition of Judges. While it is true that the theology of the book of Deuteronomy informs the contents of Judges, this does not necessitate positing a Deuteronomic author. In fact in several places the book of Judges does not reflect a Deuteronomic slant. The Deuteronomic ideology is critical of the monarchy (Deut 17:14–20), placing more faith in the prophets (Deut 18:15–19; 1 Kgs 12:22–24) as well as depicting God as transcendant residing in the temple (Deut 12:5–28; 1 Kgs 8:16–21). The book of Judges, on the other hand, reflects a positive view of the monarchy and is virtually silent about prophetic activity. There is no stress in the book on the centralization of worship that is found in Deuteronomy. In current research the focus is now on synchronic analysis, that is, reading the text as a coherent literary unity.[5]

According to Jewish tradition Samuel was largely responsible for the composition of the book of Judges. While this remains a possibility, most scholars have abandoned this view.[6] A more attractive option is the one that sees the book as composed early in the time of the

---

[3] M. Noth, *The Deuteronomistic History*, trans. D. Orton, JSOTSup (Sheffield: JSOT Press, 1981).

[4] See D. Block, *Judges, Ruth*, NAC (Nashville: B&H, 1999), 30–31, for a comprehensive discussion of the unity of the Israelite tribes in the time of the judges.

[5] See, e.g., F. E. Greenspahn, "The Theology of the Framework of Judges," *VT* 36 (1986): 395; B. G. Webb, *The Book of Judges. An Integrated Reading*, JSOTSup (Sheffield: JSOT Press, 1987); and R. O. O'Connell, *Rhetoric of the Book of Judges*, VTSup (Leiden: Brill, 1996).

[6] E.g., G. L. Archer argues that either Samuel or one of his disciples was responsible for the compiling the contents of the book (*A Survey of Old Testament Introduction*, 3rd ed. [Chicago: Moody, 1994], 303).

monarchy as the author either combined or utilized the earlier sources and traditions about individual judges.[7]

Several factors favor a date of composition early in the history of Israel. According to Judg 1:21 the Jebusites were still living in Jerusalem when Judges was written. These circumstances describe a historical reality before David's capture of the city in 2 Sam 5:6–10. In Judg 1:29 it is reported that the Canaanites occupied Gezer. This set of circumstances reflects a time before the city was given as a gift to Solomon by Pharaoh (970 BC; 1 Kgs 9:16). Also Sidon is mentioned before Tyre in Judges 3:3, indicating that it was the superior Phoenician port. It is virtually universally accepted however that beginning in the twelfth century BC. Tyre became the superior Phoenician port. These facts, along with passages such as Judg 18:1 and 19:1 which suggest that there was not yet a king in Israel, may all indicate that the book was written early in the Israelite monarchy. Critical to the discussion of the time of composition of the book is the editorial reference in Judg 18:30 that the descendants of Jonathan, the grandson of Moses,[8] served as priests to the Danites "until the day of the captivity of the land" (NASB). The latter phrase has been taken to refer to the defeat of the northern kingdom in 722 BC, the captivity of the southern kingdom in 586 BC, or the fall of Shiloh in 1 Sam 4:10–11. All of these suggestions are defensible. However, the latter has contextual support as the statement "all the time that the house of God was at Shiloh" (until c. 1104 BC)[9] in the following verse (Judg 18:31) might be viewed as parallel and thus explanatory to the phrase "until the day of the captivity of the land."

Possibly, however, the narratives of individual judges may have had a prior independent existence. These written sources would have been produced shortly after the events they describe, and were later joined together by the author. Even critics concede that the written source documents for the book of Judges would have been composed before the period of David and Solomon.[10] It seems that the contents of the book were known to other biblical writers at a very early period (1 Sam 12:9–11; 2 Sam 11:21; Pss 68:8–15; 83; Isa 9:3; Hos 9:9; 10:1).

ANCIENT NEAR EASTERN BACKGROUND

During the time of the judges, when the nation of Israel was frequently engaged in conflicts with neighboring countries, the major ANE powers were preoccupied with their own difficulties. This providential set of circumstances left the Israelites and the remaining Canaanites virtually undisturbed.

The Assyrian king Asshur-uballit (1365–1330 BC) occupied the throne at the beginning of the period of the judges, but he was apprehensive about the Kassites to the south and the Mitannian Hurrians to the west. The Hittite power, which was weakening during the time of the judges, came to the end of its existence with the Sea Peoples providing the knockout blow in about 1200 BC. The Egyptian power had a virtual "hands-off" policy toward the land of Canaan during this time, as indicated by the continual calls from Canaanite authorities for Egyptian aid in the Amarna letters. Thus the Israelites in the hill country and the Canaanites in the coastal regions and lowlands were not threatened or influenced by the major foreign powers during the time of the judges.[11]

---

[7] R. K. Harrison, *Introduction to the Old Testament* (Grand Rapids: Eerdmans, 1969), 690.

[8] Some textual evidence suggests that the name is Manasseh rather than Moses.

[9] E. Merrill, *Kingdom of Priests* (Grand Rapids: Baker, 1987), 176.

[10] E.g., Sellin and Fohrer, *Introduction to the Old Testament*, 208.

[11] See Merrill, *Kingdom of Priests*, 152–58.

CHRONOLOGY OF THE JUDGES

The number of years of the successive reigns of the 12 judges totals 410.[12]

3:8	Israel served Cushan-Rishathaim	8 years
3:9–11	Deliverance by Othniel; land rests	40 years
3:14	Israel served Eglon	18 years
3:20,30	Deliverance by Ehud; land rests	80 years
4:2–3	Oppression by Jabin	20 years
5:31	Deliverance by Deborah; land rests	40 years
6:1	Oppression by Midian	7 years
8:28	Deliverance by Gideon; land rests	40 years
9:22	Abimelech reigned over Israel	3 years
10:2	Tolah judged Israel	23 years
10:3	Jair judged Israel	22 years
10:8	Oppression by Ammon	18 years
12:7	Jephthah judged Israel	6 years
12:9	Izban judged Israel	7 years
12:11	Elon judged Israel	10 years
12:14	Abdon judged Israel	8 years
13:1	Oppression by Philistines	40 years
15:20; 16:31	Samson judged Israel	20 years
		410 years

If one adds to this number the 40 years in the wilderness, the 40 years under Eli (1 Sam 4:18), 20 years for Samuel (1 Sam 7:2,15), 40 years of David, and 4 for Solomon (1 Kgs 6:1), one would have to place the exodus in the year 1524 BC.[13] This chronology fits neither the early nor the late date for the exodus and the conquest. The normal solution for this chronological dilemma has been to acknowledge that many of the judges had authority over only a restricted region and that many of the judges overlapped in time. Arranging overlapping rulerships in a consecutive sequence has been demonstrated in other written documents of the ANE.[14]

THE ROLE OF THE JUDGES

A casual reading of the book of Judges reveals that the main characters of the book, the judges, were not engaged primarily in legal disputes but rather functioned more like military leaders.[15] Moreover, Judg 2:16, the introductory summation to the period, explicitly states that the judges *saved* (yāša') the Israelites from the foreign oppressors that had been sent by God to afflict the Israelites for their disobedience.[16] The view that the judges were actually deliverers is also apparent in what might be considered the conclusion of the period of the judges when Samuel stated that the

---

[12] Shamgar, mentioned in 3:30, is considered by many expositors as a judge. However, Block notes that the word "judge" is never used of Shamgar and that his name is not Semitic (*Judges, Ruth,* 172–75).

[13] This excludes the years for the problematic reign of Saul (1 Sam 13:1).

[14] See E. Merrill, "Paul's Use of 'About 450 Years' in Acts 13:20," *BSac* 138 (1981): 254.

[15] Only in the case of Deborah is their mention of anything like a judicial decision or arbitration (4:4–5).

[16] The root *yāša'* is used in various contexts in reference to Othniel (3:9), Ehud (3:15), Shamgar (3:31), Gideon (6:15; 8:22), Tola (10:1), Jephthah (12:3), and Samson (13:5).

judges had been sent by the Lord to deliver the Israelites (1 Sam 12:10–11).[17] The Hebrew word *šôpēṭ* ("judge") is thus broader than the normal English meaning, as indicated for example by its parallel occurrence with *mlk* ("king") in Isa 33:22. The broader usage is borne out by the cognate uses of the root *špṭ* in Akkadian, Ugaritic, and Phoenician.[18]

PURPOSE OF THE BOOK

The reason the book of Judges was written can be determined from the two major refrains of the book: "The Israelites did what was evil in the Lord's sight" (Judg 2:11; 3:7,12; 4:1; 6:1; 10:6; 13:1) and "In those days there was no king in Israel; everyone did whatever he wanted" (17:6; 21:25). Taking these two statements together shows that the book is concerned with describing Israel's relationship to God between the period of Joshua and the monarchy. It shows the outworking of Israel's covenant relationship with God where obedience to the Law resulted in blessing and peace, whereas disobedience led to hardship and oppression. The overall effect would be a call to Israel to return to her God from her idolatrous ways as her position as a holy nation was in jeopardy.[19] Focusing primarily on the second refrain, many argue that the purpose of the book is to demonstrate that a centralized kingship was necessary for the well-being of the covenant community.[20] Boling maintains that the structure of the work, which he argues focuses on the abortive attempt to establish the monarchy at Shechem, supports this theme.[21]

THE OUTLINE AND STRUCTURE OF THE BOOK

Outline

I. **Israel's Failure in the Holy War (1:1–3:6)**
   A. Failure to Remove the Canaanites (1:1–2:5)
   B. Introduction to Cycles of Apostasy (2:6–3:6)

II. **Cycles of Apostasy and Deliverance (3:7–16:31)**
   A. Othniel (3:7–11)
   B. Ehud (3:12–31)
   C. Deborah (chaps. 4–5)
   D. Gideon (chaps. 6–8)
   E. Abimelech (chap. 9)
   F. Tola and Jair (10:1–5)
   G. Jephthah (10:6–12:7)
   H. Ibzan (12:8–10)
   I. Elon (12:11–12)
   J. Abdon (12:13–15)
   K. Samson (chaps. 13–16)

III. **Depths of the Failure of Israel (chaps. 17–21)**
   A. Breakdown of Religious Life (chaps. 17–18)
   B. Breakdown of Social Order (chaps. 19–21)

---

[17] See P. House, *Old Testament Theology* (Downers Grove, IL: InterVarsity, 1998), 221–22.

[18] See Block, *Judges, Ruth*, 24–25 for a fuller discussion.

[19] See Block, *Joshua, Ruth*, 58; House, *Old Testament Theology*, 225.

[20] E.g., Harrison, *Introduction to the Old Testament*, 692; R. Rendtorff, *The Old Testament Introduction*, trans. J. Bowden (Philadelphia: Fortress, 1986), 169.

[21] R. Boling, "Judges, Book of," in *ADB*, 3:1110.

Structure

The two-part prologue and the two-part epilogue form the frame of the book and include several correspondences. Both involve all the Israelite tribes, feature all the tribes in military action, inquire of God who is to lead in battle, choose Judah to lead in battle (1:1–2; 20:18), depict the Israelites weeping and offering sacrifices (2:1–5; 20:23–26), feature the theme of obtaining wives (1:11–15; 19:1–30; 21:1–25), and refer to Bethel and Jerusalem (1:7–8, 21–26; 19:10–14; 20:18–28).[22] The first prologue section corresponds with the second epilogue while the second prologue corresponds to the first epilogue. This correspondence may be demonstrated as follows:[23]

A   Foreign wars of subjugation with the *herem* being applied (1:1–2:5)
   B   Difficulties with religious idols (2:6–3:6)
   B¹   Difficulties with religious idols (chaps. 17–18)
A¹   Civil wars with the *herem* being applied (chaps. 20–21)

Yet there are contrasts between these sections that underscore the author's message. While in the prologue Judah is successful (1:1–2), in the epilogue Judah is defeated (20:18). Also while there is tribal unity in the prologue, in the epilogue the tribes attack Benjamin.

Within the main section (3:7–16:31) the narratives have been arranged geographically by tribes, ranging from Judah in the south (Othniel, 3:9) to Benjamin (Ehud, 3:15), to Ephraim in the center (Deborah, 4:5), and then to Manasseh (Gideon, 6:15), Gilead (Jephthah, 11:1) and finally to Dan in the north (Samson, 13:2). This corresponds to the order the tribes are presented in the prologue (1:1–36).[24] Virtually every tribe contributed a judge at some point in this period, and no tribe contributed more than one. As for the seven major judges of this section the important judge Gideon occupies the central position:

A   Othniel (3:7–11)
   B   Ehud (3:12–31)
      C   Deborah, Barak, Jael (chaps. 4–5)
         D   Gideon (6:1–8:32)
      C¹   Abimelech (8:33–10:5)
   B¹   Jephthah (10:6–12:15)
A¹   Samson (chaps. 13–16)

While Gideon is the only judge who opposed idolatry, the moral decline in Gideon's own life is a reflection of the nation's spiritual decline as a whole. After the 40 years of peace following Gideon's victory, no more periods of peace are mentioned in the rest of the book (3:11,30;

---

[22] D. A. Dorsey, *The Literary Structure of the Old Testament* (Grand Rapids: Baker, 1999), 118.

[23] See K. Lawson Younger Jr., "Judges 1 in Its Near Eastern Literary Context," in *Faith, Tradition, and History: Old Testament Historiography in Its Near Eastern Context*, ed. A. Millard, J. Hoffmeier, and D. Baker (Winona Lake, IN: Eisenbrown, 1994), 224.

[24] W. Dumbrell, "In Those Days There Was No King In Israel," *JSOT* 25 (1983): 25; D. M. Gunn, "Joshua and Judges," in *The Literary Guide to the Bible*, ed. R. Alter and F. Kermode (Cambridge: Harvard University Press, 1987), 105; Block, *Judges, Ruth*, 59.

4:17; 6:23–24). From the time of Gideon to the end of the book the Israelites were increasingly engaged in internal conflict.[25]

THE CONTENTS OF THE BOOK

I. Israel's Failure in the Holy War (1:1–3:6)

The book of Judges, like the book of Joshua, opens with a reference to the passing of the dominant figure of the previous book: Moses (Josh 1:1) and Joshua (Judg 1:1). The prologue has two parts (1:1–2:5; 2:6–3:6); both of which begin with the report of the tribes taking possession of the land and both of which make reference to the death of Joshua. The first section of the prologue deals primarily with Israel's military failure, giving the narration from the point of view of the Israelites. The second section of the prologue deals with only the nation's moral failure and is perceived from God's viewpoint.

As mentioned in the discussion on the book of Joshua, Israel's military failure is not inconsistent with the book of Joshua as even in that book there were hints that the conquest had not been exhaustive (Josh 11:22; 13:2–6; 15:63; 16:10; 17:12–13). Yet to the degree that this first section does in some sense clash with the overall thrust of Joshua, this initial failure does prepare the reader for the spiritual lapses that typify the rest of the book of Judges. The conquest would be put on hold so that the nation could be tested (Judg 2:20–3:4).[26] The survey of the victories and defeats of seven tribes in Judges 1 begins with victory but quickly moves to defeat. The tribal episodes are arranged in a south-to-north direction, foreshadowing the orientation of the Judges cycle in Judg 3:7–16:31.[27]

After the mention of the death of Joshua in Judg 1:1, the tribe of Judah will be at the forefront in leading the nation to complete the conquest (1:2). While the tribe of Judah subsequently succeeds in seizing their allotted inheritance (1:2–20), the other tribes fail in their efforts to obtain theirs (1:21–36).

Judges 2 further prepares for the main body of the book, 3:7–16:31, by summarizing the almost cyclical nature of the history of the judges. The cycle moves from sin (2:11), to God's wrath (2:14), to foreign oppressors (2:14), to God's mercy (2:18), to deliverance/rest (2:16), to renewed sin (2:19). Most of the narrative units in the next section begin with the statement introducing the cyclical pattern: "The Israelites did what was evil in the Lord's sight" (2:11; 3:7; 4:1; 6:1; 10:6; 13:1). Exceptions to the overall pattern cause discontinuity and are thus of consequence. For example in the Samson narrative there is no cry for God's deliverance and Samson himself dies in the hands of the enemy.

The worship of other gods was a threat to Judah. The Israelites repeatedly followed after Baal, Ashtoroth, as well as other pagan gods (2:11–13,17,19; 3:7; 8:33; 10:6, etc.). The book of Judges particularly addressed the Israelites' devotion to Baal, the god that was believed to be the god of war, thunder, and the storm. Throughout the book idolatry brought defeat and humiliation.[28] Yet, as Block has noted, even in this description of Israel's failure there is every indication of Israel's special relationship to Yahweh. This relationship is based on three impor-

---

[25] For helpful discussion see J. R. Vannoy, "Judges, Theology of," *NIDOTTE*, ed. W. VanGemeren (Grand Rapids: Zondervan, 1997), 4:830.

[26] R. B. Chisholm, *Interpreting the Historical Books* (Grand Rapids: Kregel, 2006), 94.

[27] W. J. Dumbrell, *The Faith of Israel: A Theological Survey of the Old Testament*, 2nd ed. (Grand Rapids: Baker, 2002), 76.

[28] Chisholm, *Interpreting the Historical Books*, 96.

tant truths. (1) God is the God of the Israelite patriarchs (2:12). (2) God delivered Israel from the land of Egypt (2:10,12). (3) God established a covenant with Israel at Mount Sinai.[29]

Thus the first section of the book establishes the fact that Israel has failed to rid the land of Canaan of the Canaanites. This failure led to the apostasy that characterizes the book of Judges.

II. Cycles of Apostasy and Deliverance (3:7–16:31)

The first judge, Othniel, is the only judge who is mentioned prior to his becoming a judge. He captured Debir (Kiriah-sepher) and was given his niece Achsah (Caleb's daughter) as a wife (1:12–13). Othniel was from the tribe of Judah, and he was one of the few exemplary judges (3:7–11). God raised up Othniel to deliver the Israelites form Cushan-rishathaim, king of Mesopotamia. This account uniquely contains all the components in the cycle of the judges: sin (3:7), God's wrath (3:8), foreign oppressor (3:8), God's mercy (3:9), deliverance/rest (3:10–11), and renewed sin (3:12).

The second judge, Ehud, defeated the Moabites by secretly stabbing Moab's obese king Eglon[30] in Eglon's chambers (3:15–30). The text specifies that Ehud was left-handed (3:15). Since most people were right-handed, the assumption may be that if a search for a weapon was made the left side was probably not searched as carefully as the right.

Judges 4–5 records the account of Deborah, Israel's only female judge. Her victory over the Canaanites is the last Canaanite battle in the period of the Judges and could be considered the end of the conquest of Canaan.[31] But the fact that Deborah functioned as a judge, particularly when considered along with Jael's heroic feat, raises questions about the male leadership in Israel. This concern is accentuated by the fact that Barak and the next judge Gideon balk at the idea of their assuming leadership (Judg 4:6–9; 6:1–40). Without adequate male leadership the Lord is forced to use women. That all was not well even in Deborah's victory is also indicated in her victory song, considered one of the oldest poems in the Bible (5:1–31). The song includes denunciations against tribes who did not join in the battle (5:15b–18,23). This lack of unity foreshadows the intertribal disunity recorded in the last chapters of the book.

The Gideon account played an important role in the author's purpose. Unique to this period is what approaches a revival of religious faith in Yahweh as Gideon pulled down the altar of Baal and cut down the Asherah (6:28). The eradication of pagan idols constituted what the nation was to have been doing all along (Deut 7:5), so only here were the people obedient to the command given by Moses and Joshua to the people. Also, unlike the other Judges' narratives here is a lengthy description of how the Israelites were to overcome the Midianites (Judg 7:1–18). And yet, in the end Gideon proved not to be a good example for the nation, for he led the nation into idolatry, fashioning a golden ephod from the people's gold (8:24–27)—"a situation too much like the golden calf incident for theological comfort."[32] Like Aaron, who collected jewelry to erect a gold calf (Exod 32:1–4), Gideon took gold earrings to make an ephod. Accumulating gold for this undertaking ran counter to the Mosaic law, which stated that the king was not to amass gold for himself (Deut 17:17).[33] From this point on in the narrative the Israelites became adversarial to fellow Israelites (Judg 9:5,34–54; 12:1–6; 15:9–13).

---

[29] Block, *Judges, Ruth*, 38.

[30] The name Eglon sounds like the Hebrew word for calf (*'egel*), suggesting that he would be slaughtered like a sacrificial calf.

[31] Y. Kaufmann, *History of the Religion of Israel*, 4th ed., 4 vols. (Jerusalem: Bialik and Dvir, 4 (1956):101 (in Hb.).

[32] P. House, *Old Testament Theology* (Downers Grove, IL: InterVarsity, 1998), 219.

[33] The people seem to have been requesting that Gideon be king (Judg 8:22–23).

This unscrupulous inclination toward apostasy and unfaithfulness is certainly evident in the next generation as Abimelech, Gideon's son, murdered 69 of his brothers and accepted the invitation to become king (9:6). This experiment in monarchical rule (a concern of the author from the formulaic refrains) resembles a pagan Canaanite king rather than an obedient Israelite monarch (Deut 17:14–20). Now Israel's oppression did not come from a foreign neighbor but from one of her own judges.

The next judge, Jephthah, was the only major judge from the Transjordan region. Unlike the other judges Jephthah was called in a time of crisis by the popular demand of the people. He was promised to be the designated ruler if he successfully completed the mission against the Ammonites (Judg 11:5–11). Although God's Spirit was on him (11:29), he made an unwise vow to the Lord that he would sacrifice what first came from his house (11:31). Returning home, he had to sacrifice his only daughter to fulfill the vow.[34]

The last of the major judges is Samson, who perhaps even more than Gideon is a portrait of the nation in miniature as he blatantly violated God's instructions. In contrast with the other judges Samson's dealings with the Philistines seem to almost be of a personal nature rather than having anything to do with his tribe or Israel at large.

One of the ways the Israelites were to prevent the emergence of idolatry in the land was by avoiding mixed marriages (3:6; Exod 34:16; Deut 7:3). Samson, however, was involved with at least two relationships with foreign women (Judg 14:1–20; 16:1). In doing so he stands in contrast to Othniel, the first judge who displayed virtue and courage in his marriage to Achsah (1:12–15). This contrast illustrates the moral and spiritual decline of the judges themselves. The moral and spiritual decline of the judges seems to reach its climax with Samson. Samson demonstrates one who "did whatever he wanted" (17:6; 21:25). The prologue of the book announced that God raised up the judges and was with them (2:18). But things had become so perverse by Samson's day that he did not realize that the Lord had departed from him (Judg 16:20). Samson was also the only judge who was a Nazirite, but he seems to have violated Nazirite vows by having contact with the dead, cutting his hair, and perhaps drinking wine (Num 6:1–21).

III. Depths of the Failure of Israel (chaps. 17–21)

The period of the Judges began with Israel fighting enemies it should have annihilated, continued with Israel engaged with foreign enemies because of her apostasy, and concluded with Israel fighting among themselves.[35] The spiritual condition of the inhabitants of the land at the end of the book is no different from the pagan inhabitants the Israelites were to remove from the land at the beginning of the book.

The first epilogue records the migration of the tribe of Dan and Micah's idolatry (chaps. 17–18), while the second epilogue reports the rape of a Levite's concubine and the near anni-hilation of an Israelite tribe as a result of intertribal warfare (chaps. 19–21). Several events illustrate the depth to which Israel has departed from the commandments of the Mosaic law. The sins include theft (17:1–2), idolatry (17:5), immorality (19:2), homosexuality (19:22),

---

[34] The alternative view is that he devoted his daughter to perpetual virginity (see E. J. Young, *An Introduction to the Old Testament* ([Grand Rapids: Eerdmans, 1949], 175); Archer, *A Survey of Old Testament Introduction to the Old Testament*, 306; and D. Marcus, *Jephthah and His Vow* (Lubbock: Texas Tech Press, 1986).

[35] D. M. Howard Jr., *An Introduction to the Old Testament Historical Books* (Chicago: Moody, 1993), 99. The fact that the first episode of the appendix deals with the tribe of Dan forms a connection to Samson, the last mentioned judge, who was from the tribe of Dan.

and abduction (21:23). Micah assumed he would receive God's blessing because he procured a Levite to preside over the worship of his manufactured idol (17:13). The accounts in the epilogue illustrate in a more graphic way Israel's tendency toward idolatry and scandal that was seen earlier in the book.

Within this final section the young Levite who journeyed to the hill country of Ephraim (17:7–8) is counterbalanced by the Levite who traveled in the hill country of Ephraim to Bethlehem (chap. 19). There his concubine was raped and killed, stated in language remarkably similar to the account of Sodom and Gomorrah in Genesis 19. In both accounts men of the city surrounded the home of the guest, called for the visitors to come out to engage in homosexual relations, and were offered virgin daughters as a consolation.[36] Comparing the activity of the Israelites to the sin of Sodom and Gomarrah, the paradigm of abominable behavior in the OT, shows how low Israelites have stooped in their conduct. As a consequence of this deplorable event, Israel engaged in a civil war in which one of the tribes was in danger of becoming extinct (Judg 20). The holy war that was to be directed toward the Canaanites was directed toward one of their own tribes. "At the beginning of the book, Israel was prepared to unite against the common Canaanite foe. At the end of the book, the original ideal had failed to materialize and the tribes were uniting against one of their own brothers."[37] In the record of this internecine battle is the only mention of complete national cooperation as well as the only mention of the holiest national object, the ark of the covenant (20:27–28).

THE THEOLOGY OF THE BOOK

Political Leadership

When the Lord raised up judges, He did not give up His position as the supreme judge (Gen 18:25), a fact observed by Jephthah (Judg 11:27). Yahweh is the divine warrior on whom all of Israel's battles depend. He delivered the nation when they were under foreign oppression just as He did in the exodus.[38] Moreover, the spiritual decline and chaos demonstrated by many of the judges shows the need for another judge who would come and "judge Your people with righteousness" (Ps 72:2; see also Isa 11:4).

That future leader will emerge from the tribe of Judah, which already held a place of prominence in the book of Judges as the first tribe to encounter the Canaanites (Judg 1:2), and later the Benjamites (20:18), and the tribe to produce the first effective judge (3:7–11). The future leader of Israel would thus emerge from Judah (1:2–20) and not Benjamin (i.e., Saul).[39] The tribe of Benjamin was the first tribe that failed to complete the conquest (1:21). Gibeah in Benjamin, the hometown of King Saul, was compared to Sodom and Gomorrah, and the immorality of the tribe of Benjamin led to an internecine war with the rest of the nation.[40]

The future king from Judah will be a king, not a judge (17:6; 18:1; 19:1; 21:25). This king will be a covenant-keeper, who will read the Law (Deut 17:14–20) and promote the

---

[36] See Block, *Judges, Ruth*, 533–34.

[37] Chisholm, *Interpreting the Historical Books*, 96.

[38] The root *z'q*, "to cry out," occurs in Exod 2:23 as in Judg 3:9,15; 6:6–7; 10:10.

[39] While David and Saul are never mentioned in the book of Judges, their character and behavior are exhibited by their respective tribes, Judah and Benjamin. This indicates that David would have the character to be an effective God-fearing leader. See J. A. Groves, "Judges," in *Theological Interpretation of the Old Testament*, ed. K. J. Vanhoozer (Grand Rapids: Baker Academic, 2008), 96.

[40] For the many terminological parallels between the Gibeah incident (Judges 19) and Sodom and Gomorrah (Genesis 19) see Block, *Judges, Ruth*, 533–34.

acknowledgement of God (4:9,32–40).[41] The remaining pages of the OT anticipate the coming of this national leader, who will lead His people and serve as a faithful king.

Covenant

The book of Judges records an early description of the outworking of the covenant relationship between God and Israel. God is always faithful to His covenant commitment to the nation Israel, and both judgment and deliverance stem from God's absolute covenant faithfulness (Deut 4:31; Judg 2:18–20). A dominant theme in Judges is Israel's failure to remain faithful to God's covenant demands. This failure may be illustrated by the contrast to the covenant renewal that took place at Shechem at the end of the book of Joshua (chap. 24) with the slaughter of Abimelech's halfbrothers at the same location (Judg 8:30–31; 9:5). The people had drifted away from their covenant commitment to the Lord. By contrast, God remains faithful and continues to remember His covenant promise by responding to Israel's cries for deliverance. He is the real "hero" of the book.

THE TEXT OF THE BOOK

The text of the book of Judges has been very well preserved. The book has fewer variants than any other book of the Bible outside the Pentateuch.

THE NEW TESTAMENT AND THE BOOK

The events and the people in the book of Judges are rarely mentioned in the rest of the OT. In the few allusions to this period in the OT mention is made of the covenant failure that characterized this dark period (1 Sam 12:8–12; Neh 9:22–27; Pss 78:54–64; 106:34–39). The OT also refers to particular events such as the victory over Midian in Judges 7–8 (Ps 83:1–12; Isa 9:4; 10:26), the moral failure of Gibeah in Judges 19 (Hos 9:9; 10:9), and Abimelech's death in Judges 9:50–55 (2 Sam 11:21).[42]

In the historical survey of Israel's history Paul referred to the period of the judges and the fact that the length of the time of the conquest was "about 450 years" (Acts 13:19–20). In the honor roll of faith the author of Hebrews referred to the four judges of Gideon, Barak, Samson, and Jephthah as those who demonstrated a genuine trust in God (Heb 11:32–34).

STUDY QUESTIONS

1. What was Martin Noth's contribution to the history of composition for the book of Judges?
2. What are some indications the book of Judges was composed relatively early in Israel's history?
3. What was the general international scene among ANE nations during the time of the judges?
4. What is the chronological problem with the history of the judges?
5. What is the solution to the chronological problem of the judges?
6. What was the role of the Israelite judge?
7. What is the purpose of the book of Judges?
8. What is the basis for the arrangement of the tribes in the main section of the book of Judges?

---

[41] Groves, "Judges," 96.
[42] Ibid., 93.

9.   Which judge seems to be highlighted in the structural analysis of the major judges?
10. What tribe is designated for leadership in Judges 1?
11. What gods did the Israelites worship in the book of Judges?
12. How do we see the covenant relationship between God and Israel operate in the book of Judges?

FOR FURTHER STUDY

Block, Daniel. *Judges, Ruth*. Nashville: B&H, 1999.

Boling, Robert. *Judges*. Garden City, NY: Doubleday, 1975.

———. "Judges, Book of." In *ABD*, ed. D. N. Freedman, 3:1107–17. New York: Doubleday, 1992.

Burney, C. *Judges and Kings*. Rep. ed. New York: Ktav, 1970.

Chisholm, R. B. *Interpreting the Historical Books*. Grand Rapids: Kregel, 2006.

Cundall, A. E., and L. L. Morris. *Judges and Ruth*. TOTC. Downers Grove, IL: InterVarsity, 1968.

De Vaux, R. *The Early History of Israel*. Philadelphia: Westminster, 1978.

Dorsey, D. *The Literary Structure of the Old Testament*. Grand Rapids: Baker, 1999.

Dumbrell, W. J. "In Those Days There Was No King in Israel." *JSOT* 2 (1983): 25.

———. *The Faith of Israel: A Theological Survey of the Old Testament*. 2nd ed. Grand Rapids: Baker, 2002.

Groves, J. A. "Judges." In *Theological Interpretation of the Old Testament*. Edited by K. J. Vanhoozer, 92–101. Grand Rapids: Baker Academic, 2008.

House, P. *Old Testament Theology*. Downers Grove, IL: InterVarsity Press, 1998.

Howard, D. M., Jr. *An Introduction to the Old Testament Historical Books*. Chicago: Moody, 1993.

Kaufmann, Y. *History of the Religion of Israel*, Vol. 4 (in HB). 4th ed. Jerusalem: Bialik and Dvir, 1956.

Lilley, J. "A Literary Appreciation of the Book of Judges." *TynBul* 18 (1976): 94–102.

Mazar, B. ed. *Judges*. Vol. 3 of *The World History of the Jewish People*. Tel-Aviv: Massada, 1971.

Merrill, E. H. *Kingdom of Priests*. Grand Rapids: Baker, 1987.

Millard, A. R. "Story, History, and Theology." In *Faith, Tradition, and History: Old Testament Historiography in Its Near Eastern Context*. Edited by A. R. Millard, J. K. Hoffmeier, and D. W. Baker, 37–64. Winona Lake, IN: Eisenbrauns, 1994.

Noth, M. *The Deuteronomistic History*. Translated by D. Orton. JSOTSup 15. Sheffield: JSOT Press, 1981.

O'Connell, Robert. *Rhetoric of the Book of Judges*. VTSup. Leiden: Brill, 1996.

Vannoy, J. Robert. "Judges, Theology of." *NIDOTTE*, ed. W. VanGemeren, 4:827–37. Grand Rapids: Zondervan, 1997.

Webb, Barry. *The Book of the Judges: an Integrated Reading*. JSOTSup. Sheffield: JSOT Press, 1987.

Weippert, Manfred. *The Settlement of the Israelite Tribes in Palestine*. Naperville, IL: Allenson, 1971.

Wood, Leon. *The Distressing Days of the Judges*. Grand Rapids: Zondervan, 1975.

Younger, K. Lawson. "Judges 1 in Its Near Eastern Literary Context." In *Faith, Tradition, and History: Old Testament Historiography in Its Near Eastern Context*. Edited by A. R. Millard, J. K. Hoffmeier, and D. W. Baker. Winona Lake, IN: Eisenbrauns, 1994.

CHAPTER 17

THE BOOK OF RUTH

MARK F. ROOKER

THE BOOK OF Ruth narrates one of the best-known stories in the Bible. The book focuses on God's work to provide for an impoverished family in the time of the judges and provides a strong contrast to the covenant unfaithfulness that pervades the book of Judges. Moreover, through this faithful family God established the immediate ancestry of Israel's greatest king, King David.

THE DATE AND AUTHORSHIP OF THE BOOK

Many twentieth-century critics and commentators regard the book of Ruth as a product of the postexilic period. This late-date position has been advocated by such notable OT scholars as Otto Eissfeldt, Robert Pfeiffer, Gerhard Sellin, Georg Fohrer, W. O. E. Oesterley, and Bernard Robinson. The primary reasons for the late date include (1) the language of the book, (2) the matter of mixed marriages described also in Ezra and Nehemiah, (3) the relationship of the legal prescriptions in the book to pentateuchal law, and (4) the explanatory statement in 4:7 which seems to indicate that a great amount of time had elapsed between the events of the book and the book's composition.[1]

These arguments for the late dating of the book have not convinced all critics. Stalwart nonconservative scholars including S. R. Driver, Edward Campbell, Gillis Gerlemen, and Derek Beattie have maintained that the criteria for the postexilic dating are invalid, and thus they prefer the earlier preexilic date for the book.[2] The language argument is disputed because of a more sober assessment of the significance of the occurrence of Aramaisms in the OT. Scholars early in the twentieth century tended to view alleged Aramaisms as evidence of late writing.

---

[1] Two of these criteria have recently been stated in more recent treatments. Bush has dated the work late because of the language of the book, while Bandstra and Mathews and Moyer have argued that the work is postexilic because it confronts the endogamous doctrine argued vehemently by Ezra and Nehemiah (F. W. Bush, *Ruth, Esther,* WBC [Dallas: Word, 1996], 20–30; B. Bandstra, *Reading the Old Testament* [Belmont, CA: Wadsworth, 1995], 453; and V. Mathews and J. Moyer, *The Old Testament: Text and Context* [Peabody: MA: Hendrickson, 1997], 234).

[2] Hans Hertzberg, Gillis Gerleman, and Wilhelm Rudolph are among recent commentators who have argued that Ruth was composed in the preexilic period.

This line of argument has weakened considerably because of the fact that the Aramaic language and influence was operative earlier in the biblical period than was once assumed. Moreover, other scholars such as Robert Gordis and Weinfeld have asserted that Ruth in no way reflects a polemical spirit against the reforms of Ezra and Nehemiah. The book reflects an entirely different milieu than what is found in Ezra and Nehemiah. It is extremely difficult to prove that the book's purpose was to counter the reforms of those books.

Other proposals regarding the composition of the book of Ruth contend that the composition underwent various stages (Herman Gunkel, George Glanzman). These stages are said to have developed from an original fertility myth (Sheehan), or a poetic core (Myers). These hypotheses have not won acceptance among conservative or nonconservative scholars.

According to the Talmud, Samuel wrote the book of Ruth (*Baba Babthra* 14b). This tradition has been rightly contested since Samuel died before David became king (1 Sam 28:3), and Ruth 4:22 presupposes that David was a well-known historical figure at the time of writing. It does suggest that the book of Ruth had a long-standing tradition of being viewed as a preexilic composition. The fact that Solomon is not mentioned in the genealogy (4:18–22) would lend support to the view that the work was composed during David's lifetime before he ascended to the throne (2 Sam 2:1–4:12). The book would then provide the immediate ancestry for King David and connect him to the Judahite line (David Hubbard).[3]

In the order of the biblical books in the LXX, Ruth follows Judges. This ancient tradition lends support to the idea that the work was written early in the history of biblical Israel.[4] Another ancient tradition included Ruth in the Writings section of the OT either as the first book of the Writings, followed immediately by Psalms, or alternatively, following the book of Proverbs. The reason for the former arrangement was apparently to introduce David, the main contributor to the Psalms, while the latter is because Proverbs ends with a discussion of the noble woman (Prov 31:10–31) of which Ruth, the primary subject of the following book, is the best illustration (Ruth 3:11).[5]

THE CONTENTS OF THE BOOK

The book of Ruth opens with the family of Elimelech, a Judahite from Bethlehem, venturing into Moab to find relief from a Palestinian famine during the time of the Judges (Ruth 1:1–2).[6] In Moab Elimelech died and then his two sons died prematurely after they married the Moabite women Orpah and Ruth (1:3–5).[7] After Elimelech's widow, Naomi, heard that the famine in Israel was over, she planned to head back to her home land and advised her daughters-in-law to go to theirs (1:6–14). Orpah heeded Naomi's advice, but Ruth in her unswerving loyalty, vowed that she would accept Naomi's people and their God as her own (1:15–17).[8] Chapter 1 ends with Naomi returning with Ruth to Bethlehem at the beginning

---

[3] This purpose is clearly preeminent although it might be argued that secondary themes do exist, such as acceptance of foreigners into Israel and rewards for faithfulness.

[4] In addition in the Jewish enumeration of the Old Testament with 22 canonical books, Judges and Ruth were combined (see R. Beckwith, *The Old Testament Canon of the New Testament Church* [Grand Rapids: Eerdmans, 1985], 252–56).

[5] The Hebrew expression *ʾēšet ḥayil* is used to describe the excellent wife (Prov 31:10) and the character of Ruth (3:11). The adjective *ḥayil* is also used to characterize Boaz (2:1), thereby indicating that Ruth and Boaz were a perfect match.

[6] The Moabites, who occupied a part of the Transjordan region east of the Dead Sea, were related to the Israelites as they were descendants of Abraham's nephew Lot (Gen 19:37). For the history of Israel's checkered relationship with the Moabites see Numbers 21–25; 1 Sam 22:3–4; and 2 Sam 8:2.

[7] According to the Aramaic Targum the deaths resulted from the intermarriages.

[8] This speech, Ruth's first speech in the book, may reflect treaty language wherein Ruth officially became an Israelite (Mathews and Moyer, *The Old Testament: Text and Context*, 234).

of the barley harvest with Naomi being bitter about what had taken place in her life since she left for Moab with her family (1:19–22).

Chapter 2 opens with Ruth requesting permission from her mother-in-law to go into the fields of Bethlehem and glean among the ears of grain (Ruth 2:2; see Lev 19:9–10). Ruth ventured[9] into the field of Boaz, kinsmen of Naomi (Ruth 2:1). Boaz had heard of what Ruth had done for her mother-in-law and invited her to glean only in his field with his workers (vv. 8–11). After Boaz fed her and sent her home, Ruth reported to Naomi what had transpired and presented her with an ephah of barley (2:14–23).

In chapter 3 Naomi devised a plan for Ruth to present herself to Boaz at the threshing floor at the end of the barley harvest. Naomi told Ruth to dress and wash herself, indicating that her time of mourning for her husband had come to an end (3:1–4; 2 Sam 12:20). Ruth's encounter with Boaz was to press the issue of marriage, as is clear from her request, "Spread your cloak over me" (Ruth 3:9).[10] Boaz was agreeable to the proposal and told Ruth that he would confront the nearer kinsman to see if the nearer kinsman would take on the responsibility of next-of-kin (3:10–15). The chapter closes with Ruth reporting to Naomi what had taken place, along with presenting Naomi with six measures of barley as a gift from Boaz (3:16–18). Thus this chapter, like the previous two, ends with a reference to the harvest.

Chapter 4 begins with Boaz pulling aside the nearer kinsman at the city gate and confronting him before the leaders of the city about Naomi's desire to sell her land (4:1–4).[11] Initially the nearer kinsman agreed to make the purchase, but when Boaz reported that he would also have to marry Ruth, he refused and thereby gave legal authority to Boaz to carry out the role of the kinsman redeemer (4:5–6). Probably the unnamed relative had other children and the potential offspring from Ruth would not only have a claim on the land the kinsman purchased but would also proportionately diminish his own children's inheritance. After foregoing his right to buy the land, the nearer redeemer took off his shoe, indicating that he was abandoning his right to the land (4:7–8).[12] Boaz then married Ruth, who bore Obed, the grandfather of King David (4:9–22). The quick meeting, romance, marriage, and pregnancy contrasts with the 10 years of barrenness in the land of Moab (1:4).

Tischler has provided a helpful outline of the contents of the work as composed of five scenes:
Introduction (1:1–5)
Act 1: The Exodus (1:6–18)
Act 2: At Bethlehem (1:19–22)
Act 3: Boaz Introduced (2:1–23)
Act 4: The Plan (3:1–18)
Act 5: The Public Pronouncement (4:1–12)
Postlude (4:13–22)[13]

---

[9] It is clear from the overall context of the book that God indeed led Ruth to the field of Boaz.

[10] See Ezek 16:8. The Aramaic Targum explicitly comments that Ruth's request is one of marriage.

[11] As heir of Elimelech, Naomi apparently had the right to redeem the property of her husband by repurchasing it from its buyers. Elimelech had probably already sold the land before leaving for Moab. A kinsman would have the responsibility of buying the property back for Naomi who was relinquishing the obligation-right to redeem the land (Ruth 4:3).

[12] See R. de Vaux, *Ancient Israel* (New York: McGraw, 1961), 1:169. In Nuzi, India, and Egypt a similar symbolic gesture involving a shoe was utilized (R. Gordis, "Love, Marriage, and Business in the Book of Ruth: A Chapter in Hebrew Customary Law," in *A Light Unto My Path: Old Testament Studies in Honor of Jacob M. Myers* [Philadelphia: Temple University Press, 1974], 247).

[13] N. M. Tischler, "Ruth," in *A Complete Guide to the Bible*, ed. L. Ryken and T. Longman III (Grand Rapids: Zondervan, 1993), 152–53.

THE LITERARY FORM OF THE BOOK

The historical events of Ruth have long made the work one of the favorite narratives of the Bible. Also the way the story is told has greatly added to its effectiveness. The narrative introductions and transitions are described with swift strokes of the brush, whereas the dialogues of the main scenes move at a much slower and measured pace. The plot is advanced mainly through these dialogues. Fifty-five of the eighty-six verses of the book record conversations between two of the main characters of the book, the highest ratio of dialogue to narrative of any narrative book.

Also the author effectively used a wide range of symmetry in communicating the contents of the work. This is noted through the literary symmetry between chapters[14] as well as through words that are used infrequently or on only two occasions.[15] Many have noted how chap. 1 shares corresponding themes with chap. 4 while chaps. 2 and 3 are parallel.[16]

The occurrence of key terms marks the movement from conflict to restoration. Dommershausen has pointed out the key *Leitworte* which both characterize and bind each of the major scenes or chaps. together. These include *šûb* ("return," chap. 1), *lqṭ* ("glean," chap. 2), *gōren* ("threshing floor," chap. 3), *g'l* ("redeem") and *qnh* ("buy" chap. 4). In the final genealogy of 10 names (4:18–22) the first five (Perez to Nashhon) represent the pre-Exodus generations, while the next five (Salmon to David) represent the royal line after the exodus. Boaz, the main male hero of the book, occupies the strategic seventh position in the genealogy.

Another device masterfully used by the author is one of characterization. This is seen from the development of Naomi's character from chap. 1 to chap. 4 as well as the contrast between Orpah with Ruth and the unnamed relative with Boaz. Both pairs demonstrate how Ruth and Boaz demonstrate *ḥesed* ("loyalty") in going the extra mile and that they are right for each other (2:1; 3:11). These features suggest an overall unity in a work written by a literary genius.[17]

THE LANGUAGE OF THE BOOK

Overall the Hebrew text of the book of Ruth has been well preserved. There are a few textual variations that are of some significance (e.g., *qānîtāy* in 4:5) although it is generally admitted the text has been faithfully transmitted as evidenced by the agreement with the DSS.

There is some discussion, however, regarding the late language of the book of Ruth. Bush has argued that the language of the book of Ruth reflects postexilic Hebrew because the book contains a number of features which seem more at home in the postexilic period than in the preexilic period.[18] Weinfeld, on the other hand, has ably argued that while the book may contain features that differ from preexilic Hebrew it in no way reflects the language of Esther, Ezra–Nehemiah, and Chronicles. For this reason, the book should be seen as early. The language variations may be due to dialectal differences rather than chronological changes

---

[14] P. Trible, "Ruth, Book of," in *ABD*, ed. D. N. Freedman (New York: Doubleday, 1992), 5:843–45.

[15] The key terms include child/children (1:5; 4:16), *ḥesed* (1:8; 2:20; 3:10), security (1:9; 3:1), cling (1:14; 2:8,21,23), lodge (1:16; 3:13), brought back/restore (1:21; 4:15), empty (1:21; 3:17), covenant brother (2:1; 3:2), noble (2:1; 3:11); wing(s) (2:12; 3:9) (see E. Campbell, *Ruth* [Garden City, N. Y.: Doubleday, 1975], 13–14; and Y. Zakovitz, *Ruth: Introduction and Commentary* [Jerusalem: Magnes, 1990], 12–13 [in Hb.]).

[16] S. Bertman, "Symmetrical Design in the Book of Ruth," *JBL* 84 (1965): 165–67.

[17] Campbell, *Ruth*, 10.

[18] Bush, *Ruth/Esther*, 20–30. Not a small number of the late language features are clustered in Ruth 4:7 which is possibly a late language gloss provided to describe an ancient custom (see A. Hurvitz, "On 'Drawing off the Sandal' in the Book of Ruth," *Shnaton* 1 [1975]: 45–49 [in Hb.]).

(Weinfeld, Segal). Driver and Campbell based their preexilic dating of the book on the book's early linguistic features.

Campbell has detected use of archaic language in the speeches of Boaz and Naomi, which plays an exegetical role in distinguishing their generation from Ruth's. However, these archaic features such as paragogic nuns and second-person singular perfects with final *yods* are archaic to preexilic Hebrew as well and thus cannot be brought forth as evidence of a postexilic writer attempting to make his language appear to be preexilic Hebrew. The assignation of the language of the book to the preexilic period fits well with the book's purpose, to provide the background for the political history of King David.

THE PENTATEUCHAL LAW AND THE BOOK

A matter of great debate in the study of the book of Ruth is the apparent combination of the pentateuchal laws regarding redemption of land (Leviticus 25) and Levirate marriage (Deuteronomy 25) in Boaz's announcement to the unnamed kinsman in Ruth 4. These laws are not elsewhere combined, and this has led some to doubt that what is found in Ruth is an attestation to the legal practice of redemption and levirate marriage. The strongest argument in favor of understanding that Boaz's proposal was one of combining land redemption and levirate marriage comes from the stated purpose of his union with Ruth: "to perpetuate the man's name on his property" (4:5). This stated purpose is taken from the established purpose of levirate marriage in Deut 25:7. Moreover, the result of Boaz's union with Ruth in Ruth 4:11 "to build up his brother's house" is identical to that of levirate marriage (Deut 25:9).

A connection between land redemption and levirate marriage should be assumed as the issue of property ownership is critical to both. To raise an heir for a deceased man's name means to raise the owner of inherited property. The purpose of the levirate marriage was not only that of raising offspring for a widow, but also maintaining of the estate within the larger family: the first born of the levirate marriage would inherit the estate of the deceased brother. It is true that Deut 25:5 mentions only brothers in regard to this concept, but this may be because this was the normal way this obligation would have been realized as families were relatively large.[19] That the brother had the primary responsibility is understood not only by Naomi's statement in Ruth 1:11 but also the absence of disgrace for the unnamed kinsman when he refused his responsibility (4:1–12).[20] In conclusion, the application of biblical laws may have had broader application than the precise circumstance dictated.[21] Ancient law codes were neither exhaustive nor comprehensive.

Other illustrations of obedience to the law include Ruth's desire to glean in the fields and Boaz's provision for the poor in the land (Lev 19:9–10; 23:22; Deut 24:19–22).

---

[19] In Genesis 38 Judah, the father-in-law ultimately carries out the role. Perez, like Obed, was born of levirate marriage, but in both cases it was not the brother-in-law or nearest relative who carried out the responsibility. In Assyrian and Hittite law the brother had the first responsibility, but if he failed in this role the responsibility was carried out by the deceased brother's father (*ANET*, 182 [par 33], 196 [par 193]). Levirate marriage was also practiced among the Hurrian and Ugaritic civilizations (de Vaux, *Ancient Israel*, 1:38). For an exhaustive defense of the view that both laws of redemption and levirate marriage were combined in Ruth 4, see D. Leggett, *The Levirate and Goel Institutions in the Old Testament with Special Attention to the Book of Ruth* (Cherry Hill, NJ: Mack, 1974), 209–53. The question of the Sadducees in Matt 22:25–28 implies that the levirate law was binding in the first century AD.

[20] Reference to levirate marriage is also implied by Boaz in Ruth 3:10, when he stated that Ruth's last display of *ḥesed* (willingness to fulfill the levirate responsibility) was greater than the first.

[21] See G. Fee and D. Stuart, *How to Read the Bible for All Its Worth*, 2nd ed. (Grand Rapids: Zondervan, 1993), 155. This may also be illustrated by the application of Leviticus 25 in Jer 32:8–15, where the application of the law would not necessarily be predictable from the legal prescription alone.

THE THEOLOGY OF THE BOOK

As noted previously, the book of Ruth is about God's guidance and providence in meeting the physical needs of His faithful people and providing the theocratic rule of the Davidic dynasty. This is accomplished through God's sovereignty as He brings the famine to an end (1:6), guides Ruth to Boaz's field (2:3), and allows Ruth to conceive (4:13).

The book also stresses how God carries out His work through His people. It is Boaz who praises Ruth for taking refuge under God's wings (*kānāp*, 2:12), but it is through the agency of Boaz that Ruth finds the resolution of her needs (*kānāp*, 3:9). Boaz's first response to Ruth, "May the LORD reward you for what you have done" (2:12), expresses this theme. God is active in the book particularly in the way people act toward each other. He works through faithful people like Naomi, Boaz, and Ruth, and through their faithfulness more is accomplished than they ever knew (1:16–17; 2:12,20).

Another illustration of the faithfulness of God's people is demonstrated by the willingness of Ruth to raise an heir in giving birth (3:10; see 1 Tim 2:15). Through the determination of Tamar and Ruth God worked to provide descendants for the line of Judah.[22] These acts of allegiance foreshadow the faithfulness of Mary who rejoiced in her role of giving birth to a child born in Bethlehem, also of the tribe of Judah (Matt 1:18–2:6).

The book also underscores the fact that God welcomes non-Israelites into the covenant. Ruth left her family to follow Israel's God in language that recalls the obedience of Abraham (Ruth 2:11; Gen 12:1). Like Abraham, she was a stranger who was accepted by God through faith and thus foreshadowed God's grace that reaches out to the whole world. Yet she did so without a word of divine assurance from the Lord. Ruth joins Tamar and Rahab (all foreigners) in Matthew's genealogy (Matt 1:1–17).

As the book is largely concerned with providing an heir for the family of Elimelech, the underlying focus is on progeny and inheritance, or people and land. In the Bible an heir was given land. The book thus echoes the themes of people and land, which are salient subjects in OT history.

As God overcame human obstacles in the birth of Isaac, Jacob, Samson, and Samuel, so also David's ancestors miraculously continued his line. Moreover, the term "genealogy" *(tôlēdôt)*, a term that is a prevalent sectional marker in the book of Genesis, occurs also at the conclusion of this book and thus links David with the Israelite patriarchs. According to Jewish tradition King David was born and died on the day of Pentecost. Adherents to the Jewish faith traditionally read the book of Ruth on the day of Pentecost.

STUDY QUESTIONS

1. Why did many critical OT scholars consider the composition of the book of Ruth to be late?
2. According to the Talmud who wrote the book of Ruth?
3. Why should the book of Ruth be considered an early preexilic book?
4. In what section does the book of Ruth appear in the Hebrew Bible?
5. Why does Ruth follow Proverbs in the Hebrew Bible?
6. What was the purpose of Ruth's confronting Boaz at the threshing floor?
7. Why did the nearer kinsman redeemer refuse to marry Ruth?

---

[22] The method Ruth used to fulfill the levirate responsibility contrasts with the illicit means carried out by Ruth's ancestress, Tamar (Genesis 38). Ruth demonstrated the ethics of Israel rather than of pagan Moab.

8. What laws are in the background of Ruth 4?
9. Why do you think the book of Ruth was written?
10. How many verses in Ruth are parts of dialogues?
11. What is the pivotal event in the genealogy of Ruth?
12. The Hebrew of the book of Ruth best fits with what historical period?
13. What attribute of God is especially apparent in the book of Ruth?

FOR FURTHER STUDY

Atkinson, D. *The Wings of Refuge*. Downers Grove, IL: InterVarsity, 1983.

Block, D. *Judges, Ruth*. NAC. Nashville: B&H, 1999.

Baylis, C. P. "Naomi in the Book of Ruth in Light of the Mosaic Covenant." *BSac* 161 (2004): 413–31.

Bauckman, R. "The Book of Ruth and the Possibility of a Canonical Hermeneutic." *BI* 5 (1997): 29–45.

Beattie, D. *The Targum of Ruth*. Aramaic Targum 19. Collegeville, MN: Liturgical, 1994.

Beckwith, R. *The Old Testament Canon of the New Testament Church*. Grand Rapids: Eerdmans, 1985.

Berlin, A. *Poetics and Interpretation of Biblical Narrative*. Sheffield: Almond, 1983.

Bertman, S. "Symmetrical Design in the Book of Ruth." *JBL* 84 (1965): 165–68.

Bush, F. *Ruth/Esther*. Dallas: Word, 1996.

Campbell, E. F. *Ruth*. Garden City, NY: Doubleday, 1975.

Carasik, M. "Ruth 2, 7: Why the Overseer Was Embarrassed." *ZAW* 107 (1995): 493–94.

Cundall, A. E., and L. L. Morris. *Judges and Ruth*. TOTC. Downers Grove, IL: InterVarsity, 1968.

de Vaux, R. *Ancient Israel*. 2 vols. New York: McGraw, 1961.

Grant, R. "Literary Structure in the Book of Ruth." *BSac* 148 (1991): 424–41.

Green, B. "The Plot of the Biblical Story of Ruth. *JSOT* 23 (1982): 55–68.

Hals, R. *The Theology of the Book of Ruth*. Fortress, 1969.

Howard, D. M., Jr. *An Introduction to the Old Testament Historical Books*. Chicago: Moody, 1993.

Hubbard, R. L. *The Book of Ruth*. Grand Rapids: Eerdmans, 1988.

Leggett, D. *The Levirate and Goel Institutions in the Old Testament with Special Attention to the Book of Ruth*. Cherry Hill, NJ: Mack, 1974.

Luter, A. B., and B. Davis. *God Behind the Seen*. Grand Rapids: Baker, 1995.

Merrill, E. H. "The Book of Ruth: Narration and Shared Themes." *BSac* 142 (1985): 130–41.

Sakenfeld, K. *The Meaning of* Ḥesed *in the Hebrew Bible: A New Inquiry*. HSM. Missoula, MT: Scholars, 1978.

Tischler, N. "Ruth." In *A Complete Guide to the Bible*. Edited by L. Ryken and T. Longman III. Grand Rapids: Zondervan, 1993.

Wolde, E. V. "Texts in Dialogue with Texts: Intertextuality in the Ruth and Tamar Narratives." *BI* 5 (1997): 1–28.

Younger, K. L., Jr. *Judges, Ruth*. NIVAC. Grand Rapids: Zondervan, 2002.

Zakovitz, Y. *Ruth: Introduction and Commentary*. Jerusalem: Magnes, 1990 (in Hb.).

CHAPTER 18

THE BOOKS OF 1 AND 2 SAMUEL

EUGENE H. MERRILL

T HE DIVISION OF the book of Samuel into two parts is a product of the translation and canonical arrangement of the LXX in the second half of the third century BC. This Greek version divided the original Hebrew composition Samuel into sections called 1 and 2 Kingdoms (*Basileiōn* A and B) and also split Kings into 3 and 4 Kingdoms. However, the Jews have always called the book Samuel. The tractate *Baba Bathra* of the Babylonian Talmud states unequivocally, "Samuel wrote the book which bears his name and the Book of Judges and Ruth" (14b–15a). As we shall see, the statement that Samuel wrote the book bearing his name is at best only partially correct, but the tradition that the writing was called Samuel can hardly be denied. The English and most modern translations follow the Hebrew designation.

DATE AND AUTHORSHIP OF SAMUEL

All ancient tradition attributes at least some of the book of Samuel to the prophet Samuel himself. The most famous explicit testimony to this appears in the Talmudic text referred to above. However, this raises a serious problem in that Samuel's death is reported in 1 Sam 25:1, a fact that precludes his having authored anything beyond that point. At the most, he was responsible for the first 24 chapters of 1 Samuel, leaving chaps. 25–31 and all of 2 Samuel to other authors and/or compilers.

The developing Jewish tradition was not oblivious to this problem. The same Talmudic document adds, "[You say that] Samuel wrote the book that bears his name. But is it not written in it, Now Samuel was dead?—It was completed by Gad the seer and Nathan the prophet." Assuming that one or both of these men outlived the last datable event of 2 Samuel—the erection of David's altar at the threshing floor of Araunah (2 Sam 24:25) in about 975 BC—there is no reason to distrust the tradition. On the other hand there is no internal evidence in the book to this effect and, not even Samuel is credited with any part of the authorship.

Uncertainty about the authorship of Samuel continues to this day, but modern criticism has devoted a great deal more attention to matters of sources, composition, redaction, and the like, than to authorship.[1] A generally well-connected narrative, despite alleged unevenness of style and contradictory views, indicates rather heavy editorial activity at the completion of the process of assembling the book.[2] Clearly discernible blocks of material suggest originally independent sources that various compilers brought together to create the present product.[3] Some critics view certain of these texts as in conflict or even in contradiction to others,[4] whereas other critics argue for a greater degree of homogeneity of ideological and theological perspective.[5]

The history of modern criticism of Samuel began in the early nineteenth century with the attempt to trace the allegedly parallel strands of the Pentateuch through the historical books.[6] Various evidences of a lack of unity of the material were adduced to suggest that there are doublets, contradictions, redactional seams, and other features of Samuel that show it to be a highly composite creation. Whatever overall consistency or harmony is apparent was attributed eventually to the editorial work of the "deuteronomist," the putative creative genius who reshaped all of Joshua through 2 Kings into a massive work of history sensitive and responsive to the covenant teachings of Deuteronomy.

It is further argued that this editorial activity could not conceal the fact that separate and even opposing sources remained as constituent elements of the book. K. Budde, for example, offered the view that the J and E documents of the Pentateuch actually originated with the writers who composed the history of Saul and David. Later editions of these texts created, successively, histories of the judges, Moses, the patriarchs, and prepatriarchal times.[7]

This approach has met with little favor, for few critics are willing to extend the JEDP sources of the Pentateuch into the historical literature. Already by the end of the nineteenth century Kittel and other scholars offered compelling arguments to demonstrate that Samuel and the other historical books consist of a wide variety of compositions representing numerous genres and types such as hero stories, royal anecdotes, prophetic legends, and the like.[8] This approach, the dominant one today, was given further impetus in the work of Martin Noth[9] and Leonhard Rost especially. According to Noth, the deuteronomist (Dtr) was responsible for assembling the historical books as they stand. As for Samuel, Dtr already had at hand 1 Sam 1:1–4:1a; 4:1b–7:1; 9:1–10:16; 10:27b–11:15; 13:2–2 Samuel 2:7; 2:8–20:25; and to this he added his own material, namely, 1 Sam 7:2–8:32; 10:17–21ba; 12:1–25. Later editions of the deuteronomic history (DtrH) incorporated 2 Sam 21–24.

Rost's major contribution was the identification of 2 Samuel 13–20 + 1 Kings 1–2 as a discrete narrative often titled "History of the Succession to David," a treatise whose purpose was to answer the question as to who would follow David on Israel's throne.[10] Rost suggested that the compiler of Samuel had already at his disposal 1 Samuel 4–6 (the narrative of the ark of the covenant), 2 Samuel 6 (another Ark narrative); 7; 10:6b–11:1; and 12:26–31. These he

---

[1] A. F. Campbell and M. A. O'Brien, *Unfolding the Deuteronomistic History* (Minneapolis: Fortress, 2000), 215–19.

[2] D. M. Howard Jr., *An Introduction to the Old Testament Historical Books* (Chicago: Moody, 1993), 142–45.

[3] R. D. Bergen, *1, 2 Samuel,* NAC (Nashville: B&H, 1996), 22–24.

[4] For a number of these see J. A. Soggin, *Introduction to the Old Testament* (Philadelphia: Westminster, 1980), 186–89.

[5] B. S. Childs, *Introduction to the Old Testament as Scripture* (Philadelphia: Fortress, 1979), 271–80.

[6] For a survey of this history see O. Eissfeldt, *The Old Testament: An Introduction* (New York: Harper and Row, 1965), 268–81.

[7] K. Budde, *Die Bücher Richter und Samuel, ihre Quellen und ihre Aufbau* (Giessen: J. Ricker'sche, 1890), 169–76.

[8] R. Kittel, "Das erste Buch Samuel," in *Die Heilige Schrift des alten Testaments,* ed. E. Kautsch Tübingen; 1922), 408.

[9] Eissfeldt, *The Old Testament,* 243.

[10] L. Rost, *The Succession to the Throne of David,* trans. M. D. Rutter and D. M. Gunn (Sheffield; Almond, 1982).

edited onto the Succession narrative along with the rest of 2 Samuel 9–12. One result was the enlargement of the Succession narrative to 2 Samuel 9–20 + 1 Kings 1–2.

O. Eissfeldt proposed that Samuel consists primarily of three sources: L (Lay), J, and E.[11] The earliest of these, L, in turn embodies already existent written texts as well as creative addition and editing on the part of the compiler of the L material. In Eissfeldt's view the ark narratives (1 Samuel 4–6; 2 Samuel 6) were originally one composition, which the L redactor compiled with preexisting sources such as the lists of Saul's (1 Sam 14:49–51) and David's (2 Sam 8:16–18) royal officials, David's lament over Abner (2 Sam 3:33–34), the lists of David's sons (2 Sam 3:2–5; 5:13–15), the deeds of David's heroes (2 Sam 21:15–22), and the lists of his mighty men (2 Sam 23:8–39). Perhaps 2 Samuel 2–6 and 7 were also at L's disposal, undergoing some editing by him.

Eissfeldt suggests that J was dependent on L but also on popular tradition, the latter being exemplified by 1 Samuel 9:1–10:16 and chapter 24. On the other hand J incorporated the Succession Narrative (2 Sam 9–20 + 1 Kgs 1–2) into his corpus and he also likely included the already written lament over Saul and Jonathan (2 Sam 1:17–27). The E contribution (so Eissfeldt) was to provide a theological revision of the L + J traditions and also to derive new material from popular tradition. Some of this was so long after the event as to have little or no historical value (1 Sam 19:18–24 + 20:1a; 21:11–16), but other incidents, such as Saul's Amalekite campaign (1 Samuel 15) and his visit to the witch of Endor (1 Samuel 28), rested on reliable historical bases.

A contemporary understanding of Samuel's origin and development is that of Rolf Rendtorff.[12] Apart from offering some evidence of Deuteronomic redaction, Rendtorff has little or nothing to say about sources or about dating and provenance. He views 1 Samuel 1–7 as the story of Samuel the prophet (chaps. 1–3; 7:15–17) into which has been inserted the major part of the ark narrative (4:1–7:1). The Saul narratives that follow (chaps. 8–15) feature especially the ambivalence toward monarchy which most scholars see as evidence of conflicting ancient traditions that find unsatisfactory resolution in the book. In two narratives (9:1–10:16 and chap. 11) Saul's anointing as king is viewed positively, even by Samuel the prophet, and the monarchy thus appears to enjoy divine sanction. In chaps. 8 and 12, however, kingship is roundly condemned as a repudiation of Yahweh's rule over the nation.

Rendtorff argues that this antimonarchic stance is ancient, though there may be Deuteronomic additions that strengthen it.[13] As it stands, he points out, the positive attitude toward kingship is framed by the narratives negative toward it, thus making the latter dominant. The unfavorable view of the monarchy finds additional support in Samuel's farewell address (1 Samuel 12), especially in his implicit comparison of himself to Saul (v. 3) and his warning about the people being destroyed along with their king if they fail to keep covenant with God (vv. 14,20–25). The subsequent history of Saul vindicates the antimonarchy opinion for he turns out to be disobedient (chaps. 13, 15) and is eventually rejected (13:11–14). Rendtorff's analysis is unsatisfying for at least two reasons: (1) It does not account for the retention of the pro-kingship narratives and (2) it misses the real point, namely, that it was not kingship *per se* that was opposed but only the premature selection of Saul. This point will be argued more fully later.

---

[11] Eissfeldt, *The Old Testament*, 271–81.

[12] R. Rendtorff, *The Old Testament: An Introduction* (Philadelphia: Fortress, 1986), 170–74.

[13] Ibid., 171.

The next major unit, the "History of the Rise of David" (1 Samuel 16–2 Samuel 5), is to Rendtorff an independent piece of tradition, one interrupted with the pericope about Saul's death (1 Samuel 31). Like many critics Rendtorff sees different—even contradictory—versions of David's succession. Thus there is a secret anointing of David by Samuel (1 Sam 16:1–13), perhaps to match that of Saul (9:1–10:16), and then David went by invitation of the king to join Saul's court (16:14–23). Meanwhile David killed Goliath and afterward had to be introduced to Saul, who appears never to have met him before (17:55–58).

The second great block of material depicting David's reign is the Succession Narrative (2 Samuel 9–20 + 1 Kings 1–2), the particular matter of interest to Rendtorff being what he calls its "appendices" (2 Samuel 21–24). Between it and the preceding History of the Rise of David are "pieces of independent tradition"[14] that appear to belong to neither of the great historical narratives, having been placed there perhaps by the deuteronomists as interludes to bind them together. These include the shorter ark narrative (chap. 6); the covenant promise to David (chap. 7), which has "Deuteronomistic character";[15] and the lists of David's foreign exploits and public officials (chap. 8).

Rendtorff, like Rost and other earlier scholars, views the Succession Narrative as an originally independent document except for the intrusion of the accounts of the Ammonite war (10:6–11:1; 12:26–31), an interpolation designed to add clarity to the Bathsheba story (11:2–12:25).

In conclusion, scholars have tended in recent years to accord Samuel much more respect as to its literary (if not historical) integrity. The days of atomistically disintegrating the book into scores of literary particles have given way to a new appreciation of the clearly holistic image the book bears. Much of this, admittedly, is attributed to major, creative redaction by the "deuteronomist" and others, but much of it has come as well from new literary approaches that find cohesive artistry at work not only in separate literary blocks that hitherto were thought to have been composite but also in the book as a whole.[16] Clearly Samuel, despite its wealth of form and varying content, stands as a monument to articulate and purposeful history-writing.

THE TEXT OF SAMUEL

A history of the study of the text of Samuel, especially since the discovery of the DSS, reveals an extremely problematic MT tradition.[17] On the whole the MT of Samuel is defective compared to the rest of the Bible and also in comparison to the Qumran manuscripts (4 Q Sama and 4 Q Sam b) and the principal versions. The major flaw is the extensive occurrence of haplography, the accidental omission of words or whole phrases because of similar line endings.

The DSS materials generally support the superiority of the Hebrew texts underlying the Greek version (LXX and especially Lucian). That is, the Greek translators seem to have had access to Hebrew manuscripts of Samuel that were closer to the original than are the Masoretic readings. All this is not to say that the MT contains numerous major deviations from the hypothetical autograph or that it cannot be employed with confidence as to its historical and

---

[14] Ibid., 172.

[15] Ibid., 173.

[16] See, e.g., J. P. Fokkelman, *King David*, vol. 1 of *Narrative Art and Poetry in the Books of Samuel* (Assen: Van Gorcum, 1981).

[17] P. K. McCarter Jr., *1 Samuel*, AB (Garden City, NY: Doubleday, 1980), 5–11. For pre-Qumran scholarship see especially S. R. Driver, *Notes on the Hebrew Text of Samuel*, 2nd ed. (1912; reprint, Winona Lake, IN: Alpha, 1984), xxxiii–lxxxiii.

theological integrity. It does mean that the MT must be checked against other authoritative Hebrew and versional witnesses in order to yield the maximum fidelity to the original composition.

THE LITERARY CHARACTER OF SAMUEL

The first and certainly correct impression of those who read Samuel is that they are reading history. Matters of genre, form, style, and redaction aside, the book asserts itself as a record of Israel's national life from the birth of Samuel (c. 1120 BC) to the impending death of David (971 BC).[18] As already observed, Samuel may not be history-writing of the kind typical of the modern Western world, but that hardly disqualifies it as historiography in terms of the times and places in which it originated.[19]

The style of the great blocks of material that constitute most of the book is narrative, largely of a biographical and anecdotal kind. The book begins with the story of Samuel's birth, dedication to God, and early preparation for public ministry (1 Samuel 1–3). Somewhat intrusive, perhaps, is the Song of Hannah (2:1–10) which may have been added later but which certainly is not altogether out of place here as a response to God's having answered Hannah's prayer for a son (1:11). It hymnically anticipates the rise of Israelite monarchy (2:10), and for that reason it is usually construed to be Davidic or later in origin.[20] Whatever the case, it clearly contributes to a major theme in Samuel—the rise of David's kingship.

At this point the Samuel narrative is suspended while the historian recounts the story of the ark of the covenant, the second major block of material in the book (4:1b–7:1).[21] This section contains little biography because its focus is on the capture, fortunes, and return of the ark. It is anecdotal, a story enriched by suspense, humor, irony, and polemic, and one so self-contained and perfectly rounded off as to suggest to many scholars that it, like Hannah's hymn, is secondary to the original account of Samuel. Our own analysis below shows that this is not the case.

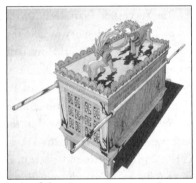

Ark of the Covenant.

The next major narrative—the History of David's Rise to Kingship (1 Sam 16:14–2 Sam 5:10)—follows the remainder of Samuel's biography (1 Sam 7:3–17), the people's demand for a king (chap. 8), the steps Samuel took to bring this request to pass in the person of Saul (9:1–11:15), and the account of Saul's tragic reign (13:1–16:13).[22] This account is introduced by Samuel's public address in which he warns the nation of the disaster that awaits

---

[18] For the literary structure and unity of the book see D. A. Dorsey, *The Literary Structure of the Old Testament* (Grand Rapids: Baker, 1999), 129–36.

[19] E. H. Merrill, "History," *Cracking Old Testament Codes,* ed D. B. Sandy and R. L. Giese Jr. (Nashville: B&H, 1995), 89–112; idem, "Old Testament History: A Theological Perspective," in *A Guide to Old Testament Theology and Exegesis,* ed. W. A. VanGemeren (Grand Rapids: Zondervan, 1997), 65–82.

[20] S. R. Driver, *An Introduction to the Literature of the Old Testament* (Cleveland: World, 1956), 174. .

[21] A. F. Campbell, *The Ark Narrative (1 Sam 4–6; 2 Sam 6): A Form-Critical and Traditio-Historical Study,* SBLDS (Missoula, MT: Scholars, 1975).

[22] B. Birch, *The Rise of the Israelite Monarchy: The Growth and Development of I Samuel 7–15* (Missoula, MT: Scholars, 1976); J. M. Miller, "Saul's Rise to Power: Some Observations Concerning 1 Sam 9:1–10:16; 10:26–11:15 and 13:2–14:46," *CBQ* 36 (1974): 157–74.

them and their new king if they fail to adhere to God's expectations (1 Samuel 12). Most of this is biographical, the exceptions being Samuel's exhortation (8:10–18), the story of Saul's Ammonite campaign (11:1–11), and, again, Samuel's farewell address (12:1–17) with a following theophany (v. 18) and popular response (vv. 19–25).

The History of David's Rise (1 Sam 16:14–2 Sam 5:10),[23] one of the longest sustained narratives in the Bible, recounts David's anointing by the Spirit (1 Sam 16:14–23), his period of favor with Saul (17:1–18:5), the years of disfavor and exile (1 Sam 18:6–2 Sam 1:27), his brief reign at Hebron (2 Sam 2:1–5:5), and his installation as king in Jerusalem (5:6–10). This largely biographical material also includes battle accounts (1 Sam 17:1–54; 27:8–12; 31:1–6; 2 Sam 2:12–17); celebratory verse (1 Sam 18:7b); death notices (1 Sam 25:1; 28:3); dirges (2 Sam 1:19–27; 3:33–34); and a brief genealogy (2 Sam 3:2–5). For the most part it is straightforward reportage with little parenesis or comment (but see the exceptions in 1 Sam 18:30; 25:28–31).

Another collection of shorter texts precedes the next major block, the "Succession Narrative" (2 Samuel 9–20 + 1 Kings 1–2). These include the description of David's establishment in Jerusalem (2 Sam 5:11–25), the (resumption of the) ark narrative (chap. 6), the prophecy of an eternal Davidic dynasty (7:1–17), David's responsive prayer (7:18–29), and a catalog of his military enterprises (8:1–14). The list of David's officials in 8:15–18 seems to be an introduction to the Succession Narrative which ends with a similar list (20:23–26). Embedded in these texts are theological observations (5:10), battle reports (5:17–25), and a prophetic oracle (7:4–16).[24]

The Succession Narrative (2 Samuel 9–20 + 1 Kings 1–2) is rightly assessed by many scholars as the crowning glory of Old Testament historiography.[25] Its thematic, stylistic, and literary cohesion gives rise to an almost universal consensus that the narrative is of one piece. The consensus does admit of differences of opinion as to the beginning of the narrative (e.g., with chaps. 6 and 7), the inclusion of 1 Kings 1–2, and even the purpose of the composition. The significance of the intervening material (2 Samuel 21–24) is also debated.

Subplots or pericopae within the Succession Narrative include the account of the Ammonite wars (10:1–11:1; 12:26–31), David's adultery (11:2–5) and subsequent murder of Uriah (11:6–25), the birth and election of Solomon (12:15b–25), the rape of Tamar and its aftermath (chaps. 13–14), the rebellion of Absalom (15:1–19:10), and David's restoration to power (19:11–20:22). Besides the anecdotal nature of the material, the book also includes various forms such as messenger reports (11:23–24), battle reports (10:15–19), a commission (11:18–21), parables (12:1–4; 14:5–7), and an "official report" (18:19–19:1).

The story of the revenge of the Gibeonites (21:1–14) has clear connections to the earlier narratives about Saul's descendants (chaps. 4, 9), perhaps forming with them a bracketing

---

[23] N. P. Lemche, "David's Rise," *JSOT* 10 (1978): 2–25.

[24] For the view that Samuel does not reflect a strict chronological approach to the David narratives see E. H. Merrill, "The 'Accession Year' and Davidic Chronology," JANES 19 (1989): 101–12.

[25] R. A. Carlson, *David, the Chosen King: A Traditio-Historical Approach to the Second Book of Samuel* (Stockholm: Almquist & Wiksell, 1964); G. W. Coats, "Parable, Fable, and Anecdote: Storytelling in the Succession Narrative," *Interp* 35 (1981): 368–82; J. W. Flanagan, "Court History or Succession Document? A Study of 2 Sam 9–20 and 1 Kings 1–2," *JBL* 91 (1972): 172–81; K. K. Sacon, "A Study of the Literary Structure of the 'Succession Narrative'," *Studies in the Period of David and Solomon and Other Essays*, ed. T. Ishida (Winona Lake, IN: Eisenbrauns, 1982), 27–54; R. N. Whybray, *The Succession Narrative. A Study of II Samuel 9–20; I Kings 1 and 2* (Naperville, IL: Allenson, 1968).

device.[26] Likewise the list of David's Philistine campaigns (21:15–22) harks back to a passage with a similar concern (5:17–25). Chapter 22 is a psalm of David, one later included in the book of Psalms (Psalm 18) with only slight variation. "The last words of David" appear in 23:1–7, followed by a list of his heroes (23:8–39). The last of the so-called "appendices" is the story of David's military census and the judgment it evoked (chap. 24). Its purpose in Samuel—and at this place in the narrative—will receive attention below.

OUTLINE OF SAMUEL

1 Samuel

I. **The Preparations for the Monarchy (chaps. 1–9)**
   A. Samuel's Birth and Childhood (chap. 1)
   B. Hannah's Song (2:1–10)
   C. The Situation at Shiloh (2:11–36)
   D. Samuel's Call (chap. 3)
   E. The Ark (chaps. 4–7)
      1. The capture of the ark (chap. 4)
      2. The power of the ark (chap. 5)
      3. The return of the ark (6:1–7:1)
      4. The restoration of the ark (7:2–17)
   F. Selection of a King (chaps. 8–9)
      1. The demand for a king (8:1–9)
      2. The nature of the king (8:10–18)
      3. The introduction of the king (8:19–9:14)
      4. The choice of the king (9:15–27)

II. **The Period of Saul (chaps. 10–31)**
   A. Saul's Ascendancy (chaps. 10–14)
      1. Saul's choice by Israel (chap. 10)
      2. Saul's first victory (chap. 11)
      3. The address by Samuel (chap. 12)
      4. Saul's first rebuke (chap. 13)
      5. Jonathan's peril (chap. 14)
   B. Saul's Rejection (chap. 15)
   C. Saul and David (chaps. 16–26)
      1. On friendly terms (chaps 16–17)
      2. On unfriendly terms (chaps 18–26)
   D. Saul's Death (chaps. 27–31)
      1. David at Ziklag (chap. 27)
      2. Saul at Endor (chap. 28)
      3. David's return to Ziklag (chaps. 29–30)
      4. The battle of Gilboa (chap. 31)

---

[26] See (without embracing all his conclusions) W. Brueggemann, "2 Samuel 21–24: An Appendix of Deconstruction?" *CBQ* 50 (1988): 383–97; Childs, *Introduction to the Old Testament as Scripture*, 273–75.

2 Samuel

ANALYSIS OF SAMUEL AS A WORK OF HISTORY

Since Noth's groundbreaking hypothesis of a Deuteronomic history, Samuel has been identified as a part of that corpus.[27] What is meant by this term is the notion that Joshua through 2 Kings is a massive history composed and/or redacted over a number of years and reaching its final form in the Jewish exile.[28] It is called "Deuteronomic" because it is thought to have been produced with the covenant principles of Deuteronomy as the standard by which Israel's history was to be understood and critiqued. This by no means presupposes the existence of the book of Deuteronomy at the beginning of the history; far from it, for Deuteronomy itself is

---

[27] M. Noth, *The Deuteronomistic History*, JSOTSup (Sheffield: University of Sheffield, 1981).

[28] F. M. Cross modifies the hypothesis by suggesting a preexilic (c. 620 BC) edition of the history (his Dtr[1]) as well as the exilic (c. 550 BC) posited by Noth (Dtr[2]). See Cross, *Canaanite Myth and Hebrew Epic* (Cambridge, MA: Harvard University Press, 1973), 274–89.

also dated by these scholars no earlier than the seventh century BC. What it does suggest is that Deuteronomy reflects ancient ideologies of belief and practice, and therefore it serves to provide a paradigm to which the nation should have conformed in its historical experience.[29]

Most scholars view Samuel as a collection of texts that are more or less reliable as records of the reigns of Saul and David but records that have been edited in places by later deuteronomists in order to present them in a certain historical and theological light. Depending on one's view of the identification of these Deuteronomic circles, the account is promonarchic or antimonarchic, pro-Davidic or anti-Davidic, pro-prophetic or anti-prophetic, or pro-priestly or anti-priestly. Such varying opinions reflect the subjectivity of a process that comes to the text with a preconceived hypothesis that has little or no objective historical basis. That is, the very existence of a Deuteronomic history (that includes Samuel) based on a late, non-Mosaic Deuteronomy is without objective evidence and therefore must be viewed with the utmost skepticism.[30]

However, it is not incorrect to suggest that Joshua–2 Kings (and all the OT, for that matter) is a consistent, even unified, presentation of Israel's history, one that reached its final, canonical form in the postexilic period. The theological, ideological, thematic, and literary evidence all points in that direction.[31] That being the case, it will be useful to see how Samuel in all its parts fits into that perspective.

The suggestion that 2 Samuel 9–20 + 1 Kings 1–2 (the "Succession Narrative") is central to Samuel has great merit for the theme of the book is clearly the establishment of the Davidic monarchy—how it originated, what forces were in danger of preventing and subverting it, and the steps taken to assure its everlasting continuation. David's sins against Bathsheba and Uriah—or, more properly, as David himself confessed, against God (Ps 51:4)—threatened to undo his monarchy and raised serious questions about his dynastic succession.

Contrary to much of modern scholarship, the message of Samuel is not antimonarchic but only against a premature choice by the masses as opposed to God's election of "a man after his own heart" (1 Sam 13:14 NIV). That man, of course, was David. The book begins with the story of Samuel (1 Samuel 1–3 + 7) for he was to be God's agent of announcing and anointing the chosen ruler. The Song of Hannah, "inserted" as it is into the Samuel story, is not some late Deuteronomic propaganda justifying Davidic kingship. Instead it was a prayer of Hannah herself (2:1) in which she anticipated an earthly messianic king (v. 10).[32] The remainder of the Samuel biography serves to authenticate Samuel's prophetic role (3:15–21) as theocratic mediator (7:3–17), advocate for legitimate kingship (8:4–22; 10:17–24; 12:6–25), facilitator of the premature and only permitted rule of Saul (9:1–10:16; 11:14–15), condemner of that rule (13:8–15; 15:1–23), and spokesman for the God-ordained selection of David (16:1–13).

The Ark Narrative (1 Sam 4–6 + 2 Sam 6?) sets the stage for the shift from the old tribal confederation to the rising monarchy and from Shiloh to Jerusalem. Its location in the text highlights the chaotic times of the judges in which Israel's religion had been largely reduced to superstition. The capture of the ark by the Philistines was in sharp contrast to its recovery over

---

[29] E. W. Nicholson. *Deuteronomy and Tradition* (Philadelphia: Fortress, 1967), 113.

[30] For a severe criticism, especially of the view that Deuteronomy and Joshua belong to DtrH, see G. Fohrer, *History of Israelite Religion* (Nashville: Abingdon, 1972), 305. K. A. Kitchen wonders whether the whole notion of "Deuteronomism" might fall under the category of "modern myth." See his "Ancient Orient, 'Deuteronomism,' and the Old Testament," in *New Perspectives on the Old Testament*, ed. J. B. Payne (Waco, TX: Word, 1970), 16–19.

[31] Childs properly understands the unity to be a product of a constantly unfolding consensus of the community regarding history and its meaning (*Introduction to the Old Testament as Scripture*, 232–38).

[32] Thus J. R. Vannoy, *1–2 Samuel*, CBC (Carol Stream, IL: Tyndale House, 2009), 54.

a century later by David (2 Samuel 6), for David, despite some mishaps, recognized the need for the ark as a symbol of his divinely originated kingship. Scholars who view 2 Samuel 5 as a continuation of the Ark Narrative are correct except in suggesting that the present text reflects the breakup of an originally unified composition.

Just as the Ark Narrative in 1 Samuel demonstrates, by contrast to that in 2 Samuel, Israel's apostate religious condition, so the stories of Saul's reign (1 Samuel 9–31) stand in opposition to the remarkable account of the rise of David. Though most literary critics locate the latter piece in 1 Samuel 16–2 Samuel 5:10, it is only the part in 2 Samuel that stands as an isolated text. Otherwise the actual decline of Saul (as opposed to its formal announcement in 1 Sam 13:14; 15:23; 16:14) is so intertwined with David's historical rise to power (as opposed to its announcement in 1 Sam 13:14; 15:28; 16:12–13) that one can hardly describe it one way or the other. Is it Saul's fall or David's rise? In line with the overall theme of the book it is perhaps best to understand it as the latter. The theme is David's rise but one that was continually under attack by antitheocratic elements.

The great treatise known as the Succession Narrative comes to the foreground. Those scholars who propose that it was created as an apologetic for Solomon's kingship certainly have a valid point (see 1 Kgs 1:5–48; 2:13–25,46), but to limit it to this is to ignore the prophetic oracle in which David's succession is assured (2 Samuel 7) and the birth account of Solomon in which the successor is at least intimated by name (2 Sam 12:24–25; cf. 1 Chron 22:9–10). Only a misguided, groundless hypothesis of Deuteronomic redaction requires that any allusions to the Davidic monarchy and its succession be assigned to a period hundreds of years after David's time. In fact the blatant disregard for David's dignity and character manifested throughout the Succession Narrative in the stories of adultery, murder, rape, intrigue, and rebellion argue strongly against its being an account long after the event, for how could such things contribute to the purpose of aggrandizing the royal family? Contrariwise, if the purpose of the deuteronomists is to denigrate that monarchy, why did they allow the glorious covenant promises of 2 Samuel 7 to remain in the record?

The literature of the "appendices" (2 Samuel 21–24) is well situated as it stands. In fact its connections to texts preceding or at the beginning of the Succession Narrative are quite striking. Thus 21:1–14 shares a common theme with chap. 9 (chap. 4); 21:15–22 is reminiscent of 5:17–25; chap. 22 (in that it is poetry) resembles 1:19–27; 23:1–7 focuses on the covenant as does chap. 7; 23:8–39 speaks of David's mighty men and their exploits, a theme also in 8:1–14; and chap. 24 narrates the account of the acquisition of Araunah's threshing-floor as a suitable place for the altar of God, a theme that echoes the Ark Narrative of chap. 6, which, among other things, presupposes the need for a sanctuary.

In conclusion, though one may and perhaps should allow for a continuing process of adaptation of the Samuel accounts long after the events recorded there, there is no need, literarily or theologically, to suppose that it is finally and primarily the product of a postexilic redaction. The material makes sense as it stands and as ancient tradition has always maintained—namely, that it work in its essence no later than its latest attested historical event.

PURPOSE AND THEOLOGY OF SAMUEL

A case can be made that Samuel's purpose is to provide a history of Israel just preceding and continuing through the reigns of Saul and David. But to limit the purpose to this as a secular matter is to fail to understand why that history had to be recounted at all. Such a rationale has to be theological in the final analysis.[33] Viewed from this perspective it seems clear that the intention of the book of Samuel is to show the why and how of the transition from a period in which "everyone did whatever he wanted" (Judg 21:25) to one in which God's kingdom rule was entrusted to one man who was "after [God's] own heart" (1 Sam 13:14 NIV).

This "kingdom theology" is not by any means limited to Samuel. The Lord had promised through Jacob that "the scepter will not depart from Judah" (Gen 49:10), and He had forced the pagan prophet Balaam to exclaim, "A star will come from Jacob; and a scepter will arise from Israel" (Num 24:17). The royal messianic thrust of these ancient texts was affirmed and their implied monarchical policies regulated by the guidelines for kingship outlined in Deut 17:14–20. Thus the way was prepared for the messianic ruler David, whose Greatest Son is to become the King of kings and Lord of lords (Rev 19:16).

STUDY QUESTIONS

1. To what main section of the Hebrew Bible does Samuel belong?
2. According to the Talmud, who wrote the book of Samuel?
3. What is the major problem with the Talmudic suggestion?
4. What is the principal significance of the Davidic covenant?
5. From whence did David finally retrieve the ark of the covenant to bring it to Jerusalem?
6. Which one of David's sons led a revolution against him?
7. From which kingdom did timber come to build David's palace?
8. Why was Saul particularly interested in Jabesh-Gilead?
9. Why was Joab so driven to kill Abner?
10. Why was David's life spared even though he had committed adultery and murder?
11. Why did David spare Saul's life though given several opportunities to take it?
12. What was the strategy behind David's selection of Jerusalem to be Israel's capital?
13. What structure eventually occupied the site of Araunah's "threshing floor"?
14. What motivated David to be reconciled to his separated wife Michal?
15. What was the main reason David's bid to build the temple was denied?

FOR FURTHER STUDY

Anderson, A. A. *2 Samuel*. WBC. Dallas: Word, 1989.
Bergen, Robert D. *1, 2 Samuel*. NAC. Nashville: B&H, 1996.
Bright, John. *A History of Israel*. 3rd ed. Philadelphia: Westminster, 1981.
Campbell, A. F., and M. A. O'Brien. *Unfolding the Deuteronomistic History*. Minneapolis: Fortress, 2000.
Chisholm, R. B., Jr. *Interpreting the Historical Books*. Grand Rapids: Kregel, 2006.
Dothan, T. *The Philistines and Their Material Culture*. New Haven, CT: Yale University Press, 1982.
Driver, S. R. *Notes on the Hebrew Text of Samuel*. 2nd ed. 1912; reprint, Winona Lake, IN: Alpha, 1984.
Fokkelman, J. P. *Narrative Art and Poetry in the Books of Samuel*. Assen: Van Gorcum, 1981.
Hamilton, V. P. *Handbook on the Historical Books*. Grand Rapids: Baker, 2001.
Hayes, J. H. and J. M. Miller. *Israelite and Judaean History*. Philadelphia: Westminster, 1977.
Hertzberg, H. W. *I and II Samuel*. Philadelphia: Westminster, 1964.
Howard, D. M., Jr. *An Introduction to the Old Testament Historical Books*. Chicago: Moody, 1993.
Kaiser, W. C., Jr. *A History of Israel*. Nashville: B&H, 1998.
Klein, R. W. *1 Samuel*. WBC. Waco: Word, 1983.

---

[33] Homer Heater Jr., "A Theology of Samuel and Kings," in *A Biblical Theology of the Old Testament*, ed. R. B. Zuck (Chicago: Moody, 1991), 115–55; E. H. Merrill, *Everlasting Dominion: A Theology of the Old Testament* (Nashville: B&H, 2006), 427–40.

Longman, T., III, and R. B. Dillard. *An Introduction to the Old Testament*. 2nd ed. Grand Rapids: Zondervan, 2006.

McCarter, P. K., Jr. *I Samuel*. AB. Garden City, NY: Doubleday, 1980.

———. *II Samuel*. AB. Garden City, NY: Doubleday, 1984.

McKenzie, Steven L. *The Chronicler's Use of the Deuteronomistic History*. Atlanta: Scholars, 1984.

Merrill, E. H. *Kingdom of Priests: A History of Old Testament Israel*. 2nd ed. Grand Rapids: Baker, 2008.

Peckham, B. *The Composition of the Deuteronomistic History*. Atlanta: Scholars, 1985.

Provan, Iain, V. Philips Long, and Tremper Longman III. *A Biblical History of Israel*. Louisville: Westminster John Knox, 2003.

Tsumura, D. T. *The First Book of Samuel*. NICOT. Grand Rapids: Eerdmans, 2007.

Vannoy, J. R. *1–2 Samuel*. CBC. Carol Stream, IL: Tyndale House, 2009.

Youngblood, R. F. *1, 2 Samuel*. EBC. Rev. ed. Edited by T. Longman and D. E. Garland, 3:21–614. Grand Rapids: Zondervan, 2009.

CHAPTER 19

THE BOOKS OF 1 AND 2 KINGS

EUGENE H. MERRILL

THE LITERARY CHARACTER OF KINGS

The Title and Canonicity of the Book

The fact that the books of 1 and 2 Kings embraces the reigns of all the kings of Israel and Judah from David's last years (c. 973–971 BC) through the tenure of Zedekiah and rehabilitation of Jehoiachin (562 BC) readily explains the modern and ancient titles of the work.[1] In the earliest Jewish traditions the books are called *mĕlākîm* ("kings") since the major figures throughout are the respective rulers of the northern and southern kingdoms. This is despite the fact that the books are included in the section of the Hebrew canon known as *nebî'îm* ("prophets"). As noted before, this latter term reflects ideas of authorship and ideology and not necessarily of content, though in the case of Kings prophets such as Elijah and Elisha played major roles. The tradition of authorship by Jeremiah (see below) delivered Kings from any dispute as to its canonicity.

In the so-called Alexandrian (or LXX) Greek canon the books of Samuel and Kings are grouped together as a vast historical collection called 1, 2, 3, and 4 Kingdoms (*Basileiōn* A, B, C, and D). Such a designation draws attention to the perspective of that third-century BC community that saw the works as fundamentally historiographical in nature and not prophetic. That is, they were historical accounts of the kingdoms of Israel and Judah from the founding of the monarchy under Saul to its demise under Zedekiah. The Vulgate followed the LXX tradition by naming the two books of Kings *Liber Regum tertius et quartus* (The Third and Fourth Book of Kings).

The Literary Forms and Genres of the Book

The overriding self-presentation of Kings is that it is history-writing. Typical of that genre at its best is the use of narrative, a dominant feature of this composition from beginning to

---

[1] For the chronology here and elsewhere in the chapter, see E. H. Merrill, *Kingdom of Priests: A History of Old Testament Israel* (Grand Rapids: Baker, 2008), 337.

end.[2] However, careful reading of the material reveals that a characterization of the composition as "mere" historiography or even narrative is overly simplistic for it is a compilation of a bewildering array of literary forms and types.[3] Such a ménage should not necessarily lead to the inference that Kings is a hodgepodge of disparate texts originally unrelated and carelessly juxtaposed (see below, pp. 321–22). Rather, the result is a marvelously crafted integration of a variety of sources and genres by a gifted historian (or historians) who has produced a satisfyingly united text without sacrificing the diversity of form that gives it such abiding interest.

Besides the rather imprecise genre of history itself, Kings shows examples of others such as reports (1 Kgs 2:1–9; 6:2–38; 20:35–43); story (2:13–25; 3:16–28; 20:1–34); petition (8:14–53; 2 Kgs 19:15–19); farewell speech (1 Kgs 2:1–9); prophetic judgment speeches (11:30–39); prophecy of punishment (13:21–22; 14:7–11); dream epiphany (3:4–15; 9:1–9); and theological review (11:1–13; 2 Kgs 10:28–31; 17:7–23; 21:9–15). All these, no matter how diverse, are woven together under the general rubric "history-writing" and by their very differences attest to (1) the variety of oral and written sources available to the historian and (2) the almost inexhaustible literary vehicles by which history may be communicated.

Recent approaches to the literature of the OT have generated an awareness that there is no such thing as an exclusively historiographic genre or set of genres.[4] That is, although history may *usually* be recorded in certain customary ways (reports, annals, chronicles, and the like), it by no means *must* be limited to these. Thus, poetry, parables, proverbs, sermons, and even fictive creations such as myths and legends may be (and, in Kings, are) used to help tell the story of Israel's past. The secret, of course, is to recognize these forms, to understand how and why the historian is using them, and to see how they contribute uniquely to the account precisely because they are outside the generally expected historical forms.

Two or three examples are given here. First Kings 2:1–9, classified by most scholars as a farewell speech or testament, consists of David's bedside charge and admonition to his son and successor Solomon.[5] Clearly the passage existed at one time as an independent piece either written by David or recorded by a witness. In any case its original intention was not to provide raw data for a history book, so it was not composed in the third person as a historian would be inclined to do. Rather, the historian appropriates the text as it stands and weaves it into his overall account because of its obviously important historical implications.

Also the prayer of Solomon in 1 Kgs 3:6–9 can hardly be classified as "historical" literature, and yet it has been creatively taken up by the historian and used as an important datum for both historical and theological purposes. Most critics deny that Solomon's very words appear here, though such judgments are entirely speculative and subjective and betray a lack of appreciation for the care with which scribes must have recorded royal utterances, even prayers.[6] However, the point here is that though a prayer is an unlikely component of historical account, it cannot be ruled "unhistorical" for that reason.

---

[2] See R. Alter, *The Art of Biblical Narrative* (New York: Basic, 1981; D. M. Gunn and D. N. Fewell, *Narrative in the Hebrew Bible* (Oxford: Oxford University Press, 1993), 3–7; E. H. Merrill, "History," in D. B. Sandy and R. L. Giese Jr., eds., *Cracking Old Testament Codes* (Nashville: B&H, 1995), 89–112; J. G. McConville, "Narrative and Meaning in the Books of Kings," *Bib* 70 (1989): 31–49.

[3] B. O. Long, *1 Kings*, FOTL IX (Grand Rapids: Eerdmans, 1984), 4–8.

[4] V. P. Long, *The Art of Biblical History* (Grand Rapids: Zondervan, 1994), 27–57; idem, "Narrative and History: Stories about the Past," in I. Provan, V. P. Long, and T. Longman III, *A Biblical History of Israel* (Louisville: WJK, 2003), 75–97.

[5] W. T. Koopmans, "The Testament of David in 1 Kings ii 1-10," *VT* 41 (1991): 429–49.

[6] B. Long, for example, describes the passage (with no objective warrant) as one "put into the mouth of Solomon" by the Deuteronomist (*1 Kings*, 65).

Particularly problematic are the so-called "tales of the prophets," stories so unusual and/ or miraculous that modern criticism assigns them the label "legend."[7] They bear this onus not because of literary criteria, however, but because they fall outside the realm of ordinary human experience. Were it not for the supernatural elements they would be classified merely as stories or anecdotes. Either way, the numerous prophetic stories—mainly of Elijah and Elisha—must indeed have circulated orally and in writing before they found their way into the canonical collection. What is relevant here is that they almost certainly were not composed at first as grist for later historians but as testimonials to God's power and faithfulness to and through his choice servants. But the sacred history of the biblical record is most interested precisely in these kinds of events. Thus brief anecdotes or cycles of anecdotes were utilized by the historian and probably with little or no effort to "bring them into line" as proper historical texts.

The Structure of the Book

Form-critical analyses of the biblical literature that have identified and offered suggestions as to the settings and purposes of genres such as those referred to above have been followed in recent years by other kinds of literary investigation bearing such terminology as "rhetorical criticism" or "new literary criticism." These methods seek not so much to find small oral and written textual units but larger compositional structures, schemes, and patterns. They generally proceed from the literature as it exists, identifying possible motifs, themes, and frameworks that provide coherent organization.

While quite persuasive in some applications—particularly in poetic and prophetic texts— efforts to find macrostructure in books like Kings have been largely unsuccessful.[8] And this ought not to be surprising for if Kings is what it claims to be, an account (albeit theological) of ancient Israel's history, only a distortion of the flow of events as they actually occurred in time and space would result were the material to be arranged according to the results of most of these analyses. On the other hand sensitivity to proper exegetical and hermeneutical intertextuality reveals such features in the Bible as historical patternism, the repetition of movements and events springing from archetypal paradigms. A view that confesses that God is the author of history can make allowance for the fact that not only can accounts of history exhibit a repetitive morphology but that history itself (at least biblical history) actually occurred in such a manner.[9]

---

[7] S. J. DeVries, *1 Kings*, WBC (Waco: Word, 1985), xxxvi–xxxviii. For a helpful critique of this notion see Long, *The Art of Biblical History*, 181–84.

[8] D. A. Dorsey offers one of the more convincing examples:

    a Solomon's reign in Jerusalem; Jerusalem's wealth; temple is built (1 Kgs 3:1–11:43)
      b Rise of northern kingdom: its first <u>seven</u> kings (1 Kgs 12:1–16:34)
        c Prophet Elijah and early Omride dynasty (1 Kgs 17:1–2 Kgs 1:18)
          d Centerpiece: Elisha's miracles of kindness (2 Kgs 2:1–8:6)
        c' Prophet Elisha and end of Omride dynasty (2 Kgs 8:7–13:25)
      b' Fall of northern kingdom: its last <u>seven</u> kings (2 Kgs 14:1–17:41)
    a' Solomon's dynasty in Jerusalem ends; fall of Jerusalem and destruction of Solomon's temple (2 Kgs 18:1–25:30)
(*The Literary Structure of the Old Testament* [Grand Rapids: Baker, 1999], 143).

[9] As a historiosophical concept see M. Eliade, *Cosmos and History: The Myth of the Eternal Return* (New York: Harper & Row, 1959), 3–48. As an aspect of biblical typology see F. Foulkes, *The Acts of God: A Study of the Basis of Typology in the Old Testament* (London: Tyndale, 1958); H. D. Hummel, "The Old Testament Basis of Typological Interpretation," *BR* 9 (1964): 38–50.

Rhetorical patternism is clearly manifested on the microlevel, examples of which have been suggested by several scholars. Burke O. Long draws attention to a great many in his study of 1 Kings, including a "concentric motival structure" in 2:29–31a:[10]

A. Solomon's order (v. 29)
    B.   Benaiah comes to Joab (v. 30aa)
        C.   Dialogue (v. 30ab)
    B[1].   Benaiah reports back to Solomon (v. 30b)
A[1].   Solomon's order reissued (v. 31)

Another, based on the recurring verb *l*, occurs in the dialogue between Ahab and Benhadad, king of Aram, in 1 Kings 20:[11]

$$
\left\{
\begin{array}{l}
\left.
\begin{array}{l}
\textbf{Ben-hadad to Ahab} \\
\textbf{Ahab to Ben-hadad}
\end{array}
\right\} \quad \textbf{vv. 2-4} \\[1em]
\textbf{Ben-hadad to Ahab} \qquad \textbf{vv. 5-6} \\[1em]
\left\{
\begin{array}{l}
\left.
\begin{array}{l}
\textbf{Ahab to elders} \\
\textbf{Elders to Ahab}
\end{array}
\right\} \quad \textbf{vv. 7-8}
\end{array}
\right. \\[1em]
\textbf{Ahab to Ben-hadad} \qquad \textbf{v. 9} \\[1em]
\left.
\begin{array}{l}
\textbf{Ben-hadad to Ahab} \\
\textbf{Ahab to Ben-hadad}
\end{array}
\right\} \quad \textbf{vv. 10-1}
\end{array}
\right.
$$

Still a third example is seen in 1 Kings 21, the story of Ahab's murder of Naboth:[12]

Ahab– to Naboth	(Speech)	vv. 1–3
Ahab	(Action)	v. 4
Ahab– to Jezebel	(Speech)	vv. 5–7
Jezebel	(Action)	vv. 8–14
Ahab– to Jezebel	(Speech)	vv. 15–16

Clearly a case can be made for a literary artistry in service to history writing, an artistry that does not in any way diminish the factuality of the accounts and in fact sometimes argues for the compositional unity of texts that previously had been considered diverse in origin.

---

[10] Long, *1 Kings*, 54.
[11] Ibid., 214.
[12] Ibid., 225.

The Outline of the Book

THE COMPOSITION OF KINGS

Authorship of the Book

The absence in Kings of any authorial ascription has led to a plethora of suggestions rang-ing from Jeremiah to the Deuteronomist(s). The Talmudic tractate *Baba Bathra* (15a) states that "Jeremiah wrote the book which bears his name, the Book of Kings, and Lamentations." "Wrote" may in this instance mean edit or compile, but even so it suggests a possibility that cannot automatically be rejected out of hand. Jeremiah was obviously literate, he lived after most (if not all) of the events recorded in the book, and he would have had good historical and theological reasons for producing such a work. He lived during and after the days of the Babylonian destruction of Jerusalem and deportation of the Jewish community and would therefore be concerned about providing a historical account of that community while there were still oral and written sources on which he could draw. Also the assessment of that history in theological terms is most compatible with Jeremiah's own undisputed testimony in both the books of Jeremiah and Lamentations.[13]

The major objections to the tradition of Jeremianic authorship are (1) the very fact that it is only tradition, that is, that it has no validation in the book itself; (2) the indisputable evidence of a variety of literary forms, genres, and sources; and (3) development in recent decades of the more likely alternative hypothesis of a Deuteronomic school that was responsible for the composition of the massive work known as the Deuteronomic History, a work encompassing Joshua through Kings.

As for (1), tradition admittedly does not constitute solid evidence but tradition of this kind, at least, deserves a more convincing alternative to it before it is rejected as impossible or even unlikely. Lack of compositional homogeneity (2) shows only that the "author" of Kings—whether Jeremiah or not—was technically such only in the sense of editor or redactor (or even collector) of historical sources that have found expression in their present canonical form. Jeremianic "authorship" in this sense even allows for exilic or postexilic redactions if, indeed, there is any evidence of such. As for (3), it simply provides another name (Deuteronomist) for the person or persons responsible for the work that older tradition attributed to Jeremiah. But it also expands the influence of the "author" much beyond Kings—in fact, all the way back to Joshua. This would seem to weaken the case for Jeremiah unless, of course, one were to identify Jeremiah as the Deuteronomist.

The Date of the Book

The last datable event in Kings is the release of King Jehoiachin from Babylonian house arrest in 562 BC, the thirty-seventh year of his having been taken prisoner (2 Kgs 25:27). However, the narrative adds that he was put on royal pension thereafter for the rest of his life (vv. 29–30), a clue to the fact that this statement, at least, was added sometime after 562, perhaps as late as 540 or so (see 2 Kgs 24:8,12). This appears to preclude Jeremiah as author of this account for the prophet began his public ministry in 627 BC (Jer 1:1–3). He could hardly have been much younger than 30 at the time and therefore would be over 90 at the time of Jehoiachin's release. Moreover, he himself had been transported to Egypt not long after the fall of Jerusalem in 586 (Jer 43:5–7), and though this need not disallow Jeremiah as the author of the end of Kings (see Jer 52:31–34) it might place the matter in some doubt.

---

[13] For support of single authorship and by Jeremiah see D. J. Wiseman, *1 and 2 Kings: An Introduction and Commentary* (Downers Grove, IL: InterVarsity, 1993), 52–55.

The Sources of the Book

Whatever may be said of the author's or final editor's role in the composition of narratives of events with which he was contemporary (commencing sometime in the reign of Manasseh, 695–642 BC), a period covered in 2 Kings 21–25, he was dependent on other sources for earlier times. Kings opens with the struggle over succession to David's throne, a struggle of about two years that finally ended with Solomon's undisputed accession in 971 BC. This pericope (1 Kgs 1–2) is generally recognized to be an independent unit,[14] the opening section of one of three major sources named in Kings itself, namely, "the Book of Solomon's Events" (1 Kgs 11:41); "Historical Record of Israel's Kings" (1 Kgs 14:19); and "the Historical Record of Judah's Kings" (2 Kgs 24:5). There is no reason to doubt the existence of such archival texts in Israel and Judah in light of their attestation among other contemporary nations, nor is there reason to doubt their historical credibility.

Within Solomon's Annals (1 Kings 1–11) there exist subunits (in addition to the struggle for succession in chaps. 1–2) such as the Gibeon sacrifice and epiphany (3:4–15); Solomon's judgment (3:16–28); his organization structure (4:1–28); his wisdom (4:29–34); preparation for and construction of the temple and other buildings (5:1–9:14); the construction of fortresses (9:15–24); Solomon's wealth and wisdom (9:25–10:29); and his spiritual, moral, and political decline (11:1–40). A framing pattern is evident in 3:1–3 and 11:41–43. A number of apparent duplications and rearrangements as compared to the LXX suggests that Solomon's Historical Records did not come to the final author as a finished product but that it was he who created the existing structure.

Kings and the Deuteronomic History

We need not repeat here what has been said previously about the Deuteronomic hypothesis. In principle it is not inimical to orthodox views of biblical authorship, especially in a work such as Kings. Its weaknesses lie in (1) assuming that Deuteronomy, the theological text and standard against which Israel's history was to be evaluated, was itself Deuteronomic and not Mosaic; (2) its denial of the account as factual history as opposed to an ideological rendition that embellished events in order to more readily accommodate a parenetic intent; and (3) the absence of any objective evidence that matters came to pass as the hypothesis demands. While it is an adequate explanation for the composition as a whole, its application in matters of detail often seems strained at best and absurd at worst. The basis for this assessment as it pertains to the Deuteronomic character of Kings will become apparent later.

Scholars are divided in their views as to the nature and extent of Deuteronomic addition to or alteration of the basic sources. And it is this very lack of consensus (as well as the assumptions made as to how the source was ideologically shaped) that should give pause to the validity of the hypothesis itself. For example in the "Solomonic" source, 1 Kgs 3:2–3,14, as well as most of chap. 8 and 11:1–13, are ascribed to the compiler and not to the original source.[15] This is because these passages have to do with the central sanctuary as opposed to local high places; with technical language based on Deuteronomy; and with the insistence on marriage only within Israel; and the impropriety of idolatry. Since all of this presupposes the existence of

---

[14] The unit is usually construed as the climax of the so-called "Succession Narrative" (2 Sam 9–20 + 1 Kgs 1–2) already discussed in chap. 19. In fact some manuscripts carry 2 Samuel all the way through 1 Kings 2. See J. Gray, *I and II Kings: A Commentary*, OTL (Philadelphia: Westminster, 1970), 1. This debate has no effect on the question of sources available to the author of Kings.

[15] So O. Eissfeldt, *The Old Testament: An Introduction* (New York: Harper and Row, 1965), 288.

the book of Deuteronomy (or at least its teachings) prior to Solomon's time—a point fatal to the documentary hypothesis based on a late Deuteronomy—the hypothesis itself dictates what could or could not have been native to the original Historical Records of Solomon.[16]

The alleged Deuteronomic features of the other two great literary blocks in Kings—the Historical Records of the Kings of Israel and of Judah—need not be addressed here. In general the supposition is the same: Any texts of a clearly ideological nature and based on the existence of a Deuteronomic written or oral corpus must be later than that corpus and hence not indigenous to those parts of the Historical Records that are pre-Deuteronomic. But some texts seem for various reasons not to be part of any of the three great sources described above. First, they are not annalistic; that is, they are not the kinds of literature one would expect to find in annals. The lengthy stories of Elijah (1 Kings 17–19; 21; 2 Kgs 1:1–2:12a) and Elisha (2 Kgs 2:12b–9:37 *passim*; 13:14–21) are the best-known examples.[17] Second, they contain elements described as legend, saga, and folk tale that, in the view of many scholars, eliminate them from consideration as serious historical source material.[18] This is true of the Elijah and Elisha stories themselves as well as many shorter tales. Thus stories such as Solomon's dream at Gibeon (1 Kgs 3:4–15), the two harlots (3:16–28), the Queen of Sheba (10:1–10), the prophet of Judah (12:32–13:32), and the exploits of Isaiah (2 Kgs 19:1–20:19) appear to be largely unhistorical or, at best, interlaced with nonhistorical embellishments.

The assumption that nonannalistic literature cannot be source material for history-writing or specifically what relates events deemed to be legendary or otherwise "unbelievable," derives from an Enlightenment view of reality that has no place in assessing ancient texts, especially biblical texts. This is not to advocate a credulous naiveté devoid of any epistemological criteria, but surely it is not unreasonable to be open to the historical reality of a book that professes from beginning to end to be the Word of God, even in those parts that contain unique and even supernatural events. By every standard of objective measurement, the book of Kings bears the stamp of authentic history.

The Text of Kings

On the whole the standard Hebrew text of Kings (the Leningradensis, or B19a, of AD 1008) has been well preserved as the DSS fragments of that book make clear (5 QK, 6 QK). Clearly the Massoretic tradition was the one most favored by the community responsible for the DSS. On the other hand, the LXX, the Greek translation of the third century BC, provides variations from the Hebrew tradition, a few of which are worth noting.[19] In the story of the selection of Jeroboam's dynasty (1 Kgs 11:26–14:20), LXX contains information after 12:24 (LXX 24a-z) not found in MT at this place but alluded to in 11:26–28,40; 14:1–18 (which is missing here in LXX); 12:1; 11:29–31; 12:3–14,16,21–24. In 1 Kgs 4:7–5:8 (Eng, 4:7–28) the MT and LXX are in different order and contain different material in certain places. Also chapters 20 and 21 are transposed in LXX so that 20 and 22 can provide a more continuous narrative, one uninterrupted by the Naboth incident of chap. 21. The chronological data of the reigns of the kings also vary considerably between the Hebrew and Greek renditions.[20] The

---

[16] J. Wellhausen, *Prolegomena to the History of Ancient Israel* (1878; reprint, Cleveland: World, 1957), 32–34, 37–38.

[17] de Vries, *1 Kings*, xxxvi-xxxviii.

[18] Long, *1 Kings*, 174-230.

[19] Gray, *I and II Kings*, 44–46.

[20] J. D. Shenkel, *Chronology and Recensional Development in the Greek Text of Kings,* HSM (Cambridge, MA: Harvard University, 1968).

remaining Greek (Hexapla, Aquila, Lucian, Symmachus, Theodotian), Syriac, and Latin (Old Latin and Vulgate) versions add little to the issue of the text complexities of Kings.

THE THEOLOGY OF KINGS

The characterization of Kings as "authentic history" is not inconsistent with the assertion that it is also theological literature. In fact its primary purpose—like that of the Bible as a whole—is to provide a record of divine revelation concerning God's person, purposes, and activities. All these, and especially the last, are the real focus of Kings. Seen from this perspective, the book is history in every sense of the term but history selected and narrated according to a theological agenda, one in and through which one can witness the outworking of God's purposes on the earth through His chosen people Israel.[21]

To the extent that Kings is viewed as a record of actual events—even in those nonannalistic sections ordinarily discounted as such—there is benefit to be derived from its description as Deuteronomic history. To this must be linked the presumption that Deuteronomy, the historical and theological point of departure for the Deuteronomic narratives, is itself anterior not only to the composition of the narratives but also to the events they describe. Otherwise Kings (and the rest of the historical corpus associated with it) reflects only a distorted, propagandistic view of Israel's past, one whose adherence to events as they actually transpired cannot be verified. Worse still, Deuteronomy, if wrested from its Mosaic moorings, becomes a pseudo-covenantal text falsely attributed to Moses and composed to justify political and theological reforms in the seventh century and later. The Deuteronomic history must then be understood as a rendition of Israel's past as seen through much later and ideologically driven lenses.

Scholars who identify Deuteronomic imprints on the Kings material provide helpful insights as to the true nature of that material, provided they recognize that those Deuteronomic assessments are based on authentic historical occurrences. The remainder of this discussion on Kings focuses on the more extensive of these texts, for they are the ones most theologically pregnant. For convenience they will be grouped around three major theological themes in Kings: (1) the sovereignty and exclusiveness of Yahweh and rejection of idolatry, (2) the centrality and exclusiveness of Jerusalem as the place of worship, and (3) the covenant as the basis of Israel's relationship to God and a standard for national life.[22]

Yahweh's exclusive claims to worship and the toleration of idols and pagan cults in Israel are contradictory ideas. To hold to the one is to reject the other. This is a central tenet of Yahwistic faith as expounded particularly in Deuteronomy and specifically in the first two commandments of the Decalogue (Deut 5:7–10; cf. 6:4–5). Solomon's classic confession of Yahweh's sole existence as God and His covenant faithfulness is clearly couched in Deuteronomic language (1 Kgs 8:22–26) as is Hezekiah's exaltation of God and his polemic against pagan deities (2 Kgs 19:14–19). These statements occur in the context of a historical pattern of idolatry and syncretism in Israel, a pattern older than the beginning of Solomon's reign (1 Kgs 3:2–3). Frequently the kings of Israel and Judah themselves introduced illicit worship or at least tolerated it, a point made with reference to Solomon in his latter years (1 Kgs 11:4–10) and continuing almost to the end (12:25–13:3; 14:9; 16:31–34; 22:53; 2 Kgs 8:26–27; 10:29–31; 16:3–4; 21:2–9,20–22). Almost invariably the people followed their leaders until at times the whole nation seems to have become apostate (1 Kgs 11:33; 14:22–24; 2 Kgs 14:4; 15:4,35; 16:3–4).

---

[21] P. R. House, *1, 2 Kings,* NAC (Nashville: B&H, 1995), 73–82.

[22] For a fuller discussion of the theology of Kings, E. H. Merrill, *Everlasting Dominion: A Theology of the Old Testament* (Nashville: B&H, 2006), 440–64.

All was not bleak and hopeless, however, for there were kings and prophets who not only verbally acknowledged the lordship of Yahweh but who also set about the reestablishment of exclusive worship of Him by destroying competing idols and shrines. Most notable are the efforts of Asa (1 Kgs 15:11–15), Jehoiada the priest (2 Kgs 11:17–18), Hezekiah (18:4), and Josiah (23:4–20). The incidents of reformation were not without theological context and underpinnings, however, for the deuteronomic insistence on the worship of Yahweh and only Yahweh at one central sanctuary clearly provided the impetus for them (Deut 12:1–14). Thus Solomon resolved to build a house "for the name of the LORD [Yahweh]" (1 Kgs 5:5; cf. Deut 12:5), and on its completion he described the Jerusalem temple as such (1 Kgs 8:12–21; cf. 9:3). That worship must be undertaken there and only there is stated repeatedly in Solomon's great temple dedication prayer (8:29,31,33,35,38,42–44,48).

The third major theological theme in Kings—that of covenant—also presupposes a Deuteronomic basis and provides in turn an explanation for the insistence that only Yahweh be recognized and worshiped as God and that such worship be carried out in one place, the "house for his name." Solomon implored the people to keep covenant, invoking in the process technical vocabulary found prominently in Deuteronomy (1 Kgs 8:57–58,61; cf. Deut 4:45; 5:1; 6:1; 7:12; etc.). Even earlier, Yahweh is said to have commissioned young Solomon to "walk in My ways and keep My statutes and commandments," again employing standard Deuteronomic terminology (1 Kgs 3:14; cf. 6:11–13; 9:4–5).

There is some evidence—all too rare—of faithful covenant-keeping (2 Kgs 18:5–6; 23:3), but on the whole the history of Israel recounted in Kings is a sorry record of covenant violation (e.g., 1 Kgs 14:7–8). In fact, this is so much the case that Israel's (and later, Judah's) fall is explained in terms of this national sin. Nowhere is Kings as *Heilsgeschichte* more clearly seen than in 2 Kgs 17:7–23,34–41. Here are found not only the facts of Israel's demise but the theological rationale. The people had gone after idolatry (17:7–14) and in doing so, had broken Yahweh's covenant with them (vv. 15–18). For these egregious violations of Deuteronomic law they had been carried off into Assyrian captivity (v. 23). Even after this, the surviving community (the product of heathen and Israelite intermarriage) continued to disregard the covenant (v. 34) by engaging in syncretistic worship (vv. 33,35) despite Yahweh's faithful reminders over the centuries to do otherwise (vv. 36–41).

CONCLUSION

The book of Kings, a history (with Chronicles) of the twin nations Israel and Judah, is much more than that alone. It is the account of a people on whom God had lavished His elective and beneficent grace but who spurned those overtures in favor of superstition and materialism. The sad tale of disobedience followed by inevitable decline and judgment stands as a paradigm against which to measure modern times and contemporary events. Surely, if Israel, the apple of God's eye, met such disastrous consequences, how can we expect any less, failing the recognition and confession of our many sins?

STUDY QUESTIONS

1. The books of Kings are associated in some circles with a large block of historical books known as what?
2. To whom does Talmudic tradition assign the authorship of Kings?
3. What is the evidence for such a position?
4. What major part of Israelite history do the books of Kings cover?

5. What role did Hiram of Tyre play in the administration of King Solomon?

6. What ancient inscription describes the conflict between Israel and Moab?

7. The "Book of the Law" was discovered during the reign of which king?

8. Who was the founding ruler of the northern kingdom of Israel?

9. What is the name of the books of Kings in the Septuagint?

10. Who was the only woman to have ruled over Judah?

11. Which king of Judah suffered from a skin disease in his latter years?

12. Which king of Israel participated in the famous battle at Qarqar against Assyria?

13. What major sin was most responsible for the exile of the northern kingdom?

14. What three cities did Solomon fortify against enemy attack?

15. What brought about the division of the United Monarchy following Solomon's death?

FOR FURTHER STUDY

Bright, J. *A History of Israel.* 3rd ed. Philadelphia: Westminster, 1981.

Campbell, A. F., and M. A. O'Brien. *Unfolding the Deuteronomistic History.* Minneapolis: Fortress, 2000.

Chisholm, R. B., Jr. *Interpreting the Historical Books.* Grand Rapids: Kregel, 2006.

Cogan, M., and H. Tadmor. *II Kings.* AB 11. Doubleday, 1988.

DeVries, S. J. *1 Kings.* WBC 12. Waco: Word, 1985.

Gray, J. *I and II Kings.* 2nd ed. Philadelphia: Westminster, 1970.

Hamilton, V. P. *Handbook on the Historical Books.* Grand Rapids: Baker, 2001.

Hayes, J. H., and J. M. Miller. *Israelite and Judaean History.* Philadelphia: Westminster, 1977.

Hayes, J. H., and P. K. Hooker. *A New Chronology for the Kings of Israel and Judah.* Atlanta: Scholars, 1988.

Hobbs, T. R. *2 Kings.* WBC 13. Waco: Word, 1985.

House, P. R. *1, 2 Kings.* NAC 8. Nashville: B&H, 1995.

Howard, D. M., Jr. *An Introduction to the Old Testament Historical Books.* Chicago: Moody, 1993.

Kaiser, W. C., Jr. *A History of Israel.* Nashville: B&H, 1998.

Long, B. O. *1 Kings with an Introduction to Historical Literature.* FOTL IX. Grand Rapids: Eerdmans, 1984.

Longman, T., III, and R. B. Dillard. *An Introduction to the Old Testament.* 2nd ed. Grand Rapids: Zondervan, 2006.

Merrill, E. H. *Kingdom of Priests. A History of Old Testament Israel.* 2nd ed. Grand Rapids: Baker, 2008.

Miller, J. M., and J. H. *A History of Ancient Israel and Judah.* Philadelphia: Westminster, 1986.

Patterson, R. D. and H. J. Austel, *1, 2 Kings.* EBC. Rev. ed. Edited by T. Longman and D. N. Garland, 3:615–954. Grand Rapids: Zondervan, 2009.

Peckham, B. *The Composition of the Deuteronomistic History.* Atlanta: Scholars, 1985.

Provan, I., V., Philips Long, and Tremper Longman III. *A Biblical History of Israel.* Louisville: Westminster John Knox, 2003.

Tetley, M. C. *The Reconstructed Chronology of the Divided Kingdom.* Winona Lake, IN: Eisenbrauns, 2005.

Thiele, E. R. *The Mysterious Numbers of the Hebrew Kings.* Grand Rapids: Eerdmans, 1965.

Unger, M. F. *Israel and the Aramaeans of Damascus.* Grand Rapids: Baker, 1957.

Wiseman, D. J. *1 & 2 Kings.* TOTC 9. Downers Grove, IL: IVP, 1993.

CHAPTER 20

THE BOOKS OF
1 AND 2 CHRONICLES

EUGENE H. MERRILL

THE LITERARY CHARACTER OF CHRONICLES

The Title of the Book

The title "Chronicles" in the English Bible follows Jerome's suggestion that the work should be called *chronikon*, that is, a record of the passing of time from the very beginning of God's revelation. Unfortunately the word "chronicles" now has a much narrower definition, one that suggests a *seriatim* collection of incidents or events with little or no comment, analysis, or interpretation. That patently fails to describe the nature of the book of Chronicles.

However, Jerome's rendition is much superior to that of the LXX, which ignored the Hebrew title *dibrê hayyāmîm* ("accounts of the days," i.e., "annals") and instead perceived the book to be only supplementary to Samuel and Kings. Thus the Greek version coined the title *Paraleipomenōn* ("things left out"). Moreover, the term *chronikon* in its classic sense also means "annal," so the English name, understood in this manner, is adequate.

Though Chronicles includes material missing in Samuel–Kings, it also omits other material found in the latter and repeats much more from those works. Therefore to see Chronicles as only supplemental to Samuel–Kings (a common misunderstanding to this day in some circles) is to fail to appreciate it as a significant and unique creation in its own right, one composed with clear historical and theological objectives in view.[1]

THE CANONICITY OF THE BOOK

The fact of the canonicity of Chronicles has never been in doubt, but its location in the various canons has fluctuated. In the earliest traditions (*Baba Bathra* 14b) the book is listed at the end of the final section of the canon (the *ketūbîm* or "writings"), but in most of the major

---

[1] W. J. Dumbrell, "The Purpose of the Books of Chronicles," *JETS* 27 (1984): 257–66.

Massoretic manuscripts it heads the list of books in that section. Its connection with Ezra–Nehemiah in terms of both canonical arrangement and in other respects will receive attention presently. The LXX, in line with its practice with regard to other books of a historiographic nature (Joshua–Kings), placed Chronicles in its second division, the books of history, usually just after the book of Kings.[2]

THE CONTENTS OF THE BOOK

The arbitrary division of Chronicles into two books came about apparently for a practical reason, the unwieldiness of such a lengthy text on a single scroll. Second Chronicles is somewhat longer, but the succession of Solomon to David seemed a sensible place to make the break so this has been the practice since the third century BC, at least in the LXX tradition. By medieval times, the major Hebrew manuscripts and codices also split the book into the halves familiar to modern readers.

The major units of Chronicles are (1) genealogies from Adam through Saul (1 Chronicles 1–9); (2) the reign of David (prefaced by that of Saul; chaps. 10–29); (3) the reign of Solomon (2 Chr 1–9); the history of the divided monarchy (chaps. 10–28:11); the history of Judah alone (28:12–36:21);[3] and a brief version of the decree of Cyrus (36:22–23). One of the striking omissions in Chronicles is any explicit reference to the Assyrian conquest of Samaria; thus the end of the divided monarchy can be located only somewhere in 2 Chronicles 28 (28:12 and 30:6 give hints of that disaster).

Unlike Kings, the book of Chronicles contains relatively few extended prophetic narratives such as those of Elijah and Elisha, but instead the focus is on the monarchy, especially that of Judah.[4] In fact the book is essentially a history of Judah with Israel entering the discussion only as a foil or as an element necessary to a full understanding of events in the southern kingdom. Few of the kings of Israel receive more than passing attention, whereas the dynasty of David is lavishly detailed, particularly in the case of Jehoshaphat (2 Chronicles 17–20), Hezekiah (chaps. 29–32), and Josiah (chaps. 34–35). When Solomon, David's first successor, is added to this (chaps. 1–9), more than half of 2 Chronicles (19 out of 36 chaps.) is devoted to four kings. Clearly the intent is to draw attention to the Davidic covenant (1 Chronicles 17) and God's faithfulness in extending its benefits to David's royal descendants.

A second dominant theme is that of the temple and worship. The temple itself was the subject of much interest in Kings, with its emphasis on Solomon's building exploits (1 Kings 6–7), but Kings has virtually nothing to say about priests, Levites, and the services of the temple. Chronicles, on the other hand, speaks extensively of David's preparations for building the temple (1 Chronicles 22, 28–29), his appointment of the various priestly and Levitical offices (chaps. 23–27), and Solomon's actual construction of the temple complex (2 Chronicles 2–4). In addition, the chronicler goes to great length to describe the service of dedication that followed the completion of the work (chaps. 5–7). Thus fully two-thirds of the account of Solomon's reign is given over to matters of the temple and its services and officiants.

The narratives about Hezekiah and Josiah are likewise preoccupied with matters of temple worship. Hezekiah's first recorded act was to reopen and repair the temple (2 Chr 29:3) after

---

[2] For various Greek canon lists see H. B. Swete, *An Introduction to the Old Testament in Greek* (Cambridge: Cambridge University Press, 1902), 201–14.

[3] The reference of 2 Chr 28:12 is arbitrary because the beginning of John's dynasty is not stated specifically in chap. 28.

[4] W. M. Schniedewind, "Prophets and Prophecy in the Books of Chronicles," in *The Chronicler as Historian*, ed. M P. Graham, K. G. Hoglund, and S. L. McKenzie, JSOTSup (Sheffield: Sheffield Academic, 1997), 204–24.

the apostate reign of Ahaz. Hezekiah then set about the work of reconsecrating the temple personnel, reestablishing worship services, reviving the celebration of Passover, and restoring the practice of presenting tithes and offerings (chaps. 29–31). The great bulk of the annals concerning Hezekiah have to do with religious affairs.

The same is true of Josiah. After purging Judah of idolatry (34:1–7), he repaired the temple (34:8–13), and on the basis of the discovery of a copy of the Torah there, he led the nation to revival and reformation (34:14–33). Then, like his godly predecessor Hezekiah, King Josiah mandated a nationwide Passover, the greatest since the days of Samuel (35:18). Of 60 verses describing Josiah's reign, all but a dozen or so are concerned with matters of the temple and worship. The book of Kings also has an inordinate interest in Hezekiah, but of three chapters detailing his reign (2 Kings 18–20) a scant four verses (18:3–6) speak of his attention to worship, and even these in a negative form, that is, the removal of competing pagan elements. In Josiah's case the Kings account does address his religious concerns more fully. In fact virtually the entire narrative (2 Kgs 22:1–23:30) is preoccupied with Josiah's temple repair and his leadership in national reformation. But this single exception in all the divided monarchy only confirms the fact that Chronicles exhibits a concern for religious life curiously lacking in Kings, at least to that extent.

Other distinctive features of the contents of Chronicles in contrast to Samuel–Kings are addressed below under "Chronicles and the 'Synoptic Problem'" (p. 337).

THE STRUCTURE OF THE BOOK

Apart from the major units just suggested, little consensus has developed as to whether Chronicles exhibits any kind of macrostructure in its composition. Various analyses have been attempted, but most are quite unpersuasive. Dorsey suggests the following scheme for the book as a whole, one that places the story of Solomon, the temple builder, at the center:[5]

A. Beginning: genealogies from Adam to the Babylonian exile and return (1 Chr 1:1–9:44)
>   B. Establishment of David's kingdom (1 Chr 10:1–22:1)
>>>   C. David assembled all Israel to make preparations for Solomon's building of the temple (1 Chr 22:2–29:30)
>>>>   D. CENTER: Solomon, the temple builder (2 Chronicles 1–9)
>>>   C.[1] Division of Israel; Judean kings from Rehoboam to good King Jehoshaphat (2 Chr 10:1–20:37)
>   B.[1] Seven kings: Jehoram to Ahaz (2 Chr 21:1–28:27)
A.[1] End: Judah's final kings: good King Hezekiah to the Babylonian exile, and a note about the return (2 Chr 29:1–36:23)

This way of arranging the material points not only to a unique literary artifice compared to the structure of Kings (see pp. 321–22), but also to the distinct theological emphases of the Chronicler. Thus as Dorsey says, "This structural highlighting of stories about the temple and its servants helps the Chronicler establish and emphasize the pattern that throughout history, when Israel did right with regard to the temple, priests, and Levites, it always prospered; conversely, when it did wrong in these areas, it always suffered."[6]

---

[5] D. A. Dorsey, *The Literary Structure of the Old Testament* (Grand Rapids: Baker, 1999), 155.
[6] Ibid., 157.

THE LITERARY FORMS AND GENRES OF THE BOOK

Like Samuel and Kings, Chronicles displays a wide variety of forms in which to communicate its message.[7] On the whole the work is narrative since its overriding purpose is to relate the history of the Davidic monarchy. The fact that it is tendentious or theological history has no bearing on its basic literary character. But the narrative itself consists of many subsidiary forms, creative ways in which the complexity of the historical/theological traditions can be laid out and clarified. At the very outset, for example, one is confronted by lengthy sets of genealogies (1 Chronicles 1–9), the structure and arrangement of which are instructive in their own right. Chapters 1 and 9 are "foundational material"[8] providing an inclusio around chaps. 2–8. The first of the tribes listed is Judah (2:3–4:22) and the last tribe is Benjamin (chap. 8). The southern kingdom is clearly made prominent by this arrangement. At the very center of the lists is Levi (chap. 6), the priestly tribe. Its location there also points to its theological centrality. Thus, in line with the theological importance of David's dynasty and temple worship is the structure of the genealogical section, one that points to this assessment.

Other common and/or important genres in Chronicles are annals (2 Chr 11:5–12), prophetic speech (2 Chr 15:2–7; 25:7–9), taunt (2 Chr 32:10–15), admonition (1 Chr 22:11–13), roster (6:16–30), hymn of praise (16:8–36), chronicle (2 Chronicles 14–16), battle report (1 Chr 4:41–43), royal narrative (2 Chr 1:2–17), oracle (1:11–12), and construction report (3:15–4:10). These suggest the variegated way in which historiography was done in ancient Israel and also the sources on which the historian (in this case, the Chronicler) drew. More often than not he seems to have taken the sources as he found them and then to have integrated them into his own work with little or no alteration.

THE OUTLINE OF THE BOOK

I. The Genealogies (1 Chr 1:1–9:44)
   A. The Patriarchal Genealogies (chap. 1)
   B. The Genealogy of Judah (2:1–4:23)
   C. The Genealogy of Simeon (4:24–43)
   D. The Genealogy of Reuben (5:1–10)
   E. The Genealogy of Gad (5:11–17)
   F. The Hagrite Campaign (5:18–22)
   G. The Genealogy of Transjordan Manasseh (5:23–26)
   H. The Genealogy of Levi (chap. 6)
   I. The Genealogy of Issachar (7:1–5)
   J. The Genealogy of Benjamin (7:6–12)
   K. The Genealogy of Naphtali (7:13)
   L. The Genealogy of Cisjordan Manasseh (7:14–19)
   M. The Genealogy of Ephraim (7:20–29)
   N. The Genealogy of Asher (7:30–40)
   O. The Genealogy of Benjamin (chap. 8)
   P. The Settlers of Jerusalem (9:1–34)
   Q. The Genealogy of Saul (9:35–44)

---

[7] S. J. DeVries, *1 and 2 Chronicles*, FOTL (Grand Rapids: Eerdmans, 1989), 426–37 *passim*.

[8] Ibid., 26.

II. **The Rise of David (1 Chr 10:1–22:1)**
  A. The Death of Saul (chap. 10)
  B. The Succession of David (chaps. 11–12)
  C. The Movement of the Ark (chap. 13)
  D. The Establishment of David's Rule (chap. 14)
  E. The Arrival of the Ark and Its Installation (chaps. 15–16)
  F. David's Concern for a Temple (chap. 17)
  G. David's International Relations (chaps. 18–20)
  H. David's Census and Its Aftermath (21:1–22:1)

III. **The Preparation for Succession (1 Chr 22:2–29:30)**
  A. David's Preparation for the Temple (22:2–19)
  B. David's Preparation of Religious and Political Personnel (chaps. 23–27)
  C. David's Great Assembly (28:1–29:22a)
  D. The Succession of Solomon (29:22b–30)

IV. **The Reign of Solomon (2 Chr 1:1–9:31)**
  A. The Assembly at Gibeon and Solomon's might (chap. 1)
  B. The Building of the Temple (2:1–5:1)
  C. The Dedication of the Temple (5:2–7:10)
  D. The Conditions of Covenant Blessing (7:11–22)
  E. Solomon's Accomplishments (chaps. 8–9)

V. **The Dynasty of David: Rehoboam to Uzziah (2 Chronicles 10–25)**
  A. The Reign of Rehoboam (chaps. 10–12)
  B. The Reign of Abijah (13:1–14:1)
  C. The Reign of Asa (14:2–16:14)
  D. The Reign of Jehoshaphat (chaps. 17–20)
  E. The Reign of Jehoram (chap. 21)
  F. The Reign of Ahaziah (22:1–9)
  G. The Interregnum of Athaliah (22:10–23:21)
  H. The Reign of Joash (chap. 24)
  I. The Reign of Amaziah (chap. 25)

VI. **The Dynasty of David: Uzziah to the Restoration Community (2 Chronicles 26–36)**
  A. The Reign of Uzziah (chap. 26)
  B. The Reign of Jothan (chap. 27)
  C. The Reign of Ahaz (chap. 28)
  D. The Reign of Hezekiah (29:1–32:33)
  E. The Reign of Manasseh (33:1–20)
  F. The Reign of Amon (33:21–25)
  G. The Reign of Josiah (chaps. 34–35)
  H. The Reigns of Jehoahaz, Jehoiakim, and Jehoiachin (36:1–10)
  I. The Reign of Zedekiah and the Fall of Jerusalem (36:11–21)
  J. The Decree of Cyrus (36:22–23)

THE COMPOSITION OF CHRONICLES

The Author of the Book

The literary diversity of Chronicles may lead to the conclusion that the composition is not so much the work of a creative author as of a compiler, collator, and redactor of texts which he selected and frequently left unchanged in the course of his use of them. While partially correct, this should not denigrate the original contribution of this unknown historian (conveniently called the Chronicler) nor mitigate his genius, for the skill with which he integrated such disparate materials leaves one with profound respect for his finished product. Close comparison of the Chronicler's rendition of history to that of Samuel-Kings, his major source, puts beyond question his ability and willingness to adapt his material in the interest of his own special approach to his task, and to do so in highly artistic ways.[9]

The issue of the "authorship" of Chronicles cannot be addressed apart from that of Ezra–Nehemiah because of their close connections in ancient tradition as well as modern scholarship. The Talmudic Baba Bathra 15a states that "Ezra wrote the book that bears his name [that is, Ezra and Nehemiah] and the genealogies of the Book of Chronicles up to his own time. . . . Who then finished it [the book of Chronicles]? Nehemiah the son of Hachaliah." The Chronicler by this view was two people—Ezra and Nehemiah, and in that order. This, of course, cannot be proved, and there appear to be compelling reasons to reject this ancient opinion.

However, the question of the connection between Chronicles and Ezra–Nehemiah still remains. In favor of their being one single composition is the fact that 2 Chr 36:22–23 (the closing of the book) is repeated almost verbatim in Ezra 1:1–3. This suggests that the canonical order at one time must have been Chronicles, Ezra–Nehemiah (as in LXX and most modern canons) and not (as in the modern Hebrew canon) Ezra–Nehemiah, Chronicles. Eissfeldt argues that Chronicles appears last in the Hebrew canon because it was canonized later than Ezra–Nehemiah, but to avoid its ending on a pessimistic note (2 Chr 36:17–21) the edict of Cyrus (vv. 22–23) was added later, thus accounting for the edict both there and at the beginning of Ezra.[10]

While this is possible, it is hardly necessary, no matter the question of the authorship and unity of the books. As matters stand, Ezra and Nehemiah continue the history begun in Chronicles and carry it forward to about 432 BC (see Neh 13:6), more than 100 years after the decree of Cyrus, the latest datable event in Chronicles. This would seem to allow for the authorship of Chronicles by Ezra as the ancient tradition suggested, but certain other data such as some of the names in the genealogies would necessitate even some post-Nehemiac additions. This of course is perfectly possible and compatible with the view that Ezra wrote Chronicles on the whole.

In recent years compelling arguments have been made against the unity of the Chronicles–Ezra–Nehemiah material. First, Chronicles exists as a separate work in the LXX (third century BC), an unlikely development in just a little over a century following the completion of Chronicles. Second, despite older contentions to the contrary, Japhet,[11] Williamson,[12]

---

[9] S. Japhet, *I & II Chronicles*, OTL (Louisville: WJK, 1993), 7. G. N. Knoppers offers the following assessment of the book as a literary oeuvre: "Given its unique literary structure and its unparalleled content, Chronicles is more than a paraphrase or literary elaboration of the primary history. Chronicles needs to be understood as its own work" (*I Chronicles 1–9*. AB [New York: Doubleday, 2004], 134).

[10] O. Eissfeldt, *The Old Testament: An Introduction* (New York: Harper and Row, 1965), 531.

[11] Japhet, *I & II Chronicles*, 4–5.

[12] H. G. M. Williamson, *1 and 2 Chronicles*, NCBC (Grand Rapids: Eerdmans, 1982), 5–11.

Knoppers,[13] and others have demonstrated quite conclusively that Chronicles differs from Ezra–Nehemiah substantially in terms of literary style, vocabulary, grammar, syntax, outlook, interests, and theology. There seems little doubt that Chronicles should be understood as a work completely separate from Ezra–Nehemiah and yet sharing with it a great many things in common. This should not be surprising, given the postexilic point of view they share.

The Date of the Book

The date of Chronicles cannot be separated from its authorship and the question of its independence from Ezra–Nehemiah. If, as Talmudic tradition suggests, Ezra wrote Chronicles for the most part, its date could not be much later than 425 BC. Ezra's last recorded act was the series of reforms he set in place following his return to Jerusalem from Susa (Neh 13:6). The book that bears his name as well as Chronicles would have to have been written at that time (458 BC) or shortly thereafter. However, along with the arguments already adduced against the unity and common authorship of Chronicles–Ezra–Nehemiah, certain other internal evidence in Chronicles itself seems to rule out authorship by Ezra (or Nehemiah, as far as that goes). First, Chronicles, in its original form, seems to have ended with the narrative about the Babylonian exile and its duration to the time of the Persians (2 Chr 36:17–21). The decree of Cyrus (vv. 22–23), even if it was not part of the original account, requires no date later than 538 BC or so. In short, the concluding narratives in Chronicles seem to preclude a date much later than 538. If Ezra were the author of Chronicles, it seems strange that he ended the book as early as he did, 80 years before his own appearance on the scene.

On the other hand there are incidental clues here and there to suggest that even if the book as a whole is pre-Persian, there were later additions and/or glosses that suggest a much later date for its final, canonical form. For example, in the chronology section (which can hardly be denied to the Chronicler) there are many names in common between the priests and Levites who are said to have returned to Jerusalem following the Babylonian exile (1 Chr 9:2–34) and those in Nehemiah who seem to be Nehemiah's contemporaries (Neh 11:3–36). Also the list of descendants of Zerubbabel (1 Chr 3:19–24), who himself returned from the Babylonian exile (Ezra 2:2), includes at least six generations.[14] At 25 years for an average generation, the last person named would have lived as late as the last quarter of the fifth century (425–400 BC).

Other incidental hints also suggest something as to dates of composition. These include a reference to the Persian coin called a drachma or daric, something unknown before 515 BC.[15] (1 Chr 29:7), and the Chronicler's quotation of Zech 4:10 (in 2 Chr 16:9; c. 520 BC). A date of c. 500 BC would accommodate these facts. At the other extreme, lack of any clear Hellenistic influence on Chronicles seems to disallow any date later than the end of the Persian period (c. 300 BC).[16] In summary, a date of 400–375 BC seems reasonable and accounts for all the literary and historical data known to this point. This being the case, Ezra can hardly be the author of Chronicles, at least as it now stands, for he lived much too early.

---

    [13] Knoppers, *I Chronicles 1–9*, 88–89.

    [14] Admittedly the list here is difficult, especially in v. 21 where the number of generations is not clear. For arguments that many of the names are contemporaries and not successive see M. J. Selman, *1 Chronicles: An Introduction and Commentary* (Downers Grove, IL: InterVarsity, 1994), 100–101. For the contrary arguments and a helpful table see J. M. Myers, *I Chronicles*, AB (Garden City, NY: Doubleday, 1965), 20–21.

    [15] M. C. Root, "Art and Archaeology of the Achaemenid Empire," in *Civilizations of the Ancient Near East*, ed. J. M. Sasson (New York: Scribner's Sons, 1995), 4:2635–37.

    [16] P. R. Ackroyd, *The Chronicler in His Age*, JSOTSup (Sheffield: JSOT, 1991), 9–11.

Chronicles and the "Synoptic Problem"

As is well known, the life and teachings of Jesus are recounted from four different perspectives in four different Gospels. Three of these writings—Matthew, Mark, and Luke—are so similar in their approaches that they are described as the "Synoptic Gospels," suggesting that though they are not identical they "see" things in essentially the same way. The effort to trace the original sayings and deeds of Jesus through comparison and contrast of these texts as well as to account for the differences among the Gospels is sometimes called the Synoptic Problem.

Analogous to this is the parallel rendition of Israel's history found respectively in Samuel-Kings and in Chronicles. As noted already, so similar are the accounts in general that the LXX assigned Chronicles the title *Paraleipomena* ("that which is left over"), betraying thereby its conviction that Chronicles merely supplemented material already found in Samuel–Kings. Such a simplistic notion has unfortunately plagued at least popular expressions of Judaism and Christianity with the result that Chronicles has been sadly neglected as an independent and indescribably rich source of historical and theological understanding.[17]

The situation has been greatly redressed in the past few decades and now Chronicles is coming into its own as literature worthy of careful study. Ironically, however, such new attention has raised a plethora of problems and questions about Chronicles and its relationship to Samuel–Kings. These include issues of common and unique sources, similarities and differences and how to explain them, and various attempts to harmonize the two traditions in such a way as to preclude contradictions and other problems.[18]

Sources

Scholars generally concede that Chronicles is a later composition than Samuel–Kings, no matter the view of the Deuteronomic history and its various redactions. If dependence can be demonstrated, Chronicles must be dependent on Samuel–Kings and not vice versa. That this is the case is apparent both from the Chronicler's citation of texts that can only be the canonical books of Samuel and Kings (1 Chr 9:1; 29:29; 2 Chr 16:11; 20:34; 24:27; 25:26; 27:7; 28:26; 32:32; 33:18; 35:27; 36:8) and from the absence of citation the other way around, that is, Samuel-Kings citing Chronicles. Though the cited texts are seldom used verbatim in Chronicles (a common practice in the ancient world), there is no doubt that the canonical books are intended by the allusion.

In addition, Chronicles refers to many other sources used in its composition such as "the Historical Record of King David" (1 Chr 27:24); "the Prophecy of Ahijah, the Shilonite, and the Visions of Iddo the Seer" (2 Chr 9:29); "the Events of Shemaiah the Prophet and of Iddo the Seer" (12:15); "the Writing of the Prophet Iddo" (13:22); "the Records of Hozai" (33:19); and "the Dirges [of Jeremiah]" (35:25).[19] These sources, no longer extant, were readily available not only to the historian but to anyone curious enough to check them independently as the recurring phrase "are written" makes clear (cf. 2 Chr 9:29; 12:15; 13:22; 16:11; 20:34; 23:18; etc.).

---

[17] E. H. Merrill, "The Chronicler: What Kind of Historian Was He Anyway?" *BSac* 165 (2008): 397–412.

[18] See, e.g., W. E. Lemke, "The Synoptic Problem in the Chronicler's History," *HTR* 58 (1965): 349–63; S. L. McKenzie, *The Chronicler's Use of the Deuteronomistic History*, HSM (Atlanta: Scholars, 1984); T. Sugimoto, "The Chronicler's Techniques in Quoting Samuel-Kings," *Annual of the Japanese Biblical Institute* 26 (1991): 30–70.

[19] A.-M. Brunet, "Le Chroniste et ses sources," *RB* 60 (1953): 481–508; and 61 (1954): 349–86; A. F. Rainey, "The Chronicler and His Sources—Historical and Geographical," in *The Chronicler as Historian*, 30–72.

SIMILARITIES AND DIFFERENCES BETWEEN
SAMUEL–KINGS AND CHRONICLES

Where material is unique to Chronicles it is obviously impossible to check its congruence with Samuel-Kings. However, where clear appeal to common sources or obvious dependence of Chronicles on Samuel-Kings can be shown, there is opportunity to weigh the one against the other and to draw conclusions as to similarities and differences and the implications of each respectively. For convenience' sake, these demonstrable differences will be considered under two headings: (1) difference in "factual" data and (2) difference in perspective or ideology.

The first of these pertains primarily to statistical information such as population figures and dimensions of buildings and other objects and to such things as spelling of personal names or even apparently different attribution of names. Most of the contradictions result from faulty text transmission, and others may be resolved by supposing differing ways of looking at the same phenomena. A number of scholars have addressed these and have provided harmonizations that are more or less satisfying.[20] Those few that resist solution are relatively unimportant and in no way impinge on the historical credibility of either the Chronicler or his sources.

The more significant variations pertain to (1) matters included by Samuel–Kings and lacking in Chronicles; (2) matters included in Chronicles and lacking in Samuel–Kings; and (3) matters common to both but presented differently.

As for (1) the most significant examples from Samuel are the greatly truncated story of Saul's reign (1 Samuel 9–31; cf. 1 Chronicles 10); the account of Mephibosheth (2 Samuel 9; lacking in Chronicles); and most famous, the narrative of David's adultery and murder (2 Samuel 11–12; lacking in Chronicles). As far as Kings is concerned, it is important to note that Samuel-Kings (i.e., the Deuteronomist) relates the history primarily in terms of the northern kingdom with events in Judah being recorded at times and places where they relate to Israel.[21] Thus the reigns of several of Israel's kings that are barely mentioned if at all by the Chronicler are given expansive treatment in Kings. This is notably the case with Jeroboam I (1 Kgs 11:26–40; 12:12–20,25–33; 13:33–14:31; cf. 2 Chr 13:1–2,13–19); Ahab (1 Kgs 16:29–22:40; cf. 2 Chronicles 18 [where Ahab appears only in reference to Jehoshaphat]); and Jehu (2 Kgs 9:1–10:36; cf. 2 Chr 22:7–9). As noted before, Samuel-Kings is also replete with stories about the prophets. Samuel has a dominant role there (1 Samuel 1–3; 7–13; 15–16; 28) but only passing notice in Chronicles (1 Chr 6:28,33; 9:22; 11:3; 26:28; 29:29). The same is true with Elijah (1 Kgs 17:1–21:28; 2 Kgs 1:1–2:12; cf. 2 Chr 21:12–15) and Elisha (2 Kgs 2:1–8:15; 13:14–21; not mentioned in Chronicles).

With reference to (2), the Chronicler adds little to the content of Samuel–Kings in the account of the political life of the united monarchy. His independent contribution is the elaborate preparations for the temple (1 Chr 22:2–27:15), David's bureaucracy (27:16–34), and plans for Solomon's succession (28:1–29:25). The book of Kings' treatment of the reigns of Hezekiah and Josiah is greatly augmented in Chronicles (95 verses about Hezekiah in Kings compared to 127 in Chronicles; 50 verses about Josiah versus 60 in Chronicles) and significantly altered. The changes are ideological in nature.

Regarding (3), in matters of commonality between Samuel-Kings and Chronicles the question should be viewed in two ways: differences in the ordering of events and differences in

---

[20] J. B. Payne, "Validity of Numbers in Chronicles," *NEASB* 18 (1978): 5–58; G. L. Archer, *Encyclopedia of Bible Difficulties* (Grand Rapids: Zondervan, 1982), 221–24.

[21] Gray, *I & II Kings*, 25–26.

the actual interpretation of events.[22] The latter is properly a theological matter and will be addressed under that heading. By and large Chronicles follows the narrative sequence of the Deuteronomic history, with two notable exceptions. According to 2 Samuel the securing of Jerusalem as David's capital (chap. 5) preceded his attempt to bring the ark into the city (chap. 6). Chronicles reverses the order (1 Chronicles 13–14). Also the Deuteronomist locates the list of David's heroes in the so-called "appendix" of 2 Samuel (2 Sam 23:8–39), whereas the Chronicler places it in connection with David's coronation over all Israel (1 Chr 11:10–47). This consistency puts beyond any doubt the fact that the Chronicler used Samuel–Kings as his model for narrating Israel's history.

THE TEXT OF CHRONICLES

Though the synoptic nature of Samuel-Kings and Chronicles would seem to offer a choice opportunity for text comparison, this is not necessarily the case except in lists and other non-contextual passages. The reason is the free way in which Chronicles cites its sources, thus obliterating any preciseness of comparison. Where it is certain that Chronicles is rigidly dependent on Samuel and Kings, it frequently is dependent on a text tradition different from MT, as the Qumran exemplars of Samuel and Kings demonstrate.[23] So far no significant DSS of Chronicles have come to light so it is impossible to determine the state of its Hebrew text that early.

LXX and dependent versions appear to have been based on the same Hebrew texts as MT, thus differing from the traditions reflected in the Qumran texts of Samuel and Kings.[24] Despite the apparently non-Massoretic nature of Chronicles' principal sources (i.e., Samuel and Kings), the freedom with which it departs from slavish adherence to those sources suggests that the attempt to trace its textual history is moot. The text as it stands is in good shape; its manuscript variations are extremely minimal.

THE THEOLOGY OF CHRONICLES

In light of its major themes, motifs, and emphases one can state the theology of Chronicles rather succinctly in the following terms: God, through a special covenant relationship with the Davidic dynasty, one exhibited by and centered on the temple and its cultus, will bless His elect people Israel when and as they live in obedience, and through them will extend his grace to all the world.[25]

The universalism of God's salvific intentions is apparent at the very beginning with the detailed genealogies that stretch back from the Chronicler's own time to the commencement of human history.[26] In fact the historian appropriates the Genesis genealogies almost verbatim in places and, like Genesis, does so in order to lay out the whole scope of human origins and national distribution (1 Chr 1:1–27). Very quickly he makes the connection with Abraham (1:28), Isaac (1:34), and Jacob (or Israel, 2:1), and then to Judah (2:3), who, though not the

---

[22] For the former see E. H. Merrill, "The 'Accession Year' and Davidic Chronology," JANES 19 (1989):108–12.

[23] R. Braun, *1 Chronicles,* WBC (Waco: Word, 1986), xxii.

[24] L. C. Allen, *The Translator's Craft,* part 1 of *The Greek Chronicles: The Relation of the Septuagint of I and II Chronicles to the Massoretic Text,* VTSup (Leiden: Brill, 1974); idem, *Textual Criticism,* part 2 of *The Greek Chronicles,* VTSup (Leiden: Brill, 1974).

[25] E. H. Merrill, "A Theology of Chronicles," in *A Biblical Theology of the Old Testament,* ed. R. B. Zuck (Chicago: Moody, 1991), 157–87; idem, *Everlasting Dominion: A Theology of the Old Testament* (Nashville: B&H, 2005), 465–82; J. A. Thompson, *1, 2 Chronicles,* NAC (Nashville: B&H, 1994), 32–45.

[26] M. J. Selman, *1 Chronicles,* TOTC (Downers Grove, IL: InterVarsity, 1994), 87.

eldest son of Jacob, appears first because through him would come David (2:15) and his royal descendants down to postexilic times (chap. 3).

Judah's (and David's) importance is seen also in the tribe's "monopolizing" of the genealogical content. Of nine chapters devoted to this material, about two and a half pertain to Judah (2:3–4:23). Moreover, after only scant attention to Saul and his ill-conceived regency (chap. 10), the narrator, disregarding all of David's struggles for accession that are such a major part of the Deuteronomic history, described David's glorious and uncontested assumption of kingship over all Israel (chaps. 11–12). He then spoke of David's conquests (14:8–17; chaps. 18–20), administration (26:29–27:34), preparations for and accomplishment of the retrieval of the ark of the covenant (chaps. 13; 15–16), plans for temple construction (chap. 22), establishment of levitical offices and tasks (23:1–26:28), and procedures for an orderly succession of Solomon to the throne (chaps. 28–29).

The rule of David is presented as being virtually without fault and flaw. Conspicuously missing are such matters as his adultery with Bathsheba and murder of Uriah, the rape of his daughter Tamar by her half-brother, and Absalom's rebellion and its devastating consequences. This was no effort at a cover-up; this would have been a fruitless endeavor since Samuel's account of these was public knowledge. But by not dwelling on David's faults the Chronicler was attempting to magnify God's grace and glory despite human failings.

Most important in establishing the centrality of David in the Chronicler's theology is the extensive account of the so-called Davidic covenant (1 Chronicles 17). Here the promise is that Yahweh will build a house for David (rather than vice versa), that is, a dynastic succession that will endure forever (17:9–14). This elicits from David amazement that God had elected Israel to be a special people and that He had become their God in a peculiar way (17:16–22). This relationship would continue forever if David's descendants and their subjects remained loyal to Yahweh or, failing that, repented of their sins (28:7–10; 2 Chr 6:16,24–39; 7:14; 21:7; 23:3; 24:20,24; 26:5; 28:5–7; 30:5–9; 34:29–33; 36:17–21). Despite a generally dismal history of their unfaithfulness, Chronicles ends with the optimistic note of Cyrus's decree which made possible the people's return to Jerusalem to reestablish the covenant community (36:22–23).

The second major theological theme in Chronicles is the temple and its services. Its importance lies in its being the material and visible expression of God's residence among His people as well as the focal point of their worship, praise, service, and even national existence. David was keenly aware of the significance of a central sanctuary to God's program for His chosen people, so he set about to provide for its construction and function near the very beginning of his reign after he had established his undisputed sovereignty. At first he provided a temporary facility to house the ark (1 Chr 15:1; 16:1,37–38) but then he determined to build a more permanent structure, one large and fine enough to be worthy of his great God (17:1–2). The time and circumstances were not right, however, so the task was assigned to David's son Solomon (17:12).

This did not preclude David from making preparations for the project, however, so he purchased a site (21:26–30), provided materials (22:2–5,14–16; 29:1–9), encouraged Solomon to undertake the project (22:6–13; 28:9–10,20–21), and even gave him a divinely revealed blueprint (28:11–19). All this Solomon took to heart and accomplished after his accession to kingship (2 Chronicles 2–4). Once done, he installed the ark of the covenant within the temple (5:2–10), and then he addressed the people as to its significance and their responsibility in relation to it (6:1–11). It was God's house (6:2), one located in the city He had chosen

(6:6) and by the dynasty He had elected (6:6), to provide a place where His special people Israel could encounter Him (6:5,10–11). It was also the place to which they must look in the future if and when they sinned and were exiled from the land (6:24–27,30,36–39), for God would continue to localize His presence there. Every reformation movement in Israel's subsequent history was centered on the temple and its significance and service (cf. 2 Chr 20:5–12; 23:1–11; 24:1–14; chap. 29; 34:1–22).

The temple served not only as the nexus between Yahweh and His people but also as the center of worship, the rites and ceremonies of which were essential to the proper maintenance of the covenant relationship. This necessitated a cadre of officiants—priests, Levites, and others who ministered before the Lord on behalf of the people. Thus the genealogical data relevant to the tribe of Levi exceed in length even those devoted to Judah and the monarchy (1 Chr 6:1–81; 9:10–34). Moreover, David understood the importance of the role of priests and Levites, whom he charged to escort the ark into his Zion tabernacle (15:1–15) and then to attend to its various services of song and sacrifice (15:16–28; 16:4–6,37–43). He also prepared for the future temple by prescribing orders of Levites to burn incense (23:13), assist the priests (23:28), offer sacrifices (23:31), praise God in music (25:6–7), serve as porters (26:1–19), keep charge of the treasury (26:20–28), and perform other duties (26:29–30). As with the temple itself, it was only as the temple personnel functioned freely and properly that God blessed His people; and their restoration to their God-given tasks was invariably an accompaniment to spiritual renewal (2 Chr 11:13–17; 17:7–9; 23:1–11,18–21; 29:12–36; 30:13–27; 31:2–19; 35:1–19).

There are, of course, multiple theological strands in Chronicles in addition to these two, but they all contribute to these overriding concerns. The revelation of God in Chronicles is clearly designed to demonstrate His love of the whole world (the genealogies) and His intention to effect salvation through His servant people Israel under the messianic leadership of David's royal offspring (1 Chronicles 10–29) who, with the nation, live out their role on the earth by faithful attention to the covenant apparatus that provides the framework for their work and witness.

CONCLUSION

The message that comes through clearly on a careful reading of Chronicles is that it is not merely complementary to or a slightly different version of Samuel and Kings. Instead it is a composition with its own unique way of presenting God's character and claims. With its openness to the plight of all mankind and yet its insistence on the redemptive role of one man and his dynastic succession—culminating, as Christian theology teaches, in Jesus Christ—the book offers hope of salvation for those who embrace Israel's God.

STUDY QUESTIONS

1. What is the Hebrew name for the book of Chronicles?
2. Why were David's sins of adultery and murder not recorded in Chronicles?
3. What is the latest possible date for the composition of the book of Chronicles?
4. What is the central theological idea of the book of Chronicles?
5. What is the purpose of the extensive genealogical lists in 1 Chronicles?
6. Explain the absence of reference in Chronicles to Elijah and Elisha.
7. Why does it seem necessary for Chronicles to have been included in the OT along with the books of Samuel and Kings?
8. In what section of the Hebrew OT is Chronicles found? Explain its location there.

9. Why is the reign of Saul given such scant attention in Chronicles compared to the treatment in 1 Samuel?

10. What is meant by describing Chronicles as a "synoptic" book?

FOR FURTHER STUDY

Braun, R. *1 Chronicles*. WBC. Waco, TX: Word, 1986.

Bright, J. *A History of Israel*. 3rd ed. Philadelphia: Westminster, 1981.

Chisholm, R. B., Jr. *Interpreting the Historical Books*. Grand Rapids: Kregel, 2006.

Curtis, E. L. *The Books of Chronicles*. ICC. Edinburgh: Clark, 1910.

De Vries, S. J. *1 and 2 Chronicles*. FOTL. Grand Rapids: Eerdmans, 1989.

Dillard, R. B. *2 Chronicles*. WBC. Waco, TX: Word, 1987.

Hamilton, V. P. *Handbook on the Historical Books*. Grand Rapids: Baker, 2001.

Howard, D. M., Jr. *An Introduction to the Old Testament Historical Books*. Chicago: Moody, 1993.

Japhet, Sara. *I & II Chronicles*. Louisville: Westminster/John Knox, 1993.

Kalimi, Isaac. *The Reshaping of Ancient Israelite History in Chronicles*. Winona Lake, IN: Eisenbrauns, 2005.

Knoppers, G. N. *I Chronicles 1–9*. AB. New York: Doubleday, 2004.

———. *I Chronicles 10–29*. AB. New York: Doubleday, 2004.

McKenzie, Steven L. *The Chronicler's Use of the Deuteronomistic History*. Atlanta: Scholars, 1985.

Merrill, E. H. *1, 2 Chronicles*. Grand Rapids: Zondervan, 1988.

———. *Kingdom of Priests: A History of Old Testament Israel*. 2nd ed. Grand Rapids: Baker, 2008.

Miller, J. M., and J. H. Hayes. *A History of Ancient Israel and Judah*. Philadelphia: Westminster, 1986.

Myers, J. M. *I Chronicles*. AB. Garden City, NY: Doubleday, 1965.

———. *II Chronicles*. AB. Garden City, NY: Doubleday, 1965.

Provan, I., V. P. Long, and T. Longman III. *A Biblical History of Israel*. Louisville: Westminster John Knox, 2003.

Selman, M. J. *1 Chronicles*. TOTC. Downers Grove, IL: InterVarsity, 1994.

———. *2 Chronicles*. TOTC. Downers Grove, IL: InterVarsity, 1994.

Thompson, J. A. *1, 2 Chronicles*. NAC. Nashville: B&H, 1994.

Williamson, H. G. M. *1 and 2 Chronicles*. NCBC. Grand Rapids: Eerdmans, 1982.

Yamauchi, E. M. *Persia and the Bible*. Grand Rapids: Baker, 1990.

CHAPTER 21

THE BOOK OF EZRA–NEHEMIAH

EUGENE H. MERRILL

INTRODUCTION

The justification for considering Ezra and Nehemiah as one composition and thus treating them together here as such lies in the testimony of the most ancient Hebrew and versional witnesses.[1] Though Philo and Jerome separated the two—a policy that became entrenched in the practice of the church—Judaism persisted in viewing the work as a unit until the advent of the printed Hebrew Bible in the early fifteenth century.

THE LITERARY CHARACTER OF EZRA–NEHEMIAH

The Title of the Book

Both ancient manuscripts and modern Hebrew Bibles label the book "Ezra" or "Ezra Nehemiah" where such information is available.[2] The LXX calls Ezra–Nehemiah by the title Esdras b and precedes the two by the apocryphal work known as Esdras a. The Vulgate (Latin Bible) designates Ezra by 1 Esdras, Nehemiah by 2 Esdras, Esdras a by 3 Esdras and the apocryphal Esdras by 4 Esdras. Most modern versions, especially in the Roman Catholic communities, refer to Ezra and Nehemiah by their Hebrew names, designating Esdras a as 1 Esdras and 4 Esdras as 2 Esdras. The specific content of each of these will receive attention at a later point. Suffice to say for now that Ezra and Nehemiah appear in "Protestant" versions in all languages as two separate treatises and with separate titles.

The Canonicity of the Book

The canonicity of Ezra–Nehemiah has never been the subject of serious debate. All the ancient canon lists include it, though of course with some variation as to its position in the

---

[1] For example the verse total (685) at the end of Nehemiah includes the grand total of Ezra and Nehemiah, and the Massoretic indicator of the center of the book is between Nehemiah 3:31 and 3:32.

[2] A helpful summary may be found in O. Eissfeldt, *The Old Testament: An Introduction* (New York: Harper and Row, 1965), 541–42.

canon. It has already been pointed out (p. 102) that Ezra–Nehemiah appears in the third great section of the Bible, namely, the Kethubîm (or Hagiographa or Writings). The Talmud *Baba Bathra* 14a states, "The order of the Hagiographa is Ruth, the Book of Psalms, Job, Proverbs, Ecclesiastes, Song of Songs, Lamentations, Daniel and the Scroll of Esther, Ezra and Chronicles." Absence of reference to Nehemiah—far from disqualifying it as canonical—attests to the ancient tradition of its being considered part of Ezra.

The modern Masoretic texts continue the practice of placing Ezra–Nehemiah just before Chronicles, the last of the books. The reason is quite apparent: Chronicles recounts the latest events of biblical history, events even later than those of Nehemiah. The LXX (except for A) places Ezra–Nehemiah under the category "History," specifically after Chronicles and before Esther. However, it bears the names Esdras a (for Ezra) and Esdras b (for Nehemiah), an arrangement that divides the work into two parts but which also implicitly links them with a common name. The Vulgate (and thus the Roman Catholic) canon places Ezra and Nehemiah after Chronicles in the "History" section, as do the "Protestant" traditions.[3]

The Contents of the Book

The account opens where Chronicles ends—with a Hebrew version of the edict of the Persian king Cyrus authorizing the Jews of the exile to return to their homeland (Ezra 1:1–4; cf. 2 Chr 36:22–23).[4] The narrator then recounted the preparations for return including the amassing of precious metals (Ezra 1:5–11). Next follows a list of the returnees (chap. 2), the total number of which was 42,360 (2:64). To this list should be compared a nearly identical one in Neh 7:5–73. On their return, the leaders of the community assembled with the populace to rebuild the great temple altar and to offer on it the festival sacrifices, all, so far, without the benefit of a temple (Ezra 3:1–7).

Burdened by this deficiency, Zerubbabel, the governor, and Jeshua, the priest, undertook the temple construction in the second year of the return (c. 536 BC; 3:8–13), an undertaking whose very commencement gave rise to intense local opposition (4:1–4). Having introduced the subject of opposition, the narrator (Ezra?) digressed somewhat by tracing its history up to his own time, some hundred years later (4:5–23), and then returned to his original setting, the first return under Zerubbabel (4:24). At this point the prophets Haggai and Zechariah encouraged the Jewish political leaders to press on with temple construction no matter the difficulties (5:1–5). Their positive efforts were offset by the Jews' enemies, however, who unsuccessfully tried to induce King Darius to bring the work to a halt (5:6–6:15). Instead, Darius permitted the project to go on and even provided materials to bring it to completion (6:16–22).

The scene shifts considerably and the historian addressed the arrival of Ezra the priestly scribe in Jerusalem in Artaxerxes I's seventh year (458 BC), an event greatly assisted by the Persian king (chaps. 7–8). Having arrived in Jerusalem with a large entourage, Ezra confronted a number of problems that had engulfed the Jewish state since its reestablishment 80 years earlier. Chief among these was the intermarriage of Jews with Gentiles, a matter which, after much prayer and confession (9:1–10:4), he addressed head-on by mandating divorce across the board (10:5–44).

---

[3] For the various titles, grouping, order, and the like see H. B. Swete, *An Introduction to the Old Testament in Greek* (Cambridge: University Press, 1902), 197–214.

[4] An account of the historical background of these events can be found in E. H. Merrill, *Kingdom of Priests: A History of Old Testament Israel*, 2nd ed. (Grand Rapids: Baker, 2008), 509–27.

Meanwhile Nehemiah had heard reports of these and other calamities from his vantage point in Susa and, having gotten permission from King Artaxerxes for a leave of absence to go to Jerusalem (Neh 1:1–2:8), undertook to do so (2:9–11). Once there he assessed the ruinous condition of the city (2:12–16) and determined to do something about it (2:17–20). The work of rebuilding the walls, though carried out with the most well-thought-out strategy (chap. 31), was impeded in every way possible by locals who were determined to subvert it (chap. 4). Meanwhile Nehemiah had to contend with internal problems such as the exaction of usury by one Jew against another (5:1–13), a practice much at odds with Nehemiah's own self-sacrifice even though he was governor (5:14–19). Having dealt with this, he had to continue to resist the blandishments and threats of his enemies (6:1–14) until, at last, the walls were finished (6:15–19).

The narrator now turned to the matter of stabilizing the political and religious situation of Jerusalem and vicinity (7:1–4). He described Nehemiah's research of the genealogical records in view of assigning the people their proper places of residence and responsibility (7:5–73). Having done this, Nehemiah called a convocation of all the citizens on New Year's Day, an apt time for a new beginning. Ezra now appears again in the story, this time as the chief officiant at a great service of instruction and rededication (chap. 8). The whole occasion, one lasting more than three weeks and including the Feast of Tabernacles, was climaxed by Israel's swearing to a covenant proclamation read to them by the Levites (chap. 9). The whole community pledged to serve Yahweh and to keep the terms of His covenant with them (chap. 10). There follows then a list of the families living in Jerusalem (11:1–24) and elsewhere (11:25–36) as well as lists of priests, Levites, and other religious personnel (chap. 12).

The book closes with a series of stern measures undertaken by Nehemiah to bring the Jewish community into covenant conformity. There was a need, first, to prohibit the ritually disqualified from temple worship (13:1–3). Next, while Nehemiah had been absent from Jerusalem for a number of years the priesthood had cozied up to Gentile interlopers (13:4–9, 28–31), the Levites had been denied their authorized support (13:10–14), the Sabbath had been commercialized (13:15–22), and Jews had intermarried with unbelievers (13:23–27)— all egregious violations of both the Mosaic law and the covenant the people themselves had made under Nehemiah's direction. Having rectified these abuses, Nehemiah asked God to remember him for good, a request made on previous occasions of reformation as well (13:31b; cf. 5:19; 13:14,22b).

The Structure and Unity of the Book

The reader of Ezra–Nehemiah soon realizes that the two parts give evidence of much commonality if not unity. The historical and geographical environments are the same. Ezra is said to have returned to Jerusalem from Babylon, a Persian province, in 458 BC, whereas Nehemiah did so from Susa, the Persian capital, only 14 years later, in 444. Both came under the aegis of King Artaxerxes I (464–424 BC) and with his material and political assistance. Both also provide nearly identical rosters of those who had returned in earlier years following the decree of Cyrus in 538 BC (Ezra 2:2–67; cf. Neh 7:6–69).[5] Though this latter point may

---

[5] On a comparison of the two lists and a helpful explanation of their slight differences see K. Galling, "The 'Gl-List' According to Ezra 2 // Nehemiah 7," *JBL* 70 (1951): 149–58.

suggest only that Ezra and Nehemiah drew on common sources, the fact their compiler(s) did so adds to the sense of unitary composition.[6]

Beyond this, both parts share common themes, such as the need for building or repairing Jerusalem and its surroundings (Ezra 3:1–13; 6:13–15; Neh 1:1–4; 2:1–3:22; 4:15–23; 6:15–19); dealing with opposition to those projects (Ezra 4:1–24; 5:3–6:12; Neh 4:1–14; 6:1–14); the establishment of pure worship (Ezra 6:16–22; 8:15–36; Neh 8:1–9:4; 10:28–39; 12:27–30; 13:1–22, 28–31); and reformation (Ezra 9:1–10:44; Neh 5:1–19; 9:5–10:27; 13:23–27). Moreover, Nehemiah referred to Ezra by name (but not vice versa), presenting him in a role that is consistent with that described in the book of Ezra and at a time compatible with the chronologies of both parts (Neh 8:1–18; 12:1,26,33,36; Ezra 7:1–10). To these might be added less objective signs of unity such as similar political motivations, spiritual and religious concerns, and, most elusive of all, similar literary and linguistic features.

On the other hand the authorial perspective or presentation is quite different between Ezra and Nehemiah. There is not even a hint in the former as to authorship except for the rare first-person pronoun on Ezra's lips (Ezra 7:28; 8:15–17,21–22,24–26,28; 9:3–6). All that may be suggested here is that the overall composition includes a document originally drafted by Ezra, one described by some scholars as the "Ezra Memoir." This may be limited to 7:27–9:15. As for Nehemiah, the situation is the reverse. Virtually the entire text presents itself as a creation of Nehemiah himself, possible exceptions being Neh 8:1–12:30; 12:44–47. Given the penchant in Hebrew discourse for an author to speak of himself in the third person, however, it is risky to draw too many conclusions from this data. What can be said is that it is unlikely that either Ezra or Nehemiah wrote the total works bearing their names, but that each made some original contribution which became part of the whole corpus as shaped by some anonymous author.

How this was shaped has become a matter of interest to a number of scholars but little consensus has emerged. Williamson isolates Ezra 1–6 as the first major section; the "Nehemiah Memoir" (Neh 1–7; parts of 12:27–43; 13:4–31) as the second; and the "Ezra Memoir" (Ezra 7–10; Neh 8) as the third. The rest (to be addressed later) he sees as small elements independent of these.[7] Blenkinsopp largely follows Williamson but limits the original Nehemiah material to 1:1–7:4, 7:5–10:39 (except for chap. 8) having been added to it later. With most scholars Blenkinsopp attributes Nehemiah 9 to the Ezra material.[8]

Proceeding from a more rhetorical-analytical perspective and with little or no attention to underlying sources, Dorsey offers the following compelling scheme, one that demonstrates clearly the overall unity and compositional strategy of Ezra–Nehemiah:[9]

A. Zerubbabel's return and list of returnees (Ezra 1–2)
    B. Building of temple and opposition from enemies (Ezra 3–6)
        C. Return of Ezra (Ezra 7–8)
            D. Center: Purification of people (Ezra 9–10)
        C[1]. Return of Nehemiah (Neh 1–2)
    B[1]. Building of walls and opposition from enemies (Neh 3:1–7:3)
A[1]. Zerubbabel's return and list of returnees; final reforms (Neh 7:4–13:31)

---

[6] See especially T. C. Eskenazi, "The Structure of Ezra–Nehemiah and the Integrity of the Book," *JBL* 107 (1988): 641–56.

[7] H. G. M. Williamson, *Ezra, Nehemiah*, WBC (Waco, TX: Word, 1985), xxiii–xxxiii.

[8] J. Blenkinsopp, *Ezra–Nehemiah*, OTL (Philadelphia: Westminster, 1988), 41–47.

[9] D. A. Dorsey, *Meaning and Structure in the Old Testament* (Grand Rapids: Baker, forthcoming), 273.

While this symmetrical analysis does not always cohere with clearly demarcated literary units in the text, it does show how the final composer worked these units into a deliberate and meaningful pattern.

Literary Forms and Genres of the Book

The dominant impression that emerges from even a superficial reading of Ezra–Nehemiah is that it is narrative, particularly first–person narrative. This gives rise to the common (if not altogether accurate) designation "memoir."[10] Fully half the material can be subsumed under this category as a whole, but even in the memoirs other materials of a different kind are embedded. For example Nehemiah's account about bad news from Jerusalem (Neh 1:1–11) includes within it a prayer (1:5–11) of petition and lament. Others are found in Ezra 9:6–15; Nehemiah 4:4–5; 5:19; 6:14; 9:5b–37; 13:14, 22b,29,31b, all in first-person narratives.

Other distinct literary forms are decrees (Ezra 1:2–4); inventories (Ezra 1:9–11a; 8:24–30); lists (Ezra 2:3–69; 8:1–14; 10:18–44; Neh 3:1–32; 7:6–72; 10:1–27; 11:3–12:26); historical narrative (Ezra 3:1–4:6); letters (Ezra 4:7–10, 11–16, 17–22; 5:7–17; 6:6–12; 7:11–26); genealogy (Ezra 7:1–5); benediction (Ezra 7:27–28a); itinerary (Neh 2:13–15); and a partial covenant text (within a prayer; Neh 9:6–37). Sometimes these formal units coincide with real or alleged literary sources, and sometimes they do not. It is important here, as always, to distinguish between literary types and the secondary uses to which they may be adapted.[11] Our discussion of sources will once again address this issue.

OUTLINE OF THE BOOK

Ezra

I. **Return from Exile** (chaps. 1–2)
   A. Proclamation of Permission (chap. 1)
   B. List of Returnees (chap. 2)

II. **Rebuilding of Cultus and Community** (chaps. 3–6)
   A. Preparation for Rebuilding (chap. 3)
   B. Opposition to Rebuilding (chap. 4)
   C. Continuation of Rebuilding (chap. 5)
   D. Completion of Rebuilding (chap. 6)

III. **Return of Ezra** (chaps. 7–8)
   A. Arrangements for His Return (chap. 7)
   B. Entourage with His Return (chap. 8)

IV. **Ministry of Ezra** (chaps. 9–10)
   A. Sin of the People (9:1–4)
   B. Ezra's Prayer for the People (9:5–15)
   C. Ezra's Leadership in Reformation (chap. 10)

---

[10] "Memoir" is "a history or narrative composed from or stressing personal experience and acquaintance with the events, scenes, or persons described" (K. Kuiper, ed., *Merriam-Webster's Encyclopedia of Literature* [Springfield, MA: Merriam-Webster, 1995], 749). D. J. Clines objects that the term is not altogether appropriate to this material, especially in light of Nehemiah's appeals to God to "remember me" (Neh 5:19; 13:14,22,31). This, Clines says, is more indicative of royal inscriptions or "prayers of the accused" (*Ezra, Nehemiah, Esther*, NCBC [Grand Rapids: Eerdmans, 1984], 4–5).

[11] For a description of the mélange of literary diversity found in biblical historical narrative, see B. O. Long, *1 Kings with an Introduction to Historical Literature*, FOTL (Grand Rapids: Eerdmans), 2–8.

Nehemiah

V. **Nehemiah's Dilemma (chap. 1)**
  A. Report of Jerusalem's Condition (1:1–3)
  B. Nehemiah's Prayer (1:4–11)

VI. **Nehemiah's Plan (chap. 2)**
  A. His Request of the King (2:1–8)
  B. His Return to Jerusalem and Plan to Rebuild (2:9–20)

VII. **Nehemiah's Building (chaps. 3–4)**
  A. His Organization (chap. 3)
  B. His Opposition (chap. 4)

VIII. **Nehemiah's Domestic Reforms (chap. 5)**

IX. **Nehemiah's Determination (6:1–7:4)**

X. **List of Returnees (7:5–73a)**

XI. **Covenant Renewal (7:73b–10:39)**
  A. Its Preparations (7:73b–9:4)
  B. Its Proclamation (9:5–10:27)
  C. Its Stipulations (10:28–39)

XII. **Rededication of Jerusalem (11:1–13:3)**
  A. Lists of People and Priests (11:1–12:26)
  B. Ceremony of Celebration (12:27–13:3)

XIII. **Return to Former Sins and Second Reformation (13:4–31)**

THE COMPOSITION OF EZRA–NEHEMIAH

The Authorship of the Book

Though, as noted, there are large sections of first person material, especially in Nehemiah, it is impossible to determine who collated, edited, and left the final imprint on this twofold work. That is, the authorship is anonymous and probably will never be known. This judgment is in spite of the dogmatic declaration of the Talmud that "Ezra wrote the book that bears his name [that is, Ezra–Nehemiah] and the genealogies of the Book of Chronicles up to his own time (*Baba Bathra* 15a)." As for the rest of Chronicles, the same tradition attributes it to Nehemiah. According to this assessment, Nehemiah is the Chronicler (except for most of 1 Chronicles 1–9) and Ezra is the author of Ezra–Nehemiah. This leads to two further considerations as to authorship: (1) the connection between Chronicles and Ezra–Nehemiah and (2) the relative chronological priority of Ezra and Nehemiah themselves.

The first of these issues has already received attention in the discussion of Chronicles (chap. 20). There compelling evidence was presented that precludes any Chronicles and Ezra–Nehemiah literary unity, to say nothing of common authorship. The second point does need to be addressed, however, for if either Ezra or Nehemiah had a hand in the authorship (or, more accurately, the composition) of the final form of the book, it would obviously have been done by the man who last appeared in historical sequence.

The question of the Ezra/Nehemiah chronological priority is too complicated to be fully rehearsed here, so a brief summary will suffice.[12] Before we undertake even that, it is appropriate to ask why this is an issue at all since a straightforward reading of the book leads to no other conclusion than that Ezra preceded Nehemiah. In a memoir section Ezra says that he returned to Jerusalem in the seventh year of King Artaxerxes (Ezra 7:8), that year being 458 BC. Nehemiah, on the other hand, asserts that he returned by permission of the same king 13 years later (Neh 1:1; 2:1), that is, in 445–444 BC.

A considerable scholarly opinion challenges this traditional view, however, by asserting that the Artaxerxes in view is not the same man in both instances.[13] The Artaxerxes in Nehemiah, it is said, is Artaxerxes I (464–424) but the ruler in the book of Ezra is Artaxerxes II (404–358). Ezra, according to this distinction, would have arrived in Jerusalem as late as 398 BC, some 46 or 47 years after Nehemiah's arrival. So, if either was responsible for the compilation of Ezra–Nehemiah, it would have to be Ezra.

The principal arguments favoring the Nehemiah priority seem, on close examination, to be without substance. The first is that Nehemiah returned to build walls (Neh 1:1–3) when, in fact, Ezra stated that walls were already in place (Ezra 9:9). The term Ezra used (*gdr*) probably is to be taken metaphorically of God's protection, but on the other hand it is quite possible that walls had been built since Zerubbabel's time, only to have been broken down again (cf. Ezra 4:12; 5:8–9). This would explain Nehemiah's surprise at the news of their destruction.

The second argument for the alternative view is the absence of reference to one another by both Ezra and Nehemiah, thus presupposing their noncontemporaneity.[14] However, Nehemiah does in fact mention Ezra (Neh 8:9; 12:26,36). Proponents of this view, however, allege that these references are secondary glosses. But this heavy-handed begging the question is on its face self-refuting.

The third argument is that Ezra seems to have dealt with the matter of intermarriage more severely and with greater finality than did Nehemiah (Ezra 10:10–14; Neh 13:25). However, according to the traditional sequence and dating, Ezra's reform would have occurred at about 457 BC, 25 years before Nehemiah addressed the issue. Clearly that was enough time for abuses to have erupted once more in this area of community life. Since Ezra's harsh response had been so effective, however, Nehemiah had comparatively little to do in his own, later generation.

In summary, if either Ezra or Nehemiah must be judged author of the book that bears their names, Nehemiah is clearly the more suitable candidate. As will be seen next, however, the matter is much too complicated for that either/or option. There is no doubt that much of the material is original to both these individuals, but the final product can hardly be attributed to either.

---

[12] See A. Demsky, "Who Came First, Ezra or Nehemiah? The Synchronistic Approach," *HUCA* 65 (1994): 1–20; L. McFall, "Was Nehemiah Contemporary with Ezra in 458 B.C.?" *WTJ* 53 (1991): 263–93; Merrill, *Kingdom of Priests*, 502–6; H. H. Rowley, "The Chronological Order of Ezra and Nehemiah," in *The Servant of the Lord and Other Essays on the Old Testament* (Oxford: Blackwell, 1965), 137–68; E. M. Yamauchi, "The Reverse Order of Ezra/Nehemiah Reconsidered," *Themelios* 5 (1980): 7–13.

[13] Eissfeldt, *The Old Testament: An Introduction*, 552–55.

[14] Other examples biblical of contemporaries who fail to mention one another are Haggai and Zechariah, who ministered together in the early postexilic period; and Jeremiah and Ezekiel, prophets of the late preexilic and exilic eras. See D. M. Howard Jr., *An Introduction to the Old Testament Historical Books* (Chicago: Moody, 1993), 282–83.

The Sources of the Book

The matter of determining primary and secondary sources in ancient literature is precarious at best. Materials that differ widely in terms of literary style, lexicography, grammar, and the like show evidence of coming from different authors, but when form-critical and literary-critical considerations are brought to bear, it is clear that a single author can express himself in a wide variety of manners and styles. At the best, such criteria must be used with great caution. When, however, there are clues within a text that it circulated at one time as an independent composition, there is good reason to believe it constitutes a secondary source.

On the other hand, when a composition makes an assertion about its own authorship—such as the use of the first-person pronoun—there is every reason to take such witness at face value unless and until it can be disproved. This is immediately pertinent to Ezra–Nehemiah where, as noted, large blocks are attributed to both Ezra and Nehemiah (Ezra 7:27–9:15; Neh 1:1–7:73a; 12:31–43; chap. 13). These parts at least must be considered original to these two authors even if incorporated by the final redactor.

Scholarship has reached no consensus as to the other sources of the work, but the following list is fairly representative:

- the decree of Cyrus (Ezra 1:2–4)
- the list of temple vessels (1:9–11)
- the list of Jewish returnees (2:1–67; cf. Neh 7:6–69)
- Rehum's letter (Ezra 4:11b–16)
- Artaxerxes' reply (4:17–22)
- Tattenai's letter (5:7b–17)
- Darius's reply (6:6–12)
- the decree of Artaxerxes (7:12–26)
- the list of Jews who had intermarried (10:18–43)
- the list of Jewish returnees (Neh 7:6–69)
- the list of Jewish citizens (Neh 11:3–36)
- the list of priests and Levites (Neh 12:1–26)

This analysis suggests that Ezra himself incorporated no secondary sources into his memoirs, or at least into the section so identified by first-person references. Indeed, his memoirs themselves became part of the finished product. Nehemiah, however, seems to have made use of the same register of Jewish returnees as is found in Ezra; in fact he declared unambiguously, "I found the genealogical record of those who came back first" (Neh 7:5), and he then reproduced it (vv. 6–73).[15]

The remaining material may be designated for lack of a better term, "editorial." This includes the introduction to the decree of Cyrus (Ezra 1:1; replicated in 2 Chr 36:22);[16] a narrative about the earliest return (Ezra 1:5–8); the narrative about the rebuilding of the temple (chap. 3) and opposition to it (4:1–6); introductions to various letters (Ezra 4:7–11a,17; 5:6–7a; 7:11); reactions to letters (4:23–24; 6:13; 7:27–28); narratives about the prophets Haggai and

---

[15] Nehemiah's purpose in researching the records to find the register of names was obviously to assist him in the settlement of Jerusalem (F. C. Fensham, *The Books of Ezra and Nehemiah,* NICOT [Grand Rapids: Eerdmans, 1982], 211).

[16] This repetition of so-called "catch-lines" is persuasive to many scholars of the unitary composition of Chronicles–Ezra/Nehemiah. See, e.g., M. Haran, "Explaining the Identical Lines at the End of Chronicles and the Beginning of Ezra," *BR* 2 (1986): 18–22. H. E. M. Williamson, responding to Haran's article, proposes other suggestions for the duplication, preferring what he calls a "liturgical" use of Ezra by a later hand who added the text to Chronicles to avoid the otherwise pessimistic ending of that book ("Did the Author of Chronicles Also Write the Books of Ezra and Nehemiah?" *BR* 3 [1987]: 59.)

Zechariah (5:1–5; 6:14–15); a report of Darius's search through the royal archives (6:1–5); a narrative concerning temple dedication (6:16–22); the narrative about mixed marriages and their resolution (10:1–17); the narrative about observing the Feast of Tabernacles (Neh 7:73b–8:18); the narrative about covenant renewal (chap. 9–10); the instruction to populate Jerusalem (11:1–2); the narrative about the dedication of the walls (12:27–30); and the assignment of priestly and Levitical duties (12:44–47).

The Date of the Book

Since the final collector and/or editor of Ezra–Nehemiah is unknown, it is impossible to assign any precise date *a quo*. Internally the last recorded event (granting the Ezra priority) is Nehemiah's second return to Jerusalem in Artaxerxes's thirty-second year, that is, 432 BC. (Neh 13:6). Some scholars, on the basis of the supposed intention of Ezra 1–6 to counteract the rise of the Samaritan temple and worship, date that part last and as late as 300 BC.[17] This and other attempts to date the book that late are unconvincing, in view of their lack of indisputable objective data.

Texts and Versions of the Book[18]

Though the Masoretic texts of Ezra–Nehemiah evidence relatively little complexity or variation, the situation with the Greek renditions is the opposite. There are two major versions of these, Esdras a (alpha) and Esdras b (beta). The former is also known as 1 Esdras, and the latter is the same as Ezra–Nehemiah. First Esdras is a free translation with unknown *Vorlage* and is significantly different from the three fragments of Ezra found at Qumran (4 Q Ezra), namely, Ezra 4:2–6, 9–11; 5:17–6:5. It includes 2 Chronicles 35–36; rearranges and adds to Ezra 1:1–Neh 8:13; and eliminates Neh 8:14–13:31 entirely. Esdras b is the prototype of LXXB and LXXA and apparently a translation of the *Vorlage* from which the MT itself developed. It includes all the material of the Masoretic Ezra–Nehemiah.

THE THEOLOGY OF EZRA–NEHEMIAH[19]

At perhaps no time in the long history of Israel and Judah was a theological explanation of the condition of God's elect people more necessary and more in order than that of the postexilic period in which Ezra and Nehemiah provided leadership. Ezra, the priest and scribe, functioned in those capacities but also politically; Nehemiah, governor of the restored community, exercised his office but also supplied spiritual authority and direction. Together they demonstrated that the kingdom of God could not be bifurcated between the secular and the sacred. If God's covenant promises were to find authentic fulfillment, the regathered and reconstituted Jewish state must conform in all its aspects to its covenant mandate and responsibilities.

Ezra was keenly aware of this and thus, following on the heels of Zerubbabel, Jeshua, and other leaders of the newly reborn commonwealth of faith, requested and received permission from the king of Persia to make the trek to his ancestral homeland and there to complete the

---

[17] Williamson, *Ezra, Nehemiah*, xxxv–xxxvi.

[18] See, Blenkinsopp, *Ezra–Nehemiah*, 70-72.

[19] See especially M. Breneman, *Ezra, Nehemiah, Esther*, NAC (Nashville: B&H, 1993), 50–59; W. J. Dumbrell, "The Theological Intention of Ezra–Nehemiah," *RTR* 45 (1986): 65–72; Howard, *An Introduction to the Old Testament Historical Books*, 304–10; E. H. Merrill, "A Theology of Ezra–Nehemiah and Esther," in *A Biblical Theology of the Old Testament*, ed. R. B. Zuck (Chicago: Moody, 1991), 189–205; idem, *Everlasting Dominion: A Theology of the Old Testament* (Nashville: B&H 2008), 482–87; P. E. Satterthwaite, "Ezra, Theology of," in *NIDOTTE*, ed. W. A. VanGemeren (Grand Rapids: Zondervan, 1997), 4:635–37; H. G. M. Williamson, "Nehemiah: Theology of," in *NIDOTTE*, 4:977–82.

task of reconstituting the community into the prophetic ideal of a theocratic body. Before his arrival other visionaries such as Zerubbabel, Jeshua, Haggai, and Zechariah had called the people to material rebuilding and spiritual renewal, a call that was met with only limited success. Opposition from without and lethargic indifference from within had frustrated progress toward a full accomplishment of all that was hoped for.

Now, more than 80 years after the first tentative steps at national renascence, Ezra arrived armed with both human and divine authority to complete the task (Ezra 7:27–28). Sadly he was to find his own optimistic hopes dashed because of the enormity of the problems that met him on every hand. Particularly distressing was the blatant intermarriage of the "holy people" (lit., "holy seed" Ezra 9:2) with their pagan neighbors, an act of covenant violation expressly and vigorously condemned in Torah (Exod 34:15–16; Deut 7:3–4). It was for this kind of infidelity that God had sent them into exile in the first place (2 Kgs 17:7–23; 2 Chr 36:14–16). In his great intercessory prayer Ezra rehearsed that long, sordid history of betrayal (Ezra 9:6–15), comparing his own generation to those of bygone days (9:7,10–11,13).

While he prayed before the temple, the people overheard and, smitten with remorse and repentance, pledged to do whatever was necessary to achieve God's forgiveness and an opportunity for a new beginning (Ezra 10:1–4). As evidence of their sincerity they addressed the very matter that had plunged Ezra into such despair to begin with—that of mixed marriage. At Ezra's direction they proceeded to divorce their heathen partners and thereby to recover their purity as God's covenant people (10:10–17).

Some 14 years after Ezra's ministry in Jerusalem began, Nehemiah, having heard of the distressful situation there, sought leave of King Artaxerxes to attend to its remediation. He lamented that the Jewish people were "in great trouble and disgrace" and that Jerusalem's walls were in ruins (Neh 1:3). These conditions were clearly attributable to the hostile forces Ezra had contended with (Ezra 4:7–23) as well as the spiritual decline of the people themselves (9:1–4). Nehemiah's task therefore was also twofold: to make repair of the physical infrastructure and to lead the community into spiritual reformation and restoration.

This meant that Nehemiah—presumably in partnership with Ezra—had to contend with the Samaritans and other neighboring peoples who attempted to prevent the rebuilding of Jerusalem's walls and other structures (Neh 2:19–20; chap. 4; 6:1–14). All along he knew that it was a work of God and that what God had begun through the early postexilic pioneers would be brought to final and fruitful culmination. With Ezra also, however, Nehemiah understood that the greater threat to the community was from within. It was not broken walls but broken covenant that jeopardized what God intended for the Jewish remnant. Thus the two together—priest and statesman—undertook the painful but essential task of undoing the wrong and establishing the right.

Ezra's initial attempts in this vein seem to have had only temporary effect, so Nehemiah set about again to reinforce what had been done and to introduce new reforms. He abolished the exaction of usury (Neh 5:1–13) and, probably after Ezra's decease, condemned mixed marriages as had his elder colleague (Neh 13:23–27; cf. Ezra 10:10–17). Together they called the people back to Torah, first in a great public assembly in which Ezra read the Law (Neh 7:73b–8:18), and then in a ceremony of covenant renewal (chap. 9–10). Twelve years later Nehemiah demonstrated his continuing concern for purity by preventing the contamination of the temple through admission of the cultically disqualified (13:1–9); by restoring the privileges of the Levites (13:10–14); and by correcting widespread abuse of the sabbath (13:15–22).

In conclusion the overriding theological concern of Ezra–Nehemiah was for the restoration of the postexilic Jewish community to a position of covenant purity and faithfulness so that it might take up and perpetuate its God-given privilege and task of mediating his salvific intentions to the whole world. Despite its failure in doing so as a community, Ezra and Nehemiah helped establish the conditions that could prepare the way for the One who, in the fullness of time, brought to pass the hopes and dreams of these mighty reformers.

CONCLUSION

The position of Ezra–Nehemiah after Chronicles in many canon lists leads many students of the Bible to relegate Ezra–Nehemiah to a place of little interest or even insignificance. Once the curtain had fallen on Judah's monarchic history, what was left of the drama? Of what concern could the tiny, struggling postexilic Jewish enclave be? Such questions fail to understand the open-endedness of Chronicles itself, which closes with a view toward redemption, one carried forward by the edict of a pagan king and fleshed out in the account of Ezra–Nehemiah by others who, consciously or not, found themselves God's agents in achieving His saving designs. Failure to grasp the import of Ezra–Nehemiah results also in an inability to see that God knows no "silent years," no time when He is not in process of bringing to pass His dominion over all things. The book bears witness to the bridging of the OT promises and the NT fulfillments.

STUDY QUESTIONS

1. Name one strong argument for the combination of Ezra and Nehemiah into one book?
2. What circumstances prompted Nehemiah to return to Jerusalem from Persia?
3. Under which Persian king did most of the activity of Ezra–Nehemiah take place?
4. What was Nehemiah's primary ministry on his return to Jerusalem?
5. What was Ezra's primary ministry on his return to Jerusalem?
6. Briefly elaborate the arguments for Ezra's chronological priority to Nehemiah.
7. What was Nehemiah's title or role in the postexilic community?
8. Why did Ezra command the men of the community to divorce their wives?
9. In what language did Ezra address the assembled crowd of Jews?
10. What status did postexilic Judah have with relation to the Persian Empire?

FOR FURTHER STUDY

Blenkinsopp, J. *Ezra–Nehemiah: A Commentary*. Philadelphia: Westminster, 1988.

Breneman, M. *Ezra, Nehemiah, Esther*. NAC. Nashville: B&H, 1993.

Bright, J. *A History of Israel*. 3rd ed. Philadelphia: Westminster, 1981.

Chisholm, R. B., Jr. *Interpreting the Historical Books*. Grand Rapids: Kregel, 2006.

Clines, D. J. A. *Ezra, Nehemiah, Esther*. NCBC. Grand Rapids: Eerdmans, 1984.

Fensham, F. C. *The Books of Ezra and Nehemiah*. NICOT. Grand Rapids: Eerdmans, 1983.

Hamilton, V. P. *Handbook on the Historical Books*. Grand Rapids: Baker, 2001.

Holmgren, F. C. *Ezra & Nehemiah*. Grand Rapids: Eerdmans, 1987.

Howard, D. M., Jr. *An Introduction to the Old Testament Historical Books*. Chicago: Moody, 1993.

Merrill, E. H. *Kingdom of Priests: A History of Old Testament Israel*. 2nd ed. Grand Rapids: Baker, 2008.

———. *Nehemiah*. OTSB. Springfield, MO: World Library, 2000.

Miller, J. M., and J. H. Hayes. *A History of Ancient Israel and Judah*. Philadelphia: Westminster, 1986.

Myers, J. M. *Ezra, Nehemiah*. AB. Garden City, NY: Doubleday, 1965.

Provan, I., V. P. Long, and T. Longman III. *A Biblical History of Israel*. Louisville: Westminster John Knox, 2003.

Williamson, H. G. M. *Ezra, Nehemiah*. WBC. Waco, TX: Word, 1985.

Yamauchi, E. M. *Persia and the Bible*. Grand Rapids: Baker, 1990.

CHAPTER 22

THE BOOK OF ESTHER

EUGENE H. MERRILL

FEW WRITINGS OF the OT have been as much the subject of debate as the book of Esther. Virtually everything about it—its authorship, date, historicity, canonicity, and purpose—has engendered fierce difference of opinion from almost the moment of its composition to the present time. The following discussion can address just the major issues and even then can offer only what seems to be the best solution to them. The student is encouraged to peruse the commentaries and other sources of information in order to arrive at a more complete picture.

THE TITLE AND CANONICITY OF ESTHER

All the major Hebrew manuscript traditions know the book as "Esther" (Hb. *'estēr*, probably related to Akkadian Ishtar, the goddess; *ištaru*, "goddess"; or Persian *stâra*).[1] The name is reflected in the LXX as *'Esthr* and in the Vulgate as *Esther* or *Hester*, with other major ancient and modern versions employing variations of these spellings. The Hebrew name of the heroine for whom the book is named is Hadassah (*hădassâ*), the feminine form of a word meaning "myrtle tree" (Esth 2:7).

From the beginning of Jewish oral and written tradition, the recognition of Esther as a work worthy of inclusion in the sacred collection of inspired works has been problematic.[2] Its omission so far from the manuscripts unearthed at Qumran adds fuel to the controversy, suggesting to some scholars that at least the community of the DSS rejected the canonicity of Esther. Such an argument from silence falls far short of proving anything, of course, though it certainly does raise questions as to the book's status in that context.[3]

On the other hand Josephus almost certainly included Esther in his list of 22 sacred books of Scripture).[4] If he did not, it is impossible to know what book he had in mind to take its

---

[1] C. A. Moore, *Esther,* AB (Garden City, NY: Doubleday, 1971), LI, 20.

[2] R. Beckwith, *The Old Testament Canon of the New Testament Church* (Grand Rapids: Eerdmans, 1985), 283, 288–91.

[3] Beckwith suggests that the Essenes of Qumran omitted Esther because they did not observe the Purim festival, which, among other things, conflicted with their sacred calendar.

[4] Josephus, *Ad Apionem* 1.8.

place. Moreover, he took the narrative of the book at face value as a historical record, repeatedly acknowledging that the victory achieved by the Jews through Mordecai and Esther was in the final analysis a work of God Himself.[5] In addition Josephus suggested its composition occurred in the days of King Artaxerxes (464–424 BC) at the latest,[6] a time in which, he says, canonical books were still being written.[7]

Nowhere is Esther's canonicity more tenuous than in the rabbinical debates recorded in various baraitas of the Mishnah, especially in *Baba Bathra* 14b–15a and *Megilla* 7a. The former tractate merely affirms Esther's canonical status, listing it among the Kethubîm between Daniel and Ezra–Nehemiah. Its "authorship" (probably meaning collection or even canonization) is attributed to the "Men of the Great Assembly." *Megilla*, however, recounts the controversies regarding the so-called Antilegomena, those writings of questionable authority. There were five of these in all, including Esther, that were thought to "defile the hands," that is, sacred and thus requiring ritual washings in order to be handled. The great rabbi Judah said that a predecessor, Samuel, had declared that Esther does not defile the hands, thereby denying its inspiration. Judah's response was somewhat equivocating: "It was spoken to be read, and was not spoken to be written." This comment apparently affirms at least quasi-canonicity for the book.[8]

The test of Esther's canonicity is its inclusion or exclusion in the major canon lists. It appears in virtually all the Hebrew manuscript witnesses as well as in the LXX (or Alexandrian canon), Vulgate, Clement of Alexandria, Origen, Hilary of Poitiers, Cyril of Jerusalem, Epiphanius, Rufinus, and Augustine. It is missing in other lists (most notably Melito)[9] which are incomplete in some cases and from still others of minor status—all apparently for a perceived lack of canonical authority. On the whole, however, the Jewish and Christian traditions have accorded canonicity to Esther, the few dissenting voices notwithstanding.

THE CONTENTS OF THE BOOK

Esther and Daniel are nearly unique among the OT books in that their settings are wholly outside Palestine and their principal characters are primarily foreign rulers and governments. They also share in common the background of the Achaemenid Persian empire (c. 550–330 BC), Daniel in the reigns of Cyrus (559–530), Cambyses (530–522), and Darius I (522–486); and Esther in the reign of Xerxes (486–465). Also, Daniel and Esther, for whom the books are named, played significant roles in preserving their Jewish countrymen from the persecutions and pogroms of their host countries.

The major purpose of Esther is to explain the origin of the Feast of Purim, the occasion for celebrating God's intervention on behalf of His beleaguered people (Esth 9:20–32). By the time of Xerxes (Ahasuerus in the Hebrew Bible) Persia dominated the entire Middle Eastern world. The Jews who did not return under Cyrus (538 BC and later) and other Persian rulers thus became Persian subjects instead of Babylonian. They lived in various regions of the empire including Susa, the capital at that time (1:5).

Esther's rise to prominence came about because of Xerxes's drunken request to his wife Vashti to display her charms in the royal court before his noblemen. When she refused, the king deposed her and sought a new queen. After a thorough search Esther was chosen, though

---

[5] Josephus, *The Antiquities of the Jews*, 4.6.

[6] Ibid., 11.6.13.

[7] Beckwith, *The Old Testament Canon of the New Testament Church*, 79–80.

[8] W. H. Green, *General Introduction to the Old Testament. The Canon* (1898; reprint, Grand Rapids: Baker, 1980), 132.

[9] Beckwith, *The Old Testament Canon of the New Testament Church*, 296.

her Jewish identity remained a secret. By the time Esther became queen (479 BC) Xerxes had suffered a humiliating defeat at the hands of the Greeks far to the west. Perhaps as a result of this national embarrassment some conspirators set about to assassinate the king, a plot overheard and exposed by Esther's kinsman Mordecai.

Meanwhile, Haman, a high official in the government, became enraged over Mordecai's impudence in refusing to pay him homage, and so he proposed to Xerxes a plan to purge the empire of the Jewish people who, he convinced Xerxes, were a danger to national well-being. In desperation Mordecai informed Esther of what was afoot and persuaded her to use her good offices to prevent this massacre. By now Xerxes had learned that it was Mordecai who had saved him from assassination, and so he promoted the Jew to great honor.

Esther disclosed to Xerxes what Haman was up to, and she also revealed that she was a Jew, a target of Haman's intrigue. The king ordered Haman to be hanged and then set about to arm the Jews against those who would kill them. He even authorized the Jews to take the offensive against their enemies on an appointed day, Adar 13 (Esth 9:1,17). Their foes had decided to cast lots (Hb. *pûrîm*) to determine who of the Jews should die (9:24) but now the tables had turned. The Jews now slew their tormentors in one day and rested on the next. From then on those days of slaughter and respite were to be commemorated as the joyous festival of Purim (9:26–28).

THE STRUCTURE AND UNITY OF THE BOOK

Scholars generally agree that the author of this short story has blended introduction, rise and suspense of action, climax, dénouement, and conclusion in a remarkably successful manner.[10] While it is entirely possible that parts of the work circulated independently (see "The Sources of the Book" below), the whole has been put together in such a way as to leave the reader with a clear sense of plot development and resolution. The characters are clearly delineated, their relationships are complicated but effectively interconnected, and the overall impression is one of careful literary craftsmanship.

Literary Forms and Genres of the Book

Though Esther may be described as wisdom literature,[11] its dominant literary device is narrative. It is a short story or *novella*, a description that in no way undercuts its facticity or historicity.[12] Between and within the narrative blocks (chap. 1; chap. 3; 4:4–17; 5:9–14; chaps. 6–7; 9:11–19; 9:29–10:3) are a host of other forms such as "speech" (2:2–4), "biographical record" (2:5–7), "report" (2:8–20,21–23; 4:1–3; 8:1–2; 9:1–10), "anecdote" (5:9–14), and "decree" (8:9–17; 9:20–28).[13] Besides its variety of genres, the book of Esther also exhibits a number of speech figures, most notably and effectively that of irony. Over and over again the action appears to be headed in one direction only to be overturned and reversed by a series of unexpected interventions. For example God's name nowhere occurs in the book, but no book exceeds Esther in its manifestation of God's presence and power. Esther, an undistinguished and unrecognized Jewish maiden, becomes the means of saving her people from destruction

---

[10] R. Gordis, "Studies in the Esther Narrative," *JBL* 95 (1976): 43–58. See also F. S. Weiland, "Historicity, Genre, and Narrative Design in the Book of Esther," *BSac* 159 (2002): 151–65.

[11] S. Talmon, "Wisdom in the Book of Esther," *VT* 13 (1963): 419–55.

[12] M. V. Fox, while uncomfortable with the description "novella," accedes to the book's own self-presentation as history (*Character and Ideology in the Book of Esther* [Columbia, SC: University of South Carolina, 1991]), 144–45, 148–50.

[13] R. E. Murphy, *Wisdom Literature: Job, Proverbs, Ruth, Canticles, Ecclesiastes, and Esther,* FOTL (Grand Rapids: Eerdmans, 1981), 158–70.

at the hands of powerful Persian enemies. Mordecai, the despised Jew, comes to prevail over wicked Haman who, ironically, dies on the gallows he had erected for Mordecai. The day appointed for Jewish annihilation became instead the day celebrated even now as the time God empowered His people to gain victory over their enemies.

OUTLINE OF THE BOOK

I. **Esther's Elevation to Power (chaps. 1–2)**
   A. The Demand of Xerxes (1:1–12)
   B. The Decrees of Xerxes (1:13–2:4)
   C. The Choice of Esther to Be Queen (2:5–18)
   D. The Discovery of a Plot against Xerxes (2:19–23)

II. **Esther's Role as Deliverer (chaps. 3–7)**
   A. The Decree against the Jews (chap. 3)
   B. The Vulnerability of the Jews (chaps. 4–5)
   C. The Deliverance of the Jews (chaps. 6–7)

III. **Esther's Establishment of Purim (chaps. 8–10)**
   A. The Decree Favoring the Jews (chap. 8)
   B. The Implementation of Deliverance (9:1–16)
   C. The Celebration of Deliverance (9:17–32)
   D. The Advancement of the Jews (chap. 10)

THE COMPOSITION OF THE BOOK

The Authorship of the Book

Apart from the enigmatic note in the Mishnah (*Megilla* 7a) that the "Men of the Great Assembly" wrote Esther, other early Jewish tradition has little to say on the matter. Eventually Mordecai himself was proposed by some advocates as the author, but the highly commendatory way in which he is presented (cf. 6:11; 8:15; 9:4; 10:3) makes this hardly likely. At present there is simply no way to identify the author.[14]

The Sources of the Book

Source-critical analysis has persuaded many scholars that Esther is a composite of an earlier narrative (chaps. 1–8) to which was appended a later ending (chaps. 9–10). The larger narrative itself, according to many of these studies, consists of an original "Mordecai story" and "Esther story" (and perhaps even a "Vashti story") that were joined to constitute the present account.[15] The evidence adduced—dual protagonists, alleged doublets, competing liturgical and political viewpoints, and the like—falls far short of proof of preexiting sources and in fact it only adds to the genius of the author's plot development.[16] As for the later ending, the Greek evidence does indeed betray some features pointing toward its original independence of and then integration into Esther 1–8, one result being a reshaping of parts of that work, especially chap. 8, to enable it to prepare the way for the introduction of the festival of Purim. If,

---

[14] D. M. Howard Jr. *An Introduction to the Old Testament Historical Books* (Chicago: Moody, 1993), 316–17.

[15] F. W. Bush, *Ruth, Esther*, WBC (Dallas: Word, 1996), 280–94.

[16] D. J. A. Clines, *The Esther Scroll: The Story of the Story*, JSOTSup (Sheffield: JSOT Press, 1984), 138–39, 151.

however, the MT is the product of that redactionism, it is fair to say that the MT represents the intended inspired Word of God.[17]

Of all the sources possibly presupposed by the various forms and genres already noted, none has been considered lacking in basic historicity except for the Vashti narrative (1:1–2:14), a story thought by most critics to be unalloyed fiction because of its lack of corroboration from extrabiblical accounts.[18] However, to conclude that a story is historically unreliable on the basis of silence is to deny the Bible any credence as historical source material. Nothing in the narrative is out of line with what is known of Xerxes's reign; moreover, the year of the incident (483 BC; cf. 1:3) is in a period of his monarchy about which very little is known anyway.[19]

On the other hand the Purim festival account, though usually acknowledged to have a historical basis, has traditionally been viewed by critical scholars as reflecting not an indigenous Jewish matrix but a pagan one.[20] The basis for this opinion is complex but includes a reference in Esther itself to the effect that Haman and his Persian cohorts cast *pûr* for a solid year in preparation for slaughtering the Jews of the empire (3:7). Moreover, since the word *pûr* itself is a loanword in Hebrew (probably from Akkadian *pûru*, "lot"), it likely had foreign origin along with the practice with which it was associated. Suffice to say, the use of loanwords hardly demands dependence of customs or practices described by them. More important, the use of lot casting by the Jews against their enemies underscores brilliantly the irony so common to the book. Amazing are the purposes and powers of God who can take pagan instruments of destruction and turn them on the enemies of His people, and more remarkably establish a festival named after these nefarious plans. Thus, though there may have been some kind of Persian festival involving the casting of lots, it was creatively adapted by the Jewish community for altogether different purposes.[21]

The Date of the Book

To explain the allegedly late origin of the Festival of Purim and to make the case for a Maccabean or even later date for its composition scholars have advanced many arguments such as the nature of the Hebrew of the book, its use of Persian and other foreign terms, and its purpose.[22] In response to these points, the Hebrew of the book is unlike that of late Palestinian or Mishnaic literature, and in fact it is closest to Ezekiel, Ezra–Nehemiah, and other compositions of the sixth and fifth centuries.[23] As for Persian words one should hardly be surprised by their use in view of the setting in the Persian empire. In fact the absence of any Greek words is even more telling for the date ascribed to Esther by many critics. It is not the presence of

---

[17] Bush, *Ruth, Esther*, 294.

[18] Moore, *Esther*, xlv–xlvi.

[19] J. S. Wright, "The Historicity of the Book of Esther," in *New Perspectives on the Old Testament*, ed. J. B. Payne (Waco, TX: Word, 1970), 42–43; W. H. Shea, "Esther and History," *Concordia Journal* 13 (1987): 234–48. It is impossible here to review all the arguments for and against Esther's historicity. In addition to Wright and Shea, see Fox, *Character and Ideology in the Book of Esther*, 134–39.

[20] O. Eissfeldt, *The Old Testament: An Introduction* (New York: Harper and Row, 1965), 508–9.

[21] B. S. Childs, *Introduction to the Old Testament As Scripture* (Philadelphia: Fortress, 1979), 603–5. For the idea (first proposed by G. Gerleman) that Purim is a reprise of Passover see M. G. Wechsler, "Shadow and Fulfillment in the Book of Esther," *BibSac* 154 (1997): 275–84; and idem, "The Purim-Passover Connection: A Reflection of Jewish Exegetical Tradition in the Peshitta Book of Esther," *JBL* 117 (1998): 321–27.

[22] R. H. Pfeiffer, *Introduction to the Old Testament*, (London: Adam and Charles Black, 1952), 740–42.

[23] Moore, *Esther*, lvii–lviii; cf. R. L. Bergey, "Post-Exilic Hebrew Linguistic Developments in Esther: A Diachronic Approach," *JETS* 31 (1988): 161–68.

Persian but the omission of Greek that is most fatal to the view of a late provenience.[24] Also, the case for a late date for Purim is overstated, though admittedly the festival does not seem to have enjoyed widespread favor as a major celebration until Hasmonean times.[25] In short, no good reason exists to date the book much later than 470 BC or so, the latest date suggested in the text itself (3:7).

Texts and Versions of the Book

The MT of Esther seems to be in excellent shape. According to some scholars it is perhaps virtually identical to the autograph.[26] On the other hand the matter is complicated by the evidence of the LXX and the so-called "A-text," a separate Greek translation.[27] The LXX seems to be based on a *Vorlage* related to MT, but the A-text clearly has a different model, one shorter than MT and the LXX exemplar. Both Greek translations also have minor additions to MT and interpretive comments from time to time. These differences from the MT are significant, however, only if one rejects the inherent superiority of the Masoretic tradition as a matter of principle.[28]

THE THEOLOGY OF ESTHER[29]

To speak of the "theology" of a book that lacks explicit reference to God may seem anomalous. However, no book of the Bible demonstrates more clearly the purposes and providence of the Lord than this. The major theme of the book—one culminating in the establishment of the Purim festival—is the "great reversal," that act of God that allowed the Jews to become not the victims, but the victors, not the despised but the triumphantly delivered.[30] This is in line with the irony already noted as a major literary component of the book.

Another way of describing the theology of the book is under the rubric of divine sovereignty. Under Xerxes, the Persian Empire had become the most powerful political entity of all history to that time. Encapsulated within that mighty kingdom were the impotent remnants of the Jewish Diaspora, descendants of the nation whose forebears had also known isolation and then persecution in Egypt a millennium earlier. Just as Moses had been raised up then to become the deliverer of Israel, so now God would effect another deliverance, this time through a Jewish maiden who against all odds would sit on a Persian throne as the agent of Almighty God. There would be no exodus this time, but the deliverance of the chosen people would be just as miraculous and magnificent. It would testify, as did the exodus, to Yahweh as King of kings and Lord of lords.

The specific workings of God—though veiled in the language of "happenstance" and "coincidence"—may be seen in such statements as "the young woman [Esther] pleased him [Xerxes]" (2:9), "she won more favor and approval from him" (2:17), and, most famous of all,

---

[24] E. M. Yamauchi, *Persia and the Bible* (Grand Rapids: Baker, 1990), 226–28.

[25] Wright, "The Historicity of the Book of Esther," 39.

[26] Moore, *Esther*, lxiii.

[27] K. H. Jobes, *The Alpha-Text of Esther: Its Character and Relationship to the Masoretic Text*, SBLDS (Atlanta: Scholars, 1996).

[28] Ibid., 219–21.

[29] E. H. Merrill, "A Theology of Ezra–Nehemiah and Esther," in *A Biblical Theology of the Old Testament*, ed. R. B. Zuck (Chicago: Moody, 1991), 188–205; idem, *Everlasting Dominion: A Theology of the Old Testament* (Nashville: B&H, 2008), 487–88.

[30] For this and other related themes see S. B. Berg, *The Book of Esther: Motifs, Themes and Structure*, SBLDS (Missoula, MT: Scholars, 1979).

Mordecai's challenge to Esther, "Who knows, perhaps you have come to the kingdom for such a time as this" (4:14). Subsequent events such as Mordecai's promotion by the king (6:10–12), the king's willingness to listen to Esther's pleas on behalf of her people (8:6–8), and the otherwise impossible victory of the Jews over their enemies (9:5–16) speak with eloquence of the incomparability of Israel's God. Though His name is not mentioned in the book, His signature is written all over this work of redemptive grace.

CONCLUSION

Despite early challenges to its canonicity and ongoing debate as to its literary and theological merit, the book of Esther continues to bless the church with its message of hope and victory. It speaks powerfully of the providential ways of God, whose actions may not always be publicly displayed or even recognized but which nevertheless are the only explanation for the triumph of His people in impossible adversity. The book also makes clear that it is God who promotes and deposes, accomplishing His objectives sometimes in the most surprising ways and through the most unlikely people.

STUDY QUESTIONS

1. What was the major stumbling block to the canonicity of Esther?
2. During whose reign did the narrative of Esther take place?
3. What is the major theological theme of the book of Esther?
4. What Jewish festival finds its source in the book of Esther?
5. What is the geographical setting of the book of Esther?
6. With what pagan deity is the name Esther associated?
7. Why does the book have no reference to God by name?
8. What role does Vashti play in the book?
9. What Is Esther's Hebrew name?
10. The book of Esther appears in what part of the Hebrew canon?

FOR FURTHER STUDY

Ackroyd, P. R. *Israel under Babylon and Persia.* Oxford: Oxford University Press, 1986.

Breneman, M. *Ezra, Nehemiah, Esther.* NAC. Nashville: B&H, 1993.

Chisholm, R. B., Jr. *Interpreting the Historical Books.* Grand Rapids: Kregel, 2006.

De Gobineau, J. A. *The World of the Persians.* Geneva: Minerva, 1971.

Hamilton, V. P. *Handbook on the Historical Books.* Grand Rapids: Baker, 2001.

Howard, D.M., Jr. *An Introduction to the Old Testament Historical Books.* Chicago: Moody, 1993.

Levenson, J. D. *Esther.* OTL. Louisville: Westminster John Knox, 1997.

Longman, T., III, and R. B. Dillard. *An Introduction to the Old Testament.* Grand Rapids: Zondervan, 2006.

Olmstead, A. T. *History of the Persian Empire.* Chicago: University of Chicago, 1948.

Tomasino, A. "Esther." In *Zondervan Illustrated Bible Backgrounds Commentary.* Edited by John H. Walton, 3:468–502. Grand Rapids: Zondervan, 2009.

Yamauchi, E. M. *Persia and the Bible.* Grand Rapids: Baker, 1990.

Part 6

THE PROPHETIC BOOKS

Mark F. Rooker

T HE PROPHETIC BOOKS comprise the largest section of the Bible.[1] In Jewish tradition the Prophetic division includes the Former Prophets (Joshua–Kings) and the Latter Prophets (Isaiah, Jeremiah, Ezekiel, and the Twelve). The Former Prophets have much to say about individual prophets but seldom convey messages from them; the Latter Prophets contain much of the prophetic messages but say virtually nothing about them as persons.

WHAT IS PROPHECY?

For many Christians the notion of prophecy conjures up the idea of gazing into a crystal ball to get a glimpse of the future. While it is true that prophets did predict future events, these announcements stemmed from the prophets addressing contemporary problems. The prophets were forthtellers as much as—if not more than—they were foretellers. Because of the various forms a prophetic pronouncement may take, prophecy should be defined as "an inspired proclamation of God's message."[2]

THE ROLE OF THE PROPHET

Four terms are used in the Old Testament to designate a man or a woman who performed prophetic activity. These terms are: *nābî*, "prophet," *ʾîš ʾelohîm* ("man of God"), and *rōeh* and *ḥozeh* which are both translated "seer." Some have argued that each of these terms reveals a distinctive role.[3] However, the terms often appear interchangeable (see 1 Kgs 16:7,12 with 1 Chr 29:29;

---

[1] The OT was commonly divided into three sections by the Jews: the Law, the Prophets, and the Writings (see Luke 24:44). English Bibles following the Septuagint divide the Prophets into the Historical Books and the Prophetic Books, each of approximate equal length. The Historical and Prophetical Book sections are each of more length than any other segment of the Bible.

[2] Similarly, see H. Ringgren, "Prophecy in the Ancient Near East," in *Israel's Prophetic Tradition*, ed. R. Coggins, A. Phillips, and M. Knibb (Cambridge: Cambridge University, 1982), 1.

[3] See D. L. Petersen, *The Roles of Israel's Prophets*, JSOTSup (Sheffield: JSOT Press, 1981).

2 Chr 19:2; Isa 29:10; 30:10). First Samuel 1:9 indicates that the term *nābî'* became the predominant designation at least by Samuel's time (eleventh century).[4]

Nābî' occurs over 300 times in the OT and is cognate to the Akkadian verb *nābu*, "to call." Based on this parallel scholars have concluded that the Hebrew prophet was one who had been "called by God." The prophet was one who was commissioned to speak on God's behalf, not unlike a modern-day ambassador representing his homeland.[5]

The use of the term *nābî'* took on its technical meaning with the Mosaic legal prescription (Deut 18:15–18). Although Moses was Israel's unique prophet (Exod 33:11; Num 12:6–8; Deut 34:10–12), he became the prototype for later prophets who would address the nation with the word of God. The biblical prophets, like Moses, did not volunteer to serve God, but they were called from various stations in life to proclaim God's word.[6] Like Moses, they often performed miracles (Exod 4:1–5; 1 Kgs 17:21–24; 2 Kgs 2:14–15; Isa 38:7–8). Yet their main task, as with Moses, was to announce God's message. As Deut 18:18b states, "I will put My words in his [the prophet's] mouth." Here, in the official legislation of prophecy, is a special statement about the nature of the prophetic word. As Lindbom states:

> The prophet is not in himself a politician, a social reformer, a thinker, or a philosopher; nor is he in the first place a poet, even though he often puts his sayings in a poetical form. The special gift of a prophet is his ability to experience the divine in an original way and to receive revelations from the divine world. The prophet belongs entirely to his God; his paramount task is to listen to and obey his God. In every respect he has given himself up to his God and stands unreservedly at His disposal.[7]

The prophets received the word of God through divine revelation. Visions and auditions might come to them suddenly and without premeditation (Num 12:6–18).[8] This communication of God's truth to the prophets explains the frequent occurrence of phrases such as "Thus says the LORD," "The word of the LORD came to" (1 Sam 15:10; 2 Sam 24:11; 1 Kgs 19:9; Jonah 1:1; Hag 1:1; 2:1,20; Zech 7:1,8; 8:1), "The spirit of God came on" or a slight variation thereof (Num 11:24–30; Judg 6:34; 1 Sam 10:10; Isa 61:1; Ezek 11:5), and "The hand of God was on" or a slight variation thereof (Jer 15:17; Ezek 33:22; 37:1) at the beginning of a prophetic announcement. The phrase "The word of the LORD" occurs in 221 of its 241 OT occurrences in the prophetic writings.

---

[4] The term *nābî'* ("prophet"), first occurs in Gen 20:7 in connection with Abimelech's recognition that Abraham was capable of interceding with God on his behalf. Although this intercessory role of a prophet is not absent from the rest of the OT (Exod 32:10–33; 33:12–23; 1 Sam 12:19; 1 Kgs 18:36–37; 2 Kgs 19:4 = 2 Chr 32:20; Jer 4:4; Hab 3:1–19), it does not seem to be a dominant function of the prophet.

[5] Exod 3:10; 4:13; Deut 34:11; Judg 6:8; Isa 6:8; Jer 1:7; Ezek 2:3.

[6] N. Habel, "The Form and Significance of the Call Narratives," *ZAW* 77 (1965): 297–323. The figure of Samuel is also very significant in the history of prophecy. He was a prophet-priest who served as a transitional figure from the time of the Judges to the beginning of the monarchy (1 Sam 3:19–21; 9–10). Many scholars view his ministry as marking the beginning of the prophetic movement (e.g., D. N. Freedman, "Between God and Man: Prophets in Ancient Israel," in *Prophecy and Prophets*, ed. Y. Gitay [Atlanta: Scholars, 1997]). See Acts 3:24.

[7] J. Lindblom, *Prophecy in Ancient Israel* (Philadelphia: Fortress, 1962), 1.

[8] What Eliphaz described in his speech in Job 4:12–17 is often cited as an illustration of the prophet's reception of divine revelation.

PROPHECY IN THE ANCIENT NEAR EAST

Archaeological discoveries in the ANE have revealed many parallels to Israel's institutions and practices. The same holds true with regard to prophecy. This fact should not be surprising since the Bible itself refers to individuals such as "sorcerers" (Exod 7:11; Dan 2:2), "prophets" (1 Kgs 18:19), "seers" (Numbers 22–24); "fortune tellers" (Isa 2:6); and "diviners" (1 Sam 6:2; Dan 2:2), who were not part of Israel. Individuals who carried out functions similar to those of the Israelite prophet have been identified from extrabiblical evidence in Phoenicia, Syria, Anatolia, Egypt, and Mesopotamia.[9]

Of particular interest are the Mari prophecies of western Mesopotamia from the eighteenth century BC. Among the Mari archives are many references to prophetic-like activity among a range of individuals with different titles (including *nābu* = Hb. *nābî ʾ*). One salient feature of these prophetic utterances is the introductory statement, "Thus says [the god X]" at the beginning of some of the prophetic utterances.[10] These ANE parallels may help elucidate some of the Israelite practices, but it would be a grave error to conclude that Israel learned or borrowed the practice of prophecy from her pagan neighbors.[11]

More is actually to be learned about the distinctiveness of biblical prophecy when compared to the ancient Near Eastern parallels. Most Israelite prophetic announcements address the entire nation (not just the king). The Israelite prophet confronts the people with a socioethical directive and a national purpose, threatening utter extinction as the consequence of disloyalty. This feature, unique to Israelite prophecy, is based on Israel's covenant relationship with God wherein God chose one nation and revealed Himself in His ongoing relationship with that nation. Israel's unique covenant relationship with God stands behind the prophets' words. Thus only in Israel do prophets appeal to God's holiness as the standard for measuring society. Pagan gods were often depicted as incorrigible and immoral as the people. In a very real sense, what is distinctive about Israelite prophecy is the incomparability of Israel's God. This God, unlike pagan gods, has a plan for the entire world and He controls history, guaranteeing the fulfillment of the prophetic word.[12]

THE FORM OF PROPHECY

In the evolutionary model popularized by Julius Wellhausen, the prophets were viewed as the great innovators or great theological thinkers in Israelite religion.[13] As such they were believed to be responsible for what came to be known as "ethical monotheism." The writing of

---

[9] See esp. K. A. Kitchen, *On the Reliability of the Old Testament* (Grand Rapids: Eerdmans, 2003), 383–89. The word is still out on the contribution of the Ebla findings on prophecy (H. B. Huffman, "Prophecy," *ABD*, ed. D. N. Freedman [New York: Doubleday, 1992], 5:477).

[10] The messenger formula was not predominant among the prophetic oracles at Mari, however (F. Ellermeier, *Prophetie in Mari und Israel*, Theologishe und Rientalistische Arbeiten 1 [Herzberg: Erwin Jungfer, 1968]).

[11] R. R. Wilson, *Prophecy and Society in Ancient Israel* (Philadelphia: Fortress, 1980), 90; H. Barstad, "No Prophets? Recent Developments in Biblical Prophetic Research and Ancient Near Eastern Prophecy," *JSOT* 57 (1993): 51; and E. Noort, *Untersuchungen zum Gottesbescheid in Mari: Die 'Mari-prophetie' in der alttestamentlichen Forschung*, AOAT 202 (Neukirchen-Vluyn: Neukirchener Verlag, 1977).

[12] The few possible parallels to predictive prophecy which exist in the ANE texts are to be understood as *vaticinium ex eventu*, "prophecy after the event." Also the Mari prophecies address one specific period of time and are recorded in the context of an epistolary genre. There is nothing here that resembles the centuries-long tradition of prophetic utterance and writing like that in the OT.

[13] J. Wellhausen, *Prolegomena to the History of Ancient Israel* (New York: World Publishing, 1957), 398.

the Law, which came much later, grew out of the creative views first proffered by the Israelite writing prophets.[14]

This focus on the eminent role of the Hebrew prophet led to a thoroughgoing analysis of the prophetic utterance from the earliest units of speech to its final written form. Hermann Gunkel investigated the individual life situations (*Sitz im Leben*) in which the prophets offered their oracles, as well as situations from which the forms of their oracles may have been borrowed. Later scholars argued that the prophetic utterance may have actually arisen out of a cultic context (Sigmund Mowinckel) or possibly the royal court.[15] The close association of priest and prophet is supported by the fact that many of Israel's prophets like Samuel (1 Sam 2:18–20; 3:1,19–21), Elijah (1 Kgs 18:23,30–39), Jeremiah (Jer 28:1,5), and Ezekiel (Ezek 1:3) carried out priestly functions.[16] Moreover, many of the early prophets, including Isaiah and Jeremiah, gave counsel to the king. And yet, these contacts with the temple or the palace are to be expected, as the prophets were religious people. Hence these views do not have the favor they once had in scholarly research.

Gunkel and others also examined the various literary types found in prophecy. Proposed literary classifications include such categories as: visions, biographical and autobiographical narratives, reports, prayers, dirges, lawsuits,[17] woes, promises, symbolic action reports,[18] oracles to foreign nations, and of course prophetic predictions. The oracle introduced by the messenger formula is the most frequently occurring form of the prophetic message.[19] The use of forms that may have originated in different but familiar contexts and settings may have given an initial shock to the audience but helped the prophet gain their attention.

It is now believed that the source critics went too far in giving such an innovative role to the Israelite prophet. Scholars no longer believe that the prophets were the great innovators, but were in debt to other ancient Israelite traditions. In addition, scholars increasingly are examining the prophetic literature in its final form.[20]

THE WRITING OF PROPHECY

Until late in the nineteenth century both Jews and Christians maintained that the prophets were responsible for the books that bear their names.[21] This assumption was challenged by

---

[14] Prominent nineteenth-century scholars such as H. Gunkel (1862–1932), B. Duhm (1847–1928), and G. Hölscher (1877–1955) argued that the innovative ideas presented by the prophets were not the result of theological reflection but rather of ecstatic experiences that sometimes accompanied prophetic activity. This view has few adherents among modern scholars.

[15] Prophets and priests are frequently mentioned together in the OT (Jer 23:11; 26:7,16; 29:26; Lam 2:20; Zech 7:3).

[16] The same could be said of Moses (Exod 24:4–8). See also 1 Chr 25:1–8; 2 Chr 35:15.

[17] Isa 1:2–4,18–20; 3:13–15; 41:1–5,21–29; 43:8–13,22–28; 44:6–8; 48:1–11; 50:1–2a; Jer 2:4–9; Hos 4:1–4; Mic 1:2–7; 6:1–8.

[18] Messages conveyed through symbolic actions include Isaiah walking naked (Isaiah 20); Jeremiah smashing a potter's vessel (Jeremiah 19); Ezekiel breaking through a wall (Ezekiel 12); the names of Isaiah's and Hosea's children (Isaiah 7–8; Hos 1:2–2:1); Jeremiah buying a field (Jeremiah 32); Hosea's marriage (1–3). See also 1 Sam 15:27–28; 1 Kgs 11:29–33.

[19] The expression "thus says the LORD" occurs over 350 times in the prophetic books. For use of the messenger formula in a nontheological text see Gen 32:3–5. See C. Westermann, *Basic Forms of Prophetic Speech* (Louisville: WJK, 1991).

[20] G. Tucker, "Prophecy and Prophetic Literature," in *The Hebrew Bible and Its Modern Interpreters*, ed. D. A. Knight and G. Tucker (Chico: Scholars, 1985), 356, and especially J. F. Sawyer, "A Change of Emphasis in the Study of the Prophets," in *Israel's Prophetic Tradition*, 233–49.

[21] This of course applies to the Latter Prophets who are the writing prophets. The Former Prophets are sometimes viewed as nonwriting prophets, although there is evidence that Nathan, Gad, Samuel, Shemaiah, and Iddo engaged in writing activity (1 Chr 29:29; 2 Chr 9:29; 12:15). These writings were not preserved and are not part of canonical Scripture.

source critical scholars who began to apply their methodologies to prophetic literature to distinguish between "genuine" and "non-genuine" elements in the prophetic composition.

Critical scholars have normally argued that the final forms of prophetic books resulted from a process characterized by three distinct stages: (1) short prophetic sayings were transmitted orally by the prophet's disciples, (2) collections of sayings were arranged around subject matter, and (3) smaller sections were organized into full-length books by a redactor who had the freedom to add additional material.

This approach has been strongly criticized and is now viewed with skepticism. First, there is no evidence that, apart from Isaiah, prophets had a following of disciples who preserved their oracles.[22] Second, the view that prophetic oracles were orally transmitted for generations has been hotly disputed. There is explicit evidence in the prophetic writings themselves that prophetic oracles were being committed to writing (2 Chr 21:12–15; Isa 8:16–18; 30:8; Jer 29:1; 36:2–32).[23] Gerhard von Rad and Geo Widengren have argued that the Israelite prophet lived in an environment where writing had been the natural means of communication for a thousand years.[24] In the ANE where there existed a high degree of literacy, anything of importance was committed to writing.[25] Oral transmission is thus related to dissemination, not preservation. For these reasons it would be unlikely that a generation would transpire between the life of the prophet and the final edition of his book.

THE MESSAGE OF PROPHECY

While it is admittedly a great challenge to pinpoint the theme of the entire prophetic corpus (as all the prophets were unique and lived in different times under different circumstances), there do seem to be some specific themes and issues frequently addressed by the prophets.

The overall concern of the prophets was Israel's faithfulness to her covenant responsibilities as prescribed in the Mosaic Law. The prophets' preoccupation with this concern has rightly led to their being designated as covenant-enforcement mediators.[26] The prophets repeatedly confronted the Israelites with the law, particularly its blessings and curses (Leviticus 26; Deuteronomy 26–28).[27] The preexilic prophets particularly were called by God to announce judgment for covenant violations.[28] But once the Babylonian invasion had begun and all false hopes of avoiding judgment had come to an end, the prophetic message turned to one of hope and salvation. Whereas the judgment was based on Israel's disobedience, the oracles of hope were the result of God's grace and faithfulness to His promise in the Abrahamic covenant.[29]

---

[22] See J. F. Sawyer, *Prophecy and the Prophets of the Old Testament* (Oxford: Oxford University Press, 1987), 23. The same can be said of the view that inauthentic material was later added to the collections. These suggestions are completely subjective.

[23] See also Ezek 2:10; 37:16–18; Hab 2:2.

[24] G. von Rad, *Old Testament Theology*, trans. D. Stalker (New York: Harper & Row, 1962), 2:40 n.16; and G. Widengren, *Literary and Psychological Aspects of the Hebrew Prophets* (Uppsala: Lundequist, 1948), 122. See also Barstad, "No Prophets?" 57–59.

[25] See R. K. Harrison, *Introduction to the Old Testament* (Grand Rapids: Eerdmans, 1969), 762; K. Kitchen, *The Ancient Orient and the Old Testament* (Chicago: InterVarsity, 1966), 136; and B. Waltke, "Oral Tradition," in *A Tribute to Gleason Archer*, ed. W. Kaiser Jr. and R. Youngblood (Chicago: Moody, 1986), 17–34.

[26] G. Fee and D. Stuart, *How to Read the Bible for All Its Worth*, 2nd ed. (Grand Rapids: Zondervan, 1993), 174. Elijah should be viewed as the first covenant enforcer accusing the nation of covenant violations (1 Kgs 18:21).

[27] For a listing of Pentateuchal curses which occur in Prophetic literature see Douglas Stuart, *Hosea-Jonah*, WBC (Waco, TX: Word, 1987), xxxiii–xlii.

[28] The exile was in fact a vindication of the preaching of the preexilic prophets who announced the coming doom.

[29] The Zion traditions, which may be viewed as further explicating how the Abrahamic covenant was to be fulfilled, are also an important theme in the prophets (Sawyer, *Prophecy and the Prophets*, 51).

The prophets also frequently motivated the people to action by proclaiming that the Day of the Lord was near (Isa 13:6; Ezek 30:3; Joel 1:15; 2:1; 3:14 [HB, 4:14]; Obad 15; Zeph 1:7,14).[30] In the Day of the Lord God would judge unrighteousness and bring blessing and security for the faithful (Amos 9:13–15). This anticipation of deliverance was the primary component for the development of eschatology that focuses on the future saving action of God.[31] Thus prophecy ultimately points to Jesus Christ, whose sacrifice was the basis for man's eternal redemption.

PROPHECY AND THE NEW TESTAMENT

After the OT period came to a close, Judaism maintained that prophecy had come to an end (1 Macc 4:44–46; 9:27; 14:41; *2 Apoc. Bar.* 85:1,3; *Cant Rab.* 8:9–10; *Num Rab.* 15:10; *b. Yoma* 9b; *b. Sotah* 48b; *b. Sanh.* 11a; *t. Sotah* 13:2). However, it was also held that the Messiah would usher in a new time of prophetic activity (*b. Sanh.* 93a–b).[32] According to the NT Jesus was regarded as a prophet by the people (Matt 16:14; 21:11; Mark 6:15; 8:28; 14:65; Luke 7:16; 9:8,19; John 4:19; 9:17). In one of the few sayings of Jesus preserved in all four Gospels Jesus spoke of Himself as a prophet (Matt 13:57; Mark 6:4; Luke 4:24; 13:33; John 4:44). From the NT witness there is no doubt that Jesus Christ is the Great Prophet promised by Moses (Luke 24:19; Acts 3:22–23; 7:37; cf. Deut 18:15–18).

STUDY QUESTIONS

1. What are the Former Prophets?
2. What are the Latter Prophets?
3. How many times does the term *nabî* ("prophet") occur in the New Testament?
4. What is the meaning of the related Akkadian word for *nabî* ("prophet")?
5. What legal passage prescribes the role of the Israelite prophet?
6. Where does the word *nabî* ("prophet") first appear in the Bible?
7. What is the primary role of a prophet?
8. How did the prophets receive their messages?
9. What is the relationship between written prophecy and oral transmission?
10. What is the overall concern of the prophetic message?
11. When did the Jews believe that prophecy had come to an end?
12. What is the connection between the office of prophecy and Jesus Christ?

---

[30] This announcement may have served a previous role in summoning men to battle. For war terminology used in the Prophets see Barstad, "No Prophets?" 54 n.43.

[31] This outlook is not unknown in the Pentateuch, however (Deuteronomy 18).

[32] John the Baptist and Paul performed prophetic ministries (Luke 3:10–14; 1 Cor 13:2; 14:6,37). Other prophets mentioned in the NT include Anna (Luke 2:36) and Agabus (Acts 21:10). See also 1 Cor 12:28; Eph 4:11.

CHAPTER 23

THE BOOK OF ISAIAH

MARK F. ROOKER

M ANY BELIEVERS REGARD Isaiah as the greatest of all the OT prophets. Because of the profound christological implications of his message such church fathers as Eusebius, Theodoret, Jerome, and Augustine even considered Isaiah an apostle and an evangelist.

Isaiah prophesied and ministered during the reigns of the Judean kings Uzziah, Jotham, Ahaz, and Hezekiah. He had a career of about 40 years (739–700 BC). Critical national events such as the fall of the northern kingdom of Israel (722), the Syro-Ephraimite war (734), and the siege of Jerusalem by Sennacherib (701) occurred during his lifetime. Like no other prophet of the OT his oracles were immersed in the turbulent events of his own time.[1]

According to Jewish tradition Isaiah was a cousin of Uzziah and the nephew of Amaziah (*b. Meg.* 10b). The pseudepigraphical work *Ascension of Isaiah*, written between the second century BC and the fourth century AD, asserts that Isaiah died a martyr during the reign of Manasseh, suffering the fate of being sawn in two (Heb 11:37).

THE AUTHORSHIP AND DATE OF THE BOOK

Prior to the Enlightenment it was generally held that the prophet Isaiah wrote the entire book that bears his name. With the rise of the critical approach to the study of the OT, particularly in the eighteenth century, this consensus began to change. The debate over the authorship of Isaiah was carried out with an intensity second only to the debate over the authorship of the Pentateuch. Late in the eighteenth century through the work of Julius Döderlein (1789), Johann Eichhorn (1783), and later Wilhelm Gesenius (1819) Isaiah 1–39 and 40–66 were viewed as two separate works written by two authors separated in time by about 150 years. The two authors came to be identified as Isaiah (chaps. 1–39) and Deutero-Isaiah (chaps. 40–66). Later, Bernhard Duhm (1892) presented the theory that chaps. 40–66 comprised two different works, Isaiah 40–55 and Isaiah 56–66. Isaiah 40–55 was composed during the Babylonian exile, while Trito-Isaiah, Isaiah 56–66, reflects a different historical backdrop and was

---

[1] M. H. Segal, *Introduction to the Old Testament* (Jerusalem: Kiryat Sepher, 1977), 1:272 (Hb.).

composed in Palestine in the postexilic period. Predictably, scholars later ascribed portions of Isaiah 1–39 and 40–66 to different periods. For example in Isaiah 1–39, chaps. 11; 12; 13:1–14:23; 21:1–10; 24–27; and 32–35 were often attributed to a writer other than Isaiah. Eichhorn argued for even further fragmentation. Since the Talmud placed Isaiah after Jeremiah and Ezekiel in the canonical order of the prophets (*Baba Bathra* 14b), Isaiah, like the collection of the Minor Prophets which followed the Major Prophets, was considered an anthology of prophetic oracles written by different prophets over a period of time. By the end of the nineteenth century the critical division of Isaiah into various parts and sources was taken for granted in the academic world.[2] In the twentieth century the study of Isaiah continued to be analyzed from both the form- and tradition-critical method as well as through redactional analysis, normally assuming and building on the critical consensus.[3]

Three arguments or criteria have been garnered as evidence for dividing Isaiah into three parts: internal evidence, style, and theological concepts. To assume that Isaiah, the eighth-century prophet, wrote to those who experienced the exile as well as those Israelites who later lived in postexilic times would, it is argued, be unprecedented and uncharacteristic of OT prophecy.[4]

Also internal evidence, it is argued, presents a portrait of Jerusalem in Isaiah 40–66 that is accurate only for the exilic and postexilic period. Jerusalem is depicted as ravaged and deserted (44:26; 58:12; 61:4; 63:18; 64:10) and in Isaiah 40–55 the addressees are in exile in Babylon (42:22; 50:10–11; 51:6,12–14). In chaps. 56–66 the nation is clearly living in Palestine again and Jerusalem has been rebuilt. There is no longing for deliverance from the exile, but inner community conflicts have arisen (56:9–12; 57:3–10; 65:1–7; 66:3–6). These points suggest that the author(s) wrote Isaiah 40–66 after the final deportation in 586 BC.

Those who divide Isaiah into 1–39 and 40–66 as the works of two authors maintain that the contrast in style between the two sections are so significant that they had to be composed by two separate writers. Proponents of this view often resort to lists of rare or unique words which in their minds demonstrate diversity of authorship. They also often claim that the writing of chaps. 1–39 is terse and compact while the rhetoric is solemn and restrained. In chaps. 40–66, on the other hand, subjects are developed at length and the style is flowing and the rhetoric is characterized by warmth and passion.[5]

Those who employ the theological argument for distinguishing between Isaiah 1–39 and 40–66 normally point out that the comments about God in chaps. 40–66 are longer and fuller than in chaps. 1–39. Truths that are merely affirmed in chaps. 1–39 are developed and made the subject of deeper reflection in chaps. 40–66. The author of Isaiah 40–66, it is purported, emphasized different aspects of divine truth than those found in Isaiah 1–39. It is argued that while Isaiah 1–39 focuses on the majesty of God, Isaiah 40–66 emphasizes God's infinitude. Conversely chaps. 1–39 reflect a remnant theology (6:13; 37:31–32), a concept that is completely foreign in chaps. 40–66. In short, the concept of God in Isaiah 1–39 does not reach the high plateau of Isaiah 40–66 and especially of Isaiah 40–55.

---

[2] B. Childs, *Introduction to the Old Testament As Scripture* (Philadelphia: Fortress, 1979), 317.

[3] C. Seitz, "Isaiah, Book of," in *ABD,* ed. D. N. Freedman (New York: Doubleday, 1992), 3:475–77.

[4] Childs, *Introduction to the Old Testament As Scripture,* 317.

[5] S. R. Driver, *An Introduction to the Literature of the Old Testament* (Edinburgh: T&T Clark, 1913), 238–42.

EVALUATION OF THE CRITICAL METHOD

Some argue that Isaiah could not have written chaps. 40–66 in the eighth century because these chapters seem to address a time after the Babylonian exile. But this overlooks the divine nature of biblical prophecy. This supposition denies the supernatural nature of prophecy in which God often revealed to the biblical writers what would take place in history. There are several examples of OT prophets foretelling events that did not take place until centuries later. The name of Josiah was foretold more than three centuries before his birth (1 Kgs 13:1–2). In the eighth century Micah predicted that Bethlehem would be the birthplace of the Messiah, the fulfillment of which took place in the first century AD (Mic 5:2 = Matt 2:6). Similarly Isaiah prophesied the coming of Cyrus by name (Isa 44:28; 45:1) 150 years before the event.[6] With Jerusalem almost destroyed during Sennacherib's invasion (701 BC) and with the persecution of believers in the terrorist reign of Manasseh (2 Kgs 21:16), the threat of exile would have been a real fear for the Judeans during Isaiah's ministry.[7] Isaiah's audience was unaware, however, that Manasseh would reign 54 years and Hezekiah and Josiah would introduce reforms that would postpone the exile for 150 years.

The argument that the writing style of Isaiah 1–39 differs enough from the style of the rest of the book to posit a different author is not convincing. This argument assumes that a writer may not change his writing style when he addresses a different subject or that a writer's style may not change over time (Isaiah prophesied over 40 years). Furthermore a writer's style is determined by an examination of his manner of writing. To derive an estimation of a writer's style from only a selected portion of material available and then to turn around and deny his authorship of the rest of material being examined is circular reasoning at its worst. Moreover, scholars are aware of the literary similarities between chaps. 1–39 and chaps. 40–66. In fact the trend in recent Isaiah scholarship is to treat the book as a whole based on the book's literary and structural unity. As Rolf Rendtorff has observed, "The established practice of separating the book into several discrete parts, each of which is viewed in isolation from the whole, is giving way to exploratory efforts to understand the overall unity and the theological dynamic of the Isaiah tradition."[8]

The argument that differing theological ideas suggest multiple authors rests on tenuous grounds. The argument is entirely subjective. The alleged heightened theological views of Isaiah 40–66 are not essentially different from the theological ideas of Micah, a contemporary of Isaiah.[9]

In addition to the weak evidence for multiple authorship based on these three arguments, several facts suggest that the book of Isaiah in its entirety is a unified composition composed by the prophet Isaiah in the eighth century.

The arguments for the dividing of Isaiah into two or three different books are fairly recent. No evidence whatsoever suggests that Isaiah 40–66 or Isaiah 40–55 and 56–66 circulated

---

[6] Josephus contended that in fact the reason the Jewish temple was allowed to be rebuilt was because Isaiah had mentioned Cyrus's name 210 years before his birth (*Ant.* 11. § 1–2).

[7] The exile had already been prophesied in Isaiah 1–39 (5:5,15; 10:20–24).

[8] R. Rendtorff, "The Book of Isaiah—A Complex Unity: Synchronic and Diachronic Reading," in *Prophecy and Prophets: The Diversity of Contemporary Issues in Scholarship*, ed. Y. Gitay (Atlanta: Scholar, 1997), 109. See also B. Childs, *Introduction to the Old Testament as Scripture* (Philadelphia: Fortress, 1980), 311–38; B. Webb, "Zion In Transformation: A Literary Approach to Isaiah," in *The Bible in Three Dimension: Essays in Celebration of Forty Years of Biblical Studies in the University of Sheffield*, ed. D. J. A. Clines, S. Fowl, and S. Porter (Sheffield: Sheffield Academic, 1990), 65–84; and R. O'Connell, *Concentricity and Continuity: The Literary Structure of Isaiah* (Sheffield: Sheffield Academic, 1994).

[9] G. L. Archer, *A Survey of Old Testament Introduction*, 3rd ed. (Chicago: Moody, 1994), 383.

independently of Isaiah 1–39. Nowhere in Jewish or Christian literature is there any hint that there was more than one author of the 66 chapters in the prophecy of Isaiah. The Isaiah manuscript of the DSS shows no division after chaps. 39 or 55 but does indicate a separation of space after chap. 33, perhaps indicating that this was the primary division of the book. The NT also understands Isaiah to be the author of the entire prophecy. Passages from Isaiah 40–66 are said to have their source in the prophet Isaiah in Matt 3:3; 8:17; 12:8–21; Luke 3:4; John 1:23; 12:38–41; Rom 9:27–33; 10:16–21. The citation in John 12:38–41 is particularly telling as statements from both Isaiah 1–39 and 40–66 are cited but attributed to the one prophet Isaiah. To this evidence could be added Josephus's comment that Cyrus read of himself in the prophecies of Isaiah (44:26–28; 45:1–6).[10] Moreover, since the author of Isaiah 40–66 was regarded as the most eloquent of all Hebrew prophets, how did he become lost in anonymity? As early as 1846 J. A. Alexander argued that it would be completely unprecedented for the author of Isaiah 40–66 to produce prophecies of this magnitude and then to disappear without a trace.[11]

The contents of Isaiah 40–66 actually support the contention that the author was in Palestine, not exiled in Babylon. There is virtually no evidence that the writer of this section had any familiarity with the situation and life in Babylon. When the prophetic texts do address the situation of the exiles (42:22; 51:14), they bear no resemblance to those texts that describe the life of the Jews exiled in Babylon (Jeremiah 29; Ezekiel).[12] To the contrary, mention is made of Jerusalem, the mountains of Palestine, and trees native to Palestine such as cedars, cypress, and oak, but not to Babylon (Isa 41:19; 44:14).[13] Other passages such as 40:9 indicate that Judean cities were still in existence, and 62:6 speaks of the walls of Jerusalem as standing, a fact incompatible with an exilic cultural setting for these oracles. And yet there are passages in Isaiah 1–39 such as 1:7–9; 5:13; 14:1–4; and 35:1–4 that seem to assume the exile will occur, just as there are in chaps. 40–55. Therefore it could be argued that the historical standpoint of Isaiah 1–39 is the same as that of Isaiah 40–66, thus removing the necessity of suggesting different authors. Another problem for those who hold the position that chaps 40–66 were written in or after the exile is the many references to idolatry among the Israelites (41:29; 44:9–20; 46:6–7; 48:5; 57:5; 66:3,17). Virtually all OT historians are in agreement that the commission of the sin of idolatry was dealt a decisive blow (with some isolated exceptions) at the commencement of the Babylonian exile. These passages in so-called Second Isaiah describing Israelite idolatry reflect the religious aberrations of the preexilic period rather than the sixth-century exile.[14]

Another evidence for the unity of Isaiah as well as the authorship of the book by Isaiah in the eighth century is the language of the book. The language of chaps. 40–66 is unlike the exilic language of Ezekiel or the postexilic language of Ezra and Nehemiah: Instead those chaps. represent preexilic Hebrew as does Isaiah 1–39.[15] Along similar lines, Robinson and Harrison have listed at least 42 verbal agreements and similarities in thought between chaps. 1–39 and chaps. 40–66.[16] Some of the verbal agreements are these:

---

[10] Josephus, *Ant.* 11. § 1–2.

[11] See R. K. Harrison, *Introduction to the Old Testament* (Grand Rapids: Eerdmans, 1969), 769.

[12] See J. A. Motyer, *The Prophecy of Isaiah* (Downers Grove, IL: InterVarsity, 1993), 28.

[13] See 43:14; 45:22; 46:11; 52:11, which reveal a Palestinian milieu rather than a Babylonian setting.

[14] References to idolatry in Isaiah 1–39 include 1:13,29; 2:8–22; 8:19.

[15] M. Rooker, "Dating Isaiah 40–66: What Does the Linguistic Evidence Say?" *WTJ* 58 (1996): 303–12.

[16] G. L. Robinson and R. K. Harrison, "Isaiah," in *ISBE*, ed. G. Bromiley (Grand Rapids: Eerdmans, 1986), 2:896.

1:20c	40:5c; 58:14c
11:9	65:25
11:12	56:8
14:27	43:13
19:25; 29:23	45:11; 60:21
34:8	61:2; 63:4
35:10	51:11

Thus in recent scholarship the focus has shifted back to the unity of Isaiah rather than to its composition by multiple authors.[17]

THE STRUCTURE OF THE BOOK

Numerous structural parallels in the book of Isaiah constitute an additional but distinctive argument for its basic unity. The closing verses (66:15–24) are reminiscent of the opening verses (1:1–26), sharing almost 50 words. At the beginning of the book heavens and earth are called on as witnesses (1:2), and at the end of the book the new heavens and new earth witness the beginning of God's reign (65:17–25; 66:22–24). In 1:2 and at the end of the book in 66:24 the people of God are described as those who have "rebelled" *(pāša')* against the Lord.

Chapters 6–12 correspond to chaps. 28–35. In both of these sections Isaiah grappled with two identical historical and spiritual crises. In both cases he confronted the monarch and predicted a glorious future. Moreover, chaps. 13–27 and 36–37 relate to these preceding sections in a similar way. Isaiah 13–27 fleshes out the reference to the Davidic ruler (9:7) into a universal, eschatological perspective. Chapters 36–37 refer to the power of the Lord over the mighty Assyrians when Judah was tempted to rely on earthly alliances (Isaiah 28–35).

THE OUTLINE OF THE BOOK

I. **Oracles of Judgment and Hope (chaps. 1–12)**
    A. Rebuke and Promise (chaps. 1–5)
    B. Destruction and Restoration (chaps. 6–12)

II. **Oracles against the Nations (chaps. 13–23)**
    A. Fall of Babylon and Judah's Restoration (chaps. 13–14)
    B. Moab (chaps. 15–16)
    C. Egypt and Ethiopia (chaps. 17–20)
    D. Fall of Babylon, Edom, and Arabia (chap. 21)
    E. Jerusalem and Shebna (chap. 22)
    F. Tyre (chap. 23)

III. **God's Triumph over the Nations (chaps. 24–27)**
    A. Worldwide Judgment (chap. 24)
    B. Thanksgiving for Deliverance (chaps. 25–26)
    C. Judgment and Restoration for God's People (chap. 27)

IV. **Trusting God or the Nations (chaps. 28–35)**
    A. Judah and the Assyrian Threat (chaps. 28–33)

---

[17] R. Schultz, "Isaiah," in *Theological Interpretation of the Old Testament*, ed. K. Vanhoozer (Grand Rapids: Baker, 2008), 197.

THE CONTENTS OF THE BOOK

I. Oracles of Judgment and Hope (chaps. 1–12)

The first five chapters of Isaiah, which serve as an introduction to the book, describe the present disastrous condition of the nation of Israel. These chapters seem to connect the final years of Uzziah's reign before his death to Isaiah's special call in 6:1. Isaiah 2–4 records condemnations of social practices in Judah that are reminiscent of those confronted by the prophet Amos, who also lived in the eighth century. As in Amos, the rich oppressed the poor (Isa 3:15), and many women were proud and materialistic (3:16–17,24–26; cf. Amos 4:1–3). The series of woes in Isa 5:8–23 is reminiscent of Amos 5:7,18; 6:1,4, and like Amos, Isaiah indicted the upper classes for social injustice. The call of Isaiah (chap. 6) may reflect his call to prophetic office, but in light of the dire circumstances described in chaps. 1–5 could also indicate a special commission to a specific task after Uzziah had died.[18]

Right after his divine commission (Isaiah 6), Isaiah was charged to confront Ahaz. Isaiah warned Ahaz against joining Aram and Israel in an anti-Assyrian coalition (Isaiah 7).[19] His message to the king was communicated through the names of three sign-children. The names of all three, unlike Hosea's sign-children, were positive for Israel. Shear-jashub (7:3) means "remnant restored," Immanuel (7:4) means "God with us," and Maher-shalal-hash-baz (8:3) is translated "Spoil speeds, Prey hastens." The explanatory statements illustrate the positive meanings of the names after each one (7:4,15–16; 8:4).[20] Immediately after the account of the sign-children are oracles describing a new ruler (9:1–7 [HB, 8:23b–9:6] and 11:1–9). In contrast to faithless Ahaz, this ruler will be just and faithful. Despite the fact that this section speaks of a near total destruction (6:13; 8:8; 10:32), it ends on the positive note that a new day will dawn (12:1–6). Chapter 12 is a psalm that thanks the Lord for deliverance and mentions two key terms in Isaiah, the name "Zion" and the phrase "the holy one of Israel" (12:6). Thus in this opening section Isaiah not only announced judgment on Israel, Jerusalem, and the Israelite leadership, but he also predicted the future salvation of Israel and Jerusalem, as well as the blessings associated with the Davidic dynasty. The oracles of salvation (2:1–5; 4:2–6; 9:1–6; 11:1–16) follow the announcements of judgment.

---

[18] Seitz, "Isaiah, Book of," 479.

[19] At this time the Neo-Assyrian Empire was taking its place as the first world empire in human history.

[20] However, see Excursus on Isa 7:14.

II. Oracles against the Nations (chaps. 13–23)

Isaiah's oracles against the foreign nations are the longest among the prophets (see Jeremiah 46–51; Ezekiel 25–32; Amos 1–2). This section addresses the major powers that surrounded Israel who very often were enemies of the nation. The prophetic oracles against the nations demonstrate the sovereignty of God over all nations—not only over neighboring states (Isa 14:28–17:14), but also against the powerful, ruling powers afar off (chaps. 18–21). This indicates that He is able to bring about the promises He made to Israel.

The importance of Babylon in this list is indicated by its occurrence/allusion at both the beginning and the end of the list (13:1–14:23; 21:1–10). The fall of mighty Babylon described in hyperbolic terms anticipates the fall of the entire world system that stands in rebellion against God.[21] This focus on Babylon also underscores the importance of Babylon in chaps. 40–66. It is doubtful that these oracles were ever read by the nations that were addressed. However, they communicated to Israel the nature of their transcendent God and His sovereignty over all nations. It is important for Israel to know that the Davidic dynasty will be successful (14:29) and the Zion-ideal achieved (14:32).[22]

III. God's Triumph over the Nations (chaps. 24–27)

God's sovereignty over the nations is continued in this section which declares that one day God's rule will extend throughout the earth. The description of the judgment in Isaiah 24–27 corresponds to the oracles in the previous section where the Lord will use Babylon as His agent to "lay waste the whole earth" (lit. trans., 13:5; 24:1).[23] In this section God displays His wrath against all human pride and national presumption (chap. 24). The coming punishment is the consequence both of Israel's disobedience (chaps. 1–12) and the violence of the nations as a whole (chaps. 13–23) which has polluted the earth (24:5). The description of this judgment is reminiscent of the flood, an association reinforced by the reference to "the everlasting covenant" (24:5; cf. Gen 9:16). The massive judgment threatens to cause great disorder and chaos as did the flood with the common promise to "put an end to all flesh" (Gen 6:12–13; cf. Isa 24:18–20). As in the days of Noah "the windows [of heaven] are opened from above, and the foundations of the earth are shaken" (Isa 24:18; cf. Gen 7:11). However, both accounts include a promise of final restoration (Isa 25:6–26:6; 27:2–6,12–13; cf. Gen 9:11–17), one in which Zion will have a prominent place (Isa 27:13). The oracles against the nations and their judgment in this section anticipates Isaiah 40–48.[24]

IV. Trusting God or the Nations (chaps. 28–35)

The first section of this division, chaps. 28–33, is structurally unified through the use of the introductory particle "woe" (28:1; 29:1; 30:1; 31:1; 33:1). In these oracles the leaders of Judah are admonished to place their trust only in the Lord.

Because of God's promises to Zion (cf. 2 Sam 7), the Israelites believed Jerusalem to be inviolable. Isaiah expanded their understanding of the Zion theology to include God's judgment against His own people if they continue in their faithlessness to Him (Isa 28:21; 29:1–8). The people were guilty of misplaced confidence, as they trusted Egypt instead of looking to

---

[21] Schultz, "Isaiah," 200.

[22] Motyer, *The Prophecy of Isaiah*, 37.

[23] Moreover, Schultz has pointed out the various links between Isaiah 24–27 with previous parts of Isaiah: 25:4 = 4:6; 26:1 = 12:2; 26:15 = 9:3; 27:2–5 = 5:1–7 ("Isaiah," 200).

[24] Seitz, "Isaiah, Book of," 486.

God (30:1–14; 31:1–5). Chapters 34–35 describe a coming world judgment over nations and nature,[25] one that will include a transformation of nature and a return of God's people to their land.

V. Historical Transition (chaps. 36–39)

Isaiah 36–37 is much like Isaiah 7–8. In both cases the prophet encountered the king with the word of God. The account of Israel's deliverance from the Assyrians mentioned here (37:36–38) is recorded also in 2 Kgs 18:13–19:37 and 2 Chr 32:1–21. This is also recorded in Sennacherib's royal annals. He boasted that he had reduced Hezekiah to a virtual prisoner "like a bird in a cage." However, Sennacherib did not refer to conquering Jerusalem as he did in regard to other Judean cities, indicating that he was prevented from doing so.[26] One prominent reason the Judeans were able to survive was because of the successful completion of an underground tunnel that was dug through solid rock about 550 meters long and 150 feet below the ground. This gave the city a continuous supply of water. The tunnel, referred to as Hezekiah's tunnel, was discovered in 1880. Scribbled on its wall an inscription, dated about 700 BC and known as the Siloam Tunnel Inscription, was written to celebrate the completion of the tunnel. Hezekiah was delivered from the Assyrian siege, but he had to pay tribute to Sennacherib (2 Kgs 18:13–16).

After Hezekiah was healed of his illness (Isaiah 38), he received a visit by Babylonian envoys to whom he displayed his wealth by giving them a tour of the royal palace. As a consequence this section closes with a portentous prediction of the Babylonian captivity.[27] The Babylonians would replace the Assyrians as Israel's main adversaries (39:7). The Babylonians, already prominent in chaps. 13–27; 34–35, were now the exclusive focus in chaps. 38–39. Chapters 38 and 39 begin a transition that leads up to and prepares for the Babylonian exile. This transition also indicates that the period of judgment is about over and a new day of transformation is about to dawn.[28]

VI. Oracles of Consolation (chaps. 40–66)

Promise of restoration (chaps. 40–48). These chapters reveal that the Lord is able to deliver the nation from the Babylonian captivity. The opening section focuses on God's new act of restoring Israel to Zion (40:1–11). Isaiah 43:9–44:5 is a reminder that Israel is to be a witness to a virtual reenactment of a new exodus from Babylon. In 44:6–23 Israel is to be a living testimony to the Lord, who is contrasted with the manufactured statues of the gods. Cyrus (44:28; 45:1) is the king God appointed to carry out His deliverance plan for Judah just as Assyria had carried out His judgment plan for Israel. In this section there are seven servant passages in which the servant refers to Israel (41:9–10; 42:18–19; 43:10; 44:1–2,21; 48:20). However, in another servant passage (42:1) the servant is an individual who will establish justice on the earth. In presenting his message to the Israelites in this section Isaiah frequently employed the elements or motifs of a court case (41:1–42:9; 43:9–44:5; 44:6–23; 45:21). Isaiah 48:20–21 in conclusion then underscores the urgent call to leave Babylon.

---

[25] Because the DSS manuscript IQIsaᵃ has three blank lines after Isaiah 33, many have suggested that a natural division of the book of Isaiah occurs after Isaiah 33. Isaiah 34 thus begins the second half of the book and is marked by the thematic transition as the messages of the book turn from messages of judgment to messages of salvation.

[26] See *ANET*, 288. The Greek historian Herodotus attributed the defeat of the Assyrian forces to their weapons being devoured by a horde of mice.

[27] Earlier texts have also indicated a future exile of the nation (3:24–26; 5:5–6; 6:11–13; 24:11–12; 27:13; 32:12–14).

[28] Seitz, "Isaiah, Book of," 487.

Redemption through the Servant (chaps. 49–55). The coming deliverance through God's Servant is announced. He will come and restore those in bondage, providing salvation for the Gentiles (49:1–13). As Shultz has observed; "Three passages describing the Servant's election, opposition, and vicarious suffering and exaltation (49:1–13; 50:4–11; 52:13–53:12) alternate with three extended passages describing Zion's current condition, coming comfort, and glorious future (49:14–50:3; 51:1–52:1; ch. 54)."[29] Since the Servant will deliver Israel (49:5–6), he must be viewed as an individual distinct from Israel.

Isaiah 50:1–51:8 assures the nation that God will be among His people in the restored Zion. The righteous are instructed to follow in the steps of their ancestor Abraham (51:1–3). Isaiah 51:9–52:12 is a petition to the Lord to defeat Israel's enemies and bring the people back to Zion.[30] Although the Servant has suffered, this suffering is vicarious for the nation (52:13–53:12). The Servant passages in this section (49:1–6; 50:4–9; and 52:13–53:12) should all be understood as referring to the ideal of Israel, Jesus Christ, the Davidic King (chap. 11). The section comes to a close, as did the previous one, with the refrain "there is no peace for the wicked" (57:21; see 48:22).

The Coming Anointed Conqueror (chaps. 56–66). Some of the observable topics in this section include the future glory[31] of Jerusalem, a commitment to holy living, and the vengeance of God on His enemies. The nation is denounced for idolatry (57:3–13; 65:3–6) and hypocrisy (58:1–7). In chaps. 56–57 the denunciation (56:9–57:13) is followed by the announcement of the coming of the Lord (57:14–21). Chapter 58 addresses the issue of fasting and is followed by a lament (chap. 59) and a public confession of sin (59:12–13).

Chapters 60–62 contain words of salvation. People from other nations will help rebuild Zion and the mourners will be comforted as God establishes an eternal covenant with them (60:1–3,8–9). They will then be called God's holy people as they realize the covenant ideal (62:12).[32] John Oswalt shows that the entire section is arranged in a chiastic format with the center at Isaiah 60–62 with its teaching on the messianic kingdom.[33] Chapters 65–66 speak of salvation as well as a new creation. Rendtorff has noted that the beginning (56:2–8) and ending (66:18–24) of this section refer to common themes such as the Sabbath (56:2,4,6; 66:23), the house of God and the holy mountain (56:5,7; 66:20), as well as foreigners (56:6–8; 66:18–21).[34] The latter will be incorporated into God's kingdom and present offerings to the Lord (60:3–16; 62:2; 66:18–20).

THE THEOLOGY OF THE BOOK

Isaiah based his accusations and warnings of coming judgment against the nation Israel on the Mosaic law (Exod 24:1–8; 34:10–28; Leviticus 26; Deut 29:1–32:47). This is most apparent in the first chapter of Isaiah, which discloses a covenant lawsuit in which the Lord accused the nation of rebellion.[35]

---

[29] Schultz, "Isaiah," 203.

[30] See R. J. Clifford, "Isaiah, Book of (Second Isaiah)," in *ABD*, ed. D. N. Freedman (New York: Doubleday, 1992), 3:491–97.

[31] The Hebrew word for "glory" *(kābôd)* occurs numerous times in this section (Isa 58:8; 59:19; 60:1–2,13; 61:6; 62:2; 66:11–12,18–19).

[32] Schultz, "Isaiah," 204.

[33] J. N. Oswalt, "Isaiah, Theology of," in *NIDOTTE,* W. VanGemeren (Grand Rapids: Zondervan, 1997), 4:726.

[34] R. Rendtorff, *The Old Testament: An Introduction,* trans. J. Bowden (Philadelphia: Fortress, 1985), 197.

[35] See R. B. Chisholm Jr., "A Theology of Isaiah," in *A Biblical Theology of the Old Testament,* ed. R. B. Zuck (Chicago: Moody, 1991), 307.

Zion and the establishment of the Davidic house are central topics for Isaiah and the emphasis on these themes distinguishes the prophet from all others. Also unlike any other biblical book Isaiah stresses the incomparability of God. The repeated phrase "the Holy One of Israel," which is characteristic of Isaiah, focuses on the fact that the God of Israel is totally distinct from the creation and not conditioned by it in any way (1:4; 5:16; 8:14; 10:17; 17:7; 30:11; 37:23; 43:15; 45:11; 48:17). The word "holy" *(qādôš)* occurs more often in Isaiah than in any other book of the Bible.

The influence of Isaiah on the NT writers is nothing short of profound. One hundred and ninety-four NT passages have citations or allusions to 54 of the 66 chapters of Isaiah. The NT books of Matthew, Luke, Acts, Romans, Hebrews, and Revelation are especially replete with quotations from the book of Isaiah.[36]

The book of Isaiah is also distinctive in its focus on the Messiah, viewed as both the Davidic King (Isaiah 9; 11) and the Suffering Servant (42:1–4; 49:1–6; 50:4–9; 52:13–53:12). Themes, persons, and motifs of Isaiah echoed in the NT include the following:

- John the Baptist (Isa 40:3; Matt 3:3; Luke 3:4–6; John 1:23)
- Virgin birth (Isa 7:14; Matt 1:23; Luke 1:34)
- Teaching in parables (Isa 6:9–10; 29:13; Matt 13:13–15; 15:7–9; John 12:39–40; Acts 28:24–27)
- Suffering Servant (Isa 53:1; John 12:38; Acts 8:27–33)
- Mission to the Gentiles (Isa 9:1–2; Matt 4:13–16)
- Servant spoken of by Isaiah (Isa 61:1–3; Luke 4:14–21)
- Avoidance of fame (Isa 42:1–4; Matt 12:15–21)
- Enthronement of God (Isa 6:1–3; John 12:41)
- Incorporation of Gentiles into the people of God (Isa 11:10; 65:1; Rom 10:20; 15:12)
- Remnant for Israel (Isa 1:9; 10:22; Rom 9:27–29)
- Renewal of paradise regained (Isa 65:16–66:24; Rom 8:18–25; Revelation 21–22)
- Arboreal imagery to describe Messiah and His people (Isa 4:2; 5:1–7; 6:13; 11:1–3, 10–11; John 15)
- Warnings against hypocritical practices (Isaiah 58; Matthew 23)
- Divine armor (Isa 59:17; Ephesians 6). [37]

Clearly Isaiah has influenced the NT more than any other OT book.

THE TEXT OF THE BOOK

The Hebrew text of Isaiah, on the whole, has been very well preserved. The LXX, often useful in elucidating certain difficulties, is somewhat free in its renderings. There are a total of 22 copies of Isaiah found among the DSS and nearby sites, with 1QIsaᵃ and 1QIsaᵇ being the best known. The DSS present many readings different from those in the MT. Peter Flint maintains that dozens of these reading are superior readings to the MT.[38] Yet, Eugene Ulrich still affirms that the Isaiah scrolls from Qumran along with the MT and Greek witnesses indicate a single main edition of the book of Isaiah in the Second Temple period.[39]

---

[36] Schultz, "Isaiah," 205.

[37] T. Longman III and R. B. Dillard, *An Introduction to the Old Testament*, 2nd ed. (Grand Rapids: Zondervan, 2006), 283; Oswalt, "Isaiah, Theology of," 729–31; Motyer, *The Prophecy of Isaiah*, 13–19.

[38] See M. Abegg Jr., P. Flint, and E. Ulrich, *The Dead Sea Scrolls Bible* (San Francisco: HarperSanFrancisco, 1999), 267–381.

[39] E. Ulrich, "Isaiah, Book of," in *Encyclopedia of the Dead Sea Scrolls*, ed. L. H. Schiffman and J. C. VanderKam, 2 vols (Oxford: Oxford University Press, 2000), 1:386.

EXCURSUS ON ISAIAH 7:14

In Isaiah 7 the prophet Isaiah stood before King Ahaz with the threat of a Syro-Ephraimite coalition attack looming on the horizon. Isaiah urged Ahaz to ask God for a sign. Ahaz piously refused, rejecting God's offering of a confirming sign and claiming he did not desire to tempt God (Deut 6:16). Despite his refusal, Isaiah proceeded to announce the sign anyway. The sign is that a virgin/young woman would conceive and bear a child whose name will be Immanuel (7:14). In the following announcement of judgment (vv. 14–25), the prophet announced that before the child reached the age of moral accountability, the lands of Rezin (Syria) and Pekah (Israel) would be devastated. Two important and debated issues in this prophecy pertain to the meaning of the term *'almâh* ("virgin") and the nature of the fulfillment of the passage in the NT.

Many argue that the term *'almâh* is not a technical word for "virgin" even though it is translated in the LXX as *parthenos*. It is argued that the actual meaning of the Hebrew word is "young woman" (NRSV) or "young maiden" rather than "virgin." Advocates of this position argue that if the author of Isa 7:14 had wanted to refer to a virgin he would have used the more accepted technical Hebrew term for virgin, *betûlâh*.

However, the translation of *betûlâh* as "virgin" is not as airtight as it is often alleged. Of the 50 uses of *betûlâh* in the OT, only 21 of these can confidently be translated "virgin."[40] In Deut 22:19 and Joel 1:8 *betûlâh* is used of a married woman.

The word *'almâh* occurs only seven times in the OT, and in Gen 24:43; Exod 2:8; Prov 30:19; Song 1:3; 6:8 the word clearly describes a virgin. However, it should be noted that the prophetic passage of Isaiah does not conclusively indicate that the virgin would conceive as a virgin. The point would rather be that at the time of speaking the young woman in question was unmarried and thus not sexually experienced.

The next critical issue in the interpretation of Isa 7:14 concerns its usage in the NT, specifically the identity of the virgin and her son. Three basic positions have emerged.

First, this refers only to Mary and Jesus. Support for this position is that Isaiah shifted his focus from Ahaz to the royal court as he addressed the whole house of David. From Isa 7:14 onward Isaiah consistently used the plural, indicating that he was continuing to address the whole house of David rather than only Ahaz. Isaiah thus announced that he was giving a sign to David's line, present and future. Isaiah did not use the singular number again until he once more addressed Ahaz in v. 16.

Second, this refers to Abi (2 Kgs 18:2) and her child Hezekiah. Some argue on the basis of Isa 8:8 that the vocative with reference to "your land" in reference to Immanuel would appropriately refer to the crown prince.[41] However, many are quick to point out that the difficulty with this position is one of chronology. Hezekiah was possibly six or seven years old when Isaiah gave that prophecy.

Third, Isaiah referred to his wife and their son Maher-shalal-hash-baz. According to this position the immediate fulfillment of the Immanuel prophecy is recorded in chap. 8, with the birth of Maher-shalal-hash-baz. The strength of this position is the parallelism of phraseology of 8:3–4 with 7:14–16 and the association of this child with Israel's immediate national crisis. The juxtaposition of the birth report narrative (8:1–8) of Maher-shalal-hash-baz and the birth announcement narrative (7:14–25) of Immanuel suggests a close relationship between the prophecy and the birth. Moreover, Immanuel is addressed at the conclusion of the prophecy

---

[40] Motyer, *The Prophecy of Isaiah*, 84, n. 4.

[41] W. C. Kaiser Jr., *Toward an Old Testament Theology* (Grand Rapids: Zondervan, 1978), 209–10.

(8:8) as if he were already alive. The Immanuel born in Isaiah's day would be a type of Jesus Christ, who is "God with us" in the fullest sense.[42] Thus 'almâh applies either to Shear-jashub's mother, if the term indicates "young maiden" in the nontechnical sense, or to Isaiah's wife-to-be if his previous wife had died and he was instructed to take a new wife who was a virgin at the time of speaking.[43]

Of these three positions, one and three seem to be commendable. In position one Matthew saw in the virgin birth and the naming of Jesus the fulfillment of Isa 7:14. In this view the passage is a direct prophecy of the Messiah, Jesus Christ, without any fulfillment in Isaiah's time period. Those who interpret the passage this way thus understand the passage as directly prophetic or exclusively messianic. It finds reinforcement from the immediate context. The name Immanuel was evoked in Isa 8:8,10, whereas in 9:1–7 the prophet spoke of a coming son of David who will rule forever.[44] For position three, which sees an immediate fulfillment as well as a later fulfillment in the time of Christ, the passage is considered typico-prophetic. In the birth of Jesus Christ there is a replication of the OT event and a heightening or escalation of that OT prophecy.

Whereas in the OT context the conception would refer to a woman who had been a virgin who later conceived in the conventional way, in the NT it refers to a unique virginal conception. In the OT the child's name expresses assurance that God was with the people in light of the threat of the Syro-Ephraimite war; in the NT Immanuel God is with His people but in a unique way—God incarnate will deliver His people from their sins.

STUDY QUESTIONS

1. During which time period did Isaiah utter his oracles?
2. What OT critic proposed that the book of Isaiah was written by three authors?
3. Why do some scholars believe that Isaiah has been written by authors besides the prophet Isaiah?
4. What light do the Dead Sea Scrolls shed on the issue of the number of authors of the book of Isaiah?
5. What light does the NT shed on the issue of the number of authors of the book of Isaiah?
6. What are the meanings of Isaiah's three sign-children?
7. What nation is emphasized in the oracles against the nations in Isaiah 13–23?
8. How does Isaiah 24–27 reflect the Genesis account of the flood?
9. What are the central topics for the book of Isaiah?
10. What word occurs more in Isaiah than in any other OT book?
11. What is unique about references to Isaiah in the NT?
12. What are the major ways Isaiah refers to the Messiah?
13. What are the three views regarding the fulfillment of Isa 7:14 in the NT?

FOR FURTHER STUDY

Alexander, J. A. *The Prophecies of Isaiah*. Grand Rapids: Zondervan, 1953.
Allis, O. T. *The Unity of Isaiah: A Study in Prophecy*. Nutley, NJ: Presbyterian and Reformed, 1950.

---

[42] J. N. Oswalt, *The Isaiah of Isaiah, Chapters 1–39* (Grand Rapids: Eerdmans, 1986), 213–14; and Chisholm, "A Theology of Isaiah," 315–16.

[43] However, there is no textual clue that leads to this conclusion.

[44] See G. V. Smith, *Isaiah 1–39*, NAC (Nashville: B&H, 2007), 201–16.

Childs, B. *Introduction to the Old Testament As Scripture*. Philadelphia: Fortress, 1979.

Chisholm, R. B., Jr. "A Theology of Isaiah." In *A Biblical Theology of the Old Testament*. Edited by Roy B. Zuck, 305–40. Chicago: Moody, 1991.

Clements, R. E. "The Unity of the Book of Isaiah." *Int* 36 (1982): 117–29.

Dumbrell, W. "The Purpose of the Book of Isaiah." *TynBul* 36 (1985): 111–28.

Evans, C. A. "On the Unity and Parallel Structure of Isaiah." *VT* 38 (1988): 12–47.

Hindson, B. E. *Isaiah's Immanuel*. BTS. N.p.: Presbyterian and Refirmed Publishing Co., 1978.

Lindsey, F. D. *The Servant Songs*. Chicago, Moody, 1985.

Motyer, A. *The Prophecy of Isaiah*. Downers Grove, IL: InterVarsity, 1993.

O'Connell, R. H. *Concentricity and Continuity: The Literary Structure of Isaiah*. Sheffield: Sheffield Academic, 1994.

Rendtorff, R. "Zur Komposition des Buches Jesaja." *VT* 39 (1984): 295–320.

———. "The Book of Isaiah: A Complex Unity. Synchronic and Diachronic Reading." *SBL 1991 Seminar Papers*. Edited by E. Lovering Jr. Atlanta: Scholars, 1990.

Rooker, M. "Dating Isaiah 40–66: What Does the Linguistic Evidence Say?" *WTJ* 58 (1996): 303–12.

Schultz, R. "Isaiah." In *Theological Interpretation of the Old Testament*. Edited by K. Vanhoozer, 194–210. Grand Rapids: Baker Academic, 2008.

Webb, B. G. "Zion in Transformation: A Literary Approach to Isaiah." In *The Bible in Three Dimension: Essays in Celebration of Forty Years of Biblical Studies in the University of Sheffield*. Edited by D. J. A. Clines, S. E. Fowl, and S. E. Porter, 65–84. Sheffield: Sheffield Academic Press, 1990.

Young, E. J. *The Book of Isaiah*. 3 vols. Grand Rapids: Eerdmans, 1972.

CHAPTER 24

THE BOOK OF JEREMIAH

MARK F. ROOKER

THE BOOK OF Jeremiah has the honor of being the longest prophetic book in the Bible. Moreover, the prophet Jeremiah holds the record for having the longest prophetic ministry. He was called to his ministry in 627 BC and continued to preach through the Babylonian exile in 586 BC down to about 582 BC, a ministry of some 45 years. Thus like Moses, Jeremiah had a lengthy prophetic career and faced intense opposition from the people. But unlike Moses, who led the people out of Egypt, Jeremiah was taken from the promised land to Egypt. During his tenure occurred numerous, momentous events in Israel's history, such as Josiah's reform (622 BC), the death of Josiah (609 BC), the failures and rebellions of Josiah's successors, and the final collapse of the southern kingdom in 586 BC. His ministry can be divided into three periods. The first begins with his call in 627 and ends with the death of Josiah in 609. The second period begins with the reign of Josiah's successor, King Jehoiakim, from 609 to 598, ending with the second Babylonian deportation. The third period took place between the first destruction of Jerusalem by the Babylonians (598) down to the final collapse of Jerusalem in 586 BC (see the appendix near the end of this chap.).

THE TEXT OF THE BOOK

Determining of the text of Jeremiah is perhaps the most problematic issue in OT textual criticism (see chap. 7). Substantial differences exist between the MT of Jeremiah and the LXX. In fact these differ more than in any other book of the OT. The MT contains approximately 2,700 words that have no correspondence in the LXX. The MT thus represents a text that is one-seventh longer than the LXX. However, one can discern in many cases a certain pattern in the differences.

Many of the MT additions consist of repeated words or phrases that do nothing more than embellish the text and do not lead to a different meaning. For example the MT often has the phrases "thus says the LORD," or "says the LORD," where as the corresponding verses in the LXX lack the phrase. The phrase "says the LORD" occurs 65 more times in the MT than it does in the LXX. Also the LXX translators often omitted names for God when they occur in combination.

For example the phrase "the LORD, the God of Israel" is usually shortened to "LORD" (*kyrios*) in the LXX.[1] Another difference is the MT's tendency to add the word "*prophet*" after a personal name, whereas the LXX has only the person's name. Similarly the LXX refers to Nebuchadnezzar rather than the fuller title in the MT that adds "King of Babylon." Sometimes the MT has an introductory heading that does not occur in the LXX (e.g., 2:1–2; 7:1–2; 16:1; 27:1–2). Also the MT is more apt to repeat material that had been recorded earlier in the prophecy, while the LXX is consistently more concise (e.g., 6:22–24 = 50:41; 10:12–16 = 51:15–19).

Based on these differences, many have argued that a scribe would be more likely to embellish a text or add to it rather than systematically abridge it, and thus the LXX should be generally understood as representing the more original text. This principle of textual criticism is known as *lectio brevior preferenda est*, "the shorter reading is the preferred reading." Preeminent LXX and DSS scholar Emanuel Tov argued that occurrences of the shorter readings in the LXX proves that the LXX is the earlier, more ancient text than the MT.[2] This reasoning is sound but one must also bear in mind that in some cases Tov maintains that the fulfillment of prophecies are later additions added by the MT, creating a *vaticinium ex eventu*. His view is thus open to criticism, for he does not take into account the supernatural nature of Scripture.[3] Moshe Greenberg, on the other hand, believes the shorter edition in the LXX can best be explained as resulting from the faulty manner employed by the Greek translators. He cited evidence that suggests that it was the practice of Alexandrian grammarians to have eliminated repetitions in the Ptolemaic texts of Homer. The Greeks tended to be more creative with texts they were translating and copying, unlike the Jews who consistently sought to use the best manuscripts available.[4]

In addition to the fact that the MT of the book of Jeremiah tends to add additional words and phrases not in the LXX, the order of the chapters is not the same between the MT and the LXX. This is especially apparent in the MT section of the "Oracles Against the Nations" (chaps. 46–51) that occurs in a different place in the LXX (after 25:13). Also the order of the nations is different. The order in which these foreign nations are addressed in the MT is Egypt, Philistine, Moab, Ammon, Edom, Damascus, Kedar, Elam, and Babylon, but the order of the nations in the LXX is Elam, Egypt, Babylon, Philistine, Edom, Ammon, Kedar, Damascus, and Moab. The purpose of the order in the MT was apparently for the nations to be listed in a west-to-east direction, whereas the purpose of the LXX order may have been to focus on Babylon, as that nation occupies the central position.

Because of these substantial differences, it is often suggested that the MT and the LXX represent two separate recensions of the book of Jeremiah. The four Jeremiah scrolls found among the DSS favor this premise. 2QJer follows the MT order with the oracles against the nations at the end of the book and otherwise also attests to the MT reading. 4QJer[a] and 4QJer[b] also are in agreement with the MT, although 4QJer[b] does share some readings with the LXX. Thus there is Hebrew manuscript evidence that lies behind the distinctive readings of the Greek LXX.

Abraham Kuenen argued several decades ago, however, that the two textual witnesses to Jeremiah are not so much two recensions as two different texts of the same recension in different

---

[1] See G. L. Archer, "The Relationship between the Septuagint Translation and the Massoretic Text in Jeremiah," *TJ* NS12 (1991): 149.

[2] E. Tov, "The Book of Jeremiah: A Work in Progress," *BR* 16 (2000): 34.

[3] Ibid., 35, 37.

[4] M. Greenberg, "The Stabilization of the Text of the Hebrew Bible Reviewed in the Light of the Biblical Materials from the Judean Desert," *JAOS* 76 (1956): 166 and n. 59.

stages of its history.[5] Possibly the differences between the MT and the LXX can be explained based on the fact that Jeremiah himself spent his last years in Egypt (41:16–44:30), the site of the LXX translation. The edition, which he either took with him or wrote in Egypt, could be the basis for the LXX of Jeremiah, and its existence far removed geographically from the MT in Palestine may explain the differences that developed between the texts. Evidence in the book itself shows that Jeremiah wrote at least some of his prophecies more than once (36:32). It is also possible that Baruch, who was not only a disciple of Jeremiah's but also his scribe, may have made a second collection of the book after Jeremiah had died. Based on the lack of certainty Peter Craigie rationally concluded that the data that exists does not allow for precision in creating a theory about the recensions of the Hebrew text of Jeremiah.[6] Furthermore one should always bear in mind that the LXX has its own history with a substantial amount of textual variants.

In spite of these differences, which as mentioned above are more acute than in any other OT book, the same message is conveyed whether one reads the MT or the LXX.[7] It should be noted, however, that the order of the MT seems to be more logical than what is in the LXX.[8]

THE COMPOSITION OF THE BOOK

A casual reading of the book of Jeremiah reveals that there are two main literary categories in the book, poetry and prose. In the nineteenth and early twentieth centuries critical scholars began to identify the prose and poetic sections as different sources. Bernhard Duhm in particular argued in 1901 that the separate poetic and prose sections of the book revealed different authors.[9] Adopting the Hebrew metrical system developed by Julius Ley, Duhm argued that only the poetic sections revealed the original sayings of Jeremiah. Specifically Duhm argued that Jeremiah wrote only in *qînāh* verse, the elegiac 3:2 meter. Among the prose sections he found two additional compositions. The biographical stories of Jeremiah, he argued, were written perhaps by a disciple about Jeremiah's life, while a much later writer wrote the remaining parts of the book in the postexilic period and transformed Jeremiah into a preacher of judgment and morals.[10] Justification for the two prose sources, not unlike the critical study of the Pentateuch, arose from the observation that there were two occurrences of the temple sermon in chaps. 7 and 26. The temple sermon was written in sermonic prose in chap. 7, but in chap. 26 it was composed in biographical prose. In 1914 Mowinckel designated Duhm's three sources as the A source–Jeremiah's poetic statements in chaps. 1–25, the B source–the biographic prose in chaps. 26–45, and the C source—the Deuteronomic redaction of chaps. 1–45. The Deuteronomic characteristics included the following: the struggle against idolatry, the centralization of the cult, the exodus and covenant, the belief in one God, observance of the law and obedience to the covenant, inheritance in the land, divine retribution, fulfillment of prophecy, and the choice of David's dynasty.[11] Chapters 46–52 contain later additions.

---

[5] Abraham Kuenen, quoted in S. R. Driver, *An Introduction to the Literature of the Old Testament* (Edinburgh: T&T Clark, 1913), 270.

[6] P. C. Craigie et al., *Jermiah 1–25*, WBC (Dallas: Word, 1991)

[7] B. Childs, *Introduction to the Old Testament as Scripture* (Philadelphia: Fortress, 1979), 353.

[8] Driver, *An Introduction to the Literature of the Old Testament*, 269–70; and Childs, *Introduction to the Old Testament as Scripture*, 353.

[9] B. Duhm, *Das Buch Jeremia* (Tübingen: Mohr, 1901)

[10] Ibid.

[11] M. Weinfeld, *Deuteronomy and the Deuteronomic School* (Winona Lake, IN: Eisenbrauns, 1992), 1.

Very early on there were detractors, even among the critics, to this model developed by Duhm and expanded by Sigmund Mowinckel. Both Friedrich Giesebrecht and Cornhill, for example, maintained that Duhm's theory was virtually baseless. They argued that restricting the writing of Jeremiah to mere poetry was completely arbitrary and that the work of later redactors was not near as extensive as Duhm had proposed. In more recent times John Bright has argued that there is much more historical continuity between these alleged sources than Duhm's and Mowinckel's theory will allow. He argued persuasively that there were not near so many postexilic additions, and he demonstrated that the prose of Jeremiah was distinctive from the prose of the Deuteronomist, undermining any reason for proposing a Deuteronomic editor. The so-called Deuteronomic style was actually nothing more than Hebrew rhetorical prose in existence in the seventh and sixth centuries BC.[12] If Jeremiah did reflect a Deuteronomic style, this actually meant that he was familiar with the contents of the book of Deuteronomy. Few scholars today continue to distinguish between the prose accounts in the alleged B and C sources. The great bulk of the C source that includes passages such as chaps. 1, 7, and 31 that had been designated as a postexilic retrojection is now viewed as reflecting the actual preaching of Jeremiah. This reversal illustrates how far scholars have departed from the old consensus of the three sources![13]

Jeremiah is one of only a few OT books that give a glimpse into at least how part of a biblical book was written. God instructed Jeremiah to record his prophecies in 605 BC, in the fourth year of King Jehoiakim, approximately 20 years after he began his prophetic ministry (36:1–3). Thus Jeremiah dictated his words to Baruch (36:4). The completed scroll was then read before the King Jehoiakim, who had it burned (36:9–26). Because of the king's angry response some scholars speculate that what was recorded on this scroll must have been similar to the contents of Jeremiah 1–25, which recorded many judgment oracles against the nation. After the destruction of the scroll Jeremiah repeated his words to Baruch, adding many additional words to be recorded in the new scroll (36:32).

Overall there is no reason to doubt that Jeremiah was the prominent author of the book that bears his name with assistance from his amanuensis Baruch. There is no reason to suggest that the oracles existed for many years only in an oral form and were later committed to writing. Recent studies on rhetoric and composition indicate that these documents were written immediately after they were delivered during Jeremiah's lifetime.[14]

THE HISTORICAL BACKGROUND OF THE BOOK

Jeremiah's call to prophetic ministry in 627 BC coincided or occurred shortly after the death of Asshur-banipal. Asshur-banipal was regarded as the last of the great Assyrian kings. As a consequence Babylon began to assert independence under Nabopolassar (626–605 BC). Assyria's hegemony was also diminished during this time because of the resurgence of Egypt under Psammetichus (664–610 BC). After Egypt's defeat at Carchemish (605 BC) it was

---

[12] Childs, *Introduction to the Old Testament as Scripture*, 342–43, R. K. Harrison, *Introduction to the Old Testament* (Grand Rapids: Eerdmans, 1969), 817; and J. Bright, *Jeremiah: Introduction, Translation, and Notes*, AB (Garden City: Doubleday, 1965), lxxiii.

[13] J. R. Lundbom, "Jeremiah, Book of," in *ABD*, ed. D. N. Freedman (New York: Doubleday, 1992), 3:709. See also R. R. Wilson, *Prophecy and Society in Ancient Israel* (Philadelphia: Fortress, 1980), 232–33; and Childs, *An Introduction to the Old Testament as Scripture*, 344–45.

[14] Lundbom, "Jeremiah, Book of," 711.

apparent that the Neo-Babylonian empire would be the force to reckon with in the ANE. The most important dates, which pertain to Jeremiah's prophecy, are the following:

640	Josiah became king of Judah
627	Jeremiah was called to his ministry
622	Josiah's reform
609	Josiah died at Megiddo
	Jehoahaz reigned for three months
	Jehoiakim installed as king by the Egyptians
605	Babylon gained ascendancy over Egypt at Carchemish
	Jehoiakim burned Jeremiah's scroll
598	Nebuchadnezzar attacked Jerusalem
	First deportation of Jews to Babylon
	Jehoiakim died
	Jehoiachin became king; was taken to Babylon
	Zedekiah installed as king by Babylonians
	Jeremiah confronted Hananiah
588	Jeremiah imprisoned by Zedekiah
586	Destruction of Jerusalem
	Gedaliah appointed governor of Judea
582	Gedaliah assassinated
	Jeremiah traveled to Egypt

THE FORM OF THE BOOK

The book of Jeremiah displays a greater variety of literary forms than any other book of the Bible. Jeremiah employed the legal language of the courtroom as he inveighed against the nation for her sins (2:5–9,10–13). His language displays profound emotion at the onslaught of disaster (4:29–31; 15:5–9). The book also contains prose reports of visions: the almond tree (1:11–12), the boiling pot (1:13–19), the loin cloth (13:1–7), and the basket of figs (24:1–10). Very distinctive of Jeremiah's prophecy is the inclusion of parables and object lessons. These include Jeremiah's bachelorhood (16:1–4), the potter at work (18:1–12), the broken pot (19:1–20:6), the yoke of iron (27:1–28:17), the field of purchase (32:6–44), the pile of stones (43:8–13), and the book in the river (51:59–64). An actual letter is included in chap. 29, and closing summations are recorded in 36:1–8 and 51:59–64. The clause, "I will restore you to the place I deported you from" occurs in 29:14 and seven additional times in chaps. 30–33. Prayers and their answers from the Lord are recorded in 32:16–44.[15] A number of these prayers reflect the pain and turmoil that accompanied his being a prophet of God (11:18–23; 12:1–6; 15:10–14,15–21; 17:14–18; 18:18–23; 20:7–12,14–18).

Jeremiah alluded to the creation account in predicting the coming Babylonian destruction (4:23–26) and acknowledging the Lord as sovereign over His creation (10:12–16; 27:5; 32:17; 33:2). In 2:2–9 he reflected on the exodus, the wandering in the wilderness, and the settlement in Canaan, and he seems to have echoed the Song of Moses (Exodus 15) in depicting the

---

[15] See Lundbom, "Jeremiah, Book of," 711; and L. Boadt, *Reading the Old Testament: An Introduction* (New York: Paulist, 1984), 365. For a list of expressions characteristic of Jeremiah see Driver, *Introduction to the Old Testament*, 275–77.

Mosaic era as Israel's idyllic period of history. Like Hosea, Jeremiah portrayed Judah as God's unfaithful wife (3:1–5,20; Hos 2:14–15).

THE MESSAGE AND PURPOSE OF THE BOOK

Based on the fact that judgment oracles are more concentrated in this book than any other form, the message of Jeremiah is largely one of judgment and punishment for the nation Judah. The prophet was assigned the task of confronting the nation about her sin in order to avoid the catastrophe of exile (2:1–6:30). In particular, Judah was guilty of committing the sin of idolatry, breaking the first two commandments of the Mosaic covenant. The Israelites had worshipped Baal (2:8,23; 7:9; 9:14; 11:13,17; 12:16; 19:4; 23:13,27; 32:29,35) and the Mesopotamia goddess Ishtar who was called the "queen of heaven" in Jeremiah (7:18; 44:17–19,25). Such horrendous events as child sacrifice were also taking place (19:5; 32:35). Such illicit worship practice grieved Jeremiah deeply (7:1–20:18). Other sins of the nation included oppression of the poor and the downtrodden by the rich (2:34; 5:26–28; 7:5–6) as well as empty ritualism (6:20; 14:12). The spiritual stubbornness of the people is a prominent theme spanning 26:1–36:22.

Having violated the covenant, the nation could expect the covenantal curses to be visited on them (Leviticus 26; Deuteronomy 28; cf. Jer 11:8). By the attachment of the historical appendix (chap. 52) after Jeremiah's words were concluded (51:64), the message that Israel's sins would eventuate in exile is substantiated.

And yet, based on the Abrahamic promises, Jeremiah also conveyed a message of hope. This is seen most vividly in the section entitled "the Book of Comfort" (chaps. 30–33) and scattered throughout the book (1:10; 3:15–18; 12:15–16; 16:14–15; 52:31–33). As Jeremiah was appointed over nations and kingdoms "to destroy and overthrow, to build and to plant" (1:10 NIV), these dual activities were expressed with regard to Israel (i.e., judgment and hope; 18:15–17; 24:6; 31:28; 42:10; 45:4) and to Gentile nations as well.

THE STRUCTURE OF THE BOOK

Many commentators have noted that the arrangement of the chapters in the book of Jeremiah seems to lack a clear rationale. This, however, may not be without intention. The irregular nature of the oracles may reveal that the book was composed during a time of great stress and despair. The tensions experienced by the author had their effect on his writing. While it is not easy to discern a clear chronological layout from chapter to chapter, the overall structure of the book does indicate a certain chronological order. For example Jeremiah's call to minister as a prophet comes in chap. 1. At the end of the book before the "Oracles of the Nations" the final activities of Jeremiah's life in Egypt are noted. Jeremiah 2 records Jeremiah's earliest preaching, which precedes in time his confessions that close the same major section (20:7–18). All of the oracles in chaps. 1–20 preceded in time the narratives recorded in chaps. 24–29 and 34–44.

Evidence shows that considerations other than chronology were prominent in the arrangement of the chapters of the book. The substratum of Jeremiah's confessions (chaps. 11–20) were clearly grouped because of their common literary form. Similarly in "the Book of Comfort" (chaps. 30–33) the theme of hope clearly dominates.[16]

---

[16] Lundbom, "Jeremiah, Book of," 711.

Marvin Sweeney has divided the entire book into 17 sections based on the occurrence of the phrase, "the word of the LORD came to Jeremiah."[17]

I.   Jeremiah's early oracles concerning Jerusalem and Judah (1:1–6:30)

II. Jeremiah's Temple sermon (7:1–10:25)

III. Jeremiah's lament concerning Judah's broken covenant with God (11:1–13:27)

IV. The great drought and Judah's coming punishment (14:1–17:27)

V.   The symbolic action of the potter and the jug (18:1–20:18)

VI. Jeremiah's oracles concerning the house of David and the prophets (21:1–24:10)

VII. Submission to Babylonia (25:1–29:32)

VIII. Jeremiah's Book of Consolation (30:1–31:40)

IX. Symbolic actions and oracles concerning the restoration (32:1–33:26)

X.   Jeremiah's oracle concerning King Zedekiah (34:1–7)

XI. The oracle concerning slaves (34:8–22)

XII. The fall of Jerusalem (35:1–39:18)

XIII. The assassination of Gedaliah and its consequences (40:1–43:13)

XIV. Jeremiah's oracle in Egypt (44:1–40)

XV. Jeremiah's oracle to Baruch (45:1–5)

XVI. Oracles concerning the nations (46:1–51:64)

XVII. Concluding narrative concerning the fall of Jerusalem (52:1–34)

J. Rosenberg detected a symmetry between chaps. 20–40, which may help make sense of the purported chronological problems in the book.[18]

A.	Jeremiah's first imprisonment is recounted (chap. 20)	No date given
B.	An official of Zedekiah asked Jeremiah to pray to Yahweh; broad survey of Jeremiah's dealings with various kings (chaps. 21–24)	Reign of Zedekiah
C.	Jeremiah orally summarized 23 years of preaching (25:1–14)	Fourth year of Jehoiakim's reign
D.	Cup of wine was forced on neighboring nations (25:15–38); Jeremiah's troubles with official circles are recounted (chap. 26)	Fourth year of Jehoiakim's reign

---

[17] M. A. Sweeney, *The Jewish Study Bible*, ed. A. Berlin and M. Z. Brettler (Oxford: Oxford University Press, 2004), 920.

[18] J. Rosenberg, "Jeremiah and Ezekiel," in *The Literary Guide to the Bible,* ed. R. Alter and F. Kermode (Cambridge, MA: Harvard University Press, 1987), 192–93.

E. Jeremiah predicted that nations will be enslaved to Babylon (chap. 27) — Beginning of Jehoiakim's reign

F. Jeremiah's rival Hananiah predicted short-term vindication of the nation (chap. 28) — Fourth year of Zedekiah's reign

G. Jeremiah told exiles to settle permanently in Babylonia (chap. 29) — Shortly after exile of Jehoiachin; thus beginning of Zedekiah's reign

H. "The Book of Consolation": addressed to the northern kingdom (chaps. 30–31)

G^1. Yahweh told exiles to settle permanently in Anathoth (chap. 32) — Tenth year of Zedekiah's reign

F^1. Jeremiah predicted long-term vindication of the nation (chap. 33) — Tenth year of Zedekiah's reign, slightly later than G^1

E^1. Judean slaveowners reneged on releasing slaves, and Jeremiah predicted death for them (chap. 34) — during siege of Jerusalem, but possibly earlier than G^1

D^1. Cup of wine was refused by Rechabites; authentic servants of God were praised; the nation's disobedience was renounced (chap. 35) — In the days of King Jehoiakim

C^1. Jeremiah summarized in writing 23 years of preaching (chap. 36) — Fourth year of Jehoiakim's reign

B^1. An official of Zedekiah asked Jeremiah to pray to God; Jeremiah's dealings with Zedekiah's court are set forth in detail (chaps. 37–39) — Early in Zedekiah's reign

A^1. Jeremiah's final release from prison is recounted (chap. 40) — After the Babylonian capture of Jerusalem

According to this layout of Jeremiah 20–40 the focus of the book is on the "Book of Consolation" in the center of the chiasm, with the promise of the new covenant in Jeremiah 31.

Regarding the macrostructure of the prophecy Richard Patterson has observed the following balanced structure:[19]

Call and Commission	*Jeremiah and His People*			*Jeremiah and the Nations*			*Appendix*
Chap. 1	Theme	Development	Sign	Theme	Development	Sign	Chap. 52
	2:1–3:5	3:6–23:40	24	25	26:1–51:58	51:59–64	

THE OUTLINE OF THE BOOK

I. **Judgment on Judah and Jerusalem (chaps. 1–25)**
    A. The Call of Jeremiah (chap. 1)
    B. Israel's Guilt and Punishment (chaps. 2–6)

---

[19] R. D. Patterson, "Of Bookends, Hinges, and Hooks: Literary Clues to the Arrangement of Jeremiah's Prophecies," *WTJ* 51(1989): 115. See also G. Yates, "Narrative Parallelism and the 'Jehoiakim Frame': A Reading Strategy for Jeremiah 26–45," *JETS* 48 (2005): 263–81.

    C. False Religion and Its Punishment (chaps. 7–10)
    D. The Broken Covenant and Jeremiah's Complaints (chaps. 11–15)
    E. Confessions, Symbolic Acts, and Messages to Judah (16:1–25:38).

II. **Biographical Narratives Connected with Jerusalem (chaps. 26–45)**
    A. Jeremiah's Controversy with False Prophets (chaps. 26–29)
    B. Messages of Hope and Consolation (chaps. 30–33)
    C. Events from the Days of Jehoiakim and Zedekiah (chaps. 34–39)
    D. Events after the Fall of Jerusalem (chaps. 40–45)

III. **Oracles against Foreign Nations (chaps. 46–51)**
    A. Egypt (chap. 46)
    B. Philistia (chap.47)
    C. Moab (chap. 48)
    D. Ammon (49:1–6)
    E. Edom (49:7–22)
    F. Damascus (49:23–27)
    G. Arab tribes (49:28–33)
    H. Elam (49:34–39)
    I. Babylon (chaps. 50–51)

IV. **Historical Appendix (chap. 52)**
    A. The Fall of Jerusalem and the Capture of Zedekiah (52:1–16)
    B. The Destruction of the Temple (52:17–23)
    C. The Three Babylonian Deportations (52:24–30)
    D. The Release of Jehoiachin from Prison (52:31–34)

THE CONTENTS OF THE BOOK

I. Judgment on Judah and Jerusalem (chaps. 1–25)

Chapter 1 wastes no time in identifying perhaps Judah's most troubling sin, her flagrant idolatry. The chapter also records two visions. The first vision of the almond rod relates to the prophet's call in 627 BC (1:4–12), and the second vision of the boiling pot tipped away from the north (vv. 13–16) forecasts the punishment that was to be visited on Israel from the north. Thus from the opening chapter the reader is aware of all the main themes and motifs of the book: Judah's idolatry, Jeremiah's ministry, and the coming Babylonian invasion.

Jeremiah 2 continues to discuss Judah's sin of idolatry, as Judah is compared to a harlot who has been unfaithful to her husband (2:4–3:5; 3:12–14,19–23). This metaphor may have been borrowed from Hosea, who compared Israel to a harlot because of her worship of Baal, thus violating her covenant relationship with the Lord. Having worshipped idols, Judah had become worthless (2:5). Jeremiah was forewarned that though Judah may learn of her need for repentance, she would fail to repent (3:6–4:4). Jeremiah felt the grief of the people who would soon be led to judgment (4:19–22), and he also identified with God's anger directed toward the nation's wicked ways (11:11–20).[20] Disaster was soon to come on the land from the north (4:6; see 1:13–16), since none in the land are righteous (5:1–9). Another important topic in this section is Jeremiah's temple sermon in chap. 7, in which he castigated the people

---

[20] J. G. McConville, "Jeremiah," in *Theological Interpretation of the Old Testament,* ed. K. J. Vanhoozer (Grand Rapids: Baker Academic, 2008), 214.

for their superstitious trust in the structure of the temple. This superstition trust corresponded to the nation's trust in empty ritual. They had mistaken a trust in religious institutions for true religion. If sacrifices are not offered with heartfelt devotion and obedience, they are rejected (7:22). Many of the prophets share this view about sacrifices (Isa 1:12–13; Hos 6:6; 9:4).

But Jeremiah was also a prophet to the nations (1:10). Jeremiah also reprimanded Egypt, Edom, Ammon, and Moab (9:25–26). In presenting his message of judgment Jeremiah experienced a great amount of resentment and subsequently struggled with God's will concerning the task God had given him (15:10,15–18; 20:7–10,14–18). He suffered beatings and humiliation (20:1–6) and had to stand his ground against false prophets who painted a different picture of Judah's future (6:13–14; 14:11–16).[21] In what may be an appendix to this first major section (chaps. 21–25) the prophet expressed laments, and the chapters record his preaching that is directed toward Judah's royal house and Jerusalem's ministers. At the end of this section Jeremiah predicted that the desolation, which will begin at the time of captivity, will last for a period of 70 years (25:11–12). The authors of Chronicles, Ezra, and Daniel were all aware of this 70-year period of exile from the book of Jeremiah (2 Chr 36:21; Ezra 1:1; Dan 9:2). Since the captivity ended in 539–538 BC, the 70 years is dated from the Babylonian invasion of 605 BC, which resulted in the first Babylonian deportation.

II. Biographical Narratives Connected with Jerusalem (chaps. 26–45)

Since the Babylonians would soon invade the land to judge the inhabitants of Judah, Jeremiah attempted to influence his nation's foreign policy. He reasoned with his countrymen to become a vassal of Babylon voluntarily and so be spared the horrors of the coming destruction (27:6–8). Chapter 28 records his unpopular message challenged by the false prophet Hananiah, which illustrates the rejection of the word of God by Judah's religious establishment.

Chapters 30–33 function as a subsection to this section and have often been referred to as the "Book of Consolation." Early in this section God states; "I will restore [*wešabtî*] the fortunes [*šebût*] of My people" (30:3). The alliterative phrase affirming God's promise of future deliverance is somewhat ironic as the verb *šub* used here is also the verb used to call Israel to repentance in the book of Jeremiah. This phrase "restore the fortunes" occurs seven times in this small section (30:3,8; 31:23[HB, v. 22]; 32:44; 33:7 [twice],11). God can miraculously restore His people because nothing is too difficult for Him (32:17).

After promises of restoration and healing (30:1–22) and an announcement of divine judgment (30:23–24), Jeremiah wrote of a new covenant (31:31–37). This covenant will differ from the Mosaic covenant in that special enabling (31:33) will be available to guarantee that Israel and Judah obey God's law. The notion that God Himself will renew the people's faithfulness is stated again in 32:39–40. The future obedience and faithfulness of the people will contrast with the history of Israel. This new covenant will be experienced when the southern and northern kingdoms of Israel are united once again (31:31). This covenant will never end (31:35–37). As an illustration of his ultimate confidence that God will enable the Jews to return to their land after the exile, Jeremiah purchased a portion of land in Anathoth from his cousin (chap. 32).

The next major sections record the events from the days of Jehoiakim and Zedekiah (chaps. 34–39) as well as events immediately after the fall of Jerusalem (chaps. 40–45). These accounts demonstrate the tragic consequences of Judah's unfaithfulness. Jeremiah was imprisoned for encouraging the people to submit to the authority of the Lord and to surrender to the

---

[21] See also Jer 23:9–40; 28:1–17; 29:8–9.

Babylonians (37:11–15; 38:1–13). On three occasions Zedekiah sought the prophet for a reprieve, but it was too late (37:3,17; 38:14). Judah still refused to submit to Babylon even after the exile had taken place, in complete defiance to God's explicit command (chaps. 40–44). And yet remarkably God graciously gave His word to Jeremiah for the people who had fled to Egypt (chap. 43). The people, however, continued their idolatrous practices even while suffering the exile (44:7–14) in fulfillment of the prophecy in Deut 28:64–68.

III. Oracles against Foreign Nations (chaps. 46–51)

It is clear that these oracles against 10 foreign nations were spoken and written by Jeremiah or by his amanuensis. Numerous phrases occur in previous parts of Jeremiah's prophecy. The phrase "terror is on every side" (46:5; 49:29) is found in 6:25; 20:10. "Faithless daughter" (49:4) occurs in 31:22. The simile "like a woman in labor" (49:24; 50:43) is in 6:24; 22:23; and 30:6, and the phrase "a jackals' den" (49:33; 51:37) is found in 9:11[HB, v. 10] and 10:22.[22]

The "Oracles against the Nations" especially illustrate the fact that Jeremiah was called to be a prophet to the "nations" (1:5,10; 25:13). The first address focuses on the nation of Egypt, which is somewhat expected as the preceding narrative focused on the move of many of the Jews (including Jeremiah) to Egypt (chaps. 43–44). In this earlier section judgments against Egypt were also announced in 43:8–13 and 44:30.

Because of the imminence of the Babylonian threat, which implemented the darkest hour in the nation's history, it is not surprising that the oracle against Babylon is the longest. The conclusion of this section of judgments against the nations portrays Babylon's doom. Baruch's brother, Seraiah, visited Babylon and read Jeremiah's prophecies against Babylon from the scroll and then sank the scroll into the Euphrates River. The intended message was that as the scroll sank, so Babylon's influence would dissipate (51:59–64).

Because Jeremiah's commission also included building up and planting (1:10), not all statements made about the foreign nations are negative. The restoration of Israel would bring about a positive effect on the nations (33:9–10). Moreover, God promised that Egypt, Moab, Ammon, and Elam would be restored after experiencing their respective judgments (46:25–26; 48:47; 49:6,39).

IV. Historical Appendix (52:1–34)

The final chapter of the book of Jeremiah is something like a postscript. The chapter records the fall of the city and the capture of Zedekiah (vv. 1–16), the destruction of the temple (vv. 17–27), the three Babylonian deportations (vv. 28–30), and, on a positive note, the release of Jehoiachin from prison (vv. 31–34). The chapter thus records the fulfillment of Jeremiah's prophecy and substantiates his claim as a true prophet called by God. The royal Davidic line will survive, and the promised Davidic king will one day emerge (23:5–6; 33:14–16). The appendix closely resembles the narrative of these same events in 2 Kgs 24:18–25:30.

THE THEOLOGICAL CONTRIBUTION OF THE BOOK

Covenant Relationship

More clearly than any other OT prophet Jeremiah preached the brokenness of the covenant and the Lord's resolve to restore it (2:20; 5:5; 7:5–10; 31:31–34; 32:37–41).

---

[22] The Edom oracle (49:7–17) is also found in the book of Obadiah.

God's Sovereignty

With regard to nature and the various nations God shows Himself as completely sovereign. The Lord fills the creation (23:24), sends rain (5:24; 14:22), and controls the sea (5:22). He knows the thoughts of everyone (17:5–11). He delivers nations into the hands of whomever He wishes (27:5–6). The success of Nebuchadnezzar was not because of his military prowess but because of God's will (27:6). The well-being of all nations is God's concern. The principle that explains God's relationship with all nations is stated in 18:7–10.

The Word of God

As perhaps with no other prophet, God's word is preeminent in Jeremiah. God's words have both a creative and destructive power (1:12; 4:28). They are powerful, self-authenticating, and overwhelming (23:9). Jeremiah could not resist them (20:8–9). God's word was in his mouth just as it was with Moses (1:9; Deut 18:18).

God's covenant people were to demonstrate implicit obedience to God's word (Jer 2:2; 7:1–11; 31:1–6). The knowledge of God comes through His word and is demonstrated by obedience to covenant stipulations.

THE NEW TESTAMENT AND THE BOOK

To illustrate the sovereignty of God in human affairs the apostle Paul cited the analogy of the potter from Jer 18:1–12 in Rom 9:20–24. In addition Stephen may have been alluding to Jeremiah's message when he referred to his fellow Israelites as uncircumcised in heart and ear (Acts 7:51; Jer 6:10; 9:26). Jeremiah 31:31–34 quoted in Heb 8:8–12 is the most distinctive of all the NT quotations of Jeremiah; this passage is the most extensive OT quotation in the NT.

The new covenant, God said, will supersede the old (Mosaic) covenant in that it will guarantee obedience to the law as being written on the heart. Moses anticipated this internal work of the Lord when he spoke of the hearts of God's people being transformed (Deut 6:6; 30:6).

This new covenant, which promised a united house of Judah and house of Israel, was inaugurated in the NT at the Last Supper, when Jesus said, "This cup is the new covenant established by My blood" (Luke 22:20; see 1 Cor 11:25). The church is now experiencing the benefits of the new covenant (the forgiveness of sin, Jer 31:34), but other aspects of the new covenant, particularly those promises given to the nation of Israel, will not be realized until the second coming of Christ. With that event the unconditional promises to Abraham (31:35–37) will be realized.[23]

APPENDIX—JEREMIAH 27:5–22
(MT additions in italics)[24]

(5) I have made the earth, *the man and the beasts which are upon the face of the earth*, by my great power and outstretched arm, and give it to whom I please. (6) *And now* I have given all these lands [LXX, the earth] into the hand of Nebuchadnezzar . . . (7) *And all nations shall serve him and his son and his son's son, till the time of his land comes also, and mighty nations and great kings make him their servant.* (8) And the nation and kingdom which will not *serve him,*

---

[23] See W. C. Kaiser Jr., *Toward an Old Testament Theology* (Zondervan: Zondervan, 1978), 84–89; and B. Horner, *Future Israel: Why Christian Anti-Judaism Must Be Challenged*, NACSBT (Nashville: B&H, 2007), 226–27.

[24] See W. Robertson, *The Old Testament in the Jewish Church* (New York: D. Appleton, 1892), 104.

Nebuchadnezzar, king of Babylon, and put their neck under the yoke the king of Babylon, will I punish, saith the Lord, with the sword, and with famine, *and with pestilence*, till I have consumed them by his hand. (9) Therefore hearken ye not to your prophets, . . . which say he shall not serve the king of Babylon. (10) For they prophesy lies to you to remove you from your land, *and that I should drive you out and ye should perish.* . .

(12) And to Zedekiah, king of Judah, I spake with all these words, saying, Bring your neck *under the yoke of the king of Babylon,* and *serve him and his people, and live.* (13) *Why will ye die, thou and thy people, by the sword, by famine, and by pestilence, as the Lord hath spoken against the nation that will not* serve the king of Babylon? (14) *Therefore hearken not unto the words of the prophets who speak unto you, saying, Serve not the king of Babylon;* for they prophesy lies unto you. (15) For I have not sent them, saith the Lord, and they prophesy lies in my name. . .

(16) And to the priests and to all his people [LXX, to all the people and priests] I spake saying, Thus saith the Lord, Hearken not to the words of your prophets who prophesy to you, saying, Behold the vessels of the house of the Lord shall be brought back from Babylon *now quickly,* for they prophesy a lie unto you. (17) *Hearken not unto them* [LXX, I have not sent them], *serve the king of Babylon, and live; wherefore should this city be laid waste?* (18) But if they are prophets, and if the word of the Lord is with them, let them intercede with the Lord of Hosts [LXX, with me], *that the vessels which are left in the house of the Lord, and the house of the king of Judah, and in Jerusalem, come not to Babylon.* (19) For thus saith the Lord *of Hosts concerning the pillars and the sea and the bases,* and the rest of the vessels left in this city, (20) Which *Nebuchadnezzar* the king of Babylon took not when he carried Jeconiah *son of Jehoiakim king of Judah* captive from Jerusalem *to Babylon, and all the nobles of Judah and Jerusalem;* (21) *For thus saith the Lord of Hosts, the God of Israel, concerning the vessels left in the house of God, and in the house of the king of Judah and Jerusalem;* (22) They shall be taken to Babylon, *and there they shall be unto the day that I visit them,* saith the Lord; *then will I bring them up and restore them to this place.*

STUDY QUESTIONS

1. What is the longest prophetic book in the Bible?
2. How long was Jeremiah's prophetic ministry?
3. What are some of the more important events that occurred during Jeremiah's prophecy?
4. What type of literary forms are in the book of Jeremiah?
5. What is the most frequent literary form in Jeremiah?
6. Comment on the structure of Jeremiah.
7. What flagrant sin did Jeremiah address early in the book?
8. Where did Jeremiah go after he left Israel?
9. What information do we learn from the appendix of Jeremiah?
10. What attribute of God is prominent in the book of Jeremiah?
11. What use does NT make of the prophecy of Jeremiah?
12. Where does the most extensive quotation of Jeremiah occur in the NT?

FOR FURTHER STUDY

Archer, G. L. "The Relationship Between the Septuagint Translation and the Massoretic Text in Jeremiah." *TJ* NS (1991): 139–50.

Bright, J. *Jeremiah.* New York: Doubleday, 1965.

Childs, B. *Introduction to the Old Testament as Scripture*. Philadelphia: Fortress, 1979.

Dumbrell, W. J. *Covenant and Creation*. Nashville: Thomas Nelson, 1984.

Gordon, R. P. *"The Place Is Too Small for Us": The Israelite Prophets in Recent Scholarship*. Winona Lake, IN.: Eisenbrauns, 1995.

McComiskey, T. E. *The Covenants of Promise*. Grand Rapids: Baker, 1985.

McConville, J. G. "Jeremiah." In *Theological Interpretation of the Old Testament*. Edited by K. J. Vanhoozer, 211–20. Grand Rapids: Baker, 2008.

Robertson, W. *The Old Testament in the Jewish Church*. New York: D. Appleton, 1892.

Rosenberg, J. "Jeremiah and Ezekiel." In *The Literary Guide to the Bible*. Edited by R. Alter and F. Kermode. Cambridge, Harvard University Press, 1987.

Seitz, C. R. "The Prophet Moses and the Canonical Shape of Jeremiah." *ZAW* 101 (1989): 3–27.

———. *Theology in Conflict: Reactions to the Exile in the Book of Jeremiah*. BZAW 176. Berlin: de Gruyter, 1989.

Thompson, J. A. *The Book of Jeremiah*. NICOT. Grand Rapids: Eerdmans, 1980.

Weinfeld, M. *Deuteronomy and the Deuteronomic School*. 1972; reprint, Winona Lake, IN: Eisenbrauns, 1992.

Yates, G. "Narrative Parallelism and the Jehoiakim Frame: A Reading Strategy for Jeremiah 26–45." *JETS* 48 (2005): 263–81.

CHAPTER 25

THE BOOK OF EZEKIEL

MARK F. ROOKER

EZEKIEL, SON OF Buzi, was among the 8,000 citizens of Jerusalem deported to Babylon when King Nebuchadnezzar conquered the city in 598 BC (2 Kgs 24:10–17). Ezekiel's call to be a prophet occurred five years later (the fifth year of King Jehoiachin's exile),[1] in the year 593, while he was living at Tel-abib[2] near the Chebar river in Babylon. He received his call at the age of 30 (Ezek 1:1), the year he would have begun his official duty as a priest had he still been living in Jerusalem (Num 4:3).[3] The last dated oracle occurs in the twenty-seventh year of King Jehoiachin (Ezek 29:17), thus giving Ezekiel a ministry of 22 to 23 years. Ezekiel, like Jeremiah, thus witnessed the greatest crisis in Israel's history: the final destruction of Jerusalem and the temple and the exile of the leading citizens to Babylon. He began his prophetic ministry shortly after Jeremiah began to prophesy, and like Jeremiah he called for the Jews to submit to the Babylonians (12:1–15; 17:1–21; 21:18–32).

The physical conditions of the exiles in Babylon may have been quite comfortable for many of the Jews. Unlike the Assyrians, the Babylonians were apparently happy with allowing conquered foes to maintain a civil existence providing they did not plot insurrections against their conquerors. In fact after the exile many Jews decided to remain in Babylon where they became quite successful. A Jewish academic society was established from which the Babylonian Talmud was conceived and produced.

The book of Ezekiel was considered one of the canonical books of the OT called the Antilogoumena, "disputed books." The reason some opposed its acceptance into the canon was because it seemed to conflict with the law of Moses on a number of accounts. For example the law required the offering of two bulls, seven lambs, and one ram at the new moon offering

---

[1] A Babylonian tablet listed provisions for the support of Jehoiachin as a state prisoner (*ANET*, 308; cf. 2 Kgs 25:27–30).

[2] Tel-abib means "mound of the flood," indicating an Assyrian or Babylonian tradition that a primeval deluge took place in the vicinity.

[3] The view that the thirtieth year refers to the prophet's age goes back to the time of Origen. An alternative early view is expressed in the Targum of Jonathan which relates the thirtieth year to the thirtieth year after Josiah's reform in 622 BC.

(Num 28:11). The book of Ezekiel on the other hand prescribed only one unblemished bull, six lambs, and one ram (Ezek 46:6).

THE COMPOSITION OF THE BOOK

Until the twentieth century there was a virtual consensus regarding the literary unity and integrity of the book of Ezekiel. S. R. Driver's comments well illustrate the scholarly unanimity regarding the book: "No critical question arises in connection with the authorship of the book, the whole from beginning to end bearing unmistakably the stamp of a single mind."[4] This literary unity was due in no small part to the various visions that divide the book into broad sections as well as the series of dates that suggest that the organization of the book was arranged according to an overall plan.

The consensus began to change rapidly, however, with the publication of Gustav Hölscher's work on Ezekiel in 1924.[5] Relying on recent studies such as that of Richard Kraetzschmar,[6] who argued that the first-person and third-person narratives were parallel recensions, Hölscher launched an attack on the traditional Ezekielian authorship of the book. He argued that the only material that came from Ezekiel was the poetic sayings distributed throughout the book, which was about one-seventh of the book. Later, a fifth-century redactor transformed the work into a form close to its present shape. Six years later in 1930 American scholar C. C. Torrey proposed that the book of Ezekiel was a complete fiction written in the Seleucid period (third century BC).[7] Other significant publications in the mid-twentieth century included the extreme positions of Millar Burrows, who argued that the book of Ezekiel was largely composed in the late pre-Maccabean period (shortly before 167 BC), and James Smith, who maintained the book was composed in the northern kingdom after the fall of Samaria in 722 BC. William Irwin in reaction to King Manasseh's abuses (687–642 BC),[8] on the other hand, closely followed Hölsher's method of attributing only poetic statements to Ezekiel (251 vv.) and insisted that the writing of the book took place in Jerusalem, not among the exiles in Babylon.[9] Other scholars who argued for a Palestinian origin for the composition included John Hartford, I. G. Mathews, Volkmar Herntrich, and John Smith.

After World War II the pendulum began to swing back to a more conservative position. Scholars such as G. A. Cooke, M. Schmidt, Carl G. Howie, Walther Zimmerli, Walther Eichrodt, and H. H. Rowley maintained that Ezekiel prophesied among the deported exiles, as the book attests. Carl Howie and Georg Fohrer focused on the stylistic elements of the book, including the dates and the unique subject matter of the book.[10] Still many scholars maintained that the book experienced a long history of composition and editorial activity. Sections of the book that were viewed with the most skepticism were the visions of Gog in chaps. 38–39 and the new temple and land division in chaps. 40–48. The real impetus toward the resurgence for the respect of the book, however, came from Zimmerli's two-volume commentary.[11]

---

[4] S. R. Driver, *Introduction to the Literature of the Old Testament*, 9th ed. (Edinburgh: T&T Clark, 1913), 279.

[5] G. Hölscher, *Hesekiel, der Dicter und Das Buch*, BZAW 39 (Giessen: Töpelmann, 1924).

[6] R. Kraetzschmar, *Das Buch Ezechiel* (Göttingen: Vandenhoeck & Ruprecht, 1900).

[7] C. C. Torrey, *Pseudo-Ezekiel and the Original Prophecy* (New Haven, CT: Yale University Press, 1930).

[8] M. Burrows, *The Literary Relations of Ezekiel* (Philadelphia JPS, 1925), 105; and J. Smith, *The Book of the Prophet Ezekiel* (London: SPCK, 1931), x.

[9] W. Irwin, *The Problem of Ezekiel: An Inductive Study* (Chicago: University of Chicago Press, 1943).

[10] C. G. Howie, *The Date and Composition of Ezekiel* (Philadelphia: SBL, 1950); and G. Fohrer, *Die Hauptprobleme des Buches Ezechiel* (Berlin: Albel Topelmann, 1952).

[11] W. Zimmerli, *Ezekiel*, Hermeneia, 2 vols. (Minneapolis: Fortress, 1979, 1983).

Zimmerli subjected the contents of Ezekiel to a thorough form-critical and traditio-critical investigation and was able to demonstrate that Ezekiel was the beneficiary of a long history of Israelite literary tradition, including the exodus and election themes as well as the legal sections of the Holiness Code (Leviticus 17–26). He also maintained that he could isolate Ezekiel's very words throughout the book. The later developments of the book, he explained, were because of Ezekiel's school of disciples. Thus Zimmerli's work was somewhat of a watershed study in which the pendulum swung back from the position that attributed virtually nothing to the prophet, to a position that ascribed a majority of the material to Ezekiel. Subsequent studies by Lawrence Boadt (1980), B. Lang (1981), and Moshe Greenberg (1983) went even further than Zimmerli in seeing greater unity in the book based on the literary style and historical arrangement.

There is sufficient reason for maintaining that the prophet Ezekiel composed the book of Ezekiel while in Babylon. The Hebrew language used throughout the book fits well in the language strata of the exilic period, not the postexilic period.[12] The work exhibits such homogeneity and literary coherence that it is reasonable to assert that all editorial work on the book was carried out by the prophet himself.

The occurrence of 14 historical dates attached to the beginning of many of the various oracles and prophecies of Ezekiel is another important unifying factor. The book of Ezekiel along with Haggai and Zechariah uses more dates than any other prophetic book. The dates fall into two categories. Several dates in the book introduce oracles against foreign nations, and other dates introduce major moments in Ezekiel's prophetic ministry. With a few exceptions each date is later than the preceding one, thus revealing that the book of Ezekiel is one of the most chronologically ordered books of the Bible. The following is a list of the dates that introduce various oracles in the book.

	Year	Month	Day
1:1–2	5	4	5
8:1	6	6	5
20:1	7	5	10
24:1	9	10	10
26:1	11		1
29:1	10	10	12
29:17	27	1	1
30:20	11	1	7
31:1	11	3	1
32:1	12	12	1
32:17	12		15
33:21	12	10	5
40:1	25	1	10

The occurrence of visions throughout the book (chaps. 1, 8–11, 40–48) is a strong argument in favor of the overall unity of the book. Many factors suggest that the book is a unity and, as Driver reasoned early in the twentieth century, the book bears "the stamp of a single mind."

---

[12] M. F. Rooker, *Biblical Hebrew in Transition: The Language of the Book of Ezekiel*, JSOTSup (Sheffield: JSOT Press, 1990). See E. Sellin and G. Fohrer, *Introduction to the Old Testament*, trans. D. E. Green (Nashville: Abingdon, 1968), 407.

Another argument for the unity of the book is seen in the stylistic features that occur throughout the book.

THE STYLE OF THE BOOK

Stylistic features throughout the book also argue for the unity of the book. The phrase "the son of man" occurs 93 times throughout the book as a title for Ezekiel, thus focusing on the prophet's human nature. This humble status is meant to contrast with the awesome presence of God's glory at the beginning of the book (Ezekiel 1). The expression "the hand of the LORD was upon me," which is said only of Elijah (1 Kgs 18:46) and Elisha (2 Kgs 3:15), occurs in the various major sections of Ezekiel (1:3; 3:22; 33:22; 37:1). The so-called recognition formula, "that you [or they] will know that I am the LORD," which echoes the work of the Lord in the exodus (Exod 6:6–8; 7:5; 10:2; 14:4,18), occurs 54 times in Ezekiel.[13] The introductory oracle clause, "Then the word of the LORD came to me saying," occurs 46 times in the book and alerts the reader to the beginning of a new section. The words "I, the LORD, have spoken" also occurs frequently in Ezekiel (5:13,15,17; 17:21,24; 22:14; 24:14; 26:14; 30:12; 36:36; 37:14).[14]

Another feature for which Ezekiel is well known is his performance of the following symbolic actions.

	Sign actions
3:22–27	Ezekiel's dumbness
4:1–3	Sketches Jerusalem on a brick
4:4–8	Lies on left side 390 days, on right side 40 days
4:9–17	Eats rations baked over dung
5:1–12	Shaves head and divides the hair into three parts
12:1–12	Digs through a wall with exile's baggage
21:18–23	Creates a route with crossroads for Babylonian king to decide
24:15–24	Ezekiel's wife dies
33:21–22	Ezekiel's dumbness removed

All these actions are meant to exhibit the sin of Israel and the impending siege of Jerusalem and the exile of her people.

Another literary technique employed by the prophet is one of allegory.[15] The allegories in the first major section of the book include Jerusalem as a vine (chap. 15), majestic eagles (17:1–21), Davidic dynasty as a lioness (19:1–9) and a vineyard (19:10–14), the sword as judgment (21:1–17), Oholah and Oholibah as corrupt Samaria and Jerusalem (23:1–35), and the caldron of destruction (24:1–14).[16]

---

[13] The root *yāda'* "to know," occurs in the book of Ezekiel more than in any other Bible book (W. Zimmerli, *I Am Yahweh*, trans. D. W. Scott [Atlanta: John Knox, 1982], 31).

[14] For a comprehensive list of characteristic phrases in Ezekiel see Driver, *An Introduction to the Literature of the Old Testament*, 297–98.

[15] See Sellin and Fohrer, *Introduction to the Old Testament*, 409, and D. Block, *The Book of Ezekiel, Chapters 1–24*, NICOT (Grand Rapids: Eerdmans, 1997), 15–16.

[16] W. LaSor, D. A. Hubbard, and F. Bush, *Old Testament Survey*, 2nd ed. (Grand Rapids: Eerdmans, 1996), 360.

Another characteristic of Ezekiel is the citation of previously written Scripture.[17] This is evident in the judgment oracles in chaps. 4–5, which depend heavily on the curses listed in Leviticus 26. Ezekiel is also aware of other portions of canonical Scripture including Num 18:1–7,22–23 (Ezek 44:9–16) and Zeph 3:1–4 (Ezek 22:25–29).[18]

THE TEXT OF THE BOOK

The MT and LXX of Ezekiel have several differences that have led some to conclude that the book was attested as two separate recensions as in the case of the book of Jeremiah. The LXX is estimated to be 4–5 percent shorter than the MT. Possibly the MT represents an expanded text that is later than the text represented by the Hebrew *Vorlage* of the LXX. For some scholars this means that the LXX was the earlier and more original text. On the other hand possibly the LXX translators shortened some longer passages to make them clearer for the Greek audience.

The LXX is clearly the work of more than one translator; it is not a homogeneous translation. However, it does characteristically omit repetitious words and phrases that occur in the MT. The numerous fragments of Ezekiel found among the DSS all bear a resemblance to the MT over against the LXX.

THE MESSAGE OF THE BOOK

The message of the book of Ezekiel revolves around the pivotal event in the book and in the history of Israel, namely, the fall of Jerusalem in 586 BC. Before announcing the fall of Jerusalem, Ezekiel's message is characterized by judgment. In his scathing review of Israelite history Ezekiel exposed the moral depravity and absence of spiritual concern in the nation (2:1–8; 8:7–18; chap. 13; 17:1–21; 20:1–32). Like Amos and Jeremiah Ezekiel also accused the inhabitants of Judah and Jerusalem of being guilty of sins against their countrymen (7:23; 9:9; 22:6–13,25–29). Then Jerusalem was destroyed and the nation was in exile. Ezekiel's message changed to a message of hope. He affirmed that God will give His people a new heart and a new spirit to enable them to be faithful and thus avoid a future judgment (11:17–20; 36:26–28). The Lord will establish a new temple and a new worship for the people (chaps. 40–48) once they are restored. The very arrangement of the book with the announcement of judgments in the beginning and the declaration of restoration at the end suggests that Ezekiel's message is ultimately one of hope.

THE STRUCTURE OF THE BOOK

As noted above, Ezekiel's message moves from judgment to hope after the destruction of Jerusalem in 586 BC. This destruction is announced in Ezek 33:21. The oracles of judgment against the foreign nations precede this announcement and are also part of the message of hope, as the prophet announced that Israel's perennial enemies would soon be punished. It is logical to connect chaps. 25–32 with 33–48 as the announcement of judgment on Israel's enemies (chaps. 25–32) could be a source of comfort for the nation. Thus many have suggested that the book be outlined based on a twofold division of two equal halves, chaps. 1–24

---

[17] Thus Y. Kaufmann, *History of the Religion of Israel*, vol. 3 (in Hb.) (Jerusalem: Bailik Institute-DeVir [1947]), 534–42; and B. Childs, *An Introduction to the Old Testament as Scripture* (Philadelphia: Fortress, 1979), 364. Surprisingly Job sides with Zimmerli that the author of Leviticus and Ezekiel were both relying on a common source rather than recognizing that Ezekiel was addressing the Israelites under the authority of the OT law (J. Job, "Ezekiel, Theology of," in *NIDOTTE*, ed. W. VanGemeren [Grand Rapids: Zondervan, 1997], 4:632).

[18] See Rooker, *Biblical Hebrew in Transition: The Language of the Book of Ezekiel*, 60–64.

and chaps. 25–48. It could be argued that this division was assumed by the Jewish historian Josephus, who stated that Ezekiel left behind "two books," not just one. The book records two commissioning scenes (chaps. 3 and 33), and in both passages Ezekiel's responsibility is likened to that of a watchman over Israel.[19] Like a watchman, Ezekiel was to announce warnings, whether the people followed them or not. Both of these commissioning reports also include a reference to Ezekiel's dumbness. In 3:26–27 Ezekiel was to be dumb until the day Jerusalem falls (cf. 24:25–27). And in 33:21–22 he was released from dumbness when it was officially announced that Jerusalem had fallen to the Babylonians.

Another method for dividing the prophecy is based on the series of visions in the book. In chap. 1 are visions of God, chaps. 8–11 record visions of the temple, and chaps. 40–48 convey Ezekiel's vision of the new temple.[20] In all of these visions Ezekiel saw the glory of God: first it was among the exiles in Babylon, then it was departing the city of Jerusalem (11:22–23), and finally returning to the temple from the east (43:2–4). In the final return of God's glory mention is made of the two previous appearances (43:3).[21]

Another popular way to survey the contents of the book of Ezekiel is based on a three-part division: the announcement of judgment on Judah and Jerusalem (chaps. 1–24), the oracles against the nations (chaps. 25–32), and the announcement of hope for Judah (chaps. 33–48). The backbone of all the literary divisions is the chronological framework provided by the 14 dates interspersed throughout the book.

THE OUTLINE OF THE BOOK

I. **Announcements of Judgment on Judah and Jerusalem (chaps. 1–24)**
    A. Throne-Chariot Vision and the Call of Ezekiel (1:1–3:21)
    B. Symbolic Acts of the Doom of Jerusalem (3:22–7:27)
    C. The Temple Abandoned by God (chaps. 8–11)
    D. Symbolic Acts and Prophecies of Woe against Israel (chaps. 12–24)
        1. Demonstration of the Exile (12:1–20)
        2. The False Leaders (12:21–15:8)
        3. The Spiritual History of Israel (chap. 16)
        4. The Unfaithful King (chap. 17)
        5. Individual Responsibility (chap. 18)
        6. Lamentation for Princes of Israel (chap. 19)
        7. The End Is in Sight (chaps. 20–24)

II. **Hope and Restoration for Judah and Jerusalem (chaps. 25–48)**
    A. Oracles Against Foreign Nations (chaps. 25–32)
        1. Ammon (25:1–7)
        2. Moab (25:8–11)
        3. Edom (25:12–14)
        4. Philistia (25:15–17)
        5. Tyre (26:1–28:19)

---

[19] The image of a watchman for the role of an OT prophet was common (Isa 56:10; Jer 6:17; Hos 9:8; Hab 2:1) (P. House, *Old Testament Theology* [Downers Grove, IL: InterVarsity, 1998], 330). Also the clause, "They will know that a prophet has been among them," is in Ezek 2:5 and 33:33.

[20] Josephus, *Ant.* 10.5 § 1.

[21] H. V. D. Parunak divides the entire prophecy into three sections based on the three major visions in the book ("The Literary Architecture of Ezekiel's *Mar'ôt 'Ĕlôhîm*," *JBL* 99 [1980]: 61–74).

THE CONTENTS OF THE BOOK

I. Announcements of Judgment on Judah and Jerusalem (chaps. 1–24)

The book of Ezekiel opens with a visionary appearance of God to the prophet Ezekiel who is exiled in Babylon. The prophet has a vision of God arriving in a fiery storm seated on a mobile throne with four sets of wheels supported by living creatures. With their wings the four creatures move about unrestricted. Above the throne is one seated who has the likeness of human form and is surrounded by brightness similar to a rainbow. In observing this manifestation of God Ezekiel was so overwhelmed that his description of what he saw alters his use of language. The prophet was so astounded that he used ungrammatical statements in describing God's appearance.[22] In describing what is indescribable he used phrases such as "the likeness of," "the appearance of," and "resembling." This vision assured Ezekiel and the people that though they were in a foreign land, a thousand miles from the holy city of Jerusalem, they had not been abandoned by God. The association of the presence of God with a cloud has been a common occurrence in Israel's history ever since the deliverance from Egypt. God appeared as a cloud of fire by night and a pillar of cloud by day (Exod 14:19–20,24; Num 10:11–12,34) and was manifested as a cloud and fire in the dedication of Solomon's temple (2 Chr 5:14; 7:3).

This magnificent theophany is also part of the prophet's call to his prophetic ministry. It was in the context of this vision (cf. Isaiah 6), that Ezekiel received his call. Ezekiel was instructed to consume a scroll that contains the message of "lamentations, mourning, and woe" written on both sides (Ezek 2:10). The content of this scroll indicated that Ezekiel was to be a prophet of judgment (2:3–5; 3:5–7).

The opening vision is followed by a group of four signs performed by Ezekiel in which he depicted the siege of Jerusalem (chap. 4; 5:1–4). In describing these sign-acts to indicate the nation's sinfulness Ezekiel often alluded to the covenant curses of Leviticus 26. Ezekiel 6 and 7 focus on the assurance of God's coming wrath and announce that the end has come (7:2–3,6,24).

Ezekiel's second vision of God (chaps. 8–11) occurred one year and one month after his initial chariot vision. In this vision he was transported in visions to Jerusalem (8:3) and then returned in the same way to the exiles (11:24). In this vision the four living creatures in God's chariot vision (chap. 1) are identified as cherubim (9:3). This vision has the function of formally indicting the nation for its abominations, especially in the temple. Although God was

---

[22] M. Greenberg, *Ezekiel 1–20*, AB (New York: Doubleday, 1983), 43–44.

still in Jerusalem, Ezekiel witnessed four horrible scenes of idolatrous behavior in the vicinity of the temple. This indicates that the nation had been rejected by God as He now departed from their presence.

This second great vision ends with words of hope and salvation for the exiles (11:14–21). Those who had been left behind in Jerusalem claimed that they had sole possession of the land (11:15). However, the promise of salvation was directed only to the exiles. Later in 33:23–29 the claim of those who had been left behind that the land of Israel belonged to them is again rejected and their idolatry is exposed.

After this word of hope (11:14–21) Ezekiel returned to his sign-demonstrations that depict the siege and exile (12:1–20). Chapters 12–24 should be seen as a unit. This is reinforced by the observation that Ezekiel himself was the sign at both the beginning and the end of the section (12:6,11; 24:24,27). His message was that judgment will not wait for the distant future but was at hand (12:21–13:23), and that Jerusalem had become so sinful that destruction was imminent (14:12–15:8).

In Ezekiel 18 the prophet was addressing the issue of who was responsible for the judgment the nation was experiencing. Based on the axiom that sin may be visited on one's descendants (Exod 20:5), the exiles attempted to shift the blame for their predicament to their forefathers. Ezekiel corrected this faulty teaching asserting that no individual is accountable for another's sins and that he is responsible for his own guilty deeds. Though repentance could not avert judgment on Jerusalem, it would result in life for the exilic community.

The sign-actions in chaps. 21–24 (21:9–12,23–29; 24:15–24) all indicated that the end was about to come on Jerusalem. In the last sign-action Ezekiel himself had become the sign (24:24). He was forbidden to mourn for his wife as a sign to the nation. Mourning the destruction of the nation would not be appropriate because this judgment was appropriate and deserved.[23] The sudden death of Ezekiel's wife and the Lord's instruction that he show no signs of remorse concludes the section (24:15–27).

II. Hope and Restoration for Judah and Jerusalem (chaps. 25–48)

Oracles Against the Nations

The day of God's judgment will not be visited on Judah only. Nations other than Judah will experience God's judgment. The nations fall into three groups: Judah's neighbors (chap. 25), Tyre (chaps. 26–28), and Egypt (chaps. 29–32). First, the neighbors of Judah—Ammon, Moab, Edom, Philistia—were about to experience God's judgment. These nations had mistreated Israel (25:3,8,12,15; 26:2), perhaps had profited from her recent plight, and had acted arrogantly before the Lord. In chaps. 29–32 Egypt is singled out for judgment. Egypt is isolated perhaps because it was to Egypt that Judah had often looked as an ally during the troubled times in the last days before the exile (29:16). Through this punishment the Lord's own people will be vindicated and restored. One of the purposes of the oracles against the nations is encouragement to Israel.

Seven of these oracles are dated, placing them between the tenth and twelfth years of Jehoiachin's exile (29:17–21 is the only exception). Thus the oracles were delivered at the same time Jerusalem was experiencing the Babylonian siege. The oracles presume that God's

---

[23] See T. Renz, "Ezekiel," in *Theological Interpretation of the Old Testament*, ed. K. Vanhoozer (Grand Rapids: Baker Academic, 2008), 227.

standards apply to everyone. Even amidst these judgment oracles salvation was promised to Israel (28:24–26).

Announcements of Restoration for Israel

The final major section of Ezekiel begins in chap. 33. However several clear flashbacks to the previous sections of the prophecy are integrated throughout: (a) Ezekiel 33:1–9 corresponds with 3:16–21; (b) 33:10–20 corresponds to chap. 18; (c) 33:21–22 with 3:25–27; 24:25–27; (d) 33:23–29 with 11:14–21; (e) 33:30–33 with 2:3–5 and 24:24.

In the promise of restoration the Lord assured the nation that the Davidic covenant will be renewed. This Messiah, in contrast to many of Israel's previous kings, will walk in fellowship with the Lord and His reign will be characterized by righteousness and justice (34:24; 37:15–25).

The promise of a new heart that will be responsive to God's will (36:26) has an earlier parallel in 11:19. The people will be repentant, but only God Himself can bring this about. The restoration will vindicate the Lord's name (36:22–23), and this restoration of the nation will be like a resurrection from the dead (37).[24]

The judgment announced on Gog and Magog in chaps. 38–39 differs from that of the judgment oracles against the nations in chaps. 25–32. The invasion of the land by Gog, the foe from the north (38:15; 39:2), moves beyond the simple judgment theme on a nation to an eschatological scheme that goes beyond Israel's contemporary experience and represents God's future judgment on all nations that oppose Israel. For this reason many have seen in this description the early stages of the development of apocalyptic literature.

Visions of the Restored Community

With the final glorious vision of the return of the glory of the Lord the book of Ezekiel reaches its climax. And yet this account of the vision is not surprising. Many of the themes and motifs presented in chaps. 1–39 are repeated and expanded in this final vision. The vision of the restored land and program of worship has been prepared particularly by the reference in 37:25–28. There the nation had been promised not only that they would have a sanctuary forever,[25] but that the temple would be a means by which the nations could know the Lord.

The third vision of God in Ezekiel 43 marks the return of God to His people as He returned to the newly restored temple, taking up residence with them once again. It thus corresponds to the two visions in chaps. 1–3 and 8–11. In chaps. 8–11 the prophet saw the glory of the Lord depart from the desecrated temple (11:22–23), but now the glory returned to the new holy temple through the same east gate through which it had earlier departed (43:1–2). In 40:1–43:12 the plan of the temple is described. Details are given regarding the size of the altar (43:13–17) and instructions for its dedication (43:18–27). The offerings and cultic regulations are given in 45:9–46:24.

Each of the 12 tribes is allotted an equal portion of land but with different geographical boundaries than those that were allotted in the time of Joshua (47:13–48:29). The new tribal divisions are arranged around the centralized temple (47:13–23). The sea flows down from Jerusalem and enriches the vegetation of the land. Because the Lord has returned to the temple, the prophet can declare, "The LORD is there" (48:35 NIV).

---

[24] The vision of the revival of the dead bones in 37:1–14 has a parallel in the song earlier in the book at 24:1–14. In the latter passage there is a fourfold reference to bones preparing for the vision of the dead bones.

[25] See M. Greenberg, "The Design and Themes of Ezekiel's Program of Blessing," *Int* 38 (1984): 182.

Interpretation of Ezekiel 40–48

It is clear that when the nation of Israel returned to Palestine following Cyrus's decree (539 BC) the transformation described in Ezekiel 40–48 did not take place. A temple was built, but it was not according to the plans described in this vision.[26] The tribes were not resettled according to the allotments, and the terrain of the Dead Sea did not change.

Three explanations of the interpretation of Ezekiel 40–48 are possible. One explanation is that the vision in Ezekiel 40–48 has not been fulfilled but will be fulfilled at the second advent of Jesus Christ. According to this view the prophecy will be fulfilled when Christ will reign on the earth for a thousand years in the millennium. This position is held by many, but is often criticized for not allowing for the symbolic and spiritual dimensions of the vision to have their appropriate symbolic function.

Another position is that these words were fulfilled but in an unexpected way in the postexilic period. The description of the temple and the land transformation were not to be fulfilled literally, but rather address the issue of restoration and renewed worship but in a figurative sense.[27] Advocates of this view note that this genre is early apocalyptic, and the chapters predict the messianic age in highly symbolic terms. The prophecy was fulfilled in part by the historical reconstruction of the temple, but certainly did not exhaust the transformational changes described in the vision. It will be fulfilled completely in the future.

Another approach, which focuses on the symbolic nature of the vision, takes the fulfillment literally but understands that the prophecy was actually fulfilled in the church age through the coming of Christ. The age of the church is described in terms of the temple. Jesus' use of the temple symbolism for His resurrection (John 2:18–22) and John's equating the presence of God with the temple of the New Jerusalem (Rev 21:22) are cited as support for this interpretation. Advocates of this view stress the symbolical nature of the vision, but in doing so they remove the historical nature of the prophecy.

THE THEOLOGY OF THE BOOK

Six major features of the Lord's work on Israel's behalf can be gleaned from the book of Ezekiel: (1) the Lord will regather His scattered people (11:16–17; 20:41; 34:11–13a,16; 36:24a; 37:21a); (2) the Lord will bring the nation back to their land and will cleanse it from defilement (11:17b–18; 20:42; 34:13b–15; 36:24b; 37:21b); (3) the Lord will give His people a new heart and a new spirit so they can walk in His ways (11:19–20; 16:62; 36:25–28; 37:23–24; (4) the Lord will restore the Davidic dynasty (34:23–24; 37:22–25); (5) the Lord will bless Israel with unprecedented prosperity and security in their land (34:25–29; 36:29–30; 37:26; chaps. 38–39); and (6) the Lord will establish His permanent residence in their midst (37:26b–28; chaps. 40–48).[28]

Ezekiel's distinctive clause "You will know that I am the LORD" is rooted in the tradition of the exodus and the conquest. The Lord declared to Moses "I am the LORD" to assure him that He is true to His promises. The clause is given a new twist in Ezekiel because there it is also employed in contexts to justify the Lord's wrath against Israel.

---

[26] Kraetzschmar, *Das Buch Ezechiel*, 263.

[27] See D. Block, "Ezekiel, Theology of," in *NIDOTTE*, ed. W. VanGemeren (Grand Rapids: Zondervan, 1997), 4: 627.

[28] Adapted from ibid., 625.

THE NEW TESTAMENT AND THE BOOK

Though there are not many quotations of Ezekiel in the NT, perhaps the structure of the book of Revelation, which begins with a vision of Christ, can be traced directly to Ezekiel. Also the end of the book of Revelation reflects the end of Ezekiel where a river flows from the presence of God (Ezek 47:1–12; Rev 21:1–22:5). Moreover, depicting the return of the exiles as a resurrection from the dead is analogous to Paul's concept of regeneration (Eph 2:5).[29]

STUDY QUESTIONS

1. In what country was Ezekiel living when he carried out his prophetic ministry?
2. What OT prophet was a contemporary of Ezekiel?
3. What does *Antilogoumena* mean?
4. Why did some Jews have a problem with Ezekiel being part of the canon?
5. What are some features of Ezekiel that suggest that the book of Ezekiel is a unified whole?
6. What is the pivotal event in the book of Ezekiel?
7. What is the purpose of Ezekiel's second vision?
8. How was the death of Ezekiel's wife a sign to the nation?
9. What is the purpose of the oracles against the nations in Ezekiel?
10. How does the judgment on Gog and Magog differ from the judgments on the other nations?
11. What constitutes the climax of the book of Ezekiel?
12. How does the third vision of Ezekiel correspond to the two previous visions?
13. What are the major positions regarding the understanding of Ezekiel's temple?

FOR FURTHER STUDY

Block, D. I. *The Book of Ezekiel: Chapters 1–24*. NICOT. Grand Rapids: Eerdmans, 1997.
———. *The Book of Ezekiel: Chapters 25–48*. NICOT. Grand Rapids: Eerdmans, 1997.
———. "Ezekiel: Theology of." In *NIDOTTE*. Edited by W. VanGemeren, 4:615–28. Grand Rapids: Zondervan, 1997.
Craigie, P. C. *Ezekiel*. DSB. Philadelphia: Westminster, 1983.
Fishbane, M. "Sin and Judgment in the Prophecies of Ezekiel." *Int* 38 (1984): 131–50.
Greenberg, Moshe. *Ezekiel 1–20*. AB. Vol. 22. New York: Doubleday, 1983.
———. *Ezekiel 21–37*. AB. Vol. 22a. New York: Doubleday, 1997.
Kaufmann, Y. *History of the Religion of Israel*. Vol. 3 (Hb.). Jerusalem: Bailik Institute-Devir 1947.
Kraetzschmar, R. *Das Buch Ezechiel*. Göttingen: Vandenhoeck & Ruprecht, 1900.
Levenson, J. D. *Theology of the Program of Restoration of Ezekiel 40–48*. HSM. Missoula, MT: Scholars, 1976.
Rooker, M. F. *Biblical Hebrew in Transition: The Language of the Book of Ezekiel*. JSOTSup. Sheffield: JSOT Press, 1990.
Parunak, H. V. D. "The Literary Architecture of Ezekiel's *Mar'ōt 'Ĕlōhîm*." *JBL* 99 (1980): 61–74.
Zimmerli, W. *Ezekiel*. 2 Vols. Translated by R. E. Clements. Philadelphia: Fortress, 1979, 1983.

---

[29] See Job, "Ezekiel: Theology of," 4:634.

CHAPTER 26

THE BOOK OF DANIEL

EUGENE H. MERRILL

THE TITLE OF THE BOOK

The book of Daniel derives its title not from its incipit or contents but from the name of its principal character and likely author. All ancient canonical lists and other references to the book know it by this title.

THE DATE AND AUTHORSHIP OF THE BOOK

The book of Daniel is an account set in the Neo-Babylonian and Persian periods, specifically within the reigns of the Babylonian kings Nebuchadnezzar (605–562 BC) and his minor successors Evil-Merodach (562–560), Neriglissar (560–556), Nabonidus (556–539), and Belshazzar (550–539); and of the Persian rulers Darius the Mede and Cyrus (559–530 BC). The narrative reports that Daniel, with other young Hebrews, was taken captive by the Babylonians in the third year of King Jehoiakim of Judah, which was also the first year of Nebuchadnezzar (Dan 1:1). The last events of the book cannot be dated with precision but can be no later than 530 BC, the date of the death of Cyrus, the last ruler mentioned by name (Dan 6:28). The events of the book therefore span the period from 605 to 530.[1]

Date and authorship are, of course, completely separate issues, but in the case of Daniel strong internal and external evidence exists to support his authorship of the book.[2] Internally the employment of the first-person pronoun occurs in contexts that strongly imply authorship (Dan 7:15; 8:1–8; 9:2,22; 10:2,7,10,12,15,18–19; 11:1; 12:5–8). Externally the vigorous attack against Danielic authorship by the Neo-Platonic philosopher Porphyry (third century AD) presupposes a well-nigh universal consensus that Daniel wrote the book.[3] The supreme example of such a presupposition is the testimony of Jesus, who clearly held to Daniel's

---

[1] For a comprehensive overview of this period see A. Kuhrt, *The Ancient Near East c. 3000—330 BC* (London: Routledge, 1995), 2:603–22, 647–701.

[2] E. J. Young, *An Introduction to the Old Testament* (Grand Rapids: Eerdmans, 1958), 380–93.

[3] R. M. Berchman, *Porphyry against the Christians* (Leiden: Brill, 2005), 58–59.

authorship of the book that bears his name (Matt 24:15). Only a revision of the date of the composition of Daniel based on considerations other than the testimony of the book itself can divest it of its traditional ascription to Daniel of the sixth century BC.[4]

This is precisely the issue at hand. Though the book as a whole admittedly fits well the Babylonian-Persian milieu of the sixth century, the portions that allege to be predictive prophecies are so accurate in their fulfillment that scholars who on whatever grounds are unprepared to concede the possibility of prediction-fulfillment have no recourse but to view such texts as *vaticinia ex eventu*, that is, "predictions" after the fact.[5] This obviously vitiates the historical Daniel's authorship of much of the book and requires both anonymity of authorship and dates of composition much later than the sixth century, in some cases no earlier then around 164 BC.

In addition to this objection of an epistemological nature, other objections (and responses) to an early Danielic authorship are as follows.[6]

1. The book shares the same outlook as the apocryphal and pseudepigraphical literature of the postbiblical period, particularly in its employment of apocalyptic genres. "Outlook," of course, is subjective to the extreme, and yet apocalyptic scholars now recognize that it sprang from much earlier soil than was previously thought, and in both biblical and ANE traditions. Joel and Zechariah, for example, display apocalyptic forms and motifs as does Isaiah 24–27, all of which are conceded to be exilic or even earlier.[7]

2. Daniel's place in the third part of the Hebrew canon—the Kethubîm—has compelled some to assume its lateness on that account. However, much of the wisdom literature is earlier than or contemporary with Daniel as are Lamentations, many of the Psalms, Ezra–Nehemiah, and Chronicles, all of which are in the Kethubîm. Daniel appears there not because it is late but because early Jewish tradition regarded Daniel not as a prophet but as a statesman with prophetic gifts.

3. Ben Sirach (c. 180 BC) fails to mention Daniel as a historical figure (cf. 49:4–13), but he also omits reference to Ezra, all of the judges, Mordecai, and other persons of indisputable historical reality. Lack of reference hardly constitutes proof of nonexistence.

4. Daniel 1:1 speaks of Nebuchadnezzar's invasion of Judah in Jehoiakim's third year, whereas Jer 46:2 dates it to his fourth year. This appears to suggest that the author of Daniel was too far removed from the event to know the precise date. However, the fact is that Jeremiah, in line with Jewish practice of the time, employed the non-accession-year chronology and the Babylonians (whom Daniel served) adopted the accession-year system, thus appearing to date the same events a year earlier.[8]

5. The use of the term *kasdîm* (=Chaldeans) in Dan 2:5,10; 4:7; 5:7,11,30 as a technical term to designate a wisdom class leads some scholars to conclude that the book must be late for that reason. However, the term also occurs with ethnic significance in Dan 5:30 and in Herodotus as a term for the priests of Bel in Babylon as early as the fifth century.[9]

---

[4] For some such considerations see G. L. Archer Jr., "Modern Rationalism and the Book of Daniel," *BSac* 136 (1979): 129–47.

[5] So, e.g., O. Eissfeldt, *The Old Testament: An Introduction* (New York: Harper and Row, 1965), 517.

[6] For the following and other arguments against traditional dates and authorship see ibid., 517–29. For counter arguments to these and other points see the early but still valuable work by R. D. Wilson, *Studies in the Book of Daniel* (New York: Putnam, 1917), 1938.

[7] J. J. Collins, *A Commentary on the Book of Daniel* (Minneapolis: Fortress, 1993), 70–71.

[8] A. R. Millard, "Daniel 1–6 and History," EQ 49 (1977): 68–69; D. J. Wiseman, "Some Historical Problems in the Book of Daniel" in *Notes on Some Problems in the Book of Daniel*, D. J. Wiseman, et al. (London: Tyndale, 1965), 16–18.

[9] Herodotos, *The Histories* (I. 181), trans. Aubrey de Sélincourt (Harmondsworth, UK: Penguin, 1954), 114.

6. The reference to Darius the Mede (Dan 5:30–6:1), unknown otherwise, seems to suggest either a fictitious figure or a confusion by the author with some other ruler. In response, various scholars have offered reasonable solutions to the problem of identification. Some proposals are that Darius was another name for Gubaru, a governor appointed by Cyrus and mentioned in tablets dated from 535 to 525 BC;[10] Ugbaru, a Gutian general who captured Babylon for Cyrus but who died within a few weeks;[11] or Cyrus himself.[12] In any case lack of more precise identification hardly constitutes evidence that Darius the Mede was not a historical figure.

7. The Aramaic of Daniel, once thought to be late Palestinian, is now considered by most linguists to be in the Imperial dialect like that of Ezra and the Elephantine papyri, neither of which is later than the fifth century.[13] Even the Qumran Daniel texts show evidence of the early composition of the autograph such as internal vowel-change passives (i.e., *hophal* rather than prefix *hit*). As a result, many critics now concede that Daniel 2–7 may be third century or earlier, but they continue to insist that Daniel 8–12 must be Maccabean.[14]

8. The presence of some 15 Persian loanwords has been adduced in favor of a late date for Daniel. However, the book itself makes no claim to have originated before the Persian period (539 BC), so one would expect Persian words. The three Greek words—all *Kulterwörten* and therefore universal—actually argue for an early rather than late date because by the Hellenistic period Greek was common in the Levant, so much so that one would expect many more Greek words in Daniel.[15]

The issue is thus fundamentally not one about the languages, *Weltanschauung*, or historical reliability of Daniel but its extensive incorporation of predictive prophecy. If such a phenomenon has no basis in reality, then clearly no case can be made for authorship by Daniel in the sixth century. However, if allowance can be made for a prophet of God to see in advance his outworkings in history, there remains no reason to challenge the ancient tradition of Daniel's setting and its early composition.

THE TEXT OF THE BOOK

The Masoretic tradition for both the Hebrew and Aramaic sections of Daniel is well supported in light of the ancient manuscripts and versions. Qumran attests at least eight manuscripts of Daniel, the earliest (4QDan^c) originating no later than the late second century BC. Among them they bear witness to parts at least of all 12 chapters of Daniel. The divisions between the Hebrew and Aramaic sections at 2:4b and 7:28 are also confirmed in the Qumran texts 1QDan^a and 4QDan^a and 4QDan^b respectively. Collins observes in conclusion that "the Qumran discoveries provide powerful evidence of the antiquity of the textual tradition of the MT."[16]

---

[10] J. C. Whitcomb, *Darius the Mede* (Grand Rapids: Baker, 1959), 23.

[11] W. H. Shea, "Darius the Mede: An Update," *AUSS* 20 (1982): 2237–24; idem, "The Search for Darius the Mede (Concluded), or the Time of the Answer to Daniel's Prayer and the Date of the Death of Darius the Mede," JATS 12/1 (2001): 97–105.

[12] Wiseman, "Some Historical Problems in the Book of Daniel," 12–16.

[13] F. Rosenthal, *A Grammar of Biblical Aramaic* (Wiesbaden: Otto Harrassowitz, 1963), 5–6. See also G. F. Hasel, "The Book of Daniel and Matters of Language: Evidences Relating to Names, Words, and the Aramaic Language," *AUSS* 19 (1981): 211–25.

[14] L. F. Hartman and A. A. DiLella, *The Book of Daniel*, AB (Garden City, NY: Doubleday, 1978), 13–14. See also A. J. Ferch, "The Book of Daniel and the 'Maccabean Thesis,'" *AUSS* 21 (1983): 129–41.

[15] E. M. Yamauchi, *Greece and Babylon* (Grand Rapids: Baker, 1967), 91–94.

[16] Collins, *A Commentary on the Book of Daniel*, 3. See also E. Ulrich, "Daniel Manuscripts from Qumran; Part 1: A Preliminary Edition of 4QDan^a" BASOR 268 (1987):17–37; idem, "Daniel Manuscripts from Qumran; Part 2: Preliminary

The Old Greek (OG) adds the pseudepigraphical The Prayer of Azariah and The Song of the Three Young Men after Dan 3:23. Susanna appears before Daniel 1 in Theodotion and after chap. 12 in OG and the Vulgate. Bel and the Dragon concludes Daniel in both OG and Theodotion. At some unknown (but likely pre-Christian) time Theodotion (or Proto-Theodotion) produced either a correction of OG or a fresh translation of Daniel which by Jerome's time replaced OG in the church.[17] As a result OG largely disappeared until modern times except for a few fragmentary direct or indirect vestiges.

The first Greek translation (OG) dates to the late second century BC and is known primarily through Origen's Hexapla. Now it is attested to in a pre-Hexaplaric text from the early third century AD. This manuscript adheres closely to MT in Daniel 8–12 but attests significant variations elsewhere.[18] Some scholars suggest that the differences reflect a translation of a non-MT *Vorlage*, whereas others attribute them to a highly creative impulse on the translator's part. In any case the NT cites both OG and Theodotion as does Josephus.[19]

As for other versions, the Old Latin is based mainly on Theodotion as are the Ethiopic and Coptic. The Vulgate translates MT but evidences influence from Theodotion as well. The same can be said of the Syriac Peshitta.

THE CANONICITY OF THE BOOK

The book of Daniel is absent from any list of antilegomena (books of suspicious canonicity) and is never otherwise the subject of debate in this respect, at least in pre-Christian times. This fact is incidental evidence for its early date, surely a writing emanating from the late second century BC could hardly gain canonical status by the time the earliest witnesses to the full canon appeared. Furthermore fragments of Daniel from the Cairo Genizah, Qumran, and Masada suggest both the canonicity of the book and its pre-second-century provenience. Finally, the OG translation of Daniel, originating perhaps as early as 150 BC, supports its canonicity and clearly attests to its antiquity.[20]

THE LITERARY FORMS AND STRUCTURE OF THE BOOK[21]

One of the most remarkable features of the book of Daniel is its bilingualism: 1:1–2:4a and 8:1–12:13 are in Hebrew and 2:4b–7:28 are in Aramaic. Scholars differ as to whether it was originally composed as a whole in one language or the other and then translated to its present form or existed in both languages from the beginning. At least some of those who argue for an original Aramaic whole do so because of its alleged second-century origin when Aramaic was the lingua franca of the Mediterranean littoral. Supporters of the view that the book was created as a bilingual work point out that the Aramaic dialect (so-called Imperial Aramaic) was common in the sixth century and that the Aramaic portions of Daniel were produced in that language because of their attention to matters of cosmic, universal interest. The Hebrew

---

Editions of 4QDan[b] and 4QDan,[c]" BASOR 274 (1989): 3–26.

[17] E. Tov, *Textual Criticism of the Hebrew Bible* (Minneapolis: Fortress, 1992), 145, 178–79, 316–17.

[18] See, e.g., Sharon Pace, "The Stratigraphy of the Text of Daniel and the Question of Theological *Tendenz* in the Old Greek," *BIOSCS* 17 (1984):15–35.

[19] Collins, *A Commentary on the Book of Daniel*, 9.

[20] R. Beckwith, *The Old Testament Canon of the New Testament Church* (Grand Rapids: Eerdmans, 1985), 78, 312, 355–58; T. J. Finley, "The Book of Daniel in the Canon of Scripture," *BSac* 165 (2008): 195–208.

[21] See in general D. A. Dorsey, *The Literary Structure of the Old Testament* (Grand Rapids: Baker, 1999), 259–62; D. W. Gooding, "The Literary Structure of the Book of Daniel and Its Implications," *TynB* 32 (1981): 43–79; P. A. Tanner, "The Literary Structure of the Book of Daniel," *BSac* 160 (2003): 269–82.

portions, on the other hand, were more limited to historical and eschatological Israel and thus were written in the language of Israel's other sacred texts.[22] Regardless of various opinions concerning the bilingual nature of the book, there is remarkable consensus that Daniel is a compositional unity and not the product of a long period of redactional layering.

A second noteworthy consideration of Daniel from a literary standpoint is its extensive use of apocalyptic themes and imagery. Collins defines an apocalypse as a "genre of revelatory literature with a narrative framework, in which a revelation is mediated by an otherworldly being to a human recipient, disclosing a transcendent reality which is both temporal, insofar as it envisages eschatological salvation, and spatial insofar as it involves another, supernatural world."[23] Apocalyptic literature is characterized by such features as (1) an interpreting angel, (2) symbolism to be interpreted allegorically, (3) *ex eventu* prophecy, (4) historical periodization, (5) a sense of determinism, and (6) a pattern of crisis-judgment-salvation.[24]

Daniel exhibits most of these traits but cannot on that account alone be dated late. As already observed, other biblical writings also contain some or all of these features as do extra-biblical Babylonian and other ANE writings that are indisputably preexilic, exilic, and early postexilic. Daniel's prolific use of the apocalyptic genre reflects clearly his special interest in God's plan for His people in the context of their apparent hopelessness in the thrall of Babylonian and Persian captivity.

THE OUTLINE OF THE BOOK

I. **The Narratives about Daniel and His Ministry (chaps. 1–6)**
    A. The Capture and Training of the Exiles (chap. 1)
    B. Nebuchadnezzar's First Dream (chap. 2)
    C. The Faithful Hebrews in the Fiery Furnace (chap. 3)
    D. Nebuchadnezzar's Second Dream (chap. 4)
    E. Belshazzar's Feast and the Fall of Babylon (chap. 5)
    F. Daniel and the Lion's Den (chap. 6)

II. **The Visions of Daniel (chaps. 7–12)**
    A. The Coming Kingdom of God (chap. 7)
    B. The Conquest of Persia and the Rise of Greece (chap. 8)
    C. The 70 Weeks (chap. 9)
    D. Daniel's Prayer (chap. 10)
    E. The History of the Diadochi and Its Aftermath (chap. 11)
    F. Tribulation and Deliverance of God's People (chap. 12)

THE CONTENTS OF THE BOOK

The Book of Daniel consists of two nearly equal parts—narratives about Daniel (chaps. 1–6) and his revelation and interpretation of dreams and visions (chaps. 7–12). When he was but an adolescent Daniel, with other choice and promising young men, was spirited away from Judah as part of Nebuchadnezzar's first deportation of Jews to Babylonia. There they were afforded special privileges and were offered training in the arts and sciences of the high

---

[22] For a helpful survey see R. K. Harrison, *Introduction to the Old Testament* (Grand Rapids: Eerdmans, 1969), 1132–33.

[23] J. J. Collins, *Apocalypse: The Morphology of a Genre* (Missoula, MT: Scholars, 1979), 9.

[24] Collins, *A Commentary on the Book of Daniel*, 55–56.

Babylonian culture (1:1–7). Daniel, however, refused to compromise his religious convictions by partaking of the nonkosher delicacies of the royal court. Surprisingly he was granted a special dispensation by King Nebuchadnezzar to see how he might fare by following his own regimen and trusting his own God (1:8–16). The result was that Daniel and his three likeminded friends exceeded the king's expectations and rose to positions of prestige and power for decades to come (1:17–20).

This promotion gained Daniel access to the king and to special responsibility as the king's interpreter of dreams. Early in his reign Nebuchadnezzar had a dream about a great image of multiple metals and minerals, an image which, when struck by an enormous stone, collapsed

Reconstruction of ancient Babylon.

to the ground (2:31–35). Daniel identified Nebuchadnezzar as the head of gold and the rest of the image as successive human kingdoms that would fall in submission to the kingdom of God (2:36–45). In defiance of the message of the dream Nebuchadnezzar erected a statue of himself before which all the people of his kingdom must bow in worship (3:1–7). Daniel's three friends refused, and for their impudence they were thrown into a burning furnace (3:8–23). Their God delivered them, thus prompting the king once more to recognize the superiority of Israel's God (3:24–30).

In a second dream Nebuchadnezzar saw a mighty tree that despite its size and strength was cut to the ground, leaving only a stump. As for the king, he learned that he would become like a wild beast, foraging in the open countryside until the Most High returned him to his sanity (4:4–27). When all came to pass Nebuchadnezzar once more confessed that the Lord alone is sovereign and worthy of worship (4:34–37).

Years later Belshazzar, son of Nabonidus, hosted a great banquet in which he toasted his many gods from the sacred cups of the temple of the Lord (5:1–4). This impious behavior was addressed by a secret message inscribed on the palace wall, a text only Daniel could interpret (5:5–28). The message was that the kingdom of Babylonia would fall to the Medes and Persians and that Belshazzar's own life would be taken that very night, a sobering threat that came to pass just as Daniel said (5:29–30). Thus the proud kingdom of Babylonia came to an end.

The more beneficent Persian rulers were no less hostile to the claims of Israel's God and the first of these, Darius the Mede, succumbed to the counsel of his advisers that he establish himself as a god who alone could be worshipped (6:4–9). Daniel obviously could not betray his loyalty to the Lord, and therefore he was called to account. The penalty was that he be cast into a den of lions, a fate that could not be reversed under Persian law even by the king himself (6:10–15). However, the Lord delivered Daniel so that Darius, like his Babylonian predecessors, was forced to concede that the God of Daniel is the living God (6:16–27).

The site of the ancient city of Babylon in modern Iraq.

The second half of the book consists of a series of dreams by Daniel in which the theme of the Lord's sovereignty continued to be played out. In the first of these Daniel saw a sequence of animals, the last of which defied taxonomic description (7:1–14). An angelic interpreter disclosed to him that the animals represented kingdoms, the fourth indefinable because it would come only in the distant future. It would seek to persecute God's people under the leadership of a wicked despot, but he and his kingdom would come to a calamitous end (7:15–28).

The second vision is similar, but its focus is on two animals representing two kingdoms from the second of which a little horn would sprout and become a terrifying despot (8:1–14). Daniel learned that the kingdoms were Persia and Greece and that the little horn would emerge from one of four kingdoms that followed the Greek Empire once it had fallen (8:15–27).

In view of these impending ominous events Daniel prayed a lengthy prayer of repentance on behalf of his wicked people Israel (9:3–19). His prayer was interrupted by Gabriel the archangel who assured him that God had heard his prayer and would, after 70 "weeks" of years (i.e., 490 years), bring about the beginnings of Israel's restoration (9:24–27). In a subsequent time of mourning Daniel received yet another vision in which he was told that neither he nor his people had reason to fear for the angelic armies of the Lord would achieve final victory over the principalities and powers arrayed against the God of heaven (10:1–21).

Somewhat retrospectively from a historical standpoint, Daniel saw a final vision detailing the affairs of the nations that would spring from Greece, the four vestigial remnants of Alexander's empire (11:1–4). The focus was on the "king of the south" and "the king of the north," the Ptolemies and Seleucids, respectively. They would engage in ceaseless conflict until, in Daniel's account, history had run its course and an evil ruler unprecedented in malice and power would

The ruins of the Hanging Gardens of Babylon, one of the Seven Wonders of the World.

rise up at the end of time (11:5–35). He would claim deity and universal dominion until he also came to ruin with no one to help him (11:36–45).

The book closes on the awesome note of an impending persecution of God's saints followed by their glorious vindication and even resurrection (12:1–4). To Daniel's query as to how all these things would come to pass in the final analysis, the interpreting angel informed him that he was not to know "for the words are secret and sealed until the time of the end" (12:9; cf. Rev 5:1–7). He was told to "go on your way to the end; you will rest, then rise to your destiny at the end of the days" (Dan 12:13).

THE PURPOSE AND THEOLOGY OF THE BOOK

Even a casual reading of the book of Daniel makes clear that the central theme and overarching purpose of the book is the recognition and celebration of the sovereignty of the God of Israel.[25] The temple might lie in ruins, the holy city devastated and depopulated, and the chosen people scattered to the four winds; nevertheless the Lord is God, and He will work out His purposes in both history and the eschaton. It is no coincidence that the awful judgment by God of His people and their exile from their homeland should have occurred under the Babylonians, the mightiest power on earth. Nor is it surprising that their deliverance and return should have been effected under the comparatively beneficent rule of Persia, Babylonia's even greater successor. In both instances—captivity and return—human potentates and their gods are seen for what they really are—mere instruments in the hand of the omnipotent One who used them to accomplish His judging and saving work.

The theology of Daniel is therefore God-centered. He is the director of its historical drama, the explanation for the rise and fall of its human personae, and the catalyst for the resolution of its central problem: How can Israel, the chosen people, be delivered and restored to their covenant role as a kingdom of priests and a holy nation?

It is precisely at this point that various eschatological views of the book come to the fore, views found in other OT (and NT) books, but not in such concentration and the subject of so

---

[25] E. H. Merrill, "Daniel as a Contribution to Kingdom Theology," in *Essays in Honor of J. Dwight Pentecost*, ed. S. D. Toussaint and C. H. Dyer (Chicago: Moody, 1986), 211–25; idem, "A Theology of Ezekiel and Daniel," in *A Biblical Theology of the Old Testament*, ed. R. B. Zuck (Chicago: Moody, 1991), 387–95; idem, *Everlasting Dominion: A Theology of the Old Testament* (Nashville: B&H, 2006), 547–54; J. E. Goldingay, *Daniel*, WBC (Dallas: Word, 1989), 329–34.

much scholarly discussion as here.[26] The four major positions are amillennialism, postmillennialism, historical premillennialism, and dispensational premillennialism. The first two deny a literal millennium or respectively maintain that it is already past, whereas the second two accept a literal future millennium but differ in interpretive details.

STUDY QUESTIONS

1. Under what circumstances was Daniel taken captive?
2. In what two languages was Daniel written?
3. Under what ruler did Daniel first serve in Babylon?
4. What is the traditional date of the book of Daniel?
5. Why is the date of the book contested?
6. Under what Persian king was the city of Babylon captured?
7. To what do the 70 weeks of Daniel 9 refer?
8. What king was made beastlike as punishment from the Lord?
9. Against whom did the Seleucids do battle in the prophecy of Daniel 11?
10. Define "amillennial."
11. Define "premillennial."
12. Identify Darius the Mede.
13. Who was the famous son of Nabonidus?
14. What is the language Daniel was taught as a servant of the king?
15. Who is one like the "son of man" in Daniel 10?

FOR FURTHER STUDY

Baldwin, J. G. *Daniel: An Introduction and Commentary.* Downers Grove, IL: InterVarsity, 1978.

Bright, J. *A History of Israel.* 3rd ed. Philadelphia: Westminster, 1981.

Bullock, C. H. *An Introduction to the Old Testament Prophetic Books.* Chicago: Moody, 1986.

Chisholm, R. B., Jr. *Handbook on the Prophets.* Grand Rapids: Baker, 2002.

Collins, J. J. *Daniel: With an Introduction to Apocalyptic Literature.* FOTL. Grand Rapids: Eerdmans, 1984.

————. *Daniel.* Minneapolis: Fortress, 1993.

Goldingay, J. E. *Daniel.* WBC. Dallas: Word, 1989.

Lucas, E. *Daniel.* Apollos. Downers Grove, IL: InterVarsity, 2002.

Merrill, E. H. *Everlasting Dominion: A Theology of the Old Testament.* Nashville: B&H, 2006.

————. *Kingdom of Priests: A History of Old Testament Israel.* 2nd ed. Grand Rapids: Baker, 2008.

Miller, Stephen R. *Daniel.* NAC. Nashville: B&H, 1994.

Pentecost, J. D. "Daniel." In *The Bible Knowledge Commentary, Old Testament.* Edited by J. F. Walvoord and R. B. Zuck, 1323–75. Victor, 1985; reprint, Colorado Springs, CO: Cook, 1996.

Rowley, H. H. *The Relevance of Apocalyptic.* London: Lutterworth, 1944.

Russell, D. S. *The Method and Message of Jewish Apocalyptic.* Philadelphia: Westminster, 1964.

Smith, G. V. *An Introduction to the Hebrew Prophets: The Prophets as Preachers.* Nashville: B&H, 1994.

Steinmann, A. E. *Daniel.* St. Louis: Concordia, 2008.

Tatford, F. A. *Daniel and His Prophecy: Studies in the Prophecies of Daniel.* London: Oliphants, 1953.

VanGemeren, W. A. *Interpreting the Prophetic Word.* Grand Rapids: Zondervan, 1990.

Walvoord, J. F. *Daniel: The Key to Prophetic Revelation.* Chicago: Moody, 1971.

Whitcomb, J. C. *Daniel.* Chicago: Moody, 1985.

---

[26] For a good overview see G. E. Ladd, *The Meaning of the Millennium: Four Views* (Downers Grove, IL: InterVarsity, 1977).

CHAPTER 27

THE BOOK OF HOSEA

MARK F. ROOKER

THE BOOK OF Hosea is the initial book in what is called the Minor Prophets. This compilation of 12 prophets was considered to be one book as these shorter books together were roughly equivalent in length to a major prophet and thus could all fit on one scroll. In the earliest reference to these books they were already grouped together and were known as "the twelve prophets" (Sir 49:10). Hosea heads the list as it is the longest of the 12 and was considered in Jewish tradition as the earliest: "The Lord *first* spoke through Hosea" (*Baba Bathra* 14b, 15a). According to tradition the first six of the Minor Prophets lived in the eighth century, the next three in the seventh century, and the last three were in the postexilic period.[1] An alternative explanation for the arrangement is based on thematic considerations. Hosea-Micah focuses on covenant breaking; Nahum, Habakkuk, and Zephaniah concentrated on the Day of the Lord; whereas Haggai, Zechariah, and Malachi address the coming transformation of judgment to glory.[2]

THE TEXT OF THE BOOK

The Hebrew text of the book of Hosea is regarded as one of the more difficult in all the OT. In past generations the prevailing viewpoint among critics was to attribute the difficulties in Hosea to errors in the Hebrew text. Presently more and more scholars are attributing the problems to Hosea's dialect, as the prophet is one of the few prophets from northern Israel. Because of limited familiarity with North Israelite Hebrew the difficulties should now be attributed to dialectal idiosyncrasies.[3]

Another reason the language of Hosea poses difficulties is the book's genre. Apart from the narrative sections 1:2–2:1 and 3:1–5 the book is entirely poetic.

---

[1] See R. Rendtorff, *The Old Testament*, trans. J. Bowden (Philadelphia: Fortress, 1986), 215. The dating of Joel and Obadiah are problematic, however. See discussions in chaps. 28 and 30.

[2] See P. House, *Old Testament Theology* (Downers Grove, IL: InterVarsity, 1998), 348.

[3] C. L. Seow, "Hosea, Book of," in *ABD,* ed. D. N. Freedman (New York: Doubleday, 1992), 3:292.

THE HISTORICAL BACKGROUND OF THE BOOK

The introduction to the book of Hosea states that the prophet Hosea prophesied during the reigns of Uzziah, Jotham, Ahaz, and Hezekiah, kings of Judah, and during the days of Jeroboam, king of Israel (Hos 1:1). Thus Hosea was a younger contemporary of Amos and probably began his prophetic ministry about a decade after Amos had denounced the social decay in the northern kingdom. Hosea began his ministry probably near the end of the reign of Jeroboam II (793–753) inasmuch as he confronted an unstable situation that eventually led to the downfall of Israel in 722 (7:3–7; 8:4). The period was characterized by political vacillation between obedience to Assyria and rebellion against Egypt (5:13; 7:11; 8:9–10; 12:1[HB, v. 2]). The unstable situation created by the Syro-Ephraimite war (735–732) is reflected in Hos 5:8–6:6. In addition to ministering during the latter part of the reign of Jeroboam II, Hosea ministered probably in the days of Zechariah (753), Shallum (752), Menaham (752–742), Pekahiah (742–740), Pekah (752–732), and Hoshea (732–722). During this chaotic time no fewer than six kings occupied the throne, and four of them were assassinated. Shortly following Hosea's ministry Israel was defeated by the Assyrians in 722 after Hoshea had withheld tribute from Shalmaneser V and sought Egyptian aid.

THE COMPOSITION OF THE BOOK

Most scholars believe that Hosea delivered his messages in the eighth century but that some of his prophecies were expanded over time, particularly by Hosea's disciples. Scholars such as Francis Andersen, David Freedman, Hans W. Wolff, and James Mays maintain that disciples did the actual writing of Hosea's oracles. However, as Brevard Childs states, there is no good reason to suggest that the book is a pseudepigraphic composition from late in the postexilic times.[4]

Wolff argued that the composition of the book of Hosea was the culmination of three separate traditions that have been joined together. Chapters 1–3 were composed by the prophet apart from expansions by one of his disciples. Chapters 4–11, which consist of various kerygmatic units from different time periods, were written by Hosea's disciples shortly after Hosea pronounced them. Chapters 12–14, on the other hand, are entirely a later expansion by Hosea's disciples shortly before the end of the northern kingdom. Finally a Deuteronomic redactor, at least a century later, added the superscription and updated various passages.

Other scholars are convinced that references to Judah[5] and passages predicting future blessing and deliverance for Israel[6] are later additions to the book. But suggestions that references to Judah are secondary insertions have not gone unchallenged. Otto Eissfeldt, for example, has noted in Hos 5:8–6:6 (a passage which includes reference to Judah) that extracting Judah from this passage would destroy the sense of the text.[7] Precisely the same difficulty is encountered if one maintains that the salvation oracles are secondary additions. The judgment oracles and the salvation oracles are so intertwined in the book that there are no textual clues that would lead one to the conclusion that the salvation oracles are secondary.[8] There is thus no good reason,

---

[4] B. Childs, *Introduction to the Old Testament as Scripture* (Philadelphia: Fortress, 1979), 377–80.

[5] Judah is mentioned in 1:7; 4:15; 5:5,10,13; 6:4,11; 11:12; 12:2.

[6] 1:10–2:1; 2:14–23; 3:5; 11:8–11; 14:2–9.

[7] O. Eissfeldt, *The Old Testament*, trans. P. Ackroyd (New York: Harper & Row, 1965), 387.

[8] See D. Garrett, *Hosea, Joel*, NAC (Nashville: B&H, 1997), 25.

as Francis Andersen and David Freedman argue, to deny that the book is essentially the work of a single person.[9]

Also it is not necessary to conclude that all of the prophecies of Hosea were delivered in a short time period. This is evident from reading the text itself. In the first prophecy of the book of Hosea it is announced that the dynasty of Jehu was about to come to a violent end (1:4). This prophecy must have occurred before the death of Jeroboam II in 753 BC as Jeroboam II's son Zechariah was the last king of the Jehu dynasty, reigning only six months. Chapter 5 on the other hand seems to be directed against King Menahem (752–742), whereas chap. 7 must have been written perhaps two decades later as it depicts the nation double-dealing with Assyria and Egypt, a set of circumstances not occurring until the reign of Hoshea (732–722).[10]

THE STRUCTURE AND OUTLINE OF THE BOOK

While it is clear that there is a major structural division between Hosea 1–3 and Hosea 4–14, there is little agreement regarding the subdivisions of the longer section. The primary difficulty in isolating the individual units is the lack of structural clues or formulae that begin or conclude a unit. Dorsey has proposed a chiastic arrangement for the entire book based not on structural components but rather on the thematic content of the book.[11]

A.   Israel is God's wayward wife: he will cause her to return home (1:1–3:5)
   B.   Condemnation of Israel's spiritual prostitution and idolatry (4:1–5:7)
      C.   Condemnation for political faithlessness and corruption and empty sacrifices; Yahweh's efforts to bring Israel back (5:8–6:11a)
         D.   Center: Israel has not returned to Yahweh, though he has called her to return (6:11b–7:16)
      C¹.   Condemnation for political faithlessness and corruption and empty sacrifices; Yahweh's efforts to bring Israel back (8:1–9:7b)
   B¹.   Condemnation of Israel's spiritual prostitution and idolatry (9:7c–10:15)
A¹.   Israel is God's wayward son: God invites him to return (11:1–14:9 [HB, 11:1–14:10])

Schmidt, on the other hand, found five basic sections within the two major divisions, all of which move in the same direction, from disaster to salvation:[12]

	Disaster	Salvation
Chaps. 1–3	1:2–9	1:10–2:1
	2:2–13	2:14–23
	3:1–4	3:5
Chaps. 4–14	4:1–11:7	11:8–11
	11:12–14:1	14:2–9

Apart from 4:1; 5:1; 11:11, Hosea 4–14 is devoid of structural divisional formulae in contrast to most of the other prophets. But based on the initial formula, "Hear the word of the LORD" (4:1), and the concluding formula, "the LORD's declaration" (11:11), there is warrant in view-

---

[9] F. I. Andersen and D. N. Freedman, *Hosea*, AB (New York: Doubleday, 1980), 59.

[10] G. Archer, *A Survey of Old Testament Introduction*, 3rd ed. (Chicago: Moody, 1994), 357.

[11] D. Dorsey, *The Literary Structure of the Old Testament* (Grand Rapids: Baker, 1999), 266.

[12] W. H. Schmidt, *Old Testament Introduction*, trans. M. J. O'Connell (New York: Crossroad, 1990), 202.

ing chaps. 4–11 as the second major unit, thus leaving chaps. 12–14 as the final unit. Thus there are three major units to the book, and they are structurally parallel. Each begins with an accusation and an announcement of judgment against Israel but ends with an announcement of salvation (3:5; 11:8–11; 14:2–9). Moreover, each section announces the judgment in the form of a legal dispute (*rîb*, 2:2; 4:1,4; 12:2). At the end of two oracles is a call to repent (*šub*; 3:5; 11:11; 14:2–3,8).[13]

The book may be outlined as follows:

I. **Hosea's Marriage to Gomer Reflects God's Relationship to Israel (chaps. 1–3)**
   A. Hosea's Three Children (1:2–2:1)
   B. The Lord's Marriage to Israel (2:2–23)
   C. Hosea's Marriage Restored (chap. 3)

II. **Israel's Indictment (chaps. 4–11)**
   A. Israel Has Broken the Covenant (4:1–5:7)
   B. Political Failures (5:8–7:16)
   C. Religious Failures (8:1–9:9)
   D. Israel Did Not Live Up to Its Calling (9:10–11:12)

III. **Israel's Imminent Fall (chaps. 12–14)**
   A. Israel's History of Rebellion (chap. 12)
   B. Israel's Punishment for Unfaithfulness (chap. 13)
   C. Israel's Call to Repentance and Restoration (14:1–8)
   D. Wisdom Colophon (14:9)

THE CONTENTS OF THE BOOK

I. Hosea's Marriage to Gomer Reflects God's Relationship to Israel (chaps. 1–3)

These chapters record the story of Hosea's marriage to Gomer and its analogy to God's relationship to Israel. Because of this, many have suggested that it was not an actual marriage but rather an allegory. Such well-known interpreters as Jerome, Kimchi, Ibn Ezra, John Calvin, Ernst Hengstenberg, and C. F. Keil have held this view. However, most modern interpreters maintain that this was an actual marriage, but they disagree about whether Gomer was a harlot before her marriage to Hosea or if she became unfaithful afterward (1:2). In support of the latter position it is often pointed out that it would be a violation of all moral sensibilities for God to command His prophet to marry a woman of known immoral character. Moreover, the text seems to indicate that Gomer's first child was Hosea's while the second and third children were the product of unfaithfulness. This information is used to support the position that Gomer was not promiscuous at the beginning of her marriage to Hosea. However, it seems that a straightforward reading of 1:2 indicates that Hosea was called by God to marry a woman who was known as a prostitute. Hosea is not explicitly mentioned as the father of Lo-ruhamah and Lo-ammi but this exhibits frugality of language; it does not indicate that he was not the father. The context seems to suggest that Hosea was the father of all three children.[14]

The name of Hosea's first child, Jezreel, has a double application (1:4–5). The name Jez-reel recalls Jehu's bloodguilt (2 Kgs 9:14–37) and anticipates the end of his dynasty presently

---

[13] See Rendtorff, *The Old Testament*, 216.

[14] Even if Hosea were not the father of the last two children, the understanding that God commanded him to marry a harlot is not diminished.

represented in the person of Jeroboam II (1:4). It also indicates the location of the nation's coming defeat: in the valley of Jezreel (1:5). Hosea's second child was his daughter Lo-ruhamah, meaning "Not compassion." This child's name made known to Israel that God's compassion was now withdrawn from them and forgiveness would not be attainable (1:6). The name of the third child, Lo-ammi, was especially harsh as it indicated that God was declaring Israel to be "Not My people." At the time of the exodus God had referred to the Israelites as "My people" in Exod 3:7; 6:7. This strong statement in Hosea indicates the severing of the covenant connection since the essence of the covenant relationship was found in the statement "I will be your God, and you will be My people." Furthermore, in the explanation of this dissolution of the covenant relationship there is a word play on the name of the Lord. At Sinai God was revealed as the great "I Am" (*'ehyeh*, Exod 3:14), but now because of the nation's unfaithfulness God declares that He is *lō' 'ehyeh* ("I am not (your) I am"). This is tantamount to saying that God is negating the promises given to Moses when God revealed His name to him at the burning bush (Exodus 3).

Hosea 1 and 3, which depict Hosea's marriage, function as a frame around the Lord's message to his wife Israel.[15] This arrangement places emphasis on Hosea 2 which announces God's message to Israel—the reason Hosea was to enter a marriage with an unfaithful partner in the first place.

Chapter 2 could be viewed as an extended commentary on 1:2. The Israelites sought the Baals, not realizing that it was the Lord, not Baal, who was responsible for their abundance (2:8). They were thus unfaithful in turning to the Canaanite gods (2:2–13) whose worship had been introduced by Ahab's queen Jezebel (1 Kgs 16:29–33).[16] Chapter 2 sets the pattern for the contents of the rest of the book. The judgment speech against Israel's apostasy (2:2–13) reflects the doom which so frequently characterizes chaps. 4–13, while the announcement of reconciliation (2:14–23) prepares for the other oracles of hope (3:5; 11:8–11; 14:1–9). In the restoration the valley of Achor, associated with Israel's failure at Ai, is transformed into a door of hope (2:15). The names of Hosea's children are reversed to indicate divine blessing rather than judgment. Jezreel now will represent God's bounty on the land. God will extend "compassion" to Israel and declare that they are "My people" (2:21–23).

All three of the opening chapters are bound together by the focus on marriage as the comparison to God's relationship to Israel and by Gomer's adultery as a comparison to Israel's response to God. This theme of the wife's unfaithfulness is carried throughout the book,[17] a theme also prevalent in other prophetic books such as Jer 2:1–3:5; Ezekiel 16 and 23. As the oracles of Hosea 1–3 depict the Lord's relationship with Israel in familial terms of husband and wife, in chaps. 4–14 the Lord's relationship with Israel is also expressed in terms of husband and wife and the additional familial relation of parent and child (11:1–4).[18] Like Hosea 2, the contents of Hosea 4–14 unpack the meaning of the accusation of 1:2: "the whole land has been promiscuous by abandoning the LORD."

---

[15] In Hosea 3 Hosea and Gomer somehow became estranged and apparently Gomer had become a slave. Hosea, representing God, still loves his unfaithful wife and graciously buys her back for himself.

[16] The worship of Baal included human sacrifice and ritual prostitution (Deut 23:17; Ps 106:34–41) (see Seow, "Hosea, Book of," 296).

[17] See ibid., 295.

[18] In Exod 4:22 Israel is depicted as God's son.

II. Israel's Indictment (chaps. 4–11)

In this section Hans Wolff detects 10 separate speeches marked by a new address or change of theme, beginning at 4:1,4; 5:1,8; 8:1; 9:1,10; 10:1,9; 11:1. In the introduction to the indictment (4:1–3), Israel is in clear violation of seven commandments, emphasizing the completeness and pervasiveness of their sin. Several of these sins are mentioned again in the main divisions of this section as the prophet called Israel to account for their unfaithfulness in both the religious (4:4–5:7; 8:1–9:9) and political (5:8–7:16) realms. Israel has mingled her worship of the true God with pagan fertility rites (4:11–13). She has blatantly adopted pagan worship (5:5). The land can be saved only by a comprehensive repentance (6:1–3). Obedience and true worship of God is what is necessary, not pagan sacrifices and ritual (6:6). Renewal can come only through transformed lives (6:1–6). The altars meant to be the place of forgiveness and atonement have become the very means of Israel's sin. The Israelites can no longer live in Yahweh's land (9:3).

In the last division of this section (9:10–11:12) the prophet reverts the audiences' attention back to Israelite historical traditions such as the desert period (9:10), Baal-poer (9:10), the conquest (10:1), the exodus (chap. 11), and the patriarchal traditions (chap. 12). This historical survey was meant to show that Israel's sinning had a long history, but the Lord had always remained faithful.[19] A recurring threat in this section is that Israel is on the verge of being deported back to Egypt (8:13; 9:3; 11:5; 14:1–2) or sent into exile (9:3,17; 11:5,11). Ironically God's judgment on Israel would affect the very areas believed to be under Baal's domain: agricultural prosperity (9:1–4), sexual vitality and fertility (9:10–17), altars and idols (10:1–6), and military prowess (10:9–15).[20] Appropriately, the Lord would deprive Israel of the very blessings they expected Baal to give them.

III. Israel's Imminent Fall (chaps. 12–14)

In this final section Hosea continued his pronouncement of judgments against Israel, reflecting on historical surveys to prove his point. The nation had become characterized by lies (12:1), violence (12:1), economic oppression (12:7–8), pride (13:1,6), idolatry (13:1–2), and rebellion (13:16). As a result, they, like their ancestors, will be taken back to the wilderness to live in nomads' tents as in the times of the exodus and the wilderness wanderings (12:9). Yet throughout this demonstration of faithlessness God remained true to His promise (13:4–5; 14:1–2,4–7). Now God's judgment will come on them like a ferocious animal (13:7–8). He will devastate the land through drought and deplete the treasury (13:15). Children will be dashed to pieces and pregnant women will have their bellies torn open (13:16). Yet God holds out hope for the future as the book ends on a note of covenant return (14:1–9). "His love does not respond to her deserts, but to his nature."[21] This restoration will return the land to Edenic conditions (14:5–7). Only in this final section of Hosea does the expression "the LORD your God" occur, once in each of its major divisions (12:9; 13:4; 14:1).

---

[19] See especially P. Kruger, "Hosea, Theology of," in *NIDOTTE,* ed. W. VanGemeren (Grand Rapids: Zondervan, 1997), 4:711. The historical survey of Israelite sinfulness is reminiscent of Stephen's speech in Acts 7.

[20] A. Hill and J. Walton, *A Survey of the Old Testament* (Grand Rapids: Zondervan, 1991), 363.

[21] W. J. Dumbrell, *The Faith of Israel: A Theological Survey of the Old Testament,* 2nd ed. (Grand Rapids: Baker, 2002), 184.

THE STYLE OF THE BOOK

In his prophetic ministry Hosea used many images to communicate his message. He referred to God as a jealous husband (2:2–13), a frustrated shepherd (4:16; see also 11:4; 13:6), a destructive moth and undesired rot (5:12), a ferocious lion (5:14; 13:7–8), and a trapper (7:12). On the other hand God is also depicted as a forgiving husband (3:1–5), a healing physician (6:1–2; 7:1; 11:3; 14:4), the resuscitating rains (6:3), a loving parent (11:3–4), a protecting lion (11:10–11), a life–giving dew (14:5), and a fertile pine tree (14:8).

Hosea also invoked images to describe Israel. However, all these images are negative. She was the unfaithful wife (1:2–9; 3:1–5; 9:1), the disappearing morning mist (6:4), a hot oven (7:4–7), a silly dove (7:11), a faulty bow (7:16), a wild donkey (8:9), and a withered plant (9:16). God's coming judgment on Israel is compared to harvesting the whirlwind (8:7), washing away of debris (10:7), and yoking a stubborn heifer (10:11). In addition, in this indictment the prophet is bringing against the nation, legal language abounds. Examples are words like "case" (4:1), "dispute" (4:4), "guilty" and "oath" (4:15), "judgment" (5:1), and "testifies" (5:5).[22]

THE THEMES OF THE BOOK

Idolatry

Clearly the main concern of the book of Hosea is idolatry, particularly the worship of Baal. While Amos, Hosea's older contemporary, denounced Israel for social failures, Hosea particularly emphasized Israel's failure to worship only the Lord. Hosea denounced Israel because she had gone after the Baals. In fact Hos 14:8 reinforces the notion that this had indeed been God's concern and was the *raison d'etre* for Hosea's marriage to an unfaithful woman in the first place.

Covenant Relationship and Marriage

Israel's infidelity to the Lord was forcefully driven home in Hosea through the marriage metaphor to describe God's relationship with Israel. This is one of the first times in Scripture that God's covenant with His people is compared to marriage. In one sense this had to be a carefully explained comparison since sexual prostitution was a vital part of Canaanite religion. And yet the love between a man and woman in marriage was the most intimate relationship; the only one suitable to convey God's love for Israel. As in marriage, Israel was to be exclusively faithful to her marriage partner. No rivals could be tolerated (Exod 20:1–6; Deut 4:15–31). One who was unfaithful to God was thus accused of harlotry or prostitution (Exod 34:11–16; Lev 17:7; Num 25:1; Deut 31:16; Judg 2:16–17; Jer 3:2).[23] This same analogy of the marriage relationship is developed in the NT, which pictures the church as the bride of Christ (Eph 5:22–33). The understanding of the covenant as presented in Exodus and Deuteronomy form the background to Hosea's reflections.[24]

---

[22] See R. Dillard and T. Longman III, *An Introduction to the Old Testament* (Grand Rapids: Zondervan, 1994), 360; and Hill and Walton, *A Survey of the Old Testament*, 361.

[23] See esp. R. C. Ortlund, *Whoredom: God's Unfaithful Wife in Biblical Theology* (Grand Rapids: Eerdmans, 1996), 25–45.

[24] M. Evans, "Hosea," in *Theological Interpretation of the Old Testament*, K. J. Vanhoozer (Grand Rapids: Baker, 2008), 246.

Knowledge of God

Hosea is somewhat distinct among OT books in that there is a strong emphasis on the knowledge of God (2:20; 4:1–6; 5:4; 6:6). Bullock suggests that the structure of Hosea 1–3 demonstrates that the primary problem in Israel is lack of knowledge of their covenant God.[25]

    A.   Hosea's Marriage (1:2–9)
        B.   Renewal of the Covenant (1:10–2:1)
            C.   Yahweh's Judgment on Israel (2:2–4)
                D.   No Acknowledgment of God in Israel (2:5–8)
            C^1.   Yahweh's Judgment on Israel (2:9–13)
        B^1.   Renewal of the Covenant (2:14–23)
    A^1.   Hosea and Gomer Reunited (3:1–5)

The priests who were to entrust the people with the knowledge of God's word thus come under heavy attack (4:6–9). This focus on the knowledge of God prepares for this same NT emphasis in passages such as Matt 11:27 and John 17:3,25.

THE NEW TESTAMENT AND THE BOOK

On two occasions in the book of Matthew Jesus quoted Hosea's statement that God desires mercy rather than sacrifice (Matt 9:13; 12:7; cf. Hos 6:6). Matthew 2:15 quotes Hos 11:1, "Out of Egypt I called My son," as being fulfilled in Jesus' life when Jesus was transported back to Israel from Egypt by His parents. The nation as a whole becomes a type of the ultimate Son of God. Paul (Rom 9:25–26) and Peter (1 Pet 2:10) use the phrase "no people" from Hos 1:10 and 2:23 to address the incorporation of the Gentiles into the NT church. Hosea 6:2, "He will revive us . . . on the third day," may possibly be a reference to Jesus' resurrection if in fact the nation is a type of the Messiah and is represented by Him (1 Cor 15:4). Moreover, Paul quoted Hos 13:14 in 1 Cor 15:55 in his declaration of the believer's victory over death through Jesus Christ. By loving his wife despite her unfaithfulness to him, Hosea is perhaps the ultimate example of the unconditional love God demonstrates to His people.

STUDY QUESTIONS

    1.   Which prophet was a contemporary of Hosea?
    2.   What are the major issues regarding the composition of Hosea?
    3.   How many major units are found in the book of Hosea?
    4.   Was Hosea's marriage to Gomer an actual marriage?
    5.   What are the meanings of the names of Hosea and Gomer's children?
    6.   How does Hosea 2 set the stage for the contents of the rest of the book?
    7.   What previous biblical events does Hosea allude to in Hosea 9–11?
    8.   Besides idolatry, of what sins was Israel guilty?
    9.   Comment on the literary style of the book of Hosea.
  10.   Which foreign god was Israel most tempted to worship?
  11.   What is the distinction between Hosea's and Amos's focus?
  12.   In what way did Hosea prepare for the NT?

---

[25] C. H. Bullock, *An Introduction to the Old Testament Prophetic Books* (Chicago: Moody, 1986), 93.

FOR FURTHER STUDY

Andersen, F. I., and D. N. Freedman. *Hosea*. AB. Garden City, NY: Doubleday, 1980.

Bullock, C. H. *An Introduction to the Old Testament Prophetic Books*. Chicago: Moody, 1986.

Carroll R., M. Daniel. "Hosea." In *EBC*. Rev. ed. Edited by Tremper Longman III and David E. Garland, 8:213–305. Grand Rapids: Zondervan, 2008.

Childs, B. *Introduction to the Old Testament as Scripture*. Philadelphia: Fortress, 1979.

Dorsey, D. *The Literary Structure of the Old Testament*. Grand Rapids: Baker, 1999.

Dumbrell, W. J. *The Faith of Israel: A Theological Survey of the Old Testament*. 2nd ed. Grand Rapids: Baker, 2002.

Eissfeldt, O. *The Old Testament*. Translated by P. Ackroyd. New York: Harper & Row, 1965.

Evans, M. "Hosea." In *Theological Interpretation of the Old Testament*. Edited by K. J. Vanhoozer, 244–50. Grand Rapids: Baker, 2008.

Garrett, D. *Hosea, Joel*. NAC. Nashville: B&H, 1997.

Hubbard, D. A. *Hosea: An Introduction and Commentary*. TOTC. Downers Grove, IL: InterVarsity, 1989.

Kidner, D. *Love to the Loveless: The Message of Hosea*. Downers Grove, IL: InterVarsity, 1981.

Ortlund, R. C. *Whoredom: God's Unfaithful Wife in Biblical Theology*. Grand Rapids: Eerdmans, 1996.

Seow, C. L. "Hosea, Book of." In *ABD*. Edited by D. N. Freedman, 3:291–97. New York: Doubleday, 1992.

Stuart, D. *Hosea-Jonah*. WBC. Waco, TX: Word, 1987.

Wyrtzen, D. B. "The Theological Center of the Book of Hosea." *BSac* 141 (1984): 315–29.

CHAPTER 28

THE BOOK OF JOEL

MICHAEL A. GRISANTI

THIS PROPHETIC BOOK is brief, but powerful; controversial, but important. Although it has only three short chapters, it provides a glimpse of an important set of future events encompassed by the "Day of the Lord." Scholars have long debated the date of this book, questioned whether Joel envisions an army of actual locusts or a human army, and discussed whether Joel predicted detailed events or described apocalyptic "events" that should not be interpreted in a detailed fashion. Regardless of the debate, Joel, the prophet of the Day of the Lord focused on the promise of divine judgment on covenant treachery. He also set before God's servant nation, Israel, the hope for restoration to their God-given function as His banner to the world.

THE AUTHOR AND COMPOSITION OF JOEL

The book begins with the words, "The word of the LORD that came to Joel son of Pethuel" (Joel 1:1). Where he lived or how he became a prophet is not known. All that is clear is that his name means "Yahweh is God." Because 3:4–8 shifts abruptly from poetry to prose, some scholars have suggested that a later writer added this section.[1] This is unnecessary since Joel repeatedly moved back and forth between present and future perspectives and thus between genres. As they have done with other prophetic books, some scholars have sought to divide Joel into two halves in light of their different emphases (e.g., the Day of the Lord has come, the Day of the Lord will come).[2] In reality the "historical" experience of the Day of the Lord encourages preparation for the eschatological Day of the Lord.

The book provides no chronological information about the time of its composition. Evangelicals have proposed a composition date from the ninth century to the postexilic period.[3]

---

[1] H. W. Wolff, *Joel and Amos*, Hermeneia (Philadelphia: Fortress, 1977), 74–75.

[2] See L. C. Allen, *The Books of Joel, Obadiah, Jonah and Micah*, NICOT (Grand Rapids: Eerdmans, 1976), 25–29, for an overview of these suggestions and responses.

[3] For the clearest and most thorough summaries of the date of Joel see J. A. Thompson, "The Date of Joel," in *A Light unto My Path: Old Testament Studies in Honor of Jacob M. Myers*, ed. H. N. Bream, R. D. Heim, and C. A. Moore (Philadelphia: Temple University Press, 1974), 453–64; D. A. Garrett, *Hosea, Joel*, NAC (Nashville: B&H, 1997), 286–94; I. A.

This lack of unanimity arises from the absence of clear chronological information in the book itself. The presence of a temple (1:9,13–14,16) provides one of the clearest indicators and demonstrates that the book was written either before 586 or after 515 BC. Other factors cause one to "lean" toward a date for the book's composition. Joel 3:1–2 seems to refer to the exile of God's people (primarily Judah, 3:1) as an event that had already taken place. The absence of any reference to a king along with the reference to Greek slave trade (3:6) may favor a postexilic date. Since no one can be sure of the date when Joel was written, it would be wise to remember John Calvin's words: "As there is no certainty, it is better to leave the time in which he taught undecided; and as we shall see, this is of no great importance . . . for the import of his doctrine is evident, though his time may be obscure and uncertain."[4]

THE TEXT OF JOEL

The Hebrew text of Joel is remarkably free from textual variants. An ancient copy of the Minor Prophets was found in a cave at Murabba'at in the Judean Wilderness (dating from the second century AD). The Hebrew of this ancient copy generally supports the Masoretic Text. The English text of Joel has only three chapters while the Hebrew text has four (2:28–32 in Eng. is 3:1–5 in HB, and 3:1–21 in Eng. is 4:1–21 in HB).

THE STRUCTURE OF JOEL

Commentators generally offer two alternatives for outlining the book of Joel. First, focusing on the book's content, 1:2–2:27 describes a locust plague sent by God against His covenant nation, while 2:28–3:21 presents an eschatological promise of blessing and judgment. Second, in light of the form of the passages, 1:2–2:17 serves as a lament over the locust plague, and 2:18–3:21 presents a divine oracle in response to the lament. Although both options have merit, the outline below follows the second suggestion that emphasizes the form of the passages.

THE OUTLINE OF JOEL

Superscription 1:1

I. **A Locust Invasion Signals the Day of the Lord (1:2–2:17)**
   A. A Call to Mourning and Prayer (1:2–20)
   B. The Announcement of the Day of the Lord (2:1–11)
   C. A Call to Repentance and Prayer (2:12–17)

II. **God Delivers and Vindicates His People (2:18–3:21; HB, 2:18–4:21)**
   A. The Lord's Restoration of His People (2:18–27)
   B. The Lord's Vindication of His People (2:28–3:21; HB, 3:1–4:21)
      1. The Outpouring of the Spirit (2:28–32; HB, 3:1–5)
      2. The Divine Judgment of the Nations (3:1–21; HB, 4:1–21)

Busenitz, *Commentary on Joel and Obadiah* (Ross-shire, UK: Christian Focus, 2003), 11–34; and R. B. Chisholm, "Joel," in *The Bible Knowledge Commentary, Old Testament,* ed. J. F. Walvoord and R. B. Zuck (Wheaton, IL: Victor, 1985; repr., Colorado Springs: Cook, 1996), 1409–10.
   [4] J. Calvin, *Joel, Amos, Obadiah,* trans. J. Owen (repr., Grand Rapids: Baker, 1981), xv.

SPECIAL ISSUES IN THE BOOK

Locusts or Soldiers?

Does Joel refer to actual locusts in chaps. 1 and 2, locusts in chap. 1 and human soldiers in chap. 2, human soldiers in both chapters, or does he have some supernatural creatures in mind? All of these options have been offered by various scholars, but most agree that Joel 1 describes an invasion by a swarm of locusts. There is less agreement regarding the locusts in 2:1–11. Does this section continue the account of the locust plague, or does the prophet use this vivid image to describe the sacking of a city by a human army?[5]

Scholars who say a human army is in view in 2:1–11 point out that although the terms for comparison, "like" or "as," in 2:4–7, normally compare the reality in mind to something else (e.g., he is like a rock), they can describe the fulfillment of the ideal. In other words the reality described in 2:4–7 is "the absolute fulfillment of the analog."[6] These proponents also suggest that the decimation of Gentile powers in chap. 3 implies that these Gentile nations had done something horrible to deserve this punishment, such as attacking and conquering Jerusalem like a plague of locusts. They view the language of 2:1–11 as an account of an assault by highly trained soldiers. Also, this enemy comes from the north (2:20), whereas locust plagues did not normally come from the north (whereas invasions from foreign powers did).

Although the above interpretation is possible, several features support the idea that Joel again had literal locusts in mind. First, 2:25 clearly identifies the Lord's army as locusts (cf. 2:11). Second, although the comparative preposition can present the reality described as the ideal, much more frequently it presents reality by means of an analogy. Joel used the preposition "like" seven times in four verses (2:4–7), something that supports the comparative function, carrying the idea of *similarity* and not *identity*.[7] The author was comparing the locust invasion to familiar aspects of human invasion. In other words, locusts were being compared to human armies, though human armies were not actually present.[8] Third, there are numerous statements that correspond to the features of a locust invasion: the invaders' numerical size (2:2,5), their destruction of the land (2:3), their horselike appearance (2:4), their leaping and scaling ability (2:5,7), the loud sounds they make (2:5), and their abundant number causing the sky to become dark (2:10). The decimation of these invaders parallels with eyewitness accounts of locusts in the Near East.[9] Also the literary parallels between chaps. 1 and 2 suggest that literal locusts are in view in both passages.[10]

---

[5] For a brief overview of the options and proponents see J. A. Thompson, "Joel's Locusts in Light of Near Eastern Parallels," *JNES* 14 (1955): 52–55. Garrett (*Hosea, Joel,* 298–301) views chap. 1 as referring to locusts and chap. 2 describing a human army (*Hosea, Joel,* 298–301), whereas Stuart argues that all of 1:1–2:27 has a human army in view. D. Stuart (*Hosea–Jonah,* WBC [Waco, TX: Word, 1987] 232–34); Allen (*The Books of Joel, Obadiah, Jonah and Micah,* 29–31); and Busenitz (*Commentary on Joel and Obadiah,* 113–17) also maintain that both chaps. 1 and 2 refer to actual locusts.

[6] Garrett, *Hosea, Joel,* 299. See also Chisholm, "Joel," 1410–12. In this sense this Hebrew preposition is used to indicate exactitude, a function described by grammarians as *kaph veritalis* (B. K. Waltke and M. O'Connor, *An Introduction to Biblical Hebrew Syntax* [Winona Lake, IN: Eisenbrauns, 1990], 203). For example Neh 7:2 does not say that Nehemiah's brother was like a man of integrity but that he was in every way a man of integrity.

[7] The examples of *kaph veritatis* cited in grammar reference tools are generally single occurrences, not part of a series of comparative statements.

[8] See NET Bible text note for 2:5.

[9] The overwhelming stench or putrefaction of swarms of locusts can cause outbreaks of typhus and other diseases that spread to mankind and animals (R. B. Dillard, "Joel," in *The Minor Prophets: An Exegetical and Expository Commentary,* ed. T. E. McComiskey [Grand Rapids: Baker, 1992], 1:256). For an eyewitness account of the 1915 locust invasion of Palestine see J. D. Whiting, "Jerusalem's Locust Plague," *National Geographic* (December 1915), 511–50.

[10] Some have wondered how the expressions "huge and powerful army" (2:2) can refer to locusts. Probably this is because the language of this chapter referring to "people" and "armies" is a hypocatastic description of the locusts of chap. 1.

In addition to the question of the identity of these invaders, what is the relationship of the invasion in chap. 2 to the one presented in chap. 1? While some may contend that the locusts in chap. 2 continue their destruction begun in chap. 1, the locust invasion in chap. 1 has already happened while the blight in chap. 2 had not yet arrived. Chapter 2 opens with a command to blow the trumpet and sound an alarm. The Lord demanded that all the inhabitants of the land shake with fear, because the Day of the Lord is about to come (2:1).[11] Verse 2 ends with a comparison of the past and the future to affirm that what is coming is unparalleled, but Joel employs this future locust invasion that would have horrific impact on God's people as a foreshadowing of or preparation for the future Day of the Lord.

Joel 2:28–32 and the Day of the Pentecost

As part of an explanation of what they had just seen on the day of the Pentecost (Acts 2:7–21), Peter stated, "this is what was spoken through the prophet Joel" (Acts 2:16). Then he quoted Joel 2:28–32 (HB 3:1–5) as somehow related to the unique phenomena that took place that day. Why did Peter make a connection between the outpouring of the Spirit in Acts 2 and what Joel predicted would happen as part of the future Day of the Lord? Scholars have offered three answers. First, covenant theologians affirm that the events at Pentecost represent the total fulfillment of Joel's prophecy.[12] The end times have arrived, and God is dealing with a new people involving Jews and Gentiles. There will be no return to the nation of Israel or an eschatological presence in the promised land. Second, traditional or classic dispensationalists believe that the events of Pentecost did not fulfill Joel's prophecy.[13] Peter cited Joel's prophecy as an illustration of what was taking place at Pentecost. According to Ryrie, "Peter's point was that the Holy Spirit and not wine was responsible for what these Jews had seen."[14] Third, progressive dispensationalists suggest that the events of Pentecost inaugurated the New Covenant age.[15] In an initial sense, elements of what Joel predicted found fulfillment at Pentecost, but the consummation of all that he predicted awaits the Second Coming. There is nothing in the experience recorded in Acts 2 that exactly corresponds to the earthly and heavenly signs described in Joel. Peter's words, "this is what" (2:16) presents an initial fulfillment of the Joel passage without precluding or minimizing a yet future and more exhaustive fulfillment in events associated with the return of Christ.[16]

THE THEOLOGY OF JOEL

The Day of the Lord

This section can provide only a brief summary of this important concept, a central theme of the book of Joel.[17] Every event in the book is related to this "day." It is a day that begins

---

[11] The imperatives, futuristic imperfect, and the "imminent" participle all point to something in the future, the eneaer future from Joel's wording.

[12] S. J. Kistemaker, *Exposition of the Acts of the Apostles*, NTC (Grand Rapids: Baker, 1990), 88–92; F. F. Bruce, *The Book of Acts*, rev. ed., NICNT (Grand Rapids: Eerdmans, 1988), 60–62.

[13] A. Gaebelein, *The Acts of the Apostles* (reprint, Neptune, NJ: Loizeaux, 1961), 54; C. C. Ryrie, "The Significance of Pentecost," *BSac* 112 (October–December 1955): 334–35.

[14] Ryrie, "The Significance of Pentecost," 334.

[15] D. L. Bock, "The Reign of the Lord Christ," in *Dispensationalism, Israel and the Church*, ed. C. A. Blaising and D. L. Bock (Grand Rapids: Zondervan, 1992), 47–55; idem, "Evidence from Acts," in *A Case for Premillennialism: A New Consensus*, ed. D. K. Campbell and J. L. Townsend (Chicago: Moody, 1992), 191–94.

[16] See NET Bible note on Joel 2:28.

[17] For a clear and helpful presentation of "the Day of the Lord" in Joel and the OT, see Busenitz, *Joel & Obadiah*, 36–49.

with judgment (darkness) and leads to restoration (light). The Day of the Lord signifies a time when the Lord supernaturally intervenes in the course of human history. It begins with divine judgment on wickedness and can lead to glorious restoration. Negatively (judgment), as part of this eschatological "day," God will sweep aside His enemies, and He will also bring judgment against His rebellious covenant people. Positively (blessing), the Lord will vindicate those who are loyal to Him as well as to His own righteousness.

This day is also covenant-driven. Although this set of events impacts the Gentile nations, God's primary focus is on His chosen nation, through whom He intends to impact the world. God seeks to drive His servant nation to humble submission to His absolute sovereignty. He does this to enable His chosen people to function as His nation before the surrounding nations.

Israel's experience of the Day of the Lord was part of their experience of covenant curse for their covenant treachery. The impact of the locust invasion was felt by every realm of society, especially evidenced by the discipline of sending a locust plague that destroyed the land's agricultural produce. This was a warning and foretaste of a future judgment on the Lord's Day. But for judgment to transition into restoration God requires genuine repentance of His people (2:12–17). Only this will suffice to avert God's wrath and usher in His restoration. The future invasion envisioned in chap. 2 was not an end; it was a means to an end. God desires to restore His people to an intimate relationship with Him, one that will enable them to make His surpassing character prominent before every inhabitant of the world.

God's Absolute Sovereignty and Power

The book of Joel vividly presents God as the one who controls every aspect of His creation. He controls the armies of locusts, both past (1:5–12) and future (2:1–11,25). He also determines the fate of all nations (3:1–21). He exercises sovereignty over the thunder, sun, moon, and stars (3:15–16). He is a mighty warrior (2:11) who annihilates His enemies (3:13). And He metes out justice fairly to those who are guilty (3:3–8,21).

God's Desire to Restore His Nation

Even in the midst of emphasizing judgment, God longs to restore His people and to enable them to make known His incomparable character to the entire world. The threat of judgment includes the potential of restoration (1:14; 2:12–17). However, God will not restore a nation that will not love Him with their entire being and repent of their sins (2:12–13). He will not accept hypocrisy or apathy.

Conclusion

Many of the biblical prophets graphically describe the covenant treachery that characterized the nation of Israel at many points in their history. The prophet Joel presents a powerful message to his fellow Israelites and God's servant nation. Drawing on the horrific devastation of a locust plague that decimated Israel's crops, Joel sets before God's people the stark reality of their situation. If they continue in covenant rebellion, an army of locusts such as they have never seen will overwhelm the nation and the land of promise, leaving them with nothing but hunger and barrenness, the opposite of covenant blessing. However, if they repent and turn to the Lord, He will pour out covenant blessings on them. He will also bring judgment against those nations that have oppressed His people. The Day of the Lord, a central part of Joel's message, offers both the threat of judgment and the hope for restoration. Yahweh will not condone Israel's hypocrisy and apathy, but will honor repentance and obedience. If they repent, He will enable them to carry out His intentions for them to impact the world (Exod 19:4–6; Deut 26:16–19).

STUDY QUESTIONS

1. What are the major views on the dating of Joel, and why is there such a spectrum of views?
2. What are the two primary alternatives for the structure of Joel?
3. Are the locusts in Joel 1 and 2 actual locusts or symbolic of human soldiers? Which view do you think the evidence favors?
4. What are several views on Peter's use of Joel 2 in his sermon on the day of Pentecost?
5. How do covenant theologians interpret Peter's use of Joel 2?
6. How do dispensational theologians interpret Peter's use of Joel 2?
7. What is the "Day of the Lord"?

FOR FURTHER STUDY

Achtemeier, E. *Minor Prophets I*. NIBCOT. Peabody, MA: Hendrickson, 1996.

Allen, L. C. *The Books of Joel, Obadiah, Jonah and Micah*. NICOT. Grand Rapids: Eerdmans, 1976.

Baker, D. W. *Joel, Obadiah, Malachi*. NIVAC. Grand Rapids: Zondervan, 2006.

Barton, J. *Joel and Obadiah*. OTL. Louisville: Westminster John Knox, 2001.

Bullock, C. H. *An Introduction to the Old Testament Prophetic Books*. Chicago: Moody, 1986.

Busenitz, I. A. *Commentary on Joel and Obadiah*. Ross-shire, UK: Christian Focus, 2003.

Chavalas, M. "Joel." In *Zondervan Illustrated Bible Background Commentary*. Edited by John H. Walton, 5:42–53. Grand Rapids: Zondervan, 2009.

Chisholm, R. B. *Handbook on the Prophets*. Grand Rapids: Baker, 2002.

———. *Interpreting the Minor Prophets*. Grand Rapids: Baker, 1990.

———. "Joel." In *The Bible Knowledge Commentary, Old Testament*. Edited by J. F. Walvoord and R. B. Zuck, 1408–24. Wheaton, IL: Victor, 1985; reprint, Colorado Springs: Cook, 1996.

———. "A Theology of the Minor Prophets." In *A Biblical Theology of the Old Testament*. Edited by Roy B. Zuck, 397–433. Chicago: Moody, 1991.

Crenshaw, R. L. *Joel*. AB. New York: Doubleday, 1995.

Dillard, R. B. "Joel." In *The Minor Prophets: An Exegetical and Expository Commentary*. Edited by Thomas E. McComiskey, 1:239–313. Grand Rapids: Baker, 1992.

Dyer, C., and G. Merrill. *Old Testament Explorer: Discovering the Essence, Background, and Meaning of Every Book in the OT*. Nashville: Word, 2001.

Finley, T. J. *Joel, Amos, Obadiah*. WEC. Chicago: Moody, 1990.

Garrett, D. A. *Hosea, Joel*. NAC. Nashville: B&H, 1997.

Harbin, M. A. *The Promise and Blessing: A Historical Survey of the Old and New Testaments*. Grand Rapids: Zondervan, 2005.

Hill, A. E., and John H. Walton. *A Survey of the Old Testament*. 3rd ed. Grand Rapids: Zondervan, 2009.

House, P. R. *Old Testament Theology*. Downers Grove, IL: InterVarsity, 1998.

———. *The Promise-Plan of God: Biblical Theology of the Old and New Testaments*. Grand Rapids: Zondervan, 2008.

Hubbard, D. A. *Joel and Amos: An Introduction and Commentary*. TOTC. Downers Grove, IL: InterVarsity, 1989.

Hurowitz, V A. "Joel's Locust Plague in Light of Sargon II's Hymn to Nanaya." *JBL* 112 (1993): 597–603.

LaSor, W. S., D. A. Hubbard, and F. W. Bush. *Old Testament Survey: The Message, Form, and Background of the Old Testament*. 2nd ed. Grand Rapids: Eerdmans, 1996.

Longman, T., III, and R. Dillard. *An Introduction to the Old Testament*. 2nd ed. Grand Rapids: Zondervan, 2006.

Merrill, E. H. *Everlasting Dominion: A Theology of the Old Testament*. Nashville: B&H, 2006.

Patterson, R. D. "Joel." In *EBC*. Rev. ed. Edited by Tremper Longman III and D. E. Garland, 8:307–46. Grand Rapids: Zondervan, 2008.

Sandy, D. B. *Plowshares and Pruning Hooks: Rethinking the Language of Biblical Prophecy and Apocalyptic.* Downers Grove, IL: InterVarsity, 2002.

Stuart, D. *Hosea–Jonah.* WBC. Waco, TX: Word, 1987.

Thompson, J. A. "The Date of Joel." In *A Light unto My Path: Old Testament Studies in Honor of Jacob M. Myers.* Edited by H. N. Bream, R. D. Heim, and C. A. Moore, 453–64. Philadelphia: Temple University Press, 1974.

———. "Joel's Locusts in Light of Near Eastern Parallels." *JNES* 14 (1955): 52–55.

VanGemeren, W. A. *Interpreting the Prophetic Word.* Grand Rapids: Zondervan, 1990.

———. "The Spirit of Restoration." *WTJ* 50 (1988): 81–102.

Waltke, B. K. *An Old Testament Theology.* Grand Rapids: Zondervan, 2007.

Wolff, H. W. *Joel and Amos.* Hermeneia. Philadelphia: Fortress, 1977.

CHAPTER 29

THE BOOK OF AMOS

MARK F. ROOKER

A MOS IS CONSIDERED the first of the writing prophets.[1] He was known as the
spokesman par excellence of social justice and equity among the underprivileged in
society.[2]

THE DATE OF THE BOOK

Amos prophesied during the reigns of Uzziah (also known as Amaziah) king of Judah
(792–740 BC) and Jeroboam king of Israel (793–753). This was a period of unprecedented
political expansion and economic prosperity, virtually comparable to the Davidic-Solomonic
age (2 Kgs 14:23–29).

THE ANCIENT NEAR EASTERN BACKGROUND OF THE BOOK

In the late ninth century BC (805–802), the Assyrian king Adad-nirari III (811–784),
crippled the Aramean city-states, removing Syria as a political threat to the nation Israel. The
succeeding Assyrian kings, however, became preoccupied with the advances of Urartu, a threat
that consequently greatly reduced Assyria's power over the Mediterranean world. Assyria's loss
of power coupled with Egypt's decline allowed Uzziah of Judah and Jeroboam II of Israel to
enlarge their boundaries. Jeroboam's northern border extended to Hamath, and for a while he
ruled both Damascus and Hamath (2 Kgs 14:28).

Israel carried on trade with Egypt, Arabia, Byblos, and Syria and dominated the King's
highway, creating an unparalleled prosperity especially among the well-to-do (Amos 3:15;
5:11; 6:4; 8:4–6).[3] Amos was called by God to confront the northern kingdom as prosperity

---

[1] Amos was third in the order of the Minor Prophets in the Hebrew Bible. In the LXX the book was placed after Hosea.
The Peshitta and the Vulgate follow the Hebrew order.

[2] It is incorrect to view Amos as an advocate of a Marxist order of society. He lifts up "his voice not as champion of
the oppressed, but as defender of the cause of Yahweh" (R. Bohlen, "Zur Sozialkritik der Propheten Amos," *TTZ* 95 [1986]:
297).

[3] Over 500 ivory fragments from the ninth and eighth centuries have been found at Samaria (Amos 3:15) (see also Amos
6:11; cf. 1 Kgs 21:1,18; H. Donner and W. Röelig, *Kanaanaische und Aramaische Inschriften* [Wiesbaden: Otto Harrasso-

had produced its inevitable fruits of pride, selfishness, greed, oppression, and moral decadence, probably around 760 BC.

THE PROPHET OF THE BOOK

The prophet Amos was from Tekoa (2 Sam 14:2; 2 Chr 11:6), a location still existing today as Khirbet *Tequ'*, a five-acre site about 10 miles south of Jerusalem.[4]

Until the twentieth century it had been customary to view Amos as an uneducated sheep-herder from a humble habitat. The use of the Ugaritic cognate *nqdm* (*nōqdîm*, Amos 1:1) in parallelism with an official of the priesthood, however, has forced a reevaluation of the proph-et's vocation. Now many have sought to identify Amos as an official herdsman of either the temple or the royal palace. There is a virtual consensus today that Amos was at least a member of the well-to-do class of Judah as the owner of cattle, sheep, and goats.[5]

Thus Amos was not a "prophet" when God called him to address the northern kingdom, denouncing their practices. The verbless clause of Amos 7:14–15 is best understood in the past tense: "I was not a prophet . . . but the Lord called me."[6] Without rendering a judgmental comment about the prophetic office, Amos declared that he had not formerly been a prophet, but that the Lord called him suddenly to prophesy to the northern kingdom.[7]

THE COMPOSITION OF THE BOOK

Before the latter half of the nineteenth century, it was maintained that the entire book of Amos was written by Amos of Tekoa. This assessment was radically altered when Julius Wellhausen argued that the book of Amos contained both genuine sayings of Amos and later additions from editors.

This critical approach went virtually unchallenged for a century and culminated with the publication of Hans Wolff's heralded commentary in 1977.[8] In this work Wolff argued that Amos went through six distinct stages of composition.[9] However, soon after this, a radical shift

---

witz, 1971], 216.17–20).

[4] Since first suggested by medieval commentator D. Kimchi, many scholars have adopted the view that Amos's Tekoa was in fact a northern city. This view is supported by the mention of the fact that Amos was a "dresser of sycamore trees." It is generally maintained that sycamores were abundant in the Shephelah but not around Tekoa. However, if Amos was from Judah it is possible for at least part of the year that Amos went to the western area of Judah where sycamores grew (1 Kgs 10:27). Nevertheless, restricting the growth of sycamores to the northern kingdom region is disputed (T. J. Wright, "Amos and the Sycamore Fig," *VT* 26 [1976]: 49–53).

[5] G. F. Hasel, *Understanding the Book of Amos* (Grand Rapids: Baker, 1991), 36; B. Willoughby, "Amos, Book of," in *ABD*, ed. D. N. Freedman (New York: Doubleday, 1992), 1:203–4. For the Ugaritic text see UT 62:55 = 6.6 *rb khnm/rb nqdm*, "Chief of Priests/Chief of (Temple)-herdsmen" (*ANET*, 141b).

[6] The past tense is employed by the JB, JPS, NAB, NIV, NKJV, and REB translations, whereas the CEV, JPSV, NASB, NCV, NEB, NRSV, RSV, and TEV translations use the present tense. The present tense would suggest that Amos had separated himself from the prophets of the palace, whom he considered corrupt and unable to speak for God. The past tense would suggest that Amos was not a prophet at the time of his calling, that he had no prophetic training, and that he did not turn to prophecy for economic or other ulterior motives. A growing number of scholars prefer the past tense (J. Ward, "Amos," in *IDBS*, ed. K. Crim [Nashville: Abingdon, 1976], 22).

[7] Amos viewed himself as a prophet. This is clear from the question he raises in Amos 3:8: "When God speaks, who will not prophesy?" (author's translation). Moreover Amos's high view of the prophetic calling is indicated by his well-known affirmation that "the Lord God does nothing without revealing His counsel to His servants the prophets" (3:7). Amos engaged in the activities of a prophet as noted by both himself and Amaziah (7:12–13,15). Throughout the book *nb'*, "prophecy/prophet" (verb six times, noun four times), never has a pejorative connotation.

[8] H. W. Wolff, *Joel and Amos* (Philadelphia: Fortress, 1977).

[9] Of course the prophet himself could have made adjustments to his prophecy when he returned to his homeland. This would explain for example the allusions to Judah in 3:1 and 6:1. The fact that the king of Judah is named before the king of

was beginning to take place in biblical studies. Scholars were beginning to focus on the synchronic study of books and the final shape of OT compositions. Perhaps the best illustration of this change with regard to Amos is represented by an Israeli scholar Shalom Paul, who criticized the method used by Wolff.[10] This change in viewpoint is also evident in the commentary by Francis Andersen and David Freedman, who state that they are concerned with the book's literary form as a finished product rather than with the numerous and diverse components that may have been involved in the book's composition.[11] Stanley Rosenbaum writes, "There is no compelling reason . . . for assuming the present text of Amos to be anything but largely authentic and the work of its traditional author."[12]

This change of perspective toward a more holistic reading has influenced how scholars now view the composition of Amos. The so-called doxologies (4:13; 5:8–9; 9:5–6), once widely thought to be secondary additions, are now viewed as so closely integrated within their respective contexts that their removal would create a disruption to the texts.[13] The same can be said of the epilogue in Amos 9:11–15, which had long been perceived as a later postexilic addition to the prophecy but is now being viewed as forming an integral element in the book's composition.[14]

Thus there is little reason to doubt that the prophet Amos of the eighth century was responsible for the written form of the oracles and visions attributed to him in the superscription. Recent research affirms the view that most (if not all) of the book of Amos derives from the historical Amos.[15]

THE MESSAGE OF THE BOOK

While Amos saw the guilt of the nations as arising primarily from their deeds in time of war (1:3–2:3), he regarded Israel as guilty of covenant violations against justice. Israel's breaches were immeasurably more serious, however, since she was the nation with whom above all others God was intimate (3:2). These covenant violations, particularly the abuse of the underprivileged by the upper class, were introduced in the first oracle addressed to Israel (2:6–8). The upper class gained and maintained its social status through violence (3:9–10), while they crushed the poor (4:1) and imposed heavy taxes (5:11). The poor had to sell themselves into slavery to pay off trivial debts (2:6; 8:6). The rich had increased their wealth through falsified weights (8:5) and dishonest trade (8:6). Even the courts, what would normally be reckoned as the last bastion of hope for the poor, were corrupt, as judges were bribed to cheat the poor (2:7; 5:10,12). Israel was in fact no longer capable of executing justice (3:10; cf. 5:7; 6:12) as

---

Israel (1:1) may indicate that the editor was a Judean and that the work of editing was done in Judah.

[10] S. M. Paul, *Amos: A Commentary on the Book of Amos* (Minneapolis: Fortress, 1991), 6.

[11] F. I. Andersen and D. N. Freedman, *Amos: A New Translation and Commentary* (New York: Doubleday, 1989), 3–4, 144.

[12] S. Rosenbaum, *Amos of Israel: A New Interpretation* (Macon: Ga: Mercer University Press, 1990), 84. For a discussion of similar views by Amos commentators see Hasel, *Understanding the Book of Amos*, 20–25.

[13] W. Rudolph, E. Hammershaimb, J. H. Hayes, D. Stuart, J. A. Soggin, and F. Andersen and D. Freedman, among others, argue that the hymnic material was used by Amos himself and may derive from an earlier hymn or may be the reworking of earlier hymnic elements (Hasel, *Understanding the Book of Amos*, 85).

[14] Hasel, *Understanding the Book of Amos*, 118 n.58 lists dozens of scholars, both conservative and liberal, who now accept the authenticity of 9:11–15.

[15] Ibid., 81.

truth and honesty were now hated (5:10).[16] Amos's message was to be the last beacon of hope for Israel as he admonished them to repent; otherwise God's judgment would surely come.[17]

THE OUTLINE AND CONTENTS OF THE BOOK

The book may be outlined as follows.

1. Superscription (1:1–2)
2. Eight Oracles against the Nations (1:3–2:16)
3. Five Prophetic Words (chaps. 3–6)
4. Five Prophetic Visions (7:1–9:10)
5. Epilogue Promising Blessing and Renewal for Israel (9:11–15)

Amos 1–2

The oracles against the nations are the beginning of a prophetic tradition in which the prophets addressed the foreign nations surrounding Israel (Isaiah 13–23; Jeremiah 46–51; Ezekiel 25–32; Jonah 3:4; Nahum 2–3; Zeph 2:4–15). The six oracles against the foreign nations consist of indictments for national crimes against humans and proclamations of coming judgment. The nations violated international laws.[18] The oracles cannot be placed in one specific historical context and may represent dealings these countries had with Israel over hundreds of years. All the oracles are cast in a stereotyped pattern, which in its full form includes the following elements: (1) messenger formula, (2) indictment formula, (3) specification of crime, (4) judgment formula, (5) specification of judgment, and (6) concluding formula.

The primary target of Amos's harangue is the nation of Israel as the oracles not only crisscross the northern kingdom but move from foreigners (Syria, Philistia, Tyre) to blood relatives (Edom, Ammon, Moab), to Judah, and finally, in the eighth oracle, to Israel. Step by step the message of judgment comes geographically nearer to Israel. Many in Amos's northern audience must have taken perverse delight, as they would have understood the seventh pronouncement against Judah (the longest oracle yet) as the climax of the judgment announcements. The southern kingdom is denounced for its apostasy from the Mosaic law, an offense of which the Judeans had formerly accused the Israelites (2 Chr 13:5–12). That Israel was the target of the first eight oracles of Amos 1–2 is suggested by the following observations: (1) it is the longest of the oracles, (2) the prophecy is a vision *(ḥāzâ)* concerning *Israel* (1:1), (3) at least four sins are mentioned,[19] (4) only Israel's previous blessings are mentioned (2:9–11),

---

[16] See Willoughby, "Amos, Book of," 206. Idolatry was also a sin of the northern kingdom in Amos's prophecy (2:8; 5:5,26; 7:9–13; 8:14), but this receives more extensive treatment by Hosea, Amos's contemporary. According to Segal the sanctuaries were centers of Canaanite influence (2:7–8) (M. H. Segal, *Introduction to the Bible* [Jerusalem: Kiryat Sepher, 1964 (in Hb.)], 1:465).

[17] The center of the book almost to the word is 5:14–15 which contains an appeal for repentance. Together the two verses are a capsule of the book's essential message (Andersen, Freedman, *Amos: A New Translation and Commentary*, 53).

[18] For discussion of international laws prohibiting massacre, plunder, and disturbing of the dead in the ANE see J. Barton, *Amos's Oracles against the Nations* (Cambridge: Cambridge University Press, 1980), 51–61; *ANET*, 199–206. Each of the oracles uses the word *pšʾ* (transgression) to describe the crime(s) of the nation. The essential idea of *pšʾ* is rebellion against authority (see 1 Kgs 12:19; 2 Kgs 1:1; 3:5,7; 8:22). Thus Amos viewed the nations' sins as acts of rebellion against the sovereign Lord. The crimes can be seen against the background of God's injunction to Noah, recorded in Genesis 9. Most, if not all, of the crimes in Amos 1:3–2:3 can be placed under the heading of disrespect for human life or of the image of God in human beings.

[19] M. Weiss has suggested that what the "for three, for four" formula means is simply three plus four (or seven; also the view of Luther and Calvin). The Israel oracle is the only one to actually list seven transgressions; what is meant by the "three and four" for the other oracles is the totality of transgressions (J. Limburg, "Sevenfold Structures in the Book of Amos,"

(5) only Israel is not judged by fire (2:13), (6) only Israel's sin evokes a personal reaction from God (2:13), (7) only Israel's oracle is personalized ("you"/"your," 2:10–11), (8) it is the eighth oracle (7 + 1),[20] (9) it is the last of the oracles, and (10) it is the only oracle that has the expression *ne'um Adonai* (2:16).[21]

The foreign nations will be judged for their sins, but they demonstrate to Israel that her coming judgment is irrevocable. Indeed, the sevenfold description of the warriors' demise in vv. 14–16 emphasizes the completeness of Israel's defeat, as the number seven symbolizes perfection and completion in the OT.

Amos 3–6

In the second major division of Amos, several terminological links unify the section. The three main oracles are introduced by the command *šim'û* ("listen") in 3:1; 4:1; 5:1,[22] while the two shorter oracles begin with the introductory particle *hôy* (5:18; 6:1). The three main oracles and the combined *hôy* oracles are concluded by an emphatic "therefore" (3:11; 4:12; 5:16; 6:7) that announces the nature of the judgment to follow. The sequence of the five oracles cumulatively had a hypnotic effect regarding Israel's approaching and inevitable ruin.

In this section Amos also opposed worship in temples though it be accompanied by an abundance of sacrifices and joy (4:4–5; 5:21–23). God would not tolerate their religious rituals, feasts, and sacrifices so long as the worshippers were guilty of sins toward their fellowman (see Matt 5:23–24).[23]

The purpose of Amos's preaching is seen most clearly in Amos 5 where the people are given an opportunity to reform and reorient their lives (5:14–15). This call went unheeded, for hardly a generation had passed before predictions of exile, disaster, and exile (2:13–16; 3:11–15; 4:12; 5:2–3,16–17,27; 7:9,17; 8:2–3; 9:1–4) came to fruition through the efforts of the Assyrian kings Tiglath-pileser III, Shalmaneser, and Sargon (2 Kgs 15:29; 17:3–6). In Amos 6 the particular sins associated with prosperity are addressed. Seven specific groups are in view including the corrupt political reality (vv. 12–13). Widbin has noted the unity of this entire section with the focus on the uniqueness of Israel's God:[24]

JBL 106 [1987]: 222). The x, x+1 was common in the wisdom literature of the ANE; see Prov 6:16; 30:15; *Ahiqar* vi.92 [*ANET*, 428].

[20] The 7 + 1 pattern here would have cleverly ensured a surprise effect (see Paul, *Amos: A Commentary*, 22–24 for 7 + 1 in ANE and the OT, and D. Dorsey, "Literary Architecture and Aural Structuring Techniques in Amos," *Bib* 73 [1992]: 306–7).

[21] This expression occurs 21 times in the book of Amos.

[22] The injunction to hear God's word or commands echoes the language of the covenant itself (e.g., Deut 4:1; 5:1; 6:4) and occurs regularly in covenant-lawsuit material (Isa 1:2,10; Jer 2:4; Hos 4:1).

[23] This concept is also found in 1 Sam 15:22; Isa 1:12–15; Jer 7:22–23; Hos 6:6.

[24] See R. B. Widbin, "Center Structure in the Center Oracles of Amos," in *Go to the Land I Will Show You*, ed. J. E. Coleson and V. H. Matthews (Winona Lake, IN: Eisenbrauns, 1996), 181.

   A.   Argument: Yahweh's Relationship with Israel as a Basis for Judgment (3:1–11)

     B.   Exhibit: An Image of Death and Worthless Leftovers (3:12)

       C.   Sworn Testimony: Divine Punishment of Jacob Coming (3:13–15)

         D.   Named in Indictment: Self-Indulgent Women in Mount Samaria (4:1–3)

           E.   Condemnation: Cultic Activities (4:4–5)

             F.   Past Judgments Reviewed: Significance Missed (4:6–13)

               G.   Lament: Funeral Songs in the City (5:1–3)

                 H.   Exhortation: "Seek Yahweh" (5:4–6)

                   I.   Accusation: Contempt for Innocence/Poverty (5:7)

                     J.   Hymn: He Who Creates Light and Water on the Earth (5:8a–b)

                       K   *Yahweh Is His Name* (5:8c)

                     J¹.   Hymn: He Who Flashes Destruction on the Fortress (5:9)

                   I¹.   Accusation: Contempt for the Innocent/Poor (5:10–13)

                 H¹.   Exhortation: "Seek Good" (5:14–15)

               G¹.   Lament: Funeral Songs in the City (5:16–17)

             F¹.   Present Judgment Announced: Significance Missed (5:18–20)

           E¹.   Condemnation: Cultic Activities (5:21–27)

         D¹.   Named in Indictment: Self-Indulgent Men in Mount Samaria (6:1–7)

       C¹.   Sworn Testimony: Divine Punishment of Jacob Coming (6:8)

     B¹.   Exhibit: An Image of Death and Worthless Leftovers (6:9–10)

  A¹.   Argument: Yahweh's Relationship with Israel as a Basis for Judgment (6:11–14)

Amos 7:1–9:10

The next major section of Amos has five visions with one message—Israel's judgment is at hand. The first four visions are to be grouped in pairs. In the first pair Amos initiated a dialogue interceding for the nation, with the visions depicting catastrophic events (locust plague and drought). In the second pair of visions the Lord speaks first, asking the prophet a question, while the visions concern objects (plumbline and fruit basket).[25] In the first two visions Amos interceded and destruction was stayed, but in the third and fourth visions, Amos did not intervene, for the Lord explained the verdict and announced judgment.

To be differentiated from the first four visions is vision five, the vision of the Lord. The first four visions are introduced by the phrase, "The Lord God showed me this," but the fifth vision by contrast opens with the words, "I saw the Lord" (9:1). In the last vision the object of the vision is the Lord Himself, and there is no dialogue, as the prophet remains a silent listener to God, who announces irrevocable words of judgment.

Between the third and fourth visions is the Amos-Amaziah confrontation (7:10–17). This historical interlude is evidence of the perversity of the Israelite sanctuaries (Amaziah was a priest) that were condemned in the third vision. The confrontation demonstrates that there

---

[25] The two groups of paired visions may reflect different chronological periods in Amos's ministry. In the first two visions repentance is still possible, but in visions three and four judgment was inevitable.

was no repentant spirit in Israel that could warrant a removal of God's planned destruction.[26] Amos's pronouncement against the false priest Amaziah represented a condensed version of the prophet's word of judgment to the whole nation.[27] The behavior of the high priest in rejecting Amos's message with its divine warning and denying the prophet's right to speak ends the last opportunity Israel had to repent.

Amos 9:11–15

The final section of the book turns from a message of judgment to a word of hope. The purpose of this section is to encourage and instill hope in the righteous remnant by assuring them that God's judgment is not final. The Lord will remember once again His covenant with Israel and will renew His steadfast love. Whereas in the previous climactic, fifth vision of judgment, the Lord promised to remove the sinful kingdom of Israel "from the face of the earth [land]" (*hā'ǎdāmâ* ; 9:8), now in this message of hope He promises to bring them from exile where "they will never again be uprooted from the land I have given them" (*'admātām* ; 9:15). This word of assurance was not completely unexpected, as it was anticipated by Amos's call to repentance (5:4,14–15). God would stay total destruction of Israel and would rebuild what He had torn down, making it once again a place of prominence and blessing (7:1–6; 9:11–15).[28] The day of judgment (2:16; 3:14; 8:3,9,11,13) would be transformed into a day of salvation (9:11,13).

THE LANGUAGE AND STYLE OF THE BOOK

The Hebrew text of Amos is well preserved, as there are no significant variations in the versions or the DSS. Amos's poetry and rhetorical style may be classed among the very best in Hebrew literature. The literary features employed by Amos include (1) wordplay (5:5b; 8:1–2), (2) repetitions ("you did not return to Me," 4:6, 8–11; 5:4,6,14), (3) comparisons (2:9; 5:2, 7,19), (4) metaphors (1:3; 2:13; 3:12; 9:9) (5) antithesis (2:13; 5:4–5,24), (6) exaggeration (2:6–8; 3:9–11; 4:1–3; 5:21; 6:12–13), (7) irony (5:5 [cf. Josh 4:19–24]; 5:17 [Exod 12:12]) (8) reversals (cf. 1:2; 2:9; 3:2,12; 4:1–3; 5:3,13,18–23; 9:11–15), (9) taunts (4:4–5), (10) riddles (6:12), (11) rhetorical questions (3:3–6), (11) qinah meter (5:1–3), and (12) use of the number seven.[29]

THE THEOLOGY OF THE BOOK

Sovereignty

Amos's cry for justice arose from his recognition of the very nature of God and His relationship to the world. Yahweh is the God of all nations, He has had a hand in all their destinies,

---

[26] The curses announced for Amaziah fit standard types: loss of family (Deut 28:30,41; 32:25;), occupation by enemies (Lev 26:32), and exile (Lev 26:38–39).

[27] The character of those who forbade the prophets to prophesy, so pungently condemned in the oracle against Israel (2:12), is in evidence here also in the direct address to Amaziah and may have indicated something of an official rejection of the prophet's message from God (C. H. Bullock, *An Introduction to the Old Testament Prophetic Books* [Chicago: Moody, 1986], 74).

[28] Agricultural plenty is a common motif in the prophets for describing the blessings of the eschatological future (Ezek 47; Joel 3:17–21 [HB, 4:17–21]; Zech 3:10). The "booth" has been understood as David's dynasty, his empire (so the Targum), and his capital city (Jerusalem).

[29] There are seven indictments against seven nations, the sum of three plus four (1:3–2:5). The sevenfold description of the warriors' collapse in 2:14–16 emphasizes the completeness of Israel's defeat, and there are 49 (7x7) divine speech formulas in Amos. See esp. Limberg, "Sevenfold Structures in the Book of Amos," and Willoughby, "Amos, Book of," 210.

and He holds them all equally responsible for their sins (chaps. 1–2). He measures the nations with righteousness and morality.[30] He is free to elevate one or depose another (chaps. 1–2; 6:14). He is free to go everywhere He chooses (9:2), and He is sovereign over all natural phenomena, bringing privation (4:6–10) or blessing (9:13).

Remnant

Although Amos seems to have no hope for Israel as a whole, he did announce the doctrine of the remnant (9:8), begun earlier in the Elijah account (1 Kgs 19:18) and developed fully by Isaiah (Isa 6:12–13; see also Mic 5:7–9). The doctrine was based on God's promise to maintain the nation Israel for the sake of the covenant given to the patriarchs (Lev 26:44–45).

THE NEW TESTAMENT AND THE BOOK

In his survey of Israel's history Stephen quoted Amos 5:25–27 in reference to the idolatry of the Israelites during the wilderness period (Acts 7:41–43). At the Jerusalem Council in Acts 15 James cited Amos 9:11–12 according to the LXX translation to demonstrate that Gentiles also are to be accepted as part of the new people of God (Acts 15:13–18).

EXCURSUS: AMOS AND THE LAW[31]

It has long been the position of source critical scholars of the Bible that the prophets were the great innovators of the OT religion, and that it was only near the end of the OT period that legal prescriptions in Israelite religion developed. This view is seriously undermined in the book of Amos as Amos assumed everywhere that his addressees were familiar with the legal material in the Mosaic law. The upper class of the eighth century BC were guilty primarily of a general attitude of abuse and indifference toward the less fortunate. This conduct was at odds with the spirit and letter of the Mosaic covenant (Lev 19:10,13,15,35–36; 25:25–53; Deut 15:7–11; 24:12–22; 25:13–16). More specifically, the ancient prohibitions against sexual abuse (Exod 21:7–9), debt slavery (22:24), charging interest to the poor (22:25), the misappropriation of collateral (22:26–27), corruption of the legal process (23:6–8), and fraudulent weights and measures (Deut 25:13–16) were ignored (Amos 2:6–8; 5:10–12; 8:5) among the upper class.[32]

Moreover, the divine judgments proclaimed against Israel are drawn from the lists of curses in Leviticus 26 and Deuteronomy 28 (Deut 28:22,30,39–40 = Amos 4:9; Lev 26:25; Deut 28:20–21 = Amos 4:10; Deut 28:30,39 = Amos 5:11; Deut 28:29 = Amos 5:20; Deut 28:36, 64–68; 29:27[HB, 28] = Amos 5:26; Lev 26:30–31 = Amos 7:9; Deut 29:27 [HB, 28] = Amos 7:11,17; Deut 28:29 = Amos 8:9; Deut 28:48 = Amos 8:11).[33] Von Rad has observed that

---

[30] See J. Smart, "Amos," in *IDB*, ed. G. A. Buttrick (Nashville: Abingdon, 1962), 1:120. Even though the nations did not enjoy the covenant privileges, they nevertheless knew of God's ethical demands. They heard the voice of God through nature and social convention, what has come to be called natural revelation (Bullock, *An Introduction to the Old Testament Prophetic Books*, 67).

[31] For Amos and the law see W. Möller, *Grundriss für Altestamentliche Einleitung* (Berlin: Evangelische Verlagsanstalt, 1958), 229–36. For a list of 37 uses of the Law by Amos, see the helpful chart in Jeff Niehaus, "Amos," in *The Minor Prophets*, ed. T. E. McComiskey (Grand Rapids: Baker, 1992), 1:322.

[32] See Willoughby, "Amos, Book of," 206. The covenant had emphasized equal access to land and continuity of land possession for successive generations within families (Num 26:53–56; 33:53–54; 36:1–12).

[33] For a listing of pentateuchal curses that occur in the prophetic literature see D. Stuart, *Hosea–Jonah*, WBC (Waco, TX: Word, 1987), xxxiii–xlii.

Amos ties his contemporaries down to the simple, obvious, literal sense of these laws.[34] No ritual could possibly substitute for the indifference to the high moral and ethical principles of God as revealed in the Torah. Election thus first meant a special responsibility and obligation to the Mosaic demands (Amos 3:2).

STUDY QUESTIONS

1. What is Amos best known for among the writing prophets?
2. What was taking place on the international scene at the time of Amos's prophecy?
3. What was Amos's occupation before he became a prophet?
4. Comment briefly on the history of scholarship on the composition of the book of Amos.
5. Of what transgressions were Israel's enemies guilty?
6. What nation was the primary target of Amos's oracles in Amos 1–2?
7. Which of the five visions in Amos 7–9 is distinctive?
8. What is the purpose of the placement of the passage that deals with the Amaziah confrontation?
9. What characterizes Amos's style?
10. What are the two primary theological themes in Amos?
11. Where is the book of Amos quoted in the NT?
12. What pentateuchal laws did Amos allude to?

FOR FURTHER STUDY

Andersen, F. I., and David N. Freedman. *Amos*. AB. Garden City, NY: Doubleday, 1989.

Barton, J. *Amos' Oracles Against the Nations*. Cambridge: Cambridge University Press, 1980.

Bullock, C. H. *An Introduction to the Old Testament Prophetic Books*. Chicago: Moody, 1986.

Craigie, P. C. *Twelve Prophets*. 2 vols. DSB-OT. Philadelphia: Westminster, 1985.

Dorsey, D. "Literary Architecture and Aural Structuring Techniques in Amos." *Bib* 73 (1992): 305–30.

Gerhard, F. H. *Understanding the Book of Amos*. Grand Rapids: Baker, 1991.

Niehaus, J. "Amos." In *The Minor Prophets: An Exegetical and Expository Commentary*. Edited by T. E. McComiskey, 1:315–494. Grand Rapids: Baker, 1992.

Paul, S. M. *Amos: A Commentary*. Hermeneia. Minneapolis: Fortress, 1991.

Petersen, D. L. *The Social Roles of Israel's Prophets*. Missoula, MT: Scholars, 1978.

Smith, G. V. *Amos: A Commentary*. Grand Rapids: Zondervan, 1988.

Stuart, D. *Hosea—Jonah*. WBC. Waco, TX: Word, 1987.

Widbin, R. B. "Center Structure in the Center Oracles of Amos." In *Go to the Land I Will Show You*. Edited by J. E. Coleson and V. H. Matthews, 177–92. Winona Lake, IN: Eisenbrauns, 1996.

---

[34] G. Von Rad, *The Message of the Prophets* (New York: Harpers & Row, 1962), 107. Andersen and Freedman assert that Amos's message presupposes the covenant (*Amos*, 81, 91–93, 236, etc.).

CHAPTER 30

THE BOOK OF OBADIAH

MARK F. ROOKER

MOST OF THE prophetic works in the OT begin with a notice of the period of the prophet's ministry, his homeland, and the identity of his father. The heading for the book of Obadiah, "the vision of Obadiah," is the shortest of the writing prophets, thus generating debate regarding its historical circumstance and dating.

Twelve individuals bear the name "Obadiah" in the OT. Talmudic tradition (*b. Sanh.* 39b) identifies the prophet Obadiah with the Obadiah who served in King Ahab's court and who saved many of the Lord's prophets from death (1 Kgs 18:1–16). However, few modern scholars, whether conservative or nonconservative, believe that these are the same.

Obadiah is a prophecy directed against Edom, a nation located on the southeastern shore of the Dead Sea from the Brook Zered in the north to the Gulf of Aqaba in the south. Edom was sometimes identified as Seir (Gen 32:3; 36:20–21,30; Num 24:18). Edom had a troubled relationship with Israel, one to be traced back to the womb of Rebekah in Gen 25:21–27 where her two twins, Jacob, the ancestor of the Israelites, and Esau, the father of the Edomite nation, were already engaged in a struggle.

ISRAEL AND EDOM

After the Israelites had been delivered from Egyptian bondage and were making progress toward the promised land of Canaan, the Edomites refused the Israelites passage through their territory (Num 20:14–21; Judg 11:17–18). When Israel became a significant force during the time of David, he defeated Edom and incorporated it into his empire (2 Sam 8:13–14; 1 Kgs 11:15–18). About two centuries later Edom managed to throw off Judah's control during the reign of Jehoram (2 Kgs 8:20–22). During most of the period of the divided kingdom there were occasional skirmishes with Edom, but the Edomites did not present a major threat to Israel or Judah (2 Kgs 16:5–6; 2 Chr 20:1–30; 21:8–10). However, in the reign of Ahaz the Edomites raided Judah and were able to take captives (2 Chr 28:17). But by far the most troubling event in the relationship of Israel and Edom occurred during the Babylonian siege of Jerusalem and the destruction of the temple in 586 BC. The Edomites apparently either offered assistance directly to the Babylonians or launched their own independent raids against Judah and Jerusalem. The Edomites occupied Judean villages in the Negev well into the Persian period (1 Esdr 4:50). This participation of Edom during the fall and destruction of Jerusalem seems to be the basis for Israel's enmity toward Edom in such texts as Ps 137:7; Isa 34:5–17; Lam 4:21–22; and Ezek 25:12–14; 35:1–15.

By the time of Malachi's prophecy (500–450) Edom was in ruins (Mal 1:2–4). Its demise is usually attributed to raids on the land from Arab tribes during the fifth century (see Neh 2:19; 4:7; 6:1). By the year 312 Nabatean Arabs had control of Edom and had established Petra as the capital city. This forced many Edomites to move into the Negev of Judah, a move that gave rise to the name Idumea, etymologically related to Edom.

THE DATE OF THE PROPHECY

As already observed, Obadiah revealed virtually nothing about himself or the times in which he lived. Thus the dating of the book has been hotly debated. Two major proposals have gained favor: (1) Edom's revolt against Judah early in the ninth century (2 Kgs 8:20–22; 2 Chr 21:8–20); or (2) Edomite assistance in the sack of Jerusalem in 586.

Advocates of the ninth-century dating cite two factors they believe to be critical to the discussion. First is the apparent use of Obadiah 1–14 in Jer 49:7–22, and the second is the canonical placement of Obadiah early in the order of the Minor Prophets.

With regard to the first position, it should be acknowledged that there very likely is a relationship between Obadiah 1–14 and Jer 49:7–22. However, there is no consensus that Jeremiah borrowed from the prophecy of Obadiah. Some have argued that Obadiah adapted the contents of Jer 49:7–22, while many scholars are of the opinion that both Obadiah and Jeremiah might have been influenced by an earlier source. The second factor, the occurrence of Obadiah near the beginning of the listing of the Minor Prophets, is not conclusive.[1] While it is true that chronology does play a factor in the arrangement of the Twelve (Haggai, Zechariah, and Malachi at the end of the arrangement are also probably the last books to be written), it is unclear that this is true of the order of the other books. Obadiah shares certain thematic and literary features with Amos and Joel, which might explain why it was grouped with these prophets. It has been suggested that Obadiah 16–21 reflects or was based on Amos 9:12. Also the focus on the Day of the Lord might have been the reason Obadiah was placed after Joel and Amos, which emphasize this theme as well (Joel 3:18; Amos 9:12). Jonah might have been placed after Obadiah because both prophecies are directed to foreign nations, not Israel. Moreover, while the royal palace was looted during the revolt in Jehoram's reign (2 Chr 21:17), there is no indication that Judah underwent the kind of heart-wrenching pain indicated in Obadiah 10–14.

Thus the evidence seems to be more heavily weighted toward the position that the book was written in response to and shortly after the Babylonian exile of 586 BC. The fall of Jerusalem is the only event in Israel's history that qualifies for the tragic situation pictured in Obadiah 11. In the Babylonians' assault on Jerusalem there is explicit indication of Edomite participation (Ps 137:7; 1 Esdr 4:45; see Obadiah 13–14). Other biblical references indicating Edomite participation include Lam 4:21; and Ezek 25:12; 35:10.

---

[1] In the LXX Obadiah was placed fifth, after Joel and before Jonah.

THE COMPOSITION OF THE BOOK

Even though Obadiah is the shortest book in the OT (291 Hb. words), it has not been overlooked by the critics beginning with Johann Eichhorn, who argued that vv. 17–21 could not have been composed by Obadiah and may not have been written until the first century BC. Julius Wellhausen expanded the secondary material in the book to also include vv. 15a–16 since they added eschatological elements to the prophecy calling for judgment not just on Edom but on all other nations as well. Other scholars such as Theodore Robinson, Wilhelm Rudolph, Artur Weiser, Julius Bewer, Otto Eissfeldt, and Robert Pfeiffer divided the book into further fragments stemming from various periods. Yet more recent critical scholars such as James Muilenburg have supported the essential unity of the prophecy, arguing that the transition from the historical to the eschatological is not unparalleled since it occurs in other biblical books, such as Joel and Zephaniah.[2] Leslie Allen and Douglas Stuart have also defended the essential unity of the prophecy. Hans W. Wolff and J. D. W. Watts have suggested that the contents of the book can be defended based on the liturgical or cultic background of the book. But these ideas have not gained many adherents.

THE STYLE OF THE BOOK

Obadiah is filled with vivid imagery. Edom's pride is described with such phrases as "soar like an eagle,"[3] and "make your nest among the stars" (v. 4). As a result of her pride God's coming judgment on Edom is justified and is described as the coming of thieves (v. 5). The betrayal of friends by allies, a picture found frequently in Obadiah (vv. 7,10,12–14), is also found in Amos 1:11 with reference to Edom. Edom will be destroyed just as a fire quickly destroys chaff (Obadiah 18c). It and other nations will reap God's judgment, which is pictured as drinking into oblivion (v. 16; cf. Isa 51:17,21–23; Jer 25:15–33; Hab 2:16; Rev 14:9–10; 16:19), whereas Israel, which will both be vindicated and victorious, is described as a fire and a flame (Obadiah 18a, b). Although the book has only 21 verses, it is characterized by a number of reversals:

Edom set itself on high (vv. 3–4)	God will bring Edom down (v. 4)
Edom is wise (vv. 3,8)	Edom is deceived (v. 7)
Edom violated the covenant with Judah (vv. 10–12)	Edom is overcome by its allies (v. 7)
Edom devastated Judah in the day of her calamity (vv. 11–13)	The Lord has a Day (vv. 8,15)
Edom cannot understand (v. 7)	The Lord will destroy understanding (v. 8)
The mount of Esau (vv. 8–9,19)	The mount of Zion (vv. 17,21)
Jacob's wealth carried off (vv. 11,13)	Esau's wealth will be lost (v. 6); Jacob's wealth will be restored (v. 17)
Judah's remnant cut off and delivered over (v. 14)	No remnant for Esau (v. 18); Judah's remnant restored (v. 17)[4]

---

[2] J. Muilenburg, "Obadiah, Book Of," in *IDB*, ed. G. A. Buttrick (Nashville: Abingdon, 1962), 2:579.

[3] The eagle is often portrayed as the image of strength and freedom in the OT (Exod 19:4; 2 Sam 1:23; Ps 103:5; Isa 40:31; Lam 4:19).

[4] Adapted from E. Achtemeier, *Preaching from the Minor Prophets* (Grand Rapids: Eerdmans, 1998), 51–52. See also P. Ackroyd, "Obadiah, Book of," in *ABD,* ed. D. N. Freedman (New York: Doubleday, 1992), 5:3; and D. Magary, "Obadiah: Theology of," in *NIDOTTE*, ed. W. VanGemeren (Grand Rapids: Zondervan, 1997), 4:993.

THE MESSAGE OF THE BOOK

The book of Obadiah is a condemnation of Edom for her evil treatment of Judah during the time of Judah's greatest crisis, the fall of Jerusalem to the Babylonian empire. Obadiah wrote that this display of violence would lead to Edom's own destruction (vv. 4,6,15,18), whereas Judah would be restored (vv. 17–21). The combined message of destruction for Edom and exaltation for Judah was intended to comfort those who had survived the Babylonian exile. Thus whereas the Day of the Lord was future for Edom, it was past for Judah. The book progresses from the particular to the general. The judgment of Edom is expanded to include the universal judgment of all nations (v. 15). The restoration of Israel advances to the establishment of God's kingdom (v. 21). The book thus is a reminder of the covenant love God has for His people and the promise of hope for the future.

THE OUTLINE AND CONTENTS OF THE BOOK

I. Edom Will Be Destroyed (vv. 1–9)

II. Edom's Violence against Judah (vv. 10–14)

III. The Destruction of Edom and the Restoration of Israel in the Day of the Lord (vv. 15–21)

I. Edom Will Be Destroyed (vv. 1–9)

Verses 1–4 give a summons for all nations to fight against Edom in her mountainous fortifications. The summons opens by announcing that the oracle is a "vision of Obadiah," that is, a divine communication from God to His spokesman. The content of the vision begins with an allusion to a local event in which some local tribes were conspiring to war against Edom. In this announcement Edom's complete downfall is announced (vv. 2–4), including the fact that Edom will be despised among the nations (v. 2).[5]

In vv. 5–9 the announcement of the fall of Edom is described in greater and more comprehensive detail. It is depicted as the coming of thieves and grape gatherers who strip the fields and warehouses, leaving the country without a food supply. Even Edom's allies will turn on them (v. 7).

This first section discloses that the nation of Edom is characterized by pride. The Edomites thought of themselves as immune from foreign invasion and defeat because of their seemingly indestructible capital (vv. 3–4), their renowned wise men (v. 8), and their mighty warriors (v. 9).

II. Edom's Violence against Judah (vv. 10–14)

Verses 10–14 recount the reason for the announcement of the judgment of Edom in the preceding section. The general indictment in v. 10 is that Edom is guilty of violence done to his brother Jacob.[6] Here Judah is called Jacob in order to focus on the sibling relationship and thus to accentuate Edom's treachery. During the critical time of Judah's trouble, when foreigners entered Jerusalem's gate, Edom did not respond like a brother but "stood aloof" (v. 11). To

---

[5] The same term *bzh* was used to describe Esau's disdain of his birthright in Gen 25:34.

[6] Edom's mistreatment by its friends (v. 7) is appropriate because he mistreated his brother Israel.

further underscore the act of treachery the prophet described Judah's destruction as if it were taking place while the prophet was speaking (vv. 12–14).[7]

III. The Destruction of Edom and the Restoration of Israel in the Day of the Lord (vv. 15–21)

Verse 15 is the pivotal verse in the prophecy. It opens the section announcing the coming of the Day of the Lord on all nations, thus preparing for the following verses (16–21). The second half of the verse states the principle of just retribution, connecting the verse to all that has preceded (vv. 1–14). The verse thus indicates that Edom is representative of all nations, a notion reflected in Amos 9:12 and reinforced by the observation that all the judgment oracles in the prophets have an oracle for Edom. The Edomites will learn that God's justice is universal (Joel 3:16–19; Amos 1:3–2:3).[8]

Verses 16–18 address the restoration of the nation of Israel in their land and the destruction of Esau. Edom attempted to stand in the way of Judah's survivors (v. 14), but as part of her judgment she will be without survivors (v. 18).

The next three verses (19–21) are an expansion or what Ackroyd calls an exegesis of vv. 16–18.[9] This passage reports the future land holdings in Israel and is reminiscent of the allotment of the land at the initial occupation of Canaan in the time of Joshua. Verses 19–20 begin and end with reference to the Negev, the area occupied by the Edomites after the destruction of Jerusalem in 586 BC. This is another way of giving prominence to Edom as a representative as well as the focus of the coming judgment. The prophecy closes with a resounding acclamation that the judgment of Esau will be complete and the Lord's kingdom will be established on Mount Zion (v. 21). The restoration of the nation and the preeminence of Mount Zion is the subject of other prophetic texts, including Isa 30:19–26; 31:4–9; 42:2–6; 62:1–12; Jer 30:1–33:26; Ezek 40:1–48:35; Zeph 3:14–20. Thus Edom's experience of the Day of the Lord is a foretaste of the yet great day of divine wrath on all peoples. This day will bring restoration for Israel (Joel 3:17–21; Amos 9:11–15; Mic 7:8–20).

THE THEOLOGY OF THE BOOK

Perhaps the most prominent theme in Obadiah is the justice of God. Since the Lord is holy, He would not allow Edom to go unpunished and He must execute appropriate judgment (v. 15). This principle is known as *lex talonis*, punishment commensurate to the crime. This principle is mentioned in the Law (Exod 21:23; Lev 24:19–20; Deut 19:21) as well as in Wisdom literature (Ps 7:15; Prov 26:27).

God executes His justice in the Day of the Lord (Obadiah 15). The Day of the Lord is the major issue in such prophetic texts as Isa 2:12–22; Amos 5:18–20; and Zeph 1:1–13. The Day of the Lord addresses the Lord's ultimate dominion over the world and is frequently associated with messianic expectation (Ezek 37:24–28; Dan 2:44–45; Zech 12:3–13:6).

Obadiah thus teaches that the Lord is the Ruler of all nations. As such, He demands exclusive worship and service. The oracle against Edom was expanded to an oracle against all foreign

---

[7] The imperfect form of the verb is used throughout this section (vv. 12–14). The word *'êdām* ("their disaster") in verse 13 is similar in sound to *'ādām*. Verse 14, which describes refugees from Judah fleeing the city and thronging the roads, may be commenting on the escape of King Zedekiah, who fled from Jerusalem to the east only to be overtaken in the plains of Jericho (2 Kgs 25:4–6).

[8] See P. House, "Obadiah," in *Theological Interpretation of the Old Testament*, ed. K. Vanhoozer (Grand Rapids: Baker Academic, 2008), 265.

[9] Ackroyd, "Obadiah, Book of," 3.

nations (Obadiah 15). Edom is representative of the nations of the world who oppose God and His people. The oracles against foreign nations as well as the restoration of Israel to her borders is directly related to the promises given in the Abrahamic covenant (Gen 12:3).

THE NEW TESTAMENT AND THE BOOK

Herod the Great's attempt to kill Jesus (Matt 2:16) is similar to Edom's efforts in persecuting Judah. Of interest is the fact Herod the Great was an Idumaean, a descendent of and hence a representative of Edom.

STUDY QUESTIONS

1. What information is normally included in the opening remarks of a prophetic book?
2. What nation is the primary addressee in the book of Obadiah?
3. What passage in Genesis gives the historical background to the book of Obadiah?
4. What are the two major positions on the date of the writing of the book of Obadiah?
5. What seems to be the best date for the writing of the prophecy of Obadiah?
6. What type of imagery do we find in the book of Obadiah?
7. Why did the Edomites think they were indestructible?
8. Why is Israel called "Jacob" in the book of Obadiah?
9. What is the pivotal verse in the book of Obadiah?
10. What is the connection of Edom with the Negeb?
11. What is the principle of *lex talionis*?
12. What nation should be considered as representative of all nations?

FOR FURTHER STUDY

Ackroyd, P. "Obadiah, Book of." In *ABD*. Edited by D. N. Freedman, 5:2–4. New York: Doubleday, 1992. 5:2–4.

Alexander, D. D., D. W. Baker, and Bruce Waltke. *Obadiah, Jonah, Micah*. TOTC. Downers Grove, IL: InterVarsity Press, 1988.

Allen, L. C. *The Books of Joel, Obadiah, Jonah, and Micah*. NICOT. Grand Rapids: Eerdmans, 1976.

Craigie, P. C. *Twelve Prophets*. Vol. 1. DSBOT. Philadelphia: Westminster, 1984.

House, Paul. "Obadiah." In *Theological Interpretation of the Old Testament*. Edited by K. Vanhoozer, 263–67. Grand Rapids: Baker Academic, 2008.

Magary, D. "Obadiah: Theology of." In *NIDOTTE*. Edited by W. VanGemeren, 4:992–96. Grand Rapids: Zondervan, 1997.

Ogden, G. S. "Prophetic Oracles Against Foreign Nations and Psalms of Communal Lament: the Relationship of Jeremiah 49:7–22 and Obadiah." *JSOT* 24 (1982): 89–97.

Stuart, D. *Hosea-Jonah*. WBC. Waco, TX: Word, 1987.

Watts, J. D. W. *Obadiah: A Critical and Exegetical Commentary*. Grand Rapids: Eerdmans, 1969.

Wolff, H. W. *Obadiah and Jonah: A Commentary*. Minneapolis: Augsburg, 1986.

CHAPTER 31

THE BOOK OF JONAH

MARK F. ROOKER

T HE BOOK OF Jonah is distinctive among the OT prophetic books in that it does not have a collection of the prophet's oracles. Instead it records the experience of the prophet Jonah in his mission to Nineveh. Hence the book of Jonah actually bears a closer resemblance to the narrative accounts pertaining to the prophets Elijah and Elisha in 1 and 2 Kings, who like Jonah witnessed supernatural events during the course of their prophetic ministry. The parallels between Jonah and Elijah are particularly striking: both fled from God, both encountered death, both fell into a deep sleep, both sat under a tree and asked to die, and both were associated with a 40-day activity.[1]

THE HISTORICAL BACKGROUND OF THE BOOK

Jonah was a prophet of the northern kingdom from the tribe of Zebulun who lived at Gath-hepher near Nazareth (2 Kgs 14:25). He prophesied during the reign of Jeroboam II (793–753 BC), a period of unparalleled prosperity throughout the land of Israel. Moreover, Jeroboam II had greatly expanded Israel's borders so that Israel attained the size it had been during the Davidic and Solomonic empire (2 Kgs 14:25,28). Syria was subject to Israel during this time, and Assyria was plagued both by international and external problems that allowed Israel to flourish.

THE COMPOSITION OF THE BOOK

Following the methodology made famous by the Graf-Wellhausen school, W. Böhme identified four separate strata of composition in the book of Jonah. Similarly, Ludwig Schmidt attempted to divide the work into different sources based on the occurrences of the divine names Yahweh and Elohim. Jonah's prayer (2:3–10), it has been argued, interrupted the narrative, for as a psalm of thanksgiving it seems to be an inappropriate insertion. Thus many have

---

[1] W. J. Dumbrell, *The Faith of Israel: A Theological Survey of the Old Testament*, 2nd ed. (Grand Rapids: Baker, 2002), 202.

maintained that the psalm was a secondary addition.[2] In addition, because the story reflects universalistic ideas of late postexilic wisdom theology, many have contended that it should be grouped with the latest writings of the OT period. As a result of its late ideas and apparent literary evolution, a broad consensus maintains a late postexilic date for the book. Many scholars argue that the existence of Aramaisms in the book supports this conclusion. Regarding the date, Eissfeldt will only concede that the book must have been written before the second century BC because it was clearly known to the writers of Sirach (49:10) and Tobit (14:4,8).[3]

Regarding the layers of different literary strata, Eissfeldt himself, a strong proponent for detecting literary sources in the Pentateuch, stated that the comparable attempt to find separate sources in Jonah has proved unsuccessful.[4] The argument that Jonah 2 as a psalm is secondary to the narrative portions in the rest of Jonah is also not strong. S. R. Driver argued that Jonah 2 was inappropriate to the context because what is called for in the account is a psalm of petition for deliverance rather than thanksgiving.[5] However, Jonah's first statement after the prayer—"Salvation is from the LORD" (v. 9)—does indicate that he was not crying out for deliverance. In addition, Magonet has argued that there is no real *a priori* reason why a composition must have only one genre.[6] As will be argued below, removing the psalm from the composition would destroy the symmetry between chaps. 1 and 2, and 3 and 4. The argument that the book is late because it has Aramaisms does not hold the weight it had among previous generations of biblical scholars. The Aramaic language was the diplomatic language in the Assyrian empire as illustrated by its use by Sennacherib's envoys late in the eighth century BC (2 Kgs 18:26). As Magonet has stated, many of the words designated as Aramaisms were spoken by the sailors in Jonah 1 and may have actually been technical maritime terms of Phoenician origin. Since Jonah was a prophet from the northern kingdom, one would expect him to employ Aramaic linguistic forms more than other biblical writers. The book cannnot be dated based merely on its language.[7]

THE LITERARY GENRE AND INTERPRETATION OF THE BOOK

Perhaps as with no other book in the OT, the genre of the book of Jonah is intrinsically related to its interpretation. Because of the miraculous events recorded in the book, particularly the rescue of Jonah by the great fish and the city-wide repentance of Nineveh, many critics have balked at the traditional notion of accepting the book as a historical biographical narrative and have looked for other comparative genres for its classification. The book has thus been called a fable, a legend, a didactic novel, a midrash, a novella, an allegory, a parable, a satire, a tragedy, and a didactic tract.

The proposed form of the book of Jonah, as is true of all OT books, will affect its interpretation. The three most commonly proposed classifications for genre for the book are allegory, parable, and historical.

---

[2] O. Eissfeldt, *The Old Testament: An Introduction*, trans. P. Ackroyd (New York: Harper & Row, 1965), 406. The psalm contains verses that are similar to verses in biblical psalms (see E. J. Young, *An Introduction to the Old Testament* [Grand Rapids: Eerdmans, 1949], 265; and G. Archer, *A Survey of Old Testament Introduction*, 3rd ed. [Chicago: Moody, 1994], 349).

[3] Eissfeldt, *The Old Testament: An Introduction*, 405. And yet many of these same critics will affirm the ultimate literary unity of the book in its final form as the word that as a whole communicates a uniform story (B. Childs, *Introduction to the Old Testament as Scripture* [Philadelphia: Fortress, 1979], 419).

[4] Eissfeldt, *The Old Testament: An Introduction*, 406.

[5] S. R. Driver, *An Introduction to the Literature of the Old Testament* (Edinburgh: T&T Clark, 1913), 325.

[6] J. Magonet, "Jonah, Book of," in *ABD*, ed. D. N. Freedman (New York: Doubleday, 1992), 3:938.

[7] Ibid., 940.

Allegory is the method of interpretation whereby a series of incidents illustrates another series of events that occurred at a different time period. According to this method each feature of the book of Jonah represents some aspect in Israel's history. Thus Jonah represents the nation Israel, his fleeing to Tarshish represents the nation's disobedience before the exile, his time in the fish speaks of the Babylonian exile, and his being disgorged to land suggests Israel's return from exile. However, there are absolutely no clues from the book of Jonah that indicate that the book should be understood in this way.[8]

An increasingly popular view of the book is that it is a parable. Though a parable need not be based on historical events, it communicates a lesson by means of a story. Again, there are no indications in the book of Jonah to indicate that the narrative should be understood in this way. Parables are often followed by explanations, which is not the case with the book of Jonah. Moreover, if this were a parable, it would be unparalleled for a parable to be so lengthy, covering four chapters. Furthermore, if one were to argue that this book is parabolic, there would be no reason to stop with Jonah, for this same view could be suggested for other Bible narratives.

The traditional time-honored interpretation of Jonah among both Christians and Jews views the narrative as a historically accurate record of the events of the prophet Jonah in the eighth century BC. Much as Elijah and Elisha went to Sidon and Syria, respectively (1 Kgs 17:8–24; 2 Kgs 8:7–15), so Jonah was sent by God to address the people of Nineveh (Jonah 1:1–2; 3:1–2). Few would contest that taking the book at face value leads to the traditional understanding. But was Jonah actually swallowed by a great fish, and did the entire city of Nineveh repent?

There is no evidence that large forms of marine life cannot swallow human beings, and examples of this have been reported in relatively modern history.[9] Regarding the repentance of the Ninevites, several events occurred in a relatively short amount of time during the reign of Ashur-dan III (773–756 BC), a contemporary of Jonah, which lends credibility to the openness of the king and the citizens of Nineveh to repent. First, a total eclipse of the sun occurred in 763 BC. According to Mesopotamian belief, after the eclipse of the sun the king would die, and there would be flooding, famine, and fire throughout the land. Evidence reveals that during the reign of this king (765–759 BC) famine was widespread. Moreover, during Ashur-dan III's reign Assyria experienced an earthquake that to the Assyrians was a further indication of divine wrath.[10] On top of all this, the city of Nineveh apparently had an esteemed veneration for the fish, and may have worshipped the fish goddess Nanshe.[11] If this is accurate and the report of Jonah's being swallowed by a fish preceded his arrival in Nineveh, he would have been guaranteed a thorough hearing from the Ninevite audience. While the repentance of the Assyrians was short-lived (they soon returned to their notorious violent behavior), one must not forget that Jonah's repentance (chap. 2) had an even shorter duration!

For Christians it is of great significance that Jesus Christ applied the account of Jonah within the great fish as an illustration of His own burial, and He viewed the repentance of the Ninevites as an unarguable fact (Matt 12:39–41; Luke 11:29–30). Interestingly these two incidents that modern scholars have the most trouble accepting are the very events from the book that were affirmed by Jesus Christ. This is a vivid reminder of the fact that doubting the historicity of

---

[8] See esp. R. K. Harrison, *Introduction to the Old Testament* (Grand Rapids: Eerdmans, 1969), 912.

[9] A. J. Wilson, "The Sign of the Prophet Jonah and Its Modern Confirmations," *PTR* (October 1927): 630–42; and Harrison, *Introduction to the Old Testament*, 907–8.

[10] See discussion by D. K. Stuart, *Hosea-Jonah*, WBC (Waco, TX: Word, 1987), 440.

[11] See E. Merrill, "The Sign of Jonah," *JETS* 23 (1980): 23–30.

the book of Jonah has only become widespread in our current skeptical age. The book of Jonah should thus be viewed as a historical narrative. But because it uniquely ends with a moral, it is perhaps best to view the book with Douglas Stuart as a didactic prophetic narrative.[12]

THE STRUCTURE OF THE BOOK

The book of Jonah is best viewed as consisting of seven episodes occurring in four separate geographic settings. The four settings are the Mediterranean Sea, the belly of the fish, Nineveh, and the eastern side of Nineveh. The seven episodes include Jonah's commission and flight (1:1–3), Jonah and the sailors (1:4–16), Jonah's prayer (1:17–2:10 [HB, 2:1–11]), Jonah's recommissioning and obedience (3:1–4), the Ninevites (3:5–10), Jonah's prayer (4:1–4), and the Lord's lesson for Jonah (4:5–11). The structure is evenly balanced. Chapters 1 and 3 put Jonah before a pagan audience, and in chaps. 2 and 4 Jonah is in prayer before God. Only the final episode, God's lesson for Jonah, has no early correspondent and hence it has the prominent position in the book.[13]

Also internal correspondence within the two major sections is evident.

Chapter 1
Focus on Sailors
1. Crisis: destruction by storm (1:4)
2. Response: prayer to the Lord (1:14)
3. Deliverance from storm (1:15b)
4. Sacrifice and vows (1:16)

Chapter 2
Focus on Jonah
1. Crisis: drowning in sea (1:15; 2:3)
2. Response: prayer to the Lord (2:2)
3. Deliverance from death (1:17; 2:6b)
4. Sacrifice and vows (2:9)

Chapter 3
Focus on Ninevites
1. Crisis: destruction of city (3:4)
2. Response: repentance (3:5–8)
3. The Lord changes His mind (3:10)

Chapter 4
Focus on Jonah
1. Crisis: city saved from destruction (4:1)
2. Response: anger (4:1–3)
3. The Lord wants to change Jonah's mind (4:4,6–11)[14]

THE OUTLINE OF THE BOOK

I. **Jonah's Commission and Disobedience (chaps. 1–2)**
  A. Jonah's Call and Escape (1:1–3)
  B. The Storm at Sea and Jonah's Fate (1:4–17)
  C. Jonah's Psalm of Deliverance (chap. 2)

II. **Jonah's Second Commission and Its Results (chaps. 3–4)**
  A. The Second Call and Obedience (3:1–4)
  B. The Ninevites Repentance and Deliverance (3:5–10)
  C. Jonah's Prayer (4:1–4)
  D. The Lesson for Jonah (4:5–11)

---

[12] Stuart, *Hosea-Jonah*, 435.

[13] See B. L. Woodward Jr., "Jonah," in *A Complete Literary Guide to the Bible*, ed. L. Ryken and T. Longman III (Grand Rapids: Zondervan, 1993), 348; D. Dorsey, *The Literary Structure of the Old Testament* (Grand Rapids: Baker, 1999), 290–91; and Magonet, "Jonah, Book of," 937.

[14] Adapted from G. Landes, "The Kerygma of the Book of Jonah," *Int* 21 (1962): 3–31.

THE CONTENTS OF THE BOOK

I. Jonah's Commission and Disobedience (chaps. 1–2)

The book of Jonah begins with Jonah receiving a commission from God to go deliver a message to the Ninevites (1:1–2). Instead of rising up in compliance with this commission as other biblical prophets did, Jonah rose up to go embark on a ship to Tarshish, the opposite direction from where God had instructed him to go.[15]

In response to Jonah's disobedience God sent a storm that threatened to kill the ship's crew and destroy the boat. The terror-stricken sailors called out to various gods and jettisoned much of the cargo to save the ship.[16] During all this frantic activity, however, Jonah was fast asleep below the deck. After the captain of the ship confronted Jonah about the danger, the sailors on deck decided to cast lots to determine who was responsible for the storm.[17] Through the casting of lots it was determined that it was Jonah, the Hebrew who feared the God of the sea and the dry land, who was responsible for the storm coming on the ship (1:7–9). After some fatal efforts to save ship and crew, the sailors acquiesced to Jonah's advice and threw him overboard (1:10–14). After being tossed overboard, Jonah was delivered from drowning by a great fish, which God had appointed (1:15–17). After being restored by God in the belly of the fish, Jonah, like the sailors, offered praise to God and vowed to make vows and sacrifices (2:1–9). This is the pinnacle for Jonah's faith in the book. God then directed the fish to vomit Jonah up on dry land (2:10).

II. Jonah's Second Commission and Its Results (chaps. 3–4)

The command of the first commission to Jonah in 1:2 is repeated with virtually the same language at the beginning of chap. 3 so that the LXX adds at the end of 3:2: "according to the former passage which I spoke." Jonah now agreed to go to Nineveh but apparently not with a whole heart. Nineveh was described as "an extremely large city, a three-day walk" (3:3). The latter phrase is problematic and has been understood as a reference to the breadth of the entire administrative district of Nineveh, or, as Wiseman has argued, as a reference to the fact that Nineveh was a full diplomatic city requiring a day for arrival, a day for the primary visit, and a day for the return.[18] Archaeological evidence has indicated that Nineveh was capable of maintaining a population of 120,000 individuals.[19]

At the announcement of Jonah's short proclamation—"In 40 days Nineveh will be overthrown!" (five words in Hb.; 3:4)[20]—the king issued a royal decree that called for a fast, the donning of sackcloth, and a call for each person to turn from his wickedness and violence (3:8).[21] The content of the decree (which mentions the Ninevites' "evil ways" and "violence"

---

[15] Tarshish is most frequently identified with Tartessus, a Phoenician colony on the southwestern coast of Spain. It is associated with distant lands (Ps 72:10; Isa 66:19).

[16] Pagan beliefs demanded that all physical calamities resulted from offending one of the pagan deities. For discussions of Hittite prayers made in these circumstances see *Near Eastern Religious Texts Relating to the Old Testament*, ed. W. Beyerlin, trans. J. Bowden (Philadelphia: Westminster, 1978), 166.

[17] For casting lots in determining God's will see 1 Sam 14:41–42; Prov 16:33; Acts 1:26.

[18] D. J. Wiseman, "Jonah's Nineveh," *TynBul* 30 (1979): 38.

[19] See Harrison, *Introduction to the Old Testament,* 909; and C. H. Bullock, *An Introduction to the Old Testament Prophetic Books* (Chicago: Moody, 1986), 46–47.

[20] Reference to "forty days" and "overthrow" connect this announcement with the biblical flood and the overthrow of Sodom and Gomorrah.

[21] The wording of the decree in 3:8 is a virtual quotation of Joel 2:14, perhaps an indication of the genuineness of the king's contrition.

[3:8]) reveals why Jonah had shown such resistance in going to Nineveh at the beginning of the book (see 4:2). The Assyrians were particularly known for their violence against their fellowman and against other nations. As King Asshur-banipal stated in his annals, "I tore out the tongues of those whose slanderous mouths had uttered blasphemies against my god Ashur and had plotted against me, his god-fearing prince. . . . The others, I smashed alive with the very same statues of protective deities with which they had smashed my own grandfather Sennacherib—now (finally) as a (belated) burial sacrifice for his soul. I fed their corpses, cut into small pieces, to dogs, pigs, *zi bu* birds, vultures, the birds of the sky and (also) to the fish of the ocean."[22]

Knowing their great acts of viciousness, Jonah did not want to give the Assyrians opportunity to repent. Instead he wanted the full measure of God's wrath to be visited on them for their notorious acts against humanity. When God, however, detected the seriousness of their contrition, He decided to withhold judgment against them.[23] Though Jonah's announcement seems unconditional, the repentance of the Ninevites and God's decision not to destroy them illustrates the principle for national repentance as outlined in Jer 18:7–10.[24]

In Jonah 4 Jonah once again prayed to God, this time while in dialogue with Him. Jonah expressed his regret that the Ninevites had heeded his call, and he was so distraught that he wanted to die (4:3). Just as Jonah had no regard for the lives of the pagan sailors (chap. 1), so here he actually wanted the pagan Ninevites not to heed his advice; he wished God had not been merciful in response to their repentance, and he wanted them to receive their just deserts by being destroyed.

Chronologically the account of the book of Jonah ends at 4:4 with God's question to Jonah about his anger that Nineveh was spared. The last episode (4:5–11), began with Jonah's taking up residence east of the city after his announcement of judgment. He wanted to witness God's annihilation of his despised enemies. This last account gave a lesson to Jonah and the Israelites who were like him. God provided a plant to protect Jonah from the Assyrian heat, but Jonah became upset when God appointed a worm to destroy the plant and a scorching east wind came in. If Jonah could become upset over the destruction of a plant, why can God not have compassion on creatures He made (4:9–11)? The book is instructing the Israelites of God's love and mercy for foreigners, even among Israel's enemies (see Isa 19:19–25).

THE STYLE OF THE BOOK

The author of the book of Jonah employed several techniques that aid in the effective communication of the message. First, the author was fond of repeating several key words throughout the book. This allows for "subliminal" messages to be conveyed to the alert reader. Key words which are repeated include "go down" (1:3,5; 2:7), "throw" (1:5,12,15), "great" (1:2, 4 [twice],10,12,16; 2:1; 3:2–3,5,7; 4:1,11), "appoint" (4:6–8), and "evil" (1:2,7–8; 3:8,10; 4:1).[25]

Irony is also found in the book. For example the pagan sailors' reaction to the storm contrasts with Jonah's. The sailors were doing all they could to keep from throwing Jonah over-

---

[22] *ANET*, 288.

[23] The reader has been prepared for the salvation of the heathen by the action of the sailors in Jonah 1.

[24] J. Walton is one who believes that the Ninevites did repent, but that it was short of a true conversion to Yahwism ("Jonah," in *Theological Interpretation of the Old Testament*, ed. K. J. Vanhoozer [Grand Rapids: Baker, 2008], 271).

[25] For additional discussion of the occurrence of repetition in the book see J. Magonet, *Form and Meaning: Studies in the Literary Techniques in the Book of Jonah* (Sheffield: Almond, 1983), 16–18.

board, whereas Jonah apparently could care less what happened to him or the sailors. Jonah slept during the storm while the pagans prayed. Jonah cited a creed, which reflected a heartless orthodoxy and claimed to fear God, which was belied by his actions (1:9). The pagans, however, demonstrated a genuine fear of the Lord and vowed to make sacrifices in response. A similar ironic scene occurs in the second half of the book. God had saved Jonah despite his sin (chaps. 1–2), and now Jonah wanted to stand in the way of the Ninevites being saved even though they repented (chaps. 3–4). Jonah's anger occurred precisely when God turned away His wrath. Jonah was unrepentant despite God's efforts, whereas the heathen repented with virtually no provocation.

THE THEOLOGY OF THE BOOK

Since the book of Jonah is an example of didactic narrative, as discussed earlier, the message of the book closely parallels the book's theology. The book closes with a question for the audience, leaving the reader with a challenge: "Do you want to adapt God's or Jonah's viewpoint on showing compassion for those outside the covenant community?" The book exhorts the Israelites to disassociate themselves from a narrow nationalism, which excluded other peoples, and to be mindful of their calling to bless all families of the earth (Gen 12:3) and to be a light to the Gentile world (Isa 42:6).[26] By placing the moral lesson at the end of the book the author thus concealed the book's main purpose until the book is completely read.

The power and sovereignty of God is also central to understanding the book of Jonah. God controls the forces of nature as He hurled a violent storm on the sea (1:4) and then caused it to rest when Jonah was thrown overboard (1:15). He prepared the great fish not only to swallow Jonah but also to deposit him on the dry ground to renew his mission (1:17; 2:10). God provided a plant overnight, appointed a worm to destroy it, and brought a scorching east wind on His prophet (4:6–7). In fact everything in the book obeyed God, except his prophet!

THE TEXT OF THE BIBLE

The text of the book of Jonah has been well preserved in the Hebrew text. A Hebrew manuscript of Jonah discovered in the Dead Sea regions is clearly in the MT tradition. Some of the Greek uncial manuscripts and cursives include Jonah 2 after the book of Psalms.

THE NEW TESTAMENT AND THE BOOK

Jesus made explicit reference to Jonah and the repentance of the Ninevites in His ministry (Matt 12:39–41). This reference is of critical importance to NT theology as Jesus stated that Jonah's time in the belly of the fish typified Jesus' time in the tomb and His own resurrection.

STUDY QUESTIONS

1. Compared with other prophetic books what is distinctive about the contents of the book of Jonah?
2. What tribe did Jonah belong to?
3. What were the conditions in Israel during Jonah's lifetime?
4. What is the theme of Jonah 2?
5. What are the three most frequent suggestions regarding the genre of the book of Jonah?

---

[26] The book presupposes that all peoples are aware of the need for repentance in light of a future judgment.

6. Who was most likely the Assyrian king during Jonah's ministry to Nineveh?
7. What is the best position on the question of the genre of Jonah?
8. What is the pinnacle of Jonah's faith in the book of Jonah?
9. Why did Jonah initially resist the Lord's instructions to go to Nineveh?
10. What prophetic text addresses the principle for national repentance?
11. Where does the book of Jonah end chronologically?
12. What is the ultimate message of the book of Jonah?
13. What does the book of Jonah say about the sovereignty of God?

FOR FURTHER STUDY

Alexander, D. "Jonah and Genre." *TynBul* 36 (1985): 35–59.

Allen, L. *The Books of Joel, Obadiah, Jonah and Micah*. NICOT. Grand Rapids: Eerdmans, 1976.

Berlin, A. *Poetics and Interpretation of Biblical Narrative*. Sheffield: Almond, 1983.

Dyck, E. "Jonah among the Prophets: A Study in Canonical Context." *JETS* 33 (1990): 63–73.

Eissfeldt, O. *The Old Testament: An Introduction*. Translated by P. Ackroyd. New York: Harper & Row, 1965.

Houk, C. B. "Linguistic Patterns in Jonah." *JSOT* 77 (1998): 81–102.

Kahn, P. "The Epilogue to Jonah." *JBQ* 28 (2000): 146–55.

Landes, G. "The Kerygma of the Book of Jonah." *Int* 21 (1962): 3–31.

Trible, P. *Rhetorical Criticism: Context, Method, and the Book of Jonah*. Minneapolis: Augsburg Fortress, 1994.

Walton, J. H. "The Object Lesson of Jonah 4:5–7 and the Purpose of the Book of Jonah." *BBR* 2 (1992): 47–57.

———. "Jonah." In *Theological Interpretation of the Old Testament*. Edited by K. J. Vanhoozer, 268–75. Grand Rapids: Baker Academic, 2008.

CHAPTER 32

THE BOOK OF MICAH

MARK F. ROOKER

T HE PROPHET MICAH prophesied during the reigns of Jotham (750–732), Ahaz (735–715), and Hezekiah (729–686), kings of Judah. He was a younger contemporary of Isaiah who, like Isaiah, prophesied just before and after the fall of the northern kingdom in 722 BC. Micah 1:2–7 predates the Assyrian conquest,[1] whereas 4:9–5:1 reflects the next serious crisis, Sennacherib's siege in 701. Micah ministered in a time characterized by both political and social unrest, although the period was one of the most economically prosperous times in Israel's history.

THE COMPOSITION OF THE BOOK

The critical analysis of the book of Micah began in earnest with the work of Heinrich Ewald and Bernhard Stade in the second half of the nineteenth century. Both worked at distinguishing the alleged genuine from the later secondary additions to the prophecy, and their conclusions are still highly regarded by many critics today. The critical consensus that emerged was that only chaps. 1–3 (apart from 2:12–13) are the words of Micah (from the eighth century). The oracles of hope in the remainder of the book are said to contradict these messages of judgment. As the result of Stade's analysis, it has been argued that the contents of Micah 4–5 belong to a later period, possibly as late as the postexilic period, as these chapters apparently assume the fall of Jerusalem (4:8), the exile and the dispersion (4:6–7), and the collapse of the Davidic dynasty (5:2–4 [HB, 5:1–3]). Moreover, the liturgy of chap. 7, generally regarded as a postexilic proclamation of salvation, is a totally distinct genre from the rest of the book. For Ewald, the difference of form and style between chaps. 1–5 and 6–7 alone was great enough to preclude their being written by the same author.

While assuming most of the findings of nineteenth-century scholarship regarding the study of Micah, twentieth-century critics have generally changed their focus in approaching their study of the book. Most of them accept the fact that additional contents were added to the

---

[1] The name Israel refers to the northern kingdom only in this passage (1:5). After this announcement the name Israel refers only to the southern kingdom (3:1,9, etc.).

book and focus on the book as a literary unit resulting from the process of growth over time. Many have argued that the original core of the book was expanded by later additions for liturgical and theological use by the religious community. Commentators on Micah who have adopted this general approach include James Mays, Ina Willi-Plein, A. S. van der Woude, Bernard Renaud, Hans Wolff, Joachim Jeremias, Brevard Childs, and Delbert Hillers. But the lack of agreement among these scholars regarding the way in which secondary material was incorporated into the book, as well as the inherent subjectivity of the approach, has prevented the emergence of a general consensus for the composition of the book.

The argument that Micah's oracles of hope must be dated in the postexilic period is inconsistent with what is known of Israelite prophecy in the eighth century. While it is true that Mic 2:12–13 presupposes the dispersion of Israel, it is inaccurate to assign this text to a later date since Isaiah also assumes a future dispersion of the nation (Isaiah 40–55). Just as oracles of salvation follow those of disaster in Hosea, so Micah's promises to the nation conclude his collections of threats.[2] Moreover, the doctrine of a remnant, an essential component of the hope oracles found in Mic 2:12; 4:7; 5:7; 7:18, is an important doctrine in other eighth-century prophets as well (Isa 37:32; Amos 5:15). The book's somewhat abrupt switch from oracles of doom to oracles of hope—which is the essential reason the oracles of hope have been considered secondary—may rather be because independent oracles were collected into the coherent whole which now makes up the book in its final form.[3] There is no serious reason to doubt the unity of the book or that it was composed by Micah who delivered its oracles in the eighth century.

THE MESSAGE OF THE BOOK

The message of Micah is stated explicitly in Mic 3:8. The nation was called to account by the prophet for their transgressions against the Lord. As with Amos's message somewhat earlier, this message is more specifically defined as injustice against the underprivileged (2:1–2; 3:1–3, 9–11; 6:10–11). Micah signaled out the powerful leaders who were guilty of bloodshed and violence (chap. 3).[4] As a prophet from the small village of Moreshah (1:1), Micah sympathized with the peasant classes who were oppressed by wealthy landowners and the powerful elite. Other violations in the nation included dishonest commercial practices (6:10–11), greedy priests (3:11), and loss of communal order (7:2–6).

Like the experience of Jeremiah after him, false prophets opposed Micah's message (3:5–8). They rested on the inviolability of Zion, believing that God would not judge and abandon the people He had chosen (3:11).

The consequence of the nation's violations was certain judgment. However, God would save a remnant (2:12–13; 4:6–7,8,10,11–13; 7:8–10,11–13,18–20) and provide the Davidic king to rule over them (5:2–4). The hope oracles illustrate God's faithfulness to His covenant promises, and thus while judgment must necessarily come, this did not mean that the covenant relationship had totally been severed. Micah's message was so venerated that it was remembered a century and a half later during the time of Jeremiah (Jer 26:18–19).

---

[2] W. H. Schmidt, *Old Testament Introduction*, trans. M. J. O'Connell (New York: Crossroad, 1990), 221.

[3] See B. Waltke, "Micah, Theology of," in *NIDOTTE*, ed. W. VanGemeren (Grand Rapids: Zondervan, 1997), 4:937.

[4] Micah's contemporaries Isaiah, Hosea, and Amos also laid special guilt at the feet of the upper class (Isa 5:8–12; Hos 4:6–10; Amos 2:6–8; 5:10–12).

THE STYLE OF THE BOOK

Micah was a skilled writer as can be seen through his use of wordplay and various literary forms. In 1:8–16 the names of the individual cities seem to indicate their fates. For example in v. 10 the inhabitants of Beth-le-aphrah ("house of dust") are told they will "roll in the dust." Several key terms are repeated to draw attention in the message. Micah 2:3–4 contains the repetition of the word *mûs* ("remove"), and *qûm* ("arise") occurs in 2:8,10. The same passage exhibits use of an inclusio in 2:6,11 with a reference to *ntp* ("preaching" or "speaking out"). The Hebrew term *mišpāt* is repeated three times in the same passage (3:1,8–9). Moreover, the occurrence of the verb *hipšîtû* ("strip off") in the same pericope (3:3) is similar in sound to *mišpāt*. Israel's ruler *(šopēt)* is struck with a rod *(šēbet)* (5:1). The prophet used the lament form in 7:1–6 as well as a liturgical form in 7:7–20. Legal language of the court is used in the first (1:2) and last of the major sections (6:1–2).

THE STRUCTURE OF THE BOOK

The book of Micah is arranged in three sections, each of which moves from judgment to salvation:

Section	Judgment	Salvation
1	1:2–2:11	2:12–13
2	3:1–12	4:1–5:15
3	6:1–7:7	7:8–20

The word "listen" in 1:2; 3:1; and 6:1 introduces each of these sections. The use of *ʿattâ,* "now" in chaps. 4 and 5 (4:9; 5:1[HB, 4:14]) provides a further structural clue for a division of a smaller unit within the book. Largely based on thematic concerns, chaps. 1–3 contain words of rebuke, chaps. 4–5 give words of comfort, and chaps. 6–7 start with rebuke and end with comfort.[5]

THE OUTLINE OF THE BOOK

 I. Judah's Exile and Restoration (chaps. 1–2)

 II. The Establishment of the Messianic Kingdom (chaps. 3–5)

 III. God's Charges and Promise (chaps. 6–7)

THE CONTENT OF THE BOOK

I. Judah's Exile and Restoration (chaps. 1–2)

Micah's first oracle (1:2–7) employs the image of a court trial *(rîb)* announced from the Lord's "holy temple." With notice of a coming theophany, Micah depicted the coming of the Lord to judge the idolatrous city of Samaria (1 Kgs 16:32). The announcement of judgment in the next section (Mic 1:8–16) takes the form of a lament with an introduction (1:8–9), the

---

[5] M. Segal, *Introduction to the Bible* (Jerusalem: Kiryat-Sepher, 1964), 1:482 (in Hb.). For comprehensive treatments on the style and compositional unity of Micah see K. Barker, "A Literary Analysis of the Book of Micah," *BSac* 155 (1998): 437–48; and L. Bliese, "Lexical and Numerical Patterns in the Structure of Micah," *JTT* 16 (2003) 119–43.

body (1:10–15), and the conclusion (1:16).[6] Wordplays on the names of the cities and towns have the effect of anticipating the future judgments.

Two successive speeches of doom are recorded in chap. 2 (2:1–5,6–11). Here Micah took up the cause of the oppressed landholder. The particle *hôy* ("woe"), frequently used in funeral laments (1 Kgs 13:30; Jer 22:18; 34:5; Amos 5:16), introduces these speeches. This has the effect of reinforcing the certainty of doom for the addressees. That the wealthy were guilty of violating the covenant is evident from the fact that they "covet" the possessions of others (Mic 2:2).[7]

The last two verses of this first section give a message of hope. Even though judgment must come, there will be a regathering from exile for the people of God (2:12–13; cf. 4:6–7,10). God will continue to be faithful to the remnant after the nation undergoes its just punishment.

II. The Establishment of the Messianic Kingdom (chaps. 3–5)

The first two sections of Micah include relatively long judgment speeches followed by short oracles of hope, whereas this section consists of a short judgment oracle but a lengthy oracle of comfort. The announced judgment is against the nation's leaders. The Lord would treat the rulers who had not responded to the cry of those whom they had oppressed in the same manner (chap. 3). The political leaders, prophets, and priests are depicted as those who carry out their duties only for a monetary fee (3:5,11). They had developed a false sense of security in believing that Zion and Jerusalem were untouchable (3:11).

After announcing that Jerusalem would in fact become a heap of ruins (3:12), the prophet presented seven oracles of hope focusing on the deliverance of the Messiah (chaps. 4–5). The coming of this kingdom (4:1–5; cf. Isa 2:2–4) that centers on Mount Zion announced a new beginning for Judah. In contrast to the utter ruin of Jerusalem at the end of Micah 3, Zion will be exalted above all other mountains (4:1). Many nations will gather there to worship the Lord as Jerusalem will become the spiritual center of the world.

This exaltation of Zion would be accompanied by the restoration of exiles and the birth of the coming Messiah (5:1–4). The Messiah will deliver His people, and the remnant will be preserved among the nations (5:5–9). The messianic kingdom will be an everlasting kingdom in which the earth will be cleansed from all idolatry and corruption (5:10–15).

III. God's Charges and Promise (chaps. 6–7)

In this final series of judgment and salvation oracles the nation at large, not the leaders, are primarily addressed. Chapter 6 consists of a covenant lawsuit (vv. 1–8) and a judgment speech (vv. 9–16). The people were guilty of various offenses including violence, deception, and unfair business practices.

Since the heavens and the earth had been witnesses to the ratification of the Lord's covenant with His people (Deut 4:26; 30:19; 31:28), Micah called on the mountains to observe Judah's covenant violation (Mic 6:1–2). The people were admonished to change their way by promoting justice and humbling themselves before God (6:8). Otherwise, even their worship and their offering of sacrifices would be in vain (6:6–8; cf. Isa 1:10–15; Hos 6:6; Amos 5:21–27).[8]

---

[6] The order of the cites may coincide with the route taken by Sennacherib when he invaded Judea at the end of the eighth century BC (R. Dillard and T. Longman III, *An Introduction to the Old Testament* [Grand Rapids: Zondervan, 1994], 398).

[7] The same verb is used in the tenth commandment in both accounts of the Decalogue (Exod 20:17; Deut 5:21).

[8] Schmidt suggests that the famous quotation in 6:8 reflects the essential message of the other eighth-century prophets: to do justice (Amos), to love kindness (Hosea), and to walk humbly before God (Isaiah) (*Old Testament Introduction*, 223–24).

The judgment speech of Mic 6:9–16 accuses the nation of violations in the marketplace. These infringements were prohibited in the law (Lev 19:35–36; Deut 25:13–16) and the prophets (Hos 12:7; Amos 8:5). Prominent individuals of Micah's day had exploited the poor and needy (Mic 6:10–12). Micah 7:1–7 concludes the judgment trial by alluding to all types of guilty parties within Israelite society, thereby indicating the comprehensive nature of the nation's transgression.

A new division (7:8–20) focuses on Israel's trust and restoration. Micah's prayer looks forward to the establishment of God's kingdom for the remnant.

THE TEXT OF THE BOOK

The Hebrew text of Micah is considered one of the least well-preserved books within the prophetic literature. Unfortunately little help comes from the discoveries in the Judean Desert, as the Hebrew text of the DSS of the Minor Prophets reflects the traditional MT.

THE THEOLOGY OF THE BOOK

As noted above, Micah was concerned with Judah's sin which called for divine judgment. This response on the part of God's prophet was in harmony with Israel's covenant relationship with the Lord, who promised a divine judgment on their sin (Leviticus 26; Deuteronomy 28). The unconditional oracles of hope find their theological mooring in the promises made to Abraham. Thus the juxtaposition of oracles of judgment and hope can be explained by the theology in the Mosaic and Abrahamic covenants.[9] The Mosaic covenant promised judgment and death for disobedience, whereas the Abrahamic covenant guaranteed Israel an everlasting status in God's redemptive program.[10] The positive hope for the remnant through which these Abrahamic promises would be realized are mentioned in Mic 4:6–8 and 5:7–9.

The oracles of hope are addressed to the Jewish remnant as well as to all Gentiles who submit to the Lord (4:1–4). These nations will acknowledge Judah's preeminence (4:12–13; 5:5–9; 7:10,16–17), and they will be blessed. The blessing on the Gentiles is an additional component of the promises made to Abraham (Gen 12:3; Mic 4:1–4). The affirmation that the promises would be realized by a remnant of Israel indicates that the future blessings for the nation will never be vitiated. The Davidic ruler will establish this kingdom and will thus fulfill the ideal expressed in the Davidic covenant (2 Sam 7:9–11).[11]

THE NEW TESTAMENT AND THE BOOK

Micah addressed aspects of the Messiah's ministry in both first and second advents of Jesus Christ. Micah 5:2 records the prophecy of the Messiah's birth who, like David, would be born in Bethlehem of Judea. This was fulfilled with the birth of Christ. Micah 5:2, a prophecy of the location of the Messiah's birth, was common knowledge among the Jews (Matt 2:6). Moreover, Micah stressed the fact that in the "last days" (Mic 4:1; 5:10 [HB, 9]), Jerusalem will be the center of spiritual life for the world. While these last days have already commenced with Christ's ascension (Heb 1:2), Micah's prophecy will not be realized in its entirety until all

---

[9] Stephane Schooling argues that the manner in which Micah uniquely balances the judgment and salvation oracles was the reason the book occupies the central position among the 12 Minor Prophets. See "La place du livre de Michee dans le contexte des douze Petits Prophetes," *EJT* 7 (1998) 27–35.

[10] See Waltke, "Micah, Theology of," 937–38.

[11] See Isa 9:7; Hos 3:5; Amos 9:11.

nations come to worship God in Jerusalem. This will be fulfilled in the millennial kingdom, the 1,000 years of Christ's future reign addressed near the end of the Bible (Rev 20:1–6).

STUDY QUESTIONS

1. What prophet was a contemporary of Micah?
2. What were the general conditions during the time of Micah's prophecy?
3. What doctrine is important among the eighth-century prophets?
4. Where is the message of Micah stated or referred to?
5. What may we surmise about Micah's economic status?
6. What was the general message of the false prophets?
7. How many major sections are in Micah?
8. What is the general context of the prophecy of the birth of the Messiah in Micah 5?
9. Where will the spiritual center of the world be located in the coming age?
10. Unconditional promises for Israel are connected with which OT covenant?
11. What does Micah say about the future of the nations?
12. When will Micah's prophecy finally be realized?

FOR FURTHER STUDY

Allen, L. *The Books of Joel, Obadiah, Jonah and Micah*. NICOT. Grand Rapids: Eerdmans, 1976.

Bliese, L. F. "Lexical and Numerical Patterns in the Structure of Micah." *JTT* 16 (2003): 119–43.

Dempsey, C. J. "Micah 2–3: Literary Artistery, Ethical Message, and Some Considerations About the Image of Yahweh and Micah." *JSOT* 85 (1999): 117–28.

Jacobs, M. R. *The Conceptual Coherence of the Book of Micah*. Sheffield: Sheffield University Press, 2001.

Mays, J. L. *Micah*. OTL. Philadelphia: Westminster, 1976.

McComiskey, T. E. "Micah." *EBC*. Rev. ed. Edited by T. Longman III and D. E. Garland, 8:491–551. Grand Rapids: Zondervan, 2008.

Segal, M. *Introduction to the Bible*. 2 vols. Jerusalem: Kiryat-Sepher, 1964. Vol. 1 [in Hb.].

Smith, R. L. *Micah–Malachi*. WBC. Vol. 32. Waco, TX: Word, 1984.

Waltke. B. "Micah." In *Obadiah, Jonah, Micah*. TOTC. Edited by D. J. Wiseman, 133–207. Downers Grove, IL: InterVarsity, 1988.

———. "Micah, Theology of," In *NIDOTTE*. Edited by W. VanGemeren, 4:936–40. Grand Rapids: Zondervan, 1997.

Zapff, B. M. "The Perspective of the Nations in the Book of Micah as a 'Systematization' of the Nations' Role in Joel, Jonah and Nahum: Reflections on a Context-Oriented Exegesis in the Book of the Twelve." *SBLSP* 38 (1999): 596–616.

CHAPTER 33

THE BOOK OF NAHUM

MARK F. ROOKER

NAHUM WAS FROM the city of Elkosh, the precise location of which is uncertain. The four most common suggestions are Elkesi or Il Kauze in Galilee (Jerome), the city of Capernaum (Kephar Nahum),[1] Alqush near Mosul in Assyria, and Elcesei, and a village located in the territory of Simeon midway between Jerusalem and Gaza.

The prophecy of Nahum, like that of Obadiah, is directed against one foreign nation, in this case the city of Nineveh, capital of Assyria. Nineveh came into prominence particularly through the effort of Sennacherib, king of Assyria (704–681 BC), who had laid siege against Jerusalem in 701 BC (see 2 Kgs 18:13–16). A massive wall 40 to 50 feet in height and eight miles in circumference surrounded Nineveh, enclosing about 1,800 acres. The city had a rather advanced water system that included one of the first aqueducts in the ancient world. When the royal library was discovered, it had approximately 22,000 clay tablets that included the Babylonian creation story (Enuma Elish) and the Babylonian flood account (Gilgamesh). Nineveh also had a magnificent palace with parks, a botanical garden, and a zoo.[2]

By the time of Nahum's prophecy the Assyrians' barbaric military policies had terrorized the ancient Near East for more than two centuries. It was not uncommon for enemies and prisoners of Assyria to be subject to flaying, to being burned alive, and to having body parts amputated.[3]

Nineveh was destroyed in 612 by a coalition of forces made up of Babylonians, Medes, and Scythians. According to the ancient historian Diodorus Siculus, Nineveh was destroyed when the Khosr River flooded and demolished a section of the city wall, thus allowing the enemies to penetrate the city (Nah 1:8).

---

[1] The name Kephar is a transliteration for the Hebrew word *kaphar*, which means a village. The idea would be that Elkosh was later renamed after its most famous citizen, the biblical prophet Nahum.

[2] See Chris Scarre, ed., *The Seventy Wonders of the Ancient World* (London: Thames & Hudson, 1999), 159–63, and A. Millard, "Nahum," in *Zondervan Illustrated Bible Backgrounds Commentary*, ed. John Walton (Grand Rapids: Zondervan, 2009), 5:150.

[3] See A. E. Hill and J. H. Walton, *A Survey of the Old Testament*, 2nd ed. (Grand Rapids: Zondervan, 2000), 511–12.

THE DATE OF THE BOOK

The book of Nahum must be dated between 663 and 612 BC. The prophet regarded the fall of Thebes (663) as a historical fact (3:8–10) while the thrust of his message was the future overthrow of Nineveh, an event that did not take place until 612. One cannot be more precise about the date. Many scholars point out that after the death of the last great Assyrian ruler Asshur-banipal in 627, the Assyrian Empire immediately showed signs of weakness. Nahum, it is argued, could have surmised in these circumstances that Nineveh was on its last leg. In the very next year, in fact (626), Nabopolassar, the Chaldean leader of Babylon, asserted his independence. However, the book's indication that the Assyrian empire was large and intact (1:12) may indicate that the prophecy was delivered sometime before 630.

THE MESSAGE OF THE BOOK

As the book of Nahum is devoted exclusively to the announcement of the destruction of the city of Nineveh, the prophecy gave hope to the people of Judah who had long been terrorized by Assyria's constant and ominous threat. One hundred fifty years earlier Jonah had come to Nineveh offering the Assyrians a chance to repent from their wickedness and violence. Now, after returning to her former ways, Nahum must announce to Nineveh certain judgment without any chance of repentance (see Ezek 32:22–23; Zeph 2:13–15). This twofold purpose of judgment for Nineveh and comfort for Judah is announced at the outset of the prophecy (1:7–8).

THE COMPOSITION OF THE BOOK

Modern critical study of the book of Nahum is dominated by two issues regarding the composition of the book. These have involved the relationship of the opening psalm to the rest of the contents of the book, and the *Sitz im Leben* ("life setting") in which the book originated.

The opening psalm or hymn of Nahum concerns a theophany describing an awesome appearance of God (1:2–8). The striking thing about the structure of this hymn is that the verses of the poem are arranged in an almost acrostic order, each line (starting with v. 2a) beginning with a successive letter of the alphabet.[4] Because of this structure some have suggested that the hymn had an existence independent of its use in Nahum. The poem could have existed before Nahum's time and been utilized by the prophet to introduce his prophecy, or a subsequent editor could have prefaced the hymn to Nahum's prophecies.

Being sensitive to issues raised in form-critical approaches to Hebrew literature, many critics have attempted to recreate the general setting in Israel's religious history that would have given rise to such a prophecy as Nahum. Haldar argued that the prophecy originated in cultic circles, and based on the content of the opening hymn the enemy of the nation was identified as ancient cosmic forces. Mowinckel saw in the victory over Assyria the myth and ritual elements employed in the ANE enthronement-of-God festival. Haupt believed the entire prophecy was a liturgy made up of four liturgical poems, the earliest of which did not originate until the Maccabean period. Humbert, Lods, and Sellin also saw in the prophecy a prophetic liturgy that was composed after Nineveh's fall and was employed in the accession festival celebrated in the annual fall New Year festival.

---

[4] The acrostic order goes almost halfway through the Hebrew alphabet, from *aleph* to *kaph*.

These theories have fallen on hard times among contemporary scholars, as many point out the lack of evidence for Israel's involvement in enthronement or New Year festivals.[5] Moreover, many of these theories overlook the fact that the prophecy is totally oriented to the future judgment of Nineveh and is not describing events that have already transpired (2:4–3:17). There is thus no reason to doubt that the prophet Nahum wrote this prophecy in the seventh century BC after the fall of Thebes (663) but before the destruction of Nineveh (612).

THE STYLE OF THE BOOK

As a literary craftsman Nahum has few rivals among the writers of the OT. He employed vivid imagery in the judgment announcements (1:2–8; 2:11–12; 3:15,17–18), rhetorical questions (1:6; 3:7–8,19), an elliptical sentence (3:2), apostrophe (2:11–12), metaphors and similes (1:10; 2:7,12; 3:4,12,17), assonance and alliteration (2:11), synonyms (1:6), irony (2:1,8; 3:14–15), satire (2:11–13; 3:8–13,14–19), chiasm (1:2; 3:1–7), and parallelism (3:15). His descriptions are picturesque and vivid (2:3–5,10; 3:2–3).[6]

Structure

Although there is a virtual consensus among scholars that the book of Nahum is a well-structured prophecy, there is no universal agreement as to where to divide the contents of the prophecy. Smith for example argued that the prophecy is composed of five distinct sections: (1) God's powerful wrath and goodness (1:2–8); (2) God will destroy those who afflict Judah (1:9–2:2 [HB, v. 3]); (3) Nineveh will fall (2:3–13 [HB, vv. 4–14]); (4) Nineveh will be destroyed because of its sin (3:1–7); and (5) Nineveh's end is inevitable (3:8–19).[7] More recently Dorsey has argued for a sevenfold division of the contents based on a chiastic structure:

A.   Yahweh avenges His enemies (1:2–10)
    B.   Yahweh will destroy Nineveh (1:11–15 [HB, 1:11–2:1]
        C.   Description of attack on Nineveh (2:1–10 [HB, 2:2–11]
            D.   Lament over fall of Nineveh (2:11–13) [HB, 2:12–14]
        C¹.   Description of looting of Nineveh (3:1–7)
    B¹.   Nineveh will be destroyed (3:8–13)
A¹.   Nineveh, like a destructive force of nature, will be destroyed (3:14–19)[8]

Of special interest is the employment of structural features throughout the book: opening hymn (1:2–8), messenger speech (1:12), announcement speech (1:15), battle description (2:3–12), divine announcement (2:13; 3:5), woe oracle (3:1), historical comparison (3:8), and direct address (3:18).[9]

---

[5] See B. Childs, *Introduction to the Old Testament as Scripture* (Philadelphia: Fortress, 1979), 442; and K. Cathcart, "Nahum, Book of," in *ABD*, ed. D. N. Freedman (New York: Doubleday, 1992), 4:999.

[6] See S. R. Driver, *An Introduction to the Literature of the Old Testament*, 9th ed. (Edinburgh: Clark, 1913), 336; and R. D. Patterson, *Nahum, Habakkuk and Zephaniah*, WEC (Chicago: Moody, 1991), 10–11.

[7] G. V. Smith, "Nahum," in *ISBE*, ed. G. Bromiley (Grand Rapids: Eerdmans, 1979), 3:477–78. For a defense of the book as composed of two parallel parts, see R. D. Patterson and M. E. Travers, "Literary Analysis and the Unity of Nahum," *GTJ* 9 (1988): 45–58.

[8] D. Dorsey, *The Literary Structure of the Old Testament* (Grand Rapids: Baker, 1999), 304. According to this arrangement the lament over the fall of Nineveh (2:11–13) is the main focus of the prophecy.

[9] See K. Barker and W. Bailey, *Micah, Nahum, Habakkuk, Zephaniah*, NAC (Nashville: B&H, 1999), 151.

Outline

Title Verse (1:1)

I. **Nineveh's Judge (1:2–15)**
   A. The Manifestation of God (1:2–6)
   B. The Lord's Care for Judah (1:7–12a)
   C. The Joy of Deliverance (1:12b–15)

II. **The Lord's Judgment on Nineveh (chap. 2)**
   A. Nineveh's Attackers (2:1–5)
   B. Nineveh's Defeat (2:6–13)

III. **Nineveh's Total Destruction (chap. 3)**
   A. Destruction and Humiliation of Nineveh (3:1–7)
   B. The Futility of Nineveh to Defend Itself (3:8–17)
   C. Funeral Lament (3:18–19)

THE CONTENTS OF THE BOOK

I. Nineveh's Judge (1:2–15)

As noted above, Nahum begins with a theophany depicting God as a mighty warrior. In ANE literature one often finds certain deities, particularly storm deities, portrayed as visiting the earth in the storm. Just north of Israel, in the city of Ugarit, the god Baal was portrayed as the god of the storm who also engaged in battle. As the result of the Lord's appearance, the mountains, which represent strength and stability, shake and crumble (1:5). The same phenomena occurred in other manifestations of God in the OT (Judg 5:4–5; 2 Sam 22:8; Ps 97:4–5; Mic 1:4; Hab 3:6). The manifestation of the Lord's power is significant for the interpretation of the book as a whole as it prepares for oracles announced against the city of Nineveh. The Lord is sovereign over all the creation of the earth. Thus Nineveh's claim to power is subordinated to the universal claim of the God of Israel.[10]

After briefly commemorating God's faithfulness to His servants (Nah 1:7), the Lord proceeded to describe the destruction that was about to overtake the Assyrian capital (1:8–12a). The effects of this judgment depict a reversal of creation.[11] The news of this devastation will produce a spirit of exultation and reassurance in the land of Judah (1:12b–15).

II. The Lord's Judgment on Nineveh (chap. 2)

Chapter 2 opens with a dramatic change of mood from the closing verses in Nahum 1. As the theophanic hymn of 1:2–8 established the fact that the all-powerful Lord is a God of vengeance, this attribute is now particularized with regard to the city of Nineveh. The city was notoriously known in the ANE as a harborer of cruelty and despotism. But now chap. 2 vividly describes a scene of siege and destruction of Nineveh by the scarlet-clad troops of Babylon. Nahum envisions the chariots and horsemen of Babylon storming through the streets of Nineveh, spreading the carnage of the city in their wake. The prediction that the gates of the

---

[10] Childs, *Introduction to the Old Testament or Scripture*, 443–44.

[11] See W. J. Dumbrell, *The Faith of Israel: A Theological Survey of the Old Testament*, 2nd ed. (Grand Rapids: Baker, 2002), 215.

city would be opened (2:6) was subsequently fulfilled as the Medes and the Chaldeans stormed the city when its walls were carried away by flood.[12]

The last three verses of chap. 2 describe the demise of the Assyrians through the imagery of the lion, the beast that accurately represented the ferocious inhabitants of the city of Nineveh. The use of the lion to portray Assyria is particularly appropriate, as Assyrian kings were often compared to lions.[13]

III. Nineveh's Total Destruction (chap. 3)

The final chapter of Nahum consists of three separate sections: (1) the description of the destruction and humiliation of Nineveh (3:1–7); (2) the utter futility of Nineveh to defend herself (3:8–17); and (3) a funeral lament (3:18–19).

Nahum 3:1–7 is a woe oracle over Nineveh, announcing judgment on the city.[14] Nineveh's fortunes are reversed through three wordplays. Whereas Nineveh had been characterized as having an endless supply of gold and silver, *wĕên mapneh* (2:9), she would be covered with an endless supply of corpses, *wĕên qēṣeh laggĕwiyyâ* (3:3), whose piles would replace her abundant wealth (kābōd, 2:9 [HB, v. 10]); and her numerous *(rōb)* harlotries (3:4) would lead to numerous *(rōb)* casualties (3:3).[15]

Nineveh's fate is sealed with her judgment as certain as the fall of mighty Thebes, defeated by the Assyrians in 663 (3:8–13). To describe Nineveh's fall, Nahum next used the imagery of the ravishing locust that strips the land and then moves on to greener pastures. In a similar manner the leading citizens of Nineveh would desert their city at the first sign of judgment (3:16–17).

The prophecy ends with a dirge or funeral lament that despondently informed Nineveh that it was now the time to prepare for the siege (3:18–19). The king of Assyria is fatally wounded (3:19), indicating that final and complete destruction is imminent.

THE TEXT OF THE BOOK

The Hebrew text of Nahum is well preserved. Some critics believe that there is evidence of some textual deterioration in 1:2–8 because the acrostic poem is incomplete. However, the ancient Greek and Syriac versions are in agreement with the MT.[16] The same is true of the DSS of the Minor Prophets from Wadi Murabbaʿat and the LXX of the Minor Prophets from Naḥal Ḥever. A commentary (*pesher*) of Nahum (1QpHah) was discovered among the DSS. Like the commentary on Habakkuk, the document is significant for understanding how the sect at the Dead Sea interpreted the Bible rather in determining the original text. Notice the very limited textual suggestions in favor of the DSS variants by J. J. M. Roberts in his commentary, *Nahum, Habakkuk, and Zephaniah*.[17]

---

[12] The Hebrew word *mûg*, used in reference to the "dissolving" of the palace (2:6 [HB, v. 7]), was used in 1:5 to describe the "dissolving" of the hills to indicate God's sovereignty over nations and nature.

[13] See A. Spalinger, "Assurbanipal and Egypt: A Source Study," *JAOS* (1974): 324–25. Jeremiah associated a lion with the king of Assyria in Jer 50:17. Lion hunts were at their peak during the reign of Asshur-banipal. See Gordon H. Johnston, "Nahum's Rhetorical Allusions to the Neo-Assyrian Lion Motif," *BSac* 158 (2001): 305.

[14] It is possible to view these verses not as a prediction of Nineveh's downfall but rather as a description of the city's conquests.

[15] See R. B. Chisholm Jr., *Interpreting the Minor Prophets* (Grand Rapids: Baker, 1990), 177.

[16] See T. Longman, "Nahum," in *The Minor Prophets*, ed. T. E. McComiskey (Grand Rapids: Baker, 1993), 2: 773–75.

[17] J. J. M. Roberts, *Nahum, Habakkuk, and Zephaniah* (Louisville: WJK, 1991). See also M. Fishbane, *Biblical Interpretation in Ancient Israel* (Oxford: Clarendon Press, 1985), 69, n.11.

THE THEOLOGY OF THE BOOK

Because the Lord is a holy God, it is contrary to His nature to allow sin to go unpunished. His holiness cannot allow unbridled wickedness to flourish (1:3). Thus Nahum announced that Nineveh's destruction was at hand. All nations that infringe on His moral law will receive just recompense (cf. Amos 1–2). In His judgment against Assyria the Lord is seen in His role as Divine Warrior who defeats His enemies (Nah 2:13; 3:5). His role in carrying out justice underscores His sovereignty over all nature and nations. They rise and fall based on His good pleasure (see Isa 10:5–19; 34; Jeremiah 50–51; Ezekiel 26–32). By His judgment on Assyria the Lord also illustrates His faithfulness to Israel as He defeats their enemies and preserves a remnant of His people (Nah 1:7; Gen 12:3).

THE NEW TESTAMENT AND THE BOOK

The picture of the Lord coming as the Divine Warrior to judge the wicked foreshadows the second advent of Christ when He will come to battle and defeat God's enemies (Rev 19:11–21). The judgment of the nations also anticipates the final judgment when God will recompense to all according to their works (Eccl 12:14; Rom 2:15–16).

STUDY QUESTIONS

1. What nation is addressed in the book of Nahum?
2. Which Assyrian king did the most to make Nineveh a prominent capital city?
3. Describe Nineveh at the time of Nahum's prophecy.
4. Comment on Assyria's military practices.
5. When was the book of Nahum composed?
6. When did Nahum deliver his message to Assyria?
7. What role does the opening theophany play in the interpretation of the book of Nahum?
8. What nation will destroy Nineveh in Nahum 2?
9. What animals were Assyrian kings compared with?
10. What insect is compared to the ravishing of the land of Assyria?
11. In which prophetic book of the Minor Prophets was this insect compared to the desolation of Israel?
12. What theological truths emerge from Nahum?

FOR FURTHER STUDY

Armerding, C. E. "Nahum." In *EBC*. Edited by T. Longman III and D. E. Garland, 8:553–601. Grand Rapids: Zondervan, 1985.

Baker, D. W. *Nahum, Habakkuk, Zephaniah*. TOTC. Downers Grove, IL: InterVarsity, 1988.

Barker, K., and W. Bailey, *Micah, Nahum, Habakkuk, Zephaniah*, NAC. Nashville: B&H, 1999.

Chisholm, R., Jr. *Interpreting the Minor Prophets*. Grand Rapids: Baker, 1990.

Dorsey, D. *The Literary Structure of the Old Testament*. Grand Rapids: Baker, 1999.

Dumbrell, W. J. *The Faith of Israel: A Theological Survey of the Old Testament*. 2nd ed. Grand Rapids: Baker, 2002.

Johnston, G. H. "Nahum's Rhetorical Allusions to the Neo-Assyrian Lion Motif." *BSac* 158 (2001): 287–307.

Longman, T., III. "Nahum." In *The Minor Prophets*. Edited by T. E. McComiskey, 2:765–829. Grand Rapids: Baker, 1993.

Maier, W. *The Book of Nahum*. Grand Rapids: Baker, 1959.

Patterson, R. D. *Nahum, Habakkuk and Zephaniah*, WEC. Chicago: Moody, 1991.

Sweeney, M. A. "Concerning the Structure and Generic Character of the Book of Nahum." *ZAW* 104 (1992): 364–77.

Watts, J. W., and P. House. *Forming Prophetic Literature: Essays on Isaiah and the Twelve in Honor of John D. W. Watts*. Sheffield: Sheffield Academic, 1996.

CHAPTER 34

THE BOOK OF HABAKKUK

MARK F. ROOKER

U NLIKE MOST OF the prophetic OT books, Habakkuk has no formal superscription with information about the time in which the prophet lived or his family background. In Jewish tradition he was identified as the son of the Shunammite saved by the prophet Elisha (Zohar 1:7; 2:44–45). In the apocryphal text of Bel and the Dragon he was associated with the tribe of Levi, which some have said accounts for Habakkuk's familiarity with musical notations ("Selah" occurs with 3:3,9, and 13, and 3:19 refers to "stringed instruments"). Some twentieth-century form-critics (Gerhard Sellin, J. H. Eaton, J. D. W. Watts) suggested that Habakkuk was a temple cult prophet based on the use of these and other liturgical forms. These comments are of interest but of questionable value. Although some prophets were also priests (e.g., Ezekiel and Zechariah), virtually no evidence exists for the role of cult prophets who were maintained by temple revenues.

The prophecy of Habakkuk is distinctive among prophetic books in that it provides insight into the prophet's own personal experience as seen in his dialogue with God. He described the inner agony he experienced when he realized what was in store for himself and his people (3:16). In addition Habakkuk gives insight on how a prophet prepared himself to receive a communication from the Lord (2:1–5).

THE DATE OF THE BOOK

A wide range of dates have been offered for the ministry and message of the prophet Habakkuk. These dates range from Sennacherib's invasion of Judah in 701 BC to Alexander the Great's conquest of the Near East in the fourth century BC.

Of critical importance in determining the date of the book is the exact meaning of the reference to the Chaldeans (1:5–11; 2:5,8–10), and the historical circumstance described in the opening of the prophecy (1:2–4). In response to the decadent situation in Judah (1:2–4), God announced that He would send the Chaldeans as an instrument to judge Israel's rampant unrighteousness. Since the Babylonians did not begin to gain military preeminence until 626, when they asserted their independence from Assyria, the situation described must be after this date. And yet because the announcement of the coming of the Babylonians was somewhat of a surprise to the prophet, it should be assumed that what is described was taking place before the first Babylonian invasion of Jerusalem in 605 BC. This compels a date early in the reign of Jehoiakim (608–598). Early in his rule forced labor, syncretism, idolatry, and persecution of false prophets was not unknown (Jer 23:13–19). In essence he reversed the reforms initiated by Josiah in 622 BC. The corruption described in Hab 1:2–4 probably refers to what was taking place in Jehoiakim's despotic reign.

THE COMPOSITION OF THE BOOK

As with other OT books, many critics have suggested that the book of Habakkuk went through a considerable process of editing before it reached its present form. The impetus for this approach with respect to Habakkuk can be traced to Bernhard Stade in 1884, and was continued by Julius Wellhausen in 1892. Stade argued that Hab 2:9–20 and the psalm in chap. 3 differed in style and language from other sections of the book and thus should be deemed as later additions. As expected, subsequent scholars increased the number of later additions to include 1:2–4 and 1:12–13.[1]

Under the influence of form-critical studies developed by Mowinckel and Gunkel, modern scholars reached a consensus that the book represents a coherent literary unity (although the book was not written by a single author).[2] There are sound literary reasons for associating Habakkuk 3 with Habakkuk 1–2. There is similarity of language and lexical links between the sections.[3] The psalm is connected to the vision of 2:1–4 (3:2,16) and in it God's righteousness is vindicated (1:12–17). Both sections focus on waiting on God's deliverance (2:1–5; 3:2,16) and emphasize the theme that God will bring the oppression of victimized peoples to an end. Thus Habakkuk 3 is a corroborating conclusion to the issues raised in Habakkuk 1–2. Chapter 3 affirms the promise of 2:3–5 that the Lord would act in His own time.[4] Since 1950 a number of critical scholars such as Otto Eissfeldt, William Brownlee, and Wilhelm Rudolph have suggested that nothing prevents Habakkuk himself from being the author of the psalm. Thus no demonstrable reason exists for denying the authorship of the entire prophecy to the prophet Habakkuk late in the seventh century.[5]

THE STYLE OF THE BOOK

The style of Habakkuk is shaped by its chief concern—the establishment of God's righteousness. This theme is presented through Habakkuk's conversations with God. The prophet's descriptions of the demise of the Babylonians are graphic and powerful, and the psalm of chap. 3 is not unlike the biblical psalms in its poetry and imagery. Rhetorical features of the book include proverbs (1:9; 2:6), similes (1:8b,9b,11a,14; 2:5; 3:4,14,19), metaphors (1:8a,9a, 15–17; 2:16; 3:8–11,14), allegory (2:15–16), irony (3:8), metonymy (2:5; 3:2,9), merismus (3:7), hyperbole (1:6–11; 3:6b,11), paronomasia (2:19; 3:13–14), personification (1:7–11; 2:5,11; 3:2,5,7,10), rhetorical questions (1:2; 2:13,18; 3:8), repetition (1:15b–17), synecdoche (3:7), alliteration and assonance (1:6,10; 2:6–7,15,18; 3:2), enjambment (1:13; 2:18; 3:4),

---

[1] E. Sellin and G. Fohrer, *Introduction to the Old Testament*, trans. D. Green (Nashville: Abingdon, 1965), 453.

[2] M. Sweeney, "Habakkuk, Book of," in *ABD,* ed. D. N. Freedman (New York: Doubleday, 1992), 3:3.

[3] Such as the occurrence of the term "wicked" in 1:4,13 and 3:13.

[4] C. H. Bullock, *An Introduction to the Old Testament Prophetic Books* (Chicago: Moody, 1986), 178.

[5] As with all other prophetic books, this affirmation does not demand that Habakkuk wrote the book at one sitting. The book could have been written over several years before it was joined together in its present form.

gender-matched parallelism (2:5; 3:3), staircase parallelism (3:8), climactic parallelism (3:2), pivot-pattern parallelism (1:17), chiasmus (1:2–4; 2:1,6,9,16; 3:3), and inclusio (2:4,20).[6] The book also uniquely contains wisdom terminology illustrated particularly by the occurrences of two words, "complaint" (*tôkaḥat*, 2:1) and "conflict" (*mādôn*, 1:3) that almost exclusively occur in wisdom literature in the OT.

THE STRUCTURE OF THE BOOK

Most scholars contend that Habakkuk consists of three major literary units: a dialogue between the prophet and God (1:1–2:5), a series of five woe oracles (2:6–20), and the psalm (chap. 3). Dorsey argues for seven sections, with the center focus on the divine announcement in 2:1–5:

Habakkuk's first complaint (1:2–4)
    Yahweh's first answer (1:5–11)
        Habakkuk's second complaint (1:12–17)
            Center: In the end the wicked will be punished (2:1–5)
        Yahweh's answer to second complaint (2:6–20)
    Yahweh's final answer (3:1–15)
Habakkuk's final resolution of first complaint (3:16–19)[7]

THE OUTLINE OF THE BOOK

Superscription (1:1)

I. **Questions and Answers (1:2–2:5)**
   A. Why Do the Wicked Prosper? (1:2–4)
   B. God Will Send the Chaldeans (1:5–11)
   C. Will God Use the Wicked Chaldeans? (1:12–17)
   D. The Righteous Will Live by His Faithfulness (2:1–5)

II. **Five Woes on Babylon (2:6–20)**
   A. Woe to the Violent Extortioner (2:6–8)
   B. Woe to the Greedy (2:9–11)
   C. Woe to the Murderer (2:12–14)
   D. Woe to the Drunkard (2:15–17)
   E. Woe to the Idol-maker (2:18–20)

III. **Habakkuk's Prayer (chap. 3)**
   A. Habakkuk's Petition (3:1–2)
   B. The Lord's Appearing (3:3–15)
   C. Habakkuk's Confidence (3:16–19)

---

[6] K. Barker and W. Bailey, *Micah, Nahum, Habakkuk, Zephaniah*, NAC (Nashville: B&H, 1999), 270–71.

[7] D. Dorsey, *The Literary Structure of the Old Testament* (Grand Rapids: Baker, 1999), 308. L. F. Bliese skillfully displays a structure of Habakkuk as composed of three parts, each containing seven parts ("The Poetics of Habakkuk," *JTT* 12 [1999] 47–75).

THE CONTENT OF THE BOOK

I. Questions and Answers (1:2–2:5)

The book of Habakkuk begins with the prophet's complaint about the violence and injustices he observed in his land (1:2–4). The oppression he described is similar to that depicted in the writings of such eighth-century prophets as Isaiah, Micah, and particularly Amos. While some scholars have wanted to identify these evildoers with foreign oppressors, it seems clear from the nature of these offenses, particularly the ignoring of the law (v. 4a), that the Judeans were the offenders.[8] The prophet felt that evil was not being reckoned with, and so he desired God's response.

The answer the prophet received certainly made him regret that he had asked the question! God in effect agreed with Habakkuk's assessment of the evil that existed in Judea, and so He announced that He would send the Chaldeans as His instruments to carry out the just punishment.[9]

In many of the Psalms a promise of deliverance or a salvation speech is included after a complaint or a lament is voiced. In God's response to Habakkuk's complaint, however, the method of deliverance was the coming onslaught by the Babylonian army (1:6–11).[10] The Babylonians would distribute violence (*hāmās*, v. 9) to those who had practiced violence in Judah (*hāmās*, v. 3). Those who perverted justice in Judah (*mišpāṭ*, v. 4) would be overrun by those who developed their own standard of justice (*mišpāṭ*, v. 7b).[11]

For Habakkuk, God's response to the problem of evil in Judah raised a serious dilemma. In administering His justice, how could God use a people more evil than the offenders to carry out justice against His covenant violators? (vv. 12–17). In reasoning with God about this dilemma the prophet focused on God's nature: He is eternal (v. 12a) and sovereign (v. 12b) and too pure to look upon evil (v. 13).

After stating his case, Habakkuk went to the lookout tower either to watch for the Babylonians or to receive a further answer from God (2:1). In His answer to Habakkuk's concern, God was in agreement with Habakkuk's evaluation of the wickedness of the Babylonians. They were arrogant and puffed up, whereas the righteous are to be characterized by humility and faith. The righteous remnant need not have full comprehension of God's ways, but they are to respond with integrity and faithfulness (2:2–5).

II. Five Woes on Babylon (2:6–20)

At the same time God is not blind to the Babylonians' corruption and so He announced five woes, each of which is given in three verses, on those He will first use to judge His people (2:6–20). God's answer to Habakkuk's dilemma is that wickedness will not go unpunished. The final climactic woe announced that Babylon would fall by its idolatry (2:18–20). Thus God was in agreement with Habakkuk's evaluation of their moral condition (1:11,16). The

---

[8] The wicked have been identified as Assyrians, Egyptians, Chaldeans, and Greeks (see Sweeney, "Habakkuk, Book of," 3).

[9] As a just recompense the upper classes of Judea were the first taken into captivity in the deportations of 605 and 597 BC, probably within a few years after this prophecy was delivered.

[10] The Chaldeans (1:6) were an Aramaic tribe from lower Mesopotamia that gained prominence and joined the Babylonians.

[11] See R. Rendtorff, *The Old Testament: An Introduction*, trans. J. Bowden (Philadelphia: Fortress, 1986), 233; and R. B. Chisholm Jr., *Interpreting the Minor Prophets* (Grand Rapids: Zondervan, 1990), 187. The prophets operated on the principle that God uses foreign nations to carry out His justice on the disobedient (Isa 7:18–20; 10:5–6).

idols overlaid with silver and gold are utterly lifeless (2:19). And they are contrasted to the invisible but sovereign Lord who oversees the affairs of men from His holy temple. Through all the enigmas and vicissitudes of history experienced by Habakkuk and the people of God of all ages, God remains seated in His holy temple summoning all creation to awed silence (2:20).

III. Habakkuk's Prayer (chap. 3)

Habakkuk's response to God's program to save a righteous remnant and to judge wicked oppressors (chaps. 1–2) is given in Habakkuk 3.[12] Habakkuk expressed assurance that God would deliver the Judeans just as He had majestically done in the exodus (3:3a; see Deut 33:2).[13] Habakkuk requested that God be merciful in the exercise of His wrath (Hab 3:1–2). The hymn that begins in v. 3 depicts a theophany of God who will come both to judge and to deliver, just as was announced in chaps. 1–2. Habakkuk 3:3–6 describes God's approach and its effects, and 3:7–15 depicts God's victory over His enemy in cosmic terms. Habakkuk demonstrated his confidence that God will deliver the land (3:13), thus affirming God's statement that He will deliver the righteous (2:4).[14]

The chapter ends with a concluding section that expresses Habakkuk's confidence that God will answer his petition (3:16–19). The prophet's mood turns from one of fearful awe to one of calm trust in Yahweh's intervention to judge the Babylonians. The prophet saw that the power demonstrated toward Israel so many times in the nation's past was still available to the righteous who live by faith. Though the coming invasion would carry out the covenant curses on Israel (Deut 28:31–34,49–51), Habakkuk would still exult in the Lord (Hab 3:17–19). Thus, Habakkuk illustrates what it means to live a life of integrity and faithfulness (2:4). His cry of "How long?" at the beginning of the book (1:2) has been transformed into "I must quietly wait" for the day of distress in the conclusion (3:16).

THE TEXT OF THE BOOK

The Hebrew text of Habakkuk is well preserved, although the commentary of the book found among the DSS (1QpHab) contains roughly 160 variants (most of only a minor spelling variation, however). The main contribution of this scroll is in the area of hermeneutics or interpretation and Second Temple history rather than in the determination of the original Hebrew text.[15] The LXX of the Minor Prophets represents a revision of a Greek text in harmony with the MT. The LXX and other versions are of little value in elucidating textual difficulties in the book.

THE THEOLOGY OF THE BOOK

God's righteousness (1:3) and His hatred of evil clearly permeate the book. This is seen in the prophet's concern about the corruption among his own people, among the Babylonians,

---

[12] Of interest is the relationship between the framing verses of the hymn (3:2,16) and Habakkuk's vision in 2:1–4.

[13] The prayer is according to the poetic form *šiggāyôn*, which, according to some scholars, is associated with Akkadian *šigû*, "song of lament." This term also appears in the superscription of Psalm 7, a psalm of lament. The hymnic nature of this chapter is further reinforced by the fact that this is the only place outside the Psalms in which the "Selah" rubric is found (3:3,9,13).

[14] Sweeney, "Habakkuk, Book of," 4.

[15] See M. Fishbane, "The Qumran Pesher and Traits of Ancient Hermeneutics," in *Proceedings of the Sixth World Congress of Jewish Studies*, 1 (Jerusalem, 1977), 97–114; idem, *Biblical Interpretation in Ancient Israel* (Oxford: Clarendon Press, 1985), 454 n.25; and M. J. Bernstein, "Pesher Habakkuk," *Encyclopedia of the Dead Sea Scrolls*, ed. L. H. Schiffman and J. C. Vanderkam, 2 vols. (Oxford: Oxford University Press, 2000), 2:649.

and in God's response to Habakkuk's questions. God condemned drunkenness, greed, theft, violence, oppression, debauchery, abuse of nature, and idolatry that characterized the Babylonians (2:6–20). His announcement of judgment on Babylon foreshadows the judgment of the wickedness of all nations and individuals. Whereas Jeremiah focused on the evil in Judah and God's use of the Babylonians as His instrument of judgment, Habakkuk focused more on the violence and wickedness of the instrument. In both cases God calls all wickedness to account.

Through righteousness God will preserve His own covenant people. Like Job, Habakkuk learned that he must continue to believe and trust in the promises of the Lord despite what he might encounter in his own circumstances and situations.

In the Babylonian Talmud Hab 2:4 is identified as a summary of all the 613 commandments of the Law (*b. Makkot* 23b–24a). Habakkuk 3 was read on the second day of the Feast of Weeks, which celebrates the giving of the law on Mount Sinai (*b. Meg.* 31a).

THE NEW TESTAMENT AND THE BOOK

The most famous passage in the book of Habakkuk is certainly 2:4, "The just shall live by his faith" (NKJV; cf. Rom 1:17; Gal 3:11; Heb 10:38). In the immediate context of Hab 2:4 "live" refers to physical preservation through the coming invasion (similarly in Heb 10:38). The faithfulness is contrasted and is antithetical to the haughty and arrogant attitude of the Babylonians. However, faith characterizes the remnant of Israel and the people of God. In Paul's use of the verse he focused on the initial demonstration of this faith which is pleasing to God and by which an individual "lives" before God.[16] Habakkuk has demonstrated that the law cannot restrain wickedness (1:4).

The book Habakkuk also teaches that evil will fail in the end. This teaching is given greater focus in the book of Revelation, which records the triumphal return of Jesus Christ to judge His enemies and deliver His people. Christ's return is prefigured both in the judgments on the nations and the tribulations of the people of God.[17] Habakkuk himself serves as an example of a faithful person living between the promise of the end and its arrival in the future.[18]

STUDY QUESTIONS

1. What is distinctive about the prophecy of Habakkuk?
2. When does it appear that Habakkuk was written?
3. When did critical scholars begin to see the prophet Habakkuk as the author of the book of Habakkuk?
4. What is the chief concern of the book of Habakkuk?
5. Who were the evildoers Habakkuk addressed in the opening of the prophecy?
6. Why did Habakkuk object to God using the Babylonians to discipline Judah?
7. What did God say He would do to the Babylonians?
8. What type of psalm does Habakkuk 3 resemble?
9. What was Habakkuk's mood at the end of the book?
10. What sins did God oppose in the book of Habakkuk?

---

[16] While it is true that most of the citations from the OT into the NT are from the LXX, Paul directly translated the MT of Hab 2:4 into Greek in Rom 1:17 amd Gal 3:11, while Heb 10:38 appears to adhere more to the LXX. See G. K. Beale and D. A. Carson, eds., *Commentary on the New Testament Use of the Old Testament* (Grand Rapids: Baker Academic, 2007), 608, 801, 983–84.

[17] C. Armerding, "Habakkuk," in *ISBE*, ed. G. Bromiley (Grand Rapids: Eerdmans, 1986), 2:585.

[18] B. Childs, *Introduction to the Old Testament as Scripture* (Minneapolis: Fortress, 1979), 455.

11. According to the Babylonian Talmud what is the significance of Hab 2:4?
12. Comment on the use of Hab 2:4 in the NT.

FOR FURTHER STUDY

Andersen, F. I. *Habakkuk*. New York: Doubleday, 2001.

Armerding, C. "Habakkuk." In *EBC*. Edited by T. Longman III and D. E. Garland, 8:603–48. Grand Rapids: Zondervan, 1985.

Baker, D. *Nahum, Habakkuk, Zephaniah*. TOTC. Downers Grove, IL: InterVarsity, 1988.

Bliese, L. F. "The Poetics of Habakkuk." *JTT* 12 (1999): 47–75.

Bruce, F. F. "Habakkuk." In *Commentary on the Minor Prophets*. Edited by T. McComiskey, 2:831–96. Grand Rapids: Baker, 1993.

Bullock, C. H. *An Introduction to the Old Testament Prophetic Books*. Chicago: Moody, 1986.

Patterson, R. D. "A Literary Look at Nahum, Habakkuk, and Zephaniah." *GTJ* 11 (1990): 17–27.

Rendtorff, R. *The Old Testament: An Introduction*. Translated by J. Bowden. Philadelphia: Fortress, 1986.

Robertson, O. P. *The Books of Nahum, Habakkuk, and Zephaniah*. NICOT. Grand Rapids: Eerdmans, 1990.

Smith, R. P. *Micah–Malachi*. WBC. Waco, TX: Word, 1984.

Sweeney, M. "Habakkuk, Book of." In *ABD*. Edited by D. N. Freedman, 3:1–6. New York: Doubleday, 1992.

Watts, J. D. W. *Joel, Obadiah, Jonah, Micah, Nahum, Habakkuk, Zephaniah*. CBC. Cambridge: Cambridge University Press, 1975.

Wendland, E. R. "'The Righteous Live by Their Faith' in a Holy God: Complementary Compositional Forces and Habakkuk's Dialogue with the Lord." *JETS* 42 (1999): 591–628.

CHAPTER 35

THE BOOK OF ZEPHANIAH

MARK F. ROOKER

THE AUTHOR OF THE BOOK

Zephaniah was born during the repressive reign of Manasseh (696–642 BC) and probably began his ministry shortly before the reform of Josiah (622). In all likelihood his ministry had an impact on Josiah's reformation (2 Kings 23; 2 Chronicles 34).

According to the heading of the book, Zephaniah was the son of Cushi, son of Gedaliah, son of Amariah, son of Hezekiah. This superscription is unique for two reasons. First, normally only the prophet's father's name is recorded in the introduction to the prophets (Isa 1:1; Jer 1:1; Ezek 1:3; Hos 1:1; Joel 1:1). Zephaniah, on the other hand, listed the ancestors of his four previous generations. Second, Zephaniah's great-great-grandfather was Hezekiah, the famous king of Judah who ruled from 729 to 686. This additional information was included to demonstrate that the prophet Zephaniah was of royal descent. The opening verse of Zephaniah's prophecy also states that he prophesied during the reign of Hezekiah's great-grandson, Josiah (640–609 BC). Because Josiah's reforms were intended to remove idolatry (2 Kings 22–23 [esp. 23:4–7]), the situation described in the opening verses (Zeph 1:4–6) indicates that Zephaniah began his prophetic ministry before Josiah's reforms, perhaps around 627 or 626 BC.[1]

THE COMPOSITION OF THE BOOK

The major critical issues regarding Zephaniah have revolved around the integrity and genuineness of the individual oracles in the book. Most OT critical scholars of the nineteenth and twentieth centuries have argued that Zephaniah received its present shape as a result of combining the actual writing of the prophet late in the preexilic period with a later layer of postexilic material. Otto Eissfeldt, for example, contends that the genuineness of what is recorded in 1:2–2:3 is beyond doubt. Sellin and Fohrer similarly maintained that the five sayings about Judah and Jerusalem in 1:4–5,7–9,12–13,14–16; and 2:1–3 are to be ascribed to the prophet

---

[1] This is about the same time Jeremiah began his ministry in Judah. Also the book of Zephaniah was written before 612 BC, the date of the fall of Nineveh, because in 2:13–15 the fall of Nineveh is future.

Zephaniah. Yet Sellin and Fohrer are representative of the broad critical consensus in stating that the announcements of threats (1:2–3,10–11,17–18), the announcements against foreign nations (2:5–7,8–11,12,15),[2] and the eschatological promises (3:9–10,14–15,16–18a) all find their origin in the later postexilic period.[3] Zephaniah 3 is thought to be postexilic because of the bias that assumes that eschatological descriptions of universal disaster represents a manner of thinking that did not arise until Israel returned from the exile.

In response it should be noted that this scissors-and-paste method of dividing up the contents of Zephaniah is completely subjective, reflecting a certain prejudice of understanding with regard to Hebrew prophecy as well as the religion of Israel. For example there is no reason Zephaniah could not have prophesied the final salvation of the remnant (3:8–13) and the promise of hope in 3:14–20, as both of these motifs are to be found in earlier eighth-century prophets such as Isaiah and Amos. Recently, for example, Kselman has noted that the similarity of Zeph 3:14–17 to the preexilic enthronement psalms (47, 95, and 97) is an argument against the late dating of Zephaniah 3.[4] There is really no sufficient reason for denying any section of the prophecy of the book to the prophet Zephaniah late in the seventh century.

THE STYLE OF THE BOOK

Zephaniah contains a variety of literary forms such as judgment speeches (1:2–3,4–6,8–9, 10–13,17–18; 2:4–15), exhortations (1:7; 2:1–3; 3:8), praise hymns (3:14–18a), and salvation speeches (3:5–13,18b–20). There are numerous references to the Day of the Lord, a theme central to the main argument of the book and graphically portrayed in the imagery of war, theophany, and judgment (1:14–18). Other literary devices include the use of double entendre in 2:4–7 as well as irony in 2:8–11.

Zephaniah is particularly keen in the use of word repetitions. These include: the Day of the Lord (1:7,14); the day of the Lord's wrath (1:15,18); the day of distress, of oppression, of darkness (1:14–15,17); the day of sacrifice (1:7–8); the day on which the Lord raises Himself up (3:8); or simply "that day" (1:9,15; in the introductory formulae 1:8,10; 3:11,16; cf. "at that time," 1:12; 3:19–20). Other repeated words and phrases include "in the midst or among or within" of Jerusalem (3:3,5,11–12,15,17); "seek the Lord" (1:6; 2:3); "accept instruction" (3:2,7); "worship" (1:5; 2:11; cf. 3:9–10); "fear" (3:7,15–16); "visit" (1:8–9,12; 3:7); "stretch out the hand" (1:4; 2:13); "gather" (1:2; 3:8,19–20); "remnant" (2:7,9; 3:12–13); "restore fortunes" (2:7; 3:20), "the city" (2:15; 3:1); the "arrogant" (2:15; 3:11); and *mišpāṭ* ("right") with various meanings (2:3; 3:5,8,15).[5]

THE MESSAGE OF THE BOOK

The primary focus of the book is on the city of Jerusalem. The prophet indicts the city for its idolatry and social apathy (1:4–13; 3:1–7), but holds out a message of hope as he predicts the city's eventual salvation (3:14–20), particularly for those who display devout humility and unswerving righteousness (2:3; 3:12–13). The visitation of the sins of Judah as well as the nation's deliverance are two aspects of the coming Day of the Lord, the central organizing

---

[2] S. R. Driver deviates from this consensus as he regards 3:1–8 as a genuine passage from Zephaniah. He maintains that the promise addressed to the remnant in the passage complements the denunciation of Judah in Zephaniah 1 (*An Introduction to the Literature of the Old Testament*, 9th ed. [Edinburgh: T&T Clark, 1913], 342).

[3] O. Eissfeldt, *The Old Testament: An Introduction*, trans. P. Ackroyd (New York: Harper & Row, 1965), 424; and E. Sellin and G. Fohrer, *Introduction to the Old Testament*, trans. D. Green (Nashville: Abingdon, 1968), 456–57.

[4] J. Kselman, "Zephaniah, Book of," in *ABD*, ed. D. N. Freedman (New York: Doubleday, 1992), 6:1079.

[5] R. Rendtorff, *The Old Testament: An Introduction*, trans. J. Bowden (Philadelphia: Fortress, 1986), 235–36.

principle of the book.[6] From this focus it is easy to see how Zephaniah's message was instrumental in bringing about Josiah's reformation.

THE STRUCTURE OF THE BOOK

The book of Zephaniah opens with a dramatic judgment announcement for all creation (1:2–3). This universalistic message (see also 2:4–15; 3:6–8) is combined with the particular judgment on Judah (1:4–9; 3:1–4). The covenant name Yahweh ("LORD") brackets the entire book from beginning (1:1) to end (3:20).

The message is conveyed through the three major sections of the book as seen in the following outline:

Superscription (1:1)

  I. **Prophecy against Judah (1:2–2:3)**

 II. **Prophecy against Foreign Nations (2:4–3:7)**
      A. Against Philistia (2:4–7)
      B. Against Moab and Ammon (2:8–11)
      C. Against Ethiopia (2:12)
      D. Against Assyria (2:13–15)
      E. Against Jerusalem and Judah (3:1–7)

III. **Prophecy of Salvation (3:8–20)**

THE CONTENTS OF THE BOOK

I. Prophecy against Judah (1:2–2:3)

The book of Zephaniah opens with an announcement of the coming of God's universal judgment on the world. Using language similar to that found in the flood account in Genesis (Genesis 6–7), Zephaniah announced that all life will be destroyed on the earth (1:2–3). The series of beings listed in 1:3—man, beasts, birds, and fish—is in reverse order to their creation in Gen 1:20–26 and constitutes another allusion to the biblical flood. The reversal of the order of the created beings probably indicates that God's act of judgment is an act of "anti-creation" (Hos 4:1–3).[7]

In Zeph 1:4–6 the scene shifts from world annihilation to punishment of Judah and Jerusalem for pagan practices. This included the worship of Milcom, the god of the Ammonites.[8] Zephaniah targeted the priests just as they were in the account of the Josianic reform (2 Kgs 23:4–7).

At this point in the oracle Zephaniah announced the coming of the Day of the Lord (1:7). The judgment on this day will be so thorough that God will use search lamps to reveal every sinner in every corner of the city (1:12). The focus on the "day" becomes especially intense in 1:14–16 where the term occurs at the beginning of six consecutive lines (1:15–16a) to emphasize both the intensity and comprehensiveness of the coming judgment. Chapter 1 ends as it began with reference to " the whole earth" and "all the inhabitants of the earth" (1:18).

---

[6] D. Baker, "Zephaniah, Theology of," in *NIDOTTE,* ed. W. VanGemeren (Grand Rapids: Zondervan, 1997), 4:1310.

[7] Kselman, "Zephaniah, Book of," 1078.

[8] For additional foreign deities who were the objects of Josiah's purge during the time of Zephaniah see 2 Kgs 23:4–5,13.

The first major section of the book concludes with an exhortation to the nation to seek the Lord and obey His commands (2:1–3). The appeal is specifically addressed to the humble who are normally the economically deprived in society, usually because of oppressive measures by the wealthy (Isa 29:19; 32:7; Amos 2:7; 8:4).

II. Prophecy against Foreign Nations (2:4–3:7)

Apart from Zephaniah, Amos is the only other book of the Minor Prophets that includes oracles directed toward foreign nations. The oracle against Philistia is of interest as the Philistine cities are personified as women whose fates include abandonment, spinsterhood, divorce, and barrenness (2:4–7).[9] Also in the oracle against Moab and Ammon their punishment is compared to the destruction suffered by Sodom and Gomorrah. Moab and Ammon were the product of the incestuous relationship between Lot and his daughters subsequent to their leaving Sodom and Gomorrah (Gen 19:36–38).

The woe oracle against Judah (Zeph 3:1–7) is redolent of a similar pattern in Amos 1–2, where the oracles against foreign nations were immediately followed by a judgment oracle against Judah. This oracle is distinctive as the indictments leveled at Jerusalem are more specific than in the preceding judgments against the nations. The thoroughgoing denunciation of Judah's leaders in 3:1–4 became somewhat of a model of Judah's disobedience as this passage was later employed by Ezekiel during the time of the exile (Ezek 22:25–28).[10]

III. Prophecy of Salvation (3:8–20)

The final section begins with an exhortation to wait for the Lord. The addressees of this exhortation are equated with the humble who were addressed in the earlier oracle (2:3) and the remnant of Judah addressed later in this section (3:12,20). The humble are to persevere through the judgment, which will be the first step in their final restoration.[11] The restoration will restore "pure speech to the peoples" (3:9), a reversal of the confusion of speech at the Tower of Babel (Gen 11:1–9).

Near the end of the prophecy in Zeph 3:11–19 Jerusalem is addressed in a positive manner, in contrast to the negative comments in 1:2–4 and 3:1–7. Judah is to receive mercy, and this promise is also extended to the Gentile nations that had been denounced in 2:4–15. The Gentiles will be converted to the Lord and bring tribute to Him (3:9–13; see 2:11).[12] There will be great rejoicing as Judah is restored (3:14–20).

THE TEXT OF THE BOOK

The MT of Zephaniah is generally free of textual difficulties. Two fragmentary *pesharim* on Zephaniah have been uncovered among the DSS. An additional Hebrew text of Zephaniah was uncovered from Wadi Murabba'at. These Hebrew texts, like the LXX, are very close to the MT despite minor scribal differences.

---

[9] Kselman, "Zephaniah, Book of," 1078.

[10] See M. Fishbane, *Biblical Interpretation in Ancient Israel* (Oxford: Clarendon, 1985), 461; and M. Rooker, *Biblical Hebrew in Transition: The Language of the Book of Ezekiel*, JSOTSup (Sheffield: JSOT Press, 1990), 63.

[11] R. Chisholm, *Interpreting the Minor Prophets* (Grand Rapids: Zondervan, 1990), 210.

[12] Similarly see Isa 45:14–17; 49:6; 60:5–6, 11.

THE THEOLOGY OF THE BOOK

Perhaps as no other book, Zephaniah focuses on the Day of the Lord. From it emerges the message that the Day of the Lord not only involves judgment for Israel and the nations but will also ultimately result in their restoration. VanGemeren discusses six features of the Day of the Lord found in Zephaniah: (1) the Day signified Yahweh's intrusion into human affairs; (2) the Day brings God's judgment on all creation (1:2–3); (3) the Day is historical and eschatological (1:3); (4) in the Day all creation will submit to God's sovereignty (1:7); (5) the Day does not discriminate in favor of the rich and powerful (1:18; 2:3; 3:12–13); (6) the Day signifies the day of vindication, glorification, and full redemption of the godly (3:14–20).[13]

The Day of the Lord is the vindication of God's righteousness, ultimately on a universal scale. With regard to Israel, God remains faithful to His covenant promises as He blesses the righteous remnant of Israel (2:7). A special contribution of the Day of the Lord described by Zephaniah is its focus on the conversion of the Gentiles (2:11; 3:9–10).

THE NEW TESTAMENT AND THE BOOK

The apostle Paul often mentioned the Day of the Lord as a time when God's righteousness will be vindicated (Rom 2:16; 1 Cor 1:8; Phil 1:6,10; 2:16; 2 Tim 4:8).[14] The promise that Gentiles will worship the God of Israel has begun in the church age but awaits its final fulfillment in the exaltation of Christ when He will be acknowledged by all (Phil 2:11).[15]

Zephaniah is unique among the OT books in its focus on the prominence of the humble, a theme that continues in the NT through the *Magnificat* sung by Mary (Luke 1:46–55) and Jesus' focus in the Sermon on the Mount (Matt 5:3–11).

STUDY QUESTIONS

1. What is the time frame of the book of Zephaniah?
2. What is unique about the superscription of the book of Zephaniah?
3. Why have critics argued that Zephaniah 3 was written in the postexilic period?
4. What expression in Zephaniah is central to the main argument of the book?
5. What is the primary focus in the book of Zephaniah?
6. What are the primary sins God addressed in the book of Zephaniah?
7. What parts of Genesis are alluded to in the opening oracle of Zephaniah?
8. Which book of the Minor Prophets (besides Zephaniah) has a collection of oracles against foreign nations?
9. What is ironic about the destruction of Moab and Amon being compared to Sodom and Gomorrah?
10. What is different about the oracle against Judah as opposed to the oracles against other foreign nations?
11. Which biblical prophet seems to be aware of Zephaniah's prophecy?
12. What special feature of the Day of the Lord is recorded in Zephaniah?

---

[13] W. VanGemeren, *Interpreting the Prophetic Word* (Grand Rapids: Zondervan, 1990), 174–76.

[14] Most of these NT references more specifically refer to the day of Christ, which may be the judgment seat of Christ (2 Cor 5:10).

[15] It is also likely that Rev 14:5 alludes to Zeph 3:13.

FOR FURTHER STUDY

Baker, D. *Nahum, Habakkuk, Zephaniah*. TOTC. Downers Grove, IL: InterVarsity, 1988.

Berlin, A. *Zephaniah*. Garden City, NY: Doubleday, 1994.

Craigie, P. C. *Twelve Prophets*. Vol. 2. DSBOT. Philadelphia: Westminster, 1985.

Ehud, B. Z. *A Historical-Critical Study of the Book of Zephaniah*. Berlin: de Gruyter, 1992.

Fishbane, M. *Biblical Interpretation in Ancient Israel*. Oxford: Clarendon, 1985.

Haak, R. D. "Zephaniah's Oracles Against the Nations: A Synchronic and Diachronic Study of Zephaniah 2:1–3:8." *CBQ* 59 (1997): 749–51.

House, P. R. *Zephaniah: A Prophetic Drama*. Sheffield, UK: Almond, 1988.

King, G. A. "The Remnant in Zephaniah." *BSac* 151 (1994): 414–27.

Kselman, J. "Zephaniah, Book of," in *ABD*. Edited by D. N. Freedman, 6:1077–80. New York: Doubleday, 1992.

Motyer, J. A. "Zephaniah." In *The Minor Prophets*. Edited by T. E. McComiskey, 3:897–962. Grand Rapids: Baker, 1998.

Patterson, R. D. "A Literary Look at Nahum, Habakkuk, and Zephaniah." *GTJ* 11 (1990): 17–27.

Robertson, O. P. *The Books of Nahum, Habakkuk, and Zephaniah*. NICOT. Grand Rapids: Eerdmans, 1990.

VanGemeren, W. *Interpreting the Prophetic Word*. Grand Rapids: Zondervan, 1990.

Walker, Larry. "Zephaniah." *EBC*. Rev. ed. Edited by T. Longman III and D. E. Garland, 8:649–95. Grand Rapids: Zondervan, 2008.

Watts, J. D. W. *Joel, Obadiah, Jonah, Micah, Nahum, Habakkuk, Zephaniah*. Cambridge: Cambridge University Press, 1975.

CHAPTER 36

THE BOOK OF HAGGAI

EUGENE H. MERRILL

THE TITLE OF THE BOOK

The book of Haggai takes its name from its attributed author, the prophet known elsewhere as a leading figure of the postexilic period (Ezra 5:1; 6:14). The book has never appeared under any other title, part of a larger collection known as the Book of the Twelve.[1]

THE DATE AND AUTHORSHIP OF THE BOOK

The tradition regarding both of these matters is firmly fixed and without appreciable controversy.[2] As noted, Haggai's historical existence is attested to in the book of Ezra, a source whose historical accuracy in such matters can hardly be questioned. The fact that Haggai's paternity—unlike certain other prophets—is not revealed is of no consequence to his historical reality since this omission is true of other prophets as well (i.e., Daniel, Amos, Obadiah, Micah, Nahum, Habakkuk, and Malachi). As for the meaning of his name (*haggay*, "[born of the] feast day"[3]), it is singularly appropriate in that the prophet's main burden was the restoration of the temple and the re-establishment of its worship including the festivals.

The setting of the book is Jerusalem in the second year of Darius Hystaspes of Persia (522–486 BC), some 18 years following the return of the Jews from Babylonian exile. The latest date

---

[1] The Talmud (*Baba Bathra* 14b) refers to Haggai, Zechariah, and Malachi as the last of the prophets and in the collection of "the Twelve Minor Prophets" commencing with Hosea.

[2] For instances of alleged redactional features in Haggai that suggest authorship by someone later see Michael H. Floyd, "The Nature of the Narrative and the Evidence of Redaction in Haggai," *VT* 45 (1995): 470–90. Floyd appeals to evidence such as the book's peculiar use of historical narrative compared to other minor prophets and the form-critical function of the introduction to the prophetic oracles. Like many critics, however, he overlooks the fact that writers are free to use (or even abuse) conventional literary patterns in any way they choose. It is impossible to prove that Haggai did not write the book as it stands, especially in light of universal ancient testimony that suggests that he did.

[3] L. Koehler and W. Baumgartner, eds., *The Hebrew and Aramaic Lexicon of the Old Testament* (Leiden: Brill, 2001), 1:290.

in the book is the twenty-fourth day of the ninth month (Kislev), that is, December 18, 520 (Hag 2:10,20). No reason exists to date the book much later than that.[4]

THE TEXT OF THE BOOK[5]

Both ancient Hebrew witnesses (e.g., several Qumran manuscripts and the Murabbaʿat DSS) and the principal versions differ from MT in only minor and inconsequential ways such as expansions of MT (cf. 2:9,14,21–22), arrangement of verses (1:9; 1:15–2:1; 2:15), and slight differences of reading based in some cases perhaps on a *Vorlage* different from that underlying MT (cf. 1:1,14; 2:2; etc.).

THE CANONICITY OF THE BOOK

From earliest times Haggai has been bundled together with the other so-called Minor Prophets, a collection known as "The Twelve." That collection has never been the subject of rabbinical or Christian debate as to its divine inspiration and hence its canonical authority.[6]

THE LITERARY FORMS AND STRUCTURE OF THE BOOK

Haggai's overall style is parenetic, that is, sermonic or hortatory, since he is concerned to motivate his hearers to several courses of action including the rebuilding of the temple and the restoration of the Jewish community. For the most part, his messages are straightforwardly pro-saic, but occasionally he lapses into poetic-like cadences, caught up perhaps in the sublimity of the subject matter occupying his mind and heart (1:4–6,7b–11; 2:3b–9,14b–19,21–23).[7] The structure of the book follows closely the chronological data marking different phases of the prophet's ministry, resulting in the following divisions: 1:1–15; 2:1–9; 2:10–19; and 2:20–23. The first section in turn consists of two parts, a command (1:1–11) and a response (1:12–15). Form-critically speaking, scholars have observed such patterns as judgment speech and announcement of salvation and the order of accusation (1:1–11; 2:10–17), response (1:12–14; 2:18–19), and assurance (2:1–9; 2:20–23).[8] Analytical schemes such as chiastic or other rhe-torical structures that attempt to embrace the whole composition have for the most part not been persuasive.[9]

THE OUTLINE OF THE BOOK

The outline of Haggai conforms to the structural configurations suggested by the chrono-logical notations just elaborated.

I. **Rebuilding the Temple (1:1–15)**
    A. Introduction and Setting (1:1)
    B. Exhortation to Rebuild (1:2–11)
    C. Response of God's People (1:12–15)

---

[4] E. H. Merrill, *Haggai, Zechariah, Malachi: An Exegetical Commentary* (Chicago: Moody, 1994), 3–4.

[5] R. A. Taylor and E. R. Clendenen, *Haggai, Malachi,* NAC (Nashville: B&H, 2004), 92–100.

[6] Thus Tt. Sottah 13.2. See R. Beckwith, *The Old Testament Canon of the New Testament Church* (Grand Rapids: Eerd-mans, 1985), 163, 288.

[7] For the suggestion that the entire book is poetic see D. L. Christensen, "Impulse and Design in the Book of Haggai," *JETS* 35 (1992): 445–56.

[8] Thus, e.g., J. G. Baldwin, *Haggai, Zechariah, Malachi*, TOTC (Downers Grove, IL: InterVarsity, 1972), 31.

[9] The absence of such features is clear from D. A. Dorsey's careful attention to their possibilities (*The Literary Structure of the Old Testament* [Grand Rapids: Baker, 1999], 315–16).

II. **The Glory to Come** (2:1–9)
   A. Reminder of the Past (2:1–3)
   B. The Presence of the Lord (2:4–5)
   C. Outlook for the Future (2:6–9)

III. **The Promised Blessing** (2:10–19)
   A. Present Ceremonial Defilement (2:10–14)
   B. Present Judgment and Discipline (2:15–19)

IV. **Zerubbabel the Chosen One** (2:20–23)
   A. Divine Destruction (2:20–22)
   B. Divine Deliverance (2:23)

THE CONTENTS OF THE BOOK

Because the book of Haggai is primarily a collection of addresses by Haggai to his various audiences, it has little historical or other narrative, though the prophet does allude from time to time to the historical circumstances that called forth his ministry and message and also recounts the responses of the people to his appeals. He most likely had returned to Jerusalem with his fellow prophet Zechariah and other Babylonian exiles on the heels of the edict of King Cyrus of Persia issued in 538 BC that permitted them to do so (Ezra 5:1; 6:14; cf. 1:1–4; 2 Chr 36:22–23). Eighteen years later he and Zechariah commenced their ministries of prophetic revelation and proclamation (Hag 1:1; Zech 1:1).

Haggai's burden was the indolence and indifference of the people who, having begun the process of rebuilding their own lives and institutions, had left the temple of the Lord and other matters unattended (Hag 1:3–4). What was central to the decree of Cyrus (Ezra 1:2–4) and the cause of great celebration and fervor immediately on the return from exile (Ezra 3) had degenerated into spiritual apathy and self-serving inversion of priority. While some of the people had begun not only to sink down roots in the holy city but to do so in a luxurious manner ("in paneled houses," Hag 1:4), only the foundations of the temple remained as a testimony to the initial exuberance of 18 years earlier (2:15–19).

The prophet severely rebuked his countrymen for this untoward behavior and pointed out that the natural and physical disasters that had begun to overtake them were eloquent testimony to God's displeasure as well (1:6–11). The only remedy for the agricultural and economic crises that were beginning to emerge was to put first things first—to resume work on the house of the Lord (1:8). Then and only then would the rains come and the earth become fertile and fruitful once again.

The message of the prophet found good soil and both the leaders of the community and the populace committed themselves to comply with the will of God and begin the task of temple building (1:12–15). Their joy in seeing the long-delayed project once more underway was tempered somewhat by the nostalgia of the old among them who recalled the glory and splendor of the massive temple of Solomon compared to which the present structure was "like nothing" (2:3; cf. Ezra 3:12). Nonetheless the work moved forward, prompted by the assurance of the prophet that the Lord was with them as surely as he had been with their ancestors in the glorious days of the exodus from Egypt (Hag 2:4–5). In fact, Haggai said, the glory that would fill this temple would far outweigh the glory of the temple of Solomon (2:9). Gold, silver, and other symbols of material prosperity that decorated the first temple would pale into insignificance compared to the shalom of the Lord that would fill this second temple, one that itself was only preparatory to the great eschatological temple in which the Lord Himself will dwell (Ezek 40:1–43:12; cf. Rev 21:22).

To that date the people had not been spiritually qualified to measure up to the anticipated glory of the temple (Hag 2:14). Having now recommitted themselves to the Lord and His program, they could expect His blessing (2:19), the eschatological expression of which would be the revival of the line of David through his offspring Zerubbabel, governor of the postexilic state (2:20–23). A scion of that line—a chosen one—would overthrow the kingdoms of the world and replace them with His own.

THE PURPOSE AND THEOLOGY OF THE BOOK[10]

This most singleminded of all the prophets pursued one controlling theme—the significance of the temple of the Lord and the need for the people to get at the task of rebuilding it as a symbol of both the Lord's immediate presence among them and of His promise to be their God and dwell among them in the ages to come. Such a message was especially important to postexilic Israel because it seemed that with the demise of the monarchy and the attendant destruction of Jerusalem, its seat of power, all the kingdom promises of God attached to the Davidic covenant had become null and void (Gen 49:10; Num 24:17; 2 Sam 7:8–16).

God's covenant with Israel as expressed in Deuteronomy contained the provision that the Lord would meet with His people in "the place the Lord your God chooses from all your tribes to put His name for His dwelling" (Deut 12:5). That place, of course, would be Jerusalem, the city recognized by both David and Solomon as the only suitable site for such a structure (2 Chr 3:1). The linkage between the temple and the Davidic monarchy is thus established as a crucial theological datum. Only a second temple, rebuilt on the ashes of the first, could provide assurance of the renascence of the Davidic line as well, one eventuating in a messianic figure who would rule not only Israel but the whole world forever.

STUDY QUESTIONS

1. Under what imperial regime did Haggai minister as prophet?
2. Who was Haggai's prophetic contemporary?
3. What is the main thrust of Haggai's message?
4. Who was the governor of Judah at the time Haggai was written?
5. How did the Lord show His disapproval of the sins of the Jewish community?
6. Who was the ruler of Persia during Haggai's time?
7. What is meant by "signet ring" in Hag 2:23?
8. To what is the temple of Haggai's time being compared?
9. Who was the high priest of the time?
10. To what does "final glory" refer in Hag 2:9?

FOR FURTHER STUDY

Baldwin, J. G. *Haggai, Zechariah, Malachi*. TOTC. Downers Grove, IL: InterVarsity, 1972.
Bullock, C. H. *An Introduction to the Old Testament Prophetic Books*. Chicago, Moody, 1986.
Chisholm, R. B., Jr. *Handbook on the Prophets*. Grand Rapids: Baker, 2002.
Hill, A. E. *Commentary on Haggai*. CBC. Carol Stream, IL: Tyndale, 2008.
Kaiser, W. C., Jr. *Micah–Malachi*. TCC. Dallas: Word, 1992.
Merrill, E. H. *Haggai, Zechariah, Malachi*. Chicago: Moody, 1994.
———. *Kingdom of Priests: A History of Old Testament Israel*. 2nd ed. Grand Rapids: Baker, 2008.

---

[10] E. H. Merrill, *Everlasting Dominion: A Theology of the Old Testament* (Nashville: B&H, 2006), 557–58.

Meyers, C. L., and E. M. Meyers. *Haggai, Zechariah 1–8*. AB. Garden City, NY: Doubleday, 1987.

Motyer, J. A. "Haggai." In *The Minor Prophets*. Vol. 3. Grand Rapids: Baker, 1998.

Petersen, D. L. *Haggai and Zechariah 1–8*. Philadelphia: Westminster, 1984.

Pusey, E. B. *The Minor Prophets: A Commentary*. Vol 2. Reprint, Grand Rapids: Baker, 1966.

Smith, G. V. *An Introduction to the Hebrew Prophets: The Prophets as Preachers*. Nashville: B&H, 1994.

Smith, R. L. *Micah-Malachi*. WBC. Waco, TX: Word, 1984.

Stuhlmueller, C. *Rebuilding with Hope: A Commentary on the Books of Haggai and Zechariah*. ITC. Grand Rapids: Eerdmans, 1988.

Taylor, R. A., and E. R. Clendenen. *Haggai, Malachi*. NAC. Nashville: B&H, 2004.

Verhoef, P. A. *The Books of Haggai and Malachi*. NICOT. Grand Rapids: Eerdmans, 1987.

Wolff, H. W. *Haggai: A Commentary*. Minneapolis: Augsburg, 1988.

CHAPTER 37

THE BOOK OF ZECHARIAH

EUGENE H. MERRILL

T
HE BOOK OF Zechariah, like the other canonical books of the prophets, bears the
name of its traditional author, in this case "Zechariah son of Berechiah, son of Iddo"
(Zech 1:1).[1] No reason exists to dispute the antiquity of this title and its association
with the well-known postexilic prophet of this name.[2]

THE DATE AND AUTHORSHIP OF THE BOOK

The dates of the oracles and events of Zechariah are plainly stated and easily converted to
modern calendars.[3] The earliest is the eighth month of the second year of King Darius of Persia, that is, between late October and late November, 520 BC (Zech 1:1). His so-called night
visions (1:7–6:15) commenced on the twenty-fourth day of the eleventh month (February 15,
519 BC) and the last of his revelations (7:1) took place on the fourteenth of the ninth month
of Darius's fourth year (December 5, 518 BC). However, such information provides no certainty as to the date of the composition of the book except to limit its terminus a quo to 518.
Without further information, one would suppose it reached its present form not much later
than that.

However, some scholars propose that the book originated in its present form much later than 518, a view which, if correct, obviously raises further questions about authorship.
Depending on how much later and the age of the prophet at the time, his responsibility
in the matter could be greatly diminished if not entirely eliminated.[4] The major reasons for

---

[1] Ezra 5:1 and Neh 12:16 refer to him as the son of Iddo, suggesting perhaps that his father had died and that he was
reared by his grandfather. In any event, he should not be confused with "Zechariah son of Jeberechiah" from the time of
Isaiah (Isa 8:2), an identification held by some scholars. See O. Eissfeldt, *The Old Testament: An Introduction* (Oxford: Basil
Blackwell, 1965), 435.

[2] See *Baba Bathra* 14b and chap. 38 n. 1.

[3] R. A. Parker and W. H. Dubberstein, *Babylonian Chronology 626 B. C.–A. D. 75* (Providence, RI: Brown University
Press, 1956), 33.

[4] A commonly held view is that Zechariah consists of two major parts, a First Zechariah (chaps. 1–8) to be attributed to
the prophet and a Second Zechariah (chaps. 9–14) of unknown provenance and authorship but ranging anywhere from the

dating chaps. 9–14 later than the rest (and thus likely barring Zechariah from contention as author) are as follows: (1) the reference to Greece in 9:8, (2) apparent allusions to Alexander the Great and the Diadochoi (especially the Ptolemies) in 9:1–10, and (3) alleged references to the second-century Jewish priests Simon, Menelaus, and Lysimachus in 11:4–17. While there may seem to be incidental points of contact between these late persons (points 1 and 2) and those obscurely referred to in the passages cited, the plethora of identifications suggested for them reveals how lacking in objective proof such connections really are.[5] As for the reference to Greece, this nation was already a major power in the sixth century and even earlier and therefore allusion to it poses no problem for the traditional dating of Zechariah.[6]

Strong arguments in favor of the unity of Zechariah and hence its common authorship were advanced as early as 1896 by George L. Robinson. He cited several points of comparison between the two parts of the book: (1) a shared spirituality, hope, and attitude toward Judah and the nations; (2) common "peculiarities of thought" developed in similar ways, resort to symbolic actions, and drawing on history; (3) common linguistic and stylistic features; and (4) similar citation of earlier prophets in both parts of Zechariah.[7] In more recent times Brevard Childs has also presented weighty evidence in support of the essential unity of the book, though he by no means holds to a single authorship by the prophet of 520 BC.[8]

No compelling evidence exists to overthrow ancient Jewish and Christian tradition supporting common authorship of the book of Zechariah in a period within a few years following its latest dated oracle, namely, 518 BC.

THE TEXT OF THE BOOK[9]

On the whole the MT of Zechariah seems to reflect a faithful transmission of the book's original composition, a fact supported by its few noteworthy deviations from other manuscript and versional witnesses.[10] Such differences that do exist are, in the words of H. G. Mitchell, "additions, omissions, and distortions through the fault of careless or ignorant transcribers."[11] In two places (1:16 and 4:2) the *Qere* appears superior to the received text, an improvement noted and followed respectively by LXX and several versions. In 6:14 the LXX reads "crown" (singular) in place of MT "crowns," a decidedly more fortuitous rendition.

THE CANONICITY OF THE BOOK

With the Minor Prophets in general, the canonicity of Zechariah has never been seriously challenged. All the ancient canon lists contain it (sometimes only as an assumed part of "the

---

prophet's own time to the Maccabean period or later. See C. Cornill, *Introduction to the Canonical Books of the Old Testament* (New York: Putnam's Sons, 1907), 363–71.

[5] For a more complete discussion of the wide range of identifications of persons and events in these passages see E. H. Merrill, *Haggai, Zechariah, Malachi: An Exegetical Commentary* (Chicago: Moody, 1994), 74–79.

[6] E. Yamauchi, *Greece and Babylon. Early Contacts between the Aegean and the Near East* (Grand Rapids: Baker, 1967).

[7] G. L. Robinson, *The Prophecies of Zechariah* (Chicago: University of Chicago, 1896, cited by H. G. Mitchell, *A Critical and Exegetical Commentary on Haggai and Zechariah*, ICC (Edinburgh: Clark, 1912), 242–44. Though Mitchell exposed the weakness of some of Robinson's connections, as a whole they stand unchallenged to this day.

[8] B. S. Childs, *Introduction to the Old Testament as Scripture* (Philadelphia: Fortress, 1979), 482–85. See also C. H. Bullock, *An Introduction to the Old Testament Prophetic Books* (Chicago: Moody, 1986), 314–17.

[9] See esp. (for Zech 9–14) Taeke Jansma, *Inquiry into the Hebrew Text and the Ancient Versions of Zechariah IX-XIV* (Leiden: Brill, 1949).

[10] Zechariah is attested to at Qumran in 4QXII[a], 4QXII[b], 4QXII[g], MurXII, and HevXIIgr.

[11] Mitchell, *Haggai and Zechariah*, 85.

Book of the Twelve" or "the Minor Prophets"), and the rabbinical debates never bring it up for discussion regarding its suitability for being included in the sacred Scriptures.[12]

THE LITERARY FORMS AND STRUCTURE OF THE BOOK

The book of Zechariah is comprised of three main divisions: (1) visions of the night (chaps. 1–6), (2) oracles concerning fasting (chaps. 7–8), and (3) eschatological oracles dealing with God's sovereignty and His rule over His repentant and restored people (chaps. 9–14). The fact that chaps. 7 and 8 are uttered independent of visions, lack introductory speech formulae, and are dated later than the first six is no impediment to the unity of the first eight chapters, as virtually all scholars concede. However, the consensus of critical scholars is that chaps. 9–14 are not from the hand of the prophet, but from a much later period (see previous section). Moreover, many divide this section into chaps. 9–11 ("Second Zechariah") and 12–14 ("Third Zechariah").[13] Though lacking any objective manuscript, versional, or traditional evidence whatsoever for such a view of the book's composition, most modern scholars simply accept it as a given with little or no independent investigation.[14]

As noted, the compositional and conceptual connections between chaps. 1–6 and 7–8 have been demonstrated by many scholars, thus effectively establishing the unity of the longer section, chaps. 1–8.[15] Others have dispelled the notion of a divided "Second Zechariah" by applying rhetorical methods such as chiastic structure. Paul Lamarche, for example, has demonstrated interconnectedness within chaps. 9–11 and within chaps. 12–14 and then an overarching framework binding the whole into a coherent unity.[16] However, he failed to address the larger question of a so-called "Second Zechariah" as an addendum to the undisputed work of the prophet, a lack now addressed at least partially by Joyce Baldwin, who asserts that "the chiastic pattern, though most prominent in the second part of the book (i.e. chaps. 9–14), is present in the whole."[17] She presents only a few examples of clear interconnection, however, so the unity of the whole must be established on other grounds such as its seven-part structure and its two-part arrangement of condemnation and exhortation followed by messages of future restoration, a pattern typical of other unified prophetic works.[18]

As for its literary genres, Zechariah consists of two main types: vision reports and oracles. The former, eight in number, appear in chaps. 1–6 (1:8–15,18–21; 2:1–5; 4:1–6a,10b–14; 5:1–4,5–11; 6:1–8), whereas the oracles are interspersed throughout chaps. 1–6, concentrated in brief form in chaps. 7–8 (1:16–17; 2:6–13; 3:8–10; 4:6b–10a; 6:9–15; 7:4–14; 8:1–23), and fully elaborated in two lengthy discourses in chaps. 9–14 (chaps. 9–11; chaps. 12–14). The term *maśśā'* translated "oracle," derives from the verb *nś'* ("carry, lift up"),[19] thus suggesting a burden or (more technically in prophetic contexts) a "pronouncement."[20] The term itself occurs only three times in the postexilic prophets (Zech 9:1; 12:1; Mal 1:1), setting off Zechariah 9–11, 12–14, and all of Malachi as discrete literary and conceptual units. However,

---

[12] See chap. 38 n.6.

[13] Childs, *Introduction to the OT*, 479–81.

[14] See for example D. L. Petersen, *Haggai and Zechariah 1–8* (Philadelphia: Westminster, 1984), 109; C. L. Meyers and E. M. Meyers, *Haggai, Zechariah 1–8*, AB (Garden City, NY: Doubleday, 1987), ix.

[15] See especially Meyers and Meyers, *Haggai, Zechariah 1–8*, liii.

[16] P. Lamarche, *Zacharie IX–XIV. Structure Littéraire et Messianisme* (Paris: Librairie Lecoffre, 1961), 106.

[17] J. Baldwin, *Haggai, Zechariah, Malachi*, TOTC (Downers Grove, IL: InterVarsity, 1972), 81.

[18] D. A. Dorsey, *The Literary Structure of the Old Testament* (Grand Rapids: Baker, 1999), 319.

[19] L. Koehler and W. Baumgartner, *HALOT* (Leiden: Brill, 2001), 1:724.

[20] Ibid., 1:639.

as prophetic messages introducing or responding to visions, oracles are common, especially in Zechariah (as noted above).

Claus Westermann defines oracles broadly as "words of a messenger, words that Yahweh gives to the prophet . . . so that he may speak them to the people of Israel."[21] The notion of "burden" or "load" no doubt reflects the importance (or heaviness) of the prophetic message, the awesome responsibility the prophet felt as the one called to disclose to his people the revelation of the transcendent God.

As for visions (hāzôn or māreh/mar'â/rō'eh), the terms so translated describe any communication by the Lord to His servants the prophets whether while asleep or awake.[22] These precise technical terms are lacking in Zechariah (though presupposed as the normal means of divine communication), and are replaced by phrases such as "the word of the Lord came to the prophet Zechariah" (Zech 1:7) and the like (cf. Hag 1:1: "the word of the Lord came through Haggai the prophet"). In any case the prophet was disclaiming any originality in composing and proclaiming the message, attributing the entire process to the Lord alone.

THE OUTLINE OF THE BOOK[23]

   I. **The Night Visions (chaps. 1–6)**
      A. Introduction (1:1–6)
      B. Visions (1:7–6:8)
          1. The four horsemen (1:7–17)
          2. The four horns (1:18–21)
          3. The surveyor (chap. 2)
          4. The priest (chap. 3)
          5. The menorah (chap. 4)
          6. The flying scroll (5:1–4)
          7. The ephah (5:5–11)
          8. The chariots (6:1–8)
      C. Concluding Oracle (6:9–15)

  II. **Oracles Concerning Hypocritical Fasting (chaps. 7–8)**
      A. Introduction and Concern (7:1–3)
      B. Hypocrisy of Fasting (7:4–14)
      C. Blessing of True Fasting (chap. 8)

 III. **Oracle Concerning Yahweh's Sovereignty (chaps. 9–11)**
      A. Coming of the True King (chap. 9)
      B. Restoration of the True People (chap. 10)
      C. History and Future of Judah's Wicked Kings (chap. 11)

  IV. **Oracle Concerning Israel (chaps. 12–14)**
      A. Repentance of Judah (chap. 12)
      B. Refinement of Judah (chap. 13)
      C. Sovereignty of Yahweh (chap. 14)

---

[21] C. Westermann, *Prophetic Oracles of Salvation in the Old Testament*, trans. K. Crim (Edinburgh: T&T Clark, 1991), 12; cf. idem, *Basic Forms of Prophetic Speech* (Philadelphia: Westminster, 1967); and A. Petitjean, *Les Oracles du Proto-Zacharie* (Paris: Librairie Lecoffre, 1969), viii.

[22] Jackie Naude, "חָזָה", in *NIDOTTE*, ed. W. A. VanGemeren (Grand Rapids: Zondervan, 1997), 2:58–59; idem, "רָאָה", 3:1012–13.

[23] Adapted from Merrill, *Haggai, Zechariah, Malachi*, 85–87.

THE CONTENTS OF THE BOOK

Like Haggai, Zechariah oriented his message to a specific time and situation—the second year of King Darius Hystaspes of Persia (522 BC). This was a critical period in the life of the newly returned Babylonian exiles and their re-establishment of a Jewish state as the continuation of the people of promise called to represent the Lord in the earth. As Haggai had declared, the work of restoring the community was moving with painful delay, the people having put their own selfish interests ahead of those of the Lord (Hag 1:2–6). Zechariah was obviously concerned about the same issues, but his overall focus was on the eschatological future, not on the present. The dismal conditions of the struggling state would be redressed and the people of so little apparent promise would some day see the fulfillment of all the glorious promises of God.

These promises find expression in visions interlaced with proclamations urging repentance as a precondition to blessing and with reminders that continuing obedience to covenant requirements is essential to expectations of a better tomorrow. The ancestors had failed in this respect and were duly punished (Zech 1:4–6), so the lesson to be learned is that the present generation must turn to the Lord lest they too experience exile or something even worse (1:4; cf. 5:3–4).

Future restoration of Israel will be possible only as the enemies of the Lord are put in subjection to His sovereignty (1:18–21). The vision of the horsemen (vv. 8–11) describes the universal peace that will create the climate in which the nation will grow and succeed. The temple will be rebuilt (v. 16) and the land filled with prosperous cities (v. 17). Jerusalem will once more become a populous city, one without city walls since the Lord Himself will be its protector (2:1–5). Moreover, proselytes will join themselves to Israel and will, with Israel, become the people of the Lord (2:11–12).

The cultus with its priests and other essential components will also reemerge to a position of importance as seen in the historical installation of Joshua and his priestly colleagues as portents of what will take place in the future (3:3–7). Satan will oppose this (v. 1), but he will not prevail (v. 2). He will give way to a coming messianic figure, God's servant the Branch, whom Joshua foreshadowed (v. 8). That One will be God's instrument for removing the sin of the land, thereby bringing about a paradise in which everyone will live in peace (vv. 9–10). Such revolutionary change will not be the product of human effort but will be accomplished only by the Spirit of God, symbolized in the prophet's vision by a menorah whose oil is supplied by two olive trees, "anointed ones . . . who stand by the Lord of the whole earth" (4:14; cf. vv. 6–7).

The Lord's judgment of sin will begin among His own people first (5:1–4), after which iniquity will be removed far away from them (vv. 6–9). Personified as a woman in a basket, evil will become airborne until she finds her resting-place in Shinar, the ancient name for Babylon (v. 11). This is appropriate, for sin first entered the world in Eden, itself in Shinar (Gen 2:15), and was later egregiously manifested in Shinar in the building of the tower of Babel (Gen 11:1–9; cf. 10:10).

The coming Messiah is depicted again as a Branch (Zech 6:12) following the last of the visions, one also having to do with universal peace forced on it by the sovereign God (6:1–8). Joshua, portrayed as a messianic prototype, is crowned as a priest-king, perhaps analogous to David who held such a dual office (vv. 11–13; cf. Psalm 110). With that glimpse into the kingdom to come, the visions end and the prophet's messages of condemnation of his own contemporaries for their abuse of the festivals commence (Zechariah 7), followed by the announcement of God's gracious forgiveness and eschatological renewal (chap. 8).

The setting is now two years later (7:1). A delegation of Jews from Bethel comes to the prophet to inquire about the propriety of their observance of the sacred festivals (vv. 2–3). The response cuts to the heart of the matter: How can the superficial and hypocritical way they have kept the festivals throughout the exile have any efficacy (vv. 4–7)? This is the way their ancestors had conducted themselves until finally they had gone into far-off Babylon. Now only as they obey the stipulations of the covenant can they lay any claim to true worship (vv. 8–14).

Even more than their forefathers, the Jewish nation of the future will enjoy an unparalleled display of God's grace. The Lord will return to His people and will bless them in unimaginable ways (8:1–8). They will rebuild the temple and their cities, plant crops that will yield great abundance, and will be the means of blessing all the nations as God intended them to do (vv. 9–17; cf. Gen 12:1–3). The festivals will be reinstated and observed in such a pious manner that all nations of the earth will want to join Israel in the worship of its God (Zech 8:18–23).

The final great oracles describe the coming of the great King (9:9–10) to a conquered land (vv. 1–8) that will no longer pose a threat to God's chosen ones (vv. 11–17) whom He will have gathered from throughout the earth (10:8–12). They will then have a godly leader, who by God's help will lead them to triumph (vv. 1–7). This messianic figure, in contrast to the evil kings of Israel, who like shepherds had led them astray and thus to covenant violation and kingdom division (11:1–17), will wear David's crown after a period of intense and genuine repentance (12:10–14). He will be the agent of national cleansing (13:1–2) and unification as the people of the Lord (vv. 7–9). This will trigger one more assault on the chosen people by the wicked nations of the world (14:1–2), but to no avail. Like a mighty warrior the Lord will defend His helpless ones against all odds (vv. 3–5). Even nature will ally itself with the Creator in a mighty act of judgment (vv. 6–15) following which the Sovereign God will reign supreme over not only restored and purified Israel but over all the repentant and believing nations of the earth (vv. 16–21).

THE PURPOSE AND THEOLOGY OF THE BOOK

In the throes of the Babylonian exile and the subsequent return of only a pitiful remnant of what had once been a mighty people of the Lord, serious questions arose as to the viability of the hastily formed state and the security of its future. Even more urgent was the question of the meaning and relevance of the ancient covenants and whether God, who had joined Himself to the people of Israel by means of the covenants, was now willing or even able to keep them. The three postexilic prophets (Haggai, Zechariah, and Malachi) were called to address these concerns and each did in his own way. Haggai (see chap. 38) urged the rebuilding of the temple as both a practical matter for public worship and as a symbol of the residence of the Lord God among His people. Zechariah directed his gaze more to the future, speaking of a day when the feeble structures of the present will give way to God's glorious kingdom in which Israel will once more play a central role. Malachi, some years later, bridged the gaps between the present and the future, rebuking the religious establishment for its corruption of the cultus and yet holding out hope for the realization of the promises that marked Israel's special relationship to the Lord (see chap. 40).

The theology of Zechariah in particular can be summarized by the following seven themes: (1) the disobedience of Israel, (2) the judgment of Israel, (3) the restoration of Israel, (4) the judgment of the nations, (5) the salvation of the nations, (6) the coming Messiah, and (7) the sovereignty of the Lord.[24] Historical Israel had failed to achieve God's covenant purposes for her, and even the state of the prophet's time was in jeopardy because of its lack of total commitment to His kingdom program. However, the promises of the Lord are sure, and what He has begun in world redemption He will bring to ultimate and magnificent conclusion.

STUDY QUESTIONS

1. How many "night visions" did Zechariah have?
2. What are the recorded dates of Zechariah's ministry?
3. Identify the "branch" of Zech 6:9–15.
4. What does the woman in the basket (6:5–11) represent?
5. Who was the Persian emperor at the time of Zechariah?
6. What is the major issue concerning the unity of authorship of the book?
7. To what does "Canaanite" refer in 14:21?
8. Who was Zechariah's prophetic contemporary?
9. What did the "fast of the seventh month" (8:19) commemorate?
10. Who is the Angel of the Lord in Zech 1:12?
11. What was the major issue confronting Zechariah?
12. Delineate the two chronological periods of Zechariah's ministry.

FOR FURTHER STUDY

Baldwin, J. G. *Haggai, Zechariah, Malachi*. TOTC. Downers Grove, IL: InterVarsity, 1972.

Bullock, C. H. *An Introduction to the Old Testament Prophetic Books*. Chicago: Moody, 1986.

Chisholm, R. B., Jr. *Handbook on the Prophets*. Grand Rapids: Baker, 2002.

Hill, A. E. *Zechariah*. CBC. Carol Stream, IL: Tyndale, 2008.

Kaiser, W. C., Jr. *The Book of Zechariah*. TCC. Dallas: Word, 1992.

Klein, G. L. *Zechariah*. NAC. Nashville: B&H, 2008.

Leupold, H. C. *Exposition of Zechariah*. Grand Rapids: Baker, 1971.

McComiskey, T. E. "Zechariah." In *The Minor Prophets*. Edited by T. McComiskey, 3:1003–1244. Grand Rapids: Baker, 1998.

Merrill, E. H. *Haggai, Zechariah, Malachi*. Chicago: Moody, 1994.

———. *Kingdom of Priests: A History of Old Testament Israel*. 2nd ed. Grand Rapids: Baker, 2008.

Meyers, C. L., and E. M. Meyers. *Haggai, Zechariah 1–8*. AB. Garden City, NY: Doubleday, 1987.

Petersen, D. L. *Haggai and Zechariah 1–8*. Philadelphia: Westminster, 1984.

———. *Zechariah 9–14 and Malachi*. Philadelphia: Westminster, 1995.

Pusey, E. B. *The Minor Prophets: A Commentary*. Vol. 2. Reprint, Grand Rapids: Baker, 1950.

Russell, D. S. *The Method and Message of Jewish Apocalyptic*. Philadelphia: Westminster, 1964.

Smith, G. V. *An Introduction to the Hebrew Prophets: The Prophets as Preachers*. Nashville: B&H, 1994.

Smith, R. L. *Micah—Malachi*. WBC. Waco, TX: Word, 1984.

Stuhlmueller, C. *Haggai & Zechariah*. Grand Rapids: Eerdmans, 1988.

Unger, M. S. *Zechariah: Prophet of Messiah's Glory*. Grand Rapids: Zondervan, n.d.

VanGemeren, W. A. *Interpreting the Prophetic Word*. Grand Rapids: Zondervan, 1990.

---

[24] E. H. Merrill, *Everlasting Dominion: A Theology of the Old Testament* (Nashville: B&H, 2006), 558–63.

CHAPTER 38

THE BOOK OF MALACHI

EUGENE H. MERRILL

L IKE ALL OTHER Hebrew *personal* names, this one too may be translated, in this
case as "my messenger" (Hb. *mal'ākî*). However, the question has been raised as to
whether this is the proper name of the prophet or whether it is descriptive of the role
of an otherwise anonymous prophet. The exact same form occurs in Mal 3:1, where the Lord
said, "I am going to send *My Messenger,* and he will clear the way before Me" (italics added; cf.
2:7), suggesting perhaps that the prophet is unnamed in the book. However, the eschatological tone of this passage rules out the possibility that the messenger to come is identical to the
Malachi in the title of the book. Furthermore, all other prophetic books bear the names of their
authors, so there is no reason to think this is not the case here.[1]

THE DATE AND AUTHORSHIP OF THE BOOK

Granting that the title reflects the name of the book's author, this is about all that can be
said on the matter. The prophet is named nowhere else in the Bible, and his own book says
nothing more about him than the mere fact that the Lord spoke through him (1:1). As for the
date of the book, its canonical location and ancient Jewish tradition place it in the postexilic
period (*Baba Bathra* 14b). More precisely, it is the last of the prophets and therefore postdates
Haggai and Zechariah, both of whom ministered in the last quarter of the sixth century BC
(see Hag 1:1; Zech 1:1).

The only historical note in the book is the reference to the anticipated destruction of Edom
(Mal 1:2–5). Some scholars propose that this is only an alleged prediction—one after the
event (*vaticinium ex eventu*)—and therefore refers to the fall of Edom to the Babylonians in
586 BC or a little later, a disaster to which the prophet was an eyewitness and that took place
earlier than Haggai and Zechariah by 50 years or more.[2] More likely, the prophet foresaw the

---

[1] For an exhaustive treatment of the matter of the title and a defense of the traditional authorship of the book see
A. E. Hill, *Malachi,* AB (New York: Doubleday, 1998), 15–18, 143–45.

[2] B. Dahlberg, "Studies in the Book of Malachi" (PhD diss., Columbia University, 1963), 202.

Nabataean expulsion of the Edomites in 312 BC, thus permitting him to remain the last of the prophets both chronologically and canonically.[3]

A more subjective line of reasoning proposes that Malachi is postexilic and follows Haggai and Zechariah for the following reasons:

1. The word "governor" (*pehâ*) occurs for the first time as a technical term for a Jewish official in the postexilic era (Neh 2:9; Hag 1:1,14; 2:2,21).

2. Jewish worship seems to have become regular and routine, presupposing the rebuilding of the temple and the resumption of all its rites and services (Mal 1:6–14; 2:7–9,13; 3:7–10). This clearly suggests that the exhortations of Haggai especially had been heeded and put into place and therefore that Malachi came on the scene some years later.

3. Issues such as religious impropriety, priestly corruption, hypocrisy, and divorce—matters preoccupying Malachi but of little concern to Ezra and Nehemiah (except for divorce) in the mid-fifth century or to Haggai and Zechariah in the latter sixth century—favor a date for Malachi somewhere in between the two periods. The most likely scenario is that the community had been in place long enough for these abuses to have crept in, thus calling for strong prophetic rebuke. The success of Malachi's ministry in this respect may be seen in the absence of most of these issues by the mid-fifth century except for mixed marriages and the (presumed) need for them to be terminated (Ezra 10) or at least never undertaken again (Neh 13:23–27).

In light of these considerations, a date of Malachi at c. 475 BC seems reasonable.[4]

THE TEXT OF THE BOOK

Apart from a few examples of lexical infelicities or grammatical uncertainties, the text of Malachi is remarkably well preserved and uncomplicated. The major exception is the transposition by LXX of MT 3:22–24 (Eng. 4:4–6) to 3:23,24,22. A possible rationale for this is the desire to have the book end on a more positive note.[5]

THE CANONICITY OF THE BOOK

The book of Malachi (with the remainder of the Book of the Twelve) was never the subject of canonical speculation. It is presupposed as part of that collection or specifically named in ancient canon traditions as being universally recognized as the inspired Word of God.

THE LITERARY FORMS AND STRUCTURE OF THE BOOK

Though the book exhibits some elements of poetry such as rhythm (1:11; 3:1,6–7) and figures of speech (1:6,9; 2:3,6–7; 3:2; 4:1–2), it is the least poetic of all the postexilic prophets. On the other hand no book in the OT (except possibly Isaiah) utilizes the device of the rhetorical question as commonly and effectively as Malachi. At least seven times (1:2,6–7; 2:17; 3:7–8,13) the prophet put rhetorical questions on the lips of his audience of whom he asked such questions in return (1:6,8–9; 2:10,15; 3:2). The setting therefore is almost like that of a courtroom (the so-called *rîb* pattern) in which the prosecuting attorney elicits confessions from the accused after thoroughly grilling him regarding his own protestations of innocence.[6]

---

[3] H. H. Spoer, "Some New Considerations Towards the Dating of the Book of Malachi," JQR 30 (1908):167–86.

[4] E. H. Merrill, *Haggai, Zechariah, Malachi: An Exegetical Commentary* (Chicago: Moody, 1994), 378.

[5] P. A. Verhoef, *The Books of Haggai and Malachi*, NICOT (Grand Rapids: Eerdmans, 1987), 169.

[6] Clendenen prefers the term "pseudodialogue" for the interchange between the prophet and his audience (R. A. Taylor and E. R. Clendenen, *Haggai, Malachi*, NAC [Nashville: B&H, 2004], 222). Though the book has features of the *rîb* pattern, Hill is correct in asserting that the classic elements of such a pattern are lacking (Hill, *Malachi*, 32).

A number of scholars have also drawn attention to such structures as disputation formulae and chiastic or concentric patterns. Wendland, for example, observes a diachronic structure for the book as a whole, consisting of six disputes each of which has three elements: assertion (A), objection (O), and response (R). An example of a simple form of this pattern is 1:2–5: A (v. 2a), O (v. 2b), and R (vv. 2c–5). A complex example is 3:6–12: A (vv. 6–7a), O (v. 7b), and R (vv. 8a–12), subdivided further into A (v. 8a), O (v. 8b), and R (vv. 8c–12).[7]

On a larger scale the composition reveals concentric or ring patterns (chiasm) that demarcate literary units as small as a few verses or as large as the entire book. Though one must be careful not to impose such structures on the text in the interest of proving compositional integrity, the studies of Wendland, Dorsey, and Hill have demonstrated the existence of such integrity by a sober and sensible analysis of the text itself.[8] The result is a strong case for the original literary unity of the book as a whole or at least for a coherence in its present form.

THE OUTLINE OF THE BOOK[9]

Introduction (1:1)

I. **God's Election of Israel (1:2–5)**

II. **The Sacrilege of the Priests (1:6–2:9)**
    A. The Sacrilege of Priestly Service (1:6–14)
    B. The Sacrilege of the Priestly Message (2:1–9)

III. **The Rebellion of the People (2:10–16)**
    A. The Disruption of the Covenant (2:10–13)
    B. The Illustration of the Covenant (2:14–16)

IV. **Resistance to God (2:17–4:3)**
    A. Resistance through Self-Deceit (2:17–3:5)
    B. Resistance through Selfishness (3:6–12)
    C. Resistance through Self-Sufficiency (3:13–4:3)

V. **Restoration through God (4:4–6)**

THE CONTENTS OF THE BOOK

Malachi, addressing the people as a whole, reminded them that they were God's elect, no matter the circumstances in which they found themselves as a small and struggling postexilic community (1:1–5). However, they had not acted as such, especially the priests, who, rather than leading the people in the pure worship of the Lord, have corrupted the whole worship system to their own selfish ends (1:6–14). Predictably this led to God's displeasure and would result in His severe judgment if priests and people refused to mend their ways (2:1–9). An example of the covenant disloyalty of the nation may be seen in the trifling way they regarded marriage and its significance. This is particularly apt because a common OT metaphor for the covenant relationship between the Lord and Israel is marriage (Jer 3:19–23; Ezek 16:8; 23:4; Hos 2:1–7). Israel had become adulterous, having gone after other gods (Mal 2:10–12), a

---

[7] E. Wendland, "Linear and Concentric Patterns in Malachi," *BT* 36 (1985):114.

[8] Ibid., and D. A. Dorsey, *The Literary Structure of the Old Testament* (Grand Rapids: Baker, 1999), 323; Hill, *Malachi*, xxxvi.

[9] Adapted from Merrill, *Haggai, Zechariah, Malachi*, 384.

grievous sin replicated at the human level by individuals who had divorced their wives in order to marry foreigners (2:14–16).

Despite all this, the Lord would not give up on His people whom He had chosen as His special vehicle of blessing the earth. He will send a covenant messenger, who will purify them in judgment (3:1–6). Those who have withheld the tithe and have suffered economic loss will, if they repent, be prospered beyond imagination (3:7–12), and those who renew covenant with Him will be recipients of His compassion and grace (3:13–18). In the Lord's day of eschatological wrath the wicked of the earth will be destroyed but His own precious ones, having heard and obeyed the message of repentance, will live and reign with Him forever (4:1–6).

THE PURPOSE AND THEOLOGY OF THE BOOK

The theology of Malachi oscillates between the historical reality of Israel's sinfulness, even as a chastened postexilic people, and God's elective grace that makes provision for their repentance and ultimate restoration as the pure covenant people He had called them to be.[10] Failure on the part of those whom He had chosen for salvation and service cannot nullify the certainty of His covenant promises.

STUDY QUESTIONS

1. What is the meaning of the name (word) Malachi?
2. What is the most likely date of the composition of the book?
3. What literary device does Malachi use to confront the priests?
4. What is the significance of the prophet's frequent use of the term "Lord of Hosts"?
5. What is the point to Malachi's addressing the matter of divorce (Mal 2:14–16)?
6. Who is the Elijah in 4:5?
7. What is the meaning of "a book of remembrance" in 3:16?
8. What major issue did Malachi address?
9. What was the prophet communicating by referring to Moses and Elijah (4:4–5)?
10. In what sense did the Lord love Jacob and hate Esau (1:2)?

FOR FURTHER STUDY

Baker, D. W. *Joel, Obadiah, Malachi*. Grand Rapids: Zondervan, 2006.

Baldwin, J. G. *Haggai, Zechariah, Malachi*. TOTC. Downers Gove, IL: InterVarsity, 1972.

Bullock, C. H. *An Introduction to the Old Testament Prophetic Books*. Chicago: Moody, 1986.

Chisholm, R. B., Jr. *Handbook on the Prophets*. Grand Rapids: Baker, 2002.

Hill, A. E. *Malachi*. AB. New York: Doubleday, 1998.

———. *Malachi*. CBC. Carol Stream, IL: Tyndale, 2008.

Kaiser, W. C., Jr. *Malachi: God's Unchanging Love*. Grand Rapids: Baker, 1984.

———. *Micah–Malachi*. TCC. Dallas: Word, 1992.

Merrill, E. H. *Haggai, Zechariah, Malachi*. Chicago: Moody, 1994.

———. *Kingdom of Priests: A History of Old Testament Israel*. Grand Rapids: Baker, 2008.

Pusey, E. B. *The Minor Prophets: A Commentary*. Vol. 2. Reprint, Grand Rapids: Baker, 1950.

Smith, G. V. *An Introduction to the Hebrew Prophets: The Prophets as Preachers*. Nashville: B&H, 1994.

Smith, R. L. *Micah—Malachi*. WBC. Waco, TX: Word, 1984.

Stuart, D. "Malachi." In *The Minor Prophets*. Edited by T. E. McComiskey, 3:1245–1396. Grand Rapids: Baker, 1998.

Taylor, R. A., and E. R. Clendenen. *Haggai, Malachi*. NAC. Nashville: B&H, 2004.

VanGemeren, W. A. *Interpreting the Prophetic Word*. Grand Rapids: Zondervan, 1990.

Verhoef, P. A. *The Books of Haggai, Malachi*. NICOT. Grand Rapids: Eerdmans, 1987.

---

[10] E. H. Merrill, *Everlasting Dominion: A Theology of the Old Testament* (Nashville: B&H, 2006), 563–65.

Part 7

THE POETIC BOOKS

MARK F. ROOKER

THE ROLE OF THE PSALMS IN ISRAELITE INSTITUTIONS

Introduction

Music and song played a vital role in the worship of God in ancient Israel as they did in the religious practices of Israel's neighbors in Egypt, Babylon, and Syria. Based on this comparative evidence from the ancient Near East it is likely that music and song played a crucial role in Israelite worship practices long before David's time. The biblical Psalms were employed on various everyday occasions of Israel's national life, such as in the coronation (Psalms 2, 20) or marriage of a king (Psalm 45). But it was especially with respect to the worship of the temple and the offering of sacrifice that the Psalms were primarily utilized. Several psalms report that the poet is at the sanctuary reciting the content of his psalm (Pss 5:3,7 [4,8]; 9:14 [15]; 22:22–31 [23–32]; 23:5–6; 28:2). Psalm 5:7 speaks of going to the temple while in Ps 66:13–15 the psalmist speaks of taking his burnt offerings to the temple. Psalm 116 may include typical words the Israelites spoke when they were presenting offerings at the temple. Psalms 78 and 105 appear to reflect expressions that were uttered in the context of covenant renewal, which surely was accompanied by some religious celebration.

It is thus likely that most of the psalms in the Psalter originated in connection with actual liturgical services. In the Mosaic law we find the repeated admonition requiring every male to go up to Jerusalem to participate in the three major annual feasts of Passover, Weeks, and Tabernacles (Exod 23:16; Deut 16:16–17). Psalms 120–135 are specifically associated with annual pilgrimages to these major feasts. They allude to the setting out (121), the journey (122:1), the joyful arrival (133), and the concluding evening worship (134).

Psalms 15 and 24 appear to be psalms sung by alternate or antiphonal choirs when worshipers gathered at the temple gate. Other likely antiphonal psalms of worship include Psalms 50, 95, 115, and 132. Psalms 46, 48, 76, 87, and 125 are Zion celebration hymns that extol the temple as well as Mount Zion as the special place God has chosen to make His home. Undoubtedly, these psalms were also sung on the temple grounds. The fact that directions for musical accompaniment appear in a great many of the superscriptions to the Psalms is another clear sign that the psalms played an important role in the temple for public worship. The superscriptions also indicate that there were trained musicians and organized choirs within the temple community (Psalm 84). The many activities in the worship of the temple including the singing of psalms can be seen in historical narratives such as 1 Chr 6:31; 16:4–7; 23:28; Ezra 3:10–11; Neh 12:24,27–29. The Psalms themselves bear witness to the color and excitement of temple worship (Pss 42:4; 68:24–26). They also bear witness to the various instruments and tunes that accompanied the individual psalms (see the superscriptions for Psalms 12, 22, 39, 54, 55, 57, 58, 67, 80, and 150).

Jewish tradition reveals other occasions in which the Psalms were used in Israel's worship experience. A particular psalm was associated with each day of the week and was to be read in conjunction with that day. On Sunday, Psalm 24 was used, on Monday Psalm 48, on Tuesday Psalm 72, on Wednesday Psalm 94, on Thursday Psalm 81, on Friday Psalm 93, and on Saturday the Sabbath Psalm, Psalm 92. The Levites recited the Hallel psalms (Pss 113–118) when the Passover lamb was being sacrificed. These psalms were also recited at the Feast of Tabernacles, Weeks, and Dedication (*t. Sukk.* 3:2). Psalms 120–134 were sung at the water-pouring rite on the eighth day of the celebration of the Feast of Tabernacles, the great day of the festival. The Aramaic Targums mention that Psalm 81 was sung at the Musaf (additional festival offerings) on New Year's Day during the feast of trumpets. Psalm 30 was sung, as indicated by its superscription, to celebrate the dedication of the temple on Hanukkah (Dedication). *Sopherim* 18 mentions additional psalms employed in the celebration of the feasts of Dedication, Purim, the first six days and the seventh day of the Passover, as well as the psalms sung at Pentecost and the Lamentation for the destruction of the temple on the eighth of Ab. Thus the main motivation apparently for collecting the Psalms was their employment in both the annual and daily celebrations in the calendar of Israel's holy days. In all probability the early church prayed and sang the Psalms (Eph 5:19; Col 3:16).[1]

The Provenance of the Psalms in Modern Research

The rise of form criticism in the early 20th century paved the way for attempts to focus more closely on the precise occasions that may have given rise to the Israelite psalms. Examinations and analyses were made to recover the *Sitz im Leben*, or life setting, for the original use and continued employment of individual songs. H. Gunkel, the "father" of form criticism, developed helpful categories of psalms such as lament, praise, royal, and wisdom psalms that are still utilized today. However, subsequent form-critical studies attempted to take Gunkel's work further, which led to more tenuous conclusions. S. Mowinckel, a student of Gunkel, tried to find a parallel between such psalms as Psalms 47, 93, 96–99 and Mesopotamian texts that recorded an annual enthronement of kings, celebrated at the fall new year observance. H. J. Kraus ventured to locate the Psalter as a whole in the context of a Zion festival celebrating God's choice of Jerusalem as the special place of God's dwelling. Somewhat similar was A. Weiser's contention that the psalms were used in a covenant festival celebration. While the latter two proposals of Kraus and Weiser had the advantage over Mowinckel in that they maintained that the psalms were employed in Israel's actual history, these proposals were still speculative. In the final analysis, the Bible is silent regarding any one primary ancient festival

---

[1] J. McCann Jr., "Psalms," in *Theological Interpretation of the Old Testament*, ed. K. Vanhoozer (Grand Rapids: Baker Academic, 2008), 157.

that led to the origination and liturgical use of the Psalms. E. Gerstenberger proposed an alternative form-critical position that the psalms originated from a variety of special occasions that brought families and friends together.[2] In truth it is impossible to know the precise function of every psalm in Israel's worship experience; but, as argued above, the Psalms were used in a variety of circumstances, most commonly in communal worship at the temple. Similar poetic traditions existed among the Sumerian, Mesopotamian, Egyptian, and Syrian civilizations.

THE ROLE OF WISDOM LITERATURE IN ISRAEL'S INSTITUTIONS

Introduction

Israel was part of an international conglomeration of nations that had a heritage of wisdom literature. The Sumerians as early as 3000 BC recorded proverbs not much different from the axioms found in the individual proverbs of the book of Proverbs. The Egyptians and Mesopotamians each made use of a considerable collection of instructional literature used probably for the training of children. Much of the content of the instructions in Egyptian wisdom literature, as in the book of Proverbs, is instructional wherein a prominent individual or official addresses his son.[3] Solomon's connections with Egypt were well known (1 Kgs 3:1), so it is not surprising that there may be similarities between the wisdom literature associated with Solomon and that found in Egypt. This historical tie, along with Solomon's international fame as a man of wisdom, explains Solomon's association with the wisdom literature of the Bible and the proliferation of this literature during the enlightenment of the Solomonic period (see 1 Kings 3; 4:29–34; 10:1–13).

Sages in the Ancient Near East

Much of the vast store of wisdom literature in the ancient Near East can be attributed to particular groups of individuals who became prominent citizens in their respective cultures. These special classes of intelligentsia arose as early as the third millennium BC in ancient Egypt and Mesopotamia. There is evidence for the existence of such special classes in the Bible itself which testifies to the wise men of Egypt (Gen 41:8; Exod 7:11; Isa 19:11) Babylon (Daniel), and Edom (Job). These wise men often conveyed their teaching in established schools that were either in or near temples and served as the instruments by which the Egyptian, Sumerian, and Babylonian scribes acquired the necessary skills to govern the people as well as provide services for prominent families.[4]

However, in contrast to the major Near Eastern cultures where wisdom literature played a prominent role at least among the governing officials, there is no clear evidence that the Israelites had established schools or training in wisdom. No archaeological finds of schools or scriptoriums exist in the Israelite period. Second Chronicles 17:7–19 does suggest that instruction was taking place outside the home but does not indicate that sanctioned schools had been established. Moreover, the fact that instruction and education was taking place does not mean that it was primarily occurring in the royal court or only among the elite. From the book of Proverbs it appears that the provenance of wisdom instruction was in the home (cf. Deut

---

[2] See discussion in J. Limburg, "Psalms, Book of," *ABD,* ed. D. N. Freedman (New York: Doubleday, 1992), 5:525.

[3] It is also apparent, especially in Egypt, that Wisdom literature originated and was associated with the royal court, providing instruction for governing the people and in the training of future rulers.

[4] J. Crenshaw, *Old Testament Wisdom: An Introduction,* rev. ed. (Louisville: WJK, 1998), 21.

6:4–9; 32:6; Prov 4:3).[5] The first unambiguous reference to an organized school for education occurs in the second century BC apocryphal writing Ben Sira (Sir 51:23).

However, evidence does appear in the Bible for the existence of professional sages in ancient Israel. While it could be argued that counselors of the royal court such as Ahithophel and Hushai indicate the existence of a professional wisdom class (2 Samuel 15–17; 1 Chr 27:33–34), unequivocal testimony alludes to the "men of Hezekiah" who were associated with the editing if not the writing of many Proverbs (25:1). The beginning of the rise of this class of wisdom thinkers is best traced to Solomon himself who extended his contacts throughout the world and may have been particularly influenced by what was taking place in the Egyptian royal court given his personal ties (1 Kgs 3:1; 9:16; 10:28–29).[6]

Nature of Wisdom Literature

Because wisdom literature (and many psalms) was to be passed down from generation to generation and was not time-bound, there is little concern in this literature for history and genealogy. Rather, there is a focus on the established moral and social code of conduct as well as the perennial struggle with the question of good versus evil in the world.[7]

Wisdom literature fits within the framework of a theology of creation. It rests on the belief in the goodness of God's created order.[8] The root of the biblical word for wisdom, hōkmâ, is used in the Old Testament in reference to displays of particular skill (Exod 28:3; 1 Kgs 7:14). Hence, biblical wisdom is often defined as "skillful living." The Akkadian and Egyptian terms for wisdom have a different connotation from the Hebrew word hōkmâ. These terms were often used to refer to skill in magic and ritual. In Israel, unlike other ancient Near Eastern cultures, wisdom is never far removed from reverence for God.[9]

Within the wisdom literature of the Old Testament two distinct genres emerge. On the one hand is the didactic, practical wisdom found in the book of Proverbs which is illustrated by proverbial sayings. On the other hand, there exists what scholars call skeptical or philosophical wisdom. This type of literature is best illustrated in the books of Job and Ecclesiastes.

Wisdom literature, often thought of as the step-child of Old Testament theology, is actually not different in outlook from the law as it likewise exalts sexual purity, honor of parents, and integrity towards one's neighbor.[10] While the wisdom Psalms and wisdom literature in general do not focus on redemptive history, the promises to the patriarchs, the exodus from Egypt, or the covenant at Sinai, God's sovereign control of the world and all human events is the underlying premise behind all of this vast collection of Hebrew literature. The practice of acquiring wisdom must always be associated with the "fear of the Lord" (Job 28:28; Prov 1:7; 9:10; Eccl 12:13–14).

---

[5] For a helpful discussion, see B. K. Waltke and David Diewart, "Wisdom Literature," in *The Face of Old Testament Studies*, ed. D. W. Baker and B. T. Arnold (Grand Rapids: Baker, 1999), 295-328.

[6] See D. Garrett, *Proverbs, Ecclesiastes, Song of Songs*, NAC (Nashville: Broadman, 1993), 27.

[7] See especially, V. Mathews and J. Moyer, *The Old Testament: Text and Context* (Peabody: Hendrickson, 1997), 177. This is also characteristic of so-called wisdom psalms (1, 19, 37, 49, 73, 111, 119).

[8] W. Zimmerli, "The Place and Limit of the Wisdom in the Framework of the Old Testament Theology," *SJT* 17 (1964): 148, and B. Bandstra, *Reading the Old Testament: An Introduction to the Hebrew Bible* (New York: Wadsworth, 1995), 428.

[9] J. Williams, "Wisdom in the Ancient Near East," *IDBS*, ed. K. Crim (Nashville: Abingdon, 1976), 49.

[10] C. H. Bullock, *An Introduction to the Old Testament Poetic Books*, rev. ed. (Chicago: Moody, 1988), 24.

STUDY QUESTIONS

1. What ancient cultures utilized music and song in their worship activities?
2. How were the psalms primarily utilized?
3. What three annual feasts required every man to appear in Jerusalem?
4. Which psalms were recited when the Passover lamb was being sacrificed?
5. Which psalm was used on the Sabbath day?
6. What does the phrase *Sitz im Leben* mean?
7. In critical research it was believed that the psalms originated from what type of settings?
8. Which nation had wisdom literature that may have been known by Solomon?
9. For the Israelites where did wisdom instruction take place?
10. What is the connection of wisdom literature to creation?
11. Contrast wisdom in the ANE with biblical wisdom?
12. How does wisdom literature fit into OT theology?

CHAPTER 39

THE BOOK OF JOB

MICHAEL A. GRISANTI

JOB IS A masterpiece of literature. Thomas Carlyle has said, "There is nothing written, I think, in the Bible or out of it of equal literary merit."[1] Charles Kent called Job the "Matterhorn of the Old Testament."[2] However, Job's theological value is greater than its literary value. Since everyone knows something about suffering, the book of Job has a universal appeal. A key part of Job's appeal to readers is that he or his conduct does not appear to be the cause of the suffering. This book raises the important question concerning the fairness of God's dealings with mankind.

THE DATE AND AUTHORSHIP OF THE BOOK

The book of Job does not name an author or provide explicit information on its date of composition.[3] It also offers somewhat vague evidence about the date of the events it depicts and the location of Job's existence. Because of the book's ambiguity on these issues, a host of suggestions have been made.

Date of the Events in Job's life

When did Job live, that is, what is the approximate date of the events recorded in the book? Scholars have suggested a date for the story ranging from the time of the patriarchs until as late as 200 BC. Most evangelicals date it somewhere between the time of the patriarchs and the Solomonic period (the wisdom period).

Various features suggest a patriarchal setting (and perhaps pre-Abrahamic) for the events described in the book. Job offers sacrifices without the benefit of a priest (1:5), his wealth is measured in terms of herds, flocks, and servants (1:3; 42:12), and his life span reminds the reader of life spans from the time of Genesis, after the flood (42:16). Roving bands of Sabeans

---

[1] T. Carlyle, *On Heroes, Hero Worship and the Heroic in History* (London: Chapman and Hall, 1894), 45.

[2] C. Kent, cited by V. E. Reichert, *Job* (Surrey, UK: Soncino, 1946), xiii.

[3] Jewish tradition (Babylonian Talmud *Baba Bathra* 14b) claims that Moses wrote the book of Job, but most scholars do not find this compelling.

and Chaldeans (1:15,17) suggests an early second millennium BC setting. The book makes no reference to the Mosaic law and rarely refers to God as Yahweh. Job appears to be a non-Israelite, living in the land of Uz. Scholars have debated this location, but the consensus seems to be that Uz was in the area of Edom (Gen 10:23; Lam 4:21).[4] Since these events seem to focus on a non-Israelite, it seems best to date them before the Abrahamic covenant narrowed God's primary dealings to a particular family.

The Date of Composition

Suggestions about authorship have included Job, Elihu, Moses, Solomon, Hezekiah, Isaiah, Ezra, and an anonymous author in third century BC (to name the major alternatives), ranging from the time of the patriarchs to the postexilic period. The linguistic evidence is ambiguous because it has some very old and somewhat new Hebrew words. Besides this, dating a biblical book in light of linguistic issues is generally precarious and subjective.[5] Bullock offers some helpful observations about the date of the book's composition. He points out that wisdom compositions in the ANE are as old as the second millennium BC.[6] He also affirms that since the afterlife is addressed in both Mesopotamian and Egyptian literature, scholars cannot relegate the afterlife concept to the postexilic period.[7] Bullock sees no cogent reason for denying a preexilic date for Job's composition. He concludes that a more precise decision requires more evidence than is at hand.[8] Hill and Walton state, "Evidence is extremely difficult to establish, and in any case, the timeless nature of the message makes the dating of the book a moot point."[9]

Various scholars have suggested that certain sections were later additions, including the Elihu speeches (chaps. 32–37), the hymn of wisdom (chap. 28), and God's second speech (40:6–41:34), as well as the prose prologue (chaps. 1–2) and epilogue (42:7–17). However, the book is best seen as a unified composition, even though no one can be sure when it was written.

The Text of the Book

Scholars have found fragments of a Targum of Job in Cave 11 at Qumran (11QtgJob).[10] The linguistic style appears to be closest to the 2nd century BC.[11] In general, the Qumran Targum supports the MT, including the order of chs. 24–27.[12]

Most scholars regard the Greek translation of Job (LXX) as a faithful translation of the Hebrew text. The LXX, however, is 400 lines (ca. one-sixth) shorter than the MT. Although

---

[4] D. J. A. Clines, *Job 1–20*, WBC (Dallas: Word, 1989), 10–11. Other options include Egypt, Arabia, and Israel. See R. Gordis, *The Book of God and Man* (Chicago: University of Chicago Press, 1965), 209–2, for an overview of these options.

[5] See R. L. Alden, *Job*, NAC (Nashville: B&H, 1993), 26, for some helpful comments about the ambiguous evidence of Arabic and Aramaic words in Job.

[6] C. Hassell Bullock, *An Introduction to the Old Testament Poetic Books*, rev. ed. (Chicago: Moody, 1988), 73. Cf. W. G. Lambert, who gives numerous examples of Babylonian wisdom from the second and first millennia BC (*Babylonian Wisdom Literature* [Oxford: Clarendon, 1960]).

[7] Bullock, *An Introduction to the Old Testament Poetic Books*, 73.

[8] Ibid.

[9] A. E. Hill and J. H. Walton, *A Survey of the Old Testament*, 3rd ed. (Grand Rapids: Zondervan, 2009), 404.

[10] M. Sokoloff, *The Targum to Job from Qumran Cave XI* (Ramat Gan, Israel: Bar-Ilan University, 1974). The text of Job is extant from the middle of chap. 17 through 42:11, but is quite fragmentary (John H. Hartley, *The Book of Job*, NICOT [Grand Rapids: Eerdmans, 1988], 4).

[11] M. H. Pope, *Job*, AB, 3rd ed. (Garden City, NY: Doubleday, 1979), xlv–xlvii.

[12] Hartley, *The Book of Job*, 5.

some may argue that the LXX represents a translation of an earlier form of Job, it is more likely that the Greek translator intentionally abridged the speeches.[13]

THE LITERARY FORM AND STRUCTURE OF THE BOOK

Genre

The book of Job has defied all efforts to establish its literary form or genre. Of the numerous suggestions scholars have made over time,[14] the two most significant alternatives are that Job is a lawsuit[15] or a dramatized lament.[16] These varied suggestions arise from the fact that the book employs a wide variety of literary forms. Various commentators suggest that the author of Job created a literary masterpiece that is *sui generis*, that is, of its own category. As LaSor writes, Job "must not fit into any preconceived mold. It does weep with complaint, argue with disputation, teach with didactic authority, excite with comedy, sting with irony, and relate human experience with epic majesty. But above all, Job is unique—the literary gift of an inspired genius."[17]

Structure

The structure of the book of Job is essential for grasping the message of the book. The major structural feature of the book is the clear distinction between the prose prologue (chaps. 1–2) and epilogue (42:7–17) and the poetic discourse between these sections (3:1–42:6). The prose sections delineate the narrative of Job's experience, that is, the loss and the eventual restoration of his family, possessions, and health. The poetic discourse has two main sections with a chapter (chap. 28) that serves as an interlude between them. Dialogues or disputes between Job and his three "friends" occupy chaps. 3–27. After Job's opening lament, these speeches occur in three cycles. Then 29:1–42:6 record monologues by Job, Elihu, and God Himself. Chapter 28 serves as an interlude on wisdom by Job himself (or the author of Job) that speaks to the dialogues and the misunderstanding of wisdom found in them.[18] The concluding epilogue brings a measure of resolution to the tension in Job's mind and focuses attention on God as the one whom Job (and all believers) must trust absolutely.

THE OUTLINE OF THE BOOK

I. **Prologue (chaps. 1–2)**
    A. Job's Character (1:1–5)
    B. Job's Calamities (1:6–2:13)

II. **Dialogues (between Job and Eliphaz, Bildad, and Zophar) (chap. 3–27)**

---

[13] Ibid., 4.

[14] See the helpful survey of the nine most commonly proposed genres for Job, providing bibliographic citations for each in W. S. LaSor, D. A. Hubbard, and F. W. Bush, *Old Testament Survey: The Message, Form, and Background of the Old Testament*, 2nd ed. (Grand Rapids: Eerdmans, 1996), 486–87.

[15] H. Richter, *Studien zu Hiob: Der Aufbau des Hiobbuches, dargestellt an den Gattungen des Rechtslebens* (Berlin: Evangelische Verlagsantalt, 1959), 48–58.

[16] C. Westermann, *The Structure of the Book of Job: A Form-Critical Analysis*, trans. C. A. Muenchow (Philadelphia: Fortress, 1981), 1–15.

[17] LaSor, Hubbard, and Bush, *Old Testament Survey*, 487.

[18] Scholars have long debated the composition of chap. 28 and how it fits into the structure of the book. However, those discussions are not included here.

THE CONTENTS OF THE BOOK

Prologue (chaps. 1–2)

This narrative section gives the reader an "inside look" at the causes of Job's theological dilemma. This section also vividly portrays the ultimate struggle of the universe between God, who is absolutely sovereign, and Satan, who can only do what God allows him to carry out. The opening verse describes Job as "blameless and upright" and who "feared God and shunned evil" (NIV). Five scenes (two in heaven and three on earth) delineate the course of events Job experienced. After speaking of Job's character and prosperity (1:1–5), the scene shifts to Satan's first accusation of Job before God (1:6–12). Satan declared that Job served God only "because it pays," that is, because God protected and blessed Job. God gave Satan permission to take away all those blessings. The third scene (1:13–22) records Job's experience of horrific loss and his glorious response of trust: "Naked I came from my mother's womb, and naked I will depart. The Lord gave and the Lord has taken away; may the name of the Lord be praised" (v. 21 NIV). Satan again challenged the Lord, urging him to allow Satan to afflict Job more personally by allowing him to experience painful physical affliction (2:1–6). With God's permission Satan struck Job with excruciating boils over his entire body. In spite of his wife's discouraging advice, Job exclaimed, "Shall we accept good from God, and not trouble?" (v. 10 NIV). In both responses Job did not sin. Once they heard of Job's severe affliction, three friends came to see Job, wept over his circumstances, and sat with him in silence for seven days (2:11–13).

Dialogues (chaps. 3–27)

Job's opening lament. Job spoke first, but when he did, he did not curse as Satan had predicted. Instead he spoke of his affliction as a fate worse than death. He cursed the day of his birth (3:1–10) and preferred death to continued life (3:11–26). What he said in chaps. 1 and 2 were truths he genuinely felt, but as he sifted through the rubble that was left of his life, his world made no sense at all. Questions like those that have plagued scores of others must have been swirling in his mind: Why did this happen, and why to me? Is this something I deserved? Where is God, just and merciful, in all of this? Job faced three possibilities. First, his theology was wrong. His implicit trust in the God who does good for His children is misplaced trust. Second, Job was a horrible sinner and deserved this suffering. Third, there is no moral order in the universe, and he had been caught up in one of life's many injustices. His experience did not seem to match at all what he believed about God and the way God deals with His followers. Job could not stand the thought of living in a world with no clear moral order, that is, no clear connection between righteousness and blessing.

First cycle of speeches. Chapter 4 begins the first of three cycles of speeches in which each friend spoke and Job responded to each one.[19] Eliphaz, an empiricist, based his counsel on experience. Bildad, a traditionalist, grounded his advice on the orthodoxy of the past. Zophar was a rationalist who carefully avoided any minimizing of Job's sin. In fact Zophar said Job had seen more of God's mercy than he deserved. The intensity of accusations and rebukes directed against Job increased in their intensity with each successive cycle. Also, Job's frustration intensified. An underlying problem for this entire discussion is that neither Job nor his three friends knew the reason for these misfortunes Job had experienced. They knew nothing of the developments "behind the scenes."

After rebuking Job for his lack of composure in the face of affliction, Eliphaz declared that he knew of no righteous person who has perished (chaps. 4–5). The clear implication is that Job's sin must have occasioned his suffering. Eliphaz also reminded Job of the general principle that people reap what they sow (4:7–9; cf. Gal 6:7). Eliphaz said Job needed to appeal to God and to regard his present circumstances as a divine blessing (Job 5:8,17–18). Job's reply can be characterized as a sarcastic "thanks for nothing!" (chaps. 6–7). He likened Eliphaz and the other friends to an unreliable or deceptive "wadi" or a dry riverbed that characterized many parts of the ANE. It may be full of water at certain times, but it soon dries up (6:14–17). He asked God to leave him alone, and he asked God why He made him (Job) His target or object of attention (7:11–21). The answer is obvious to Bildad (chap. 8). History makes it abundantly evident that God is a just God who punishes sinners and does not reject blameless men. What Job must do is repent. Job granted (at least theoretically) that God punishes the wicked and cares for the righteous (chaps. 9–10), but he wondered if it is even possible for a mortal man to be regarded as righteous by God (9:2). Job described God as the incomparably powerful God of the universe, but he hinted that God is arbitrary (v. 15) and perhaps capricious (vv. 16–18). Job concluded that it is impossible for him to satisfy God, and again he wished he had never been born or would be allowed to die in peace (10:18–22). Zophar (chap. 11) accused Job of idle talk and arrogance, affirming that Job's suffering is less than it could have been (because of the apparent greatness of his sin) (11:1–12). If only Job would confess his sin, his darkness would turn into light (11:13–20). Job (chaps. 12–14) directed his reply to all three friends, accusing them of arrogantly thinking that wisdom begins and ends with them (12:2). The entire universe knows that God is in control of all that happens (12:7–10). Job was not challenging God's sovereignty. Instead he longed for an opportunity to have an audience with God and defend himself (13:13–19). However, since God insisted on continuing his affliction (13:24–27), Job once again pleaded for a swift death (14:13).

Second cycle of speeches. The second cycle of speeches continues the antagonistic dialogue between Job and his three friends. Eliphaz (chap. 15) affirmed that Job's own words condemned him (15:1–6). He was self-righteous, and he was arrogant to think that his sin did not cause his suffering (15:7–16). Job's experience of fear, deprivation, and uncertainty matched what is experienced by the wicked who are hostile against God (15:21–26). Eliphaz felt Job needed to stop deceiving himself. Job (chaps. 16–17) was tired of hearing the same thing over and over, and he regarded his friends as "miserable comforters" (16:2). If only God, his witness

---

[19] The third cycle is truncated and does not have a speech by Zophar.

in heaven, would vindicate him (16:19). But Job realized that would probably not happen—he expected to go to his grave without vindication or justification (7:11–16). Bildad (chap. 18) was tired of Job's unrelenting refusal to admit to the extent of his sin. History makes it abundantly clear that the wicked do not prosper and receive what they deserve (18:5–21). In light of Job's experience of severe affliction, his spiritual condition was apparent to all. But Job was tired of his friends incessantly tormenting him with their counsel (chap. 19). Their badgering him was, however, not as painful as his conclusion that God regarded him as His enemy, reduced him to poverty, and laid siege to him (19:5–12). Job cataloged people in all levels of human relationships who have forsaken him (19:13–22). Yet Job remained convinced that his suffering was not a representation of the depth or extent of his sin. He longed for a permanent and enduring testimony of his innocence that would find validation after his death. He expected his Redeemer to vindicate him after his life ended (19:25–27). In his last interaction with Job, Zophar (chap. 20) felt that Job had dishonored him, and he reminded Job of the fleeting nature of the wicked (20:4–11). Although some wicked men have greedily accumulated abundant wealth, their enjoyment of that wealth will be quite brief and unsatisfying (implying that Job's wealth may have been gained through wicked greed) (20:20–29). Although he expected nothing but mockery in response, Job (chap. 21) pointed out that the theological belief system of his three friends had at least one major flaw: the experience of the wicked does not support it! After all, the wicked have large families, have enduring estates, and enjoy a full life, even as they openly defy God (21:7–16). Many wicked people who have gathered wealth through corrupt practices seem to enjoy bliss in life and death (21:27–33). This "reality" is not just a problem for Job's three friends; it is also a fundamental part of Job's struggle, for it does not match what he expected God to do.

Third cycle of speeches. Eliphaz's final reply to Job (chap. 22) is the most caustic yet. With dripping sarcasm he asked whether God judged Job because of his piety. Then he presented a litany of accusations that present Job as a man known to all for his injustice and lack of compassion toward the needy (22:4–11). He suggests that Job had a limited view of God since he apparently believed he could hide his sin from God (22:12–14). Eliphaz urged Job to repent and restore his relationship with God, who embraces repentant sinners (22:21–30). Eliphaz was so upset with Job's refusal to admit to great sin that he (Eliphaz) had lost objectivity. A basic theological principle for him was that a person's experience of blessing or judgment is a clear indicator of one's spiritual condition. If that is true (and all three friends drew on that principle repeatedly in the first two cycles), Eliphaz inconsistently turned his back on that principle. Now, Job's wealth and influence were just a cover for his far-reaching treachery. Job's reply to Eliphaz does not seem to be directed at Eliphaz (chaps. 23–24). Instead Job spoke to and about God. He fervently wanted to find God and lay out his case before Him, confident that God would vindicate his innocence (23:3–7). Yet God was absolutely inaccessible. Job did not feel that God cared about Job's agony; he felt God had done nothing to provide relief (23:8–17). It seemed to Job that God silently witnesses the treachery of the wicked without protecting the righteous or punishing the wicked (24:2–17). Job concluded by challenging anyone to prove that he was a liar (24:25). In his final brief word to Job (chap. 25)[20] Bildad directed his adversary's attention to the majesty of God. He wanted Job to see that no human,

---

[20] The brevity of Bildad's reply and the absence of a reply by Zophar has caused some scholars to suggest that this part of Job is somewhat "mutilated" and they rearrange passages in order to create a reply by Zophar and lengthen Bildad's reply. Others affirm that the brevity of responses by the three friends in the third cycle indicates that they have exhausted their arguments and see any further argumentation as a waste of time. Rearranging the text of Job to provide a more complete

including Job, can claim innocence before the great God. Of course all three of Job's friends seemed to have misunderstand Job's central claim. Job did not affirm that he had never committed any sin or was absolutely or perfectly innocent. He understood that everyone sins. Job's struggle was how to relate experience of intense suffering with his understanding of himself as an upright man (in accord with the description of him in chap. 1). After ridiculing the "comfort" provided by his friends (26:1–4), Job launched into a magnificent hymn that celebrates the power of God that is far beyond human control or understanding. He reveled in God's activity seen in various parts of His created world (26:5–14). Fully convinced of God's power, Job refused to give up his claim of innocence. Beyond this, he affirmed that God's sending this affliction into his life was a denial of justice to Job (27:1–6). Because of that injustice and the incessant harping by his friends, Job wished that God would bring divine condemnation against his "friends" and treat them as wicked men (27:7–23).

Through their debate with Job, the three friends represented the problematic concept of retribution theology. This false understanding of God involved "a dogmatic employment of the concept of divine retribution so that there was an automatic connection between deed and state of being."[21] It likened man's relationship to God to a business contract which has mutual claims and is binding in court.[22]

The Bible does not deny the general principle that God blesses the righteous and judges the ungodly. However, the Bible does reject a simplistic, mathematically precise and instant application of the doctrine of retribution. As Kidner points out, about nine-tenths of life is regular and manageable and quietly rewarding to those who follow the principles found in Scripture; this is the portion of life Proverbs addresses. Job and Ecclesiastes, however, address the approximately one-tenth of life that is wholly unexpected and unexplained.[23] The book of Job, in particular, rejects any airtight formula that affirms that the righteous always prosper and the wicked are always destroyed. The book teaches that there may be many reasons for suffering, and the reward (of both blessing and suffering) may be long delayed. Job's experience shows that from a human perspective the ways of God are at times difficult to understand. But even when God's purposes involve personal suffering and loss, He can be trusted because He is the all-wise and all-loving Sovereign of the universe.

Interlude on Wisdom (chap. 28)

This chapter could be included as part of a lengthy reply by Job to his three friends (chaps. 6–31). However, the flow of chap. 28 does not match the cycles of speeches that precede it and Job's monologue that follows it (chaps. 29–31). This monologue could be viewed with Job's summarizing speeches, or it may be viewed as distinctly by itself. This arrangement hopefully places a brighter spotlight on this impressive description of the unsearchable nature of divine wisdom.[24]

In stark contrast with the three "know-it-all" counselors, this beautiful wisdom poem contrasts man's successful search for riches in the normally inaccessible regions of the earth with

---

set of replies seems unnecessary. Any explanation of this brevity, though potentially valid, is conjectural and should be seen as such.

[21] G. W. Parsons, "The Structure and Purpose of the Book of Job," in *Sitting with Job: Selected Studies in the Book of Job*, ed. R. B. Zuck (Grand Rapids: Baker, 1992), 23.

[22] Although this concept may conform to human ideas of justice, it contradicts the biblical teaching of divine grace.

[23] D. Kidner, *The Wisdom of Proverbs, Job and Ecclesiastes: An Introduction to Wisdom Literature* (Downers Grove, IL: InterVarsity, 1985), 36.

[24] I have outlined chap. 28 in this manner without any consideration of authorship or date of inclusion in the book of Job. I regard it as a centerpiece of Job's message.

the absolute inability of human wisdom to find and acquire genuine wisdom. In contrast to man's ability to find gold, iron, copper, and precious gems through great ingenuity and in obscure places (38:12–20), he cannot purchase or trade great riches for true wisdom. Wisdom must come from God, the only One who knows where it can be found (v. 23).

Monologues (29:1–42:6)

Job's call for vindication (chaps. 29–31). Job began his concluding soliloquy by reflecting back on the days before his afflictions began. He remembered when his family was still intact and God was his security (29:1–5). He had enjoyed the respect of his fellow citizens (29:6–11,21–25) and had ministered to many of them in their time of need (29:6–17). He fully expected to die as a happy and blessed man (29:18–20). However, that was not meant to be. Instead he was mocked and harassed by the dregs of society (30:1–15). The galling part of Job's affliction was his belief that God authorized this suffering (30:11,16–23). He could only look forward to agony, the absence of friends, and constant mourning (30:24–31). He concluded his monologue with a final protestation of his innocence. Job's oaths and calling down curses on his conduct could have occasioned personal disaster. Curses were taken seriously by people of the ANE. To call down curses on oneself was a serious and daring thing to do. Job was so convinced of his innocence that he referred to various categories of sin and then mentioned the punishment that would be totally appropriate for those sins (31:5–34). The implication is that if he had committed these treacherous deeds, he would gladly accept the appropriate punishment. Again he demanded an audience with God, his accuser (31:35–40). He longed to know what sins he had committed that justified his suffering. He longed to clear himself of the charges made against him and to demonstrate to his three friends and fellow citizens that God is indeed arbitrary and afflicts the innocent.

Elihu's speeches (chaps. 32–37). In his monologue of four speeches, Elihu sought to correct both Job and his three friends. He was angry with Job "for justifying himself rather than God" (32:2) and with the three friends "because they had found no way to refute Job, and yet had condemned him" (32:3 NIV). In the end Elihu came no closer to solving Job's problem than the three friends who had angered him. He said he had not spoken earlier out of respect for the three older friends. Elihu showed obvious knowledge of the three cycles of speeches, but Job made no response to Elihu's words. In his first speech Elihu asked Job to listen to his words, even in spite of his (Elihu's) youth (32:6–9). Referring to Job's protestations of innocence, Elihu rebuked Job for not being content with his lot in life. He said suffering is one of the things God uses to give direction to His people (33:14–22). Affliction, he said, can be preventive as well as punitive. If it is preventive, suffering can be a clear expression of divine mercy (33:23–30). In his second speech Elihu reproached Job for questioning God's justice (34:4–15). God is just and fair because He knows everything (34:21–28). Elihu reaffirmed the clear connection between a person's experience of judgment and their sinful conduct. Through Job's accusations of divine injustice, Job had added rebellion to his long list of sins (34:37). Elihu began his third speech by pointing out a contradiction between two of Job's statements. He repeatedly had argued for his innocence and also wondered what value or profit there was in avoiding sin (35:2–3). Elihu then proposed that God's silence in certain situations indicates His recognition of the insincerity of the petitioner (35:13–16). In his final speech Elihu returned to his emphasis on God's justice and great power. God is just in the way He treats everyone, regardless of their place in society (36:1–21). This is such an amazing truth because God does not use His absolute power to treat His subjects arbitrarily or maliciously (36:22–37:13).

Beyond this the awesomeness of His power should cause every subject (including Job) to marvel at God's power and revere Him (37:14–24).

Although Elihu did not solve Job's dilemma, he seemed to have provided a transition between the adversarial debate between Job and his three friends and the next monologue, when Job's "accuser" (God) confronted Job. Elihu's concluding focus on the need for repentance and God's power and greatness prepared the way for the truths Job desperately needed to understand. In the preceding chapters Job, his three friends, and Elihu said some things that were correct and true, but they also manifested their total misunderstanding of fundamental truths about God and how He deals with His subjects. God now spoke to Job to correct his and their flawed thinking through two speeches. As Tremper Longman and Raymond Dillard said, "Human wisdom has run out; it is time for God to take the stage."[25]

God's response to Job (38:1–40:5). In the first speech, after rebuking Job for speaking "words without knowledge" (38:2 NIV), the Lord delineated His amazing control of the entire universe, focusing on the physical and animal world. The Lord, however, did not present a number of complicated assertions about the extent of His sovereignty. Instead He asked Job repeated questions about various aspects of creation questions. Here is a brief selection of these questions: "Where were you when I laid the earth's foundation?" (38:4 NIV). "Have you ever given orders to the morning, or shown the dawn its place?" (38:12 NIV). "Have you journeyed to the springs of the sea or walked in the recesses of the deep?" (38:16 NIV). "Who cuts a channel for the torrents of rain, and a path for the thunderstorm?" (38:25 NIV). "Can you bring forth the constellations in their seasons or lead out the Bear with its cubs?" (38:32 NIV). "Can you set up God's dominion over the earth?" (38:33 NIV). "Do you give the horse his strength or clothe his neck with a flowing mane?" (39:19 NIV). "Does the eagle soar at your command and build his nest on high?" (39:27 NIV). One can imagine Job, overwhelmed by these questions, responding, "I can't," "I wasn't there," "I never have," "I don't," and so forth. The point is that God's flawless dominion extends over every realm of creation. His absolute power and wisdom are incontestable. When God gave Job opportunity to reply, Job affirmed that he had nothing at all to say (40:3–5).

However, the Lord was not yet finished. He began his second speech (40:6–42:6) by challenging Job to listen carefully, pointing out that Job was totally unable to save himself or handle the affairs of others (40:6–14). God then referred to two powerful creatures, one on the land and the other on water, both of which are subject to His power and His alone—concrete examples of the extent of God's power. Behemoth[26] has powerful muscles and legs of iron (40:15–18). A raging river does not alarm him, nor is a hunter foolish enough to capture him or cause him concern (40:19–24). Leviathan is a powerful water creature that no one dares to drag out from its hiding place (40:1–2). Could Job domesticate it, or could a fisherman catch it and sell it for profit (41:5–7)? The Lord told Job that if he ever laid a hand on it, he would never do it again (41:8)! Leviathan has fearsome teeth and impenetrable armor and regards arrows and slingstones as a bit of dust (41:12–29). No animal in the world is equal to it (41:33–34). When the Lord paused after these impressive descriptions, Job affirmed God's absolute power and admitted that his verbal sparring manifested his lack of understanding. Job

---

[25] T. Longman III and R. B. Dillard, *An Introduction to the Old Testament,* 2nd ed. (Grand Rapids: Zondervan, 2006), 230.

[26] Scholars debate whether these are legendary creatures, creatures from pagan mythology, or actual animals that were part of God's creation. Some identify Behemoth as a hippopotamus and the Leviathan as a crocodile. Others liken them to dinosaurs that are now extinct. For discussion see R. B. Zuck, *Job* (Chicago: Moody, 1978), 177–83.

repented "in dust and ashes" (42:6), which signified "an outward demonstration of his inward contrition and the death of his own opinions."[27]

Epilogue (42:7–17)

God's verdict (42:7–9). Did the Lord charge Job with sins that brought on his present suffering? Did God give Job a detailed indictment? Did the Lord challenge Job's defense of his integrity? Did He even specifically respond to the "whys" and "wherefores" of Job's suffering? No, these speeches are unique in that they ask more questions than they provide answers. Furthermore the questions seem to be irrelevant to the heart of Job's concern.

Rather than addressing Job's suffering directly, God taught Job a more important truth. Even though much in the created world is incomprehensible to humans and sometimes even threatening to their existence, it is all the work of a wise God who has His own unfathomable purpose for all He does. The fundamental issue is not the existence of a *rigid* connection of conduct and experience (retribution theology). The issue is whether Job will trust God to run His universe in His way! This is as if God had said; "Job, here is the key idea. I am God and you are man. I don't have to submit my intentions to you so they can satisfy your sense of justice and equity. You need to trust that I know the eternal implications of everything I do." God reminded Job that He created the world to operate in a theocentric fashion rather than an anthropocentric one.

Job's restoration (42:10–17). God vindicated Job's righteousness and blessed him again. This blessing was not a reward for the right answer but part of God's plan for Job. Job's final blessing could not remove his suffering. Those losses would always be with him. Also the Bible says that Job's final blessing was God's gracious gift (42:10), not something he had earned by his faithfulness.

THE PURPOSE AND THEOLOGY OF THE BOOK

The key theological truth in Job is that the sole basis for a proper relationship between God and man is "the sovereign grace of God and man's response of faith and submissive trust."[28] The book of Job gives its readers a clear glimpse of God and man. God is seen as sovereign, omniscient, omnipotent, and caring. By contrast, man is seen as finite, ignorant, and sinful. And yet even in the face of suffering, man can worship God, confident that His ways are perfect (Ps 18:30) and that pride has no place before Him. The suffering believer must learn to live by faith in the sovereign Creator and Ruler of the cosmos, for His rule is righteous and wise.

THE HEBREW TEXT OF THE BOOK

The MT of Job has numerous syntactical and orthographic challenges. It is one of the most difficult Hebrew texts in the OT. Job contains more hapax legomena than most of the other OT books.[29] According to several scholars the book also evidences influence by Arabic and Aramaic. Various studies that compare Job with Ugaritic and Northwest Semitic inscriptions have contributed to understanding the philology and syntax of Job.[30] These and other factors

---

[27] Alden, *Job*, 409.

[28] Parsons, "The Structure and Purpose of the Book of Job," 22.

[29] S. Hooks, *Job* (Joplin, MO: College Press, 2007), 21.

[30] M. H. Pope, *Job*, AB (Garden City, NJ: Doubleday, 1973); A. Ceresko, *Job 29–31 in the Light of Northwest Semitic: A Translation and Philological Commentary*, BibOr (Rome: Pontifical Biblical Institute, 1980); W. L. Michel, *Job in the Light of Northwest Semitic*, BibOr (Rome: Pontifical Biblical Institute, 1987).

add to the complexity of translating and understanding the Hebrew text of this important book. Although these difficulties do not undermine confidence in the message of the book as a whole, they do make the interpretation of numerous passages complicated and difficult.

The LXX translation of the book of Job is essentially a faithful translation of the Hebrew. The LXX, however, omits almost 400 poetic lines. This has caused some to suggest that the Hebrew text (*Vorlage*) behind the LXX represents the earliest Hebrew form of Job. Because most of the omissions occur in the third cycle and the wordy Elihu speeches and because many of those lines involve recurring lines and thoughts, it seems that the Greek translator abridged the speeches intentionally.[31]

CONCLUSION

This important book has challenged and blessed its readers for centuries. People today resonate with the problem of "unjust" suffering that Job faced because they have either faced similar circumstances or have seen others experience something similar. Also anyone who reads the book of Job expecting a model of how to respond to suffering is in for a surprise. However, the heart of the book is not to be found in the cutting arguments between Job and his three friends or even in Elihu's speeches. The crescendo of the book is found in the Lord's presentation of His absolute power and self-sufficiency and in Job's recognition of God's ability to do everything that needs to be done, with justice and equity. Job had to realize that God did not have to submit His plans to Job for approval, from the perspective of human fairness. This is as if God had said this to Job: "I am God, you are mortal man; trust me to do what is right, regardless of how things might appear to you."

STUDY QUESTIONS

1. What complicates the discussion of the composition and authorship of the book of Job?
2. What two areas do scholars discuss in relation to the date and authorship of Job?
3. What is the genre and structure of the book of Job?
4. What does Satan seem to suggest is the reason Job serves God?
5. Who are Job's three "friends," and how would you summarize their counsel to Job?
6. What are the three horrifying possibilities that Job confronted as he sifted through the rubble of his life?
7. How would you describe or characterize the interchange between Job and his friends as the debate continues?
8. What is "retribution theology"?
9. How does the interlude on wisdom (chap. 28) stand apart from the discussions that precede and follow it?
10. What function do the Elihu speeches have in the flow of the book's argument?
11. How would you summarize God's response to Job?
12. What are the most important truths God taught Job (and teaches those who read it) through this book?

---

[31] J. E. Hartley, *The Book of Job*, NICOT (Grand Rapids: Eerdmans, 1988), 4. R. K. Harrison suggests that the translator "regarded any attempt to render the less intelligible passages into Greek as an exercise in futility" (*Introduction to the Old Testament* [Grand Rapids, Eerdmans, 1969], 1042.

FOR FURTHER STUDY

Alden, R. L. *Job*. NAC. Nashville: B&H, 1993.

Andersen, F. I. *Job: An Introduction and Commentary*. TOTC. Downers Grove, IL: InterVarsity, 1976.

Archer, G. L., Jr. *The Book of Job: God's Answer to the Problem of Undeserved Suffering*. Grand Rapids; Baker, 1982.

Bullock, C. H. *An Introduction to the Old Testament Poetic Books*. Rev. ed. Chicago: Moody, 1988.

Ceresko, A. *Job 29–31 in the Light of Northwest Semitic: A Translation and Philogocal Comentary*. BibOr. Rome: Pontifical Biblical Institute, 1980.

Clines, D. J. A. *Job 1–20*. WBC. Dallas: Word, 1989.

Cornelius, I. "Job." In *Zondervan Illustrated Bible Backgrounds Commentary*. Edited by John H. Walton, 5:246–315. Grand Rapids: Zondervan, 2009.

Crenshaw, J. L. *Old Testament Wisdom: An Introduction*. Atlanta: John Knox, 1981.

Dyer, C. H., and G. Merrill. *Old Testament Explorer: Discovering the Essence, Background, and Meaning of Every Book in the OT*. Nashville: Word, 2001.

Estes, D. J. *Handbook on the Wisdom Books and Psalms*. Grand Rapids: Baker, 2005.

Gordis, R. *The Book of God and Man*. Chicago: University of Chicago, 1965.

Harbin, M. A. *The Promise and Blessing: A Historical Survey of the Old and New Testaments*. Grand Rapids: Zondervan, 2005.

Harrison, R. K. *Introduction to the Old Testament*. Grand Rapids: Erdmans, 1969.

Hartley, J. E. *The Book of Job*. NICOT. Grand Rapids: Eerdmans, 1988.

Hill, A. E., and J. H. Walton. *A Survey of the Old Testament*. 3rd. Grand Rapids: Zondervan, 2009.

House, P. R. *Old Testament Theology*. Downers Grove, IL: InterVarsity, 1998.

Kaiser, W. C., Jr. *The Promise-Plan of God: Biblical Theology of the Old and New Testaments*. Grand Rapids: Zondervan, 2008.

Kidner, D. *The Wisdom of Proverbs, Job and Ecclesiastes: An Introduction to Wisdom Literature*. Downers Grove, IL: InterVarsity, 1985.

Lambert, W. G. *Babylonian Wisdom Literature*. Oxford: Clarendon, 1960.

LaSor, W. S., D. A. Hubbard, and F. W. Bush. *Old Testament Survey: The Message, Form, and Background of the Old Testament*. 2nd ed. Grand Rapids: Eerdmans, 1996.

Longman, T., III, and R. Dillard. *An Introduction to the Old Testament*. 2nd ed. Grand Rapids: Zondervan, 2006.

Merrill, E. H. *Everlasting Dominion: A Theology of the Old Testament*. Nashville: B&H, 2006.

Michel, W. L. *Job in the Light of Northwest Semitic*. BibOR. Rome: Pontifical Biblical Institute, 1987.

Parsons, G. W. "The Structure and Purpose of the Book of Job." *BSac* 138 (April-June 1981): 139–57.

———. "Guidelines for Understanding and Proclaiming the Book of Job." *BSac* 151 (October-December 1994): 393–413.

Pope, M. H. *Job*. AB. Garden City, NY: Doubleday, 1973.

Scott, R. B. Y. *The Way of Wisdom in the Old Testament*. New York: Macmillan, 1971.

Smick, E. B., and T. Longman III. "Job." In *EBC*. Rev. ed. Edited by T. Longman III and D. E. Garland, 4:675–921. Grand Rapids: Zondervan, 2010.

Von Rad, G. *Wisdom in Israel*. Nashville: Abingdon, 1972.

Waltke, B. K. *An Old Testament Theology*. Grand Rapids: Zondervan, 2007.

Walton, J. H. "Job 1: Book of." In *Dictionary of the Old Testament: Wisdom, Poetry, and Writings*. Edited by T. Longman, III, and P. Enns, 333–46. Downers Grove, IL: Inter Varsity, 2008.

Westermann, Claus. *The Structure of the Book of Job: A Form-Critical Analysis*. Translated by C. A. Muenchow, Philadelphia: Fortress, 1981.

Zuck, R. B. *Job*. EBC Chicago: Moody, 1978.

———. "A Theology of the Wisdom Books and the Song of Songs." In *A Biblical Theology of the Old Testament*. Edited by Roy B. Zuck, 207–55. Chicago: Moody, 1991.

CHAPTER 40

THE BOOK OF PSALMS

MICHAEL A. GRISANTI

I N ADDITION TO providing insight into the history of God's dealings with Israel and Israel's experience of God, the psalms serve as an impressive witness to man's nature. Man's penchant for sin is contrasted with the unparalleled character of God. William LaSor, David Hubbard, and Frederic Bush write, "Like the windows and carvings of medieval cathedrals, the Psalms were pictures of biblical faith for a people who had no copies of the Scriptures in their homes and could not have read them."[1]

THE TITLE OF THE PSALTER

The English title "the Psalms" draws on Greek and Latin versions of the Hebrew OT. The LXX used the noun *psalmos* (designating a song sung to the accompaniment of a harp) to render the Hebrew *mizmôr* (a technical word for a song sung to the accompaniment of musical instruments).[2] Jesus and Paul referred to it as "the Book of Psalms" (Luke 20:42; Acts 1:20). The Latin Vulgate renders the Hebrew term as *Psalmus* or *Psalmi*. The Alexandrinus LXX manuscript entitled the book *psaltērion* ("stringed instrument"), which provides the basis for the designation the Psalter. The Hebrew text appropriately entitled the book *tĕhillîm* ("praises"). Although the singular form of this word (*tĕhillāh*) occurs only once to designate an individual psalm (Psalm 145), it occurs a number of times in various psalms to describe praise that should be directed to Israel's incomparable God.

THE STRUCTURE OF THE BOOK

Basic Divisions

The traditional divisions of the Psalter are these:

Book I   Psalms 1–41
Book II   Psalms 42–72

---

[1] W. S. LaSor, D. A. Hubbard, and F. W. Bush, *Old Testament Survey: The Message, Form, and Background of the Old Testament*, 2nd ed. (Grand Rapids: Eerdmans, 1996), 445.

[2] The Vaticanus LXX manuscript has the title "Psalms" (Psalmoi).

Book III	Psalms 73–89
Book IV	Psalms 90–106
Book V	Psalms 107–150

Each of the first four books ends with a doxology (41:13; 72:18–19; 89:52; 106:48). The first three doxologies seem to be distinct from the message of the psalm they conclude. Psalm 150 serves as the final doxology for the fifth book and the entire collection. The fact that these doxologies belonged to the psalm in antiquity is evidenced by the presence of the doxology in 1 Chr 16:35–36, which is a slightly revised version of Ps 106:1,47. Also this five-book arrangement of the Psalter exists in all extant Hebrew manuscripts. But the order of the last two books (IV and V) differs in some of the DSS, suggesting that their *final order* was not firmly established until around the time of Christ (see section below on the canonicity of the Psalter).

Psalm Numbering

The chapter divisions used by the Hebrew and the LXX vary slightly. The Hebrew Bible has 150 psalms and Protestant Bibles follow the Hebrew numbering of the psalms. The LXX has an additional psalm and changes the numbering of the psalms. Also on two occasions it subdivides a Hebrew psalm into two psalms (MT 116 and 147 divided into LXX 114–115 and 146–147) and in two instances it fuses a pair of Hebrew psalms into one (MT 9–10 and 114–115 combined into LXX 9 and 113). The psalms that involve a numbering change are in bold font (see below):

Hebrew and Protestant Bibles	*Greek and Roman Catholic Bibles*
1–8	1–8
9	**9**
10	
11–113	10–112
114	**113**
115	
	114
116	**115**
117–146	116–145
	146
147	**147**
148–150	148–150
	151 (Greek)

Psalm Versification

The verse divisions of the Hebrew text and most English versions vary most of the time. This is because the Hebrew text includes the superscription as the first verse of the psalm.[3] Thus the Hebrew versification is regularly one number greater than the English.

---

[3] When the MT includes the superscription *together* with the first verse (as it appears in most English translations), the versification of the MT and English versions match (e.g., Psalm 78).

THE COMPOSITION OF THE PSALTER

Two separate issues merit consideration with regard to the composition of the Psalter: the authorship of the individual psalms and the composition of the Psalter as a whole. Since certain psalms claim to have been composed in the time of Moses and others were written at least as late as the divided monarchy (if not into the period after the exile), the following two conclusions are feasible. First, the composition of the entire Psalter did not take place until sometime after the exile. Second, the editor/compiler of the Psalter is to be distinguished from the authors of individual psalms.

The Process of Compilation

This process probably involved at least four stages. Obviously any precise conclusions in this area are based to some degree on conjecture. First was the writing of individual poems/ psalms. The primary use of the psalms seems to have been for temple worship (as a kind of a prayer book). When individual psalms were written, they were collected for use in regular worship. Second, the individual psalms were gathered into collections. For example, Ps 72:20 testifies to the existence of an early collection of the prayers of David. Since some psalms among the first 72 psalms are non-Davidic, this could refer to an earlier collection by David that was incorporated into this material. Second Chronicles 29:30 may suggest that in Hezekiah's day there were only two collections of psalms, that of David and Asaph. Books II and III have the following collections: "of the sons of Korah" (Psalms 42–49), "of Asaph" (Psalms 73–83), and Books IV and V have those "of David" (Psalms 138–145), "songs of Ascent" (Psalms 120– 134), and the *"hodu"* psalms (Psalms 105–107),[4] among others. Third, the smaller collections were then organized into five books. Fourth, a final edition was completed. While there may not be a traceable theme throughout the Psalter, there do appear to be traces of careful organization. Psalms 1 and 2 form a fitting introduction and psalms 145–150 a triumphant finale. Certain psalms seem to have been used as seams between the books (Psalms 41, 72, 89, 106).

The Authorship

Of the 150 psalms all but 34 have titles of some sort. Of the 116 titles, 100 might indicate authorship, often along with other information.

Moses—1 psalm (Psalm 90)
David—73 psalms (mostly in Books I and II)
Solomon—2 psalms (Psalms 72, 127)
Asaph—12 psalms (Psalms 50, 73–83)
Sons of Korah—10 psalms (Psalms 42, 44–49, 84–85, 87)[5]
Heman, the Ezrahite—1 psalm (Psalm 88)
Ethan, the Ezrahite—1 psalm (Psalm 89)

The titles that might indicate authorship have the Hebrew preposition *lamed* prefixed to the names in question. The ambiguity of the preposition complicates the issue because it can signify "of," "to," "for," or other options. It could signify authorship, dedicated to a person, or belonging to a collection. There is nothing about these citations, however, that precludes their indication of authorship. In fact the NT use of various psalms confirms Davidic authorship of a number of psalms. It simply is not something about which we can be dogmatic without indications from other passages.

---

⁴ They are called "*hodu*" psalms because they each begin with the Hb. verb *hôdû,* "give thanks."
⁵ Scholars debate whether this title indicates authorship or refers to a musical rendition.

The Titles

Over two-thirds of the psalms have titles that generally provide the following categories of information: authorship, historical origin or setting, literary features, liturgical use, and musical notations. James Thirtle has proposed that in many of the psalms certain elements of the title conclude the preceding psalm rather than introduce the psalm on which they appear as a superscription (following the example of Habakkuk 3).[6] But, this theory has received little attention in most works on the Psalms.

THE CANONICITY OF THE PSALTER

The book of Psalms belongs to the division called the Writings in the third division of the Hebrew Bible, as part of the poetic or wisdom literature of the OT. The Psalter holds an unquestioned place in the OT canon.

Fragments of biblical psalms have been found in Caves 1–6, 8, and 11 of the DSS, and scrolls that include a number of psalms were found in Caves 4 and 11.[7] The Psalms Scroll found in Cave 4 (4 QPs[a]) contains all or parts of Psalms 6–69, generally in canonical order. The Psalms Scroll found in Cave 11 (11 QPs[a]) contains part or all of Psalms 93, 101–103, 109, 118–119, 121–146, and 148–50 (35 psalms). It also contains three additional psalms: 151, 154, and 155 (Psalm 151 may lie behind the final psalm of the LXX). The scroll generally confirms the text of the MT even though the order of the psalms differs significantly from the order in the MT. The Psalms Scroll adds more Davidic headings and attributes, new psalms, and has a prose statement celebrating David as a prophet and the author of 4,050 psalms and songs.[8] Since most scholars date the copying of 11QPs[a] to AD 30–50,[9] various suggestions have been made about the significance of this for the development of the canon. While some suggest that it indicates that the text, order, and number of psalms had not yet been finalized, others say that the collection of psalms present in 11QPs[a] could suggest a kind of Qumran prayer book. Evidence based on these Psalms scrolls is insufficient to make a final decision. Other factors (see chap. 6 for a discussion of the canon of the OT) suggest that the OT canon was closed in the fourth century BC.

THE LITERARY FORMS AND GENRES OF THE BOOK

The psalmists themselves provided a number of different terms in the superscriptions that at that time were some kind of helpful designation for the type or content of the psalm (e.g., *mizmôr, higgayon, miktām, tᵉpillāh, tᵉhhillāh, maśkîl*). The meaning of those terms is less clear to modern scholars. The psalms are generally categorized in accord with their content, function, or some combination of the two. Some refer to categories such as national, historical, royal, messianic, wisdom, and imprecatory psalms. Others refer to the psalms based on their type or

---

[6] J. Thirtle, *The Titles of the Psalms, Their Nature and Meaning Explained* (London: Henry Frowde, 1904). See also B. K. Waltke, "Superscripts, Postscripts, or Both," *JBL* 110 (1991): 583–96.

[7] At least 30 partial copies of the Psalter have been discovered in the caves around Qumran, more than for any other biblical book. These 30 copies have fragments of at least 115 of the biblical psalms (W. L. Holladay, *The Psalms Through Three Thousand Years: Prayerbook of a Cloud of Witnesses* [Minneapolis: Fortress, 1993], 100). Cf. J. A. Sanders, *The Dead Sea Psalms Scroll* (Ithaca, NY: Cornell University Press, 1967), 9–14. Also see P. W. Flint, *The Dead Sea Psalms Scroll and the Book of Psalms: Studies on the Texts of the Desert of Judah*, vol. 17, ed. F. G. Martinez and A. S. Van Der Woude (New York: Brill, 1997).

[8] G. H. Wilson, *Psalms*, NIVAC (Grand Rapids: Zondervan, 2002), 20. Wilson says that the Qumran scroll "davidizes" the Psalter.

[9] Holladay, *The Psalms Through Three Thousand Years*, 100.

genre, some of which are hymns, community laments, songs of the individual, laments of the individual, and royal psalms.

Primary Kinds of Psalms

Although scholars have proposed a number of psalm types, three categories encompass a large number of psalms: praise, lament, and thanksgiving.[10]

Praise. Praise psalms contain an appeal (to oneself or others) to praise God, accompanied by numerous descriptions of His praiseworthy name, deeds, attributes, and character. They focus their attention on God's surpassing character and His role in history as the Creator, Sustainer, and Stabilizer of the universe. His care for the world gives His subjects the only reliable basis for hope and encouragement. These psalms express great confidence in God's sovereignty and incomparability. Some examples of praise psalms are Psalms 8, 29, 33, and 146–150.

Lament. The lament psalms also direct their appeal to God Himself, but in stark contrast to the praise psalms they seek deliverance from terrifying circumstances. While the praise psalms seem to present a world with no suffering or disorder, lament psalms arise from personal experience with suffering and injustice. One of the challenges faced by the psalmists is that they had experienced suffering while living under the umbrella of God's control. Thus they wonder, "Is He really in control? Does He really care for my particular circumstances?" The psalmists longed for God to act on their behalf. Lament psalms can refer to individual or national affliction. Generally, these psalms open with a cry to God and then present the psalmist's lament (referring to the foes, himself, and God). After a confession of trust, the psalmist pleads for divine intervention (e.g., hear, save, punish). The psalm concludes with a vow or expression of praise. Psalms 22, 74, 88, and 130 are examples of lament psalms.

Thanksgiving. The psalms demonstrate a clear understanding of suffering and injustice. However, this perspective differs from the lament psalms. Rather than describing suffering as a present and ongoing experience, they describe suffering and pain as a past reality. The psalmists affirm their fervent gratitude for God's intervention in their difficult circumstances. These expressions of gratitude or praise duplicate those found in praise psalms. A thanksgiving psalm can be distinguished from a praise psalm by its clear reference to past suffering. Psalms 104, 107, 116, and 136 are examples of this category.

Other Types of Psalms

Four other categories of psalms are not designated by form or structural issues but are classified according to their content.

Royal psalms. As stated below (see "The Theology of the Book"), the Psalter places great emphasis on God's rule over His creation and His covenant nation in particular. These psalms focus on the king of Israel and depict him as God's representative through whom He rules over His chosen people. They refer to the king and also present him as the anointed one (*mašiah*—Psalms 2, 18, 20, 45, 89, 132).[11] As Walther Zimmerli affirmed, "The king of Israel makes the dominion of Yahweh visible on earth."[12] He epitomizes God's reign. As the king goes, so goes the nation. These psalms present God's intentions for all the descendents of David who

---

[10] Wilson, *Psalms*, 65–66. For a helpful explanation of these primary types of psalms as well as the other categories, see C. H. Bullock, *Encountering the Psalms: A Literary and Theological Introduction* (Grand Rapids: Baker, 2001), 121–238; and idem, *An Introduction to the Poetic Books*, rev. ed. (Chicago: Moody, 1988), 135–42.

[11] In addition to these psalms, 21, 72, 101, 110, and 144 are generally regarded as royal psalms.

[12] W. Zimmerli, *Old Testament Theology in Outline*, trans. D. E. Green (Atlanta: John Knox, 1978), 92.

would rule over God's servant nation. And in the ultimate sense they serve "as a witness to the messianic hope which looked for the consummation of God's kingship through his Anointed One."[13]

Royal psalms draw attention to the anointed king who belongs to the line of David (Psalms 89, 132; cf. 2 Samuel 7). Some of the psalms refer to some high point in the monarch's reign, such as his coronation (Psalm 2), his wedding (Psalm 45) or his going into battle (Psalms 20, 144), as well as his anticipated coming in conquest (Psalm 110) and his glorious reign (Psalm 72).

These psalms set a high standard for every Davidic descendant who would become king. They envision an "ideal Davidic ruler." In addition to focusing on different key periods of a king's reign, they place great emphasis on this king's unflinching commitment to ruling with justice and compassion over his subjects (see Psalm 72 in particular). However, no Davidic descendant measured up to this divine standard. This "nonfulfillment" in the reigns of all the Davidic kings who ruled over Israel created an expectation of some future king who might rule in this manner. So although these psalms refer to the human Davidic rulers who would rule over Israel they pave the way for a "messianic" expectation. Their anticipation of an ideal Davidic king eventually led to a messianic anticipation that found fulfillment in Jesus (see figure below).

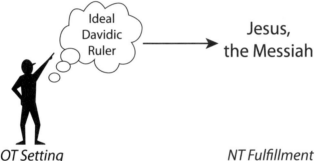

Ideal Davidic Ruler Figure

Enthronement psalms. Although these six psalms (Psalms 93, 95–99) are similar to royal psalms in light of their emphasis on kingship, they are distinct in that they focus on God's kingdom and rule. Some call them *Yahweh malak* (i.e., "Yahweh rules") psalms because that Hebrew expression begins Psalms 93, 97, and 99 (cf. 96:10). Tradition historians conclude that these psalms describe an annual enthronement festival, much like the Akitu festival in Babylon, which symbolized the re-enthronement of Yahweh.[14] However, there is no biblical evidence for this kind of festival.[15] Even if there was some kind of enthronement festival, for Israel to model a festival after a pagan fertility and cultic procession would violate biblical teaching in other parts of the OT. The so-called "enthronement" psalms[16] are better seen as eschatological

---

[13] B. S. Childs, *Introduction to the Old Testament as Scripture* (Philadelphia: Fortress, 1979), 517.

[14] S. Mowinckel, *The Psalms in Israel's Worship*, trans. D. R. Ap-Thomas (Nashville: Abingdon, 1962), 1:115.

[15] Israel had fall festivals, but they were associated with the Day of Atonement, the Feast of Tabernacles, and the New Year.

[16] Bullock calls these psalms "kingship of Yahweh psalms" (*Encountering the Psalms,* 188).

psalms, looking forward to the time when the Lord will actually come to establish His king-dom and reign.[17]

Wisdom psalms. Like the book of Proverbs, these psalms describe the way a person can enjoy a "good life," as defined in Scripture. They are also identified with "Torah Psalms," which expound the wisdom of following the law. They emphasize the theme of "two roads" through numerous "sayings": "Better" sayings (Ps 119:72), numerical sayings (Ps 62:11–12a), admonition to "sons" (Ps 34:11), blessing formulas (Ps 1:1), and an emphasis on the law (Psalm 119). Some of the psalms that fit in this category are 1, 37, 73, 112, 119, and 127.

Messianic psalms. The Psalter repeatedly refers to an anointed ruler from the line of David, who will rule over his kingdom with justice and compassion. So several royal psalms are also regarded as messianic psalms. Different psalms describe his divine placement on the throne (Psalm 2), the affliction a king would experience (Psalms 16, 22), and the incomparable nature of his reign (Psalm 72). Obviously the One who brings all this to fulfillment is Jesus Christ (the Messiah). But what is the primary focus of these psalms? Do they focus on their present and near future (history) or the distant future (eschatology)? Are these psalms exclusively or primarily messianic, typologically messianic, or indirectly messianic?[18] Another factor to consider is the NT's use of a psalm. The NT quotes from this group of psalms (royal) at least 15 times (Psalms 2 [six times], 18, 45, 110 [seven times]). Psalm 110 "had the future Messiah as its center of gravity."[19] It is primarily messianic. Other psalms are typological, like Psalm 22, where the psalmist's intense suffering foreshadowed Christ's suffering. The terms used by the psalmist to describe the intensity of his own suffering provide a pattern that the Gospel writers utilized. Most of the royal psalms are indirectly messianic because they were written to describe what God intended for all kings who would rule over Israel, and the nonfulfillment of those expectations gave rise to an anticipation of the one who will provide ultimate fulfillment, namely Jesus Christ.

WHAT ABOUT IMPRECATORY PSALMS?

What Are They?

The imprecatory psalms have occasioned considerable debate. How are the statements in these psalms to be understood? Can similar language be used today against those who oppose believers and the spread of the gospel? The word "imprecation" (derived from the Latin verb *imprecārī*) means "the action of invoking evil, calamity, or divine vengeance upon another, or upon oneself, in an oath or adjuration: cursing."[20] Imprecatory language, then, signifies calling down divine judgment on an enemy of the psalmist.[21] This sobering language occurs in 18

---

[17] These psalms include epiphany (appearance) language that is drawn from the Sinai event and used by the biblical prophets to anticipate the great Day of the Lord.

[18] F. Delitzsch proposed five types of messianic psalms: purely prophetic (only Psalm 110), eschatological (Psalms 96–99), typological-prophetic (Psalm 22), indirectly messianic (Psalms 2, 45, 72), and typically messianic (Ps 34:20; 69:1–36) (*Psalms, Commentary on the Old Testament* [reprint; Grand Rapids: Eerdmans, 1976], 1:66–71).

[19] Bullock, *Introduction to the Poetic Books,* 137.

[20] J. A. Simpson and E. S. C. Weiner, eds., "Imprecation," in *Oxford English Dictionary,* 2nd ed. (Oxford: Clarendon, 1989), 7:737.

[21] Imprecatory language also occurs in other parts of the OT outside the Psalter. A few examples are Num 10:35; Judg 5:31; Jer 11:20; 15:15; 17:18; 18:21–23; 20:12.

psalms, but does not characterize any psalm entirely.[22] To call them "imprecatory psalms" is unfortunate because that does not accurately describe each psalm as a whole.

What Is the Problem?

The primary interpretive debate revolves around the relationship of imprecatory language to the language of the NT (e.g., Matt 5:44—"love your enemies and pray for those who persecute you"). Beyond the "love ethic" of the NT, scholars also point to examples of imprecatory language in the NT (Acts 13:10–11; 23:3; 1 Cor 16:22; Gal 1:8–9; 5:12). Some imprecatory statements in the psalms are quoted in the NT (e.g., Acts 1:20 cites Pss 69:25 and 109:8). Scholars have offered different ways to explain the language found in these psalms.[23]

What Is the "Big Picture" for These Psalms?

One can only understand the language in the imprecatory psalm if he maintains an awareness of the larger OT theological and covenantal context. Two observations may be made.

Israel enjoys an intimate covenant relationship with Yahweh. In the Abrahamic covenant God declared that He would make the descendants of Abraham into a nation, give them a land, and bless them (Gen 12:1–3). Demonstrating His sole responsibility for the prosperity of Abraham and his descendants, God blessed His covenant subjects with abundance. Later, when Israel camped on the plains of Moab at the brink of the promised land, Moses said God had done exactly as He had promised (Deut 10:21–22). In the Mosaic covenant, established when Israel camped at the base of Mount Sinai, the Lord made His relationship with the descendants of Abraham more concrete, welding them into a fledgling nation.[24] He pledged to be their God and demanded that they be His people. He required that they love Him wholeheartedly (Deut 6:5), leading lives of absolute loyalty. As the God who redeemed them from Egypt and formed them as a nation, He had the right to expect them to live in a way that put His incomparable character on display before each other as citizens of Israel as well as before the nations of the world.

Covenant curses (and blessings) are an integral part of that covenant relationship. When God initiated this covenant relationship with Abraham and his descendants, covenant blessings and curses were linked with the way the nations treated God's chosen nation (Gen 12:3). The concept of covenant blessings and curses reached fuller expression in the Mosaic covenant. Leviticus 26 and Deuteronomy 27–28 delineate the covenant sanctions promised to those who committed covenant treachery. Prophetic predictions of coming judgment on the nation drew on the covenant-curse language of the Mosaic covenant: illness and death, drought and famine, defeat by an enemy, eviction from the land, and so forth.[25] The Psalter "forms a songbook of a people bound in covenant to their God."[26] Meredith Kline pointed out, "The Psalter

---

[22] Of the 368 verses in these psalms, only 95 verses can be called imprecatory (c. 17 percent). In the three psalms that have the most imprecatory language (Psalms 35, 69, 109), the imprecations represent only about one-fourth of those psalms. The most commonly cited imprecatory psalms are Psalms 5, 10, 28, 35, 40, 55, 59, 69, 79, 109, and 137.

[23] See Bullock, *Encountering the Psalms,* 228-32; and J. C. Laney, "A Fresh Look at the Imprecatory Psalms," *BSac* 138 (January–March 1981): 37–40, for helpful overviews of the most common interpretive suggestions.

[24] God's giving Israel the law in the wake of the 10 plagues, the crossing of the Red Sea, and His repeated miraculous provision of their physical needs served to transform this loose collection of ethnically related individuals into a nation with the Mosaic covenant as their "constitution."

[25] As D. Hillers points out, "They were not indulging a morbid imagination but were fundamentally like lawyers quoting the law; this is just what the covenant curses had said would happen" (*Covenant: The History of a Biblical Idea* [Baltimore: John Hopkins University Press, 1969], 134).

[26] A. M. Harman, "The Continuity of the covenant Curses in the Imprecations of the Psalter," *RTR* 54 (1995): 69.

served broadly as a cultic instrument in the maintenance of a proper covenant relationship with Yahweh. The Psalter's function in covenant confession suggests it may be regarded as an extension of the vassal's ratification response, which is found in certain biblical texts as well as extra-biblical covenants as part of the treaty text."[27]

To understand the imprecatory language of various psalms correctly one must correctly understand the larger theological backdrop. Israel enjoyed a covenant relationship with God that demanded their exclusive allegiance and required that they treat each other with justice and compassion. Disobedience of the covenant and the refusal to live as loyal subjects before Him provided just grounds for Him to bring covenant curses against His rebellious subjects. In other words to refuse God the total allegiance He demanded or to treat one's fellow citizens wickedly was more than bad conduct: it was high treason and abhorrent treachery.

What Are Some Key Factors to Consider?

What other factors help correctly understand the imprecatory language in the Psalter? Five responses may be given.

First, vindication of God's righteousness rather than vengeance for the afflicted psalmist is the central issue. This imprecatory language is not about personal "payback," getting a "pound of flesh." Although the psalmist had personally experienced some kind of horrific treatment by these "enemies," personal vengeance was not the point of this language. Imprecatory language witnesses to the psalmists' concern for God's just character. They were *at least* as concerned for God's reputation as they were for their own welfare. Since they firmly believed that God is the just and compassionate ruler over all creation, He must intercede on behalf of the innocent and oppressed. Deuteronomy 10:18 presents Him as one who "defends the cause of the father-less and the widow, and loves the alien" (NIV). In Ps 58:11 the psalmist wrote that after God intervenes on behalf of the oppressed, "Surely the righteous still are rewarded; surely there is a God who judges the earth" (NIV). The "enemy's" treatment of the psalmist was not just a violation of conventional standards; it also revealed their rebellion against God. However, even though the psalmists prayed for the demise of the wicked, they left the *doing* of that prayer in God's hands, whether in this life or the next. They refused to take matters into their own hands; instead they trusted God to do what He deemed best and right as their righteous judge.

Second, God's kingship is prominent. For example Ps 5:2 refers to "my King and my God." God "King forever and ever" (10:16) and "is enthroned from long ago" (55:19 [HB, v 20]). He is the Lord God of Hosts (59:5; 69:6). The entire psalter's emphasis on God's kingship and role as the suzerain of Israel must not be ignored (see section below) on the theology of the Psalter. Since He is the supreme king, any violations of His demands represent acts against Him.

Third, there is a covenantal basis for a curse on Israel's enemies. Though the word "covenant" (*bᵉrît*) rarely occurs in the Psalter, various other covenantal terms occur with regularity (e.g., "choose," "know," "law" "statues," "Your people"). Many of these psalms (as well as others throughout the Psalter) review the history of the nation's relationship by means of their covenant with God. They make frequent use of the name of Yahweh, which highlights His capacity as covenant maker and keeper. They also commend or condemn conduct with language reminiscent of the Mosaic covenant. Psalm 109 makes explicit reference to covenant blessing and cursing (vv. 17–19,28).

---

[27] M. G. Kline, *The Structure of Biblical Authority* (Grand Rapids: Eerdmans, 1972), 63.

Fourth, the enemies referred to in these psalms are ultimately God's enemies. They rebelled against God (5:10b), they hurled insults at Him (69:7,9), they have no room for God (10:4), and they have no fear of God (55:19b). This language of wrath does not arise from some personal offense; instead it deals with a rejection of God's authority.

Fifth, imprecatory language must be interpreted in light of the message of the entire Psalter as well as the OT.[28] One must not view the psalms' imprecatory language as expressing anger and frustration against those who oppose their intentions and plans. Instead the imprecatory language must be seen in light of Israel's covenant relationship with God and the cursing that was an integral part of that covenant allegiance.

Can Believers Pray Imprecatory Prayers Today?

As those who have a faith relationship with God who makes and keeps covenant (through the new covenant and not the Mosaic covenant), believers should be just as passionate about demonstrating the surpassing nature of God's character to the world as were the psalmists. Believers should also be just as offended by acts of treachery against God's sovereignty. To long that God would punish the wicked so as to vindicate His righteousness is totally proper. The imprecations in the psalms were "motivated by a desire to promote righteousness (Ps 7:6–11), to demonstrate God's sovereignty (58:11; 59:13), to cause the wicked to seek the Lord (83:16–18), and to provide an opportunity for the righteous to praise God (7:17; 35:18,28)."[29] Also one must remember that these imprecations were pronounced against unbelieving Israelites and Gentiles who, as it were, shook their fists in the face of the God of Israel.

THE THEOLOGY OF THE BOOK

As part of any attempt to understand the theology of the Psalter, one must recognize several facts about the nature of the book of Psalms: its literary features, its theological character, and its unique makeup. First, one can loosely divide OT biblical literature into two categories. The vast majority of the OT claims to be God's direct revelation to mankind through a divinely chosen, human messenger. A smaller portion of Scripture is singular in that it presents itself as a primarily human creation (not revelation). It concerns both a vertical and a horizontal relationship, that is, a relationship between Israel (as well as mankind in general) and God, or between human beings. The Psalter belongs to this latter category. Second, the Psalter does not present a "catechism of doctrine." Instead of making abstract and "systematic theology" statements, the various psalms make affirmations that emerge from a knowledge of God that is rooted in a relationship. Third, the Psalter consists of a large number of component parts (different kinds [genres] of individual psalms). Although they were probably collected along major theological themes, the theology they present is not exhaustive.

The psalmists set forth the Lord as king of the universe, who is establishing His just rule on the earth in and through His people. According to Robert Chisholm, "As the Creator of all things, God exercises sovereign authority over the natural order, the nations, and Israel, His unique people. In His role as universal King God assures order and justice in the world and among His people often by exhibiting His power as an invincible warrior. The proper response to this sovereign King is trust and praise."[30]

---

[28] Harman, "The Continuity of the Covenant Curses in the Imprecations of the Psalter," 72.

[29] Laney, "A Fresh Look at the Imprecatory Psalms," 44.

[30] R. B. Chisholm Jr., "A Theology of the Psalms," in *A Biblical Theology of the Old Testament*, ed. R. B. Zuck (Chicago: Moody, 1991), 258.

From a human perspective, as vassals of the great King, the psalmists praised God for who He is (His attributes) and what He does (His activity). They longed and prayed for the comprehensive establishment of His sovereign rule over the earth, and they lamented its present incompleteness. Thus three primary elements or categories should be considered in synthesizing the theology of the Psalms: the great King (the suzerain), mankind (His vassals), and the relationship between the two (God's rule).

God, the Almighty King

God is the most prominent figure in the Psalter. All the psalms describe Him or humanity in relationship to Him. He is the supreme King, sovereign over all. The psalmists teach much about God's attributes and activities.

His attributes. One of the most obvious aspects of God's surpassing character involves His sovereignty. Since the rule of God is a significant motif throughout the Scriptures, it is no surprise that God's sovereignty is a frequent and important motif in the Psalter. The so-called "enthronement psalms" (Psalms 47, 93, 96–99) demonstrate most pointedly that God has ruled (47:2–6 [HB, vv. 3–7]), does rule (Psalm 93), and will rule (47:7–8 [HB, vv. 8–9]). Holiness is also a prominent divine attribute throughout the Scriptures. It denotes Yahweh's apartness/separation from everything that is common or profane. He is supramundane, majestic, and transcendent (29:2; 7:22; 89:36; 96:9; 103:1; 111:9). As in the rest of the OT, many other attributes of God are present in the Psalter, a few of which are immutability (90:2–6; 102:24–26 [HB, 25–27]), omnipresence, and omniscience (Ps 139), eternality (90:1–4 [HB, 2–5]), steadfast love (*ḥesed*—25:10; 62:12; 136; emphasizing God's faithfulness to His covenant), righteousness and justice (33:5; 37:28; 145:17), and love (*'āhēb*—47:4; 78:68; 87:2).

His activity. First, He is the Creator God. He created the universe and all that it includes (33:15; 74:16–17; 95:5; 96:5; 100:3; 104:19; 136:4–9). This creation is not only the product of His decree and power; it is also a revelatory vehicle of His character (19:1–4). By virtue of His creation He stands as the absolute Sovereign over everything outside of Himself (Psalm 33). His creative activity also sets Him on a plane different from impotent idols (86:8; 95:3; 96:4–5; 135:5). He is also the all-controlling God. Second, the historical psalms (68, 78, 105–106, 135–136) clearly depict His involvement in history as the planner and executor of all events. The most common figure used to express His sovereignty is kingship. Third, He is the redeeming God. His role as the Savior represents a key theological element both outside of the Psalter (Exod 3:8–10; Isa 43:1–3; Jer 14:8) and within it (Pss 7:10; 18; 19:14). Thanksgiving and praise and petitions and laments often revolve around the appreciated or anticipated redemptive activity of God. Fourth, He is the judging God. Because God is King and God, He is also Judge, vindicating and delivering the faithful and punishing the wicked (35:25–26; 48:4–10 [HB, vv. 5–11], 50:6; 89:17).

Mankind, the Privileged Subjects

As stated above, all of God's creation is subject to His rule. Even though mankind in general, as the crowning climax of God's creation, receives attention in certain psalms (e.g., Psalm 8), two distinct groupings of people receive special attention throughout the Psalter: the obedient or cooperative vassals and the rebellious ones.

Obedient subjects. In general those who are in a proper relationship with God are those who trust in Him (34:8; 37:5; 62:8). Many terms are used to describe these subjects: afflicted (*'ānî*—poor, humble, needy, 18:27 [HB, v. 8]; 22:24 [HB, v. 25]; 34:6 [HB, v. 7]; 72:4,12), righteous (*ṣaddîqîm*—34:15,19,21 [HB, vv. 16,20,22]; 146:8), godly or faithful (*ḥᵃsîdîm*—4:3 [HB, v. 4]; 16:10; 32:6; 145:9 [HB, v. 10]), and holy (*qᵊdôšîm*—16:3 [HB, v. 4]; 34:9 [HB, v. 10]). These subjects are in no way perfect. However, when they sin, they must turn to God for mercy and restoration (37:24; 40:11–13 [HB, vv. 12–14]). These obedient vassals are normally part of Israel, but Gentile inclusion is a feature that broadens the scope of this category (47:9 [HB, v. 10]; 96:7; 97:6; 98:2).

Rebellious subjects. These rebels are pictured as "enemies" in the Psalter. They are always the enemies of God, but they are also the enemies of the chosen nation (Psalms 44, 60, 79) as well as certain individuals (often the psalmist himself, e.g., Psalm 37). As enemies of one of God's children, they represented the enemies of all God's children. This results from the covenant relationship that existed between God and His children. Some of the appellations given them are these: persecutors (7:1 [HB, v. 2]; 31:15 [HB, v. 16]; 55:3 [HB, v. 4]), false witnesses (27:12; 35:11), insolent (31:18 [HB, v. 19]), proud (36:11 [HB, v. 12]), and bloodthirsty (54:23 [HB, v. 24]; 59:2 [HB, v. 3]). The psalmist depicted them as seeking his life (35:4), mocking him (31:11 [HB, v. 12]; 35:16), plotting against him (37:12), and repaying evil for good (35:12; 38:20 [HB, v. 21]).

God's Sovereign Rule

God's rule describes the intersection between the great God of the universe and His subjects. Throughout the Bible the Lord clearly presents Himself as the Creator and Sustainer of the universe. He rules over everyone and everything. This may be called God's universal rule or kingdom. In addition, the way the Mosaic covenant delineates the relationship between God and His chosen nation as a *suzerain-vassal relationship* also helps us understand God's rule. More specific and more concrete than God's universal rule, the Lord manifests Himself as the one and only true God, whose rule impacts history. This takes a concrete form in His relationship with the nation Israel as well as in His dealings with Gentile nations. God gave the Mosaic covenant as a vehicle to govern His relationship with Israel for a number of reasons. A fundamentally important reason for the Mosaic covenant was to enable God's chosen people to understand how to live in a way that would vividly, accurately, and clearly manifest His surpassing character before the entire world (Exod 19:4–6; Deut 26:16–19). His ultimate goal, throughout the entire Bible and manifested in the Psalter as well, is that His rule would extend over all creation and would be gladly accepted by all people (by means of a faith relationship with Him).

The earthly focal point of His rule. God had planned that the earthly administrative center of His rule would be in Zion, that is, Jerusalem. Jerusalem is celebrated as the city of God, the religious and civic center of the theocracy. God dwells in Zion (Ps 76:1–3). From there He controls all other nations (2:1–6; 46:4–7; 48:4–8 [HB, vv. 5–9]; 76:12 [HB, v. 13]), and in Zion He will be exalted over all the earth (46:8–11 [HB, vv. 9–12]; 48:11–14 [HB, vv. 12–15]; 87:5 [HB, v. 6]). The pilgrim songs (Psalms 102–134) celebrate Jerusalem as the center of the theocracy and focus on the festivals established by the Lord.

The chosen Administrator of His rule. God ordained that His anointed Servant, the ideal Davidic ruler/king should conduct the earthly administration of His theocracy. The royal psalms (Psalms 2, 20, 21, 45, 72, 89, 101, 110, 144) present the ideal Davidic king in the foreground. The king was both the representative of the people as well as the administrative representative of God. The statements made about the king in these psalms apply to him, but they also look forward to the future and final King, God's anointed Son.

The impact of His rule on His subjects. God's dealings with His servants are always related to the covenant He established with them. The blessings they enjoy, the hope they possess, the faith they exercise, the salvation they experience, and the praise they utter are all related to the covenant God established with them.

God's rule over His servants also presents certain *demands* on Yahweh's subjects. On the one hand, all of mankind, whether rebellious or obedient is required to live in accord with God's law. On the basis of an individual's conformity to that law or lack of it, blessing and vindication or punishment and condemnation can be expected (Psalms 1; 18:24–26 [HB, v. 27]). On the other hand, although the general rule was blessing for obedience and cursing for disobedience, many times the wicked seemed to prosper and the righteous suffered. The wisdom and Torah psalms (1, 37, 49, 73, 91, 112, 119, 127–128, 133, 139) were written to guide God's obedient servants in the face of this apparent inequity. These psalms remind the righteous that it is necessary to live in the light of God's law, and the psalms exhort them to trust in their God who will accomplish His purposes (regardless of what their present situations might suggest).

The psalms also state that His subjects should *respond* to His compassionate and just rules praising Him and trusting Him. Elements of praise are located in every psalm but are most prominent in the hymns (19, 100, 104), historical psalms (78, 105), and thanksgiving psalms (32, 65, 66, 118). Certain psalms include declarative praise where there is a distinct call to praise. More often, descriptive praise is found where God is praised for who He is and what He does. Besides praising God for His past actions, His present deliverances, His answers to prayer, and His sovereign rule, Yahweh received praise for what He will yet do. His ultimate control over creation (Psalm 121) and the nations (Psalms 125, 126) from Zion (46:3–11 [HB, vv. 4–12]; 84:1 [HB, v. 2]) is anticipated and praised (in the psalms of Zion and pilgrim psalms). His promise of kingship is acclaimed in the royal psalms. The present and future exercise of His rule is praised in the "enthronement psalms."[31]

The second kind of response God expects is implicit trust. Praise and faith are the head and tail of the same coin (cf. 71:5–6). One will not be present without the other. In the Psalter, faith (trust, confidence, and security) is especially present in the context of some difficulty or crisis. Besides being a key element in laments (see below), trust and confidence form a major focus in psalms of confidence (a subcategory of psalms of lament—e.g., 3, 4, 11 16, 23, 27, 62, 121). People experience security, peace, and joy (4:9; 16:8; 23:6) because of the character of God, His past deeds of faithfulness, and the privilege of enjoying a relationship with Him.

The Psalter also presents a human response to God's rule that is not demanded by Him but that arises out of genuine life experience, namely, lament. When life did not seem to measure up to what God promised and the psalmist's faith was tested, he turned to his God to seek a resolution to his difficulty. If personal sin was the cause of his problem, the psalmist would repent in order to receive forgiveness (penitential psalms—e.g., 6, 32, 38, 51, 102). If there was no known occasion for the tribulation, deliverance from this distress was sought (e.g., 17, 35, 59, 69). At times imprecations were uttered against the psalmist's enemies with the desire that God's righteousness be vindicated (58:6–11). However, these laments were not the epitome of futility; they were uttered because the speaker had confidence in God's ability and intention to deliver him.

---

[31] Scholars debate whether the phrase "the Lord reigns" expresses confidence ("the Lord will reign") or is a stative idea ("the Lord reigns").

God's rule over His creation also envisions a certain *destiny* for his subjects. For His obedient servant, the realization of God's promises had clear implications for the future life. God has great things in store for the nation (see discussion of the royal, Zion, and enthronement psalms). The individual had a belief in life after death, but details of that existence were lacking. Sheol was a place that almost denoted nonexistence (39:13), for it was a place of silence and darkness (31:8; 35:6; 69:3,15; 94:17) where no more communion with God was possible (6:5; 30:9 [HB, v. 10]; 88:4–5 [HB, vv. 5–6]; 10–12 [HB, vv. 11–13]). The prayers for deliverance from Sheol (16:10; 49:15 [HB, v. 16]) are best regarded as appeals for deliverance from a premature death and not a plea for resurrection. While the concept of resurrection is not found in the Psalter, the seed or germ form of the concepts of eternal life and resurrection are to be recognized (based on the NT usage of the psalms).

The Psalter gives a glimpse of God at work in the life of His children, as seen in the past and present, and hopefully to be seen in the future. His subjects, both the obedient ones and the rebellious ones, are encountered. The rule of God, which operates in relation to the covenant He established with His children, is praised in light of its past and present operation. And the ultimate and comprehensive establishment of His rule is the longing and prayer of all God's children.

CONCLUSION

The Psalter stands distinct from the rest of the OT. Because of its size and diversity, the book of Psalms covers a wide scope of theology and life experiences. The book teaches much about Yahweh and His covenantal demands on His chosen people as well as the world at large. Also God's subjects respond to His rule in a variety of ways, from gratitude and submission to arrogance and rebellion. The "direction" of the Psalter is also unique. Most of the psalms delineate the praise, thanksgiving, lament, and beliefs of the writers as opposed to a customary presence of divine revelation. One of the most powerful truths in this important book involves its description of Yahweh as the incomparable God of the universe, who reigns with perfect justice and compassion over creation that desperately needs His mercy and praise.

STUDY QUESTIONS

1. What must be understood about the numbering and versification of the psalms?
2. What were some of the stages involved in the process of compiling the psalms?
3. How can the authorship of each psalm be determined?
4. What are three major kinds of psalms, and what is the focus of each one?
5. What is the key role of the royal psalms, and how do they relate to OT theology?
6. What is the key function of the enthronement psalms, and how have critics misunderstood them?
7. What are some of the ways evangelical scholars have interpreted the messianic psalms?
8. What are the imprecatory psalms, and what problem does the language of these psalms create?
9. What must one keep in mind as the biblical and theological backdrop for imprecatory psalms?
10. What are the three central elements of the theology of the psalter?

FOR FURTHER STUDY

Allen, Leslie C. *Psalms 101–150*. Rev. ed. WBC. Nashville: Thomas Nelson, 2002.

Allen, R. B. *Lord of Song: The Messiah Revealed in the Psalms*. Portland, OR: Multnomah, 1985.

———. *Praise: A Matter of Life and Breath*. Nashville: Thomas Nelson, 1980.

Brown, W. P. *Seeing the Psalms: A Theology of Metaphor*. Louisville: Westminster John Knox, 2002.

Broyles, C. C. *Psalms*. NIBCOT. Peabody, MA: Hendrickson, 1999.

Bullock, C. H. *Encountering the Psalms: A Literary and Theological Introduction*. Grand Rapids: Baker, 2001.

———. *An Introduction to the Old Testament Poetic Books*. Rev. ed. Chicago: Moody, 1988.

Chisholm, R. B., Jr. "A Theology of the Psalms." In *A Biblical Theology of the Old Testament*. Edited by Roy B. Zuck, 256–304. Chicago: Moody, 1991.

Craigie, P. C., and M. E. Tate. *Psalms 1–50*. WBC. 2nd ed. Dallas: Thomas Nelson, 2004.

Day, J. N. *Crying for Justice: What the Psalms Teach Us about Mercy and Vengeance in an Age of Terrorism*. Grand Rapids: Kregel, 2005.

Delitzsch, F. *Psalms*. Commentary on the Old Testament. Reprint, Grand Rapids: Eerdmans, 1976.

Estes, D. J. *Handbook on the Wisdom Books and Psalms*. Grand Rapids: Baker, 2005.

Firth, D., and P. S. Johnson, eds. *Interpreting the Psalms: Issues and Approaches*. Downers Grove: IL: InterVarsity, 2005.

Futato, M. D. *Interpreting the Psalms*. HOTE. Grand Rapids: Kregel, 2007.

Goldingay, J. *Psalms*. BCOTWP. 3 vols. Grand Rapids: Baker, 2006–2008.

Grogan, Geoffrey. *Psalms*. Two Horizons. Grand Rapids: Eerdmans, 2008.

Harrison, R. K. *Introduction to the Old Testament*. Grand Rapids: Eerdmans, 1969.

Hilber, J. W. "Psalms." In *Zondervan Illustrated Bible Backgrounds Commentary*. Vol. 5. Edited by J. H. Walton, 5:316–463. Grand Rapids: Zondervan, 2009.

Hill, A. E., and J. H. Walton. *A Survey of the Old Testament*. 3rd ed. Grand Rapids: Zondervan, 2009.

House, P. R. *Old Testament Theology*. Downers Grove, IL: InterVarsity, 1998.

Kaiser, W. C., Jr. *The Journey Isn't Over: The Pilgrim Psalms for Life's Challenges and Joys*. Grand Rapids: Baker, 1993.

———. *The Promise-Plan of God: Biblical Theology of the Old and New Testaments*. Grand Rapids: Zondervan, 2008.

Keel, O. *The Symbolism of the Biblical World: Ancient Near Eastern Iconography and the Book of Psalms*. New York: Seabury, 1978.

Kidner, D. *Psalms 1–72*. TOTC. Downers Grove, IL: InterVarsity, 1973.

———. *Psalms 73–150*. TOTC. Downers Grove, IL: InterVarsity, 1975.

Kraus, H. J. *Theology of the Psalms*. Translated by Keith Crim. Minneapolis: Fortress, 1992.

Laney, J. C. "A Freshs Look at the Imprecatory Psalms." *BSac* 138 (January–March 1981): 35–45.

LaSor, W. S., D. A. Hubbard, and F. W. Bush. *Old Testament Survey: The Message, Form, and Background of the Old Testament*. 2nd ed. Grand Rapids: Eerdmans, 1996.

Longman, T., III. *How to Read the Psalms*. Downers Grove, IL: InterVarsity, 1988.

———, and R. Dillard. *An Introduction to the Old Testament*. 2nd ed. Grand Rapids: Zondervan, 2006.

Merrill, E. H. *Everlasting Dominion: A Theology of the Old Testament*. Nashville: B&H, 2006.

Miller, P. D. *They Cried Out to the Lord: The Form and Theology of Biblical Prayer*. Minneapolis: Fortress, 1994.

Sabourin, L. *The Psalms: Their Origin and Meaning*. Expanded ed. New York: Alba House, 1974.

Tate, M. E. *Psalms 51–100*. WBC. Dallas: Word, 1990.

VanGemeren, W. A. "Psalms." In *EBC*. Rev. ed. Edited by Tremper Longman III and David E. Garland, 5:21–1011. Grand Rapids: Zondervan, 2008.

Waltke, B. K. *An Old Testament Theology*. Grand Rapids: Zondervan, 2007.

Westermann, C. *Praise and Lament in the Psalms*. Translated by K. Crim and R. N. Soulen. Atlanta: John Knox, 1981.

Wilcock, M. *The Message of Psalms 1–72: Songs for the People of God*. BST. Downers Grove, IL: InterVarsity, 2001.

———. *The Message of Psalms 73–150: Songs for the People of God*. BST. Downers Grove, IL: InterVarsity, 2001.

Wilson, G. H. *Psalms*. NIVAC. Grand Rapids: Zondervan, 2002.

CHAPTER 41

THE BOOK OF PROVERBS

MARK F. ROOKER

L IKE OTHER WRITINGS of the ANE, the book of Proverbs begins with a title, *mišlê šĕlōmōh*,[1] "the proverbs of Solomon." The English title "Proverbs" is derived from the Latin Vulgate title *Liber Proverbiorum*.

THE COMPOSITION OF THE BOOK

Because of the association of Solomon's name with the book of Proverbs a large percentage of the contents of the book has been traditionally attributed to him.[2] With the rise of critical scholarship late in the eighteenth century and early in the nineteenth century, however, this consensus began to change.

Liberal critics such as Otto Eissfeldt, Sellin, Fohrer, Toy, and S. R. Driver saw the book of Proverbs as a literary anthology of discourses and sayings, which came from various periods of Israel's history. They questioned whether Solomon was involved in writing the book; they assigned large portions of the book (esp. chaps. 1–9) to the exilic and postexilic periods. One criterion for the late dating included the presupposition that lengthy discourses were late developments in Israelite wisdom writing.[3] Hermann Gunkel argued that there was a process of development from the two-line wisdom sayings to the developed discourse found in chaps. 1–9. The notion was that the short pithy sayings in Proverbs reflected an earlier writing development and the tendency was to later expand shorter sections into the lengthy discourses. Another supposition for the general late character of the book pertained to the use of personification of wisdom motifs in Proverbs 1–9. Critical scholars were in general agreement that this personification of wisdom betrayed a later Greek influence. Thus they suggested that chaps. 1–9 could have been the latest section added to the anthology of proverbs that were being collected and combined. Critics also said that other clearly identifiable sections, such as the word

---

[1] The same phrase begins the sections 10:1–22:16 (10:1) and 25:1–29:27 (25:1).

[2] The Talmud says that Hezekiah's men were responsible for the contents of the book (*Baba Bathra* 15a). This may mean no more than the fact that they collected portions of the book or were in some way responsible for editing them.

[3] Many critics conceded that Solomon may have had a part in the writing of the shorter proverbs in 10:1–22:16.

of Agur (30:1–14), the words of Lemuel (30:1–9), and the virtuous wife (31:10–31), were added to the book in the postexilic period. Thus it was argued that Proverbs did not reach its present form until sometime between the sixth and third centuries BC.

Because of the relatively recent uncovering of comparative wisdom material from the ANE the critical consensus that prevailed just a few short generations ago has now collapsed. The position that the shorter sayings in Proverbs preceded the writing of the longer discourses has been undermined from what has been found in comparative wisdom writings from Egypt and Mesopotamia. In these ANE writings the longer discourse was a prevalent wisdom genre long before Solomon.[4] Thus the length of a proverb can no longer be used as a criterion for dating. In addition the personification of wisdom is also evident in early Egyptian writings, while other early personifications are evident in Canaanite, Hittite, Hurrian, and Babylonian literature, thereby undermining the notion that this practice had been borrowed from the Greeks late in Israel's history. To the contrary, Israel's wisdom tradition presented in Proverbs very much resembles the *Maxims of Ptahhotpe* and the *Teaching for Merikare*, early instructional literature that has survived from ancient Egypt. Based on careful comparison of Proverbs with the Egyptian wisdom literature, British Egyptologist Kenneth Kitchen concluded that the collection of Proverbs 1–24 should be assigned to the beginning of the first millennium BC, the precise time of Solomon's reign.[5] Scholars have now abandoned any notion of a Hellenistic background to the book of Proverbs in favor of an ANE milieu from the time of Israel's monarchy and even before.[6]

In contrast to earlier critics who argued that the book of Proverbs went through an evolutionary development of form, William McKane argued that the Proverbs went through historical changes based on ideational development. He argued that three distinct stages can be discerned from (a) profane or secular proverbs used for educational purposes, to (b) the use of proverbs in the larger community, to (c) the religious use of proverbs based on Yahwistic reinterpretations.[7] The weakness of this explanation is the simple fact that there is no evidence that Israel experienced such a religious evolution. In other words the existence of the nation as well as its relationship with God was based on the covenant indicating that the nation was religious from its conception.

According to 1 Kgs 4:29–34 Solomon's knowledge and wisdom surpassed all the other wise men and sages of the ANE. He is credited with uttering 3,000 proverbs and 1,005 songs, many of which are included in the books of Proverbs and Psalms (e.g., Psalms 72, 127). Thus the association of Solomon in the various titles of Proverbs (1:1; 10:1; 25:1) is plausible, and the final arrangement of the book suggests that the book is to be associated with King Solomon. Based on his studies in Canaanite thought and literature of the second millennium BC, William Albright concluded that the book of Proverbs contains a nucleus of material that should be attributed to Solomon who stood at the fountainhead of Israel's wisdom traditions. The poetic forms common to Proverbs have much in common with the Ugaritic literature of the second millennium BC and are to be contrasted with the wisdom *Sayings of Ahiqar* of the

---

[4] R. N. Whybray, "Proverbs, Book of," in *IDBS*, ed. K. Crim (Nashville: Abingdon, 1976), 702, and J. Crenshaw, "Proverbs, Book of," in *ABD*, ed. D. N. Freedman (New York: Doubleday, 1992), 5:514.

[5] K. A. Kitchen, "Proverbs and Wisdom Books of the Ancient Near East," *TynBul* 28 (1977): 69–114.

[6] See B. K. Waltke and D. Diewert, "Wisdom Literature," in *The Face of Old Testament Studies: A Survey of Contemporary Approaches*, ed. D. W. Baker and B. T. Arnold (Grand Rapids: Baker, 1999), 302.

[7] See D. J. Estes, *Handbook on the Wisdom Books and the Psalms* (Grand Rapids: Baker, 2005), 214; and Waltke and Diewert, "Wisdom Literature," 309.

seventh century BC.[8] There thus should be no reason for denying the sayings attributed to Solomon in the book. In about 700 BC the men of Hezekiah collected other proverbs attributed to Solomon (chaps. 25–29).[9] Thus it is fair to claim that Solomon was the author of Proverbs 1–29.[10] Perhaps later, contributions of other wisdom teachers such as Agur and Lemuel were added to the Solomonic collection (as he was the patron of the Israelite wisdom tradition), thus giving the book its final form. Agur and Lemuel may possibly have been members of the sages, which along with priests, prophets, and kings constituted the four major leadership classes in Israelite society (Jer 18:18; Ezek 7:26–27). Recent scholars, including especially literary critics, appreciate the early preexilic nature of the contents of the book of Proverbs.[11]

Thus Proverbs is part of Israelite wisdom literature, which shares an affinity with other ancient literature from Egypt and Mesopotamia. These early texts had similar genres of literature and often overlap in content. This connection is best illustrated by the similarity of many of the Proverbs with the Egyptian account of *The Wisdom of Amenemope,* dated from 1070 to 945 BC, roughly contemporaneous with Solomon.

Amenemope	*Proverbs*
Give your ear and hear what is said, Give your heart to understand it. Putting them in your heart is worthwhile (1).	Listen closely, pay attention to the words of the wise, and apply your mind to my knowledge. For it is pleasing if you keep them within you and if they are constantly on your lips (22:17–18).
Better is bread when the heart is happy, than riches with sorrow (6).	Better a little with fear of the Lord than great treasure with turmoil (15:16).
Do not carry off the landmark at the boundaries of the arable land (6).	Don't move an ancient property line, and don't encroach on the fields of the fatherless (23:10).
the [riches] have made themselves wings like geese and are flown away to the heavens (8).	It disappears, for it makes wings for itself and flies like an eagle to the sky (23:5b).

---

[8] W. F. Albright, "Canaanite-Phoenician Sources of Hebrew Wisdom," in *Wisdom in Israel and the Ancient Near East,* ed. M. Noth and D. W. Thomas, VTSup (Leiden: Brill, 1955), 1–15. See also S. Blank, "Proverbs, Book of," in *IDB,* ed. G. A. Buttrick (Nashville: Abingdon, 1976), 3:939.

[9] Hezekiah also had an interest in other parts of the OT including the Psalms and the prophets (2 Chr 29:25–30; Isaiah 37).

[10] B. Waltke, "Proverbs, Theology of," in *NIDOTTE,* ed. W. VanGemeren (Grand Rapids: Zondervan, 1997), 4:1080–82. Support for Solomonic authorship of most of the book is supported by the language and vocabulary used in most of the book. See A. Steinmann, "Proverbs 1–9 as a Solomonic Composition," *JETS* 43 (2000): 659–74. Also some of the preexilic prophets seem to have been aware of Israelite wisdom teaching (see Isa 1:2–3; 11:2; 28:3–4; Amos 6:12).

[11] B. Childs, *Introduction to the Old Testament as Scripture* (Philadelphia: Fortress, 1979), 548. Indeed L. Boadt has noted that the book of Proverbs contains a number of sayings as old as the wisdom literature from the Sumerian civilization in 3000 BC and there is no reason these could not have been collected under Solomon's directive (*Reading the Old Testament: An Introduction* [New York: Paulist, 1984], 479).

| One thing are the words said by men, | Many plans are in a man's heart, |
| another thing is what the god does (18). | but the LORD's decree will prevail (19:21). |

Do not eat bread before a noble, nor lay	When you sit down to dine with a ruler,
on thy mouth at first. If thou art satisfied	consider carefully what is before you,
with false chewings, they are a pastime	and stick a knife in your throat
for thy spittle. Look at the cup which is	if you have a big appetite;
before thee, and let it serve thy needs (23).	don't desire his choice food,
	for that food is deceptive (23:1–3).

The numerous connections between these two accounts suggest either that one source influenced the other or that they both may have borrowed their common sayings from an earlier source. The majority of scholars believe Proverbs was dependent on *Amenemope*. While recognizing some truth in the Egyptian account, the biblical author would have transformed the account by placing it in the book of Proverbs with its Yahwistic faith. This would not be too much different from Moses making use of an oral tradition in writing Genesis. Under the influence of the superintending of the Holy Spirit the biblical author would recognize the truth in the account and include the inspired account in Scripture. As part of wisdom literature the writing of Proverbs was not given face to face (as with Moses) or through vision or audition (as with a prophet). Instead the authors often made observations based on creation and human behavior and, inspired by faith, they recorded their observations (Heb 1:3).[12]

THE LITERARY FORM OF THE BOOK

The Hebrew word for proverb is from the root *mŝl*, which may designate a wide range of literary forms that are illustrated in the book. The rhetorical devices that accompany these proverbs include allegory, taunt, lament, simile, repetition, alliteration, and assonance. As already noted, the form of the proverbs in chaps. 1–9 is somewhat distinctive from the rest of the book for it contains lengthy discourses around particular subjects. The rest of the book includes proverbs that are pithy sayings characterized by great brevity. These sayings are remarkably compact, which is even more striking in the Hebrew text. Normally about a dozen English words are needed to translate only about five to eight words in the Hebrew text.[13]

The most frequently occurring form in the book is the two-line proverb (distich). These proverbs are normally constructed as parallel lines and exhibit different types of parallelism in communicating instructions. The six constructions include synonymous, antithetical, synthetic, comparative, emblematic, and formal parallelism. Synonymous parallelism occurs when the second line repeats virtually the sense of the first line. The second line may present some form of intensification, or move from the general to the specific:

Pride goes before destruction,

And a haughty spirit before stumbling (16:18 NASB).

In antithetical parallelism the second line states virtually the opposite meaning of the first line:

The integrity of the upright will guide them,

But the crookedness of the treacherous will destroy them (11:3 NASB).

---

[12] Waltke, "Proverbs, Theology of," 1079.

[13] R. Van Leeuwen, "Proverbs," in *A Complete Literary Guide to the Bible*, ed. L. Ryken and T. Longman III (Grand Rapids: Zondervan, 1993), 263.

In synthetic parallelism the second line extends the sense of the first line in expanded or modified form:

He who conceals hatred has lying lips,

And he who spreads slander is a fool (10:18 NASB).

In comparative parallelism a practical truth is illustrated from nature or practical experience:

Good news from a distant land

is like cold water to a parched throat (25:25).

Emblematic parallelism occurs when one line gives an illustration of the other line:

An endless dripping on a rainy day

and a nagging wife are alike (27:15).

Formal parallelism occurs when the second line completes the thought of the first line:

The hearing ear and the seeing eye—

the LORD made them both (20:12).

The different sections of the book are characterized by distinctive forms:

1:8–9:18	Discourse proverbs
10:1–15:33	Mostly two-line proverbs in antithetical parallelism
16:1–22:16	Two-lines either in synonymous or synthetic parallelism
22:17–24:22	Various forms occur, though four-line proverbs are most dominant
24:23–34	Two-line, four-line, and discourse proverbs
25:1–29:27	Mostly two-line, three-line, and four-line proverbs with comparative and synthetic parallelism (chaps. 25–26) and antithetic parallelism (chaps. 28–29)
30:1–33	Two-line, four-line, and numerical proverbs
31:2–9	Two-line and four-line proverbs
31:10–31	Alphabetic acrostic poem[14]

The form of Proverbs 1–9 with extended sapiential discourses differs from what appears to be the random arrangement of proverbs in chaps. 10–24 and chaps. 25–29. This apparent disorderly arrangement may serve a didactic purpose. The order may demonstrate that while truth and reality are not arbitrary, neither do they easily comply to human systematization. The somewhat haphazard arrangement in these sections may well mirror the way people encounter the issues addressed. No doubt there is a reason for their arrangement just as there is a reason that all proverbs of similar content have not been gathered in the same context.[15]

THE PURPOSE OF THE BOOK

The purpose of the book of Proverbs, stated in the introduction (1:2–7), is delineated through the use of five infinitive verbs: to know, to discern, to receive, to give, and to understand. Thus the book is like an instructional manual to lead people in righteous living before God. Issues on the execution of sacrifices and worship, so important in other aspects of Israel's religious life, receive little attention (7:14; 15:8,29; 17:1; 21:3,27; 28:9), though the fundamental theological presuppositions of biblical wisdom do not differ in any respect with those

---

[14] Adapted from C. H. Bullock, *An Introduction to the Old Testament Poetic Books* (Chicago: Moody, 1988), 161.

[15] See D. Garrett, *Proverbs, Ecclesiastes, Song of Songs*, NAC (Nashville: B&H, 1993), 48.

of the law and the prophets. The presupposition behind the instruction and the wisdom to be attained is the fear or reverence of God, a commitment to put the Lord as the center of one's life (1:7). Thus commitment to the Lord is the appropriate starting point for the acquiring of wisdom. Fearing the Lord determines one's progress in wisdom and is characterized by obedience.[16]

THE OUTLINE AND CONTENTS OF THE BOOK

The Book's Outline

Based on the analogy of the division of the Mosaic law into five books, some have argued for a fivefold division of the book of Proverbs. Michael Fox divides Proverbs into the following five divisions: (1) The proverbs of Solomon, son of David (chaps. 1–9); (2) the proverbs of Solomon (10:1–22:16); (3) the words of the sages (22:17–24:22); (4) additional words of the sages (24:23–34); and (5) proverbs of Solomon that the men of Hezekiah copied (chaps. 25–29).[17]

The division that begins each new section based on the occurrence of a new title seems to be the neatest division of the book. This leads to the following sevenfold division:

I. Solomon's Reflections on the Way of Wisdom (chaps. 1–9)

II. Proverbs of Solomon (10:1–22:16)

III. Anonymous Wise Sayings (22:17–24:22)

IV. More Anonymous Sayings (24:23–34)

V. More Proverbs of Solomon (chaps. 25–29)

VI. Sayings of Agur (chap. 30)

VII. Sayings of Lemuel (chap. 31)

Each of the three major sections (points I, II, and V) has the same title, "The proverbs of Solomon." This fact along with the title of the book clearly indicate why the book is viewed as primarily a work of Solomon.

The Book's Contents

I. Reflections on the Way of Wisdom (chaps. 1–9)

As already noted, the stated purpose of the book of Proverbs is given in the introduction (1:2–7). These verses introduce not only the first major section (1:8–9:18) but also the book as a whole. The statement that the fear of the Lord is the beginning of wisdom (1:7) is repeated

---

[16] Ibid., 54.

[17] *The Jewish Study Bible*, ed. Adele Berlin and Marc Zvi Brettler (Oxford: Oxford University Press, 2004), 1449. Also Alex Luc divides Proverbs into five parts: 1:1–9:18; 10:1–24:32; 25:1–29:27; 30:1–33; and 31:1–31 ("The Titles and Structure of Proverbs," *ZAW* 112 [2000]: 252–55).

toward the end of the first section in 9:10, thereby setting up an inclusio for the first section. These chapters present life as a "structured world of boundaries."[18]

In this first major section several speeches open with the teacher addressing the pupil as his son (1:8; 2:1; 3:1), thus giving a parental tone to the entire section. No consensus has emerged regarding the number of individual units in 1:8–9:18. Suggestions have ranged from 10 to 17 individual divisions in this first major section. Longman divides the section into 17 divisions:

Superscription (1:1)
1. The Purpose of the Book (1:1–7)
2. Avoid Evil Associations (1:8–19)
3. Don't Resist Woman Wisdom (1:20–33)
4. The Benefits of the Way of Wisdom (chap. 2)
5. Trust in the Lord (3:1–12)
6. Praising Wisdom (3:13–20)
7. The Integrity of Wisdom (3:21–35)
8. Embrace Wisdom! (4:1–9)
9. Stay on the Right Path (4:10–19)
10. Guard Your Heart (4:20–27)
11. Avoid Promiscuous Women; Love Your Wife (chap. 5)
12. Wisdom Admonitions: Loans, Laziness, Lying, and Other Topics (6:1–19)
13. The Danger of Adultery (6:20–35)
14. Avoid Promiscuous Women; Part II (chap. 7)
15. Wisdom's Autobiography (chap. 8)
16. The Ultimate Encounter: Wisdom or Folly (9:1–6,13–18)
17. Miscellaneous Wisdom Sayings (9:7–12)[19]

Ten of the discourses are introduced with the phrase "my son" (1:8; 2:1; 3:1,21; 4:1,10, 20; 5:1; 6:20; 7:1). Throughout the section only two options are given: the way of wisdom or the way of folly. Wisdom is presented not as an abstract ideal, but as a practical companion for those who would choose her path. While praising the virtues of pursuing wisdom, the teacher continually warns the pupil about the ways of folly that lead to destruction. These foolish ways include violence (1:10–19; 4:14–19), hastiness (6:1–5), laziness (6:6–11), dishonesty (6:12–15), and particularly sexual immorality (2:16–19; 5:3–20; 6:23–35; 7:4–27; 9:13–18).

While wisdom is thrice personified as a respectable and attractive woman (1:20–33; 8:1–36; 9:1–6), folly is depicted as an immoral woman who tries to seduce the young and naive to their death (7:6–27; 9:13–18).[20] Wisdom is also personified as a tree of life (3:18), a way (4:10–19), and a craftsman (8:22–31).[21] In harmony with his fivefold division of the book as a whole Fox observes five interludes in chaps. 1–9: (1) Lady wisdom's condemnation of fools (1:20–23), (2) praise of wisdom (3:13–20), (3) four epigrams on various follies and evils (6:1–19),

---

[18] R. Van Leeuwen, "Proverbs," in *Theological Interpretation of the Old Testament*, ed. K. Vanhoozer (Grand Rapids: Baker Academic, 2008), 175.

[19] T. Longman III, *How to Read Proverbs* (Downers Grove, IL: InterVarsity, 2002), 23.

[20] The personification of foolishness as a prostitute is analogous to the prophetic description of the nation as whoring after foreign gods (Jer 3:1–13; 5:7–9; Hos 1:2; 2:13; 4:12–15).

[21] W. J. Dumbrell, *The Faith of Israel: A Theological Survey of the Old Testament*, 2nd ed. (Grand Rapids: Baker, 2002), 268.

(4) Lady wisdom's self-praise (chap. 8), and (5) Lady wisdom's and Lady folly's invitations (chap. 9).[22]

II. Proverbs of Solomon (10:1–22:16)

In marked contrast to 1:1–9:18, Prov 10:1–22:16 consists of 375 single proverbial sayings, arranged in no apparent order. The arrangement is not completely haphazard, however, as Proverbs 1–9 provides the theological worldview for understanding the various proverbs in Proverbs 10–29.[23] As noted above, this second major section of the book consists of observations about life presented in distich form. The section continues the contrast between the righteous and the wicked as well as the inevitable consequences of each lifestyle. The contrast between the righteous and the wicked parallels the contrast between wisdom and folly in chaps. 1–9.

This section is sometimes divided into two subsections of 10:1–15:33 and 16:1–22:16. Proverbs 10–15 may be further divided into six subsections, each introduced by an admonition to pay attention to wisdom (10:1,23; 12:1; 13:1; 14:2; 15:2). Chapters 10–15 exhibit antithetic parallelism and emphasize the way things usually occur, while 16:1–22:16 is primarily made up of synonymous parallelisms and presents far more cases of exceptions to the general rules.[24] Whereas chaps. 10–15 focus on practical issues, 16:1–22:16 has more of a religious overtone (see e.g., 16:1–9). Proverbs 15:33–16:9, where the Yahweh sayings are concentrated, might be considered as the center or heart of this section.[25] As mentioned, the seemingly haphazard arrangement of these proverbs may reflect the seemingly indiscriminate order in which people deal with these life issues.

III. Anonymous Wise Sayings (22:17–24:22)

This section has been divided into 29 or 30 proverbial poems that consist of two or three verses each. Many of these short poems include an exhortation or a warning followed by a description of the consequences. The pattern in 22:17–23:12 is almost identical to the Egyptian *Teaching of Amenemope*, which was probably composed around 1000 BC very close to the time of Solomon. About one-third of the section bears resemblance to the *Amenemope* text. The similarities between the texts may be explained by the international character of wisdom that is recognized in the Bible itself (1 Kgs 4:29–34). The royal court of Egypt influenced Solomon's court through marital and other ties. If this account was borrowed from this Egyptian source, it has been adapted to the parameters of the Israelite Yahwistic faith. This brief section includes concise proverbs (e.g., Prov 22:26) as well as longer discourses (22:30–34).

IV. More Anonymous Sayings (24:23–34)

This section records additional wisdom sayings from Israelite sages. The wise men who generally have been associated with the royal court must have been a prominent class in ancient Israel (Job 15:18; Prov 1:6; 22:17; 24:23; Jer 18:18). These men, like Hezekiah's men (Prov 25:1), may have been royal scribes commissioned with the task of collecting axioms and proverbial sayings about the practical aspects of life.

---

[22] See M. V. Fox, "Ideas of Wisdom in Proverbs 1–9," *JBL* 116 (1997): 616.
[23] Van Leeuwen, "Proverbs," 175.
[24] See Van Leeuwen, "Proverbs," 261.
[25] Thus R. Rendtorff, *The Old Testament: An Introduction*, trans. J. Bowden (Philadelphia: Fortress, 1985), 256.

V. More Proverbs of Solomon (chaps. 25–29)

This more lengthy section of Solomon's proverbs is frequently subdivided into two sections, chaps. 25–27 and chaps. 28–29. The first subsection has parallel lines, which are mostly synthetically parallel, and includes numerous similes and also rules based on practical experience. Chapter 25 has some topical collections that come closest to the longer discourse forms in 1:8–9:18 than in any other portion of the book. The second section (chaps. 28–29) exhibits mostly antithetical parallelism as well as sayings that could be considered more religious in tone. Also contrasts between the rich and the poor are more frequent in these two chapters than in other sections of the book.

Two juxtaposed verses in this section have fomented debate from antiquity. Proverbs 26:4–5 reads, "Don't answer a fool according to his foolishness, or you'll be like him yourself. Answer a fool according to his foolishness, or he'll become wise in his own eyes."

Sayings such as these caused Jewish leaders to challenge the canonicity of the book of Proverbs. Some argued that Proverbs should not be in the canon because these sayings created alleged contradictions (*b. Šabb.* 30b). However, the two verses simply indicate that at times it is appropriate to respond to a fool but at other times it is not. These verses thus qualify each other.

The collection of these proverbs during the reign of Hezekiah (715–687 BC) may reflect his focus on effecting a religious reform during his reign (2 Kings 18–20; Isaiah 36–39). Of particular importance in this section is a focus on the responsibility of the king to fear the Lord and live in obedience before Him.

VI. Sayings of Agur (chap. 30)

In 30:15–33 are graded numerical sayings with three observations that allude to the four types of persons mentioned in 30:11–14.[26] This x, x + 1 pattern is attested elsewhere in the OT (Amos 1–2; Mic 5:5) and in Ugaritic literature.

VII. Sayings of Lemuel (chap. 31)

This chapter has small sections (31:2–9) that address social issues reminiscent of theme addressed elsewhere in the book. This is followed by an acrostically arranged poem that describes the virtuous woman (31:10–31). The two sections are connected by a reference to women (vv. 3,10), a concern for noble character (*ḥayil*; vv. 3,10) as well as a concern for the poor (vv. 9,20).[27] The virtuous woman displays the wise character and qualities emphasized throughout the book. Possibly this positive portrayal of the virtuous woman is intended to counter the many references elsewhere in the book to the wayward woman who tries to seduce young men. The virtuous woman exemplifies the fear of the Lord (vv. 27–31), the prerequisite for wisdom. Thus the end of the book with its focus on wisdom returns to the theme with which the book began in 1:7.

These last two sections of Proverbs (chaps. 30–31) return to themes mentioned earlier in the book, especially drunkenness, sexual immorality, and control of the tongue. Nothing is known of Agur and Lemuel apart from their being mentioned here at the end of Proverbs. Many scholars connect them with the northern Arabian tribe of Massa, one of Ishmael's sons (Gen 25:14; 1 Chr 1:30).

---

[26] Crenshaw, "Proverbs, Book of," 517.
[27] See Waltke, "Proverbs, Theology of," 1084.

THE TEXT OF THE BOOK

The Hebrew text of the book of Proverbs has survived in remarkably good condition. The LXX of Proverbs on the other hand has not survived as well; it has suffered numerous corruptions. The LXX has some of the sections in an order different from that in the MT. Following Prov 22:16 the sequence in LXX is as follows: 22:17–24:22; 30:1–14; 24:23–34; 30:15–33; 31:1–9; 25:1–29:27; 31:10–31. In addition the LXX includes extra material near the end of various collections (at 9:12,18; 15:27,29,33; 16:1–9; 24:22; 27:24–27). The LXX has about 130 more lines than the MT, which tend to harmonize with other Jewish wisdom books.

THE THEOLOGY OF THE BOOK

The focus on the fear of the Lord in the introduction to the book is the proper theological and hermeneutical grid through which the contents should be read (1:7; 2:5; 8:13; 9:10; 10:27; 14:27; 15:33; 19:23; 22:4). All the proverbs should be read against this backdrop. Read in this way, Proverbs is in harmony with the other major portions of the OT. The basic identity between Deut 19:14 and Prov 23:10 well illustrates that wisdom literature and the law overlap. Links such as this have led a number of scholars to see a tight connection between the admonition of the book of Proverbs with the Mosaic law. Apart from the prohibition of idolatry and the law of the Sabbath all the principles found in the Ten Commandments can be illustrated from Proverbs. The proverbs spell out the impact of the covenant relationship on each individual Israelite's life before God. This focus is maintained even though the actual history of the nation Israel is virtually ignored in the book. God promised in the law that violation of the covenant would result in the dispensing of covenant curses for the nation (Leviticus 26; Deuteronomy 28). Also Proverbs assumes a retribution theology in which individuals are held accountable for their actions by being judged appropriately (10:2–3,6–7,25,27,30; 11:4–6). Covenant loyalty and faithfulness is the standard for the godly life in Proverbs. At the same time the proverbs present general guidelines, not absolute promises or inflexible laws for every specific situation.[28] Because of their brevity the proverbial sayings do not provide qualifications or exceptions to the rules. The life context determines a proverb's meaning and truth.[29]

In the book of Proverbs God is viewed as the Creator (3:19; 8:22–31). Wisdom literature is concerned with the relationship of creation to God and the implications of this relationship on human conduct in the everyday affairs of life.[30] God is also seen in the book of Proverbs as ruler of the earth (10:30–32; 16:1–9) provider (2:6–8), judge (3:11–12; 5:21; 6:16–19; 10:3, 29; 11:1,28; 12:2), and revealer of truth (2:6; 6:23; 8:22–36).[31]

THE NEW TESTAMENT AND THE BOOK

Wisdom literature addresses all human beings in the cosmos and should be considered as a feature of common grace. It addresses the spirituality of everyday life (1 Cor 6:20).

Many of the axioms from the book of Proverbs are repeated in the NT and reflect the same application they have in their OT context. The admonition to accept discipline in Heb 12:5–6 quotes Prov 3:11–12; the motivation for humility in Jas 4:6 and 1 Pet 5:5 is based on Prov 3:34; the necessity of judgment in1 Pet 4:18 is taken from Prov 11:31; an admonition address-

---

[28] P. House, *Old Testament Theology* (Downers Grove, IL: InverVarsity, 1998), 448.

[29] Waltke and Diewert, "Wisdom Literature," 310.

[30] Leeuwen, "Proverbs," 173.

[31] House, *Old Testament Theology*, 440.

ing vengeance in Rom 12:20 is taken from Prov 25:21–22; and instruction about returning to folly in 2 Pet 2:22 is borrowed from Prov 26:11.[32]

In addition Jesus Christ is associated with the wisdom of God (Luke 11:31; 1 Cor 1:30; Col 2:3). The book of Proverbs supplies the theological and contextual background for this NT truth.

STUDY QUESTIONS

1. Why was Proverbs 1–9 thought to reflect late composition?
2. What is Solomon's connection to Proverbs?
3. What is the name of the Egyptian text that has many parallels to Proverbs?
4. What is the most frequent form in the book of Proverbs?
5. What is parallelism?
6. Which section of Proverbs has the highest concentration of antithetic parallelism?
7. What is the purpose of the book of Proverbs?
8. What is the fundamental theological presupposition of biblical wisdom in the book of Proverbs?
9. How many sections are in the preferred outline of the book of Proverbs?
10. What is the range of divisions suggested for Proverbs 1–9?
11. What chapter outside Proverbs 1–9 best resembles the collection of Proverbs 1–9?
12. Which of the Ten Commandments are not found in the book of Proverbs?
13. Comment on the theology of Proverbs.

FOR FURTHER STUDY

Atkinson, D. *The Message of Proverbs.* Downers Grove, IL: InterVarsity, 1996.

Bullock, C. H. *An Introduction to the Old Testament Poetic Books.* Chicago: Moody, 1988.

Clifford, R. J. *Proverbs.* OTL. Philadelphia: Westminster John Knox, 1999.

Crenshaw, J. "Proverbs, Book of." In *ABD.* Edited by D. N. Freedman, 5:513–20. New York: Doubleday, 1992.

Dumbrell, W. J. *The Faith of Israel: A Theological Survey of the Old Testament.* 2nd ed. Grand Rapids: Baker, 2002.

Estes, D. J. *Handbook on the Wisdom Books and the Psalms.* Grand Rapids: Baker, 2005.

Fox, M. "Ideas of Wisdom in Proverbs 1–9." *JBL* 116 (1997) 613–33.

———. *Proverbs 1–9.* AB. New York: Doubleday, 2000.

Garrett, D. *Proverbs, Ecclesiastes, Song of Songs.* NAC. Nashville: Broadman, 1993.

House, P. *Old Testament Theology.* Downers Grove, IL: InterVarsity, 1998.

Kidner, D. *The Proverbs: An Introduction and Commentary.* TOTC. Downers Grove, IL: InterVarsity, 1964.

Kitchen, K. "Proverbs and Wisdom Books of the Ancient Near East." *TynBul* 28 (1977): 69–114.

Longman, T., III. *How to Read Proverbs.* Downers Grove, IL: InterVarsity, 2002.

———. *Proverbs.* Grand Rapids: Baker Academic, 2006.

McKane, W. *Proverbs: A New Approach.* OTL. Philadelphia: Westminster, 1970.

Mouser, W. E. *Walking in Wisdom: Studying the Proverbs of Solomon.* Downers Grove, IL: InterVarsity, 1983.

Murphy, R. E. *Proverbs.* WBC. Nashville: Word, 1999.

Parsons, G. W. "Guidelines for Understanding and Proclaiming the Book of Proverbs." *BSac* 150 (April–June 1993): 151–70.

Scott, R. B. Y. *Proverbs, Ecclesiastes.* AB. Garden City, NY: Doubleday, 1965.

Van Leeuwen, R. C. "Proverbs." In *Theological Interpretation of the Old Testament.* Edited by K. Vanhoozer, 171–78. Grand Rapids: Baker Academic, 2008.

von Rad, G. *Wisdom in Israel.* Translated by J. Martin. Abingdon, 1972.

---

[32] See D. A. Hubbard, "Proverbs, Book of," in *ISBE*, ed. G. Bromiley (Grand Rapids: Eerdmans, 1986), 3:1020.

Waltke, B. K. "Proverbs, Theology of." In *NIDOTTE*. Edited by W. VanGemeren, 4:1079–94. Grand Rapids: Zondervan, 1997.

———. *The Book of Proverbs: Chapters 1–15*. NICOT. Grand Rapids: Eerdmans, 2004.

———. *The Book of Proverbs: Chapters 15–31*. NICOT. Grand Rapids: Eerdmans, 2005.

——— and D. Diewert. "Wisdom Literature." In *The Face of Old Testament Studies: A Survey of Contemporary Approaches*. Edited by D. W. Baker and B. T. Arnold, 295–328. Grand Rapids: Baker, 1999.

Westermann, C. *Roots of Wisdom*. Louisville: Westminster John Knox, 19.

Whybray, R. N. *Proverbs*. NCB. Grand Rapids: Eerdmans, 1994.

Chapter 42

The Book of Ecclesiastes

Mark F. Rooker

THE TITLE OF THE BOOK

The book of Ecclesiastes is attributed to Qoheleth, a name or term which in fact occurs only in Ecclesiastes (1:1–2,12; 7:27; 12:8–10). The noun Qoheleth is based on the verb *qhl*, which means "convoke and assemble," or simply "to assemble." This verb occurs frequently in 1 Kings 8 in reference to Solomon's gathering the people to dedicate the newly constructed temple (1 Kgs 8:1–2,14,22,25), and its use in Ecclesiastes would evoke the memory of Solomon. For the title of the book the LXX used the Greek word *'Ekklēsiastēs*, which is derived from *ekklēsía*, "assembly, congregation, church."

THE COMPOSITION OF THE BOOK

Many critics of past generations thought the contents of the book of Ecclesiastes revealed a late pessimistic attitude and was influenced by Greek philosophy. They also maintained that the text had an extended period of composition. In 1898 Karl Siegfried argued that the final form of the book resulted from the combination of nine different sources beginning with a Greek philosopher and later expanded by a Sadducean Epicurean. In 1911 P. Volz proposed that in an earlier stage of the composition of the book, Ecclesiastes was thoroughly skeptical in nature and many theological interpolations (3:15b; 5:6b,18–19; 7:18b,29; 8:5–6,12–13; 9:7b; 11:9b; 12:1a,13–14) were added by a later editor to reinforce the biblical notion of divine retribution as well as proper reverence for God. Otto Eissfeldt located later insertions in 2:26; 3:17; 7:26b; 8:5,12b,13a; 12:7b,13–14. Wilhelm Schmidt later suggested that the composition of the book went through three successive stages: (1) the first person discourse in 1:12–6:9 was the original introduction to the collection of the sayings of Qoheleth; (2) the first epilogist added 12:9–11; and (3) the second epilogist added his final remarks in 12:12–14.[1]

In recent scholarship on Ecclesiastes the assumed Greek influence on the book has been undermined. It is now more and more recognized that the alleged Greek ideas actually had

---

[1] W. H. Schmidt, *Old Testament Introduction*, trans. M. O'Connell (New York: Crossroad, 1990), 329.

their source in ANE thought over a millennium before the Greek language and culture came into prominence. Critics such as George A. Barton argued that the resemblance between Ecclesiastes and Stoicism was artificial and in fact the philosophies represented in the works were in complete opposition. Since Barton's study the attempts to link Ecclesiastes with Greek philosophy have met stern rebuttals from the academic community. The issues pondered by Qoheleth are thoroughly Semitic and totally independent of Greek influence. Moreover, there are no clear Greek constructions or idioms in the book and not one Greek word. In addition, Brevard Childs has noted the drift of modern scholarship is to view the book as a unified composition of one author.[2] This trend began early in the twentieth century when S. R. Driver recognized that the epilogue should be attributed to the author of the whole book.

THE AUTHORSHIP OF THE BOOK

The authorship of Ecclesiastes has generally been attributed to King Solomon because of the information given in the first verse of the book, "son of David, king in Jerusalem." At face value this title most naturally refers to Solomon. Notable exceptions to this consensus, however, included Martin Luther's refusal to credit the contents of the book to Solomon. Many reasoned that the internal evidence of the book seems to indicate a time different from that of the united monarchy. The author described his time as a time of misery (1:2–11), and the splendor of the Solomonic age seems to have been past (1:12–2:26). Moreover, others have proposed that the language of the book betrays a stratum of the Hebrew language characteristic of the postexilic period and beyond.

However, the contents of the book do not conclusively rule out Solomonic authorship of the book.[3] Many scholars note that the Hebrew of Ecclesiastes differs from the Hebrew of any other OT book. The book fits into no known period of the history of the Hebrew language. Yet Daniel Fredericks has convincingly shown that the language reflects an earlier stage in the history of the Hebrew language.[4] Clearly the language can certainly not be classified with later postexilic and postbiblical Hebrew works. The unique language style may reflect the common vernacular in Solomon's day.

On the positive side, the traditional profile of Solomon as a wise man and a writer of wisdom literature is clearly reflected in passages such as 1 Kgs 4:29–34 (HB 5:26–32); 10:23–29; and 2 Chr 1:7–13. These passages are harmonious with the character of the author of Ecclesiastes who is described as unrivaled in wisdom (1:16), one who explored carnal pleasure (2:1–3), who made impressive accomplishments (2:4–6), and who was unequalled in wealth (2:7–10).

THE PURPOSE AND MESSAGE OF THE BOOK

The book of Ecclesiastes brings into focus the mystifying existence of mankind. Man cannot know what God is doing and why. The message of the book is not unlike the book of Job, where Job is challenged to trust and surrender to God, not knowing where God may lead him.

The mystery of life is to a large part conveyed by the frequent occurrence of a key term in Ecclesiastes, the word *hebel*, most familiarly translated as "vanity." This term occurs 38 times

---

[2] B.Childs, *Introduction to the Old Testament as Scripture* (Philadelphia: Fortress, 1979), 582.

[3] The phrase in 1:12 may be translated "I became king," while the phrase "all who were over Jerusalem before me" (1:16) may refer to wisdom teachers who preceded Solomon rather than a long line of monarchs (W. Beecher and C. Armerding, "Ecclesiastes, Book of," in *ISBE*, ed. G. Bromiley [Grand Rapids: Eerdmans, 1979], 2:13).

[4] D. Fredericks, *Qoheleth's Language: Re-evaluating Its Nature and Date* (Lewiston, NY: Edwin Mellen, 1988).

in the book, more than half of its total occurrences in the Old Testament.[5] The concrete meaning is "vapor" or "breath" (see Job 7:16; Pss 39:5,11 [HB, vv. 6, 12]; 62:9 [HB, v. 10]). *Hebel* conveys notions of transience and insubstantiality. Some occurrences of the term in Ecclesiastes may carry the concrete connotation (Eccl 3:19; 6:12; 7:15; 9:9; 11:8), but the term has several other possible nuances in the book as well. The meaning of "transitory" or "unable to be controlled" seem to be the most dominant nuance (1:15; 2:11,17,26; 4:4,16; 6:9). The idea that everything in human experience is ultimately beyond human control is one of the primary motifs conveyed.

Duane Garrett sums up three main motifs that occur throughout the book: (1) one must recognize that he is mortal, (2) one should enjoy life as a gift from God, and (3) one must revere God.[6] The author encourages his readers to exercise faith in God as the only possible basis for meaning and significance in a life lived under the sun. Life without God has no meaning.

THE STYLE OF THE BOOK

The style of Ecclesiastes is as distinctive as its language. The book has numerous aphorisms (1:12–15,16–18; 5:1–7 [HB, 4:16–5:6]; 5:8–9 [HB, 5:7–8]), metaphors (7:26), comparisons (11:5), rhetorical questions (2:19,25), autobiographical narrative (2:1–11), woe sayings and benedictions (10:16–17), admonitions (7:9–10,13), hyperboles (6:3,6), and rhymes (10:11). It also exhibits numerous "better" sayings (4:3,6,9,13; 5:5 [HB, v. 4]; 6:3,9; 7:1–3,5,8; 9:4,16,18) as well as the characteristic expression "under the sun," which occurs 29 times in Ecclesiastes but nowhere else in the Bible.[7]

THE STRUCTURE OF THE BOOK

The structure of Ecclesiastes is one of the mysteries of modern-day biblical scholarship. No analysis of its design has gained widespread scholarly support. It seems that determining where a unit begins and ends is open to debate throughout the contents of the book. If one examines the commentaries and other aids, it is clear that no common consensus has emerged. R. Rendtorff opines that the structure of Ecclesiastes comes close to that of Proverbs, wherein one largely finds a collection of individual sayings with no apparent progression of thought.[8] Yet some profound observations have been made about the way the book is organized. First, some similarities exist between the beginning of the book and the way the book ends. The beginning (1:2) and the conclusion (12:8) of Qoheleth's teaching form an expressed inclusio. Only these two verses use the superlative construct *hăbēl hăbālîm* (lit., "vanity of vanities"). Moreover, as Schmidt has noted, 1:3–11 and 11:9–12:7 both address the issue of succession of generations and growing old and thus seem to be corresponding sections at the beginning and the end of the book.[9] Thomas Krüger has proposed an even simpler outline of the contents of the book:[10]

---

[5] Some have argued that the term occurs 37 times in the book, the numerical equivalent of the Hebrew consonants *hbl*. The total number of verses in Ecclesiastes is 222 verses, 37 x 6.

[6] Garrett, *Proverbs, Ecclesiastes, Song of Songs*, NAC (Nashville: B&H, 1993), 278.

[7] See ibid., 271; and J. Crenshaw, "Proverbs, Book of," in *ABD*, ed. D. N. Freedman (New York: Doubleday, 1992), 2:275.

[8] R. Rendtorff, *The Old Testament: An Introduction*, trans. J. Bowden (Philadelphia: Fortress, 1985), 265.

[9] Schmidt, *Old Testament Introduction*, 329.

[10] T. Krüger, *Qoheleth*, trans. O. C. Dean Jr. (Minneapolis: Fortress, 2004), 5.

1:1   Title
1:2   Motto
1:3–12:7   Corpus of the book
12:8   Motto
12:9–11   Epilogue

THE OUTLINE OF THE BOOK

While there are numerous options in the literature for the outline of Ecclesiastes, a simple four-part outline may be suggested here.

Superscription (1:1)

I. Theme (1:2–11)

II. Quest for the Meaning of Life (1:12–6:9)
   A. Everything Is Temporary (1:12–4:16)
   B. Coping with Uncertainty (5:1–6:9)

III. Wisdom Admonitions (6:10–12:8)
   A. Earthly Goods Do Not Satisfy (6:10–8:17)
   B. God Will Deal with Injustices (9:1–12:8)

IV. Epilogues (12:9–14)

This outline makes particular use of Addison G. Wright's observations about the structure of the book. According to Wright a single refrain, "all is absurd and striving after wind," is the key structural divider in the first half of the book (1:12–6:9), yielding the following subunits (2:1–11; 2:12–17; 2:18–26; 3:1–4:6; 4:7–16; 5:1–6:9). Wright then suggests that major structural indicators in 6:10–11:6 are revealed by the repeated phrases "not discover" and "who can discover," which mark out subunits 7:1–14; 7:15–24; 7:25–29; and 8:1–17, while the phrase "does not know" concludes 9:1–12; 9:13–10:15; 10:16–11:2; and 11:3–6.[11]

Conceptually speaking, the subsections of the book conclude by expressing one of four ideas: (1) the weakness or transience of man's accomplishments, (2) man's uncertain fate, (3) the impossibility of obtaining true knowledge in this world, and (4) the need to enjoy life.[12] The book can thus be roughly divided into two equal halves with the first half focusing on the apparent pointlessness of life (1:12–6:9) and the second half giving various maxims regarding prudent behavior (6:10–12:8).

THE CONTENTS OF THE BOOK

I. Theme (1:2–11)

The first major section of Ecclesiastes serves as an introduction to the book, announcing its main theme. Qoheleth began his quest by searching for human significance. The section illustrates the endless and apparently meaningless cycles of life in both nature and history. Man's toil is said to be of no profit (1:3).

---

[11] A. G. Wright, "The Riddle of the Sphinx: The Structure of the Book of Qoheleth," *CBQ* 30 (1968): 313–34. In addition, according to the Masoretic notes Eccl 6:9 marks the halfway point in the book of Ecclesiastes.

[12] See R. Gordis, *Koheleth—The Man and His World*, 2nd ed. (New York: Bloch, 1955), 252.

II. Quest for the Meaning of Life (1:12–6:9)

This section is written in the form of an autobiographical narrative, clearly alluding to the unique and privileged experience of King Solomon. Ecclesiastes 1:12–26 reports Solomon's experiences and reflections in his investigation of what is best for people to do during the limited days of their life (2:3).[13] This section opens with the rather depressing note that an increase of wisdom results in an increase in sorrow because it does not provide comprehensive answers to life (1:12–18). From this point the narrative addresses various experiences of life that are believed to lead to happiness but in fact do not bring ultimate satisfaction and meaning. These include such experiences as pleasure (2:1–11), wisdom and toil (2:12–27), wealth (2:18–26), toil and time (3:1–4:6), friendship (4:7–16), and religion and wealth (5:1–6:9).

The meaning of life cannot be determined by experience or observation. This conclusion was derived empirically by Israel's greatest king, Solomon, who was in the best position to master life and know by wisdom the meaning to life through many quests (1 Kgs 4:23–28; chaps. 5–9; 10:1–11:3). And yet this all led to futility. Even human wisdom, which is superior to folly, is limited and in the end is as helpless as folly when faced with death (Eccl 2:15). Only God knows the meaning of the interaction of life's events (3:1–9). The awareness of time and eternity on the part of humanity does not bring fulfillment, for the desire to know the eternal cannot be quenched (3:11). Wisdom is no guarantee to peace and happiness. Yet God blesses people with gifts that allow them to forget their hardships (5:18–20; see also 2:24–26).

III. Wisdom Admonitions (6:10–12:8)

After an opening statement expressing man's inability to know what the future will bring (6:10–12), this third major section records a number of adages for appropriate behavior. The next subsection contains a collection of sayings that address such issues as wisdom, politics, and religion (7:1–14). This is followed by a section dealing with the function of wisdom relative to justice and wickedness (7:15–24). Next is a short section that addresses immorality and man's propensity to sin (7:25–29). Ecclesiastes 8:1–17 discloses how wisdom displays itself along with the reminder that the righteous are quickly forgotten. Ecclesiastes 9:1–12 records reflections about the enjoyment of life and the issue of time and chance, and 9:13–10:15 includes illustrations and sayings about the limitation of wisdom. Ecclesiastes 10:16–11:6 addresses various issues, including how to behave before the king as well as the uncertainty of human industry. This section concludes with instruction addressing the issue of youth and old age (11:7–12:8). In this subunit the author returned to the futility of his toil that he mentioned at the beginning of the book (1:2–11).

Scholars disagree on the meaning of the contents of 12:1–8. Some of the major proposals have included a description of the aging process, a description of a funeral procession, or eschatological symbolism. The last verse of the section before the refrain observes that the human spirit will return to the Lord who created it, a description of life after death (12:7). This notion from a book of wisdom is also found in Psalms 49, 72, 73, as well as Job 19:23–27; Isa 26:19; and Dan 12:1–3. Since all life comes from God (Eccl 12:1), it also must return to God.

---

[13] The Aramaic Targum translation of Eccl 1:12 relates these experiences to Solomon and also identifies Solomon with Qoheleth. See T. Longman III, *The Book of Ecclesiastes*, NICOT (Grand Rapids: Eerdmans, 1998), 3.

IV. Epilogues (12:9–14)

The book closes with two epilogues, the first describing Qoheleth's activities as a wise man (12:9–10), followed by instructions to the reader to be satisfied with the sayings of the wise (vv. 11–12).

THE TEXT OF THE BOOK

The Hebrew text of Ecclesiastes is in relatively good condition. The LXX translation is of limited value because the translator(s) in his (their) penchant for literalism in the translation has produced a work that has violated the norms of the Greek language. Among the DSS, portions of Ecclesiastes 5–7 have been uncovered, dated to the second century BC. These manuscripts create no real variants to the traditional reading of the MT.

THE THEOLOGY OF THE BOOK

For all the skepticism expressed in the book of Ecclesiastes, Qoheleth never denied the reality of God (2:24; 3:11,13–14), the monotheistic faith, or a meaningful role for humankind in the world. This notion may be reinforced by the fact that while the key term *hebel* occurs 37 or 38 times in the book, *ʾĕlōhîm*, the name of God, occurs 40 times. Even though man and the creation are temporal, God is sovereign (2:26; 3:14; 7:13–14; 8:16–9:1; 11:5). God's sovereignty is indicated by two fundamental concepts: "all that is done under the sun is the work of God" and "humans do not understand the work of God" (see 3:11; 8:17; 11:5; 12:14).[14] He is the Creator (11:5; 12:1,7; see also 3:11,14,20; 7:14; 8:17), judge (3:17–18; 11:9), controller of events (3:11; 5:18–6:2; 7:13–14), benefactor (11 times the subject of the verb "give" [2:24–26; 3:13; 5:18–20]), one to be feared (3:14; 5:1–7; 7:18; cf. 12:1) and obeyed (5:4; 7:26), and is ultimately beyond human comprehension (3:11; 8:16–9:1).[15] Qoheleth's affirmation of joy is an expression of his belief in creation. It is an affirmation of life as God made it.[16]

At the same time wisdom cannot penetrate the mystery of life or the purpose of life's diverse experiences. Qoheleth held to the retribution principle found in Proverbs, namely, that obedience will be rewarded and disobedience judged (3:16–18; 8:10–14), but like Job he was conscious of exceptions to this rule. Man can live and even flourish apart from having all the answers he craves.[17] The final verdict is that man should enjoy life (2:24–25; 3:12–13,22; 5:18; 8:15; 9:7; 11:8–9; 12:1) and fear God (12:13–14).

The teaching of Ecclesiastes presumes that the reader is aware of the creation and fall of Genesis 1–3. Genesis and Ecclesiastes both assume an order in the world, and God fixed this order. Human beings have a sense of eternity (3:1–14) as they are created in the image of God (Gen 1:26–31). Yet man has limited knowledge since he is made from dust (Eccl 3:20; 12:7; Gen 2:7; 3:19). Furthermore, the fact that God has decreed that man must toil for food (Gen 3:17–19) is everywhere assumed in Ecclesiastes with its focus on human toil (Eccl 1:3,13; 2:3; 3:9–10). The desire of Qoheleth to have comprehensive knowledge parallels Eve's desire, which led her into sin. Everything about this world is marred by the tyranny of the curse that the Lord placed on all creation (Gen 3:17–19). God made the human race upright, but they have

---

[14] See R. E. Murphy, "Qoheleth and Theology?" *BTB* 21 (1991): 32.

[15] D. Fredericks, "Ecclesiastes, Theology of," in *NIDOTTE*, ed. W. VanGemeren (Grand Rapids: Zondervan, 1997), 4:553.

[16] C. Bartholomew, "Ecclesiastes," in *Theological Interpretation of the Old Testament*, ed. K. Vanhoozer (Grand Rapids: Baker, 2008), 183.

[17] Beecher and Armerding, "Ecclesiastes, Book of," 2:12.

all sinned (Eccl 7:20, 26–29; Genesis 3). For Qoheleth, life is in many ways a curse, and this curse is especially acute not only in labor and toil but also in mental anguish (Eccl 1:13; 2:23; 3:11; 4:7–8; 8:17; Gen 3:17,19). The difficulty shared by Qoheleth in the entire book can be credited to sin and its consequences.[18] Death is the inevitable conclusion to man's existence and God often seems absent and hidden from sinful human beings (Gen 2:15–17; 3:1–5).[19]

THE NEW TESTAMENT AND THE BOOK

Paul took up the issue of the curse on creation in Rom 8:19–21 where he emphasized that the consequences of man's actions will affect the created order. In fact, the word translated "futility" in Rom 8:20 is the Greek translation of the Hebrew term *hebel* ("vanity") in the LXX of Ecclesiastes. Moreover, the repeated emphasis in Ecclesiastes—that one should enjoy life and the simple gifts of life even though he does not have the answers to all of life's issues—finds an echo in NT teaching. Man is to dedicate all his actions to the glory of God, even in the daily routine of eating and drinking (1 Cor 10:31; Col 3:17), since God has given humankind everything for its enjoyment (1 Tim 6:17).

Ecclesiastes exposes the futility of seeking to find meaning in life apart from God. Qoheleth had attempted to find satisfaction in knowledge, riches, pleasure, work, fame and sex, but was disappointed. He came to realize that only the person who is God-centered and sees the simple things in life as a gift from God can truly understand the meaning of life. Man is not created just to enjoy life; he is to enjoy life and fear God.

STUDY QUESTIONS

1. Was Ecclesiastes influenced by Greek philosophical thought?
2. In what way does the author of Ecclesiastes appear to be Solomon?
3. The message of Ecclesiastes is like the message of what OT book?
4. Where else does the characteristic phrase "under the sun" appear in the OT?
5. Where are the main divisions in the book of Ecclesiastes?
6. What is Qoheleth's view of the reality of God?
7. What attributes of God are addressed in Ecclesiastes?
8. How is Ecclesiastes similar to Proverbs?
9. How is Ecclesiastes similar to Job?
10. What part of Genesis does Qoheleth seem to be aware of?
11. What key term in Ecclesiastes does Paul use in Romans?
12. What key term in Ecclesiastes is used in Genesis 4?

FOR FURTHER STUDY

Bartholomew, C. "Ecclesiastes." In *Theological Interpretation of the Old Testament*. Edited by K. Vanhoozer, 179–85. Grand Rapids: Baker Academic, 2008.

Eaton, M. *Ecclesiastes*. Downers Grove, IL: InterVarsity, 1983.

Fredericks, D. *Qoheleth's Language: Re-evaluating Its Nature and Date*. Lewiston, NY: Edwin Mellen, 1988.

———. "Ecclesiastes, Theology of." In *NIDOTTE*. Edited by W. VanGemeren, 4:552–55. Grand Rapids: Zondervan, 1997.

---

[18] The predominance of the word *hebel* also alludes to Genesis, as Abel's name in Genesis 4 is composed of the same consonants as *hebel*. Abel became the paradigm of those whose life was cut short; he lived a transitory life. See D. M. Clemens, "The Law of Sin and Death: Ecclesiastes and Genesis 1–3," *Themelios* 19 (1994): 5–8; and P. House, *Old Testament Theology* (Downers Grove, IL: InterVarsity, 1998), 467.

[19] See A. Caneday, "Qoheleth: Enigmatic Pessimist or Godly Sage?" *GTJ* 7 (1986): 21–56; and Garrett, *Proverbs, Ecclesiastes, Song of Songs*, 279.

Garrett, D. *Proverbs, Ecclesiastes, Song of Songs*, NAC. Nashville: B&H, 1993.

Ginsburg, C. D. *The Song of Songs and Coheleth*. New York: KTAV, 1970.

Gordis, R. *Koheleth—The Man and His World*. 2nd ed. New York: Bloch, 1955.

Krüger, T. *Qoheleth*. Translated by O. C. Dean Jr. Minneapolis: Fortress, 2004.

Longman, T. *The Book of Ecclesiastes*. NICOT. Grand Rapids: Eerdmans, 1998.

Ogden, G. *Qoheleth*. Sheffield, UK: JSOT Press, 1987.

Seow, Chung-Leong. *Ecclesiastes*. Garden City, NY: Doubleday, 1997.

———. "Qoheleth's Eschatological Poem." *JBL* 118 (1999): 209–34.

———. "Beyond Mortal Grasp: The Usage of Hebel in Ecclesiastes." *ABR* 48 (2000): 1–16.

Whybray, R. N. *Ecclesiastes*. NCBC. Grand Rapids: Eerdmans, 1989.

Wright, A. G. "The Riddle of the Sphinx: The Structure of the Book of Qoheleth." *CBQ* 30 (1968): 313–34.

Zuck, Roy B. "God and Man in Ecclesiastes." *BSac* 148 (1991): 46–56.

———. *Reflecting with Solomon: Selected Studies on the Book of Ecclesiastes*. Grand Rapids: Baker, 1994.

CHAPTER 43

THE BOOK OF THE SONG OF SONGS

MARK F. ROOKER

THE TITLE OF THE BOOK

The title of the book, Song of Songs, is taken from the opening phrase of the book, *šîr haššîrîm*, variously rendered "Song of Solomon," "The Song," or "Best Song." It is sometimes called Canticles based on the title of the book in the Vulgate, *Canticum Canticorum*, lit., "Song of Songs."

THE COMPOSITION OF THE BOOK

Until recent times the Song of Songs had been attributed to Solomon, the last king of the united monarchy of Israel. This is for good reason since Solomon's name appears seven times in the book (1:1,5; 3:7,9,11; 8:11–12). In harmony with Solomonic authorship is the fact that the book seems to reflect conditions in Israel before the division of the kingdom, such as the place names Jerusalem, Carmel, Sharon, Lebanon, Engedi, Hermon, and Tirzah. There is no indication that Israel had been divided into northern and southern kingdoms.

Other indicators of Solomonic authorship appear as well. The reference to 21 varieties of plant life and 15 species of animals throughout the book harmonizes perfectly with the massive knowledge of Solomon, who was an expert in such matters (1 Kgs 4:33). In addition the comparison of the bridegroom to "a company of horses in Pharaoh's chariots" seems to harmonize with the introduction of horses from Egypt during Solomon's reign (1 Kgs 10:28). Support for the notion that the book was written by a single individual emerges from the unity of style and themes exhibited by the relatively widespread occurrence of repetition of words and phrases throughout the book. Previous arguments for a date later than Solomon, based on what were thought to be late language factors in the book, have fallen out of favor among contemporary scholars.[1]

However, many scholars, including some contemporary evangelicals, do not agree that the opening of the book indicates Solomonic authorship. They argue that Solomon's prolific sexual experience (700 queens and 300 concubines [1 Kgs 11:3]) would disqualify him from

---

[1] See M. H. Pope, *Song of Songs*, AB (New York: Doubleday, 1977), 33–34.

expressing the romantic love and devotion for one woman indicated in the book. Proponents of the Solomonic authorship respond by asserting that the Shulamite woman was the one true love of Solomon's life (and perhaps the first), and that the book may have been written early in Solomon's life.

THE INTERPRETATION OF THE SONG OF SONGS

The correct understanding of the Song is one of the real enigmas in the history of the interpretation of the Bible. As Ernst Sellin and Georg Fohrer have summarized, "The history of interpretation of the Song of Solomon is no feather in the cap of biblical exegesis."[2] Many different approaches have been proposed as the correct model for its interpretation, three of which—the allegorical, cultic, and lyric/dynamic—are discussed here.

The Allegorical Interpretation

Many consider the allegorical interpretation as the oldest method of interpreting the Song. This approach attempts to find a spiritual meaning behind the descriptive passages about the love relationship between a man and a woman. According to Jewish allegorists, the love expressed between the man and the woman is actually a way of conveying God's love for Israel. This link is not far-fetched since the OT frequently uses the human love relationship as a metaphor for Israel's relationship with God (Isa 54:4–8; Jer 2:1–2; Ezekiel 16, 23; Hosea 1–3). Similarly Christian allegorists such as Origen, Jerome, Athanasius, Augustine, Luther, and Calvin argued that the Song of Songs conveyed the love between Christ and His church. This great distinction between the Jewish and Christian allegorical approach to the book as well as the inherent subjectivity of the interpretation is the greatest drawback to the allegorical view.

This subjectivity can be illustrated from the interpretation of Song 1:13: "My love is a sachet of myrrh to me, spending the night between my breasts." Both Rashi and Ibn Ezra said this phrase refers to the tabernacling of God over the ark of the cherubim, while Cyril of Alexandria proposed that the verse referred to the two Testaments. Bernard of Clairvaux believed the verse referred to the crucifixion of Christ, which strengthens the believer in sorrow and joy.[3] The allegorical approach was undermined by these variant interpretations as well as by the fact there is no hint in the Song itself that the male-female relationship should be understood as referring to anything else. In other words, nothing in the book indicates that it was intended to be read as an allegory. Moreover, as Duane Garrett has stated, the strongest argument against the allegorical method is the sexual nature of the Song itself. The explicit language in the book would be an inappropriate way to portray the love between God and His people.[4] While the allegorical interpretation was dominant throughout much of the history of interpretation of the Song, it began to be abandoned by interpreters on a large scale in the middle of the nineteenth century. Many scholars turned their attention from the allegorical method to the cultic and lyrical/dramatic interpretations.

The Cultic Interpretation

The cultic interpretation of the Song understands the love poetry and expressions of love in the book as referring to a *hieros gamos* ("a sacred marriage") in which the sexual union of two gods (such as Ishtar and Tammuz) was enacted cultically by a priestly couple. According to the

---

[2] E. Sellin and G. Fohrer, *Introduction to the Old Testament*, trans. D. Green (Nashville: Abingdon, 1968), 300.

[3] See N. Gottwald, "Song of Songs," in *IDB*, ed. G. A. Buttrick (Nashville: Abingdon, 1962), 4:422.

[4] See esp., Song 7:7–8 (D. Garrett, *Proverbs, Ecclesiastes, Song of Songs* [Nashville: B&H, 1993], 357).

myth this union would ensure the production of crops on the earth for another year. Since the law of Moses condemned such pagan notions, it was believed that the Song became acceptable to the Jewish people at a time when the earlier pagan and mythological connections of the book were forgotten. While many scholars believe this interpretation best explains the sexual content of the Song, it is difficult to imagine that the association of the contents of the book with a blatantly pagan ritual, even if dimly remembered, would not have disqualified the book as a candidate for the OT canon.

The Lyrical/Dramatic Interpretation

The lyrical/dramatic interpretive method has several variations, each one attempting to interpret the Song in a more literal fashion. The dramatic method actually has two variations, one which views the Song as describing the love relationship between two characters, Solomon and the Shulamite woman, and the other which discerns an additional character, the Shulamite shepherd. In the two-character drama the book extols the joys of conjugal love in the person of Solomon with the only pure romance of his life, the Shulamite woman. In the three-character drama, the Shulamite shepherd is the true love of the woman's life, and Solomon takes on the character of a villain or a scoundrel. Beginning in the nineteenth century both dramatic interpretations have had many adherents. Those who argued that three characters are presented in this love story suggest that the contents of the Song require three individuals, including two males. Otherwise Solomon is described as a shepherd (1:7; 6:2–3) who visits the Shulamite in her country home (2:8–13) and in the closing scene appears with her not in the royal palace but in her native village (8:5). This, it is maintained, is not only improbable but would be at odds from what is known of Solomon from the historical narratives in 1 Kings and 2 Chronicles. Thus it seems logical to understand the existence of a Shulamite shepherd. Moreover, it would be unsuitable for a man who had multiple queens and concubines to voice such expressions to one woman. Andrew Hill and John Walton, who promote the three-character position, believe the book discusses these three characters in a series of sequential events:

I. The Shulamite Maiden in Solomon's Harem (1:2–3:5)

II. Solomon Woos the Shulamite Maiden (3:6–7:9)

III. The Shulamite Maiden Rejects King Solomon (7:10–8:4)

IV. The Shulamite Maiden and the Shepherd-Lover Are Reunited (8:5–14)[5]

The difficulty with the three-character view is that it often leads to an unannounced and abrupt division of the dialogue. In this view the sentiments of warm affection are assigned to the shepherd, and the more formal speeches are assigned to Solomon. Thus one must assume that 4:8–15 abruptly inserts the shepherd's speech, while the previous paragraph (4:1–7) is clearly to be assigned to Solomon. This is one illustration of a frequently cited weakness of the dramatic view, namely, the difficulty of assigning individual passages to specific characters and convincingly tracing the plot of the story. But even more than this, the dramatic view is rejected by many because no other examples of such a genre are attested anywhere else in the ANE. Because of these difficulties, many contemporary interpreters, both liberal and conservative, have argued for a purely lyrical approach that asserts that the book is merely a collection

[5] A. Hill and J. Walton, *A Survey of the Old Testament*, 2nd ed. (Grand Rapids: Zondervan, 2000), 375.

of love poems that give evidence to no particular plot and celebrate the love between a man and a woman in a conjugal arrangement designed by God. Among those who understand the book to be a collection of love poems, the number of love poems in the book ranges from 20 to 40 separate poems.

THE PURPOSE OF THE BOOK

The interpretive method one adopts for the Song of Songs has a direct effect on the perceived purpose and message of the book. Yet the book clearly appears to celebrate the joyful and mysterious love between a man and a woman within the created order designed by God. It extols the God-ordained goodness and virtue of sexual love in marriage (7:8–12). The book was thus placed in the canon to teach the purity and sanctity of the marriage estate which God had established. It is thus an extended commentary on the creation of man and woman as male and female in the image of God in Genesis 1–3.[6] More specifically, the book expands on the perfect marital harmony in the garden (2:25). As such the Song was used in wedding ceremonies or betrothals. The Song was recited at the observation of the Passover and is still recited by many Jews every Friday evening as part of the *kabbalat šabbat*, "the welcoming of the Sabbath."

THE STYLE OF THE BOOK

The uniqueness of the Song of Songs has already been indicated in the discussion of its contents and interpretation. The same distinctiveness applies equally to style. Because of the uniqueness of the book's contents, there are 49 terms that occur only in the Song. In expressing the mutual love of the man and woman, the author employed the imagery of nature more than any other writer of the Bible. Doves hide in the clefts of the rock (2:14), lovers rest beside the water brook (5:12), and gazelles leap over the mountains (2:8–9) or feed among the lilies (4:5). No other book is as replete with images of flora, fauna, perfumes, and spices. The author also utilizes metaphors such as these: "Behind your veil, your eyes are doves" (4:1), "Your hair is like a flock of goats streaming down Mount Gilead" (4:1), and "Your nose is like the tower of Lebanon looking toward Damascus" (7:4). Through the use of simile and metaphor, sexual intimacy is expressed in a tasteful and appropriate way. The author also employed the devices of alliteration and poetic parallelism.

THE STRUCTURE OF THE BOOK

The author apparently arranged the work in a chiastic manner that gives the Song an overall unity.[7] Dorsey has divided the Song into seven major units, which are arranged symmetrically:

A.   Opening words of mutual love and desire (1:2–2:7)
  B.   Young man's invitation to the young woman (2:8–17)
    C.   Young woman's nighttime search (3:1–5)
      D.   Center: their wedding day (3:6–5:1)
    C¹.   Young woman's nighttime search (5:2–7:11 [HB, 5:2–7:10])
  B¹.   Young woman's invitation to the young man (7:12–8:4 [HB, 7:11–8:4])
A¹.   Closing words of mutual love and desire (8:5–14)

---

6 B. Childs, *Introduction to the Old Testament as Scripture* (Philadelphia: Fortress, 1979), 574–76; and F. Landy, "The Song of Songs and the Garden of Eden," *JBL* 98 (1979): 513–28.

7 For a comprehensive survey of recent analyses regarding the chiastic nature of the Song see R. Davidson, "The Literary Structure of the Song of Songs *Redivivus*," *JATS* 14 (Fall 2003): 44–65.

Each of the units begins with a change of perspective. Dorsey also notes that each unit begins with the lovers separated and experiencing tension but closes with the lovers reunited with a sense of tranquility.[8] The first and last sections of the book are in correspondence as indicated by the metaphor of the vineyard in 1:6b and 8:11–12, as well as the speech of the brothers in 1:6b and 8:8–9. Also correspondence exists between 2:6 and 8:3 as well as the longer sections of 2:10–15 with 7:10–13. Moreover, a number of terms such as "henna" (1:14; 4:13; 7:11) and "choicest fruits" (4:13,16) (terms found rarely outside the Song of Songs) are dispersed within different sections of the book contributing to the overall unity. Roland Murphy argues that even though there are several unsolved issues concerning the structure and unity of the Song, there is a discernible thrust toward its unity.[9] Craig Glickman's chiastic analysis on the macro and micro level of the book as a whole leaves no doubt as to the unity and coherence of the book (see appendix). A helpful outline that exhibits a unified structure is the following:

I. **Love Is Anticipated** (1:2–2:7)

II. **Found, and Lost—and Found** (2:8–3:5)

III. **Love Is Consummated** (3:6–5:1)

IV. **Lost—and Found** (5:2–8:4)

V. **Love Is Affirmed** (8:5–14)

Each of these sections begins with the anticipation of love and the arrival of one of the lovers (1:2; 2:8; 3:6; 5:2; 8:5–6).[10]

Whether from the chiastic arrangements or the outline, the central section and the highpoint of the book is the lover's consummation in marriage in 3:6–5:1.[11] This central section supports the view that the book deals with only two characters. "It seems appropriate to interpret Solomon as the groom here given the verse's linking of the woman's desire for her beloved in 3:1–5, Solomon's arrival in 3:6–11, and the comment about the king's wedding day and gladness of heart in 3:11."[12]

TEXT

In spite of the fact that the Song of Songs has a unique style and vocabulary, resulting in making the Hebrew difficult in places, the major versions follow the MT rather closely. The same may be said of the fragments of the Song among the Dead Sea Scrolls where variants of the MT are minor and without significance.[13]

---

[8] D. Dorsey, *The Literary Structure of the Old Testament* (Grand Rapids: Baker, 1999), 200. A viable alternative is to divide the Song into five sections based on the occurrence of the concluding refrain, "I adjure you, O daughters of Jerusalem" (2:7; 3:5; 5:8; 8:4 NASB).

[9] R. E. Murphy, "Song of Songs, Book of," in *ABD*, ed. D. N. Freedman (New York: Doubleday, 1992), 6:152.

[10] See G. Carr, "Song of Songs," in *A Literary Guide to the Bible*, ed. L. Ryken and T. Longman III (Grand Rapids: Zondervan, 1993), 291–92.

[11] Similarly Davidson has argued that the climax of the Song is to be found in Song 4:16–5:1, which is the exact center of the Song (60 verses on either side). Davidson, "The Literary Structure of the Song of Songs *Redivivus*," 62–64.

[12] P. House, *Old Testament Theology* (Downers Grove, IL: InterVarsity, 1998), 606 n. 7.

[13] Only in Song 4:8 and 7:10 do the versions appear to have a superior reading. See D. Garrett and P. House, *Song of Songs/Lamentations*, WBC (Nashville: Thomas Nelson Publishers, 2004), 15–16.

THE THEOLOGY OF THE BOOK

The Song of Songs is best understood as a commentary on the establishment of marriage in Genesis 1–2. In some ways it could be argued that it amplifies the first recorded words about the human race: "This one, at last, is bone of my bones and flesh of my flesh" (2:23). As such, monogamy is the assumed ethic behind the entire account (see Prov 5:18; Eccl 9:9; Mal 2:14).

The Song could also be considered a corrective against all forms of sexual perversity. God has created sex, and it is not evil when enjoyed within the confines He has established (Gen 1:26–28; 2:20–25; Matt 19:1–12). The candor with which sexual desire and gratification are discussed within the book does not indicate a low standard of morality. The language is not lewd or crudely sensate. The love the man and the woman have for one another displays integrity, commitment, and faithfulness. The book's inclusion in the canon of Scripture frustrates any attempt to denigrate human sexuality. It also may serve as a corrective to asceticism.[14] Its canonical status could be viewed as a fulfillment of the creation covenant, as well as a reenactment of the love relationship between the first man and woman. Without the Song the Bible could be seen as incomplete as it would include prohibitions about illicit sexual relations but lack the positive instructions that enable the reader to discover the joy of healthy love.[15] The fact that Solomon himself may not have paid particular heed to his own advice in no way undermines this message.

THE NEW TESTAMENT AND THE BOOK

The apostle Paul uses the picture of the love between the man and woman reflected in the Song of Songs to speak of the relationship between Christ and His church (Eph 5:22–23). And interestingly the ultimate union of a believer with the Lord is described as a wedding (Rev 19:6–8).

APPENDIX: GLICKMAN'S CHIASTIC SYMMETRY OF THE SONG OF SOLOMON[16]

Section A: Beginning of Story (1:2–2:7)
> a: Shulamith, Solomon and the daughters of Jerusalem (1:2–4)
>> b: her brothers, their vineyards, and her appearance (1:5–6)
>>> c: Shulamith's character and beauty (1:7–11)
>>>> d: love's expression (1:12–2:5)
>>>>> e: refrains conclude section A and begin Section B (2:6–7)

Section B: Invitation to Enjoy Spring Day (2:6–17)
> a: refrains of longing and patience (2:6–7)
>> b: his invitation to come enjoy spring, leaving *from* her house (2:8–15)
>>> c: refrains of unity and invitation to her breasts (2:16–17); transition

---

[14] Gottwald, "Song of Songs," 425, and F. Knutson, "Canticles," in *ISBE*, ed. G. Bromiley (Grand Rapids: Eerdmans, 1986), 1:608.

[15] Garrett, *Proverbs, Ecclesiastes, Song of Songs*, 367, 378.

[16] See S. C. Glickman, *Solomon's Song of Love* (West Monroe, LA: Howard, 2004), 240.

SECTION C: NIGHT SEPARATION PRECEDING WEDDING (3:1–4)

> a: Shulamith is awakened, alone and longing for Solomon (3:1)
>> b: leaves home to find him (3:2)
>>> c: is found by guards (3:3)
>>>> d: asks for help (3:3b)
>>> c¹: finds Solomon (3:4)
>> b¹: returns home with him (3:4b)
> a¹: is reunited with him through the night (3:4b); transition—*refrain* of patience

SECTION D: WEDDING DAY AND NIGHT (3:6–5:1)

> a: songwriter's own words (3:6–11)
>> b: celebration of the wedding's beginning (3:6–11)
>>> c: wedding night (4:1–5:1); refrain answering invitation to enjoy breasts (4:6)
>> b¹: celebration of wedding's consummation (5:1b)
> a¹: songwriter's own words (5:1b)

SECTION C¹: NIGHT OF SEPARATION FOLLOWING WEDDING NIGHT (5:2–7:9)

> a: Shulamith is awakened, alone and reluctant (5:2–8)
>> b: gives tenfold praise (5:9–16)
>>> c: aware of Solomon's presence in the garden (6:1–3)
>>>> d: receives his praise in the garden (6:4–9)
>>> c¹: recounts her journey to the garden (6:11–12)
>> b¹: receives tenfold praise (7:1–5)
> a¹: they delightfully make love, together drift off to sleep (7:6–9)

SECTION B¹: INVITATION TO ENJOY SPRING DAY (7:10–8:4)

>>> c¹: enjoyment of breasts and refrain of unity (7:7–8,10); transition
>> b¹: her invitation to come enjoy spring, returning *to* her house (7:11–8:2)
> a¹: refrains from longing and patience (8:3–4)

SECTION A¹: COMPLETION OF STORY (8:3–14)

>>>> e¹: refrains conclude section B' and begin section A' (8:3–4)
>>> d¹: love's devotion (8:5–7)
>>> c¹: Shulamith's character and beauty (8:8–9)
>> b¹: her brothers, their vineyards, and her appearance (8:10–12)
> a¹: Shulamith, Solomon, and Shulamith's companions (8:13–14); refrain to enjoy breasts

STUDY QUESTIONS

1. How many times does Solomon's name occur in the Song of Songs?
2. What chapter in Kings describes the extent of Solomon's knowledge?
3. What are the three main interpretive approaches to the Song of Songs?
4. What seems to be the oldest interpretive approach to the Song of Songs?
5. What is *hieros gamos*?
6. Who are the three individuals in the three-character dramatic interpretation?
7. What is the difficulty of the three-character view in the dramatic interpretation?
8. In which Israelite festival is the Song of Songs recited?

9. What type of imagery does the author of the Song of Songs employ more than anyone else in the OT?
10. What is the five-section outline to the Song of Songs?
11. What section functions as the highpoint of the Song of Songs?
12. The Song of Songs is a commentary on what OT passage?

FOR FURTHER STUDY

Akin, D. L. *God on Sex*. Nashville: B&H, 2003.

Caird, G. B. *The Language and Imagery of the Bible*. Philadelphia: Westminster, 1980.

Carr, G. L. *The Song of Solomon*. TOTC. Downers Grove, IL: InterVarsity, 1984.

———. "Song of Songs." In *A Literary Guide to the Bible*. Edited by L. Ryken and T. Longman III. Grand Rapids: Zondervan, 1993.

Davidson, R. M. "Theology of Sexuality in the Song of Songs: Return to Eden." *AUSS* 27 (1989): 1–19.

———. "The Literary Structure of the Song of Songs *Redivivus*." *JATS* 14 (Fall 2003): 44–65.

Dorsey, D. "Literary Structuring in the Song of Songs." *JSOT* 46 (1990): 81–96.

Fox, M. V. *The Song of Songs and the Ancient Egyptian Love Poetry*. Madison: University of Wisconsin Press, 1985.

Garrett, D. *Proverbs, Ecclesiastes, Song of Songs*. Nashville: B&H, 1993.

——— and Paul House. *Song of Songs/Lamentations*. WBC. Nashville: Thomas Nelson, 2004.

Ginsburg, C. D. *The Song of Songs and Coheleth*. Jersey City: KTAV, 1970.

Gledhill, T. *The Song of Songs*. CBC. Cambridge: Cambridge University Press, 1975.

Glickman, S. C. *Solomon's Song of Love*. West Monroe, LA: Howard, 2004.

Hess, R. S. *Song of Songs*. BCOTWP. Grand Rapids: Baker, 2005.

Hubbard, D. A. *Ecclesiastes, Song of Solomon*. TCC. Waco, TX: Word, 1993.

Landy, F. "The Song of Songs." In *The Literary Guide to the Bible*. Edited by R. Alter and F. Kermode. London: Grafton, 1987, 305–19.

Longman, T., III. *The Song of Songs*. NICOT. Grand Rapids: Eerdmans, 2001.

Murphy, R. E. *The Song of Songs*. Heremeneia. Philadelphia: Fortress, 1990.

Ohlsen, W. *Perspectives on Old Testament Literature*. New York: Harcourt, Brace, 1978.

Parsons, G. W. "Guidelines for Understanding and Utilizing the Song of Songs." *BSac* 156 (1999): 399–422.

Pope, M. H. *Song of Songs*. AB. New York: Doubleday, 1977.

Provan, I. *Ecclesiastes and Song of Songs*. NIVAC. Grand Rapids: Zondervan, 2001.

Schwab, G. *The Song of Songs' Cautionary Message concerning Human Love*. New York: Lang, 2002.

Seerveld, C. *The Greatest Song*. Amsterdam: Trinity Penyasheet Press, 1967.

Tanner, J. P. "The History of Interpretation of the Song of Songs." *BSac* 154 (1997): 23–46.

———. "The Message of the Song of Songs." *BSac* 154 (1997): 142–61.

Webb, B. "The Song of Songs: A Love Poem and as Holy Scripture." *RTR* 49 (1990): 91–99.

CHAPTER 44

THE BOOK OF LAMENTATIONS

MARK F. ROOKER

THE TITLE OF THE BOOK

The English title "Lamentations" derives from the Greek *(thrēnoi)* and Latin *(threni)* versions' translation of Hb. *qînôt*, "laments" (*b. Baba Bathra* 14b). In the Jewish tradition the name of the book was taken from the first word of the book, *'êkâ* (sometimes spelled *'êk*), an interjection meaning "how" or "alas." This term occurs also at the beginning of Lamentations 2 and 4 as well as the opening line of other funeral dirges (2 Sam 1:19; Isa 14:12). Because the book records the lamentation of the Israelites over the destruction of Jerusalem and the temple, it is often compared to similar Sumerian laments composed about 1,000 years earlier that record the response to the fall of prominent cities such as Ur and Accad.

THE COMPOSITION OF THE BOOK

Unlike most of the other OT books, Lamentations has evaded radical notions regarding its origin and composition. A few critics have suggested that Lamentations 5, being somewhat distinct from the other four chapters, may have been composed at a later time. But even these exceptions suggest that the chapter was composed no more than a generation after chaps. 1–4 had been completed. Beyond this, as Childs has noted, if any later editing was done on the book, it was probably so minor that what exists in the final form of the book is essentially its original form.[1] Because there is also unanimity regarding the theme of the book—the grief over the defeat of Judah by the Babylonians in 586 BC (2 Kings 25; Jeremiah 52) and the conditions of Jerusalem after the conquest—the book had to have been written soon after the exile began. Moreover, it was completed before 538 when the Persians allowed the Jews to return to their homeland. More to the point, the author of the book was completely unaware of King Jehoiachin's discharge from prison in 562 (2 Kgs 25:27–30). Thus a very small window of opportunity remains for the editing and redacting of the book. This is not to say that the individual poems may not have had a separate independent existence. Also this is not to

---

[1] B. Childs, *Introduction to the Old Testament as Scripture* (Philadelphia: Fortress, 1979), 593–94.

say that a motivating factor for collecting the five poems (chaps.) was not for festive use in the remembrance of the destruction of Jerusalem. But it has been the custom of critical biblical scholars, particularly modern ones, not to speculate about layers of tradition in Lamentations but to study the book in its present form.

THE AUTHORSHIP OF THE BOOK

Both Jewish and Christian tradition attests that the prophet Jeremiah was the author of Lamentations. Support for the Jeremianic authorship of the book comes from a number of different angles. First, the LXX not only places Lamentations after Jeremiah and before Ezekiel, but it also includes an opening introduction to the book in the first verse, attributing the composition of the book to Jeremiah. Moreover, the Aramaic Targum, the Peshitta, the Vulgate, and the Babylonian Talmud, as well as early church fathers such as Origen and Jerome, all attest that Jeremiah was the author. Another line of support comes from the book of Chronicles, which states that Jeremiah had written laments (*qînôt*) with reference to King Josiah (2 Chr 35:25). In addition, stylistic similarities between Jeremiah and Lamentations suggest a common authorship. Some phrases that occur in both books are these:[2] "among her lovers she has none to comfort her" (Lam 1:2; Jer 30:14), "the wine cup of God's judgment" (Lam 4:21; Jer 49:12), "the virgin daughter of Judah" (Lam 1:15; Jer 14:17), "the prophet's eyes flow down with tears" (Lam 1:16a; Jer 9:1,18b; 13:17b), "fears and terrors surround" (Lam 2:22; Jer 6:25; 20:10), and appeal to God for vengeance (Lam 3:64–66; Jer 11:20). Also notable is the use of one of Jeremiah's characteristic words, *šeber* ("disaster" Jer 4:20), in Lam 2:11,13; 3:47–48; 4:10.

The disaster that overtook Judah is attributed to the same causes in both books. The southern kingdom's ruin had resulted from national sin (Lam 1:5,14,18; 3:42; 4:6,22; 5:7,16 with Jer 14:7; 16:10–12; 17:1–3), corrupt prophets and priests (Lam 2:14; 4:13–15 with Jer 2:8; 5:31; 14:13; 23:11–40), and reliance on ineffective foreign allies (Lam 1:2,19; 4:17 with Jer 2:18,36; 30:14; 37:5–10). Added to this evidence is the fact that Lamentations was certainly written by an author who must have been an eyewitness to the events (as was Jeremiah) that occurred in Judah's final days before her exile.

Arguments against the Jeremianic authorship of Lamentations include the different orientation reflected by the two books. They appear to reflect different attitudes toward the foreign nations and King Zedekiah (Lam 4:20). But the fact that Jeremiah was written to encourage the people to accept the coming disciplinary judgment by the Babylonians whereas Lamentations was written after the destruction had taken place could certainly account for any apparent inconsistency on the part of the prophet. It must be concluded, therefore, that the traditional attribution of the authorship of the book to Jeremiah has strong support. However, the book does not say this explicitly, and recognizing a contemporary of Jeremiah as the author, while not exactly necessary, would in no way lead to a different interpretation of the book's contents.

THE PURPOSE AND MESSAGE OF THE BOOK

Lamentations records the pathos and pain that took place at the fall of Jerusalem to the Babylonians in 586 BC (2 Kings 24–25). All five poems of the book address the tragic downfall of the city and are united in stating that the reason for this tragedy was God's punishment for Israel's sins. The content of the book is dominated by the theme of complaint as the remnant

---

[2] Author's translations.

of God's people wrestled with the disaster that had overtaken their city and holy place. This collection of laments was read annually in Jewish liturgy on the ninth of Ab (in July or August) to remember the destruction of the first temple in 586 BC and the second temple in AD 70.

THE STRUCTURE OF THE BOOK

The book of Lamentations consists of five poems, each of which makes up one chapter. Chapters 1, 2, and 4, which all begin with the interrogative *'êkâ/'êk* ("how"), are funeral dirges (cf. 2 Sam 1:19,25,27; Isa 1:21), and chaps. 3 and 5 are lamentations and record the nation's complaint. This unique combination of funeral dirges with laments allowed the people to convey their deeply personal and tragic account in the form of a complaint and lament to God.[3] Gottwald argues for a chiastic arrangement for the entire book with chaps. 1 and 5 providing summaries of the disaster and chaps. 2 and 4 supplying the details of the death and devastation. Chapter 3 occupies the central pivotal position in form and content as it distinctively encouraged the people to depend on the goodness of God.[4] This chap. functions as both the literary and theological center of the book.

The actual chapter lengths are similar, even though chap. 3 has 66 verses; however, each of the stanzas is proportionately shorter than what is found in the other four chaps. The clarity of the structure of the book is virtually universally recognized among scholars, a rarity in the field of OT studies.[5] The book may be outlined as follows.

I. Jerusalem Is Devastated (chap. 1)

II. The Reasons for God's Wrath (chap. 2)

III. The City Laments Its Devastation (chap. 3)

IV. Zion's Ancient Glory and Present Misery (chap. 4)

V. Israel Calls for God's Mercy (chap. 5)

THE STYLE OF THE BOOK

Chapters 1, 2, and 4 are acrostic poems. In such a piece each verse begins with a successive letter of the Hebrew alphabet. Chapter 3, the central and longest poem, is a triple acrostic. Each line of the 22 sections begins with a successive letter of the alphabet.[6] Chapter 5, the final and only nonacrostic chapter, nevertheless shares an affinity with the other chapters since it too has 22 verses (the number of letters in the Hb. alphabet), so the last poem has the same number of verses as chaps. 1, 2, and 4. The allusion to the entire alphabet in the chapters may have been for memory purposes, but more likely it conveyed the idea of completeness. The similar structure between the chaps. may also convey the notion that with the repetition the poems all reflect on the most tragic event in Israel's history, the fall of Jerusalem.

A second stylistic feature of the book is the use of the *qînâh* meter throughout the poems. The *qînâh* meter, in which the second colon of a parallel line is consistently shorter than the

---

[3] N. Gottwald, "Lamentations, Book of," in *IDB*, ed. G. A. Buttrick (Nashville: Abingdon, 1962), 3:61.

[4] Ibid., 62. For an even more intricate chiastic structure for the entire book see D. A. Dorsey, *The Literary Structure of the Old Testament: A Commentary on Genesis–Malachi* (Grand Rapids: Baker, 1999), 251.

[5] Childs, *An Introduction to the Old Testament as Scripture*, 591.

[6] The first chapter is the only chapter that follows the normal order of the Hebrew alphabet. In chaps. 2, 3, and 4 the letter *pe* precedes the letter *'ayin* in contrast to chap. 1.

first, is characteristic of the lament genre. The meter is described as 3:2 meter rather than the more balanced 3:3 meter. It has been speculated that this unbalanced rhythm creates the sensation of limping or halting and may have reflected the irregular gait of attendants at a funeral procession.[7] Lamentations 5, the only poem of the book that does not follow the acrostic pattern, is also the only poem that does not follow the *qinah* rhythm pattern.

A third characteristic feature of the style of Lamentations involves the use of personification. The nation is portrayed as an abandoned woman (1:1–2), and possibly as a persecuted man (3:1). Jerusalem itself is portrayed as a sick body (1:13; 3:4; cf. Isa 1:5–6).

THE ANALYSIS OF THE BOOK

Since each of the five poems in Lamentations addresses the fall of Jerusalem, it does not appear that there is any necessary progression of thought in the book. In this regard, the individual poems of the book resemble the book of Psalms whose arrangement follows no apparent evolvement. Yet many of the same themes appear dispersed throughout the book. Detailed information is provided about the destruction of the temple (1:10; 2:6–7,20; 5:18), the sinfulness of Jerusalem (1:8; 3:39,42; 4:6; 5:16), the horrors of famine (2:11–12,19; 4:4,9–10), and the hope of retribution against the enemy (1:22; 3:64,66; 4:21).[8] The content of each of the major poems is summarized in the opening lines of each chapter, which in effect function as a kind of title.

I. Jerusalem Is Devastated (chap. 1)

Chap. 1 depicts the anguish of Zion, moving from the eyewitness account expressed in the form of a funeral dirge (1:1–11) to the lament and outcry of the city itself (1:12–22). Jerusalem is compared to a woman who has been abandoned by her "lovers" and "friends" (1:2), an illusion to Judah's dependence on foreign alliances rather than on the Lord. The phrase "there is no one to comfort" Jerusalem functions as a refrain in this chapter, occurring five times (1:2,9, 16–17,21). All the principal themes of the book are introduced in this first chapter including the causes of the suffering, the rejection of God's people, and the paradox created by God's turning against His own people and His temple.[9]

II. The Reasons for God's Wrath (chap. 2)

In Lamentations 2 the source of the nation's calamity is traced back to the Lord Himself. Hardly a verse in the first half of this poem omits the fact that these horrible conditions have come on the nation as the result of God's will (2:1–11,17). He has become like Israel's enemy (2:4–5). The prophets, priests, and kings have led the people astray (2:6–14) and the conditions were so severe that mothers had to resort to cannibalism with their own offspring (2:20).

III. The City Laments Its Devastation (chap. 3)

Chapter 3, unlike chaps. 1 and 2, is written in the first person; this possibly represents the city through personification, as noted above. The author described his suffering as though he personally suffered along with his countrymen (Lam 3:14,53–57,61–62). Thus the chapter opens like an individual lament from the Psalms (Psalms 6, 88), describing his predicament

---

[7] See M. Brown, "Lamentations, Theology of," in *NIDOTTE*, ed. W. VanGemeren (Grand Rapids: Zondervan, 1997), 4:887.

[8] Childs, *Introduction to the Old Testament as Scripture*, 594.

[9] D. Hillers, "Lamentations, Book of," in *ABD*, ed. D. N. Freedman (New York: Doubleday, 1992), 4:137.

(Lam 3:1–18) and then looking to God for relief (3:19–21). He then confessed his faith in the goodness and compassion of God in what sounds almost like a creedal statement (3:22–24; cf. Exod 34:6–7; Num 14:18; Ps 86:15). The steadfast mercies of the Lord engender hope (Lam 3:23).[10] In 3:40–47 the author shifted to the plural form, and the poem takes on the form of a national lament. In the last part of the poem the mood has changed to the extent that God is no longer the enemy but is now an ally (3:58) who supports the nation against their enemies. The poet speaks with the confidence of the deliverance as though it had already happened (3:61–66).

IV. Zion's Ancient Glory and Present Misery (chap. 4)

The horrors of the siege are depicted in chap. 4. The former splendor of Jerusalem is contrasted with the present humiliation of her inhabitants (4:1–10). As in chaps. 1 and 2, the horrors of famine have been visited on the city. Jerusalem was worse off than immoral Sodom, which was destroyed "in an instant" (4:6). The prophets and the priests, the spiritual leaders, are specifically mentioned as guilty of corruption (4:12–16). The chapter ends with an imprecation against the Edomites and a blessing on Judah (4:21–22).

V. Israel Calls for God's Mercy (chap. 5)

The final poem begins with the words, "Yahweh, remember what has happened to us" (5:1), and thus takes the form of a prayer. The author asked that the city be delivered from its misery (5:2–18) and restored to its former glory (5:19–22). This chapter thus takes the form of a communal lament. Like the communal psalms, it concludes with an appeal to God for help (Psalms 44, 60, 74, 79, 80, 83, 89). Lamentations 5:19–20 may be thought of as a summary of the entire book.

THE TEXT OF THE BOOK

The Hebrew text of the book of Lamentations has been well preserved. The few variations that exist with the LXX possibly reveal corruption within the transmission of the LXX and certainly do not indicate that the LXX translator translated a text that was substantially different from the MT.

THE THEOLOGY OF THE BOOK

The people lost their land and sanctuary (Lam 1:10) because the nation had rebelled and broken the covenant. There was thus no question among the Israelites that they deserved the punishment inflicted by the Babylonians as God's agent (1:5,14,22; 4:13). Lamentations 1:5, 14 and 2:17 acknowledge that the covenant curses resulted from Israel's covenant disobedience (Leviticus 26; Deuteronomy 28). God was right to punish the sin (Lam 1:18,22; 2:14; 3:40–42; 4:13,22; 5:7) and unleash His wrath (1:12–14; 2:1–9,20–22; 3:1–18; 4:6,11). There is thus no doubt that God was ultimately responsible for the destruction since the Babylonians are never mentioned by name.

The message is not entirely one of judgment, however. Hope is expressed in 3:22–33 that the Lord will respond to those who turn to him. The people were still God's covenant people, and God had been faithful in bringing destruction, as promised, on the covenant violators.

---

[10] See W. J. Dumbrell, *The Faith of Israel: A Theological Survey of the Old Testament*, 2nd ed. (Grand Rapids: Baker, 2002), 297.

The complaint of the lament of the city is similar to Job's complaint (Lam 3:14; cf. Job 30:9). However, in contrast the author of Lamentations nowhere protests that the city is innocent (Lam 3:39–40).

THE NEW TESTAMENT AND THE BOOK

The primary themes found in the book of Lamentations are also found in the writings of the NT. God still disciplines His children for disobedience (Heb 12:5–11), and those who continue in persistent rebellion can expect to be judged by God (1 Cor 11:30) and to reap the consequences (Gal 6:7).

STUDY QUESTIONS

1. What is unique about the critical views on the history of composition of the book of Lamentations?
2. What is the basis for the view that the book of Lamentations was composed before 538 BC?
3. What are the major reasons for insisting that Lamentations was written by Jeremiah?
4. What are the major transgressions in Lamentations that led to the defeat of Jerusalem?
5. What is the stated reason for the fall of Jerusalem?
6. Which chapter of Lamentations has the most verses?
7. What is unique about the critical views on the structure of Lamentations?
8. What is an acrostic poem?
9. What is the qînâh rhythm pattern?
10. What is the meaning of the image of Judah being compared to a woman in Lamentation 1?
11. What type of psalm is Lamentations 3 compared to?
12. Who was responsible for the destruction of Jerusalem?

FOR FURTHER STUDY

Albrektson, B. *Studies in the Text and Theology of Lamentations*. Lund: Gleerup, 1963.
Berlin, A. *Lamentations*. Louisville: Westminster/John Knox, 2002.
Dorsey, D. A. *The Literary Structure of the Old Testament: A Commentary on Genesis–Malachi*. Grand Rapids: Baker, 1999.
Dumbrell, W. J. *The Faith of Israel: A Theological Survey of the Old Testament*. 2nd ed. Grand Rapids: Baker, 2002.
Ellison, H. L. "Lamentations." *EBC*. Edited by F. Gaebelein, 6:693–734. Grand Rapids: Zondervan, 1986.
Gordis, R. *The Song of Songs and Lamentations*. Rev. ed. New York: KTAV, 1947.
Heater, H. "Structure and Meaning in Lamentations." *BSac* 149 (1992): 304–15.
Hillers, D. R. *Lamentations*. AB. Garden City, NY: Doubleday, 1972.
Marcus, D. "Non-recurring Doublets in the Book of Lamentations." *HAR* 10 (1986): 177–95.
Provan, I. *Lamentations*. NCBC. Grand Rapids: Eerdmans, 1991.
Renkema, J. "The Meaning of the Parallel Acrostics in Lamentations." *VT* 45 (1995): 379–83.
Scott, R. B. Y. *The Way of Wisdom*. New York: Macmillan, 1971.
Tepox, A. "Translating Acrostics as Acrostics." *BT* 55 (2004): 233–43.

EPILOGUE

EUGENE H. MERRILL

A T THE END of an endeavor like this, it is good as authors to reflect again on its rationale, this time not in anticipation of what should or will be done but in assessment of what has in fact been done. We have attempted to demonstrate an awareness of the latest and best scholarship in the realm of Old Testament criticism without slavishly aping it or polemically reacting to it. Our intention has been to examine objectively and abstractly the various themes and topics that constitute the genre and to employ all available evidence in as fair-minded and even-handed a manner as possible. Readers of the work will have to determine whether or not we have succeeded in achieving these goals.

At the same time, as evangelicals we are not loath to concede that our work is informed by an a priori and confessional stance that obviously colors our method and its outcome. This approach (often not acknowledged by scholars) is not unique to evangelicalism because, as is commonly recognized, presupposition is endemic to virtually all areas of the humanities, particularly those of biblical and theological scholarship. One's traditions and worldviews can hardly be eliminated from his scholarly pursuits. If this is a crime, we must plead guilty.

We view our presentation—though similar in many respects to other works in the field—to be unique and necessary precisely because most others have omissions that render them less than ideal for graduate theological education. While matters like text criticism, canonicity, and historical and cultural backgrounds receive scattered attention in some works of this nature, few if any devote entire chapters to comprehensive and cohesive explorations of these very important introductory issues. We have therefore addressed this lack by including nine chapters of prolegomena consisting of (1) introduction, (2) the historical setting of the Old Testament, (3) the cultural world of the Old Testament, (4) ancient Near Eastern literature and the Old Testament, (5) composition of the Old Testament, (6) canonicity of the Old Testament, (7) transmission and textual criticism of the Old Testament, (8) development of the historical-critical method, and (9) the present state of scholarship. We are persuaded that no adequate understanding of the nature and content of the Old Testament is possible without attention to these ancillary adjuncts to the Bible itself.

These sections (commonly referred to as "general introduction") recur greatly abbreviated in the chapters dealing with each section and book of the Old Testament ("special introduction"), but there against the backdrop of the issues as a whole as well as in their peculiar historical, cultural, and canonical contexts. This "double exposure" enhances the likelihood of a more informed grasp of the holistic nature of the biblical revelation. The prolegomena are thus not disconnected essays but reservoirs of information which the student can tap in order to understand better how critical portraits that are special to particular books can be viewed against a broader canvas. Each book has its own introduction dealing with its own interests and tailored to its author(s) own life situation and the needs of the community.

We frequently address the theology of each book and section as well for in the final analysis the theology of the Old Testament ought to be the capstone of its study. It has been said that "the theology of a scholar is in direct relationship to the bibliology of that scholar." That is, one cannot disconnect the one from the other and claim to have given the text its due respect. The purpose of Old Testament introduction (or criticism) is to understand the origin, nature, transmission, and canonicity of the Word of God, thus presenting it to the theologian as the "raw material" upon which and with which he must labor in order to derive a cohesive, self-consistent understanding of the revelation of God which the text is intended to yield. If this foundational groundwork is flawed in its presuppositions and subsequent methodology, the theological practitioner who adheres to it as his basis of theological authority is bound to generate a theology that itself is flawed. Yet, no one work can embrace both a full body of introductory detail and a comprehensive theology that is sensitive to all the parts of the biblical canon. It is our judgment that they must be done in tandem, the introduction providing the underpinning for the theology. We pray that the foundation attempted here will prove to be a worthy basis for future theological projects.

Finally, we have done our work with an eye to the New Testament and the church. One must therefore ask, In what sense can an enterprise like this be open-ended to the New Testament part of the whole canon? First, a position that maintains that the whole is equally the Word of God cannot escape the compulsion to view Old Testament introduction as also foundational to the New. The Christian scholar is thus obliged to approach the Old Testament for what it is—the anteroom to the great chamber of truth to be found in the living Word, Jesus Christ. Second, Jesus and the apostles embraced the Old Testament as Scripture, sacred texts which they and normative Judaism with them confessed to be God's Word on the terms of the Old Testament tradition itself. Thus, for example, Moses wrote the Torah, Isaiah wrote all 66 chapters of the book named for him, and Daniel lived and ministered in a Babylonian-Persian world. What the Old Testament anticipated, the New Testament brought to fruition or at least seconded and clarified.

Any project dedicated to the study of Scripture should embody the notion of applicability. How does the Bible relate to the faith and to me in particular? This question is particularly acute when addressed to the Old Testament. We have undertaken our task with a pastoral frame of mind that has asked of us over and over, How does our wrestling with this or that issue contribute to the spiritual well-being of the body of the church and each of its parts? Paul noted that "All Scripture is inspired by God and is profitable for teaching, for rebuking, for correcting, for training in righteousness" (2 Tim 3:16). For Paul, the Scripture, of course, was the Old Testament. An introduction to the Old Testament that denies or ignores Paul's assessment of the essence, worth, and applicability of the ancient text has failed to grasp its God-intended purpose. We pray that what we have attempted here has not been found wanting in this respect but, to the contrary, will shore up and make even more perspicuous this former part of the Word of God

Name Index

Subject Index

Scripture Index

MAP 1

MEDITERRANEAN SEA

AMMON

MOAB

LOWER
EGYPT
Goshen

Great
Bitter
Lake

Wilderness
of Zin

EDOM

Little
Bitter
Lake

Wilderness
of Paran

30 N

30 N

Faiyum

Gulf
of
Suez

Sinai

MIDIAN

Area
enlarged
below

Bahariya

Wilderness
Of Sin

Farafra

UPPER
EGYPT

Ed-Dakhla

Abydos

Western Desert

Thebes

Eastern Desert

El-Kharga

Edfu

Sahara

Elephantine   Ombos

Desert

First cataract

Buhen   Abu Simbel

RED

Second cataract

Nubia

SEA

Soleb

20 N

Third cataract

Fourth
cataract

Nile River

Gebel
Barkal
(Napata)

Fifth cataract

Cush

Atbara River

Sixth cataract

Khartoum

Blue Nile

White Nile

0   100   200   300 Miles

0   100   200   300 Kilometers

Inset map

N

0   40   80   120   160   200 Miles

0   40   80   120   160   200 Kilometers

MEDITERRANEAN SEA

Megiddo

Edrei

Beth-shan

Jordan River

AMMON

Shechem

Shittim

Rabbah

Jericho

Heshbon

Medeba

Sais

Hebron

Gaza

LOWER
EGYPT

Arad

Dibon

Baal-zephon   Sile

Beersheba

MOAB

Raamses

DEAD SEA

Kir-hareseth

Bubastis

Succoth

Ismalia

Tamar

On (Heliopolis)   Pithom

Goshen

Great
Bitter
Lake

Wadi el-Arish

Wilderness
of Zin

Punon

EDOM

Giza

Little
Bitter
Lake

Kadesh-
barnea

Arabah

Petra

Noph

FAIYUM

Wilderness
of Paran

Ain Hawarah

Serabit el-
Khadim

Taba

Ezion-geber

Abu Zeneimeh

Gulf
of
Aqaba

Nile River

Sinai

Nuweiba

Gulf
of Suez

Ain Khadra

Rephidim

Dahab

Hermopolis

Wilderness
of Sin

MIDIAN

Akhetaten

RED SEA

Legend

EGYPT: LAND OF BONDAGE

- • City
- ○ City (uncertain location)
- • City (modern name)
- ≋ Cataract

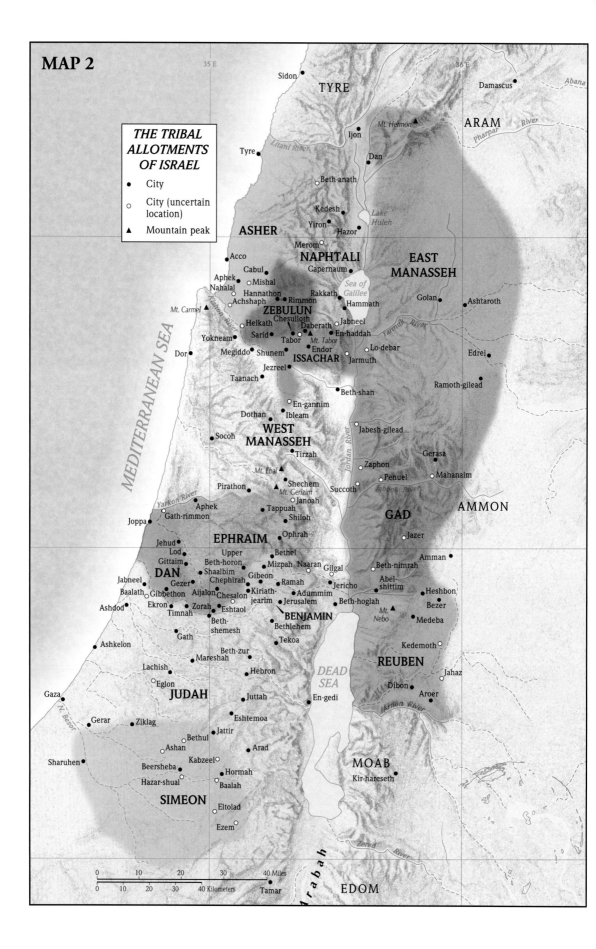

MAP 2

THE TRIBAL
ALLOTMENTS
OF ISRAEL

- • City
- ○ City (uncertain location)
- ▲ Mountain peak

Sidon
TYRE
Damascus
ARAM

Ijon
Mt. Hermon ▲
Tyre
Dan
Pharpar River
Abana

Beth-anath
Litani River

Kedesh
Lake Huleh
Yiron
Hazor
ASHER
Merom
Acco
NAPHTALI
Capernaum
EAST MANASSEH
Cabul
Aphek
Mishal
Sea of Galilee
Nahalal
Hannathon
Rakkath
Golan
Ashtaroth
Achshaph
Rimmon
Hammath
Mt. Carmel ▲
Kishon River
ZEBULUN
Chesulloth
Jabneel
Helkath
Daberath ▲
En-haddah
Yokneam
Sarid
Tabor
Mt. Tabor
Yarmuk River
Dor
Megiddo
Shunem
Endor
Lo-debar
Edrei
ISSACHAR
Jarmuth
Jezreel
Ramoth-gilead
Taanach
Beth-shan
En-gannim
Dothan
Ibleam
Jabesh-gilead
WEST
MANASSEH
Socoh
Tirzah
Gerasa
Zaphon
Mt. Ebal ▲
Penuel
Mahanaim
Pirathon
Shechem
Succoth
Mt. Gerizim ▲
Janoah
Tappuah
GAD
AMMON
Aphek
Shiloh
Joppa
Gath-rimmon
Ophrah
Jazer
EPHRAIM
Jehud
Upper
Bethel
Amman
Lod
Beth-horon
Mizpah
Naaran
Beth-nimrah
Gittaim
Shaalbim
Gibeon
Gilgal
DAN
Chephirah
Ramah
Jericho
Abel-shittim
Jabneel
Gezer
Kiriath-
Heshbon
Baalath
Gibbethon
Aijalon
Chesalon
jearim
Adummim
Bezer
Ashdod
Ekron
Zorah
Eshtaol
Jerusalem
Beth-hoglah
Timnah
Beth-
Mt. Nebo ▲
Medeba
Gath
shemesh
Bethlehem
Ashkelon
Beth-zur
Tekoa
Kedemoth
Mareshah
DEAD
SEA
REUBEN
Lachish
Hebron
Jahaz
Eglon
Dibon
Gaza
JUDAH
Juttah
En-gedi
Aroer
Gerar
Eshtemoa
Arnon River
Ziklag
Jattir
Bethul
Arad
Sharuhen
Ashan
Kabzeel
MOAB
Beersheba
Hormah
Kir-hareseth
Hazar-shual
Baalah
SIMEON
Eltolad
Ezem
Zered River
EDOM
Tamar

MEDITERRANEAN SEA

Jordan River

Yarkon River

N. Besor

Jabbok River

BENJAMIN

0   10   20   30   40 Miles
0 10 20 30 40 Kilometers

35 E
36 E

Arabah

MAP 3

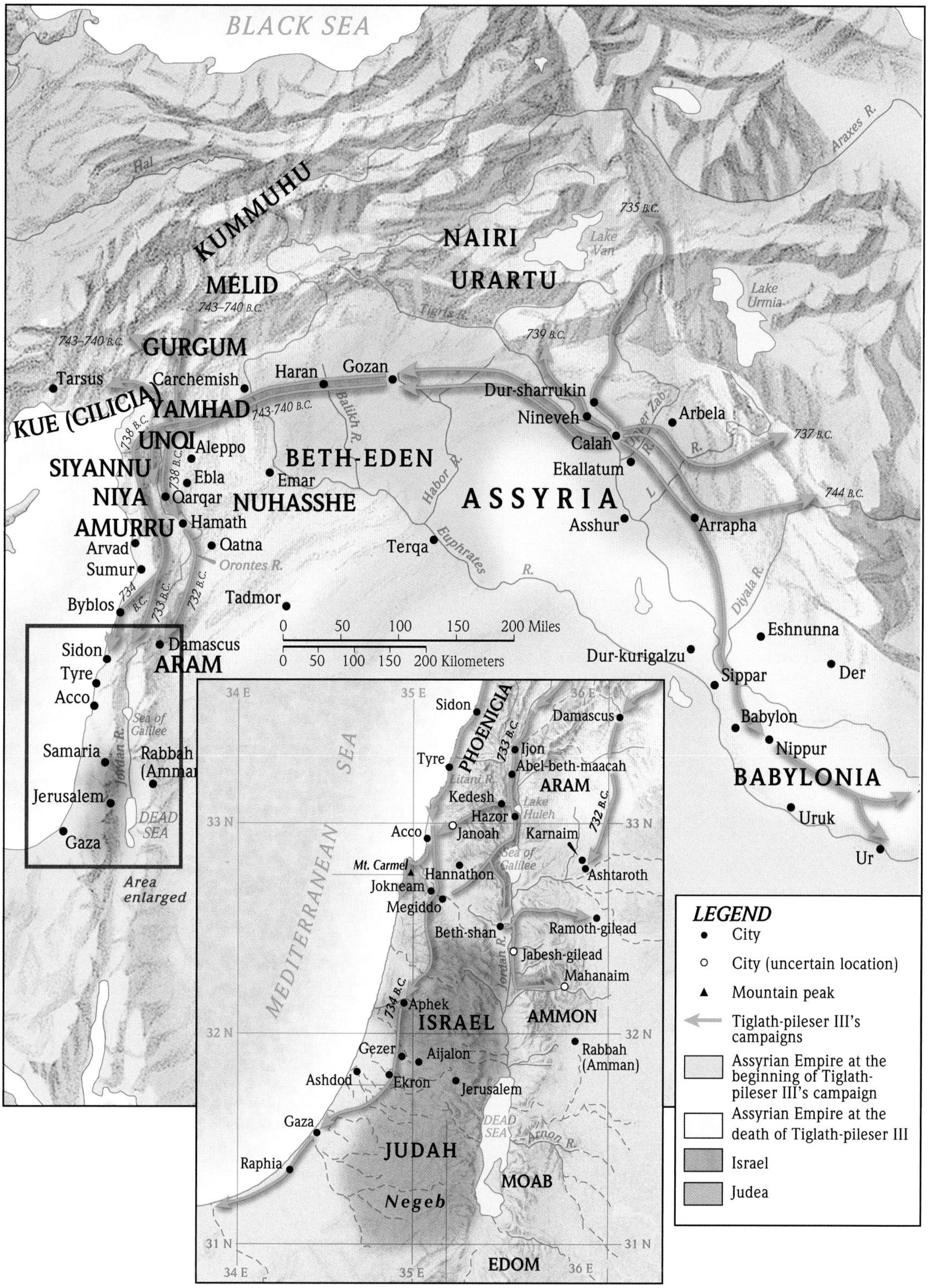

BLACK SEA

KUMMUHU

NAIRI

MELID
743-740 B.C.

URARTU
735 B.C.

Lake Van

Lake Urmia

GURGUM
743-740 B.C.

Tarsus
Carchemish
Haran
Gozan
739 B.C.

Dur-sharrukin
Nineveh
Arbela
737 B.C.

KUE (CILICIA)
YAMHAD
743-740 B.C.

UNQI
Aleppo
BETH-EDEN
Calah
Ekallatum

SIYANNU
Ebla
Emar
738 B.C.

NIYA
Qarqar
NUHASSHE
ASSYRIA

AMURRU
Hamath
Asshur
Arrapha
744 B.C.

Arvad
Qatna
Terqa

Sumur
Orontes R.
Euphrates R.

Byblos
734 B.C.
733 B.C.
732 B.C.
Tadmor
Eshnunna

Sidon
Damascus
Der

Tyre
ARAM
Dur-kurigalzu
Sippar

Acco
Sea of Galilee
Babylon
Nippur

Samara
Rabbah (Ammar
BABYLONIA

Jerusalem
DEAD SEA
Uruk

Gaza
Ur

Area enlarged

0   50   100   150   200 Miles
0   50   100   150   200 Kilometers

Inset map (Area enlarged)

34 E   35 E   36 E

Sidon
PHOENICIA
733 B.C.
Damascus

Tyre
Ijon
Abel-beth-maacah

Litani R.
Kedesh
ARAM
732 B.C.

Acco
Hazor
Janoah
Karnaim

Mt. Carmel
Hannathon
Ashtaroth

Jokneam
Megiddo
Beth-shan
Ramoth-gilead

Jabesh-gilead
Mahanaim

734 B.C.
Aphek
AMMON

ISRAEL
Gezer
Aijalon
Rabbah (Amman)

Ashdod
Ekron
Jerusalem

Gaza
DEAD SEA

Raphia
JUDAH
MOAB

Negeb

EDOM

34 E   35 E   36 E

LEGEND

- • City
- ○ City (uncertain location)
- ▲ Mountain peak
- → Tiglath-pileser III's campaigns
- ▢ Assyrian Empire at the beginning of Tiglath-pileser III's campaign
- ▢ Assyrian Empire at the death of Tiglath-pileser III
- ▢ Israel
- ▢ Judea

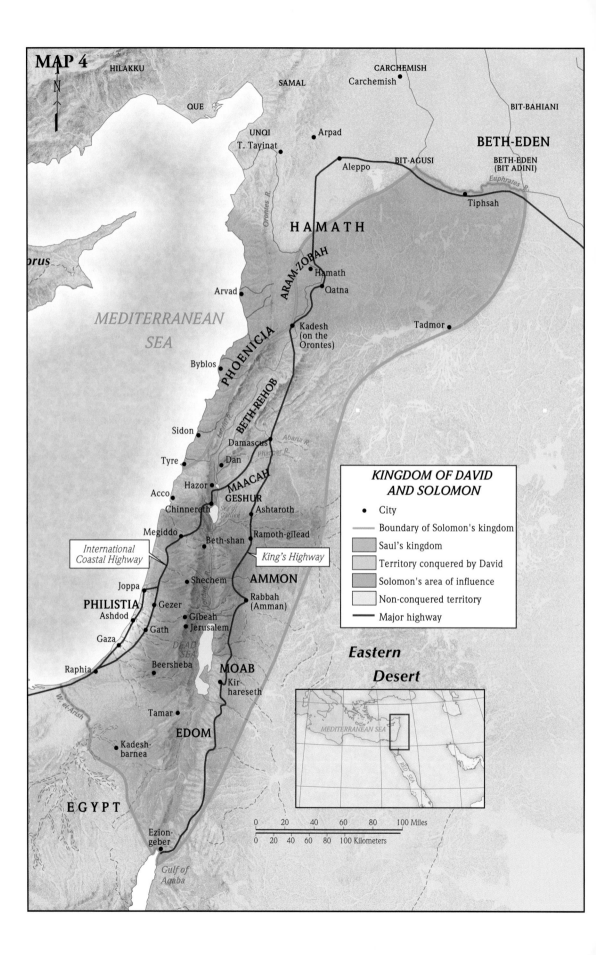

MAP 4

N

HILAKKU

QUE

SAMAL

CARCHEMISH
Carchemish

BIT-BAHIANI

UNQI
T. Tayinat

Arpad

Aleppo

BIT-AGUSI

BETH-EDEN

BETH-EDEN
(BIT ADINI)

Euphrates R.

Tiphsah

Orontes R.

H A M A T H

ARAM-ZOBAH

Hamath

Qatna

Arvad

Tadmor

MEDITERRANEAN
SEA

Kadesh
(on the
Orontes)

Byblos

PHOENICIA

BETH-REHOB

Sidon

Litani R.

Damascus

Abana R.

Pharpar R.

Tyre

Dan

Hazor

MAACAH

Acco

GESHUR

Chinnereth

Ashtaroth

Megiddo

Ramoth-gilead

*International
Coastal Highway*

Beth-shan

King's Highway

Joppa

Shechem

AMMON

PHILISTIA

Gezer

Rabbah
(Amman)

Ashdod

Gibeah

Gath

Jerusalem

Gaza

*DEAD
SEA*

Raphia

Beersheba

MOAB

W. el-Arish

Tamar

Kir-
hareseth

EDOM

Kadesh-
barnea

E G Y P T

Eziongeber

*Gulf of
Aqaba*

Eastern

Desert

**KINGDOM OF DAVID
AND SOLOMON**

• City

Boundary of Solomon's kingdom

Saul's kingdom

Territory conquered by David

Solomon's area of influence

Non-conquered territory

Major highway

MEDITERRANEAN SEA

RED SEA

0   20   40   60   80   100 Miles

0   20   40   60   80   100 Kilometers

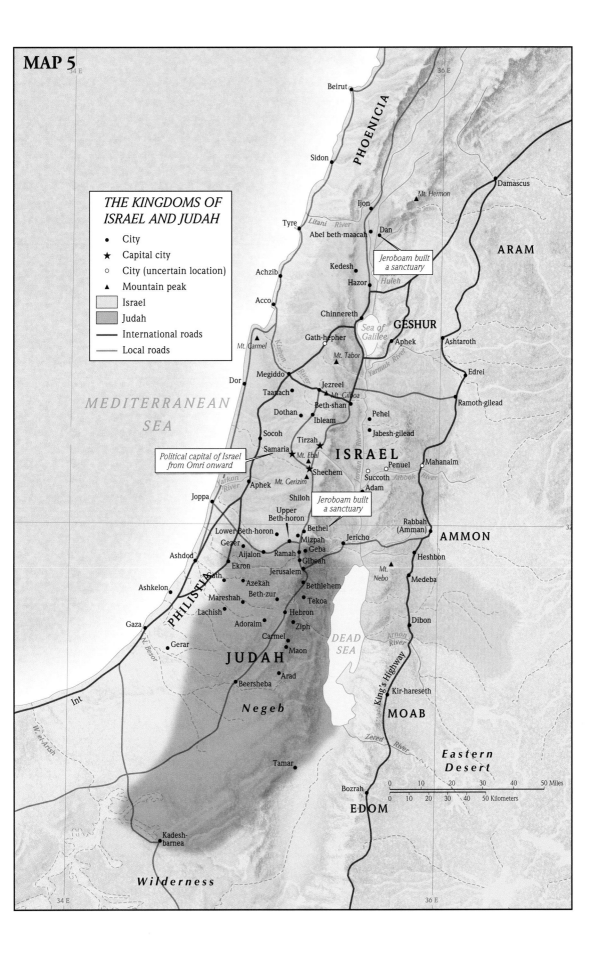

MAP 5

THE KINGDOMS OF
ISRAEL AND JUDAH

● City
★ Capital city
○ City (uncertain location)
▲ Mountain peak
  Israel
  Judah
── International roads
── Local roads

MEDITERRANEAN
SEA

PHOENICIA

Beirut

Sidon

Mt. Hermon ▲

Damascus

Ijon

Tyre   Litani   River

Abel beth-maacah   Dan

*Jeroboam built
a sanctuary*

ARAM

Kedesh

Achzib

Hazor   Huleh

Acco

Chinnereth   GESHUR

Mt. Carmel ▲   Gath-hepher ○   Sea of
                                      Galilee

Aphek

Ashtaroth

Kishon River   Mt. Tabor ▲

Edrei

Dor   Megiddo   Jezreel
                               Mt. Gilboa ▲   Ramoth-gilead
           Taanach   Beth-shan   Yarmuk River

           Dothan   Ibleam   Pehel

                                      Jabesh-gilead

           Socoh   ISRAEL

*Political capital of Israel
from Omri onward*

           Samaria   Tirzah ★   Mahanaim
           ★ Mt. Ebal ▲   Penuel
                      Shechem   Succoth
Joppa   Aphek Mt. Gerizim ▲   Adam
                                   Jordan River   Jabbok River
           Yarkon
           River   Shiloh
                                      *Jeroboam built
                     Upper   a sanctuary*
                     Beth-horon
                                                 Rabbah
           Lower Beth-horon   Bethel   (Amman)   AMMON
           Gezer   Mizpah   Jericho
Ashdod   Aijalon Ramah Geba   Heshbon
           Ekron   Gibeah   Mt.
           Jerusalem   Nebo ▲   Medeba
Ashkelon   Azekah   Bethlehem
       PHILISTIA Gath
           Mareshah Beth-zur   Tekoa
           Lachish   Hebron   Dibon
Gaza   Adoraim   Ziph
           N. Besor   Carmel   Arnon River
       Gerar   Maon   DEAD
                                      SEA
                    JUDAH   King's Highway
                              Arad
              Beersheba   Kir-hareseth
                                                 MOAB
Int   N e g e b

                                   Zered   River

                                      Eastern
                                      Desert

           Tamar
W. el-Arish   0   10   20   30   40   50 Miles

                    Bozrah   0 10 20 30 40 50 Kilometers

                                      EDOM

           Kadesh-
           barnea

W i l d e r n e s s

MAP 6

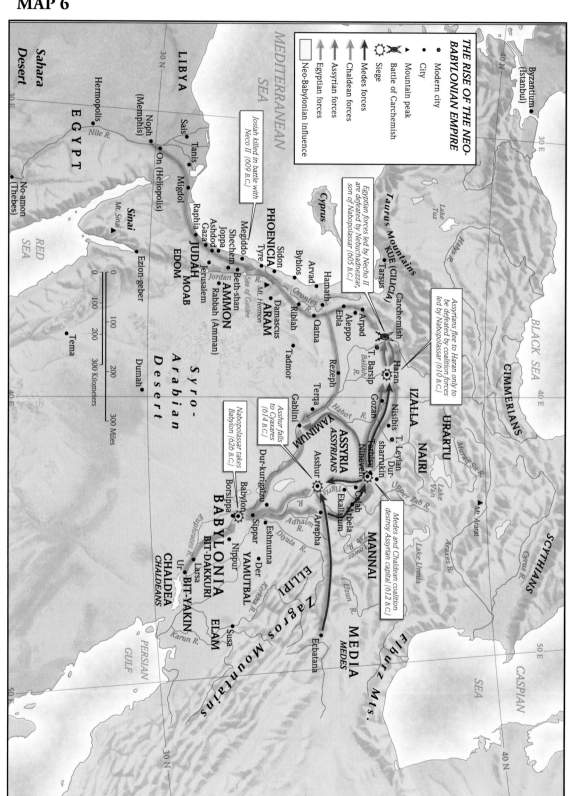

THE RISE OF THE NEO-
BABYLONIAN EMPIRE

- ● Modern city
- ● City
- ▲ Mountain peak
- ⚔ Battle of Carchemish
- ☼ Siege
- ⬆ Medes forces
- ⬆ Chaldean forces
- ⬆ Assyrian forces
- ⬆ Egyptian forces
- ☐ Neo-Babylonian influence

Josiah killed in battle with
Neco II (609 B.C.)

Egyptian forces led by Necho II
are defeated by Nebuchadnezzar,
son of Nabopolassar (605 B.C.)

Assyrians flee to Haran only to
be defeated by coalition forces
led by Nabopolassar (610 B.C.)

Asshur falls
to Cyaxares
(614 B.C.)

Nabopolassar takes
Babylon (626 B.C.)

Medes and Chaldean coalition
destroy Assyrian capital (612 B.C.)

Byzantium
(Istanbul)

MEDITERRANEAN
SEA

Sahara
Desert

LIBYA

EGYPT

Hermopolis
Noph
(Memphis)
Sais
Tanis
On (Heliopolis)
Migdol
No-amon
(Thebes)

RED
SEA

Sinai
Mt. Sinai ▲

Ezion-geber

Tema

Dumah

Syro-
Arabian
Desert

PERSIAN
GULF

Karun R.

Zagros Mountains

Raphia
Gaza
Ashdod
Joppa
Shechem
Megiddo
Beth-shan
Jerusalem
Rabbah (Amman)
EDOM
MOAB
AMMON
JUDAH
Jordan R.
Sea of Galilee
Mt. Hermon
Damascus
Tadmor
Riblah
Qatna
Hamath
Orontes R.
PHOENICIA
Tyre
Sidon
Byblos
Arvad
ARAM

Cyprus

Taurus Mountains
KUE (CILICIA)
Tarsus
Arpad
Aleppo
Ebla
Rezeph
Carchemish ⚔
T. Barsip
Balikh R.
Haran
Gozan
sharruken
Dur-
Nisibis
T. Leilan
URARTU
Lake
Tuz
Halys R.

BLACK SEA

GIMMERIANS

SCYTHIANS

Elburz Mts.

CASPIAN
SEA

Mt. Ararat ▲
Araxes R.
Cyrus R.
Murat Su R.

IZALLA
NAIRI
MANNAI
Lake
Van
Lake Urmia

Terqa
Gablini
Khabur R.
AMMINUM
ASSYRIA
ASSYRIANS
Asshur
Nineveh
Calah
Arbela
Ekallatum
Upper Zab R.
Lower Zab R.
Tigris R.
Arrapha
Eshnunna
Der
Diyala R.
Adhaim R.
Dur-kurigalzu
Babylon ☼
Borsippa
Sippar
Nippur
BABYLONIA
YAMUTBAL
BIT-DAKKURI
CHALDEA
CHALDEANS
BIT-YAKIN
Ur
Larsa
Euphrates R.
Kebar R.
ELAM
Susa
Ecbatana
MEDIA
MEDES
ELLIPI
Uzun R.

0   100   200   300 Kilometers
0   100   200   300 Miles

30 E
30 N
40 N
40 E
50 E
50 N
30 N
40 N

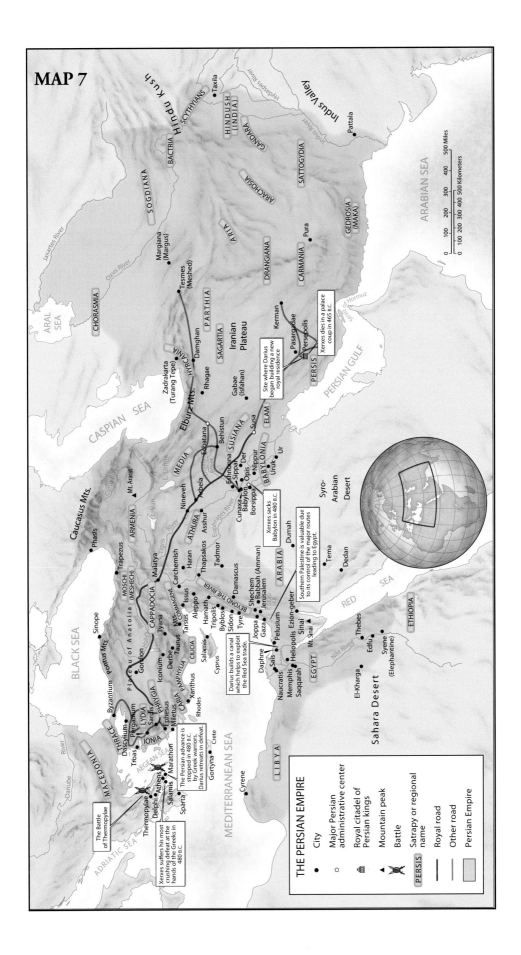

MAP 7

THE PERSIAN EMPIRE

- • City
- ○ Major Persian administrative center
- 🏛 Royal citadel of Persian kings
- ▲ Mountain peak
- ⚔ Battle
- PERSIS Satrapy or regional name
- —— Royal road
- —— Other road
- ▨ Persian Empire

The Battle of Thermopylae

Xerxes suffers his most crushing defeat at the hands of the Greeks in 480 B.C.

The Persian advance is stopped in 480 B.C. by Greek warriors. Darius retreats in defeat.

Darius builds a canal which helps to exploit the Red Sea trade.

Southern Palestine is valuable due to its control of the major routes leading to Egypt.

Xerxes sacks Babylon in 480 B.C.

Site where Darius began building a new royal residence

Xerxes dies in a palace coup in 465 B.C.

ADRIATIC SEA
MEDITERRANEAN SEA
AEGEAN SEA
MACEDONIA
THRACE
Troas
Pergamum
Dascylium
Byzantium
Sinope
BLACK SEA
Pontus Mts.
Trapezus
Phasis
Caucasus Mts.
Mt. Ararat ▲
ARMENIA
MOSCHI (MESHECH)
Malatya
CAPPADOCIA
Plateau of Anatolia
Gordion
Sardis
LYDIA
PHRYGIA
Iconium
Tyana
Derbe
Taurus Mts.
CILICIA
Tarsus
Issus
CARIA
PAMPHYLIA
Xanthus
Rhodes
Ephesus
Miletus
IONIA
Marathon
Athens
Delphi
Thermopylae
Salamis
Sparta
Gortyna
Crete
Gortyn
Cyrene
LIBYA
Salamis
Cyprus
CILICIA
COMMAGENE
Carchemish
Haran
Thapsakos
Aleppo
Hamath
Tripolis
Byblos
Sidon
Tyre
Damascus
Shechem
Rabbah (Amman)
Jerusalem
Joppa
Gaza
BEYOND THE RIVER
ATHURA
Nineveh
Asshur
Arbela
Eshnunna
Behistun
Ecbatana
MEDIA
Euphrates River
Tigris River
Cunaxa
Sippar
Opis
Der
Babylon
Borsippa
Nippur
Uruk
Ur
BABYLONIA
Susa
ELAM
SUSIANA
Dumah
ARABIA
Tema
Dedan
Syro-Arabian Desert
RED SEA
Daphne
Sais
Naucratis
Memphis
Saqqarah
EGYPT
Heliopolis
Pelusium
Ezion-geber
Sinai
Mt. Sinai ▲
El-Kharga
Edfu
Syene (Elephantine)
Thebes
Sahara Desert
ETHIOPIA
Nile River
CASPIAN SEA
CHORASMIA
ARAL SEA
Jaxartes River
Oxus River
SOGDIANA
BACTRIA
SCYTHIANS
Hindu Kush
Taxila
Hydaspes River
HINDUSH (INDIA)
GANDARA
Indus River
Indus Valley
Pattala
ARACHOSIA
SATTOGYDIA
GEDROSIA (MAKA)
ARABIAN SEA
CARMANIA
Pura
DRANGIANA
ARIA
Margiana (Margus)
Tesmes (Meshed)
PARTHIA
Damghan
Zadrakarta (Turang Tepe)
HYRCANIA
Rhagae
Gabae (Isfahan)
SAGARTIA
Iranian Plateau
Kerman
Pasargadae
Persepolis
PERSIS
PERSIAN GULF
Strait of Hormuz
Elburz Mts.
Lake Urmia
Danube
Euphrates River

0 100 200 300 400 500 Miles
0 100 200 300 400 500 Kilometers

MAP 8

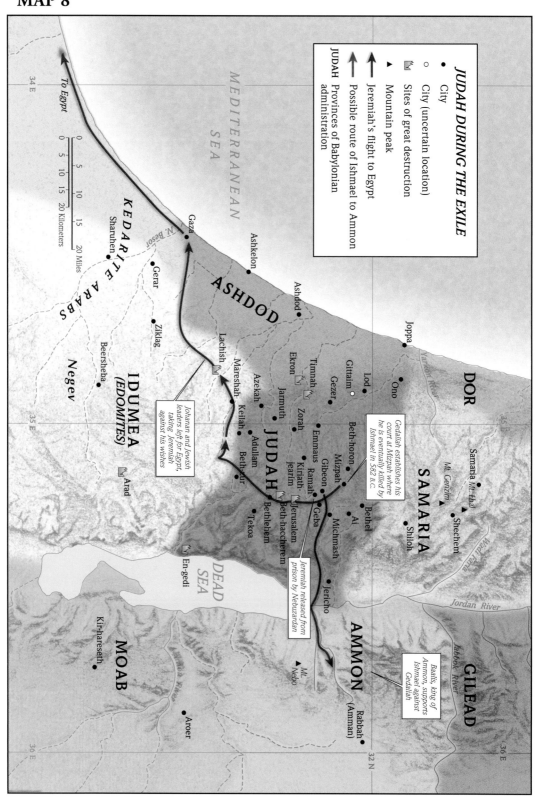

JUDAH DURING THE EXILE

- • City
- ○ City (uncertain location)
- ⚔ Sites of great destruction
- ▲ Mountain peak
- ⬆ Jeremiah's flight to Egypt
- ⬆ Possible route of Ishmael to Ammon
- JUDAH Provinces of Babylonian administration

MEDITERRANEAN SEA

To Egypt

0 5 10 15 20 Miles
0 5 10 15 20 Kilometers

34 E

N. Besor

Gaza

Ashkelon

Ashdod

ASHDOD

Joppa

DOR

SAMARIA

Samaria (Mt. Ebal)
Mt. Gerizim ▲
▲ Shechem

Shiloh

Bethel

Ai

Michmash

Jericho

Jordan River

Wad Fara

Yarkon River

Jabbok River

GILEAD

AMMON

Rabbah
(Amman)

KEDARITE ARABS

Sharuhen
Gerar

Ziklag

Beersheba

Negev

IDUMEA
(EDOMITES)

⚔ Arad

Lachish ⚔
Mareshah
Azekah
Keilah
Adullam
Bethzur

Jarmuth
Zorah
Emmaus
Kiriath-jearim
Bethlehem
Beth-haccherem
Tekoa

JUDAH

Gezer
Timnah ⚔
Ekron
Gittaim
Lod
Ono

Beth-horon
Gibeon
Mizpah
Ramah
Geba
Jerusalem

DEAD SEA

En-gedi

Kir-hareseth

MOAB

Aroer

▲ Mt. Nebo

35 E

35

36

36 E

32 N

Gedaliah establishes his court at Mizpah where he is eventually killed by Ishmael in 582 B.C.

Johanan and Jewish leaders left for Egypt, taking Jeremiah against his wishes

Jeremiah released from prison by Nebuzardan

Baalis, king of Ammon, supports Ishmael against Gedaliah

MAP 9

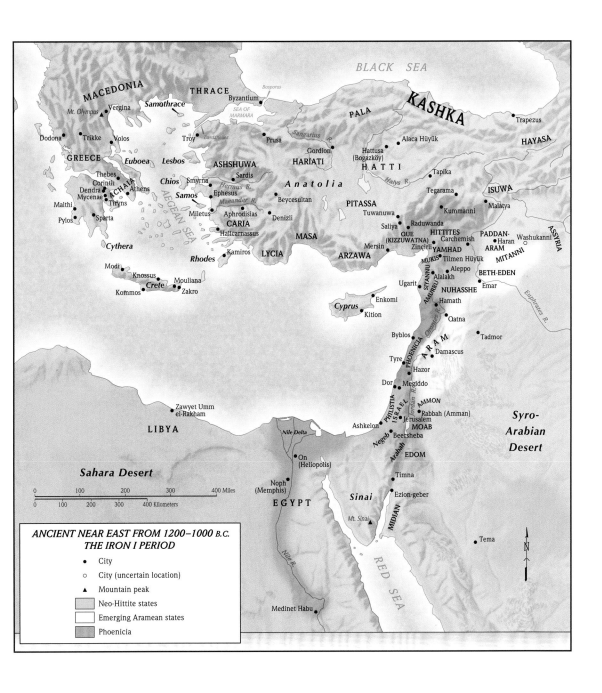

BLACK SEA

MACEDONIA
THRACE
Mt. Olympus ▲ • Vergina
Samothrace
Byzantium
Bosporus
SEA OF MARMARA
PALA
KASHKA
• Trapezus

Dodona • • Trikke Volos •
Troy • *Dardanelles*
Prusa •
Sangarius R.
Gordion •
Alaca Hüyük •
HAYASA

GREECE
Euboea
Lesbos
ASHSHUWA
Sardis •
HARIATI
Hattusa (Bogazköy) •
Tapika •
ISUWA

Thebes • Corinth
Chios Smyrna •
Hermus R.
Ephesus •
Anatolia
H A T T I
Tegarama •
Kummanni •
Malatya •

Dendra • Athens
ACHAIA
Samos
Maeander R.
Beycesultan •
PITASSA
Tuwanuwa •
HITTITES

Malthi • Mycenae • Tiryns
Miletus •
Aphrodisias •
CARIA
Denizli •
Saliya •
Raduwanda •
QUE (KIZZUWATNA)
Carchemish
PADDAN-ARAM
Washukanni •

Pylos • Sparta •
Halicarnassus
Mersin •
Zincirli •
• Haran
ASSYRIA

Cythera
Kamiros •
LYCIA
MASA
ARZAWA
SIYANNU
YAMHAD
Tilmen Hüyük •
Aleppo •
BETH-EDEN
MITANNI

Modi •
Rhodes
MUKIS
AMURRU
Alalakh •
NUHASSHE
Emar •
Euphrates R.

Knossos •
Mouliana •
Ugarit •
Hamath •

Kommos • *Crete* Zakro •
Cyprus
Enkomi •
Kition •
Qatna •

Byblos •
Orontes R.
Tadmor •

AEGEAN SEA
Tyre •
A R A M
Damascus •

Dor • Hazor •
Jordan R.

Zawyet Umm el-Rakham •
Megiddo •
AMMON
Rabbah (Amman) •

LIBYA
Nile Delta
Ashkelon •
PHILISTIA
ISRAEL
Jerusalem •
MOAB

Syro-Arabian Desert

On (Heliopolis) •
Negeb
Beersheba •
Arabah
EDOM

Sahara Desert

Noph (Memphis) •
Timna •

Sinai
Ezion-geber •

EGYPT
Mt. Sinai ▲
MIDIAN

Tema •

RED SEA

Medinet Habu •

Nile R.

Scale:
0 — 100 — 200 — 300 — 400 Miles
0 — 100 — 200 — 300 — 400 Kilometers

N ↑

ANCIENT NEAR EAST FROM 1200–1000 B.C.
THE IRON I PERIOD

- • City
- ○ City (uncertain location)
- ▲ Mountain peak
- Neo-Hittite states
- Emerging Aramean states
- Phoenicia

PHOENICIA

MAP 10

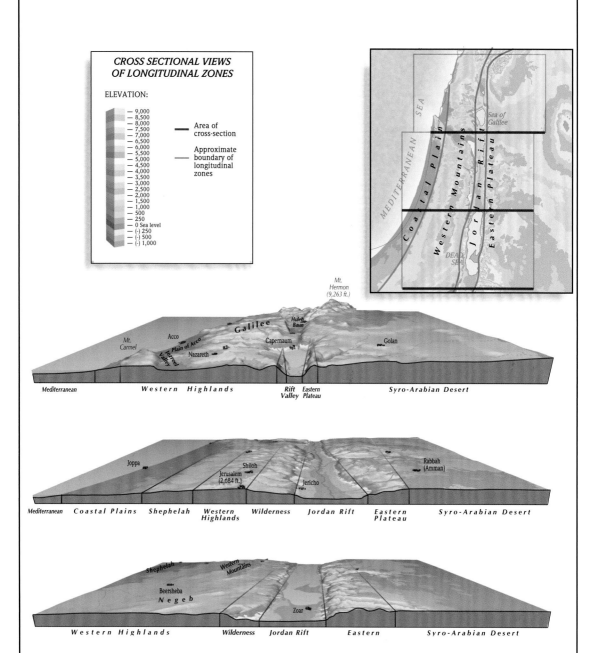

CROSS SECTIONAL VIEWS OF LONGITUDINAL ZONES

ELEVATION:

— 9,000
— 8,500
— 8,000
— 7,500
— 7,000
— 6,500
— 6,000
— 5,500
— 5,000
— 4,500
— 4,000
— 3,500
— 3,000
— 2,500
— 2,000
— 1,500
— 1,000
— 500
— 250
— 0 Sea level
— (-) 250
— (-) 500
— (-) 1,000

Area of cross-section

Approximate boundary of longitudinal zones

MEDITERRANEAN SEA

Coastal Plain

Western Mountains

Jordan Rift

Eastern Plateau

Sea of Galilee

DEAD SEA

Mt. Hermon (9,263 ft.)

Galilee

Huleh Basin

Acco

Plain of Acco

Nazareth

Capernaum

Golan

Mt. Carmel

Jezreel Valley

Mediterranean   Western Highlands   Rift Valley   Eastern Plateau   Syro-Arabian Desert

Joppa

Jerusalem (2,684 ft.)

Shiloh

Jericho

Rabbah (Amman)

Mediterranean   Coastal Plains   Shephelah   Western Highlands   Wilderness   Jordan Rift   Eastern Plateau   Syro-Arabian Desert

Shephelah

Western Mountains

Beersheba

Negeb

Zoar

Western Highlands   Wilderness   Jordan Rift   Eastern   Syro-Arabian Desert

MAP 11

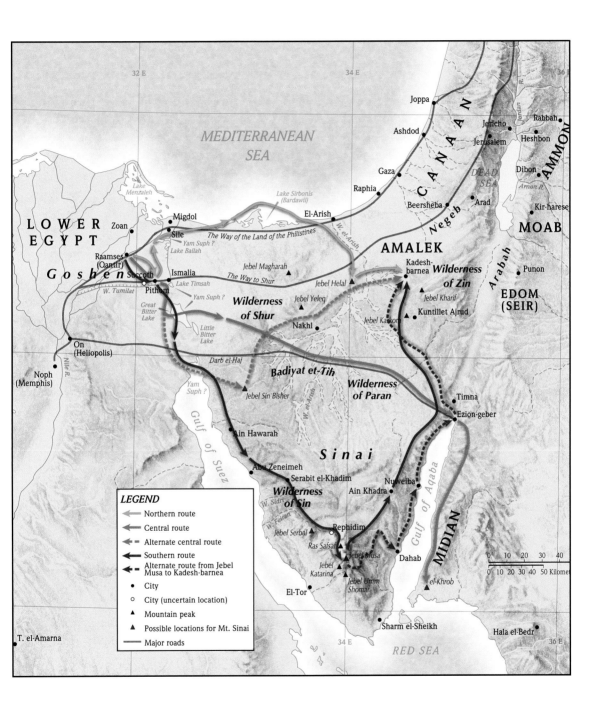

MEDITERRANEAN
SEA

Lake Menzaleh

LOWER
EGYPT
Zoan
Migdol
Sile
Yam Suph ?
Lake Ballah
Raamses
(Qantir)
Goshen
Succoth
Pithom
Ismalia
Lake Timsah
W. Tumilat
Yam Suph ?
Great Bitter Lake
Little Bitter Lake
On
(Heliopolis)
Nile R.
Noph
(Memphis)

Lake Sirbonis
(Bardawll)

El-Arish

The Way of the Land of the Philistines

Jebel Magharah ▲

The Way to Shur

Jebel Helal ▲

**Wilderness
of Shur**

Jebel Yeleq ▲

Nakhl

Darb el-Haj

Yam Suph ?

Jebel Sin Bisher ▲

Badiyat et-Tih

W. et-Arish

**Wilderness
of Paran**

Joppa

Ashdod

Gaza

Raphia

Beersheba

W. et-Arish

AMALEK

Kadesh-
barnea

Jebel Kharif ▲

Jebel Karkom ▲

Kuntillet Ajrud

**Wilderness
of Zin**

Jericho
Jerusalem

Rabbah
Heshbon

DEAD SEA

Dibon
Arnon R.

Kir-hareseh

MOAB

Punon

**EDOM
(SEIR)**

Arabah

Negeb

CANAAN

Jordan R.

Arad

Ain Hawarah

Abu Zeneimeh

Serabit el-Khadim

**Wilderness
of Sin**

W. Sidri

W. Feiran

Jebel Serbal ▲

Ras Safsaf ▲

Rephidim ○

Jebel Musa ▲

Jebel Katarina ▲

Jebel Umm Shomar

El-Tor

S i n a i

Ain Khadra

Nuweiba

Dahab

Timna

Ezion-geber

Gulf of Aqaba

Gulf of Suez

MIDIAN

el-Khrob

Sharm el-Sheikh

Hala el-Bedr

RED SEA

T. el-Amarna

LEGEND
→ Northern route
→ Central route
⇢ Alternate central route
→ Southern route
⇢ Alternate route from Jebel Musa to Kadesh-barnea
• City
○ City (uncertain location)
▲ Mountain peak
▲ Possible locations for Mt. Sinai
— Major roads

0 10 20 30 40
0 10 20 30 40 50 Kilometers

MAP 12

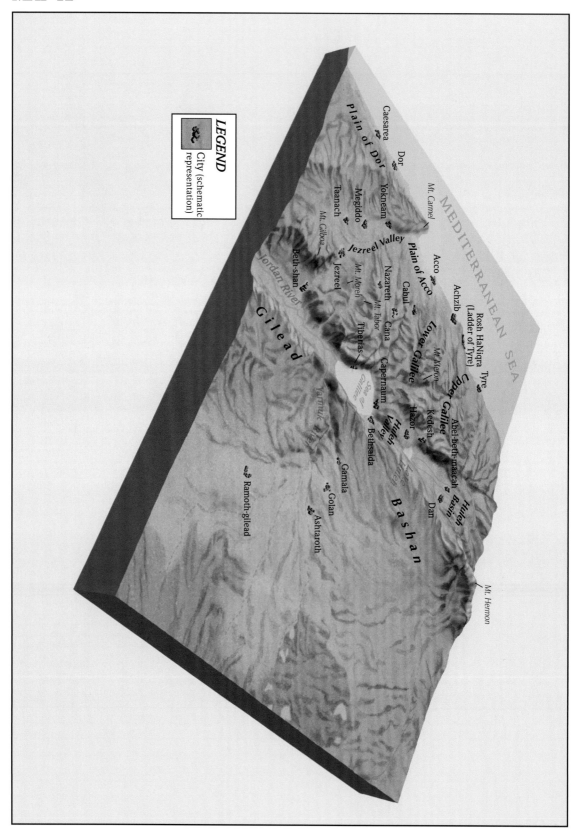

LEGEND

City (schematic representation)